COLE PORTER

A Biography

Also by Charles Schwartz
Gershwin: His Life and Music

W. H. ALLEN · LONDON
A Howard & Wyndham Company
1978

COLE PORTER

A Biography

by Charles Schwartz

Copyright © 1977 by Charles Schwartz

First British edition, 1978

Printed and bound in Great Britain by
Redwood Burn Limited, Trowbridge & Esher
for the Publishers, W. H. Allen & Co. Ltd,
44 Hill Street, London W1X 8LB

ISBN 0 491 02292 1

Book design by Holly McNeely

Acknowledgments

Grateful acknowledgment is made for permission to use the following copyrighted Cole Porter lyrics.

"The Blue Boy Blues" copyright © 1922 by Chappell & Co. Ltd., copyright renewed; "It's De-Lovely" copyright © 1936 by Chappell & Co., Inc., copyright renewed; "Ridin' High" copyright © 1936 by Chappell & Co., Inc., copyright renewed; "Down in the Depths" copyright © 1936 by Chappell & Co., Inc., copyright renewed; "At Long Last Love" copyright © 1937, 1938 by Chappell & Co. Inc., copyright renewed; "From Alpha to Omega" copyright © 1938 by Chappell & Co., Inc., copyright renewed; "My Heart Belongs to Daddy" copyright © 1938 by Chappell & Co., Inc., copyright renewed; "Get Out of Town" copyright © 1938 by Chappell & Co., Inc., copyright renewed; "I Concentrate On You" copyright © 1939 by Chappell & Co., Inc., copyright renewed; "But In the Morning, No" copyright © 1939 by Chappell & Co. Inc., copyright renewed; "Let's Not Talk About Love" copyright © 1941 by Chappell & Co., Inc., copyright renewed; "You'd Be So Nice To Come Home To" copyright © 1942 by Chappell & Co., Inc., copyright renewed; "I Love You" copyright © 1943 by Chappell & Co., Inc., copyright renewed; "Ev'ry Time We Say Goodbye" copyright © 1944 by Chappell & Co., Inc., copyright renewed; "Hasta Luego" copyright © 1942 by Chappell

To My Parents

Preface

Perhaps consistent with my having been a professional musician since the age of fourteen, I have long admired Cole Porter's songs and have performed them on numerous occasions. I have also long admired the public image of the man. But that is hardly enough reason for another Porter biography. So much material has already been published on him that one might reasonably ask, "What more can be said about him?" But I should also note that I had entertained a similar thought when I started doing serious research on George Gershwin some years earlier, out of a desire to learn as much as I could about the man and his work. Ultimately that research on Gershwin led to my book on the composer, published in 1973. In doing research on Gershwin I soon found that most of the books and other published material on him were not as comprehensive or as objective as they might have been, and that a substantive biography on the composer was wholly in order.

That same conclusion evolved, too, from my Cole Porter research. I discovered that many publications about Porter were not as factual as I would have liked, whether in dealing with major matters relating to his basic personality or with perhaps less crucial items such as the physical appearance of his father and mother, or his World War I military record, or even the actual location of his burial site. Porter, moreover, was a considerably more complicated character than has generally been presented; so, too, was his wife, Linda. Their relationship was a unique one by almost any standard, but many of the important nuances of their individual lives, as well as their life together, have been glossed over or not even touched on in previous biographies. In addition, details about Porter's musical training, his work habits, and even his songs themselves have not always been presented as accurately as they might have been. For all these reasons, plus the perspective that the passage of time adds to an artist's life and work, it seemed to me that Cole Porter and everything he represented needed reappraisal.

In doing my research I have tried to draw on prime sources wherever possible and have examined innumerable personal documents, musical manuscripts, photos, and memorabilia. I have interviewed dozens of Porter's—and his wife's—friends, many of whom are mentioned in the text. Since the list is too long to do justice to all involved, I would like to thank them collectively for their wonderful cooperation, especially in helping to fill in many of the highly personal details in Porter's life (understandably, the sources for such intimate details are generally not specifically identified, out of consideration for their wishes). I would like, too, to express my appreciation to James Omar Cole (Cole Porter's second cousin and heir, who answered many questions and kindly placed Porter family photos at my disposal), John F. Wharton (Porter's lawyer and trustee of the Cole Porter Musical and Literary Property Trusts), Florence Leeds and John Breglio (of the Cole Porter Trusts), Harold G. Rader (of Worcester Academy), Grant Robley (registrar of Yale University), Stephen M. Bernardi (of the Harvard Law School), Guibert Lassalle (chief of information for the French Foreign Legion), Colonel Marchal (of the French Military Administration), Richard Warren (curator of Yale's Historical Sound Recordings), Joseph Fuchs, Donna Brown and Barbara Eick (of Yale's library staff), Helen Brundage (in charge of the Porter archives in Peru, Indiana), Donald Madison (of the New York Public Library), as well as the staffs of Yale University, the Music Division of the Library of Congress, the Museum of the City of New York, and of the Music and Theater collections of the New York Public Library at Lincoln Center.

I owe a debt of thanks as well to Honoria Murphy Donnelly, Virgil Thomson, Philip Claflin, Henry Burke, Dr. Dana W. Atchley, Anita Loos, Billy Baldwin, Bella Spewack, Robert Kimball, Alexander Steinert, Archibald MacLeish, Robert Russell Bennett, Ben Sturges, Arnold Whitridge, Nicolas de Gunzburg, and Madeline P. Smith. Finally, my gratitude also goes to my family, for their persistent devotion and encouragement; to Maxine Groffsky, for her many helpful comments in connection with my manuscript; to Joyce Engelson, my editor at The Dial Press, for her strong support and critical acumen; and to Red and Pick Heller, Morris Golde, Patricia Nash, Lee and Betty Lee Kolker, Ted and Rhoda Weiler, Ray Gottlieb, Joseph Machlis, and Lee Wurlitzer for their steadfast interest in my research and my findings.

Only through the cooperation of many was this book possible, and I am much indebted to all of them.

Charles Schwartz

Contents

Preface   ix

1   Background   1

2   The Roots   6

3   Growing Up   13

4   College Days   22

5   The Expatriate   34

6   Married Life   49

7   On the Move   62

8   Venetian Period   75

9   Rising Star   88

10   Decade's End   100

11   Naughty Thirties   111

12   Anything Goes   124

13   Jubilee   138

14   Hollywood Resident   149

15   Red, Hot and Blue!   161

16   The Accident   172

17 Back in Harness 182

18 Buxton Hill 195

19 Inner Turmoil 204

20 Night and Day 214

21 Kiss Me, Kate 224

22 Going Strong 238

23 Amputee 250

24 Journey Home 260

Appendix 1: Works by Cole Porter 271

Appendix 2: Alphabetical List of
Cole Porter Songs
and Other Musical Works 294

Appendix 3: A Selected Cole Porter
Discography 324

A Selected Bibliography 334

Index 345

Illustrations

Cole Porter's grandparents, J. O. and Rachel Cole.
Grandfather Cole.
Kate Porter, Cole's mother.
Samuel Fenwick Porter, Cole's father.
Cole, as an infant.
Cole, as a young boy, tuning his violin.
Cole, at age eight.
Cole, in a play in prep school.
Cole, cheerleading at Yale, 1912.
Linda Lee Thomas, 1910.
Linda at the time she married Cole, 1919.
William Crocker at Cap d'Antibes, 1921.
Sara and Gerald Murphy and children, 1922.
The Murphys dressed for a costume ball in Paris.
Irving Berlin and wife Ellin, 1926.
Cole and Ed Tauch, 1933.
Cole and Monty Woolley.
Ethel Merman in *Anything Goes*, 1934.
Moss Hart.
Cole in Hollywood, 1937.

Cole, Howard Sturges, and Ed Tauch, 1937.
Cole and Elsa Maxwell, 1938.
Photo portrait of Cole by Alfredo Valente, 1938.
Elsa Maxwell dressed for her role in the film *Riding Into Society*, 1940.
"Black-Jack" Bouvier and daughter Jacqueline, 1947.
Cole and Bella Spewack during rehearsals for *Kiss Me, Kate*.
Bella Spewack, Cole, and Jack Wilson.
Cole and Linda together, 1948.
Monty Woolley, Pert Kelton, and Anne Seymour.
Ed Sullivan and Cole.
One of the last photos of Cole and Howard Sturges together, 1955.
Cole's final resting place, Peru, Indiana.
Mabel Mercer and Jimmy Lyon in a musical tribute to Cole, 1975.

COLE PORTER

A Biography

1

Background

It was a bleak, raw day in the fall of 1964, the winds from Lake Michigan swirling about in volatile bursts of energy, when a small group of Cole Porter's relatives and friends came together in Peru, Indiana, sixty-five miles north of Indianapolis, to pay their last respects to him. Cole had been born seventy-three years earlier in Peru to a well-to-do family, but he had left in his mid-teens to go to prep school in Massachusetts. He came back to Peru only infrequently after that. Instead, he went on to Yale, Harvard, and life as an expatriate American in France during and after World War I, before eventually achieving international fame as a popular songwriter. Along the way Cole also became an indomitable world traveler. But in death he was once again a Hoosier son, as his body was brought back home to Peru for burial alongside his ancestors in the local cemetery.

The majority of the small group of mourners at the funeral were natives of Peru, and related to Cole in some way. As solid, substantial midwesterners, they represented Peru well indeed. Like Cole, they were descendants of pioneer stock who had settled in Peru in the previous century. Like Cole, too, they had their early roots and training in Peru. Yet for all that, Cole's relatives had little in common with him. In contrast to Cole, they had settled in Peru or its environs, had made their lives there and formed their values there, whereas his ties had essentially been severed decades earlier. As the world had come to know him, Cole epitomized big-city sophistication. His name conjured up all the accouterments of international glamour: elegantly dressed people, sumptuous homes, fancy cars, many servants. For years he had moved in the best circles, both at home and abroad. With style and grace, he was was often an arbiter of fashion and taste. Cole was definitely one of the beautiful people of his time. The contrast between the life-style he represented and that of the relatives who mourned him could not have been more extreme.

Even while he was growing up in Peru, differences could be noted between Cole and his peers, largely because of the emphasis he placed on music. His mother, Kate, whom he adored, strongly encouraged his musical bent, and by the time he left for prep school he was a reasonably accomplished pianist, violinist, and composer. But it was as a composer and lyricist rather than as a performer that Cole made his musical mark. Little is known of his musical achievements at prep school, but at Yale he was one of the outstanding members of his class, by virtue of the many songs and musicals he wrote and performed for the students. Because of the great success he and his music enjoyed at Yale, it was perhaps inevitable that Cole would concentrate on a career as a songwriter despite opposition from his maternal grandfather, the power in the family, who wanted him to become a lawyer. As a concession to his grandfather, after graduating from Yale in 1913 Cole even studied briefly at Harvard Law School, with dismal results. But since popular music was always Cole's first love, it is not surprising that his brief fling at studying law turned out to be a fiasco.

A number of Cole's cronies at Yale, like Monty Woolley and Leonard Hanna, remained his close, lifelong friends. As collegians and then as Yale alumni, they helped spread the word of Cole's songwriting talent. But mainly through Cole's own persistence, in 1916 he had the distinction of having one of his musicals, *See America First*, open on Broadway. By 1919 he also had a hit song, "Old-Fashioned Garden," to his credit. Slowly at first, but then gaining in momentum, Cole's songs, from a variety of musicals with which he was associated—such as *Paris* (1928), *Wake Up and Dream* (1929), *Fifty Million Frenchmen* (1929), *The New Yorkers* (1930), *Gay Divorce* (1932), *Anything Goes* (1934), *Jubilee* (1935), and *Red, Hot and Blue!* (1936) —caught on with the public. From about 1928 on, hit songs came so regularly—among them "Let's Do It, Let's Fall in Love" (1928), "What Is This Thing Called Love?" (1929), "You Do Something to Me" (1929), "Love for Sale" (1930), "Night and Day" (1932), "I Get a Kick Out of You" (1934), "You're the Top" (1934), "Blow, Gabriel, Blow" (1934), "Begin the Beguine" (1935), and "It's De-Lovely" (1936), to name a few—that he and his tunes became internationally known by the mid-thirties.

At their best, Cole's songs blended fresh, witty, urbane lyrics and highly singable melodies into a sparkling, irresistible combination. Cole's lyrics in particular were models of ingenuity and sophistication. They set new standards of invention and craftsmanship that helped to spell the downfall of the mundane June-moon-croon approach that had been prevalent in popular music for so long. Once the public had gotten to appreciate the special brand of genius that set Cole's lyrics apart from those of his competition, it was largely unwilling to settle for the prosaic any longer.

Cole left for France in 1917, shortly after the United States entered World War I, and remained in France when the war ended in 1918. While there he met Linda Lee Thomas, a beautiful and wealthy American divorcée living in Paris, and married her in 1919. Linda was eight years older than Cole and socially very prominent. As a collegian Cole had invariably gravitated to the rich and high-born, and his marriage to Linda reflected that pattern. They both loved amusing parties, gossip, and mingling with nobility and high society. They did all that and more after their marriage, living on a scale so grand—including residences in Venetian palazzos and lavish parties for hundreds at a time—that they were soon the talk, and perhaps the envy, of the international set.

Another important tie between the two was the fact that Linda was extremely supportive of Cole's talent and did everything she could to further his career. Even though their marriage was, sexually, really one in name only since Cole was a homosexual, the two had an exceptional relationship. Save for a brief period in 1937 when Linda left Cole after a major disagreement, they were essentially devoted to each other until her death in 1954.

Linda's devotion to Cole was clearly demonstrated when he severely injured his legs in a horseback-riding accident on Long Island in 1937. There was a strong possibility that they would have to be amputated. Linda was then separated from Cole and living in Paris. When she learned of the accident she immediately returned to New York to be with him. During the crucial early period of treatment, Linda's insistence that

Cole's legs be saved encouraged doctors to stave off amputation with numerous operations and to have him walking again with the aid of braces and a cane.

Following the accident Cole resumed his songwriting career with a vengeance. He turned out a string of hit Broadway shows in the next decade or so: *Leave It to Me* (1938), *DuBarry Was a Lady* (1939), *Panama Hattie* (1940), *Let's Face It* (1941), *Something for the Boys* (1943), *Mexican Hayride* (1944), and *Kiss Me, Kate* (1948), unquestionably his finest score. Many of Cole's best-known tunes came from these shows, among them "My Heart Belongs to Daddy" *(Leave It to Me)*, "Get Out of Town" *(Leave It to Me)*, "Do I Love You?" *(DuBarry Was a Lady)*, "Friendship" *(DuBarry Was a Lady)*, "Well, Did You Evah! *(DuBarry Was a Lady)*, "But In the Morning, No" *(DuBarry Was a Lady)*, "Let's Be Buddies" *(Panama Hattie)*, "Make It Another Old-Fashioned, Please" *(Panama Hattie)*, "Ev'rything I Love" *(Let's Face It)*, "Let's Not Talk About Love" *(Let's Face It)*, "I Love You" *(Mexican Hayride)*, "Wunderbar" *(Kiss Me, Kate)*, "So in Love" *(Kiss Me, Kate)*, "Why Can't You Behave?" *(Kiss Me, Kate)*, and "Always True to You in My Fashion" *(Kiss Me, Kate)*.

Besides writing for Broadway, Cole was also active in Hollywood. His movie credits from the mid-thirties through the forties include the scores for the films *Born to Dance* (1936), *Rosalie* (1937), *Broadway Melody of 1940*, *You'll Never Get Rich* (1941), *Something to Shout About* (1943), and *The Pirate* (1948). Between Broadway shows and Hollywood films, Cole's career kept him sufficiently busy that he found it necessary to maintain residences on both coasts—a large apartment at the Waldorf Astoria in New York, and a luxurious mansion in California. He lived in them alternately during the year. But along with his work, Cole also found loads of time to play, enjoying a very full social life and extensive traveling.

Cole's emphasis on play caught the fancy of the media relatively early in his career. His diversions made for interesting reading, judging from the numerous articles that appeared telling of his fun-and-games approach to life. Since Cole traveled so widely these stories abounded in descriptions of the exotic places he visited and the hordes of glamorous people he knew. These reports also claimed that many of his best musical ideas resulted from his global diversions, whether floating down the Rhine in a *faltboat*, or witnessing native dances in Morocco's Marrakesh, or at Kalabahai in the Dutch East Indies. Some of these tales, as we shall see, may have been more fanciful than real, but at least they captured much of the joie de vivre and sophistication of the man and his songs.

While he was still around to savor the experience, Cole had the unusual satisfaction of seeing his life portrayed on screen in the 1946 movie, *Night and Day*, with no less an actor than Cary Grant playing the lead. Though *Night and Day* was far from an accurate depiction of Cole's life, there apparently was enough glitter in the film to make it seem the real thing to the public. Since the media had invariably portrayed Cole as larger than life, Hollywood's distortions did little to alter that image, and hundreds of thousands flocked to see the film.

Because of his exciting existence, heredity, and conscious concern with his appearance, Cole remained surprisingly youthful most of his life, despite the trauma, pain, and crippling effects of his 1937 accident. There were, to be sure, low periods for him, especially in his later years, when he questioned whether he had lost his creative spark. But even in his sixties Cole looked remarkably young for his age—and turned out successful scores for Broadway musicals (*Can-Can* [1953] and *Silk Stockings* [1955]) and for films (*High Society* [1956] and *Les Girls* [1957]).

But all that changed in 1958, when Cole's long struggle to save both legs finally ended with the amputation of his right leg close to the hip. Linda by then had died, and Cole was somehow not able to make the adjustment to the loss of the leg on his own. As an aftermath of the amputation Cole stopped writing songs. His health, too, declined from then on. He died in October of 1964, in California, and was buried in Peru at his own request.

Cole's death left a void in American musical theater that is still felt today. The world also lost a remarkable personality whose life, as it was known, was indeed a fascinating one. Perhaps even more fascinating, however, were many of the key aspects of Cole's life that the public knew little about, though they add to the full dimensions of the man. They are surely, therefore, worth the telling.

2

The Roots

Today Peru, Indiana, could be any one of thousands of small, bustling communities practically anywhere in the United States. Its main street, Broadway, despite its many especially ornate, turn-of-the-century buildings and a particularly wide thoroughfare, differs little from other such downtown districts. It has the well-scrubbed look and the usual assortment of shops, metal storefronts, and signs that are the trademark of countless thriving American cities. Once away from Peru's downtown business section, however, its rolling farms and grazing livestock epitomize rural America, except for the intrusion of nearby Grissom Air Force Base, a remnant of World War II, with its screaming jets.

Before the turn of the century, of course, farms were more plentiful in Peru, but its Broadway already had the look of get-up-and-go. Its streets may not have been paved yet, but Peru's Broadway, nonetheless, was the miniscule counterpart of its big-city equivalent to the east: It was a place for shopping, banking and investing, and even socializing—particularly after Sunday church services, when families paraded up and down the street in their finery.

Though Congress created the territory of Indiana in 1800 and admitted Indiana into the Union as a state in 1816, Peru was not formally incorporated as a city until after the end of the Civil War, on February 25, 1867.

But despite its relatively short existence as an incorporated city, Peru had a lot to be proud of. It started out as a one-cabin frontier settlement; when homesteader John McGregor built his home there in 1827, he was the first white man to do so. That same year a trading post was also established by Samuel McClure, and Peru was on its way—not as Peru, but as Miamisport, in deference to its location on the Wabash River and in Miami Indian territory. But for reasons that are not entirely clear, the settlement came to be called Peru, after the country of the Incas. By 1837, when the town's first newspaper, the *Peru Forester*, appeared, there was no reference to the former name of the town.

Three years before the birth of the *Peru Forester*, Albert Cole, Cole's maternal great-grandfather, a tanner and shoemaker by trade, came to the town with his six-year-old son, James Omar Cole. The elder Cole, an easterner from Connecticut born in 1790, had fought under Andrew Jackson in Louisiana during the War of 1812 before eventually migrating to Peru by way of Zanesville, Ohio, and Goshen, Indiana, to seek his fortune. Concentrating mainly on farming and merchandising, Albert gradually built up a fairly sizable estate; one that would pass on, in the normal course of events, to his son, James Omar—or J.O., as he was known.

However, instead of remaining in Peru, J.O., like his father before him, sought to make his own fortune. So in 1850, at the age of twenty-two, after only a meager grade-school education and some work experience as a farmer and a clerk, he headed west for California, where gold had been discovered two years earlier at Sutter's Mill, northeast of Sacramento.

J.O. found California jumping with activity. Once news leaked out of the finding of gold on John A. Sutter's vast domain in 1848, other Californians eagerly began looking for gold themselves. By 1849 the gold rush was on. Adventurers and fortune seekers and the simply greedy from all over the United States and other parts of the globe descended on California. They came in droves by boat, prairie schooner, and horseback, looking for the golden dust that would make them wealthy. California's population, which had been somewhat over ten thousand before the discovery of gold, swelled to one hundred thousand by 1850. With such a marked population increase and little in the way of law enforcement (the country was then without an effective, organized territorial government), murder, gambling, claim jumping, and other forms of lawlessness and vice were rampant among the hordes of gold prospectors.

In such an aggressively competitive and lawless setting, where fortunes could be made or lost at the turn of the dice or the strike of a pick, the value of gold cheapened the value of human life: One had to be hard and rough simply to survive. It says much about J.O.'s tough hide and character that he not only survived in this hostile jungle of gold; he prospered greatly—though it was only tangentially from gold mining.

After a year in Maryville, California, working as a mining assistant and a clerk, he accumulated about seven hundred dollars and went into business for himself, operating a general store. Responding to the need for drinking water, he also helped build a water conduit between Maryville and Sacramento, a distance of forty miles. Between his mercantile business and the income derived from the conduit, he ultimately amassed about thirty thousand dollars, a small fortune in those days. But J.O. did not stop there. He parlayed his California stakes to several million dollars by subsequently operating a brewery and an ice and cold-storage company in Peru and a large sawmill in Cincinnati, and by investing widely in timberland in Indiana, Illinois, Ohio, Kentucky, and West Virginia. The West Virginia holdings proved particularly profitable because of the high yield of coal and gas found on the land.

Because of the wealth he accrued and the power it wielded, one must credit J.O. with the establishment of the family dynasty in Peru after returning from California. Albert Cole may have preceded his son to Peru, but it was J.O. who became the dominant force there.

As is true of many self-made millionaires, J.O. had great confidence in his judgment of men and money. Business for him was all-encompassing; it was both play and work. He drove himself hard and expected others to be no less unrelenting in the pursuit of wealth. He also had a terrible temper, easily provoked when things did not go his way, and, above all, an absolute loathing for wasteful living.

Yet in spite of his obsession with making money, his temper tantrums, and his tyrannical behavior, J.O. could be inordinately tender and generous where the women in his family were concerned. For along with his accumulation of wealth, in 1860 J.O. had married a pretty, gentle Peru woman, Rachel Henton, whom he adored. They had two children: a daughter, Kate, in 1862, and a son, Louis, in 1865. Though father and son were reasonably close, J.O.'s relationship with Rachel and Kate was considerably warmer. For J.O. the sun rose and set on his women, as he lavished affection upon them, pampered them indiscriminately, and indulged their every whim. J.O. would spend hours looking at Rachel's face, particularly as she slept, mawkishly referring to her in public as "the rose of Indiana." As for Kate, he considered her perfection itself, though others possibly more objective might have found excessive J.O.'s estimation of his small, slim, perky, dark-eyed, brown-haired daughter.

Consistent with J.O.'s concern for material goods and his background as an entrepreneur and investor was the small regard he had for what were to him only cultural niceties: music, theater, and dance. For him these were little more than diversions for the idle or topics of conversation at women's tea parties. While tolerant of women dancing at balls or singing at church functions or in the nursery, he had contempt for their pursuit of artistic careers. As for men in the arts—whether actors, musicians, or the like—he considered them essentially ne'er-do-wells, sexually suspect, or both. In his estimation, men had more important things to do in life than romp onstage or play an instrument in public.

But if J.O. had reservations about artistic matters beyond his ken, they did not intrude upon his overall plans for bringing up Kate in a manner befitting the daughter of one of Indiana's wealthiest, most prominent citizens. He saw to it that she was dressed in the height of fashion, almost from the moment she outgrew her baby garments; he also hired the finest instructors to teach her singing, piano, and French; enrolled her in dancing classes with the children of Peru's best families; and sent her abroad while she was still a teenager to add some foreign polish to her very American, very midwestern personality. For her general education, once she was past the primary grades J.O. sent her first to Colby Academy in New London, Connecticut, and then to Brooks Seminary in Poughkeepsie, New York, which was a finishing school for young women of good families.

Bright and winsome, Kate should have been ready for marriage on her return to Peru from school. J.O. even attempted to help the process along by sponsoring a lavish coming-out party for her to announce to the world that she was of marriageable age. But Kate at that point had not found a young man who really interested her. She was hard to please and rather headstrong, especially since her father had never denied her anything. J.O., moreover, despite his apparent interest in seeing that she married well, always seemed to have some reservations about the young men she knew. As J.O. voiced it, they often seemed more interested in his money than his daughter, or they had some basic character quirks that boded badly for the future, or their professional goals did not lend themselves to supporting a wife and family in proper style. Considering J.O.'s worshipful attitude toward his daughter, perhaps no man would have fully satisfied him as a potential husband for her.

Notwithstanding her father's overly solicitous involvement with assuring the finest marital prospects for her, Kate finally settled, surprisingly, for someone almost completely antithetical to everything J.O. looked for in a son-in-law. For the young man she chose, Samuel Fenwick Porter, was a shy druggist of limited means and unprepossessing appearance with a modest gift for telling tall stories. Contrary to published reports, which have somehow depicted him as handsome and Kate as plain, the fact is that he was not particularly good-looking while Kate was very attractive. Sam Porter had come to Peru from rural Vevay, Indiana, to better his fortune, and perhaps Kate represented the fortune he sought. At any rate, she responded to his diffidence, his homespun looks, his love for poetry and literature, his humorous stories, and his serious study of horticulture as a means of improving plant life rather than for its commercial potential.

Possibly no man Kate could have married would have differed so markedly from the male role-model her father set for her. And because of this difference, one might readily speculate that Kate's choice of Sam as a husband constituted a rebellion, conscious or otherwise, against her father, with his rough-and-ready background and lack of appreciation for the arts and the more esoteric things in life. In a larger community Kate undoubtedly would have had more men to choose from, and we can only guess at how much insight she had into her own motives. But in Peru, Sam evidently was the only one that Kate—finishing-school education and all—could find with the qualities she was looking for in a man.

If Kate thought she had found a soul mate in Sam, their courtship did not proceed without its share of difficulties. For J.O., as was to be expected, had reservations about Sam. But Kate stood her ground, and J.O. slowly relented—obviously his love for Kate exceeded his distaste for Sam. She and Sam were quietly married on April 9, 1884, in her father's large house on East Second Street, with only a few guests present—not exactly the wedding expected of J.O.'s daughter.

Now that he had the responsibility of a wife, Sam intensified his attempts to do well as a druggist. As a matter of fact, even on their brief honeymoon in Indianapolis, Sam—as reported in the Peru press—concentrated on business by purchasing new drugs for his store. With J.O.'s remarkable drive to the top as a model and stimulus for improving his own financial status, Sam spent long hours at his store and even launched an advertising campaign in Peru's newspapers boosting himself and his drugstore. Resorting to aggressive, give-'em-hell tactics, Sam alleged in his ads that the town's other druggists "stole" from the public by their high, "monopoly" prices, while he sold his drugs "dirt cheap." "Porter the druggist," as he called himself, "does not steal from you," he announced in his ads. (Irrespective of such claims, Sam showed a somewhat more larcenous side many years later by selling bootleg whiskey on the sly during Prohibition.) These ads may not have endeared Sam to his opposition or the more conservative townspeople, who resented the tone of his accusations, but they *did* improve his business. Yet despite increased sales it did not take long for Sam to realize that no matter how hard he tried, he not only could never come close to achieving the success of J.O., but he could never support Kate in the style her father had accustomed her to. Once Sam had accepted this fact, one might have expected him to severe his, and Kate's, ties in Peru and to try to make an independent go of it elsewhere. But Sam chose to remain in Peru— perhaps out of fear that he would not do any better elsewhere. This decision says much about his character. It also helps explain to a large extent his ultimate failure as a husband.

Under the shadow of J.O.'s wealth and power, Sam never emerged as a figure of consequence even in his own household. Often he seemed a family afterthought; in a way, the equivalent of a drone selected for mating with the queen bee. To begin with, Kate, after her marriage, still depended on her father's largess: She still had the finest clothes to wear and servants to look after her. In going along with this arrangement Sam's position was compromised from the start. As for J.O., he comported himself reasonably well in his relations with Sam, presumably for Kate's sake. If he never fully accepted Sam, he at least appeared friendly enough on the surface. From time to time, however, undercurrents of resentment toward Sam would emerge if he botched some financial deal or spent too much time on his horticultural hobby or reading and writing poetry. But whatever the effort on both sides, J.O. and Sam were so far apart in their makeup and interests that their differences could never even remotely be reconciled. With such an intense polarization of personality between the two men, it was inevitable that Kate would emerge as a key figure, the focus of a *modus operandi* that evolved among them. Thus, for instance, when J.O. eventually built a beautiful home for the Porters on his property, Westleigh Farms, it was Kate who helped trigger this generosity, but it was Sam who reaped much of the benefit.

Along with the Porters' inevitably high quota of marital tensions went the problems of childbearing and raising. For Kate suffered the loss of two infants in quick succession: A son, Louis, died shortly after birth in 1888, and a daughter, Rachel, died at the age of two in 1890. It was in such a climate of loss, uncertainty, and inherent family difficulties that Cole Porter was born in his parents' home at 102 East Third Street on June 9, 1891: the only child of a weak, ineffective father and an excessively indulged mother, and the grandson of a crusty, powerful, unpredictable despot of a grandfather.

3

Growing Up

As a rather fragile, exceptionally tiny infant, Cole undoubtedly needed an extra amount of care. But he soon grew into a healthy, unusually alert and active child, though he was small for his age. Nevertheless, Kate hovered over him protectively. Perhaps her ties to Cole were intensified because he was her only living child, and a son at that. But mother and son also closely resembled each other. Like Kate, Cole was small of frame and stature, with a large mouth, ready smile, brown hair, and dark eyes; like her, he was spunky and willful.

Just as Kate had always been the apple of her father's eye, so too was Cole his mother's pride and joy. She was ambitious for him, denied him nothing, spoiled him shamelessly. She also tried to instill in her son her notions of upper-class refinement (which she had presumably—and unsuccessfully—sought in Sam, and which were so sorely lacking in her father). Whether covered like an oriental potentate in velvets and silks as he tossed in his crib, or dressed in lace cuffs and waistcoats as a boy of seven or so, Cole was hardly a typical Indiana boy. Kate saw to it that he had his own Shetland pony, a private tutor for French lessons, and a working familiarity with the social graces expected of one of society's elite, including dancing classes, music instruction, and Sunday churchgoing (less for religious beliefs than for a sense of communal participation).

Kate frowned upon contact sports and excessive physical activity as being unworthy of a gentleman, so Cole did little of either, generally limiting his exercise to walking, swimming, and horseback riding.

Cole began studying piano and violin at the age of six. He barely tolerated the violin, for he found its case cumbersome to carry and also disliked the harsh, squeaky sounds he made on it. The piano, however, was more to his liking, though he hated the two-hours-daily practice his mother insisted upon. Fortunately, when practice got too tedious Kate would often revive his interest by accompanying herself as she sang popular tunes of the day for him in satirical fashion. Singing at the top of her voice, Kate would burlesque such well-known tunes as "Ben Bolt" by broadly distorting the text, to Cole's amusement and delight. In Kate's renditions the English language would be vigorously assaulted as she ludicrously stretched out a phrase like "don't you remember" to a ponderous "dough-oughnt yoo-ooh ree-uh-mem-em-buh." Cole's subsequent witty and satirical approach in many of his own works, from college musicals like *The Pot of Gold* to such famous tunes as "Miss Otis Regrets" and "Friendship," may very well stem from his delight in his mother's musical burlesques.

Under Kate's supervision and with local lessons, Cole received enough of the basics of piano playing to be able to meet his subsequent professional songwriting needs. As a budding violinist, however, he did not fare so well, for he hardly seemed to be making any progress. To help improve his ability on the instrument, Kate decided to look outside Peru for instruction, finally settling on a "conservatory" in Marion, Indiana, some thirty miles away.

For several years, plainly out of obedience to his mother, Cole suffered the ordeal of train trips to Marion for the hateful violin lessons. He even accommodated her by serving as a less-than-inspired violin soloist with the Marion student orchestra in a number of annual concerts they gave in Peru at the behest of Kate, who helped absorb the expenses of the concerts in return for the guarantee of Cole's solo appearances. That Cole fulfilled his mother's expectations may be deduced from an undated review in the Peru press that she saved of his debut performance as violin soloist. "Master Cole," noted the review, "completely charmed his audience with sweet music and the gracefulness of rendition." It also reported that "the elite of the city" attended the concert "in response to invitations extended by Mr. and Mrs. S. F. Porter as an introductory for their son, Cole. . . . The affair was the occasion of one of the grandest social gatherings ever held in the city." The world may have lost a great soloist when Cole packed away his violin case for the last time as a teenager. But he later claimed that one redeeming feature—in addition to pleasing his mother—resulted from his violin experiences: During the course of his train trips to and from Marion in quest of higher musical knowledge, Cole discovered that candy vendors sold more than sweets. They were also the purveyors of those spicy, naughty books that have always been the forbidden fruit of young people. Cole soon made a point of stocking up on these books, secretly stashing them away in his violin case for reading when no one was around. Later in life Cole even maintained—without being specific—that his delight in the excitement and titillation of these books was eventually to find its way into his lyrics. Perhaps he had in mind tunes like "Love for Sale," "My Heart Belongs to Daddy," and "But in the Morning, No," all of whose lyrics, as we shall see, have rather explicit sexual overtones.

Besides piano and violin lessons, Kate apparently also encouraged Cole to compose, judging from a brief piano piece titled "Song of the Birds" that he dedicated to her in 1901, when he was ten. Interspersed in the manuscript, all of it written in Cole's childish hand, are programmatic comments above each of the six sections of the piece to help convey its story. The comments, in the order they occur, are these: "Mother's Cooing," "The Young Ones Learning to Sing," "One Bird Falls from the Nest," "The Cuckoo Tells the Mother Where the Bird Is," "The Bird Is Found," and finally, "They Fly Away." Though hardly indicative of a major musical talent, "Song of the Birds" is a charming memento of Cole's childhood and his devotion to his mother.

Kate's devotion to Cole, in turn, is manifest in connection with his next composition, another "bird" piece for piano written the following year. Titled "Bobolink Waltz," this little tune has the distinction of being Cole's first published work—a distinction tempered somewhat by the fact that it was Kate who had one hundred copies of the waltz published at her own expense to distribute to her friends and relatives. Proudly printed in large type on the cover of the piece is its title and composer. At the bottom of the page, printed in small type, the legend indicates that the waltz was "published for the author" by S. Brainard's Sons of New York and Chicago, a vanity press for music. The piece itself indicates little of the future songwriting talents of its creator. Like the "Song of the Birds," the artistic potential inherent in "Bobolink Waltz" is less apparent than its historical value as an extant sampling of Cole Porter musical juvenilia. Clearly revealed, however, is the encouragement and nurturing Cole got from his mother, as well as their exceptionally close relationship.

The interest Kate showed in Cole's youthful musical achievements was shared by neither her father nor her husband. (Kate's mother, Rachel, died in 1890 before Cole was born; her stepmother—J.O.'s second wife, Bessie—never played a major role in Cole's life.) J.O., of course, considered his grandson's musical training a waste of time, money, and energy —for Cole and everyone else. In J.O.'s estimation, a youth's training was expected to prepare him for manly responsibilities—being the head of a household, raising a family, and coping successfully with the life of business—*not* what he considered the sissified pursuit of a musical career. Out of deference to his beloved Kate, however, J.O. did not take as firm a stand as he might have. Instead of continually badgering Kate and the boy in an attempt to get them to mend their ways, J.O. somewhat impatiently restrained himself, hoping that Cole would eventually outgrow his youthful folly. But as a calculated means of helping to shape his goals for Cole, of winning him over to his way of thinking, J.O. would make a point of dressing up stories of his own past glories during the frontier days or of his exploits on the gold battlefields of California, so that he emerged as a hero of Herculean dimension. J.O. also took another, severer, tack in his efforts to put Cole straight. From time to time he would take the boy horseback riding with him to explore the beautiful land around them. Inevitably on these trips J.O. would point to an ugly, large, gray frame building that marred the horizon. "You'll end up there, Cole, in the county poorhouse," J.O. would sternly warn the boy, "if you're not careful in preparing for the future." Considering J.O.'s powerful personality, one might assume that his warnings and machinations must have had considerable effect on the boy's still-immature psyche. But in retrospect, it seems that J.O.'s efforts made Cole draw ever closer to his mother and all that she wished to, or did, represent to him.

Sam Porter's role as father, too, must have left its mark on his son. But unlike J.O., who tried to do something about Cole's upbringing, Sam Porter made no real effort to change the status quo. He seemed resigned to being a second-class citizen in his own household and faded into the background where Cole was concerned, letting Kate rule by default. To be sure, Sam and Cole shared some moments of mutual interest, usually in connection with a story or poem they both liked and discussed. But these occasions were few. By and large there was so little interaction between father and son that Cole was later to claim—possibly out of an unconscious need to repress the relationship—that he remembered little about Sam, who died on August 18, 1927, at the age of sixty-nine, from complications resulting from a prolonged nervous breakdown.

With Kate as his major influence, Cole passed his youthful years in Peru going to school, keeping up with his music lessons, and generally following the day-to-day routines his mother approved of for him. Among the activities he particularly enjoyed during this period were visits to the Great Wallace Show, a circus which wintered in Peru. Cole especially loved to wander in the menagerie of the circus, with its exotic animals and pungent smells, as well as among the quarters of the side-show members. Cole visited the circus often enough to come to know a number of its employees by name, including the animal keepers, the massive fat lady, the strong man, and several of the midgets.

Cole's summers were usually spent at Lake Maxinkuckee, forty miles to the north, swimming, sunning himself, and watching the local lake steamer dock and depart. Winters, Kate would invariably take Cole to Chicago for two weeks of theater- and opera-going. His eager anticipation of these Chicago trips may have been an early indication of his love for the stage. One of Cole's favorite memories of these jaunts was the sight of a huge tenor inside a makeshift boat drawn by a large, very obviously man-made white swan, in Richard Wagner's *Lohengrin*. This was Cole's first exposure to opera and he was amused by the sight of the tenor pouring out volumes of sound while being towed across the stage by a less-than-invisible and sweaty-looking stage crew. Eventually Cole developed a lifelong interest in opera. But the farcical thrust of some of his own works—especially his college musicals—may very well have been influenced by the ludicrousness of the *Lohengrin* stage effects he remembered from his childhood.

Some years before Cole had even come close to completing his grammar school education, Kate had already decided she would send him to a prestigious eastern prep school, one that would serve as a springboard to a good Ivy League college. She eventually chose Worcester Academy, a boys' school in Worcester, Massachusetts, with a reputation for emphasizing the classics. However, despite Kate's plans for Cole, J.O. balked at the thought of a classical education for the boy. Cole, he thought, was physically underdeveloped, small and weak for his age. He needed some toughening up to prepare for life's hard knocks. J.O. proposed instead that Cole should go to a military academy closer to home that would make a man out of him, or to a business school, or even that he take a complete break from school for a while and learn about farming and the respon-

sibilities of managing the family's various interests. Just as she had
refused to budge in the face of her father's opposition to her marriage to
Sam Porter, so, too, Kate remained adamant about sending Cole to
Worcester.

Kate had her way, but the struggle was not without its aftereffects. For
when Cole left Peru for Worcester in 1905 he did not return home again
until shortly before his senior year at prep school. Whether this hiatus
occurred because Kate wanted to keep Cole away from J.O.'s influence
or because she felt the need to shield the boy from the repercussions of
a rift that had presumably developed between herself and her father over
the school issue—or possibly because of other reasons—is not clear. What
is clear is that Cole's ties with his home base in Peru, whatever the cause,
were irrevocably altered during his time at Worcester. For though Cole
always remained close in spirit to his mother and corresponded with her
frequently, he never again stayed at Westleigh Farms for any great length
of time. Peru became a place for Cole to visit during Christmas or summers, but never again more than that. In a sense, Cole's Worcester period
marks a break with his Indiana childhood and the start—though small,
a prophetic one—of his life as a sophisticate of the world.

After enrolling as a student at Worcester in September, 1905, Cole
quickly entered into the spirit of being on his own for the first time, away
from the restrictions at home. He seemed to adjust completely to life at
school and gave little indication that he missed Kate or anyone else from
Peru. He may have been inwardly lonely on occasion, but he seldom
mentioned his family, nor did he receive any visits from them. Some of
his classmates, as a matter of fact, thought Cole was an orphan because
of his reticence in speaking about his family. From this silence one might
deduce that the hateful aspects of Peru—especially everything J.O. represented—outweighed the benefits of home, where he was so indulged by
Kate. This silence, too, may have been Cole's way of playing down his
small-town background (even at his young age, considering how much of
a social creature and snob he ultimately became, he surely must have been
aware of the differences between the East and Peru), as well as of avoiding
questions about his family, especially his ineffectual druggist father.

Though Cole had been somewhat of a loner and had had few friends
in Peru, he soon became a favorite of students and faculty at the academy.
His sparkling eyes and personality and quick smile undoubtedly played
a part in his swift acceptance. Cole's elfin size and agile mind may have
also helped to endear him to students and faculty, especially since he was

thought to be twelve and just about the youngest in his class. Actually Cole was fourteen when he enrolled at Worcester. But his age had mysteriously been lowered by two years for the school records. One must assume that Kate had had a hand in this deception, possibly to make Cole seem more precocious than he really was, or possibly in the hope that fewer demands would be made on him. Certainly we know she was not above changing the record for Cole's benefit. For example, he had not been given a middle name at his christening. He was simply called Cole Porter, after the surnames of his mother and father. However, when he was six years old Kate had been advised by a gypsy fortune teller that he should have a middle name so that his three initials would spell out a word, which was considered to be a lucky omen. Following this advice, Kate quickly had the official records changed so that Cole's middle name became Albert, after his maternal great-grandfather. The initials, now spelling CAP, fulfilled the fortune teller's requirements.

At Worcester Cole followed a prescribed classical curriculum in preparation for college entrance: four years of English and mathematics; three of Greek and Latin; two of French, history and science; plus two of manual training. He applied himself to his studies and did well enough to rate as an honor student, with at least one A and no grade lower than B, for most of his semesters there.

But it was not all work and no play for Cole at the academy. Though he generally avoided athletics and sports, he participated in numerous other extracurricular activities; he belonged, for instance, to Sigma Zeta Kappa (SZK), the school's highly prestigious debating society, and also the dramatic, mandolin, and glee clubs. Moreover, as one of the wealthier students at Worcester, with a monthly allowance to match, he had his own upright piano in his living quarters and played and sang popular tunes for his classmates at every chance. Cole often amused his friends with his musical takeoffs on the more obvious idiosyncracies of faculty members as well as with renditions of risqué tunes of his own, like "The Bearded Lady," "The Tattooed Gentleman," and "Fi, Fi, Fifi." From all reports these early smutty songs were particular favorites with Cole's peers, though, unfortunately, no copies of them exist. With more and more emphasis given to playing the piano and composing for his own and his friends' amusement, Cole had less and less time for the violin, and finally gave up that instrument completely in his senior year.

The headmaster of Worcester while Cole studied there was Dr. Daniel Webster Abercrombie, who doubled as the school's teacher of Greek. Harvard-trained, with a reputation among Worcester students and faculty as an enlightened but demanding pedagogue, Abercrombie turned out to be an important influence on Cole; in fact, practically a godsend for the youngster. Not only did Abercrombie respond to Cole's avid attention in class and polite ways by taking a personal interest—almost as a substitute father would—in his progress at school and his development as a human being, but he also influenced the youth's future work as a lyricist-composer. Looking back on his stay at Worcester after he had established himself in the popular music field, Cole freely admitted that it was Abercrombie who first made him aware, by example, of the close correlation between meter and verse in the epic poems of Homer and other great Greek poets; of the importance of unifying music and text in his own popular songs. Speaking about the lesson learned from Abercrombie as it related to his own work, Cole said: "Words and music must be so inseparably wedded to each other that they are like one." Cole's songs are a testament to this philosophy.

Cole's grades as a student under Abercrombie are a testament to the headmaster's motivation of the youth, as well as to his influence on him. For Cole not only did well under Abercrombie; his grades in Greek, in his senior year, were higher than any of his other grades during his four years at Worcester.

By the end of the spring semester of 1909, Cole, through his extracurricular activities, general good fellowship, and school work, had so ingratiated himself with the faculty and students at Worcester that he was chosen valedictorian of his graduating class. On learning the good news Cole immediately wired his mother. Cole's other achievements at Worcester, noted on his academic record, included him winning the Dexter Speaking Prize in 1908 and second honors at his graduation commencement. His record at Worcester also shows that he served as treasurer of SZK, director of the mandolin club, and monitor of his senior class.

Cole's accomplishments at Worcester, plus his graduation, were duly reported in the Peru press. Under the banner heading CLASS VALEDICTORIAN, one local news item stated that "Cole Porter, son of Mr. and Mrs. S. F. Porter, has been chosen the valedictorian of his class at Worcester." The announcement then went on to say that "Cole is probably the youngest boy in the class, which numbers at least fifty students, and his selection is quite a distinction." In view of the misinformation about Cole's age in the announcement, plus the emphasis on his precocity, one might reasonably assume that Kate's intense motherly pride and protectiveness had some influence on the press, who apparently accepted the comment about Cole's age without question.

One might reasonably assume, too, that the strong reservations that J.O. had originally voiced about Cole attending Worcester were somewhat dissipated by the boy's excellent record at the school, judging by this announcement in the home press: "J. O. Cole, of Peru, has awarded to his grandson Cole Porter, son of Mr. and Mrs. S. F. Porter, an extended tour of Europe as a present, the young man having won high honors in graduating from Worcester Academy. Cole Porter is a deserving young man."

The announcement also noted that Cole would be entering Yale the following fall. Whatever J.O.'s true feelings may have been about Cole's upbringing and education, his public posture—in this instance, at any rate—appeared to sanction the course Cole, and Kate, had chosen to take. Privately, in a brief message to Cole at Worcester dated May 20, 1909, J.O. unbent sufficiently to write: "The news [about the valedictory] we all rejoice in. This fixes the Paris trip."

And so during the summer of 1909 Cole's graduation present—a present he had requested—took him to the Continent for the first time. He was joined on the trip by several Worcester classmates, and they went immediately to Paris. Cole had wanted to go there since his childhood French lessons with a private tutor, which he had followed up with French studies at Worcester. By 1909 he had a good working knowledge of the language and a great curiosity about France and its people. After a brief stay in Paris with a French family, who helped familiarize him with the sights, customs, and vernacular of this great city, Cole, along with his classmates, toured the French countryside before going on to Switzerland and Germany.

Clearly this vacation had a profound effect on Cole. Though Worcester may have represented the first flexing of his wings away from the home nest, this European jaunt unquestionably reinforced Cole's need for independence. He also discovered an intense enjoyment of travel, and he repeated the trip, or its equivalent, almost every year of his adult life.

4

College Days

Cole returned to Peru from his European holiday just in time to get ready for Yale. Late August of 1909 was a hectic period for him, mainly because of all the time spent shopping for what he and Kate considered a suitable wardrobe—suits, ties, shirts, sweaters, shoes, and so forth. Along with the new collegiate clothes went a definite transformation in Cole's appearance. For when Cole arrived in New Haven for freshman indoctrination and the start of fall classes, he no longer had the rather rumpled, tousled look of one of Dr. Abercrombie's prep-school scholars. His hair was now slicked down and parted in the middle like a French gigolo on the make, and he wore, according to all reports, outlandishly garish shirts, ties, and accessories.

Cole's dress may have had all the sartorial razzmatazz of a later age's Joe College, but it was hardly the look Yale then expected of its men, especially an incoming freshman. Nor did Cole's manner of dress change very much after he had been there awhile. A description of how he looked in 1911 has been supplied by Gerald Murphy, an important campus figure at Yale while Cole was there. According to Murphy, Cole struck him as "a little boy from Peru, Indiana, in a checked suit and a salmon tie, with his hair parted in the middle and slicked down, looking just like a westerner all dressed up for the East." Yet in spite of this description, Murphy and many other properly dressed easterners, who then constituted the bulk of the student leaders, came to accept Cole as one of their own on the basis of his many positive attributes—especially his musical talent—and pretty much overlooked his ludicrous clothes, youthful appearance, and small-town background.

Together with the many pieces of luggage that arrived with Cole at Yale was an upright piano. As at Worcester, Cole had his own piano in his Yale quarters. Wherever he lived during his four years at the university—whether at Garland's Rooming House, at 242 York, during his freshman year; or at 112 Welch, 499 Haughton, or 31 Vanderbilt as an upperclassman—the piano went with him. As at Worcester, too, Cole kept busy writing tunes that he played and sang for his classmates at every opportunity. But by now the number of tunes he wrote had dramatically increased. By his own estimate, Cole wrote over three hundred songs while at Yale, many of them now lost.

Cole, of course, did not simply sing and play his way through Yale's ivy-covered halls while he was there. But he hardly made a dent as a scholar, nor did he aspire to. For, contrary to his fine academic record at Worcester, Cole barely survived the intellectual demands made on him in New Haven, mainly because he was so busy socially and musically. In his freshman year, for instance, Cole took courses in English and history plus three languages: French, German, and Latin. At the end of the year Cole could look back at a dismal record: one F (in history), five D's (two each in Latin and German; one in history), and grades of C and B for both of the semesters of English and French. Continuing with English, French, and history in his sophomore year, but substituting Spanish and geology for German and Latin, Cole did little better. He managed to squeak out a B for his first semester in Spanish, but he failed geology twice that year and his remaining sophomore grades were D's and C's. In apparent desperation to make up the F's on his record, Cole added several music courses—basic harmony, introduction to music history, and applied piano—to his already full program in his junior and senior years. Though Cole did not do very much better in music than in his other courses, he at least passed them (with four D's, two C's, and two B's). With three hours of credit for extracurricular activities that the university somehow allowed to be added to his course grades, Cole was able to fulfill Yale's academic requirements and graduated on schedule with the class of 1913.

Despite his poor level of scholarship, Cole did very well at Yale from a variety of other standpoints. Socially, for example, Cole had a field day in New Haven. He seemed to have been a member, at one time or another, of practically every club, large or small, devised by Yale men, among them the Whiffenpoofs, the Hogans, the Grill Room Grizzlies, the Pundits, the Mince Pie Club, the Wigwam and Wrangler Debating Club, the Corinthian Yacht Club, the Dramatic Association, and the University Club. In his sophomore year, moreover, he was elected to Delta Kappa Epsilon (DKE), a top fraternity, and as a junior he was tapped for the coveted Scroll and Key, undoubtedly the most social of the secret societies on campus. Cole also managed to be a football cheerleader, an actor in several school productions (he played the role of Mistress Melinda in *The Recruiting Officer*), and to serve as singer-pianist-conductor of the university glee club.

It was as a composer-lyricist, however, that Cole really made his mark at Yale. Besides writing songs for his own and his friends' pleasure, he also kept his eyes open for chances to have his works published and performed. In short order he got Remick's, a well-known Tin Pan Alley publisher, to put out "Bridget," a simple waltz he wrote as a freshman about the marriage of an Irish scullery maid, Bridget McGuire, to Patrick O'Brien, her beau. Though "Bridget" was never a big hit—even when sung with a heavy Blarney Stone accent, popular in show business at the time—its publication established Cole as a professional composer and lyricist.

Cole had better luck with another freshman creation, "Bingo Eli Yale," a football song. He submitted it in a Yale football-song competition in the fall of 1910, and it quickly became the rage of that football season. Its rah-rah spirit (with lines like "Bingo, bingo, bingo, that's the lingo" and "Fight, fight, fight, with all your might") came through on and off Yale's football field and helped make Cole a big musical man on campus. To fulfill the demand for his gridiron tunes after the success of "Bingo Eli Yale," Cole wrote a number of others while at New Haven, among them "Bull Dog" ("Bull dog, bull dog, bow, wow, wow"), "Beware of Yale," "Eli," and "Fla De Dah," all now considered Yale classics. By his senior year Cole had become so closely associated with the Yale football team because of his tunes—including "A Football King," a solo piece which extolled the virtues of being a gridiron hero—that he was chosen chairman of the football song-selection committee, to help pass on others' contributions. Thus Cole found his own way to support the team—as chairman of the song-selection committee, as cheerleader, and as composer-lyricist—a very clever way for someone of limited athletic aptitude and diminutive size (he was five foot six), and with an abhorrence of physical exertion.

Cole's status as a musical figure of consequence at Yale was undoubtedly enhanced by his own renditions of his tunes. He had a knack for putting them over, even though his high tenor voice by any standard was far from extraordinary, and his piano playing was at best only serviceable. But by dint of an exuberant personality, expressive hands and eyes, an assortment of facial expressions, body English, and a wonderful sense of timing and mimicry, he did very well as an entertainer.

Since his renditions were so good and he loved doing them every chance he could, it was perhaps inevitable that Cole was thrust into the spotlight as a performer while at Yale. It was as a member of the university glee, banjo, and mandolin clubs that Cole had his widest exposure. For these clubs would frequently combine their talents and resources for concerts on campus as well as for tours, especially during Christmas, when they would give a dozen or so concerts in as many different cities within a ten- to twelve-day period. During their Christmas tour of 1911, for example, they started with a concert in Brooklyn on December 21 and then visited Pittsburgh, Cincinnati, Louisville, Knoxville, Atlanta, Jacksonville, Savannah, and Richmond before winding up their travels with a concert in Washington, D. C., on New Year's Day.

During these tours Cole received favorite-son treatment from Yale alumni everywhere he went; audiences went wild over his act and reviewers spoke glowingly of his performances. "The glittering star of the concert was Cole Porter," went one press notice, while adding that "this young man has a singing pianologue act that would easily make good in 'big time' vaudeville. He is a born comedian, both facially and vocally; plays the piano very well, and writes most of his own 'stuff,' which is unusually clever." The press comments continued to be laudatory, especially during Cole's senior year, when as director of the glee club he was featured even more prominently in the concerts. Among the audience favorites on these tours were Cole's renditions of "Antoinette Birby," the sad tale of a provincial maid "done wrong" by a Yale man, "Yellow Melodrama," a takeoff on silent-screen villains sung to the accompaniment of sinister piano chords, and "The Motor Car," a humorous look at the travails of automobile driving. At any rate, Cole invariably had the satisfaction of returning from these whirlwind trips with the ring of audience adulation in his ears and, as an additional ego boost, a pocketful of good press clippings.

Along with the frenetic pace of touring, performing, fulfilling social and academic obligations, and writing tunes for the football team and glee club, Cole still managed to turn out the scores and lyrics for four full-blown musical comedies during his junior and senior years: *Cora, And the Villain Still Pursued Her, The Pot of Gold,* and *The Kaleidoscope.* Since they were all written rather quickly for college smokers under the pressure of deadlines, it is not surprising that all four had a number of elements in common: They were each in two acts, consisting of approximately twenty musical numbers, including an opening chorus, a finale, and a variety of solos, duets, and ensemble pieces in between; their plots, which caricatured many of the foibles associated with college life, were ludicrously broad or almost nonexistent, and often incidental to the musical numbers; they were each dependent on Yale students performing both male and female roles in a farcical, larger-than-life fashion; and they each required a minimum of scenery, costumes, and staging. They were also written for either one of the two key Yale student groups with which Cole was affiliated: the Delta Kappa Epsilon fraternity or the Dramatic Association. For instead of presenting already established musical-comedy fare for their smokers, both organizations called on Cole—reflecting one of the important fringe benefits of his active social and musical life on campus—to come up with original productions for two years running, between the fall of 1911 and the spring of 1913. Cole jumped at the chance.

Drawing on many of his friends at school to perform roles in the productions, Cole shaped his work to suit their abilities and personalities. As Cole put it in a letter to Almet Jenks, a fellow student and the scriptwriter for *The Pot of Gold,* "My only means of making songs relevant is by writing verses which give the idea of belonging to the persons that sing them." In line with that policy Cole easily came up with fitting material for classmate Arnold Whitridge, tall and mature in appearance, who was chosen to play essentially middle-aged parts: a father in *Cora;* a cruel uncle in *And the Villain Still Pursued Her;* a Russian nihilist, Levin Dostokoff, in *The Pot of Gold;* and Mr. Snake in *The Kaleidoscope.* Another friend, Johnfritz Achelis, was suitable for female roles. He was cast as a rich heiress, Arabella, in *And the Villain Still Pursued Her,* and as Mrs. Whitney in *The Kaleidoscope.*

Cole also had to take into account multiple roles. For example, Archibald MacLeish, the poet, not only recited the Prologue to *The Kaleidoscope,* he also played the part of a baby, Butler, in the same musical. Nor did Cole overlook his own performing capabilities. Consistent with his relative position of power in the mounting of the productions, he saw to it that he had some plums for himself: the role of Dick Devereaux in *Cora;* and the romantic lead, Lawrence Thorne, in *The Pot of God.*

Some idea of the less-than-inspired scripts Cole had to work with can be inferred from the book for one of them, *The Pot of Gold,* which was based on the familiar phrase, At the foot of the rainbow there is a pot of gold. The script was summarized in the printed playbill for the show under the heading "arguement":

> The scene of the play is laid in the Hotel Rainbow, which is owned and managed by Oliver Delor. Through long neglect and ill management the house has gradually become shabby and poverty-stricken, until Mr. Delor's only assets are a certain latent cleverness and a young daughter. Lawrence Thorne, coming to the hotel to meet a wealthy uncle whom he has not seen since boyhood, falls in love with the girl. But her father's consent can be gained only under the condition that Thorne shall in some way change the falling fortunes of the Rainbow. In order to accomplish this, Thorne endeavors to create a scandal in the place, which, he believes, will, in making the hotel conspicuous, draw the attention and the patronage of the public.
>
> At the same time, there are two Nihilists plotting in the lobby, looking for their chief, whom they have come to meet at the Rainbow. Presently, Thorne's uncle, General Harrison, arrives with a friend and begins to look for his nephew, and in the confusion of a motor accident, one of the Nihilists is mistaken for the nephew, while the Russians believe they have found their chief.
>
> In the meantime, Thorne, having succeeded in rejuvenating the Rainbow, further confuses matters by informing Delor that General Harrison is mentally enfeebled, and the ensuing actions of Delor and the mistake in nephews proceed to an almost fatal conclusion.

If the script for *The Pot of Gold* by Almet Jenks was a hopeless mishmash, Cole's lyrics for the show were surprisingly fresh, as these lines from the chorus of the tune, "My Salvation Army Queen" (sung in the show by Cole himself, as Lawrence Thorne) bear out:

> My little Salvation Army queen,
> My little Salvation Army queen.
> She was so seraphic

That she blocked the traffic
When she beat that tambourine.
And like an angel, divinely tall,
She shouted, "Down with King Alcohol!"
So when I once found she flirted
I was very soon converted
By my blue-eyed Christian soldier,
My Salvation Army queen.

The lines from another number in the show, "My Houseboat on the Thames," also show Cole's way with words as a collegian:

On my houseboat (on the) Thames,
On my houseboat (on the) Thames,.
It's a jolly ripping vessel to relax on,
For its deuced dull and deadly Anglo-Saxon.
We have Punch on board, I think,
One to read, and one to drink.
And when we're bored and feeling undone,
We can wander up to London
On my houseboat on the Thames.

Though much of Cole's material for his Yale shows has disappeared, most of his manuscript score for *The Pot of Gold* is still extant. It is thus possible to approximate how this smoker entertainment came off when it was first produced at the DKE fraternity house at Yale on November 26, 1912, and—presumably to meet public demand—at New Haven's Hotel Taft the following December 4. Cole himself has described the overture to *The Pot of Gold*, which contains a good sampling of the musical numbers that follow, in this rather convoluted manner:

It begins with the motif—Chlodoswinde's [Chlodoswinde Delor, the heroine] yearning for Larry [Lawrence Thornton]; then follows the waltz representing her pangs on finding him false, ending in the motif of supreme happiness, which appears again at the end of the play. Following this comes Larry's love song. Then a thing in 5/4 time introducing the foreign influence on the hotel, modulating into a death march representing the monotony and decadence of the place. This is connected with the opening chorus by a movement which grows more excited as it progresses.

Irrespective of Cole's quasitechnical analysis of leitmotifs in *The Pot of Gold* worthy of a poor-man's Wagner, the music for the show as a whole is quite good, particularly for a twenty-one-year-old. It reflects elements of Gilbert and Sullivan, Viennese operetta, Russian folk song (for the Russian characters in the show), and Broadway, tastefully combined with bright lyrics. Among the numbers written for *The Pot of Gold*, two of them saw extra duty, a practice Cole followed whenever feasible. For instance, when one of the numbers, "If I Were Only a Football Man," was deleted from the show, it became instead, "A Football King," one of Cole's most popular solo pieces with the school glee club. Another number, "When I Used to Lead the Ballet," which did appear in *The Pot of Gold*, Cole also incorporated into his first professional Broadway production, *See America First*, in 1916.

In getting his musicals ready for their New Haven premieres, Cole had a hand in practically every aspect of their production—staging, costuming, lighting, scriptwriting, and so on. For as is often the case in musical comedy, the opening-night curtain reflects the close collaboration of many minds and talents and the give and take that implies. However, once he had completed the score—usually after much consultation with his peers—Cole's prime responsibility was to prepare the cast for their singing roles. Coaching at the piano—singing, playing, demonstrating—Cole gradually got his fellow students, many of whom could barely carry a tune, to project his lyrics and melodies with the seeming confidence of professionals. It was fine training for all concerned, especially for Cole, who was learning his craft by doing it. When one musical phrase or line of text didn't work, he simply substituted another. That the end justified the means for Cole might be inferred from the review of his contributions to *The Kaleidoscope* that appeared in the *Yale News* on May 7, 1913: "Let it be said at the outset that Cole Porter's music . . . has all the swing, dash, 'whistly' and catchy qualities necessary for musical comedy. It makes your feet tingle and shuffle, and your eyes close in the ecstasy that people who sit at classical concerts sometimes imitate."

Most of Cole's friends at Yale, like Arnold Whitridge, Almet Jenks, Johnfritz Achelis, Gerald Murphy, and Monty Woolley, either participated in his school musicals or were fellow members of one or more of the various clubs and fraternities to which he belonged. In many respects Cole and his friends were cut from the same cloth. They were invariably bright and personable and came from good, well-to-do families, though a number of them—like Robert Lehman, probably best known now for his contribution of the widely publicized Lehman wing and art collection to the Metropolitan Museum of Art, of the investment-banking family, or Leonard Hanna, son of the Cleveland industrialist, or Vanderbilt Webb, of the Vanderbilt clan—were definitely upper crust in terms of family wealth and prestige.

As one of Yale's brightest lights on campus, Cole came to know an enormous number of students, including those not in his class. As he came to know everybody who was anybody on campus, Cole was invited to the best homes in New Haven and out of town and became a regular at the "best" parties given by his club and fraternity members and other friends. Just as his mother made a big social splash in Peru—judging by press accounts—from his solo appearances as a child violinist, so, too, Cole, practically from the moment he set foot in New Haven, used his musical talents to better his social standing. With his songwriting and performing abilities, plus his sparkling wit and repartee, Cole came to be in great demand at social events.

Cole particularly loved to trade small talk and gossip at the various shindigs he attended. "What's the latest dirt?" became one of Cole's catch-phrases at Yale and remained with him the rest of his life, as did his habit of rather heavy smoking and drinking in social situations.

Little is known about when or where Cole's homosexuality began, though it would not be unreasonable to assume that he had manifested it in some manner while attending all-male schools away from home. As a matter of fact, in view of Cole's later well-documented preference for virile, big-muscled men, one might question whether his association in various capacities with the Yale football team was not such a manifestation. Yet as one of Cole's Yale classmates has stated, "Cole would be seen just as often with women as with men on social occasions. Even if one had suspected something because of his close friendship with Monty Woolley and Leonard Hanna, both clearly homosexual, there was nothing, really, to confirm those suspicions. Besides, Cole was so bright and talented, one expected him to be a little different."

And he was. For though Cole's family background may have been solidly small-town, grass-roots Middle America, he came to be accepted in collegiate circles as the personification of eastern, big-city sophistication. Cole, moreover, doted on being a collegiate celebrity and on the life that went with it. He made a point of writing to his mother regularly with news of his musical and social triumphs. Kate, in turn, avidly followed his ever-increasing eminence at Yale by keeping a scrapbook devoted to him. In it she pasted press clippings and memorabilia of all kinds connected with his exciting collegiate goings-on. She empathized so closely with Cole that presumably every accolade for him became one for herself.

Besides the personal satisfaction she derived from her burgeoning scrapbook on Cole, Kate also used the material in it as leverage on J.O., who often complained that his grandson was wasting time at college with all his foolish musical activities. If Kate did not completely pacify J.O. with her tactics, she at least kept him from cutting off his financial support for Cole at school, something he had threatened to do. J.O. kept the generous monthly checks coming to Cole, but his grumbling persisted. He even tried to get Cole to do heavy manual farm labor during the summers away from Yale, so as to learn about managing the family's interests from the ground up. But Cole and Kate strongly rebelled at the idea, and J.O. backed down. But Cole and Kate's united front could not persistently go counter to J.O.'s wishes, especially since he controlled the family's finances. So when J.O. strongly indicated his desire for Cole to go on to law school after college and concentrate on a legal career, both mother and son reluctantly acceded to his plan. J.O. had too much financial clout to be denied.

With a future law career hanging over his head, Cole—thanks to Kate serving as a buffer between himself and J.O.—still continued to lead the good life at Yale, doing what pleased him most. That included regular visits to Broadway to keep abreast of the latest trends in musical comedy and to savor the hustle and bustle of the big town. It also included the propagation of a number of tall stories about himself on the Yale campus that boosted his stock as a worldly musical figure. For example, the Sunday *New Haven Register* of November 12, 1911, contained a long article on Cole writing "Bingo Eli Yale" and other school football songs. In discussing Cole's talents, the article alleged that "some of the peculiar and distinctive features of his work have been explained by the fact that he spent several years in the mountains of Rumania, and heard many strange birds while up there." The *Register* article may have had little to do with actual fact, but it made interesting reading. That Cole, perhaps in emulation of Kate's lying in his behalf, planted the exotic reference to Rumania in the article for his own interests can be readily deduced. For many other highly romantic, if inaccurate, stories about himself, as we shall see, subsequently emanated from his fertile brain as well.

But Cole could also change the record to suit himself on less exalted levels than the Rumanian caper. At Yale, for instance, Cole claimed that his father was no longer active in business. Sam Porter was thus described in Cole's graduating yearbook as retired, rather than as an unglamorous Peru pharmacist. Nor did Cole own up to his real age at Yale, for he continued to make himself two years younger than he actually was. Even after Kate—for reasons that are not clear—signed a notarized affidavit in Peru in 1919 formally attesting to the fact that he was born on June 9, 1891, Cole still tampered with his age. On his 1933 passport, for example, Cole took off a year, claiming he was born in 1892. By 1949, however, on another passport, he was back to deducting two years from his age. On both passports, moreover, he conveniently added two inches to his height, listing himself as five-eight rather than his actual five-six.

While maintaining his hectic involvement with Yale's musical and social life, Cole was on reasonably good terms with most of his peers. True, some students found him a bit of an oddball with his loud dress and extraordinary interest in things theatrical: His graduating class, as a matter of fact, considered him one of their most eccentric members, while voting him the most entertaining in their group. But Cole invariably displayed great tact in his campus dealings. He scrupulously avoided arguments and confrontations, and went out of his way not to ruffle other people's feelings. In later life these traits stood him in good stead in his relations with temperamental, high-powered actors, directors, musicians, and other Broadway and Hollywood professionals. He would ordinarily try to express himself as diplomatically as possible. In fact, after he had established his reputation in the music field, Cole would frequently use the ruse of having an intermediary speak for him at rehearsals. That job often fell to Dr. Albert Sirmay, a well-trained musician who had studied at the Royal Academy of Music in Budapest. Sirmay was Cole's close friend and his music editor for many years at the publishing firms of both Harms and Chappell. It would be Sirmay's duty to suggest changes in tempo, phrasing, orchestration, and so on during rehearsals. In a few cases Cole would speak up and make suggestions himself, but usually only after first claiming that he was doing so at Sirmay's bidding. But whether Sirmay or Cole was involved, this approach generally worked out very smoothly. However, Robert Russell Bennett, the famous orchestrator who has been closely associated with many of Cole's musicals, recalls one instance when Cole's tactics not only backfired, but revealed him to be rather cowardly. During an out-of-town tryout of one of his shows prior to a Broadway opening, the musical director became so exasperated with Cole's many suggestions that he dramatically threatened—in jest—to take a gun out of his pocket and shoot Cole if he didn't desist. The musical director even made a gesture toward his pocket, as though he had a gun there. Cole took him at his word and was so intimidated by the threat that he hired a burly bodyguard to be near him whenever he had to deal with the musical director. Though Cole never found out that he had been duped, many in the know had a big laugh at his less-than-heroic behavior.

Cole graduated from Yale in the spring of 1913. To commemorate the occasion there was the usual rash of graduation parties, as well as the commencement itself, in which Cole and a small contingent of Yale's most illustrious seniors led the class march. There was also the inevitable exchange of promises among the departing men to keep in touch with each other. In Cole's case these assurances were not idly given, for he had already agreed to write material for future smokers at the school, even though he expected to be attending Harvard the following fall. For despite his spectacularly poor academic record as a collegian, Cole was accepted at Harvard Law School.

Since first coming East from Peru as a fourteen-year-old (masquerading as a twelve-year-old), Cole had made great strides, particularly at Yale, and he could look back at four years of extraordinary creative ferment. After arriving at the campus as an undersized, overdressed freshman, he had made his presence felt in remarkably short order with his football songs, glee-club renditions, smoker musicals, social activities, and friendships. At Yale, too, Cole had become an ambitious sophisticate. He could also thank the university for lending direction to his life, though less from the result of scholarly pursuits than from the opportunity it had afforded him to develop as a composer-lyricist. But because of the many chancy elements involved in making a successful career in musical theater outside Yale's cloistered halls, Cole undoubtedly left with mixed feelings, especially since with the start of fall classes at Harvard Law School almost upon him, the question of whether he could survive Cambridge's perhaps forbidding scholarly demands and yet manage to follow his own artistic inclinations still had to be resolved.

As a graduation gift during that summer and as a balm for any qualms he might have had about his immediate future, Kate had gotten J.O to agree to a vacation trip to England. There he explored the glorious countryside with several of his Yale chums. On his return home Cole was too busy preparing for Harvard to ponder his future. But as it turned out, the answer was not too long in coming.

5

The Expatriate

For at least a month or two after starting classes at Harvard's venerable law school in September, 1913, Cole went through the motions of being a dutiful student. During this initial period he attended lectures fairly regularly and often stayed up late poring over his texts and fulfilling school assignments. He even thought enough of one of his completed assignments—a sample brief in which he, as counsel, argued for the plaintiff in a slander case—to send a copy of it to Peru, presumably for J.O. and Kate's delectation. It didn't take Cole too long, however, to see that the courses required of a first-year law student—"Agency," "Civil Procedure at Common Law," "Contracts," "Criminal Law and Procedure," "Property," and "Torts"—were not to his liking, and that he had neither the ability nor the inclination to be a lawyer. With that realization came a concomitant slackening of interest in legal matters at Harvard. Where he had started out at a moderate running pace in quest of the law degree that would please J.O., he soon slowed down to a deliberate walk. Cole and law didn't seem to mix, and he knew it.

But Cole and songwriting continued to be as compatible as ever. For in almost inverse proportion to his declining enthusiasm for a career as a lawyer, his affection for musical theater seemed to be steadily increasing. Unquestionably Cole's fondness for musical comedy was stimulated by his being in such great demand as a composer-lyricist for Yale smoker entertainments. Once he had resolved against a future legal career, he concentrated on his major area of interest, turning his attention and his talent to writing the score for another Yale musical. The sound of Cole's piano now emanated most consistently from his room in Craigie Hall on Harvard's campus as he applied himself to his chosen task. Legal briefs were forgotten.

With T. Lawrason Riggs, his roommate at Craigie Hall, Cole collaborated on a two-act musical farce for Yale's Dramatic Association. Riggs, a Scroll and Key fraternity brother of Cole's from the Yale class of 1910, was then taking graduate courses in English literature. Their plot, as befitting one for a Yale smoker, was typically nonsensical. It concerned itself with Cyril Chester, the fictional undergraduate president of the Yale Dramatic Association (YDA), who finds himself in the mythical kingdom of Paranoia, remotely located in the Balkan peninsula between Scutari and Montenegro. While in Paranoia, Chester falls in love with Princess Vodka, the king's daughter. He also rallies the military to help save the country from falling into the hands of conspirators. When King Trszchka (laughingly pronounced Tosh, according to Cole and Riggs) of Paranoia abdicates in favor of his daughter, Chester marries Princess Vodka and winds up as king himself. The curtain comes down with Paranoians reveling in the knowledge that a Yale man is now king of their country.

Originally called *The Belle of the Balkans,* Cole and Riggs ultimately settled on the more ludicrous title, *Paranoia, or Chester of the Y.D.A.,* for their musical. Though both were credited as joint creators of their "melopedrama in two acts" in the printed program, it is reasonable to assume that the music and lyrics were mainly Cole's, while the book was essentially Riggs's. The lyrics in particular have many of the impudent, offbeat qualities of the early Porter. From the opening chorus, in which Paranoia is described as "a kingdom behind the beyond," to the finale, with its salute to the new Paranoian king and queen ("Hail, hail to Cyril, unconquerable king! Hail, hail to Vodka, her praises loudly sing!"), there are the numerous touches, deft and saucy, that are unmistakably Cole's. Especially praiseworthy—as well as prophetic, for it anticipated somewhat Cole's subsequent life-style—was the number "I've a Shooting Box in Scotland," which extolled the pleasures of collecting country places all over the globe: a chateau in Touraine; a chalet in the Interlaken Valley;

a hacienda in Spain; or a villa close to Rome. The number ended reassuringly on a self-satisfied note. "When traveling," went the lyrics, "it's really quite a comfort to know that you're never far from home."

Cole, as with his other Yale musicals, took an active part in preparing *Paranoia* for its showing in New Haven on April 24, 1914, at the Hotel Taft. Cole had again tailored his score to the personalities and abilities of the participants. Most of the key parts in *Paranoia* were performed by students who had proven themselves in previous smoker entertainments by Cole. The role of Princess Vodka, for example, went to senior Rufus King, who had successfully played women's parts in *And the Villain Still Pursued Her* and *The Kaleidoscope*. Similarly, seniors Newbold Noyes and Stoddard King, as Cyril Chester and King Trszchka respectively, had also previously demonstrated what they could do. Archibald MacLeish, too, had a part in *Paranoia*—that of a Nubian slave—while Edgar Montillion Woolley, now better known as Monty Woolley, the villain of *And the Villain Still Pursued Her* and the newly appointed head of the Dramatic Association, produced and directed the show.

With Woolley sparing no expense—at least, for a Yale smoker—in putting *Paranoia* on the boards, the Dramatic Association decided to go public in order to help defray mounting costs. Instead of limiting its audience solely to its members, who were admitted free, the association democratically opened its doors to Yale's general student body, but for a price: one dollar admission. A large student turnout stayed to cheer, attesting to value received. "The most elaborate and entertaining smoker-play that the Dramat has ever given," was the verdict of the *Yale News*, while adding, "Mr. Porter has never written more 'whistleable' tunes." As for the team of Riggs and Porter, the *News* labeled them "the Gilbert and Sullivan combination of college dramatics."

Hardly had the cheers for *Paranoia* died down before Cole was involved in another Yale musical, this time for an alumni group, the Western Federation of Yale Clubs, whose annual reunion was scheduled to be held in Cincinnati in May of 1914. This group had heard so much about Cole's musicals for the Dramatic Association smokers that he and a nucleus of the association were invited to come to Cincinnati to perform at the alumni reunion. As incentive for Cole and his cohorts to make the trip west, the alumni group promised to entertain them in high style.

Cole and his friends—and they included Monty Woolley, Johnfritz Achelis, and Newbold Noyes—were wined and dined, invited to all the best parties, and generally feted as though they were royalty. In return,

Cole came up with a wildly incongruous two-act burlesque of Mexican revolutionaries and Yale campus life that he and his associates performed to a turn at the Gibson House in Cincinnati on the evening of May 22, 1914. With the audience holding their sides from laughter, the musical, entitled *We're All Dressed Up and We Don't Know Huerta Go*, focused first on Mexico and its tyrannical, real-life revolutionary, Huerta. By the second act Huerta had captured the United States and had conveniently moved the capitol from Washington, D. C., to the Yale campus in New Haven. The farce ended with the performers grouped around the Old Yale Fence singing, in best collegiate fashion, "In Cincinnati," newly written for the occasion, in honor of the host city.

The Huerta opus was received so favorably by the alumni group that Cole and the Dramatic Association performers were invited back a few years later to take part in another of their annual reunions, this time in Cleveland. Though Cole could not attend the festivities on this occasion, he did contribute a new number for the entertainment, and in highly dramatic fashion. He sent a voluminous—and expensive—telegram containing all the lyrics for the new song, "Cleveland," to the Dramat performers at the very last moment, just before they entrained for their destination—which meant they had to learn the song's lines en route. These lyrics for "Cleveland" are one of the two key mementos (the other is the song, "In Cincinnati") that still exist of Cole's contributions to the Ohio reunions of Yale's Western alumni group. All his other numbers for their shindigs, unfortunately, have been lost.

While he was turning out songs for Yale and its alumni during his first year at Harvard, Cole did not hesitate to inform Kate of his musical activities. He and she carefully held back the news from J.O., however, with the result that Cole kept getting his regular monthly allowance from Peru with no questions asked, just as if he were conscientiously attending law classes. To further appease J.O., Cole did not break ties with Harvard as a second-year graduate student. For at the suggestion of a Harvard Law School dean, Ezra Ripley Thayer, who had heard Cole perform his songs at a Cambridge smoker, he switched—again without telling J.O., only Kate knew of the move—to the Harvard Graduate School of Arts and Sciences for the academic year 1914–15, presumably to major in music. But once more Cole did not apply himself very diligently to his studies. Enrolling in only two courses during the year—one in music appreciation and the other in basic harmony—Cole's work as a graduate music student still left much to be desired. The few harmony and counterpoint

exercises that exist of his Harvard music studies are often more interesting for his assorted doodles of women—dressed and undressed—than for
the exercises themselves.

During his second year in Cambridge Cole moved from his dormitory
room in Craigie Hall to a house at One Mercer Circle, which he shared
with a contingent of former Scroll and Key members, including Riggs
and Dean Acheson, studying then at Harvard. There were the usual
quota of parties at the house, for Cole loved to be in the social swim, and
partying—usually of the most imaginative kind—would invariably happen where he was. Monty Woolley, for example, tells of the time when
he and Cole, as students at Yale, dreamed up a "Prince of Wales" party.
They contacted about fifty of their closest Yale friends and invited them
to meet the prince at an inn near New Haven. Each student was asked
to assume the name and rank of a member of British nobility and to dress
in an appropriate costume, complete with decorations. On the appointed
day horse-drawn carriages with liveried drivers, all hired for the event,
brought the costumed students to meet the prince, who, it turned out,
was Cole himself in an Eton collar and knee pants. He played the princely
role to the hilt, acknowledging the introductions with grace and appropriate comments, as perhaps might be expected from someone who later
became known for his elegant, even royal, demeanor.

Not all of Cole's student parties, of course, were quite so genteel.
Occasionally, for instance, he and Woolley would take their chances at
crashing the Marie Antoinette, a hotel on upper Broadway operated by
Woolley's father, a successful hotel entrepreneur. Stealing a pass key,
Woolley would smuggle Cole and other friends into a large, unoccupied
suite at the hotel, from which they would telephone room service for an
assortment of delicacies, along with chilled champagne. They would then
have a merry time eating and drinking on the house; that is, except when
management got wind of their shenanigans and broke up the party before
it got off the ground.

Cole was in great demand at parties because of his ebullience and wit,
plus his reputation as a personality. When he was in stimulating company, Cole's charm was awesome. His dark eyes would light up; his
white, even teeth would be framed in a stunning smile; and ideas would
pour forth with extraordinary rapidity, betraying a slight lisp as he
spoke. He literally glowed in any exchange that interested or amused
him. Just as quickly, if the going became slightly tedious, he would
become almost another person: nervous and withdrawn, the glow gone,
the eyes clouded. This side of Cole was not especially noticeable when

he was a young man, for he was too adroit and politic, and still terribly concerned with making his way in the world and of showing a proper face. As his fame and social commitments increased, however, his low boredom threshold could hardly be disguised. In a roomful of elegantly dressed people, chattering away, he would turn inward if he was bored, and become completely oblivious to the crowd.

Cole also had other ways of coping with boredom. When things became too dull for him at parties, he would frequently leave quietly and unobtrusively, without a word to his host; he considered any farewell gestures or remarks in such cases wholly superfluous. As a host himself, especially after he had become famous, he would think nothing of extending his hand without warning when a party's momentum had slackened and imperiously say good-bye to his guests. That signaled the end of the gathering.

But no matter which approach Cole used, he was constantly concerned with avoiding ennui. As Cole himself once stated, "I have spent my life escaping boredom, not because I am bored, but because I do not want to be."

Yet contrary to that reassuring statement, Cole presumably must have experienced great boredom (when and why is not clear. Did it first happen, for example, while he was a child in Peru, or was it later?) for him to be so fearful of its consequences. That hypothesis is indirectly supported by one of Cole's lesser-known numbers, "Poor Young Millionaire." Written during the twenties and never published or performed in any show, this song emphasizes boredom so noticeably that its lyrics—which focus on the words *tired* and *bored*—seem to have evolved from bitter personal experience.

> After hunting all over for pleasure
> With some measure of success,
> I've decided the pace known as rapid
> Leads to vapid nothingness.
> And I'm tired of betting,
> Tired of sporting,
> Tired of flirting,
> Tired of courting,
> Tired of racing,
> Tired of yachting,
> Tired of loafing,
> Tired of rotting,

Tired of dining,
Tired of wining,
Tired of being,
Tired, tired, tired.
Oh won't somebody care
For a poor young millionaire.
If you knew what blues meant
You'd find me amusement.
I've had every thrill
From a Rolls-Royce to a Ford.
And there's no concealing
The fact I'm feeling
Bored, bored, bored.

Fortunately, Cole had little chance to be bored during his Yale and Harvard days, due, in good part, to his frequent social rounds with a continually widening circle of wealthy and influential friends. As his social parameters broadened Cole became a great favorite of the New York and Easthampton society set, who fell madly in love with his pixie-ish ways and sparkling songs.

Among this socially prominent group, Elisabeth "Bessie" Marbury proved especially helpful in launching Cole's career on Broadway. Miss Marbury, who apparently knew all of society's elite and doubled as a theatrical producer and agent, took a strong personal interest in Cole's career. Through her Cole not only met important socialites but also numerous Broadway professionals, like comedian-producer Lew Fields and composers Jerome Kern and Sigmund Romberg. She was also instrumental in getting a Porter song, "Esmeralda," interpolated into a Romberg musical, *Hands Up.* This show ran for only fifty-two performances after opening at the Forty-fourth Street Theater on July 22, 1915, and "Esmeralda" died with it, but at least Cole could claim he had made Broadway.

Bessie Marbury had a hand, too, in placing another of Cole's songs, "Two Big Eyes," with lyrics by John Golden, in a Jerome Kern musical, *Miss Information,* which opened at the George M. Cohan Theater on October 5, 1915. Like *Hands Up,* this musical, along with Cole's song, disappeared after only forty-seven performances. What mattered to Cole, though, was his expanding contacts as a songwriter, for he now felt emboldened enough by his new professional affiliations to speak out about it to his grandfather. "Tell grandad," Cole urged Kate in a wire to her on May 25, 1915, "that Lew Fields gave me fifty dollars for each song I sold him and [eventually] four cents on each copy [of published music]." Though it is not clear which songs Cole referred to in his wire, his pride in getting paid is what comes through in the message. At long last he had realized an income, although a modest one, from his songs, which was an important consideration in J.O.'s eyes, and Cole made certain that his grandfather learned of the news.

Cole also made certain that Kate and J.O. learned of Bessie Marbury's interest in producing a show of his on Broadway the following season. "Tell grandad," Cole wired Kate on December 15, 1915, that "unless something extraordinary happens [the] show will go into rehearsal in a few weeks." The show in question was *See America First*, a spoof of flag-waving musicals (presumably of the kind associated with George M. Cohan, like *Little Johnny Jones* of 1904, and *George Washington, Jr.* of 1906, which contained such Cohan flag-waving numbers as "Yankee Doodle Boy" and "You're a Grand Old Flag") that Cole and Lawrason Riggs had collaborated on. Drawing on earlier Porter songs, mainly from *Paranoia, or Chester of the Y.D.A.* of 1914, plus newly written ones, Cole and Riggs devised a hodgepodge of a plot for *See America First* similar to the zany scripts that had titillated countless Yale men at smoker entertainments. The book touched on many bases: the Wild West; an English duke disguised as a cowhand; a wealthy American politician, Senator Huggins, and his daughter, Polly, at odds with each other because he loved everything American and she did not; cowboys and Indians; and a mélange of other characters, ideas, and settings.

The strange mixture that constituted the plot for *See America First* also characterized the way Bessie Marbury produced the show. Putting it bluntly, the production ingredients that went into *See America First* reflected her social and theatrical background, but so combined as to make an indigestible mess. To begin with, she chose Dorothie Bigelow, a young, pretty Englishwoman of impeccable social credentials lacking in experience as a singer and an actress, to play Polly, the female lead. Dorothie Bigelow first came to Bessie Marbury's attention after she had arrived in New York from London in 1915. She had been sent to the United States by her highly placed English family to escape the turmoil and strife of Great Britain during World War I. New York society quickly took to Dorothie on her arrival, especially wealthy Mrs. O. H. P. Belmont, who announced her intention of producing a musical dealing with the suffragette movement that would star the young Englishwoman. When that musical did not pan out, Bessie Marbury claimed Dorothie

Bigelow for her own show. She surrounded her with some role-hardened professionals like Felix Adler as the Indian chief, Blood-in-His-Eye, but most of the cast members were new to Broadway, including Clifton Webb, originally a ballet dancer from Indianapolis, who was making his debut as an actor. Nor did the director, Benrimo, have much experience. If to this mixed bag of talent one added the relatively unknown team—outside of Yale circles, that is—of Porter and Riggs in their first attempt at creating a full-scale musical for Broadway, it is easy to see why the betting odds did not favor a successful opening-night curtain.

Bessie Marbury's undue emphasis on the social rather than the purely professional aspects of theatrical producing was especially noticeable in her financing of *See America First*. In getting backing for her show she turned to many of her society friends for financial support, among them feminist Anne Morgan of the Morgan banking family and Elsie de Wolfe, an amateur actress who became famous as a decorator. As a matter of fact, in order to accommodate the large social contingent interested in the show, Miss Marbury decided to present the initial Broadway performance of *See America First* to a veritable who's who of society before opening the show's doors to the press and general public. Thus, after a series of out-of-town tryouts between February 22 and March 23, 1916, the show opened to the bravos of society's blue bloods on March 27, 1916, at the Maxine Elliott Theater. Dorothie Bigelow and the other performers, as well as Cole and Riggs, could do no wrong in the eyes of the select audience that evening, and all concerned with the production of *See America First* were cheered enthusiastically.

It was another story when New York's first-line theater critics reviewed the new comic opera, as it was now called, after it officially opened at the Maxine Elliott the following night, on March 28. Almost unanimously, the critics found fault with nearly all aspects of the production. Dorothie Bigelow "looked very pretty, but her singing voice was inadequate in volume, small in range and not very beautiful in quality," carped the *Herald*'s critic. He also found fault with Cole's and Riggs's contributions. "Its plot is silly, its music unimpressive," wrote the *Herald* reviewer of *See America First*, while conceding that "it would be delightful as a college play, with the 'boys' rah-rahing and the audience consisting of fond relatives." The *Tribune* critic made a similar assessment: "Gotham is a big town," went the review, "and it may be that the sisters, aunts, and cousins of its Yale men will be sufficient to guarantee prosperity for *See America First*. Therein, at all events, lies its best chance." Though there were a number of positive comments in the reviews about the performances of Felix Adler, Clifton Webb, and several other members of the cast, as well as about the quality of Cole's lyrics and the similarities in approach between the Riggs-Porter team and Gilbert and Sullivan, the consensus of the press was highly unfavorable. With the reviewers lined up so solidly against it, the play lasted only fifteen performances.

The failure of *See America First* has been explained differently by two of its key participants. Dorothie Bigelow, for one, has laid the blame squarely on Riggs and his book for the show. Conversely, Riggs, in an underhanded slap at Dorothie Bigelow, attributed the demise of the show largely "to the fact that the composer and I consented to complete transformation of the piece to meet the capabilities of its interpreters and the supposed taste of the public." Riggs went on: "We suffered, in addition to our disappointment, the unsatisfactory feeling that nothing had been proved as to the worth of our efforts. But we are wiser as well as sadder, and for myself I have done with attempts at dramatic composition, so far as I can foresee." Riggs, as it turned out, lived up to this declaration, made in a letter to Yale's alumni magazine, by completely giving up the musical theater after *See America First*. He subsequently converted to Roman Catholicism, joined the priesthood, and became a chaplain at Yale.

Despite the quick demise of *See America First* and the doom-and-gloom ramifications inherent in such a failure, many of those associated with the show, including Cole, went on to greater glory. For example, Walter Wanger, a young production assistant from Dartmouth, eventually became a famous movie producer, while Clifton Webb, after a fine career on Broadway as a song-and-dance man, became even better known as a Hollywood actor. Some substantial benefits, both direct and indirect, accrued to Cole. One of the more significant direct gains was the publication by G. Schirmer of thirteen of the show's songs, including the title tune and four numbers originally written for *Paranoia*: "I've a Shooting Box in Scotland," "Prithee Come Crusading with Me," "The Language of Flowers," and "Slow Sinks the Sun." Still another published number, "When I Used to Lead the Ballet," had originally been performed in *The Pot of Gold* of 1912. Of the published numbers, one of them—"I've a Shooting Box in Scotland"—was even recorded for Victor, in 1916, by the Joseph C. Smith Orchestra. It is the first commercial recording of Cole's songs.

But perhaps the most important benefit for Cole from *See America First* derived indirectly from the show and was a long-term financial one. For on December 6, 1916, J.O. set up a trust for Cole to receive income from his grandfather's one-half interest in real estate holdings in West Virginia and Kentucky, which he had purchased with a partner, Clinton Crane. The trust, called the Cole and Crane Real Estate Fund, provided for Cole to get a substantial annual income from J.O.'s holdings after the death of the two partners. Inasmuch as both partners were in their eighties at the time the trust was set up, it is reasonable to assume that J.O. anticipated that Cole would receive the money fairly soon. It is also reasonable to assume that the setting up of the trust so soon after the opening of *See America First* indicated that J.O. had reconciled himself to his grandson's songwriting pursuits—in spite of his previous tirades against a musical career—and had given up on Cole ever being a lawyer or a businessman.

Many reports, especially those circulated by Cole himself in later years, have supported the notion that he was so depressed by the poor critical reception of *See America First* that he hid himself from his friends, refusing to see them, and joined the French Foreign Legion not long after the show's closing. Actually Cole did not leave the United States until almost a year and a half after *See America First* hit the dust, and was as much a bon vivant as ever during this period. Elsa Maxwell, the famous party-giver, described in her 1954 autobiography, *R.S.V.P.*, her first impressions on being introduced to Cole at a party in 1916, after *See America First* had closed. She hardly paints a portrait of someone depressed. For on meeting Cole, in her words,

> I felt antagonistic toward him. I thought he was trying to be excessively cute, and I've always been allergic to that approach in men and women, adults and children. Further, he was dressed too immaculately for a young composer who had been roasted by the critics. I had seen too many gigolos in Europe to be taken in by fine feathers. I pegged him for a phony, easily the worst snap judgment I made. . . .
>
> "You must be flat broke or else you wouldn't dress so well," I said rudely in my annoyance.
>
> Cole waved airily, "All on tick, grandpa's tick." I saw that he was tight and that, too, rubbed me the wrong way. I've never been able to tolerate people who drink too much, although I must confess that Cole made a large dent in that prejudice in later years. . . .
>
> The buzz of conversation in the room went on when Cole sat at the piano and played a few bars from *See America First*. The music was unfamiliar and so was the first number he sang, but at the end of it everyone was straining to catch the droll nuances of his lyrics. He held a critical audience enraptured. . . .

Cole wove a spell with his songs on many other party audiences while deciding on his next move. For a while he lived at the Yale Club in New York before taking an apartment on East Nineteenth Street, ostensibly, so far as his family was concerned, to study serious composition with Pietro Alessandro Yon, an eminent Italian musician, then organist at St. Francis-Xavier's in Manhattan. But, not unexpectedly, Cole's apartment turned out to be the scene of numerous glittering parties rather than a place for concentrated musical study.

Cole might have continued the partying indefinitely had not World War I interfered. For on April 6, 1917, after nearly three years of proclaimed neutrality in the European war between the Allies and the Central Powers, the United States Congress declared war on Germany when its submarines began sinking American ships as a protest against American shipments of arms and goods to the Allies. As America aligned itself with England and its other allies in "fighting the Boche," and began converting to a full wartime status, Congress passed the Selective Service Act of May, 1917, authorizing President Wilson to draft one million men between the ages of twenty-one and thirty for military service. Before long, as the need for a larger army increased, the age range for military conscription was extended from eighteen to forty-five years. Inasmuch as Cole was going on twenty-six—or twenty-four, according to his school records—at the initiation of the military draft he was presumably eligible for service. Cole, however, never served a day in the American armed forces, nor is it even clear that he registered for the draft. For in July of 1917, along with a zither (unlike most zithers, this specially-made instrument had a small piano keyboard and was thus practically a portable piano) strapped to his back, he sailed for France.

Just as Cole had come to expect special treatment for himself in other respects—whether in getting through college, or in having Kate intercede with J.O. on his behalf, or in his sparkling, continual-round-of-parties life-style—he apparently did not feel compelled to conform to the man-in-the-street mentality where military service was concerned. Whereas most of his friends—like Arnold Whitridge, who became a captain on General Pershing's staff—quickly enlisted for military duty or involved themselves directly with the American war effort, Cole took a somewhat different route. Social-minded to the core, Cole associated himself with an organization founded by Nina Larre Smith Duryea, an American society woman he knew, to help distribute food supplies in wartime France. So instead of the prospects of deadly combat as an American soldier, Cole opted for the more glamorous job of doing volunteer humanitarian work with the social Duryea Relief Party, as no less than the personal aide to the president and founder of the group.

In a letter to Kate, which she passed on to the Peru press—who published it on October 5, 1917, under the heading LETTER FROM COLE PORTER AT THE FRONT—Cole related some of his experiences as a Duryea assistant. Dated September 4, 1917, and emanating from Roye-sur-Somme in France, Cole's letter told of his interviewing over a thousand people in connection with his relief mission and of seeing French aviators and German caterpillars (antiaircraft torches that enveloped planes in flame) in action.

Cole also described coming upon an old French farmwoman living alone in an underground dirt air shelter. She had an interesting story to tell: After her husband and son had been killed by the Germans, she had been taken prisoner by them and sent to Prussia. There she became ill and was brought back to France. Finding her home and property gone on her return, she settled for living with her few prized possessions in the underground shelter, where Cole found her.

Despite her age and infirmities, she impressed Cole with her charm and gaiety. Commented Cole, "I love this French race. They're so attractive, so amusing, so wonderfully brave, and so simple—just like children, all of them." Cole added this practical note as well: "We being without a cook, and I being tired of opening canned beans, asked her if she could cook. And she said, 'Oh, Monsieur, of course I can cook.' So I said, 'Pack up your things and jump in this motor.' So here she is, this extraordinary old sport, living in the house with us, working like a Trojan, and cooking delicious omelettes, rabbit chops, and compotes. And she has forgotten her trouble and we've forgotten ours!"

Save for that published letter to Kate, little is known of Cole's involvement as a Duryea aide. Nor is the full scope of his wartime activities in France during 1917 and 1918 very clear. From numerous accounts Cole at least looked the part of a military man, for he often wore a French army uniform of one kind or another. Mysteriously, the uniforms were frequently inconsistent. One day he might be seen in a captain's uniform, another day in a corporal's. To add to the confusion, a wartime Yale alumni report announced that Cole had joined the American Aviation Forces in France. Cole himself maintained that he joined the French Foreign Legion not long after arriving in France, out of disillusionment with the failure of *See America First* and as a gesture of futility.

In describing how he joined the Legion, Cole stated, "I went to a little office in Paris for my physical examination after having asked to enlist.

There was an officer of the Legion there and several soldiers." In laconic, true blood-and-guts fashion, Cole then alleges, "The officer looked up my name and then asked me to get on the scales. After I had been weighed he said to me, 'Now you're in the Foreign Legion.' That was all there was to it and afterwards I was sent immediately to Limoges to go through preliminary training before being sent to the front."

Notwithstanding Cole's statement, nor the numerous published reports—all stemming from Cole—that appeared during his lifetime and after his death about his experiences as a World War I legionnaire, nor the military portrait of him depicted in the 1945 supposedly biographical Porter movie, *Night and Day*, there is *no* evidence that he was actually a member of the French Foreign Legion. Contrary to Cole's allegation of legion affiliation, a careful and extensive search of their records indicates that he was never a member of their ranks. Cole's so-called stint with the legion may have made interesting and glamorous news, but it was entirely fabricated.

Equally fictional are the widely reported accounts of Cole's service in the French army. In these stories, also circulated by Cole himself, he is not only supposed to have served in the French military during World War I after his legion stint, but also to have received the Croix de Guerre from the French government for these services. Cole, however, never served in the French army or, for that matter, in any other army; there are no records to support claims that he did. It is highly questionable whether anyone who needed a bodyguard as protection to cope with a vexed musical director would have been temperamentally suited for active military duty, much less seek out such an assignment.

There have been many allegations bruited about, moreover, concerning Cole's good life in wartime France, that further weaken the tales linking him with the French military. Archibald MacLeish, for example, tells of the time he ran into Cole in Paris in 1917 (not long after MacLeish was to fight in the crucial second battle of the Marne). MacLeish reports that Cole was then "comfortably settled in a house of his own, or at least I assumed it was." As for Cole's reputed army affiliations, MacLeish states, "It never occured to me that he was in military service." Another friend, the late Lt. Col. Sir Rex Benson, who served as a wartime liaison officer between the English and the French, also recalled seeing Cole in Paris, at 22 Place Vendôme. Cole frequently entertained Benson and other friends there during 1917 and 1918 by playing and singing his songs at the piano. As a matter of fact, Cole even managed to have some of his songs performed in London musicals during 1918. One of the numbers,

"Alone with You," written in conjunction with Melville Gideon, was included in the show *Very Good Eddie,* while a second tune, "Altogether Too Fond of You," coauthored by Cole, Gideon, and James Heard, found its way into the production *Telling the Tale.*

By the end of October, 1918, the combined Allied forces, including nearly a million and a half Americans who had seen service in France, had so battered the German military machine and its lines of communication that an end to war seemed imminent. On November 11, shortly after Kaiser Wilhelm II had abdicated, the holocaust officially ended as Marshall Ferdinand Foch, the Allied supreme commander, granted Germany the armistice that country had petitioned for.

With the war's end American servicemen by the shiploads eagerly looked forward to their return home, away from the scenes of battle. Not so Cole. Unlike the doughboys and other American military personnel who often had had to slug it out to the death in the muddy trenches near no-man's-land or in equivalent air and sea battles, Cole had had too interesting a time in Paris and its environs to want to rush home. In certain respects Cole had had the best of all possible worlds in Paris, for he had been where all the excitement was without sharing in the danger of the war itself. He had avoided the constraints and hazards of military service while enjoying some of the thrills, glamour, heroism, and even the pathos inherent in war, and at the same time he had still been prominent on the social scene, had still managed to keep active writing and performing his songs, and had even scored professional points by getting some of his numbers accepted for London productions. Moreover, as a result of his lengthy stay in France, he had come to love the country and its gallant, charming people. Cole and France got along famously. And he intended to savor more of this delicious part of the world before returning to the States.

6

Married Life

Cole took great pleasure in running into old Yale friends like Arnold Whitridge and Archibald MacLeish during his stay in wartime France. Indeed, almost wherever Cole went throughout his life, Yale and his fellow alumni never seemed to be far away. Cole especially saw a lot of heavyset, rumpled, extroverted Monty Woolley during the eight months Woolley spent in France in 1918 as a newly commissioned lieutenant. Resourceful and articulate, Woolley somehow always managed to finagle passes from his superiors on an as-needed basis to join Cole in Paris. Such was their cordial relationship that Cole would inevitably break into loud, affectionate laughter at the mere mention of his friend's name. For years after Yale, Cole and Woolley kept in constant touch by telephone, whether close at home or oceans and continents apart, laughing and chatting away like two schoolboys.

As if permanently seeking the status of undergraduate life, the two also played practical jokes on each other, particularly Cole on Woolley. Knowing, for example, that Woolley was an exceptionally restless sleeper who often looked as if he had been tossed about by a hurricane, Cole made a point of collecting photos—many of them taken himself—of Woolley snoozing to show to friends for laughs. Cole and Woolley also fabricated stories for each other's amusement. Once, in 1939, while in Boston for the tryout of *DuBarry Was a Lady*, Cole called Woolley in New York to ask if he would consider appearing in a musical. "What would be required?" asked Woolley, falling for the bait. "You'll have to do some singing, but waltzing would be even more important," replied Cole. After Woolley had assured Cole he could waltz satisfactorily, he innocently asked what his role would be. "A whoremonger," Cole quickly replied from left field, hanging up amid gales of laughter. Such manic goings-on were typical of the two in action.

Almost the opposite of Woolley's booming-voiced extrovertism was tall, thin, and elegantly debonair Howard Sturges, another of Cole's close companions in wartime France. Born in Providence, Rhode Island, in 1884 to an eminent banking and investing family, Sturges had spent years in France after graduating from Yale in 1908. Like Cole, Sturges was a homosexual. He was also completely at home with the international social set and *au courant* with all the latest society gossip. Like Cole, too, Sturges had started out as a young violinist, but had given up the instrument by the time he went to college. His love for music, though, particularly opera, remained with him all his life, as did his great zest for travel and the cultivation of friendships. Except during his periodic bouts with acute alcoholism, Sturges was warm, amiable, tactful, and generous. He often seemed to live to give pleasure to others. He also had the knack of bringing out the best in people, including Cole. George Santayana, the philosopher and poet, who knew Sturges well, described him as "host and hostess in one, who held court in a soft nest of cushions, of wit, and of tenderness, surrounded by a menagerie of outcast dogs, a swarm of friends and relations, and all the luxuries of life." Sturges was clearly an unusual person. He and Cole soon became fast, lifelong friends after meeting in Paris.

Cole also came to know a beautiful American divorcée, Linda Lee Thomas, who was a leading social figure in Paris. She had moved to France in 1912 shortly after divorcing Edward Russell Thomas, the scion of a prominent, affluent publishing family. Rumor has it that after her divorce she was for a time the mistress of the Spanish Duke of Alba. He had apparently been interested in marrying her, but, as a devout Catholic, he could not. Nonetheless, Linda and the duke remained on good terms even after he had married someone else. Through Linda, as a matter of fact, Cole, too, later became a good friend of the duke's.

When Cole first met Linda in early 1918 at a wedding reception at the Ritz for socialites Ethel Harriman and Henry Russell, she easily qualified as wealthy. Her origins, though, were somewhat more humble. She had been born on November 16, 1883, one of three daughters of William Paca Lee, a Louisville, Kentucky, banker beset with financial problems. Her long-established southern ancestry, however, included a signatory of the Declaration of Independence. Despite her father's monetary problems, the beautiful and poised Linda, as a young belle, went to the best parties and mingled with the finest Kentucky families. Through her social connections she eventually met the handsome and highly sought after Thomas, whose reputation as a sportsman and playboy was well known. After a brief courtship, they were married in Newport shortly before Linda's eighteenth birthday, in the summer of 1901.

As Thomas's wife, Linda wanted for nothing. She was surrounded by enough opulence to stagger the imagination: jewels, servants, yachts, racehorses, and an assortment of homes. Though she was young, Linda proved equal to the task of running the various houses, of handling the servants, and of coping with the vast resources and power put at her disposal. On paper Linda's marriage was literally one in a million, the kind that dreams are made of. She and her husband were both young, attractive, popular, and apparently very much in love—at least at first.

Yet the marriage did not work out, and Thomas must share a good deal of the responsibility for its failure. He was too much the *macho* personality for Linda; too bullheaded, too aggressive. He would just as soon run over a sporting opponent or business competitor as run around him (that trait also surfaced behind the wheel of an automobile, for he was reputedly the first man in the United States to kill someone with a car). Nor did marriage inhibit Thomas's philandering ways; rumors of his escapades with numerous showgirls continually reached the ears of Linda and her friends. To complicate matters further, Linda suffered from a recurring bronchial-asthmatic condition that necessitated her going to a dry climate—and away from Thomas—for relief. These absences only heightened the differences between the two and weakened the relationship further.

Their incompatibility was temporarily overlooked in 1908, when Thomas was threatened with a possible leg amputation (by an interesting coincidence, both of Linda's husbands suffered the threat of leg amputation) as a result of a car accident. Linda stood resolutely by him and helped nurse him back to health. But this reunion was short-lived. After a series of estrangements and reconciliations that appeared doomed to failure from the start, Linda and Thomas finally agreed to divorce in 1912. The settlement called for Linda to receive over a million dollars in stocks, bonds, and other holdings.

When Cole met Linda in 1918 she was truly in her prime. At the age of thirty-five, eight years older than Cole, she was an exquisite woman: tall and slender, with light blue eyes, finely chiseled features, and a husky, smoke-tinged voice (the result of smoking for years in spite of her respiratory problems). Her normally brownish-blonde hair was tinted to a lustrous golden hue—she was one of the first in her set to lighten her hair —that accented her fair skin and blue eyes.

She dressed superbly, with a minimum of frills. Her favorite outfit was a simple black dress set off by just a bit of jewelry. She has been described as one of the outstanding beauties of her time; she was also bright and amusing, had impeccable manners and exceptional taste, and knew all the people considered "right" in her circle: those with real achievement and those with purely social prestige.

Cole and Linda hit it off from the very beginning, helped in part by their many mutual friends as well as their common love of the social scene. Even before they met Cole had learned about Linda's wealth, beauty, and social standing, just as she had known about his gift with words and music. Hearing Cole play and sing only confirmed all that Linda had been told about his talent: Everything stopped when Cole sat down at the piano to entertain at a party. When he took off on one of his merry, witty flights of fancy, nothing was sacred. He would sing his numbers in their original versions and would often also parody them, using off-color and humorous lyrics. He would do the same with tunes by other composers, including Jerome Kern's lovely, rather sentimental number, "They Didn't Believe Me." In Cole's hands this tune became a comic "War Song," which satirized fighting on the front in World War I with lines like:

> And when they ask us how dangerous it was
> We never will tell them, we never will tell them,
> How we fought in some café
> With wild women night and day,
> 'Twas the wonderfullest war you ever knew.

Nor were Cole's close friends immune to his satiric, risqué barbs. His sly allusion, for example, to "playing on Anne Morgan's organ" in one of the parodies would greatly amuse the cognoscenti, aware of its reference to the reputed lesbian relationship among Anne Morgan, Bessie Marbury, and Elsie de Wolfe. But whether Cole performed his numbers straight or parodied them, his talent made a strong impression on Linda.

Linda made an equally strong impression on Cole. Her looks, her clothes, her demeanor and personality, and her sophistication all had a great impact on him. He was especially taken with her grand style of life: the battalion of servants, the chauffeur-driven cars, the lavish homes. Linda may have started out with a somewhat down-at-the-heels, though distinguished, southern lineage, but she could now qualify as wealthy "old money," thanks to Thomas's handsome divorce settlement. And she made the most of it: She collected first-rate antiques and art objects, particularly old Chinese art; she gave the most delightful and lavish parties; she mingled with ease among nobility and royalty; and she cultivated and counted as friends many of the most distinguished minds of the time, among them George Bernard Shaw, John Galsworthy, Winston Churchill, and Bernard Berenson (who not only admired Linda's looks, manners, and dress, but was particularly struck by her almost infallible artistic sense in relation to painting, sculpture, and architecture).

In retrospect, it would appear that Cole and Linda responded so strongly to each other largely because of their many common interests. Moreover, they both had money—Linda's was already at hand, and Cole's was expected in the near future, on a regular basis, from the Cole and Crane trust set up by his grandfather. Cole and Linda undoubtedly also responded to each other's special qualities—Linda to Cole's talent, youthfulness, charm, and sparkling irreverence; Cole to Linda's looks, maturity, worldly sophistication (considerably more advanced than his own), and exquisite taste. Linda, furthermore, had learned from bitter experience that the rip-roaring *machismo* mentality of a Thomas was not to her liking, and Cole represented no threat to her on that count. He liked to be seen in the company of beautiful women, but it would be naive to think that Linda was not aware of Cole's sexual leanings. Since both were highly liberated people ahead of their time in terms of sexual mores, one must assume that Linda essentially accepted Cole on his own terms, though both were discreet enough not to make a big issue of it. Linda also felt completely at home with Cole's closest chums (many of whom were originally her friends), as they did with her. Thus, from a variety of standpoints—social, sexual, aesthetic, and so on—Linda and Cole complemented each other beautifully.

By early 1919 Cole and Linda knew each other well enough to consider marriage, even though Cole was not in a financial position to take a wife until he became eligible for his full inheritance. In an attempt to improve his finances, Cole decided to return to the States to discuss with J.O. the feasibility of realizing his trust-fund income sooner or, at the very least, getting an increase in his monthly allowance—which his grandfather had cut from five hundred to one hundred dollars a month, presumably out of disapproval of what he considered Cole's lack of direction. On the boat back to America Cole was fortunate enough to meet Raymond Hitchcock, a popular comedian and producer then planning the third of his annual *Hitchy-Koo* revues for Broadway. Cole played about a dozen of his songs for him. Hitchcock sat stony-faced during the performance, without comment. Cole naturally feared the worst. But when he finished Hitchcock then and there commissioned Cole to write the music and lyrics for *Hitchy-Koo of 1919*, which became Cole's second complete score for Broadway. Perhaps even more important, Hitchcock also introduced Cole to Max Dreyfus, head of T. B. Harms, one of the most prestigious music publishers in Tin Pan Alley.

Dreyfus, a talented musician himself, had been connected with Tin Pan Alley as a pianist, song plugger, arranger, composer, and publisher. Born in Germany in 1874, he came to New York as a youth to work in the music field. By 1901 he had advanced far enough to purchase a twenty-five percent interest in Harms, a young and floundering publishing company. Through astute signing of composing talent, Dreyfus made Harms a major publishing voice in Tin Pan Alley and became a millionaire many times over along the way. Dreyfus had the rare gift of recognizing the potential of composers early in their careers, among them Jerome Kern, Sigmund Romberg, Rudolf Friml, Vincent Youmans, George Gershwin, Kurt Weill, and Richard Rodgers. On hearing Cole's music, shrewd Dreyfus soon added Porter's name to his list of composers. From 1919 on he published most of Cole's songs.

When *Hitchy-Koo of 1919* opened on Broadway at the Liberty Theater on October 6 of that year it was well received. "The music and lyrics are the work of Cole Porter, who has made a particularly clever job of the lyrics and a good tinkling one of the music," wrote the *Times* critic. Though others responded equally favorably, *Hitchy-Koo* lasted only fifty-six performances on Broadway (however, it later made a year's tour of America's hinterlands).

Regardless of the short New York run for *Hitchy-Koo*, one of Cole's numbers in it, "Old-Fashioned Garden," quickly caught on and became his first big hit. The song had been written at the behest of Hitchcock and his backers, who had cheaply acquired a slew of surplus flower costumes from producer Florenz Ziegfeld, of *Follies* fame. Utilizing the name of his mother's former home in Peru, Old Fashioned Garden Farm, in the title and lyrics, Cole created a lilting tune that played up the flower motifs of the costumes. The number was also uncharacteristically senti-mental—perhaps because of its association with Kate—as it spoke of "the dear days of yore," and highly erroneous as well. It told of phlox, hol-lyhocks, violets, eglantines, columbines, and marigolds all blooming at the same time—an unlikely possibility. Cole eventually realized a small fortune in royalties from the song, as the American public, responding to the gushy sentiments in it, bought thousands of copies of sheet music for it. The tune, on the other hand, never did well in England, perhaps because the British, presumably more savvy to the blooming periods of flowers, reacted adversely to Cole's inaccurate lyrics. Nonetheless, "Old-Fashioned Garden" may have convinced Cole that there was money to be made from sentimental tunes, for, as we shall see, he subsequently wrote others.

The success of "Old-Fashioned Garden" advanced both Cole's reputa-tion as a songwriter and his immediate cash reserves, but it did not put him in the financial position he sought. He had long since gotten used to living high on the hog. Indeed, he had never lived any other way! Yet at the age of twenty-eight, with the imminent prospect of marrying the wealthy (and very classy) Linda Lee Thomas, he was still dependent on a monthly allowance from home. In actuality, this was hardly different from the position he had been in during his school years. Nor did his grandfather agree to increase his monthly allowance or advance the trust-fund income—presumably out of disapproval of Cole's plans to marry when he really had neither solid career nor means of his own for support-ing a wife. Fortunately Kate, as she had done many times before, came to Cole's rescue by promising to augment his allowance as much as she could.

With Kate's help, plus income from the sheet-music sales of "Old-Fashioned Garden" (supplemented by continual advances from Max Dreyfus on projected royalties for the song), and loans coming to more than ten thousand dollars, which Cole eventually paid back, from Yale chum William Crocker of the San Francisco railroad and banking family, Cole apparently felt justified in going ahead with his marriage plans. He returned to Paris in the fall of 1919 and married Linda on December 18, before a French civilian official. A few close friends attended the couple during the brief, nonreligious ceremony. The Paris *Herald* of December 19, 1919, carried this announcement about the wedding: "The marriage of Mr. Cole Porter of Peru, Indiana, who served with the French Army [*sic*] during the war, and Mrs. Lee Thomas [*sic*] of Louisville, Ky., was celebrated yesterday at the Mairie of the Eighteenth Arrondissement.

After a brief visit to cities in the south of France, Mr. and Mrs. Porter will make their home in Paris." (Actually, Cole and Linda visited Italy as well, going as far south as Sicily.)

It seems probable that their honeymoon in France and Italy was one more of the spirit than the flesh, but it set the pattern that Cole and Linda pursued, of traveling frequently and extensively. In the years following their marriage, London, Venice, Monte Carlo, Biarritz, Berlin, Morocco, and Rome, among other places, became favorite stopping-off points on their journeys. The Porters, furthermore, invariably traveled royally (made possible, at least initially, by Linda's money), with a host of friends in their entourage plus several servants, including Cole's valet and Linda's personal maid. One of their more ambitious trips took place in early 1921, when they charted a large riverboat, the *Chonsu,* for a two-month journey up the Nile (similar to one Linda had made with her first husband in 1909). Guided by distinguished English Egyptologists Howard Carter and Lord George Edward Carnarvon (whose excavations in the Valley of the Kings led to the discovery of the tomb of Tutankhamen in 1922), Linda and Cole, with guests Howard Sturges and Martha Hyde, visited temples and excavations at Abydos, Luxor, and Karnak, and additional venerable cities along the Nile. Thanks to Linda and Cole's way of doing things, the trip combined all the luxuries of fine hotel living on the *Chonsu* with exposure to Egyptian history, artifacts, and monuments —a truly civilized way of absorbing culture!

Equally civilized were Linda's musical plans for Cole. Ambitious for him and convinced that his talent extended to serious music as well as popular, Linda tried to interest Serge Diaghilev, the famed impresario of the Ballets Russes, in a ballet by Cole, but nothing came of it. She was unsuccessful, too, in getting Igor Stravinsky to teach Cole harmony and composition; the Russian master quickly declined the suggestion. Nor did her literary friends George Bernard Shaw, John Galsworthy, and Arnold Bennett respond to her offer to pay each of them handsomely for a libretto that Cole could fashion into an opera. Nonetheless, Linda's persistence in seeking to widen Cole's musical horizons was presumably responsible for motivating him in 1920 to attend classes for a short time in orchestration and counterpoint at the Schola Cantorum in Paris, the renowned music school founded in 1894 by composer Vincent d'Indy. Among the mementos of Cole's studies are some brief notes dealing with the elements of a fugue ("la fugue," in Cole's description) and the instruments of a symphony orchestra. Cole also scored for large orchestra a movement apiece from Robert Schumann's first and second piano sonatas as part of his student work there. But evidently little of Cole's exercises at the Schola had any long-range value for him, as he never orchestrated any of his own music or wrote any fugues. In the single instance in which Cole wrote a serious composition—the score for the 1923 ballet, *Within the Quota*—Charles Koechlin, a French musician, orchestrated the piece for him. Probably the most substantial benefit that Cole derived from the Schola was not so much a musical as a public relations one. Over and over in later years he would speak pridefully, for press purposes, of his studies at the Schola and his work with Vincent d'Indy, each of which were minimal at best.

Besides getting Cole to take additional music lessons and to consider writing serious compositions, Linda exerted her influence on him by her smooth and efficient running of her household staff. Under Linda's direction her staff wasted no motions in its gardening, food preparation (of *cordon bleu* quality), or handling any one of hundreds of basic tasks on a regular basis. Moreover, Linda punctiliously kept to a time schedule and expected others to do the same. She had little patience with latecomers at social events. On her orders, food would be served when originally planned, irrespective of the tardy ones.

Cole soon adjusted to Linda's clockwork precision and made it part of his own life pattern, even exceeding her concern with punctuality in some respects. In later years he would often set up arbitrary and rigid timetables from which he would not deviate, or perhaps could not escape. If Cole asked guests to join him for lunch or a trip to the country at, say, 12:53 P.M., he expected them to be there at the appointed time or he would proceed without them. As a privileged person Cole did not hesitate to set rules for others to follow, especially when he thought he could get away with it.

Linda also did not hesitate to make her own rules, but these usually dealt with fashion. With a flawless eye for decoration, form, and detail, she liked to mix together seemingly incongruous things: invaluable antique furniture subtly combined with art deco objects; old paintings hung alongside contemporary ones; simply tailored clothes counterbalanced by priceless jewelry. Her uncommon mixtures were not done merely to be different or for shock value; she had too much taste for that. She did enjoy setting new styles, however. Just as she was the first in her group to tint her hair, to smoke, to flaunt a bright yellow Rolls Royce phaeton in which a huge Old English sheepdog would ride up front with the chauffeur, so, too, Linda led the way in fashion. At a time when Americans were not always socially acceptable, Parisians loved Linda for her adventuresome chic and took to Cole as well, at first, largely because of her. So entrenched did the two become in Parisian society that they were invariably referred to as the *Coleporteurs*, practically never as *Mr. and Mrs.*, which was certainly a cachet of a kind.

After their marriage Cole and Linda lived for a while in her small, attractive house at 3 rue de la Baum in Paris, and also kept a suite at the Ritz, which they maintained for years. Linda, however, soon sold her home for a larger one at 13 rue Monsieur, surrounding a courtyard on a quiet street in the fashionable *quartier des Invalides*. This exquisite house, purchased at the reputed price of a quarter of a million dollars, became the Porters' French base for the remainder of their lives. It evolved, also, into a Parisian showplace, thanks to Linda's furnishings and decorations. Chinese art, mainly statues, lacquered tables, and bowls, predominated, but English and French antiques, many of them traceable to royalty, were also in evidence. The broad circular entrance, complete with a white-and-black marble floor and imposing white marble columns and staircase, set the tone for the house. Close by, the immense drawing room, with its grand piano, white wainscoting, silk taffeta hangings, and richly upholstered cut-velvet sofas and armchairs added to the aura of elegant wealth. There were decorating surprises practically everywhere in the house: platinum wallpaper in one room; zebra-skin floor covering in another; red-lacquered chairs upholstered in white kid in still another.

In this seemingly inexhaustible treasure trove of visual adornments, embellishments, and creature comforts, Cole and Linda had their apartments—separate ones—on the second floor of the residence. In another part of the house Howard Sturges had an apartment as well. Though the three got along beautifully together, their living arrangements hardly constituted a *ménage à trois* in the usual sense, for in no way was it a sexual triangle. Sturges was perhaps Cole's closest confidant; they had many friends—male and female—in common and shared numerous intimate secrets in connection with their homosexuality (they were not, however, lovers). Sturges was also closely attached to Linda and she to him. They had been warm friends before either had met Cole, and often visited art galleries and auction houses together. If Linda was ill—and she had periodic respiratory difficulties—Sturges, rather than Cole, usually looked after her. Linda, in turn, took it upon herself to oversee Sturges's alcoholic problems, particularly since he would disappear for days during a drinking bout without remembering what had transpired. To avoid any harm coming to him in his drunken state (purportedly Linda once found him lying in the gutter while intoxicated), she would stop whatever she was doing and run to his side when word reached her that Sturges was in his cups. After much persuasion, she finally got him to go to a sanitarium for treatment. From then on, except for an occasional lapse, he seldom drank. He ultimately stopped completely in 1933, on learning that his younger sister, Dorothy, had died during a routine appendicitis operation. Shocked by the news of this incredible waste of life, Sturges vowed never to drink again, and kept his word.

Shortly before he married Linda, Cole, in collaboration with Melville Gideon, turned out "I Never Realized" and "Chelsea," both used in the 1919 English production of *The Eclipse*. Presumably to get further mileage from these same tunes in the States, Cole also included them in two New York shows: "I Never Realized" was interpolated into *Buddies*, a 1919 production, while "Chelsea," with a change of lyrics and title—to "Washington Square"—was heard in *Buddies* and in *As You Were*, in 1920. In 1920, too, Cole and Clifford Grey cowrote three songs—"Look Around," "Our Hotel," and "Why Didn't We Meet Before?"—performed in the British show *A Night Out*, which ran for 309 performances. Though none of these numbers caught on, Cole hardly seemed to notice. He continued to keep himself busy creating music and lyrics, presumably in the hope that one of the new songs would be a hit. As Elsa Maxwell has noted, even when Cole "was cutting capers all over Europe, he was working hard and steadily, six hours a day, writing songs, experimenting with lyrics, polishing his technique . . . [and] building up a large inventory of songs."

Cole, of course, was able to do as he pleased because of Linda's wealth. For despite his new status as a married man he had few, if any, of the financial responsibilities that ordinarily went with it. Linda saw to that. She adored Cole and his work and did whatever she could to smooth the way for him. Since Cole had not yet come into his share of J.O.'s fortune, Linda simply absorbed the bulk of the enormous expenses that their life-style entailed. In many respects Linda was very much a close replica of Kate: an indulgent, accepting, totally giving, older, rich woman. Linda represented, therefore, what Cole was used to—a mother indulging him, spoiling him, making the world adapt itself to him. Cole obviously needed someone like Linda, and he was clever enough to fulfill that need through marriage to her. She may have been younger, taller, prettier, and more sophisticated than Kate, but as with his mother, Cole could practically do no wrong in Linda's eyes. (Linda and Kate, incidentally, always got along well together. To begin with, both were very socially oriented and could thus appreciate the other's good social points. In addition, Linda was consistently deferential toward Kate and kept in frequent touch—by letter and by telephone—with her. But perhaps the strongest unifying bond between them was their mutual adoration of Cole.)

Even after Cole and Linda had been married for years, friends recall that Cole was not above acting like a willful, prankish child in her presence; yet Linda loved it. Alexander Steinert, a musician friend of the Porters, tells of the time he last saw Cole and Linda together, shortly before she died in 1954. (She had been ill for a number of years and few traces of her former beauty remained. She was then bent over with a slight hunchback and walked with the aid of a cane.) Steinert remembers that Cole, while talking to Linda, suddenly put his hands into a bowl of colored pills and started popping them into his mouth like candy as she looked on in dismay. Cole obviously knew that the pills could not harm him, but it amused him that he had startled her. When she realized what had happened, Linda merely laughed it off. She recognized Cole's prank for what it was: the childish exhibitionism of an extraordinary and special figure.

Linda's reaction in this instance typified her great devotion to Cole. Because of her all-consuming interest in him plus her many outstanding attributes as a person, many of the Porters' friends considered Linda as perfect a wife for Cole as any woman could be. Anita Loos, who knew the Porters for many years, tells of one incident that points up Linda's concern for Cole's well-being. Miss Loos remembers how surprised she was when Linda, with all her money, started to economize drastically— even on small items, like lunches—not long before she died. When questioned about it, Linda confided: "I want to leave Cole an even two million dollars when I go." Linda came close to the goal she set for herself; she left a gross estate of $1,939,671—all to Cole. Linda had Cole in mind even in the matter of her funeral: She requested that simple services be held at St. Bartholomew's, around the corner from the Waldorf Astoria, where the Porters lived, so that Cole would be inconvenienced as little as possible.

This same solicitude was noticeable when Linda first put herself at Cole's service to aid his career. Through her contacts she opened many doors for him. She also backed up her confidence in his abilities with money and her special gifts of personality and instinct.

In return, Linda got immense satisfaction from being the wife of an outstanding talent. Her marriage to Cole also fulfilled her nurturing needs as a wealthy, indulgent, childless woman while allowing her to use her special social gifts within a pleasant, respectable, and interesting— though sexless—ambience. For apparently Linda had been sufficiently repelled by the aggressive, freewheeling personality of her first husband —a philandering cad more at home in the male-dominated settings of sports and business than in truly sophisticated social situations—so that the sexual side of marriage was not something that particularly appealed to her. In connection with the sexless aspect of her marriage to Cole, some of Linda's friends have speculated that she may have been a latent lesbian, though they have no proof to support that hypothesis. But perhaps Linda's greatest gratification from her marriage to Cole came when he bloomed as a creator and got the recognition that went with it. When the world showered him with the kudos he deserved, Linda exulted in them as much as he. Few knew her sentiments, however, for she always remained in the background where Cole's career was concerned. Yet the brief epitaph on her gravestone is remarkably revelatory of her feelings. It reads only, "Linda Lee, wife of Cole Porter."

7

On the Move

Cole and Linda quickly made their home at 13 rue Monsieur the scene of some of the best soirees in France. One could always count on something special—like the first Charleston lessons in Paris—happening there. Linda was especially adroit at inviting hordes of interesting people to her home, many of whom had the potential for helping Cole's career. Interspersed with the society stalwarts, members of nobility, painters, sculptors, and literary figures at these gatherings would be popular entertainers and theatrical producers whose friendship and esteem Cole and Linda solicited. Nor did they overlook impresarios, managers, conductors, and performers from the serious-music field. Like stockbrokers spreading their risks to protect investments, Cole and Linda kept on the best of terms with both camps of the music fraternity. At the Porters' it was quite common for highbrow musicians such as singer Mary Garden, pianist Artur Rubinstein, composer Igor Stravinsky, and conductor Vladimir Golschmann to rub elbows congenially with popular entertainers like Fanny Brice and Beatrice Lillie.

As social leaders Cole and Linda always tried to be as selective as possible in choosing the company they kept. They were helped in this regard by Elsa Maxwell, who had come to Paris after the war because of the large contingent from the international set who now lived there.

Starting out with no money or family connections to speak of, Elsa had made a fantastic name for herself among New York's wealthy by her masterminding of society charity affairs for the benefit of the Allies during World War I. Soon her reputation as an upper-echelon social director extended to Paris, where many of her "clients" now resided, one satisfied patron telling another of her party-arranging skills. She had almost immediate access to heads and near-heads of state, as well as to people like the Rothschilds and the Aga Khan. So formidable were her social contacts that she would frequently be given carte blanche by the wealthy to organize parties of all kinds for them, ranging from very elaborate costume balls to informal scavenger hunts. At her say-so palatial homes, large staffs, and mountains of food, drink, and decorations would immediately be made available to her in the interests of a good party. Governments, too, sought her out for her special brand of expertise. When the principality of Monaco wanted to promote Monte Carlo as a summer resort in 1927, its representatives came to Elsa Maxwell for assistance, just as Italy in 1923 made use of her services to help put the Lido, the beach resort near Venice, on the social map. Her imprimatur of social acceptability carried so much weight that the Waldorf Astoria gave her a suite rent-free when it opened in New York in 1931 at the height of the Depression, hoping to attract rich clients because of her. Even the Ritz, a Parisian institution long before the Waldorf was built, allowed Elsa to run up bills there at will rather than chance offending her. Similarly, the world-famous Maxim's never gave her a check when she dined there.

It was perhaps inevitable that Elsa and the Porters would be drawn to each other in postwar Paris because of their mutual social interests, since for Elsa the social scene provided financial support, while for the Porters it was a means of meeting new and important people. But still another reason for their coming together was a musical one. For Elsa was a good, self-taught musician who was in demand as a piano accompanist and soloist, and also happened to be a great champion of Cole's music. She had been taken with his work from the first time she had heard it in 1916, and made a point of performing and boosting his songs at every chance. As much as anyone, Elsa Maxwell deserves credit for spreading the word about Cole in the early days, with the result that he became a kind of cause célèbre among the elite considerably before the masses knew about him.

Cole and Elsa made an unusual pair—wholly mismatched—when seen together. She was a lesbian, squat, jowly, masculine-looking, exceedingly plain; a bundle of blubber at first glance. She gave little thought to dress —possibly because it did little for her five-by-five, army-tank frame—and none to trimming down. In comparison with Elsa, Cole was on the effeminate side, especially when seen in early photos taken at the beach, wearing bathing trunks and a woman's necklace or holding a woman's parasol over his head. Unlike Elsa, Cole was very much concerned with appearance. He draped his lithe, lean body in the finest clothes and invariably wore a carnation in his buttonhole as an added punctilio of dash and verve. Though far from a matinee idol, Cole worked hard at maintaining his looks. For years the first thing he did on awakening was to have his valet bring him chilled witch hazel, which he carefully applied around his eyes to keep the area, with its telltale signs of age, as taut as possible. He also kept his skin well oiled, his teeth brightly polished, swallowed an assortment of pills daily, and took regular afternoon naps, all in the interests of good health and appearance.

The Porter-Maxwell alliance, for all its mutual benefits, also had its share of difficulties: Cole and Linda did not always approve of Elsa's schemes for making pocket money for herself between paid social assignments. One of Elsa's favorite devices was to inveigle friends into playing bridge or Mah-Jongg for small stakes, on the pretext that it added interest to the games. Inevitably, she would win. Another of her contrivances was to approach someone with the sad tale of her mother's recent death. Would they help her meet funeral expenses? Without fail, funds would quickly be forthcoming. This scheme might have continued indefinitely had not several of her friends compared notes and found that they had all contributed to the same funeral. To add insult to injury, Elsa's mother turned out to be very much alive.

Notwithstanding these peccadillos, Elsa's friends readily conceded that she generally gave great value, in terms of being socially useful as well as amusing, for any sums she took from them under false pretenses. They laughed off their losses while praising her ingenuity. Even Cole, who had an intermittent love-hate relationship with Elsa because of one grievance or another (he often called her Miss Liar to her face), remained lifelong friends with her on the strength of her support of his music, her outgoing personality, and her social contacts.

Postwar Paris as Cole, Linda, and Elsa found it continually teemed with excitement. A large part of this excitement was endemic to the city itself, with its beauty, gaiety, and historical tradition. Paris, however, added still another important dimension to its special qualities when it emerged relatively unscathed from the "war to end all wars." After four difficult years—from 1914 to 1918—of valiantly resisting the onslaughts of a powerful enemy, Paris now stood proud and free, a symbol of mankind's hope for the future. Perhaps because of the symbolic factor, combined with its long-established reputation as a leading cultural center, postwar Paris quickly became the mecca for artists all over the world, both established and still unknown, like Ernest Hemingway, Aaron Copland, James Joyce, Virgil Thomson, and F. Scott Fitzgerald.

In this creative setting experimentation became the vogue. "New" music, "new" painting, "new" sculpture, and "new" literature emerged steadily from artists' studios. Some artistic reputations were made overnight on the basis of novelty, and some lost just as quickly for being old hat. Especially caught up in the novelty syndrome were many of the international set who had flocked to Paris at the war's end to renew their acquaintance with the city and to keep up with the times. Along with sampling the customary French staples, fashion and food, they also experienced the cultural explosion firsthand. Their exposure to an atmosphere that often played up newness for its own sake at the expense of the traditional undoubtedly affected the outlook of many of them. Certainly among those with whom Cole, Linda, and Elsa frequently mingled, it was apparent that a free-swinging, devil-may-care attitude of living for the moment was pervasive. For Cole, Linda, Elsa, and their friends, pleasure, no matter how derived, frequently became the end itself. As one might expect under the circumstances, these sybarites—a motley crew ranging from aristocrats to show-business personalities—invariably had the time and money to gratify their appetites. Promiscuity—of the heterosexual, homosexual, or bisexual variety—placed high among their indulgences, as did gossip. Every juicy tidbit that made the rounds would be fondly savored, chewed over with care, and then quickly regurgitated at an appropriate moment for others to enjoy. As one story gained currency—about this prominent mustachioed lesbian or that famous cubist bisexual—it would soon be superceded by another.

Consistent with this emphasis on variety, Cole and Linda, at the suggestion of Mary Garden, rented a large villa at Cap d'Antibes on the French Riviera for the summer of 1921. They spent several months of isolated splendor there, in a marked change of pace from their normally hectic Paris schedule. The Riviera had not yet become a tourist spot, and Antibes was then still a small, provincial town. The main sources of entertainment for its few residents were a movie house that opened only once a week and a local casino. Telephone service reflected the town's leisurely way of doing things. It came to a halt at noon while the operator had lunch, and stopped completely after seven in the evening. The natural beauty of the place, nevertheless, more than made up for the lack of big-city amenities. The Porters' stately, ivy-covered house and surrounding gardens were situated on top of a precipitous, rocky cliff affording a breathtaking view of the Mediterranean. At the bottom of the bluff there was a pristine, seaweed-covered beach, La Garoupe, where the Porters and their guests bathed and sunned themselves. Close by was Angel's Bay, whose calm, clear waters were perfect for boating and canoeing.

Among the guests who visited the Porters at Antibes were Cole's classmate, Gerald Murphy, and his wife, Sara. After graduating from Yale in 1912, Murphy spent five years working at Mark Cross, the famous New York store, which was owned by his father. While he was employed at the store, he married Sara, the eldest of three pretty daughters of Frank B. Wiborg, a successful Cincinnati ink manufacturer. At the start of World War I, Murphy joined the army for training as an aviator, but the war ended before he had a chance to go overseas. Rather than return to his job, which did not interest him, Murphy opted for studying landscape architecture at Harvard. For the next two years he took courses in botany and landscape architecture. But this, too, did not fulfill his needs. In the spring of 1921, dissatisfied with life in America and still not sure of his future goals, Murphy sailed for Europe with his wife and three small children—a daughter, Honoria, aged three, and sons Baoth, two, and Patrick, eight months.

The Murphys, like many other Americans of their generation who went abroad, soon settled in Paris. Shortly after their arrival Murphy saw cubist paintings by Picasso, Braque, and Gris that were a revelation to him. They made so strong an impression that he immediately decided, at the age of thirty-three, to become a painter himself. In the eight years—until 1929—that he worked at perfecting his skills, he turned out a small body of outstanding paintings which combined cubist abstraction and primitive realism in a highly personal way. These canvases are now recognized as significant American art for their period.

At the time he and Sara visited the Porters at Antibes, however, Murphy had not yet gotten into painting with full seriousness. But the same spontaneous enthusiasm Murphy showed for painting also surfaced at the sight of Antibes and its unspoiled beauty. He and Sara quickly fell in love with the town and ended up buying a summer home there. It was a small hillside chalet overflowing with exotic plants and trees, to which they returned again and again. The Porters, on the other hand, never went back to Antibes after their initial stay, presumably because there were other summer places that had more appeal—or perhaps greater novelty—for them.

The Murphys, as did the Porters, had a wonderful flair for living. Gerald and Sara had come to France with enough inherited income between them to be able to do as they wanted. Both had been disappointed by the many vapid people they mingled with at home. Gerald often made fun of them, particularly in cahoots with Monty Woolley. When he and Woolley got together they would play a game of their own invention called stomach touch, which ridiculed all the stuffy, wealthy, corpulent men—especially Yale men—they knew. In the game, Murphy and Woolley would face each other, their stomachs vastly extended and touching. Along with this stance went pompous, inane bits of conversation in appropriately out-of-breath voices: their biting commentary on the American success story. Murphy was so down on many of the people he had grown up with he even cautioned his young daughter, Honoria, about ever marrying a Yale man; he would be too dull for her.

When the Murphys arrived in Paris from the States they quickly volunteered to be unpaid apprentices for Diaghilev's Ballets Russes on learning that most of the dance company's scenery had been destroyed by fire. As apprentices, the Murphys reported to the company's atelier daily to assist in painting scenery and to make themselves generally useful. Through their volunteer work the Murphys were able to attend rehearsals regularly, and also went to all the openings and parties of the Ballets Russes. They were such a wonderfully attractive, dedicated couple—Sara, wholesome and open, who always said what came to mind; Gerald, handsome and circumspect, with his quick intelligence and wit—that they were soon on the best of terms with Diaghilev, Picasso, Braque, Stravinsky, and other prominent figures associated with the company. As their contacts expanded the Murphys invited to their home many of the important artists involved in the creative life of Paris. Hemingway, Picasso, Léger, Dos Passos, MacLeish, and Fitzgerald became close friends of theirs. Fitzgerald, as a matter of fact, modeled Dick and Nicole Diver, his two key characters in *Tender Is the Night,* on the Murphys (though Fitzgerald's story was not of the Murphys), and dedicated the book to them as well.

In short order the Murphys, like the Porters, became a social force in Paris. One of the Murphys' parties that caused a sensation and helped solidify their reputation as hosts took place in June of 1923, after the premiere of Stravinsky's *Les Noces* by the Ballets Russes. The meticulously planned champagne-dinner, held on a docked barge on the Seine, lasted until dawn and glittered with the presence of many of the leading figures in the arts, including Jean Cocteau, Stravinsky, Picasso, Diagh-ilev, and Princess Edmond de Polignac (née Winnaretta Singer, of the Singer sewing machine fortune, a major patroness). With Cocteau masquerading as the barge's captain (he would regularly announce that it was sinking), Stravinsky doing a flying leap through a huge laurel wreath, and Picasso creating "art" on the spot out of children's toys, all on board had a wonderful time cavorting about. The party was the talk of Paris for weeks, for its novelty and brilliance.

In Antibes, too, the Murphys were social leaders, but with a difference. For the slower pace of the Riviera garden spot lent itself to a simpler way of life, which they actually preferred. The Murphys had come to Paris largely because of their dissatisfaction with the artificiality of their existence in the United States. In their hearts they had always strongly identified with the Emersonian-Whitmanesque idealization of the American spirit. Unfortunately, because of family and outside pressures, the Murphys had found it difficult to realize in their own country the purity and strength of purpose inherent in the America envisaged by Emerson and Whitman. It was another story, however, in Antibes. The sunny, unhurried setting on the Riviera stimulated the Murphys to devise an almost idyllic world for themselves, one that drew them close to the natural environment and that also encouraged an appreciation of technological advances, intellectual and artistic pursuits, good taste, beauty, and congeniality. As symbolic gestures toward the native land of their dreams, the Murphys called their chalet Villa America and affixed an abstraction of the American flag to a wall near its entrance.

The Murphys soon attracted many of their Parisian friends—the Hemingways, the Fitzgeralds, the Légers, and others—to their Riviera domain. The Eden-like world of the Murphys encompassed both the latest jazz records from America and traditional Provençal dishes (prepared with fruits and vegetables from their garden); relaxed daily picnics on the beach and intense, solitary, creative work. It was a world that was neither completely American nor completely French; not entirely up to date nor rooted in the past. Rather, it was a unique synthesis of many components, and the Murphys thrived on the mixture; especially Gerald, whose painting made remarkable strides in Antibes.

The Murphys' blissful sojourns in southern France ended suddenly in October, 1929, when they learned that their youngest son, Patrick, had developed tuberculosis. They dropped everything, closed the Villa America, and left for Montana-Vermala in the Swiss Alps, where the boy was being treated. Focusing all his energies on Patrick in an attempt to improve his health, Murphy stopped painting completely. Nor did he ever go back to it. The Depression, which followed the stock market crash of October 29, 1929, quickly began devastating businesses left and right. Mark Cross, too, felt the economic crunch. In order to meet family obligations Murphy returned to the business world he hated as head of Mark Cross. Referring to himself sarcastically as Merchant Prince, Murphy soon turned the organization around financially. By using his taste and imagination to add new lines to the inventory, and by moving the store to a prime location (at 707 Fifth Avenue), Murphy made Mark Cross a more profitable enterprise than ever before.

While bravely coping with business and family exigencies, the Murphys were staggered by enervating calamities that followed in quick succession. Within the space of two years both their sons died: Baoth in 1935 of spinal meningitis and Patrick in 1937 of tuberculosis. Each boy was just sixteen at his death. Though he was overwhelmed by events beyond his control, Murphy still managed to meet life head-on, but gave up painting. He turned inward, refusing to discuss his paintings or even to have them mentioned. Yet they obviously remained important to him. In a deeply anguished letter to Scott Fitzgerald in 1935 after the death of Baoth, Murphy conceded that "only the invented part of our life—the unreal part—has had any scheme, any beauty. Life itself has . . . blundered, scarred and destroyed."

The pathetic turn of Murphy's life, explicit in his remarks, had few parallels in his circle of friends. Among them perhaps only Cole suffered the deep tragedy of withdrawing from his art, in his last years, as a consequence of psychic trauma. As with Murphy, it was almost as though fate were exacting retribution from Cole for happier days.

While staying on top of the latest social and artistic trends and gossip in Paris, Cole kept turning out songs and playing them at every opportunity for his friends at parties. He also visited London and New York (where the Porters had a Fifth Avenue apartment) so that he could maintain his contacts in the theater and the music publishing world. Cole placed over a dozen of his songs in three 1922 revues on both sides of the Atlantic: two London failures, *Mayfair and Montmartre* and *Phi-Phi*, and the Broadway-bound *Hitchy-Koo of 1922*, which closed out of town. Unfortunately, when the three shows folded, Cole's tunes disappeared along with them. To the extent that the songs were a little too advanced for their time, Cole must share some of the responsibility for their quick demise. As composer-author-critic Deems Taylor put it on hearing Cole perform several of these numbers at a party in New York shortly after their premieres, "[the] tunes were far too tricky and . . . [the] lyrics much too sophisticated to have any popular success." As used by Taylor, the word "tricky" presumably meant that Cole's songs were too problematic from a musical standpoint for the general public. That viewpoint is supported by Cole's treatment of "The Blue Boy Blues," from *Mayfair and Montmartre.*

The stimulus for writing the song came from the London press's denunciation in 1922 of the sale of Gainsborough's famous painting, "The Blue Boy," owned by the Duke of Westminster, to American railroad magnate Henry E. Huntington for a reputed price of $620,000. Art dealer Sir Joseph Duveen, the middleman in the sale, triggered the press outcry when he arranged, as a publicity gesture, a special showing of "The Blue Boy" at London's National Gallery before the painting left England. As Britishers by the thousands lined up to see the Gainsborough for the last time, the press played up what they considered a national disgrace. Cole quickly jumped into the fray with his "Blue Boy Blues," in which he had the painting itself tell of its sad plight. The lyrics of the verse began lugubriously enough:

> As a painting you must have heard a lot about me,
> For I lived here for many happy years;
> Never dreaming that you could ever do without me,
> Till you sold me in spite of all my tears.
> It's a long way from gilded galleries in Park Lane
> To the Wild West across the winter sea.
> If you don't know quite what I mean,
> Simply ask Sir Joseph Duveen
> And he'll tell you what he gave 'em for me.

In the refrain, the painting continued lamenting its move across the ocean:

> For I'm the Blue Boy, the beautiful Blue Boy,
> And I am forced to admit I'm feeling a bit depressed.
> A silver dollar took me and my collar
> To show the slow cowboys
> Just how boys
> In England used to be dressed.
> I don't know what I shall do

So far from Mayfair:
If Mister Gainsborough knew, I know he'd frown.
As days grow fewer, I'm bluer and bluer,
For I am saying "goodbye" to London town.

A blues section—a kind of second refrain—followed the initial refrain.
It closed the song in honky-tonk fashion, while repeating the title, "Blue
Boy Blues," again and again in its text:

We've got those Blue Boy blues,
We've got those doggone Blue Boy blues.
We fairly feel it oozing from our heads down to our shoes.
So won't you tell us what to do, boy?
We've got the Blue Boy blues,
We've got those Blue Boy blues,
We've got the doggone Blue Boy blues.
We fairly feel it oozing from our heads down to our shoes.
So won't you tell us what to do, boy?
We've got the Blue Boy blues.

As presented in *Mayfair and Montmartre* at London's New Oxford
Theatre, "The Blue Boy Blues" came off as an effective production number. English singer-dancer Nellie Taylor impersonated Blue Boy, costume and all. In a solo rendition of the tune's verse and refrain, against
a backdrop reminiscent of Gainsborough's painting, she told of Blue
Boy's sad plight. Stepping out of the Gainsborough setting into one
representing America's Wild West, she was joined by a chorus of Indians
and cowboys belting out the blues. The contrast between the propriety
of a Gainsborough figure intermeshed with a jazzed-up version of rural
Americana projected with stunning theatricality, and the audience responded accordingly: Night after night they roared their approval of the
number.

Solely as a song, "The Blue Boy Blues" also had much to commend it
to an audience, especially its fashionable allusions to jazz, which was then
sweeping England and the Continent as a spin-off from its success in
America, and its topicality. Problematic from the public's point of view,
however, were the song's demanding melodic contours, extensive range
(an octave and a half), and relatively convoluted harmony. Moreover,
instead of the usual introductory verse and complementary thirty-two-
bar refrain (a songwriting formula widely used from Tin Pan Alley to

Drury Lane), the tune ended with an extra twenty-four-measure blues section. For these musical reasons, plus its "arty" textual association with Gainsborough, "The Blue Boy Blues" did not lend itself to easy accessibility by a broad public outside of its stage context. When *Mayfair and Montmartre* ended its run after seventy-seven performances, "The Blue Boy Blues" quickly fell by the wayside.

In attempting to cash in on the controversy surrounding the sale of the famed painting, Cole merely followed a basic principle of popular songwriting: Publicity of any kind can be helpful in generating interest in a tune. His resourcefulness in trying to capitalize on a topical matter also points up the way he generally created his tunes. Unlike most songwriters, who compose their melodies first and then have them fitted with words, frequently by a separate lyricist, Cole invariably started out with a nonmusical concept before putting a note down on paper. In describing his creative process, Cole stated, "I like to begin with an idea and then fit it to a title. I then write the words and music. Often I begin near the end of a refrain, so that the song has a strong finish, and then work backwards. I also like to use the title phrase at the beginning of a refrain and repeat it at the end for a climax." About his penchant for reiterating words of similar sounds in unusual rhyming schemes to heighten intensity, Cole readily conceded that "writing lyrics is like doing a crossword puzzle"; solutions could often best be achieved by juggling material around. Cole's great concern in his songs with ideas and the manipulation and repetition of text for dramatic purposes, rather than simply emphasizing the music, is quite apparent from his comments.

After *Hitchy-Koo*—the third of his 1922 revues—closed in Philadelphia in the fall of that year without ever reaching Broadway, Cole began casting about for his next move. He and Linda were in New York at the time renewing acquaintances, developing contacts, and catching up on the latest Broadway shows. Cole did not wait long to make up his mind. As had happened many times before, Cole's grandfather helped to influence his decision. J.O., who was then approaching ninety-four (he had been born on December 23, 1828), was beginning to show the effects of age. He was still the same irascible person and the dominant force in the family, but he had reduced the scope of his activities. Toward the end of January the infirmities of old age finally caught up with him and he was confined to bed. After a lifetime of being constantly on the go, ten days in bed proved to be too much for the old man. On the evening of February 3, 1923, a month and ten days after his ninety-fourth birthday, J.O. died in his home in Peru.

The Peru press, as was to be expected, gave major attention to J.O.'s death. Extolling his "reputation for sterling integrity" as a civic leader and businessman, the press recounted in detail how he made his fortune, worth millions, by dint of "ceaseless activities . . . thrift and business management." Calling him one of the last of the pioneers, the press noted that "of perhaps half a dozen men who might be chosen for reason of power and activities in this city during the last half century, the late Mr. J.O. Cole would probably deserve first mention." The lavish press encomiums contrasted sharply with the modest Episcopalian funeral services for J.O. in his home. Save for a casket-covering of red roses, a sentimental gesture toward his first wife, Rachel, "the rose of Indiana," J.O. was interred in the family plot in Peru's Mount Hope cemetery with a minimum of ceremony.

Overlooking past disagreements with J.O. and in deference to Kate, Cole—joined by Linda—hurried to Peru to be with his mother for the funeral. Practical considerations also prompted the visit. The trust fund for Cole, set up in 1916 by J.O., became operative only after the deaths of the old man and his business partner. J.O. had outlived Clinton Crane, and with his death the last stumbling block vanished. Cole soon learned that he would be entitled to a large income from the trust, which was based on coal, gas, and timber sales. Though the amounts would vary annually depending on the total sales involved, Cole, as a kind of absentee landlord, would realize enormous sums of money from the operators of mines and timberlands on the family properties in Kentucky and West Virginia. But Cole's windfall did not end there. The old man's will divided the bulk of his large estate between Kate and her brother's family (J.O.'s son, Louis, had died in 1903 during a hernia operation, leaving behind a wife and four children). Included in J.O.'s estate was approximately one million dollars in cash, of which Kate received half. Always looking out for Cole's best interests, Kate split her share of the cash with her son.

With Cole's inheritance added to Linda's already ample fortune, the Porters had even more money to spend on themselves than before. They had always lived lavishly, but Cole's newfound wealth only increased the degree of their self-indulgence. Like Dionysian votaries caught up in ever-changing hedonistic rites, the Porters now turned to Venice as a site for fresh pleasures. Their choice was largely influenced by the knowledge that Elsa Maxwell had been hired by the Italian government to promote the Lido as a beach resort. Casting their lot with Elsa's, Cole and Linda rented a huge, four-story palazzo for the summer of 1923—the Palazzo

Barbaro—fronting Venice's Grand Canal. They resided in two other imposing palazzos during the next four summers that they spent there. When not in Venice they were either in Paris, London, New York, or on assorted side trips all over the Continent. They practically never stayed in one place long enough for ennui to set in. Perhaps their solid American roots stimulated their quest for excitement and titillation on a global basis. But clearly Cole and Linda were almost a breed apart in their pursuit of the glamorous and the novel on an international scale.

8

Venetian Period

Long set apart from the world's other major cities by the unique chain of Adriatic islands connected by an intricate network of canals and bridges, Venice had also distinguished itself as a religious, cultural, and trade center and as the site of fabulous churches, palazzos, and art treasures. Titian and Tintoretto painted and flourished there, as did the Gabrielis, who wrote much of their majestic antiphonal music for pageant-filled Venetian civic ceremonies as well as for performance in the multiple choir galleries of Saint Mark's Church. Unlike Rome, there was little of a devotional and ascetic quality about life in Venice, despite its ties with the church. Venice's centuries-old trade with the East may have had something to do with it; Venice's spirit was always rather open and extroverted, perhaps even flamboyant. The people of Venice took religion less seriously—or at least the distinctions between the religious and the secular were less clear—than did those in the stronghold of Roman Catholicism to the south.

Until World War I intruded, Venice had been a visitor's paradise for many years. When the war ended, Venice, like Paris, once again became a place to see and to be seen in, especially for the international set, who began to return there in ever-increasing numbers. The allure of ornate ducal palaces, gondolas and gondoliers, resplendent, masterful murals, the city's *piazzetta,* and other reminders of a romantic past—a past seemingly untouched by the hurly-burly intrusions of the twentieth century —proved irresistible for those who could afford it. An additional inducement was the fact that the Italian lira was then relatively cheap, assuring excellent value in most currency exchanges. For several thousand American dollars a month it was possible to rent a large palazzo complete with gilded, carved ceilings and walls; cavernous chambers; exquisite, museum-quality tapestries, furniture and paintings; plus a large staff. It was in such magnificent palazzos that the Porters, joined by Howard Sturges, lived while in Venice. In 1923 they resided at the enormous Palazzo Barbaro before moving on to more stately quarters as their social contacts broadened. The following year they stayed at the even larger Palazzo Papadopoli, and from 1925 to 1927 they spent their summers at the Palazzo Rezzonico, the famed Venetian home of Robert and Elizabeth Barrett Browning. The Rezzonico was so immense that its grand ballroom could accommodate close to a thousand guests.

Venice's sunny, bright, summer days were made to order for lolling on the broad Lido beach. With Elsa Maxwell and the Porters spreading the word, more and more prominent figures like Tallulah Bankhead, Noel Coward, Fanny Brice, Billy Reardon, Lady Diana Cooper, Elsie de Wolfe, and Sir Charles Mendl came to the beach to enjoy its amenities. For those so inclined there was no shortage of daytime activities at the Lido, including beach-ball games and other group sports, swimming, or simply chitchatting. Venice in the evening was another matter, for the city appeared to close down once it became dark. Although Venice, with the sun reflecting on its surrounding waters, sparkled during the day, it became dull and gloomy at night; unless, that is, ways could be found to liven it up. Fortunately, Elsa Maxwell, the Porters, and their friends had a flair for dreaming up scintillating parties, treasure hunts, and similar amusements. Members of their group would take turns as hosts, so that nearly every night of the week something exciting would be in the offing. Hard drinking was commonplace at these festivities, as was the use of drugs of all kinds, including opium, cocaine, and hashish. A greater sensualist than most of his friends (than Linda, too), Cole never hesitated trying drugs or practically anything else for kicks while socializing. After excessive dissipation had left its mark in the way of pronounced black circles under his eyes and a puffiness in his face, Cole would immediately call a halt to his indulgences or limit them, for he was very concerned with his appearance and health. In no time at all he would bounce back as chipper as ever, his smooth-faced, boyish looks belying any dissolute acts. Evidently the tough, long-lived genes that helped J.O. reach his mid-nineties also coursed through Cole's body.

But quick recuperative powers or not, reports have it that Cole was forced to leave Venice at the invitation of its police when, in the summer of 1927, they raided the Palazzo Rezzonico. The police found a party in full swing in which a slew of handsome Italian boys dressed in Linda's fancy clothes (she was away at the time) were cavorting for Cole and several of his friends. To the dismay of the police chief who conducted the raid, his own son was among the boys in drag at the party. To protect his own interests the police chief quickly hushed up the affair, but he made it very clear to Cole that it would be best if he left Venice. Cole, of course, had little choice but to comply.

Cole invariably spoke most favorably of Venice and the wonderful times he had there. He would also tell how he first fell in love with Venice as a child, when he saw a large painting of the Grand Canal in a Peru theater. Little did he realize then that he would live in palazzos and be one of the first to drive a speedboat on that very same canal, or that he would sponsor some of the most spectacular parties ever held in Venice. At one of these shindigs Diaghilev's ballet company danced for the gathering to the accompaniment of a large orchestra. The background consisted of a fifty-foot statue of Venus, thousands of glowing candles, and fireworks. At another affair, a "red and white" ball held at the Rezzonico, a corps of gondoliers dressed in red and white stood stiffly at attention along a winding marble stairway, lit torches in hand, as hundreds of guests entered the palazzo. Exploiting the color motif further, the Porters then distributed specially made red-and-white paper costumes representing four key periods of the nineteenth century to all the guests. Swirling ballroom lights playing on the costumes also emphasized the kaleidoscopic mixture, as did a battery of colored beacons focused on tightrope walkers who entertained high up in the courtyard. The combination of brilliant colors, lively entertainment, and a carnival atmosphere made the event unforgettable.

The ball was particularly memorable for Mrs. Cecilia vom Rath, a close friend of the Porters, for reasons even more extraordinary. Before the ball Cole had told Mrs. vom Rath that the Rezzonico was reputed to be haunted by the ghosts of the Brownings. Mrs. vom Rath remembers returning to the grand ballroom late in the evening, after a short stay away from it. As she walked along a deserted corridor leading to the ballroom, she suddenly saw a couple, exactly like the Brownings in dress and appearance, embracing in a desolate spot. Convinced that she had seen the ghosts, Mrs. vom Rath rushed to tell the Porters. When she returned to the spot with Cole and Linda in tow, there was no sign of the couple. In retrospect, Mrs. vom Rath has not been able to decide whether she had actually seen the Browning ghosts, or had simply been the victim of a practical joke by Cole.

One of Cole's most talked-about events in Venice borrowed a page from Gerald and Sara Murphy's social book. In a setting reminiscent of the Murphys' 1923 *Les Noces* party, Cole's festivities, too, took place on a barge. The first inkling Venetians had of what was in store for them came from a July, 1926, press announcement. "One of the charms of Venice is that it is never dull," began the news item in self-congratulatory fashion. "Just when one begins to feel the need of an innovation," continued the announcement, "out of the hat, like a rabbit, it springs. This time it is out of the heads of four members of the younger set in Venice, Count Andrea Robilant, Marquis di Salina, Baron Franchetti, and Mr. Cole Porter, who are successfully launching the Dance Boat." The news squib noted that "a large barge, which has been specially constructed, containing facilities for serving supper, will float out into the lagoon and, on still nights, even into the open sea. A Negro jazz orchestra is being brought from Paris to play and there will be dancing." The announcement concluded with the information that "invitations have been sent to a number of members of the summer colony, and the subscription list is to be limited to 150 members, with the proceeds going to several Venetian charities."

The combination of the press item and word that the Leslie "Hutch" Hutchinson band, one of the hottest black jazz groups in Paris, would be performing at the festivities soon had all the socialites in Venice vying with each other for invitations to the opening-night party on the barge. At the appointed time the lucky ones (including the Porters and many of their friends), dressed in all their finery, boarded the vessel, its wine cellar, French chef, and jazz band in readiness, in anticipation of a gala affair. The night started promisingly enough with dinner and dancing as the barge drifted slowly into the lagoon. But trouble entered the picture when the normally calm lagoon waters started acting up. Before long many members of the party became seasick, and since no one had thought of installing toilet facilities when the craft had been converted to a floating nightclub, the elegant guests had no choice but to retch en masse from the sides of the barge as it returned to dock. Never again did the vessel move about freely in Venetian waters. Henceforth, it always remained moored close to shore, to avoid such a catastrophe as had befallen it on its maiden voyage.

As a leader among Venice's summer colony, Cole's name often came up in local conversation; but not always in flattering terms. Some considered him *persona non grata* because of his flamboyant ways, extravagant parties, and persistent drive to be fashionable. The dance-boat affair particularly triggered a number of outbursts against Cole and what he represented. In a letter one complainant, possibly more outspoken than others, grumbled that "the whole of Venice is up in arms against Cole Porter because of his jazz and his Negroes. He has started an idiotic night club on a boat . . . and now the Grand Canal is swarming with the very same Negroes who have made us all run away from London and Paris. They are teaching the 'Charleston' on the Lido Beach! It's dreadful! . . . Their [the Porters'] renting [of] the Palazzo Rezzonico is . . . characteristic of nouveaux riches." The complaints about Cole could be applied to many of the people in his circle. Like Cole, they were generally attractive, sophisticated, and had money and prestige. But they were also frequently snobbish, spoiled, inwardly cold and cruel, interested mainly in self-gratification in one form or another. As a group they seemed to lack a most important quality: concern for others. Life for them was one big treasure hunt, dance, masked ball, and indulgence of their appetites. Cole, too, clearly exhibited a number of these unattractive attributes—he was at times manipulative, snobbish, disinterested in the rest of the world, untruthful, overly concerned with self-gratification, and a phony. Fortunately, though, as a compensating factor, he had a major saving grace: talent.

In 1923, through the good offices of Gerald Murphy, Cole had an opportunity to demonstrate his talent—not as a songwriter, as it turned out, but as a composer for the ballet. Murphy, who had many friends in the dance as a result of his volunteer work with Diaghilev's Ballets Russes, had been asked by Rolf de Maré, the Swedish impresario of the young Ballets Suédois company, then based in Paris, to come up with an idea for an "American" ballet. Murphy gladly agreed to write the scenario for the ballet and to create appropriately American scenery and costumes as well. Knowing of Linda's ambitions for Cole to write serious works, Murphy recommended him as the composer for the ballet score. When Maré went along with the recommendation, Cole jumped at the chance of doing a large-scale piece. So that he and Gerald could start on the project as soon as possible, Cole invited the Murphys to Venice that summer, where they spent three weeks at the Palazzo Barbaro. There Gerald and Cole collaborated on the ballet, titled *Within the Quota*.

The plot that Murphy devised for the ballet revolved around a Swedish immigrant, newly arrived in the United States, who has a series of adventures with a wide variety of American types: a cowboy; a sheriff; a madcap heiress with a long string of pearls; a black vaudevillian; a Hollywood goodie-goodie movie star, à la Mary Pickford; a shimmying, seductive "jazz baby"; a social reformer; and a prohibition agent. The immigrant is continually thwarted, for one reason or another, in his encounters with these assorted characters, until the ballet's end, when he is warmly welcomed and kissed by the "Sweetheart of the World," a movie star. As cameras grind away, immortalizing the scene on celluloid, the immigrant finds that he has not only finally been accepted in his new land but has also become a movie celebrity in the bargain. His is the American success story personified.

Murphy's plot, which broadly satirized contemporary American life, was helped by his costumes. They appropriately evoked the period, the locale, and the people represented. Perhaps Murphy's major contribution to the ballet, however, was his backdrop: a huge, parodistic likeness of the front page of an American daily, similar to ones put out by the Hearst press. Murphy's newspaper likeness was complete with sensational but nonsensical headlines like UNKNOWN BANKER BUYS ATLANTIC, EX-WIFE'S HEART-BALM LOVE-TANGLE, and RUM RAID LIQUOR BAN, and a "photo" of a mammoth ocean liner upended next to the Woolworth building. Murphy's hyperbolic and cynical view of American news headlines—all the ballet's action took place in front of them—set the tone for the entire work. As Murphy explained his parody of a tabloid front page, "the object [was] to get the quintessence of Americanism out of its newspapers."

Cole's music for *Within the Quota*, too, had its satiric moments and share of Americanisms, especially ragtime and jazz. By 1923 numerous serious composers in America and abroad, among them Igor Stravinsky, Charles Ives, John Alden Carpenter, and Darius Milhaud, had incorporated ragtime and jazz into their music. Cole followed suit. His score abounds in syncopations, rifflike punctuations, and bluesy inflections. The music also alludes to such diverse elements as a fox trot, a Swedish waltz, a Salvation Army chorale, silent-movie piano accompaniment, and Manhattan taxi horns. The eighteen-minute piece, in one continuous movement, closely matched Murphy's scenario and consisted of an "opening" and a "finale," with a number of sections in between labeled for various characters in the ballet—like "Heiress," "Heiress-Reformer," "Colored

Gentleman," "Colored Gentleman-Reformer," "Jazz Baby," "Jazz Baby-Reformer," "Cowboy," and "Sweetheart of the World."

Though the work was obviously intended for orchestra, Cole's score is written on four to six staves, as if it were to be performed by two or three pianos. There are no clues in the score as to Cole's instrumental ideas. Perhaps he had none. The actual orchestration of the piece was left to Charles Koechlin, a renowned French musical pedagogue of the old school who had distinguished himself by his erudition and theoretical knowledge. In the words of Darius Milhaud in his 1953 autobiography, *Notes Without Music,* the union of Koechlin and Porter was an "odd partnership between the technician of counterpoint and fugue and the brilliant future 'King of Broadway.'"

Milhaud's own composition, the now-famous *La Création du monde,* received its premiere by the Ballets Suédois at the same time that *Within the Quota* did, on October 25, 1923, at the Théâtre des Champs-Élysées. The pairing of these two jazz-influenced ballets worked out beautifully. Both ballets, and the music that went with them, enjoyed instant success with the audience—a mixture of international society, the French artistic community, and the Parisian general public—and the press. The normally staid *Figaro* was moved to describe the reception accorded *Within the Quota* as "triumphal," while the Paris edition of the *New York Herald* gave the work a rave. Equally generous was a cable dispatch to New York's *Sun* and *Globe.* "Cole Porter, Yale's musical prodigy," went the dispatch, "scored a satirical touchdown."

A month after the highly touted premiere of *Within the Quota,* the Ballets Suédois began an American tour and included the work in its repertoire. New Yorkers had a chance to hear the music for *Within the Quota* for the first time on November 28, 1923, when the ballet company opened its tour with a series of performances at the Century Theater. Unlike Paris, the New York reviews for *Within the Quota* were less than enthusiastic. The comments of *Tribune* critic Francis D. Perkins were typical. Noting that the music sounded more French than American to his ears, Perkins alleged that Cole had "drunk deeply of the Milhaud-Honegger spring." According to Perkins, Cole's "jazz smacked of . . . Darius Milhaud rather than George Gershwin." Nonetheless, Perkins conceded that the piece "had effective moments, some lively syncopated measures, and clever interweaving of a sentimental waltz into more modernistic strains." Deems Taylor, in the *World,* also had reservations about the work. "[It] did not mark the beginning of a new epoch in music,"

Mr. Taylor derisively wrote of the score, while acknowledging that it "comprised some very good jazz and some polytonal dissonances that were evidently meant to be as funny as they sounded."

Possibly Cole's strongest support from the press came from Paul Rosenfeld, one of the most highly respected and demanding of America's music critics. In his "Musical Chronicle" report in the April, 1924, issue of the renowned Chicago publication, *The Dial*, Rosenfeld had mainly complimentary things to say about Cole's ballet score (unfortunately, though, Rosenfeld's comments were published some five months after the New York critics had roasted *Within the Quota*, so that they had little effect on countering the negative reviews). "*Within the Quota* is very good burlesque indeed," observed Rosenfeld. He added, "Cole Porter's music brings a talented and original humorist to light. The snoring of New York with the horns of taxi-dom faintly blowing; the fatigued and exaggerated suggestiveness of the jazz-baby's undulations; and the finale, when the orchestra becomes an electric piano, and the trumpet sobs with soulfulness, would be creditable to any living musician, and gives one great hopes for this new composer." Rosenfeld's reservations about the work centered entirely on the fact that Cole had not orchestrated it himself. In Rosenfeld's opinion, Koechlin's orchestration of the piece "made Debussy out of it: very charming, but not in character." As advice for Cole's future consideration as a serious composer, Rosenfeld made the point that "any student of music can learn to orchestrate competently." Concluded Rosenfeld with some emphasis, "a composer who does not know his instruments, today, is nobody at all."

Barely had the Ballets Suédois completed its tour before Cole made known his intentions of writing another ballet score, despite the many negative comments about *Within the Quota* in the American press. Knowing the value of publicity in molding public and professional opinion, and as a stimulus for the project he had in mind, Cole had an unusual press item printed in the Paris *Herald* in early 1924. Presumably the news story was Cole's handiwork, for it had all the earmarks of his zany humor. Moreover, instead of blatantly announcing his ballet plans, Cole skillfully planted them in the context of a human-interest story that was practically guaranteed to pique readers' curiosity. CANINE FAVORITE OF STAGE IS LOST the story proclaimed in its heading. The news item then reported that a shaggy black and white dog named Jack Hamlet, with theatrical ambitions, had disappeared on New Year's Day from Cole's apartment at the Ritz. The dog's name, the story revealed, had been bestowed on it by none other than John Barrymore. "Mr. Cole Porter, who wrote the music of

'Within the Quota,' the American immigrant story given in Paris last November [*sic*] by the Swedish Ballets and afterwards taken to America by them," the press item disclosed, "is at work on a new ballet with M. Léon Bakst, the Russian designer, and was planning to put the dog in the show." Continuing the tie-in between Jack Hamlet and Cole's future plans, the story went on to say that "the owner is offering a reward to anyone who will restore the fugitive Hamlet to his home and his career."

It is not clear whether Jack Hamlet was ever returned to Cole (perhaps the dog—if there really was one—was never lost). But notwithstanding the press announcement, Cole's plans for another ballet score came to naught. Cole may have had hopes of having his projected ballet music performed by the Ballets Russes when he released the Jack Hamlet item for publication. For Bakst, along with Diaghilev and choreographer Fokine, had helped found that famed company in 1909. With Bakst as a collaborator, Cole presumably had the inside track on a Ballets Russes production, even though there is no music extant to support the published announcement that he was actually "at work on a new ballet" with Bakst. Unfortunately for Cole's plans, however, Bakst died in 1924, not long after the printing of the shaggy-dog story. With Bakst's death went Cole's key contact with the Ballets Russes and any hopes of a production by the company. Nor did Cole have any better luck with the Ballets Suédois. This company folded in 1924, following its American tour.

The demise of the Ballets Suédois, coupled with Bakst's death, ended Cole's serious-music plans. Never again did he write a large-scale ballet score or, for that matter, any music geared specifically for the concert hall or the opera house. The world may have lost an important voice in the serious-music field when Cole turned his back on it to concentrate on getting ahead as a popular songwriter. On the basis of his score for *Within the Quota*, Cole showed himself capable of handling a large-scale piece with considerable charm and skill. The music is witty and tuneful, and rather fastidiously put together.

What the score does not have is the blazing vitality of a *Rhapsody in Blue*, George Gershwin's crude but highly original composition "for jazz band and piano," which first burst on the scene in February of 1924, less than four months after the premiere of *Within the Quota*. Where the *Rhapsody* has a strong, outgoing musical profile—despite passing nods to a number of nineteenth-century composers from Chopin to Tchaikovsky— *Within the Quota* is more subtle and less grandiose, undoubtedly due to differences in origin, temperament, and upbringing between rich, midwestern-WASP Cole and lower East Side Jewish-boy-made-good Gershwin. The *Rhapsody*, moreover, had been written from the outset for concert-hall performances by the celebrated Paul Whiteman ensemble; that is, the piece was expected to be heard and judged solely as music. Cole's *Within the Quota*, on the other hand, depended for its life from the very first on ballet productions. Without such continued productions to keep it before the public, the *Within the Quota* score fared poorly, notwithstanding its many real charms.

Cole himself did not help matters by mislaying his manuscript draft of the work once there was no demand for it. He must have had inward reservations about the piece to have allowed such an oversight to happen; for years he claimed that the score was irrevocably lost. Not until after Cole's death was the manuscript found among the music and memorabilia that he had willed to Yale University. At the news that the manuscript had been located, the American Ballet Theater undertook to mount a new production of the work choreographed by Keith Lee, a young member of the company. Changing the title to *Times Past*, and with a new orchestration by American composer William Bolcom, the company presented their version of the work in New York on July 1, 1970, some forty-seven years after its premiere. Though the ballet received respectable reviews—perhaps more out of deference to Cole's memory than anything else—it did not set the world on fire. Nor has it entered the repertoire of the American Ballet Theater or any other dance company. A two-piano concert version of *Within the Quota*, performed by pianists Peter Basquin and Herbert Rogers at New York's Whitney Museum of American Art on November 19, 1975, in the Composers' Showcase series directed by this author, managed to create something of a stir. Nevertheless, as things now stand, *Within the Quota* is more readily accepted as a curiosity piece of the twenties—one that shows a side of Cole that the public is unfamiliar with—than as a delightful work on its own.

In addition to its musical-historical value, the saga of *Within the Quota* represents an important turning point in Cole's personal life, especially when seen in the perspective of his relationship with Gerald Murphy. When Cole and Murphy began their collaboration on the ballet in 1923, they had many interests in common, especially their desire to utilize as fully as possible their innate creative gifts. They had been close companions from college days, ever since Murphy, a year ahead of Cole and an important figure on the Yale campus, had befriended the elfin wonder from Peru. Among other things, Murphy had used his considerable influence at school to get Cole elected to the DKE fraternity. Moreover, as manager of the university glee club at about the time Cole first started with the group, Murphy saw to it that Porter songs—with the composer-lyricist as performer—were well represented in glee club concerts. Murphy also helped to promote Cole's DKE smoker entertainments at New Haven. As was true of most of Cole's Yale cronies, Murphy had every confidence that Porter would eventually be famous, and did what he could from the very beginning to push his friend's career along.

Following their graduation from Yale, Cole and Murphy—aided by the fact that Murphy's wife, Sara, was particularly fond of Cole—continued their friendship. When Cole married Linda, however, something of a strain developed, chiefly because Sara and Linda did not get along very well. The two women were dissimilar in many respects. Unlike Linda, with her meticulously coiffed and tailored look, Sara avoided unnecessary frills. She was a natural beauty, with little interest in clothes and hairstyles. Outgoing, direct, and unpretentious, Sara, furthermore, was very much involved with her children and the day-to-day routines of raising a family. She found Linda too imperious, too stuffy, and too ego-involved. Though many of Linda's friends, attuned to her interests and needs, swore by her many positive attributes, Sara reacted quite differently.

Yet in spite of Sara's reservations about Linda, the Murphys saw much of the Porters—socially active expatriates like themselves—when they came to France in 1921. Cole and Gerald's subsequent collaboration on *Within the Quota* brought the two couples closer together than ever before. But after *Within the Quota* and the Ballets Suédois had run their parallel course, the Porters and the Murphys essentially went their separate ways, though they remained on good terms for the rest of their lives. Cole even volunteered to be Honoria Murphy's godfather when he learned that the young girl's original godfather—her uncle, Fred—had died; Honoria was then about ten. Just as the Murphys and the Porters responded differently to Antibes—in contrast to the gallivanting Porters, the Murphys made this sleepy Riviera town the focus of their existence during the period they spent in France—so, too, they differed in other ways as well, especially in regard to the goals they set for themselves and the people they mingled with. The Murphys became more directly involved with the Parisian art movement of the twenties through Gerald's efforts as a painter. He started exhibiting at the Salon des Indépendants in 1923 and continued showing there through 1926. In addition, he began to get attention as a painter in avant-garde publications and the European edition of the *New York Herald*. Their circle of friends reflected this change in their lives, and more and more the Murphys associated with the artists and intellectuals they most admired. That the Murphys benefited from their contacts with the likes of Picasso, Léger, Stravinsky, Hemingway, Fitzgerald, and Dos Passos is beyond question. But they apparently also gave as much as they received from these luminaries, judging by, among other things, the recurring image of Sara Murphy among Picasso's drawings and the general similarities between the Murphys and the protagonists in Fitzgerald's *Tender Is the Night*.

While the Murphys gravitated to the artistic and the intellectual, the Porters were drawn ever more to social and theatrical pursuits following their *Within the Quota* experience. That is not to say that the Porters suddenly abjured artists and intellectuals. A sprinkling of concert and opera performers, painters, writers, and similar types could still be seen at the Porters' fabulous parties. Nonetheless, when Cole gave up on serious music, presumably because of the lack of opportunities for him as a longhair composer, the Porters, in turn, reconsidered their priorities. It was only natural that they should cultivate those interests that had the greatest appeal for them and could be most beneficial for Cole's career. But it was not a complete about-face on their part. Linda was and remained an avid reader and book collector (at her death her fine library comprised over twenty-five hundred volumes, many of them first editions of modern American, English, and French literature). Also, both she and Cole had always liked opera, which they followed with scores, and they still continued to attend opera performances whenever they could. Cole even tried his hand at painting—mainly quixotic, angular figures, painted on glass—during 1926 and 1927, before giving it up for good, presumably to devote more time to songwriting. Cole, too, frequently listened to classical music, a habit he followed most of his life. In connection with that practice, an interesting observation has been made by valet Henry Burke, who served Cole for about five years, until Cole's death. According to Burke, Cole would invariably listen to classical music in his free moments, except when he lived in the Hollywood area, where he had a home from 1935 on. As a Hollywood resident, Burke notes, Cole's musical tastes changed radically, for he would listen *only* to popular music, often of the most unsophisticated kind. It was almost as though these less-than-exalted musical products helped Cole become more readily attuned to the environment of moviedom.

Be that as it may, Cole's goals and way of life crystallized after *Within the Quota* and remained reasonably constant from then on. It is conceivable that Cole might have been quite another person had he become a composer of symphonies, concertos, and other large-scale works. Cole himself once confessed to Ginny Carpenter, the daughter of composer John Alden Carpenter, that he envied her father's skill and talent. In Cole's words, "I have little knowledge. John is a serious composer, and I would give my soul if I could believe that I was." By concentrating on popular songwriting, however, he never really had to face the decision of whether he *could* develop as a serious composer. But since character so often *is* destiny, the direction Cole took was presumably the right one for him, especially in view of his preference for the "fun" aspects of life. The world, too, is probably the richer for his taking the path that he did, considering the fantastic legacy of popular songs that Cole left behind.

9

[illegible faded text from previous page showing through]

Rising Star

In the inimitable way he had with descriptive phrases (which we see so well in his songs), Cole once told an interviewer, "I must play to work and I must work to play. It's all bound together." The sweep of the statement and its emphasis on play and work fit Cole like a glove, for he kept turning out an almost endless supply of songs while luxuriating in new sights and experiences as he moved about in grand style from city to city and port to port. Cole's approach to life comes through in a letter he sent to his mother from Paris in February, 1927. "I have written a lot of new songs, and I believe excellent ones," he confidently told Kate. He also reported, "I'm happy as a lark, and so is Linda. We are staying here until the last week in March, when we leap in the motor and go all over Spain, ending up at Seville, at the Albas [Duke and Duchess of Alba], for an Easter house-party. The Prince of Wales is going too, and it will be very gay." Thinking ahead to his stay in Venice after visiting Spain, Cole asked Kate, perhaps rhetorically, "Do you want me to come over in the spring and bring you to Venice?"

Due to her husband's illness and death on August 18, 1927, from complications following a prolonged nervous breakdown, Kate could not follow through on Cole's offer even if she wanted to. Among the numerous people, however, who did accept his invitation to come to Venice was

Fanny Brice, who visited the Porters in the summer of 1926. She was then one of the world's most famous stage personalities. Cole and Linda openly admired her talent and showered her with their hospitality. Miss Brice reciprocated by asking Cole to write some material for her. Keeping in mind her Yiddish-inflected, jewel-in-the-rough, comic personality, as demonstrated by her famous rendition of "Second-Hand Rose" from *The Ziegfeld Follies of 1921,* Cole tailored a song for her called "Hot-House Rose," about a poor Jewish factory girl, Rose Rosenbaum. As the story unfolded it told how Rose, who lived in an oppressive, ill-ventilated basement room, had a recurring dream in which she visited a beautiful rose garden. The lyrics for the song's initial refrain tell much of Rose's sad story:

> I'm hot-house rose from God knows where,
> The kind that grows without fresh air.
> The whistle blows and work is done
> But it's too late for me to get the sun.
> They say that when you dream a lot,
> You always dream of what you haven't got,
> That's why I dream of a garden, I s'pose,
> 'Cause I'm only a hot-house rose.

This mawkish text may not have fully suited Fanny Brice's comic talents, for she never sang the song. Nonetheless, she never tired of telling friends of the circumstances surrounding her first exposure to it, when Cole demonstrated the tune for her on a grand piano in the immense ballroom of the Rezzonico, with paintings by Tiepolo looking down upon them from the palazzo's walls. The inconsistency between the royal setting and the woeful tale of the poor factory girl made an indelible impression on her.

Another song that Cole wrote for Fanny Brice did not fare much better despite her interest in it. Titled "Weren't We Fools," the song touched on an ill-starred romance and the remorse of two lovers over their past mistakes. Miss Brice liked the tune well enough to schedule it for performance at the Palace Theater in the fall of 1927. But when the opening date arrived it was decided that "Weren't We Fools" was too autobiographical for comfort. Miss Brice was then having her own problems of the heart with gambler Nicky Arnstein, and the song seemed to allude to those difficulties.

The fate of "Hot-House Rose" and "Weren't We Fools" was not atypi-

cal for many of Cole's songs up until then. For with the exception of his
1919 hit, "Old-Fashioned Garden," none of Cole's songs had yet made a
big splash with the public. After he had achieved international acclaim
as a composer-lyricist of the first water, Cole alleged that he "had given
up all hope [by the mid-twenties] of ever being successful on Broadway
and had taken up painting" because of what he considered a lack of
recognition for his efforts. Just as Cole's story about joining the French
Foreign Legion on account of the failure of *See America First* does not pass
muster, so, too, his gloom-and-doom statement that nearly all was lost in
terms of his career—an appraisal made years after the fact—is not entirely accurate either. (Surprisingly, for all his sophistication as a personality and as a songwriter, Cole had an unmistakably maudlin and
overdramatic streak not really appropriate for a secure and comfortable
WASP from middle America. That side of Cole is particularly noticeable
in some of his more sentimental lyrics as well as in his need to make
exaggerated claims.)

To be sure, Cole in the early days of his career had had moments of
self-doubt about his work and his future as a songwriter. He also had had
his share of impatience; making his mark was slow going. But such
doubts and impatience hardly deterred him from leading the life of a
Continental dandy while pursuing his career practically on his own
terms. All his life Cole had almost always had everything he wanted.
Why, then, should he not expect special treatment as a songwriter as
well? Unlike the rank and file of Tin Pan Alley and Broadway songwriters, who would be out hustling daily, trying to break down the doors of
music publishers, theatrical producers, and others affiliated with the
popular-music field for the opportunity of demonstrating their ditties,
Cole did his "selling" in more leisurely fashion and with greater panache
and flair. Though he was not averse to visiting Max Dreyfus at Harms
for the purpose of showing him his latest songs while getting the low-
down on forthcoming Broadway productions, Cole did not make this the
regular routine that most songwriters did. It was not his style. Instead
of enduring the steady grind of promoting himself and his songs through
standard channels, Cole often as not used his parties and social connections as a means of making points with those who could be helpful to him.
It was simpler for him—and more effective—to deal with Fanny Brice or
some other key personage on his own turf rather than through persistent
visits to music and theatrical offices. Cole uniquely combined the ability
for getting his songs heard by the right people with high-flying living.

Cole could indulge himself in this inimitable approach by virtue of his money and social position. If to these factors one adds his Yale and Harvard background, his family roots that went back to pioneer days, and his life-style, it is clear that Cole hardly fit the stereotype of popular songwriters. In contrast to Cole, a good many songwriters—as well as the men who ran the New York music-publishing houses—came from newly emigrated Middle and Eastern European Jewish stock. They did not share the luxury of poor grades at Yale: There was seldom much formal education for these men. And they nearly always had a common goal: to make a killing in a field where, through perseverance and a little luck, it was possible to reap immense financial rewards. Cole had no less a desire to get ahead, but he was not in a do-or-die situation. For a large number of songwriters, a hit tune or two could mean financial security and upward social mobility—not exactly crucial considerations for Cole, since he had both in ample supply—and so they drove themselves hard in a highly competitive field. Cole, on the other hand, had been conditioned from childhood on to expect that practically anything he wanted he could have (to Kate he was always a king; and Cole no doubt saw himself in that light). He could thus be somewhat more sanguine about realizing his goals, though at no time did Cole ever simply sit back and wait for the world to seek him out. In his own very special way, Cole was always in there pitching, but never in the more obvious fashion of his competitors.

Shortly after *Within the Quota* had had its last performance by the Ballets Suédois, Cole, through friends, met stage director John Murray Anderson in Paris when Anderson visited France in 1924. At that time Anderson was considered a promising talent in the theater because of his flair for mounting spectacular productions; he later became famous for his direction of Billy Rose's colossal circus show, *Jumbo*, at the Hippodrome in 1935.

On hearing Cole perform some of his songs at a Paris party, Anderson asked him to write the score for the sixth edition of the *Greenwich Village Follies*, an annual revue with which Anderson was associated. Besides Cole, Anderson assembled an assortment of talent for the revue, among whom were the comedy team of Moran and Mack (known as The Two Black Crows), the singing Dolly Sisters, and the Vincent Lopez Orchestra. Unfortunately, none of the numbers that Cole wrote for the *Greenwich Village Follies* caught on right away, despite the revue's respectable run of 127 performances after opening at the Shubert Theater on September 16, 1924. One of the tunes for the show, "Two Little Babes in the Wood" (the Dolly Sisters portrayed the Babes), eventually became popular, largely because of Cole's inclusion of it in the score for a later musical, *Paris*. But the big hit of the *Greenwich Village Follies* turned out to be a tune that Cole had given up for lost. In a letter to his mother in 1927, Cole told how the song, "I'm in Love Again," gained its new lease on life:

> Three years ago, when I was writing the *Greenwich Village Follies*, I gave them a tune called "I'm in Love Again." This tune I had written before and had sung it around Paris, and always with howling success, as the melody was very simple and the sentiment appealed to everyone. The great powers of the *Greenwich Village Follies* thought less than nothing of this song. . . . So it lay in a drawer at Harms, and I thought it was dead for ever. But one thing very funny about that little song, no matter where I traveled to, I'd always hear someone singing it. Last year, in New York, I heard it at Maurice's cabaret. They played it over and over again, simply the one refrain, as no one knew the verse. I went to the band leader and asked him who wrote it, and he said "Oh a Harlem nigger wrote it." Everybody in Paris knows it, and it's almost as well known in London and in Rome. But practically no one knows that I wrote it. Now, suddenly out of a clear sky, comes a wire from Harms, offering me an excellent royalty to publish this song and do everything they can to make a big hit out of it. . . . As Harms usually only publish songs in productions, and never launch a song unless they make a big hit of it, I shall be surprised if I don't make a lot of money out of it. Don't you think it's a funny story, that poor little deserted song suddenly landing on her feet.

The direct appeal of "I'm in Love Again" derives largely from its simple, pithy lyrics. The opening lines of the song's refrain set the tone for the entire number:

> I'm in love again
> And the Spring is comin',
> I'm in love again,
> Hear my heart strings strummin',
> I'm in love again,
> And the hymn I'm hummin',
> Is the "Huddle Up, Cuddle Up Blues!"

"I'm in Love Again" was only one of a steady profusion of hits that began to command the public's attention from about 1928 on. But that was still several years away from the closing of the *Greenwich Village Follies*. In the intervening years Cole kept sharpening his tools as a composer-lyricist while dividing his time, as he put it, between play and work. The eventual emergence of the finely honed, mature Porter song style, with its music wedded to lyrics that are a graceful mixture of sexual innuendoes, topicality, offbeat humor, alliteration, rhyming ingenuity, colloquialism, social parody, and references to celebrated people and exotic places, are in large part a result of the fact that Cole never stopped writing even as he shuttled back and forth between Paris, Venice, New York, and other places of interest.

Following the *Greenwich Village Follies*, Cole's next theatrical affiliation smacked of old-home week, inasmuch as he contributed three numbers in 1925 to a Yale Dramatic Association play, *Out o' Luck*, directed by Monty Woolley and performed—as in Cole's collegiate days—by Yale students. Another Yale man, Tom Cushing, of the class of 1902, wrote the play, a comedy-melodrama about some World War I doughboys and a pretty French girl. Cole's three numbers—"Butterflies," "Mademazelle," and "Opera Star," a ludicrous takeoff on opera divas—were hard during the second act of the play as part of an impromptu entertainment put on by the soldiers. With Cole's name—he was by then, of course, a celebrated Yale alumnus—adding an element of glamour to the production, *Out o' Luck* did so well in its initial performances in New Haven and out of town during the Christmas week of 1925 that the Dramatic Association toured with the work a year later, again with great success.

Cole was never reluctant to seek professional help in promoting his work. He approached Louis Shurr, a highly respected theatrical and press agent who represented many of the top Broadway and Hollywood names, early in 1927. Shurr, who was familiar with Cole's career and liked his songs, quickly accepted the assignment and arranged for Cole to perform some of his tunes for the Broadway producing team of Alex Aarons and Vinton Freedley. Aarons, an ex-clothing salesman, and Freedley, a former song-and-dance man, had first gained wide recognition as a team with their 1924 production of Gershwin's *Lady, Be Good*, one of Broadway's biggest hits of that season. After *Lady, Be Good* Aarons and Freedley went on to become Gershwin's most important producers, for they subsequently brought to Broadway his *Tip-Toes* (1925), *Oh, Kay!* (1926), *Funny Face* (1927), *Treasure Girl* (1928), *Girl Crazy* (1930), and *Pardon My English* (1933). So quickly did the Aarons-Freedley fortunes rise as a result of producing Gershwin shows that by the end of 1927, after three years or so of partnership, they could boast of owning their own Broadway theater, the Alvin (it still exists today), immodestly named after themselves: *Al*, from Alex, and *Vin*, from Vinton. But as quickly as they rose to prominence, Aarons and Freedley skidded downhill even more rapidly. In 1932, as one of the consequences of the Depression, they lost their theater for lack of business. The following year, under the pressure of mounting debts, they were forced to dissolve their partnership when their production of Gershwin's *Pardon My English* closed after only forty-six performances. To escape from creditors Freedley even left the United States for a while until things quieted down. *Pardon My English* was Aarons's last Broadway production, for he never fully recovered from the effects of that show's failure. Freedley, on the other hand, bounced back quickly enough. His 1934 production of *Anything Goes*, with a Porter score, was a tremendous hit, and he and Cole soon became two of the hottest personalities on Broadway. Nevertheless, at the time that Louis Shurr first approached Aarons and Freedley about sponsoring a Porter musical, they both were disinclined to do so. They listened politely to Cole performing a sampling of his tunes, but offered little encouragement. Why switch from Gershwin to Porter, they reasoned, when they were making a bundle of money with Gershwin.

Persisting in his efforts to get a show assignment for Cole, Shurr put in a pitch for him with E. Ray Goetz, a colorful, extroverted Broadway figure who had his hand in many theatrical pies as producer, playwright, and tunesmith, among other things. Goetz, it turned out, was thinking of asking Richard Rodgers and Lorenz Hart to write the score for a musical he intended to produce with Gilbert Miller, the son of England's famous actor-manager Henry Miller. The show was to be built around the talents and French accent of the vivacious musical-comedy star Irene Bordoni, who also happened to be Goetz's wife. She had built up a reputation for singing slyly suggestive tunes like Gershwin's "Do It Again" (1922) and "I Won't Say I Will But I Won't Say I Won't" (1923) in a naughty, insouciant, Gallic manner. When Goetz learned that Rodgers and Hart were not available for his show (they were then involved in readying *A Connecticut Yankee* for its Broadway opening in the fall of 1927), he readily accepted Shurr's suggestion that Cole, doubling as composer and lyricist, substitute for them. Goetz had long been familiar with Cole's work—they had been colyricists for "Washington Square," a little-known tune performed in *As You Were*, a 1920 revue—and had every confidence that Cole's songs would be assets for the production.

Cole had a chance to learn more about the forthcoming musical, *Paris,* during the summer of 1927 when Goetz visited Venice. While enjoying the Porters' hospitality at the Rezzonico and the sun and the surf at the Lido, Goetz outlined key aspects of the production—including, of course, the plot—for Cole to keep in mind when shaping his songs. Besides sharing some of the amenities of Venice together, their meeting allowed for a free and full exchange of ideas, which proved beneficial for both of them. But perhaps most important, at least from Cole's standpoint, was the psychological boost of being involved with a show that gave every indication, judging from Goetz's extraordinary enthusiasm for the project, of being a winner. By the time Goetz left Venice Cole was fired up more than ever with the idea of returning to Broadway.

The book concocted for *Paris* by scriptwriter Martin Brown was little more than window dressing for Irene Bordoni to show off her wardrobe and ingratiating stage presence. The story told of a young, handsome, and very proper Bostonian, Andrew Sabot (presumably the fictional equivalent of a real, blue-blooded Cabot), who has fallen in love with a svelte Parisian actress, Vivienne Rolland, and wants to marry her. The young man's snooty, straitlaced mother, on learning of his romantic attachment, rushes to Paris to see for herself whether the actress is worthy of her darling son. As was to be expected, the mother wastes little time in disapproving of the actress as a wife for a Sabot. After a series of comic entanglements in which the mother, under the influence of alcohol, is transformed from a holier-than-thou, stuffy dowager to a passionate sex creature, the show ends with the actress turning down young Sabot for her own tried-and-true stage partner, one Guy Pennell.

Before bringing *Paris* to New York, Goetz tried out the show in a number of other cities over more than a six-month period. Starting in Atlantic City on February 6, 1928, before going on to Philadelphia, *Paris* also opened in Boston in May of that year as well as in Washington, D. C., at the end of September. While *Paris* had its shakedown stints out of town, Cole accepted the invitation of Edmond Sayag, the manager of Les Ambassadeurs, a well-known Parisian nightspot, to write the score for an American revue that Sayag wanted to present at the club in May of 1928.

The prospect of being involved simultaneously with two productions on both sides of the Atlantic hardly deterred Cole. Continent-hopping had become routine for him by then. Cole, moreover, was delighted at the prospect of working with the exceptionally brilliant group of Americans who were at Sayag's disposal, among them Morton Downey, Evelyn

Hoey, Buster and John West, Frances Gershwin (the sister of George; at opening night, on May 10, George accompanied her at the piano as she sang a medley of Gershwin numbers), and Fred Waring and his orchestra. Nevertheless, of the nearly twenty numbers he fashioned for Sayag's show, titled simply *La Revue des Ambassadeurs,* only one song had much success. The tune, "Looking At You," was used again by Cole in *Wake Up and Dream,* a 1929 production. But even if the score did not represent Cole at his best, his association with the revue was enough to bring out Paris's social elite. They cheered mightily for their hero and followed that up with a whole string of lavish parties in his honor, a ritual that delighted Cole. Over the years, no matter how many shows accrued to his credit, Cole never tired of the social hubbub that went along with an opening. The festivities that went hand in hand with a premiere were at least as important to Cole as his role of composer-lyricist in a production.

When *Paris* finally opened in New York on October 8, 1928, at the Music Box Theater, the show had been whipped into great shape after months of playing in the hinterlands. The sparkling cast and spiffy production more than compensated for the humdrum book, with the result that the normally hard-boiled, blasé New York press could hardly contain their delight with the show. They fell over themselves praising Irene Bordoni as the Parisian actress and the other leads (Eric Kalkhurst's performance of Andrew Sabot, the mother-cum-sexpot role of Mrs. Sabot undertaken by Louise Closser Hale, and Arthur Margetson's rendition of Guy Pennell) plus Irving Aaronson's "Commanders," a versatile band that monopolized the show's second act with their exuberant playing, singing, and dancing. Cole's songs also received their share of approbation. Though producer Goetz had included some of his own tunes in the show along with Cole's, it was Cole's that stood out. As Richard Watts of the *Herald Tribune* put it, Cole "was the flaming star of the premiere of 'Paris.' " While noting somewhat caustically that Cole was "a wealthy American living abroad who occasionally finds the time to sit down in his Riviera chateau and write a song," Watts willingly conceded that Cole's tunes were "the triumph" of the show. The *New Yorker*'s drama critic, Charles Brackett was equally complimentary, maintaining that "no one else now writing words and music knows so exactly the delicate balance between sense, rhyme, and tune." In Brackett's estimation, Cole's "rare and satisfactory talent makes other lyrists [*sic*] sound as though they'd written their words for a steam whistle." And so it went, in review after review.

Of the five Porter songs in *Paris,* two of them—"Let's Do It, Let's Fall in Love" and "Two Little Babes in the Wood"—had the greatest public appeal. Almost as if in retribution for its rather lukewarm reception in the *Greenwich Village Follies* of 1924, "Two Little Babes in the Wood" had audiences yelling their approval throughout the show's Broadway run of 195 performances as Irene Bordoni related the delightful tale of how two pretty girls, left to die in the woods by their cruel uncle, were saved by

> A rich old man in a big sedan,
> And a very, very fancy beard.
> He saw those girls and cheered,
> Then he drove them down to New York town,
> Where he covered them with useful things,
> Such as bonds, and stocks, and Paris frocks,
> And Oriental pearls in strings,
> And a show case full of rings.

"Let's Do It, Let's Fall in Love" was an even bigger hit. This number, sung winningly by Irene Bordoni and Arthur Margetson, had all the magic ingredients of Porter songs at their best. "Let's Do It" combined melodic pizzazz with highly inventive lyrics. Conceived as an extolment of the virtues of lovemaking, the song cunningly suggested that every couple "do it," since so many of nature's creations—people, birds, sea creatures, insects, and animals—do it too. In Cole's hands, "Let's Do It" was indeed a tour de force as it convincingly demonstrated that—among others—Finns, electric eels, barnyard fowls, refined ladybugs, and heavy hippopotami all do it. Typical are these lines from one of its refrains:

> The dragon flies, in the reeds do it,
> Sentimental centipedes do it,
> Let's do it, let's fall in love.
> Mosquitos, heaven forbid, do it,
> So does ev'ry katydid, do it,
> Let's do it, let's fall in love.
> The most refined ladybugs do it,
> When a gentleman calls,
> Moths in your rugs, do it,
> What's the use of moth balls?
> Locusts in trees do it, bees do it,
> Even highly educated fleas do it,
> Let's do it, let's fall in love.

With *Paris* Cole finally arrived as a composer for Broadway. At the age of thirty-seven, with years of social and professional experience behind him, Cole could no longer be thought of simply as a wealthy, smarty-pants, Yale and Harvard man whose songs—especially the lyrics—were just too highfalutin for the public to grasp. Cole still hardly fit the mold for popular songwriters, but with a solid hit show under his belt, he now had to be taken seriously. Moreover, Cole had never shied away from publicizing the glamorous aspects of his life. It was no secret that, while other songwriters were involved in the nitty-gritty of hacking out a career on their home turf, Cole was usually off somewhere living it up in a Riviera chateau or a Venice palazzo. Almost as the raison d'être for his sophisticated songs, Cole would gladly speak out about some of his interesting adventures—from fictional French Foreign Legion and World War I escapades to impressive soirees with potentates—for the press to pass on to the hoi polloi.

All this emphasis on the glamorous life might not have been taken too seriously when Cole was considered only a wealthy songwriting dilet-tante still trying to find himself. However, once he became a much-talked-about composer-lyricist of hit songs, his exciting global adventures not only were taken at their face value, but they also worked to his advantage. Cole now epitomized for the masses, too, the suave man of the world, and his urbane and polished songs were more readily accepted on that basis.

Cole, furthermore, had always had a flair for getting the press to print practically any story he fed them. Just as he got the *New Haven Register* in 1911 to print the claim that his talent for writing collegiate songs derived from the years he spent in the Rumanian mountains listening to the strange birds there, and was able to disseminate the news story in 1924 of the loss of his dog, Jack Hamlet, in connection with his ballet plans, so, too, Cole shrewdly used the communications media now to build up his glamorous image. It is not often that legends are shaped by the very person they describe, but, as much as anyone, Cole—aided, of course, by press agents and other media personnel—can take credit for promul-gating the portrait of himself that the world has come to know and accept.

Consistent with the chi-chi public image of Cole are some of the whim-sical descriptions of him published by various friends. Writer Michael Arlen combined surrealistic fantasy with deadpan humor in his portrait of Cole:

Every morning at half past seven, Cole Porter leaps lightly out of bed and, having said his prayers, arranges himself in a riding habit. Then, having written a song or two, he will appear at the stroke of half past twelve at the Ritz, where leaning in a manly way on the bar, he will say: "Champagne cocktail, please. Had a marvelous ride this morning!" That statement gives him strength and confidence on which to suffer this, our life, until ten minutes past three in the afternoon when he will fall into a childlike sleep.

Noted gadabout and columnist Lucius Beebe also helped to further the carefully nurtured Porter image when he observed, rather enviously:

It is really the simple things of life which give pleasure to Mr. Porter —half-million-dollar strings of pearls. Isotta motor cars, cases of double bottles of Grand Chambertin '87, suites at Claridge's, brief trips aboard the *Bremen*, a little grouse shooting.

Beebe, himself a flamboyant fashion plate and self-styled connoisseur of high living, doffed his top hat in admiration as he listed a few of Cole's other achievements:

He is on all the first-night lists. Leon at L'Aperitif salutes him as 'Highness,' he is reputed to travel with his own linen sheets, punkah-wavers, court chamberlains, and sauce cooks.

Fanciful descriptions, these, of Cole. And yet they are evocative of the man and his way of life. Since Cole made such wonderful copy, it was inevitable that more and more would be written about him in a veritable snowball effect as he and his songs became better known. His increased fame, in turn, helped to open up opportunities for his particular talents. Fortunately for the world, Cole made the most of his opportunities, as his long string of successful musicals for the stage and films will attest. But it was the good showing of *Paris* that really gave the first major boost to Cole's career.

Decade's End

Cole's career was now moving at an accelerated pace. His next show, *Wake Up and Dream*, opened at the London Pavilion in March of 1929 while *Paris* was still running on Broadway. The producer of *Wake Up and Dream*, Charles B. Cochran, had previously employed Cole for the 1922 London revue, *Mayfair and Montmartre*, which included "The Blue Boy Blues" in its score. Not one to let near-boorish behavior becloud his judgment of talent, Cochran called on Cole to write the score for *Wake Up and Dream* despite some personal slights from him. For on several occasions Cochran had been dismayed when Cole, during the course of a conversation, would peremptorily end the discussion and leave. Nor was Cochran alone in receiving such treatment. Other acquaintances of Cole complained of him suddenly staring at them with a look of disgust when he apparently had had enough of their company. Before they knew it Cole, without a word of explanation, would bolt from the room as if to avoid the plague.

Idiosyncratic or not, Cole's closest friends accepted him on his own terms with the greatest of affection. Among these friends must be counted amateur actress-turned-professional-decorator Elsie de Wolfe, the noted society figure, and Sir Charles Mendl, a very correct Englishman who was always something of a mystery.

On the surface Mendl was English to the core, with an accent so heavily British it was often difficult to understand what he said. The aura of secrecy surrounding him derived largely from a lack of information about his early background. Reputedly his forebears were Lebanese Jews who had emigrated to England. Supposedly, in 1880 or so, when he was seventeen, Mendl left England to seek his fortune in South America. When he returned to Great Britain some years later, Mendl had attained the directorship of a number of Latin American railroads, including ones in Argentina and Paraguay. Mendl subsequently became head of the British Embassy press bureau in Paris and was also knighted for invaluable services to his government, though the exact nature of these services was never spelled out.

In 1926 Mendl married Elsie de Wolfe, whom he had known for a long time. Both were then in their sixties. A very distinguished-looking couple (Elsie was tiny and slim, Mendl was tall and more amply proportioned) with much in common, there were also inherent differences in their makeup: Elsie's name had long been linked with lesbian groups while Sir Charles's reputation was that of a womanizer. (Ironically, F. Scott Fitzgerald modeled the homosexual Campion in *Tender Is the Night* on Mendl; it was an inaccurate and unflattering portrayal.) Since sexual relations—in view of their inclinations and advanced ages—presumably had nothing to do with their decision to marry, it always amused their friends when Elsie would banteringly protest in company that Sir Charles had married her for her money (she was by far the wealthier of the two), while he in turn would retort that she had married him for his title. Even in jest, both protestations had a ring of truth to them.

At any rate, such marriages of convenience—whatever the convenience—as the Mendls' were often the rule rather than the exception in Cole's circle, as the partners were usually not only sophisticated but highly individual ("liberated" might be the better word, for the upper class has always been able to afford liberation) in their sexual mores as well. A setup such as the Mendls' allowed for great personal freedom within the framework of marriage as a bulwark of social respectability and family responsibility. When the arrangement worked out—as was true with the Mendls and the Porters—both partners benefited.

In Cole and Linda's case there was a solid base of understanding and devotion underlying the marriage. Cole's sexual drives may have been male-oriented, but that in no way altered the fact that he was deeply attached to Linda and she to him. Little is known of Linda's basic sexual inclinations. Perhaps they were so deeply hidden or so heavily sublimated that she herself was not completely aware of them. Whatever they were—and some of her friends, as already stated, have speculated that she may have been a latent lesbian—they certainly did not interfere with her marriage to Cole. For clearly Cole's career and well-being meant everything to Linda, and she gave of herself accordingly, encouraging and supporting him and helping in any way she could. So intense was her interest in Cole's professional advancement, she scrupulously maintained hordes of scrapbooks dealing with his various productions. In each of the scrapbooks she pasted all kinds of pertinent material—reviews, programs, photographs, published interviews and stories, telegrams, and letters—as mementos of these important events. Apparently nothing of potential value as a keepsake escaped her notice, judging by the extensive amount of material she ultimately accumulated in these books (which are now housed at Yale University).

Linda showed her intense interest in Cole's career in other ways, too. Early in his professional life Linda started the practice of giving him a valuable, inscribed cigarette case with the opening of each new production. No two cases were alike. They generally reflected different aspects of the shows involved, and varied in design and construction. For the most part the cases were made of gold, silver, or leather, though many of them were also studded with precious stones. As was true of the scrapbooks, Linda's cigarette cases evidenced her great concern with detail. She would make it a point, for example, of checking the design of the cases with Kate and others close to Cole for their reactions before showing the design to him. Once Cole had given his approval, Linda, on her own, would make the final decision as to the actual finish of the case. By taking this final step Linda helped to maintain an element of surprise in what might have become a somewhat routinized—though highly personal and loving—form of gift-giving.

Also in connection with Cole's productions, Linda invariably had a hand in the planning of the festivities that accompanied opening nights. Usually the Porters would have a small dinner party for close friends preceding the opening-night curtain, and Linda would oversee the affair from the sending of the invitations to the determination of what was served. Like a commander marshalling forces for greatest effect, Linda would see to it, too, that the Porter party arrived at the theater at the most propitious moment, and shortly before the lights went down they would sweep into the theater in a wave of furs, formal attire, perfume, and laughter. As all eyes focused on them they would wend their way slowly to their seats up front, stopping from time to time to chat and exchange greetings with friends and well-wishers.

No sooner had the opening-night curtain rung down than the Porters would once again be caught up in the whirl of social activities attendant on a new production. Typical of such occasions was the party in Cole's honor given by Lady Cunard, a good friend of the Porters, when *Wake Up and Dream* opened in London on March 27, 1929. Typical, too, of the hoopla surrounding Cole's opening nights was the press attention that Lady Cunard's party received. Under the heading COLE PORTER NIGHT the London press noted that "last night Lady Cunard gave a brilliant supper party in honor of Cole Porter, the American composer of the music and lyrics of the new Cochran revue. Her salons in 7, Grosvenor Square, were crowded with celebrities after the first night, itself a distinguished assembly." Among the celebrities at Lady Cunard's affair were Sir Charles and Lady Mendl, who came from Paris for the opening of the revue so that they might, in the words of the press, share with the Porters "the thrills of a London debut." Like many others in the Porter circle, the Mendls thought nothing of traveling great distances to attend a significant social event. Moreover, the Mendls' presence at the premiere of *Wake Up and Dream* helped to make the show's opening one of London's most glittering social occasions, a cachet not lost on the London press.

Cole's score for *Wake Up and Dream* included a number of tunes he had written earlier, such as "Looking At You" from *La Revue des Ambassadeurs* of 1928 and "Let's Do It, Let's Fall in Love," the big hit of *Paris*. Cole had been especially concerned that the unremitting emphasis on lovemaking in "Let's Do It" might make the song too risqué for British tastes. He was therefore considerably relieved when, on meeting England's Lord Chamberlain during the tryout of *Wake Up and Dream* in Manchester, the venerable gentleman congratulated him on the song's wonderful lyrics and the extensive research that had gone into naming the myriad creatures who "do it." The London public evidently agreed with their Lord Chamberlain, for they, too, responded positively to the song. Another favorite of theirs was Cole's "What Is This Thing Called Love?" which received exotic treatment—in keeping with the song's quick shifts from the major to the minor, an unusual and exotic musical device for the time —in *Wake Up and Dream*. As staged in the revue, dancer Tilly Losch gyrated sensuously to the persistent beat of tom-toms before an African idol while Elsie Carlisle sang the number, whose refrain went:

What is this thing called love?
This funny thing called love?
Just who can solve its mystery?
Why should it make a fool of me?
I saw you there one wonderful day.
You took my heart and threw it away.
That's why I ask the Lord in heaven above,
What is this thing called love?

Like "Let's Do It," "What Is This Thing Called Love?" has since become one of Cole's most famous songs. As for the show itself, it essentially got mixed reviews from the London critics but still managed to achieve a profitable run of 263 performances—enough to make producer Cochran overlook Cole's occasionally errant behavior.

On the basis of the revue's good showing, Cochran brought *Wake Up and Dream*, with most of the original cast intact, to Broadway at the end of its London engagement. Contrary to its lengthy run in London, *Wake Up and Dream* lasted for only 136 performances after opening at Broadway's Selwyn Theater on December 30, 1929. The New York critics' mixed reviews undoubtedly took their toll on box-office receipts. For the Broadway critics—like their London counterparts, but apparently with more damaging effect—had at least as many bad things to say about the show as good.

But perhaps one of the more interesting aspects of their evaluation of the show, aside from the overall consistency of viewpoint on both sides of the Atlantic, was the almost complete turnabout of Richard Watts and Charles Brackett in their opinion of Cole. Where both had extolled Cole to the skies for his songs in *Paris*, they each now had decided reservations about the score for *Wake Up and Dream*. In his *Herald Tribune* review Watts took an indirect swipe at "Let's Do It" along with his general carping about the score. He wrote:

A number of us who long have admired the lyrics of Mr. Cole Porter and had wished that he would write a whole score without demonstrating his passion for zoology had our wish last night, but it hardly can be said that we were altogether satisfied. There is not one reference in "Wake Up and Dream" to the sex habits of the beaver and the gnu, but, on the other hand, there is little of the brilliant style to be found in his better songs.

Granting that "What Is This Thing Called Love?" is "charming in every way," Watts complained that "the rest of the score, as well as the remaining lyrics, seemed . . . less than striking." Brackett, in his *New Yorker* critique, dismissed *Wake Up and Dream*—and Cole's score with it—as "one of the dullest revues ever put on the local boards." An important press voice, however, who more than made up for Watts's and Brackett's snipings by speaking out strongly in Cole's behalf, was Walter Winchell. He acclaimed *Wake Up and Dream* and Cole's score for it in his column, particularly singling out "What Is This Thing Called Love?" as an example of the newest breed of love songs. With Winchell rallying to his support, Cole and his songs ended up becoming better known than ever before as a result of the publicity.

Adding to the momentum of Cole's rising career at this juncture was the rash of productions which appeared in quick succession with his songs in them. For shortly before *Wake Up and Dream* began its Broadway run, two other productions containing tunes by Cole opened almost simultaneously in November of 1929: *Fifty Million Frenchmen*, a stage musical put on by E. Ray Goetz, and *The Battle of Paris*, a film released by Paramount Pictures. Of these two new productions, *The Battle of Paris* represented something of a departure for Cole, since it was his first film assignment. Yet it was inevitable that he would receive a film offer. After all, early talking pictures of the twenties placed great emphasis on music. To the film moguls of that era, sure-fire talkie entertainment for the masses invariably meant singing and dancing on the silver screen. With such a formula in mind they fashioned *The Jazz Singer* (1927) and *The Singing Fool* (1928), two early and very successful talkies which featured Al Jolson as singer. Once it was clear that the formula worked, the film industry quickly began hiring songwriters, and talkie after talkie was turned out with music. Before long, talkie production—not only of the musical, but of the nonmusical variety as well—was literally on a round-the-clock basis in studios on both coasts to satisfy the voracious appetite of the masses for films of all descriptions.

By far the busiest of the East Coast studios was the Paramount lot in Astoria, Long Island. There talkies were turned out by the carload, using such Broadway stars as Eddie Cantor, Lillian Roth, Fanny Brice, and Ann Pennington, plus the talents of relative newcomers like Edward G. Robinson and Claudette Colbert. To keep up with the heavy demand for talkies, the studio was run with almost clockwork precision: Feature films were made on weekdays, tests were done at night, and short subjects were shot over the weekend. Supervising the production at the Astoria lot was none other than Walter Wanger, who in 1916, fresh from Dartmouth, had been a production assistant for Cole's first Broadway show, *See America First*. Wanger had always been partial to Cole's songs. As a production supervisor for Paramount he was in a position to call on Cole's services, particularly since Cole was now a figure of consequence in popular music, someone whose name would make a welcome addition to any talkie.

With Wanger putting in a good word for him, Cole was asked to write several songs for Paramount's *The Battle of Paris*, starring Gertrude Lawrence, the darling of the Broadway and London stage. Selected to direct the movie was Robert Florey, who had scored an incredible triumph with his brilliant direction of the Marx Brothers in the film version of *The Cocoanuts*. (Originally a hilarious and highly successful stage vehicle for the Marxes, *The Cocoanuts* became even more hilarious and more successful when it was transferred to the screen.) Unfortunately, Florey had little sympathy with Gene Markey's vapid script for *The Battle of Paris*, which did little more than demonstrate that Gertrude Lawrence had a charming British accent. When Florey tried to get out of directing the film, Paramount ruled against him—he was under contract to them, and they had the final say in the matter. Besides Florey's lack of interest in the project, there was a further complication: The shooting schedule at the Astoria studio had become so crowded that Florey had no choice but to film at night, between eight in the evening and five in the morning.

For all these reasons, *The Battle of Paris* never had a chance. It was a film so mired down by a variety of ineptitudes that it never got off the ground. Lost in the ensuing shuffle were Cole's two songs for the film: "Here Comes the Bandwagon" and "They All Fall in Love." As one reviewer pointed out, "The songs in this banal musical comedy—it just missed being a floperetta—won't knock anyone cold." In retrospect, except for the publicity that went along with the release of *The Battle of Paris* on November 30, 1929, Cole had little to show for his first screen credit.

It was another story, however, with the stage musical *Fifty Million Frenchmen*. Where *The Battle of Paris* collapsed from its own dead weight, Goetz's *Fifty Million Frenchmen* was as light and airy as a master chef's soufflé. The book for *Frenchmen*, by Herbert Fields (the son of comedian-producer Lew Fields, one of Cole's first important Broadway contacts) had a lot to do with capturing the frothy Gallic essence implicit in the title, as did the near-perfect cast headed by William Gaxton, Genevieve Tobin, and Helen Broderick, and the sure-handed direction of Cole's good friend, Monty Woolley (*Frenchmen* was the first of several Porter shows that Woolley was involved with on Broadway). The plot for *Frenchmen* concerned one Peter Forbes (William Gaxton), a wealthy young American expatriate in Paris, who has been smitten with Looloo Carroll (Genevieve Tobin), a pretty young thing from Indiana. At the instigation of friends, Peter bets that he can win over Looloo in a month's time solely through his own ingenuity, without drawing on his immense financial resources. While courting Looloo and simultaneously trying to secure his bet, Peter is forced to support himself by a string of odd jobs: as a tour guide, racetrack tout, gigolo, master of ceremonies, and magician. The pie-in-the-face type of travails that befall Peter in his efforts are the sum and substance of Fields's waggish script. Adding to the belly laughs were the uninhibited antics of Violet Hildegarde (Helen Broderick), an American department-store buyer of fur coats, who is continually on the prowl for the earthier aspects of Parisian life, from provocative French postcards to love-'em-and-leave-'em roués.

Complementing the book, cast, direction, and overall lavishness of Goetz's production was Cole's score for *Frenchmen*, his most comprehensive one for a Broadway show up to then. Though twenty of Cole's songs —a sizable lot—were actually used in the show, he wrote approximately twice that number for Goetz's consideration. The score, moreover, showed Cole in top form, particularly in the way he skillfully delineated character and mood. Whether writing the now-famous "You Do Something to Me," in which Peter first expresses his love for Looloo, or jazz-influenced numbers like "The Happy Heaven of Harlem" and "You've Got That Thing," or French-flavored tunes such as "You Don't Know Paree" and "Paree, What Did You Do to Me?" (there is even a subtle melodic reference to "La Marseillaise," the French national anthem, in the latter number), Cole's coupling of music and lyrics is masterly. Nor are the songs in the show mere set pieces that have little to do with the continuity of the show. Rather, they are highly integrated parts of the production as a whole.

The special Porter touch comes through in most of the songs. A case in point is the emphasis on the sound "oo" ("do do that voodoo that you do so well") in the lyrics of "You Do Something to Me," the big hit of the show. Another recognizable Porter characteristic in the *Frenchmen* score is the use of musical quotations from diverse sources, a practice Cole had followed since college days. Just as he had not hesitated to quote the opening measures of "Onward Christian Soldiers" (to correspond with the text, "by my blue-eyed Christian soldier") in the refrain of "My Salvation Army Queen," from *The Pot of Gold* of 1912, so, too, Cole felt free to quote briefly from "Dixie," "Stars and Stripes Forever," "Yankee Doodle," and Elgar's *Pomp and Circumstance, No. 1* in the *Frenchmen* score. There are even minuscule references in the score to Gershwin and Youmans (in the long, 192-measure production number "Do You Want to See Paris?" a musical discourse on the sights of Paris, Cole quotes briefly from Gershwin's highly popular " 'S Wonderful," dating from 1927, and Youmans's less familiar "Hallelujah" of 1918).

Where there were qualifications for Cole's *Frenchmen* score, they centered mainly on his witty tune, "The Tale of the Oyster." Some critics, especially Gilbert Seldes, considered the song "disgusting" because of its graphic description of a "social-climbing" oyster being eaten by a rich society dame, who then regurgitates it as a result of seasickness. Some of the key lines of the song that triggered the outcry are:

> See that bi-valve social climber
> Feeding the rich Mrs. Hoggenheimer,
> Think of his joy as he gaily glides
> Down to the middle of her gilded insides.
> Proud little oyster!
> After lunch Mrs. H. complains,
> And says to her hostess, "I've got such pains,
> I came to town on my yacht today,
> But I think I'd better hurry back to Oyster Bay."
> Scared little oyster!
> Off they go thru the troubled tide,
> The yacht rolling madly from side to side,
> They're tossed about till that poor young oyster
> Finds that it's time he should quit his cloister.
> Up comes the oyster!

Ultimately, to appease criticism of its "disgusting" lyrics, the song was dropped from the show (for years it was virtually ignored; only recently has it been performed to some extent, as well as recorded).

All in all, however, the score for *Fifty Million Frenchmen* convincingly demonstrated Cole's ever-increasing skills as a composer-lyricist—an opinion shared by many of his admirers, including Irving Berlin, a composer-lyricist of the first rank. In an advertisement for the show Berlin was quoted as saying that the *Frenchmen* score was "one of the best collections of song numbers I have ever listened to." As a further plug for Cole, Berlin volunteered that it was "worth the price of admission to hear Cole Porter's lyrics."

Berlin's public endorsement, added to other praise for the show (from Walter Winchell and Gilbert Gabriel, among others), helped to trigger interest in *Frenchmen* despite the generally mixed reviews that followed its Broadway opening on November 27, 1929, at the Lyric Theater. Taking their lead from Berlin and other boosters of the show, the public turned out in sufficient numbers to keep *Frenchmen* open for 254 performances—enough to put the production in the black. Warner Brothers, who had backed the show in order to secure the film rights for it, eventually made a Technicolor movie of it in 1931 (in getting the film rights, Warners agreed to shoot the movie in color). By that time, unfortunately, the craze for film musicals had abated somewhat, with the result that the *Fifty Million Frenchmen* movie put out by Warners, with William Gaxton and Helen Broderick of the original Broadway cast in it, was not a musical. The movie eliminated Cole's vocal score, though it drew on it for instrumental background music.

When the stage version of *Fifty Million Frenchmen* began its run, Cole had the unique satisfaction of knowing that a total of three of his American productions would be opening within a five-week period: *Frenchmen* and *The Battle of Paris*, starting on November 27 and 30 respectively, and *Wake Up and Dream* on December 30, 1929. Considering that the bottom had fallen out of the American economy with the Wall Street crash of October 29, 1929, with a resultant constriction of public spending, the almost simultaneous opening of three Porter musicals was an extremely impressive achievement.

The final days of 1929 that ended the fabulous decade of the roaring twenties saw Cole's professional standing attaining new heights. His prospects for the thirties and beyond seemed most promising, as his work was increasingly in demand. Thus it was with a decidedly optimistic outlook for the future that Cole took off on New Year's Day of 1930—almost immediately after the festivities for the opening of *Wake Up and Dream*, the last of his 1929 New York musicals—to tour the Far East and Europe for six months with Linda and several friends. Cole had every reason to be gratified with his progress. No matter that his life-style emphasized play at least as much as work. In his own way, Cole had paid his dues to his profession—and in substantial fashion—by continually striving to write the best songs he knew how. It was perhaps fitting, therefore, that with the start of the thirties Cole had the security of knowing that he, with his songs, was a decided success.

11

Naughty Thirties

It didn't take much to bring out the puckish side of Cole. But at times it seemed that Cole would go to greater lengths than usual to bring off a stunning practical joke or some other inspired bit of outlandishness when he was traveling, if only because new experiences invariably stimulated his brand of tomfoolery. Like a swashbuckling film star whose nearly every gesture, both on and off the screen, was calculated to show his heroic dimensions as grist for the publicity mills, so, too, Cole's actions while on the move were often the kind of which stories—especially wire-service ones—are made. One such instance occurred during Cole's travels to the Far East in 1930. Dissatisfied with the regular Japanese train service of that period, Cole simply hired an entire private train for himself and his party to take them to their destination. Not unexpectedly, when the story got out it made Japanese headlines.

Cole made capital, too, of his 1933 beer-drinking escapade with Monty Woolley, judging by the number of times the story made the rounds in the press. According to Cole, he and Woolley were drinking heady, dark beer in Munich in the summer of 1933 when they suddenly decided, in the interests of science, to ferret out the lightest beer they could find. Approaching their task with the objective detachment of the Louis Pasteurs of the world, Cole and Woolley went from city to city and pub to pub, checking out beer samples firsthand. Several weeks later—and considerably heavier for their guzzling efforts—Cole and Woolley finally found light-beer Nirvana in Pilsen, Czechoslovakia's famous beer-producing city, located many miles from where they had started. Their joy at discovering Pilsen's extraordinary beer more than compensated for their hangovers and the extra inches around their waists, which they considered line-of-duty consequences for such an undertaking.

Besides their Munich-to-Pilsen jaunt, Cole and Woolley made many other trips together. Often on these expeditions one would try to top the other in all sorts of pranks. But no matter who came out on top, both would have a hearty laugh at the shenanigans before starting the cycle all over again. Typical of their capers was the stunt Cole once pulled on Woolley in New York after Woolley had become famous as the red-bearded and irascible Sheridan Whiteside in *The Man Who Came to Dinner* —the George S. Kaufman–Moss Hart 1939 stage spoof based on the life of Alexander Woollcott. In celebration of his good Broadway notices as the fictional counterpart of Woollcott, Woolley decided to give a party. Without warning Woolley what he was up to, Cole appeared at the height of the party with an attractively gowned and mysteriously veiled woman. At a signal from Cole she quickly removed her veil to reveal a long, flowing beard, at least the equal of Woolley's in size and conformation. As Woolley looked on in chagrin, Cole went around the room introducing the bearded lady—whom he had hired from the circus just for the party—to everyone he met as Woolley's sister.

Linda delighted in Cole's exuberance and whimsical turn of mind as much as anyone, and lent tacit support to most of his carryings-on with Woolley and other chums. She spoke up, however, if she felt Cole overstepped the bounds of fair play and good taste. Not surprisingly, then, it was Linda who cautioned Cole about being more prudent in the future when the Japanese press in 1930 played up his extravagance in renting an entire train for his party at a time when the Depression was devastating vast areas of the world. It was Linda, too, who quashed Cole's brainstorm for surprising Woolley with a gift-wrapped baby elephant placed in front of his door. The idea had occurred to Cole at the sight of elephants in Ceylon, following the Japan visit. But Linda soon talked him out of this surprise for Woolley when she pointed out the possibility of adverse reaction from the Ceylonese press if they got wind of the plan. The danger of antagonizing the Ceylonese, in Linda's estimation, outweighed the fun aspects of Cole's surprise gift.

It was not often that Linda put a damper on Cole's activities. They were each too savvy and had too much respect for one another to impose any consistent restraints on their marital arrangement. Just as Cole and Linda always had separate bedrooms, they had the flexibility of going their separate ways in other respects as well. That is not to say that they didn't do many things together. But Cole and Linda also believed in freedom of choice on a variety of levels. Their choices, however, were often predicated on the differences in their physical makeup. Unlike Cole, who was in the prime of his life in the 1930s, Linda was not only eight years older than Cole, but she had a recurring respiratory problem that limited what she could do physically. This meant that she did not always have the stamina for the extensive traveling and moving about that so appealed to Cole. Consequently, if Cole was interested in boating on the Rhine or hiking through the Dolomites and Linda was not up to it, Cole could still make the trip knowing that he had Linda's blessings. On those occasions when Cole went off without her, Linda would usually remain in their Paris home or take a rest-cure for her bronchial-asthmatic condition in the Swiss Alps or a similar place with good, dry air. During these separations Linda could look forward to a spate of droll stories from Cole on his return. As might be expected from someone with Cole's performance and theatrical background, he told the stories with such verve and gusto that Linda hardly felt deprived at not having joined him.

Save for their six-month journey to the Far East and Europe in 1930 and two cruises to the South Seas, one in 1935 and the other in 1940, Cole and Linda's trips together were generally shorter. The bulk of Cole's pleasure trips, however, were made with one or more of his close friends—like the Munich-to-Pilsen beer trek with Monty Woolley; or the German *faltboat* tour in 1933 with Ed Tauch, a handsome young architect; or the German-Austrian hiking expedition in 1937 with Tauch and Howard Sturges. Almost as a corollary to Cole's trips without Linda, there were certain hush-hush areas in his life that he felt were better left untalked about as far as she was concerned. Yet as a highly sophisticated and sensitive woman, she was unquestionably aware of them. But even with her insights into what was going on, she and Cole were both so discreet in their dealings—he in not volunteering information that went beyond the pale, she in not prying—that the smooth exterior of their relationship was hardly ruffled by any unsavory undercurrents.

The swept-under-the-rug aspects of Cole's life mainly concerned the strong homosexual drive that often involved him with a motley assortment of characters on a casual basis. This drive, for whatever reason, was not as noticeable when he was a younger man—or at least little information has come down about this side of Cole in his early years. It was not until he became famous and successful in his profession that stories began to leak out about homosexual escapades.

From all reports, Cole was physically attracted to tall and burly truck-driver and sailor types, whom he would seek out in some very seedy places, like shabby waterfront bars near the Hudson River in Manhattan or similar places on the West Coast or abroad. The contrast between Cole's more usual environment and the waterfront dives that he would go to is formidable. Nonetheless, this facet of Cole's personality asserted itself time and again. As a matter of fact, one might speculate that these strong drives for sexual encounters with cruder men of a different social class were external manifestations of some basic inner need, and that when satisfied, these drives served as important creative stimulants for him. This hypothesis is supported by the emphasis he placed on the fulfillment—often through the most casual encounters—of his sexual appetite; an enormous, practically insatiable one, according to those who knew him. Nor did Cole shy from boasting of his gluttonous sexual appetite to close friends; only in later years, shortly before he died, did he express concern that some might think of him "as an old queen" because of his past exploits. Some idea of the way in which many of Cole's sexual arrangements were made can be gotten from a story told by one of Cole's friends. It seems that Cole and Monty Woolley were driving in Manhattan one evening in the thirties, in an open car. They were cruising for some action—a "fucking party," as they called it—when they stopped for a light. Spotting a young, virile-looking sailor standing at the corner, they motioned to him to come to the car. When he approached them, Woolley quickly spoke up and invited the sailor into the car. Taken somewhat aback by the tone of the invitation, the sailor retorted, "What are you, cocksuckers?" Without batting an eyelash, Woolley wittily replied, "Well, now that the preliminaries are out of the way, why don't you jump in the car and we can discuss the matter further."

Besides such fucking parties, Cole and Woolley frequently made use of procurers to supply them with the physical types that appealed to them. For a price (during the Depression it was usually ten dollars for a white man, five dollars for a black), Cole and Woolley would get sailor and truck-driver types—or any other they desired—simply by contacting any one of the various pimps at their disposal. In New York these pimps were usually Jack Alexander, Harry Glynn, Matty Costello (also known as Nomad, because he was constantly on the run and changing telephones to throw the police off his track), and Clint Moore. Except for Moore, who kept a stable of black male prostitutes in his Harlem "house," all the other pimps generally supplied white men. So often did Cole and Woolley use the services of these pimps that the two devised a simple but ingenious scheme to get the "call men" into their fancy hotels without making it appear too obvious to the hotel employees. At Cole and Woolley's suggestion, the "call men" would come to their apartments in the guise of delivery people, with empty packages in their hands, before getting down to the business they had come for.

In addition to their sexual forays together and their warm personal relationship, Woolley and Cole continued their professional association beyond *Fifty Million Frenchmen*. For after directing *Frenchmen* in the late 1920s, Woolley directed *The New Yorkers*, Cole's very first musical of the new decade. Other key *Frenchmen* alumni besides Cole and Woolley also helped to put *The New Yorkers* on the boards. Heading the list was E. Ray Goetz. He not only produced the musical, but he helped, too, in concocting—along with cartoonist Peter Arno—the basic idea of the show: to satirize Gotham and some of the types who inhabit it, from high society, Park Avenue matrons to petty con men and crooks. Adding his own special touch to *The New Yorkers* was another *Frenchmen* recruit, scriptwriter Herbert Fields, who came up with all sorts of local-color lines appropriate for Gotham residents for the cast, which included Jimmy "Schnozzle" Durante and his madcap cohorts, Lou Clayton and Eddie Jackson, who played three hoods. With Durante setting the lead by deftly murdering the English language—as he pronounced it, "potato" became "patata" and "inventor" "inventorer"—and verbally assaulting everyone on stage practically nonstop, an unmistakable New York flavor permeated the production. In line with its emphasis on New York characters and their lingo, *The New Yorkers* was characterized in its printed program and promotional material as a "sociological musical satire." But in actuality, judging by the comments of Brooks Atkinson of the *New York Times*, the show "kept as far away from sociology as boisterous entertainment can." As Atkinson described *The New Yorkers*, it managed "to pack most of the madness, ribaldry, bounce and comic loose ends of giddy Manhattan into a lively musical show."

In a calculated attempt to counteract the Depression blues and show a profit at the same time, Goetz went all out in making *The New Yorkers* as bright and sparkling as possible—from the variegated costumes and the Arno settings to the large and dynamic cast, which included Ann Pennington and socialite-actress Hope Williams, in addition to the

Clayton-Jackson-Durante trio. Goetz also featured a young group that had never appeared on Broadway and had not yet made any commercial recordings as the stage band for the show: Fred Waring and his Pennsylvanians (the same ensemble that had played in the 1928 Paris production of *La Revue des Ambassadeurs*). Goetz had been introduced to the Pennsylvanians in Los Angeles, and had been so impressed with their talent that he signed them for *The New Yorkers*. Possibly the most unique quality of the Pennsylvanians was their clean-cut, collegiate looks. Moreover, they all sang as well as played instruments, a policy that Waring had initiated when he founded the group while he was an architecture student at Pennsylvania State College. With so much going for them, it was perhaps only inevitable that the Pennsylvanians would go on to bigger and better things after their exposure in *The New Yorkers*. They soon signed a recording contract with Victor, their number of engagements increased, and they eventually became one of America's most popular musical ensembles.

Among the earliest recordings that Waring's group made for Victor was "Love for Sale," Cole's big hit from *The New Yorkers*. As originally staged in the show, "Love for Sale" was sung by Kathryn Crawford, as May, a young white woman of the streets, who hawked her wares and availability ("appetizing young love for sale") to the vocal accompaniment of three sister streetwalkers. On the whole, the audience attending the Broadway opening of the show on December 8, 1930, at the B. S. Moss Broadway Theater took the song's ribald message in stride. One important press voice, however, took exception to the number. In his review of *The New Yorkers* in the *World*, drama critic Charles Darnton excoriated "Love for Sale" and its treatment as being "in the worst possible taste." Apparently America's radio executives agreed with Darnton, for they banned the tune from the air. The lyrics included these lines:

> Love for sale.
> Who will buy?
> Who would like to sample my supply?
> Who's prepared to pay the price
> For a trip to paradise?
> Love for sale.

as well as these

> If you want to buy my wares
> Follow me and climb the stairs,
> Love for sale.

Nor was the concern about the song's lewdness limited solely to radio. As a reaction to Darnton's indictment of "Love for Sale," and out of fear that the song might offend the general public and affect ticket sales, the production staff of *The New Yorkers* quickly changed the tune's setting. Instead of the original street scene with a white protagonist, the setting was shifted to the famous Cotton Club in Harlem, where a black woman sang the tune as part of her night-club act; the 1930s morality considered it less controversial to have a black woman as a streetwalker than a white woman.

The radio ban of "Love for Sale" and the song's change of treatment in *The New Yorkers* was not a complete surprise. Reviewer Percy Hammond, writing in the *Herald Tribune* after the opening of the show, had worried about how "Love for Sale" would be received. Though Hammond had reacted positively to the song and its treatment, he made this point in his review: "When and if we ever get a censorship, I will give odds that it will frown upon such an honest thing."

Fortunately for Cole, despite the censorship there were enough printed accounts and word-of-mouth reports about "Love for Sale" during the Broadway run—168 performances—of *The New Yorkers* that recordings of the tune by Waring's Pennsylvanians and others were in great demand. Interest in "Love for Sale" got an additional boost from live renditions by dance bands and night-club performers, so that the tune soon became one of Cole's biggest hits.

Aside from its earthy lyrics, the song's popularity was unquestionably also helped by its plaintive, minor-tinged melody. Richard Rodgers commented on that melody and a number of others by Cole, in his autobiography, *Musical Stages.* Rodgers tells of meeting Cole for the first time in 1926, while visiting Venice that summer. At Cole's invitation, Rodgers joined Cole, Linda, and Noel Coward for dinner one evening at the fabulous Rezzonico. After dinner they all retired to the palazzo's enormous music room for the men to play a selection of their songs for each other. Rodgers, wholly unfamiliar with Cole's songs until then, was very much impressed with what he heard, and could not understand why Cole's work was not better known. However, in speaking with Cole, Rodgers was surprised to learn that Cole had finally found the formula for writing hit songs. It was simplicity itself. Since many of the hit tunes up to then had been written by Jewish composers—Jerome Kern, Irving Berlin, and George Gershwin among them—Cole had evidently decided that all one had to do, as he put it, was to "write Jewish tunes." On hearing Cole's formula, Rodgers's immediate response was to laugh at what he assumed was a joke, but he was soon convinced that Cole was in earnest. According to Rodgers, moreover, Cole eventually followed that formula. "Just hum," suggests Rodgers, "the melody that goes with 'Only you beneath the moon and under the sun' from 'Night and Day,' or any of 'Begin the Beguine,' or 'Love for Sale,' or 'My Heart Belongs to Daddy,' or 'I Love Paris.' These minor-key melodies are unmistakably eastern Mediterranean."

It is easy to quibble with Rodgers's description of these minor-tinged melodies as eastern Mediterranean, as well as to wonder whether Cole might not have been jesting with Rodgers, one of the more successful of the Jewish composers, by this indirect slap at the domination of American popular music by Jews (implicit, too, in Cole's "Jewish" formula were undercurrents of anti-Semitism, especially since Cole's really close friends were invariably *not* Jewish; nor did he have much to do with Jews socially), though Rodgers himself accepted Cole's formula at face value. In Rodgers's opinion, "It is surely one of the ironies of the musical theatre that despite the abundance of Jewish composers, the one who has written the most enduring 'Jewish' music should be an Episcopalian millionaire who was born on a farm [*sic*] in Peru, Indiana."

One of the tunes labeled Jewish by Rodgers, as it happened, became Cole's next big hit after "Love for Sale." The tune, "Night and Day," part of Cole's score for the 1932 musical *Gay Divorce*, was written specifically for Fred Astaire. At that point he and his sister Adele were two of the biggest names in show business. Both Astaires had begun dancing and singing together as children in Nebraska under their original name, Austerlitz. By 1917, with a name change to Astaire and an accumulation of experience as a team, they made their Broadway debut to respectable reviews in a Sigmund Romberg musical, *Over the Top*. The Astaires' first big break came in 1922, when they starred on Broadway in *For Goodness Sake*, an Alex Aarons production. Everything they had been working toward from childhood on finally fell into place when they appeared in *Lady, Be Good* in 1924 and *Funny Face* in 1927, both produced by the Alex Aarons-Vinton Freedley combine and brimful of exceptional Gershwin songs. Just when the Astaires were at the height of their fame as a brother-and-sister act, Adele left the team, after marrying an English lord in 1932, to devote herself to her husband and her home. In the best tradition of the stage, Fred carried on as before. But rather than take a new partner in Adele's place, Fred resolved to try to make a go of it on his own, as a single.

He didn't have long to wait for a suitable role. For Cole had just been engaged to write the score for *Gay Divorce*, and both he and Dwight Wiman, one of the producers of the show, felt that Astaire would be perfect as the male lead. As an inducement to get Astaire to take the part, Cole invited him to his exquisite Paris home to hear a sampling of the music that had been written for the show. After hearing Cole play only one number, "After You, Who?" Astaire agreed to take the role of a writer who is mistaken by a pretty young woman (Claire Luce) for a correspondent hired to compromise her so that she can obtain a divorce. The comic interactions of the bogus gigolo and the young lovely, aided by the irreverent byplay of the real correspondent (Erik Rhodes), the wife's caustic friend (Luella Gear), a bungling, obtuse lawyer (G. P. Huntley, Jr.), and a host of other waggish characters, were the main pegs upon which scriptwriter Dwight Taylor hung his lightweight confection. The plot may have been little more than a harmless spoof of the complications involved in getting a divorce (a fairly sophisticated subject for the early 1930s), but so well did all the components of the production mesh—the casting, the score, the staging, the settings—that hardly anyone noticed how trite and simplistic Taylor's book really was. For despite the script, *Gay Divorce* carried the day when it opened at New York's Ethel Barrymore Theater on November 29, 1932. The show, moreover, did so well on Broadway—248 performances' worth—that it was brought to London the following year for an additional run.

An important factor in keeping *Gay Divorce* on the boards for substantial Broadway and London runs was, of course, Cole's score, particularly the standout tune, "Night and Day." So quickly did this number catch on that *Variety* reported it as one of the leaders in American record and sheet-music sales for January of 1933, little more than a month after *Gay Divorce* had opened on Broadway. In January, too, Irving Berlin complimented the song in a letter he sent to Paris, where Cole had gone to catch up with the European scene after the Broadway opening of *Gay Divorce*: "I am mad about NIGHT AND DAY, and I think it is your high spot. You probably know it is being played all over, and all the orchestra leaders think it is the best tune of the year—and I agree with them."

Professional courtesies aside, Berlin's sentiments reflected the good relationship that seemed to exist between Cole and this Russian-born Jew reared on the lower East Side, especially after Berlin's highly publicized marriage in 1926 to Linda's good friend, wealthy socialite Ellin Mackay (the daughter of Clarence Mackay, president of Postal Telegraph). One might speculate that Berlin's compliments of Cole's songs, though presumably sincere, may have also been stimulated by his marriage to a friend of Linda's. Not only was Berlin's social prestige enhanced by the marriage, but now he and Cole had more in common than the fact that they were both leading composer-lyricists in a tough field.

In writing "Night and Day" with Astaire in mind, Cole followed a practice he had started years earlier at Yale of tailoring his songs for the students who performed in his musicals. By shrewdly playing up the strong points and minimizing the weak ones of his cast, Cole invariably got excellent results—relative, that is, to the talents he had to work with. In Astaire's case Cole was dealing with a magnificent dancer and stage personality, but an only so-so singer whose voice was limited in range and quality. It was undoubtedly because of these vocal limitations that Cole tried to make things as easy as possible for Astaire by emphasizing repeated notes in a comfortable range in "Night and Day." By cleverly stressing reiterated sounds like the "beat, beat, beat" of a tom-tom; the "tick, tick, tock" of a clock; and the "drip, drip, drip" of raindrops in the lyrics, Cole came up with a viable means for using a similar approach in the melody as well. Thus, to simulate the desired pulsating effects in the opening sixteen-measure verse, Cole employed only three notes a half-step apart in the middle register (where the quality of Astaire's voice was best) for the entire verse. The first of these notes was repeated a total of forty-six times in the verse, the second, eleven times, and the third, five times—hardly demanding from a vocal standpoint. Even when Cole opened up the melody in the song's forty-eight-measure refrain (unlike most popular songwriters of the time, Cole often used refrains that were longer than the usual thirty-two measures) to encompass a range of an octave and a half, he still saw to it that many of the most prominent notes —again, in a comfortable range for Astaire—were frequently repeated.

Cole subsequently proved on numerous occasions that he could use the vocal idiosyncracies of other famous stars to good advantage. Bert Lahr, for example, had a way of spitting out his words when talking and singing so that they seemed to spray the audience. In the 1939 musical *DuBarry Was a Lady*, Cole took that peculiarity into account when he wrote "It Ain't Etiquette" for Lahr and ended the lyrics to the verse of the song with the phrase, "now for instance Snooks." As Lahr mouthed that phrase it came out "now for ninstance Snooks," full of sibilants and moisture-laden enough to drench the last row in the balcony. Ethel

Merman, too, got special treatment from Cole. She had first rocked the world with her full-voiced, brassy rendition of Gershwin's "I Got Rhythm" in her Broadway debut in *Girl Crazy*, a 1930 Aarons-Freedley production. She brought down the house each night with that song as she held a high note almost interminably while the orchestra tried desperately to hold its own with her. From *Girl Crazy* on there was no mistaking that she had the lung power to inflate the Graf Zeppelin and the volume to match it. Cole, cognizant of all this, made certain that many of his songs for her (like "Blow, Gabriel, Blow," from *Anything Goes*) gave her voice enough latitude to ring out, and that the tunes ended on held notes. He also tried to include in his lyrics for her words like "terrific" (so prominent in the line, "that would bore me terrific'ly too," from the song "I Get a Kick Out of You," which she sang in *Anything Goes*), that allowed her to roll out the r's with the force of a TNT charge. Cole considered her in a class by herself in singing such words. (Cole did not limit himself solely to musical matters when focusing on Ethel Merman's special qualifications. During the road tour of the 1936 musical *Red, Hot and Blue!* which starred Ethel Merman, Jimmy Durante, and Bob Hope, numerous changes had to be made in the show's script to get it ready for Broadway. Rather than hire a stenographer to transcribe all the script changes, Cole called on Ethel, since she had been a secretary-stenographer before going into show business. Cole would dictate all the script changes to her and she would quickly take them down in shorthand. "Among the best stenographers I ever had," was Cole's flattering description of her.)

Included in Cole's score for *Gay Divorce* were three numbers from an earlier musical, E. Ray Goetz's *Star Dust* of 1931, which somehow never went into production. Inasmuch as Cole made it a practice never to waste good material, he simply drew on the three tunes—"I Still Love the Red, White and Blue," "I've Got You On My Mind," and "Mister and Missus Fitch"—in fashioning his *Gay Divorce* score. In the case of the "Fitch" tune, Cole had the benefit of extensive publicity even before *Gay Divorce* opened. For after writing the song Cole decided to have some fun at the expense of the press by passing off the invented Fitches as a real couple. Notices suddenly appeared in various newspapers, especially the Paris edition of the *New York Herald*, detailing the myriad social activities and travels of the heretofore unknown S. Beach Fitches of Tulsa, Oklahoma. One account had them dining with the Cole Porters; another told of their charity interests; still another had them leaving for Carlsbad to take the cure. It was even reported that an audience had been arranged for them with the pope. Since "Fitch" also sounded off regularly in the "Letters to the Editor" column of the *Herald* on a variety of inane subjects dear to the heart of "a 100 percent American," as he described himself, it was not long before he and his wife were among the best-known members of the international set. So smoothly and skillfully did Cole (aided by several friends, principally Elsa Maxwell and Elsie Mendl) carry off the saga of the Fitches that many were surprised to learn that the couple never existed. Cole revealed the hoax shortly before *Gay Divorce* began its Broadway run to two of his press favorites, Walter Winchell and society columnist Cholly Knickerbocker. They duly reported the Fitch caper to their readers, at the same time giving Cole full credit for his adroit handling of the entire wild scenario. Yet despite the extensive press attention the tune received, it never really caught on. Perhaps its rather prosaic melody plus its subject matter—the Fitches themselves—had something to do with the song's lack of popularity. For the Fitches come off in the song as a young, pushy, new-money, farming couple who throw their weight around after striking it rich in oil, as these lines from the tune's refrain indicate:

> When they called for champagne,
> Champagne arrived.
> An aeroplane,
> The plane arrived.
> A private train,
> The train arrived.

But popular or not, "Mister and Missus Fitch" still deliciously ridiculed —almost as inventively as Cole's scheme to foist the couple that never was on society—all the *nouveaux riches* of the world.

Once *Gay Divorce* had opened (in late November of 1932 at the Ethel Barrymore Theater on Broadway) and had settled down for what promised to be a relatively long stand, Cole, as was his wont, took off on a jaunt. For the 1932–33 trip Cole's itinerary included stopovers in Paris, Vienna, Carlsbad, and other parts of Europe. As was his custom, too, Cole kept professionally active even on his tours, particularly since he and his songs were now so frequently in the news that there was no dearth of assignments to consider. By the beginning of 1933, as a matter of fact, Cole had already accepted an offer from English producer Charles B. Cochran to write the score for a musical based on James Laver's rather scandalous novel, *Nymph Errant*, about an English lass hell-bent on losing her virginity. The projected musical gave every indication of being a very exciting one, so, perhaps more than ever, Cole could look forward to an unusually interesting work schedule in the year ahead to complement his normally frenetic play routines.

12

Anything Goes

Taking his cue from the script for *Nymph Errant*, which detailed a schoolgirl's amorous flings in such offbeat places as a sheik's desert tent, the Parisian "Follies," a Turkish harem, and a nudist camp, Cole created an extraordinary score for the show that not only kept pace with the heroine's global philanderings but added some wonderfully suggestive overtones of its own. Typical of Cole's breezy suggestiveness was the tune "Experiment," with its admonitions to "be curious" and to "experiment" —presumably in things sexual. Also freewheeling in approach was Cole's "Si Vous Aimez Les Poitrines," a number glorifying the size and shape of Parisian women's breasts over other women's, including women in Poona, Bali, Spain, and similar romantic Edens of the world. Sung in the show by Iris Ashley, as Madeleine, a well-endowed Parisian cocotte, the tune served as a titillating reminder to mankind that "when zat feeling comes astealing," Madeleine was the one to "call on." Another tune that showed Cole at his wicked best was "The Physician," a humorous anatomical inventory of the heroine's body from the viewpoint of an overzealous medical man who also happens to be one of the schoolgirl's long line of lovers. As recounted by Evangeline, the English schoolgirl, played by Gertrude Lawrence, the song deftly enumerated all the parts of her body that the physician adored: her bronchial tubes, her epiglottis, her medulla oblongata, her pancreas, and so on. Unfortunately, as the song makes very clear in the last line of the refrain ("but he never said he loved me"), the doctor was too carried away with the individual parts of Evangeline's anatomy to love her for herself.

Cole's sexual sophistication and worldliness radiates, of course, from many of his lyrics (he was light-years ahead of most of his colleagues in that regard), but perhaps never more so than in his score for *Nymph Errant*. Cole himself considered that score the best one he had ever written. Other cognoscenti agreed. As one reviewer put it in discussing the score, there was a "witty inference of every intonation and a sting in every verse's last line." Yet despite the brilliant score, the gifted cast, the animated choreography by Agnes de Mille (her first important choreographic work), the forceful book and staging by Romney Brent, and the sheen of the overall production by Charles B. Cochran, *Nymph Errant* lasted only 154 performances after opening at London's Adelphi Theatre on October 6, 1933. Largely responsible for the rather quick closing of the show was its basic theme: the multifarious sexual adventures of a nymphomaniac—not exactly typical English stage fare.

Despite the short stand of *Nymph Errant*, Cole's name was almost constantly in the English news during the time of its run. For shortly after *Nymph Errant* began its run, *Gay Divorce* (with Fred Astaire and Claire Luce still in their starring roles) opened at London's Palace Theatre on November 2, 1933. The combination of the two shows running simultaneously, plus the opening-night celebrations that went with each of the productions, guaranteed that Cole would not be neglected by the London press.

Especially festive and newsworthy was the *Nymph Errant* premiere. Word had gotten around beforehand, of course, about the show's emphasis on the sexual peregrinations of its heroine (played by everyone's favorite, Gertrude Lawrence), with the result that fashionable people from far and wide came running to be where the fun and scandal were. This assured a lustrous opening-night audience, in which Society and Nobility rubbed elbows with ambassadors from France, America, and other major powers. Following the performance, Lady Cunard—as she had done after Cole's previous English production, *Wake Up and Dream* —gave a fabulous supper party at her home for the Porters and their guests. The party and everything else that preceded it made the *Nymph Errant* premiere one of the most notable social events of the London season.

Before starting on his *Nymph Errant* score, Cole had asked to see the script for the show so that his songs could closely match the written dialogue; it was a practice he had adhered to since his college days. (Few scores for musicals up to then were well integrated with their scripts. But then the scripts themselves were often terribly inane, since they were not really concerned with plot and character development, but merely served as loose framework for the singing and dancing onstage. A major exception would be the book for Jerome Kern's *Show Boat* of 1927, by Oscar Hammerstein II, which tackled such "heavy" topics for a musical as unhappy marriages, miscegenation, and the harsh life of southern blacks. However, even within the limitations of the scripts he generally had to work with, Cole was invariably most conscientious in trying to match his songs to them—a practice that became more common in the 1950s with such "story" shows as *Guys and Dolls* and *My Fair Lady*.) Inasmuch as Romney Brent, the scriptwriter and director for the show, had only just begun the process of transforming the original *Nymph Errant* novel by James Laver into a vehicle for the stage, Cole suggested that the two work closely together while the script was being prepared. Cole followed up that suggestion by inviting Brent to join Linda and him at Carlsbad, where they were planning to take the cure.

Accepting the invitation gave Brent the unique opportunity of observing the Porters at close range. There were, to be sure, the usual trappings of wealth and glamour surrounding them—the great stacks of matched luggage and the sizable retinue of servants that went with them when they traveled; the many rooms and compartments that they reserved for themselves and their party on trains and at hotels; and their overall civility, particularly Linda's southern belle charm, quiet solicitude, and aristocratic style. Of the two Porters, Brent found Cole, of course, the more dynamic, with his expressive eyes, charming smile, and incisive wit and repartee. But like many others who had dealings with Cole, Brent was exasperated by his strange quirk, in the presence of company, of leaving a room quickly, without explanation, when he was bored with the conversation. (Linda, of course, was aware of this quirk of Cole's and had come to accept it; as she saw it, Cole had always been like that, and there was no reason to try to change him.)

Brent was also amazed at Cole's great concern with his looks and physical well-being. Though Cole seemed to be in the pink of condition, he would go through a daily ritual of ministering to his health and appearance. So ingrained had this ritual become that Cole would think nothing of discussing script matters with Brent while applying lotions to his skin, swallowing a variety of pills, spraying his throat, and indulging himself in other similar routines. Brent was surprised, too, at Cole's involvement with bodily functions as well as his lack of reticence in that connection. Early each morning Cole would drink great quantities of Carlsbad's mineral waters before taking a walk with Brent to talk over the *Nymph Errant* script. Invariably Cole would excuse himself several times during their walk to relieve himself at one of the many toilets located en route. Each time Cole rejoined Brent he would casually take up the conversation where he had left off. (Nor was this focus on basic intestinal-colonic processes noticeable only at Carlsbad. For many years one of the first things Cole would do in the morning, while still in bed, would be to take a suppository—which he inserted himself—to induce a bowel movement.) Notwithstanding, however, all the emphasis on health, looks, and bodily functions, and his peculiarities of personality, Brent found Cole to be an exceptional collaborator. He was always receptive to new ideas and wonderfully imaginative in integrating his score with the script. Brent was impressed, too, at how hard Cole worked at creating his music and lyrics. At Carlsbad Cole would set aside at least three hours each morning, when he was at his freshest, to concentrate on his songs, and would freely spend more time on them whenever it became necessary.

At about the time Cole created his *Nymph Errant* score, he also wrote two songs that became among his most requested numbers when he entertained friends at private parties. One of the tunes, "Thank You So Much, Mrs. Lowsborough-Goodby," caricatured the prim and proper English woman—long hyphenated name and all—who is a deadly hostess, but persists in inviting guests for weekends to the point where they can't refuse her. The song is a good example of Cole's sardonic flair for presenting two comically opposed strands of thought simultaneously in straight-faced fashion. In the tune Cole writes an imaginary letter to Mrs. Lowsborough-Goodby describing one of her long weekends, replete with cold baths, damp rooms, hot cocktails, boring conversation, and horrendous food, while still managing the nicety of thanking her for the invitation.

An even more popular number with Cole's friends was his "Miss Otis Regrets," a kind of high-class version of the woman-done-wrong classic, "Frankie and Johnnie." "Miss Otis" evolved very casually one day when Cole was at a party at the New York apartment of his Yale classmate, Leonard Hanna. A cowboy lament he heard on the radio sounded so bad to Cole that he immediately sat down at the piano to improvise a lament of his own, burlesquing the cowboy tune. As he simulated a cowboy twang with suitably shrill, nasal tones, "Miss Otis Regrets"—music and lyrics—began to take shape. Before long Monty Woolley, who was also present at the party, jumped into the fray. Borrowing a silver tray and a morning coat from Hanna, Woolley assumed the guise of a butler to help put the song over. With Cole accompanying him at the piano, Woolley's stentorian voice could be heard telling the humorous-sad tale of why "Madam," Miss Otis, could not keep her luncheon appointment. Like the "Mrs. Lowsborough-Goodby" tune, "Miss Otis Regrets" ludicrously projects two diametrically different attitudes played against each other. No matter that Miss Otis is about to be strung up for gunning her wayward lover down; she is still the paragon of good manners and upbringing. Just before she dies for her indiscretion, her last gasp reveals the one thought uppermost in her mind: "Miss Otis regrets she's unable to lunch today."

Woolley's rendition of "Miss Otis Regrets" was so well received at Hanna's house that it rapidly became a fixture on the party circuit, especially at Elsa Maxwell's shindigs. All that winter of early 1934 at Miss Maxwell's fun-filled parties in her large, rent-free suite at the Waldorf Astoria, Woolley would make a meticulously planned entrance as a butler and launch into "Miss Otis Regrets," to the delight of the hostess and her guests. Helped by word-of-mouth reports that circulated after these parties, "Miss Otis Regrets" soon became a favorite among New Yorkers and abroad. It never became popular, though, in the hinterlands of America, probably because its juxtaposition of propriety and indiscretion is too offbeat and sophisticated for general American tastes. So quickly was interest in "Miss Otis Regrets" generated overseas, it was sung in the 1934 English musical, *Hi Diddle Diddle,* and also recorded that year on English Decca by Douglas Byng, who performed it in the show.

Presumably in gratitude to Elsa Maxwell for her aid in getting the song known, as well as for her friendship, Cole dedicated "Miss Otis Regrets" to her. Presumably, too, because of the humorous ramifications inherent in the song, many amusing stories have been told over the years which have drawn on its tag line. Perhaps the bitchiest of these stories is the one by Truman Capote published in the November, 1975, issue of *Esquire.* As Capote tells it, Cole was attracted to a dark, sexy Italian wine steward, known as Dixie because he originally came from southern Italy. Dixie worked in one of the fancy New York restaurants Cole frequented. One day Cole invited Dixie to his apartment on the pretense that he needed advice in installing a new wine cellar. Once in his apartment, Capote relates, "Cole kisses this fellow on the cheek, and Dixie grins and says:

'That will cost you five hundred dollars, Mr. Porter.' Cole just laughs and squeezes Dixie's leg. 'Now that will cost you a thousand dollars, Mr. Porter.' Then Cole realized this piece of pizza was serious; and so he unzippered him, hauled it out, shook it and said: 'What will be the full price on the use of that?' Dixie told him two thousand dollars. Cole went straight to his desk, wrote a check, and handed it to him. And he said: 'Miss Otis regrets she's unable to lunch today. Now get out.' "

Toward the end of 1934, as often seemed to happen with Cole as his fame increased, two new productions using his music opened almost concurrently. The first of these, *The Gay Divorcee*, a movie version of *Gay Divorce*, with Fred Astaire and Ginger Rogers in the leads, was released by RKO-Radio Pictures on October 12, 1934, to considerable critical acclaim. The second production, the musical *Anything Goes*, featuring Ethel Merman, William Gaxton, and Victor Moore, opened on Broadway at the Alvin Theater on November 21, 1934, to rave notices. In the case of *The Gay Divorcee*, its two key beneficiaries were unquestionably its stars, Fred Astaire and Ginger Rogers. They complemented each other so beautifully in this film—their first one as a singing and dancing team—that between 1935 and 1939 they appeared together in seven more films for RKO: *Roberta* (1935), *Top Hat* (1935), *Follow the Fleet* (1936), *Swing Time* (1936), *Shall We Dance* (1937), *Carefree* (1938), and *The Story of Vernon and Irene Castle* (1939). In selecting Astaire to play the same role in the film that he had played on the stage, Hollywood studio heads made what might be considered an obvious choice. Nonetheless, they had not always gauged Astaire's screen capabilities so well. For in 1928, after Fred and his sister Adele had gotten smash notices for their roles in the Gershwin musical *Funny Face* on Broadway, both were tested by Paramount for a proposed film version of that show. Legend has it that Paramount's adverse evaluation of Fred's screen test (reputedly their report on Fred stated: "Can't act; can't sing; balding; can dance a little!") quickly scotched their film plans for *Funny Face*.

On getting the heave-ho from Hollywood, Astaire returned to the stage as before, but not without keeping an eye open for future film prospects. When *Gay Divorce* catapulted him into the limelight once again, Astaire saw his chance and asked his agent, Leland Hayward, to try to wangle a film offer for him. Through Hayward, Astaire got a small part—playing himself—in MGM's *Dancing Lady*, starring Joan Crawford and Clark Gable, which was released in 1933. That same year Astaire began his long association with RKO by appearing in *Flying Down to Rio*, a rickety musical travelogue that segued precipitously between extolling the delights of Latin life in Rio and air travel there on the Sikorsky-designed clipper ships of Pan Am (it was hardly coincidence that the head of RKO, Merian C. Cooper, also happened to be a member of Pan Am's board of directors). In a part that only hinted at his future stardom, Astaire played second fiddle—with commensurate billing—to fair-haired Mr. Clean himself, Gene Raymond. It was Raymond, not Astaire, who got the chance to crush in his manly arms the star of the whole shebang: sloe-eyed, tawny Delores del Rio.

Astaire's future partner, Ginger Rogers, had the somewhat innocuous role of a band vocalist in the film. Despite having made a substantial number of shorts and feature films—mainly playing sassy gold-digger types—from 1929 on, she had still not achieved major-star status at the time *Flying Down to Rio* was shot. As a matter of fact, she had gotten the part in the movie only when Dorothy Jordan, who had originally been cast, left the production to honeymoon with her new spouse, RKO studio head Merian C. Cooper (Cooper, on the strength of his fabulous success with the movie *King Kong,* replaced David O. Selznick as RKO studio chief when Selznick joined his father-in-law, Louis B. Mayer, at MGM). But if neither Ginger Rogers nor Fred Astaire was especially outstanding in *Flying Down to Rio,* they did impress studio bigwigs with their potential as a team in a scene where they danced together briefly to "The Carioca," a fast, tangolike number by Vincent Youmans, who wrote the score (this number was probably the best thing about the film). So strong an impression did Astaire and Rogers make with the upper echelon at RKO that the studio soon decided to star them in a film of their own.

In making the decision to go with the new team, RKO was motivated by its desperate financial position. The company, in receivership, had to come up with a winning formula. As a possible salvation RKO decided to go into the production of film musicals full-blast. For their first film starring Astaire and Rogers as a team, producer Pandro S. Berman chose *The Gay Divorcee* over another film, *Down to Their Last Yacht,* about several zany socialites stranded somewhere in the South Pacific. Berman had seen Astaire in the London production of *Gay Divorce* and had liked the show sufficiently to buy the movie rights for twenty thousand dollars, a low figure even then. Berman, however, might not have been in a sufficiently strong position at RKO to decide in favor of *The Gay Divorcee* over the other film if Merian C. Cooper had not suffered a heart attack (possibly an aftermath of honeymooning with his considerably younger starlet wife). While Cooper took a long leave of absence to recuperate, Berman became acting head of production at RKO and, in that position of power, gave the green light to a movie version of *Gay Divorce* that included a title change to *The Gay Divorcee* for added sophistication. As director of the film Berman chose young Mark Sandrich, a former physicist whose three-reeler, *So This Is Harris,* had won an Academy Award in 1932. Like their two stars, Berman and Sandrich turned out to be a winning combination. After *The Gay Divorcee,* Berman went on to produce all seven of the additional Astaire-Rogers films for RKO, while Sandrich directed four of them: *Top Hat, Follow the Fleet, Shall We Dance,* and *Carefree.* Perhaps more than anything else, the Astaire-Rogers films proved to be the magic formula that RKO needed to turn itself around financially, and the studio became one of the most affluent giants of the industry thanks to a gamble that paid off.

Of Cole's original score for *Gay Divorce,* only "Night and Day" was incorporated into *The Gay Divorcee.* The song became a standout number. In the original musical, besides singing the tune, Astaire had also danced to it with Claire Luce. She was a fine dancer, but a completely different personality from Astaire's original partner—his sister, Adele. To match Miss Luce's more sinuous stage personality, Astaire tried to come up with a new dancing approach. Whereas most of his dances with Adele were lively, outgoing affairs, his choreographic concept for "Night and Day" was a relatively slow and seductive one—the first such dance in his career. In adapting the dance for the screen, Astaire continued the languorous, romantic approach. At the start of the number he and Ginger Rogers are shown alone in a ballroom at night. Again and again he sidles up close to her and pulls her to him, but she draws away. His persistence, however, wins out in this evocation of the mating game played to the hilt. As the dance ends she is wrapped in his arms, the two of them as one, gazing entranced into each other's eyes.

Though "Night and Day" was already a popular classic when *The Gay Divorcee* was released, the number became even better known because of the film and the dance built around it. The song that got the lion's share of attention in *The Gay Divorcee,* however, was not Cole's "Night and Day" but Con Conrad's "The Continental" (with lyrics by Herb Magidson). Conrad's tune had the benefit of a long dance sequence in the film —some seventeen minutes' worth—in which a large group dressed in black and white sashayed about doing the Continental, a follow-up dance to the Carioca, which had become enormously popular as a result of its exposure in *Flying Down to Rio.* RKO also did its part to build up the tie-in between the Continental and the Carioca by advertising Astaire and Rogers in *The Gay Divorcee* as "The King and Queen of Carioca." In addition, an extensive press campaign was launched to popularize the Continental by outlining and illustrating movements of the dance in newspapers across America. With all this promotion, it is not surprising that "The Continental" became an almost instant success and received an Academy Award as the Best Film Song for 1934—the first movie tune to be so honored. But as history has subsequently shown, after all the build-up and the hoopla had died down, "The Continental" and the dance that it inspired quickly faded. On the other hand, Cole's "Night and Day" continues as popular as ever. ASCAP, for example, rates "Night and Day" among its top money earners of all time. Even now, decades after it was first written, "Night and Day" still earns approximately ten thousand dollars each year in ASCAP royalties—a phenomenal amount by any standard.

If there was any doubt in the public's mind about whether Cole or Conrad took the songwriting honors for *The Gay Divorcee*, there was no such doubt in connection with *Anything Goes* since Cole wrote the complete score for it. And it was a beauty. But then so was the show, produced by Vinton Freedley. The idea for *Anything Goes* first came to Freedley while he was lazily fishing in the Pacific Ocean, near the Pearl Islands, where he had gone to escape the creditors hounding him after the Broadway failure of *Pardon My English* in 1933. As he fished, Freedley began to plot his return to show business. In those days it was not unusual for a producer to sign up several stars for a musical even before a script had been written, and then have the score and book shaped around their stage personalities. As he plotted out the strategy for his next Broadway show, Freedley determined that his projected stage venture would have built-in safeguards to guarantee him an automatic hit. For the stars of his dream musical, Freedley settled on three of the most coveted names in show business: William Gaxton, Victor Moore, and Ethel Merman. Gaxton and Moore, of course, had already made theater history with their loony characterizations of Wintergreen and Throttlebottom in the Pulitzer Prize-winning musical *Of Thee I Sing*. Ethel Merman, too, had made her own kind of history with her stunning debut as Frisco Kate, the rough-and-tumble barroom gal in Aarons and Freedley's 1930 smash *Girl Crazy*. To create the book for these stars, P. G. Wodehouse and Guy Bolton, the scriptwriters for another Aarons-Freedley hit *(Oh, Kay!)* and masters at turning a comical phrase, immediately came to Freedley's mind. Finally, to handle the score assignment, Freedley thought of Cole, since the Gershwins, perhaps the most logical choice, from his past associations with them, were not available because of their commitment to write the opera *Porgy and Bess.*

Once his financial situation had cooled off sufficiently for Freedley to return to the States with impunity, though he had little money at his disposal, on the basis of his past track record as a producer Freedley managed to sign up the stars, the librettists, and Cole. To get the project moving Freedley suggested—stimulated by his own experiences on numerous boat trips—that Bolton and Wodehouse devise a lively script about a pleasure ship wrecked at sea with several screwball characters on board. The two writers complied, but when they turned in their finished script in mid-August of 1934, Freedley was disappointed. It lacked the light touch—one of the "success guarantees"—he was looking for. As a further complication, several weeks later, on September 8, 1934, the *Morro Castle*—a prototype of the pleasure ship Freedley had in mind—was wrecked off the New Jersey coast and went down in flames with a loss of over one hundred lives as it returned from a seven-day cruise to Havana. The grim reality of a shipwreck—one of the worst of its kind —so close to home made Freedley's original story idea untenable for a Broadway musical meant to entertain. Inasmuch as Bolton and Wodehouse were both out of the country at the time and script changes had to be made at once, Freedley in desperation turned for help to Howard Lindsay, the director of the show, who had also just authored *She Loves Me Not,* a reasonably successful play. Because of the emergency at hand, Lindsay—later to become famous as the father in *Life With Father* as well as coauthor of that show and others—reluctantly agreed to double as writer and director, provided he had a collaborator for the scriptwriting chores. As his partner for the revisions, Howard Lindsay chose Russel Crouse, the head of public relations for the Theatre Guild and the joint creator in 1933 of the book for *Hold Your Horses,* which starred the famous Joe Cook, the zany master of inconsequential patter.

The two collaborators plunged right into the task of devising a new script, but, as Lindsay and Crouse later readily admitted, it was tough going. At the start of rehearsals only a portion of the first act had been completed, and the second act had not even been written yet. Everything was in such a state of flux that the show was still without an ending for its Boston tryouts. Even as the show headed for its opening night, wholesale revisions continued. It was during this period of panic and pandemonium that the show's ultimate title was bestowed on it. First known as *Hard to Get* and then as *Bon Voyage,* the show was finally christened *Anything Goes*—a fitting title for a production born and nurtured in the line of fire.

When the curtain went up at the Alvin Theater for *Anything Goes* on November 21, 1934, all the bits and pieces of the production that had been so terribly askew for weeks on end suddenly fell into place. What might easily have been another Broadway casualty came up a winner instead, and the reviewers responded accordingly: they lavished praise on the score, the book, the direction, the casting, the scenery, and indeed anything else they could think of. The plot that Lindsay and Crouse contrived for *Anything Goes* was full of merriment from start to finish and set the tone for the show. While the book did not abandon Freedley's idea for a ship setting, there now was not the slightest allusion to a disaster at sea (even with this major change in conception, Bolton and Wodehouse shared program credits with Lindsay and Crouse as the creators of the script). The three leads—Gaxton, Merman, and Moore—were, of course, at the heart of the hilarity on stage. Cast in the improbable role of Public Enemy Number 13—and a superstitious one to boot, itching to get off that unlucky number by moving ahead in ranking—was soft-voiced, sad-faced, cherubically rotund Victor Moore, complete with a machine gun stashed away in his ever-present saxophone case. To make his escape from the authorities, Moore boards an ocean liner disguised as a clergyman, the Reverend Dr. Moon. Also on the boat is Ethel Merman, as a former evangelist turned nightclub singer, Reno Sweeney; and William Gaxton, playing a Wall Street type, Billy Crocker (named after Cole's Yale chum William Crocker, of the San Francisco banking and railroad family, who had been such a good friend when he'd needed money). Crocker (Gaxton) has stowed on board to be near his society sweetheart, Hope Harcourt (Bettina Hall), and, like Moore, is forced to disguise himself to avoid being put in the brig. One of the many funny spots in *Anything Goes* has Gaxton disguised in a makeshift beard of dog's hair that he had shorn only moments earlier from a lady's precious Pomeranian without her knowledge. On seeing the impressive hirsute face, the dog's mistress innocently asks him, "What are you, Spanish?" "No, Pomeranian," was Gaxton's instantaneous reply. There were loads of other such jolly—though perhaps not uproarious by today's standards—moments in the production, and they added up to a really good evening in the theater.

Of the songs Cole wrote for *Anything Goes,* five quickly became major hits—a record not matched by any of his other scores. These five tunes

—"Blow, Gabriel, Blow," "All Through the Night," "I Get a Kick Out of You," "You're the Top," and the title song, "Anything Goes"—and the score they were part of helped to keep *Anything Goes* on Broadway for 420 performances, Cole's longest-running show up to that point. If there were any doubts before *Anything Goes* about Cole's music and lyrics being of the very first rank, those doubts were certainly dissipated after the show opened. And even in retrospect it is easy to see why Cole's *Anything Goes* score received the praise it did. In masterly fashion, Cole's tunes more than matched the saucy impudence of the spirited cast, the uninhibited double entendres of the Lindsay-Crouse script, and the lavish glitter of the entire fast-moving production. The show typified the naughty thirties by the degree of its freewheeling, no-holds-barred spirit. As Cole stressed in his title tune, the world—and it was unmistakably the world of the thirties that he spoke of—had done an about-face in its values. Clearly, *everything* was now acceptable—from four-letter words to parties in the nude. The opening lines of the song's initial refrain enunciate Cole's viewpoint:

> In olden days, a glimpse of stocking
> Was looked on as something shocking,
> But now, God knows,
> Anything goes.
> Good authors, too, who once knew better words
> Now only use four-letter words,
> Writing prose,
> Anything goes.

"You're the Top" also had the trappings of the thirties, with its sprightly and topical references to Pepsodent, Waldorf salad, Mickey Mouse, and Mae West, among its long list of rhymed superlatives, including these:

> You're the top!
> You're Mahatma Ghandi.
> You're the top!
> You're Napoleon brandy.
> You're the purple light of a summer night in Spain,
> You're the National Gall'ry,
> You're Garbo's sal'ry,
> You're cellophane.

In number after number, Cole's score somehow caught the essence of the period. Like a mirror to the world, it laid bare many of the foibles and inconsistencies of the period—but always with wit and imagination.

There was enough impetus from the original production of *Anything Goes* to stimulate Paramount Pictures to release a movie of it in 1936, starring Bing Crosby and Ethel Merman. Exactly twenty years later, in 1956, another movie of *Anything Goes*—but with the story changed considerably—was put out by Paramount with Bing Crosby again in the lead. This time his compatriots included Donald O'Connor, Mitzi Gaynor, and Jeanmaire. In both films, however, save for Cole's songs, much of the effervescence and bounce of the original show was lost in the transition to the screen. A. H. Weiler summed it up in his review in the *New York Times* of the second movie version: "Mr. Porter is still the most inventive contributor to 'Anything Goes.' "

Cole was also the key personage in a series of four records—his only commercial ones—that he made for Victor in late 1934 and early 1935 that included three tunes from *Anything Goes*. Accompanying himself at the piano, Cole sang "You're the Top" on one of the records (Victor 24766), coupled with his famous party song, "Thank You So Much, Mrs. Lowsborough-Goodby." On another record (Victor 24825) Cole performed "Anything Goes" and the earlier number, "Two Little Babes in the Wood." The third record (Victor 24843) contained Cole singing "Be Like the Bluebird," an attractive but little-known tune from *Anything Goes*, as well as "I'm a Gigolo," from *Wake Up and Dream*. The final record (Victor 24859) consisted of two numbers from *Nymph Errant*: "The Physician" and "The Cocotte." In these four records Cole's rather prissy, high-pitched way with the tunes may not have established him as a threat to Bing Crosby, but he did sing the numbers with a fine sense of style and undeniable authority.

Cole's recording of tunes from *Anything Goes* was just one of the many bonuses that came his way after the show's outstanding triumph. Among the others were the publication of the show's complete vocal score and voluminous royalties from sheet-music and record sales. But perhaps the major benefit for Cole was the extraordinary amount of media coverage he got after *Anything Goes* exploded on Broadway. More than ever before, he was besieged by journalists who pleaded for the privilege of telling the world about those special tidbits that set him apart from other personalities.

Typical of the coverage was the article, "It's All in Fun," in the April, 1935, issue of *American Magazine*. Cole, it was said, liked "hunting, swimming, parties, food, drink, composing . . . cats, voyages." "I'm not cynical or acid or anything of that kind," Cole was quoted as saying. "I'm a hard-working boy from Indiana, and I'm engaged in the business of entertaining myself, which enables me to entertain, as much as I can, the world." His play-work routine, it was revealed, consisted of partying all night, catching some sleep between sunup and ten in the morning, working from eleven o'clock on, then dining, doffing his top hat, and stepping out into the night for another round of the same.

Presenting himself to the *American Magazine* interviewer, Hubert Kelley, as he wanted the world to see him, Cole—not unexpectedly—expounded on his fleeing to the French Foreign Legion after his first Broadway flop, *See America First*. He had fled to the Legion, he confided, expecting it to be a haven for strong but heartbroken men, failures in business and in love. But instead of a grim and dismal crew, Cole claimed he found the legionnaires to be a hard-fighting and fast-living bunch who, as they marched through war-torn France, roistered when they were high and sang when they were low. Warming up to his subject, Cole elaborated further on his fictional World War I military experiences. He told of being transferred from the legion to a French army artillery school for the purpose of teaching French gunnery methods to American troops when they arrived in France. Before long, he confessed, the French government awarded him the Croix de Guerre, not—and here Cole added an exquisitely modest touch worthy of the greatest of con artists—for bravery, but for his personality and good comradeship. "They really gave it to me," Cole stated finally with humility, "because I was the only American in a French company."

The media professionals took Cole at his word—apparently no one ever bothered to check his story with the legion or the French army—and reported the tall tales he fed them about his French war service with as much relish as he evidently took in dishing it out. Since Cole's fictional military experiences made for exciting news, stories about these experiences proliferated over the years and added to the aura of glamour and sophistication that already surrounded him. Just as Cole from childhood on had had his own way in so many other aspects of his life, he had his own way with this canard by pulling it off so smoothly. He must have chuckled again and again at getting away with it. Or perhaps, as often happens with tellers of tall tales, he came to believe his own fictions. Who can tell?

13

Jubilee

COLE PORTER OFF FOR SOUTH SEAS TO HUNT A TUNE, the *Herald Tribune* of
January 12, 1935, proclaimed in bold print. A subhead to the long story that
followed added: "Ballader, With Moss Hart, to Pass 5 Months Seeking
New Musical Comedy." The news item noted that Cole, "heir apparent
to the throne of Jerome Kern as the nation's top ballader," had just sailed
from New York for the South Seas with playwright Hart on the Cunard
liner *Franconia,* and that the two planned to collaborate on a new show
as they traveled. Thirty-year-old Hart already had two big stage hits to
his credit: *Merrily We Roll Along* and *As Thousands Cheer,* both written with
George S. Kaufman. Joining Cole, described by the *Herald Tribune* as the
composer of the "current Broadway grand slam," *Anything Goes,* and a
"shy, smallish, black-haired, urbane young man . . . [who] carefully keeps
his birthday out of all the who's whos," and Hart on the trip were Linda,
Monty Woolley, Howard Sturges, and travel writer William Powell,
Leonard Hanna's most intimate friend.

Hart had met Cole nearly two years earlier in France. Armed with a
letter of introduction from Irving Berlin, Hart had sought out Cole in
Paris. The two met for the first time at the Ritz Bar shortly before
Christmas. Though neither had seen each other before, Hart recognized
Cole at once and waved to him, for he looked so much like one of his

songs. As Hart tells it, there was the dazzling smile, "the small, lithe figure beautifully turned out, the intensely alive face, the immense dark eyes wonderfully set off by the brilliant red carnation in the lapel of his suit—it could not possibly be anyone else." Along with Berlin's letter Hart had brought a small Christmas package for Cole from dancer George Hale. On opening the red leather, satin-lined box, Cole found two gold garters with his initials on them from Cartier's. As Hart looked on in astonishment, Cole lifted his trousers, removed the gold garters he was wearing, and replaced them with the new ones. Then, calling to the barman, Cole casually tossed the old garters to him as a gift. Perhaps nothing else Cole could have done would have impressed itself so firmly on young, Brooklyn-bred Hart than this sublimely simple yet overtly theatrical gesture. Cole further strengthened the impact he made on the young man by inviting him to join Linda and him for dinner at their home.

Hart dined with them twice during his brief stay in Paris and quickly became enamored of the Porters and everything they represented. "They were rich, they were gifted, and they moved about with infinite ease and lightheartedness in two worlds—the world of fashion and glitter and the pantaloon world of the theater," Hart has said of his initial impressions of them. He was especially taken with the Porters' exquisite home and with Linda. He found her to be "a woman of immense delicacy, with an enchanting turn of mind, as easily beguiled by a chorus girl as by a duchess and equally at home with both." It was while dining with the Porters that the thought came to Hart of doing a musical with Cole. He dismissed the idea, however, because, as he recalled, "I was a mere neophyte—barely out of Brooklyn and my first play—and Cole Porter was already one of the most sought-after of all composers."

Hart openly expressed his idea some eighteen months later as he lunched in New York with Cole shortly after *Anything Goes* had stormed Broadway. But Hart also made clear that he wanted to take time off from work for a long trip around the world. "Why not do both?" Cole had replied. He liked Hart's idea for a musical and suggested that the two collaborate on the projected show while traveling together. It was thus that the plan was set for their trip on the *Franconia* in the early part of 1935.

Cole came well prepared for his end of the collaboration. As the *Franconia* pulled out to sea, his beautifully appointed stateroom contained a piano-organ, a metronome, a phonograph and records, a typewriter, two dozen sharpened pencils, a quire of music paper, and three cases of his favorite champagne. Besides these mainly professional items and various personal necessities, Cole's cabin could also boast of accommodating a most unusual woman. As a practical joke on Cole, Howard Lindsay and Russel Crouse had had a large crate delivered to his stateroom before the *Franconia* left port. On opening the crate Cole found a huge, grotesque, wooden statue of an amply proportioned woman—all bulges and curves. Instead of tossing his uninvited guest overboard in the dead of night as others might have been tempted to do, Cole took delight in her presence. He had her dressed in outlandish costumes and gave extravagant parties in her honor.

But Cole did not spend his time on board simply feting his Amazonian companion. When there was a musical job to be done, he was all seriousness. As Hart saw it, "Cole Porter 'worker' and Cole Porter 'playboy' were two different beings. . . . The secret of those marvelously gay and seemingly effortless songs was a prodigious and unending industry. He worked around the clock." In these efforts Cole was greatly aided by Linda. According to Hart, Linda "was as stern and jealous a guardian of that work as Cole Porter himself." When he was caught up in creative labors, Cole would withdraw from everyone around him. In Hart's words, Cole's "withdrawals were not confined to the moment when he entered his cabin to sit at the small upright piano; they spilled over the luncheon table, the dinner table, and even onto some of the sightseeing tours when the boat docked." No matter what else was happening, Cole would often withdraw within himself to concentrate on his work. This habit sometimes put a strain on his social relations. One day during rehearsals in 1936 of *Red, Hot and Blue!* Cole passed Russel Crouse—coauthor, with Howard Lindsay, of the show's script—numerous times without speaking or acknowledging him in any way. Crouse couldn't imagine what he had done to cause this rebuff, when Cole suddenly blurted out to him, "In my pet pailletted gown." Only then did Crouse realize that Cole's strange behavior had resulted from him trying to come up with a suitable line for "Down In the Depths," one of the key songs in the show.

The leisurely trip on the *Franconia* lasted about four and a half months. When the boat returned to New York on May 31, 1935, it had logged approximately thirty-four thousand miles and had docked around the globe for sightseeing, including stopovers in California, Hawaii, New Zealand, New Guinea, Rio de Janeiro, Cape Town, Ceylon, and Singapore. The voyage was a press agent's dream. All along the way stories would reach the press telling of the progress Cole and Hart were making on their show and the places they had visited. Typical of the coverage was this report in the *Herald Tribune* of April 28, 1935:

> From Durbar, British East Africa, last week, Cole Porter cabled the Sam H. Harris office that he and Moss Hart are far ahead of schedule on the musical show, which is likely to inaugurate a new season for Mr. Harris. Mr. Hart is now completely finished with the book for the entertainment, according to Mr. Porter, while virtually all his songs are assembled and comprise what he considers his best sequence of musical comedy ditties. The globe-trotting collaborators will be in Cape Town this week.

The story went on to say that after Cape Town, Cole and Hart would sail across the south Atlantic before finally returning to Broadway at the end of May.

As a follow-up to the various news items dealing with the trip, the press reported on June 1, 1935, after the *Franconia* had tied up in New York, that Cole and Hart had been "met by Sam H. Harris, who is to produce the new show and who is to have it read and sung to him by the authors. . . . Casting will probably begin immediately and if it proceeds without difficulty it is possible that the piece will be presented out of town in August." The public also learned that Cole and Hart had finished their collaboration five weeks earlier and each had begun other work: Hart a new play, and Cole a new score.

As a testament to Cole's fame in 1935, everywhere he and his party went aboard the *Franconia* they were bombarded with renditions—frequently very bad ones—of Porter tunes, especially "You're the Top" and "I Get a Kick Out of You," from *Anything Goes*. It was the fate of Cole and his entourage, as Hart remembers it, "to be plagued by hotel orchestras hidden behind potted palms manfully blaring out 'You're the Top' in Bombay, in Zanzibar, in Rio, and even—by what miracle of communication no one of us could fathom—in Tahiti and Bali." But aside from such moments, the trip was almost pure bliss for Cole, for it allowed him to indulge in sightseeing. He has been described by Hart as

> an indefatigable sightseer, a tourist to end all tourists. Everything held an interest for him. No ruin was too small not to be seen, particularly if it meant a long climb up a steep hill; no ride into the interior was too much or too far, if it was a broiling hot day and there was a piddling waterfall at the end of it. Even the flora and fauna

fascinated him, and he would drive miles to gape at a native shrub or an animal that flourished only in a particularly disagreeable part of whatever country we were in.

Yet it was through this insatiable curiosity about the world around him that Cole derived many of his ideas for songs. The first number he wrote on the *Franconia* trip evolved just that way. At the first stopover—Kingston, Jamaica—Cole had been intrigued by an unusual bird-sound while on a guided tour. The song and its title fell into place almost immediately when he learned that the bird was called a kling-kling and that it often inhabited the tropical divi-divi tree; thus, "The Kling-Kling Bird on the Divi-Divi Tree."

Since Cole was continually writing songs wherever he traveled, it was inevitable that the origins of many of his tunes were as varied as the places he visited. Cole even made a point of claiming an exotic source as the stimulus for a song even when it may not have been the case. Thus he claimed on a number of occasions—including for publication in a *New Yorker* article—that he had been inspired to write "Night and Day" on hearing the monotonous wail of Moroccan music. But as is often the case with inventors of tales, Cole did not always keep his stories straight. Instead of attributing a Moroccan influence in the creation of "Night and Day" when interviewed for a *World-Telegram* article published on November 26, 1938, Cole rather matter-of-factly said,

I wrote the piece for a spot in *Gay Divorce*. I wasn't trying to plumb any depths or interpret mass psychology of the times. . . . I was living down at the Ritz-Carlton when the song was put together. I put the tune on paper, I remember, on a Saturday and wrote the lyric the next day while lying on a beach in Newport.

Cole also gave more than one version of how his famous "Begin the Beguine" had evolved. He originally alleged that he wrote the song on the *Franconia* voyage after witnessing a native dance at Kalabahai, a small village on the island of Alor (one of the Sunda Islands of the Dutch East Indies). Hart has supported this allegation, and remembers that he first heard the tune "sung by Cole Porter himself, sitting at the upright piano in his cabin as the boat sailed toward the Fiji Islands" on its global tour. In a personal letter dated June 12, 1944, to a Stanford King of Williamsburg, Virginia, who had inquired about the origins of the song, Cole gave a somewhat different story. He admitted that he had "first discovered the dance [the beguine] in Paris in 1933. There was a special dance hall on the left bank where French negroes from Martinique used to dance every night and I went often to see them." In another letter, dated March 23, 1945, to a Frank Colby of Houston, Texas, who had also inquired about the song, Cole's reply once again gave Paris as the first geographic stimulus for the tune, while giving credit to Kalabahai as an additional influence:

I was living in Paris at the time and somebody suggested that I go to see the Black Martiniquois, many of whom lived in Paris, do their native dance called The Beguine, in a remote nightclub on the left bank of the Seine. This I did quickly and I was very much taken by the rhythm of the dance, the rhythm was practically that of the already popular rumba but much faster. The moment I saw it I thought of BEGIN THE BEGUINE as a good title for a song and put it away in a notebook, adding a memorandum as to its rhythm and tempo.

About ten years later while going around the world we stopped at an island in the Lesser Sunda Islands, to the west of New Guinea, at a place called "Kalabahi." My spelling of Kalabahi is entirely phonetic. A native dance was stated for us, the melody of the first four bars of which was to become my song.

I looked through my notebook, and found again, after ten years, my old title BEGIN THE BEGUINE. For some reason the melody that I heard and the phrase that I had written down seemed to marry. I developed the whole song from that.

More important, of course, than the inconsistencies in Cole's stories is the quality of the songs involved. Whether "Night and Day" was a product of the Ritz-Carlton rather than a Moroccan setting, or whether "Begin the Beguine" first evolved in Paris instead of Kalabahai, is certainly less crucial than the end result. However, the obvious discrepancies that emerge from Cole's stories relating to "Night and Day" and "Begin the Beguine" also make some of his other claims questionable. If one were to take Cole's word at face value, "You're the Top" was written in a *faltboat* as he floated down the Rhine; "What Is This Thing Called Love?" was suggested by a native dance in Marrakesh; and on and on. What is true and what is not? With Cole's vivid imagination, impishness, and love of practical jokes, one can't always be sure, though the stories are invariably as delightful as the man responsible for them.

Irrespective of the origins of the songs Cole came up with for Moss Hart's script, the score as a whole was one of Cole's finest. Besides the "Beguine" song, the score also included such favorites as "A Picture of Me Without You," "Why Shouldn't I?" and "Just One of Those Things." Except for the latter, all of Cole's other key numbers were finished by the end of the *Franconia* voyage. "Just One of Those Things" was written the following September when Cole and Hart visited Leonard Hanna's farm in Ohio as a breather before the start of rehearsals. While walking through the Ohio countryside Hart suggested that a major song was still needed for the second act. Cole agreed and immediately fell silent, obviously concentrating on the problem at hand. By the next morning he had completed the entire verse and chorus of "Just One of Those Things."

Jubilee, the musical that resulted from Cole and Hart's collaboration, drew passing inspiration from the actual silver anniversary celebrations for the reign of England's ruling monarch, George V. Even before *Jubilee* began its Boston tryout, the British Foreign Office had expressed fear that the musical might cast an unfavorable light on the English royal family. Like the real-life equivalent, *Jubilee* evoked considerable pomp and ceremony in its story about a king and queen of a mythical, though anglified, country. But there ended any resemblance to the real thing.

Jubilee was too much of a delightful comic romp to be taken seriously. It told of a king and queen of an unspecified country, tired of the formalities of court, who use the ruse of a possible revolution at home to leave their Feathermore Castle and go out into the world as simply "Mr. and Mrs. Smith," taking with them their two oldest children, Prince James and Princess Diana. As ordinary citizens they are able to let their hair down and indulge themselves in those fancies denied them as members of the royal household. The king concentrates on his major passion, rope tricks; the queen is attracted to a swimming champion who plays a jungle man, Mowgli, on the screen; Princess Diana is smitten with Eric Dare, a celebrated and brilliant young playwright; while James wins dancing prizes as the partner of a shapely blonde nightclub beauty, Karen O'Kane. Interwoven into the plot's playful spoof of royalty were caricatures of Johnny Weissmuller (the famous screen Tarzan; the "Mowgli" of the show), Noel Coward (in the guise of Eric Dare), and Elsa Maxwell (represented by the character Eva Standing, a party-giver without peer). *Jubilee* made fun, too, of George Gershwin, whose legendary reputation for hogging the piano at parties to play his own music was best summed up by a remark once made by the always acidulous George S. Kaufman: "I'd bet on George anytime in a hundred-yard dash to the piano." In

Jubilee perennial hostess Eva Standing boasts pridefully that Gershwin has promised *not* to play the piano at one of her elaborate parties.

Heading the large *Jubilee* cast in the role of the effusive and sentimental queen was Hollywood's own Mary Boland. Playing her mouselike spouse with enough regal diffidence and reserve to make the part amusing was famed British actor Melville Cooper. The supporting cast effectively added to the proceedings: June Knight was the decorative Karen O'Kane, Charles Walters and Margaret Adams played the royal siblings James and Diana with enthusiasm and energy, and Derek Williams, Mark Plant, and May Boley kept the pace lively performing Eric Dare, Mowgli, and Eva Standing respectively. In the small role of a child prince was young Montgomery Clift of later Hollywood fame. Crucial to the entire production was Hassard Short's staging, which expertly blended the splendiferous ceremonial trappings of high royalty with lowbrow comic relief. The show was a treat for both the eye and the funny bone. As the *New York Times* reported of the show's Boston opening on September 21, 1935, *Jubilee* was "big, beautiful, amusing, spectacular and for the most part in admirable taste." The *Times* report from Boston found *Jubilee* "setting new standards," while noting, too, that "Hart's book mingles satire, sentiment and humor in good proportion. Porter's score and lyrics are original and tuneful."

Perhaps influenced by the good advance word from Boston, New York's reviewers could hardly contain themselves when *Jubilee* opened on Broadway at the Imperial Theater on October 12, 1935. "Probably the most beautiful production in pretty nearly any playgoer's memory," gushed Gilbert Gabriel in his *New York American* review. "It is the ultimate of the post-Ziegfeld period. It is an extravaganza extraordinary, raised by its lovely scenery and clothes, and by all its gay staging, to realms almost fabulous." Even the usually more reserved Brooks Atkinson of the *Times* pronounced *Jubilee* "the aristocrat of American festivals in music."

It was natural to expect that *Jubilee* would have a reasonably long life on Broadway. Yet the $150,000 production—an exceptionally expensive one for the period—folded after only 169 performances, without coming close to recouping the money invested in it. Lost in the shuffle was Cole's personal investment of eighteen thousand dollars. Like the rest of the show's angels (among them MGM studios, the major backer), he had invested in *Jubilee* with the expectations of turning a tidy profit. Why did the show close when it did? A major factor in the debacle was the dissatisfaction of star Mary Boland with the continual grind of appearing nightly. She had gotten used to the soft life in Hollywood and was not up to the rigors of regular live appearances. This was compounded by a drinking problem that caused her to miss a number of performances. After spending approximately four months on Broadway, she was finally released from her contract and was replaced by Laura Hope Crews. Fine actress though she was, Miss Crews did not have a glamorous enough image to attract paying customers, with the result that box-office receipts dropped precipitously.

To all these complications one must add the effects of a depressed economy on theatrical ventures in general. There were about fifty fewer productions on Broadway when *Jubilee* opened than the year before, and most shows lost money. Of the ten musicals that opened on Broadway during the 1935–36 season, none turned out to be financial successes—not even Billy Rose's long-running (233 performances) supercolossal, *Jumbo*. Legitimate theater was in such an economic bind at this point that President Franklin D. Roosevelt in 1935 initiated the Federal Theater Project as part of his New Deal, to help bring shows to the public at prices they could afford, while subsidizing employment for theatrical professionals. Viewed in the light of these extenuating circumstances, it is easy to see why *Jubilee* closed when it did despite its promise. Though the loss of his own investment in the show hardly made a dent in Cole's almost limitless pocketbook, he was sufficiently disenchanted by the experience to vow never to invest in Broadway productions again—especially those in which he was involved.

Neither "Begin the Beguine," "Just One of Those Things," nor any of the other outstanding songs from *Jubilee* became overnight successes. As was often the case with Cole's tunes, it took a while for them to catch on. That was exactly Gilbert Gabriel's conclusion in his *New York American* review of *Jubilee*. "You hear a song of his for the first time and say, 'Oh yes!' or something as ungrateful as that," said Gabriel of Cole's way with a tune, "but by the fourth or fifth time you hear it you realize—as everybody else from Manitoba to Mississippi has already realized by then —that it's a honey." Waxing prophetic, Gabriel singled out "Begin the Beguine" as "probably that kind of honey." And Gabriel's prediction, of course, turned out to be a reasonably accurate one, though it took far more than just four or five hearings for the song to catch on. The major problem with the tune, in terms of accessibility, was its inordinate length —108 measures' worth. Simply remembering the complete tune became a major hassle for the public. Nor has that built-in problem ever been completely resolved. Even now most people can not sing "Begin the Beguine"—the longest of Cole's hit tunes—from beginning to end without messing up somewhere along the line. But going a long way toward making the song popular was clarinetist Artie Shaw's recorded instrumental version of the tune, in July of 1938, for Bluebird (B-7746). This colorful swing treatment, arranged by Jerry Gray, not only made Shaw and his band world-famous almost instantaneously; it also did the same for the tune.

While he was involved in the preparations for the premiere of *Jubilee* shortly after returning from the *Franconia* voyage with Hart, Cole already knew that a British version of *Anything Goes* was to open at London's Palace Theatre on June 14, 1935. The American production was still going strong on Broadway. Save for an English cast and some minor changes in the lyrics and the book to conform to British humor and topicality, *Anything Goes*, London style, had a strong resemblance to the Broadway production. Mounted by Charles B. Cochran, Cole's most significant English producer, *Anything Goes* had enough of a draw for British audiences to run for 261 performances—enough to temper any of Cole's misgivings about the fate of *Jubilee* because of factors beyond his control.

In spite of the fine results of their joint creative effort, Cole and Hart never collaborated again after *Jubilee;* though Hart, along with a slew of other writers, did contribute some sketches for Billy Rose's *Seven Lively Arts*, for which Cole wrote the score, in 1944. From time to time Cole and Hart discussed doing another complete musical together, but nothing ever came of it. "Shows either happen or they don't happen," is the explanation Hart has given, without elucidating further on the subject. Clearly, however, the peak of their friendship was reached as they worked together on *Jubilee*. After this project, although they kept in touch, essentially they took separate paths. This divergence may have been caused by Cole pushing the issue of homosexuality with Hart. Apparently feeling that Hart was straddling the sexual fence and a potential convert, Cole, supported mainly by Monty Woolley, would often proselytize on behalf of the gay cause when he was with Hart. "You haven't been laid until you've been laid by a man who knows the ropes," or "nothing takes the place of a good man," would be freely and teasingly proferred as advice to Hart, according to Cole's friends. Hart apparently never took the advice nor was influenced by Cole's evangelizing. What is clear is that Hart went on to greater glory as a playwright—as the cocreator, with George S. Kaufman, of *You Can't Take It With You* (1936), and the author of *Lady In the Dark* (1941), among other shows—after *Jubilee;* that he married singer-actress Kitty Carlisle in 1946; and that the two were a close-knit couple until Hart's death in 1961. Nonetheless, Hart's ties to Cole evidently remained strong even if they saw each other rather infrequently after their *Jubilee* collaboration had ended. Nearly a quarter of a century after that show had opened on Broadway, Hart readily conceded in print that Cole "was an early hero of mine and he has remained a late one." Cole, in turn, always spoke warmly of Hart. Thanks to *Jubilee* and the memories they shared in connection with it, a common bond united the men as long as they lived.

14

Hollywood Resident

Accepting the bad with the good in his professional life, Cole stoically endured the usual quota of musicals that somehow never got produced. In 1931 E. Ray Goetz had asked Cole to write the score for *Star Dust* but for one reason or another this musical never got on the boards. Two years or so later Gilbert Miller's planned production of *Once Upon a Time* also came a cropper, knocking out Cole's score for it as well. A similar fate befell *Adios Argentina,* a movie planned for release by Fox in 1935. Unfortunately, Fox shelved its plans for *Adios Argentina* before it ever got to the filming stage. However, in nearly all such catastrophes Cole managed to rescue a portion of his material for use in other productions so that he, at least, had something to show for his creative efforts. Several of Cole's best-known songs were originally castoffs from musicals that never went into production. The famous "Mister and Missus Fitch" tune had first been part of the *Star Dust* score before Cole incorporated it into *Gay Divorce.* "I Get a Kick Out of You" was another reject from *Star Dust* prior to becoming one of Cole's biggest hits in *Anything Goes.* But perhaps the most popular song that Cole salvaged from among his discarded scores was "Don't Fence Me In," a casualty of *Adios Argentina.* After lying dormant for years this tune eventually became a phenomenal success.

In 1934 Lou Brock, a top producer at RKO, lost much of his power at that studio when Pandro S. Berman took over as acting chief of production in place of Merian C. Cooper, who had suffered a heart attack. Unhappy with the turn of events at RKO, Brock—the man most responsible for bringing Fred Astaire to RKO and for teaming him with Ginger Rogers—began casting about for a new studio affiliation. When RKO did not renew his contract, he signed with Fox.

As part of his production itinerary at Fox, Brock asked Cole to create the score for *Adios Argentina*, a projected cowboy musical, and suggested that for it Cole consider writing a cowboy lament on a poem, "Don't Fence Me In," by a Montana cowhand, Bob Fletcher. On acquiring the rights to the poem from Fletcher for two hundred dollars, Cole wrote the simple, wistful "Don't Fence Me In," based on the poem's title and some of its text, as one of the numbers for his *Adios Argentina* score. Once the film project was abandoned Cole did little to promote any of his tunes for it, including "Don't Fence Me In," and soon lost contact with Brock. (Such is the tenuousness of a Hollywood career, Brock ultimately died in obscurity. From a position of power at RKO and Fox, Brock ended up as a night clerk in a Hollywood hotel.)

After languishing unnoticed and unwanted for some ten years, "Don't Fence Me In" finally made it to the screen in a World War II musical potboiler, *Hollywood Canteen*, released in 1944 by Warner Brothers.

One of many flimsy musicals put out during the war period as morale boosters for the general public and servicemen, *Hollywood Canteen* had little in the way of plot or visual interest. Drawing on moviedom's famous servicemen's center as its major focus, the film served mainly as a showcase for a mixed bag of Hollywood talent to strut before the camera as if they were actually entertaining at the canteen. Through a stroke of good luck for Cole, Walter Gottlieb, producer of *Hollywood Canteen*, learned about the neglected "Don't Fence Me In" and thought it a perfect song for cowboy star Roy Rogers, who was to appear in the film. With Roger's adding his imprimatur of authenticity to the rather banal tune, with such lines as "Give me land, lots of land under starry skies above" and "Let me straddle my old saddle underneath the western skies," "Don't Fence Me In" had almost instant appeal. At a time when Adolf Hitler and Nazi Germany were threatening the existence of the free world, the song had a reassuring ring to it, epitomizing as it did all that was American, pure, and rural. Aided by recordings by Roy Rogers, the Andrews Sisters, Bing Crosby, and other established artists, "Don't Fence Me In" quickly became one of Cole's biggest money-makers.

Besides its amazing rags-to-riches history, "Don't Fence Me In" is unusual in other respects. In terms of both the life-style it espouses and simply as a song, it is the complete antithesis of everything that Cole stood for. "Don't Fence Me In" and Cole were worlds apart, and probably no one knew that better than he. Perhaps symptomatic of his feelings about the tune is the fact that even after "Don't Fence Me In" had become a big smash he referred to it as "that old thing."

Long before Cole hit the jackpot with "Don't Fence Me In," his film fortunes, after starting so precariously, had taken an upswing. The first movie using his songs, Paramount's *The Battle of Paris* of 1929, starring Gertrude Lawrence, was so tepid that his two tunes in it, "Here Comes the Bandwagon" and "They All Fall in Love," were virtually ignored. Cole's second film affiliation, Warners' 1931 version of *Fifty Million Frenchmen*, was also disastrous for him, for it completely eliminated the vocal score he had written for the original 1929 stage production. *Adios Argentina* fared even worse, since it never got beyond the drawing-board stage. But Cole's reputation as a writer of hit tunes for the theater remained impeccable. Also, the impact of "Night and Day" in RKO's 1934 release of *The Gay Divorcee*, which saw Fred Astaire and Ginger Rogers blossom as a team, was enormous. By 1935 Cole's position as a composer-lyricist was so strong that MGM called him to Hollywood to write a film score. To clinch the deal MGM offered him a handsome seventy-five-thousand-dollar fee for approximately twenty weeks' work, an offer too generous for Cole to refuse, especially at a time when the theater was in desperate straits because of the Depression.

Cole had frequently visited Hollywood prior to signing with MGM, but he had never actually lived there. His contract with MGM changed all that. As a working member of the movie colony, he found it more advantageous to live there. Cole was but one of a long line of top Broadway songwriters who moved to Hollywood, including Irving Berlin, Jerome Kern, and George Gershwin. They made the trek westward in the thirties because of better opportunities there. While millions of Americans were unemployed and dependent on welfare for subsistence, Hollywood of the Depression era was thriving as never before, turning out celluloid fantasy for a public that could not seem to get enough of it. For a modest admission price endless numbers sought surcease from their economic woes in the make-believe projected from the screens of darkened movie houses across the nation. With the theater floundering and offering only token competition, film production zoomed ahead in the thirties as the unqualified leader in the entertainment industry. Helping to promote film production was the impact made by *42nd Street*, released by Warner Brothers in early 1933. For about two years, between 1931 and 1932, most film musicals had not done very well at the box office. The public, perhaps because at first it found them too artificial in comparison with the harsh realities of the Depression, generally avoided them. But just as Jolson's *The Jazz Singer* and *The Singing Fool* gave great impetus to films in the late twenties, so, too, did *42nd Street* give a boost to movies of the thirties, especially musicals. With singing and dancing now once again considered an important ingredient for attracting paying customers, Hollywood studios resumed their production of musicals with a vengeance. It was because of this that Cole and other prestigious songwriters were so greatly coveted by the big film studios, who lured them west by wads of cash and promises of the good life in Hollywood's sunny climate.

For his first residence in Hollywood Cole chose a large, luxurious home complete with well-manicured lawns, tennis courts, and a big swimming pool, as befitted a visiting celebrity from Broadway. He and Linda rented their impressive home from silent-film star Richard Barthelmess, one of the fortunate few of his breed to survive the transition to the talkies, but not without some dubbing help. As a means of capitalizing on Barthelmess's fame in the period immediately following Hollywood's conversion from silent films to talkies, his studio, First National Vitaphone, had announced to the world that Barthelmess would not only talk but would also sing and play the piano in their 1929 production of *Weary River*, described in publicity releases as "an epic of a down-and-outer whose plaintive music reaches through prison's bars to find love and a new life a thousand miles away." As an enticement for Barthelmess's fans to see their hero in a talkie, Vitaphone's extensive advertising campaign proudly enunciated his multiple talents:

> All these years the wealth of Richard Barthelmess' rich voice has been concealed. Now, VITAPHONE unearths this hidden treasure for you to enjoy. VITAPHONE brings you a Barthelmess so much greater it's like discovering a NEW STAR. A voice so sensationally fine he could have won stardom on it alone.

The ads also stressed that Barthelmess would play the piano in the new talkie. What Vitaphone judiciously did not say in their publicity blurbs was that the singing and the piano playing were dubbed into the film. While Barthelmess mouthed the words, a hired singer, John Murray, actually did the singing. Similarly, pianist Frank Churchill did the playing out of camera range as Barthelmess emoted at the keyboard.

The chicanery and dishonesty so evident in Vitaphone's promotion of Barthelmess and *Weary River* also typified the mentality common to the movie industry when Cole first arrived in Hollywood. The studio chieftains of the mid-thirties, as of the twenties, were hardly paragons of virtue and integrity. Most of them were of the same mold: ill-mannered, bullying tyrants of humble origins and limited education who had somehow gravitated to the movie industry when it was still in its infancy, and had risen to the top at least as much from aggression and *chutzpah* as talent. They ran their big studios with iron fists and corps of yes-men who catered to their overblown egos. When these studio rajahs roared, all came to attention, for they chopped off heads of underlings as readily as they chomped on the big Havana cigars that seemed to be their trademark. Some indication of how these moguls, rolling in money and power, operated, and the overall professional climate in Hollywood of the thirties, can be deduced from notes Cole kept of a series of meetings he had with MGM officials in connection with his first film for them.

Shortly after arriving in Hollywood in December, 1935, Cole had his initial studio conference, on December 20, with Sam Katz, executive producer at MGM, and screenwriters Sid Silvers and Jack McGowan. Katz quickly laid out the plan for the new musical. He wanted the movie based on the highly publicized shenanigans of the aging John Barrymore and an aspiring young actress, Elaine Barrie. As Katz envisaged it, Clark Gable would play Barrymore and Jean Harlow would be Elaine Barrie. By January 6, however, at his next meeting with Katz and his writers, Cole learned that the Barrymore-Barrie escapade had now been discarded as a potential plot and that Gable and Harlow were no longer being considered for the leads since neither could sing. No new plot had as yet been developed, but Katz exhorted his writers to "try to think of a story within a reasonable time," while giving Cole this reassurance: "Now, Cole, don't worry about authors, because I can spend two hundred thousand dollars on authors to give you the right script." Katz ended the conference with, "Good-bye, Cole, come back in a few weeks."

A week later Cole met with Jack Cummings, the producer of the film, identified by Cole as a member of "The Family"—meaning that he was related to MGM head Louis B. Mayer, as were many others in key positions on the studio payroll. Cummings, who was accompanied to the meeting by writer Eric Hatch, told Cole that Silvers and McGowan had been dropped from the project because of exhaustion from work on another movie, but that an idea for a plot for Cole's film had germinated anyhow. The new concept revolved around a young couple—reporters for rival newspaper syndicates—in love, though in competition with each other to win the Pulitzer Prize for the year's best newspaper story. By banding together, however, they write the prize-winning story.

Cole's notes indicate that he liked Cummings's concept "much better than anything that had been suggested so far." Nonetheless, on the very next day, January 14, in a conference with Sam Katz and his cohorts, Cole learned that everything Cummings had told him no longer applied. Hatch was no longer on the film, while Silvers and McGowan were back in. Moreover, head man Louis B. Mayer had passed the word to Katz that he definitely wanted the movie to be a revue so that all of his MGM stars could appear in it. The problem was that no one had a suitable idea to tie the revue together. When Cole proposed that perhaps the revue could be based on different sections of a newspaper, Katz and his sidekicks almost fell over themselves with enthusiasm. In Cole's words, "They all leaped at this, as if I had suddenly discovered radium, and Sam suggested that after such a great idea I should go to the desert and take three weeks' rest."

But as had happened previously with other suggestions, the notion of a revue soon went out the window. At a January 17 meeting, after several general plot ideas—including ones about a six-day bike race and a radio show—had been rejected, Silvers recalled that he, McGowan, and Buddy De Sylva, a lyricist and producer, had worked on a play several years earlier about a hostess of a lonely-hearts club and two sailors. Katz liked the idea. When McGowan reminded him that De Sylva would probably have to be paid substantially for his rights to the property, Katz replied airily, "Oh, that's all right, boys; don't let that stop you." Katz, though, did have one request to make of his writers. "Give me," he asked, "one character and one scene that I have always clung to: the character—a female wharf rat who can sing torch songs; and the scene—two battleships, one full of boys and one full of girls." As before, however, once the meeting ended little seemed to be accomplished in resolving details about the movie's plot. When Cole called Katz on January 21 to find out how the story was progressing he was told, "Don't worry, my boy, we will find an idea in a few weeks. In the meantime, take advantage of California and get a lot of health."

Two days later, however, Katz telephoned Cole to say that De Sylva had sold the rights to his play for $17,500, and by mid-February it was rather clear to all that the film would be about a lonely-hearts club and sailors even if all the details were not yet resolved (while planning was still going on Katz made a point of reminding his staff that he had not lost interest in "a scene showing two battleships, one covered with boys and one covered with girls"). After further communication with Katz and company, Cole had completed several numbers for the movie by early March, among them "Goodbye, Little Dream, Goodbye." This song was never used in the film, but when Cole performed it for Katz and his group on March 12 they enjoyed it so much they couldn't restrain themselves from singing it again and again. Katz in particular was so transported by the tune he was moved to say, "You know, Cole, that song is beautiful, it's—why, it's Jewish." Nor did Katz limit his enthusiasm for the number to those comments. For the following day, March 13, Cole was told by his agent, Arthur Lyons, that "Goodbye, Little Dream, Goodbye" had stirred up so much excitement on the Metro lot that it had been rumored that MGM wanted him back for another movie the following year, but for a higher fee—$100,000 rather than the $75,000 he was then getting.

The high regard Katz and his crew had for Cole, as manifested by agent Lyons's message, was occasionally offset by disquieting moments during the additional conferences Cole attended in March, April, and May. Such an instance occurred on May 11 when Katz suddenly said, "Now, Cole, I want you to write a skating waltz. We haven't enough beauty in this picture and I want to sign Sonja Henie for an ice ballet." Taken aback, Cole asked where the ice ballet would fit into the movie, to which Katz replied, "Well, instead of taking the male lead and the Broadway star to a nightclub, we will take them to a skating rink." At this news, Cole left the conference, as he put it, "feeling very happy about the picture as a whole, but definitely worried as to Sonja Henie and the skating waltz." Luckily, Cole never had to write the skating waltz Katz requested, as negotiations with Miss Henie ultimately fell through. Cole, moreover, was so adroit in his dealings with Katz and his entourage that awkward incidents were kept to a minimum in the planning stages of the film. Cole's finesse in handling MGM personnel is readily apparent from his own comments about a meeting at his home with Katz's staff on May 19: "They all came to the house. I plied them with whiskies and sodas, and then played the entire score. Even if the score had been awful, none of them would have known it, as they all felt so well, but they left saying it was the greatest thing they had heard in years."

By the end of May, Cole's score was virtually set, most of the cast had been signed, and shooting of the film was geared to start on June 15 in anticipation of an October 1 release date. Cole also had this assurance from Katz about the quality of the film: "We are going to have a swell picture. It is going to be a million-dollar picture, maybe it will cost a million and a half." Despite these encouraging words, Katz asked Cole to play the entire score for Louis B. Mayer and Irving Thalberg, the driving forces at Metro, for their final approval. On June 3 Cole appeared at the studio with the score plus copies of the lyrics for distribution and proceeded to play and sing his songs for Mayer, Thalberg ("looking more dead than alive," in Cole's estimation), Katz, and other MGM bigwigs. Before long it became clear to Cole "that the atmosphere was friendly." As he described it, Mayer "began jumping around the room whispering to people" and Thalberg "suddenly became a different person and began smiling." After the finale, Thalberg, in Cole's words, "leaped out of his seat, rushed over to me, grabbed my hand and said, 'I want to congratulate you for a magnificent job; I think it's one of the finest scores I have ever heard.'" Mayer, too, responded warmly by putting his arms around Cole and asking, "Cole, how about coming into the next room and signing your contract for next year?" With everyone in a jubilant mood, Mayer then addressed the assemblage: "Now, Sam [Katz], this material is so fine that I don't want you to take any chances with it. I want every lyric heard, and in order to assure that, I want you to make rushes of these numbers and then show them in theaters as shorts to find out whether the audiences can understand every word. And another thing, this finale is so brilliant that I want you to go to town and spend $250,000 on that number alone." At the conclusion everyone hugged and kissed everyone else, and no sooner had Cole left the meeting than Mayer, still exuberant, put through a call to agent Arthur Lyons to discuss Cole doing a second film for MGM. Less than a week later Cole had signed to write another score for Metro beginning December 1, 1936. His new fee: $100,000.

After this start on the right track with the top brass as a Metro songwriter, Cole never had very much trouble with Mayer or other movie bigwigs. Cole invariably dealt from strength with them. After all, his glamorous and highly publicized reputation as a world traveler, bon vivant, French Legionnaire, and Yale-Harvard man had preceded him to Hollywood, as had his outstanding track record as a writer of hit songs. Cole was so different from the usual run of Hollywood professionals, by virtue of his independent wealth, background, and personality, that he made a strong impression on these ill-educated, rapacious, ex-clothing salesmen and furriers who now headed the movie empires. From his precise, almost British-sounding voice, to the smooth, urbane way he handled himself in their presence, Cole was a breed apart from the Hollywood norm. The Hollywood brass cottoned to him, and he, apparently, to them, though one can detect a certain looking-down-the-nose attitude on Cole's part in his notes. Never again did Cole comment so extensively for the record on the ramifications of movie-making and the personalities who ran the film industry. But clearly Sam Katz emerges as a first-class *schlemiel*, and many of the others Cole dealt with also come off poorly, including Louis B. Mayer, who, in Cole's description, literally oozed unctuousness from every pore. Cole may have welcomed Mayer's flattering comments about his work, but his notes also reveal a certain amount of contempt for the man.

Cole seemed to bloom in Hollywood, mainly because working there was a heady new experience for him, and he had always welcomed new experiences. Also, it was a marvelous ego boost for him to be in such great demand for the relatively new medium of film while being paid so handsomely for his services. Writing for films, moreover, almost automatically guaranteed a vast exposure of his work to millions of people throughout the world and added an extra dimension to his career that he welcomed. In the interest of professional advancement it was easy enough for him to put up with the grossness of many of the Hollywood types. He may inwardly have looked down his nose at people like Louis B. Mayer, but at the same time he was greatly impressed with the immense power of such cinematic tycoons as well as by the highly professional—if not necessarily artistic—quality of the products they turned out.

Cole's reactions to Hollywood were so favorable that, when asked by columnist Dorothy Kilgallen whether he liked the place, he replied: "When I first came here they told me, 'You'll be so bored you'll die; nobody talks about anything but pictures.' After I was here a week, I discovered I didn't want to talk about anything else myself."

Besides getting caught up in the repartee, glamour, and tinsel of the movie colony, Cole became enamored of Hollywood's summery climate (in the thirties, after all, the word "smog" had not even entered the vocabulary) and the life-style that went with all that sunshine. Cole would spend hours lounging around his swimming pool, tanning himself to a nut-brown finish while intermittently swimming, drinking, bantering with friends, and carrying on a variety of social and business telephone conversations (for, like many others of the Hollywood set, he had a phone at poolside). There were, too, the usual quota of evening affairs on his agenda for fulfilling social obligations and bolstering professional ties. Cole mingled easily with the movie people at these parties, freely trading gossip and shop talk with them as though he had known them all his life. These were often hard-drinking, rowdy affairs, where it was not uncommon for some of the most famous names in the colony to revert to the gutter manners of their early origins.

Cole took all this in stride, and, as many people do, probably derived an unconscious satisfaction from the more outrageous of these incidents out of relief that it was not *he* making a spectacle of himself in public. Linda, who was not so directly involved as Cole in her dealings with the Hollywood crowd, was much less sanguine about these displays of vulgarity. Although there was little that she could do about it when she was in someone else's home, in her own home, as she had always done, she kept to a fixed schedule for serving dinner, after allowing enough time for her guests to have a maximum of two drinks before eating. She would be punctilious about having dinner served at the precise time called for, irrespective of latecomers (in so doing she cleverly lessened the excessive drinking before dinner that was typical of so many Hollywood gatherings). Linda had another social idiosyncrasy that was unusual for Hollywood: She deplored the custom at these parties of the women disappearing to the powder room after dinner to gossip while the men remained behind for the "serious" talk. To avoid this and to maintain a consistent level of conversation at her parties, Linda would close down the large ladies' room on the main floor of her home and keep open only a small bathroom upstairs for their use.

However, not all of the Porters' Hollywood parties required such adroit handling of their guests, for Cole and Linda would also hold intimate gatherings pretty much exclusively for their close friends, whose style was more their own. Anita Loos recalls that when she was in Hollywood while the Porters were there, their intimate parties stood out like oases in a barren desert. With close friends like Anita Loos, Howard Sturges, and the Fred Astaires present, these soirees were generally models of the best in civilized living.

Responding as positively as he did to living in Hollywood, Cole made it a practice of returning to the movie colony for approximately four to six months each year for the rest of his life—even when he was not involved in film work. Undoubtedly the substantial success of his initial movie as a Hollywood resident played a part in his decision. The movie, *Born to Dance*, starring dancer Eleanor Powell and actors James Stewart, Virginia Bruce, Una Merkel, Frances Langford, and Buddy Ebsen, followed the scheme that had been worked out between Cole and Sam Katz and his staff. The plot revolved around Nora Paige (Eleanor Powell), a hostess in a New York lonely-hearts club, and sailor Ted Barker (James Stewart). As often happens in the movies, the two fall almost instantly in love after meeting at the club. Their romance runs into a snag, however, when Broadway musical-comedy star Lucy James (Virginia Bruce) visits Ted's ship for publicity purposes. While on the ship Lucy's dog falls overboard and is rescued by Ted. Lucy's press agent seizes on the incident to build up a romance between the two. On reading about the affair in the papers, Nora, stunned by the news, refuses to see Ted. Heartbroken, he goes all-out to win her back, but in a rather convoluted way. First he arranges for Nora to be Lucy's understudy in a forthcoming show, without either woman knowing of his machinations. Then, playing up to Lucy, he complains to her about all the publicity their affair has gotten. She takes him at his word and tells her press agent that she won't open in the new show if another line is printed about Ted and herself. Shortly before the opening Ted telephones a leading columnist with a manufactured story about himself and Lucy, which appears in print. Infuriated at having her wishes disobeyed, Lucy walks out of the show. Nora steps into her part, becomes an instant star, and is reunited with Ted at the movie's end.

Born to Dance reflected the no-expenses-spared approach that Sam Katz and Louis B. Mayer had led Cole to expect, with seemingly the entire American fleet and an army of shapely chorus girls shown singing and dancing on the screen in lavish production numbers. Of the assorted songs by Cole that were featured in the movie, two—"Easy to Love" and "I've Got You Under My Skin"—became classics. "Easy to Love" had originally been written for William Gaxton in *Anything Goes*. When he complained that the song did not lie properly for his voice and was not to his liking, Cole substituted "All Through the Night" for him instead. After Cole had resurrected "Easy to Love" for *Born to Dance*, the song was assigned to James Stewart, who had no voice to speak of (while Stewart was still being considered for the film, Cole had noted that "he sings far from well," though he thought him perfectly suited for the role of a clean-cut sailor). Nor did Stewart's rendition of the tune disprove Cole's original assessment of his voice, for his pipsqueak though earnest tenor did little justice to the song. Nonetheless, the pithy lyrics, flowing melody, and tasteful harmony of "Easy to Love" easily survived Stewart's assault, and the song went on to receive great acclaim. The other hit of *Born to Dance*, the beguinelike "I've Got You Under My Skin," is also beautifully written. Despite its unconventional length (fifty-six measures) and form (consisting essentially of seven eight-measure phrases, all of them somewhat different from each other), the tune readily caught on, especially since Virginia Bruce—unlike Stewart—sang it reasonably well in the film.

In connection with Cole's and Linda's opposite reactions to Hollywood —he liked the colony; she had many reservations about it, mainly because of its residents—absurd claims have been made that she had urged him to leave and break his artistic ties with the place, and that when he did not a crisis resulted in their relationship. Linda was far too supportive of Cole and his career to have carried on so about a place with which he was professionally associated. If Cole wanted to stay in Hollywood and she did not, this difference in outlook would hardly have precipitated a schism between them. They had often gone their separate ways before, and could have done so again without any major hassle. Their warm regard for each other and their common goal—furthering Cole's career —had always been unifying factors in their lives, in spite of the minor differences and frictions that inevitably arise between two people. Moreover, during the years Cole spent in Hollywood, Linda, except for those periods when she was physically not up to it, would always look forward to joining him there, for no other reason than to be with him. She may have been cool to those who lived and worked there, but Cole took precedence over such matters, and she would jump at the chance of going there at his bidding (Anita Loos remembers how excited and pleased Linda would invariably be at the thought of joining Cole in Hollywood *because he had asked her to*).

Yet Hollywood *did* help trigger an estrangement between Linda and Cole, but for more basic reasons than merely their innately different responses to the colony and its inhabitants. For Cole developed fresh personal interests in Hollywood which cut into their ties and established relationship. As a consequence, he saw less of Linda and had less need of her support. Under these circumstances, where such a noticeable change took place, it was inevitable that a major upheaval would occur in their lives—but more about this turn of events later.

15

Red, Hot and Blue!

In 1936, a remarkably active period for Cole, MGM released *Born to Dance*; Paramount put out its version of *Anything Goes*, starring Ethel Merman and Bing Crosby; and Cole started work on the score for *Rosalie*, a Metro remake of the Sigmund Romberg–George Gershwin stage musical of the same title. That year, too, Cole kept active on Broadway by doing the songs for *Red, Hot and Blue!* which opened at the Alvin Theater on October 29, 1936. If to all the hoopla generally attendant on these Hollywood and Broadway productions one adds the generous amount of media attention consistently showered on Cole and his songs, there is no mistaking that Cole at this point was one of the notables of the world.

Cole had really never been diffident about himself or his talent while he was on the way up, but now that he had made his mark and was a celebrity, easily recognized and fawned over everywhere he went, he exuded the confidence and authority expected of a famous personage. The change in Cole was essentially one of degree, since from childhood on he had come to expect preferential treatment. His celebrity status only heightened this expectation, for he could now stretch the rules of the game or throw his weight around with the impunity reserved for the very famous. Cole, for example, had always loved to exchange juicy gossip items with his close friends. As a celebrity, however, he did not always feel inclined to trade such tidbits on a one-to-one basis. As the mood moved him he would proclaim royally to individual friends, "Amuse me!" signaling that he wanted to hear the latest dirt told as divertingly as possible, but not necessarily that he would reciprocate in kind. As an additional privilege, Cole would not hesitate to cut his informant short and go on to something else if the gossip were not titillating enough.

Another early trait of Cole's that remained with him all his life was his great snobbishness. From prep school and college on he assiduously cultivated the wealthy—including the Vanderbilts and the Morgans—and the highly placed as his social peers. It was one thing for Cole to get along with many of Hollywood's louts for purely professional reasons, or to satisfy his sexual appetite with less than exalted types, but it was another for Cole to accept as social equals those who did not have money, position, or some cachet that would set them apart from the ordinary.

One story that helps to illuminate Cole's snobbishness—as well as his orneriness—concerns a luncheon he gave at his home for friends, when he was already a celebrity. Shortly before the luncheon was to take place, Cole called one of the invited guests to ask him to bring an extra friend whom he thought would be an attractive addition to the luncheon group. Without the extra guest, Cole explained, he would have a total of thirteen people for luncheon and he considered that an unlucky number. Furthermore, a man was needed to balance the number of women who were to be present. Cole's friend quickly invited to the luncheon a tall, handsome young westerner who was an editor for a leading publisher and a great fan of Cole's. But fan or not, the young westerner immediately incurred Cole's displeasure by requesting a cocktail after Cole had announced that luncheon was to be served, displaying a lack of familiarity with the Porter household dictum that the drinking of cocktails stopped when food was to be served. Cole, however, took no account of the young editor's unfamiliarity with this rule and showed his annoyance by hovering over him impatiently while he was attempting to drink the cocktail, forcing him to gulp it down. Only then did Cole lead his guests into the dining room. During lunch, moreover, the young man aggravated the situation by not understanding any of the French that was spoken. Shortly after the guests had left Cole telephoned the friend who had invited the editor to complain about the young man's manners and his backwardness in regard to French. Cole stressed in no uncertain terms that the young westerner was never to be invited to his home again. "He simply will not do," was Cole's curt appraisal of the editor. To reinforce this appraisal Cole added, "Besides, he wore brown shoes."

This unattractive side of Cole was not limited to purely social matters. He could be difficult in his professional dealings, especially after he had become a major celebrity. Cole not only showed up late for the start of work in New York on *Red, Hot and Blue!* (the delay was caused when Cole, on his way East by car from Hollywood, decided to visit the home of the famous Dionne quintuplets in Collander, Ontario; unfortunately, even Cole was not able to wangle permission to see the five little girls privately), but he also proved to be very testy during the out-of-town tryouts of the show, when the production was plagued with a host of problems ranging from a book that was too long and did not mesh very well with the score to musical arrangements that left much to be desired. In desperation producer Vinton Freedley made numerous suggestions for overhauling the show. Most of those involved in reshaping the musical accepted Freedley's production ideas in good faith. Cole did not. He refused to cooperate even when Freedley pleaded with him to "play ball with us for another ten days." Cole reacted so negatively to what he considered Freedley's excessive carping that he sent the producer a wire stating, "I have lost all heart and have stopped work." He requested that Freedley "please address all further complaints" to his agent, Richard Madden. Incensed at Cole's arbitrary behavior, Freedley speedily wired this strong reply to Madden: "Staging a musical comedy without a composer is not easy. He is acting outrageously to the authors and me. Why can't he take it like a man and not hide behind your skirts?" As further ammunition for his cause Freedley's wire alluded to the early demise of Cole's previous Broadway show. "If he does not do something drastic," Freedley reminded Madden, "he has another *Jubilee* to his demerit. Can he afford this?" This presumably made Cole reconsider the tenuousness of his position; he relented and resumed work on revising the score to both his and Freedley's satisfaction.

Unpleasant as this interchange between Cole and Freedley was, it was not the only personality clash that afflicted *Red, Hot and Blue!* Even before the show went into production, an ego conflict developed between two of its principals. In anticipation of repeating the success of *Anything Goes,* Freedley had asked Ethel Merman and William Gaxton, as well as Cole, Howard Lindsay, and Russel Crouse (key alumni from the former show) to lend their names to his forthcoming production, which would also star Jimmy Durante. At first all of these talents seemed amenable. Gaxton, however, immediately became disenchanted with the production when he overheard Lindsay and Crouse telling Ethel Merman about the large part she would have in the script they were preparing. Gaxton's ego was so easily bruised that he quickly withdrew from the show rather than chance the possibility that Ethel Merman would outshine him on stage.

With Bob Hope brought in to replace Gaxton and the casting now virtually set, another hitch developed in the production, this time because of a hassle over billing between Jimmy Durante and Ethel Merman. Speaking through their agents, Durante and Merman each insisted on having their names listed boldly on the left side, above the show's title. For a while it appeared as though the production would be bogged down indefinitely in this top-billing battle, for neither star would accede to the other's demands. Fortunately, the impasse was finally broken when Cole came up with a solution that allowed Jimmy Durante and Ethel Merman to share the billing by having their names crisscross above the show's title. By alternating the position of their names every few weeks, no one would have any advantage. The basic arrangement that was finally settled on looked like this:

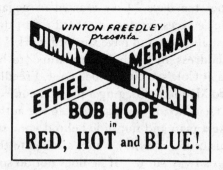

Originally called —*but Millions!* then *Wait for Baby!* before being titled *Red, Hot and Blue!* the show told about the search for a missing heiress with an unusual imprint on her backside. Eighteen years earlier, at the age of four, she had sat on a hot waffle iron by mistake and was branded for life with its grid design. Intermeshed with this search for the heiress with a rare bottom went a supply of satirical barbs aimed at such topical American sources of humor as the incompetence of the fuddy-duddies who sit on the Supreme Court, the coddling of prisoners in jail, and the lack of money in the United States treasury. Presumably these barbs by Lindsay and Crouse were intended to emulate the lampooning of the American political scene that playwrights George S. Kaufman and Morrie Ryskind had so brilliantly introduced into the George and Ira Gershwin musical, *Of Thee I Sing*, the winner of the Pulitzer Prize for drama in 1932. But where the political spoofing in *Of Thee I Sing* was impudently fresh for its time, the satirical thrusts of Lindsay and Crouse often seemed stale and thrice-told in *Red, Hot and Blue!* In his review of *Red, Hot and Blue!* in the *Herald Tribune*, Richard Watts carped that the book for the show "does not exactly reveal Howard Lindsay and Russel Crouse, its authors, in their most hilarious manner." Watts found that the show was "by no means all pure gold. There are, in fact, times when its tale . . . drifts off into what can be vaguely described as the doldrums." Watts noted, too, that "the anatomical jokes grow a trifle feeble upon occasion."

Drama critic Brooks Atkinson of the *New York Times* also criticized the plot, singling out its makeshift connecting links. For Atkinson these links consisted mainly of "I was looking for you" and "Oh, hello, Bob." In answer to such criticism, Crouse humorously tried to explain the plot. "The whole thing, of course, is done in symbols," Crouse said of his and Lindsay's brainchild. "Even the orchestra is composed entirely of symbol players. For instance, Ethel Merman, you will find, is playing a wealthy young widow. But if you look behind Miss Merman—I mean, if you look behind Miss Merman's characterization—you will find that she represents much more than wealth and youth and widowhood. She is really in the play as a symbol of the class struggle between freshmen and sophomores. The same applies to Jimmy Durante. When Mr. Durante says 'Hot-cha-cha!' he doesn't mean 'Hot-cha-cha!' at all, but something much more intangible, something that reaches to the very core of industrial life today, something fine and good and true, something you can put away and forget about."

Nevertheless, the New York press thought the plot for *Red, Hot and Blue!* was clearly the weakest part of the show. Nor did Cole's score win over many reviewers. Richard Watts probably best summed it up when he characterized the score as being in Cole's "second-best vein." While admitting that on hearing a number in the show sung by the likes of Ethel Merman one is "forced into the conviction that it is a masterpiece," Watts also made the point that "it is only as an afterthought that you begin to realize that it may have been merely a pretty good piece, raised into the major leagues by Miss Merman's exciting rendition." According to Watts, "it is only by comparing the score to earlier ones of the same composer that you begin to grow captious." Besides praising Ethel Merman's dynamic rendition of the part of "Nails" O'Reilly Duquesne, a young, sentimental widow, Watts also had only kind words for Jimmy Durante as "Policy" Pinkie, the captain of the polo team at Lark's Nest Prison, the state penal institution. When Durante sang Cole's "A Little

Skipper from Heaven Above," in which he confessed that he was not really a man but a woman about to become a mother, Watts considered the result "a comic masterpiece."

Cole was always a model of composure at the opening of his musicals. He had a very long memory indeed for reviewers whom he felt were not especially sympathetic to his work or lacked critical acuity (apparently Richard Watts qualified as a leading candidate in both respects for Cole, judging by remarks he made privately over the years to close friends), but one would hardly guess that by the way he comported himself in public on opening nights. He invariably looked as though he were thoroughly enjoying himself at these affairs. Meticulously dressed in evening clothes and surrounded by friends of long standing, Cole would be the picture of relaxation as he smilingly walked down the aisle to his front seat before the curtain went up. During the show itself he would be totally immersed in the stage action, laughing heartily at each bright spot as if he were hearing and seeing it for the first time. Nor would he be shy about commenting favorably about something he himself had created. "Isn't it great?" or similar phrases would often be used by Cole to describe his work.

In an article entitled "Notes on the Morning After an Opening Night" that Cole wrote for the *New York Times* shortly after *Red, Hot and Blue!* had begun its Broadway run, Cole candidly discussed his behavior at opening nights. Beginning the article with the rather startling question, "Am I made wrong?" Cole then responded to the question by elaborating on his opening-night behavior. "While Russel Crouse," wrote Cole,

was pacing back and forth in the lounge of the Alvin Theater during the opening performance of "Red, Hot and Blue!" giving a perfect take-off on all of the ten million ghosts, and Howard Lindsay was somewhere on his New Jersey estate getting quarter-hourly reports from his wife, I was in as good a seat as the management would give me, and, flanked by Mary Pickford and Merle Oberon, was having a swell time watching the actors. Russel claims this is being as indecent as the bridegroom who has a good time at his own wedding. . . . The reason for my behavior isn't that I'm confident of the play's success or that I'm totally without nerves. I'll put up my nerves against the best of them. But, for some reason, the moment the curtain rises on opening night, I say to myself: "There she goes," and I've bid good-bye to my baby.

Cole summed up his behavior:

> During the months of preparation the piece itself has a way of
> becoming something of a person to me—not always a nice person
> perhaps, but at least some one that I've grown fond of. The minute
> it is exposed to its premiere audience, however, I feel that it's no
> longer mine. It belongs to the performers. And I become just another
> $8.80 customer. That is why I take my friends along and make a night
> of it afterward.

Though Cole gave every indication of having had a fine time at the
Broadway premiere of *Red, Hot and Blue!* he had little cause for rejoicing
after reading the decidedly mixed reviews. The show did reasonably well
at the box office, though, primarily because of the drawing power of its
outstanding array of big-name talent, and remained on Broadway until
April 10, 1937, for a respectable run of 183 performances. Among the
assorted Porter tunes in the show, one of them, "It's De-Lovely," caught
on almost immediately and became one of Cole's biggest hits. In retrospect, it is easy to see why the song did so well. Not only was the melody
of its refrain—with its simple ascending scale to start it off—a very catchy
one, but the lyrics that went with the melody were truly exceptional in
the way they combined the very conventional with the unexpected, especially in their imaginative use of the concocted word "de-lovely" and
derivatives of it. Cole's coupling of the conventional and the unexpected
in the song's lyrics is noticeable at once, for the rather prosaic beginning
of the refrain,

> The night is young, the skies are clear,
> So if you want to go walking, dear,

is immediately follwed by the decidedly unusual phrase, "It's delightful,
it's delicious, it's de-lovely." This sets the tone for the entire refrain,
including the outstanding tag ending, in which Cole really lets loose with
a barrage of "de" words:

> So please be sweet, my chickadee,
> And when I kiss you, just say to me,
> "It's delightful, it's delicious,
> "It's delectable, it's delirious,
> "It's dilemma, it's delimit, it's deluxe, it's de-lovely."

Prior to Cole's including "It's De-Lovely" in his *Red, Hot and Blue!*
score, he had suggested the tune to Sam Katz and his staff at MGM for
consideration in *Born to Dance*. When the song was not used in the film,
Cole found a place for it in *Red, Hot and Blue!* as a duet between Ethel
Merman and Bob Hope that traces their romance over the course of five
choruses from their first kiss to their marriage, their honeymoon, and the
engagement of their first-born many years later. Actually Cole had conceived "It's De-Lovely" some months before either *Born to Dance* or *Red,
Hot and Blue!* on the boat trip he and Moss Hart made to the South Seas
so that they could collaborate on *Jubilee*.

But as often happened, Cole gave more than one version of how "It's
De-Lovely" came about. In one account Cole related how he, Hart, and
Monty Woolley had partaken of the delectable mangosteen melon while
visiting Java on their world tour and were so taken with the fruit that
when Hart exclaimed, "It's delightful," Cole chimed in with, "It's delicious" and Woolley added, "It's de-lovely," which became the title of
the song. In still another version of the tune's creation, Cole changed the
setting somewhat and substituted Linda for Hart as the third party in the
story. In this second account Cole claimed that he, Linda, and Woolley
were so moved by the sight of Rio de Janeiro at dawn during their world
tour aboard the *Franconia* that Cole cried out, "It's delightful," to which
Linda replied, "It's delicious," and Woolley followed with, "It's de-
lovely." Unlike the discrepancies in his stories about the creation of a
number of his other famous tunes, Cole's two accounts of the genesis of
"It's De-Lovely" are—save for some minor differences—essentially the
same, though neither version can be considered definitive. Both accounts,
moreover, credit Monty Woolley with originating the key phrase "It's
de-lovely," on which the song is based.

Besides "It's De-Lovely," several more of Cole's songs for *Red, Hot and
Blue!*—especially the ones he wrote for Ethel Merman—managed to do
well. These numbers included "Ridin' High," "Down in the Depths,"
and the title song. When Miss Merman proclaimed forthrightly in the
latter number her dislike of the classics and her love for tunes that are
"red, hot and blue," everyone sat up and took notice, just as they responded enthusiastically when she trumpeted, in "Ridin' High,"

> Life's great, life's grand,
> Future all planned.
> No more clouds in the sky,
> How'm I ridin'? I'm ridin' high.

She was equally convincing singing the doleful "Down in the Depths." In this song she showed still another facet of her dramatic capabilities by conveying great dejection, that resulted, as she explained it, because "the one I've most adored is bored with me." Despite the most elegant of surroundings, high above the roar and glitter of Manhattan, she was the epitome of gloom and doom as she admitted,

> I'm deserted and depressed
> In my regal eagle nest
> Down in the depths on the ninetieth floor.

So well was Cole served by Ethel Merman that soon after *Red, Hot and Blue!* opened in New York he publicly declared, "I'd rather write for Ethel than anyone else in the world." Elaborating further, Cole stated, "Every composer has his favorite, and she is mine. Her voice, to me, is thrilling. She has the finest enunciation of any American singer I know. She has a sense of rhythm which few can equal. And her feeling for comedy is so intuitive that she can get every value out of a line without ever overstressing a single inference. And she is so damned apt." Responding to Cole's generous tribute, Ethel Merman returned the compliment with equal fervor, saying unequivocally, "I'd rather sing his songs than those by any other writer." They also demonstrated their high regard for each other by their long, close friendship, which lasted up until Cole's death, and their extended professional ties. For after *Red, Hot and Blue!* Miss Merman—or La Merman, as Cole frequently referred to her in tribute to her uniqueness—also performed in these Broadway musicals by Cole: *DuBarry Was a Lady* (1939), *Panama Hattie* (1940), and *Something for the Boys* (1943).

Whether writing for Ethel Merman or any one of the dozens of performers who appeared in his musicals, Cole always tried to shape his songs to fit specific vocal and dramatic capacities. To familiarize himself as much as possible with the talents of potential performers for his shows, Cole would regularly attend casting sessions and kept notes on all who auditioned, with information about the way they moved, their voice qualities and ranges, their looks, and whether they could dance. Cole would often simply put a "no" next to various names on his list; of the many who received the designation, most have not been heard from since. But then there would be the exception, like Wally Cox, who received a "no" when he auditioned for *Out of This World* in 1950 and then went on to make a big name for himself as a television personality. Theodore

Uppman, who subsequently became a Metropolitan Opera singer, did a little better when he, too, auditioned for *Out of This World*. Instead of "no" Cole put down these comments: "Very fine baritone. Pleasing personality. 6 feet. 28 years old. Blonde curly hair." Cole, however, ended his description of Uppman with the negative "but can't move."

Cole's written comments on performers included such other barometers of disapproval as "can't sing," "too cute," "too fat." Cole's notes also stressed favorable attributes, such as "striking personality," "fine voice," "good figure," and "interesting face." But irrespective of whether a performer suited him, Cole, on the surface, would be extremely generous in his appraisals. "*Dee*-vine," or "*mah*-velous," were the most frequent expressions he used after someone had auditioned for him. Invariably these expressions indicated his disinterest, unless they were followed with additional comments or questions. But, inasmuch as those performers who did not fit the bill were not privy to Cole's real assessment of their talent, they would usually leave the audition with their self-esteem and hope still intact.

Cole's method of writing songs did not fit the common mold any more than his method of handling auditions and his comportment at opening nights. In creating his tunes for a production, or merely in writing songs for his own pleasure, Cole, unlike most popular composers of his generation, did not start out by doodling at the piano. He generally first thought through the basic lyrics and melody of a song away from the piano. Only after he was satisfied with his material did he try it out at the piano. Cole could work this way because of his rather substantial musical training and experience—for a popular songwriter, that is—and his good ear. This is not to imply that Cole used the piano infrequently when he was working. On the contrary, Cole would often play the piano in his home until the early hours of the morning while he was working on something. As a matter of fact, Cole had acoustical "mud" installed in his Waldorf Astoria apartment (he lived at the Waldorf from 1935 on, having followed Elsa Maxwell there during the Depression, when the Waldorf management offered him a large apartment at the hotel for a nominal rental) to deaden the sounds he made at the piano at night, so as not to disturb his neighbors. And yet, with all of Cole's musical training and professional experience, he was dependent on a number of musical aides to assist him in putting the finishing touches to his songs. Several times a week Cole would meet with either Dr. Albert Sirmay (Cole's music editor, first at Harms and then at Chappell), Alexander Steinert, or any one of several others who served as his musical secretaries over the years, to play his tunes for them at the piano. Cole would at that point have fully worked out the lyrics and the melody for a particular song, but not, as a rule, the harmony or the rhythmic patterns that made up the accompaniment. After playing a song for his aides, they would play it back for him fully harmonized and embellished. Cole would then make comments on what he heard, such as "make the bass line stand out," or "there should be more movement in the inner voices," or "give more drive to the accompaniment." Cole was quite precise in what he wanted, and his instructions would be closely followed. When Cole was finally satisfied, the song would be notated to reflect his wishes. The end result of these sessions would be a highly polished product for voice and piano that was essentially ready for publication as it stood, and also suitable for arrangement purposes.

Commuting as frequently as he did between Broadway and Hollywood from the mid-1930s on, Cole utilized the services of his musical aides on both coasts, usually paying them twenty dollars an hour for their help. When Cole was in Hollywood and specifically wanted the services of Alexander Steinert, who might be back East, Cole would bring Steinert to the West Coast—at Cole's expense—and pay him, in addition, a salary of about five hundred dollars weekly for as long as his assistance was needed.

In spite of the increased professional pressure on Cole because of Hollywood as well as Broadway deadlines, he still found time for diversion during and between assignments. Long travel trips, however, now had to be planned far more in advance to allow for his intensified professional schedule. Thus when he returned to Hollywood only a month after the Broadway premiere of *Red, Hot and Blue!* and the near-simultaneous release by MGM of *Born to Dance* (the two events, of course, made rather extensive demands on Cole's time), he was already thinking ahead to a long vacation in Europe that following summer, as soon as he had completed work on *Rosalie* for Metro. He had not taken a walking tour on the Continent for several years and was looking forward to the prospect with great relish. Unfortunately, it was to be the last walking tour he would ever make.

16

The Accident

The sheer vitality that Cole exhibited by alternating so rapidly between Broadway and Hollywood assignments in the mid-thirties says much about his physical constitution then. At the age of forty-five, when he started work on his *Rosalie* score in December of 1936, Cole was in excellent health and looked at least ten years younger than he really was, with his trim figure, large, vibrant eyes, virtually unlined face, boyish grin, and full crop of dark hair. Remarkable specimen that he was, Cole also had the stamina to match his appearance. He thrived on working hard and playing hard, and had the recuperative power of someone half his age. After expending enormous amounts of energy on his various activities, Cole would be ready for more of the same after a reasonably quick breather.

In direct contrast to Cole's vigor, exuberance, and youthful appearance, Linda, at fifty-four, clearly showed her age. Alongside Cole some might have taken her for his mother. She was still a handsome woman in her way, who still dressed as elegantly as ever, but her recurring bronchial-asthmatic condition and the passage of time had taken their toll, both on her basic energy level and on her appearance. The finely chiseled face of her younger days had been replaced by considerably broader features. Her nose was now wider and longer than before, and the rest of her face had coarsened to match. Nor was her figure willowy any longer. Though Linda always remained small-boned, her body, instead of being slenderly curvaceous as in the past, now had the boxlike look of an elderly dowager's. Linda, moreover, shrank in size as she got older. She was not yet bent over in 1936—as was true prior to her death, in 1954—but she was definitely shorter than when she had married Cole. Then, in her heels, she was slightly taller than Cole. But by the mid-1930s, Cole was taller than Linda by an inch or two.

Considering Cole's inordinate concern with his appearance and with remaining perennially youthful (as evidenced by, among other things, his refusal to own up to his real age), and his great vitality, it was indeed inevitable that his relationship with Linda would be affected by her physical deterioration. Just as Cole now often made trips or did other things on his own because Linda was physically not up to them, so, too, he could no longer turn to her for the chic glamour she had once contributed to their partnership. From his Yale days on Cole had always loved to be seen with stylish, alluring women, and Linda for years had filled the bill beautifully. With her looks now a thing of the past, Linda was quite delighted when Mary Pickford and Merle Oberon, both friends of hers, accepted Cole's invitation to be his guests at the Broadway opening of *Red, Hot and Blue!* It was with Linda's blessing that Cole escorted the two movie stars—one on each side of him—to the opening, as all eyes in the theater were upon them. As a further supportive gesture, Linda that same evening presented Cole with her usual gift of a cigarette case —this time a two-tone eighteen-karat affair with a zigzag reeded design, from Cartier's—to commemorate the opening of a new production. Unknown to Linda, Cole, as a token of his gratitude, had had an extraordinarily elaborate platinum cigarette case made up for her for just this occasion. Thus, when she presented him with her gift, he had the pleasure of surprising her with an even more lavish—but similar—gift of his own. Linda's cigarette case had as its major motif a diamond sunburst; it practically sparkled with solar energy, covered as it was with diamonds, sapphires, and gold-inlaid stars. Linda treasured the gift all her life, at least as much for the memory of the pleasant surprise associated with it as for its beauty and Cole's thoughtfulness in ordering it for her.

About a month after *Red, Hot and Blue!* opened, Linda presented Cole with still another eighteen-karat two-tone cigarette case from Cartier's as a memento of MGM's release of *Born to Dance*. But then, inexplicably, Linda did not give Cole her customary gift when Metro put out his *Rosalie* film in 1937. It was not until the New Haven tryout, in March of 1938, of

Cole's subsequent stage musical, *You Never Know*, that Linda resumed giving Cole a cigarette case for each of his new productions.

The reason for Linda's divergence from her regular gift-giving pattern in connection with *Rosalie* is not completely clear, but it is presumably related to a schism that developed between Cole and her in mid-1937. For in the spring of that year, at just about the time Cole had finished work on *Rosalie*, Linda left him and Hollywood to return to her Paris home. Published claims made after their deaths have asserted that Linda had urged Cole to cut his professional ties with the movie colony because she did not like the place, and that his refusal brought about a break between them. These allegations, as already stated, do not hold water simply because Linda was far too supportive of Cole and his career to have made such demands on him. Besides, evidence has shown that she was only too happy to be in Hollywood if Cole wanted her there. As long as Linda felt that Cole needed her and that she could be useful to him, she would have been content to remain in Hollywood, or anywhere else, her health permitting. By the same token, they often went their different ways and still remained united by their common interests and high regard for each other.

But whether in close proximity to each other or not, Linda and Cole were inextricably bound together just as long as the fine line that often separates mutual trust and concern from doubt and suspicion was reasonably maintained in their relationship. For Linda, then, to have reacted as she did and leave Cole while he was in Hollywood, it is obvious that *he*, rather than the movie colony itself, had somehow altered the delicate balance on which their very special marriage partnership was predicated.

And he had. For Cole became so enamored of Hollywood and all the treats it offered that he went overboard in his indulgences. Like a child in a fantasy world of charlotte russes and chocolate sundaes, all there just for the taking, Cole partook fulsomely of the delights—particularly sexual—at his disposal. Hollywood, after all, has always served as a magnet for the physically attractive with movie ambitions. Consequently, as the movie colony grew in size and prestige, it was perhaps inevitable that a large homosexual contingent would evolve there because of the colony's great emphasis on appearance, the body, and the sensual life.

Included in the gay enclave were some of the biggest names in films as well as bit players and extras. In a community where press-agentry and the big build-up are the rule rather than the exception, this sexual side of its life has, understandably, been consistently kept under wraps. It would hardly have served the interests of Hollywood if word got out that

Top: Cole Porter's grandfather, J. O. Cole, as a young man, with his wife Rachel, whom he referred to as "the rose of Indiana." *Left:* Grandfather Cole in his later years. *Right:* Young and attractive Kate Porter, Cole's adored mother. (Photos: Cole Porter collection.)

Above: Cole, far right, as he appeared in a production of Sheridan's *The Rivals* at Worcester Academy, the prep school he attended between 1905 and 1909. (Courtesy Worcester Academy.)

Opposite: (Upper left) Samuel Fenwick Porter, Cole's father, shown with daughter Rachel. She died at the age of two, in 1890, before Cole was born. *(Upper right)* Cole, as an infant, dressed in velvet, silk, and fur; not unlike a young prince. *(Lower left)* Cole, who started studying the violin at the age of six, is shown tuning his instrument. *(Lower right)* Cole, as he looked at about the age of eight. (Photos: Cole Porter collection.)

Above: During his Yale years, Cole devoted considerably less time to his studies than to his social activities, including a close association with the Yale football team, as songwriter and cheerleader. He is shown here, at the left, with his fellow cheerleaders for the 1912 season. (Courtesy Yale University.)

Opposite: (Upper left) Linda Lee Thomas Porter, as she looked circa 1910. A heavy smoker even at this early date, she can be seen holding a cigarette in her right hand. *(Upper right)* Linda, considered an outstanding beauty, as she looked at about the time she married Cole, in 1919. (Photos: Cole Porter collection.)

(Lower left) Cole's good chum, Yale man William Crocker, of the San Francisco railroad and banking family, is seen showing off in the gardens of the large villa at Cap d'Antibes that Cole and Linda rented in the summer of 1921. (Courtesy Yale University.)

(Lower right) A family photo of Sara and Gerald Murphy, good friends of the Porters, taken in 1922, not long after the Murphys had arrived in France. On the donkey are the Murphys' children— sons Baoth, left, Patrick, right, and daughter Honoria, in the middle. (Courtesy Honoria Murphy Donnelly.)

Left: Like the Porters, the Murphys became social leaders in France shortly after their arrival there in the twenties. They are shown dressed for a costume ball in Paris, given by the Comte and Comtesse Etienne de Beaumont. (Courtesy Honoria Murphy Donnelly.) *Below left:* Cole's fellow songwriter, Irving Berlin, and his wife Ellin, aboard the liner *Leviathan*, shortly after their marriage on January 4, 1926. By his marriage to wealthy Ellin Mackay, a member of New York society, Berlin's social position was undoubtedly enhanced with the very socially conscious Porters.

Opposite: (Upper left) A shot of Cole and friend Monty Woolley taken during one of their numerous jaunts together. (Courtesy Honoria Murphy Donnelly.) *(Upper right)* Indomitable traveler Cole and his friend Ed Tauch raise their glasses in a toast during a German *faltboat* tour they made together in 1933. (Courtesy Yale University.) *(Below)* Ethel Merman, Cole's favorite singer, shown with William Gaxton in the 1934 production of *Anything Goes*.

Left: Moss Hart. He and Cole traveled to the South Seas together in 1935 while collaborating *on Jubilee.* (Courtesy Museum of the City of New York.) *Below:* In the summer of 1937 Cole went on a European walking tour with Howard Sturges (middle) and Ed Tauch (right). This walking tour was Cole's last, for shortly afterward both his legs were badly smashed in a horse-back-riding accident. (Courtesy Yale University.)

Cole in his Hollywood home (rented from actor Richard Barthelmess) in 1937, when he worked on the score for the film *Rosalie*. It was during this period that Linda abruptly left him and Hollywood to return to Paris. (Courtesy Museum of the City of New York.)

Above: On January 17, 1938, less than three months after Cole's accident, Elsa Maxwell gave a large party for him at the Waldorf so that many of his friends could toast his health. Cole and Elsa Maxwell are shown at the party raising their glasses. (Wide World Photos.) *Left:* A photo portrait of Cole, circa 1938, by Alfredo Valente. (Courtesy Mrs. Alfredo Valente.)

As a result of the fame she achieved for her social talents, Elsa Maxwell eventually became a show-business personality as well as an author and newspaper columnist. She is shown here dressed as an equestrienne for her role in a 1940 Warners' film, *Riding Into Society*.

Top: Cole and playwright Bella Spewack exchange smiles during a light moment in the preparatory rehearsals of *Kiss Me, Kate.* (Courtesy Bella Spewack.) Judging by the expressions of Bella Spewack, Cole, and director Jack Wilson (on the right), *Kiss Me, Kate* is encountering some rough going in rehearsal. As an outgrowth of their collaboration on this show, Cole and Wilson allegedly became very intimate friends. (Courtesy Bella Spewack.)

Cole and Linda together in 1948. In comparison to Cole's rather youthful appearance, Linda was now stooped and shrunken, looking almost old enough to be his mother. (Wide World Photos.)

Left: Yale man "Black-Jack" Bouvier, of whom Cole reputedly spoke most enthusiastically, is shown with daughter Jacqueline in 1947, shortly before her eighteenth birthday. Jacqueline, of course, subsequently achieved international fame as the wife of John F. Kennedy, and then of Aristotle Onassis.
(Wide World Photos.)

Opposite: (Upper right) After Monty Woolley's outstanding success on Broadway in 1939 in *The Man Who Came to Dinner*, he was in great demand as an actor. He is seen here with Pert Kelton, left, and Anne Seymour, center, performing in *The Magnificent Montague*, a radio series heard on NBC from 1950 until 1951. (Courtesy NBC.) *(Upper left)* Ed Sullivan, on his "Toast of the Town" television series, devoted two programs—February 24 and March 2, 1952—to Cole and his songs. Sullivan and Cole are shown here discussing these programs. (Courtesy CBS.) *(Bottom)* One of the last photos of Cole and Howard Sturges together, taken in 1955 in Provence, France. Sturges died shortly afterward. Seated between them is Jean Howard, the former wife of Hollywood agent Charles Feldman.
(Courtesy Jean Howard.)

Above: Cole's final resting place. He lies buried between his father and Linda(*not* between his mother and Linda, as many have erroneously claimed) in the family plot at Mt. Hope Cemetery, in Peru, Indiana. *Below:* The inimitable song stylist, Mabel Mercer, accompanied by pianist Jimmy Lyon, as she participated in a musical tribute to Cole presented by Composers' Showcase—a music series directed by the author—at the Whitney Museum of American Art on November 19, 1975. (Photo by Hank O'Neal.)

some of its best-known film heroes were homosexual, as were many of the rank and file who lived and worked there. With this wall of silence as a buffer to shield the colony from the outside world, it has been very rare indeed for any news to be printed that touched on the sex life of prominent Hollywood gays. When dashing Ramon Navarro, for example, was the heartthrob of women throughout the world in the twenties and thirties as a leading movie idol, only Hollywood insiders knew of Navarro's gay escapades. It was not until years after Navarro had retired from the screen that the world learned about his homosexuality, and then only under the most tragic circumstances. The story made headlines when Navarro was found dead in his home, the victim of two young male hustlers he had picked up one evening. When apprehended, the two young men confessed to torturing and mutilating Navarro, in a fit of pique and passion, before killing him.

The Hollywood that Cole knew had more than its share of the virile he-men types who appealed so strongly to him, and he came to know many of them while he was there. With a friend of his, an actor's agent, serving as a kind of procurer or sexual middleman for Cole, he had practically his pick of the Hollywood gays. Through this agent, who had a wide acquaintance with movie-colony homosexuals (especially young actors hopeful of moving ahead in films), Cole would be introduced to the most attractive of them at parties specifically arranged for that purpose.

For those young men Cole took a fancy to, life would take a bountiful turn, for they would frequently be rewarded with gifts, money, and other tangible evidence of Cole's interest in them. It was not unusual for Cole to buy a car or some other luxurious item as a present for a young man he liked. One such young man, who also served as Cole's masseur for a period, even sought legal redress after Cole died for money he claimed Cole had promised him. The masseur produced two checks totaling $17,500 signed by Cole, from two different New York banks. Unfortunately for the masseur, the banks from which the money was to be drawn no longer existed. The two banks had consolidated and changed their individual names to a collective one approximately ten years before the dates indicated on the respective checks. Because of these obvious inconsistencies, the masseur had little choice ultimately but to drop his claim. But irrespective of the masseur's legal rights to the money he sought from Cole's estate, the signed checks typified Cole's largesse with young men he favored. We can only guess whether Cole's numerous paid dalliances were symptomatic of an unceasing need for a male figure to serve as a surrogate for his own father, with whom he could not relate.

Cole, moreover, did not limit his sexual involvement solely to men whose affections and favors he helped buy with cash and gifts. Some of Cole's most intense affairs were with men from distinguished families, with considerable money of their own. Cole, for instance, was reported to have been very much taken at one time with "Black-Jack" Bouvier. Flamboyant and handsome, John Vernou Bouvier III was, like Cole, a Yale man of the class of 1914, and later the father of Jacqueline Kennedy Onassis. "I'm just mad about Jack," Cole is supposed to have enthused about him to his very close friends at the height of his relationship with Bouvier. However, like many other of Cole's similarly intense affairs, this one allegedly petered out before too long, though Cole and Bouvier remained on amicable terms for the rest of their lives.

Between his numerous dalliances, "fucking parties" (as he called them), and other social and sexual activities during the period he was working on *Rosalie*, Cole had little time left for Linda, and bright woman that she was, she soon sized up the situation. Though normally she and Cole discreetly avoided discussing matters that might prove embarrassing to either of them, Linda reputedly was sufficiently distressed by Cole's actions at the time to speak out. Aside from any resentment that she may have felt about Cole paying less attention to her than usual, Linda's main concern was with what she considered his too obvious public display of homosexual involvement. She feared that if word got out to the media of how he was carrying on, it would be terribly damaging to his reputation and career (this was, after all, before there was such a thing as a gay liberation movement; nor had society's taboos relating to homosexuality changed very much from the time Oscar Wilde had been imprisoned on morals charges some forty years earlier). Responding to Linda's persuasiveness, Cole readily agreed to mend his ways. However, he was not normally used to constraints where his personal pleasure was concerned, and before long he had pretty much resumed his previous life-style. This time when Linda got wind of it she was so disturbed by the news that she quickly left Hollywood for Paris.

Just prior to Linda's departure, Cole had virtually completed the score for *Rosalie*; judged by normal Porter standards, it was not one of his best. The book for the film by William Anthony McGuire and Guy Bolton undoubtedly contributed to the lackluster quality of the score. McGuire and Bolton had originally written their script for a 1928 musical of the same title, for which Sigmund Romberg and George Gershwin had written the songs. Even by 1928 standards the plot for *Rosalie* had left much to be desired. It told about a princess from the mythical kingdom of

Romanza who meets an army lieutenant from West Point while visiting the United States. The two fall in love, but then the princess must return to Romanza. Hardly deterred by the ocean that now separates them, the lieutenant flies across the Atlantic in a plane—as Lindbergh did in 1927 —in pursuit of his love. Credibility gaps aside, the lieutenant and his princess are reunited in mutual bliss as the musical comes to its inevitable frothy conclusion.

The movie version of *Rosalie* was no less innocuous than the stage production, notwithstanding a better-than-average cast that featured Nelson Eddy and Eleanor Powell as the romantic leads and Frank Morgan and Edna May Oliver playing two royal heads of state. Among the tunes Cole wrote for the film, "Why Should I Care?" stood out more for its minor-key "Jewishness"—Cole's "hit-tune" formula, according to Richard Rodgers—than for any other qualities. But if "Why Should I Care?" and most of the other numbers for *Rosalie* did little to enhance Cole's reputation as a songwriter, two of the film's tunes did become big hits. One of them, "In the Still of the Night," was incorporated into the film against the objections of Nelson Eddy. Eddy complained that the song's long, seventy-two-measure refrain was put together in such a strange fashion (there are four sections to the refrain; the first two and the last are each sixteen measures in length, while the third section is an unusual twenty-four bars long) that he found the number difficult to sing and asked Cole to create another one for him in its place. Under normal circumstances Cole would have gone along with such a request out of deference for the performer involved. This time, however, Cole had sufficient faith in the song that he resolved to play it for L. B. Mayer himself and let the big man make the ultimate decision. On hearing Cole perform the tune, with its rather prosaic text ("Do you love me as I love you? Are you my life to be, my dream come true?"), Mayer was so touched by the song's sentiments that he could not hold back his tears. The sight of Mayer bawling over this tune remained one of Cole's most cherished memories. ("Imagine making L. B. Mayer cry," Cole would often tell his friends pridefully. "What could possibly top that?") However, more important for the song's future was Mayer's decision that "In the Still of the Night" *had* to be retained in the film. On hearing this, Eddy quickly did an about-face and willingly lent his voice to the song.

Mayer also used his clout in connection with the title tune for *Rosalie*. After hearing Cole perform the film's entire score for him, Mayer observed: "I like everything in the score except that song 'Rosalie.' It's too highbrow." Speaking with the weight of his position at Metro, Mayer suggested, "Forget you are writing for Nelson Eddy and simply give us a good popular song." Mayer's pronouncement came after Cole had already gone all-out to come up with as strong a number as possible for the key title slot in the film. Only after discarding five versions of the tune as not being good enough had he settled on the sixth. To say, then, that Cole was taken aback because his title tune did not pass muster would be a mild understatement, but, of course, he had little choice but to comply with Mayer's request. As Cole put it, "I took 'Rosalie No. 6' home and in hate wrote 'Rosalie No. 7.'" On hearing this version, Mayer, according to Cole, "was delighted with it, but I still resented my 'No. 6' having been thrown out, which to me seemed so much better." Nonetheless, this seventh version of "Rosalie" quickly caught on and became a major hit, despite insipid lyrics and an uninspired melody to match (one report even has it that Cole deliberately set out to write the worst song he could, to spite Mayer). With the passage of time Cole eventually took kindly to the tune, perhaps as a result of a remark Irving Berlin made to him shortly after "Rosalie" had become popular. "Listen, kid," Berlin had pragmatically told him, "never hate a song that has sold a half-million copies."

Once his work on *Rosalie* was behind him, Cole left Hollywood in June to visit Linda in Paris at 13 rue Monsieur before starting the European walking tour that he had been contemplating for some time. If Cole had any hopes of a reconciliation with Linda prior to coming to Paris, they were quickly thwarted, for she remained cool to him. Though they shared the same house she generally kept to herself and went her own way while he was there. After several weeks of this silent treatment Cole was only too happy to join Howard Sturges and architect Ed Tauch on a walking tour of Germany, Austria, Yugoslavia, and Italy before going on to the Scandinavian countries. As was Cole's custom on these trips, he took numerous photos en route; judging by those photos in which he appears, he showed little effects of Linda's estrangement from him. He looked very much his usual affable, confident self, whether hiking up mountain trails with a pack strapped to his shoulders or seated at a table drinking beer with his friends. By the end of the summer, as a matter of fact, Cole had already made plans for his next Broadway show, starring Clifton Webb, which was to start rehearsals in the late fall. In line with that assignment Cole left Europe (Linda stayed behind in Paris) on October 4, 1937, for his return to the States.

On his arrival in New York Cole lost no time in starting on the score for the projected Clifton Webb musical. But neither did Cole neglect his leisure activities. He had been back only briefly when he accepted an invitation to spend a weekend with several friends at the home of Countess Edith di Zoppola (the former Edith Mortimer, a New York socialite) in Oyster Bay, Long Island, the residence for many of the upper crust's horsey set. While at Countess di Zoppola's, Cole, joining in the spirit of the locale, decided to do some horseback riding, and asked a few friends to accompany him. Together they headed for the nearby Piping Rock Club in Locust Valley. Despite not having ridden for months, the often impetuous, willful Cole chose an extremely high-spirited horse against the advice of the horse's groom, who warned that the skittish animal might be difficult to handle. (In light of what followed, one might question whether Cole was courting disaster here out of some deep-rooted guilt feelings—perhaps in connection with Linda's estrangement from him and the subconscious need to cause bodily harm to himself so that he could get her back to mother him. The possibilities for interpreting Cole's actions in this instance are infinite and fascinating.) As Cole and his party rode along the bridle path, Cole's horse, apparently frightened by an unexpected noise or object, or by something Cole precipitately did, suddenly reared up and fell on its side, taking Cole, who wasn't able to extricate himself quickly enough from the stirrups, with him. In its fall the animal landed on one of Cole's legs, shattering it. As the terrified animal tried to right itself, it fell again, on its opposite side, smashing Cole's other leg. When the horse finally freed itself and got to its feet, Cole lay on the ground dazed, though conscious, too stunned by what had happened to be aware that he had been severely injured. (He even later made the outlandish claim that, as he awaited help, he took out a pencil and paper to work on the lyrics for "At Long Last Love," one of the songs for the Clifton Webb show.)

The first member of the riding party to reach the scene of the accident, Benjamin Moore, took one look at Cole and decided that he was badly hurt, notwithstanding Cole's assurances to the contrary. While other members of the party remained behind to look after Cole, Moore returned immediately to the clubhouse to summon an ambulance. A frantic call to the local North Country Hospital quickly determined that they had none available. Fortunately the Locust Valley Fire Department's ambulance was at hand, and it was in this vehicle that Cole, in a state of shock, was brought to the hospital. There he alternated between unconsciousness and delirium for the next day or so. Nonetheless, shortly after he came to Cole showed that he had lost none of his impish wit. One of the first remarks he made on opening his eyes was, "I know now that fifty million Frenchmen can't be wrong; they eat their horses instead of riding them."

Despite the gravity of Cole's condition, press accounts gave little indication of how seriously he had been hurt. In describing the accident, the *New York Times* of October 25, 1937, stated merely that Cole had suffered compound fractures of both legs the previous day, that "he appeared to have no other injuries . . . and that he was resting comfortably." This report and others like it simply reflected the medical information given out by Dr. Joseph B. Connolly, who was then treating Cole. For public consumption Dr. Connolly played down the extent of Cole's injuries. In a private telephone conversation with Linda in Paris, Dr. Connolly was more blunt. Both of Cole's legs were so severely impaired, he told her, that the right leg, and possibly the left, would probably have to be amputated. On hearing the news, Linda, putting Cole's well-being first and completely overlooking her previous differences with him, requested that the doctor delay making any final determination until she returned to New York. Without saying so, she had already made up her mind that amputation was out of the question—or at least was the last resort. She knew how much stock Cole placed on his looks and felt that any maiming of his body through amputation would have such a damaging effect on his morale that it would undoubtedly kill him. As further support for her decision Linda could look back on an episode that had occurred some thirty years earlier, when her first husband's leg had been threatened with amputation as a result of a car accident, yet had been ultimately saved. Why might not the same hold true for Cole as well? Moreover, in a long-distance telephone discussion with Kate in Indiana, Cole's mother strongly urged Linda to prevail on the doctors treating Cole to save his legs at all cost.

No sooner had Linda arrived in New York than she brought in Dr. John J. Moorhead, a distinguished and highly recommended bone specialist, to get another medical opinion on Cole's condition. After examining Cole, Dr. Moorhead agreed to delay amputation for the time being out of respect for Linda's wishes, but warned that if Cole developed any complications, such as a high fever, he would have no alternative but to remove either or both legs. Dr. Moorhead also cautioned that even if Cole's legs could be saved, the rebuilding process would be long and painful, and there would be no guarantee that there would not be many setbacks along the way. Would Cole accede to the uncertain course inherent in Dr. Moorhead's bleak prognosis? In view of Cole's generally optimistic nature and the emphasis he placed on his appearance, he obviously had little difficulty making up his mind, especially where his only other alternative was amputation. Furthermore, no one could have foreseen at that point that as a consequence of the attempts at rebuilding his shattered legs he would be in almost continual pain for the rest of his life and that, despite more than thirty operations, his right leg would ultimately be amputated close to the hip—considerably higher than it would have been if doctors had removed it earlier—because of bone and tissue deterioration. As he lay, then, in his hospital bed awaiting further treatment for his leg injuries, it was with a reasonable degree of optimism that he looked forward to the day when he would be moving about under his own steam and on his own two legs. Moreover, as one of the more positive results of the accident, he now had Linda back by his side to bolster his spirits and as a buffer for the rough going ahead. Their lives had been closely intermeshed for almost two decades before the accident, while Cole's career proliferated and Linda basked in the reflected glory that accrued to her as his wife. They had had much to be thankful for in the past. Would not their future together be equally salutary?

17

Back in Harness

During the months immediately following the accident, Cole spent most of his time at Doctors' Hospital in Manhattan, under heavy sedation to ease his intense pain as Dr. Moorhead worked desperately at trying to save his legs. Despite the sedation and having both legs in plaster casts for much of this period, Cole still suffered excruciating pain, especially in the right leg, because of nerve damage that resulted from the riding mishap. Cole often described the agony he felt in Geraldine, the name he playfully gave to his crippled right leg, as that of many sharp knives jabbing away at him. His injured left leg, the one he called Josephine (interestingly, Cole gave feminine names to both legs), proved less troublesome, though it, too, would act up on occasion. Some idea of the torture Cole went through at this point can be gotten from a series of notes he wrote while being treated. The writing was done at the suggestion of Dr. Moorhead, who felt that it would be good therapy for Cole to freely express himself regarding the pain he experienced. Moorhead also believed that the notes might serve as a guide for subsequent medical treatment for Cole. In any event, Cole discussed the pain in his right leg in a fanciful and often epigrammatic sequence of notes that he collectively titled "A Few Illusions Caused by an Injured Anterior Popliteal Nerve." These notes, in which Cole referred to himself as "a toe dancer, but a toe dancer who dances only on the toes of his right foot," were recently uncovered by this writer among Cole's papers, and are published here for the first time:

I'm a toe dancer, but a toe dancer who dances only on the toes of his right foot. The music in the orchestra pit is charming and it's very pleasant hopping around and around to that gay tinkling strain. But after a while I realize that my toes are tired and, risking the reprimand of the ballet master, I decide to drop to the ball of my foot and give them a rest. But, lo and behold, try as I may, I cannot do it, for my ballet-slipper has been made in such a way that I must stay always on the tips of my toes. So, long after the curtain has gone down, the music has stopped and I'm alone in the theatre, I watch the sad shadow I make as I go on and on, doomed forever to hop around on those poor tilted toes.

It's a relief to wake up and be no longer a toe dancer. But it's an awful bore to have this tremendous new pressure on the sole of my foot, which forces it up with such incredible insistence that I feel, as if, at any moment, the tendons of my ankle would break. Gradually I get used to this, however, as it continues pushing and pushing, but I must say I become rather discouraged when late at night I look at my toes to find that they are as far away as they ever were from the shin bone.

The toes on my right foot are having a delightful time under the covers; they are tapping up and down on the cast and then resting from their exertions by stretching, and stretching so completely that each is separate from the other. This is such a pleasant feeling that it seems too good to be true. So I pull up the covers. It is *not* true.

My right leg stretches, slanting upwards before me, like the side of a hill, the summit of which is my toes. From the ankle down—and approaching me—any number of small, finely, and sharply-toothed rakes are at work. Each one has about the same routine. For instance, the rake that has been allotted to the inside of the leg begins at the ankle, proceeding slowly toward the knee, and digs as deeply as it can into the skin, at times much deeper than at others, and, consequently varying in its painfulness. It goes slowly on in this manner until it reaches a point just a little short of the knee, then retraces its tracks until it finds the spot where it was able to penetrate the most, at which point it settles down to dig to its heart's delight. The same procedure takes place over the entire leg and continues until I yell for a hypo.

The toes on my right foot are tapping against the cast again and once more stretching happily in the morning sun—that is, until I look at them and find that they aren't. A little later the rakes go to work, but for some reason they have reversed their procedure and instead of beginning at the ankle and digging toward the knee, they start from just below the fracture and wind up at the toes. Those that mount the sole of the foot have great difficulty digging under the nails of the smaller toes, which are so close to the skin, but they finally succeed and the result is a most interesting new form of torture.

In the late afternoon I notice that the right foot is doing its best to fit into a shoe that is much too short for it, but it persists and persists until some one inserts, inside the cast, a jagged glass shoehorn that extends from the inner heel all the way around to the little toe, but it is sadly ineffective and only adds to the confusion. Even after a shot of dilaudid has started to calm everything down, and the jagged glass shoehorn has changed into a rough stone shoehorn, it is obvious that that foot will never fit into that shoe.

I wake up to find that the rough stone shoehorn has changed back into a jagged glass one again, so the future looks pretty precarious, especially as, during the night, a long sock has been put on my foot. It's a very unusual sock in that it's made of finely woven wire mesh, highly charged with electricity, thus giving the surface of the skin an infinite series of shocks. For some reason, some one is trying to pull this sock as high up on my leg as possible, and at moments, the strain upon some of the minute wires is so great that they break, at the same time branding that spot of the leg with a burning little blister. What with the sock being pulled up, and the glass shoehorn helping the foot to push its way down into that absurd shoe, the conflict is very interesting indeed.

A procession of little men with picks over their shoulders choose a spot on the inner side of the instep of my right foot, near the ankle, and start digging a hole. The hole becomes fairly deep until one of them spots a site nearer the center, deserts his co-workers and begins to dig there. Gradually, all of them desert the first location for the second, and dig as if their lives depended upon their tunneling through to the sole of the foot. Then a sudden desertion again by one of them for another spot, and the same story is repeated. They finally reach a place just this side of the third toe and it looks as if all the other pits had been permanently abandoned, when unexpectedly from below the outer ankle appears at least a hundred more little men, who surround all the holes that lie quietly recovering from the picks, that a few minutes ago were attacking them, and start digging, and digging so furiously that soon the whole foot feels like a tortured cushion.

There are several small, long-handled knives with heart-shaped blades, the bulge of the heart being nearest the handle, which are working on the lower parts of my toes. The job seems to be to make more space between the second and third toes, the third and fourth toes and the fourth and fifth toes. After a few knives have worked quite a while on the area between the second and third toes, a small, rough-surfaced cord is drawn between these toes—yet there still isn't enough room for easy play back and forth, so the knives go to work again. Finally this space has been made adequate, at which the knives move over to the space between the third and fourth toes, where the same process is repeated, then later to the fourth and fifth toes. The area between the fourth and fifth toes, however, seems to be much tougher than the other areas, and gouge as they may, the knives never seem to make enough space for a cord to play easily between them. At times I become discouraged at the inadequacy of the effort, for it's going to be so pleasant when the job is finished, to have those four rough-surfaced cords playing back and forth between the toes.

Cole's notes end here, possibly because there was little else he could say about the intense and persistent pain in his right leg. At the height of the agony, which lasted for several months after the accident, Cole was on such heavy dosages of painkillers that there was fear that he might become addicted to the drugs. Eventually, however, his pain reached more reasonable proportions, until finally he was taking only minimal amounts on an as-needed basis. But even when his pain was at its most intense, Cole was a model patient. All who treated him marveled at his remarkable fortitude. He seldom complained no matter how severe the pain, and put up with the many inconveniences that a lengthy hospital confinement entails with enormous poise and forbearance. He was so exceptional a patient, as a matter of fact, that one might speculate whether his ability to cope with such a high degree of physical agony was not but another manifestation—or variation—of his unusually high tolerance for physical pleasure.

Cole took his hospital stay and his medical treatment completely in stride, accepting them with the magnanimity usually reserved for more pleasurable pursuits. If ever Cole demonstrated strength of character—a character molded, no doubt, by the combination of his pioneer-stock background and genteel, upper-class upbringing—in the face of adversity, he did so as he underwent the remedial program that sought to save his legs. In enduring so heroically the trauma resulting from his accident, Cole was enormously helped by being able to resume writing songs just as soon as he was no longer under the stultifying effects of heavy sedation. It was Dr. Moorhead's belief that creative activity would be Cole's best therapy, and it was at the doctor's urging that Cole resumed work on the score for the Clifton Webb show, titled *You Never Know*, which was to begin rehearsals in early February of 1938, as well as on *Greek to You*, a musical suggested by Vinton Freedley; unfortunately, the latter never got produced.

During this recuperative period, too, Cole learned that *Break the News*, a film by French director René Clair, was soon to be released in England with one of his tunes, "It All Belongs to You," in it. Thus both in the hospital and out, Cole was again involved with his career, slowly at first, then gaining in momentum by the start of 1938. Cole even had his piano at his Waldorf apartment raised on blocks so that he could move his wheelchair close to it as he tried out his songs. Cole also gradually resumed his social activities, despite having both legs in casts. Not only did he celebrate Christmas and New Year's of 1937 with Linda and his friends (as a memento of this holiday period Linda presented Cole with a special gold cigarette case set with sapphires in which was inscribed, to Cole's legs, "Merry Christmas and Happy New Year to Joe and Geraldine. Linda."), but he was also guest of honor at a large party Elsa Maxwell gave for him at the Waldorf on January 17, 1938. Some five hundred of New York's most elegant social and theatrical figures eagerly attended Elsa's shindig to toast Cole's health and to wish him well.

Cole, however, needed considerably more than good wishes to temper the tepid response to *You Never Know* during its out-of-town tryouts, which began in New Haven on March 3, 1938, before moving on to

Boston, Washington, D.C., Philadelphia, Pittsburgh, Detroit, Chicago, Des Moines, Indianapolis, Columbus, Buffalo, and Hartford. A good portion of the blame for the show's lack of popularity must rest with its book, a rather humdrum concoction about a butler pretending to be his master in order to win over a grande dame, only to discover that the woman in question is a maid herself. The plot had originally been devised by playwright Siegfried Geyer for his 1929 show *Candle Light*, which met with little success despite a cast headed by Gertrude Lawrence and Leslie Howard. Nonetheless, when a German musical version of Geyer's brain-child, *Bei Kerzenlicht*, did sufficiently well at the Deutsche Volkstheatre in Vienna after opening on April 10, 1937, the Shubert theatrical organization decided to mount an American production of the show with a score by Cole. It was so obvious that *You Never Know* was in deep trouble as it played out of town that the Shuberts brought in theatrical wizard George Abbott in an attempt to beef up the show in Philadelphia. For a while it was thought that the Abbott touch might pull the show through, but by the end of its spring tryout run—which included a three-day stint between May 23 and May 25, 1938, at the English Theater in Indianapolis—it was clear that further revisions were needed if *You Never Know* was to open on Broadway that following September.

In conjunction with the show's Indianapolis stop, plans had been made by a number of leading Indiana citizens to honor Cole, one of their state's best-known sons. Except for occasional Christmas visits to see his mother and a preference for Arnold's "So-Good Fudge"—a hometown candy product that Cole had shipped regularly to him no matter where he was—Cole had had little to do with Indiana ever since he left Peru as a schoolboy. That Cole's ties to Indiana had been minimal for years did not deter the committee responsible for feting Cole. Apparently the combination of Cole's fame, sympathy for his accident, and the unusual showing of a Porter musical so close to his birthplace helped to spark the kind of chauvinistic spirit endemic to such festivities. The public's first inkling of all this was from Indianapolis newspaper headlines on April 23 announcing a celebration in tribute to Cole, to take place on May 23, the day *You Never Know* opened in town. The scope of this celebration was revealed shortly afterward, when Indiana's Governor M. Clifford Townsend proclaimed May 23 as Cole Porter Day throughout the state. Speaking out, too, in Cole's honor was another distinguished Hoosier son, the venerable Booth Tarkington: "Of course it's something to be a Hoosier who becomes a New York and Hollywood celebrity; but when a New York and Hollywood celebrity becomes so celebrated that he's known in

Indiana, too, he touches the mantle of fame itself. Mr. Cole Porter of Indiana, New York and Hollywood and several continents receives honor from his native state for being an honor to it."

Adding to the excitement surrounding the event was the distinct impression that Cole himself would be present. Before the announcement of the celebration had even been made public, Cole had been sounded out to find out if the project met with his approval. When he indicated that it did, the machinery was set in motion for making May 23 a day to be proud of. As the day approached, however, Cole declined to attend, claiming that his health would not permit it. Whether or not this was actually the case (Cole was able to get around at this point), Cole was represented at the affair by another prominent Hoosier close to him—his mother, Kate. The committee in charge of the festivities also got this message of thanks from Cole:

Seven months ago I had my legs knocked from under me by a very unkind and inconsiderate horse. Tonight, I find my wind knocked out of me by so much attention, and even if I were actually with you I should still be speechless. Luckily my mother, who, like all good mothers, has so often borne the brunt of her son's misdeeds, is here to face the music for me and I wish her much joy and happiness. It's probably the only sensation that can compare with my own deep gratitude to you for this signal honor.

Despite this cordial message, Cole was considerably less gracious in communicating with the sponsoring officials once all the shouting was over. For in settling their accounts after the May 23 festivities, the committee members found themselves very much in the red and asked Cole if he would intercede with the Shuberts about having them reduce their tariff for the showing of *You Never Know* so that the committee could save some money and possibly end up in the black. In answering that request Cole clearly showed what a tough sonofabitch he could be if he put his mind to it. "As regards the Shuberts, and your funds deficiency, I regret that I have no authority and can do nothing to help you," he coldly replied. Claiming that he had asked the Shuberts "numerous times . . . that they communicate with you in regard to this matter," Cole washed his hands of the problem by stating unequivocally that "if they have failed to do so, I can offer no further solution."

Cole's solution, on the other hand, for his own most immediate problem—that of his legs—was to keep himself busily occupied, as Dr. Moorhead had suggested. With the Indiana festivities out of the way and summer now upon him, Cole continued his work in New York by staying on top of the revisions made on *You Never Know* to get it ready for Broadway while simultaneously creating a score for a new Vinton Freedley production that was to open in the fall. Cole was thus once again as active as ever writing songs, in spite of a physical setback that occurred when he slipped on a marble stairway and reinjured his left leg as he celebrated his forty-seventh birthday on June 9, 1938. (By coincidence, and possibly as a sympathetic response to Cole's leg injuries, the two most important women in his life also fell and hurt themselves at about the same time: Kate fell and broke her right hip two weeks before Cole's birthday mishap, while Linda slipped and fractured her arm the following August.) Since Cole could not leave New York that summer because of professional commitments and medical treatment, he and Linda rented a home at nearby Lido Beach, Long Island, that offered the attractive features of seashore living as well as many of the civilities that they had come to expect from residing at the Waldorf Astoria. Besides bringing their regular staff with them to Long Island, the Porters were even visited twice weekly by a truck from the Waldorf. Though the sight of this truck making its weekly stop at the home of the glamorous Porters was a source of considerable speculation on the part of the local townspeople, the truth of the matter was that soiled linen was picked up on the first trip and brought back freshly laundered on the second.

The revised *You Never Know* opened at the Winter Garden Theater on September 21, after a brief tryout in Hartford. Joining Clifton Webb in the production were throaty-voiced Libby Holman, dance satirists Paul and Grace Hartman, and the tempestuous Mexican movie star Lupe Velez, who was making her Broadway musical debut. Notwithstanding their talent and efforts, the show left New York's reviewers cold. Even Walter Winchell, usually favorably disposed to Cole's musicals, labeled the show "draggy" and complained "that nothing exciting occurs, for instance, until the amusing Hartmans enter, which is forty-seven minutes after the overture." John Mason Brown and Richard Watts voiced similar sentiments. Brown found the original 1929 version of the show dull and *You Never Know* "considerably duller," while for Watts the production suffered "from plot feebleness and anemia of jokes."

With the handicap of such a trite book, Cole's score, too, made little headway with the critics. As John Mason Brown put it, Cole, for him, was "so adroit a lyricist and so satisfying a musician that one expects much of him. The major trouble with his score for 'You Never Know' is that it forces one to keep on expecting, without getting much during the evening." It was a foregone conclusion that *You Never Know* would have a very limited life span; after running for only fourteen weeks on Broadway, the show rang down its final curtain at the conclusion of its seventy-eighth performance.

Though Cole's total score for *You Never Know* did not register with the reviewers, several of the show's individual songs did extremely well for themselves, especially "At Long Last Love," which became a big hit. This tune's refrain cleverly juxtaposes a romantic, highly singable melody with the kind of bright, coolly sophisticated lyrics that one had come to expect from a good Porter song. In fact, the lyrics exhibited what had become almost a cliché for Cole after "You're the Top," from *Anything Goes*: a list of clever comparisons. For example, the opening two lines of the refrain,

> Is it an earthquake or simply a shock?
> Is it the good turtle soup or merely the mock?

are followed by such contrasts as "right" with "wrong" and "Bach" with a "Cole Porter song":

> Have I the right hunch or have I the wrong?
> Will it be Bach I shall hear or just a Cole Porter song?

"From Alpha to Omega," another of the show's better-known numbers, also used this comparison-list approach in its lyrics, almost to distraction. Thus, one finds such references as

> From left hooks by Dempsey to Braddock's upper-cuts,
> From Jericho to Kokomo, not to mention from soup to nuts,

as well as

> From love songs by Schumann to hits by Jerry Kern,
> From Sarawak to Hackensack, not to mention from stem to stern,

in the tune's various refrains. In essence, this song was a compilation of numerous metaphoric allusions to love that had already been similarly stated—and possibly with greater effect—in "You're the Top," but without that number's catchy melodic qualities. Nonetheless, even if they were not prime Porter, practically all the tunes in *You Never Know* had enough of the sheen and worldliness associated with Cole's work to set it apart from the general run of theater songs of that period.

Another factor that set Cole and his songs apart from their competition was the sheer number of Porter productions following each other in quick succession. This was particularly true in the fall and winter of 1938. So much attention was showered on Cole in connection with the Broadway opening of his next musical, *Leave It to Me*, and MGM's release of *Rosalie* that the public quickly forgot about the failure of *You Never Know*.

Especially gratifying for Cole was the critical acclaim accorded *Leave It to Me* so soon after *You Never Know* had flopped. A major reason for this reversal was the fine book for the new production by Samuel and Bella Spewack. Both Spewacks had served as foreign correspondents for New York newspapers in the 1920s and had drawn on this experience in writing their script. Originally titled *First in the Hearts*, *Leave It to Me* was based on the Spewacks' successful 1932 comedy *Clear All Wires*, a satire dealing with an American correspondent in Moscow. In *Leave It to Me*, however, instead of focusing on the newspaper man, the Spewacks made the American diplomatic corps the butt of their humor. Their plot revolved around a naive but wealthy businessman, Alonzo P. "Stinky" Goodhue from Topeka, Kansas, who has been appointed ambassador to the Soviet Union, though he would much prefer staying in Topeka and pitching horseshoes. Hoping to be recalled, Goodhue pulls such undiplomatic stunts as kicking the German ambassador, a Nazi, in the stomach and taking a potshot at the Russian commissar of Foreign Affairs, who turns out to be a counterrevolutionary. Much to Goodhue's dismay, instead of falling from grace he is widely acclaimed for these actions. Only when Goodhue finally takes his job seriously and tries to promulgate an international peace plan which advocates the interchange of troops between various countries does he run into trouble. The idea that Goodhue would be so foolhardy as to propose a United States of Europe is enough for his superiors to bring him back home to Topeka and his horseshoe pitching.

In the role of Stinky Goodhue, all bumbling innocence, was none other than Victor Moore, known for his rotund form and soft-voiced helplessness. Just as he had had audiences laughing themselves silly when he played Vice President Alexander Throttlebottom in *Of Thee I Sing* and Reverend Dr. Moon—really "Public Enemy Number 13"—in *Anything Goes*, so, too, Moore was the comic hit in *Leave It to Me*. Cast as his socially ambitious, domineering wife who gets him appointed ambassador by making a sizable contribution to the presidential campaign was Sophie Tucker, departing from her usual image as a "red-hot mamma." The other key lead in the production, that of the fast-talking American newspaper man, Buckley Joyce Thomas, went to William Gaxton. Veteran musical-comedy star that he was, Gaxton added the necessary bite and drive to the show to counter Moore's lethargically paced amiability. But even in the company of such veteran performers it was Mary Martin, a newcomer to the Broadway scene, who drew an inordinate amount of attention in the cameo role of Dolly Winslow, a blithe young spirit on the loose in Russia, now stranded in a freezing Siberian railroad station. Urged on by a group of bundled-up Russians (one of whom was Gene Kelly, another Broadway novice), Mary Martin stopped the show each night by her demure singing of Cole's insinuating "My Heart Belongs to Daddy," embellished by a girlishly modest striptease made all the more provocative by its seeming innocence. Yet for all her suggestiveness on stage, Cole remembers Mary Martin as a "dreary little girl who appeared to be the last word in scared dowdiness" when as an unknown she first auditioned for him, producer Vinton Freedley, the Spewacks, and other members of the production. Cole, who was reclining on a couch at the time, responded to her request to sing four numbers somewhat sardonically with, "Carry on, on all fours"—a remark hardly geared to make her feel welcome. But on hearing her sing, Cole admits the occasion was "marked with five stars in my head; it was the finest audition I had ever heard." On his orders to "dress her up," she returned for additional testing and quickly got the part, and went on to score such a major triumph with her small role that by February, 1939, a mere three months after making her Broadway debut, she was receiving featured billing in the production.

Among the many reviewers who responded favorably to Mary Martin when *Leave It to Me* opened at Broadway's Imperial Theater on November 9, 1938, was Richard Watts, ordinarily a tough man to please. Besides praising her striptease, Watts loved nearly everything else in the production. "The local musical comedy stage is in proper shape again," announced Watts in his *Herald Tribune* review of the show. He also lauded Sophie Tucker for putting "over all her songs with characteristic effectiveness," and William Gaxton, whom he described as "an energetic, enthusiastic and expert performer." Watts, however, saved his strongest commendations for Victor Moore and Cole. He described Moore as "the hero of the evening" in his best role ever and said that the music and

lyrics for *Leave It to Me* constituted "one of Cole Porter's choicest scores."
For Watts this score was "a continuously delightful series of songs in the
best Porter vein." The majority of New York's other reviewers agreed,
and *Leave It to Me* had 307 performances at the Imperial before going on
a road tour on October 16, 1939.

Mainly on the basis of the tremendous amount of media coverage of
Mary Martin's rendition of the doleful-sounding "My Heart Belongs to
Daddy" and the striptease that went with it, this number caught on
almost immediately and became Cole's big hit in *Leave It to Me*. When
Mary Martin, with wide-eyed innocence, confessed,

> If I invite
> A boy, some night,
> To dine on my fine finnan haddie,
> I just adore
> His asking for more,
> But my heart belongs to Daddy.

the song's sexual overtones seemed only that much more explicit and
added to its impact on the public. Moreover, though the tune's use of a
Jewish-like cantillation ("Da-da, da-da-da, da-da-da, dad!") may have been
offensive to some people because of its possibly intentional implications
that Mary Martin's "Daddy" was a rich and powerful Jew, the song as
a whole came off so strongly that these parodistic Jewish references were
largely overlooked or ignored.

Other songs in the show that came in for their share of praise were
"Most Gentlemen Don't Like Love," "Tomorrow," "From Now On,"
"Far Away," and especially "Get Out of Town." This latter tune, with
its sultry melody full of repeated notes, has eventually become just about
as popular as "My Heart Belongs to Daddy," despite lyrics that are filled
with ambiguities when taken out of the context of the show. The text
includes lines that seem both welcoming and hostile:

> Get out of town,
> Before it's too late, my love.
> Get out of town,
> Be good to me, please.
> . . . . .

Just disappear,
I care for you much too much,
And when you are near,
Close to me, dear,
We touch too much.

Thanks to all the hoopla surrounding the opening of *Leave It to Me* and MGM's release of *Rosalie,* Cole's professional standing at the end of 1938 was as high, if not higher, than it had been before his riding accident only one year earlier. Cole's battered legs may have continued to be a persistent and painful reminder of the mishap, but instead of being overwhelmed by his bad luck, Cole was now back in professional harness, creating music and lyrics of quality as readily as ever. He was managing, too, to lead a relatively normal life, in spite of having to wear braces on both legs. Cole even found time for vacations. During Christmas of 1938 he and Linda visited Cartagena, Colombia (as a memento of the trip Linda gave Cole still another cigarette case as a gift), and the following February, as he had done earlier the previous year, Cole spent a month in Havana taking large doses of sun and somewhat smaller doses of nightlife. In 1939, too, Cole visited the Machu Picchu ruins in Peru and, despite his leg braces, even had himself hoisted on a horse in order to visit the site of the ruins. This radical turnabout from a position of anguish and physical incapacity to a resumption of a life-style not too dissimilar to one he had always led in so short a period says much about Cole's recuperative powers and his zest for living. It is also indicative of Cole's inner fortitude at this crucial point in his life.

18

Buxton Hill

Almost as if to prove that his accident had not impeded his songwriting, Cole turned out five major Broadway hit shows in a row between December, 1939, and January, 1944. These five smashes—*DuBarry Was a Lady, Panama Hattie, Let's Face It, Something for the Boys,* and *Mexican Hayride*—got good reviews and ran for over four hundred performances each, with *Panama Hattie* and *Let's Face It,* both topping five hundred. At about the same time, Cole also wrote the film scores for MGM's *Broadway Melody of 1940* and Columbia's *You'll Never Get Rich* and *Something to Shout About* of a year or two later. What with his writing for Broadway and Hollywood and his busy-as-ever social schedule, it is clear that Cole's work and play routines had not changed drastically as a result of his accident, despite braces on both legs and the occasional need to use canes.

Even Cole's active sex life was hardly slowed down by the riding mishap. For a year or so after the accident, Cole led a rather passive (at least for him) sex life as he built up confidence in getting about on his own. But even in his passivity Cole did not abstain completely. Just as soon as he was up to it and could move around, he arranged with black procurer Clint Moore to visit his house of male prostitution in Harlem —not as an active participant, however, but as an observer. Inasmuch as Cole—like Monty Woolley—had always found black men sexually stimulating, it evidently was enough for Cole at that point to secretly watch the action taking place in another room through peepholes. Yet for all Cole's sexual interest in black men, it is noteworthy that his friendship with Woolley was seriously affected in later years when Woolley took a black manservant as his lover. It apparently was one thing for Cole to pay for sex with black men and another to accept them as social equals.

In connection with social class levels in relation to sex, there is an amusing story about the time Leonard Hanna invited Cole and Woolley to a Cleveland Indians baseball game. As the scion of a prominent Cleveland family, Hanna closely followed the exploits of the Indians on the baseball field and knew all the players on a first-name basis. Aware of Cole and Woolley's predilection for virile, athletic types, and afraid that the two might take a fancy to some members of the Indians team and possibly proposition them, Hanna laid down the law before inviting his friends to the game. As Hanna made clear, Cole and Woolley could be as genial as they wanted when introduced to the players on the field before the game, but under no circumstances were they to visit the players' locker room afterward (as presumably they might have been tempted to do). Besides his fuddy-duddy attitude in regard to the Indians, Hanna was also more straitlaced than Cole and Woolley as far as paid sex was concerned. Whereas Cole and Woolley freely made use of procurers and male prostitutes, Hanna proudly boasted that he had never paid cash to a man for sexual favors. What Hanna neglected to mention, however, was that he paid in other respects—with cars, clothes, and other expensive items—for these very same favors.

But such differences aside, Hanna remained one of Cole's—and Woolley's—best chums. And it was on the basis of this tried-and-true relationship that Hanna on January 20, 1940, joined Cole, Linda, and several other close friends for a leisurely trip to Cuba, the Panama Canal Zone, Mexico, and the South Seas. Prior to the trip Cole had labored on the scores for *Broadway Melody of 1940* and *DuBarry Was a Lady,* and had also contributed a song, "What Am I to Do," to the George S. Kaufman–Moss Hart hit play, *The Man Who Came to Dinner,* starring Monty Woolley, which opened on Broadway in the fall of 1939. The play incorporated Cole's tune into its script as the product of one Beverly Carlton (played by John Hoysradt), a Noel Coward type. In keeping with the tune's resemblance to Coward's style, Cole signed his name to the song as "Noel Porter." Though the song never caught on with the public, Cole at least was the recipient of a wonderful memento of his association with the play: As a gesture of thanks to Cole for creating the song, Hart and Kaufman presented him with an elegant silver and enamel cigarette case on which his name, in large gold letters, surrounded engraved caricatures of Woolley, Hart, Kaufman, and John Hoysradt.

In 1939 Cole had a number of hit tunes to serve as reminders of his creative endeavors. The first of these 1939 productions, the *Broadway Melody* film, occupied a good portion of Cole's time during the spring and summer of that year while he and Linda were living in Hollywood. This movie, the fourth in MGM's *Broadway Melody* series (the initial *Broadway Melody* of 1929, the first talkie to win an Academy Award, helped to set the stage for similarly titled films released by MGM—in 1936, 1938, and 1940), featured Fred Astaire and Eleanor Powell in a rather insipid tale about an emotionally unstable heel, King Shaw (George Murphy), who lands a job as the dancing partner of Broadway favorite Clare Bennett (Eleanor Powell) through the coaching and selflessness of Johnny Brett (Fred Astaire). When King becomes drunk and is not able to perform on opening night, Johnny dons King's costume and mask and dances in his place, receiving rave reviews, the critics, of course, assuming that it is King performing. The good notices only make King more conceited and difficult than ever. On realizing, however, that Clare really loves Johnny rather than him, King shows up at the theater in a drunken stupor to announce that he is leaving the show for another job, and suggests that Clare ask Johnny to be her regular dancing partner in his place. The movie ends on a spectacular if somewhat incongruous note as the three dancers are reunited in a colorful and spirited rendition of Cole's "Begin the Beguine."

Though the story for *Broadway Melody of 1940* was easily forgettable, the lavish dance treatment of "Begin the Beguine" was not. Moreover, of the new tunes Cole created for the movie, "I Concentrate on You" also had considerable lasting power. Over the years it has become one of Cole's best-known numbers. Dispensing completely with an introductory verse to go directly to the refrain (several other famous Porter tunes, like "I've Got You Under My Skin," "In the Still of the Night," and "Begin the Beguine," are also without an orthodox opening verse), "I Concentrate on You" exudes melodic verve, harmonic chic, and rather unusual form (the basic sixty-four-measure tune, in five sections, concludes with an additional—and uncommon—eight-measure coda that is derived from the opening section).

The song's text is also an example of prime Porter versificatio often been cited for its relatively complicated rhyming scheme several levels of rhymes are operative throughout the tune. On there is the rhyme pattern around "me" ("Whenever skies look gray to me"; "When Fortune cries 'Nay, Nay!' to me"; "And so when wise men say to me"). On another level there are the rhymes related to "brew" ("And trouble begins to brew"; "I concentrate on you"; "And people declare 'You're through!' "; and "That love's young dream never comes true"). There are, as well, the rhymes that evolve from "strong" ("Whenever the winter winds become too strong"; "Whenever the blues become my only song"; and "To prove that even wise men can be wrong"). These rhyming devices can be broken down even further, so that in the "me" lines one finds, too, an inner rhyming pattern of "skies . . . gray," "cries . . . 'Nay,' " and "wise . . . say." Moreover, if to these various rhymes one adds the simple rhymes for the more prosaic middle part, or release, of the song (in which "tender" is rhymed with "surrender," and "decline" with "intertwine"), it becomes clear that the overall rhyming scheme is rather intricate, as the complete lyrics for "I Concentrate on You" will bear out:

> Whenever skies look grey to me
> And trouble begins to brew,
> Whenever the winter winds become too strong,
> I concentrate on you.
> When Fortune cries "Nay, Nay!" to me
> And people declare "You're through!"
> Whenever the blues become my only song,
> I concentrate on you.
> On your smile so sweet, so tender,
> When at first my kiss you decline.
> On the light in your eyes, when you surrender,
> And once again our arms intertwine.
> And so when wise men say to me
> That love's young dream never comes true,
> To prove that even wise men can be wrong,
> I concentrate on you.
> I concentrate and concentrate on you.

Ingenious as these lyrics were, Cole's way with words worked at least as well in his songs for *DuBarry Was a Lady*, his next production. As evidenced by such numbers as "Well, Did You Evah!" "But In the Morning, No," "Do I Love You?" and "Friendship," there was no mistaking that Cole was at the height of his powers as a lyricist as well as a composer, and the public and many reviewers alike responded accordingly.

Cole's songs for *DuBarry Was a Lady* were immeasurably helped by the outstanding performing talents of Ethel Merman and Bert Lahr, among others, in addition to the delightful script for the show by Herbert Fields and Buddy De Sylva (De Sylva also produced this musical). The plot for *DuBarry Was a Lady* was a fanciful concoction of the old and the new as it shifted between the eighteenth-century court of Louis XV and the Club Petite, a gaudy, contemporary Manhattan nightclub. This switch between pre-Revolutionary France and up-to-date New York is precipitated when Louie Blore (Bert Lahr), a washroom attendant at the Club Petite, who is madly in love with the club's singer, May Daley (Ethel Merman), mistakenly drinks a Mickey Finn that he had tried to foist on Alex Batin (Ronald Graham), May's boyfriend, in an attempt to thwart their romance. Under the influence of the knockout potion, Louie dreams that he is Louis XV of France and that May is his mistress, Madame DuBarry. But just as in real life at the nightclub, the king does not get very far with his mistress, for DuBarry has a lover on the side. However, it was the frenetic working out of this love triangle—both at the French court at Versailles and the Club Petite—that made *DuBarry Was a Lady* such a fun show. As John Mason Brown pointed out, the musical was a "rowdy, boisterous, high-spirited extravaganza which stops at just this side of nothing."

Opening at the 46th Street Theater on December 6, 1939, *DuBarry Was a Lady* had the distinction of being the final Broadway musical of the year as well as of the decade. By a strange coincidence, Cole's *Wake Up and Dream*, in its American production, had also closed out the previous decade for Broadway musicals with its opening at the Selwyn Theater on December 30, 1929. But *Wake Up and Dream* and *DuBarry Was a Lady* had as little in common as the two periods they represented. A major factor that set the two decades apart was the ominous threat of a world war that was so much in the news at the conclusion of the 1930s, especially after Hitler's Wehrmacht had invaded Poland on September 1, 1939, and Great Britain and France had retaliated by declaring war against Germany two days later. And in the light of the mounting international hysteria and tension at the time *DuBarry Was a Lady* opened, it is perhaps easy to understand why the show's boisterous, bawdy humor was such a delightful palliative for the crowds who flocked to see it. When Bert Lahr and Ethel Merman, in their eighteenth-century courtly getups, sang the gavottelike, risqué "But In the Morning, No," full of double entendres, audiences were beside themselves. Some important media voices like the

New Yorker may have complained that "But In the Morning, No" was "dirt without wit," but the public adored it when La Merman asked such innocent questions in the song as

> Can you do the crawl, my dear?
> Kindly tell me, if so.

and Lahr responded deftly with

> I can do the crawl, my dear,
> But in the morning, no.
> When the sun through the blind
> Starts to burn my poor behind
> That's the time when I'm in low.

Equally appreciated were the simple love sentiments in the ballad "Do I Love You?" (sung by Ethel Merman and Ronald Graham) and the abrasive social comments of "Well, Did You Evah!" (performed by Betty Grable, in her Broadway debut, and Charles Walters). It was, however, the humorous, pseudohillbilly expressions of fealty and comradeship in "Friendship" that seemed to have the greatest audience appeal. The avowals of eternal friendship by Bert Lahr and Ethel Merman invariably had audiences cheering this tune and its delightful lines, among them "If you're ever down a well, ring my bell," or "If you ever lose your teeth and you're out to dine, borrow mine," or "If they ever put a bullet through your brain, I'll complain."

Just as "But In the Morning, No" and "Friendship" reflected two wholly different worlds, Cole's score as a whole for *DuBarry Was a Lady* had touches of the old and the new. Thus, for the dream portion of the show at the court of Louis XV, Cole subtly incorporated elements of eighteenth-century French dance styles into numbers like "Mesdames and Messieurs," "Gavotte," a purely instrumental selection, and "But In the Morning, No." There is even an oblique reference to "La Marseillaise" in the tune "Give Him the Oo-La-La." On the other hand, Cole captured an unmistakable contemporary flavor in "Come On In," a celebration of girly striptease shows; in the sprightly one-step, "Katie Went to Haiti"; and in the jazzy "When Love Beckoned." Yet so successfully did Cole bring off this mixed bag of musical styles that looked backward and forward almost simultaneously that this very diversity proved to be one of the score's most appealing features and undoubtedly contributed to the long run (408 performances) of the show. (Some of the production's strong points were also captured in a 1943 MGM film of *DuBarry*, which starred Lucille Ball and Red Skelton.)

While New York audiences were enjoying the antics of Bert Lahr, Ethel Merman, and the rest of the *DuBarry Was a Lady* company, the European theater of war was continually expanding as Russia took over Finland in March of 1940 and Germany invaded Denmark and Norway in April and then attacked and quickly overwhelmed Belgium, Luxembourg, and the Netherlands in May. By May 29 the British Expeditionary Force, which had rushed to the Continent to try to stop Hitler, was forced to begin its heroic evacuation from Dunkirk. Shortly afterward Italy declared war on Great Britain and France, and by June 22 France, in utter collapse, capitulated to the Germans, allowing them to occupy two thirds of their country and also agreeing to let Marshall Pétain organize a French state at Vichy that would be subservient to Hitler's Reich.

With Europe, particularly France, in such a turmoil, Linda's Paris home was, of course, out of bounds for Cole and her. Actually, Linda had anticipated that she and Cole would not make much use of the house on learning of Cole's accident in 1937. For on November 23, 1937, shortly after the mishap, Linda had four vans of household items from 13 rue Monsieur, containing furniture, glass, china, ornaments, silver, and books, shipped to the United States aboard the liner *Wisconsin*. Moreover, in early 1939, because of the ominous international situation, Linda closed the house completely and disposed of the extensive wine collection there. Presumably these precautions were taken as temporary measures until the war situation had brightened. However, even after the war had ended and the house was once again in Linda's possession, neither she nor Cole ever lived in it again. At the war's end Linda turned the house over to a private school. When she died the house became Cole's, in conformance with the terms of Linda's will, and he subsequently sold it.

Undoubtedly one of the key reasons that the Porters' ties to 13 rue Monsieur were so radically affected by its wartime closing was that they had purchased another home in its place, to alternate with their New York and Hollywood residences. In June of 1940 Linda was so taken with a lovely two-hundred-acre country place, Buxton Hill, in Williamstown, Massachusetts, that she and Cole ended up buying it. The facilities at Buxton Hill included a large, ivy-covered fieldstone house atop a six-hundred-foot incline overlooking meticulously arranged lawns and gardens. The house had a glorious view of nearby Greylock mountain and the surrounding meadows and trees of the Berkshire countryside. At the bottom of the hill was a small guest house, which Cole later appropriated for his own use to work in, as well as a caretaker's cottage. To Buxton Hill Linda brought her exquisite taste and many of the furniture items and artifacts that had been shipped to America from 13 rue Monsieur. In Linda's hands Buxton Hill became a Williamstown showplace that afforded many of the niceties of country life—including outdoor swimming in a large, specially built pool—within an easily accessible setting only several hours by car or train from the heart of Manhattan. Because of this accessibility and its numerous amenities, Cole and Linda would visit Buxton Hill all year round, especially as a weekend retreat, when they were staying at the Waldorf, and frequently invited their close friends to join them.

But if Buxton Hill turned out to be a treasured retreat for the Porters, it also triggered some minor annoyances for them at first. Linda was particularly embarrassed in the early stages of negotiating for Buxton Hill. She had decided to sell some jewels, which she had received years earlier as a divorce settlement, to help pay for the place. As Baron Nicolas de Gunzburg, a close friend of Linda and Cole's, recalls, she went to her vault to pick up the jewels in order to bring them to Cartier's for an appraisal. At Cartier's, however, she was horrified to learn that the jewels she had brought in were fake, and virtually worthless. The situation was soon rectified when she realized that she had mistakenly exchanged the real jewels for paste copies. Like many other women in her circle, Linda often wore imitations of her good jewels for social occasions and kept the real ones in her vault. In this instance she had mistakenly done it the other way around.

In contrast to Linda's almost immediate attachment to Buxton Hill, Cole had little love for the place at first, mainly because he found its imposing main house a little too old-fashioned and somber. But before long he was won over by the lovely Berkshire setting as well as by the property's small guest house, which Linda imaginatively converted to a work cottage for him. This cottage, with its piano and simple but elegant and attractively arranged furnishings, became forbidden territory to everyone but Cole and those he specifically invited there. To reinforce this privacy he had a NO TRESPASSING mat placed at the entrance to the cottage, with the result that it came to be known as "No Trespassing." So fond did Cole become of his cottage that after Linda's death he had the main house razed—it was much too large and problematic for him to handle on his own—and the cottage moved six hundred feet uphill and installed on the site of the big building, over its original cellar. Cole also added a wing to the cottage in its new site, and had the entire house redone by Billy Baldwin, the famous decorator, whose talents had been highly praised by Linda. In describing the cottage Baldwin had spoken enthusiastically of how light and airy all of its rooms were and how large arrays of freshly cut flowers, as when Linda lived, would fill each room. Reminiscent of Linda's touch, too, was the emphasis the cottage placed on comfort and practicality, from its deeply cushioned chairs and book-lined shelves to its functional reading lights and strategically placed record collection. Thus, even in its new guise, Buxton Hill still reflected much of Linda's spirit, if not her actual presence. And that was perhaps only fitting, for Buxton Hill, as was true of many other important aspects of Cole's life, would clearly have not come about without her.

19

Inner Turmoil

The European war intensified during 1940. Japanese troops occupied the northern part of French Indochina in July of that year, soon after the fall of France. Japan followed up that move with an alliance between Germany, Italy, and itself in September of 1940, in which all three countries agreed to assist one another in case any of them was attacked by a major power (obviously the United States) not then directly involved in the European or Asian conflicts. But any pretense of a defensive alliance against America by the Japanese-German-Italian axis went out the window with Japan's surprise attack on Pearl Harbor on December 7, 1941. The following day, at the urging of President Roosevelt, who described the attack as one "which will live in infamy," the American Congress passed a formal declaration of war against Japan. Germany and Italy, in turn, under the terms of their treaty with Japan, declared war on the United States on December 11. America retaliated that same day with a resolution of war against Germany and Italy. And so within a five-day period between December 7 and 11, after months of intense political acrimony and maneuvering on an international scale, as well as continually expanding military hostilities, global war emerged as an indisputable fact of life.

In girding for the war effort America was quickly forced to mobilize its vast industrial, agricultural, financial, and manpower resources fully and to coordinate them with its military needs. So successful were the results that by the war's end in 1945, America had equipped nearly twelve million men and women serving military duty all over the globe with the necessary ships, planes, tanks, guns, and ammunition, and, in addition, had sent approximately thirty-three billion dollars' worth of war materials to its allies through lend-lease arrangements.

While America concentrated on supplying its armed forces and its allies with the arms and equipment needed to wage war, civilian life in the United States reflected the wartime economy by various austerity measures, such as the rationing of butter, meat, sugar, and gasoline. But if rationing in theory was meant to apply equally, without favoritism, to the entire American populace, it did not work out that way in practice. Cole, for one, somehow managed to obtain as much of the rationed items as he wanted, war or no war. Even hard-to-get gasoline presented no problem for Cole. Not only was there always enough for Cole's regular driving needs, as before the war, but he even had no difficulty getting enough gasoline to bus crews of attractive, amenable young men to join friends and himself for weekend trips to the country. As a further boost for wartime morale, Cole would take groups of young men out to dinner at fancy restaurants. Like Oscar Wilde at his most indulgent, Cole would often show up at a fancy restaurant with half a dozen or so handsome young men in tow, all of them actively vying for the attention of their host.

Cole made other contributions to the war effort by giving generously to numerous social causes that aided war relief. He also wrote two songs in 1942 specifically for the armed forces. They were "Glide, Glider, Glide" and "Sailors of the Sky"; neither of them made much of a dent with the public or the military when they were published in 1943. Yet despite these financial and artistic contributions, Cole often seemed disappointed that he was not more actively involved in the war effort. He particularly admired the way Irving Berlin's *This Is the Army* show of 1942 not only generated loads of goodwill and made lots of money for the United States Army but also served as a wonderful vehicle for promoting Berlin—who appeared in the show—and his songs. Cole would frequently speak glowingly of this show, going so far as to suggest that Berlin was worthy of the Congressional Medal of Honor for creating it. Nonetheless, even with such outward praise for an old friend, there may very well have been some undercurrents of resentment on Cole's part for all the attention Berlin got from *This Is the Army*. For a variety of reasons,

206 | COLE PORTER

including possibly Cole's frustrations at his limited role in the war, the psychological damage from his accident, the onset of male menopause, the aftereffects of years of heavy drinking, and the narcissistic fear of growing old—he began to exhibit some personality changes as the war continued. He would become irritable more easily than before and would also have periods of depression and aimlessness. When it was suggested that he seek psychiatric help, both Cole and Linda thought it was unnecessary, claiming that he would soon bounce back to normal. And in essence they were right, for Cole continued to follow his usual regime of work and play all during the war years and beyond, in spite of occasional lapses into depression and irritability.

In 1951, however, at the age of sixty, these symptoms increased, and Cole showed unmistakable signs of irrationality. At a time when his annual income from his songs and his family business interests was well up into six figures, Cole would spend sleepless nights worrying how he would make ends meet. He complained that high taxes were ruining him and that he didn't have enough money to pay his medical bills, much less his usual living expenses. He became withdrawn and argumentative, and suffered from severe headaches. He was consumed, too, with fear that he had written himself out. So bad were Cole's symptoms that it was necessary for him to be hospitalized for a series of electric-shock treatments. After several months of continued medical supervision, Cole's condition had improved sufficiently so that, except for intermittent lapses, he was able to resume his usual life-style. Still, it was close to three years—between *Out of This World* in 1950 and *Can-Can* in 1953—before Cole had another show on Broadway.

Prior to the surfacing of these changes in personality, Cole had written the score for *Panama Hattie*, which opened at New York's 46th Street Theater on October 30, 1940, less than two months before the Japanese attack on Pearl Harbor. Like the successful *DuBarry Was a Lady*, *Panama Hattie* starred Ethel Merman performing in a tale written by Herbert Fields and Buddy De Sylva, with the latter again doubling as producer. As in *DuBarry*, too, Ethel Merman played a hard-boiled nightclub singer, Hattie Maloney. This time, while she is working in the Canal Zone she falls in love with Nick Bullett (James Dunn), an American government official stationed there. Between carrying a torch for Nick and finally marrying him, Hattie was almost center-stage all evening long, whether in thwarting a plot to blow up the Panama Canal or in getting drunk—while belting out "Make It Another Old-Fashioned, Please"—because of unrequited love. She was also front and center singing "Let's Be Buddies," the hit of the show, with Nick's small daughter Geraldine (Joan Carroll). The song may have been downright corny, with such prosaic lyrics as "What say, let's be buddies, what say, let's be pals," and a sentimental melody to match, but audiences loved it. As Brooks Atkinson pointed out in his review of the show, the number was presented so movingly that "gruff old codgers are going to choke a little this winter when tot and temptress sing 'Let's Be Buddies' and bring down the house."

Nonetheless, some critics were not so easily won over to this and other tunes in Cole's score. Writer John O'Hara had this to say in print of Cole's score for *Panama Hattie*: "Who'd have thought we'd live to see the day when Cole Porter—*Cole Porter!*—would write a score in which the two outstanding songs are called 'My Mother Would Love You' and 'Let's Be Buddies'? And written straight too; no kidding." O'Hara explained away Cole's decline to sentimentality by, "Ah, well, he had a bad riding accident a year or two ago."

O'Hara's caustic comments constituted a minority opinion among reviewers and had little effect on ticket sales. *Panama Hattie* was a big, brassy, fast-moving show that had all the necessary ingredients—especially Ethel Merman and such fine supporting talents as Arthur Treacher, Rags Ragland, and Betty Hutton—for countering the problems of war and survival that afflicted the world, as the production's long New York run of 501 performances would bear out. Even after making its mark on Broadway, *Panama Hattie* had enough going for it to be able to withstand a so-so 1942 MGM movie version of it starring Red Skelton and Ann Sothern and still go on to run for 308 performances in London after opening at the Piccadilly Theatre there on November 4, 1943.

Once *Panama Hattie* had settled down for its long stay on Broadway, Cole returned to Hollywood in the spring of 1941 to fulfill a movie commitment for Columbia Pictures. In his two previous films for MGM—*Born to Dance* and *Broadway Melody* of 1940—Cole had gotten along famously with Louis B. Mayer and his underlings, mainly because they were all so deferential to him. In his dealings with Columbia, Cole was again given VIP treatment by the studio staff, except that now he had Harry Cohn, the head of the studio, to contend with. The notorious Cohn, whose reputation for ruthlessness, shady dealings, and taking sexual advantage of many of the beautiful women who worked for him, had become legendary in the industry. He pulled rank on Cole by insisting that his songs be tried out on Columbia's office crew—specifically Cohn's secretary and telephone girls—to see what they thought of them, before being used in a film. Fortunately, Cole's songs easily met this test, so that this one-upmanship stunt by Cohn never really impeded upon Cole's working relationship with the Columbia production staff.

Moreover, any temporary annoyance with Cohn was more than compensated for by Cole's delight with Hollywood and the idea of being involved in another film, *You'll Never Get Rich,* with Fred Astaire. As Cole expressed it in a letter from Hollywood in June of 1941 to Dr. Sirmay in New York, "It is heaven here and it seems incredible that people are willing to stay in New York when it is so simple to come to California." About his film assignment for Columbia, Cole added, "I'm working very hard and believe I have some good new numbers. In any case, it's a most interesting job." Yet despite this implicit optimism and the singing and dancing of Fred Astaire and his glamorous co-star, Rita Hayworth, *You'll Never Get Rich* never rose above its cliché-ridden love-triangle plot. Cole's score for the film also came off poorly, for not one of the numbers—and they included "Since I Kissed My Baby Goodbye," "So Near and Yet So Far," and "Dream Dancing"—became a hit. In later years, as a matter of fact, Cole freely conceded that "it was a bad score" but an even "worse picture."

The numerous negative aspects of *You'll Never Get Rich,* however, were somehow blunted by the good showing of *Let's Face It,* Cole's next Broadway musical, which opened at the Imperial Theater on October 29, 1941, just about a week after Columbia had released *You'll Never Get Rich.* Produced by Vinton Freedley and starring Danny Kaye, *Let's Face It* was based on a 1925 farce, *The Cradle Snatchers.* But instead of the original plot in which three discontented, middle-aged wives go on a spree with some young gigolos, the script for *Let's Face It* by Herbert Fields and his sister Dorothy called for three young servicemen—more in keeping with the wartime conditions of the period—to have a fling with the three married women. With the irrepressible Danny Kaye as one of the soldiers (the other two were played by Benny Baker and Jack Williams) setting the pace, *Let's Face It* proved to be, in the words of John Mason Brown, "an exuberant and irresistible show." Yet in its out-of-town tryouts *Let's Face It* hardly seemed destined for success; so many of its production details seemed to be so terribly out of kilter that Cole had pretty much given up on the show.

Adding to Cole's less-than-optimistic outlook for the show was a rather persistent pain in his left leg because of a bone growth. In order to remove the growth Cole went into Doctors' Hospital ten days before the Broadway premiere of *Let's Face It* for surgery on his left leg (after the

series of major operations following his accident, the subsequent operations on his legs—like this one for the removal of a bone growth—were
usually corrective measures that were less serious and painful than the
initial surgery), which precluded his doing any further work on the show.
Nonetheless, once the curtain went up at the Imperial on opening night,
everything went so smoothly onstage that both the critics and the public
loved the results, especially the performances of Danny Kaye and his
soldier sidekicks, as well as those of Eve Arden, Edith Meiser, and Vivan
Vance as the three wives on a spree. Cole's tunes, too, were well received,
particularly the simple, somewhat mawkish ballad "Ev'rything I Love"
(whose opening lines of the refrain, "You are to me ev'rything, my life
to be, ev'rything," were typical of the rather pedestrian lyrics that followed), which soon became the hit of the show. Among the other songs
that stood out were "A Lady Needs a Rest," which enumerated the many
—and exhausting—duties expected of a woman; "Farming," a lively
spoof of celebrities who turn to the soil to be fashionable; and "Let's Not
Talk About Love," a perfect number for Danny Kaye to display his
virtuosity at handling—at lightning speed—lines like,

> Let's check on the veracity of Barrymore's bibacity
> And why his drink capacity should get so much publacity,
> Let's even have a huddle over Ha'vard Univassity.

It was precisely because of such foolishness by Danny Kaye that *Let's
Face It* was able to compile a total of 547 performances—a longer run
than any of Cole's previous shows—on Broadway. In addition, a London production of the show which opened at the Hippodrome Theatre
on November 19, 1942, did well enough with English audiences to have
a run of 348 performances.

As might be expected, the enthusiastic response to *Let's Face It* had a
tonic effect on Cole's spirits at a time when his lapses into periods of
depression and irritability first became noticeable. Also helpful for Cole's
state of mind was the continued demand for his services, both on Broadway and in Hollywood. Thus, by the spring of 1942, with *Let's Face It*
behind him, Cole was again back in California with a contract for still
another movie for Columbia. When he signed with the studio Cole knew
little more about the film than that William Gaxton, Don Ameche, Janet
Blair, and Jack Oakie were expected to be in it and that the movie would
be produced and directed by Russian-born actor-turned-producer-
and-director Gregory Ratoff. However, in a telegram from Ratoff dated

June 22, 1942, Cole finally learned what the title of the film would be. In his wire Ratoff inquired:

> Will you write a very optimistic song under the title "Something to Shout About"? This will be the stock phrase of Billy Gaxton as a producer. All through the picture he will be saying "I want the kind of a show that there'll be something to shout about." Columbia sales organization here begs me to call the picture "Something to Shout About." They know the pulse of the picture-going public and they are always looking for a saleable title.

Cole, of course, quickly complied with Ratoff's request. He also quickly complied with the request of the Hollywood Production Code, made by Joseph I. Breen, that changes be made in the lyrics of "Hasta La Vista," a tune Cole wrote for the film. By revising the title of that number to "Hasta Luego" and simply altering an inoffensive line like

> Down in Argenteena,
> In a tango bar,

to an even more innocuous one, like

> In a small canteena,
> On an island far,

Cole easily met the demands of the Production Code.

On hearing Cole's score for *Something to Shout About*, Ratoff—whom Cole privately characterized as "full of charm" but "much madder than any hatter I ever met"—felt that it was Cole's "best since *Anything Goes.*" Singling out one tune, Ratoff confided to Cole, "You'll be thrilled to hear that every electrician and everyone on the set is whistling 'I Can Do Without Tea in My Teapot.' "

Despite Ratoff's apparent enthusiasm for the number, it was never used in the film. Another equally inaccurate assessment by Ratoff was his boast to Cole that "the entire Columbia studio front office and back lot are of the opinion that *Something to Shout About* is not only the best musical Columbia ever made, but one of the best musicals that was ever produced by any studio." Contrary to Ratoff's estimation, the movie was a pleasant, innocent-enough affair, capable of mildly titillating audiences during a depressing war period—but hardly more than that. From Cole's standpoint *Something to Shout About* was something, in his words, "to cry about," for all his tunes in it save one were quickly forgotten or overlooked. The sole tune that caught on, "You'd Be So Nice to Come Home To," evoked enough of a feeling of togetherness in its wistful melody and lyrics to have almost instant appeal for the millions who were then separated from their loved ones because of the war. The simple lyrics to the song's refrain are:

> You'd be so nice to come home to,
> You'd be so nice by the fire,
> While the breeze on high,
> Sang a lullaby,
> You'd be all that I could desire.
> Under stars chilled by the winter,
> Under an August moon burning above,
> You'd be so nice,
> You'd be Paradise
> To come home to and love.

Alternating, as had become his custom, between films and the stage, Cole concentrated on a Broadway production after completing the score for *Something to Shout About.* For his next stage musical he again had the benefit of a book by Herbert and Dorothy Fields and the talent and box-office draw of Ethel Merman, performing in her fifth and final Porter show. He also had the benefit of the drive and imagination of producer Michael Todd, who took over the show when Vinton Freedley bowed out of it because of differences with the Fields team and Cole over the book and score. Todd, who had made a major impact on Broadway with his 1939 production of *The Hot Mikado* (based on Gilbert and Sullivan's *The Mikado* but with an all-black cast) was clearly a man on the run. He had clawed his way to the top by being both tough and shrewd, and, in that respect easily fit the mold of many of the Hollywood executives with whom Cole got along so well. Cole and Todd quickly hit it off, for the cigar-chomping Todd was greatly impressed not only with Cole's quota of hit tunes but also with his sophistication and urbanity; while Cole respected Todd's pugnacity and what might be called his gutter instincts (it was those instincts that enabled Todd in 1939 to dream up the idea of hanging a large banner advertising his own *The Hot Mikado* close to the theater of a competing production, *The Swing Mikado*, obscuring his rival's marquee from view). Todd's instincts, too, drew him to Cole's new musical. He saw in it a chance for a major Broadway success and was only too happy to mount the production when Freedley would not.

Titled *Jenny Get Your Gun* before eventually being called *Something for the Boys*, the new musical had Ethel Merman playing a defense worker capable of receiving radio messages by means of fillings in her teeth. This fanciful notion by the Fields duo may not have had enough substance upon which to build a complete evening's entertainment, but Miss Merman's presence was enough to turn what might have been dross into pure gold. Aided by such seasoned professionals as sour-faced Allen Jenkins and lively Paula Laurence, Ethel Merman romped through her part to the delight of reviewers and the public. *Something for the Boys* was sufficiently praised by the media at its Broadway opening on January 7, 1943, at the Alvin Theater, to ultimately tally 422 performances.

But along with the praise for Ethel Merman and the show, a number of dissenting voices could also be heard expressing reservations about the quality of the songs Cole was now turning out. Reviewer Louis Kronenberger lamented in *PM* that "Mr. Porter isn't the composer he once was." George Freedley, drama critic of the *Morning Telegraph*, was even more biting in his criticism. "Cole Porter's last few shows," he complained, "have been most disappointing and this one perhaps most of all. The songs are pleasant and amusing as you listen to them, but that's all." He found that *Something for the Boys* had "none of the tunes that you go out of the theater whistling or that you could remember an hour later. That is the real test of a musical and in that respect Cole Porter has fallen down in all his latest shows. In this one he also fails as a lyricist, usually his strongest facet in the theater, for there is little that is unusual or specially amusing in the rhymes which go with his songs."

These comments did not come as a complete surprise to those who had closely followed Cole's career. For despite five long-running, highly touted Broadway shows in a row (*Leave It to Me, DuBarry Was a Lady, Panama Hattie, Let's Face It,* and *Something for the Boys*), the number of hits Cole was writing had slowly but steadily declined. Especially noticeable was the fact that none of Cole's tunes for *Something for the Boys* came even close to being a major hit. It was one thing for audiences at the Alvin to applaud vociferously when Ethel Merman and Paula Laurence, cavorting on stage as two Indian squaws, told of sharing a husband in "By the Mississinewah," but it was another to remember the number after the curtain had rung down. And like "By the Mississinewah," none of Cole's other songs for *Something for the Boys* (among them "Could It Be You?" "He's a Right Guy," and the title tune) had those special, memorable qualities needed for a smash. Moreover, the decline in the number of Cole's hit tunes and the onset of his periods of depression and irritability occurred in such close proximity that one might reasonably assume that they were interrelated in some way—though one can't be certain, as Cole shunned psychiatric help and his available medical records do not shed light on the matter. One must also assume that these unsettling elements in Cole's psyche were not only early clues to his subsequent mental deterioration, but were related to the total abandonment of songwriting in his final years, as well. On the surface, however, Cole's life at the time of *Something for the Boys* seemed to be as full and rewarding, socially and professionally, as ever.

20

Night and Day

In the spring of 1943, in making what had practically become their annual trek to California, Cole and Linda could look forward to residing in a lovely new home at 416 North Rockingham in Beverly Hills that they had rented from interior decorator William Haines, formerly a well-known movie actor of the twenties and thirties. Like the Porters' first California residence, the Barthelmess home, or their second one, the house of actor Richard Cromwell, which they had rented between 1940 and 1942, the Haines house was so luxurious that few but highly paid movie actors could afford to own it. Unlike their relatively limited stays in their other Hollywood homes, the Porters were to use the Haines house as their regular West Coast residence for the rest of their lives.

Besides moving into the Haines home in the spring of 1943, several months after *Something for the Boys* had opened on Broadway, Cole also started work on the score for a new film, *Mississippi Belle*, for Warner Brothers. The producer of the film was Arthur Schwartz, who had come to Hollywood in 1938 as a songwriter himself but had branched out into producing. Almost from Cole's first dealings with Schwartz, there was an undercurrent of friction between the two, especially since Schwartz continually suggested changes in Cole's songs for the film. Possibly if Schwartz himself were not a songwriter, Cole might have taken more kindly to these suggestions. But since inherent in Schwartz's carpings and Cole's negative responses were ego factors heightened by artistic differences, it was perhaps inevitable that a blowup should occur. At last, after Schwartz had dropped a series of Cole's tunes from the projected film and called for new songs, Cole was so angered that he complained to studio head Jack Warner and other executives, with the result that Schwartz was forced to soften his position, promising Cole that the bulk of his songs would be retained in the film after all. But once the dust had settled, the *Mississippi Belle* project was shelved—though not before Cole had gleefully told friends how the studio had backed down under his pressure. As Cole saw it, the tougher he got with Hollywood chieftains the better they liked it and the more they respected him.

Almost concurrent with the *Mississippi Belle* fracas, Cole had a chance to demonstrate his toughness in connection with still another Warners film, this one about his own life. The idea for the film originated with Irving Berlin. He felt that the spirit Cole had shown in surmounting his horrible leg injuries would make a wonderful focal point for a movie and also serve as inspiration for those who had similar obstacles to overcome —particularly military casualties. When Cole gave him the green light on the project, Berlin immediately called Jack Warner to broach the subject with him. Warner, too, liked the idea and arranged to meet with Cole to discuss the matter further. A telegram from Warner to Cole dated May 15, 1943, pretty much spells out what transpired as a result of the meeting:

> After our very lovely luncheon talk the other day, I was sure that we would be able to get together and quickly close the deal on the screening of your life. . . . But the terms that are being outlined by Arthur Lyons [Cole's agent], which Steve Trilling [Warner's assistant] has transmitted to me, are so tough that I am sure that it was not your intention to set it up on such a prohibitive plane. Therefore I think you should talk this over with Arthur and tell him to bring it down to a realm of possibility as we want to go ahead to make what I know will be one of the most important pictures and a great tribute to yourself and your fine spirit.

Despite Warner's pitch, it was not until the following August that he and Cole finally reached an agreement that resulted in the fictional *Night and Day*, but only after Warner had promised to pay Cole $300,000 for the film rights to his life.

Yet even with this contractual commitment, the actual filming of *Night and Day* was delayed for two years until 1945, mainly because of casting problems and difficulty in arriving at a suitable script. In the interim Cole was represented during 1944 by two productions on Broadway—*Mexican Hayride* and *Seven Lively Arts*—and by the movie *Hollywood Canteen*, from which his tune "Don't Fence Me In," written ten years earlier for the unproduced *Adios Argentina*, emerged as a major hit. The first of these Broadway shows, *Mexican Hayride*, reunited Cole with producer Mike Todd, staging and lighting expert Hassard Short, and scriptwriters Herbert and Dorothy Fields, all from *Something for the Boys*. Joining this group was comedian Bobby Clark, with his ubiquitous cigar, painted-on eyeglasses, and mile-a-minute patter. As Joe Bascom, an American numbers racketeer fleeing from justice, Clark ends up in Mexico, where he continues his wicked ways, including fixing a national lottery and assuming various disguises, both male and female. Cast as Clark's comedic foil was pretty, blonde June Havoc, playing the role of Montana, a female bullfighter. Between the two of them there was no shortage of comic invention when *Mexican Hayride* opened at Broadway's Winter Garden on January 28, 1944. The staging, lighting, and costuming for the show, too, were up to the best Broadway standards. The book and score for *Mexican Hayride*, on the other hand, did not come off very well. As the *Morning Telegraph* phrased it, the show had a "bad book and an indifferent score" and ventured the opinion that Cole's talent had "very nearly reached the vanishing point." But these harsh sentiments had little or no effect on ticket sales. There was enough gaiety and sparkle in the way *Mexican Hayride* was put together that it still managed to play to packed houses for months on end, and had a total run of 481 performances.

Besides the show's lengthy stay on Broadway, Cole had the satisfaction of winning a bet from Monty Woolley because of a hit tune in the production. While *Mexican Hayride* was still in its formative stage, Woolley had challenged Cole to write a hit number titled "I Love You," in which that banal phrase would be repeated again and again. Woolley felt that even Cole's gift with words and music would not be enough to surmount such a handicap and backed up that opinion with a small wager. Rising to the challenge (and at this point, Cole may have needed Woolley's goading to bring out the best in him), Cole came up with a languid refrain whose lyrics begin:

> "I love you,"
> Hums the April breeze.
> "I love you,"

Echo the hills.
"I love you,"
The golden dawn agrees
As once more she sees daffodils.

As sung by big-voiced Wilbur Evans in the show, "I Love You" quickly caught on, enabling Cole to win the wager while adding still another number—the only one in *Mexican Hayride* to become popular—to his long list of hit songs.

Before 1944 was out, and with *Mexican Hayride* still on the boards, Cole's next production, *Seven Lively Arts*, opened at the Ziegfeld Theater under the aegis of the diminutive Billy Rose, whose size was often derided by George S. Kaufman, one of the writers for the show. Invariably when someone asked Kaufman, "What's Rose up to?" he would almost instantaneously retort, "Your waist." But if Rose was small in stature he did have a colossal ego and the same-size approach to show business, as typified by his 1935 circus spectacular, *Jumbo*. As Rose conceived it, *Seven Lively Arts* also had mammoth proportions, for it attempted to explore a wide spectrum of the arts ranging from ballet and opera to modern painting, within the context of an evening's entertainment. The show featured such diverse performers as Beatrice Lillie and Bert Lahr, dancers Alicia Markova and Anton Dolin, and jazz clarinetist Benny Goodman.

In addition to Cole's songs, Rose had also commissioned Igor Stravinsky to write a fifteen-minute orchestral ballet suite, *Scènes de Ballet*, for dancers Markova and Dolin. In connection with that piece, Stravinsky tells an amusing story about Rose's attempt to change the Russian modernist's original, rather advanced (by Broadway standards) orchestral sound to a more palatable commercial one. For shortly after *Scènes de Ballet* had been tried out in Philadelphia, Stravinsky received this telegram from Rose:

YOUR MUSIC GREAT SUCCESS STOP COULD BE SENSATIONAL SUCCESS IF YOU WOULD AUTHORIZE ROBERT RUSSELL BENNETT RETOUCH ORCHESTRATION STOP BENNETT ORCHESTRATES EVEN THE WORKS OF COLE PORTER.

Without delay Stravinsky wired back this laconic reply:

SATISFIED WITH GREAT SUCCESS.

Just as Rose attempted artistic suggestions beyond his ken with Stravinsky, he also tried to control nearly all other aspects of the production of *Seven Lively Arts*. He more than met his match in Cole, however, when he did not give him what he considered suitable billing on the theater marquee and display signs when the show played Philadelphia before coming to New York. On learning of this slight Cole directed his agent, Richard Madden, to complain to Rose at once. Only after Rose had wired Madden the assurance that the question of billing would "be handled in New York precisely in conformity your telegram," did Cole drop the matter. But then, where billing and publicity for his productions were concerned, Cole took a back seat to no one. (Typical of his reaction to promotional slights is the letter he sent to agent Irving Lazar, who represented him for the MGM film, *High Society*, released in August, 1956. In the letter to Lazar dated January 11, 1956, Cole lamented, "So many people have spoken to me about the lack of publicity I am getting on *High Society*. Everyone else connected with it gets almost daily publicity, including Sol Siegel [producer of the film]." Cajoled Cole, "Maybe you have some Irving Lazar method by which this could be solved?")

In originally planning *Seven Lively Arts* Rose had envisaged using a full-length script about a group of young people who come to New York to make their fortunes in the arts. Interwoven into the plot were to be references to Rose's major show-business ventures from *Jumbo* on, including his productions of *Carmen Jones* and *Aquacade*, and his proprietorship of the Diamond Horseshoe nightclub. When a full-length script proved too unwieldy, Rose settled for a series of sketches by a gaggle of writers, most prominent of whom were George S. Kaufman and Moss Hart, and a running commentary by Ben Hecht. But even as a revue *Seven Lively Arts* still made so much of the pint-sized showman that *Variety* grumbled that portions of the show "could be called 'Glorifying the American Rose.'" As an added boost for his image, Rose opened *Seven Lively Arts* in New York at his newly acquired Ziegfeld Theater, before a glittering audience that had paid a top price of twenty-four dollars a ticket, an extraordinarily steep price then. In an attempt to further appropriate the lustrous Ziegfeld mantle, Rose threw a lavish champagne party at the show's premiere and also attended the event with Ziegfeld's widow, actress Billie Burke, on one arm, and his own wife, swimmer Eleanor Holm, on the other.

So much took place at the premiere of *Seven Lively Arts* on December 7, 1944, that reviewer Lewis Nichols made the point that Rose had "piled a little bit of everything but the kitchen sink" both on and off the stage of the Ziegfeld. And, in essence, that was the common plaint made by New York reviewers. There was just too much show and not enough art in *Seven Lively Arts* to make it prime entertainment. Rose, however, was not one to take such critical blows without fighting back. He desperately tried to salvage the sinking production by script changes, personnel cuts, and an extensive advertising campaign, but nothing seemed to help. *Seven Lively Arts* was too far gone to recover from its initial critical onslaught and went under after a modest run of only 183 performances.

If Cole had any apprehensions about how his score for *Seven Lively Arts* would be received, he may have been reassured by a communication from Dr. Sirmay written the day *Seven Lively Arts* was to open at the Ziegfeld.

In your new show, you are giving again a most delightful evidence of your great talent. Instead of declining, your imagination, the freshness of your ideas and your skill both as a composer and lyricist are all on the increase. I myself have a personal affair with your song "Ev'ry Time [We Say Goodbye]." It chokes me whenever I hear it, it moves me to tears. This song is one of the greatest songs you ever wrote. It is a dithyramb to love, a hymn to youth, a heavenly beautiful song. It is not less a gem than any immortal song of a Schubert or Schumann. Contemporaries usually fail to recognize real values. I don't care what critics may say, this song is a classic and will live forever as many others of your songs.

Though this assessment of Cole's talent might not be considered wholly objective because of Sirmay's close friendship with Cole, it does show exceptional acumen and foresight by singling out "Ev'ry Time We Say Goodbye" from the score. Of all the numbers Cole wrote for Rose's extravaganza, only this song survived the show's early demise to become a hit. Its simple, elegaic, repeated-note melody—a Porter characteristic—and cogent harmony beautifully complement a superior text. One example of how closely Cole correlated words and music in this song can be seen by his switch from primarily major to minor harmony to correspond with the phrase "from major to minor" in the lyrics for the refrain:

> Ev'ry time we say goodbye
> I die a little.
> Ev'ry time we say goodbye
> I wonder why a little.
> Why the gods above me,

Who must be in the know,
Think so little of me
They allow you to go.
When you're near there's such an air
Of spring about it,
I can hear a lark somewhere
Begin to sing about it.
There's no love song finer,
Yet how strange the change from major to minor
Ev'ry time we say goodbye.
Ev'ry single time we say goodbye.

It took months for the tune to really become a hit, however, and by the time it did, *Seven Lively Arts* had passed into history. In any case, its eventual success hardly made up for the many critical barbs directed against Cole and his score for Rose's mammoth flop. Cole was particularly vexed by the numerous press innuendoes that he was now only a shell of his former creative self. Cole himself probably suffered from some inner doubts about whether his creative faculties were as vivid as years before, but he was sufficiently annoyed by these public carpings to join forces with Rose in the latter's advertising campaign to save *Seven Lively Arts* (and indeed his self-doubt may have added to his anger at the show's failure). Though Cole privately denigrated Rose as a producer and as a person, he was only too happy to supply the bantam showman with derogatory press quotes about earlier Porter tunes that ultimately became world-famous in order to show that reviewers had been wrong in their judgment before and were wrong again in their evaluation of *Seven Lively Arts.* But like everything else connected with *Seven Lively Arts,* this advertising brainstorm had little effect on the fate of the show.

Another annoyance for Cole that practically coincided with his bad press for *Seven Lively Arts* was the report from Warner Brothers on December 27, 1944, that tunesmith Ira Arnstein, a persistent litigant in the courts against famous American songwriters, had threatened suit, presumably over the studio's planned production of Cole's movie biography. According to the studio's legal department, Arnstein claimed that Cole had plagiarized a number of his compositions and submitted various manuscripts as well as printed material to support this allegation. In their report Warner Brothers made clear that they considered Arnstein's claim "absolutely ridiculous," but warned that "if Arnstein follows his usual course he can become an awful nuisance." And Arnstein did. He sued

Cole for a million dollars, claiming plagiarism. In the two-week-long jury trial that followed, Monty Woolley, Deems Taylor, and Sigmund Spaeth all appeared in Cole's defense to support his contention that he had never taken material from Arnstein. Cole also testified that he neither knew Arnstein nor was familiar with his work. When the case finally went to the jury it was dismissed as being without merit after a deliberation of nearly two hours. But though Cole won the case, it was perhaps as a result of the experience gained from this trial that, when asked if he ever went out without a carnation in his boutonniere, Cole answered, "Only when I'm being sued, because a carnation in the buttonhole never helps your case before a jury."

While Cole was still involved with *Seven Lively Arts* and the Arnstein suit, he also took a hand in the shaping of his movie biography. His key contact for *Night and Day* was Arthur Schwartz, who had been assigned by Warners to produce it. In contrast to the acrimony that had developed between Cole and Schwartz over *Mississippi Belle*, there was virtual harmony between the two in connection with *Night and Day*. Schwartz had little choice but to defer to Cole, and frequently, in the planning of a production virtually built around Cole's life. As early as August 26, 1944, Schwartz wrote Cole to say that he considered it important that such stars as Fred Astaire, Mary Martin, Danny Kaye, Sophie Tucker, Jimmy Durante, and Bert Lahr do numbers from previous Porter musicals. The strategy, as Schwartz outlined it, was for Cole to personally ask the stars to appear in the film because, as Schwartz phrased it, "of your great contribution to their success." Schwartz felt that even if the stars had conflicting contractual obligations, especially to other film companies, they "would surely be more receptive if approached by you rather than the studio" since "an entirely different color would be given to the request." But despite this attempt to dress up the film with loads of name entertainers, presumably all working for "reasonable" fees out of deference to Cole, of the group Schwartz sought, only Mary Martin actually appeared in *Night and Day*; as was to be expected, she sang her signature number, "My Heart Belongs to Daddy." High production costs for *Night and Day* ultimately made the inclusion of the other name performers impossible. Cast in the film as a composite of several of these stars who had first introduced some of Cole's most famous numbers was vocalist Ginny Simms. This substitution of Ginny Simms for the actual personalities is indicative in a small way of the extent to which *Night and Day* deviated from the true Porter story.

Perhaps the most outlandish example was in the casting of Cary Grant as Cole. True, Cole had requested Grant for the part, and in getting him for the role was able to realize a fantasy shared by many men—from President John F. Kennedy to mobster Lucky Luciano—of being portrayed on the screen by him (even Grant, some say, has illusions of seeing himself played in films by Cary Grant). But from the moment tall, handsome, fortyish Grant is shown in *Night and Day* as a carefree Yale student leading a chorus of Eli men in the Porter college song, "Bull Dog," credibility quickly vanished. In addition to such incongruities as showing the Porter family mansion in Indiana staffed by black servants from the Deep South and having Cole's tunes presented completely out of the contexts and time periods in which they were written, *Night and Day* piled one fictitious episode on top of another. Typical of the film's fabrication was the scene showing Cary Grant, as Cole, composing "Night and Day." Against an inordinately loud sound track of falling rain and a ticking clock, Grant, at the piano, announces to Alexis Smith, in the role of Linda: "I think I've got it." He then proceeds to give birth to the tune, with its emphasis on the "tick, tick, tock of the stately clock" and the "drip, drip, drip of the raindrops," with all the creative ease that only Hollywood can muster.

There was no improvement in the film's stress on Cole's war record. In contrast to reality, he is portrayed as a soldier-hero overseas during World War I who is badly wounded by an exploding bomb. From beginning to end, *Night and Day* was a tissue of fabrications neatly wrapped in technicolor and Hollywood gloss and lavishly bound together by a bejeweled string of over a dozen Porter classics, including "I've Got You Under My Skin," "You're the Top," "Begin the Beguine," "My Heart Belongs to Daddy," "Easy to Love," and the title tune.

Just as Cole chose Cary Grant to represent him on screen, so, too, lovely and elegant Alexis Smith was Linda's choice as her movie counterpart. Monty Woolley was also brought into the production by a Porter request. For at Cole's say-so, Woolley—complete with beard and bluff *Man-Who-Came-to-Dinner* mannerisms—was given a role in the film; that of a Yale law professor who prefers the stage to the classroom. Besides Grant, Alexis Smith, Woolley, Ginny Simms, and Mary Martin playing herself, the cast for *Night and Day* also featured Jane Wyman portraying a New Haven chorus girl who knew Cole when he first started songwriting, and Eve Arden as a French prima donna. Overseeing the whole shebang was Hungarian-born Michael Curtiz, a very gifted but overly demanding screen director whose tyrannical behavior on the set so infuriated the usually debonair Grant that he finally exploded when the shooting of *Night and Day* had concluded. "If I'm ever stupid enough to be caught working with you," roared Grant before the startled crew, "you'll know I'm either broke or I've lost my mind." Notwithstanding this outburst by Grant, Curtiz's direction of *Night and Day* so pleased studio head Jack Warner that on November 20, 1945, he wired Cole this enthusiastic message:

HAVE FINALLY COMPLETED PICTURE. GOING ON RECORD WITH YOU HAVE MOST IMPORTANT MUSICAL EVER PRODUCED.

Several months later, on February 12, 1946, after the scoring and editing of the film had been completed, Warner sent Cole another glowing, though somewhat more modest, appraisal in which he reported the results of a sneak preview of *Night and Day* before a Beverly Hills audience:

REACTION WAS EVERYTHING ONE WOULD DESIRE. WE HAVE AN IMPORTANT FILM AND ONE I KNOW YOU WILL BE VERY PROUD OF AND ALSO A SUCCESS WHICH I KNOW IS WHAT COUNTS.

Cole's public response on seeing *Night and Day* later that spring was equally enthusiastic, for he sent cordial wires of thanks to Warner, Curtiz, Cary Grant, Alexis Smith, and practically everyone else who had a hand in the film. Cole's wire to Curtiz reflected the genial tone of all the messages he sent:

BELOVED MIKE, LINDA AND I SAW NIGHT AND DAY PICTURE FRIDAY NIGHT AND YOU HAVE OUR ETERNAL GRATITUDE FOR TREATING US SO BEAUTI-FULLY. WHAT A GREAT DIRECTOR YOU ARE AND HOW LUCKY WE WERE TO HAVE BEEN PUT IN YOUR HANDS.

Off the record, however, Cole was considerably more critical of the film, despite its exceptional success at the box office. "None of it is true," Cole would freely admit to his friends. As a matter of fact, when the film began to be shown on television years after it had first been released, Cole would watch it at every opportunity so that he could have a good time laughing at the many plot absurdities concocted by a string of Hollywood hacks. Yet considering the numerous fibs about himself that Cole had foisted on an unsuspecting public for decades, one could hardly expect a Hollywood film biography to come any closer to the truth. But then, when you get down to it, Cole wouldn't have wanted the truth told anyway!

21

Kiss Me, Kate

The inconsistencies between the "real" Cole and the one depicted in *Night and Day* were perhaps no more diverse than the inconsistencies that actually coexisted in Cole's makeup. How else, then, can one reconcile Cole's unmistakable maudlin streak with his even more pronounced unsentimental one? To see this all one has to do is compare such refreshingly cool and sophisticated gems as "Let's Do It," "You're the Top," and "Anything Goes" with some of Cole's more mawkish, heart-on-the-sleeves tunes like "Old-Fashioned Garden," "Hot-House Rose," and "Let's Be Buddies." Also indicative of this sentimentality—especially surprising in one normally considered the personification of worldliness, savoir faire, and even cynicism—was Cole's habit of listening to the radio soap opera *Stella Dallas*. Cole would lap up the tear-jerking insipidities that were regularly and liberally dished out on this program as it told of the trials and tribulations that befell Stella and her daughter, Lolly-Baby. So addicted was Cole to this soap opera that he would stop whatever he was doing in order to listen to the program every chance he could.*

Another contrast existed between the hard-as-nails Cole who manifested his toughness in his financial arrangement with Jack Warner in connection with *Night and Day,* or his refusal to extend himself to help the financially troubled sponsoring committee of the 1938 Cole Porter

Day festivities in Indiana, and the generous Cole who gave money and expensive presents to young men who struck his fancy. Cole's tender side also asserted itself in relation to his mother and various mother-surrogates. Ginny Carpenter, the daughter of composer John Alden Carpenter, recalls several incidents which reveal this more compassionate side of Cole's personality. She remembers on one occasion how Cole generously arranged for her to sit for artist Marie Laurencin so that she might surprise her mother with a gift of a portrait of herself. In another instance Cole quickly offered to make an unannounced visit to Ginny's mother, in the hopes of cheering her up, on learning she was ill. Where Cole's own mother, Kate, was concerned, he was even more solicitous. He not only kept in close touch with her wherever he was and invited her to all his Broadway openings, but he made a point, too, of feting her on her birthdays as well as of sending her gifts from the various places he visited on his travels. In fact, while working on a production in Europe one year, Cole suddenly realized that his mother's birthday was upon him and that he had not done anything about it. He immediately wrote out a long, sentimental message that he cabled to her in Indiana, telling her how much he and Linda loved her and asking her to let them know how she was doing. Almost as if to offset Cole's sentimental effusiveness, Kate the very next day cabled back a one-word reply: "Okay."

There were numerous other contradictions in Cole's personal life, made all the more fascinating by their extremes. One has merely to contrast the shabby waterfront bars where Cole on occasion sought the burly truck-driver and sailor types that so appealed to him with the beautiful homes and estates that were his more usual setting to appreciate the degree of inconsistency in his makeup. Moreover, these contradictions covered a broad psychological and physical spectrum. For example, in creating his tunes Cole was the model of tidiness and efficiency. He would insist that certain customary objects always be close at hand as he worked: sharpened pencils, disposable tissues, cigarettes, cough drops, trash baskets, and an assortment of language and rhyming dictionaries, reference books, and geographical guides. Also, Cole would chart the script layout of a production in advance so as to be able to follow a fast number with a slow tune and a romantic song with a humorous one. In addition, he kept his songs—both finished and unfinished—neatly arranged in folders and looseleaf notebooks for easy accessibility. Yet with all this outward display of well-oiled efficiency and tidiness, Cole's handwriting, by contrast, was invariably labored and often sloppy, presumably as a result of his contorted way of writing. For as a left-hander, Cole had developed the bad habit of getting into an awkward, convoluted stance, with his shoulders hunched and his left arm arched at an impossible angle, when he wrote. This evidently affected the end result, though no doubt experienced psychiatrists and calligraphers might have other explanations for the discrepancy between Cole's smooth-as-silk work routine and his labored handwriting.

Also contradictory was the lack of gray in the mature Cole's hair. If someone were indiscreet enough to inquire about this when he was in his sixties and older, Cole would say that he came from long-lived stock with a predilection for retaining natural hair coloring. What Cole did not mention was that he colored his hair regularly as he got on in years. As a matter of fact, Cole's hairdresser, a Parisian named Rowland, had worked out a formula for dyeing Cole's hair that Cole carried with him whenever he traveled, so that he could pass on the information to hairdressers wherever he was. The Rowland formula was quite specific about hair-coloring brands and particular shades that would best suit Cole. Describing Cole's hair coloring as "dark ash blonde," Rowland specified in his formula that "if Inecto is used, it is number 6; if Roux is used, it is number 106."

As was true of his hair, Cole's teeth, too, were not quite what they seemed. Though Cole's broad smile, complete with an even set of white, shiny teeth, had always been one of his most attractive features, nearly all of his teeth—especially as he advanced in age—were false; he had an extensive set of bridges to replace what had been lost. However, except for Cole's valets, who were used to seeing Cole without teeth when he took out his bridgework for daily cleaning, few knew that Cole's luminescent smile derived largely from dentures. Cole's artificial teeth were also indirectly responsible for revealing Cole's state of mind to Henry Burke, Cole's valet for the last five years or so of his life. Burke recalls that Cole, always fastidious, regularly cleaned his false teeth—except, that is, for a period of about a year before he died. In that final year Cole completely stopped cleaning his dentures. When that happened Burke knew that Cole, normally so concerned about his appearance, had given up on living and had resigned himself to death.

Considerably before Cole had stopped cleaning his dentures, his big, contagious smile—and white, shiny teeth—could be seen in published ads endorsing various products like Rheingold beer and Camel cigarettes. These endorsements reached their peak after Cole's great success with *Kiss Me, Kate* in the late forties. "My beer is Rheingold the *dry* beer!" and "Camels have been a hit with me for years!" were typical statements attributed to Cole in these ads. But the claims had little basis in fact, as was often the case in connection with Cole's *public* personna. Though Cole, for instance, was a heavy smoker, he normally did not smoke Camels (he preferred Murads and Helmars; smoother—and more expensive —brands). Nor did Cole drink very much Rheingold, or any other beer, for he usually imbibed stronger stuff, particularly Scotch, in vast quantities. Yet even if the ads were inconsistent with actuality, Cole received so much money and publicity from them he was only too delighted to bend the truth.

The kind of truth-stretching that Cole did so readily apparently came even more easily to Orson Welles, the author, director, and major driving force behind *Around the World in Eighty Days*, Cole's next Broadway production after *Seven Lively Arts*. Welles's gift for telling tall stories proved especially useful in getting financial support for *Around the World*. At one point, when he had completely run out of funds for the project, Welles telephoned movie czar Harry Cohn in Hollywood to tell him of a wonderful idea he had for a movie. Was Cohn interested? When he indicated that he was, Welles ad-libbed a plot over the phone—which he subsequently forgot—that helped to raise the needed cash for the production. But so highly respected was Welles for his stage, radio, and film achievements that he could get away with such hanky-panky. For as early as 1934, at the age of nineteen, Welles, his face covered by a false beard, was playing Tybalt on Broadway in Katherine Cornell's *Romeo and Juliet*, and giving a good account of himself. Three years later Welles, in conjunction with John Houseman, had formed the now-famous Mercury Theatre, whose initial production, a modern-dress rendition of Shakespeare's *Julius Caesar*, took New York by storm. Going on to do radio drama as well, Welles in 1938 made front-page headlines with his alarmingly realistic broadcast of H. G. Wells's *The War of the Worlds*, which had hundreds of thousands of Americans believing that Martians had invaded Earth and the world was coming to an end. When Welles turned his attention to films, his production of *Citizen Kane*, released in 1941, with its vivid portrayal of a ruthless newspaper tycoon whose life closely paralleled that of William Randolph Hearst, brought him great acclaim. With such a record of accomplishments Welles had little difficulty persuading Cole to write the score for a 1946 musical based on Jules Verne's famous novel of 1873, *The Tour of the World in Eighty Days*.

At the start of Welles's *Around the World* project, Mike Todd had evinced interest in producing the show. He soon bowed out of the venture, however, when it became clear that Welles not only expected to act in it, but he really wanted to produce the musical himself, and oversee all other aspects of the show. "Written, produced, directed, and performed by Orson Welles," was typical of the sort of credits that the world had come to expect from practically anything Welles, now thirty, touched, and Welles had enough confidence in himself—and the ego to go with it—to insist on having complete control of any show under his imprimatur. And in retrospect, it was this attempt by Welles to live up to his reputation as a theatrical superman that proved to be the undoing of *Around the World*. Despite Welles's Herculean efforts—toiling for days on end with little food or sleep—the final result left much to be desired. The show was just too full of excesses, from its enormous cast to its tons of props, costumes, and sets, to really work.

Despite Welles's description of the production as "an extravaganza in two acts and thirty-four scenes," the audience was not quite ready for the extravagances that took place at the Adelphi Theater when *Around the World* opened in New York on May 31, 1946. Drama critic Howard Barnes noted that "Welles has never been a stage artist to do things in half measures." For Barnes, Welles's creation combined "silent movies, Hoboken melodramatic satire, a magic show and Olsen and Johnson japes in a singular potpourri." While praising Arthur Margetson, as the English adventurer, Phileas Fogg, and other leads in the show—among them Larry Laurence (now better known as Enzo Stuarti), Julie Warren, Mary Healy, and Victoria Cordova—Barnes had little that was positive to say about Cole's score ("the Porter songs are not in the finest Porter tradition") or Welles's various contributions to the production, including his portrayal of Dick Fix, a stool pigeon. About Welles the actor Barnes complained that "he takes over all sorts of redolent roles at the drop of a hat, rushing around the stage with six-shooters, or out into the audience to grab a protesting duck from the vest pocket of a protesting patron." Barnes's ultimate verdict of *Around the World* excoriated Welles: "It is a very uneven musical which the producer-author-actor must answer for. In this instance he is more often exhibitionistic than entertaining."

Barnes's critique of *Around the World* accurately reflected the general reactions of the public and the media; the production closed after only seventy-five performances. This quick closing lent support to the growing belief that Cole was no longer the composer he used to be, especially since none of his songs for the show was even remotely a hit. Nor was Cole's reputation helped by having two Broadway flops in a row (*Seven Lively Arts* and the Welles extravaganza).

But if *Around the World* was a professional bust for Cole, it did at least give him a chance to work with Welles. Cole, in fact, was so impressed with the multifaceted talents of Welles that during the Boston tryout of *Around the World* he wrote to a friend extolling Welles as "a tower of strength" who "never loses his temper or his power to surmount almost impossible difficulties." Even "if the show flops," Cole admitted, "I shall at least have had a great experience with a wonderful guy." However, as the Broadway premiere of *Around the World* drew near, Cole became sufficiently disenchanted with Welles and the show that he left for California before the opening—an unusual move for Cole, but one presumably made to soften the critical blows that he anticipated being heaped on the show. (Yet if the Jules Verne classic did not succeed as a Welles stage musical, it subsequently became a major smash, in 1956, as a big, colorful, non-musical film—featuring David Niven and Cantinflas in the leads—without benefit of the Mercury Theatre wunderkind. Ironically, Mike Todd, who walked away from Welles's stage treatment of *Around the World in Eighty Days,* came up with the winning movie formula that showed how viable the Jules Verne story could be in the right hands.)

Cole's next production, *The Pirate,* did not do any better as a movie than it had on the stage. In its 1942 stage version *The Pirate* had been presented on Broadway as a vehicle for the widely beloved husband-and-wife acting team of Alfred Lunt and Lynn Fontanne. Yet even with the brilliant Lunts in it, *The Pirate* got only so-so reviews and lasted a mere 177 performances. As produced on Broadway by the Theatre Guild, in conjunction with the Playwrights' Company, *The Pirate,* an adaptation by S.N. Behrman of a 1911 farce by German dramatist Ludwig Fulda, was carefully tailored for the Lunts. The story tells of a highborn damsel who is wooed by the leader of a band of nondescript traveling acrobats. To impress the lady he pretends to be a famous swashbuckling pirate. When the real buccaneer enters the picture, complications, of course, develop. But since *The Pirate* was little more than a make-believe period piece with colorful costumes and derring-do substituted for plausibility, these complications were soon resolved in the interests of a happy ending.

As a movie by MGM, *The Pirate* drew on Behrman's adaptation, but also added a score by Cole, filming in technicolor, singing and dancing, the directorial skills of Vincente Minnelli, and the box-office appeal of Judy Garland and Gene Kelly in the roles formerly undertaken by the Lunts—all to no avail, however. With all the talent in it and the millions spent on production, *The Pirate* as a film still emerged as a cloddish affair, no more inspired than the Broadway play. As a consequence, Cole's score for *The Pirate* never had a chance. Though not one of his better ones, this score did have its moments in such tunes as the charmingly optimistic "You Can Do No Wrong" or the bittersweet "Be a Clown." But since the overall film results were so ponderous and leaden, Cole unfortunately had the stigma of still another flop on his hands when MGM released *The Pirate* in the spring of 1948.

Unhappy and chagrined by this all-too-regular and widely noted series of flops, Cole was desperate enough at this point to consider doing a score for a script by a writer of soap operas, Elaine Carrington. Cole's rationale for contemplating this move was that soap operas—as evidenced by the enormous popularity of many daily radio serials—had great audience appeal, and he, for some reason, no longer seemed to have the touch for reaching a broad public. Elaine Carrington's idea centered around a Miss America contest. But before the project got very far, Cole left it to concentrate instead on what ultimately became his most important work for the theater: *Kiss Me, Kate.*

Cole did not switch his energies to *Kiss Me, Kate* without many reservations. When he had first been asked to do the score for a musical based on Shakespeare's *The Taming of the Shrew*, Cole was apprehensive that such a production might be too highbrow for Broadway. Nor did he feel that his style would lend itself readily to Shakespeare. Also figuring in his apprehension was the poor showing he had made on Broadway and in Hollywood in recent years. The last thing he needed was another flop, notwithstanding the fact that five of his numbers had just been ranked among the thirty-five most popular song favorites of all time in the United States: "What Is This Thing Called Love?" "Night and Day," "I Get a Kick Out of You," "Begin the Beguine," and "Just One of Those Things."

The initial impetus for *Kiss Me, Kate* came from a young stage manager, Arnold Saint Subber. After hearing Alfred Lunt and Lynn Fontanne bicker offstage while appearing in *The Taming of the Shrew*, Subber conceived the notion of a musical using the Shakespearean work as part of a play-within-a-play format. Subber got Lemuel Ayers, a bright young designer of sets and costumes, to join him in trying to mount the musical on Broadway. As one of their first moves the tyro producers approached writer Bella Spewack about doing the script for their show. Bella minced no words with the two would-be producers. She told them she had always hated *The Taming of the Shrew*, and considered it one of the bard's worst plays. Nonetheless, she promised to give some thought to a script that would be suitable for a Broadway musical, and told them she would let them know if anything worthwhile developed.

Approximately six weeks later Bella had not only overcome her distaste for *The Taming of the Shrew*, but, more important, she had devised a most ingenious script for the new show. But now the question was, who would write the score? As their first choice the two young producers leaned toward Burton Lane, the composer of *Finian's Rainbow*. However, when he was not immediately available because of other assignments, Bella opted for asking Cole, despite less-than-enthusiastic reactions from Subber and Ayers, who pointed out that Cole had not had a hit musical in a number of years. Bella refused to back down on her choice, with the result that Subber and Ayers had to go along with her.

On meeting with Cole to discuss the project, Bella was immediately rebuffed by him. Cole wanted no part of the show and clearly articulated his objections: The basic plot was too esoteric; his own style would not be appropriate for a Shakespearean musical; he did not think that the show had the potential for being a hit. But Bella refused to be put off by Cole's negative response and persisted in speaking up for the show. For every objection Cole raised Bella countered with an argument of her own. The basic notion of the show, she maintained, was not too esoteric. It simply concerned theater folk, much like people they both knew, who had their own private lives away from the theater but who also took on new personality characteristics once onstage. As for the use of a Shakespearean work as a subplot, well, *The Taming of the Shrew*, as Bella explained it, was really a Yiddish play at heart. According to Bella the basic premise of the *Shrew*—that a younger sister (Bianca) can't marry until the older one (Kate) does—was clearly a Jewish religious custom that was at the core of many Yiddish shows that had played on Second Avenue in Manhattan for audiences who could not get enough of them. If the Yiddish theater had been able to make money from such a basic premise, Bella argued, why not a Broadway show? And in retrospect it may very well have been this tie-in between *Kiss Me, Kate* and Jewish custom—and its financial success on stage—that ultimately won Cole over to the project, considering his own theory about writing hit songs, with its implications—verging on the anti-Semitic—of Jewish domination of the popular-music field. At any rate, after much give and take between Bella and Cole, he finally relented.

Once he was committed to *Kiss Me, Kate*, Cole went all-out in trying to come up with a score that would be both genuinely good Broadway and good Shakespeare. He succeeded magnificently. Some of his numbers, like the rousing "Another Op'nin', Another Show," or the cynical "Always True to You in My Fashion," or the tender "So in Love," or the importuning "Why Can't You Behave?" had all the earmarks of Porter Broadway tunes at their best. But at the same time Cole did not neglect the world of the bard; Cole's "We Open in Venice," "Tom, Dick or Harry," and "I Hate Men," though not specifically Shakespearean in tone, still managed to convey the spirit of *The Taming of the Shrew.* As a more overt link to Shakespeare, however, Cole's "I've Come to Wive It Wealthily in Padua" (sung by Alfred Drake, as the swaggering Petruchio, in the *Shrew* sequence) was fashioned from these lines by Shakespeare:

> I come to wive it wealthily in Padua;
> If wealthily then happily in Padua.

Cole's "I Am Ashamed That Women Are So Simple" and "Where Is the Life That Late I Led?" were derived, too, from Shakespeare. Similarly, "Were Thine That Special Face" was based on these lines spoken by Bianca in *The Taming of the Shrew*:

> Believe me, sister, of all the men alive,
> I never yet beheld that special face
> Which I could fancy more than any other.

Also tied to the bard were Cole's deliberate malapropisms in "Brush Up Your Shakespeare." As mouthed by two hoods (portrayed by Harry Clark and Jack Diamond), the tune's lyrics spoof the ignoramuses of the world with assaults on the English language:

> Just declaim a few lines from "Othella"
> And they'll think you're a helluva fella,
> If your blonde won't respond when you flatter 'er
> Tell her what Tony told Cleopaterer,
> If she fights when her clothes you are mussing,
> What are clothes? "Much Ado About Nussing."

Equally satirical in its own way, though neither Shakespeare nor show business, was "Wunderbar," a wonderful spoof of Viennese waltzes. This tune had first been written around 1933 for Gilbert Miller's *Once Upon a Time,* which never got produced. In its original state the tune had been known as "Waltz Down the Aisle." Using that same title, Cole had incorporated the number into his scores for *Anything Goes* and *Jubilee,* but the number was dropped from both. Not one to waste material, Cole then revised the song for *Kiss Me, Kate*, with excellent results. From the opening lines of the song's verse,

> Gazing down on the Jungfrau
> From our secret chalet for two,

it is clear that the number is meant to be satirical, since one could hardly gaze down from a chalet on the Jungfrau, one of the tallest peaks in the Alps. Adding to the song's spoof of Viennese waltzes are Cole's use of such *gemütlich* phrases in his lyrics as "Liebchen mein" and, of course, "wunderbar." Musically, moreover, the song literally drips *Alte Wien* sentiment, from the parody in its verse of melodic clichés associated with Johann Strauss, Jr., the waltz king, to its emphasis on a stolid, oom-pah-pah waltz accompaniment throughout its verse and refrain.

The final script for *Kiss Me, Kate*, devised by Bella Spewack in conjunction with her husband Samuel, revolved around Fred Graham, the leading man and director of a second-rate acting company, and his ex-wife, Lilli Vanessi, the female lead in the company. Though their marriage has been dissolved and they argue frequently, Fred and Lilli are still romantically attached to each other. Also connected with the company are the secondary romantic characters, Lois Lane and Bill Calhoun, whose marriage plans are continually being thwarted by their bickering over her questionable fidelity and his compulsive gambling. As the Spewacks' plot unfolds, Fred, Lilli, Lois, and Bill come to terms with themselves while performing *The Taming of the Shrew* (in which Fred portrays Petruchio, Lilli is Kate, and Lois and Bill are Bianca and Lucentio respectively) in Baltimore. By means of this play-within-a-play framework, with its interweaving of the different worlds of sixteenth-century Padua and twentieth-century America, the four leading characters resolve their own offstage differences through the insights they gain from their onstage roles in the *Shrew*.

Almost from the moment *Kiss Me, Kate* was conceived, Alfred Drake was earmarked for the Fred Graham–Petruchio role. Despite four Broadway failures in a row prior to *Kate*, he was chosen as the show's male lead mainly on the basis of the strong impression he had made five years earlier as Curly in Rodgers and Hammerstein's *Oklahoma*. Compared to Drake, Patricia Morison, his female counterpart in *Kate*, was practically unknown. Her last appearance in a New York musical had been some ten years earlier in a less-than-exalted production called *The Two Bouquets* (by coincidence, Drake, too, had had a part in that show). When Broadway did not work out for her, Miss Morison then shifted to Hollywood, where she was seen in a number of B pictures, without much distinction. Yet when she tried out for the Lilli Vanessi–Kate role in *Kiss Me, Kate*, she made such a marvelous impression, first on Cole and then on the Spewacks, that she landed the job. Rounding out the quartet of principals in *Kate* was beauteous Lisa Kirk, in the Lois Lane–Bianca role, and Harold Lang, a former American Ballet Theater dancer, as Bill Calhoun–Lucentio.

In trying to raise the necessary backing—$180,000—for *Kiss Me, Kate*, producers Subber and Ayers found it rough going at first, largely because potential investors were skeptical about tying up their money with unknown producers. Investors also questioned the value of Cole's name linked with the production, in view of his series of Broadway flops prior to *Kate*. Complicating matters further was a Treasury Department ruling not long before *Kate* went on the boards that changed the tax structure for theatrical investments: Instead of being considered capital gains, income from such investments were now to be taxed as regular profits. For all these reasons, plus the paucity of big names as stars, the prospects for getting the necessary funding for *Kate* seemed so unpromising that John "Jack" C. Wilson, an old friend of Cole's, was brought in as an additional producer to help raise cash for the show. Eventually Wilson switched from producing to directing *Kate*, after a slew of backers' auditions had helped to raise sufficient funding from seventy-two angels to mount the production.

Cole had known Jack Wilson since the mid-twenties, in his Venice days. He had first met him through Noel Coward, whose practically inseparable companion the handsome, charming Wilson was in the twenties and thirties. At the time of *Kiss Me, Kate* Wilson, like Cole, had long been connected with the theater, as Coward's manager. Wilson had also invested with Coward in a number of Lunt and Fontanne shows presented by the Theatre Guild, among them *The Taming of the Shrew* (1935), *Idiot's Delight* (1936), and *Amphitryon 38* (1937). In 1942 Wilson, in conjunction with Alfred Lunt, had helped stage the Lunt-Fontanne production of *The Pirate* that served as the basis for the later movie with Gene Kelly and Judy Garland.

Besides their affinity for the theater Cole and Wilson had other things in common. Both were polished, urbane men; both were heavy drinkers and smokers; both were gay, with virtually insatiable sexual appetites; and both had married beautiful, regal-looking women. In the case of Wilson's wife, however, the association with royalty was not simply a question of personality and appearance, for Natasha "Natalie" Wilson, née Paley, had actually been born a Russian Romanov princess (her grandfather was Emperor Alexander II, who ruled Russia from 1855 to 1881). Rumor has it that Queen Mary, the wife of England's George V, had been so taken with Natasha's beauty and grace that she had considered her as a possible bride for her second son, Albert, who became King George VI on the abdication of his older brother, Edward VIII (who then became the Duke of Windsor), in 1936. Instead of Albert, Natasha ended up marrying first Lucien Lelong, the famous Parisian couturier, and then, after divorcing Lelong, the dapper and dashing Wilson, in 1937.

Just as Cole and Wilson had much in common, so, too, did Linda and Natasha. In addition to their innate beauty and regal bearing, and their safe, sexless marriages to ambitious, forceful, homosexual men, Linda and Natasha each generally shunned the limelight (in the thirties, however, Natasha had tried, unsuccessfully, to break into films as an actress), while doing what they could behind the scenes to push their husbands' careers along. Both women were also inclined to follow ambiguous and frequently dangerous routines with respect to their health and beauty. Linda, for example, in spite of her chronic respiratory problems, smoked regularly and excessively, with harmful effect. Yet along with this clearly self-destructive habit, Linda also spent time in various American and European sanitariums located in dry, invigorating climates to try to cut down the ravages of her illness. Natasha, too, followed a contradictory routine. Though she seemed hell-bent on destroying herself by immoderate amounts of drinking (for years she was a chronic alcoholic) she was still sufficiently concerned with her looks, dress, and grooming to go on occasional abstinence programs.

Considering Linda's and Natasha's somewhat similar backgrounds and affinities, it is not surprising that they remained on good terms over the years. But what *is* perhaps surprising is that Cole and Wilson, along with their professional ties to *Kiss Me, Kate,* reputedly became lovers as well, without in any way impinging on the friendship they had with each other's wives or affecting the friendship that Linda and Natasha had for each other. Cole and Wilson were sufficiently discreet about their affair not to flaunt it before Linda and Natasha. Nor is there any indication that Noel Coward, whose lover Wilson had evidently been for years, was aware of the relationship between the two men, even though they were presumably on intimate terms for many months as an outgrowth of their collaboration on *Kiss Me, Kate.*

Some evidence of the mutual esteem that Cole, Linda, and the Wilsons had for each other—irrespective of the intimacies between the men involved—can be seen in the fact that a portrait of Natasha by the Russian-American painter Pavel Tchelitchew hung in the Porters' residence at the Waldorf in tribute to the Russian princess. (As one of the provisions of Cole's will, and as a reminder of past ties, he bequeathed the portrait to Natasha on his death.) Another manifestation of the cordial relationship between the Porters and the Wilsons was the gift Cole gave Natasha after Linda's death: As mementos of the long friendship between the two women, Natasha received two of Linda's jeweled bracelets and a clip. Wilson, too, showed his high regard for Linda (and by so doing, for Cole also) by his solicitous concern for her health and well-being and by his overall cordiality toward her. Wilson's feelings for Linda can be readily perceived from a note that he sent her shortly before *Kiss Me, Kate* opened for its Philadelphia tryout. "Darling Linda," began Wilson, "who could have foreseen on the Lido in 1925 a Cole Porter *Kiss Me, Kate* staged by John C. Wilson!" Wilson then added, "I am so proud and happy about it all and Cole aside from simply being a genius is the sweetest, kindest person in show business." In an oblique reference to his staging of the production, Wilson concluded with, "And even if some of the lights don't work—they will by Saturday. All my love, Jack."

The worries Wilson implied in his note to Linda were soon dispelled by the warm reception Philadelphians gave the show. By the time *Kate* opened at the New Century Theater in New York on December 30, 1948, word had already gotten out that a major hit was in the making. And New York's press corps pretty much reaffirmed that prognosis with rave reviews and by honoring the show, through the aegis of the Newspaper Guild, with their Page One Award for theatrical excellence. As additional honors for *Kate*, the theatrical community bestowed several Tonys on the show: for the best musical production, the best book, and the best score of the 1948–49 season.

As the kudos and honors poured in for *Kate*, it was evident that so exceptional a show was bound to be around for a long time. But the extent of its longevity has exceeded even the most optimistic expectations. Not only did the original production of *Kate*, by virtue of its 1,077 performances, become Cole's longest-running musical by far in New York, but other productions of the show have continued year after year since its premiere. In 1949 a national company of *Kate* began a three-year tour of major theaters across the United States, and on March 8, 1951, a British production of the show, with Patricia Morison repeating her original role, opened at London's Coliseum for a run of 400 performances. There have been so many performances of *Kate* throughout the world (in Poland, for example, it played over 200 performances to capacity houses) that it has been a financial bonanza for its creators and investors, with royalties pouring in almost unceasingly. The show has been presented in approximately twenty languages, under such titles as *Embrasse-moi Catherine; Baciami, Caterina;* and *Kuss mich Kätchen,* in numerous countries in Europe, Scandinavia, Latin America, the Near and Far East, and behind the Iron Curtain. *Kate* also did well as a 1953 MGM movie starring Kathryn Grayson and Howard Keel. Nor is there an end in sight: Helped along by many recordings of its songs and a published version of the complete vocal score put out by Buxton Hill Music, named after Cole's Williamstown estate (this company was originally formed in the 1940s as a branch of Chappell to publish and distribute Cole's music, but was subsequently purchased by Harms, which assumed that function), *Kate* is still in almost constant demand by amateur and professional theatrical groups for productions in an assortment of settings ranging from college campuses to opera houses throughout the world.

Apparently anticipating a smash, Cole had invited a large party of ninety-seven guests, costing him more than a thousand dollars for tickets alone, to join him for *Kate*'s Broadway opening and the festivities that followed. Cole was so enthusiastic about the premiere that he returned with other guests to see the show fourteen more times in the space of several weeks. And it is easy to see why Cole enjoyed himself so much at a show for which he had expressed so many doubts at first. For his songs had all the Porter earmarks of twentieth-century sophistication and topicality, even within the context of Shakespeare's *The Taming of the Shrew.* For example, "Bianca," sung by Bill Calhoun–Lucentio as a commentary on his love for Lois Lane–Bianca, has these wonderful lines so typical of Cole in the refrain:

> To win you, Bianca,
> There's nothing I would not do,
> I would gladly give up coffee for Sanka,
> Even Sanka, Bianca, for you.

If only for these lines alone, Cole would have left his imprint on *Kate* for years to come. But so wonderfully has Cole's *complete* score for *Kate* stood the test of time that, some three decades after the show's premiere, the score is still as fresh and as incisive as ever.

22

Going Strong

Shortly after *Kiss Me, Kate* had settled into the New Century Theater, its future on Broadway relatively assured, Cole and Linda decided to visit Europe; it was to be their first trip there since Cole's accident nearly twelve years earlier. As *Time* magazine of January 31, 1949, described the trip projected for that spring, the Porters' first stop was to be Paris, where they would stay at the Ritz, as Linda's house at 13 rue Monsieur was now occupied by a school. According to *Time* Cole's itinerary would then take him from Paris "to Rome and, naturally, on to Venice. From Italy he will fly to Athens. Then he will take a yacht—already charted—and trace a lazy course among the sunny Greek islands of the Aegean."

But as so often happens to the best of plans, this European trip did not materialize. Linda happened to have caught cold, which developed into pleurisy, during the Philadelphia tryout of *Kate*. Her lungs, always a source of trouble for her, became congested, and it was decided that she should go to Arizona's dry climate to regain her health. When it was apparent that her recovery would take longer than expected (she remained in Arizona until the end of April), Cole canceled the European trip and went to California instead so that he could look after his professional interests while visiting Linda in Arizona every few weeks. If ever Cole demonstrated his warm attachment to Linda—as well as reciprocating her devotion to him after his accident—it was from this period until her death in 1954. For during these years her health was more precarious than ever, and Cole showed by action and deed his deep affection for her and his concern for her well-being.

When Cole was not visiting Linda in Arizona in the spring of 1949, he would regularly write chatty letters to her, giving all the dirt about mutual acquaintances, to keep her spirits up. Cole also arranged for Howard Sturges, Leonard Hanna, and other close friends to spend time with Linda in Arizona during her convalescence, so that she always had plenty of company. After Linda had recovered sufficiently to return East to Williamstown for the summer, Cole continued keeping in frequent touch with her from California by telephone and letters.

While all this was going on Cole still managed to be on top of his own affairs. One matter that was especially close to his heart was the question of whether his *Kate* score was getting sufficient publicity. He made no bones about his concern to Max Dreyfus, his publisher, and he may have been assuaged by a letter from Dreyfus on April 13, 1949, discussing his promotion of the *Kate* songs. As Dreyfus explained it, except for "Too Darn Hot" (with such lines in it as "I'd like to fool with my baby tonight, break ev'ry rule with my baby tonight"), which had limited promotional potential because it had been banned from the air by the major networks, the rest of the *Kate* score was getting Dreyfus's undivided attention. In Dreyfus's words, "Be assured, Cole, that we are giving all our efforts to the songs from 'KISS ME KATE' and be further assured that I am on the job and in back of the boys [song-pluggers] every minute."

That spring and summer in California Cole also had his hand in the casting of the national *Kate* company, which began its three-year American tour in Los Angeles on July 11, 1949. He was involved as well with other professional chores. One of them was the MGM film *Adam's Rib*, starring Katharine Hepburn, Spencer Tracy, Judy Holliday, and David Wayne. On being asked to write a tune for the movie, Cole simply dug into his grab bag of previously unpublished numbers and discards and came up with a tune he had written in 1940 while he was on a boat trip to the South Seas. Then the song had been called "So Long, Samoa," and never got very far. Its text for the refrain went this way:

> So long, Samoa,
> Lovely land so sweet, so serene.
> So long, Samoa,
> I've got to go back to the old routine.

But when the next time they tell me,
That my income tax is overdue,
'Stead of cursing F.D.R. as befoa,
Sweet Samoa, I'll return to you.

By essentially keeping the "Samoa" melody intact but completely revising the lyrics (and eliminating the smart-aleck references to F.D.R. and taxes), Cole devised "Farewell, Amanda" with no one the wiser. The new lyrics for the refrain of "Amanda" now were:

Farewell, Amanda,
Adios, Addio, Adieu.
Farewell, Amanda,
It all was great fun but it's done, it's through.
Still now and then, fair Amanda,
When you're stepping on the stars above,
Please recall that wonderful night on the veranda,
Sweet Amanda, and our love.

Despite these revisions "Farewell, Amanda" ultimately got lost within the context of the film and hardly made a dent on the public. Nor did Cole realize any money from the tune, for he gave his share of the profits from it to the Damon Runyon Cancer Fund. But if nothing else, Cole's association with *Adam's Rib* did deepen his friendship with Katharine Hepburn. As he noted in a letter to Linda, "I think the nicest thing that has happened to me this summer has been getting to know Kate much better. She has great quality and I am devoted to her."

Besides his number for *Adam's Rib*, Cole spent time that spring and summer doing preparatory work on the score for his next Broadway musical, initially called *Amphitryon*, which was to be produced by the *Kiss Me, Kate* team of Saint Subber and Lemuel Ayers. Like the Lunt-Fontanne production in 1937 of *Amphitryon 38* (the reason for the number in the title was that French dramatist Jean Giraudoux had whimsically claimed that his adaptation of the Amphitryon legend, upon which the Lunt-Fontanne production was based, was the thirty-eighth such attempt made), Cole's projected musical concerned Jupiter's amorous relationship with a mortal woman, and its consequences.

In addition to the amatory complications in the tale, complications also arose in regard to the basic script for the show. At first the adaptation of the Amphitryon legend into a script for a Broadway musical was left solely in the hands of Dwight Taylor, the author of Cole's 1932 hit, *Gay Divorce*. However, it soon became clear that his adaptation was too literal, for there was not enough comical invention or love interest in it. In an attempt to lighten Taylor's plot, Subber and Ayers then brought in Betty Comden and Adolph Green, the writers of some of the wittiest lyrics, stories, and screenplays for Broadway and Hollywood. Their script was not only lighter than Taylor's, but it also had little relationship to its original Greek source, for instead of emphasizing the affair between a god and a contemporary mortal, the plot had now become a baseball story.

Since that approach was deemed unsuitable, Subber and Ayers now turned for assistance to playwright Reginald Lawrence, perhaps best known for his antiwar play, *If This Be Treason*. Between Lawrence and Dwight Taylor a script was ultimately fashioned that was considered tenable. Nonetheless, so much time had elapsed between the initial impetus for the musical and the completion of a satisfactory script that the production, now called *Out of This World* (its other previous titles, besides *Amphitryon*, were *Heaven on Earth* and *Cloudburst*), was not ready for its Philadelphia tryout until November 4, 1950, some eighteen months after Cole had first started on the score.

Almost as soon as *Out of This World* opened in Philadelphia, it was apparent that the show, directed by Agnes de Mille, was in trouble. As the Philadelphia *Evening Bulletin*'s critic delicately put it, the production was "big, beautiful, opulent; but it must be admitted . . . just a trifle tedious." To speed up the action for Broadway, the producers, in desperation, hired George Abbott and comedy writer F. Hugh Herbert as behind-the-scenes play doctors. Though Agnes de Mille still remained the official director, Abbott and Herbert were pretty much given the freedom to shape the production as they saw fit. As a consequence, they made wholesale revisions both in Philadelphia and during the show's three-week stand in Boston, with complete scenes eliminated and new ones substituted at will. Caught up in the revision frenzy were Cole's tunes; several of them were hastily dropped—among them the now-famous "From This Moment On"—in the interests of a smoother production. In Boston Cole also had to quickly add a number, "I Sleep Easier Now," to conform to spur-of-the-moment changes.

But not all of the revisions imposed on *Out of This World* in Philadelphia and Boston resulted from purely artistic decisions. On opening in Boston the show was notified by Beatrice J. Whelton, a censor in the city's Licensing Division, that certain aspects of the production were considered officially objectionable, including the scanty dress worn onstage by some cast members and a sexually evocative ballet sequence at the end of the first act. As good measure, censor Whelton complained, too, about the irreverent use of the word "god" in the script, as well as such phrases in Cole's songs as "nobody's goosing me" (from "Nobody's Chasing Me") and "quieting all my urgin's for several vestal virgins" (from "They Couldn't Compare to You"). Since Whelton's complaints were tantamount to orders if *Out of This World* was to continue its Boston run, revisions were made at once to comply with her requests—but not before the New York press was alerted to the enforced cutting of "blue" material. Producers Subber and Ayers, through the press, promised New York theatergoers that all the lewd material eliminated in Boston would be restored when the production came to Broadway.

The combination of the Boston censoring and the good showing of another Subber-Ayers-Porter production on Broadway (*Kiss Me, Kate* was still going strong then; but at the Shubert Theater, rather than the New Century) was enough to spur an advance ticket sale of over $500,000. Things looked sufficiently rosy for *Out of This World* that a *Herald Tribune* report on December 17, 1950, indicated that the chances that the show would recoup its budgeted cost of $220,000—unlike what had happened with *Kiss Me, Kate*, angels practically fell over themselves in the rush to invest in *Out of This World*—were reasonably good. Cole, too, spoke up favorably for the production in advance of its premiere. "I'm a pushover for anything that has to do with magic and magician's craft," Cole told Ward Morehouse of the *New York Telegram*, while adding, "That's why I love this new show; there are so many tricks in it."

The tricks Cole referred to were mainly visual, especially the simulation, through imaginative lighting and mechanical contrivances, of Greek gods floating on air. Other striking visual elements were producer Lemuel Ayers's celestial-looking sets and costumes and choreographer Hanya Holm's pseudo-Grecian dances. But the show was also loaded with talented performers, among them comedienne Charlotte Greenwood as Juno, the jealous wife of Jupiter, and big-voiced George Jongeyans as her straying spouse. Standouts, too, were William Redfield in the role of Mercury; David Burns playing an American gangster hiding out in Greece; Priscilla Gillette as the pretty American mortal favored by Jupiter; and William Eythe as her strutting, *macho*, reporter husband, Art O'Malley. Cole's own favorite was the long-legged, high-kicking and angular Charlotte Greenwood, whose numerous film roles had made her internationally known. He had talked her into taking the Juno role on hearing her sing a few of his songs, despite her not having been on Broadway since *Le Maire's Affairs* in 1926.

Evidently Cole was sufficiently optimistic about the chances of *Out of This World* to invite an exceptionally glittering array of guests to the show's Broadway opening at the New Century on December 21, 1950. Joining Cole and Linda at the premiere were the Duke and Duchess of Windsor, Mrs. William Randolph Hearst, the Gilbert Millers, the John Wilsons, Merle Oberon, André Kostelanetz, Lily Pons, and numerous other luminaries.

As he entered the theater with his party, Cole was his usually composed self. Inwardly, however, he may have been suffering from some of the tension that had built up over an incident that had promised to get out of control. For shortly before the premiere of *Out of This World*, Cole learned that leading man William Eythe had been picked up in a subway men's room on charges of committing a sexual act with another man. There was thus the horrible possibility that not only would the news get out—to the detriment of the show—but that Eythe would not be able to perform as scheduled. Fortunately the charges against Eythe were quietly squashed, reportedly through payoffs to the "right" people. And so when the opening-night curtain went up for *Out of This World*, Cole and the entire audience at the New Century saw the production as originally planned, with Eythe portraying the swaggering reporter, Art O'Malley.

The New York reviews of this fanciful blend of Greek mythology and contemporary life were decidedly mixed, ranging from Robert Coleman's unqualified rave in the *Daily Mirror* to carpings in the *Times* and *Herald Tribune*. The *Times* man, Brooks Atkinson, conceded that the production was visually attractive, but thought that the show "looks a lot better than it turns out to be." For Atkinson the striking visual aspects of *Out of This World* were negated by the old-fashioned "sex pranks that used to set the customers to giggling nervously many long years ago." Though conceding that Cole's score contained some fine numbers, Atkinson felt that *Out of This World* did "not get far outside the Broadway library of second-rate operetta routines." Similarly, the *Herald Tribune* critic, Otis Guernsey, complimented the color, glitter, and energy of the show. But he also noted that "there is not so much wit, nor as much melody lurking here as the decor and enthusiasm would pretend." As Guernsey summed it up: " 'Out of This World' does not ascend very far into the empyrean, but the pink clouds and purple passions create a minor diversion."

So effectively did these carping comments dry up interest in *Out of This World* that even with the show's sizable lot of presold tickets, it closed after only 157 performances and lost money for its investors. A few of Cole's songs for the show, however, had a life of their own, particularly the dreamy "Use Your Imagination" and, to a lesser extent, the vivacious "Nobody's Chasing Me" as well as the ballad "I Am Loved." This carryover beyond the show's quick demise was helped to some extent by a recording of numbers from *Out of This World* issued by Columbia Records (OL-4390) in January of 1951. For on the basis of Columbia's success with an original-cast LP album of *Kiss Me, Kate* (thanks to the development of the LP in the forties, record companies were able to release relatively complete scores of a musical on only two sides of a record; *Kiss Me, Kate* was the first LP release of a Broadway musical by Cole), it had arranged to record the score of *Out of This World* as performed by the show's original cast. But the most popular by far of Cole's songs for *Out of This World* was "From This Moment On," which had been dropped from the show before its Broadway opening. The song was published nonetheless and performances of it were heard with increasing frequency. It was subsequently included in the 1953 movie version of *Kiss Me, Kate* and has since gone on to become one of Cole's most popular numbers, with a refrain that begins:

> From this moment on,
> You for me, dear,
> Only two for tea, dear
> From this moment on.
> From this happy day,
> No more blue songs,
> Only whoop-dee-doo songs,
> From this moment on.

In 1951—almost concurrent with the demise of *Out of This World*—a noticeable change occurred in Cole. At a time when the condition of Cole's legs appeared to have stabilized, though he still got about with the aid of braces and a cane, periods of depression and irritability that he had occasionally exhibited before, now seemed to fuse into a relatively consistent personality change. He became obsessively convinced that he had lost his creative flair. Tense and drawn, he suffered from severe headaches and sleepless nights, and would burst into anger with little provocation. Though he was as wealthy as ever, he was now so pessimistic and concerned with loss that he would irrationally claim—despite reassurances from all sides—that he was going broke. Yet he refused to consider psychiatric help for his condition, believing—and in this he was supported by Linda—that such help constituted an invasion of his and, indirectly, Linda's, privacy.

Linda was a tower of strength during these tribulations, notwithstanding her own delicate health. In the hopes of improving his spirits, she and Howard Sturges accompanied Cole to Mexico for several weeks in June of 1951 for a change of scenery. He enjoyed himself sufficiently in Mexico that the following September, at Linda's bidding, Cole, accompanied only by his valet, left by plane for a six-week stay in Paris for another change of scenery. But after only a week or so in France, Cole felt so miserable and depressed that he returned to the States.

On getting back to New York, Cole was quietly placed under medical supervision at Doctors' Hospital, with every precaution taken to keep the news away from the press. Medical tests showed that physically Cole was in relatively good shape, save for an overactive thyroid. In an attempt to alleviate his tremendous depression, he underwent a series of electric-shock treatments. After approximately a month of such therapy, Cole was allowed to leave the hospital for continued medical supervision at home. By the end of February of 1952, except for recurring headaches, which were subsequently diagnosed as being caused by a chronic catarrh condition, for which little could be done, Cole had shown enough improvement to be able to leave for his customary California sojourn.

An important factor in Cole's improvement was the news that producers Cy Feuer and Ernest Martin, the men responsible for bringing *Where's Charley?* and *Guys and Dolls* to Broadway, were interested in having him write the score for a new musical set in Montmartre in the 1890s. Abe Burrows, the director and scriptwriter for the previous two Feuer-Martin hits, was assigned the same tasks for the new show, and he and Cole began collaborating in earnest on the production by the early summer of 1952. The score was slowly beginning to take shape when Cole suddenly received word that his mother had been stricken by a cerebral hemorrhage.

Though Kate was ninety when the stroke occurred, she had been in reasonably good health up to that point; she had even advised Cole not to make too much of his own ailments, for it would only bore people. As had been her custom for many years, she had visited Cole in New York that previous winter and the two had engaged in their usual good-natured bantering. Cole, for example, with tongue-in-cheek deference would often refer to her in public as "The Great Katie," while she would smilingly accuse him of checking up to see how late she got in each evening from her social rounds. After spending enough time in New York seeing friends and catching up on the latest movies and Broadway shows, Kate, as part of the routine, would announce that she had to return to Peru "to do the spring planting." That, of course, meant that she was restless to go back home. Respecting Kate's wishes, Cole would then fondly bid her adieu until her next visit. But the visit of the winter of 1951 was the last.

At the news of his mother's stroke, Cole immediately left for Peru with his valet and Howard Sturges. Linda could not make the trip to Indiana because of illness, but she was kept apprised of Kate's condition. When Cole arrived at the family home in Peru, his beloved mother was in a deep coma and sinking steadily. There was thus little he could do for her except stoically await her death (out of the necessity to keep himself occupied as he sat on the porch of his mother's home waiting for her to die, Cole intermittently worked on his new score for Feuer and Martin). Kate never regained consciousness and died in her bed at Westleigh Farms, in the large house her father had built for her, on the morning of August 3, 1952. After a simple funeral service she was buried in the family plot at Mount Hope Cemetery in Peru, next to her husband, Sam. In death as in life, Cole's interests had remained paramount to her. Except for cash bequests of $12,100 to relatives and friends, Kate left everything she had to Cole, including her beautiful home.

Between Kate's death, Linda's rather persistent illness, and his own physical and mental ups and downs, Cole tried to keep himself occupied professionally and socially. And, in general, he succeeded beautifully, seeming to be the old, dapper Cole, very much involved with life. When his guard was down, however, he would own up to friends that he couldn't help feeling depressed that those dearest to him had either died or were dying. But even in discussing someone as close to him as Linda, Cole could vary between displaying great tenderness and being quite cold-blooded. His softer side appeared in his message to Sara Murphy on February 23, 1953, thanking her for writing to Linda: "You will never know how much good your letter to Linda did. It made her very happy, and she smiled for the first time in so long, and said: 'Look at the wonderful letter I got from Sara.' It was the beginning of her getting better; and last night was the best she has had so far." On the other hand, Cole could be surprisingly testy in speaking of Linda's illness, such as the time he wrote to a friend that Linda was thinking of buying lots of new clothes because she happened to be feeling much better. "This will definitely kill her, but it is a beautiful way to die, I suppose," is the icy way Cole put it. Going on to mention two very social friends of hers—Mrs. Ogden Mills and Mrs. Hamilton Rice—who had died under similar circumstances, Cole then noted somewhat sarcastically, "Perhaps Linda has become socially ambitious."

Socially ambitious or not, Linda was too ill to attend the Broadway premiere of Cole's show for Feuer and Martin. Titled *Can-Can*, its production had been delayed for months, principally because the script for this nostalgic look at Parisian music-hall life before the turn of the century took longer to create than expected. It was not until May 7, 1953, that *Can-Can* opened at New York's Shubert Theater. By that time Linda's health had deteriorated to the point where she seldom went out at night. Seated in her place at the opening, next to Cole, was Mrs. Lytle Hull, an old friend of Linda's. Except for that change, Cole's opening-night routine for *Can-Can* was similar to many of his previous New York premieres. He invited a select group to his Waldorf apartment for a pre-theater snack (the group included his cousin Jules Omar Cole and his wife, as well as close friends Elsa Maxwell, Helen and Lytle Hull, Countess Edith di Zoppola, Millicent Hearst, Duke Fulco di Verdura, and Baron Nicolas de Gunzburg), and then joined them and others for more elaborate festivities after the opening-night curtain had rung down. But if Linda was not with Cole and his party in body that evening, she was at least there in spirit. As was her custom, she saw to it that Cole received a new cigarette case for the opening of the show. This case, which was gold, with a monogram of *Can-Can* superimposed on it, was designed by Duke di Verdura, who created a number of other cases for Cole. It was the last one Linda gave Cole. She died before his next show, *Silk Stockings*, opened.

The book for *Can-Can*, a breezy, lightweight affair, revolved around the attempts of the Parisian constabulary to shut the café operated by La Mome Pistache (Lilo) because of indecent dancing by the young women employed there, particularly one Claudine (Gwen Verdon). But the inconsequential story was so wonderfully embellished by Michael Kidd's exciting choreography (it helped to catapult Gwen Verdon to stardom), Abe Burrows's lively direction, and Cole's highly melodic, Gallic-flavored score that a large public turned out to cheer on *Can-Can* and its Parisian naughtiness. Audience demand for *Can-Can* was such that it was kept on the boards for 892 performances, making it Cole's second-longest-running musical on Broadway (surpassed only by *Kiss Me, Kate*). When shown at London's Coliseum Theatre beginning on October 14, 1954, *Can-Can* added still another 394 performances to its total. Nor did interest in *Can-Can* end there. In 1960, 20th Century-Fox released a successful movie version of *Can-Can* starring Frank Sinatra, Shirley MacLaine, Maurice Chevalier, and Louis Jourdan.

Thanks to the power of recordings (especially the release of an original-cast album of *Can-Can* by Capitol Records in June of 1953) some of Cole's numbers for the show became big hits in a matter of months, despite severe criticism of the entire *Can-Can* score by many powerful press people, not least among them Brooks Atkinson. For Atkinson the score was practically devoid of humor or originality. Yet by the end of 1953 five songs from the show—the rather melancholic "I Love Paris," plus "It's All Right with Me," "C'est Magnifique," "Allez-Vous-En," and "I Am in Love"—were listed by *Variety* as being among the top tunes of the year. As further tribute to the popularity of Cole's numbers for *Can-Can*, the complete vocal score for the show was published, presumably to meet public demand (as was also true for such smashes as *Kiss Me, Kate* and *Anything Goes*).

On the basis of its substantial hit-tune quota and long run, *Can-Can* was unquestionably one of Cole's most winning ventures on Broadway. But at the start of the show's Broadway stand he was quite vexed by the degree of hostility shown by top reviewers. One after another of them suggested that Cole's work had seen much better days. Another sore point resulted from his frustration at not getting any recognition from the French government for his espousal of things Gallic—"I Love Paris" is the most obvious example—in *Can-Can*. As he confided to friends, he was plainly disappointed that the French government completely ignored his paean to France in *Can-Can*, though it had often honored many others for lesser contributions.

Cole had little opportunity to dwell on these frustrations, however, under the pressure of professional commitments that required his attention; among them, another score for Feuer and Martin. Even before *Can-Can* had opened on Broadway, Cole had agreed to do a new score for the show's producers, but the public did not learn any details about the projected musical until July of 1953. While Cole was on the West Coast overseeing the filming of *Kiss Me, Kate* (he left New York for California on May 9, two days after the *Can-Can* premiere; Linda remained in the East because she was not up to making the trip), Lewis Funke reported in the *New York Times* on July 26, 1953, that the new musical would be based on Melchior Lengyel's satire on contemporary Soviet life from which MGM, in 1939, had fashioned *Ninotchka,* a most hilarious and profitable film starring Greta Garbo. In his *Times* report Funke also revealed that George S. Kaufman and his wife, Leueen MacGrath, were adapting the Lengyel satire for Feuer and Martin in expectation of a spring opening in 1954.

Cole, then, in 1953, at the age of sixty-two, was still going strong. He had been able to weather the death of his mother, Linda's prolonged illness, and his own physical and psychological problems without being overwhelmed in the process (would one expect Kate's son and Linda's husband to react any differently?). Cole had the admiration of those who knew him well for his spunk and drive under very difficult circumstances. But few outside his immediate circle were aware of the ramifications involved. Cole himself preferred it that way.

23

Amputee

As Linda's health deteriorated, few traces of her former beauty remained; occasionally her mind would wander, as well. Bent over and somewhat hunchbacked now as a result of age and infirmity, Linda seemed to be barely hanging onto life. As an additional complication she developed emphysema, which often made breathing extremely difficult for her. To facilitate the intake of oxygen into her lungs, shortly before her death Linda's bedroom at the Waldorf was practically turned into one big oxygen tent. But even under these conditions she and Cole would lunch together at the Waldorf whenever she felt up to it—through long habit it had become a kind of ritual for them. The two had had separate but adjacent apartments on the forty-first floor of the Waldorf for many years. During this final period in Linda's life, these lunches together gave them a chance to affirm their warm regard for each other while also exchanging the latest gossip, which they both loved to do.

Linda died on May 20, 1954; she was not quite seventy-one. At the end she was completely bedridden and in such great agony because of breathing difficulty that she welcomed death. Cole, of course, was by her side when the end came. He was in California on business when he learned that she had taken a turn for the worse, and immediately flew back to be with her. In compliance with Linda's wishes, Cole saw to it that brief services for her were held on May 22 at St. Bartholomew's, near the Waldorf, as she had requested. Her body was then taken to Peru for burial in the Porter family plot at Mount Hope cemetery. As a memorial gesture for Linda, Cole got horticulturists to develop an especially large pink rose in her name. This exquisite "Linda Porter rose," for which Cole obtained a patent, was a wholly fitting memorial for one who had always loved flowers, particularly roses. As a matter of fact, some of Linda's friends had frequently joked that she was the only woman they knew who could hold two dozen extremely long-stemmed roses in her arms as though it were the easiest and most natural thing to do. Another description of Linda commonly made by her friends was that she had never opened a door in her life; presumably, in her imperious way, she had always gotten men to do it for her.

Linda had hoped to leave Cole an even two million dollars when she died. Though she made a concerted effort toward that end by economizing as much as possible shortly before her death, she didn't quite reach the figure she had aimed for. Her gross estate, all left to Cole, was assessed at $1,939,671 (undoubtedly this assessment was on the low side for income-tax purposes). Linda's legacy to Cole included two homes—the Buxton Hill property and the Paris house at 13 rue Monsieur—in addition to all her exquisite furniture, thousands of books, jewelry, works of art, and other valuables.

Besides this substantial legacy, Linda left her imprint on Cole in at least one other tangible way. Not long before she died Linda had met decorator Billy Baldwin, through Howard Sturges. She was so impressed with Baldwin's talents that she strongly urged Cole to consider moving to a new and larger apartment at the Waldorf—both she and Cole had often felt he could use more space there—and to have Baldwin decorate it. Since Linda in the past had invariably had the final say on how their homes were decorated (Cole freely admitted that he always deferred to her in such matters, for her decorative sense was infinitely stronger than his), it was perhaps inevitable that her suggestion would ultimately be carried out.

In the fall of 1954, some six months after Linda's death, Baldwin recalls that he received a call from Cole requesting him to decorate his new nine-room bachelor apartment on the thirty-third floor of the Waldorf. On meeting with Cole to discuss the assignment, Baldwin was asked to draw on Linda's superb collection of antique French furniture, most of which she had had shipped to the United States in 1937 from 13 rue Monsieur because of threatening war conditions, for installation in the new apartment. With only minor exceptions, Baldwin was given carte blanche. "Don't forget, I'm Broadway," was Cole's first admonition to him. Secondly, Cole asked that his bed be huge and colored a bright, fire-engine red. Cole insisted, too, that there not be any bells in the apartment; instead, bulbs were used—blue for the telephone, white for the back door, and red for the front entrance. Also, since Cole was left-handed, he wanted all the major mechanical appurtenances like the high-fidelity and air-conditioning systems to be operated from switches to the left of his favorite chairs.

Closely adhering to Cole's wishes but freely adding his own decorative flair, Baldwin worked on the apartment for nearly four months, from mid-February to early June of 1955, while Cole was visiting Switzerland, Italy, Monaco, Spain, Portugal, France, and Greece. When Cole returned home on June 7, 1955, he was amazed. The subtly underplayed decorative touches in Cole's previous Waldorf apartment had now been changed to Baldwin's more outgoing ones, which ingeniously combined rare French furniture and parquetry with English heirlooms, valuable Chinese art, and contemporary accouterments into a dramatic blend of color, design, and functionalism. Room after room reflected this bold transformation. The foyer was completely mirrored except for the black-and-beige marble floor; the lavish study had tortoiseshell leather walls and shiny tubular brass bookshelves, upon which reposed Linda's—and now Cole's—vast collection of books, and so on. So spectacular were the results that *Vogue* gave prominent attention to the apartment and Baldwin's role in decorating it in its November, 1955 issue. Soon other publications followed suit. Baldwin, as a matter of fact, is quick to concede that he not only got his greatest share of publicity from decorating Cole's apartment, but that it was his most pleasurable and challenging assignment as well. As a further bonus, Cole commissioned Baldwin to redecorate Buxton Hill. Baldwin completed the job in 1957, once Linda's big house on the property had been razed and Cole's cottage, with a wing added, placed on its site.

Prior to Cole's 1955 European sojourn during the period his Waldorf apartment was being decorated, he was very much involved with his second musical for Feuer and Martin. *Silk Stockings* went into rehearsal on October 18, 1954—approximately six months later than had originally been planned—and began its out-of-town tryouts in Philadelphia on November 26. A week before that opening date Cole arrived at Philadelphia's Hotel Barclay with his valet, chauffeur, Howard Sturges, and the slew of supplies that he invariably brought with him for such out-of-town tryouts. Besides a long list of drug items (including suppositories, assorted pills, and six large bottles of witch hazel for dabbing the skin around his eyes every morning), songwriting necessities (such as music manuscript paper, a writing board, and dozens of pencils), and hordes of miscellaneous items (like a portable urinal, a pepper mill, two cocktail shakers, a New York telephone directory, and a number of cooking utensils), Cole also brought a variety of art objects for sprucing up his hotel suite (among them two drawings by Lyonel Feininger and a small painting by Grandma Moses). As an adjunct to the musical items he took along to Philadelphia, Cole also requested that the hotel management supply him with a Steinway baby grand for his work.

Cole particularly had need of the piano during his Philadelphia stay, for the play and its score underwent many revisions. Though the Philadelphia critics took kindly to *Silk Stockings*, Feuer and Martin were convinced that the show was a dud as it stood, mainly because of its book and direction. Both of these responsibilities were being handled by the celebrated George S. Kaufman (he shared the scriptwriting chores with his wife, Leueen MacGrath, but was the sole director), yet Feuer and Martin felt that the show was not snappy enough for Broadway. The two producers, who were tough and hard, worked in tandem, with the short and aggressive Feuer perfectly complemented by the tall and superficially more amiable Martin. They kept exhorting Kaufman to add more and more gags and stage business to the show until finally, his patience and strength exhausted, Kaufman and his wife bowed out of the production. As their replacements, Feuer and Martin had Abe Burrows handle the book revisions while Feuer himself took over the direction. Fortunately, by the time *Silk Stockings* opened at the Imperial Theater in New York on February 24, 1955, the production had had enough of a shakedown out of town (besides Philadelphia, the show also played in Boston and Detroit) to smooth out many of its rough edges. As Walter Kerr stated in reviewing the Broadway premiere, the show was "the end-product of a fabulous out-of-town sortie in which the authors were changed, the choreographers were changed, and the changes were changed. What has been wrought in all this travail? Well, not a miracle, certainly. But not precisely a clambake, either."

The overall plot for *Silk Stockings* closely resembled the one for MGM's *Ninotchka*. In the role that Greta Garbo made famous, Feuer and Martin cast the German star Hildegarde Neff (originally spelled "Knef," her last name was simplified for American audiences) as the Russian commissar with the heart of stone who is sent to Paris to see for herself why a famous U.S.S.R. composer has not returned to his homeland. While in Paris the commissar gradually loses her icy facade as she becomes romantically attached to a fast-talking American actors' agent (Don Ameche), and he to her, despite their different political ideologies. For besides its basic theme of international romance, *Silk Stockings* poked fun at many of the clichés and foibles associated with Communist and Capitalist dogmas. Unlike the gossamer touch of film director Ernst Lubitsch in *Ninotchka*, however, Feuer and Martin's attempts at high humor were often bogged down by overly predictable Capitalism-versus-Communism platitudes and heavy-handed bits of stage business. But as John Chapman commented in his review, "whenever the plot shows the merest sign of taking over more than its share, Cole Porter shoulders it aside with some of his best melodies, lyrics, and rhythms."

Even if one concedes that Chapman's praise of Cole was excessively generous, there is still no question about the fact that Cole's score played a large part in keeping *Silk Stockings* running on Broadway for 478 performances and in helping to recoup the immense production expenses for the show (brought in at a cost of $370,000, *Silk Stockings* was considered one of Broadway's most expensive musicals for its time). Cole's score, too, was a stimulus for RCA Victor to issue an original-cast album (LOC-1016) of the production in March of 1955 and for MGM to buy the show's film rights. The movie, with Fred Astaire and Cyd Charisse in the leads, was released by MGM in July of 1957 and, like the stage production, did very well. The big hit for Cole in both the stage and movie versions was clearly "All of You," in which the hero suggests a geographic exploration of Ninotchka, with these lines in the song's refrain:

> I love the looks of you, the lure of you,
> I'd love to make a tour of you,
> The eyes, the arms, the mouth of you,
> The East, West, North, and the South of you.

But other numbers in *Silk Stockings* also made an impact, among them the lugubrious-sounding title tune as well as "Paris Loves Lovers," a duet for the two romantic leads in which the hero plays up Paris's charms while Ninotchka denigrates them with such Red-inspired words as "capitalistic," "imperialistic," and "militaristic." "Siberia," too, came off effectively (with three Communist agents humorously describing Siberia's good points: no unemployment, plenty of ice for cocktails, loads of salt for beer), as did "Stereophonic Sound" (a takeoff on the many novel technical devices like cinemascope and stereophonic sound that have been introduced into films as a means of attracting paying customers). The sum total of all of Cole's numbers for *Silk Stockings* added up to a good —if not prime—Porter score; one that he could certainly be pleased with.

Cole did not attend the Broadway opening of *Silk Stockings* on February 24, 1955, for he had left five days earlier for his European jaunt. But even without being present at the show's premiere, Cole received his usual opening-night cigarette case. For in commemoration of the show's premiere and as a memorial gesture for Linda, Cole's and Linda's close friends Howard Sturges, Baron de Gunzburg, Duke di Verdura, Jean Howard (the former wife of Charles Feldman, a famous Hollywood agent), and Natasha Wilson presented him with a handsome gold case adorned with two Russian gold coins (in keeping with the Russian theme of *Silk Stockings*). Inasmuch as *Silk Stockings* turned out to be Cole's final Broadway show, this gift ultimately took on extra significance, especially since Cole added only one more cigarette case to this special collection.

The last cigarette case in Cole's collection was one that he had made up for himself, using diamonds from a brooch of Linda's, to commemorate the 1956 release of his film *High Society*. Though it was released in August of 1956, most of Cole's work on *High Society* was completed in Hollywood during the summer and fall of 1955, not long after he had returned to the States from his European trip. Before leaving for California that summer, on June 12 Cole participated in commencement ceremonies at Williams College in Williamstown, where he was given an honorary doctorate. Whether this honorary degree was precipitated by Cole's decision to give his entire Buxton Hill property to the school after his death is not clear. What is clear is that no matter what helped trigger the honor, Cole was eminently worthy of it. As President James P. Baxter III of Williams College put it in conferring the degree on Cole, "In the words of one of your own songs, *You're the Top.*" At any rate, along with all the other songwriting credentials that he brought to *High Society*, he now had an extra something that few of his confreres could match: a doctorate. Nor did it stop there. By January of 1956, while writing to his agent, Irving Lazar, about *High Society* matters, Cole was able to reveal that "there is a possibility that Yale will give me an honorary degree this summer." The Yale degree, however, was not conferred on him until several years later, on June 9, 1960, Cole's sixty-ninth birthday.

In signing to do the *High Society* score for MGM, Cole knew that the film would be a musical treatment of *The Philadelphia Story*, the highly successful Philip Barry play originally written for Katharine Hepburn and the Theatre Guild. Katharine Hepburn had been especially careful in choosing *The Philadelphia Story* as a Broadway stage vehicle, for she had been practically hooted off the boards some years earlier in *The Lake*, a 1933 fiasco that prompted Dorothy Parker to remark that Miss Hepburn's emotions ran the gamut from A to B. After a long out-of-town tryout *The Philadelphia Story* opened in New York under the Guild's sponsorship on March 28, 1939, to ecstatic reviews. The play, a fluffy comedy of manners, was a personal triumph for Katharine Hepburn, and she repeated that success in a 1940 movie version of it. Both the play and the movie emphasized a lot of sophisticated banter about divorce, the special qualities of champagne, swimming in the nude, and the like among Philadelphia's smart set. *High Society*, too, emphasized gloss over content, but changed the locale from Philadelphia to Newport.

Somewhat changed, too, was the portrayal of the leading character, the well-heeled and sumptuously gowned Tracy Lord. Instead of auburn-haired Katharine Hepburn's rather biting conception of a divorcée about to remarry, Tracy Lord was now more languidly played by golden-hued Grace Kelly. Carrying the musical brunt of the film were such stalwarts as Bing Crosby (in the role of Tracy's former happy-go-lucky sportsman husband, C. K. Dexter-Haven, who ultimately wins her back), Frank Sinatra (as reporter Mike Connor), Celeste Holm (Connor's female side-kick, Liz Imbrie), and Louis Armstrong (playing himself). Though not known for her vocal ability, Grace Kelly did a highly respectable job singing the nostalgic "True Love," aided by Bing Crosby. The song was the hit of the film and one of Max Dreyfus's all-time favorites. Dreyfus expressed his admiration for this number in a letter he wrote to Cole dated November 12, 1956, after the song had become a smash. "In all my sixty-odd years of music publishing," began Dreyfus, "nothing has given me more personal pleasure and gratification than the extraordinary success of your 'TRUE LOVE.' It is truly a simple, beautiful, tasteful composition worthy of a Franz Schubert." Dreyfus then added this warm, personal note: "This also gives me a chance to tell you something that you must have known—that I have loved my association with you through all these years."

Among Cole's other songs for *High Society* that effectively stood out and helped to make the film a big moneymaker were "You're Sensational," "I Love You, Samantha," and "Well, Did You Evah!" that caustic commentary on the social scene first heard in *DuBarry Was a Lady*. Save for minor textual changes, "Well, Did You Evah!" closely resembled the 1939 version, with its ludicrous references to characters like Mimmsie Starr (who "just got pinched in the Astor Bar") and Professor Munch (who "ate his wife and divorced his lunch"). And it was just such zany commentary that got MGM to contact Cole's lawyer, Robert H. Montgomery, to worriedly inquire whether clearances were needed from the people mentioned before the song could be used in the film. Only when Cole assured MGM that those referred to in "Well, Did You Evah!" were fictional characters did the studio relax enough to feature the number—brilliantly performed by Bing Crosby and Frank Sinatra—on the screen.

While he was still busy with production details for *High Society*, Cole learned in October of 1955 that Howard Sturges had died suddenly in Paris. Sturges had apparently been in fine health when, without warning, he suffered a fatal heart attack at the breakfast table. With Kate and Linda now gone, Sturges's death meant that still another of Cole's important ties with life had been severed, and he was greatly saddened by the news. But even with this loss, Cole was able to laugh at an incident connected with his dear friend's demise. Sturges, an inveterate traveler like Cole, had often chafed at the delays he encountered with American Customs agents. Cole was amused to learn that Sturges, ironically, was delayed by Customs after death as he had often been in life. It seems that Sturges's body had been cremated in France and his ashes brought back to the States. Mysteriously, however, the ashes were misplaced by Customs. Just when it appeared that the final remains of Sturges were lost forever, they turned up just as mysteriously as they had vanished.

As one means of countering the bad news about Sturges, Cole saw to it that there was no letup in his busy schedule. After spending some time in Peru, New York, and Buxton Hill during the fall and winter of 1955–56, Cole took off in mid-February of 1956 for Europe and the Near East, including a cruise of the Greek islands aboard the yacht *Eros*, belonging to Stavros Niarchos, the Greek shipping magnate. Cole had also been a guest on *Eros* the previous year, and as a way of showing his gratitude for such hospitality he contributed ten thousand dollars to the Greek Archdiocese of North and South America, one of Niarchos's favorite charities. Barely had Cole gotten back to New York in early June of 1956 before he was on his way to California to do two films for MGM: *Silk Stockings* and *Les Girls*. Of the two, *Silk Stockings* required practically no effort on Cole's part, for with the exception of two new numbers—"Fated to Be Mated" and "Ritz Roll and Rock," neither of which made much of a splash—the score consisted of tunes Cole had previously written for the stage version. *Les Girls* was another matter. Cole started from scratch on this score and came up with over a dozen songs, five of which were used in the film; one of them, "Ça, C'est l'Amour," quickly caught on.

The plot for *Les Girls* by John Patrick (he also did the screenplay for *High Society*) was a sprightly trifle about the shenanigans of a singing-dancing troupe consisting of Gene Kelly, Mitzi Gaynor, Kay Kendall, and Taina Elg. Years after the troupe had disbanded, its members are brought together in court because of a libel suit over the memoirs by one of their number, now Lady Wren (Kay Kendall). Through a series of flashbacks in which conflicting testimony is given about the troupe's early days, the story of *Les Girls*, directed by George Cukor, unfolds with great wit and style. So wonderfully integrated were the various elements of music, dance, and plot that it was inevitable that the film would do well with reviewers and the public. *Les Girls* has also had remarkable lasting power. To this day most viewers agree that it is one of the most delightful treats turned out by Hollywood.

On returning East after a summer and fall in California readying the scores for *Silk Stockings* and *Les Girls*, Cole began to experience occasional sharp stomach pains. At the end of December, 1956, he entered Columbia–Presbyterian Hospital for a complete checkup under the supervision of Dr. Dana W. Atchley, one of the hospital's leading physicians. Examination showed that Cole, probably as one of the consequences of his extensive drinking over a long period, had developed a large stomach ulcer, approximately two centimeters in size, that penetrated to his pancreas. There was considerable inflammation around the ulcerous tissue, though examination revealed no sign of cancer. On January 8, 1957, Dr. Milton Porter (no relation to Cole) corrected the condition through surgery, and two weeks later Cole was discharged from the hospital. He then left for Montego Bay in the West Indies for a brief recuperative stay.

Cole seemed to be his old self again on resuming his usual activities in New York, including frequent weekends at Williamstown with close friends. In April Cole also went to Italy for a month, prior to heading for California, where he worked that summer on the score for a television special: a musical adaptation of *Aladdin*, set in China, with a script by S. J. Perelman.

Before actually tackling the score, Cole, as was his custom, did a lot of preparatory work to familiarize himself with the people, customs, and topography of China of an earlier era. And Cole's songs for *Aladdin*—especially their lyrics—reflected that meticulous attention to detail. But unfortunately there was little else—like memorable melodies—to commend the score, or the production itself. Despite the efforts of Cole and an exceptional cast, with such famous names in it as Cyril Ritchard, Dennis King, Basil Rathbone, and Una Merkel, *Aladdin* was a flop when it was shown on CBS on February 21, 1958, as part of DuPont's "Show of the Month" series. Nor did a live version of *Aladdin* presented in London the following year do any better. For, both live and televised, *Aladdin* was noticeably lacking in those special magical qualities that are part of its story.

Cole never wrote anything else after *Aladdin*. It is indeed ironic that someone who had contributed so many musical hits to the world should end his songwriting career on such a dismal note. But Cole was so overwhelmed by the turn his life now took that he lost interest in writing songs. For on January 14, 1958, approximately a month before *Aladdin* received its television premiere, Cole was once again admitted to Columbia–Presbyterian Hospital. He was extremely nervous and tense, and very much bothered by his right leg as well as by intermittent stomach pains. Examination revealed that the upper part of his intestine, at the duodenum, was ulcerated and that he was suffering from chronic osteomyelitis (a bone inflammation) of the right upper tibia. The right leg, too, was badly ulcerated, with the foul smell of rotting flesh emanating from it.

Cole's intestinal ulcer responded to treatment, but his right leg, which was too far gone by then, did not. Out of fear that Cole's entire system would be contaminated by the degenerating limb, it was decided to amputate it. On April 3, 1958, orthopedic specialist Dr. F. M. Smith, assisted by Dr. Frank Stinchfield, successfully performed the operation, removing the leg close to the hip. That May Cole was able to leave the hospital, but as an amputee. After years of valiantly fighting to save the leg, the battle had now been lost. It was such a tremendous blow to Cole that he never got over it.

24

Journey Home

When Cole had healed sufficiently he was fitted with an artificial leg and instructed in its use at the Institute for the Crippled and Disabled on East Twenty-fourth Street in Manhattan. Gradually his walking ability improved, though he often claimed that he found the artificial limb heavy, cumbersome, and uncomfortable. In addition to the difficulties involved in learning to walk smoothly, Cole experienced phantom pains for many months, mainly aching and itching, where his right leg had previously been. But perhaps the most pressing problem for Cole was in adjusting to what he considered the horrible maiming of his body. For one who had always taken pride in his appearance, it was difficult for him to adapt to the small stump that remained where his right leg had been. Perhaps if Kate and Linda were still around to see him through this difficult period —as they had been after his accident in 1937—Cole might have been able to make a better adjustment. Despite all the attention and sympathy he received from close friends and devoted employees like Madeline P. Smith, his secretary since 1947, or Paul Sylvain, his long-time valet, Cole could never really accept the amputation. Again and again in his despondent moments Cole would bemoan, "I'm only half a man now."

As one of the consequences of this inability to cope, Cole's health began to decline steadily, particularly since he now lost interest in food. Where previously Cole had normally enjoyed eating—chile and other heavily spiced foods were favorites of his—he now usually nibbled at the things put before him and often substituted liquor for food. This, combined with his persistently heavy smoking, had a decidedly deleterious effect on his health. It is not surprising, then, that between the time of the amputation in 1958 and his death in 1964, practically no year went by without him being hospitalized for one reason or another. While in California in the summer of 1959, for example, Cole had to be treated for a kidney obstruction. The following year, on November 26, 1960, Cole was admitted to Columbia–Presbyterian Hospital desperately ill with pneumonia (hospital records show that his lungs were in very bad shape) and suffering also from malnutrition and depression. It was not until July 4, 1961, more than seven months later, that Cole was considered fit enough to be discharged. Cole was hospitalized again from April to August of 1963 for burns that resulted from falling asleep while smoking. Usually Cole's valet would be standing by when he was smoking in bed to prevent such a calamity; in this instance a temporary valet had not taken that precaution. A year or so later, in a state of depression, Cole returned to Columbia–Presbyterian because of a bladder infection, severe anemia (due to substituting alcohol for food), and an impacted fracture of the right hip that was sustained by a fall three days earlier, on his birthday. After a fifteen-day stay at the hospital, from June 12 to June 27, 1964, Cole was released. By the following September 22, however, while in California, Cole was hospitalized once more: at St. John's Hospital in Santa Monica. He had originally gone into St. John's for treatment of a minor case of hemorrhoids. But in the hospital he developed a bladder infection and pneumonia. On October 13 he was operated upon for removal of a kidney stone. Two days later he was dead. An autopsy report by Cole's attending physician, Dr. William Weber Smith, to Cole's cousin, Jules Omar Cole, disclosed the following:

> Our gross examination revealed chronic nephrosclerosis (degeneration of the kidneys, due to hardening of the arteries). His tissue in general showed some evidence of heart weakness and heart failure. There was rather far advanced arteriosclerosis.
>
> I feel his cause of death was the severe bronchopneumonia in his chest. He suffered from a chronic over-expansion of the lungs, called emphysema, which would make it very difficult to overcome infections, in spite of antibiotics and other aids.

In the six years between the amputation of his leg and his death, Cole, when not hospitalized or otherwise incapacitated, tried to maintain some semblance of the life-style he had long followed. He would thus alternate during each year between living on the East and West coasts and frequently giving small, elegant dinner parties for his old friends. Even though he no longer wrote songs (or even played the piano), he still kept abreast of professional matters that concerned him, including 20th Century-Fox's movie of *Can-Can* released in 1960. In connection with that film Cole gave his approval for the inclusion of an "Adam and Eve" ballet sequence based on his famous "I Love Paris" tune. In 1960, too, Cole gave his blessings to a gala in his honor titled "Salute to Cole Porter" held at the Metropolitan Opera House on May 15 for the benefit of the Children's Asthma Research Institute (Cole did not attend, but the affair, with stars like Beatrice Lillie, Celeste Holm, Lilo, William Gaxton, and Lisa Kirk participating, did well enough to gross sixty-five thousand dollars for the charity).

Several weeks after the Metropolitan gala, Yale University awarded Cole an honorary doctorate. Inasmuch as Cole had hoped to receive this degree as far back as 1956, it is obvious that the groundwork for the honor had been prepared long in advance. There may have been a tie-in between the degree and Cole's decision to leave all his original manuscripts and other memorabilia to the university after his death. At any rate, on Cole's birthday—June 9—university officials converged on Cole's Waldorf apartment to award him the degree of Doctor of Humane Studies. The ceremony was held at the Waldorf to spare Cole the trip to New Haven for the regular commencement ceremonies a few days later. As Cole sat on a large sofa in his study, very properly dressed in an academic robe, Provost Norman S. Buck of Yale, also robed, hung a blue velvet hood on Cole and read this citation conferring the degree on him:

> As an undergraduate, you first won acclaim for writing the words and music of two of Yale's perennial football songs. Since then, you have achieved [a] reputation as a towering figure in the American musical theater. Master of the deft phrase, the delectable rhyme, the distinctive melody, you are, in your own words and your own field, the top.
>
> Confident that your graceful, impudent, inimitable songs will be played and sung as long as footlights burn and curtains go up, your Alma Mater confers upon you the degree of Doctor of Humane Letters.

Just as the conferring of this degree coincided with Cole's birthday, another milestone in Cole's life was celebrated on that date two years later. The media gave much attention to the festivities that took place on June 9, 1962, at the off-Broadway Orpheum Theater on lower Second Avenue, where a revival of *Anything Goes* was then playing. With Elsa Maxwell serving as hostess for the occasion, some three hundred invited guests—among them many show-business personalities like Zsa Zsa Gabor, Margaret O'Brien, Lillian Roth, Red Buttons, Faye Emerson, Carol Bruce, Dolores Gray, and Kaye Ballard—showed up for a special midnight performance of *Anything Goes* and to wish Cole well on his seventieth birthday. "This will be a real shot in the arm for Cole," Elsa Maxwell announced from the stage to the assemblage, who then toasted Cole with champagne and sang "Happy Birthday" in his honor. Cole himself did not attend the festivities; he remained instead at Williamstown. But he was undoubtedly pleased by the sentiments expressed and by the vast coverage the event got in the press (paper after paper headlined the event). He also must have been amused that his seventieth birthday was celebrated a year later than it should have been and that evidently no one—including his good friend Elsa Maxwell—knew the difference.

The vanity implicit in Cole not owning up to his right age at that late point in his life also helps to explain why he absented himself from the "seventieth" birthday party in his honor at the Orpheum and the earlier "Salute to Cole Porter" gala at the Metropolitan. Though he was physically up to attending both celebrations, he did not, presumably because he felt an artificial leg reflected on and diminished his public image. Cole's vanity also comes through in this final period in such personal matters as the regular dyeing of his hair (actually, he had little hair left to dye, for by the last decade of his life his hair had thinned out considerably in front and he was quite bald in the back) and in the retention of a year-round tan, frequently with the aid of a sunlamp. But besides being manifestations of Cole's vanity, these cosmetic concerns also reflected his desire to maintain a fairly steady routine. Cole had always abhorred boredom and had organized his time so as to keep himself busy both at work and at play. Now, even though he no longer worked at creating songs and his leisure activities were limited by his health and sensitivity over the amputation of his right leg, he still held to a prescribed routine, including hair-dyeing and suntanning, as a means of avoiding boredom.

Cole's valet for most of the final period of his life was Henry Burke, an Englishman. He shared the duties of looking after Cole with another

Englishman, Eric Lindsay, and was hired after Cole's faithful valet, Paul Sylvain, died in July of 1959 (in appreciation of Sylvain's long and zealous service, Cole subsequently set up a seventy-five-thousand-dollar trust fund in his will to assist Sylvain's two young daughters). Burke was not only a devotee of the theater who could discuss it knowledgeably with Cole; he was also talkative and amusing (Cole especially liked Burke's takeoff on Eleanor Roosevelt; in an approximation of her breaking voice and awkward mannerisms, Burke would espouse a variety of outlandish "liberal" causes considerably to the left of Cole's rather conservative political leanings, among them a law requiring all blacks and whites to sleep together). As Cole's personal valet, Burke attended Cole daily and was privy to the most intimate details of his regular routine. On the basis of information supplied by Burke, it is possible to reconstruct Cole's general daily routine, from the time he got up in the morning until he went to bed.

Cole would arise at eleven A.M. (he would usually get to bed at three or four A.M.) and ring for Burke, who would bring him cold witch hazel and cotton swabs. The first thing Cole did was apply witch hazel around his eyes in the belief that it kept the skin there taut and minimized telltale crow's feet. Once this was done, Cole would flash his brightest smile.

Cole would then be given a suppository, which he inserted himself, and would also utilize his portable urinal, which he kept close to his bed.

Breakfast in bed—which consisted only of a cup of tea—would follow.

Cole would now be lifted on a wheelchair and brought to the bathroom sink to wash his face and clean his teeth (as previously noted, Cole gave up cleaning his teeth during the last year of his life). When Burke first started working for Cole he would leave him alone in the bathroom so that he might have more privacy. But after Cole fell while washing—his short stump made it difficult for him to balance himself, even when seated—and almost cracked his skull, Burke made a point of being present for all of Cole's bathroom needs, including his bowel functions, which followed immediately after the face-washing and teeth-cleaning rituals.

Cole would next be taken by wheelchair to the shower and lifted onto a special seat in the shower stall which enabled him to wash himself.

On being dried, Cole would be dressed in a white cotton bathrobe (the only kind of bathrobe he ever wore) in preparation for exercise and massage. In California a masseur would handle these activities out in the open, next to the pool. At Cole's Waldorf apartment, however, the exercise and massage were done in Cole's bedroom and the door was always closed. The New York masseur, a personal friend of Cole's, was often referred to as "the pervert" by Cole's other employees, who felt that there was a physical relationship between the two (rumor had it that the masseur could sustain an erection almost indefinitely). That belief was supported when word got out that Cole, in addition to paying the masseur a handsome annual salary for almost no work at all, also rewarded him with substantial bonuses of money and gifts, including a car. From time to time Cole would complain that the masseur "was acting up again"; presumably meaning that he wanted extra money or a special gift. Yet if for any reason the masseur did not show up as scheduled, Cole would go into a deep melancholy.

After exercise and massage it would now be about one P.M. Cole would then be attended by a barber, who took care of cutting and dyeing his hair and applying a sunlamp to his entire body (in California Cole would usually be outside sunning himself at this point; his barber would come in the evening, shortly before dinner, instead).

At one thirty P.M. it was time for lunch. Cole would be joined for lunch by his secretary, Madeline Smith, so that they could discuss his correspondence and diverse business matters. Cole would invariably nibble at his food, but he would always have something to drink. Initially, Cole drank only Scotch. But then Burke devised the ruse of telling Cole that doctors preferred that he drink gin or vodka, the idea being that the liquor content could be diluted with tomato juice if Cole were served Bloody Marys. The ruse helped to cut down Cole's intake of Scotch at lunch, though he would often insist on drinking it at other times.

At three P.M. Cole returned to his bedroom to rest.

He would be awakened at four thirty P.M. Cole's artificial leg would now be put on him and he would be dressed for going out. He would then be driven to the Institute for the Crippled and Disabled for what was supposed to be physical therapy (on the West Coast, except for the last year of his life, Cole followed a similar routine). Cole actually spent little time in physical therapy, for he would invariably find some excuse to sit down, smoke, and carry on small talk with the hospital staff. Cole, however, went through the charade of participating in physical therapy because it was part of his daily regimen, and it gave him something to do in the late afternoon.

By six P.M. Cole would be back home. He would soon resume drinking and also look at the evening newspaper (sometimes, from all the drinks, Cole would conk out while reading the paper). There would now also be a regular ritual in connection with the feeding of Pepi (full name: Pépin le Bref), Cole's small black dog; Merle Oberon had given him this pedigreed schipperke as a gift years earlier. In the dog-feeding ritual, Pepi's food would be placed in his dish and brought to where Cole was; Pepi, of course, would be close behind the dish. The food would be held away .from Pepi until he barked three times. That was the signal to give him his food. (Pepi died in May of 1963 at a relatively ripe old age.)

At seven P.M. Cole would be brought back to his bedroom, undressed, and his leg taken off so that he could rest.

Cole would be awakened at eight P.M. and his leg put on again. He would then be dressed for dinner, the inevitable carnation inserted in his lapel, and brought to the living room. He would be placed on a deep couch there, with his legs propped on it, to await his dinner guests, who would usually arrive at eight thirty (his guests were invariably old friends: socialites, famous show-business personalities, and so on). When things went smoothly these dinners were very attractive affairs. Cole would be a charming host who superbly complemented the excellent food (in New York the meals were prepared by the Waldorf staff), the fine company, and the sophisticated banter. But often Cole would be less than charming because of excessive drinking. For though Cole hardly ate anything during the meal, he still joined his guests in drinking the wine served with the food. This, combined with the liquor consumed before dinner and Cole's general physical deterioration, caused inebriation. Moreover, as one of the consequences of all this drinking, Cole would have to urinate fairly frequently. Rather than be taken to the bathroom, his guests would be asked to leave the room while his portable urinal was brought to him. To complicate matters further at these affairs, Cole sometimes wet his clothes before his urinal was brought to him. Out of their love and deep respect for Cole, his guests, of course, made little of these incidents, though they no doubt registered deeply with them. These incidents unquestionably also had their effect on Cole and added to his misery over the amputation.

Cole's dinner guests would leave around midnight. He would then watch a late show on television, while continuing his drinking. By three or four A.M. Cole would be ready for bed and would ask for a sleeping pill. Sometimes he would ask for a second pill, but Burke always refused that request out of fear of mixing too many sleeping pills with all the liquor and wine Cole had consumed.

This daily routine was essentially the one Cole followed both in New York and California. When he was in Williamstown on weekends, however, his schedule was somewhat more leisurely and flexible, mainly because there were fewer social and professional demands made on him

there. Another difference between Buxton Hill and Cole
dences was that at Williamstown he would usually be join
for the entire weekend, rather than simply for dinner. B
amputation his friends had always looked forward to join
these weekends in Massachusetts. That attitude changed in Cole's final
years because of his boorish behavior. Almost from the moment Cole and
his guests left New York for Williamstown he would usually be drunk,
and would remain that way practically all weekend. Whereas meals at
Williamstown had previously been served on schedule, they were now
frequently served hours late because Cole's drunkenness prevented him
from joining his guests on time. Between drunkenness and periods of
long, morbid silences when he completely ignored his guests, Cole was
hardly a gracious host. After a weekend spent in this Williamstown
"torture chamber," many of Cole's guests would somehow find an excuse
for not accepting another invitation.

Guest attrition became so bad that Burke recalls one occasion when
Cole could get no friends to join him for a weekend at Buxton Hill. Cole
then designated Burke as his weekend guest. On the way to Williamstown Burke sat in the back of the car with Cole instead of sitting up front,
as he normally would, with the chauffeur and Cole's dog, Pepi. But
Burke's status as guest did not remain that for long. Once at Williamstown Burke assumed the uneasy dual roles of employee and guest. Consequently, he would alternate between serving Cole his meals as an
employee and then joining him at the dining table as his guest.

In his final year Cole's health had deteriorated to the point where he
frequently became incoherent as well as incontinent; both were the result
of poisons that collected in his body because of bladder and kidney mal-
functions. Interestingly, Cole's old crony Monty Woolley suffered, too,
from a kidney disorder, undoubtedly from the effect of years of heavy
drinking, before he died on May 6, 1963 (toward the end Cole and Woolley
seldom saw each other, mainly because Cole had reacted so negatively to
Woolley taking a black manservant as a lover; many times Cole would not
even return Woolley's calls). Life had generally become so unbearable for
Cole by then that he would often say, "I wish I were dead." Consistent
with this death wish, Cole not only stopped cleaning his teeth in his final
year, but he also practically gave up wearing his artificial leg.

Yet there were still moments when Cole seemed to rally and be his old
exuberant self again. One such instance occurred when Cole was seen
being passionately soul-kissed in his Waldorf apartment on his "fucking"
couch—a deep couch he had had made for such purposes years earlier—

by a handsome young actor who was playing up to him. Cole's teeth may not have been the cleanest at that point, but that evidently did not deter the actor. For in addition to whatever intrinsic satisfaction he got from this and presumably other similar interactions with Cole, he was also well rewarded with various gifts, including a car, for his affections.

Save for these few intermittent pleasantries, Cole's physical and psychological burdens had become too much for him to bear, and he looked forward to death. He finally got his wish when his worn-out, illness-ridden body stopped functioning at 11:05 P.M. on October 15, 1964. When word got out about his death in a Santa Monica hospital, an avalanche of tributes to him poured forth. "The supreme sophisticate of American song," "an international legend," and "one of the giant songwriters in the American musical theater" were typical of the encomiums heaped on Cole. (Though indeed deserving of high praise for his songwriting gifts, one still has to wonder whether these tributes might have been a bit tempered if the world knew the real man, with all his personal imperfections, rather than the public image of him that had evolved over the years. If nothing else, Cole raises anew the age-old question—a philosophically sophisticated and difficult one—of whether an accomplished artist is to be judged somewhat differently—morally, ethically, and practically every other way—from his less-talented counterparts.) Many of the laudations commented that Cole's songs particularly captured the spirit of the twenties and thirties, but that they would unquestionably be around for many years to come. Cole himself had once been asked by a reporter whether he thought his songs would last. "I never gave it a thought," he replied. "My enjoyment was in writing them." And it was that very enjoyment that rubbed off on his songs and made them so contagious—then and now.

In compliance with Cole's wishes there was a minimum of pomp and ceremony in connection with his funeral. He had been very specific about funeral arrangements in his will, which he had had drawn up and signed some two years earlier. Cole's instructions were:

I direct my Executors to arrange for my burial in Peru, Indiana. I further direct my Executors to arrange for no funeral or memorial service, but only for a private burial service to be conducted by the Pastor of the First Baptist Church of Peru, in the presence of my relatives and dear friends. At such service I request said Pastor to read the following quotation from the Bible, "I am the resurrection and the life; he that believeth in me, though he were dead, yet shall

he live; and whosoever liveth and believeth in me shall never die,"
and to follow such quotation with the Lord's Prayer.

I request that the foregoing be substantially the entire burial service, and that neither said Pastor nor anyone else deliver any memorial address whatsoever. I particularly direct that there be no service
of any kind for me in New York City.

These instructions were followed to the letter. Cole's body was sent home
to Peru from Santa Monica, and, after simple services, buried in Mount
Hope Cemetery between the graves of Linda and—ironically, since Cole
was not very close to him in life—his father. (Many reports have erroneously—and rather romantically—claimed that Cole is buried between the
two most important women in his life: Kate and Linda. Whatever sentimental justification there may be for this claim, it is wholly inaccurate.)
And so in essence Cole's life had come full circle, ending as it had started.
Cosmopolite Cole had returned to his basic Indiana roots at death. A
small, simple gravestone (it lists only his name and dates of birth and
death), similar to those of his pioneer-stock Hoosier ancestors who lie
nearby, marks Cole's final resting place.

Despite Cole's lavish living and his frequent worries—especially when
he was in a depressed mood—that he was going broke, he left a gross
estate of close to six million dollars. And it is easy to see why his estate
was so large. Besides his inheritances from Kate and Linda, his own
earnings were enormous. For example, in the year immediately preceding his death, even though he had not written any new songs since the
amputation, he still earned over five hundred thousand dollars in royalties and income from his music and lyrics. If to that figure one adds the
monies he received from his family's business interests, it is clear that the
total amount he earned for that year was in the high six figures. With so
much money, plus additional assets at his disposal, it was perhaps to be
expected that Cole had many bequests to make in his twenty-nine-page
will, including gifts of paintings, jewelry, and memorabilia to old friends,
as well as cash bequests, mainly ten thousand dollars each, though a few
got lesser amounts, to employees and others close to him. Cole also made
generous bequests to Williams College and Yale University. But the bulk
of Cole's estate went to his first cousin, Jules Omar Cole, and Jules's son,
James. Between them they were awarded, among other things, Cole's
property in Peru and half the income from Cole's copyrighted music.
The other half-interest in Cole's copyrighted music went, surprisingly,
not to a relative or an institution, but to a friend, Ray C. Kelly, and his

children. No explanation was given by Cole for this generosity to Kelly, nor has Kelly publicly discussed the matter. As far as can be learned, Cole knew Kelly over a long period of time, though they seldom saw each other in Cole's final years (according to Henry Burke, Kelly visited Cole only twice, at Williamstown, during the entire period that Burke worked for Cole as valet). Considering the enormity of this legacy to Kelly, it is understandable that speculation abounds as to why Kelly was so favored. But, like many other aspects of Cole's life that have been shrouded in secrecy, it is unlikely that all the ramifications involved in this rather unusual bequest will ever be known.

Cole's popularity since his death has been as strong as ever, as evidenced by the numerous television specials in his honor, the many revivals of his shows, the extensive performances of his individual songs, and the quantity of material that is continually being published about him. Cole was a unique character when he lived, and a unique character he has remained. We may never see the likes of him again. He left such a strong imprint on our hearts and minds that he is still with us—as saucy as he always was—in spirit. Long may that continue!

Schwartz, C. Cole Porter: A Biography (N+1 filler London, 1978)

Appendix 1:

Works by Cole Porter

(* denotes publication of individual works as well as vocal scores from shows)

1901

Song of the Birds (for piano)

1902

*Bobolink Waltz (for piano; published for Cole Porter by his mother)

1905–09
(songs written at Worcester Academy; all the manuscripts are lost)

The Bearded Lady
Class of 1909 Song
Fi, Fi, Fifi
The Tattooed Gentleman

1910

*Bingo Eli Yale
*Bridget
Perfectly Terrible
When the Summer Moon Comes 'Long

1911

*Beware of Yale (c. 1911)
*Bull Dog
*Eli
*Fla De Dah
*Hail to Yale (lyrics by Cole Porter; music by Arthur Troostwyck)
Miss Chapel Street
The Motor Car
No Show This Evening
Yellow Melodrama

Cora. Book by T. Gaillard Thomas II. Directed by Thomas and Peter C. Bryce. Presented by the Phi Opera Company at the Delta Kappa Epsilon fraternity house at Yale, November 28, 1911; one performance. The cast included Thomas, Cole Porter, Leonard Hanna, Arnold Whitridge, H. H. Parsons, Fletcher Van W. Blood, and Reginald LeG. Auchincloss.

Poker
Concentration
Saturday Night
Hello, Miss Chapel Street
Cora, the Fair Chorine
My Home Town Girl
Queen of the Yale Dramat
We're Off
Goodbye Boys
Cablegram
The Old Rat Mort
Ma Petite Ninette
Le Reve d'Absinthe
Far, Far Away
Fair One
Rosebud
Rolling, Rolling
Mother Phi

1912

And the Villain Still Pursued Her. Book by T. Gaillard Thomas II. Directed by Thomas and Cole Porter. Presented by the Yale Dramatic Association at the New Haven Lawn Club, April 24, 1912, and at the Yale Club in New York City, May 10, 1912; two performances. The cast included Monty Woolley (as "The Villain"), Rufus F. King, Johnfritz Achelis, Arnold Whitridge, Irving G. Beebe, Lawrence M. Cornwall, and Joseph E. Brown.

We are the Chorus of the Show
Strolling
The Lovely Heroine
The Villain
Twilight
Llewellyn
That Zip Cornwall Cooch
Charity
Queens of Terpsichore
Leaders of Society
Submarine
My Little Barcelona Maid
Silver Moon
Dear Doctor
Anytime
Come to Bohemia
Dancing
Fare Thee Well

The Pot of Gold. Book by Almet F. Jenks, Jr. Directed by Jenks and Cole Porter. Presented at the Delta Kappa Epsilon fraternity house at Yale, November 26, 1912, and at the Hotel Taft in New Haven, December 4, 1912; two performances. The cast included Cole Porter, Arnold Whitridge, H. H. Parsons, T. Gaillard Thomas II, A. Clark, and Fletcher Van W. Blood.

At the Rainbow
Bellboys
Longing for Dear Old Broadway
When I Used to Lead the Ballet
My Houseboat on the Thames
She Was a Fair Young Mermaid
What An Awful Hullabaloo (finale,
  Act I)
What a Charming Afternoon
Since We've Met
Exercise
We Are So Aesthetic
Scandal
I Wonder Where My Girl Is Now

My Salvation Army Queen
It's Awfully Hard When Mother's Not
  Along
I Want to Be Married (to a Delta
  Kappa Epsilon Man)
Ha, Ha, They Must Sail for Siberia
I Love You So
Loie and Chlodo
So Let Us Hail
Not Used:
If I Were Only a Football Man
  (became "A Football King")
That Rainbow Rag
(Miscellaneous Songs)
Antoinette Birby (c. 1912)
A Football King
I Want to Be a Yale Boy
It Pays to Advertise
Mercy Percy (c. 1912)
Music with Meals
When I'm Eating Around with You

1913

The Kaleidoscope. Author and director not credited in the program. Presented by the Yale Dramatic Association at the Hotel Taft in New Haven, April 30, 1913, and at the Yale Club in New York City, May 7, 1913; two performances. The cast included Rufus F. King, Newbold Noyes, Archibald MacLeish, Arnold Whitridge, Johnfritz Achelis, Stoddard King, Daniel L. McCoy, and Henry J. Wiser.

At the Dawn Tea
We Are Prom Girls
Chaperons
In the Land Where My Heart Was
  Born
Meet Me Beside the River
Beware of the Sophomore
Rick-Chick-a-Chick
Goodbye My True Love
On My Yacht

We're a Group of Nonentities
Flower Maidens
Absinthe
Absinthe Drip
Maid of Santiago
As I Love You (became
  "Esmeralda" in 1915)
Duodessimalogue
Oh, What a Pretty Pair of Lovers
A Member of the Yale Elizabethan
  Club
Moon Man
My Georgia Gal

1914

Paranoia, or Chester of the Y.D.A.
Book, music, and lyrics by Cole Porter and Thomas Lawrason Riggs. Produced and directed by Monty Woolley. Presented by the Yale Dramatic Association at the Hotel Taft in New Haven, April 24, 1914; one performance. The cast included Rufus F. King, Newbold Noyes, Stoddard King, Archibald MacLeish, William S. Innis, Percival Dodge, and Thomas W. Enright.

Paranoia
Funny Little Tracks In the Snow
  (national anthem)
Innocent, Innocent Maids
Oh, What a Lonely Princess
Won't You Come Crusading with Me
  (became "Prithee Come
  Crusading with Me" in *See
  America First*)
I Want to Row on the Crew
What Love Is
Down In a Dungeon Deep
Slow Sinks the Sun
The Prep School Widow
Idyll
I've a Shooting Box in Scotland
Down Lovers' Lane

Flower Song (became "The Language of Flowers" in *See America First*)
Dresden China Soldiers
Naughty, Naughty
Hail, Hail to Cyril

We're All Dressed Up and We Don't Know Huerta Go. Presented by the Yale Dramatic Association at the Hotel Gibson in Cincinnati, Ohio, May 22, 1914, for the annual reunion of the Western Federation of Yale Clubs. Included in the cast were Cole Porter, Monty Woolley, Johnfritz Achelis, Newbold Noyes, Phelps Newberry, Lawrence Cornwall, and Hay Lagenheim. With the exception of "In Cincinnati," all the other numbers for the show are unknown and presumed lost.

Class of 1913 Song (written for the first annual reunion, in June of 1914, of Yale's class of 1913)

1915

Esmeralda (based on "As I Love You" from *The Kaleidoscope;* included in *Hands Up,* a Sigmund Romberg musical, that opened at the 44th Street Theater, July 22, 1915, and ran for 52 performances)
Two Big Eyes (with lyrics by John Golden; included in *Miss Information,* a Jerome Kern musical, that opened at the George M. Cohan Theater, October 5, 1915, and ran for 47 performances)

1916

Cleveland (c. 1916; written for an annual reunion of the Western Federation of Yale Clubs held in Cleveland, Ohio)

See America First. Book, music, and lyrics by Cole Porter and T. Lawrason Riggs. Staged by Benrimo. Produced by Elisabeth Marbury at the Maxine Elliott Theater, March 28, 1916 (after tryouts in Schenectady, Albany, Rochester, New Haven, and Providence, starting February 22, 1916, and a New York preview, March 27, 1916, for members of society); 15 performances. The cast included Dorothie Bigelow, John Goldsworthy, Felix Adler, Clifton Webb, Clara Palmer, and Jeanne Cartier.

Dawn Music (incidental music)
Indian Girls' Chant
Bad Men
To Follow Every Fancy
Indian Maidens' Chorus
* *Something's Got to Be Done*
* *I've Got an Awful Lot to Learn*
Beautiful, Primitive Indian Girls
Hold-Up Ensemble
* *See America First*
* *The Language of Flowers*
* *Prithee Come Crusading with Me*
The Lady I've Vowed to Wed
Hail the Female Relative (finale, Act I)
Mirror, Mirror
* *Ever and Ever Yours*
* *Lima*
Will You Love Me When My Flivver Is a Wreck?
Woodland Dance
* *Buy Her a Box at the Opera*
* *I've a Shooting Box in Scotland*
* *When I Used to Lead the Ballet*
Not Used:
Bichloride of Mercury
Dinner
If In Spite of Our Attempts
Lady Fair, Lady Fair

Love Came and Crowned Me
*Oh, Bright Fair Dream
*Pity Me Please
Revelation Ensemble
Serenade
*Slow Sinks the Sun
The Social Coach of All the
Fashionable Future Debutantes
Step We Grandly
Strolling Quite Fancy Free
Sweet Simplicity
Wake, Love, Wake
When a Body's In Love

1918

It Puzzles Me So (c. 1918)
Katie of the Y.M.C.A. (c. 1918)
War Song (c. 1918; a parody of
Jerome Kern's "They Didn't
Believe Me")
*Alone with You (lyrics by Cole
Porter; music by Melville
Gideon; included in the 1918
English production of Very Good
Eddie)
*Altogether Too Fond of You
(co-authored by Cole Porter,
James Heard, and Melville
Gideon; included in the 1918
English production of Telling the
Tale and the 1919 New York
production of Buddies)

1919

Oh, Honey (c. 1919)
Widow's Cruise (c. 1919)
Tired of Living Alone (c. 1919)
Chelsea (lyrics by Cole Porter;
music by Melville Gideon;
included in the 1919 English
production of The Eclipse)
*I Never Realized (lyrics by Cole
Porter; music by Melville
Gideon; included in the 1919
English production of The Eclipse

and the 1919 New York
production of Buddies)
*Washington Square (the same tune
as "Chelsea"; lyrics by Cole
Porter and E. Ray Goetz, music
by Melville Gideon; included in
Buddies of 1919, as well as in As
You Were of 1920)

Hitchy-Koo of 1919. Book by George
V. Hobart. Staged by Julian Alfred.
Produced by Raymond Hitchcock at
the Liberty Theater, October 6, 1919
(after tryouts in Atlantic City and
Boston starting August 18, 1919); 56
performances (followed by a year's
tour of the United States by members
of the company). The cast included
Raymond Hitchcock, Joe Cook, Lil-
lian Kemble Cooper, Charles Witzell,
Sylvia Clark, Mark Sullivan, and
Waneta Means.
Pagliacci
When Black Sallie Sings Pagliacci
*I Introduced
*In Hitchy's Garden
*When I Had a Uniform On
*I've Got Somebody Waiting
*Peter Piper
I'm An Anaesthetic Dancer
*My Cozy Little Corner in the Ritz
*Old-Fashioned Garden
*Bring Me Back My Butterfly
Not Used:
Ah Fong Low
*Another Sentimental Song
Since Ma Got the Craze Espagnole
*That Black and White Baby of Mine

1920

A Table for Two (c. 1920)
Venus of Milo (c. 1920)
You Make Up (c. 1920)

A Night Out. This English production opened at London's Winter Gar-

den Theatre on September 18, 1920; 309 performances. Three Cole Porter numbers (with lyrics by Clifford Grey) were included in the show.

*Look Around
* Our Hotel
* Why Didn't We Meet Before?

1922

Mayfair and Montmartre. Book by John Hastings Turner. Produced and staged by Charles B. Cochran at London's New Oxford Theatre, March 9, 1922; 77 performances. This revue, whose cast included Alice Delysia, Nellie Taylor, Nikitina, and Joyce Barbour, used three Cole Porter numbers.

*The Blue Boy Blues
* Cocktail Time
* Olga (Come Back to the Volga)
Not Used:
The Bandit Band
The Sponge
Wond'ring Night and Day

Phi-Phi. This Charles B. Cochran production opened at the London Pavilion, August 16, 1922, and included one Porter number: *"The Ragtime Pipes of Pan."

Hitchy-Koo of 1922. Book by Harold Atteridge. Directed by J. C. Huffman, under the supervision of J. J. Shubert. Produced by Lee and J. J. Shubert at Philadelphia's Sam S. Shubert Theater, October 10, 1922; closed in Philadelphia after a run of less than two weeks, without reaching New York. The cast included Raymond Hitchcock, Jack Pearl, Benny Leonard, Edythe Baker, Jack Squires, May Boley, El Brendel, Florence Bert, and Helen Dahlia.

Maryland Scene
Oh, Mary
Ah Fong Low
* When My Caravan Comes Home
* The American Punch
Play Me a Tune
* Love Letter Words
* The Bandit Band
The Sponge
* The Harbor Deep Down In My Heart
Not Used:
The Old-Fashioned Waltz
Pitter-Patter
Scotch Twins
South Sea Isles
Twin Sisters

1923

Within the Quota. A jazz ballet presented by the Ballets Suédois, with music by Cole Porter (orchestrated by Charles Koechlin); libretto, costumes, and scenery by Gerald Murphy. The world premiere took place at Paris's Théâtre des Champs-Élysées, October 25, 1923; the American premiere at New York's Century Theater, November 28, 1923.

1924

Greenwich Village Follies. Book by Lew Fields, Irving Caesar, William K. Wells, and others. Production devised and staged by John Murray Anderson. Produced by A. L. Jones and Morris Green at the Shubert Theater, September 16, 1924 (after a one-week tryout in Atlantic City); 127 performances. The cast included Moran and Mack, the Dolly Sisters, Bobbe Arnst, George Hale, Dorothy Neville, Don Barclay, Vincent Lopez and his orchestra, George Rasley, and Julia Silvers.

*Brittany
I Want Twins
The Dollys and their Collies
Toy of Destiny
* Two Little Babes in the Wood
Bring Me a Radio
Broadcast a Jazz
* Wait for the Moon
Syncopated Pipes of Pan
* My Long Ago Girl
* Make Every Day a Holiday (not
  related to "Ev'ry Day a Holiday"
  in Dubarry Was a Lady)
* I'm In Love Again
Not Used:
The Life of a Sailor
Understudies

1925

Out O' Luck. Book by Tom Cushing.
Directed by Monty Woolley. Presented by the Yale Dramatic Association during a 1925 Christmas tour of
various cities in the East and Mid-
west. The tour was so successful that
it was repeated the following Christmas. The cast included John McA.
Hoysradt, Henry C. Potter, Theodore S. Ryan, Roger V. Stearns, and
Edward R. Wardwell.

Butterflies
Mademazelle
Opera Star

(Miscellaneous Songs)
* Hot-House Rose
The Scampi (later revised to become
  "The Tale of the Oyster")
Don't Tell Me Who You Are
  (written in the 1920s, but date
  uncertain)
I'm Dining With Elsa (written in
  the 1920s; date uncertain)
Italian Street Singers (written in the
  1920s; date uncertain)

Love 'Em and Leave 'Em (written in
  the 1920s; date uncertain)
Poor Young Millionaire (written in
  the 1920s; date uncertain)
That Little Old Bar at the Ritz
  (written in the 1920s; date is
  uncertain)

1927

* The Laziest Gal in Town (not used
  until 1950; performed in Stage
  Fright by Marlene Dietrich)
* Let's Misbehave
Sex Appeal (c. 1927)
* Weren't We Fools

1928

La Revue des Ambassadeurs. Directed by Bobby Connolly. Produced
by Edmond Sayag at Les Ambassadeurs, a Parisian nightclub, May 10,
1928 (the number of performances is
not known). The cast included Morton Downey, Fred Waring and his
orchestra, Buster and John West,
Evelyn Hoey, and Frances Gershwin.

Keep Moving
* The Lost Liberty Blues
Omnibus
* Pilot Me
* In a Moorish Garden
* Almiro
* You and Me
* Fish
* Military Maids
* Blue Hours
* Alpine Rose
Gershwin Specialty
Excelsior (Boulevard Break)
* Hans
* Baby, Let's Dance
* Old-Fashioned Girl (Old-Fashioned
  Boy)

*Fountain of Youth
*Looking At You

Paris. Book by Martin Brown. Directed by W. H. Gilmore. Produced by Gilbert Miller in association with E. Ray Goetz at the Music Box Theater, October 8, 1928 (after tryouts in Atlantic City, Philadelphia, Boston, and Washington, D.C., starting February 6, 1928); 195 performances. The cast included Irene Bordoni, Eric Kalkhurst, Louise Closser Hale, Irving Aaronsons's Commanders, and Arthur Margetson.

*Two Little Babes in the Wood
*Don't Look at Me that Way
*Let's Do It, Let's Fall in Love
*Vivienne
*The Heaven Hop
  Not Used:
  Dizzy Baby
*Let's Misbehave
*Quelque-Chose
*Which

1929

Wake Up and Dream. Book by John Hastings Turner. Staged by Frank Collins under the supervision of Charles B. Cochran. Produced by Cochran at the London Pavilion, March 27, 1929 (after a tryout at Manchester's Palace Theatre starting March 5, 1929); 263 performances. Cochran also produced the show at New York's Selwyn Theater, December 30, 1929; 136 performances. The English cast included Jessie Matthews, Sonnie Hale, Tilly Losch, William Stephens, Toni Birkmayer, Elsie Carlisle, and Tina Meller. In the American production Jack Buchanan replaced Sonnie Hale.

*Wake Up and Dream
  I've Got a Crush on You
*I Loved Him But He Didn't Love
  Me
*Looking At You
*The Banjo That Man Joe Plays
  Dance of the Crinoline Ladies (dance music)
  Dance of the Ragamuffins (dance music)
  Entrance of Emigrants (instrumental march)
*Aqua Sincopada Tango
*What Is This Thing Called Love?
  Wait Until It's Bedtime
  Operatic Pills
  After All, I'm Only a Schoolgirl
*Let's Do It, Let's Fall in Love
*I Dream of a Girl in a Shawl
  Night Club Opening
*I'm a Gigolo
*I Want to Be Raided by You
*Which
  Not Used:
  The Extra Man
  The Lady I Love
  My Louisa

Fifty Million Frenchmen. Book by Herbert Fields. Directed by Monty Woolley. Produced by E. Ray Goetz at the Lyric Theater, November 27, 1929 (after a tryout in Boston, starting November 14, 1929); 254 performances. The cast included William Gaxton, Genevieve Tobin, Helen Broderick, Betty Compton, Jack Thompson, and Evelyn Hoey.

  A Toast to Volstead
*You Do Something to Me
  The American Express
*You've Got That Thing
*Find Me a Primitive Man
  Where Would You Get Your Coat?
  Do You Want to See Paris?
  At Longchamps Today

Yankee Doodle
* The Happy Heaven of Harlem
Why Shouldn't I Have You?
Somebody's Going to Throw a Big
   Party
It Isn't Done
* I'm in Love
The Tale of the Oyster (based on
   "The Scampi" of 1926; dropped
   from the show)
* Paree, What Did You Do to Me?
* You Don't Know Paree
* I'm Unlucky at Gambling
* Let's Step Out (added after the New
   York opening)
The Boy Friend Back Home (added
   after the New York opening)
Not Used:
Down With Everybody But Us
The Heaven of Harlem
* I Worship You
My Harlem Wench
* Please Don't Make Me Be Good
* The Queen of Terre Haute
The Snake in the Grass (ballet music)
That's Why I Love You
Watching the World Go By
Why Don't We Try Staying Home?

The Battle of Paris (film). Screenplay
by Gene Markey. Directed by Robert
Florey. Produced by Paramount Pictures; released November 30, 1929.
The cast included Gertrude Lawrence, Charles Ruggles, Gladys Du
Bois, Walter Petrie, Joe King, and Arthur Treacher.

* Here Comes the Bandwagon
* They All Fall in Love

1930

What's My Man Gonna Be Like?
(included in The Vanderbilt
Revue, which opened at New
York's Vanderbilt Theater,
November 5, 1930, and ran for 13
performances)

The New Yorkers. Book by Herbert
Fields, based on a story by Peter
Arno and E. Ray Goetz. Directed by
Monty Woolley. Produced by E. Ray
Goetz at the Broadway Theater, De-
cember 8, 1930 (after tryouts in Phila-
delphia and Newark starting Novem-
ber 12, 1930); 168 performances. The
cast included Hope Williams, Jimmy
Durante, Charles King, Ann Pen-
nington, Lou Clayton, Eddie Jackson,
Marie Cahill, Frances Williams,
Fred Waring and his Pennsyl-
vanians, Richard Carle, and Barrie
Oliver.

Go Into Your Dance
* Where Have You Been?
Say It With Gin
Venice
* I'm Getting Myself Ready for You
* Love for Sale
* The Great Indoors
Sing Sing for Sing Sing
* Take Me Back to Manhattan
* Let's Fly Away
* I Happen to Like New York
Not Used:
* Just One of Those Things (not the
   famous song from Jubilee)
Mona and Her Kiddies
My Louisa
The Poor Rich
We've Been Spending the Summer
   With Our Families
Why Talk About Sex?
You're Too Far Away
You've Got to Be Hard-Boiled

1931

Fifty Million Frenchmen (film).
Screenplay by Joseph Jackson, Al
Boasberg, and Eddie Welch; based on

the 1929 musical by Herbert Fields. Directed by Lloyd Bacon. Produced by Warner Brothers. The cast included William Gaxton, Helen Broderick, Olsen and Johnson, Claudia Dell, Lester Crawford, John Halliday, Vera Gordon, and Bela Lugosi. Cole Porter's original vocal score for the 1929 stage musical is *not* included in this film except as instrumental background accompaniment.

Star Dust. Unproduced stage musical (with a book by Herbert Fields), which E. Ray Goetz had intended to present in 1931.

Auf Wiedersehen
But He Never Says He Loves Me
  (revised to become "The
  Physician" in *Nymph Errant*)
Die Schöne Wirtstochter
I Get a Kick Out of You
I Still Love the Red, White and Blue
It's Probably Just as Well
I've Got You On My Mind
I Worship You
Mister and Missus Fitch
Mysteriously
Pick Me Up and Lay Me Down

1932

Gay Divorce. Book by Dwight Taylor. Directed by Howard Lindsay. Produced by Dwight Wiman and Tom Weatherly at the Ethel Barrymore Theater, November 29, 1932 (after tryouts in Boston and New Haven, starting November 7, 1932); 248 performances. The cast included Fred Astaire, Claire Luce, Eric Blore, Luella Gear, Erik Rhodes, G. P. Huntley, Jr., Taylor Gordon, and Betty Starbuck. A London production, with Fred Astaire and Claire Luce in the leads, opened at the Palace Theatre, November 2, 1933; 180 performances.

*After You, Who?
Why Marry Them?
Salt Air
I Still Love the Red, White and Blue
*Night and Day
*How's Your Romance?
What Will Become of Our England?
*I've Got You On My Mind
*Mister and Missus Fitch
*You're in Love
I Love Only You (only in the
  London production)
Never Say No (only in the London
  production)
Waiters v. Waitresses (only in the
  London production)
Not Used:
Fate
A Weekend Affair

1933

Nymph Errant. Book by Romney Brent (based on the novel by James Laver). Directed by Brent, under the supervision of Charles B. Cochran. Produced by Cochran at London's Adelphi Theatre, October 6, 1933 (after a tryout in Manchester, starting September 11, 1933); 154 performances. The cast included Gertrude Lawrence, Iris Ashley, Moya Nugent, Queenie Leonard, Doris Carson, Elizabeth Welch, and Austin Trevor.

*Experiment
*It's Bad for Me
Neauville-Sur-Mer
The Cocotte
*How Could We Be Wrong?
They're Always Entertaining
Georgia Sand
*Nymph Errant
Ruins

*The Physician
*Solomon
Back to Nature
Plumbing
Si Vous Aimez Les Poitrines
*You're Too Far Away
Casanova
Not Used:
My Louisa
Sweet Nudity
*When Love Comes Your Way

Once Upon a Time (Ever Yours). Unproduced stage musical. Book by Guy Bolton based on a novel by Lily Hatvany. Gilbert Miller had intended to present this in late 1933 or early 1934.

Auf Wiedersehen
Coffee
Die Schöne Wirtstochter
Gypsy Song
Ilsa's Song
It All Seems So Long Ago
Lead Me On
The Night of the Ball
Once Upon a Time
Success
Technique
Thank You
Waltz Down the Aisle (eventually
  became "Wunderbar" in Kiss Me,
  Kate)
When Love Comes Your Way
Yours

1934

*Miss Otis Regrets (included in the
  English production Hi Diddle
  Diddle)
*Thank You So Much, Mrs.
  Lowsborough-Goodby
Java (written in the 1930s; date
  uncertain)
How Do They Do It? (written in the
  1930s; date uncertain)

Maybe Yes, Maybe No (written in
  the 1930s; date uncertain)
The Upper Park Avenue (written in
  the 1930s; date uncertain)

The Gay Divorcee (film). Screenplay by George Marion, Jr., Dorothy Yost, and Edward Kaufman; based on the 1932 musical Gay Divorce, by Dwight Taylor. Directed by Mark Sandrich. Produced by Pandro S. Berman for RKO; released October 12, 1934. The cast included Fred Astaire, Ginger Rogers, Edward Everett Horton, Alice Brady, Erik Rhodes, Eric Blore, and William Austin. Only "Night and Day" from Cole Porter's original score for Gay Divorce was heard in the film.

*Anything Goes. Book by Guy Bolton and P. G. Wodehouse; revised by Howard Lindsay and Russel Crouse. Directed by Howard Lindsay. Produced by Vinton Freedley at the Alvin Theater, November 21, 1934 (after a tryout in Boston starting November 5, 1934); 420 performances. The cast included Ethel Merman, Victor Moore, William Gaxton, Bettina Hall, Leslie Barrie, and Vivian Vance. A London production by Charles B. Cochran opened at the Palace Theatre, June 14, 1935; 261 performances.

*I Get a Kick Out of You
Bon Voyage
*All Through the Night
*There'll Always Be a Lady Fair
Where Are the Men?
*You're the Top
*Anything Goes
Public Enemy Number One
*Blow, Gabriel, Blow
Be Like the Bluebird

*Buddie Beware
*The Gypsy in Me
Not Used:
Kate the Great
There's No Cure Like Travel
*Waltz Down the Aisle
What a Joy to Be Young

Adios Argentina. Unproduced movie that Fox Studios had originally planned to film in late 1934 or early 1935.

Adios Argentina
The Chiripah
Don't Fence Me In (based on a text by Bob Fletcher)
If You Could Love Me
The Side Car
Singing In the Saddle

1935

Jubilee. Book by Moss Hart. Staged and lit by Hassard Short. Produced by Sam H. Harris and Max Gordon at the Imperial Theater, October 12, 1935 (after a tryout in Boston starting September 21, 1935); 169 performances. The cast included Mary Boland, Melville Cooper, June Knight, Charles Walters, Derek Williams, May Boley, Mark Plant, Margaret Adams, and Montgomery Clift.

Our Crown
We're Off to Feathermore
*Why Shouldn't I?
Entrance of Eric
*The Kling-Kling Bird on the Divi-Divi Tree
*When Love Comes Your Way
What a Nice Municipal Park
When Me, Mowgli, Love
Gather Ye Autographs While Ye May
My Loulou
*Begin the Beguine

Cabinet Music (incidental music)
Good Morning, Miss Standing
My Most Intimate Friend
*A Picture of Me without You
Ev'rybod-ee Who's Anybod-ee
The Judgment of Paris (dance music)
Swing that Swing
Sunday Morning, Breakfast Time
Mr. and Mrs. Smith
Six Little Wives
Beach Scene (incidental music)
*Me and Marie
*Just One of Those Things
Jubilee Presentation
Not Used:
Greek Scene (incidental music)
Sing Jubilee
There's Nothing Like Swimming
Waltz Down the Aisle
Yours

1936

Born to Dance (film). Screenplay by Jack McGowan and Sid Silvers; based on an original story by McGowan, Silvers, and B. G. "Buddy" De Sylva. Directed by Roy Del Ruth. Produced by Jack Cummings for MGM; released in November, 1936. The cast included Eleanor Powell, James Stewart, Virginia Bruce, Sid Silvers, Una Merkel, Raymond Walburn, Frances Langford, Alan Dinehart, and Buddy Ebsen.

*Rolling Home
*Rap-Tap On Wood
*Hey, Babe, Hey
Entrance of Lucy James
*Love Me, Love My Pekinese
*Easy to Love
*I've Got You Under My Skin
*Swingin' the Jinx Away

Anything Goes (film). The first of two Paramount movie versions of the 1934 stage musical. The cast included Bing Crosby, Ethel Merman, Charles Ruggles, and Ida Lupino. Many of the numbers from the original score were incorporated into the film.

Red, Hot and Blue! Book by Howard Lindsay and Russel Crouse. Directed by Howard Lindsay. Produced by Vinton Freedley at the Alvin Theater, October 29, 1936 (after tryouts in Boston and New Haven starting October 7, 1936); 183 performances. The cast included Ethel Merman, Jimmy Durante, Bob Hope, Vivian Vance, Dorothy Vernon, Thurston Crane, and Grace and Paul Hartman.

At Ye Olde Coffee Shoppe in Cheyenne
It's a Great Life
*Perennial Debutantes
*Ours
*Down in the Depths
Carry On
*You've Got Something
*It's De-Lovely
*A Little Skipper from Heaven
  Above
Five Hundred Million
*Ridin' High
We're About to Start Big Rehearsin'
Hymn to Hymen
*What a Great Pair We'll Be
*You're a Bad Influence on Me
*The Ozarks are Callin' Me Home
*Red, Hot and Blue
Not Used:
Bertie and Gertie
*Goodbye, Little Dream, Goodbye
Lonely Star
That's the News I'm Waiting to Hear
When Your Troubles Have Started
Where?
Who, But You

*Goodbye, Little Dream, Goodbye
(though not used in *Red, Hot and Blue!* it was included in the 1936 English production of *O Mistress Mine*)

1937

Rosalie (film). Screenplay by William Anthony McGuire; based on the 1928 musical by McGuire and Guy Bolton. Directed by W. S. Van Dyke. Produced by McGuire for MGM; released December 24, 1937. The cast included Nelson Eddy, Eleanor Powell, Edna May Oliver, Frank Morgan, Ilona Massey, and Ray Bolger.

*Close
*In the Still of the Night
It's All Over but the Shouting
*I've a Strange New Rhythm in My
  Heart
*Rosalie
Spring Love Is in the Air
*Who Knows?
*Why Should I Care?
Entrance of Prince Paul
To Love or Not to Love
Not Used:
A Fool There Was
I Know It's Not Meant for Me

Break the News (film). Screenplay by Geoffrey Kerr. Directed by René Clair. Produced by Clair in England in 1937 for Monogram Pictures; released in 1938 (in the United States, in 1941). The film starred Maurice Chevalier, Jack Buchanan, and June Knight, and included the Cole Porter number, *"It All Belongs to You."

Greek to You. Unproduced stage musical (with an unfinished book by Howard Lindsay and Russel Crouse), which Vinton Freedley had intended to present in 1937 or 1938.

Greek to You
It Never Entered My Head
Melos, That Lovely Smiling Isle
Wild Wedding Bells

1938

You Never Know. Book by Rowland Leigh; based on Siegfried Geyer's play, *Candle Light.* Directed by Leigh. Produced by Lee and J. J. Shubert in association with John Shubert at the Winter Garden, September 21, 1938 (after tryouts in New Haven, Boston, Washington, D.C., Philadelphia, Pittsburgh, Detroit, Chicago, Des Moines, Indianapolis, Columbus, Buffalo, and Hartford, starting March 3, 1938); 78 performances. The cast included Clifton Webb, Libby Holman, Lupe Velez, Rex O'Malley, Toby Wing, and Charles Kemper.

I Am Gaston
Au Revoir, Cher Baron
*Maria
*You Never Know
*What Is That Tune?
*For No Rhyme or Reason
*From Alpha to Omega
Don't Let It Get You Down
*What Shall I Do?
*At Long Last Love
Yes, Yes, Yes
Good Evening, Princess
Not Used:
By Candlelight
Ha, Ha, Ha
I'll Black His Eyes
I'm Back in Circulation
I'm Going in for Love
I'm Yours
It's No Laughing Matter
Just One Step Ahead of Love
What a Priceless Pleasure

Leave It to Me. Book by Bella and Samuel Spewack. Directed by Samuel Spewack. Produced by Vinton Freedley at the Imperial Theater, November 9, 1938 (after tryouts in New Haven and Boston starting October 13, 1938); 307 performances. The cast included William Gaxton, Victor Moore, Sophie Tucker, Mary Martin, Tamara, and Gene Kelly.

How Do You Spell Ambassador?
We Drink to You, J. H. Brody
Vite, Vite, Vite
*I'm Taking the Steps to Russia
*Get Out of Town
When All's Said and Done
*Most Gentlemen Don't Like Love
Comrade Alonzo
Recall Goodhue (recitative)
*From Now On
*I Want to Go Home
*My Heart Belongs to Daddy
*Tomorrow
*Far Away
To the U.S.A. from the U.S.S.R.
Not Used:
As Long as It's Not About Love
Information Please
Just Another Page in Your Diary
There's a Fan
When the Hen Stops Laying
Wild Wedding Bells

*River God (interpolated in the English production of *The Sun Never Sets,* based on a book by Guy Bolton and Pat Wallace.

1939

Broadway Melody of 1940 (film). Screenplay by Leon Gordon and George Oppenheimer; based on a story by Jack McGowan and Dore Schary. Directed by Norman Taurog. Produced by Jack Cummings for MGM; filmed during 1939, but released February 9, 1940. The cast included Fred Astaire, Eleanor Powell, George Murphy, Frank Morgan, Ian Hunter, Florence Rice, Lynne Carver, and Douglas McPhail.

*Please Don't Monkey with Broadway
*Between You and Me
*I've Got My Eyes on You
*I Concentrate on You
*Begin the Beguine
Not Used:
*I Happen to Be in Love
I'm So in Love with You (the same tune as "I've Got My Eyes on You," but with different lyrics)

DuBarry Was a Lady. Book by Herbert Fields and B. G. De Sylva. Directed by Edward MacGregor. Produced by De Sylva at the 46th Street Theater, December 6, 1939 (after tryouts in New Haven, Boston, and Philadelphia starting November 9, 1939); 408 performances. The cast included Ethel Merman, Bert Lahr, Ronald Graham, Charles Walters, and Betty Grable. A London production opened at His Majesty's Theatre October 22, 1942; 178 performances.

Where's Louie?
*Ev'ry Day a Holiday
It Ain't Etiquette
*When Love Beckoned
*Come On In
Dream Song
Mesdames and Messieurs
Gavotte
*But In the Morning, No
*Do I Love You?
Danse Victoire (dance music)
Danse Erotique (dance music)
DuBarry Was a Lady (finale, Act I)
Danse Tzigane (dance music)
*Give Him the Oo-La-La
*Well, Did You Evah!

*It Was Written in the Stars
L'Après-Midi d'un Boeuf
*Katie Went to Haiti
*Friendship
Not Used:
In the Big Money
What Have I?
Zombie Dance (instrumental music)

At Last In Your Arms (written for the MGM movie Balalaika, but not used)
What Am I to Do (included in the Broadway production of The Man Who Came to Dinner)

1940

Panama Hattie. Book by Herbert Fields and B. G. De Sylva. Directed by Edward MacGregor. Produced by De Sylva at the 46th Street Theater, October 30, 1940 (after tryouts in New Haven and Boston starting October 3, 1940); 501 performances. The cast included Ethel Merman, Arthur Treacher, James Dunn, Rags Ragland, Joan Carroll, Betty Hutton, Frank Hyers, and Pat Harrington. A London production opened at the Piccadilly Theatre, November 4, 1943; 308 performances.

A Stroll On the Plaza Sant'Ana
Join It Right Away
*Visit Panama
*My Mother Would Love You
*I've Still Got My Health
*Fresh as a Daisy
Welcome to Jerry
*Let's Be Buddies
They Ain't Done Right By Our Nell
I'm Throwing a Ball Tonight
We Detest a Fiesta
*Who Would Have Dreamed?
*Make It Another Old-Fashioned, Please
*All I've Got to Get Now Is My Man

You Said It
God Bless the Woman
Not Used:
Americans All Drink Coffee
Here's to Panama Hattie

So Long, Samoa (written during a cruise to the South Seas; it eventually became "Farewell, Amanda" and was used in the 1949 film *Adam's Rib*)

1941

You'll Never Get Rich (film). Screenplay by Michael Fessler and Ernest Pagano. Directed by Sidney Lanfield. Produced by Samuel Bischoff for Columbia Pictures; released October 23, 1941. The cast included Fred Astaire, Rita Hayworth, Robert Benchley, and Martha Tilton.

*Boogie Barcarolle
*Dream Dancing
*Shootin' the Works for Uncle Sam
*Since I Kissed My Baby Goodbye
*So Near and Yet So Far
*The Wedding Cake-Walk
Not Used:
A-Stairable Rag (instrumental music)

Let's Face It. Book by Herbert and Dorothy Fields. Directed by Edward MacGregor. Produced by Vinton Freedley at the Imperial Theater, October 29, 1941 (after a tryout in Boston, starting October 9, 1941); 547 performances. The cast included Danny Kaye, Eve Arden, Benny Baker, Edith Meiser, Mary Jane Walsh, Sunnie O'Dea, Vivian Vance, Jack Williams, and Nanette Fabray. A London production opened at the Hippodrome Theatre, November 19, 1942; 348 performances.

Let's Face It
Milk, Milk, Milk
A Lady Needs a Rest
*Jerry, My Soldier Boy
*Farming
*Ev'rything I Love
*Ace in the Hole
*You Irritate Me So
Baby Games
*Rub Your Lamp
I've Got Some Unfinished Business with You
*Let's Not Talk About Love
*A Little Rumba Numba
*I Hate You, Darling
Get Yourself a Girl
Not Used:
Aladdin Dance (instrumental music)
Fairy Tale (instrumental music)
Make a Date With a Great Psychoanalyst
Pets
Revenge
Up to His Old Tricks Again
What Are Little Husbands Made Of
The Whip Dance (instrumental music)
You Can't Beat My Bill

1942

Panama Hattie (film). Screenplay by Jack McGowan and Wilkie Mahoney (based on the original book by Herbert Fields and B. G. De Sylva). Directed by Norman Z. McLeod. Produced by Arthur Freed for MGM. The cast included Red Skelton, Ann Sothern, Ben Blue, Rags Ragland, Marsha Hunt, Dan Dailey, Alan Mowbray, Jackie Horner, Virginia O'Brien, and Lena Horne. "Let's Be Buddies" and other numbers from the original score were incorporated into the film.

Something to Shout About (film). Screenplay by Lou Breslow and Edward Eliscu. Directed by Gregory Ratoff. Produced by Ratoff for Columbia Pictures; filmed during 1942 but released in February, 1943. The cast included Don Ameche, Janet Blair, William Gaxton, and Jack Oakie.

*Hasta Luego
* I Always Knew
* Lotus Bloom
* Something to Shout About
Through Thick and Thin
* You'd Be So Nice to Come Home To
Not Used:
Couldn't Be
I Can Do Without Tea in My Teapot
* It Might Have Been
Let Doctor Schmet Vet Your Pet
Take It Easy

Glide, Glider, Glide (written for the armed forces)
Sailors of the Sky (written for the armed forces)

1943

Something for the Boys. Book by Herbert and Dorothy Fields. Staged and lit by Hassard Short. Produced by Michael Todd at the Alvin Theater, January 7, 1943 (after a tryout in Boston, starting December 18, 1942); 422 performances. The cast included Ethel Merman, Paula Laurence, Allen Jenkins, Bill Johnson, Anita Alvarez, Betty Garrett, and Betty Bruce.

Announcement of Inheritance (prologue)
* See That You're Born in Texas
* When My Baby Goes to Town
* Something for the Boys
When We're Home on the Range
* Could It Be You?

* Hey, Good Lookin'
* He's a Right Guy
Assembly Line
* The Leader of a Big-Time Band
* I'm in Love with a Soldier Boy
There's a Happy Land in the Sky
* By the Mississinewah
Not Used:
Oh, How I Could Go for You
Riddle Diddle Me This
So Long, San Antonio
Texas Will Make You a Man
Washington, D.C.
Well, I Just Wouldn't Know
Wouldn't It Be Crazy

DuBarry Was a Lady (film). Screenplay by Irving Brecher (based on the original book by Herbert Fields and B. G. De Sylva). Directed by Roy Del Ruth. Produced by Arthur Freed for MGM. The cast included Lucille Ball, Red Skelton, Gene Kelly, Virginia O'Brien, Rags Ragland, Zero Mostel, Donald Meek, Douglas Dumbrille, George Givot, Louise Beavers, and the Tommy Dorsey Band. Many of the numbers from the original score were incorporated into the film.

Mississippi Belle. Unproduced film. Cole Porter worked on the score for Warner Brothers in 1943. In 1944 the project was abandoned, with none of his numbers used.

Amo Amas
Close to Me
Hip, Hip Hooray for Andy Jackson
I Like Pretty Things
I'm Not Myself at All
In the Green Hills of County Mayo
Kathleen
Loading Song
Mamie Magdalin
Mississippi Belle

My Broth of a Boy
School, School, Heaven-Blessed School
So Long
When a Woman's in Love
When McKinley Marches On
When You and I Were Strangers
Who'll Bid

1944

Mexican Hayride. Book by Herbert and Dorothy Fields. Staged and lit by Hassard Short. Produced by Michael Todd at the Winter Garden Theater, January 28, 1944 (after a tryout in Boston starting December 29, 1943); 481 performances. The cast included Bobby Clark, June Havoc, Wilbur Evans, George Givot, Luba Malina, and Corinna Mura.

Entrance of Montana
*Sing to Me Guitar
* The Good-Will Movement
*I Love You
*There Must Be Someone for Me
*Carlotta
*Girls
What a Crazy Way to Spend Sunday
*Abracadabra
*Count Your Blessings
Not Used:
He Certainly Kills the Women
Hereafter
Here's a Cheer for Dear Old Ciro's
A Humble Hollywood Executive
I'm Afraid I Love You
I'm So Glahd to Meet You
* It Must Be Fun to Be You
It's a Big Night
It's Just Like the Good Old Days
It's Just Yours
Octet
Put a Sack over Their Heads
A Sight-Seeing Tour
Tequila

That's What You Mean to Me
We're Off for a Hayride in Mexico

Seven Lively Arts. Sketches by Moss Hart, George S. Kaufman, Robert Pirosh, Joseph Schrank, Charles Sherman, and Ben Hecht. Staged and lit by Hassard Short. Produced by Billy Rose at the Ziegfeld Theater, December 7, 1944 (after a tryout in Philadelphia, starting November 24, 1944); 183 performances. The cast included Beatrice Lillie, Bert Lahr, Benny Goodman, Alicia Markova, Anton Dolin, Dolores Gray, Teddy Wilson, Red Norvo, and Nan Wynn.

Big Town
*Is It the Girl? (Or Is It the Gown?)
*Only Another Boy and Girl
* Wow-Ooh-Wolf
Drink, Drink, Drink
* When I Was a Little Cuckoo
*Frabngee-Pahnee
Dancin' to a Jungle Drum
*Ev'ry Time We Say Goodbye
*Hence, It Don't Make Sense
*The Band Started Swinging a Song
The Big Parade
Not Used:
Café Society Still Carries On
Dainty, Quainty Me
I Wrote a Play
If I Hadn't a Husband
Pretty Little Missus Bell
Where Do We Go From Here?
Yours for a Song

*Don't Fence Me In (included in the Warner Brothers' film, *Hollywood Canteen;* sung by Roy Rogers)

1945

Night and Day (film). Screenplay by Charles Hoffman, Leo Townsend, and William Bowers; adapted by Jack Moffitt. Directed by Michael Curtiz. Produced by Arthur Schwartz for Warner Brothers; film completed in 1945 but released in 1946. The cast included Cary Grant, Alexis Smith, Monty Woolley, Ginny Simms, Jane Wyman, Mary Martin, Eve Arden, Henry Stephenson, and Victor Francen. Among the many famous Cole Porter songs heard in the film were "Night and Day," "Begin the Beguine," "I've Got You Under My Skin," "Old-Fashioned Garden," "Miss Otis Regrets," "What Is This Thing Called Love?" "You're the Top," and "My Heart Belongs to Daddy."

1946

Around the World in Eighty Days. Book by Orson Welles; based on the Jules Verne novel. Directed by Welles. Produced by Welles for the Mercury Theatre at the Adelphi, May 31, 1946 (after tryouts in Boston, New Haven, and Philadelphia starting April 28, 1946); 75 performances. The cast included Orson Welles, Arthur Margetson, Julie Warren, Mary Healy, Larry Laurence (Enzo Stuarti), Victoria Cordova, and Stefan Schnabel.

*Look What I Found
* There He Goes, Mr. Phileas Fogg
Suttee Procession
Suez Dance
Sea Chantey
*Should I Tell You I Love You?
*Pipe Dreaming
Oka Saka Circus (incidental music)
California Scene Dance (ballet music)

*If You Smile at Me
* Wherever They Fly the Flag of Old England
(A variety of incidental music not listed on the program may have been used)
Not Used:
Missus Aouda
Slave Auction
Snagtooth Gertie

The Gold Dusters Song (written for the Gold Dusters, a Vassar College singing group)

1948

The Pirate (film). Screenplay by Albert Hackett and Frances Goodrich; based on S. N. Behrman's adaptation of Ludwig Fulda's 1911 farce. Directed by Vincente Minelli. Produced by Arthur Freed for MGM; released March 24, 1948. The cast included Judy Garland, Gene Kelly, Walter Slezak, Gladys Cooper, and Reginald Owen.

*Be a Clown
*Love of My Life
*Mack the Black
*Nina
*You Can Do No Wrong
Not Used:
Manuela
Martinique
Voodoo

Kiss Me, Kate. Book by Bella and Samuel Spewack. Directed by John C. Wilson. Produced by Saint Subber and Lemuel Ayers at the New Century Theater, December 30, 1948 (after a tryout in Philadelphia, starting December 2, 1948); 1,077 performances. The cast included Alfred

Drake, Patricia Morison, Harold Lang, Lisa Kirk, Harry Clark, Jack Diamond, Lorenzo Fuller, and Annabelle Hill.

*Another Op'nin', Another Show
* Why Can't You Behave?
* Wunderbar
* So in Love
* We Open in Venice
* Tom, Dick or Harry
* I've Come to Wive It Wealthily in
  Padua
* I Hate Men
* Were Thine That Special Face
  I Sing of Love
  Kiss Me, Kate (finale, Act I)
  Tarantella (instrumental music)
* Too Darn Hot
* Where Is the Life That Late I Led?
* Always True to You in My Fashion
* Bianca
* Brush Up Your Shakespeare
* I Am Ashamed That Women Are So
  Simple
  Not Used:
  If Ever Married I'm
  I'm Afraid, Sweetheart, I Love You
  It Was Great Fun the First Time
  We Shall Never Be Younger
  What Does Your Servant Dream
  About?
  A Woman's Career

1949

Adam's Rib (film). Screenplay by Ruth Gordon and Garson Kanin. Directed by George Cukor. Produced by Lawrence Weingarten for MGM; released in 1949. The cast included Spencer Tracy, Katharine Hepburn, Judy Holliday, David Wayne, and Tom Ewell. One Cole Porter number was used in the film: *"Farewell, Amanda" (a revised version of "So Long, Samoa," written in 1940).

1950

Out of this World. Book by Dwight Taylor and Reginald Lawrence. Directed by Agnes de Mille. Produced by Saint Subber and Lemuel Ayers at the New Century Theater, December 21, 1950 (after tryouts in Philadelphia and Boston starting November 4, 1950); 157 performances. The cast included Charlotte Greenwood, William Eythe, David Burns, George Jongeyans (George Gaynes), Priscilla Gillette, William Redfield, and Barbara Ashley.

Prologue
  I Jupiter, I Rex
* Use Your Imagination
  Hail, Hail, Hail
  I Got Beauty
  Maiden Fair
* Where, Oh Where?
* I Am Loved
  They Couldn't Compare to
  You
  What Do You Think About
  Men?
  I Sleep Easier Now
* Climb Up the Mountain
* No Lover
* Cherry Pies Ought to Be You
* Hark to the Song of the Night
* Nobody's Chasing Me
  Not Used:
  Away from It All
* From This Moment On
  Hush, Hush, Hush
  Midsummer Night
  Oh, It Must Be Fun
  To Hell with Everything but Us
  Tonight I Love You More
  We Shall Never Be Younger
  We're on the Road to Athens
* Why Do You Want to Hurt Me
  So?
  You Don't Remind Me

1953

Can-Can. Book by Abe Burrows. Directed by Burrows. Produced by Cy Feuer and Ernest Martin at the Shubert Theater, May 7, 1935 (after a tryout in Philadelphia starting March 23, 1953); 892 performances. The cast included Lilo, Peter Cookson, Hans Conried, Gwen Verdon, Erik Rhodes, and Phil Leeds. A London production opened at the Coliseum Theatre, October 14, 1954; 394 performances.

Maidens Typical of France
* *Never Give Anything Away*
* *C'est Magnifique*
Quadrille (dance music)
* *Come Along with Me*
* *Live and Let Live*
* *I Am in Love*
* *If You Loved Me Truly*
* *Montmart'*
The Garden of Eden (dance music)
* *Allez-Vous-En*
Never, Never Be an Artist
* *It's All Right with Me*
Every Man Is a Stupid Man
Apache Dance (dance music)
* *I Love Paris*
* *Can-Can*
Not Used:
Am I in Love?
Her Heart Was in Her Work
I Do
I Shall Positively Pay You Next Monday
If Only You Could Love Me
Laundry Scene
The Law
A Man Must His Honor Defend
Nothing to Do but Work
To Think That This Could Happen to Me
What a Fair Thing Is a Woman
When Love Comes to Call
Who Said Gay Paree?

Kiss Me, Kate **(film).** Screenplay by Dorothy Kingsley; based on the play by Bella and Samuel Spewack. Directed by George Sidney. Produced by Jack Cummings for MGM; released in 1953. The cast included Howard Keel, Kathryn Grayson, Ann Miller, Keenan Wynn, James Whitmore, and Kurt Kaznar. Most of the numbers from the original score were used in the film. In addition, "From This Moment On," (dropped from *Out of this World*) was incorporated into the score.

1955

Silk Stockings. Book by George S. Kaufman, Leueen MacGrath, and Abe Burrows. Directed by Cy Feuer. Produced by Feuer and Ernest Martin at the Imperial Theater, February 24, 1955 (after tryouts in Philadelphia, Boston, and Detroit starting November 26, 1954); 478 performances. The cast included Don Ameche, Hildegarde Neff, Gretchen Wyler, George Tobias, David Opatoshu, Julie Newmar, and Leon Belasco.

Too Bad
* *Paris Loves Lovers*
* *Stereophonic Sound*
* *It's a Chemical Reaction, That's All*
* *All of You*
* *Satin and Silk*
* *Without Love*
Hail Bibinski
* *As On Through the Seasons We Sail*
* *Josephine*
* *Siberia*
* *Silk Stockings*
The Red Blues
Not Used:
Art
Bebe of Gay Paree

Boroff's Ode (instrumental music)
Give Me the Land
If Ever We Get Out of Jail (the same
  music but different text as "As
  On Through the Seasons We
  Sail")
I'm the Queen Thamar
Keep Your Chin Up
Let's Make It a Night
The Perfume of Love
Theme: Ode to a Tractor
  (instrumental music)
There's a Hollywood That's Good
Under the Dress
What a Ball
Why Should I Trust You?

1956

High Society (film). Screenplay by
John Patrick; based on Philip Barry's
play The Philadelphia Story. Directed
by Charles Walters. Produced by Sol
C. Siegel for MGM; released August
3, 1956. The cast included Bing
Crosby, Grace Kelly, Frank Sinatra,
Celeste Holm, John Lund, Louis
Armstrong, Louis Calhern, and Sid-
ney Blackmer.

*High Society Calypso
* I Love You, Samantha
* Little One
* Who Wants to Be a Millionaire?
* True Love
* You're Sensational
* Now You Has Jazz
* Well, Did You Evah! (slightly
  revised version of the original
  number)
* Mind If I Make Love to You?
Not Used:
Caroline
Hey Sexy
Let's Vocalize
So What?
A Step Montage

Anything Goes (film). This second of
two movie versions (screenplay by
Sidney Sheldon; directed by Robert
Lewis; produced by Robert Emmett
Dolan) by Paramount Pictures has little in common with the 1934 stage musical, save for the title and some Cole
Porter songs from the original score.
The cast included Bing Crosby, Donald O'Connor, Jeanmaire, Mitzi Gaynor, Kurt Kaznar, and Phil Harris.
Besides Porter songs, three numbers
by Sammy Kahn and Jimmy Van
Heusen were incorporated into the
film.

1957

Silk Stockings (film). Screenplay by
Leonard Spigelgass and Leonard
Gershe. Directed by Rouben
Mamoulian. Produced by Arthur
Freed for MGM; released in July,
1957. The cast included Fred Astaire,
Cyd Charisse, and Janis Paige. Most
of the numbers from the original
score were used in the film. In addition, two new Cole Porter numbers—
*"Fated to Be Mated" and *"Ritz Roll
and Rock"—were incorporated into
the score.

Les Girls (film). Screenplay by John
Patrick. Directed by George Cukor.
Produced by Sol C. Siegel for MGM;
released in November, 1957. The cast
included Gene Kelly, Kay Kendall,
Mitzi Gaynor, Taina Elg, Jacques
Bergerac, and Henry Daniell.

*Ca, C'est l'Amour
* Les Girls
  Ladies in Waiting
* Why Am I So Gone About That Gal?
* You're Just Too, Too!
Not Used:
Drinking Song

High Flyin' Wings on My Shoes
I Could Kick Myself
Is It Joy?
My Darling Never Is Late
My Little Piece o' Pie
Per Favore
What Fun
You're the Prize Guy of Guys

1958

*Aladdin (television musical). Book by S. J. Perelman. Directed by Ralph Nelson. Produced by Richard C. Lewine for CBS Television's "DuPont Show of the Month," February 21, 1958. The cast included Cyril Ritchard, Dennis King, Basil Rathbone, Una Merkel, Sal Mineo, and Anna Maria Alberghetti. A London stage production opened at the Coliseum Theatre, December 17, 1959, for a brief run.

*Trust Your Destiny to a Star
* Aladdin
* Come to the Supermarket in Old Peking

*I Adore You
* Make Way for the Emperor
* No Wonder Taxes Are High
* Opportunity Knocks But Once
* Wouldn't It Be Fun!
 Genie's Theme (instrumental music)

1960 .

Can-Can (film). Screenplay by Dorothy Kingsley and Charles Lederer. Directed by Walter Lang. Produced by Jack Cummings for 20th Century-Fox; film completed in 1959, but released in 1960. The film score incorporated key numbers from the 1953 stage musical as well as such Cole Porter plums as "Just One of Those Things" and "You Do Something to Me." Incorporated in the score, too, was an "Adam and Eve" ballet sequence based on the song "I Love Paris." The cast included Shirley MacLaine, Frank Sinatra, Maurice Chevalier, and Louis Jourdan.

Appendix 2:

Alphabetical List of Cole Porter Songs and Other Musical Works

ABRACADABRA
Mexican Hayride, 1944

ABSINTHE
The Kaleidoscope, 1913

ABSINTHE DRIP
The Kaleidoscope, 1913

ACE IN THE HOLE
Let's Face It, 1941

ADIOS ARGENTINA
Adios Argentina (unproduced film),
1934–35

**AFTER ALL, I'M ONLY A
SCHOOLGIRL**
Wake Up and Dream, 1929

AFTER YOU, WHO?
Gay Divorce, 1932

AH FONG LOW
Hitchy-Koo of 1922

ALADDIN
Aladdin, 1958

ALADDIN DANCE
Let's Face It (not used), 1941

**ALL I'VE GOT TO GET NOW
IS MY MAN**
Panama Hattie, 1940

ALL OF YOU
Silk Stockings, 1955

ALL THROUGH THE NIGHT
Anything Goes, 1934

ALLEZ-VOUS-EN
Can-Can, 1953

ALMIRO
La Revue des Ambassadeurs, 1928

ALONE WITH YOU
Very Good Eddie (English
production), 1918

ALPINE ROSE
La Revue des Ambassadeurs, 1928

ALTOGETHER TOO FOND OF
YOU (co-authored by James Heard
and Melville Gideon)
Telling the Tale (English
production), 1918, and *Buddies* (New
York production), 1919

ALWAYS TRUE TO YOU IN
MY FASHION
Kiss Me, Kate, 1948

AM I IN LOVE?
Can-Can (not used), 1953

THE AMERICAN EXPRESS
Hitch-Koo of 1922

AMERICANS ALL DRINK
COFFEE
Panama Hattie (not used), 1940

AMO AMAS
Mississippi Belle (unproduced
film), 1943–44

ANNOUNCEMENT OF
INHERITANCE
Something for the Boys, 1943

ANOTHER OP'NIN',
ANOTHER SHOW
Kiss Me, Kate, 1948

ANOTHER SENTIMENTAL
SONG
Hitchy-Koo of 1919 (not used)

ANTOINETTE BIRBY
Performed with the Yale Glee
Club, c. 1912

ANYTHING GOES
Anything Goes, 1934

APACHE DANCE
Can-Can, 1953

AQUA SINCOPADA TANGO
Wake Up and Dream, 1929

ART
Silk Stockings (not used), 1955

AS I LOVE YOU
The Kaleidoscope, 1913

AS LONG AS IT'S NOT ABOUT
LOVE
Leave It to Me (not used), 1938

AS ON THROUGH THE
SEASONS WE SAIL
Silk Stockings, 1955

ASSEMBLY LINE
Something for the Boys, 1943

A-STAIRABLE RAG
You'll Never Get Rich (not used), 1941

AT LAST IN YOUR ARMS
Balalaika (MGM film; not used),
1939

AT LONG LAST LOVE
You Never Know, 1938

AT LONGCHAMPS TODAY
Fifty Million Frenchmen, 1929

AT THE DAWN TEA
The Kaleidoscope, 1913

AT THE RAINBOW
The Pot of Gold, 1912

AT YE OLDE COFFEE SHOPPE
IN CHEYENNE
Red, Hot and Blue! 1936

AU REVIOR, CHER BARON
You Never Know, 1938

AUF WIEDERSEHEN
Star Dust, 1931, and *Once Upon a
Time*, 1933–34 (unproduced musicals)

AWAY FROM IT ALL
Out of This World (not used), 1950

BABY GAMES
Let's Face It, 1941

BABY, LET'S DANCE
La Revue des Ambassadeurs, 1928

BACK TO NATURE
Nymph Errant, 1933

BAD MEN
See America First, 1916

THE BAND STARTED
SWINGING A SONG
Seven Lively Arts, 1944

THE BANDIT BAND
Hitchy-Koo of 1922

THE BANJO THAT MAN JOE
PLAYS
Wake Up and Dream, 1929

BE A CLOWN
The Pirate, 1948

BE LIKE THE BLUEBIRD
Anything Goes, 1934

BEACH SCENE
Jubilee, 1935

THE BEARDED LADY
Written at Worcester Academy
sometime between 1905 and 1909

BEAUTIFUL, PRIMITIVE
INDIAN GIRLS
See America First, 1916

BEBE OF GAY PAREE
Silk Stockings (not used), 1955

BEGIN THE BEGUINE
Jubilee, 1935

BELLBOYS
The Pot of Gold, 1912

BERTIE AND GERTIE
Red, Hot and Blue! 1936

BETWEEN YOU AND ME
Broadway Melody of 1940

BEWARE OF THE
SOPHOMORE
The Kaleidoscope, 1913

BEWARE OF YALE
Yale football song, c. 1911

BIANCA
Kiss Me, Kate, 1948

BICHLORIDE OF MERCURY
See America First (not used),
1916

THE BIG PARADE
Seven Lively Arts, 1944

BIG TOWN
Seven Lively Arts, 1944

BINGO ELI YALE
Yale football song, 1910

BLOW, GABRIEL, BLOW
Anything Goes, 1934

THE BLUE BOY BLUES
Mayfair and Montmartre, 1922

BLUE HOURS
La Revue des Ambassadeurs,
1928

BOBOLINK WALTZ
Piano piece, 1902

BON VOYAGE
Anything Goes, 1934

BOOGIE BARCAROLLE
You'll Never Get Rich, 1941

BOROFF'S ODE
Silk Stockings (not used), 1955

THE BOY FRIEND BACK
HOME
Fifty Million Frenchmen, 1929

BRIDGET
Written at Yale, 1910

BRING ME A RADIO
Greenwich Village Follies, 1924

BRING ME BACK MY
BUTTERFLY
Hitchy-Koo of 1919

BRITTANY
Greenwich Village Follies, 1924

BROADCAST A JAZZ
Greenwich Village Follies, 1924

BRUSH UP YOUR
SHAKESPEARE
Kiss Me, Kate, 1948

BUDDIE BEWARE
Anything Goes, 1934

BULL DOG
Yale football song, 1911

BUT IN THE MORNING,
NO
DuBarry Was a Lady, 1939

BUTTERFLIES
Out o' Luck, 1925

BUY HER A BOX AT THE
OPERA
See America First, 1916

BY CANDLELIGHT
You Never Know (not used), 1938

BY THE MISSISSINEWAH
Something for the Boys, 1943

ÇA, C'EST L'AMOUR
Les Girls, 1957

CABINET MUSIC
Jubilee, 1935

CABLEGRAM
Cora, 1911

CAFE SOCIETY STILL
CARRIES ON
Seven Lively Arts (not used),
1944

CALIFORNIA SCENE
DANCE
Around the World in Eighty Days,
1946

CAN-CAN
Can-Can, 1953

CARLOTTA
Mexican Hayride, 1944

CAROLINE
High Society (not used), 1956

CARRY ON
Red, Hot and Blue! 1936

CASANOVA
Nymph Errant, 1933

C'EST MAGNIFIQUE
Can-Can, 1953

CHAPERONS
The Kaleidoscope, 1913

CHARITY
And the Villain Still Pursued Her,
1912

CHELSEA
The Eclipse (English production),
1919

CHERRY PIES OUGHT TO BE
YOU
Out of This World, 1950

THE CHIRIPAH
Adios Argentina (unproduced film),
1934-35

CLASS OF 1909 SONG
Written at Worcester Academy,
1909

CLASS OF 1913 SONG
Written for the first reunion of the
Yale class of 1913; 1914

CLEVELAND
Written for an annual meeting
of the Western Federation of
Yale Clubs held in Cleveland,
c. 1916

CLIMB UP THE MOUNTAIN
Out of This World, 1950

CLOSE
Rosalie, 1937

CLOSE TO ME
Mississippi Belle (unproduced film),
1943–44

COCKTAIL TIME
Mayfair and Montmartre, 1922

THE COCOTTE
Nymph Errant, 1933

COFFEE
Once Upon a Time (unproduced
musical), 1933–34

COME ALONG WITH ME
Can-Can, 1953

COME ON IN
DuBarry Was a Lady, 1939

COME TO BOHEMIA
And the Villain Still Pursued Her, 1912

COME TO THE
SUPERMARKET IN OLD
PEKING
Aladdin, 1958

COMRADE ALONZO
Leave It to Me, 1938

CONCENTRATION
Cora, 1911

CORA, THE FAIR CHORINE
Cora, 1911

COULD IT BE YOU?
Something for the Boys, 1943

COULDN'T BE
Something to Shout About (not used),
1942

COUNT YOUR BLESSINGS
Mexican Hayride, 1944

DAINTY, QUAINTY ME
Seven Lively Arts (not used), 1944

DANCE OF THE CRINOLINE
LADIES
Wake Up and Dream, 1929

DANCE OF THE
RAGAMUFFINS
Wake Up and Dream, 1929

DANCIN' TO A JUNGLE
DRUM
Seven Lively Arts, 1944

DANCING
And the Villain Still Pursued Her, 1912

DANSE EROTIQUE
Du Barry Was a Lady, 1939

DANSE TZIGANE
DuBarry Was a Lady, 1939

DANSE VICTOIRE
DuBarry was a Lady, 1939

DAWN MUSIC
See America First, 1916

DEAR DOCTOR
And the Villain Still Pursued Her, 1912

DIE SCHÖNE WIRTSTOCHTER
Star Dust, 1931, and *Once Upon a
Time*, 1933–34 (unproduced musicals)

DINNER
See America First (not used), 1916

DIZZY BABY
Paris (not used), 1928

DO I LOVE YOU?
DuBarry Was a Lady, 1939

DO YOU WANT TO SEE
PARIS?
Fifty Million Frenchmen, 1929

THE DOLLYS AND THEIR
COLLIES
Greenwich Village Follies, 1924

DON'T FENCE ME IN
Adios Argentina (unproduced
musical), 1934–35, and *Hollywood
Canteen*, 1944

DON'T LET IT GET YOU
DOWN
You Never Know, 1938

DON'T LOOK AT ME THAT
WAY
Paris, 1928

DON'T TELL ME WHO YOU
ARE
Written in the 1920s (not used)

DOWN IN A DUNGEON
DEEP
Paranoia, 1914

DOWN IN THE DEPTHS
Red, Hot and Blue! 1936

DOWN LOVERS' LANE
Paranoia, 1914

DOWN WITH EVERYBODY
BUT US
Fifty Million Frenchmen (not used),
1929

DREAM DANCING
You'll Never Get Rich, 1941

DREAM SONG
DuBarry Was a Lady, 1939

DRESDEN CHINA SOLDIERS
Paranoia, 1914

DRINK, DRINK, DRINK
Seven Lively Arts, 1944

DRINKING SONG
Les Girls (not used), 1957

DUBARRY WAS A LADY
DuBarry Was a Lady, 1939

DUODESSIMALOGUE
The Kaleidoscope, 1913

EASY TO LOVE
Born to Dance, 1936

ELI
Yale football song, 1911

ENTRANCE OF EMIGRANTS
Wake Up and Dream, 1929

ENTRANCE OF ERIC
Jubilee, 1935

ENTRANCE OF LUCY JAMES
Born to Dance, 1936

ENTRANCE OF MONTANA
Mexican Hayride, 1944

ENTRANCE OF PRINCE PAUL
Rosalie, 1937

ESMERALDA
Hands Up (a Sigmund Romberg
musical; the first Broadway
production to use a Cole Porter
song), 1915

EVER AND EVER YOURS
See America First, 1916

EVERY MAN IS A STUPID
MAN
Can-Can, 1953

EV'RY DAY A HOLIDAY
DuBarry Was a Lady, 1939

EV'RYBOD-EE WHO'S
ANYBOD-EE
Jubilee, 1935

EV'RYTHING I LOVE
Let's Face It, 1941

EV'RY TIME WE SAY
GOODBYE
Seven Lively Arts, 1944

EXCELSIOR (BOULEVARD
BREAK)
La Revue des Ambassadeurs, 1928

EXERCISE
The Pot of Gold, 1912

EXPERIMENT
Nymph Errant, 1933

THE EXTRA MAN
Wake Up and Dream (not used), 1929

FAIR ONE
Cora, 1911

FAIRY TALE
Let's Face It (not used), 1941

FAR AWAY
Leave It to Me, 1938

FAR, FAR AWAY
Cora, 1911

FARE THREE WELL
And the Villain Still Pursued Her,
1912

FAREWELL, AMANDA
Adam's Rib, 1949

FARMING
Let's Face It, 1941

FATE
Gay Divorce (not used), 1932

FATED TO BE MATED
Silk Stockings (film), 1957

FI, FI, FIFI
Written at Worcester Academy
between 1905 and 1909

FIND ME A PRIMITIVE MAN
Fifty Million Frenchmen, 1929

FISH
La Revue des Ambassadeurs, 1928

FIVE HUNDRED MILLION
Red, Hot and Blue! 1936

FLA DE DAH
Yale football song, 1911

FLOWER MAIDENS
The Kaleidoscope, 1913

FLOWER SONG
Paranoia, 1914

A FOOL THERE WAS
Rosalie (not used), 1937

A FOOTBALL KING
Yale football song, 1912

FOR NO RHYME OR REASON
You Never Know, 1938

FOUNTAIN OF YOUTH
La Revue des Ambassadeurs, 1928

FRAHNGEE-PAHNEE
Seven Lively Arts, 1944

FRESH AS A DAISY
Panama Hattie, 1940

FRIENDSHIP
DuBarry Was a Lady, 1939

FROM ALPHA TO OMEGA
You Never Know, 1938

FROM NOW ON
Leave It to Me, 1938

FROM THIS MOMENT ON
Out of This World (not used), 1950,
and *Kiss Me, Kate* (film), 1953

FUNNY LITTLE TRACKS IN
THE SNOW
Paranoia, 1914

THE GARDEN OF EDEN
Can-Can, 1953

GATHER YE AUTOGRAPHS
WHILE YE MAY
Jubilee, 1935

GAVOTTE
DuBarry Was a Lady, 1939

GENIE'S THEME
Aladdin, 1958

GEORGIA SAND
Nymph Errant, 1933

GERSHWIN SPECIALTY
La Revue des Ambassadeurs, 1928

GET OUT OF TOWN
Leave It to Me, 1938

GET YOURSELF A GIRL
Let's Face It, 1941

GIRLS
Mexican Hayride, 1944

GIVE HIM THE OO-LA-LA
DuBarry Was a Lady, 1939

GIVE ME THE LAND
Silk Stockings, 1955

GLIDE, GLIDER, GLIDE
Written for the armed forces,
1942

GO INTO YOUR DANCE
The New Yorkers, 1930

GOD BLESS THE WOMEN
Panama Hattie, 1940

THE GOLD DUSTERS SONG
Written for the Gold Dusters, a
Vassar College singing group,
1946

GOOD EVENING, PRINCESS
You Never Know, 1938

GOOD MORNING, MISS
STANDING
Jubilee, 1935

GOODBYE BOYS
Cora, 1911

GOODBYE, LITTLE DREAM,
GOODBYE
Red, Hot and Blue! (not used) 1936,
and *O Mistress Mine* (English
production), 1936

GOODBYE MY TRUE LOVE
The Kaleidoscope, 1913

THE GOOD-WILL MOVEMENT
Mexican Hayride, 1944

THE GREAT INDOORS
The New Yorkers, 1930

GREEK SCENE
Jubilee (not used), 1935

GREEK TO YOU
Greek to You (unproduced musical),
1937–38

THE GYPSY IN ME
Anything Goes, 1934

GYPSY SONG
Once Upon a Time (unproduced
musical), 1933–34

HA, HA, HA
You Never Know, 1938

HA, HA, THEY MUST SAIL
FOR SIBERIA
The Pot of Gold, 1912

HAIL BIBINSKI
Silk Stockings, 1955

HAIL, HAIL, HAIL
Out of This World, 1950

HAIL, HAIL TO CYRIL
Paranoia, 1914

HAIL THE FEMALE RELATIVE
See America First, 1916

HAIL TO YALE (music by Arthur Troostwyck)
Yale football song, 1911

HANS
La Revue des Ambassadeurs, 1928

THE HAPPY HEAVEN OF HARLEM
Fifty Million Frenchmen, 1929

THE HARBOR DEEP DOWN IN MY HEART
Hitchy-Koo of 1922

HARK TO THE SONG OF THE NIGHT
Out of This World, 1950

HASTA LUEGO
Something to Shout About, 1942

HE CERTAINLY KILLS THE WOMEN
Mexican Hayride (not used), 1944

THE HEAVEN HOP
Paris, 1928

THE HEAVEN OF HARLEM
Fifty Million Frenchmen (not used), 1929

HELLO, MISS CHAPEL STREET
Cora, 1911

HENCE, IT DON'T MAKE SENSE
Seven Lively Arts, 1944

HER HEART WAS IN HER WORK
Can-Can (not used), 1953

HERE COMES THE BANDWAGON
The Battle of Paris, 1929

HEREAFTER
Mexican Hayride (not used), 1944

HERE'S A CHEER FOR DEAR OLD CIRO'S
Mexican Hayride (not used), 1944

HERE'S TO PANAMA HATTIE
Panama Hattie (not used), 1940

HE'S A RIGHT GUY
Something for the Boys, 1943

HEY, BABE, HEY
Born to Dance, 1936

HEY, GOOD LOOKIN'
Something for the Boys, 1943

HEY SEXY
High Society (not used), 1956

HIGH FLYIN' WINGS ON MY SHOES
Les Girls (not used), 1957

HIGH SOCIETY CALYPSO
High Society, 1956

HIP, HIP HOORAY FOR ANDY JACKSON
Mississippi Belle (unproduced film), 1943–44

HOLD-UP ENSEMBLE
See America First, 1916

HOT-HOUSE ROSE
Written for Fanny Brice (not used), 1926

HOW COULD WE BE WRONG?
Nymph Errant, 1933

HOW DO THEY DO IT?
Written during the 1930s (not used)

HOW DO YOU SPELL AMBASSADOR?
Leave It to Me, 1938

HOW'S YOUR ROMANCE?
Gay Divorce, 1932

A HUMBLE HOLLYWOOD
EXECUTIVE
Mexican Hayride (not used), 1944

HUSH, HUSH, HUSH
Out of This World (not used), 1950

HYMN TO HYMEN
Red, Hot and Blue! 1936

I ADORE YOU
Aladdin, 1958

I ALWAYS KNEW
Something to Shout About, 1942

I AM ASHAMED THAT
WOMEN ARE SO SIMPLE
Kiss Me, Kate, 1948

I AM GASTON
You Never Know, 1938

I AM IN LOVE
Can-Can, 1953

I AM LOVED
Out of This World, 1950

I CAN DO WITHOUT TEA IN
MY TEAPOT
Something to Shout About (not used),
1942

I CONCENTRATE ON
YOU
Broadway Melody of 1940

I COULD KICK MYSELF
Les Girls (not used), 1957

I DO
Can-Can (not used), 1953

I DREAM OF A GIRL IN A
SHAWL
Wake Up and Dream, 1929

I GET A KICK OUT OF YOU
Anything Goes, 1934

I GOT BEAUTY
Out of This World, 1950

I HAPPEN TO BE IN LOVE
Broadway Melody of 1940 (not used)

I HAPPEN TO LIKE NEW
YORK
The New Yorkers, 1930

I HATE MEN
Kiss Me, Kate, 1948

I HATE YOU, DARLING
Let's Face It, 1941

I INTRODUCED
Hitchy-Koo of 1919

I JUPITER, I REX
Out of This World, 1950

I KNOW IT'S NOT MEANT
FOR ME
Rosalie (not used), 1937

I LIKE PRETTY THINGS
Mississippi Belle (unproduced film),
1943–44

I LOVE ONLY YOU
Gay Divorce (English production),
1933

I LOVE PARIS
Can-Can, 1953

I LOVE YOU
Mexican Hayride, 1944

I LOVE YOU SAMANTHA
High Society, 1956

I LOVE YOU SO
The Pot of Gold, 1912

I LOVED HIM BUT HE DIDN'T
LOVE ME
Wake Up and Dream, 1929

I NEVER REALIZED
The Eclipse (English production),
1919, and *Buddies* (New York
production), 1919

**I SHALL POSITIVELY PAY
YOU NEXT MONDAY**
Can-Can (not used), 1953

I SING OF LOVE
Kiss Me, Kate, 1948

I SLEEP EASIER NOW
Out of This World, 1950

**I STILL LOVE THE RED,
WHITE AND BLUE**
Gay Divorce, 1932

I WANT TO BE A YALE BOY
Written at Yale, 1912

**I WANT TO BE MARRIED (TO
A DELTA KAPPA EPSILON
MAN)**
The Pot of Gold, 1912

**I WANT TO BE RAIDED BY
YOU**
Wake Up and Dream, 1929

I WANT TO GO HOME
Leave It to Me, 1938

**I WANT TO ROW ON THE
CREW**
Paranoia, 1914

I WANT TWINS
Greenwich Village Follies, 1924

**I WONDER WHERE MY GIRL
IS NOW**
The Pot of Gold, 1912

I WORSHIP YOU
Fifty Million Frenchmen (not used),
1929

I WROTE A PLAY
Seven Lively Arts (not used), 1944

IDYLL
Paranoia, 1914

IF EVER MARRIED I'M
Kiss Me, Kate (not used), 1948

IF EVER WE GET OUT OF JAIL
Silk Stockings (not used), 1955

IF I HADN'T A HUSBAND
Seven Lively Arts (not used), 1944

**IF I WERE ONLY A FOOTBALL
MAN**
The Pot of Gold (not used), 1912

**IF IN SPITE OF OUR
ATTEMPTS**
See America First (not used), 1916

**IF ONLY YOU COULD LOVE
ME**
Can-Can (not used), 1953

IF YOU COULD LOVE ME
Adios Argentina (unproduced film),
1943–44

IF YOU LOVED ME TRULY
Can-Can, 1953

IF YOU SMILE AT ME
Around the World in Eighty Days,
1946

I'LL BLACK HIS EYES
You Never Know (not used), 1938

ILSA'S SONG
Once Upon a Time (unproduced
musical), 1933–34

I'M A GIGOLO
Wake Up and Dream (1929)

I'M AFRAID I LOVE YOU
Mexican Hayride (not used), 1944

**I'M AFRAID, SWEETHEART, I
LOVE YOU**
Kiss Me, Kate (not used), 1948

I'M AN ANAESTHETIC
DANCER
Hitchy-Koo of 1919

I'M BACK IN CIRCULATION
You Never Know (not used), 1938

I'M DINING WITH ELSA
Written in the 1920s (not used)

I'M GETTING MYSELF READY
FOR YOU
The New Yorkers, 1930

I'M GOING IN FOR LOVE
You Never Know (not used), 1938

I'M IN LOVE
Fifty Million Frenchmen, 1929

I'M IN LOVE AGAIN
Greenwich Village Follies, 1924

I'M IN LOVE WITH A
SOLDIER BOY
Something for the Boys, 1943

I'M NOT MYSELF AT ALL
Mississippi Belle (unproduced film),
1943–44

I'M SO GLAHD TO MEET
YOU
Mexican Hayride (not used), 1944

I'M SO IN LOVE WITH YOU
Broadway Melody of 1940 (not used)

I'M TAKING THE STEPS TO
RUSSIA
Leave It to Me, 1938

I'M THE QUEEN THAMAR
Silk Stockings (not used), 1955

I'M THROWING A BALL
TONIGHT
Panama Hattie, 1940

I'M UNLUCKY AT GAMBLING
Fifty Million Frenchmen, 1929

I'M YOURS
You Never Know (not used), 1938

IN A MOORISH GARDEN
La Revue des Ambassadeurs, 1928

IN CINCINNATI
*We're All Dressed Up and We Don't
Know Huerta Go*, 1914

IN HITCHY'S GARDEN
Hitchy-Koo of 1919

IN THE BIG MONEY
DuBarry Was a Lady (not used), 1939

IN THE GREEN HILLS OF
COUNTY MAYO
Mississippi Belle (unproduced film),
1943–44

IN THE LAND WHERE MY
HEART WAS BORN
The Kaleidoscope, 1913

IN THE STILL OF THE
NIGHT
Rosalie, 1937

INDIAN GIRLS' CHANT
See America First, 1916

INDIAN MAIDENS' CHORUS
See America First, 1916

INFORMATION PLEASE
Leave It to Me (not used), 1938

INNOCENT, INNOCENT
MAIDS
Paranoia, 1914

IS IT JOY?
Les Girls (not used), 1957

IS IT THE GIRL? (OR IS IT
THE GOWN?)
Seven Lively Arts, 1944

IT AIN'T ETIQUETTE
DuBarry Was a Lady, 1939

IT ALL BELONGS TO YOU
Break the News, 1938

IT ALL SEEMS SO LONG AGO
Once Upon a Time (unproduced
musical), 1933–34

IT ISN'T DONE
Fifty Million Frenchmen, 1929

IT MIGHT HAVE BEEN
Something to Shout About (not used),
1942

IT MUST BE FUN TO BE YOU
Mexican Hayride (not used), 1944

IT NEVER ENTERED MY
HEAD
Greek to You (unproduced musical),
1937–38

IT PAYS TO ADVERTISE
Written at Yale, 1912

IT PUZZLES ME SO
Written around 1918 (not used)

IT WAS GREAT FUN THE
FIRST TIME
Kiss Me, Kate (not used), 1948

IT WAS WRITTEN IN THE
STARS
DuBarry Was a Lady, 1939

ITALIAN STREET SINGERS
Written in the 1920s (not used)

IT'S A BIG NIGHT
Mexican Hayride (not used), 1944

IT'S A CHEMICAL REACTION,
THAT'S ALL
Silk Stockings, 1955

IT'S A GREAT LIFE
Red, Hot and Blue! 1936

IT'S ALL OVER BUT THE
SHOUTING
Rosalie, 1937

IT'S ALL RIGHT WITH ME
Can-Can, 1953

IT'S AWFULLY HARD WHEN
MOTHER'S NOT ALONG
The Pot of Gold, 1912

IT'S BAD FOR ME
Nymph Errant, 1933

IT'S DE-LOVELY
Red, Hot and Blue! 1936

IT'S JUST LIKE THE GOOD
OLD DAYS
Mexican Hayride (not used), 1944

IT'S JUST YOURS
Mexican Hayride (not used), 1944

IT'S NO LAUGHING MATTER
You Never Know (not used), 1938

IT'S PROBABLY JUST AS WELL
Star Dust (unproduced musical), 1931

I'VE A SHOOTING BOX IN
SCOTLAND
Paranoia, 1914, and *See America First*,
1916

I'VE A STRANGE NEW
RHYTHM IN MY HEART
Rosalie, 1937

I'VE COME TO WIVE IT
WEALTHILY IN PADUA
Kiss Me, Kate, 1948

I'VE GOT A CRUSH ON YOU
Wake Up and Dream, 1929

I'VE GOT AN AWFUL LOT TO
LEARN
See America First, 1916

I'VE GOT MY EYES ON YOU
Broadway Melody of 1940

I'VE GOT SOME UNFINISHED
BUSINESS WITH YOU
Let's Face It, 1941

I'VE GOT SOMEBODY
WAITING
Hitchy-Koo of 1919

I'VE GOT YOU ON MY MIND
Gay Divorce, 1932

I'VE GOT YOU UNDER MY
SKIN
Born to Dance, 1936

I'VE STILL GOT MY HEALTH
Panama Hattie, 1940

JAVA
Written in the 1930s (not used)

JERRY, MY SOLDIER BOY
Let's Face It, 1941

JOIN IT RIGHT AWAY
Panama Hattie, 1940

JOSEPHINE
Silk Stockings, 1955

JUBILEE PRESENTATION
Jubilee, 1935

THE JUDGMENT OF PARIS
Jubilee, 1935

JUST ANOTHER PAGE IN
YOUR DIARY
Leave It to Me (not used),
1938

JUST ONE OF THOSE
THINGS (not the famous song)
The New Yorkers (not used), 1930

JUST ONE OF THOSE
THINGS
Jubilee, 1935

JUST ONE STEP AHEAD OF
LOVE
You Never Know (not used), 1938

KATE THE GREAT
Anything Goes (not used), 1934

KATHLEEN
Mississippi Belle (unproduced film),
1943–44

KATIE OF THE Y.M.C.A.
Written around 1918 (not used)

KATIE WENT TO HAITI
DuBarry Was a Lady, 1939

KEEP MOVING
La Revue des Ambassadeurs, 1928

KEEP YOUR CHIN UP
Silk Stockings, 1955

KISS ME, KATE
Kiss Me, Kate, 1948

THE KLING-KLING BIRD ON
THE DIVI-DIVI TREE
Jubilee, 1935

LADIES IN WAITING
Les Girls, 1957

LADY FAIR, LADY FAIR
See America First (not used), 1916

THE LADY I LOVE
Wake Up and Dream (not used),
1929

THE LADY I'VE VOWED TO
WED
See America First, 1916

A LADY NEEDS A REST
Let's Face It, 1941

THE LANGUAGE OF
FLOWERS
See America First, 1916

L'APRES-MIDI D'UN BOEUF
DuBarry Was a Lady, 1939

LAUNDRY SCENE
Can-Can (not used), 1953

THE LAW
Can-Can (not used), 1953

THE LAZIEST GAL IN TOWN
Written in 1927, but not used until
Marlene Dietrich performed it in
Stage Fright in 1950

LEAD ME ON
Once Upon a Time (unproduced
musical), 1933–34

THE LEADER OF A BIG-TIME
BAND
Something for the Boys, 1943

LEADERS OF SOCIETY
And the Villain Still Pursued Her, 1912

LE REVE D'ABSINTHE
Cora, 1911

LES GIRLS
Les Girls, 1957

LET DOCTOR SCHMET VET
YOUR PET
Something to Shout About (not used),
1942

LET'S BE BUDDIES
Panama Hattie, 1940

LET'S DO IT, LET'S FALL IN
LOVE
Paris, 1928, and *Wake Up and Dream,*
1929

LET'S FACE IT
Let's Face It, 1941

LET'S FLY AWAY
The New Yorkers, 1930

LET'S MAKE IT A NIGHT
Silk Stockings (not used), 1955

LET'S MISBEHAVE
Performed at Les Ambassadeurs
nightclub in 1927, and included in
the score for *Paris,* 1928, but not
used.

LET'S NOT TALK ABOUT
LOVE
Let's Face It, 1941

LET'S STEP OUT
Fifty Million Frenchmen, 1929

LET'S VOCALIZE
High Society (not used), 1956

THE LIFE OF A SAILOR
Greenwich Village Follies (not used),
1924

LIMA
See America First, 1916

LITTLE ONE
High Society, 1956

A LITTLE RUMBA NUMBA
Let's Face It, 1941

A LITTLE SKIPPER FROM
HEAVEN ABOVE
Red, Hot and Blue! 1936

LIVE AND LET LIVE
Can-Can, 1953

LLEWELLYN
And the Villain Still Pursued Her,
1912

LOADING SONG
Mississippi Belle (unproduced film),
1943–44

LOIE AND CHLODO
The Pot of Gold, 1912

LONELY STAR
Red, Hot and Blue! (not used),
1936

LONGING FOR DEAR OLD
BROADWAY
The Pot of Gold, 1912

LOOK AROUND (lyrics by
Clifford Grey)
A Night Out (English production),
1920

LOOK WHAT I FOUND
Around the World in Eighty Days,
1946

LOOKING AT YOU
La Revue des Ambassadeurs, 1928, and
Wake Up and Dream, 1929

THE LOST LIBERTY BLUES
La Revue des Ambassadeurs, 1928

LOTUS BLOOM
Something to Shout About, 1942

LOVE CAME AND CROWNED
ME
See America First (not used), 1916

LOVE 'EM AND LEAVE 'EM
Written in the 1920s (not used)

LOVE FOR SALE
The New Yorkers, 1930

LOVE LETTER WORDS
Hitchy-Koo of 1922

LOVE ME, LOVE MY
PEKINESE
Born to Dance, 1936

LOVE OF MY LIFE
The Pirate, 1948

THE LOVELY HEROINE
And the Villain Still Pursued Her, 1912

MA PETITE NINETTE
Cora, 1911

MACK THE BLACK
The Pirate, 1948

MADEMAZELLE
Out o' Luck, 1925

MAID OF SANTIAGO
The Kaleidoscope, 1913

MAIDEN FAIR
Out of This World, 1950

MAIDENS TYPICAL OF
FRANCE
Can-Can, 1953

MAKE A DATE WITH A
GREAT PSYCHOANALYST
Let's Face It (not used), 1941

MAKE EVERY DAY A
HOLIDAY
Greenwich Village Follies, 1924

MAKE IT ANOTHER
OLD-FASHIONED PLEASE
Panama Hattie, 1940

MAKE WAY FOR THE
EMPEROR
Aladdin, 1958

MAMIE MAGDALIN
Mississippi Belle (unproduced film),
1943–44

A MAN MUST HIS HONOR
DEFEND
Can-Can (not used), 1953

MANUELA
The Pirate (not used), 1948

MARIA
You Never Know, 1938

MARTINIQUE
The Pirate (not used), 1948

MARYLAND SCENE
Hitchy-Koo of 1922

MAYBE YES, MAYBE NO
Written in the 1930s (not used)

ME AND MARIE
Jubilee, 1935

MEET ME BESIDE THE
RIVER
The Kaleidoscope, 1913

MELOS, THAT LOVELY
SMILING ISLE
Greek to You (unproduced musical),
1937–38

A MEMBER OF THE YALE
ELIZABETHAN CLUB
The Kaleidoscope, 1913

MERCY PERCY
Written at Yale, c. 1912

MESDAMES ET MESSIEURS
DuBarry Was a Lady, 1939

MIDSUMMER NIGHT
Out of This World (not used),
1950

MILITARY MAIDS
La Revue des Ambassadeurs, 1928

MILK, MILK, MILK
Let's Face It, 1941

MIND IF I MAKE LOVE TO
YOU?
High Society, 1956

MIRROR, MIRROR
See America First, 1916

MISS CHAPEL STREET
Written at Yale, 1911

MISS OTIS REGRETS
Hi Diddle Diddle (English
production), 1934

MISSISSIPPI BELLE
Mississippi Belle (unproduced film),
1943–44

MISSUS AOUDA
Around the World in Eighty Days (not
used), 1946

MISTER AND MISSUS FITCH
Star Dust (unproduced musical), 1931,
and *Gay Divorce*, 1932

MONA AND HER KIDDIES
The New Yorkers (not used), 1930

MONTMART'
Can-Can, 1953

MOON MAN
The Kaleidoscope, 1913

MOST GENTLEMEN DON'T
LIKE LOVE
Leave It to Me, 1938

MOTHER PHI
Cora, 1911

THE MOTOR CAR
Written at Yale, 1911

MR. AND MRS. SMITH
Jubilee, 1935

MUSIC WITH MEALS
Written at Yale, 1912

MY BROTH OF A BOY
Mississippi Belle (unproduced film),
1943–44

MY COZY LITTLE CORNER IN
THE RITZ
Hitchy-Koo of 1919

MY DARLING NEVER IS
LATE
Les Girls (not used), 1957

MY GEORGIA GAL
The Kaleidoscope, 1913

MY HARLEM WENCH
Fifty Million Frenchmen (not used),
1929

MY HEART BELONGS TO
DADDY
Leave It to Me, 1938

MY HOME TOWN GIRL
Cora, 1911

MY HOUSEBOAT ON THE
THAMES
The Pot of Gold, 1912

MY LITTLE BARCELONA
MAID
And the Villain Still Pursued Her, 1912

MY LITTLE PIECE O' PIE
Les Girls (not used), 1957

MY LONG AGO GIRL
Greenwich Village Follies, 1924

MY LOUISA
Wake Up and Dream (not used), 1929

MY LOULOU
Jubilee, 1935

MY MOST INTIMATE FRIEND
Jubilee, 1935

MY MOTHER WOULD LOVE
YOU
Panama Hattie, 1940

MY SALVATION ARMY
QUEEN
The Pot of Gold, 1912

MYSTERIOUSLY
Star Dust (unproduced musical), 1931

NAUGHTY, NAUGHTY
Paranoia, 1914

NEAUVILLE-SUR-MER
Nymph Errant, 1933

NEVER GIVE ANYTHING
AWAY
Can-Can, 1953

NEVER, NEVER BE AN
ARTIST
Can-Can, 1953

NEVER SAY NO
Gay Divorce (English production),
1933

NIGHT AND DAY
Gay Divorce, 1932

NIGHT CLUB OPENING
Wake Up and Dream, 1929

THE NIGHT OF THE BALL
Once Upon a Time (unproduced
show), 1933–34

NINA
The Pirate, 1948

NO LOVER
Out of This World, 1950

NO SHOW THIS EVENING
Written at Yale, 1911

NO WONDER TAXES ARE
HIGH
Aladdin, 1958

NOBODY'S CHASING ME
Out of This World, 1950

NOTHING TO DO BUT WORK
Can-Can (not used), 1953

NOW YOU HAS JAZZ
High Society, 1956

NYMPH ERRANT
Nymph Errant, 1933

OCTET
Mexican Hayride (not used), 1944

OH, BRIGHT FAIR DREAM
See America First (not used), 1916

OH, HONEY
Written around 1919 (not used)

OH, HOW I COULD GO FOR
YOU
Something for the Boys (not used),
1943

OH, IT MUST BE FUN
Out of This World (not used), 1950

OH, MARY
Hitchy-Koo of 1922

OH, WHAT A LONELY
PRINCESS
Paranoia, 1914

OKA SAKA CIRCUS
Around the World in Eighty Days,
1946

OLD-FASHIONED GARDEN
Hitchy-Koo of 1919

OLD-FASHIONED GIRL
(OLD-FASHIONED BOY)
La Revue des Ambassadeurs, 1928

THE OLD-FASHIONED WALTZ
Hitchy-Koo of 1922 (not used)

THE OLD RAT MORT
Cora, 1911

OLGA (COME BACK TO THE
VOLGA)
Mayfair and Montmartre, 1922

OMNIBUS
La Revue des Ambassadeurs, 1928

ON MY YACHT
The Kaleidoscope, 1913

ONCE UPON A TIME
Once Upon a Time (unproduced
musical), 1933–34

ONLY ANOTHER BOY AND
GIRL
Seven Lively Arts, 1944

OPERA STAR
Out o' Luck, 1925

OPERATIC PILLS
Wake Up and Dream, 1929

OPPORTUNITY KNOCKS BUT
ONCE
Aladdin, 1958

OUR CROWN
Jubilee, 1935

OUR HOTEL (lyrics by Clifford
Grey)
A Night Out (English production),
1920

OURS
Red, Hot and Blue! 1936

THE OZARKS ARE CALLIN'
ME HOME
Red, Hot and Blue! 1936

PAGLIACCI
Hitchy-Koo of 1919

PARANOIA
Paranoia, 1914

PAREE, WHAT DID YOU DO
TO ME?
Fifty Million Frenchmen, 1929

PARIS LOVES LOVERS
Silk Stockings, 1955

PER FAVORE
Les Girls (not used), 1957

PERENNIAL DEBUTANTES
Red, Hot and Blue! 1936

PERFECTLY TERRIBLE
Written at Yale, 1910

THE PERFUME OF LOVE
Silk Stockings (not used), 1955

PETER PIPER
Hitchy-Koo of 1919

PETS
Let's Face It (not used), 1941

THE PHYSICIAN
Nymph Errant, 1933

PICK ME UP AND LAY ME
DOWN
Star Dust (unproduced musical),
1931

A PICTURE OF ME WITHOUT
YOU
Jubilee, 1935

PILOT ME
La Revue des Ambassadeurs,
1928

PIPE DREAMING
Around the World in Eighty Days,
1946

PITTER PATTER
Hitchy-Koo of 1922 (not used)

PITY ME PLEASE
See America First, 1916

PLAY ME A TUNE
Hitchy-Koo of 1922 as well as *The
Dancing Girl* (a Sigmund Romberg
musical), 1923, and *One Dam Thing
After Another* (English production),
1927

PLEASE DON'T MAKE ME BE
GOOD
Fifty Million Frenchmen (not used),
1929

PLEASE DON'T MONKEY
WITH BROADWAY
Broadway Melody of 1940

PLUMBING
Nymph Errant, 1933

POKER
Cora, 1911

THE POOR RICH
The New Yorkers (not used), 1930

POOR YOUNG MILLIONAIRE
Written in the 1920s (not used)

THE PREP SCHOOL WIDOW
Paranoia, 1914

PRETTY LITTLE MISSUS
BELL
Seven Lively Arts (not used), 1944

PRITHEE COME CRUSADING
WITH ME
See America First, 1916

PROLOGUE
Out of This World, 1950

PUBLIC ENEMY NUMBER ONE
Anything Goes, 1934

PUT A SACK OVER THEIR
HEADS
Mexican Hayride (not used), 1944

QUADRILLE
Can-Can, 1953

THE QUEEN OF TERRE
HAUTE
Fifty Million Frenchmen (not used),
1929

QUEEN OF THE YALE
DRAMAT
Cora, 1911

QUEENS OF TERPSICHORE
And the Villain Still Pursued Her, 1912

QUELQUE-CHOSE
Paris (not used), 1928

THE RAGTIME PIPES OF
PAN
Phi-Phi (English production), 1922

RAP-TAP ON WOOD
Born to Dance, 1936

RECALL GOODHUE
Leave It to Me, 1938

THE RED BLUES
Silk Stockings, 1955

RED, HOT AND BLUE
Red, Hot and Blue! 1936

REVELATION ENSEMBLE
See America First (not used), 1916

REVENGE
Let's Face It, 1941

RICK-CHICK-A-CHICK
The Kaleidoscope, 1913

RIDDLE DIDDLE ME THIS
Something for the Boys (not used), 1943

RIDIN' HIGH
Red, Hot and Blue! 1936

RITZ ROLL AND ROCK
Silk Stockings (film), 1957

RIVER GOD
The Sun Never Sets (English
production), 1938

ROLLING HOME
Born to Dance, 1936

ROLLING, ROLLING
Cora, 1911

ROSALIE
Rosalie, 1937

ROSEBUD
Cora, 1911

RUB YOUR LAMP
Let's Face It, 1941

RUINS
Nymph Errant, 1933

SAILORS OF THE SKY
Written for the armed forces,
1942

SALT AIR
Gay Divorce, 1932

SATIN AND SILK
Silk Stockings, 1955

SATURDAY NIGHT
Cora, 1911

SAY IT WITH GIN
The New Yorkers, 1930

THE SCAMPI
Written in 1926 (later became THE
TALE OF THE OYSTER)

SCANDAL
The Pot of Gold, 1912

SCHOOL, SCHOOL,
HEAVEN-BLESSED SCHOOL
Mississippi Belle (unproduced film),
1943–44

SCOTCH TWINS
Hitchy-Koo of 1922 (not used)

SEA CHANTEY
Around the World in Eighty Days,
1946

SEE AMERICA FIRST
See America First, 1916

SEE THAT YOU'RE BORN IN
TEXAS
Something for the Boys, 1943

SERENADE
See America First (not used),
1916

SEX APPEAL
Written around 1927 (not used)

SHE WAS A FAIR YOUNG
MERMAID
The Pot of Gold, 1912

SHOOTIN' THE WORKS FOR
UNCLE SAM
You'll Never Get Rich, 1941

SHOULD I TELL YOU I LOVE
YOU?
Around the World in Eighty Days,
1946

SI VOUS AIMEZ LES POITRINES
Nymph Errant, 1933

SIBERIA
Silk Stockings, 1955

THE SIDE CAR
Adios Argentina (unproduced film), 1934–35

A SIGHT-SEEING TOUR
Mexican Hayride (not used), 1944

SILK STOCKINGS
Silk Stockings, 1955

SILVER MOON
And the Villain Still Pursued Her, 1912

SINCE I KISSED MY BABY GOODBYE
You'll Never Get Rich, 1941

SINCE MA GOT THE CRAZY ESPAGNOLE
Hitchy-Koo of 1919

SINCE WE'VE MET
The Pot of Gold, 1912

SING JUBILEE
Jubilee (not used), 1935

SING SING FOR SING SING
The New Yorkers, 1930

SING TO ME GUITAR
Mexican Hayride, 1944

SINGING IN THE SADDLE
Adios Argentina (unproduced film), 1934–35

SIX LITTLE WIVES
Jubilee, 1935

SLAVE AUCTION
Around the World in Eighty Days (not used), 1946

SLOW SINKS THE SUN
Paranoia, 1914, and *See America First* (not used), 1916

SNAGTOOTH GERTIE
Around the World in Eighty Days (not used), 1946

THE SNAKE IN THE GRASS
Fifty Million Frenchmen (not used), 1929

SO IN LOVE
Kiss Me, Kate, 1948

SO LET US HAIL
The Pot of Gold, 1912

SO LONG
Mississippi Belle (unproduced film), 1943–44

SO LONG, SAMOA
Written in 1940 (not used; later became FAREWELL, AMANDA)

SO LONG, SAN ANTONIO
Something for the Boys (not used), 1943

SO NEAR AND YET SO FAR
You'll Never Get Rich, 1941

SO WHAT?
High Society (not used), 1956

THE SOCIAL COACH OF ALL THE FASHIONABLE FUTURE DEBUTANTES
See America First (not used), 1916

SOLOMON
Nymph Errant, 1933

SOMEBODY'S GOING TO THROW A BIG PARTY
Fifty Million Frenchmen, 1929

SOMETHING FOR THE BOYS
Something for the Boys, 1943

SOMETHING TO SHOUT
ABOUT
Something to Shout About, 1942

SOMETHING'S GOT TO BE
DONE
See America First, 1916

SONG OF THE BIRDS
Piano piece, 1901

SOUTH SEA ISLES
Hitchy-Koo of 1922 (not used)

THE SPONGE
Hitchy-Koo of 1922

SPRING LOVE IS IN THE AIR
Rosalie, 1937

A STEP MONTAGE
High Society (not used), 1956

STEP WE GRANDLY
See America First (not used), 1916

STEREOPHONIC SOUND
Silk Stockings, 1955

A STROLL ON THE PLAZA
SANT'ANA
Panama Hattie, 1940

STROLLING
And the Villain Still Pursued Her, 1912

STROLLING QUITE FANCY
FREE
See America First (not used), 1916

SUBMARINE
And the Villain Still Pursued Her,
1912

SUCCESS
Once Upon a Time (unproduced
musical), 1933–34

SUEZ DANCE
Around the World in Eighty Days,
1946

SUNDAY MORNING,
BREAKFAST TIME
Jubilee, 1935

SUTTEE PROCESSION
Around the World in Eighty Days,
1946

SWEET NUDITY
Nymph Errant (not used), 1933

SWEET SIMPLICITY
See America First (not used), 1916

SWING THAT SWING
Jubilee, 1935

SWINGIN' THE JINX AWAY
Born to Dance, 1936

SYNCOPATED PIPES OF PAN
Greenwich Village Follies, 1924

A TABLE FOR TWO
Written around 1920 (not used)

TAKE IT EASY
Something to Shout About (not used),
1942

TAKE ME BACK TO
MANHATTAN
The New Yorkers, 1930

THE TALE OF THE OYSTER
Fifty Million Frenchmen, 1929

TARENTELLA
Kiss Me, Kate, 1948

THE TATTOOED
GENTLEMAN
Written at Worcester Academy
between 1905 and 1909

TECHNIQUE
Once Upon a Time (unproduced
musical), 1933–34

TEQUILA
Mexican Hayride (not used), 1944

TEXAS WILL MAKE YOU A MAN
Something for the Boys (not used), 1943

THANK YOU
Once Upon a Time (unproduced musical), 1933–34

THANK YOU SO MUCH, MRS. LOWSBOROUGH-GOODBY
Written in 1934 (and published that year as an independent song)

THAT BLACK AND WHITE BABY OF MINE
Hitchy-Koo of 1919 (not used)

THAT LITTLE OLD BAR AT THE RITZ
Written in the 1920s (not used)

THAT RAINBOW RAG
The Pot of Gold (not used), 1912

THAT ZIP CORNWALL COOCH
And the Villain Still Pursued Her, 1912

THAT'S THE NEWS I'M WAITING TO HEAR
Red, Hot and Blue! (not used), 1936

THAT'S WHAT YOU MEAN TO ME
Mexican Hayride (not used), 1944

THAT'S WHY I LOVE YOU
Fifty Million Frenchmen (not used), 1929

THEME: ODE TO A TRACTOR
Silk Stockings (not used), 1955

THERE HE GOES, MR. PHILEAS FOGG
Around the World in Eighty Days, 1946

THERE MUST BE SOMEONE FOR ME
Mexican Hayride, 1944

THERE'LL ALWAYS BE A LADY FAIR
Anything Goes, 1934

THERE'S A FAN
Leave It to Me (not used), 1938

THERE'S A HAPPY LAND IN THE SKY
Something for the Boys, 1943

THERE'S A HOLLYWOOD THAT'S GOOD
Silk Stockings (not used), 1955

THERE'S NO CURE LIKE TRAVEL
Anything Goes (not used), 1934

THERE'S NOTHING LIKE SWIMMING
Jubilee (not used), 1935

THEY AIN'T DONE RIGHT BY OUR NELL
Panama Hattie, 1940

THEY ALL FALL IN LOVE
The Battle of Paris, 1929

THEY COULDN'T COMPARE TO YOU
Out of This World, 1950

THEY'RE ALWAYS ENTERTAINING
Nymph Errant, 1933

THROUGH THICK AND THIN
Something to Shout About, 1942

TIRED OF LIVING ALONE
Written around 1919 (not used)

TO FOLLOW EVERY FANCY
See America First, 1916

TO HELL WITH EVERYTHING BUT US
Out of This World (not used), 1950

TO LOVE OR NOT TO LOVE
Rosalie, 1937

TO THE U.S.A. FROM THE
U.S.S.R.
Leave It to Me, 1938

TO THINK THAT THIS
COULD HAPPEN TO ME
Can-Can (not used), 1953

A TOAST TO VOLSTEAD
Fifty Million Frenchmen, 1929

TOM, DICK OR HARRY
Kiss Me, Kate, 1948

TOMORROW
Leave It to Me, 1938

TONIGHT I LOVE YOU MORE
Out of This World (not used), 1950

TOO BAD
Silk Stockings, 1955

TOO DARN HOT
Kiss Me, Kate, 1948

TOY OF DESTINY
Greenwich Village Follies, 1924

TRUE LOVE
High Society, 1956

TRUST YOUR DESTINY TO A
STAR
Aladdin, 1958

TWILIGHT
And the Villain Still Pursued Her,
1912

TWIN SISTERS
Hitchy-Koo of 1922 (not used)

TWO BIG EYES (lyrics by John
Golden)
Miss Information (a Jerome Kern
musical), 1915

TWO LITTLE BABES IN THE
WOOD
Greenwich Village Follies (1924) and
Paris, 1928

UNDER THE DRESS
Silk Stockings (not used), 1955

UNDERSTUDIES
Greenwich Village Follies (not used),
1924

UP TO HIS OLD TRICKS
AGAIN
Let's Face It (not used), 1941

THE UPPER PARK AVENUE
Written in the 1930s (not used)

USE YOUR IMAGINATION
Out of This World, 1950

VENICE
The New Yorkers, 1930

VENUS OF MILO
Written around 1920 (not used)

THE VILLAIN
And the Villain Still Pursued Her,
1912

VISIT PANAMA
Panama Hattie, 1940

VITE, VITE, VITE
Leave It to Me, 1938

VIVIENNE
Paris, 1928

VOODOO
The Pirate (not used), 1948

WAIT FOR THE MOON
Greenwich Village Follies, 1924

WAIT UNTIL IT'S
BEDTIME
Wake Up and Dream, 1929

WAITERS v. WAITRESSES
Gay Divorce (English production),
1933

WAKE, LOVE, WAKE
See America First (not used), 1916

WAKE UP AND DREAM
Wake Up and Dream, 1929

WALTZ DOWN THE AISLE
Once Upon a Time (unproduced
musical), 1933–34, *Anything Goes* (not
used), 1934, and *Jubilee* (not used),
1935 (later became WUNDERBAR)

WAR SONG
Written around 1918 (a parody of
Jerome Kern's THEY DIDN'T
BELIEVE ME)

WASHINGTON, D.C.
Something for the Boys (not used),
1943

WASHINGTON SQUARE (lyrics
by Cole Porter and E. Ray Goetz,
and music by Melville Gideon)
Buddies, 1919, and *As You Were*, 1920
(the same tune as CHELSEA)

WATCHING THE WORLD GO
BY
Fifty Million Frenchmen (not used),
1929

WE ARE PROM GIRLS
The Kaleidoscope, 1913

WE ARE SO AESTHETIC
The Pot of Gold, 1912

WE ARE THE CHORUS OF
THE SHOW
And the Villain Still Pursued Her,
1912

WE DETEST A FIESTA
Panama Hattie, 1940

WE DRINK TO YOU J. H.
BRODY
Leave It to Me, 1938

WE OPEN IN VENICE
Kiss Me, Kate, 1948

WE SHALL NEVER BE
YOUNGER
Kiss Me, Kate (not used), 1948

THE WEDDING CAKE-WALK
You'll Never Get Rich, 1941

A WEEKEND AFFAIR
Gay Divorce (not used), 1932

WELCOME TO JERRY
Panama Hattie, 1940

WELL, DID YOU EVAH!
DuBarry Was a Lady, 1939, and *High
Society* (revised lyrics), 1956

WELL, I JUST WOULDN'T
KNOW
Something for the Boys (not used), 1943

WERE THINE THAT SPECIAL
FACE
Kiss Me, Kate, 1948

WE'RE A GROUP OF
NONENTITIES
The Kaleidoscope, 1913

WE'RE ABOUT TO START BIG
REHEARSIN'
Red, Hot and Blue! 1936

WE'RE OFF
Cora, 1911

WE'RE OFF FOR A HAYRIDE
IN MEXICO
Mexican Hayride (not used), 1944

WE'RE OFF TO
FEATHERMORE
Jubilee, 1935

WE'RE ON THE ROAD TO
ATHENS
Out of This World (not used), 1950

WEREN'T WE FOOLS
Written for Fanny Brice and
published in 1927; dropped from her
show at the Palace Theater

WE'VE BEEN SPENDING THE
SUMMER WITH OUR
FAMILIES
The New Yorkers (not used), 1930

WHAT A BALL
Silk Stockings (not used), 1955

WHAT A CHARMING
AFTERNOON
The Pot of Gold, 1912

WHAT A CRAZY WAY TO
SPEND SUNDAY
Mexican Hayride, 1944

WHAT A FAIR THING IS A
WOMAN
Can-Can (not used), 1953

WHAT A GREAT PAIR WE'LL
BE
Red, Hot and Blue! 1936

WHAT A JOY TO BE YOUNG
Anything Goes (not used), 1934

WHAT A NICE MUNICIPAL
PARK
Jubilee, 1935

WHAT A PRICELESS
PLEASURE
You Never Know (not used), 1938

WHAT AM I TO DO
Written for *The Man Who Came to
Dinner*, 1939

WHAT AN AWFUL
HULLABALOO
The Pot of Gold, 1912

WHAT ARE LITTLE
HUSBANDS MADE OF
Let's Face It (not used), 1941

WHAT DO YOU THINK
ABOUT MEN?
Out of This World, 1950

WHAT DOES YOUR SERVANT
DREAM ABOUT?
Kiss Me, Kate (not used), 1948

WHAT FUN
Les Girls (not used)

WHAT HAVE I?
DuBarry Was a Lady (not used), 1939

WHAT IS THAT TUNE?
You Never Know, 1938

WHAT IS THIS THING
CALLED LOVE?
Wake Up and Dream, 1929

WHAT LOVE IS
Paranoia, 1914

WHAT SHALL I DO?
You Never Know, 1938

WHAT WILL BECOME OF OUR
ENGLAND?
Gay Divorce, 1932

WHAT'S MY MAN GONNA BE
LIKE?
The Vanderbilt Revue, 1930

WHEN A BODY'S IN LOVE
See America First (not used), 1916

WHEN A WOMAN'S IN LOVE
Mississippi Belle (unproduced film),
1943–44

WHEN BLACK SALLIE SINGS
PAGLIACCI
Hitchy-Koo of 1919

WHEN I HAD A UNIFORM ON
Hitchy-Koo of 1919

WHEN I USED TO LEAD THE
BALLET
The Pot of Gold, 1912, and *See America
First*, 1916

WHEN I WAS A LITTLE
CUCKOO
Seven Lively Arts, 1944

WHEN I'M EATING AROUND
WITH YOU
Written at Yale, 1912

WHEN ALL'S SAID AND
DONE
Leave it to Me, 1938

WHEN LOVE BECKONED
DuBarry Was a Lady, 1939

WHEN LOVES COME TO CALL
Can-Can (not used), 1953

WHEN LOVE COMES YOUR
WAY
Nymph Errant (not used), 1933, and
Jubilee, 1935

WHEN McKINLEY MARCHES
ON
Mississippi Belle (unproduced film),
1943–44

WHEN ME, MOWGLI, LOVE
Jubilee, 1935

WHEN MY BABY GOES TO
TOWN
Something for the Boys, 1943

WHEN MY CARAVAN COMES
HOME
Hitchy-Koo of 1922

WHEN THE HEN STOPS
LAYING
Leave It to Me (not used), 1938

WHEN THE SUMMER MOON
COMES 'LONG
Written at Yale, 1910

WHEN WE'RE HOME ON THE
RANGE
Something for the Boys, 1943

WHEN YOU AND I WERE
STRANGERS
Mississippi Belle (unproduced film),
1943–44

WHEN YOUR TROUBLES
HAVE STARTED
Red, Hot and Blue! (not used), 1936

WHERE?
Red, Hot and Blue! (not used), 1936

WHERE ARE THE MEN?
Anything Goes, 1934

WHERE DO WE GO FROM
HERE?
Seven Lively Arts (not used), 1944

WHERE HAVE YOU BEEN?
The New Yorkers, 1930

WHERE IS THE LIFE THAT
LATE I LED?
Kiss Me, Kate, 1948

WHERE, OH WHERE?
Out of This World, 1950

WHERE WOULD YOU GET
YOUR COAT?
Fifty Million Frenchmen, 1929

WHERE'S LOUIE?
DuBarry Was a Lady, 1939

WHEREVER THEY FLY THE
FLAG OF OLD ENGLAND
Around the World in Eighty Days,
1946

WHICH
Paris (not used), 1928, and *Wake Up
and Dream*, 1929

THE WHIP DANCE
Let's Face It (not used), 1941

WHO, BUT YOU
Red, Hot and Blue! (not used), 1936

WHO KNOWS?
Rosalie, 1937

WHO SAID GAY PAREE?
Can-Can (not used), 1953

WHO WANTS TO BE A MILLIONAIRE?
High Society, 1956

WHO WOULD HAVE DREAMED?
Panama Hattie, 1940

WHO'LL BID
Mississippi Belle (unproduced film), 1943–44

WHY AM I SO GONE ABOUT THAT GAL?
Les Girls, 1957

WHY CAN'T YOU BEHAVE?
Kiss Me, Kate, 1948

WHY DIDN'T WE MEET BEFORE? (lyrics by Clifford Grey)
A Night Out (English production), 1920

WHY DO YOU WANT TO HURT ME SO?
Out of This World (not used), 1950

WHY DON'T WE TRY STAYING HOME?
Fifty Million Frenchmen (not used), 1929

WHY MARRY THEM?
Gay Divorce, 1932

WHY SHOULD I CARE?
Rosalie, 1937

WHY SHOULD I TRUST YOU?
Silk Stockings (not used), 1955

WHY SHOULDN'T I?
Jubilee, 1935

WHY SHOULDN'T I HAVE YOU?
Fifty Million Frenchmen, 1929

WHY TALK ABOUT SEX?
The New Yorkers (not used), 1930

WIDOW'S CRUISE
Written around 1919 (not used)

WILD WEDDING BELLS
Greek to You (unproduced musical), 1937–38

WILL YOU LOVE ME WHEN MY FLIVVER IS A WRECK?
See America First, 1916

WITHIN THE QUOTA
Ballet score, 1923

WITHOUT LOVE
Silk Stockings, 1955

A WOMAN'S CAREER
Kiss Me, Kate (not used), 1948

WOND'RING NIGHT AND DAY
Mayfair and Montmartre (not used), 1922

WON'T YOU COME CRUSADING WITH ME
Paranoia, 1914

WOODLAND DANCE
See America First, 1916

WOULDN'T IT BE CRAZY
Something for the Boys (not used), 1943

WOULDN'T IT BE FUN!
Aladdin, 1958

WOW-OOH-WOLF
Seven Lively Arts, 1944

WUNDERBAR
Kiss Me, Kate, 1948

YANKEE DOODLE
Fifty Million Frenchmen, 1929

YELLOW MELODRAMA
Written at Yale, 1911

YES, YES, YES
You Never Know, 1938

YOU AND ME
La Revue des Ambassadeurs, 1928

YOU CAN DO NO WRONG
The Pirate, 1948

YOU CAN'T BEAT MY BILL
Let's Face It (not used), 1941

YOU DO SOMETHING TO ME
Fifty Million Frenchmen, 1929

YOU DON'T KNOW PAREE
Fifty Million Frenchmen, 1929

YOU DON'T REMIND ME
Out of This World (not used), 1950

YOU IRRITATE ME SO
Let's Face It, 1941

YOU MAKE UP
Written around 1920 (not used)

YOU NEVER KNOW
You Never Know, 1938

YOU SAID IT
Panama Hattie, 1940

YOU'D BE SO NICE TO COME
HOME TO
Something to Shout About, 1942

YOU'RE A BAD INFLUENCE
ON ME
Red, Hot and Blue! 1936

YOU'RE IN LOVE
Gay Divorce, 1932

YOU'RE JUST TOO, TOO!
Les Girls, 1957

YOU'RE SENSATIONAL
High Society, 1956

YOU'RE THE PRIZE GUY OF
GUYS
Les Girls (not used), 1957

YOU'RE THE TOP
Anything Goes, 1934

YOU'RE TOO FAR AWAY
Nymph Errant, 1933

YOURS
Once Upon a Time (unproduced
musical), 1933–34, and *Jubilee* (not
used), 1935

YOURS FOR A SONG
Seven Lively Arts (not used), 1944

YOU'VE GOT SOMETHING
Red, Hot and Blue! 1936

YOU'VE GOT THAT THING
Fifty Million Frenchmen, 1929

YOU'VE GOT TO BE
HARD-BOILED
The New Yorkers (not used), 1930

ZOMBIE DANCE
DuBarry Was a Lady (not used), 1939

Appendix 3:

*A
Selected Cole Porter
Discography*

Many hundreds of recordings of Cole Porter songs have been made over the years, and new ones are being released all the time. As a consequence, a selected discography can at best only barely touch the surface of what has become a veritable deluge of Porter recordings. Within the limits of this discography, two listings are given. The first focuses on relatively recent releases (from 1965 on, though quite a few of these releases derive from recordings from an earlier period) that are presumably available. The second listing concentrates on record-ings—many of them 78 rpm collectors' items of very doubtful availability—that have some historical relevance to Cole Porter's career.

RELATIVELY RECENT RELEASES, PRESUMABLY AVAILABLE

"Bobby Short Loves Cole Porter" A two-record album by Bobby Short (sup-ported by bassist Beverly Peer and drummer Richard Sheridan) of twenty-two numbers, among them such Porter chestnuts as "Just One of Those Things," "At Long Last Love," and "Do I Love You?" The album also includes such little-known tunes as "Why Don't We Try Staying Home?" *(Fifty Million Frenchmen)*, "Once Upon a Time" (from the unproduced musical by the same title), and "By Candlelight" *(You Never Know)*, as well as two songs Cole wrote for Fanny Brice: "Hot-House Rose" and "Weren't We Fools." Atlantic SD 2–606.

"Born to Dance" Eleanor Powell, James Stewart, Virginia Bruce, Frances Lang-ford, and Buddy Ebsen, among others, are heard singing (from the original sound track of this 1936 film) "Rolling Home," "Rap-Tap On Wood," "Hey, Babe, Hey," "Love Me, Love My Pekinese," "Easy to Love," "I've Got You Under My Skin," and "Swingin' the Jinx Away." C.I.F. 3001.

"Broadway Melody of 1940" Fred Astaire, Eleanor Powell, George Murphy, and others, sing (from the original sound track of this film) "Please Don't Monkey with Broadway," "Between You and Me," "I've Got My Eyes on You," "I Concentrate on You," and "Begin the Beguine." C.I.F. 3002.

"Cole" One of several recordings by that title, this is a two-record album of a 1974 entertainment based on Cole Porter's work that was presented at London's Mermaid Theatre. This album contains a broad sampling of Porter numbers, ranging from an orchestral version of the early piano piece, "Bobolink Waltz" (1901), to Yale songs, to tunes from Broadway and Hollywood musicals, among them "You Don't Know Paree," "Love for Sale," "I Happen to Like New York," "Night and Day," "Anything Goes," "In the Still of the Night," and "Be a Clown." The performers are Ray Cornell, Lucy Fenwick, Peter Gale, Bill Kerr, Julia McKenzie, Rod McLennan, Kenneth Nelson, Elizabeth Power, Angela Richards, and Una Stubbs. RCA LRL2–5054.

"Cole" This English release features Elaine Stritch, Patricia Routledge, Ian Carmichael, Susannah McCorkle, and the Mike Sammes Singers performing twenty-one of Cole Porter's better-known numbers, among them "Night and Day," "I Get a Kick Out of You," "True Love," "In the Still of the Night," "I'm in Love Again," "Thank You So Much, Mrs. Lowsborough-Goodby," "Don't Fence Me In," "Why Can't You Behave?" "Begin the Beguine," "Anything Goes," "Miss Otis Regrets," "Easy to Love," "You'd Be So Nice to Come Home To," "You're the Top," and "Let's Do It, Let's Fall in Love." EMI EMC–3049.

"Cole" On side 1 of this album Cole Porter himself is heard—in a recording made not for commercial distribution, but to demonstrate to performers how his numbers were to be done—singing and playing nine selections from *Jubilee*: "A Picture of Me Without You," "Entrance of Eric," "The Kling-Kling Bird on the Divi-Divi Tree," "When Love Comes Your Way," "What a Nice Municipal Park," "When Me, Mowgli, Love," "Ev'rybod-ee Who's Anybod-ee," "Sunday Morning, Breakfast Time," and "Me and Marie." On the reverse side Porter reminisces about his career and introduces Mary Martin, Danny Kaye, and Ethel Merman, who sing "My Heart Belongs to Daddy" (Mary Martin), "Most Gentlemen Don't Like Love" (Mary Martin), "Let's Not Talk About Love" (Danny Kaye), "Farming" (Danny Kaye), "You're the Top" (Ethel Merman), and "I Get a Kick Out of You" (Ethel Merman). Columbia KS-31456.

"Cole Porter—1924–1944" A two-record album of thirty-two Porter numbers, spanning a twenty-year period. Porter himself is heard singing and playing eight numbers (taken from the only commercial recordings he ever made, in 1934 and 1935). They are: "Two Little Babes in the Wood," "I'm a Gigolo," "The Physician," "The Cocotte," "Thank You So Much, Mrs. Lowsborough-Goodby,"

"You're the Top," "Be Like the Bluebird," and "Anything Goes." Other performers include Ethel Merman, Fred Astaire, Frances Langford, Martha Tilton, Benny Goodman, and the Paul Whiteman Orchestra doing numbers from *Anything Goes, Jubilee, Born to Dance, Red, Hot and Blue!, Panama Hattie, Let's Face It, You'll Never Get Rich, Something for the Boys,* and *Seven Lively Arts*. JJA 19732 (a limited edition, available only at Music Masters, Inc., in New York City).

"Cole Porter (Music and Lyrics)" Twenty-one selections from *Red, Hot and Blue!, DuBarry Was a Lady, Panama Hattie, Mexican Hayride, Seven Lively Arts,* and *Around the World in Eighty Days* performed by Ethel Merman, Bert Lahr, Bob Hope, June Havoc, Wilbur Evans, and others. JJA 19745 (a limited edition, available only at Music Masters, Inc., in New York City).

"Cole Porter Revisited" Fourteen lesser-known Porter numbers are performed by David Allen, Kaye Ballard, Ronny Graham, Bibi Osterwald, and Bobby Short (musical arranger for the album is Norman Paris). The songs: "Come On In" *(DuBarry Was a Lady)*, "A Little Skipper from Heaven Above" *(Red, Hot and Blue!)*, "You're a Bad Influence on Me" *(Red, Hot and Blue!)*, "I've Still Got My Health" *(Panama Hattie)*, "But In the Morning, No" *(DuBarry Was a Lady)*, "Since I Kissed My Baby Goodbye" *(You'll Never Get Rich)*, "By the Mississinewah" *(Something for the Boys)*, "I'm Throwing a Ball Tonight" *(Panama Hattie)*, "Far Away" *(Leave It to Me)*, "Solomon" *(Nymph Errant)*, "It Ain't Etiquette" *(DuBarry Was a Lady)*, "The Tale of the Oyster" *(Fifty Million Frenchmen)*, "I Worship You" *(Fifty Million Frenchmen)*, and "Red, Hot and Blue" *(Red, Hot and Blue!)*. Painted Smiles PS–1340.

"The Decline and Fall of the Entire World as Seen Through the Eyes of Cole Porter" Twelve numbers and a finale from this 1965 Ben Bagley production, based largely on lesser-known Porter songs, are performed by Kaye Ballard, Harold Lang, Carmen Alvarez, William Hickey, and Elmarie Wendel. The songs: "I Introduced" *(Hitchy-Koo of 1919)*, "I'm a Gigolo" *(Wake Up and Dream)*, "The Leader of a Big-Time Band" *(Something for the Boys)*, "I Loved Him But He Didn't Love Me" *(Wake Up and Dream),*. "I Happen to Like New York" *(The New Yorkers)*, "What Shall I Do?" *(You Never Know)*, "Tomorrow" *(Leave It to Me)*, "Farming" *(Let's Face It)*, "Give Him the Oo-La-La" *(DuBarry Was a Lady)*, "Make It Another Old-Fashioned, Please," "Down in the Depths," and "Most Gentlemen Don't Like Love" *(Leave It to Me)*. Columbia COS–2810.

"Ella Fitzgerald Sings the Cole Porter Songbook" A recent reissue of an earlier recording that has not been available for some years. This two-record album features Ella Fitzgerald, accompanied by Buddy Bregman and his orchestra, singing thirty-two of Porter's best-known numbers, among them "Night and Day," "You're the Top," "Easy to Love," "Begin the Beguine," "Miss Otis Regrets," and "Don't Fence Me In." Verve 2683044.

"Ella Loves Cole" Ella Fitzgerald, accompanied by Nelson Riddle and his orchestra, sings thirteen Porter numbers: "I Get a Kick Out of You," "Down in the

Depths," "At Long Last Love," "I've Got You Under My Skin," "So Near and Yet So Far" *(You'll Never Get Rich)*, "All of You," "Without Love" *(Silk Stockings)*, "My Heart Belongs to Daddy," "Love for Sale," "Just One of Those Things," "I Concentrate on You," "Anything Goes," and "C'est Magnifique." Atlantic SD–1631.

"The Great Hits of Cole Porter" The Ray Ellis Strings, conducted by Ray Ellis and Johnny Douglas, perform "Night and Day," "C'est Magnifique," "You'd Be So Nice to Come Home To," "I Love Paris," "In the Still of the Night," "Easy to Love," "Begin the Beguine," "True Love," and "I Get a Kick Out of You." RCA CAS–2522.

"Lee Wiley Sings George Gershwin and Cole Porter" Lee Wiley originally recorded the eight Porter songs in this album in 1939 and 1940, for Liberty Records. Cole Porter was so pleased with the results that he sent his congratulations to Miss Wiley. The Porter songs in this reissue are: "Looking At You," "Let's Fly Away," "Why Shouldn't I?" "Hot-House Rose," "You Do Something to Me," "Find Me a Primitive Man," "Easy to Love," and "Let's Do It, Let's Fall in Love." Monmouth-Evergreen MES–7034.

"Meyer Davis Plays Cole Porter" Thirty-six of Cole Porter's best-known tunes, among them "Just One of Those Things," "I've Got You Under My Skin," "It's All Right with Me," "Why Can't You Behave?" "From This Moment On," "All of You," "You Do Something to Me," "I Get a Kick Out of You," "Wunderbar," "So in Love," and "In the Still of the Night," are performed in a series of medleys by a "society" orchestra (a fitting ensemble for Porter numbers) under Meyer Davis's supervision. Monmouth-Evergreen MES–6813.

"The Music of Cole Porter" Frank Chacksfield and his orchestra perform "Night and Day," "Begin the Beguine," "I Love Paris," "My Heart Belongs to Daddy," "Ev'ry Time We Say Goodbye," "Wunderbar," "Just One of Those Things," "You'd Be So Nice to Come Home To," "Friendship," "In the Still of the Night," and "Blow, Gabriel, Blow." London SP–44185.

"Paul Whiteman—Volume 1" The album contains numbers by various composers (among them George Gershwin and Cole Porter) that the Paul Whiteman Orchestra recorded between 1920 and 1934, including this Porter medley from *Anything Goes*: "Anything Goes," "I Get a Kick Out of You," "You're the Top," "Waltz Down the Aisle," and "All Through the Night." RCA (Vintage Series) LPV–555.

"Unpublished Cole Porter" Fifteen little-known Porter numbers, many of them not used in the shows they were written for, are performed by Carmen Alvarez, Blossom Dearie, Edward Earle, Laura Kenyon, Karen Morrow, Alice Playten, and Charles Rydell. The songs are "Get Yourself a Girl" *(Let's Face It)*, "When Love Comes to Call" *(Can-Can)*, "After All, I'm Only a Schoolgirl" *(Wake Up and Dream)*, "If Ever Married I'm" *(Kiss Me, Kate)*, "Kate the Great" *(Kiss Me, Kate)*,

"What Does Your Servant Dream About?" *(Kiss Me, Kate)*, "Oh, It Must Be Fun" *(Out of This World)*, "Pets" *(Let's Face It)*, "Si Vous Aimez Les Poitrines" *(Nymph Errant)*, "To Think That This Could Happen to Me" *(Can-Can)*, "A Humble Hollywood Executive" *(Mexican Hayride)*, "I Know It's Not Meant for Me" *(Rosalie)*, "Where Would You Get Your Coat?" *(Fifty Million Frenchmen)*, "I Could Kick Myself" *(Les Girls)*, and "Give Me the Land" *(Silk Stockings)*. Painted Smiles PS–1358.

RECORDINGS OF HISTORICAL RELEVANCE TO COLE PORTER'S CAREER
(Many of Doubtful Availability)

"See America First" (1916) The Joseph C. Smith Orchestra performs "I've a Shooting Box in Scotland." Victor 18165 (this is the first known commercial recording of a Porter number).

"The Eclipse" (English production) (1919) Nancy Gibbs and F. Pope Stamper, of the original cast, sing "Chelsea" and "I Never Realized" (lyrics by Cole Porter; music by Melville Gideon). Columbia (English) F–1033.

The Garrick Theatre Orchestra performs selections from the show, including "Chelsea" and "I Never Realized." Columbia (English) 783.

"A Night Out" (English production) (1920) Lily St. John and Leslie Henson, of the original cast, sing "Why Didn't We Meet Before?" (lyrics by Clifford Grey; music by Cole Porter). Columbia (English) F–1061.

The same artists perform "Look Around" (lyrics by Clifford Grey; music by Cole Porter). Columbia (English) F–1062.

"Greenwich Village Follies" (1924) In a recording made some ten years after the original production, Cole Porter sings and plays "Two Little Babes in the Wood." Victor 24825 (this rendition is included in the album "Cole Porter—1924–1944").

"Paris" (1928) Irving Aaronson's Commanders play and sing "Let's Misbehave." Victor 21260.

Irene Bordoni and Irving Aaronson's Commanders perform "Don't Look at Me that Way." Victor 21742.

Irving Aaronson's Commanders play and sing "Let's Do It, Let's Fall in Love." Victor 21745.

"Wake Up and Dream" (1929) In a recording made some five years after the original production, Cole Porter sings and plays "I'm a Gigolo." Victor 24843 (this rendition is included in the album "Cole Porter—1924–1944").

George Metaxa, of the original cast, sings "What Is This Thing Called Love?" and "Wake Up and Dream." HMV B–3016.

Leslie "Hutch" Hutchinson sings and plays (piano) "Looking At You" and "Let's Do It, Let's Fall in Love." Parlophone F–242, R–342.

Hutchinson also sings and plays "What Is This Thing Called Love?" and "I'm a Gigolo." Parlophone F–243, R–343.

The Leslie Hutchinson Orchestra performs selections from the show. Parlophone E–10869.

"The New Yorkers" (1930) Fred Waring's Pennsylvanians (and the Three Waring Girls) perform "Where Have You Been?" and "Love for Sale." Victor 22598 ("Love for Sale," by the same ensemble, is also on Victor 25080).

"Gay Divorce" (1932) Fred Astaire, accompanied by the Leo Reisman Orchestra, sings "I've Got You on My Mind" and "Night and Day." Victor 24193 ("Night and Day," by Astaire and the Reisman Orchestra, is also on Victor 24716).

From the 1933 English production, Astaire sings "After You, Who?" and "Night and Day." Columbia (English) DB-1215, FB-1255.

"Nymph Errant" (1933) In a recording made a year or so after the original production, Cole Porter sings and plays "The Cocotte" and "The Physician." Victor 24859 (these renditions are included in the album "Cole Porter—1924–1944").

Gertrude Lawrence, of the original cast, sings "Experiment" and "The Physician." HMV B-8029, Victor 25224.

Gertrude Lawrence performs "How Could We Be Wrong?" and "It's Bad for Me." HMV B-8030, Victor 25225.

Gertrude Lawrence sings "Nymph Errant," and Elisabeth Welch, of the original cast, performs "Solomon." HMV B-8031, Victor 25226.

The five numbers—"Experiment," "The Physician," "How Could We Be Wrong?" "It's Bad for Me," and "Nymph Errant"—that Gertrude Lawrence recorded on three 78 rpm records for HMV and Victor were later reissued on one ten-inch LP: Victor LRT-7001.

"Anything Goes" (1934) Cole Porter sings and plays "You're the Top." Victor 24766.

Porter performs "Anything Goes." Victor 24825.

Porter sings and plays "Be Like the Blubird." Victor 24843 (Porter's renditions of "You're the Top," "Anything Goes," and "Be Like the Bluebird" on three 78 rpm records for Victor are included in the LP album "Cole Porter—1924–1944").

The "Anything Goes Foursome," from the show, perform "There'll Always Be a Lady Fair" and "The Gypsy in Me." Victor 24817 (these renditions are included in the album "Cole Porter—1924–1944").

Ethel Merman, of the original cast, sings "I Get a Kick Out of You" and "You're the Top." Brunswick 7342, Liberty L-261.

Ethel Merman performs "I Get a Kick Out of You" and "You're the Top." Decca 24451.

Ethel Merman sings "Blow, Gabriel, Blow." Decca 24453.

Ethel Merman's renditions of "I Get a Kick Out of You" and "You're the Top" (on Brunswick) are included in a recent "Cole" (LP) album. Columbia KS-31456.

" 'Party' Songs" (**1934**) Cole Porter sings and plays "Thank You So Much, Mrs. Lowsborough-Goodby." Victor 24766 (this rendition is included in the album "Cole Porter—1924–1944").

Douglas Byng performs "Miss Otis Regrets" (this song was used in the 1934 English production of *Hi Diddle Diddle*, of which Byng was a cast member). Decca (English) F-5249.

"Jubilee" (**1935**) Cole Porter sings and plays nine selections from *Jubilee*—"A Picture of Me Without You," "Entrance of Eric," "The Kling-Kling Bird on the Divi-Divi Tree," "When Love Comes Your Way," "What a Nice Municipal Park," "When Me, Mowgli, Love," "Ev'rybod-ee Who's Anybod-ee," "Sunday Morning, Breakfast Time," and "Me and Marie"—to demonstrate to performers how his numbers were to be done (though not originally recorded for commercial distribution, these renditions are included in a recent "Cole" album). Columbia KS-31456.

Artie Shaw and his orchestra perform "Begin the Beguine." This recording was made in July of 1938, nearly three years after the show opened (the first recording of the number was by the Xavier Cugat Orchestra; Victor 25133), but it helped to make the song famous. Bluebird B-7746.

"Born to Dance" (**1936**) Frances Langford, of the original cast, sings "I've Got You Under My Skin" and "Rap-Tap On Wood." Decca 939.

Frances Langford performs "Easy to Love" and "Swingin' the Jinx Away." Decca 940.

Virginia Bruce, of the original cast, sings "I've Got You Under My Skin" and "Easy to Love." Brunswick 7765.

As previously mentioned, a relatively recent LP release—taken from the original sound track of this film—features singing by Eleanor Powell, James Stewart, Virginia Bruce, Frances Langford, Buddy Ebsen, and others, of "Rolling Home," "Rap-Tap On Wood," "Hey, Babe, Hey," "Love Me, Love My Pekinese," "Easy to Love," "I've Got You Under My Skin," and "Swingin' the Jinx Away. C.I.F. 3001.

"Red, Hot and Blue!" (**1936**) A performance of "It's De-Lovely" by Ethel Merman and Bob Hope, of the original cast, is included in the recent LP release, "Cole Porter (Music and Lyrics)," mentioned earlier. JJA 19745.

"O Mistress Mine" (**English production**) (**1936**) Yvonne Printemps and Pierre Fresnay, of the original cast, perform "Goodbye, Little Dream, Goodbye." HMV DA-1539 (this rendition is included in the album "Cole Porter—1924–1944").

"Leave It to Me" (**1938**) Mary Martin, of the original cast, performs—with Eddie Duchin's Orchestra—"My Heart Belongs to Daddy" and "Most Gentlemen Don't Like Love." Brunswick 8282.

Mary Martin's renditions of "My Heart Belongs to Daddy" and "Most Gentlemen Don't Like Love" (on Brunswick) are included in a recent "Cole" album. Columbia KS-31456.

"The Sun Never Sets" (English production) (1938) Todd Duncan, of the original cast, sings "River God." Columbia (English) DB-1778.

"Broadway Melody of 1940" (1939) As already stated, the original sound track of this film is the basis for a recent LP release which highlights Fred Astaire, Eleanor Powell, George Murphy, and others from the cast, singing "Please Don't Monkey with Broadway," "Between You and Me," "I've Got My Eyes on You," "I Concentrate on You," and "Begin the Beguine." C.I.F. 3002.

"DuBarry Was a Lady" (1939) A performance of "Friendship" by Ethel Merman and Bert Lahr, of the original cast, is included in the LP release, "Cole Porter (Music and Lyrics)."

"Panama Hattie" (1940) Ethel Merman, of the original cast, sings "Let's Be Buddies" (with Joan Carroll), "Make It Another Old-Fashioned, Please," "My Mother Would Love You," and "I've Still Got My Health." Decca 203.

Ethel Merman performs "Let's Be Buddies" (with Joan Carroll) and "Make It Another Old-Fashioned, Please." Decca 18187.

Ethel Merman sings "My Mother Would Love You" and "I've Still Got My Health." Decca 23200.

Ethel Merman's renditions of "Let's Be Buddies" (with Joan Carroll), "Make It Another Old-Fashioned, Please," "My Mother Would Love You," and "I've Still Got My Health," on Decca, are included in the LP album "Cole Porter— 1924–1944."

A performance of "I'm Throwing a Ball Tonight," by Ethel Merman, is included in the LP album "Cole Porter (Music and Lyrics)."

"You'll Never Get Rich" (1941) Martha Tilton, of the original cast, sings "The Wedding Cake-Walk." Decca 4029 (this rendition is included in the album "Cole Porter—1924–1944").

Fred Astaire, of the original cast, performs selections from the film. Vocalion VL-3716.

Fred Astaire sings "So Near and Yet So Far" and—with the Delta Rhythm Boys—"Since I Kissed My Baby Goodbye." Decca 18187 (the rendition of "Since I Kissed My Baby Goodbye" is included in the album "Cole Porter—1924–1944").

Fred Astaire performs "Dream Dancing" and—with the Delta Rhythm Boys —"The Wedding Cake-Walk." Decca 18188.

"Let's Face It" (1941) Mary Jane Walsh, of the original cast, sings "Farming" and "I Hate You, Darling." Liberty L-343.

Mary Jane Walsh performs "Ev'rything I Love" and "Ace In the Hole." Liberty L-344 (Miss Walsh's renditions of "Farming," "I Hate You, Darling," "Ev'rything I Love," and "Ace In the Hole" are included in the album "Cole Porter— 1924–1944").

Danny Kaye, of the original cast, sings "Let's Not Talk About Love." Columbia 36582.

Danny Kaye performs "Farming." Columbia 36583.

Danny Kaye's renditions—on two 78 rpm sides—of "Let's Not Talk About Love" and "Farming" are included in a recent "Cole" album. Columbia KS-31456.

"Something for the Boys" (**1943**) Paula Laurence, of the original cast, performs "Something for the Boys" and—with Betty Garrett—"By the Mississinewah." Decca 23363 (these renditions are included in the album "Cole Porter—1924–1944").

Ethel Merman, of the original cast, performs, with Bill Johnson, "Something for the Boys," "Could It Be You?" "Hey, Good Lookin'," and "He's a Right Guy" (these renditions, taken from a transcription disc made for radio broadcast, are included in the album "Cole Porter—1924–1944").

"Mexican Hayride" (**1944**) Corinna Mura, of the original cast, performs "Sing to Me Guitar" and "Carlotta." Decca 23336.

Wilbur Evans, of the original cast, sings "I Love You" and "Girls." Decca 23337.

June Havoc, of the original cast, performs "There Must Be Someone for Me" and "Abracadabra." Decca 23338.

June Havoc performs "Count Your Blessings" and a chorus sings "What a Crazy Way to Spend Sunday." Decca 23339. The eight numbers—"Sing to Me Guitar," "Carlotta," "I Love You," "Girls," "There Must Be Someone for Me," "Abracadabra," "Count Your Blessings," and "What a Crazy Way to Spend Sunday"—on four 78 rpm Decca records, are included in the LP album "Cole Porter (Music and Lyrics)."

"Seven Lively Arts" (**1944**) Benny Goodman, of the original cast, and his quintet perform "Ev'ry Time We Say Goodbye" (with vocalist Peggy Mann) and "Only Another Boy and Girl" (with vocalist Jane Harvey). Columbia 36767.

Teddy Wilson, of the original cast, and his quintet perform "Ev'ry Time We Say Goodbye" (with vocalist Maxine Sullivan). Musicraft 317 (the Benny Goodman rendition of "Only Another Boy and Girl" on Columbia, and the Teddy Wilson recording of "Ev'ry Time We Say Goodbye" on Musicraft, are included in the album "Cole Porter—1924–1944").

"Around the World in Eighty Days" (**1946**) Larry Laurence (Enzo Stuarti), of the original cast, sings "Should I Tell You I Love You?" and "Look What I Found." Real 1195A-B.

Larry Laurence performs "If You Smile at Me" and "Pipe Dreaming." Real 1195C-D. The Laurence renditions of "Should I Tell You I Love You?" "Look What I Found," "If You Smile at Me," and "Pipe Dreaming" are included in the album "Cole Porter (Music and Lyrics)."

"The Pirate" (**1948**) Judy Garland and Gene Kelly, of the original cast, sing "Be a Clown." MGM 30097.

Judy Garland performs "Love of My Life" and "You Can Do No Wrong." MGM 30098.

Gene Kelly sings "Nina" and Judy Garland performs "Mack the Black." MGM 30099.

The renditions by Judy Garland and Gene Kelly of "Be a Clown," "Love of

My Life," "You Can Do No Wrong," "Nina," and "Mack the Black" are included in one LP: MGM E-3234.

"Kiss Me, Kate" (1948) Alfred Drake, Patricia Morison, Lisa Kirk, Harold Lang, and others from the Broadway production perform in an original-cast album (LP) of the score. Columbia OL-4140, OS-2300 (1949), and S-32609 (1973 reissue).

The original cast recorded another album of the score in 1959. Capitol TAO-1267, STAO-1267.

"Out of This World" (1950) Charlotte Greenwood, Priscilla Gillette, William Redfield, Barbara Ashley, George Jongeyans (George Gaynes), and David Burns, from the Broadway production, perform in an original-cast album of the score. Columbia OL-4390, COL-4390.

"Can-Can" (1953) Lilo, Peter Cookson, Gwen Verdon, and others from the Broadway production perform in an original-cast album of the score. Capitol DW-452, S-452.

"Kiss Me, Kate" (film) (1953) Howard Keel, Kathryn Grayson, Ann Miller, and others perform in an original-cast album of the score, taken from the sound track of the film. MGM E-3077 and Metro M-525, S-395.

"Silk Stockings" (1955) Hildegarde Neff, Don Ameche, and others from the Broadway production perform in an original-cast album of the score. RCA Victor LOC-1016 and LOC-1102, LSO-1102 (1965 reissues).

"High Society" (1956) Bing Crosby, Frank Sinatra, Grace Kelly, and others perform in an original-cast album of the score taken from the sound track of the film. Capitol W-750, SW-750.

"Silk Stockings" (film) (1957) Fred Astaire, Cyd Charisse, and others perform in an original-cast album of the score, taken from the sound track of the film. MGM E-3542.

"Les Girls" (1957) Gene Kelly, Kay Kendall, Mitzi Gaynor, and Taina Elg perform in an original-cast album of the score, taken from the sound track of the film. MGM E-3590.

"Aladdin" (1958) Cyril Ritchard, Dennis King, Anna Maria Alberghetti, and others perform in an original-cast album of the score. Columbia CL-1117.

"Can-Can" (film) (1960) Frank Sinatra, Shirley MacLaine, Maurice Chevalier, and Louis Jourdan perform in an original-cast album taken from the sound track of the film. Capitol W-1301, SW-1301.

A Selected Bibliography

The amount of published material on Cole Porter is voluminous, for he was so much in the news while he lived. Even after his death much continues to be written about him. If, in addition to all this material, one considers the great amount of personal documents, manuscripts, memorabilia, and music relating to him that is found at such repositories as Yale University, the Porter archives in Peru, Indiana, and the Cole Porter Musical and Property Trusts in New York, then it is obvious that a "complete" Porter bibliography begins to reach overwhelming proportions. For reasons of manageability, the bibliography compiled here represents a culling of published books and articles that have some bearing on Cole Porter's life, career, and the period he lived in. It is far from complete, but it should give the interested Cole Porter reader a good bibliographic base.

Abbott, George. *Mister Abbott.* New York: Random House, 1963.

Allen, Frederick Lewis. *Since Yesterday.* New York: Harper, 1940.

Anderson, John Murray, and Hugh Abercrombie Anderson. *Out Without My Rubbers.* New York: Library Publishers, 1954.

Arnold, Elliott. *Deep in My Heart* [biography of Sigmund Romberg]. New York: Duell, Sloan and Pearce, 1949.

Astaire, Fred. *Steps in Time.* New York: Harper, 1959.

Atkinson, Brooks. *Broadway Scrapbook.* New York: Theatre Arts, 1947.

———. *Broadway.* New York: Macmillan, 1970.

Austin, William W. *Music in the Twentieth Century.* New York: Norton, 1966.

Baldwin, Billy. *Billy Baldwin Decorates.* New York: Holt, Rinehart and Winston, 1972.

———. *Billy Baldwin Remembers.* New York: Harcourt Brace Jovanovich, 1974.

Baral, Robert. *Revue: The Great Broadway Period* (revised edition). New York: Fleet, 1970.

Bartholomew, Marshall (editor). *Songs of Yale.* New York: Schirmer, 1934.

——— (editor). *Songs of Yale.* New York: Schirmer, 1953.

———. *The First Hundred Years, 1861–1961: The Story of the Yale Glee Club.* New Haven, Conn.: Yale University, 1960.

Beard, Alexander Humphrey, Albert Beecher Crawford, Anson Blake Gardner, and James Edward Meeker (editors). *The Yale Banner and Pot Pourri: The Annual Yearbook of the Students of Yale University.* New Haven, Conn.: Yale University, 1913.

Blesh, Rudi. *Modern Art USA.* New York: Knopf, 1956.

Blum, Daniel. *A Pictorial History of the American Theater.* New York: Crown, 1969.

Boardman, Fon W., Jr. *The Thirties.* New York: Walck, 1967.

Bolton, Guy R., and Pelham Grenville Wodehouse. *Bring on the Girls!* New York: Simon and Schuster, 1953.

Broder, Nathan. "Cole Porter." *Die Musik in Geschichte und Gegenwart* (volume X), columns 1476–77. Basel, London, New York: Bärenreiter, 1962.

Brown, John Mason. *The Art of Playgoing.* New York: Norton, 1936.

———. *Two On the Aisle.* New York: Norton, 1938.

———. *Broadway in Review.* New York: Norton, 1940.

Bruccoli, Matthew J., Scottie Fitzgerald Smith, and Joan P. Kerr (editors). *The Romantic Egoists: A Pictorial Autobiography from the Scrapbooks and Albums of Scott and Zelda Fitzgerald.* New York: Scribner's, 1974.

Burton, Jack. *The Blue Book of Tin Pan Alley.* New York: Century, 1950.

———. *The Blue Book of Hollywood Musicals.* New York: Century, 1953.

———. *The Blue Book of Broadway Musicals* (with additions by Larry Freeman). New York: Century, 1969.

Capote, Truman. "La Côte Basque, 1965." *Esquire* (November 1975), pp. 110–18, 158.

Chase, Gilbert. *America's Music from the Pilgrims to the Present* (2nd edition). New York: McGraw-Hill, 1966.

"Cole Porter's Apartment: Country House on the 33rd Floor." *Vogue* (November 1, 1955), pp. 130–33.

Cole Porter Song Album. New York: Harms, 1935.

The Cole Porter Song Book (foreword by Moss Hart). New York: Simon and Schuster, 1959.

Coward, Noel. *Present Indicative.* New York: Doubleday, Doran, 1937.

———. *Future Indefinite.* New York: Doubleday, 1954.

Congdon, Don (editor). *The '30's—A Time to Remember.* New York: Simon and Schuster, 1962.

Conrad, Earl. *Billy Rose: Manhattan Primitive.* Cleveland: World, 1968.

Croce, Arlene. *The Fred Astaire and Ginger Rogers Book*. New York: Outerbridge and Lazard (distributed by Dutton), 1972.

De Groot, R. A. "Cole Porter's Dinner for Edward VIII." *Esquire* (January 1973), pp. 102–06, 170–74.

De Mille, Agnes. *Dance to the Piper*. Boston: Little, Brown, 1952.

Dietz, Howard. *Dancing in the Dark: An Autobiography*. New York: Quadrangle, 1974.

Dos Passos, John. *The Fourteenth Chronicle* (letters and diaries of Dos Passos). Boston: Gambit, 1973.

Downer, Alan S. (editor). *American Drama and Its Critics*. Chicago: University of Chicago, 1965.

Duke, Vernon. *Passport to Paris*. Boston: Little, Brown, 1955.

———. *Listen Here!* New York: Obolensky, 1963.

Eames, John Douglas. *The MGM Story: The Complete History of Over Fifty Roaring Years*. New York: Crown, 1975.

Eells, George. *The Life That Late He Led: A Biography of Cole Porter*. New York: Putnam, 1967.

Ellis, Edward Robb. *A Nation in Torment*. New York: Coward, McCann & Geoghan 1970.

Engel, Lehman. *Planning and Producing the Musical Show* (revised edition). New York: Crown, 1966.

———. *Words with Music*. New York: Macmillan, 1972.

———. *The American Musical Theater* (revised edition). New York: Collier (paperback), 1975.

Eustis, Morton. *Broadway, Inc.!* New York: Dodd, Mead, 1934.

Ewen, David. *The Story of Irving Berlin*. New York: Holt, 1950.

———. *Panorama of American Popular Music*. Englewood Cliffs, N.J.: Prentice-Hall, 1957.

———. *The World of Jerome Kern*. New York: Holt, Rinehart and Winston, 1960.

———. *The Life and Death of Tin Pan Alley*. New York: Funk and Wagnalls, 1964.

———. *The Cole Porter Story*. New York: Holt, Rinehart and Winston, 1965.

———. *New Complete Book of the American Musical Theater*. New York: Holt, Rinehart and Winston, 1970.

———. *Great Men of Popular Song*. Englewood Cliffs, N.J.: Prentice-Hall, 1972.

Farnsworth, Marjorie. *The Ziegfeld Follies*. New York: Bonanza, 1956.

Ford, Corey. *The Time of Laughter*. Boston: Little, Brown, 1967.

Fowler, Gene. *Schnozzola* [biography of Jimmy Durante]. New York: Viking, 1951.

Freedland, Michael. *Irving Berlin*. New York: Stein and Day, 1974.

Freedley, George, and John A. Reeves. *A History of the Theater*. New York: Crown, 1968.

Fuld, James J. *American Popular Music, 1875–1950*. Philadelphia: Musical Americana, 1955.

———. *The Book of World Famous Music* (revised edition). New York: Crown, 1971

Fuller, John Grant (editor). *Baker's Roaring Twenties Scrapbook*. Boston: Baker's Plays, 1960.

Gaige, Crosby. *Footlights and Highlights*. New York: Dutton, 1948.

Gassner, John. *Producing the Play*. Hinsdale, Ill.: Dryden (division of Holt, Rinehart and Winston), 1941.

———. *The Theater in Our Times*. New York: Crown, 1954.

Gilbert, Douglas. *Lost Chords: The Diverting Story of American Popular Song*. New York: Doubleday, Doran, 1942.

———. *American Vaudeville: Its Life and Times*. New York: Dover (paperback; a reissue of the 1940 book), 1963.

Gill, Brendan. "Profiles" (Cole Porter). *The New Yorker* (September 18, 1971), pp. 48–64.

Goldberg, Isaac. *Tin Pan Alley: A Chronicle of American Popular Music*. New York: Ungar (paperback; a reissue of the 1930 book), 1961.

Goodale, G. Frank (editor). *The New Yale Song-Book*. New York: Schirmer, 1918.

Gordon, Max, and Lewis Funke. *Max Gordon Presents*. New York: Geis, 1963.

Gordon, Ruth. *Myself Among Others*. New York: Atheneum, 1971.

Gottlieb, Polly Rose. *The Nine Lives of Billy Rose*. New York: Crown, 1968.

Green, Abel, and Joe Laurie, Jr. *Show Biz from Vaude to Video*. New York: Holt, 1951.

Green, Stanley. *The Rodgers and Hammerstein Story*. New York: Day, 1963.

———. *Ring Bells! Sing Songs!: Broadway Musicals of the 1930's*. New Rochelle, N.Y.: Arlington House, 1971.

———. *The World of Musical Comedy* (3rd edition). Cranbury, N.J.: A.S. Barnes, 1974.

Hall, James B., and Barry Ulanov. *Modern Culture and the Arts*. New York: McGraw-Hill, 1967.

Handlin, Oscar. *The Uprooted*. Boston: Little, Brown, 1951.

Harriman, Margaret Case. "Profiles" (Cole Porter). *The New Yorker* (November 23, 1940), pp. 24–34.

Hart, Dorothy (editor). *Thou Swell Thou Witty: The Life and Lyrics of Lorenz Hart*. New York: Harper and Row, 1976.

Hart, Moss. *Act One: An Autobiography*. New York: Random House, 1959.

Hatlin, Theodore W. *Orientation to the Theater*. New York: Appleton-Century-Crofts, 1962.

Hellman, Lillian. *An Unfinished Woman*. Boston: Little, Brown, 1969.

Hewitt, Bernard. *Theater U.S.A., from 1668 to 1957*. New York: McGraw-Hill, 1959.

Heylbut, Rose. "You're the Top, Cole Porter." *Etude* (September 1956), pp. 23, 56–57.

Higham, Charles. *Ziegfeld*. Chicago: Regnery, 1972.

Hirschfeld, Al. *Show Business Is No Business*. New York: Simon and Schuster, 1951.

Hitchcock, H. Wiley. *Music in the United States* (2nd edition). Englewood Cliffs, N.J.: Prentice-Hall, 1974.

Houghton, Norris. *Advance from Broadway*. New York: Harcourt, Brace, 1941.

"The House of Mrs. Cole Porter in Paris." *Vogue* (August 1, 1925), pp. 56–58.

Houseman, John. *Run-Through: A Memoir.* New York: Simon and Schuster, 1972.

Howard, John Tasker. *Our American Music: A Comprehensive History from 1620 to the Present* (4th edition). New York: Crowell, 1965.

Howard, John Tasker, and George Kent Bellows. *A Short History of Music in America.* New York: Crowell, 1957.

Hubler, Richard G. *The Cole Porter Story* (introduction by Arthur Schwartz). Cleveland: World, 1965.

Hudson, Lynton. *Life and the Theater.* New York: Roy, 1954.

Hughes, Glenn. *A History of the American Theater.* New York: French, 1951.

Jablonski, Edward. "The American Musical." *Hi-Fi Music at Home* (October 1958), pp. 43–55.

Jordan, Philip D., and Lillian Kessler. *Songs of Yesterday: A Song Anthology of American Life.* New York: Doubleday, Doran, 1941.

Kahn, Ely Jacques, Jr. *The Merry Partners: The Age and Stage of Harrigan and Hart.* New York: Random House, 1955.

————. *The World of Swope.* New York: Simon and Schuster, 1965.

Katkov, Norman. *The Fabulous Fanny* [biography of Fanny Brice]. New York: Knopf, 1953.

Kazin, Alfred. *On Native Grounds.* New York: Harcourt, Brace, 1942.

Kelley, Hubert. "It's All in Fun." *American Magazine* (April 1935), pp. 62–63, 96, 99–102.

Kernodle, George R. *Invitation to the Theater.* New York: Harcourt, Brace and World, 1967.

Kerr, Walter. *Thirty Days Hath December.* New York: Simon and Schuster, 1969.

Kimball, Robert. "The Cole Porter Collection at Yale." *The Yale University Library Gazette* (July 1969), pp. 8–15.

———— (editor). *Cole* (with a biographical essay by Brendan Gill). New York: Holt, Rinehart and Winston, 1971.

———— (editor). *The Unpublished Cole Porter.* New York: Simon and Schuster, 1975.

Knef, Hildegarde. *The Gift Horse: Report on a Life.* New York: McGraw-Hill, 1970.

Knox, Donald. *The Magic Factory.* New York: Praeger, 1973.

Kobal, John. *Gotta Sing Gotta Dance: A Pictorial History of Film Musicals.* London: Hamlyn, 1971.

Kreuger, Miles. "From Fortune to Fame: The Unconventional Cole Porter— His Life and Works." *The American Record Guide* (September 1966), pp. 584–87, 666.

————. "Not One But Two Books (Both Full of Misinformation) About Cole Porter." *The American Record Guide* (September 1966), pp. 56–60.

———— (editor). *The Movie Musical: From Vitaphone to "42nd Street."* New York: Dover, 1975.

Krutch, Joseph Wood. *American Drama Since 1918.* New York: Random House, 1939.

Lahr, John. *Notes on a Cowardly Lion* [biography of Bert Lahr]. New York: Knopf, 1969.

Langner, Lawrence. *The Magic Curtain.* New York: Dutton, 1951.

Laufe, Abe. *Anatomy of a Hit.* New York: Hawthorn, 1966.

———. *Broadway's Greatest Musicals.* New York: Funk and Wagnalls, 1969.

Laver, James. *Between the Wars.* London: Vista 1961.

Lawrence, Gertrude. *A Star Danced.* New York: Doubleday, 1945.

Leighton, Isabel (editor). *The Aspirin Age.* New York: Simon and Schuster, 1949.

Lesley, Cole. *Remembered Laughter: The Life of Noel Coward.* New York: Knopf, 1976.

Levant, Oscar. *A Smattering of Ignorance.* New York: Doubleday, Doran, 1940.

———. *The Memoirs of an Amnesiac.* New York: Putnam, 1965.

———. *The Unimportance of Being Oscar.* New York: Putnam, 1968.

Levin, Martin. *The Phoenix Nest.* New York: Doubleday, 1960.

Lewine, Richard, and Alfred Simon. *Encyclopedia of Theater Music.* New York: Random House, 1961.

———. *Songs of the American Theater.* New York: Dodd, Mead, 1973.

Lewis, Allan. *American Plays and Playwrights of the Contemporary Theater.* New York: Crown, 1965.

Lewis, Emory. *Stages.* Englewood Cliffs, N.J.: Prentice-Hall, 1969.

Little, Stuart W., and Arthur Cantor. *The Playmakers.* New York: Norton, 1970.

Loos, Anita. *A Girl Like I.* New York: Viking, 1966.

———. *Kiss Hollywood Good-By.* New York: Ballantine (paperback), 1975.

Lounsberry, Fred. "Cole Porter's Lively Lyre." *Saturday Review of Literature* (April 26, 1952), pp. 43–45, 60.

——— (editor). *103 Lyrics of Cole Porter.* New York: Random House, 1954.

Lubbock, Mark. *The Complete Book of Light Opera.* New York: Putnam, 1962.

Maloney, Russell. "Profiles" (Monty Woolley). *The New Yorker* (January 20, 1940), pp. 25–29.

Mander, Raymond, and Joe Mitchenson. *Musical Comedy: A Story in Pictures.* New York: Taplinger, 1970.

Maney, Richard. *Fanfare.* New York: Harper, 1957.

Mantle, Burns (editor). *The Best Plays* (annual volumes; from 1919–47). New York: Dodd, Mead.

Mantle, Burns, and John Gassner (editors). *A Treasury of the Theater.* New York: Simon and Schuster, 1935.

Mantle, Burns, and Garrison P. Sherwood (editors). *The Best Plays of 1909–1919.* New York: Dodd, Mead, 1933.

Marchant, William. *The Privilege of His Company: Noel Coward Remembered.* New York: Bobbs-Merrill, 1975.

Marks, Edward Bennet. *They All Had Glamour—From the Swedish Nightingale to the Naked Lady.* New York: Messner, 1944.

Martin, Mary. *My Heart Belongs.* New York: Morrow, 1976.

Marquand, John P. *Thirty Years.* Boston: Little, Brown, 1954.

Marx, Samuel, and Jan Clayton. *Rodgers and Hart.* New York: Putnam, 1976.

Mattfeld, Julius. *Variety Music Cavalcade.* Englewood Cliffs, N.J.: Prentice-Hall, 1962.

Maxwell, Elsa. *Elsa Maxwell's Etiquette Book.* New York: Bartholomew House, 1951.

———. *R.S.V.P.: Elsa Maxwell's Own Story.* Boston: Little, Brown, 1954.

———. *How to Do it; or the Lively Art of Entertaining.* Boston: Little, Brown, 1957.

———. "That Cole Porter Magic." *The American Weekly* (March 16, 1958), pp. 10–13.

———. *The Celebrity Circus.* New York: Appleton-Century, 1963.

McSpadden, J. Walker. *Light Opera and Musical Comedy.* New York: Crowell, 1939.

———. *Operas and Musical Comedies* (revised edition). New York: Crowell, 1951.

Melchinger, Siegfried. *The Concise Encyclopedia of Modern Drama.* New York: Horizon, 1964.

Mellers, Wilfrid. *Music in a New Found Land.* New York: Knopf, 1965.

Meredith, Scott. *George S. Kaufman and His Friends.* New York: Doubleday, 1974.

Merman, Ethel, and Pete Martin. *Who Could Ask for Anything More?* New York: Doubleday, 1955.

Mersand, Joseph. *The American Drama Since 1930.* Port Washington, N.Y.: Kennikat Press, 1949.

Meyer, Hazel. *The Gold in Tin Pan Alley.* Philadelphia: Lippincott, 1958.

Michel, Artur. "Swedish Ballet Celebrated Folk Form." *Dance Magazine* (April 1943), pp. 10, 37–38, 40.

Milford, Nancy. *Zelda.* New York: Harper and Row, 1970.

Milhaud, Darius. *Notes Without Music: An Autobiography.* New York: Knopf, 1953.

Millstein, Gilbert. "Words Anent Music by Cole Porter." *The New York Times Magazine* (February 20, 1955), pp. 16, 55.

Mockridge, Norton. "Broadway Hit-Makers" (Feuer and Martin). *World-Telegram and Sun Saturday Magazine* (July 9, 1955), pp. 10–11, 19.

Montgomery, Elizabeth R. *The Story Behind Popular Songs.* New York: Dodd, Mead, 1958.

Mooney, H. F. "Songs, Singers and Society, 1890–1954." *American Quarterly* (Fall 1954), pp. 221–32.

———. "Popular Music Since the 1920's." *American Quarterly* (Spring 1968), pp. 67–85.

Morehouse, Ward. *Forty-Five Minutes from Broadway.* New York: Dial Press, 1939.

———. *George M. Cohan: Prince of the American Theater.* Philadelphia: Lippincott, 1943.

———. *Matinee Tomorrow.* Philadelphia: R. West, 1975 (reprint of 1949 edition).

———. *Just the Other Day.* New York: McGraw-Hill, 1953.

Morley, Sheridan. *A Talent to Amuse* (Noel Coward). New York: Doubleday, 1970.

Morris, Lloyd. *Postscript to Yesterday.* New York: Random House, 1947.

————. *Curtain Time.* New York: Random House, 1953.

Moses, Montrose J., and John Mason Brown (editors). *The American Theater as Seen By Its Critics, 1752–1934.* New York: Norton, 1934.

Murray, Nicholas, and Paul Gallico. *The Revealing Eye.* New York: Atheneum, 1967.

Music and Lyrics by Cole Porter: A Treasury of Cole Porter (introduction by Robert Kimball). New York: Chappell and Random House, 1972.

"Musical Spoofs Russians." *Life* (March 21, 1955), pp. 93–96.

Nathan, George Jean. *Testament of a Critic.* New York: Knopf, 1931.

————. *The Intimate Notebooks of George Jean Nathan.* New York: Knopf, 1932.

————. *Passing Judgments.* New York: Knopf, 1935.

————. *The Theater of the Moment.* New York: Knopf, 1936.

————. *The Morning After the First Night.* New York: Knopf, 1938.

————. *Encyclopedia of the Theater.* New York: Knopf, 1940.

————. *The Entertainment of a Nation.* New York: Knopf, 1942.

————. *The Theater Book of the Year* (annual volumes; from 1944–51). New York: Knopf.

————. *The Theater in the Fifties.* New York: Knopf, 1953.

————. *The Popular Theater.* Rutherford, N.J.: Fairleigh Dickinson University, 1971.

" 'Night and Day' vs. Cole Porter." *Life* (August 5, 1946), pp. 101–07.

O'Hara, Frank Hurburt. *Today in American Drama.* Chicago: University of Chicago, 1959.

Oppenheimer, George (editor). *The Passionate Playgoer.* New York: Viking, 1958.

————. *The View from the Sixties.* New York: McKay, 1966.

Othman, Frederick C. "The Beard that Talks Like a Man" (Monty Woolley). *The Saturday Evening Post* (September 4, 1943), pp. 12–13, 44–48.

Paris, Leonard A. *Men and Melodies.* New York: Crowell, 1954.

Parks, Melvin. *Musicals of the 1930's.* Museum of the City of New York, 1966.

Parsons, Schuyler Livingston. *Untold Friendships.* New York: Houghton Mifflin, 1955.

Perelman, S. J. *The Dream Department.* New York: Random House, 1943.

Phillips, Cabell. *From the Crash to the Blitz, 1929–1939.* New York: Macmillan, 1969.

Prideaux, Tom. "Beyond Question the Good Turtle Soup: Cole Porter." *Life* (February 25, 1972), pp. 71–72.

"Presentation: Cigarette Cases and Boxes, from the Collection of the Late Cole Porter." New York: *Parke-Bernet Catalogue* (May 17, 1967).

"The Professional Amateur" (Cole Porter). *Time* (January 31, 1949), pp. 40–44.

Quinn, Arthur Hobson. *A History of the American Drama.* New York: Appleton-Century-Crofts, 1936.

Raph, Theodore (editor). *The Songs We Sang: A Treasury of American Popular Music.* Cranbury, N.J.: A. S. Barnes, 1964.

Reed, Joseph Verner. *The Curtain Falls.* New York: Harcourt, Brace, 1935.

Reif, Rita. "Cole Porter's Bookshelves: They're So Nice to Come Home To." *The New York Times* (March 1, 1967), p. 46.

Rice, Elmer. *The Living Theater.* New York: Harper, 1959.

Richman, Harry, and Richard Gehman. *A Hell of a Life.* New York: Duell, Sloan and Pearce, 1966.

Rigdon, Walter (editor). *The Biographical Encyclopedia and Who's Who of the American Theater.* New York: Heineman, 1965.

Robbins, Richard Whitfield (editor). *History of the Class of 1913, Yale College* (volume 1). New Haven, Conn.: Yale University, 1913.

Roberts, Vera Mowry. *On Stage, a History of Theater.* New York: Harper and Row, 1962.

Rodgers, Richard. *Musical Stages.* New York: Random House, 1975.

Rosenfeld, Paul. "Musical Chronicle." *The Dial* (April 1924), pp. 388–90.

Rubin, William, and Carolyn Lanchner. "The Paintings of Gerald Murphy" (foreword by Archibald MacLeish). New York: *Catalogue of the Museum of Modern Art,* 1974.

Sablosky, Irving L. *American Music.* Chicago: University of Chicago, 1969.

Salsini, Paul. *Cole Porter, Twentieth Century Composer of Popular Songs* (pamphlet). Charlotteville, N.Y.: Story House (SamHar Press), 1972.

Sandburg, Carl. *The American Songbag.* New York: Harcourt, Brace, 1927.

Santayana, George. *The Last Puritan.* New York: Scribner's, 1936.

Saylor, Oliver M. *Our American Theater.* New York: Brentano's, 1923.

Schwartz, Charles. *Gershwin: His Life and Music.* New York: Bobbs-Merrill, 1973.

Seldes, Gilbert. *The Seven Lively Arts.* New York: Harper, 1924.

Settle, Ronald. *Music in the Theatre.* London: Jenkins, 1957.

Severo, Richard. "Cole Porter Wasn't Perfect, Only Incomparable." *The New York Times Magazine* (October 10, 1971), pp. 18–19, 99–102.

Shannon, David A. (editor). *The Great Depression.* Englewood Cliffs, N.J. Prentice-Hall, 1960.

Siebert, Lynn Laitman. *Cole Porter: An Analysis of Five Musical Comedies and a Thematic Catalogue of the Complete Works.* Unpublished Ph.D. Dissertation, City University of New York, 1974.

Sillman, Leonard. *Here Lies Leonard Sillman.* Secaucus, N.J.: Citadel, 1959.

Skinner, Cornelia Otis. *Life with Lindsay and Crouse.* New York: Houghton Mifflin, 1976.

Smit, Leo. "The Classic Cole Porter." *The Saturday Review* (December 25, 1971), pp. 48–49, 57.

Smith, Cecil. *Musical Comedy in America.* New York: Theatre Arts, 1950.

———. *Worlds of Music.* Philadelphia: Lippincott, 1952.

Smith, Harry B. *First Nights and First Editions.* Boston: Little, Brown, 1931.

Smith, Madeline P. "Cole Porter: A Personal Memory." *The Peru Tribune* (June 9, 1976), pp. 1–2.

Sobel, Bernard. *Broadway Heartbeat.* New York: Hermitage House, 1953.

Sobol, Louis. *The Longest Street.* New York: Crown, 1968.

Spaeth, Sigmund. *Read 'Em and Weep: The Songs You Forgot to Remember.* New York: Doubleday, Page, 1926.

———. *Weep Some More, My Lady.* New York: Doubleday, Page, 1927.

———. *The Facts of Life in Popular Song.* New York: McGraw-Hill, 1934.

————. *A History of Popular Music in America.* New York: Random House, 1948.

————. *Fifty Years with Music.* New York: Fleet, 1959.

Spears, Jack. *Hollywood: The Golden Era.* Secaucus, N.J.: Castle, 1971.

Spewack, Samuel and Bella. *Kiss Me, Kate: A Musical Play.* New York: Knopf, 1953.

————. "The Complete Text of *Kiss Me, Kate.*" *Theatre Arts* (January 1955), pp. 33–57.

Stagg, Jerry. *The Brothers Shubert.* New York: Random House, 1968.

Stambler, Irwin. *Encyclopedia of Popular Music.* New York: St. Martin's, 1965.

Stearns, Marshall W. *The Story of Jazz.* New York: Galaxy (paperback), 1970.

Stillman, Edmund. *The American Heritage History of the 20s and 30s.* Boston: American Heritage, 1970.

Stravinsky, Igor, and Robert Craft. *Dialogues and a Diary.* New York: Doubleday, 1963.

Taubman, Howard. "Cole Porter Is 'The Top' Again." *The New York Times Magazine* (January 16, 1949), pp. 20–23.

————. *The Making of the American Theater.* New York: Coward, McCann & Geoghan, 1965.

Taylor, Deems (editor). *A Treasury of Gilbert and Sullivan.* New York: Simon and Schuster, 1941.

————. *Some Enchanted Evenings: The Story of Rodgers and Hammerstein.* New York: Harper, 1953.

Taylor, John Russell, and Arthur Jackson. *The Hollywood Musical.* New York: McGraw-Hill, 1971.

Teichmann, Howard. *George S. Kaufman: An Intimate Portrait.* New York: Atheneum, 1972.

Terkel, Studs (editor). *Hard Times.* New York: Pantheon, 1970.

Thomas, Bob. *King Cohn.* New York: Putnam, 1967.

————. *Thalberg: Life and Legend.* New York: Doubleday, 1969.

Thomson, Virgil. *The Musical Scene.* New York: Knopf, 1945.

————. */American Music Since 1910.* New York: Holt, Rinehart and Winston, 1970.

Tomkins, Calvin. *Living Well Is the Best Revenge.* New York: Viking, 1971.

Trewin, J. C. *The Turbulent Thirties.* London: Macdonald, 1960.

Turnbusch, Tom. *Complete Production Guide to Modern Musical Theater.* New York: Richards Rosen Press, 1969.

Tyler, Parker. *Screening the Sexes: Homosexuality in the Movies.* New York: Holt, Rinehart and Winston, 1972.

Ulanov, Barry. *A History of Jazz in America.* New York: Viking, 1952.

Untermeyer, Louis (editor). *A Treasury of Laughter.* New York: Simon and Schuster, 1946.

Vallance, Tom. *The American Musical.* Secaucus, N.J.: Castle, 1970.

Vernon, Grenville (editor). *Yankee Doodle-Doo: A Collection of Songs of the Early American Stage.* Detroit: Singing Tree Press, 1973 (reprint of 1927 edition).

Waldau, Roy S. *Vintage Years of the Theatre Guild: 1928–1939.* Cleveland, Ohio: Case Western Reserve University, 1972.

Waters, Edward. *Victor Herbert: A Life in Music.* New York: Macmillan, 1955.

Whiting, Frank M. *An Introduction to the Theater.* New York: Harper, 1954.

Wilder, Alec. *American Popular Song: The Great Innovators, 1900–1950.* New York: Oxford University Press, 1972.

Wilk, Max (editor). *The Wit and Wisdom of Hollywood.* New York: Atheneum, 1971.

Williamson, Audrey. *Gilbert and Sullivan Opera: A New Assessment.* New York: Macmillan, 1953.

Wilson, Edmund. *The Twenties.* New York: Farrar, Straus and Giroux, 1975.

Woollcott, Alexander. *The Story of Irving Berlin.* New York: Putnam, 1925.

Wright, Edward B., and Lenthiel H. Downs. *A Primer for Playgoers.* Englewood Cliffs, N.J.: Prentice-Hall, 1958.

Zadan, Craig. *Sondheim and Co.* New York: Macmillan, 1974.

Zolotow, Maurice. *Stagestruck: The Romance of Alfred Lunt and Lynn Fontanne.* New York: Harcourt, Brace and World, 1964.

Index

Aarons, Alex, 93–94, 118, 121, 132
Aaronson, Irving:
  "Commanders," 96, 278
Abbott, George, 187, 241
Abercrombie, Daniel Webster, 19–20
Achelis, Johnfritz, 26, 29, 36, 272, 273, 274
Acheson, Dean, 38
Adams, Margaret, 145, 282
Adler, Felix, 42, 43, 274
Aga Khan, 63
Alba, Duchess of, 88
Alba, Duke of, 50, 88
Alexander, Jack, 114, 115
Ameche, Don, 209, 254, 287, 291, 333
American Ballet Theater, 84
American Magazine, 136–137
Anderson, John Murray, 91, 276
Andrews Sisters, 150
Antibes, 65–67, 68, 85
Arden, Eve, 209, 222, 286
Arlen, Michael, 98–99

Armstrong, Louis, 256, 292
Arno, Peter, 115, 279
Arnstein, Ira, 220–221
Arnstein, Nicky, 89
Ashley, Iris, 124, 280
Astaire, Adele, 118, 131
  For Goodness Sake, 118
  Funny Face, 118, 129
  Lady, Be Good, 118
  Over the Top, 118
Astaire, Fred, 118–119, 129, 131, 150, 158, 221
  Broadway Melody of 1940, 197, 285, 325, 331
  Carefree, 129, 131
  Dancing Lady, 129
  Flying Down to Rio, 129–130
  Follow the Fleet, 129, 131
  For Goodness Sake, 118
  Funny Face, 118, 129
  Gay Divorce, 118, 119, 120, 125, 130, 131, 280, 329
  The Gay Divorcee, 129, 130, 131, 151, 281

Lady, Be Good, 118
Over the Top, 118
recordings, 325, 326, 329, 331, 333
Roberta, 129
Shall We Dance, 129, 131
Silk Stockings, 254, 292, 333
*The Story of Vernon and Irene
    Castle,* 129
Swing Time, 129, 131
Top Hat, 129, 131
You'll Never Get Rich, 208, 286
Astaire, Mrs. Fred, 158
Atchley, Dr. Dana W., 258
Atkinson, Brooks, 115, 145, 165,
    207, 243, 248
Ayers, Lemuel: *Kiss Me, Kate,*
    230, 231, 234, 242, 289
    Out of This World, 240, 241, 242,
    290

Baker, Benny, 208, 209, 286
Bakst, Léon, 83
Baldwin, Billy, 203, 251–252
Ball, Lucille, 201, 287
Ballard, Kaye, 263, 326
ballet score. See *Within the Quota*
Ballets Russes, 56, 67, 77, 79, 83
Ballets Suédois, 79–81, 82, 83, 85,
    279
Bankhead, Tallulah, 76
Barnes, Howard, 228
Barrie, Elaine, 153
Barry, Philip: *The Philadelphia
    Story,* 255, 292
Barrymore, John, 153, 209
Barthelmess, Richard, 152–153
Basquin, Peter, 84
Baxter, James P., III, 255
Beebe, Lucius, 99
Behrman, S. N., 229, 289
Belmont, Mrs. O. H. P., 41
Bennett, Arnold, 56
Bennett, Robert Russell, 32–33,
    217
Benrimo, 42, 274
Benson, Lt. Col. Sir Rex, 47
Berenson, Bernard, 53

Berlin, Irving, 108–109, 118,
    119–120, 138, 151, 178, 215
    This Is the Army, 205
Berlin, Mrs. Irving (Ellin
    Mackay), 120
Berman, Pandro S., 130–131, 150,
    281
Bigelow, Dorothie, 41–42, 43, 274
Blair, Janet, 209, 287
Boland, Mary, 145–146, 282
Bolcom, William, 84
Boley, May, 145, 282
Bolton, Guy: *Anything Goes,* 132,
    133, 134, 281
    Oh, Kay!, 132
    Once Upon a Time (Ever Yours),
    281
    Rosalie, 176–177, 283
    The Sun Never Sets, 284
Bordoni, Irene, 94, 95, 96, 97,
    278
Bouvier, John Vernou, III
    ("Black Jack"), 176
Brackett, Charles, 96, 104, 105
Braque, Georges, 66, 67
Breen, Joseph I., 210
Brent, Romney, 125, 126–127, 280
Brice, Fanny, 62, 76, 88–89, 90,
    105
    "Second-Hand Rose," 89
Brock, Lou, 149–150
Broderick, Helen, 106, 107, 109,
    278, 280
Brown, John Mason, 189–190,
    199, 208
Brown, Martin, 95, 278
Bruce, Carol, 263
Bruce, Virginia, 158, 159, 160, 282
Buck, Norman S., 262
Burke, Billie, 218
Burke, Henry, 86, 226, 263–64,
    265, 267, 270
Burns, David, 242, 290
Burrows, Abe, 245, 247, 253, 291
Buttons, Red, 263
Buxton Hill, 201–203, 251, 252, 257,
    258, 266–267

given to Williams College, 255, 269

Buxton Hill Music, 237

Byng, Douglas, 128, 330

Cantinflas, 229
Cantor, Eddie, 105
Capote, Truman, 128–129
Carlisle, Elsie, 103–104, 278
Carlisle, Kitty, 147–148
Carnarvon, Lord George Edward, 56
Carpenter, Ginny, 87, 225
Carpenter, John Alden, 80, 87, 225
Carrington, Elaine, 230
Carroll, Joan, 207, 285, 331
Carter, Howard, 56
Chapman, John, 254
Chappell Music Company, 32, 170, 237
Charisse, Cyd, 254, 292, 333
Chevalier, Maurice, 248, 293
Churchill, Frank, 153
Churchill, Winston, 53
Clair, René, 186, 283
Clark, Bobby, 216, 288
Clark, Harry, 232, 290
Clayton, Lou, 115–116, 279
Clift, Montgomery, 145, 282
Cochran, Charles B., 100
    Anything Goes, 147, 281
    Mayfair and Montmartre, 100, 276
    Nymph Errant, 122–123, 125, 280
    Wake Up and Dream, 100, 103, 104, 278
Cocteau, Jean, 68
Cohn, Harry, 207–208, 227
Colbert, Claudette, 105
Colby, Frank, 143
Cole, Albert, 7, 8
Cole, James, 269
Cole, James Omar (J.O.), 7–13 passim, 16
    and daughter, Kate, 8–13 passim, 18, 31, 33, 37, 40, 45, 73

death, 72–73
    and grandson, Cole, 16, 18, 21, 31, 33, 34, 37, 40, 41, 44, 55; allowance, 31, 37, 54, 55; trust fund, 43–44, 53, 55, 59, 73, 206, 269
Cole, Mrs. James Omar (Bessie), 16
Cole, Mrs. James Omar (Rachel Henton), 8, 16, 73
Cole, Jules Omar, 247, 261, 269
Cole, Mrs. Jules Omar, 247
Cole, Louis, 8, 73
Coleman, Robert, 243
Columbia Pictures: and Porter, 207–208, 209; Something to Shout About, 4, 195, 209–211, 287; You'll Never Get Rich, 4, 195, 208, 286
Columbia Records: Kiss Me, Kate, 244, 333
    Out of This World, 244, 333
Comden, Betty, 241
Connolly, Dr. Joseph B., 180
Conrad, Con: "The Continental," 131–132
Cook, Joe, 133
Cooper, Lady Diana, 76
Cooper, Melville, 145, 282
Cooper, Merian C., 130, 150
Copland, Aaron, 65
Cordova, Victoria, 228, 289
Cornell, Katherine: Romeo and Juliet, 227
Costello, Matty (Nomad), 114, 115
Coward, Noel, 76, 117, 144, 196, 234, 235
Cox, Wally, 169
Crane, Clinton, 43–44, 73
Crawford, Joan, 129
Crawford, Kathryn, 116
Crews, Laura Hope, 146
Crocker, William, 55, 134
Cromwell, Richard, 214
Crosby, Bing, 150
    Anything Goes, 136, 161, 282–283, 292
    High Society, 256, 257, 292, 333

Crouse, Russel, 140
  Anything Goes, 133, 134, 135, 281
  Greek to You, 283
  Hold Your Horses, 133
  Red, Hot and Blue!, 140, 163, 164, 165, 166, 283
Cukor, George, 258, 292
Cummings, Jack, 153–154, 282, 284, 293
Cunard, Lady, 103, 125
Curtiz, Michael, 222–223, 289
Cushing, Tom, 93, 277

Darton, Charles, 116–117
de Mille, Agnes, 125, 241, 290
De Sylva, B. G. ("Buddy"), 154, 199, 206, 282, 285, 287
de Wolfe, Elsie (Lady Mendl), 42, 52, 76, 100, 101, 103, 122
del Rio, Dolores, 130
Diaghilev, Serge, 56, 67, 68, 77, 79
The Dial, 82
Diamond, Jack, 232, 290
Dietrich, Marlene, 277
d'Indy, Vincent, 56, 57
Dionne quintuplets, 163
Dolin, Anton, 217, 288
Dolly Sisters, 91, 92, 276
Dos Passos, John, 67, 86
Downey, Morton, 95, 277
Drake, Alfred, 232, 233, 290, 333
Dreyfus, Max, 54, 55, 90, 239, 256
Dunn, James, 206, 285
Durante, Jimmy, 221
  The New Yorkers, 115–116, 279
  Red, Hot and Blue!, 121, 163, 164, 165–166, 283
Duryea, Nina Larre Smith, 45, 46
Duveen, Sir Joseph, 70

Ebsen, Buddy, 158, 282
Eddy, Nelson, 177, 283
Edward VIII, King. *See* Windsor, Duke of
Elg, Tanya, 258, 292, 333

Emerson, Faye, 263
Evans, Wilbur, 217, 288, 326
Eythe, William, 242, 243, 290

Federal Theater Project, 146
Feininger, Lyonel, 253
Feldman, Charles, 255
Feuer, Cy: *Can-Can*, 245, 246, 248, 291
  Guys and Dolls, 126, 245
  Silk Stockings, 252, 253, 254, 291
  Where's Charley?, 245
Fields, Dorothy: *Let's Face It*, 208, 286
  Mexican Hayride, 216, 288
  Something for the Boys, 211, 287
Fields, Herbert, 106
  DuBarry Was a Lady, 199, 206, 285, 287
  The New Yorkers, 115, 279
  Fifty Million Frenchmen, 106, 115, 278, 280
  Let's Face It, 208, 286
  Mexican Hayride, 216, 288
  Panama Hattie, 206, 285
  Something for the Boys, 211, 287
  Star Dust, 280
Fields, Lew, 40, 41, 106, 276
Figaro, 81
Film industry, 105–106, 151–152, 153, 156, 157–158
  homosexuality, 174–175
  See also Hollywood; individual studios
Films (music by Porter): *Adam's Rib*, 239–240, 286, 290
  Adios Argentina (not produced), 149, 150, 151, 216, 282
  Anything Goes (1936), 136, 161, 282–283
  Anything Goes (1956), 136, 292
  The Battle of Paris, 105, 106, 109, 151, 279
  Born to Dance, 4, 153–154, 155–156, 158–160, 161, 168, 171, 173, 207, 282, 330

Break the News, 186, 283
Broadway Melody of 1940, 4, 195, 196, 197–198, 207, 284–285, 330
Can-Can, 248, 262, 293, 333
DuBarry Was a Lady, 201, 287
Fifty Million Frenchmen, 109, 151, 279–280
Funny Face (not produced), 129
The Gay Divorcee, 129, 130–132, 151, 281
Les Girls, 5, 257–258, 292–293, 333
High Society, 5, 218, 255–257, 292, 333
Hollywood Canteen, 150, 216, 288
Kiss Me, Kate, 237, 244, 248, 291, 333
Mississippi Belle (not produced), 214–215, 221, 287–288
Night and Day, 5, 47, 215–216, 220–224, 288–289
Panama Hattie, 207, 286
The Pirate, 4, 229–230, 289, 332–333
Rosalie, 4, 161, 171, 172, 173, 174, 176, 177–178, 191, 283
Silk Stockings, 254, 257, 292, 333
Something to Shout About, 4, 195, 209–211, 287
You'll Never Get Rich, 4, 195, 286, 331
see also Recordings; Songs
First National Vitaphone: *Weary River*, 152–153
Fitzgerald, F. Scott, 65, 67, 68, 69, 86
Tender Is the Night, 67, 86, 101
Fitzgerald, Mrs. F. Scott (Zelda), 68
Fletcher, Bob, 150, 282
Florey, Robert, 106, 279
Fokine, Michel, 83
Fontanne, Lynn: *Amphitryon 38*, 234, 240
Idiot's Delight, 234
The Pirate, 229, 234

Fox Studios, 150
Adios Argentina (not produced), 149, 150, 151, 216, 282
see also 20th Century-Fox
Franchetti, Baron, 78
Freedley, George, 212
Freedley, Vinton, 93–94
Anything Goes, 94, 132–133, 281
Funny Face, 93, 118
Girl Crazy, 93, 121
Greek to You, 186
Lady Be Good, 93, 118
Leave It to Me, 189, 192, 284
Let's Face It, 208, 286
Oh, Kay!, 93
Pardon My English, 93, 94
Red, Hot and Blue!, 163, 164, 283
Something for the Boys, 211
Tip-Toes, 93
Treasure Girl, 93
Friml, Rudolf, 54
Fulda, Ludwig, 229, 289
Funke, Lewis, 248–249

Gable, Clark, 129, 153
Gabor, Zsa Zsa, 263
Gabriel, Gilbert, 109, 145, 146
Galsworthy, John, 53, 56
Garbo, Greta, 249, 253
Garden, Mary, 62, 65
Garland, Judy, 229, 234, 289, 332–333
Gaxton, William, 262
Anything Goes, 129, 132, 134, 159, 281
Fifty Million Frenchmen, 106, 107, 109, 278, 280
Leave It to Me, 192, 284
Of Thee I Sing, 132
Red, Hot and Blue!, 163–164
Something to Shout About, 209, 210, 287
Gaynor, Mitzi, 136, 258, 292, 333
Gear, Luella, 119, 280
George V, King, 144
George VI, King, 235

Gershwin, Frances, 96
Gershwin, George, 54, 93–94, 96,
    118, 144–145, 151
    "Do It Again," 94
    Funny Face, 93, 118, 129
    Girl Crazy, 93, 121, 132
    "I Got Rhythm," 121
    "I Won't Say I Will But I
        Won't Say I Won't," 94
    Lady, Be Good, 93, 118
    Of Thee I Sing, 132, 164–165, 191
    Oh, Kay!, 93, 132
    Pardon My English, 93, 94, 132
    Porgy and Bess, 133
    Rhapsody in Blue, 83–84
    Rosalie, 161, 176
    "'S Wonderful," 108
    Tip-Toes, 93
    Treasure Girl, 93
Gershwin, Ira, 133
    Of Thee I Sing, 132, 164–165, 191
Geyer, Siegfried: *Candle Light*,
    187, 284
Gideon, Melville, 48, 59, 275
Gillette, Priscilla, 242, 290, 333
Giraudoux, Jean, 240
Glynn, Harry, 114, 115
Goetz, E. Ray, 94
    Fifty Million Frenchmen, 105,
        106, 107, 278
    The New Yorkers, 115, 116, 279
    Paris, 94, 95, 96, 278
    Star Dust, 121, 149, 280
    "Washington Square," 94, 275
Golden, John, 40, 274
Golschmann, Vladimir, 62
Goodman, Benny, 217, 288, 326,
    332
Gottlieb, Walter, 150
Grable, Betty, 200, 285
Graham, Ronald, 199, 285
Grant, Cary, 5, 222–223, 289
Gray, Dolores, 263
Gray, Jerry, 147
Grayson, Kathryn, 237, 291, 333
Green, Adolph, 241
Greenwood, Charlotte, 242–243,
    290, 333

Grey, Clifford, 59, 276
Gris, Juan, 66
Guernsey, Otis, 243
Gunzburg, Baron Nicolas de,
    202, 247, 255

Haines, William, 214
Hale, George, 139
Hale, Louise Closser, 96, 278
Hall, Bettina, 134, 281
Hammerstein, Oscar, II:
    Oklahoma, 233
    Show Boat, 126
Hammond, Percy, 117
Hanna, Leonard, 30, 138, 196, 272
    and Cole, 2, 30, 127, 128, 144,
        196, 239
Harlow, Jean, 153
Harms Company, T. B., 32, 54,
    92, 170, 237
Harris, Sam H., 141
Hart, Lorenz, 94
    A Connecticut Yankee, 94
Hart, Moss, 147–148
    As Thousands Cheer, 138
    Jubilee, 138, 139, 141, 144, 145,
        147, 148, 282
    Lady in the Dark, 147
    The Man Who Came to Dinner,
        112, 196–197
    Merrily We Roll Along, 138
    and Porter, 138–142, 147, 148,
        168; *See also* Jubilee *above*
    Seven Lively Arts, 147, 218, 288
    You Can't Take It With You, 147
Hartman, Grace, 189
Hartman, Paul, 189
Harvard University, 1, 2, 31, 33–38
    passim, 40, 91
Hatch, Eric, 153
Havoc, June, 216, 288, 326, 332
Hayward, Leland, 129
Hayworth, Rita, 208, 286
Healy, Mary, 228, 289
Heard, James, 48, 275
Hearst, William Randolph, 227
Hearst, Mrs. William Randolph
    (Millicent), 243, 247

Hecht, Ben, 218, 288
Hemingway, Ernest, 65, 67, 68, 86
Hemingway, Mrs. Ernest, 68
Henie, Sonja, 155
Hepburn, Katharine: *Adam's Rib*, 239–240, 290
The Lake, 256
The Philadelphia Story, 255–256
Herbert, F. Hugh, 241
Hitchcock, Raymond, 54, 275, 276
Hoey, Evelyn, 95–96, 277
Hollywood: Cole/Cole and Linda, 4, 86, 151–160 *passim*, 162, 171, 172, 174–179 *passim*, 195, 197, 201, 207–211 *passim*, 214, 215, 238, 239, 240, 245, 248, 250, 255, 258, 264, 265, 266
homosexuality, 174–175
See also Film industry; individual studios
Holm, Celeste, 256, 262, 292
Holm, Eleanor, 218
Holm, Hanya, 242
Holman, Libby, 189, 284
Hope, Bob, 326
Red, Hot and Blue!, 121, 164, 168, 283, 330
Houseman, John, 227
Howard, Jean, 255
Howard, Leslie, 187
Hoysradt, John, 196, 197
Hull, Lytle, 247
Hull, Mrs. Lytle (Helen), 247
Huntington, Henry E., 70
Huntley, G. P., Jr., 119, 280
Hutchinson, Leslie ("Hutch"), 78, 328, 329
Hutton, Betty, 207, 285
Hyde, Martha, 56

Ives, Charles, 80

Jackson, Eddie, 115–116, 279
Jeanmaire, 136, 292
Jenkins, Allen, 212, 287
Jenks, Almet F., Jr., 26, 27, 29, 272

Jolson, Al: *The Jazz Singer*, 105, 152
The Singing Fool, 105, 152
Jongeyans (Gaynes), George, 242, 290, 333
Jordan, Dorothy, 130
Jourdan, Louis, 248, 293
Joyce, James, 65

Kalkhurst, Eric, 96, 278
Katz, Sam, 153–159 *passim*, 168
Kaufman, George S., 144, 217
As Thousands Cheer, 138
The Man Who Came to Dinner, 112, 196–197
Merrily We Roll Along, 138
Of Thee I Sing, 132, 164–165, 191
Seven Lively Arts, 217, 218, 288
Silk Stockings, 249, 253
You Can't Take It With You, 147
Kaye, Danny, 208, 209, 221, 286, 331, 332
Keel, Howard, 237, 291, 333
Kelley, Hubert, 137
Kelly, Gene: *DuBarry Was a Lady*, 287
Les Girls, 258, 292, 333
Leave It to Me, 192, 284
The Pirate, 229, 234, 289, 332–333
Kelly, Grace, 256, 292, 333
Kelly, Ray C., 269–270
Kendall, Kay, 258, 292, 333
Kern, Jerome, 40, 54, 118, 138, 151, 190
Miss Information, 40
Show Boat, 126
"They Didn't Believe Me,"
Porter parody on, 52, 275
Kerr, Walter, 253
Kidd, Michael, 247
Kilgallen, Dorothy, 157
King, Dennis, 258, 293, 333
King, Rufus F., 36, 272, 273
King, Stanford, 142–143
King, Stoddard, 36, 273
Kirk, Lisa, 234, 262, 290, 333
Knickerbocker, Cholly, 122
Knight, June, 145, 282

Koechlin, Charles, 57, 81, 82, 276
Kostelanetz, André, 243
Kronenberger, Louis, 212

Lahr, Bert, 221, 326
  DuBarry Was a Lady, 120, 199,
    200, 201, 285, 331
  Seven Lively Arts, 217, 288
Lane, Burton: Finian's Rainbow,
  231
Lang, Harold, 234, 290, 326, 333
Langford, Frances, 158, 282, 330
Laurence, Larry. See Stuarti,
  Enzo
Laurence, Paula, 212, 287
Maurencin, Marie, 225
Laver, James, 122–123, 126, 280
Lawrence, Gertrude: The Battle
  of Paris, 106, 151, 279
  Candle Light, 187
  Nymph Errant, 124, 125, 280, 329
Lawrence, Reginald: If This Be
  Treason, 241
  Out of This World, 241, 290
Lazar, Irving, 218, 255
Lee, Keith, 84
Léger, Fernand, 67, 68, 86
Léger, Mme. Fernand, 68
Lehman, Robert, 29–30
Lelong, Lucien, 235
Lengyel, Melchior, 248–249
Lillie, Beatrice, 62, 217, 262, 288
Lilo, 262, 333
Lindsay, Eric, 263–264
Lindsay, Howard, 140
  Anything Goes, 133, 134, 135, 281
  Greek to You, 283
  Life with Father, 133
  Red, Hot and Blue!, 140, 163,
    164, 165, 166, 283
Loos, Anita, 60, 158, 160
Lopez, Vincent: Orchestra, 91,
  276
Losch, Tilly, 103, 278
Lubitsch, Ernst, 254
Luce, Claire, 119, 125, 131, 280

Lunt, Alfred: Amphitryon 38, 234,
  240
  Idiot's Delight, 234
  The Pirate, 229, 234
  The Taming of the Shrew, 230,
    234
Lyons, Arthur, 155, 156, 215

McGowan, Jack, 153–154, 282
MacGrath, Leueen, 249, 253, 291
McGuire, William Anthony,
  176–177, 283
MacLaine, Shirley, 248, 293, 333
MacLeish, Archibald, 26, 36, 47,
  49, 67, 273
Madden, Richard, 163, 218
Magidson, Herb, 131
Marbury, Elisabeth ("Bessie"),
  40, 41–42, 52, 274
Maré, Rolf de, 79
Margetson, Arthur, 96, 97, 228,
  278, 289
Markey, Gene, 106, 279
Markova, Alicia, 217, 288
Martin, Ernest: Can-Can, 245,
  246, 248, 291
  Guys and Dolls, 126, 245
  Silk Stockings, 252, 253, 254, 291
  Where's Charley?, 245
Martin, Mary, 192, 193, 221, 222,
  284, 330
Marx Brothers: The Cocoanuts,
  106
Mary, Queen, 235
Maxwell, Elsa, 62–64, 65
  and Cole, 44, 59, 63, 64, 122,
    128, 144, 247, 263
  Cole and Linda, 62, 63, 64, 65
  Venice's Lido promoted by,
    63, 73, 76
  Waldorf Astoria suite, 63, 128,
    170
Mayer, Louis B., 130, 153
  and Porter, 154, 156, 157, 159,
    177–178
Media. See Press
Meiser, Edith, 209, 286

Mendl, Sir Charles, 76, 100, 101, 103
Mendl, Lady. *See* de Wolfe, Elsie
Merkel, Una, 158, 258, 282, 293
Merman, Ethel, 120–121, 169
  Anything Goes, 121, 129, 132, 134, 136, 161, 281, 282–283, 329
  DuBarry Was a Lady, 169, 199, 200, 201, 206, 285
  Girl Crazy, 121, 132
  Panama Hattie, 169, 206, 207, 285, 331
  recordings, 326, 329, 330, 331, 332
  Red, Hot and Blue!, 121, 163–164, 165, 168–169, 283, 330
  Something for the Boys, 169, 211, 212, 287, 332
MGM (Metro-Goldwyn-Mayer), 129, 130
  Broadway Melody of 1929, 197
  Broadway Melody of 1936, 197
  Broadway Melody of 1938, 197
  Dancing Lady, 129
  Ninotchka, 249, 253, 254
  and Porter, 151–160 *passim*, 177–178; *Adam's Rib*, 239–240, 286, 290; *Born to Dance*, 153–154, 155–156, 158–160, 161, 168, 171, 173, 207, 282, 330; *Broadway Melody of 1940*, 4, 195, 196, 197–198, 207, 284–285, 330; *DuBarry Was a Lady*, 201, 287; *Les Girls*, 5, 257–258, 292–293, 333; *High Society*, 5, 218, 255–257, 292, 333; *Jubilee* backed by, 145; *Kiss Me, Kate*, 237, 244, 248, 291, 333; *The Pirate*, 4, 229–230, 289, 332–333; *Rosalie*, 4, 161, 171, 172, 173, 174, 176, 177–178, 191, 283; *Silk Stockings*, 254, 257, 292, 333
Milhaud, Darius, 80, 81
  La Création du monde, 81
Miller, Gilbert, 94, 149, 232, 243, 281

Miller, Mrs. Gilbert, 243
Miller, Henry, 94
Mills, Mrs. Ogden, 247
Minnelli, Vincente, 229, 289
Montgomery, Robert H., 257
Moore, Benjamin, 179
Moore, Clint, 114–115, 195
Moore, Victor: *Anything Goes*, 129, 132, 134, 281
  Leave It to Me, 191, 192, 284
  Of Thee I Sing, 132, 191
Moorhead, Dr. John J., 180, 182, 186, 188–189
Moran and Mack, 91, 276
Morehouse, Ward, 242
Morgan, Anne, 42, 52
Morgan, Frank, 177, 283
Morison, Patricia, 233–234, 236, 290, 333
Moses, Grandma, 253
Movies. *See* Film industry; Films
Murphy, Baoth, 66, 69
Murphy, George, 197, 285
Murphy, Gerald, 66, 67, 68–69, 85–86
  and Cole, 22–23, 29, 66, 79, 84–85; *Within the Quota*, 79–81, 84, 85, 276
  in Fitzgerald's *Tender Is the Night*, 67, 86
  painting, 66, 68, 69, 85
Murphy, Mrs. Gerald (Sara), 66, 67, 68, 85–86
  in Fitzgerald's *Tender Is the Night*, 67, 86
  Linda and Cole, 66, 79, 85, 246
Murphy, Honoria, 66, 67, 85
Murphy, Patrick, 66, 68–69
Murray, John, 152–153
Music publishers: Buxton Hill Music, 237
  Chappell Music Company, 32, 170, 237
  T. B. Harms Company, 32, 54, 92, 170, 237

G. Schirmer, Inc., 43
vocal scores of musicals, 248
Musicals and plays, 14, 17, 163
auditions and casting, interest
in, 169–170
and critics, 166, 220; bad
reviews, 42–43, 69–70, 106,
189, 199–200, 216, 220; good
reviews, 25, 36, 54, 81, 82, 96,
115, 125, 134, 145, 192–193, 199,
208, 236, 254; mixed reviews,
81, 104–105, 109, 165–166, 167,
207, 212, 228, 243, 248, 253
material re-used, 149, 232–233
opening night: cigarette cases
as gifts, 102, 173, 186, 194, 197,
247, 255; festivities and
parties, 96, 102, 103, 125, 237,
243, 247; Porter's
comportment, 166–167, 170
out-of-town tryouts, 252–253
principals: material tailored
to, 29, 36, 120–121, 125–126, 169;
tact and diplomacy in
dealings with, 32
scripts, 126; material
integrated with, 29, 125–126,
127
See also Press, publicity;
Recordings; Songs
Musicals and plays—list: And the
Villain Still Pursued Her, 26, 36,
272
Aladdin, 258–259, 293, 333
Anything Goes, 2, 94, 121, 129,
132–136 passim, 138, 139, 141,
147, 149, 159, 163, 190, 191, 232,
248, 263, 281–282, 329
Around the World in Eighty
Days, 227–229, 289, 332
As You Were, 59, 94
Buddies, 59, 273
Can-Can, 5, 206, 245, 246,
247–248, 291, 333
Cora, 26, 27, 272
DuBarry Was a Lady, 4, 49–50,
120, 169, 195, 196, 198–201, 206,
212, 256, 285, 331

The Eclipse, 59, 275, 328
Fifty Million Frenchmen, 2,
105–109 passim, 115, 278–279
Gay Divorce, 2, 118–122 passim,
125, 130, 131, 241, 280, 329
Greek to You (not produced),
186, 283–284
Greenwich Village Follies, 91–92,
93, 276–277, 328
Hands Up, 40, 274
Hi Diddle Diddle, 128, 281, 330
Hitchy-Koo of 1919, 54, 275
Hitchy-Koo of 1922, 69, 72, 276
Jubilee, 2, 138, 139, 141, 144–148
passim, 163, 232, 282, 330
The Kaleidoscope, 26, 29, 36, 273
Kiss Me, Kate, 4, 226, 230–239
passim, 242, 247, 248, 289–290,
333
Leave It to Me, 4, 191–194, 212,
284, 330
Let's Face It, 4, 195, 208–209, 212,
286, 331–332
The Man Who Came to Dinner,
196, 285
Mayfair and Montmartre, 69,
70–72, 100, 276
Mexican Hayride, 4, 195, 216–217,
288, 332
Miss Information, 40, 274
The New Yorkers, 2, 115–117, 279,
329
A Night Out, 59, 275–276, 328
Nymph Errant, 122–127 passim,
136, 280–281, 329
O Mistress Mine, 283, 330
Once Upon a Time (Ever Yours).
(not produced), 149, 281
Out o'Luck, 93, 277
Out of This World, 169–170, 206,
240–244, 290, 333
Panama Hattie, 4, 169, 195,
206–207, 212, 285–286, 331
Paranoia, or Chester of the
Y.D.A., 35–36, 41, 43, 273–274
Paris, 2, 92, 94–100 passim, 103,
104, 278, 328
Phi-Phi, 69, 276

The Pot of Gold, 14, 26, 27–29, 43, 108, 272–273
Red, Hot and Blue!, 2, 121, 140, 161, 163–169, 171, 173, 283, 330
La Revue des Ambassadeurs, 95–96, 103, 116, 277–278
See America First, 2, 29, 41–43, 44, 46, 90, 106, 274–275, 328
Seven Lively Arts, 147, 216–221 *passim*, 228, 288, 332
Silk Stockings, 5, 248, 252–255, 291–292, 333
Something for the Boys, 4, 169, 195, 211–213, 214, 287, 332
Star Dust (not produced), 121, 149, 280
The Sun Never Sets, 284, 331
Telling the Tale, 48, 275
The Vanderbilt Revue, 279
Very Good Eddie, 48, 275
Wake Up and Dream, 2, 96, 100, 103–105, 109, 125, 136, 199, 278, 328, 329
We're All Dressed Up and We Don't Know Huerta Go, 37, 274
You Never Know, 173–174, 178, 179, 186–187, 189–191, 284

Navarro, Ramon, 175
Neff, Hildegarde, 253, 291, 333
New Haven Register, 31, 98
New York: Cole/Cole and Linda, 4, 45, 69, 72, 170, 201, 202, 250, 251–252, 257, 264, 265, 266
New York American, 145, 146
New York *Daily Mirror*, 243
New York *Globe*, 81
New York *Herald*, 42
New York *Herald Tribune*, 96, 104–105, 117, 138, 141, 192–193, 242, 243
New York *Morning Telegraph*, 212
New York *Sun*, 81
New York Times, 54, 115, 136, 145, 165, 166, 180, 243, 248–249
New York *Tribune*, 42, 81

New York *World*, 81–82, 116
New York *World-Telegram*, 142, 242
New Yorker, 96, 104, 105, 142, 199–200
Newspaper Guild, 236
Niarchos, Stavros, 257
Nichols, Lewis, 218–219
Night and Day (film), 5, 47, 215–216, 220–224, 288–289
Niven, David, 229
Noyes, Newbold, 36, 273, 274

Oakie, Jack, 209, 287
Oberon, Merle, 166, 173, 265–266
O'Brien, Margaret, 263
O'Connor, Donald, 136, 292
O'Hara, John, 207
Oliver, Edna May, 177, 283
Onassis, Jacqueline Kennedy, 176

Paris, 62, 64–65, 67–68
  Cole/Cole and Linda, 1, 3, 45–69 *passim*, 88, 201, 238, 251–252
  Maxim's, 63
  Ritz, 58, 63
Paramount Pictures, 105
  Anything Goes (1936), 136, 161, 282–283
  Anything Goes (1956), 136, 292
  The Battle of Paris, 105, 106, 109, 151, 279
  Funny Face (not produced), 129
Paris *Herald*, 81, 82, 85, 122
Parker, Dorothy, 256
Pennington, Ann, 105, 115, 279
Pépin le Bref (Pepi), 265–266
Perelman, S. J., 258, 293
Perkins, Francis D., 81
Philadelphia *Evening Bulletin*, 241
Picasso, Pablo, 66, 67, 68, 86
Pickford, Mary, 166, 173
Plant, Mark, 145, 282
PM, 212
Polignac, Princess Edmond de (Winnaretta Singer), 68

Pons, Lily, 243
Porter, Cole Albert: age, fiction about, 19, 32, 33, 45, 173, 263
anti-Semitism, 118, 193, 231
biographical film, *Night and Day*, 5, 47, 215–216, 220–224, 288–289
birth and early life, 12–18 *passim*
cigarette cases, collection of, 102, 173, 186, 194, 197, 247, 255
classical music, fondness for, 17, 86
and criticism, professional, 166, 220
death, 250, 261, 268; burial, 1, 5, 268–269; estate, 269; will, 236, 255, 268–269, 269–270; will—Williams College, bequest to, 255, 269; will—Yale University, bequest to, 84, 102, 262, 269
descriptions of, 13, 18, 25, 32, 126, 138, 139, 172
drinking habits, 30, 44, 206, 226, 227, 234, 258, 261, 265, 266, 267
drugs, use of, 76
education: Harvard, 1, 2, 31, 33–38 *passim*, 40, 91; local, 17, Worcester Academy, 1, 2, 17, 18–20, 23, 271; Yale, 1, 2, 14, 17, 21–33 *passim*, 84–85, 91, 271–273 (*See also* Yale University)
family background, 1–2, 7, 8, 91
and father, 16–17, 18, 175, 269
finances, 91, 206; from commercial endorsements, 226–227; estate at death, 269; from grandfather, 31, 37, 43–44, 53, 54, 55, 73, 206, 269; irrational worry over, 206, 244–245, 269; from mother, 55, 73, 269; from own music, 41, 55, 145, 146, 206, 269; from wife, 51, 52, 53, 55, 56, 58, 59, 60, 73, 251, 269

friendships. *See* Hanna, Leonard; Murphy, Gerald; Sturges, Howard; Woolley, Monty
gossip, fondness for, 3, 30, 161–62, 250
and grandfather, 16, 18, 21, 31, 33, 34, 37, 40, 41, 44, 45. *See also* finances *above*
health, 172; concern for, 76, 126–127, 252–253, 264; headaches, 206, 244, 245; insomnia, 244; personality changes and psychological problems, 5, 69, 181, 206, 209, 213, 244–245, 246, 249, 259; ulcers and operations, 258, 259
health—leg injuries in accident, 3–4, 51, 179–181; aftermath, 4, 5, 181–189 *passim*, 194, 195, 206, 208–209, 215, 244, 249; removal of right leg and problems, 5, 69, 181, 226, 259, 260–261, 263–267 *passim*
homosexuality, 3, 30, 50, 58, 77, 101, 113–114, 128–129, 147, 162, 174, 175–176, 195–196, 205, 225, 234, 265, 267–268
honors: Cole Porter Day in Indiana, 187–188, 224–225; on his death, 268; honorary degrees from Williams and Yale, 255, 262; "Salute to Cole Porter," 262, 263; "seventieth" birthday party, 263
and mother: as adult, 45, 46, 55, 59, 60, 73, 88, 91, 92, 180, 187, 188, 225, 245–246; during college, 21, 22, 30–31, 33, 34, 37, 40–41; early life, 2, 13–21 *passim*; money from, 55, 73, 269

name, 19
painting, 86, 90
personal characteristics, 2, 32,
98, 99, 180, 224–227; boorish
or rude, 39, 100, 126, 140, 162,
267; boredom, 38–40, 126, 263;
charm, 18, 38, 53; spunky and
willful, 13, 179, 249;
practical jokes, fondness for,
49–50, 60, 78, 111, 112, 143
publicity, fondness for and
use of, 4, 31, 44, 72, 78, 82–83,
98, 99, 105, 111, 121–122, 125,
136–141 passim, 161, 218,
226–227, 239
smoking, 30, 226, 227, 234, 261
snobbishness, 18, 79, 90, 162
social life, 3, 45, 90; Harvard,
38, 40; in last years, 258, 266,
267; Yale, 23–24, 25, 26, 29, 30,
32, 33, 38
travel, fondness for. See
Travel
truth often tampered with, 4,
31, 44, 46–47, 79, 90, 98,
121–122, 137, 142–143, 168, 223,
227; age, 19, 32, 33, 45, 173, 263;
French Foreign Legion, 44,
46–47, 90, 98, 137
vanity and concern over
appearance, 2, 14, 64, 76,
126–127, 173, 180, 181, 226, 253,
259, 260, 263–267 passim;
dress, 2, 22, 32, 44, 64
World War I, 3, 44–48 passim,
90, 98, 137
World War II, 205, 206
See also Films; Musicals and
plays; Songs
Porter, Mrs. Cole (Linda Lee
Thomas), 3, 50–53, 235
and Cole's mother, 59–60, 102,
180
death, 5, 60, 61, 201, 250–251;
estate and will, 60, 251, 269
descriptions of, 52, 53, 172–173
finances, 51, 52, 53, 55, 56, 58, 59,
60, 73, 251, 269
health: fractured arm, 189;
respiratory problems, 51, 52,
58, 60, 113, 160, 172, 173, 235,
238, 245–250 passim
marriage to Edward Thomas,
50, 51, 53, 61, 180
personal characteristics, 51, 52,
53, 57–58, 60–61, 85, 86,
101–102, 126, 139, 235, 251; taste,
52, 53, 57, 58, 202, 203, 251, 252,
253
Porter, Cole and Linda
cigarette cases, gifts of, 102,
173, 186, 194, 247
Cole's accident, 3–4, 180, 181,
201
"Linda Porter rose," 251
marriage, 55–56
meeting and courtship, 50, 52,
53, 55
relationship, 3, 60, 86, 101,
112–113, 160, 174, 181, 238–239,
250
residences. See Antibes;
Buxton Hill; Hollywood;
New York; Paris; Venice
separation, 3, 160, 173–174, 176,
178, 179
social life, 2, 3, 4, 18, 39, 86, 96;
Hollywood, 158; Paris and
Antibes, 48, 52, 57, 58, 62, 63,
64, 65, 69; opening nights,
96, 102, 103, 125, 237, 243, 247;
Venice, 76, 77, 78, 79
travel, fondness for. See
Travel
Porter, Samuel Fenwick, 10–11,
12, 13, 31–32, 88, 246
and Cole, 16–17, 18, 175, 269
Porter, Mrs. Samuel Fenwick
(Kate Cole), 8–13 passim, 88, 189
cerebral hemorrhage and
death, 245, 246, 249
and Cole: as adult, 45, 46, 55,
59, 60, 73, 88, 91, 92, 180, 187,

188, 225, 245–246; during
college, 21, 22, 30–31, 33, 34,
37, 40–41; early life, 2, 13–21
passim; money given to, 55,
73, 269
and father, 8–13 *passim,* 18, 31,
33, 37, 40, 45, 73
and Linda, 59–60, 102, 180
Powell, Eleanor: *Born to Dance,*
158, 159, 282, 330
Broadway Melody of 1940, 197,
285, 331
Rosalie, 177, 283
Powell, William, 138
press: publicity, and Porter's use
of, 4, 31, 44, 72, 78, 82–83, 98,
99, 105, 111, 121–122, 125, 136–141
passim, 161, 218, 226–227, 239
See also Musicals and plays,
and critics
Ragland, Rags, 207, 285, 287
Rath, Mrs. Cecilia vom, 77–78
Rathbone, Basil, 258, 293
Ratoff, Gregory, 209–210, 287
Raymond, Gene, 130
RCA Victor: "I've a Shooting
Box in Scotland," 43, 328
"Love for Sale," 116, 329
recordings by Porter, 136, 325,
326, 328, 329, 330
Silk Stockings, 254, 333
See also Recordings

Reardon, Billy, 76
Recordings: "Begin the
Beguine," 147, 330
Can-Can, 248, 333
discography, 324–333
"Don't Fence Me In," 150
"I've a Shooting Box in
Scotland," 43, 328
Kiss Me, Kate, 244, 333
"Love for Sale," 116, 117, 329
"Miss Otis Regrets," 128, 330
Out of This World, 244, 333
by Porter: "Anything Goes,"
136, 326, 329; "Be Like the

Bluebird," 136, 326; "The
Cocotte," 136, 325, 329; "I'm a
Gigolo," 136, 325, 328; "The
Physician," 136, 325, 329;
"Thank You So Much, Mrs.
Lowsborough-Goodby," 136,
325, 330; "Two Little Babes
in the Wood," 136, 325, 328;
"You're the Top," 136, 325,
329
Silk Stockings, 254, 333
Redfield, William, 242, 290, 333
Rhodes, Erik, 119, 130, 280
Rice, Mrs. Hamilton, 247
Riggs, T. Lawrason, 35, 38, 43
*Paranoia, or Chester of the
Y.D.A.,* 35, 36, 273
See America First, 41, 42, 43, 274
Ritchard, Cyril, 258, 293, 333
RKO-Radio Pictures, 149–150
Carefree, 129, 131
Flying Down to Rio, 129–130
Follow the Fleet, 129, 131
The Gay Divorcee, 129, 130–132,
151, 281
King Kong, 129
Roberta, 129
Shall We Dance, 129, 131
*The Story of Vernon and Irene
Castle,* 129
Swing Time, 129
Top Hat, 129, 131
Robilant, Count Andrea, 78
Robinson, Edward G., 105
Rodgers, Richard, 54, 94, 117–118
A Connecticut Yankee, 94
Oklahoma, 233
Rogers, Ginger, 130, 150
Carefree, 129, 131
Flying Down to Rio, 130
Follow the Fleet, 129, 131
The Gay Divorcee, 129, 130, 131,
151, 281
Roberta, 129
Shall We Dance, 129, 131
*The Story of Vernon and Irene
Castle,* 129

Swing Time, 129
Top Hat, 129, 131
Rogers, Herbert, 84
Rogers, Roy, 150, 288
Romberg, Sigmund, 40, 54
Hands Up, 40, 274
Over the Top, 118
Rosalie, 161, 176
Roosevelt, Franklin D., 146, 204
Roosevelt, Mrs. Franklin D., 264
Rose, Billy: *Aquacade,* 218
Carmen Jones, 218
Jumbo, 91, 146, 217, 218
Seven Lively Arts, 147, 217–218,
218–219, 220, 288
Rosenfeld, Paul, 82
Roth, Lillian, 105, 263
Rowland, 226
Rubenstein, Artur, 62
Russell, Henry, 50
Russell, Mrs. Henry (Ethel
Harriman), 50
Ryskind, Morrie: *Of Thee I Sing,*
132, 164–165, 191

Saint Subber, Arnold: *Kiss Me,
Kate,* 230, 231, 234, 242, 289
Out of This World, 240, 241, 242,
290
Salina, Marquis di, 78
Sandrich, Mark, 131, 281
Santayana, George, 50
Sayag, Edmond, 95, 96, 277
Schirmer, Inc., G., 43
Schwartz, Arthur, 214–215, 221,
289
Seldes, Gilbert, 108
Selznick, David O., 130
Shaw, Artie, 147, 330
Shaw, George Bernard, 53, 56
Short, Hassard, 145, 216, 282, 288
Shubert, J. J., 187, 188
Shubert, John, 187, 188
Shubert, Lee, 187, 188
Shurr, Louis, 93, 94
Silvers, Sid, 153–154, 282
Simms, Ginny, 221, 222, 289

Siegel, Sol, 218, 292
Sinatra, Frank: *Can-Can,* 248,
293, 333
High Society, 256, 257, 292, 333
Sirmay, Dr. Albert, 32, 170, 208,
219
Skelton, Red, 201, 207, 286, 287
Smith, Alexis, 222, 289
Smith, Joseph C.: Orchestra, 43,
328
Smith, Madeline P., 260, 265
Songs, 2–3, 87, 268
lyrics, 3, 27, 28, 35, 88, 93, 98;
Porter on, 72;
sentimentality, 55, 90, 207,
224; sexual innuendo, 15, 19,
52, 116–117, 124, 125, 135, 192,
193, 199, 242; sophistication,
3, 70, 190, 224, 237; topicality,
72, 93, 135, 237; wit and
satire, 3, 14, 93, 135–136
music, 3, 29, 70; background
and training, 2, 13–17 *passim,*
19, 23, 37–38, 56–57; elements
from other composers, 29,
107–108, 200, 233; "Jewish
tunes," 117–118, 177, 231;
parodies of other
composers, 52; serious
composition, 56–57
Porter as performer, 25, 136
working habits, 59, 140,
225–226; creative process, 72,
170; material integrated with
script, 29, 125–126, 127;
material re-used, 149, 232–233;
material tailored to
performers, 29, 36, 120–121,
125–126, 169; musical aides,
170–171
See also Films; Music
publishers; Musicals and
plays; Press, publicity
Songs—lists, 271–323
"After You, Who?," 119, 280
"All of You," 254, 291

"All Through the Night," 135, 159, 281

"Allez-Vous-En," 248, 291

"Alone with You," 48, 275

"Altogether Too Fond of You," 48, 275

"Always True to You in My Fashion," 4, 231, 290

"Another Op'nin', Another Show," 231, 290

"Antoinette Birby," 25, 273

"Anything Goes," 135, 136, 224, 281

"At Long Last Love," 179, 190, 284

"Be a Clown," 230, 289

"Be Like the Bluebird," 136, 281

"The Bearded Lady," 19, 271

"Begin the Beguine," 3, 118, 142–143, 144, 146–147, 197, 222, 230, 282, 285

"Beware of Yale," 24, 271

"Bingo Eli Yale," 24, 31, 271

"Blow, Gabriel, Blow," 3, 121, 135, 281

"The Blue Boy Blues," 70–72, 100, 276

"Bobolink Waltz," 15, 271

"Bridget," 24, 271

"Brush Up Your Shakespeare," 232, 290

"Bull Dog," 24, 222, 271

"But In the Morning, No," 4, 15, 198, 199, 200, 285

"Butterflies," 93, 277

"By the Mississinewah," 212, 287

"Ça, C'Est l'Amour," 257, 292

"C'Est Magnifique," 248, 291

"Chelsea," 59, 275

"Cleveland," 37, 274

"The Cocotte," 136, 280

"Come On In," 200, 285

"Could It Be You?," 212, 287

"Do I Love You?," 4, 198, 200, 285

"Do You Want to See Paris?," 108, 278

"Don't Fence Me In," 149, 150–151, 216, 282, 288

"Down in the Depths," 140, 168, 169, 283

"Dream Dancing," 206, 286

"Easy to Love," 159, 221, 282

"Eli," 24, 271

"Esmeralda," 40, 273, 274

"Ev'ry Time We Say Goodbye," 219–220, 288

"Ev'rything I Love," 4, 209, 286

"Experiment," 124, 280

"Far Away," 193, 284

"Farewell, Amanda," 239–240, 286, 290

"Farming," 209, 286

"Fated to Be Mated," 257, 292

"Fi, Fi, Fifi," 19, 271

"Fla De Dah," 24, 271

"A Football King," 24, 29, 273

"Friendship," 4, 14, 198, 200, 285

"From Alpha to Omega," 190, 284

"From Now On," 193, 284

"From This Moment On," 241, 244, 290

"Gavotte," 200, 285

"Get Out of Town," 4, 193–194, 284

"Give Him the Oo-La-La," 200, 285

"Glide, Glider, Glide," 205

"Goodbye, Little Dream, Goodbye," 155, 283

"The Happy Heaven of Harlem," 107, 279

"Hasta Luego," 210, 287

"Here Comes the Bandwagon," 106, 151, 279

"He's a Right Guy," 212, 287

"Hot-House Rose," 89–90, 224, 277

"I Am Ashamed That Women Are So Simple," 232, 290
"I Am in Love," 248, 291
"I Am Loved," 244, 290
"I Can Do Without Tea in My Teapot," 210, 287
"I Concentrate on You," 197–198, 285
"I Get a Kick Out of You," 3, 121, 135, 141, 149, 230, 281
"I Hate Men," 232, 290
"I Love Paris," 118, 248, 262, 291, 293
"I Love You," 4, 216–217, 288
"I Love You, Samantha," 256, 292
"I Never Realized," 59, 275
"I Sleep Easier Now," 241, 290
"I Still Love the Red, White and Blue," 121, 280
"I'm a Gigolo," 136, 278
"I'm in Love Again," 92–93, 277
"In Cincinnati," 37, 274
"In the Still of the Night," 177, 197, 283
"It Ain't Etiquette," 120
"It All Belongs to You," 186, 283
"It's All Right with Me," 248, 291
"It's De-Lovely," 3, 167–168, 283
"I've a Shooting Box in Scotland," 35–36, 43, 273, 274
"I've Come to Wive It Wealthily in Padua," 232, 290
"I've Got You on My Mind," 121, 280
"I've Got You Under My Skin," 159–160, 197, 222, 282
"Just One of Those Things," 144, 146, 230, 282
"Katie Went to Haiti," 200, 285
"The Kling-Kling Bird on the Divi-Divi Tree," 142, 282

"A Lady Needs a Rest," 209, 286
"The Language of Flowers," 43, 274
"Let's Be Buddies," 4, 206–207, 224, 285
"Let's Do It, Let's Fall in Love," 3, 96–97, 103, 104, 224, 278
"Let's Not Talk About Love," 4, 209, 286
"A Little Skipper from Heaven Above," 165–166, 283
"Look Around," 59, 276
"Looking at You," 96, 103, 278
"Love for Sale," 3, 15, 116–117, 118, 279
"Mademazelle," 93, 277
"Make It Another Old-Fashioned, Please," 4, 206, 285
"Mesdames and Messieurs," 200, 285
"Miss Otis Regrets," 14, 127–128, 281
"Mister and Missus Fitch," 121, 149, 280
"Most Gentlemen Don't Like Love," 193, 284
"The Motor Car," 25, 271
"My Heart Belongs to Daddy," 4, 15, 118, 192, 193, 221, 222, 284
"My Houseboat on the Thames," 28, 272
"My Mother Would Love You," 207, 285
"My Salvation Army Queen," 27–28, 107–108, 273
"Night and Day," 3, 118, 119, 120, 131, 132, 142, 143, 151, 222, 230, 280, 281
"Nobody's Chasing Me," 242, 244, 290
"Old-Fashioned Garden," 2, 54–55, 90, 224, 275
"Opera Star," 93, 277

"Our Hotel," 59, 276
"Paree, What Did You Do to Me?," 107, 279
"Paris Loves Lovers," 254, 291
"The Physician," 124–125, 136, 280
"A Picture of Me Without You," 144, 282
"Poor Young Millionaire," 39–40, 277
"Prithee Come Crusading with Me," 43, 273
"Ridin' High," 168, 283
"Ritz Roll and Rock," 257, 292
"Rosalie," 177, 283
"Sailors of the Sky," 205
"Si Vous Aimez Les Poitrines," 124, 281
"Siberia," 254, 291
"Silk Stockings," 254, 291
"Since I Kissed My Baby Goodbye," 208, 286
"Slow Sinks the Sun," 43, 275
"So in Love," 4, 231, 290
"So Long, Samoa," 239–240, 286, 290
"So Near and Yet So Far," 208, 286
"Something for the Boys," 212, 287
"Something to Shout About," 210, 287
"Song of the Birds," 15, 271
"Stereophonic Sound," 254–255, 291
"The Tale of an Oyster," 108, 277
"The Tattooed Gentleman," 19, 271
"Thank You So Much, Mrs. Lowsborough-Goodby," 127, 128, 136, 281
"They All Fall in Love," 106, 151, 279
"They Couldn't Compare to You," 242, 290
"Tom, Dick or Harry," 232, 290

"Tomorrow," 193, 284
"Too Darn Hot," 239, 290
"True Love," 256, 292
"Two Big Eyes," 40, 274
"Two Little Babes in the Wood," 91–92, 97, 136, 277, 278
"Use Your Imagination," 244, 290
"War Song," 52, 275
"Washington Square," 59, 94, 275
"We Open in Venice," 232, 290
"Well, Did You Evah!," 4, 198, 200, 256–257, 285, 292
"Were Thine That Special Face," 232, 290
"Weren't We Fools," 89–90, 277
"What Am I to Do," 196, 285
"What Is This Thing Called Love?," 3, 103–105, 143, 230, 278
"When I Used to Lead the Ballet," 29, 43, 272, 274
"When Love Beckoned," 200, 285
"Where Is the Life That Late I Led?," 232, 290
"Why Can't You Behave?," 4, 232, 290
"Why Didn't We Meet Before?," 59, 276
"Why Should I Care?," 177, 283
"Why Shouldn't I?," 144, 282
"Wunderbar," 4, 232–233, 290
"Yellow Melodrama," 25, 271
"You Can Do No Wrong," 230, 289
"You Do Something to Me," 3, 107, 278
"You Don't Know Paree," 107, 279
"You'd Be So Nice to Come Home To," 210, 287
"You're Sensational," 256, 292
"You're the Top," 3, 135, 136, 141, 143, 190, 222, 224, 281

"You've Got that Thing," 107, 278
Sothern, Ann, 207, 287
Spaeth, Sigmund, 221
Spewack, Bella: *Clear All Wires*, 191
  Kiss Me, Kate, 230–231, 233, 234, 289
  Leave It to Me, 191, 192, 284
Spewack, Sam: *Clear All Wires*, 191
  Kiss Me, Kate, 233, 234, 289
  Leave It to Me, 191, 192, 284
Steinert, Alexander, 60, 170, 171
Stewart, James, 158, 159, 160, 282
Stinchfield, Dr. Frank, 259
Stravinsky, Igor, 56, 62, 67, 68, 80, 86
  Les Noces, 67
  Scènes de Ballet, 217–218
Stuarti, Enzo (Larry Laurence), 228, 289, 332
Sturges, Dorothy, 59
Sturges, Howard, 50, 58–59
  and Cole, 50, 56, 113, 178, 239, 245, 246, 252, 255
  Cole and Linda, 58, 76, 138, 158
  death, 257
  and Linda, 58–59, 239, 251, 255
Sylvain, Paul, 260, 264

Tarkington, Booth, 187–188
Tauch, Ed, 113, 178
Taylor, Deems, 69–70, 81–82, 221
Taylor, Dwight, 119, 240–241, 280, 290
Taylor, Nellie, 71
Tchelichew, Pavel, 236
Thalberg, Irving, 156
Thayer, Ezra Ripley, 37
Thomas, Edward Russell, 50, 51, 53, 61, 180
Thomson, Virgil, 65
Time, 238
Tobin, Genevieve, 106, 107, 278
Todd, Michael, 211
  Around the World in Eighty Days, 227, 229

The Hot Mikado, 211
Mexican Hayride, 216, 288
Something for the Boys, 211–212, 216, 287
Townsend, M. Clifford, 187
travel, 1, 4, 56, 74, 88, 126, 171
  Cole alone or with male friends, 21, 33, 113, 122, 173, 178, 245, 252, 257, 258
  Cole's love of sightseeing, 141–142
  (1909), Europe, 21
  (1913), England, 33
  (1919), Italy, 56
  (1921), Egypt, 56
  (1927), Spain, 88
  (1930), Europe and Far East, 109, 111, 112, 113
  (1932–33), Europe, 113, 122, 126, 127
  (1935), South Seas, 113, 138, 139–141, 168
  (1937), Cuba, 194; Europe, 113, 171, 178
  (1938), Cuba and South America, 194
  (1940), Central America and South Seas, 113, 196
  (1949), Europe, planned, 238
  (1951), Mexico, 245
  (1955), Europe, 252
  (1956), Europe and Near East, 257
  (1957), Italy, 258
Treacher, Arthur, 207, 285
Trilling, Steve, 215
Tucker, Sophie, 191–192, 221, 284
20th Century-Fox: *Can-Can*, 248, 262, 293

Uppman, Theodore, 169–170

Vance, Vivian, 209, 286
Variety, 119, 218, 248
Velez, Lupe, 189, 284
Venice, 63, 75–76, 77
  Cole and Linda, 3, 73–74, 76, 77–79, 88, 95

Elsa Maxwell's promotion of the Lido, 63, 73, 76
Verdon, Gwen, 247, 291, 333
Verdura, Duke Fulco di, 247, 255
Verne, Jules, 227, 229, 289
Victor. *See* RCA Victor

Waldorf Astoria: Cole/Cole and Linda, 4, 170, 201, 202, 250, 251–252, 257, 264, 265, 266
Maxwell, Elsa, 63, 128, 170
Wales, Prince of. *See* Windsor, Duke of
Walters, Charles, 145, 200, 282, 285
Wanger, Walter, 43, 106
Waring, Fred: Pennsylvanians, 96, 116, 117, 277, 279, 329
Warner, Jack, 215, 223, 224
Warner Brothers: *42nd Street*, 151–152
and Porter, 214–215, 220–221; *Fifty Million Frenchmen*, 109, 151, 279–280; *Hollywood Canteen*, 150, 216, 288; *Mississippi Belle* (not produced), 214–215, 221, 287–288; *Night and Day*, 5, 47, 215–216, 220–224, 288–289
Warren, Julie, 228, 289
Watts, Richard, 96, 104–105, 165, 166, 189, 192–193
Webb, Clifton, 43
See America First, 42–43, 274
You Never Know, 178, 179, 186, 189, 284
Webb, Vanderbilt, 30
Weiler, A. H., 136
Weill, Kurt, 54
Weismuller, Johnny, 144
Welles, Orson: *Around the World in Eighty Days*, 227–228, 228–229, 289
Citizen Kane, 227
Julius Caesar, 227
Romeo and Juliet, 227
The War of the Worlds, 227

West, Buster and John, 96, 277
Whelton, Beatrice J., 241–242
Whiteman, Paul: Orchestra, 84, 327
Whitridge, Arnold, 26, 29, 45, 49, 272, 273
Wilde, Oscar, 176, 205
Williams, Derek, 145, 282
Williams, Hope, 115, 279
Williams, Jack, 208, 209, 286
Williams College: Buxton Hill left to, 255, 269
honorary degree from, 255
Wilson, John C. ("Jack"), 234, 235–236, 243, 289
Wilson, Mrs. John C. (Natasha Paley Lelong), 234–235, 235–236, 243, 255
Wiman, Dwight, 119, 280
Winchell, Walter, 105, 109, 122, 189
Windsor, Duchess of, 243
Windsor, Duke of, 88, 235, 243
Within the Quota (Times Past) (ballet score), 57, 79–86 *passim*, 276
Wodehouse, P. G.: *Anything Goes*, 132, 133, 134, 281
Oh, Kay!, 132
Woollcott, Alexander, 112
Woolley, Monty (Edgar Montillion), 67
And the Villain Still Pursued Her, 36, 272
death, 267
as director: *Fifty Million Frenchmen*, 106–107, 278; *The New Yorkers*, 115, 279; *Paranoia, or Chester of the Y.D.A.*, 36, 273; *Out o' Luck*, 93, 277
homosexuality, 30, 114, 115, 147, 195, 267
The Man Who Came to Dinner, 112, 196, 197
Night and Day, 222

and Porter, 2, 29, 30, 38, 49–50, 114, 115, 128, 147, 196, 216, 221, 267; travels, 111–112, 113, 138, 168
We're All Dressed Up and We Don't Know Huerta Go, 274
Worcester Academy, 1, 2, 17, 18–20, 23, 271
World War I, 3, 44–48 *passim,* 90, 98, 137
World War II, 199, 201, 204–205, 206
Wyman, Jane, 222, 289

Yale *News,* 36
Yale University, 1, 2, 14, 17, 21–33

passim, 84–85, 91, 271–273
honorary degree from, 255, 262
manuscripts and memorabilia left to, 84, 102, 262, 269
music written for groups after graduation, 35–37, 85, 93, 273–274
Yon, Pietro Alessandro, 45
Youmans, Vincent, 54
"The Carioca," 130, 131
"Hallelujah," 108

Ziegfeld, Florenz, 54
Zoppola, Countess di (Edith Mortimer), 179, 247

Comparative Labour Law
and
Industrial Relations

EDITOR: BLANPAIN, R.

Aaron, B.
Barbagelata, H.
Birk, R.
Cella, G.
Clarke, O.
Cordova, E.
Gamillscheg, F.
Goldman, A.
Hanami, T.
Hepple, B.

Monat, J.
Oechslin, J.
Pankert, A.
Rojot, J.
Schnorr, G.
Schregle, J.
Treu, T.
Valticos, N.
Windmuller, J.

THIRD EDITION

KLUWER LAW AND TAXATION PUBLISHERS
Deventer · Antwerp · London · Frankfurt · Boston · New York

Distribution in the USA and Canada
Kluwer Law and Taxation Publishers
101 Philip Drive
Norwell, MA 02061
USA

Library of Congress Cataloging in Publication Data

Comparative labour law and industrial relations.

   Includes indexes.
   1. Labor laws and legislation. 2. Industrial
relations. I. Blanpain, R. (Roger), 1932-
II. Aaron, Benjamin.
K1705.6.C65   1987   344'.01   87-17078
ISBN 90-6544-316-9   342.41

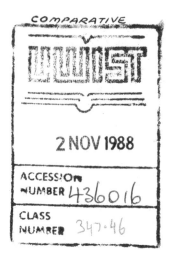
D/1987/2664/68
ISBN 90 6544 316 9

Table of Contents

		Page
Notes on Contributors		vii
Editor's Preface		ix
List of Abbreviations		xi

INTRODUCTION

Chapter 1. Comparativism in Labour Law and Industrial Relations   3
            R. Blanpain
Chapter 2. Documentation   25
            F. Gamillscheg
Chapter 3. Industrial Relations in a Changing Economic Environment:
            The Post War Experience of Advanced Market Economies   39
            O. Clarke
Chapter 4. Labour Law and Industrial Relations in the Third World   57
            J. Schregle

INTERNATIONAL DEVELOPMENTS

Chapter 5. International Labour Law   77
            N. Valticos
Chapter 6. Conflict of Laws in Employment Contracts and Industrial
            Relations   95
            F. Gamillscheg
Chapter 7. European Communities   113
            G. Schnorr
Chapter 8. Guidelines for Multinational Enterprises and Labour
            Relations   133
            R. Blanpain
Chapter 9. The International Trade Union Movement   149
            J.P. Windmuller

COMPARATIVE STUDIES

Chapter 10. Freedom of Association   173
            A. Pankert
Chapter 11. National Trade Union Movements   197
            G. Cella and T. Treu
Chapter 12. Employers' Organisations   229
            J. Oechslin

Chapter 13. Employee Participation in the Workshop, in the Office
and in the Enterprise   249
T. Hanami and J. Monat
Chapter 14. The Attitudes of Employers and Trade Unions towards
the Quality of Working Life Movement   287
J. Rojot
Chapter 15. Collective Bargaining   307
E. Córdova
Chapter 16. Settlement of Disputes over Rights   337
B. Aaron
Chapter 17. Settlement of Disputes over Interests   361
A. Goldman
Chapter 18. Industrial Conflict: Perspectives and Trends   383
R.O. Clarke
Chapter 19. Industrial Conflict: The Law of Strikes and Lock-Outs   401
R. Birk
Chapter 20. Different Categories of Workers and Labour Contracts   427
H. Barbagelata
Chapter 21. Equality and Prohibition of Discrimination in Em-
ployment   453
R. Blanpain
Chapter 22. Security of Employment   475
B. Hepple
Chapter 23. Labour Relations in the Public Sector   503
J. Schregle

Authors Index   517

Geographical Index   518

Subject Index   522

Notes on Contributors

Benjamin Aaron is Professor of Law and Research Associate of the Institute of Industrial Relations, University of California, Los Angeles.

Hector-Hugo Barbagelata is Professor of Labour Law in the Faculty of Law at Montevideo.

Rolf Birk is Professor of Labour Law in the Faculty of Law of the University of Trier (FR Germany) and Director of the Institute for Labour Law and Industrial Relations in the European Community (Trier).

Roger Blanpain is Professor of Labour Law at the Catholic University of Leuven (Belgium) and Visiting Professor at the European Institute of Business Administration, Fontainbleau (INSEAD) (France).

Gian Primo Cella is Professor of the Theory of Trade Unions and Social Conflict at the University of Trieste.

R. Oliver Clarke is a Principal Administrator in the Social Affairs and Industrial Relations Division of the Organisation for Economic Cooperation and Development (OECD).

Efren Córdova, formerly Professor of Labour Law at the Universities of Havana and Puerto Rico, has been Chief of the Labour Law and Labour Relations Branch of the International Labour Organisation since 1975.

Franz Gamillscheg is Professor of Labour and International Private Law at the University of Göttingen.

Alvin Goldman is Professor of Law at the University of Kentucky.

Bob Hepple is Professor of Law in the University of London, at University College.

Tadashi Hanami is Professor of Labour Law at Sophia University, Tokyo, where he was also Dean of the Law School.

Jacques Monat is Head of the Participation Program of the International Institute for Labour Studies (Switzerland).

Jean-Jacques Oechslin is Chairman of the Executive Committee of the International Organisation of Employers.

Alfred Pankert is Head of the Labour-Management Relations Section of the International Labour Organisation.

Jacques Rojot is Professor of Management at the University of Rennes and Associate Professor in Industrial Relations at the European Institute of Business Administration, Fontainebleau (INSEAD) (France).

Gerhard Schnorr has been Professor ordinarius at the University of Innsbruck since 1967. He is also Director of the Institute for Labour Law and Social Security at that university.

Johannes Schregle is a former Director of the Industrial Relations and Labour Administration Department of the ILO, Geneva; Honorary Professor for International and Comparative Labour Law, University of Salzburg; Secretary-General of the International Society for Labour Law and Social Security, Geneva.

Tiziano Treu is Professor ordinarius in Labour Law at the University of Pavia, as well as holding an appointment in the Department of Economics at the Catholic University of Milan.

Nicolas Valticos is Secretary-General of the Institute of International Law; formerly Assistant Director-General at the International Labour Organisation and Associate Professor at the Faculty of Law of the University of Geneva.

John Windmuller is Martin P. Chaterwood Professor in the New York State School of Industrial and Labour Relations at Cornell University since 1951, specialising in international and comparative labour relations.

Editor's Preface

Comparativism is no longer a purely academic exercise but has increasingly become an urgent necessity for industrial relations and legal practitioners due to the growth of multinational enterprises and the impact of international and regional organisations aspiring to harmonise rules. The growing need for comprehensive, up-to-date and readily available information on labour law and industrial relations in different countries led to the publication of the *International Encyclopaedia for Labour Law and Industrial Relations*, in which almost 50 international and national monographs have thus far been published.

This book, *Comparative Labour Law and Industrial Relations*, goes a step further than the *Encyclopaedia* inasmuch as most of the 24 chapters provide comparative and integrated thematic treatment. Our aim is to describe the salient characteristics and trends in labour law and industrial relations in the contemporary world. However, this work is more than a set of papers written by individual authors. For the first edition (1982) twelve of the nineteen contributors, the associate editor, and the publisher were able to meet to discuss the chapters, carefully evaluating, reviewing and co-ordinating our collaborative efforts. The meeting was exceptionally informative and productive. It was sponsored by and took place at Insead (Fontainebleau) with the additional support of the Catholic University of Leuven and Kluwer Publishers. I thank them for their courtesy and assistance. This close contact was maintained in the development of the second edition.

Our book obviously is not exhaustive with respect to the coverage of countries and topics. For example, in order to continue our efforts within the area of our greater expertise, the comparative chapters in the second and third editions do not examine the collectivist economies. For the second and third editions, however, more attention has been given to developing countries, and to the public sector. Also, an attempt has been made to strike a better balance between labour law and industrial relations.

Encouraged by the warm reception of the first two editions, we hope that also the third edition will serve as a textbook and reference work to facilitate the task of teachers and students of comparative labour law and industrial relations. We hope, too, that the book will provide labour lawyers with the necessary insights to cope with a world which is increasingly international.

The English language does not have a personal pronoun which is gender neutral and we find the form s/he somewhat inelegant. Accordingly, where the authors have used the form he, this should be taken to refer also to the feminine gender, unless the context indicates otherwise.

Finally, my warm personal thanks go to all those who made the first as as well as the second and third editions of Comparative Labour Law and Industrial Relations possible: to Dr. Frances Millard who was very much involved in the rewriting and editing of the first edition and to Prof. I. Christie and the staff of the Institute of Labour Relations in Leuven: Dr. O. Vanachter, M. Vranken, Mrs. Theuwissen, J. Van Rijmenant, and G. Van Staeyen.

R.B.
Leuven, January 1987

List of Abbreviations

AAFLI	Asian–American Free Labor Institute (AFL–CIO)
AALC	African–American Labor Center (AFL–CIO)
ACAA	Australian Conciliation and Arbitration Act
ACAC	Australian Conciliation and Arbitration Commission
ACAS	Advisory, Conciliation and Arbitration Service (UK)
ACSPA	Australian Council of Salaried and Professional Associations
ACTU	Australian Council of Trade Unions
AFL	American Federation of Labor
AFL–CIO	American Federation of Labor–Congress of Industrial Organizations
AFRO	African Regional Organisation (ICFTU)
AIFLD	American Institute for Free Labor Development (AFL–CIO)
ARO	Asian Regional Organisation (ICFTU)
ASAP	Association of Petrochemical Plants (Italy)
ASEAN	Association of South East Asian Nations
AUCCTU	All Union Central Council of Trade Unions (USSR)
AUEW	Amalgamated Union of Engineering Workers (UK)
BATCO	British American Tobacco Company
BATU	Brotherhood of Asian Trade Unionists (WCL)
BDA	Bundesvereinigung der Deutschen Arbeitgeberverbände
BDI	Bundesverband der Deutschen Industrie
BIAC	Business and Industry Advisory Committee (OECD)
BIM	British Institute of Management
CAC	Central Arbitration Committee (UK)
CCO	Confederatión de Comisiones Obreras (Spain)
CEEP	Centre Européen des Entreprises Publiques
CFDT	Confédération Française Démocratique du Travail
CFTC	Confédération Française des Travailleurs Chrétiens
CGC	Confédération Générale des Cadres (France)
CGD	Christlicher Gewerkschaftsbund Deutschlands
CGIL	Confederazione Generale Italiana del Lavoro
CGT	Confédération Générale du Travail (France)
CIFE	Counseil Industriel des Fédérations Européennes
CIO	Congress of Industrial Organizations (USA)
CISC	Confédération Internationale des Syndicats Chrétiens
CISL	Confederazione Italiana Sindacati del Lavoratori
CLAT	Central Latino Americana de Trabajadores (WCL)
CNPF	Conseil National du Patronat Français
CNV	Christelijk Nationaal Vakverbond (The Netherlands)

COCCEE	Comité des Organisations Commerciales de la Communauté Economique Européenne
COGECA	Comité Général de Coopératives Agricoles (EC)
Comintern	Communist International
COPA	Comité des Organisations Professionnelles Agricoles (EC)
COPE	Committee for Political Education (AFL–CIO)
CSC	Confédération des Syndicats Chrétiens (Belgium)
DAG	Deutsche Angestelltengewerkschaft
DBB	Deutscher Beambtenbund
DGB	Deutscher Gewerkschaftsbund
DOMEI	Japanese Confederation of Labour
EC	European Communities
EEOC	Equal Employment Opportunity Commission (USA)
EFA	European Federation of Agricultural Workers
ELC	Employers' Liaison Committee (UNICE)
EMF	European Metalworkers' Federation
EO	European Organisation (WCL)
EP	European Parliament
EPCA	Employment Protection (Consolidation) Act (UK)
ERO	European Regional Organisation (ICFTU)
ESC	Economic and Social Committee (EC)
ETUC	European Trade Union Confederation
ETUI	European Trade Union Institute
FCA	Federal Court of Australia
FMCS	Federal Mediation and Conciliation Service (USA)
FNV	Federatie Nederlandse Vakbeweging
FR Germany	Federal Republic of Germany
HMS	Hind Mazdoor Sabha (Indian Trade Union Congress)
ICC	International Chamber of Commerce
ICEF	International Federation of Chemical, Energy and General Workers Unions
ICFTU	International Confederation of Free Trade Unions
IELL	International Encyclopaedia for Labour Law and Industrial Relations
IFTU	International Federation of Trade Unions
ILO	International Labour Organisation Office
IME	Committee on International Investment and Multinational Enterprises (OECD)
IMF–JC	International Metalworkers Federation – Japanese Council of Metal Workers Unions
INTUC	Indian National Trade Union Congress
IOE	International Organisation of Employers

ITS	International Trade Secretariat
ITT	International Telephone and Telegraph Corporation
LO	Landsorganisationen (Denmark, Norway, Sweden) (Central Confederation of Employees)
MNE	Multinational Enterprise
NLRB	National Labor Relations Board (USA)
NVV	Nederlands Verbond van Vakverenigingen
OATUU	Organisation of African Trade Union Unity
OAU	Organisation of African Unity
OECD	Organisation for Economic Co-operation and Development
OEEC	Organisation for European Economic Co-operation
OB	Official Bulletin of the European Communities (ILO)
ORIT	Interamerican Regional Organization of Workers (ICFTU)
PAWC	Pan-American Workers Congress (WCL)
PR of China	People's Republic of China
QWL	Quality of Working Life
RILU	Red International of Labour Unions
SAF	Svenska Arbetsgivareföreningen (Swedish Employers' Confederation)
SE	Societas Europeae
SOHYO	General Council of Trade Unions of Japan
TCO	Tjänstemanns Centralorganization (Sweden) (Central Organization of Salaried Employees)
TGWU	Transport and General Workers' Union (UK)
TUAC	Trade Union Advisory Committee (OECD)
TUC	Trade Union Congress (UK)
TUI	Trade Union International (WFTU)
UAW	United Automobile Workers (USA)
UIL	Unione Italiana del Lavoro
UIMM	Union des Industries Métallurgiques et Minières (France)
ULA	Union der Leitenden Angestellten (FR Germany)
UN	United Nations
UNIAPAC	International Christian Union of Business Executives
UNICE	Union des Industries de la Communauté Européenne
WCL	World Confederation of Labour
WFTU	World Federation of Trade Unions

Introduction

Chapter 1. Comparativism in Labour Law and Industrial Relations

R. Blanpain

'The use of the comparative method requires a knowledge not only of the foreign law, but also of its social, and above all its political context. The use of comparative law for practical purposes becomes an abuse only if it is informed by a legalistic spirit which ignores this context of the law.'
O. Kahn-Freund, 'On Uses and Misuses of Comparative Law', *The Modern Law Review*, 1974, p. 27.

I. IN SEARCH OF A DEFINITION

1. 'In every country, North and South', Schregle points out, 'workers, employers and governments have both common and divergent interests, short term and long term. The divergent interests must be accommodated and reconciled.... . The way in which such interests are expressed and reconciled is the subject of industrial relations. It will of necessity vary from country to country. International comparison must bring out and explain the differences and similarities of national industrial relations systems'.[1] Schregle's statement, which obviously also applies to labour law, brings us to the two schools of thought concerning the development of comparative labour relations. One is the *convergence* school, which holds that the spread of industrialisation would gradually bring labour relations systems closer to one another. This view was first expounded by Dunlop in his classic book on *Industrial Relations Systems*[2] and further elaborated by other American scholars such as Harbison, Coleman and Kerr. The other school of thought, the *divergence* school, maintained that labour relations are a subsystem of political systems and mostly reflect prevailing national conditions and cultural values. This view has gained momentum in recent years as a result of the efforts made by developing countries to depart from Western systems, inherited from colonial times and to mould their own labour relations system in the light of their own development requirements.

---

1. J. Schregle, 'Comparative Industrial Relations: Pitfalls and Potential', *International Labour Review*, 1981, p. 27.
2. J. Dunlop, *Industrial Relations Systems*, New York, 1958.

2. Coming back to Schregle's point one can consequently say that comparing labour law and industrial relations consists of the study of the labour laws and industrial relations systems of different countries. As Valticos puts it: 'The basic aim of comparative labour law can be said to be essentially *scientific* in nature – namely to gain a *more extensive knowledge of the law of nations'*.[3] This is to say that it involves first, a scientific analysis of law and practice in order to set them side by side, and by doing so note the similarities and the differences, secondly an attempt to explain those similarities and differences; and thirdly an effort to perceive eventual trends and overall developments, which operate across national boundaries.

II. USES OF THE COMPARATIVE METHOD

3. It goes without saying that the knowledge gained by this examination on a comparative basis can serve several purposes which do not exclude each other but on the contrary may very well and do indeed go together.

A. *Better Insight into One's Own National System*

4. Comparative law is undoubtedly an excellent tool of education. It has thereby often been stressed that the analysis of foreign systems entails the enormous benefit of putting one's own national experience into perspective; that when studying other systems one often experiences a (cultural) shock in discovering that a similar problem is resolved in another country in a completely different way, such that one cannot help but initiate the analysis and evaluation of one's own system again, but now from another angle, from an enriched point of view, from a new insight.

Comparativism consequently contributes to the better perception of one's own national system; besides, it 'enriches one's own approach to and understanding of industrial relations, and improves one's own skills in analysing a variety of industrial relations'.[4]

5. Comparativism may also facilitate the penetration of the national system through the sapping of the 'interpretations' as advanced in foreign doctrines, which can be a source of renewed intellectual stimulation.

We must, however, recognise that comparing the labour law of different countries is for many, if not most lawyers of no explicit practical value for their daily work. No doubt there are many labour lawyers, extremely busy and successful, for whom national law and developments are plentiful and more than sufficient. Most lawyers have rarely or never been exposed to

---

3. 'Comparative Law and the International Labour Organisation', *Comparative Labour Law*, 1977, p. 274.
4. Schregle, *op. cit.*, p. 24.

another legal system, except perhaps when travelling as a tourist and experiencing the legal procedures involved in a car accident, loss of luggage and the like. Many lawyers, if so asked, would certainly argue that they see no compelling reasons to engage in comparative work and that they are more than busy keeping up with national developments . . .

The fact is that most national systems in our industrialised European countries are more or less mature and capable of resolving the cases, which the legal profession in a given country has to deal with.

6. Except for dramatic circumstances, as a consequence of wars, or drastic revolutions, massive transfers of legal systems do no longer take place. Rarely are there, in actual times, such dramatic legal gaps in a given country, that a wholesale transfer is needed, advocated and carried through, although this may partially occur e.g. as in *Spain*, when during the post Franco period the *Italian* Statute of Workers' Rights of 1970 was often referred to in the elaboration of the Spanish Estatuto de los Trabajadores of 1980.

Those occasions currently being rare, references to a foreign system, are in many countries not frequent for purposes of day to day practice.

There are however very important exceptions. For example in *Austria* and *Switzerland* where the influence of German doctrine is reported to be overwhelming, given inter alia the fact of a common language and also arising from the fact that the evolution of German labour law is more advanced in the *FR Germany* than in *Switzerland*.

Comparativism is a frequently used method in *Poland* but this is a consequence of the co-existence of legal rules and concepts of the prewar and post-war systems, which clearly involves the difficulties of using concepts which were formulated upon the basis of an ideology and a context which is no longer present.

In *judgements* themselves comparison plays a role only in exceptional cases, although e.g. in *FR Germany* the comparative method is recognised as a valid method of interpretation.

It is only when countries have a common problem – e.g. when a labour relationship transcends national boundaries, or when a given organisation has an international, supranational or multinational jurisdiction – that the knowledge of more systems becomes mandatory.

B. *International Private Labour Law*

7. Knowledge of another legal system is obviously required in the application of *international private labour law*. There is no need to expand on this, except for saying that due to the growing internationalisation of business and the expanding free movement of labour across national boundaries, as e.g. in the European Common Market, the phenomenon of employees involving different national jurisdictions, has become a normal fact of life.

One should recognise however that judges, when confronted with international private labour law problems, may tend to apply their own national system and that lawyers confronted with those problems frequently rely on a report given by a foreign colleague, without themselves striving to discover the foreign solution.

C. Multinational Enterprises and International Unions

8. Multinational enterprises, which by their very nature, operate – in a more or less centralised way – in different countries, clearly have more than a vested interest in studying and comparing labour law of the home country and of actual or potential host countries.

Labour relations are in essence national in the multinational enterprise in the sense that subsidiaries have to follow national rules and practice,[5] at least up to a certain point, since a national system may have a lot of manoeuvre for multinational input; national labour law and practice may constitute an important factor in deciding where to invest and disinvest.[6] In central and regional headquarters specialists attentively follow developments in the different countries, in which operations take place, or might take place as well as developments in international organisations, like the ILO, the OECD, the EEC.

One can foresee that the growing development of international labour relations, namely relations between headquarters in one country and employees in one or more other countries, on issues such as the co-responsibility of the parent for the debts of the daughter or the 'access to real decision makers' will grow in importance in the years to come.

In *international trade unions* the same interest exists in comparing and following developments in different countries, this is obviously in order to defend the interests of workers, especially those employed in multinational enterprises. Some unions also closely follow collective bargaining developments in different countries, in order to advise their members and coordinate certain actions.

D. Forecast of Further Developments

9. Moreover if comparative analysis allows us to acknowledge certain trends and developments, then the exercise will enable the comparative scholar 'to find out to *what extent our own national system is synchronised with such*

---

5. Paragraph 7 of the Introduction of the OECD Guidelines for Multinational Enterprises (1976). See further chapter 8 of this Handbook. A similar principle is laid down in the Tripartite Declaration of Principles Concerning Multinational Enterprises and Social Policy of the ILO (no. 8).

6. R. Blanpain, *The OECD Guidelines for Multinational Enterprises and Labour Relations 1976–1979*, pp. 15–16.

6

trends, or whether it precedes them, lags behind or even moves in a different direction. This opens up fascinating prospects'.[7]

By the same token comparativism may help to forecast future developments as ideas and concepts do indeed, more than before, due to the growing internationalisation of our world, cross national and regional boundaries; and what may happen to us may already be inscribed in the labour relations in other countries.

E. To Guide or Promote Social Change at Home – Assistance

10. Another use of comparativism is to promote at home a social change which foreign law or practice is designed either to express or to produce[8] which obviously involves difficulties of transplantability to be discussed below.

11. Many examples could be given to illustrate this use. When 'temporary work' was introduced in Europe and national legislators were taking measures to regulate this new social phenomenon, national measures were, in many countries, inspired by regulations elaborated in other countries.[9]

12. Other examples can be given, showing that this is not without problems. Thus one may cite the Spanish case, when due to the fact that the workers' statute (Statuto de los Trabajadores) was close in name and apparent content to the Italian Statuto dei Lavoratori (1970), raised expectations to Spanish workers which to some extent could not be met. In some Latin American countries the use of the Labour Code of a more advanced country (e.g. the influence of the Columbian Labour Code on Honduran legislation also entailed some difficulties of implementation).

Another example can be found in the adoption of the Australian system of compulsory arbitration by some developing countries, like Singapore, which resulted in the establishment of an Industrial Court vested with relatively wide powers. The Industrial Courts model, as developed in Kenya, Singapore, Trinidad and Tobago, has been applied in turn in other developing countries, e.g. Zambia, Sierra Leone and Malaysia.

13. A distinction may be made between developing countries and developed countries. In the former transplantation has been used as a tool of modernisation or industrialisation. Here, too, there are two sides to the coin. The positive side is the easiness in the introduction of industrial change; less advantageous is the fact that those countries may suffer from inconsistencies between the system introduced and the social context of that country.

7. Schregle, *op. cit.*, p. 24.
8. O. Kahn-Freund, 'On Uses and Misuses of Comparative Law', *op. cit.*, p. 2.
9. R. Blanpain, (ed.), *Temporary Work and the Law*, Deventer, 1978, 544 pp.

14. Another use for comparativism lies in the area of advice and assistance given to specific countries, either by international organisations or in a bilateral framework.

F. As an Instrument in the Formulation and the Application of International Labour Standards: Horizontal and Vertical Comparison

15. Valticos underlines rightly that the formulation of international minimum standards or international labour law is often quoted as one area where the use of the comparative method has been the most extensive.[10] Here not only the international labour conventions and recommendations elaborated in the framework of the ILO come naturally to mind, but also the European Social Charter as the harmonization of social standards in the Member States of the Council of Europe, next to United Nations Instruments and the European Human Rights Convention, to name only the most important.

In addition mention should be made of the Charter of Social Rights, adopted by the *Organization of American States* in 1948 (Bogota), and the Conventions adapted by the *Arab Labour Organisation*.

1. The International Labour Organisation

16. The ILO Conventions are, by far, the main source of international labour law. This is due not only to their number (from 1919 to 1986, more than 160 conventions and more than 170 recommendations were reproduced apart from 5,100 (Dec. 1983) ratifications by more than 130 countries and over 1000 declarations of applications in respect of 30 non-metropolitan territories) but also their detailed character and the increasingly broad field they cover.[11]

17. It is self-evident that the first step in the formulation of international legislation and practice is to collect information on national legislation and practice: international standards are indeed not created out of the blue, but should relate as much as possible to national experience. It is therefore only natural that before the governing body of the ILO decides to place an item on the agenda of the International Labour Conference with the aim of adopting an international instrument, the Office must place before it 'a concise statement of the existing laws and practice in the various countries relative to that item'.

---

10. *Op. cit.*, p. 273.
11. N. Valticos, 'International Labour Law', in *International Encyclopedia for Labour Law and Industrial Relations*, pp. 43, 229.

18. Valticos describes the formulation process as follows: 'Once it has conducted this general survey of the state of current legislation throughout the world, the Governing Body decides whether or not to place the item on the agenda of the Conference. If the item is placed on the agenda, a second, more detailed comparative study must be carried out. The ILO prepares "a preliminary report setting out the law and practice in the different countries" and any other useful information. The report draws attention to generally accepted guiding principles in the field concerned, usually under several headings, and to the various national regulations on the subject . . .

Together with this comparative survey of law and practice, the ILO sends governments a questionnaire with the request that they should give reasons for their replies. On the basis of the replies from governments, the ILO prepares a further report indicating the principal questions which require consideration by the Conference so as to be able to reach conclusions as to the general, or at least the majority, view. This report forms the basis of an initial discussion by the Conference. Following this first discussion, which leads to the adoption of conclusions with a view to an international instrument, a second series of consultations is carried out by the ILO, which then drafts one or more Conventions or Recommendations on which governments are invited to comment, whereupon the matter is again placed before the Conference, which adopts the final texts'.[12]

19. The comparative method is also used for the examination of the application of the international minimum standards. 'In the context', Valticos indicates, 'it generally takes the form of a comparison between the international standard and the national legislation of countries that have ratified the Convention concerned – though also sometimes of countries which have not ratified it. At times, too, the international standards may even be compared with all known national laws on the subject'.[13]

2. The Council of Europe and the European Communities

20. Mention should obviously also be made of the *European Social Charter*, promulgated by the *Council of Europe* in 1961 and up to now ratified by thirteen of the twenty-one Member States of the Council (Austria, Cyprus, Denmark, France, FR Germany, Iceland, Ireland, Italy, Norway, Spain, Sweden, The Netherlands, The United Kingdom). The supervision of the application of the 19 articles of the Charter is mainly in the hands of a Committee of Independent Experts, which examines the two-yearly reports the Governments are required to submit.[14]

12. 'Comparative Law and the International Labour Organisation', *Comparative Labour Law*, 1977, pp. 279–80.
13. Ibid, pp. 284–286.
14. O. Kahn-Freund, 'The European Charter' in F.G. Jacobs ed., *European Law and the Individual*, Amsterdam, 1976, pp. 181–211.

Equally important are certain articles (4 – 10 – 11) of the *European Convention of Human Rights and Fundamental Freedoms*, adopted in 1950.

21. Comparativism is also at the heart of the harmonisation of labour laws which takes place within the framework of the *European Economic Community*. One of the goals of the Community consists of the development of a social policy aiming to promote improvement in the living and working conditions of labour so as to permit the equalisation of such conditions in an upward direction. This development, the EEC treaty indicates, 'will result not only from the functioning of the Common Market which will form the harmonisation of social systems, but also form the approximation of (legislative and administrative) provisions' (Article 117). Harmonisation of labour laws is, however, not a goal of the EC. It is only where 'different, territorial limited, legal systems disturb the realisation of the goals of the treaty' that the Community is entitled to propose a measure favouring harmonisation.[15]

22. Jörn Pipkorn, a civil servant at the European Communities, gives a clear description of the use of the comparative method in the drafting of harmonised EC rules. 'When an action for harmonising social and labour law is envisaged under those circumstances, the competent service of the Commission (for example, the Directorate General for Social Affairs) asks qualified experts in all the Member States (in most cases professors of social and labour law) to prepare reports on the legal situation in the respective Member State as to the subject to be covered by the envisaged harmonisation. One such expert is entrusted with summarising these reports and evaluating their findings with a view to indicating possible trends towards harmonisation. This general rapporteur has to ensure, in cooperation with the competent officials of the EEC Commission, that the national reports have a common structure and a coherent approach to the relevant problems, as is necessary for the comparative study. To these ends, the general rapporteur and the EEC officials prepare a questionnaire which is then discussed with the national rapporteurs before it serves as a basis for their reports. Those reports, as well as the draft synthetic report of the general rapporteur, are discussed among all rapporteurs, in order to clarify the relevant problems.'

23. If the problems to be solved do not appear so difficult to the competent EEC officials, they may, however, simplify the preparatory work, entrusting one or two experts with the comparative research for all the nine Member States.

Whether one or nine experts do the comparative research, the result will inevitably reflect certain inconsistencies or some overemphasis due to the personality of the author. But those imperfections are revealed, in both cases, in the subsequent stages of the procedure.

15. J. Pipkorn, 'Comparative Labour Law in the Harmonisation of Social Standards in the European Community', *Comparative Labour Law*, 1977, p. 263.

When the synthetic report is ready, the responsible Directorate General of the Commission sends it to the employer and union organisations, UNICE and ETUC. Those organisations send the report to their affiliated organisations in all the Member States and prepare a paper reflecting the joint opinion of their affiliates. Both organisations send their papers to the Commission and discuss them with the responsible service.

The responsible service of the Commission then convenes a working party of experts nominated by the Governments of the Member States to discuss the synthetic report and possible measures of harmonisation. The Governments normally send to this working party officials of their competent departments. Those officials are generally the same persons who will subsequently represent their Governments on the working party of the Council when the Commission eventually submits its proposal to that body. But at this earlier stage of the process, the officials are not meant to express the views of their Governments but to give a reasoned opinion as experts. The responsible services of the Commission then prepare a draft proposal of a directive or a regulation embodying the envisaged harmonisation measure on the basis of the article of the Treaty of Rome relevant to this measure. This draft proposal is discussed in the same way as the synthetic report before it is finalised and formally adopted by the Commission.

24. The proposal of the Commission is submitted to the Council, the Community's main legislative body. Before the Council examines the proposal, formal consultation with the European Parliament (EP) and the Economic and Social Committee (ESC) takes place, as provided for in the respective article of the Treaty. The opinions of these bodies are prepared in special committees with technical help from the officials of the EP and sometimes from outside experts (for example specialists of UNICE and ETUC in the case of the ESC consultation).

When the European Parliament and the Economic and Social Committee have given their opinions, the Commission revises its original proposal . . . The crucial and decisive stage is reached when the Council discusses the modified proposal of the Commission . . .

This discussion within the Council has of course much 'feed-back' with the national employer and labour organisations and their legal and socioeconomic framework. This process offers the maximum guarantees for making available all arguments of comparative law for the political discussion.[16]

G. As an Instrument for Theory Formulation

25. The important contribution to comparativism of theory formulation and theorising in industrial relations reveals another area of the possible uses of comparativism in industrial relations.

16. *Op. cit.*, pp. 264–267.

Professor John Dunlop, in his seminal work *Industrial relations systems*, was one of the first to articulate the need to adopt a comparative approach in order to acquire theoretical insight in industrial relations. As he and others[17] have explained, comparativism could and should be used as an instrument to verify *a priori* hypotheses or to produce abstract generalisations derived from research findings in a variety of national contexts.[18]

As Walker rightly points out however, comparativism used for such purposes should transcend the descriptive approach to foreign industrial relations systems, and concentrate upon the explanation of the functioning of industrial relations systems, in order to identify the role, importance and interaction of the different factors shaping and influencing industrial relations systems in a variety of national contexts.

26. One of the most prominent examples of theoretical studies, where comparativism was the main underpinning method, is the research project known as 'the Inter-university study of Labor problems in economic development', from which originated major works such as *Industrialism and Industrial man, Labor in developing economics*.[19]

A further review of the industrial relations literature provides us with many other examples, where comparativism appears as a vital instrument for theory formulation.

We refer in this context to a number of theoretical contributions, which cover the various subfields of the industrial relations discipline, and which fruitfully used comparativism for the study and theoretical explanation of industrial relations problems such as strike trends and industrial conflict, collective bargaining, trade-unionism etc.

Ross and Hartmann,[20] for example, used the comparative method to confirm the famous 'withering away' hypothesis; they also contributed to theory formulation by identifying the different factors which explained the (decreasing) level of strikes, caused by factors such as the development of labour parties with close trade-union affiliations, the growing importance of the state as the major institution influencing workers' welfare, changing employers' policies etc.

27. Finally, it might be of interest to note that comparativism has retained much of its prominence as a research method for theory formulation in

17. J. Porter, 'Quelques observations sur les études comparées', in: *Bulletin International Institute for Labour Studies*, 1967, p. 97.
    M. Shalev, Industrial Relations theory and the comparative study of industrial relations and industrial conflict, *BJIR*, vol, XVIII, March 1980, p. 26.
18. K. Walker, L'étude comparée des relations professionalles, in *Bulletin International Institute for Labour Studies*, no. 3, 1967, p. 213.
19. C. Ken, J. Dunlop, F. Harbison, C. Meyers, *Industrialism and Industrial Man*, London, 1962.
    W. Galenson, (ed.), *Labour and Economic Development*, New York, 1959.
20. A. Ross and P. Hartmann, *Changing Patterns of Industrial Conflict*, New York, 1960.

industrial relations, as is illustrated by the new International Institute for Labour Studies, a Geneva programme for comparative industry studies. Some of the research objectives of this project also provide us with a good example of the possible use of comparativism for theory formulation. They were defined as follows: a) to use the international variations in the strength of certain factors to assess the manner and extent of the influence of those factors upon industrial relations in the industry under study; b) to establish which characteristics of industrial relations in a particular industry are sufficiently powerful to withstand the pressure of national industrial relations systems in the countries compared, thus helping to identify and clarify the role of certain strategic factors in industry level industrial relations systems; c) to advance, through the comparison of a number of industries across a number of countries, an understanding of the operation of strategic factors in industrial relations systems, as a further step towards the development of a general theory of industrial relations.[21]

III. WHAT AND HOW TO COMPARE?

A. Comparison of Functions rather than of Institutions

28. In order to compare what is in fact comparable one needs to compare the functions institutions perform, rather than institutions themselves. Indeed similar institutions, e.g. works councils, labour courts, union delegations, may perform different functions in different countries. One is interested in what is going on, thus in the functions rather than in institutions as such. Schregle illustrates this point by considering three examples: labour courts and labour disputes, collective agreements and collective bargaining, and workers' participation. Let us limit ourselves to Schregle's third example: workers' participation. 'There is much confusion and disagreement over this term. Whatever the expression "workers' participation" may mean in the terminology and context of a given country, I propose to use it here in its wide sense as encompassing various arrangements by which workers and their representatives have a say in the decision-making process at the enterprise level . . . Again we must guard against falling into the trap of a purely institutional comparison. A tabular listing of the respective rights of, say the *French* works council, the *Austrian* or *Federal German* works council, the *Belgian* or *Dutch* works council, the *Indian* works committee or the recently created employees' councils in public enterprises in *Sri Lanka* may be of some informative usefulness but it does not permit of any meaningful evaluative comparison. It is certainly interesting to see what the respective rights of such bodies are as regards, for instance, management decisions on personnel questions, social and welfare matters, terms and

---

21. M. Derber, 'Strategic Factors in Industrial Relations Systems, the metal working industry'. *Labour and Society*, 1976, p. 18.

conditions of employment, as well as in the fields of production, marketing, finance and investment ... Such charts or tabular listings do not allow a comparative evaluation of the respective degree of workers' influence on management decisions in different countries. At first sight it might appear that in the Federal Republic's highly institutionalised system of works councils with far-reaching statutory co-determination rights, workers' influence would be greater than in a country where there are no such bodies. However, it may well be that in fact the influence which workers can exercise on management decisions is much stronger under a system of enterprise-level collective bargaining, as is the case in the United States.

Here again – and this cannot be repeated too often – we must compare functions and not institutions. Whether the worker's representatives on the supervisory boards of the Volkswagen Company who help to take important investment decisions in the boardroom really have a greater or lesser influence on management than the trade unions in Italy, which as a matter of principle and policy reject the very idea of workers' representation on company boards but have secured agreement on large-scale FIAT investments in the south of Italy through collective bargaining with the management in Turin, would be an interesting subject for comparative industrial relations research.'[22]

B. Comparison of what is 'going on'

29. From what has been said thus far concerning the comparison of functions, it follows self-evidently that the comparative scholar should try to find out what is 'going on', look for 'reality'. It is therefore not sufficient to compare the text of the legislation of different countries, as they e.g. appear in the Legislative Series of the ILO; one should also look at collective agreements, works rules in the enterprise, tacit understandings, customs and past practice. It is above all important to find out whether and how laws are applied, how institutions function in practice. It is not interesting to know whether the Belgian works councils do in fact get the abundant information they are by legislation entitled to? A recent investigation showed that the implementation of that legislation is far from adequate.

30. It is, to give another example, equally relevant not only to examine the law on trade-union freedom, but also to know whether there are trade-unions in a given country, what rights they enjoy in reality, how they are structured and the like. It is certainly interesting to know that the Belgian labour courts in practice deal almost exclusively with individual disputes of dismissed employees; this raises challenging questions such as why this is so and what happens to grievances of employees still at work.

22. Schregle, *op. cit.*, p. 22–23.

C. Looking for 'Models'

31. One of the best means of obtaining the benefits of the comparative method is the comparison of 'models', a model being a distinctive way of approaching a given problem, and by illustrating how a given 'model' functions in one or more countries. Such a method enables us to get a panoramic view of the different ways in which similar problems are solved, how one's system relates to these models, and to note differences, similarities and trends.

32. Let us illustrate how this might be done in the field of job security. One can obviously distinguish different systems or models for promoting job security, e.g.:
   – through lifetime employment;
   – government action: permission by a government official, e.g. a director of the employment office, is needed before an employer can dismiss an employee;
   – through workers' representatives (e.g. a works council) who may oppose dismissal;
   – through legal obligation upon the employer to respect a term of notice;
   – through the application of various criteria for selection for redundancy such as: last hired – first fired (the seniority system);
   – by means of the rule that employment may not be terminated unless there is a valid reason connected with the capacity or the conduct of the employee or based on the operational requirements of the enterprise, establishment or service . . .

33. These different systems of securing employment could then be illustrated by referring to experience in one or more countries where one or more models are in operation. The lifetime employment model is obviously to be represented by the Japanese practice; while the role of the government could be depicted by e.g. the Dutch or the French experience; for the evaluation of the role of the representatives of employees one could refer to the competence of the works council in the FR Germany or of the local union (union delegates) in Sweden. The obligation to respect a term of notice could be best illustrated by the Belgian example of the (rather long) terms of notice to be given in the case of a dismissal of a white collar employee. Seniority could be depicted on the basis of the American system, as it is elaborated in collective agreements, while the justification of dismissal could be illustrated by a number of countries, which follow the widely applied ILO Recommendation (No. 119) of 1963 as further elaborated by Convention No. 154 of 1981 on the same subject concerning the Termination of Employment at the Initiative of the Employer.

34. One could further look for models in the area of the remedies designed to achieve employment security, namely compensation, reinstatement, (penal) sanctions, then again look for countries where such models are in operation.

35. Another example can be easily found in the area of workers' participation, used in the sense of the influence by labour on management decision-making. Here the models (functions) are obvious: information, consultation, co-decision making, possibly self-government. The question is whether and how these functions are fulfilled in different countries by examining the role of collective bargaining, of representative bodies of employees in the enterprise (works councils, union delegates, shop stewards, committees for hygiene, . . .); the role of employees sitting on company boards, the effect of job enrichment schemes, semi-autonomous work groups and the like.

D. An Integrated and Global Approach

36. This heading covers different points. It goes without saying that if comparativism aims not only at the discovery of similarities and differences, of common or opposing trends but also at explaining why different systems operate the way they do in a given country, one can study a given problem only within the overall context of the industrial relations' system, or even the society taken as a whole, both in its contemporary as in its historic dimension. In order to understand and appreciate the role of a labour director (an employee sitting on the management board of a company) in the *Federal Republic of Germany*, one has to relate this form of workers' participation not only to the works council(s) – which are established – but also at plant level and at enterprise or company level, to the economic committee; also to the 'Vertrauensleute' (trusted men) at enterprise level, (in the metal working industry); as well to collective bargaining, which takes place at the industrial level of the different States. This leads us in turn to the role of German trade unions, which are not active at the level of the plant or the enterprise, just as one needs insight into this unique German character of order and discipline one has to know that workers' participation started long before the Second World War . . . and that it is the outcome of a long and evolutionary process, brutally interrupted by the Nazis and first reintroduced in the coal, iron and steel industry by Allied Command, after the Second World War. This is obviously not an easy task.

37. It is clear, then, that comparing labour laws and industrial relations' systems involves much more than setting side by side summaries of legislation from different countries on a given number of subjects. This is only part of the material needed. What is necessary is a thorough knowledge of the different industrial relations' systems, seen within a wider societal framework, i.e. a knowledge of what is going on and why this is so. The real comparative work starts when one writes on 'one subject comparing and contrasting the law and practice' in all countries covered. This I would call

the *integrated approach*: not country reports in succession, but a concentration on issues across national boundaries. It is obvious that this constitutes an ideal which can only be fully be obtained in rather exceptional circumstances, namely within the framework of collective scholarship.

E. Group Collaboration

38. The best way to reap the full benefits of the comparative method as a tool for research is obviously the group approach used e.g. by the European Communities as mentioned earlier; namely to start with national reports, written by national experts, prepared on the basis of a common outline; then on the basis of those reports a comparative report is written. Both the national reports as well as the general report are discussed by the members of the expert group. In doing so one develops a framework guaranteeing the best use of national expertise and insight, ensuring that the reports are clear and understood by the different members of the group and that the general report is a true reflection of similarities, differences, trends and explains the nature of and reasons for particular developments.

39. This method is used at least in part by a number of international societies, such as the International Society for Labour Law and Social Security. The collective method was also used by the Comparative Labour Law Group, now no longer in existence, which involved six professors from Britain, France, Italy, Sweden, the USA and FR Germany respectively. In his personal appraisal of their work Aaron writes: 'The strongest single conviction produced by my participation in the work of the Comparative Labour Law Group is that our various methods of conducting our research represent a unique and lasting contribution to comparative research. I knew at the start that no one person could learn within a reasonable time, if ever, as such about the system in any other country as was already known by a competent scholar from the country. Hence, we began with the national reports. But preparing a series of national reports is really not comparative research; it may sometimes be essential, but it is never sufficient. Accordingly, we moved to the next step: each member writing on one subject but comparing and contrasting the law and practice in all six countries. This was the real thing . . . .'[23]

F. Educational Visits

40. Of course, this does not imply that individual scholars cannot effectively engage in comparative work, but this obviously should not, except for purely

---

23. 'The Comparative Labour Law Group: A Personal Appraisal', *Comparative Labour Law*, 1977, p. 235.

technical issues, be limited to a 'desk study'. It is especially necessary in the case of individual research involving foreign countries to make frequent visits to the countries in question and to inquire with the aid of extensive interviews with local scholars and practitioners (lawyers, employers, trade unionists) about the realities of the situation. An example of successful research is the study which *Herbert Sherman* undertook concerning 'Seniority and the Harmonisation Goal of the EEC'.[24]

IV. THE TRAPS

A. *Language and Terminology*

41. One of the main difficulties, which presents a real pitfall for the comparative scholar, is the fact that the identical words in different languages may have different meanings, while the corresponding terms may embrace wholly different realities.

42. Examples are easy to find. Let's limit ourselves to an *English–French* interchange and start with the word 'eventually', in French 'éventuellement'. Although both words are identical they convey a different, almost opposite meaning: 'eventually' means 'ultimately', while the French 'éventuellement' means 'possibly'. I must to my shame confess that I have used the English 'eventually' for more than ten years with the French meaning in mind.

Another example constitutes the word 'arbitration' – in French 'arbitrage'. To my great surprise I learned when participating in an EEC Working Group on 'The Prevention and Settlement of Industrial Disputes' as general rapporter,[25] that the word 'arbitration' (arbitrage) which usually means a binding decision by an impartial umpire, signifies in Luxemburg a recommendation by a government conciliator to the conflicting parties.

When discussing the competence of works councils in different European countries with *Goldman*, and more specifically the 'economic' and 'social' competence of the councils we found that the words 'economic' and 'social' carry different meanings in the American and European contexts: in the USA, wages and benefits are looked upon from the financial side and are consequently classified under the heading 'economic' competence, while in Europe wages and benefits relate to the social conditions of the employee and are by that logic filed under the heading 'social competence'. Another example concerns the American 'public company' and the French 'Enterprise Publique'. The latter is a state-owned enterprise while the American Public Company is a private company, the shares of which are however public . . . The list is endless.

24. *Comparative Labour Law*, 1981, p. 26–56.
25. See: 'Settlement of industrial disputes in the EEC Countries', *Bulletin of the Industrial Law Society*, 1979, pp. 10–24.

43. The traps set by language are minor compared to those which arise in connection with terminology. Schregle rightly points out that 'comparative industrial relations faces a tremendous problem of terminology . . . as concepts, expressed in words, are laden with values, emotions, past experiences and future expectations'[26] which make comparativism almost a mission impossible. He recalls that Hanami, in his book on *Labor Relations in Japan Today* (1979) pointed out that 'applying Western terminology to Japanese phenomena . . . has led to confusion'.

B. Parochialism and Ideological Hangovers

44. A major danger for comparativism lies undoubtedly in the possibility that the researcher may be overly-influenced by the system in his/her own country. He may attempt to analyze another country's system by continuously identifying, assimilating and evaluating practices there with local familiar experiences. 'Comparative industrial relations must liberate us from emotions and prejudices inherent in our own national systems and from the idea that our own system should be a model for others.'[27]

45. A second threat is constituted by ideological hangovers, which can hamper exchanges of ideas, and consequently comparative work. One example may suffice to illustrate this point. The debate on workers' participation has been extremely confused since those involved in the debate depart from different ideologies and expectations.

Some see workers' participation or industrial democracy as a fundamental political goal and want, by introducing more democratic schemes, fundamentally to change the socio-econoic system of society, striving e.g. at self-government by workers, on the Yugoslav model. Others refuse to discuss the possibility of having employees on supervisory boards of companies, since this conflicts with their theories of class struggle as it promotes the 'integration of the working class in neo-capitalist society'. Still others view workers' participation in terms of efficiency and point out that certain participatory devices are necessary to engage the enthusiastic participation of employees in furthering the goals of the company. A number of others see workers' participation in terms of the humanisation of the workplace and think inter alia in terms of job-enrichment schemes (advocated by some to keep unions out) and semi-autonomous work groups. Still others think of 'participation' in terms of profit-sharing, which was General De Gaulle's approach to the 'participation' problem. Thus ideological perceptions provide a serious obstacle to fruitful comparative analysis.

46. It is only when one tackles the problem of workers' participation independent from ideology by simply stating that whatever system or model of

26. Schregle, *op. cit.*, p. 26.
27. *Ibid.*

workers' participation is considered, its entails greater power for labour to influence managerial decision-making, that comparativism becomes possible.

Obviously, ideology cannot be ignored – on the contrary – for ideology will inter alia, help us to find us out why things evolve in a certain way. It is also crucial since at the end of the day each individual will have to decide what sort of participative society is desirable. But again, ideology *should not* hinder us from taking reality as it stands or from engaging in open discussion.

V. THE TRANSPLANTABILITY ISSUE

47. In his unforgettable 'Uses and Misuses of Comparative Law'[28] *Kahn-Freund* formulated and analysed the transplantability issue in a few pages which everyone engaged in comparative work must read. Kahn-Freund in his unique, penetrating and all-embracing way, said it all in a way no one can match. Kahn-Freund makes the following point: 'we cannot take for granted that rules or institutions are transplantable . . . ; any attempt to use a pattern of law outside the environment of its origin continues to entail the wish of rejection'.[29] Indeed, 'labour law is a part of a system, and the consequences of change in one aspect of the system depends upon the relationship between all elements of the system. Since those relationships may not be similar between the two societies, the effects of similar legislation may differ significantly as between the two differing settings'.[30]

This does not however mean that we cannot adopt solutions which have proved successful in other countries, nor that there is no case for introducing rules which will not be rejected, but integrated. There are indeed 'degrees of transferability'.[31]

48. The degree of (non) transplantability depends largely on the relationship to the distribution of power in society. In considering this one must constantly bear in mind that labour relations are in essence power relations; that in any labour relations system the main question is who has the power to take decisions. It is obvious that the answer to that question has to do with the political system of the country involved: whether one lives in a pluralist system, where different groups share power or in a country where considerable power is concentrated in the hands of one group – e.g. the political party. It is obvious that the role of trade unions, of collective bargaining (the autonomy of labour-management), of the right to strike, let alone the influence of labour on management decision-making, fun-

---

28. *The Modern Law Review*, 1974, pp. 1–27.
29. *Op. cit.*, p. 27.
30. Meyers, *op. cit.*, p. 243.
31. Kahn-Freund, *op. cit.*, p. 6.

damentally differ according to the type of political system. This is clearly demonstrated by the recent Polish experience and the development of the free trade union 'Solidarity'. It is also obvious that independent trade unions, sharing power, do not fit into the socialist model of the Eastern European countries. The political arrangements in a given country are a determining factor affecting the transfer of rules which might have an impact on the power relations in that country.

49. This is so even in countries which share more or less the same social, economic, political structures as do, for example, the Member Countries of the EEC. The balance of power – however evolving – in a given country between all organized groups, not only business, trade unions, farmers, the self-employed, political parties, but also cultural groups, consumer organizations, religious groups, universities and the like – is indeed so delicate that any change effecting that package will be most cautiously considered and runs a high chance of being rejected.

50. This is why the proposed directive providing for more workers' participation in the ten EEC Member Countries, the so-called proposed Vth directive, although already put forward in 1972 is still not on the books: it affects the power relationship in the enterprises. This is why a real battle has taken place, both in the European capitals and in the European headquarters of Brussels and Strasbourg (the European Parliament), concerning the proposed (1980) directive on information and consultation of employees in transnational enterprises and in enterprises with a complex structure: multinational enterprises fear that trade unions may find in that directive a platform for international collective bargaining and thus affect the overall managerial flexibility multinational headquarters enjoy at international level. The conclusion is clear: rules relating to the power relations in the industrial relations systems and also in society as a whole will be the most difficult to transplant. Even if transplanted under dramatic circumstances, as with the transfer of the American collective bargaining (plant – enterprise bargaining) model to Japan after World War II, the foreign model will be completely absorbed and transformed into a new and unique system as the Japanese experience so abundantly illustrates.

51. This point becomes crystal clear if one analyses the success of the ratification of the ILO Conventions and the impact of its Recommendations, which, as Kahn–Freund puts it, constitute a 'gigantic enterprise of transplantation'. The fact is that the bulk of ILO instruments do not relate to elements of power in the industrial relations systems but to protect standards, such as industrial safety and hygiene, holidays, forced labour, discrimination in employment, employment policies, general conditions of work (hours of work, weekly rest, paid leave) women's work, children, older workers . . . migrant labour and the like. The conventions relating to trade union freedom and collective bargaining, although extremely important, constitute exceptions. They are, moreover, drafted in very cautious and flexible terms: the obligation to promote collective bargaining to be implemented by 'measures appropriate to national conditions' and only 'where necessary'.[32]

52. To put it otherwise, collective labour law (trade union freedom, workers' participation, including collective bargaining, the right to strike and the rules concerning lock-out, as well as the procedures concerning settlement of industrial disputes – conciliation and arbitration) is resistant to transplantation, while individual labour law (categories of contracts, rules on leave, hours, sickness, discrimination, job security and the like) lends itself much more easily to transplantation.[33]

VI. The Status of the 'Academic Art'

53. Academic curricula are usually not in the forefront of legal developments. Rather they develop with caution, moderation and a certain element of conservatism. This may be one of the reasons, why comparativism in general and comparative labour law specifically are not yet prominent in the list of obligatory or even optional courses for law students in a number of countries; why a comparative touch is mostly also lacking, when national labour law is taught. In certain countries, we might recall, (national) labour law is not even part of the obligatory curriculum.

In a number of countries there are, however, *encouraging signs* and a growing interest can be noticed.

In *Italy*, for example, nine universities provide *courses* in *comparative labour* law focussing on trade-unions, collective bargaining, industrial relations systems, and the like.

In *Belgium* every law school is obliged to have a number of *optional* comparative courses in its programme, among which are included comparative labour law, and each student has to choose one comparative course.

In other countries comparative teaching seems less widespread. In *Switzerland* the University of Geneva has had a comparative labour law course since 1963; in FR *Germany* there are some optional courses, inter alia at Göttingen. In the *Netherlands* there is a regular course in *Tilburg*, . . . There are plans to start a comparative course on labour law in the *Nordic* Countries.

54. Also in the area of *research* encouraging signs can be reported. Besides studies by the international organsiations, like the ILO, the OECD and the EEC, as reported by F. Gamillscheg, there are a number of informal groups which engage in interesting comparative work, such as the International

---

32. *Ibid.*, p. 22.
33. *Ibid.*, p. 21.

Society for Labour Law and Social Security, or the International Industrial Relations Association, where in fact the main comparative task is performed by the general rapporteurs.

It is also interesting that many *Ph.D.'s in labour law* have a comparative aspect and that in *Switzerland*, to give an example, each Ph.D. must testify to comparative work.

VII. The Comparatione Ferande: Guidelines

55. Where does all this lead us into?

There is no doubt that comparativism is an excellent tool for education and research, for the understanding and better solving of problems. On the other hand we see even from our sketchy 'state of the art' that the role of comparativism can be improved upon in teaching, research and also problem solving. Here our International Society could contribute by setting some guidelines for the promotion of comparativism in labour law, which I submit for your consideration.

A. Teaching

(1) Each labour law course should provide on certain topical issues some comparative insights, in order to open the students' minds toward comparative thinking.
(2) Each law school should provide an 'optional course' or 'seminar' of comparative labour law.
(3) Each law library should have a minimum of comparative labour law materials.

B. Research

(1) *Doctoral theses* should, whenever possible and appropriate, make use of the comparative method.
(2) The International Societies should favour the creation of *informal working groups*, which should be able to present the result of their comparative work at the regional and worldwide congresses

Conclusions

56. There is no doubt that the need for comparativism is growing, as our world becomes more and more our village, as people and ideas cross boundaries as easily as they do due to the ever-expanding communications, and information technology, as international cooperation develops and multinational investment and free movement of labour increases, for all entail enormous cross-fertilization.

57. Comparativism is, however, a very demanding discipline. The comparative student not only needs to know about labour law and industrial practice, he also needs an insight into the history, the culture, the political system, and the prevailing values of a society in order to be able to grasp the essentials of any industrial relations system. There are the necessary skills of knowledge of languages, as well as an awareness of the traps and the pitfalls.

58. This may raise for many the question of whether comparativism is not reserved for a happy few, the international civil servants, the jet-setting professors, constantly travelling and exposed to foreign experience, with ample time and money. The answer to that question is a resounding and categoric no! Otherwise it would be like saying that tennis is reserved for professionals, for the Borgs, McEnroes and the Connors; not taking into account that even those with much less physical, psychological and time facilities do enjoy and benefit from a (good) game of tennis. This does not alter the fact that comparativism requires long practice and experience, perhaps more so than in other branches of law and industrial relations. Moreover comparativism remains even for the professionals an ideal which can only partly be realised. For all of us comparativism is finally an exercise in modesty as we are constantly and overwhelmingly confronted with the richness and diversity of so many different cultures.

SELECT BIBLIOGRAPHY

B. Aaron, 'The Comparative Labour Law Group: A Personal Appraisal', *Comparative Labour Law*, 1977, pp. 228–237.
IELL (International Lâbour Law), 1979, 268 p.
J. Pipkorn, 'Comparative Labour Law in the Harmonisation of Social Standards in the European Community', *Comparative Labour Law*, 1977, pp. 260–272.
J. Schregle, 'Comparative Industrial Relations: Pitfalls and Potential', *International Labour Review*, 1981, pp. 15–30.
N. Valticos, 'Comparative Law and the International Labour Organisation', *Comparative Labour Law*, 1977, pp. 273–288.
F. Meyers, 'The Study of Foreign Labour and Industrial Relations' in S. Barkin et al. (eds.), *International Labour*, New York, 1967.

Chapter 2. Documentation*

F. Gamillscheg

I. Documentation

1. Of all areas of law, labour law can claim to have the richest reserves of foreign legal materials at its disposal. These will now be set forth, though it is not our intention to draw up a fully comprehensive list.

A. ILO Publications

2. Most important of all are the materials which we owe the *International Labour Office*. Since its inception it has given us an edition of collected laws, a large number of monographs, and much information in other forms on all areas of working life. These various publications have appeared since 1945 in the three official languages English, French and Spanish, sometimes also in German and Russian; German held the place of Spanish between 1920 and 1936. The publication of labour law statutes and regulations had in fact already been started by the Office's predecessor, the (private) International Labour Institute in Basle.

The *Legislative Series* provides us, in three annual instalments, with translations in English, French and Spanish of the most important labour laws from throughout the world. The reader thus gains access to laws passed in countries that would otherwise be out of reach due to the language barrier. It is possible that the choice of laws published is occasionally determined by translation difficulties. A *Chronological Index* (1984) reviews the contents of these volumes by subject matter (and within each subject matter, country by country) from 1919 to 1983. Since 1983 the laws are automatically processed.

3. The most important journal of the International Labour Office is the bimonthly *International Labour Review*, also in three languages. It is well known that the International Labour Organisation is not only concerned with labour and social law, but also with society in the broadest sense; the journal accordingly deals with a broad range of specialised topics, with a wealth of information on the facts of working life. One notes that the Third World is given wide coverage. It also contains a selection of reports on court

* O. Clark (OECD), A. Pankert (1LO) and G. Zingone (EC) helped us in updating this chapter for which our sincere thanks (ed. note).

25

decisions and book reviews; as always in such cases, the editors' choice sometimes may be open to question. The authors are mostly officials of the International Labour Office.

A quarterly journal, the *Social and Labour Bulletin*, contains short reports on world developments, which are taken from a large number of different sources, including newspapers. The bulletin *Women at Work* is exclusively devoted to questions concerning the economic and social contribution of women to society.

A *Bulletin of Labour Statistics* containing the relevant figures appears quarterly, and a *Yearbook of Labour Statistics* is published annually.

The preparatory work for the Annual General Meetings of the ILO also yields a wide range of materials. These are mainly represented by the law and practice reports prepared for the initial discussion of an item and the subsequent reports which contain government responses to official questionnaires together with research undertaken by members of the ILO and others. The wealth of this material can hardly be exaggerated; the various countries concerned naturally make careful checks to see that their legal systems are correctly reported, thus providing as a rule a guarantee of accuracy of information. One should also mention the voluminous *Reports on the Application of Conventions and Recommendations* which are published annually for discussion by the Conference Committee on the Application of Conventions and Recommendations. They contain very detailed information on national legislation and practice, including the most recent changes and developments. The *Official Bulletin* of the ILO gives in *Series A* information on the activities of the ILO, texts adopted by the International Labour Conference and other official documents; *Series B* contains reports of the Committee on Freedom of Association of the Governing Body of the ILO and related material. – The *Judgments of the Administrative Tribunal* of the ILO are published every year in two or three issues.

In addition, the ILO also publishes a large number of books on all kinds of subject matters related to labour questions. Let us cite just one title as an illustration: the essay on 'Collective Bargaining in Industrialised Market Economies' (1987), in which the International Labour Office with the assistance of Prof. Windmuller of New York made a general comparison of the basic structures of collective labour law in the major western industrial countries. Whereas industrial safety regulations were the prime topic in the early days, collective labour law is now increasingly becoming the main focus of interest. This is also shown by the appearance of the special '*Labour-Management Relations Series*', of which 64 issues have appeared to date.

Currently one programme of the ILO is devoted to *multi-national enterprises*; some 45 working papers have been published containing most valuable information.

The ILO also arranges *regional conferences* (in Africa, Asia, America and Europe) which deal with the particular problems of these areas, and it publishes their reports.

4. The library of the International Labour Office must contain more books than any other labour law library in the world, although the present writer has never counted them. The acquisitions of the library are reported in the monthly *International Labour Documentation*, which notes books, selected articles from journals, congress reports etc. It does not merely contain a catalogue of titles, but also headings indicating their content; in this way the reader can place any publication in its appropriate category, even if it is written in a foreign language.

With 159 conventions and 169 recommendations the ILO has made a great contribution to labour law that is in itself an object of comparative study. The conventions and recommendations have been collected in a handy book: *International Conventions and Recommendations 1919–1981.*

5. The *International Institute for Labour Studies* (Geneva) is closely connected with the International Labour Office. Founded in 1960, this research institute is relatively unknown. Between 1966 and 1975 it published a *Bulletin* in twelve parts that were to give a broad view of society by means of short essays and reports. In 1976 it instituted a quarterly *Labour and Society* in place of the *Bulletin*. Monographs on selected topics come out as part of a *Research Series*, about 78 of which have been published to date. A *Bibliography Series* contains among others a sequence of five selected bibliographies on workers' participation in management, covering the years from 1950 to 1983. A *Directory of Institutes for Labour Studies* lists some 300 institutes worldwide, includes entries in English, French or Spanish, provides information on aims, administrative structure, staff size, programmes and activities, publications, facilities. One third of the entries are updated each year and new entries added regularly.

B. Other International Sources

6. The European Communities are also active in the publication and promotion of the comparative treatment of labour law; their scope is of course not so wide, and is not intended to be so. Most noteworthy of these is a series entitled '*Sammlung des Arbeitsrechts*' (Collection of Labour Law), edited by the European Community for Coal and Steel. The series contains research on the following topics: sources of labour law, stability of the work relationship (i.e. protection against dismissal), workers' rights of co-determination in plants and companies, strikes and lock-outs. Each volume consists of reports from individual countries and a general summary. A wider ranging volume on contracts of employment, and one on professional associations, came out in 1966, followed in 1968 by another on the jurisdiction of labour tribunals. This series also contains details of the reports and proceedings of a Study Congress on Co-determination held in Luxemburg. The languages are German, French, Italian and Dutch.

The EC is also responsible for the publication of a collection entitled

27

Studies, *Social Policy Series*, comprising to date a total of about 40 issues. Some cover a good deal of ground (e.g. No. 26 on educational leave), others less (e.g. No. 35 on professional training in the Netherlands). Amongst the most recent ones, one should mention:

- The protection of young workers in the Member States of the European Communities – 1977;
- Problems and prospects of collective bargaining in the EEC Member States – 1979;
- Model of an European Individual Employment contract;
- The prevention and settlement of industrial conflict in the Community Member States – 1981;
- The law of collective agreements in the Countries of the European Community – 1982;
- Protection of workers in Member countries of the Community in the event of rationalisation within Undertakings – 1983;
- Labour Markets in the Member States of Community – 1985;
- Labour law and industrial relations in small- and medium-sized enterprises – 1986.

Mention should also be made of the *Annual Social Report*. New studies are now being published under EC auspices on: collective bargaining, problems and perspectives (1979), prevention and settlement of industrial disputes (1982).

Finally, the EC began recently to publish a new information bulletin on the impact of new technology on labour relations (*Changement social + technologie en Europe*, 1981) as well as a bulletin 'Social Europe' (1983).

Most of the publications of the institutions of the EC – monographs, series, bibliographies, periodicals, information papers etc., too many to be listed up here – are recorded in an annual polyglot catalogue; supplements are published in the monthly 'Bulletin of the European Communities' and other monthly information papers. One tries to make use of the new technologies. – *Information offices* of the EC exist not only in the member states but also in other countries. *Depositary libraries*, one or more in each member state, and *European Documentation Centres* in 13 European countries collect all EC publications.

For further activities of the EC see chapter 7.

Another useful source are the two yearly reports of the *Committee of Independent Experts*, which supervise the application of the European Social Charter, promulgated by the *Council of Europe* in 1965 and up to now ratified by thirteen of the twenty-one Member States of the Council.

7. The Organisation for Economic Co-operation and Development (OECD), and its predecessor organisation the Organisation for European Economic Co-operation (OEEC) have produced a considerable number of comparative studies of industrial relations, in English and French, particularly on economic aspects. Publications include Socially Responsible Wage Policies and Inflation (1975); The Development of Industrial Relations

Systems; Some Implications of Japanese Experience (1977); Policies for Life at Work (1977); Labour Disputes (1979); Job Security and Industrial Relations (1979); and Collective Bargaining and Government Policies (and its companion volume, Collective Bargaining and Government Policies in Ten OECD Countries (1980)); Employment in the Public Sector (1982); M.R. Cooper, The Search for Consensus, 1982; R.B. McKersie and W. Sengenberger, Job Losses in Major Industries, 1983; B. Grais, Lay-offs and Short-time Working, 1983; Lay-offs and Short-time Working in Selected OECD Countries (1983); The Employment and Unemployment of Women in OECD countries (1984); R.A. Hart, Shorter Working Time: a Dilemma for Collective Bargaining, 1984; Employment Growth and Structural Change, 1985. The OECD has also done work in connection with its Guidelines on Multinational Enterprises, notably A. Morgan and R. Blanpain, 'The Industrial Relations and Employment Impact of Multinational Enterprises' (1977) and The OECD Guidelines for Multinational Enterprises (1986). See also Blanpain, The OECD Guidelines for Multinational Enterprises and Labour Relations 1976–1979 (1979), – 1979–1982 (1983) – 1982–1984 (1985).

C. Private Collections

8. Szladits C. of the Parker School of Foreign and Comparative Law (Columbia University, USA) publishes a *Bibliography on Foreign and Comparative Law. Books and Articles – Compiled and annotated* (Oceana Publications). This bibliography covers now the years since 1790 and comprises all books and articles in the English language with non-common law, legal systems and with general subjects bearing upon the comparative study of law.

The *Hungarian Academy of Science* has published a series in English and French containing important material on labour law in socialist countries. I would like to cite Garancsy's book on termination of employment[1] and Troscanyi's on the jurisdiction of the labour courts.[2]

9. Private institutes also publish similar collections of articles. A good example is the now dissolved *International Institute for Temporary Work* in Brussels which has produced a work on this subject. The first volume is devoted to labour law, containing twelve reports from different countries, one article on the international law of temporary work, and five summaries.[3] There are also regular cahiers in this series.

1. G. Garancsy, *Labour Law Relation and Its Termination in Hungarian Law*, Budapest, 1973.
2. Trocsanyi, *Le droit de procédure en matière de conflits du travail dans les Pays Socialistes Européens*, Budapest, 1974. In this connection also Weltner, *Fundamental Traits of Socialist Labour Law with Special Regard to Hungarian Legislation*, Budapest, 1970; L. Nagy, *The Socialist Collective Agreement*, Budapest, 1984.
3. W. Albeda, R. Blanpain and G. Veldkamp, 'Temporary Work in Modern Society', Part I: *Temporary Work and the Law*, Deventer, 1978, 544 pp.; Part II: *Temporary Work within a Socio-Economic Framework*, Deventer, 1978, 332 pp.; Part III: *Proceedings of the International Conference*, Geneva, 2–3 May 1978, Deventer, 1979, 285 pp.

Kahn-Freund once said that a week is a long time in labour law. Many publications, such as the collection edited by the European Coal and Steel Community are out of date almost as soon as they come out. This is due partly to the rapidity of new developments and partly to the tardiness of their authors. A lawyer seeking up-to-date information will therefore most likely use a text-book or notes published in the country itself, provided that he knows its language.

A loose-leaf system is one solution. It is not popular with librarians, and persons of conservative temperament, such as the present writer, also prefer to work with properly bound books.[4] But it is a solution nevertheless. Two important private collections already employ this format: In *Jura Europae*, we have to date two volumes offering a comprehensive treatment of the labour law of Germany, Belgium, France, Italy, Luxembourg, the Netherlands and Denmark, in both German and French.[5] The interested reader will be particularly grateful for the information on the smaller countries.

10. A second and considerably more ambitious collection has been brought out by Roger Blanpain, editor of the *International Encyclopaedia for Labour Law and Industrial Relations*. The complete work will comprise some fifteen volumes, covering the present state of labour law and 'Industrial Relations' in 60 countries. The reports on the various countries concerned are in English and set in a common framework that makes it easier for the reader to find his way, yet still enables each author to do justice to the particular characteristics of his own nation. We should also mention that the *Bulletin of Comparative Labour Relations* (sixteen issues to date), which Blanpain edits under the auspices of the Institute for Labour Law at Leuven University, is also devoted to comparative labour law. Each issue normally focuses on one general topic, e.g. women and labour law in 1978, job security in 1981, new technologies in 1983, equality and prohibition of discrimination, 1985. No. 6 (1975) contains an international bibliography of publications in English and French on labour law and labour relations in those countries where English and French are not the official languages (66 countries are covered).

11. The *International Encyclopaedia of Comparative Law*, edited under the auspices of the International Association of Legal Sciences by Ulrich Drobnig and his staff of the Hamburg Max-Planck-Institut für ausländisches und internationales Privatrecht, also has as its objective the comparison of the laws of the whole world. One volume will be devoted to labour law. It is clear that it cannot (and will not) compete in any respect with details of information available to the reader in the fifteen volumes of Blanpain's collection. But that is not the Encyclopaedia's intention. Its aim is to draw general conclusions, to identify basic common features and differences, and to put a scientific legal framework at the disposal of all future legislations.

4. When one thinks of the technological advances that promise to bring books that will do no more than flicker on a television screen, then even loose-leaves begin to take on a certain charm.

5. *Droit du travail – Arbeitsrecht*, vols. I and II, Munich and Paris, 1971, 16th Supplement 1981.

12. A programme of useful information for American investors in Europe is offered in the published record of a colloquium entitled '*The Supranational Corporation and Western Labor*', and organised by *A. Kamin*, Professor of Labour Law at Loyola University, Chicago, in 1968, in the course of which American practising lawyers and European academics discussed all kinds of questions both general and particular. Supranational and European labour law as well as the conflict of laws in the field of the employment contract and the collective labour law are the subject of two handbooks which appeared in France: *Gerard and Antoine Lyon-Caen, Droit social international et européen*, fifth ed. 1981, and *Ribas, J.J., M.-J. Jonczy and J.-Cl. Séché, Traité de droit social européen* (1978). Mention should also be made of *International Labour Law*, (1979, suppl. 1984) by N. Valticos. The following publications too deserve full attention: A. Blum's *International Handbook of Industrial Relations. Contemporary Developments and Research*, 1981, covering some 27 countries; *Introduction aux institutions du droit du travail en Amérique Latine*, 1980, by H. Barbagelata, as well as H.C. Jain's, *Worker Participation. Success and Problems*, 1980. Detailed information on many aspects of industrial relations is contained in a series of books by Hildegard Waschke: *Gewerkschaften in Westeuropa. Nationale Besonderheiten, Organisationen und Zielsetzungen im Ausland*, Köln 1975; *Zentrale wirtschaftspolitische Beratungsgremien im Ausland. Eine Skizze der Wirtschaftsräte in: Frankreich, Italien, den Niederlanden, Belgien, Luxemburg, Dänemark, Großbritannien, Kanada und USA*, Köln 1977; *Supranationale Gewerkschaftspolitik. Ziele und Wege der internationalen Gewerkschaftsbewegung*, Köln 1978; *Gewerkschaften in der Europäischen Gemeinschaft*, Köln 1978; *Amerikas Arbeitsbeziehungen sind anders. Eine Skizze des Tarifvertragswesens der USA*, Köln 1980; *Gewerkschaften und Arbeitsbeziehungen in Skandinavien. Ein Überblick über die Systeme in Schweden, Dänemark und Norwegen*, Köln 1980; *Mitbestimmungssysteme im Ausland. Ein Überblick über die Mitwirkung ausländischer Gewerkschaften in Betrieb, Unternehmen, Gesamtwirtschaft*, Köln 1982; *Japans Arbeitsbeziehungen zwischen Tradition und Moderne*, Köln 1982; *Großbritanniens Arbeitsbeziehungen im Wandel*, Köln 1983.

D. Reports and Reviews

13. The division between countries that have codes and those that have Common Law has long been inappropriate to labour law. German law today is widely based on judge-made law, not only in areas where the legislator has expressly stated that the law should be determined by court decisions – as for example in the law concerning freedom of association and industrial disputes –, but also in areas where norms have already been laid down. Great Britain has in recent years moved in the opposite direction with an increasing number of statutes restricting the scope of Common Law. In the United States, too, the great majority of decisions has recently been based on statute law, even where this, as in the case of the National Labor Relations Act, consists basically of not more than a few general provisions.

So comparative labour law involves the comparison of court decisions. This field, however, has been scarcely cultivated. An 'International Collection of Labour Law Decisions' published by the ILO was not continued after 1945.

However, one should mention the *Summary of Judicial Decisions* published twice yearly by the International Labour Review. Each article comprises a summary of some 25 important court decisions on various labour problems in all parts of the world. In addition, one should note the international collection of court decisions: I refer to the *International Labour Law Reports*[6] recently taken in hand by the president of the National Labour Court in Israel, Zvi H. Bar-Niv, in company with a number of well-known legal experts. The first volume appeared in 1978 and reported 66 decisions from 10 different legal systems (the European Community, France, Germany, Great Britain, Israel, Italy, Japan, the Netherlands, Sweden and the United States) together with details of the relevant legislation and with brief commentaries. It is clear that the authors have had to limit themselves, for reasons of space, to broad statements of principle and brief notes, and that a basic problem has been that of selection.

A new publication, coordinated by R. Blanpain, called *International Labour Law. Case Law* will contain the 'judgments' in the area of Labour Law, which emanate from international bodies such as the *European Court of Justice*, the *European Commission* and the *European Court of Human Rights*, set up in the framework of the Council of Europe and the International Court of Justice. It will also include the cases which have been dealt with by the *OECD* under the follow-up procedures of the Guidelines for Multinational Enterprises, as well as the recommendations of the *Committee on Freedom of Association*, set up by the Governing Body of the *ILO*, which has dealt now with over 1300 cases affecting a wide range of aspects of freedom of association.[7]

14. This brings us directly to the leading question: a *'Journal of Comparative Labour Law'*? Here we have a blank spot on a map that is otherwise so well populated. Apart from the International Labour Review, which is, as previously stated, primarily an organ of the International Labour Office, we have no really representative journal. Attempts have been made: *Renato Balzarini*, Professor of Labour Law at Trieste University, started a *Rivista di Diritto Internazionale e Comparato del Lavoro* in 1953 which failed to flourish; however, it was revived in 1961 – in a 'New Series' –, but has unfortunately led only a shadowy existence until now.

Comparative Labor Law is another delicate plant, a slender journal of about 280 pages per volume published by the American Section of the International Society for Labor Law. It first appeared in 1976. In 1985 a new comparative journal was launched under the title: The International Journal of Comparative Labour Law and Industrial Relations with A. Neal as editor. Since then three issues have appeared.

6. Kluwer, Deventer, The Netherlands.
7. *International Labour Law Reports*, Vol. I: 1978, 383 pp.; vol. 2: 1979, 356 pp.

15. In the main, however, foreign and international labour law depend on the general labour law journals. It is of course not true to say that they have no place whatsoever they can call their own: European topics are in creasingly dealt with in British journals, for example. The German journal *'Recht der Arbeit'* devoted its entire September 1978 issue to the IX International Congress on Labour and Social Law, and printed its three General Reports in English, German and French. Italian journals also often print articles from abroad. One may also include specifically the *Modern Law Review*, the *Industrial Law Journal*, and the *Giornale di Diritto del Lavoro e delle Relazioni Industriali*. The USA Department of Labor's Bureau of Labor Statistics publishes valuable labour profiles.

Useful and up-to-date information can also be found in different private monthly publications, like the *European Industrial Relations Review*, *Industrial Relations Europe* and *Intersocial*.

16. De comparatione ferenda all this is of course still insufficient. We are living in a time of international co-operation, and lawyers should stop wasting their energies doing a little here and a little there, without any sensible consultation or co-operation. What is needed is an *institute of international calibre* with a solid financial basis provided by a foundation, and with a director of energy and dedication: an institute which would become the centre for the exchange of news and experiences.

Its most important task would be the publication of a *journal* that would be truly international in terms of both content and source. This journal would have the primary function of providing accurate information concerning events in major countries in the form of national reports on all relevant developments, including statutes, court decisions and bibliographies. Secondly, the journal would provide reports and arguments on selected topics – employment contract, agreements in restraint of trade, redundancy provisions, transfer of ownership of plant, industrial disputes and the like. The editors would need to have a long-term programme covering both aspects; the contents of a journal should not have to depend on the possibility of receiving a manuscript worth printing. It would be up to the editors to seek the collaboration of foreign specialists as correspondents – not just big names to decorate the front page and increase prestige, but real experts who would take this work seriously. The editors for their part would need to have a firm enough hand to be able to ask them to send a report on something important when the correspondent fails to do so. They would also have to overcome the aversion that many editors feel towards the possible printing of specialist articles from other journals (of course with the agreement of the publishers) in translation. Important material that cannot be published immediately and in full should appear in the form of short reports, and the editors, who have the original in their possession should offer a service providing full details to any subscriber requiring them. If such a journal were to gain the reputation of a trusty helper in the labyrinth of social legislation, it will also gain a loyal readership and, in the end, financial success. The interest and the need are already there; all that is missing is an organising hand.

II. INTERNATIONAL SOCIETIES AND MEETINGS

17. Comparative law could not, of course, exist without personal meetings at congresses, colloquia and so on. Labour law is no exception to this rule.

The *International Academy for Comparative Law* at the eleven congresses it has held to date has given some space to labour law topics (The Hague 1937: 'Methods in the Drawing Up of Conditions of Work'; Teheran 1974: 'Co-Determination'; 'Foreign Workers'[8]; Budapest 1978: 'Mass Dismissals'; 'Protection of Minors at Work'; 'The Payment of Salaries: Additional Expenses'; Caracas 1982: Conflict of Laws in Labour Relations; Administration and Judicial Control of Labour Unions and Social Security of Artists and Authors).

But such general congresses do not constitute a sound base. Compartmentalisation into a large variety of different areas stretching from tax law to public international law effectively prevents any wider exchange of views. Nor does any attempt seem to be made to seek general, overriding principles out of the multiplicity of disciplines on display.

A representative association of labour and social lawyers (professors, judges, industrial and union lawyers, legal officials, practising lawyers etc.) is constituted by the *International Society for Labour Law and Social Security* (Geneva). It was established at the congress in Brussels in 1958 as a result of the amalgamation of the 'International Association for Social Law' which had held its first congress in Sao Paulo in 1954, and the 'International Congress for Labour Law', which had met in Trieste in 1951 and in Geneva in 1957. The Society is made up of national representative committees and private members. Following the Foundation Congress in Brussels, further congresses were held in Lyon (1963), Stockholm (1966), Warsaw (1970), Brindisi (1974), Munich (1978), Washington (1982) and Caracas (1985); the next one will take place in Madrid (1988). They provided regular opportunities for labour lawyers to meet and discuss pertinent issues in an informal atmosphere. Lawyers from Eastern Europe have always taken an active part in these meetings, despite the differences in economic systems: many contacts were made in this way, and misunderstandings removed. The 1974 congress was preceded, at Sweden's suggestion and with its help, by a colloquium in Geneva on labour law topics in the developing countries, attended by about 30 Third World experts, who then came on to the Brindisi congress. This experiment was repeated in 1978, with the financial support of the Federal Republic of Germany. 32 labour lawyers from the developing countries were again invited to the congress, which had been hitherto characterised by a certain European/American bias, and broadened its horizons.

18. These congresses have for some time now followed a fixed pattern: an advance committee decides on three main themes, one of which always

---

8. Cf. *Rapports Généraux au IXe Congrès international de Droit comparé*, Téhéran, 27 Septembre–4 Octobre 1974, Bruxelles, 1977, 880 pp.

concentrates on the laws of social insurance. The participating countries are invited to submit national reports (97 were received in 1985); these are then processed by a General Reporter and put before the assembled congress in summary form. The various speakers of the different countries are regularly asked before the discussion to refrain from simply setting forth their own country's point of view, but to make points of general interest; as at other congresses, this request is seldom obeyed. But dramatic contrasts from other countries can often cast an interesting light on one's own legal system.

In this way the congresses of the last twenty years have seen the discussion of many important topics; in Munich, for example, papers were given on 'The Settlement of Labour Law Disputes in the Courts or by Arbitration', 'Sickness in Labour Law and in the Law of Social Security', and 'The Codification of Labour Law'.[9] The Washington Conference dealt with the following important subjects: Worker Participation in Management Decisions, Employment Termination and Position of Women in Labour and Social Security.[10] The Caracas Congress had on its agenda collective bargaining at the enterprise level, atypical employment relationships and employment injuries.

Lately the International Society has been organising very successful Regional Conferences in Asia[11] and Europe. The First European Congress met in Szeged (Hungary) in 1984. One of the topics which were discussed as the methodology of comparativism in labour law. The Second European Congress was held in Jesolo (Italy) in 1986.[12] The Third Asian Congress was held in January 1985 in Bangkok; the fourth in Singapore, 1987.

19. National reports such as the above-mentioned ones do of course vary in quality. Together with brief reports of a type that one would normally expect to find in works of the popular science type, we find articles that are of most excellent quality. Let us take an example from the Munich congress: few subjects are so obscure to continental lawyers as the present system of jurisdiction in English labour law, where competence is distributed between the ordinary courts, the industrial tribunals and various official bodies with names that are difficult to decipher like ACAS and CAC. The article by Paul Davies on this subject deserves by virtue of its clarity and conciseness to find a prominent place even in the law literature of its country of origin.

---

9. Cf. G. Müller and F. Gamillscheg, ed., *Reports and Proceedings*, International Society for Labour Law and Social Security, 9th International Congress, Munich, 12–15 September 1978.
10. B. Aaron and D.F. Farwell, eds., *Reports and Proceedings, International Society for Labor Law and Social Security*, 10th International Congress, Washington, D.C., 7–10 September 1982, 3 vols., Washington, D.C., 1984.
11. F.R.P. Romero, ed., *First Asian Congress of Labor Law and Social Security*, Under the Auspices of the International Society for Labor Law and Social Security, Manila, 12–16 December 1980, Quezon City 1982; Chi Sun Kim, ed., *Second Asian Congress of Labor Law and Social Security*, Seoul, 14–16 September 1983, Seoul, 1984.
12. The materials of the First and Second European Congresses of Labour Law and Social Security, will be published soon.

20. The leading international association in the area of industrial relations is the *International Industrial Relations Association* (IIRA), the Secretariat of which is also in Geneva. The IIRA, founded in 1964, has already held six international congresses (Geneva, London, Paris, Kyoto, Hamburg). The next one will take place in Brussels in 1989. IIRA meetings have discussed a broad array of labour relations issues from worker participation to industrial relations and political systems. Papers and communications submitted to IIRA meetings are available at the Secretariat of the Association in Geneva. The IIRA organises also regional congresses. The next ones take place in Israel (1987) and Canada (1988).

21. An organisation such as the *Institute for International Law* does not exist for comparative labour law. The International Society has an Executive Committee of about 50 members, but this performs exclusively administrative functions. It has not yet been suggested that it should be built up into a body of academic status, and this would probably fail for lack of funds. Yet, at its meeting in September 1981, the committee, following the proposal of its General Secretary Dr. Johannes Schregle, – after ample discussion of a variety of administrative issues – devoted the last of the three days of the meeting to a discussion of the methodology of comparative law: a happy precedent for the future.

22. The lesser offerings in the field, for example papers given at colloquia, are too numerous and hardly interesting enough to be put on record. But two examples are outstanding enough to deserve mention: the Luxembourg meeting of the EEC on the question of co-determination[13] and a colloquium organised by the Max-Planck-Institute for Foreign Public Law and International Law, held in Heidelberg in 1978 on the question of industrial relations, to which 20 national reports and five reports on international norms and institutes were submitted.[14]

23. A further example of informal scholarly co-operation is provided by the *Comparative Law Group*. Benjamin Aaron reported on its work: Following a suggestion of Kahn-Freund, he secured the services of a number of scholars (Giugni, Italy; Ramm, FR Germany; Wedderburn, England; Blanc-Jouvan, France; and Folke Schmidt, Sweden) for a joint contribution on the 'Settlement of Disputes in Labour Law'. After about two years – years which were not without their financial problems – the first results were published: Aaron (ed.), Labor Courts and Grievance Settlement in Western Europe (1971), including reports on France, Italy, FR Germany and

---

13. *Die Arbeitgeber-Arbeitnehmer-Beziehungen im Betrieb und Unternehmen – Formen und Funktionen*, Studientagung vom 4. – 6. Oktober 1965 in Luxemburg: Sitzungsberichte und Dokumente, Luxemburg, 1967.
14. *The Freedom of the Worker to Organise. Comparative Law and International Law*, 2 vols., Berlin 1980.

Sweden and a general introduction written by the editor. The length and scope of the English contribution led to its publication as a book in its own right. The theme of the second joint project, commenced in 1969, was industrial conflict. This time the authors abandoned the country-by-country report form, dividing the material instead into subject categories in such a way that each one of them had to write a genuinely comparative study.[15] The authors dealt with their next topic, discrimination, in the same way; the report appeared in 1978.[16] This was the final work produced by the group. *Aaron's* personal appraisal is a unique example of the sociology of comparative law. With pleasing frankness, he makes no secret of the difficulties and disappointments that are necessarily involved in requiring colleagues 'to give priority to our projects over all others in which they are constantly engaged'. But it becomes also obvious to the reader that it is an intolerable state of affairs when a scholar of Ben Aaron's calibre is forced to squander time and energy on questions of finance and organisational details.[17]

24. We come at last, at the end of this long list, to the private research scholar of comparative law. To give details of this kind of work would turn the present Report into an unsuitably long bibliography.

25. Our final *conclusion* is by no means discouraging: The foundations for a reasonable version of comparative law – an all-embracing, global discipline would be too much to expect all at once – have to a large extent already been laid. To use these foundations well, to build on them, means to be able to open a window outwards and away from the solipsistic contemplation of one's own law and legal doctrines. This applies above all to students. International disciplines are rare in the option lists of university law departments, and are thus beyond most students' imagination; but it should be possible to find a select few and convince them of the great opportunities for professional success and personal satisfaction that exist in the study and practice of foreign and international law.

15. B. Aaron and K.W. Wedderburn, eds., *Industrial Conflict: A Comparative Legal Survey*, London 1972.
16. F. Schmidt, ed., *Discrimination in Employment*, Stockholm 1978.
17. B. Aaron, The Comparative Labour Law Group: a Personal Appraisal, *Comparative Labour Law*, 1972, p. 228.

Chapter 3. Industrial Relations in a Changing Economic Environment: The Postwar Experience of Advanced Market Economies

O. Clarke

O. Clarke

I. THE POSTWAR DEVELOPMENT OF INDUSTRIAL RELATIONS SYSTEMS

1. The main influences shaping the structure and operation of industrial relations systems may be identified as economic, social, and technological. The nature and strength of these influences varies according to circumstances – as does which of them is in the ascendant at a particular time. This chapter will pay regard to all three influences but will give particular attention to the economic, which has confronted many industrial relations systems with their most serious challenge in the postwar era.

2. The countries taken into account here are all but the smallest of the 24 OECD market-economy countries except, for the earlier years, Greece, Portugal, Spain and Turkey, these omissions having regard to the special political developments which these countries have experienced. This said, in the countries covered, apart from Italy, the bases of present industrial relations systems were in place by around 1952, as postwar reconstruction drew to its conclusion.

3. The industrial relations systems of 1952 differed widely from one another. The United States maintained its pre-war predominantly enterprise bargaining and market-oriented unionism. Japan developed an entirely new system under mainly American influence but building nevertheless on the important Japanese concepts of 'lifetime' employment and the seniority wage system and based largely on enterprise unionism; (the practice of the coordinated 'Spring Labour Offensive' was to come later). The continental European systems tended to make a distinction between negotiation and consultation, with negotiation being conducted on a national or regional industry-wide basis, and consultation and worker representation being the province of works councils, with unions virtually excluded from the enterprise. European unions, though divided on political or confessional grounds

39

in Belgium, France, Italy and the Netherlands, had largely developed close links with political, mainly social democratic, parties, though the largest union centres in France and Italy were associated with communist parties. Exceptionally, the Federal Republic of Germany had instituted worker representation not only through works councils but also on supervisory boards in many companies, and, in the case of the coal, iron and steel industries, on management boards. In the United Kingdom, while national industry-wide collective bargaining remained the norm, workplace bargaining was slowly developing – particularly in some major industries – as national agreements, often keyed to what the less efficient firms could afford, failed to satisfy workers whose shopfloor bargaining power had greatly increased in strength. (The growth in influence of shop stewards was a corollary of this.) British unions continued their traditional close relationship with the political Labour Party. Australia retained its centralised, judicial-type, arbitration machinery in preference to collective bargaining (though some bargaining nevertheless took place), but more emphasis was coming to be placed on conciliation by the Commonwealth and State Conciliation and Arbitration Commissions. On the employers' side, central and industry-wide employers' associations continued, or were newly established, in almost all of the countries, though playing a less significant role in North America than elsewhere. There were to be few major structural changes in the following 20 years in these industrial relations systems, although, as is made clear in section IV, the product and operation of the systems changed considerably. The most significant structural differences were in the levels of collective bargaining, and its coverage and content, and in the strengthening of workers' participation in managerial decisions.

II. The Economic Environment Since the Second World War

4. The development of the economic environment since the second world war falls clearly into three parts: 1948–1973, 1974 to 1979, and the nineteen-eighties. The first of these periods was characterised by economic growth of unprecedented levels, duration and near continuity, widely accompanied by more or less full employment. Though growth rates varied between countries it was possible to maintain the regime of fixed exchange rates instituted at Bretton Woods near the end of the war, until the end of the 1960s, and the economies of the major countries moved roughly in line over most of the period.

5. At the end of 1973 the massive increase of oil prices hit a world economic system which was not only unprepared for such a move but which already contained an ominous constellation of circumstances which of themselves

would have been likely to have a serious effect on most economies. Taken together,[1] these factors heralded the onset of major difficulties.

6. Inflation had been a present or lurking problem in most countries throughout.the period of growth[2] but most particularly (apart from the time of the Korean war) from 1970 on.[3] With the economic events of 1973–4 it came to grow towards high and obdurate levels. What was additionally serious was that this inflation was frequently accompanied by slow or even no growth and by rising unemployment – the phenomenon of 'stagflation'.

7. In the new economic environment it seemed fairly clear to governments generally that their first concern must be to roll back inflation, even though some of the restrictive measures commonly deemed necessary for this purpose were unfortunately likely both to discourage growth and to increase unemployment. But there was, at the time, a widespread belief that such measures were likely to be of relatively short duration: there had been an economic check but when it had been surmounted the customary growth pattern would be resumed.

8. In the cold economic climate prevailing after 1973 a wide measure of agreement emerged between the governments of the advanced industrial countries as to the economic policies which should be pursued. When inflation had been beaten, or at least had fallen back to the levels prevalent in the sixties, the way would be clear to concentrate on growth, and with that, to reduce unemployment. To give priority to growth and thereby make an earlier immediate attack on unemployment would, it was thought, be likely to exacerbate inflation. High unemployment now was, at least, preferable to higher unemployment in the future.

9. But it was not long before it became apparent that if a future return to pre-1974 growth levels was still possible it would not be quick or easy to accomplish. Meanwhile, though most countries, in most years, were achieving some growth, even if usually much less than in the sixties, unemployment was rising, and industrial profitability and investment were commonly at low levels. The international prescription for public policy was viewed as to dampen inflation, necessitating continuing tight monetary and fiscal policies; to discourage rising wage levels, and to stimulate business initiative by encouraging profitability and investment.

10. Towards the end of the seventies, understanding grew that the economic check of 1974 was much more than a brief halt but rather marked the end of

1. P. McCracken, *et al.*, *Towards Full Employment and Price Stability*, OECD, Paris, 1977, for a review of causation, resultant problems and prospective remedies.
2. W. Fellner, *et al.*, *The Problem of Rising Prices*, OEEC, Paris, 1961.
3. *Inflation, the Present Problem*, OECD, Paris, 1970.

one economic phase and the beginning of a more difficult one, in which most countries would have to struggle to achieve even small economic growth, by postwar standards. Governments saw the need to think more and more about medium and long-term as well as short-term correctives. They started to examine the rigidities which had crept into their countries' economies over the years, asking, for example, whether their existing industrial structures were optimal for future needs and whether undesirable obstacles to efficient mobility and utilisation of labour had grown up in their labour markets. The implications for employment of the vastly increased payroll-based charges which employers had come to be called upon to pay, and of the more stringent and detailed provisions introduced to improve workers' safety and to ensure healthy working conditions, also came under review.

11. In addition the economic pinch was being felt in public expenditure generally. Through the long years of growth public spending had been rising steadily in nearly all countries, usually more rapidly than the portion of national income going to private expenditure. In particular social expenditure, with the extension of provision for education and the establishment and growth of the Welfare State, had risen steeply. The cost of providing for the growing proportion of elderly people and the large numbers of unemployed in most countries was becoming increasingly difficult to meet, not to mention the rocketing costs of many health services.

12. Patterns of world trade too were changing and the old advanced industrial countries were faced with growing competition from newly industrialising countries – who were sometimes offering financially very attractive 'free trade zones' – with relatively low costs, and with a tendency by multinational enterprises to put down new plants or extend production in developing countries rather than in their home countries.

13. The second massive rise in oil prices, around the end of 1979, exacerbated the problems of the non-oil producing countries. But this time, though their economic performances were more widely dispersed, so far as collective bargaining was concerned most countries were markedly more successful than they had been in 1974 in preventing, largely by using non-accommodating monetary policies, what was in effect an external tax on them from passing through into inflationary wage increases. By then, however, the industrialised countries were entering the most serious recession since the 1930s and the high level of unemployment, low order books and poor profitability had a depressive effect on wage increases and on inflation. If the changes did not lead to any fundamental change in the structure of industrial relations systems they certainly led to changes in how the systems were operating. Though by 1983 countries were generally emerging from the recession a "return to the sixties" came to seem increasingly unlikely.

14. As things stood at the beginning of 1987, the industrialised countries were achieving some (though mainly modest) economic growth, and inflation had declined almost everywhere. In September 1986 the twelve-month rate of increase of consumer prices stood at 2.5% for the OECD as a whole – the lowest inflation since 1964. The black spot now was unemployment, still standing at near record post-war levels in many OECD countries, with an OECD-wide average of $8\frac{1}{4}\%$. Particularly noticeable were the differences between the U.S. and Japan, on the one hand, and the European countries on the other, the U.S. and Japan having lower unemployment and inflation than the corresponding averages for OECD European countries. This again focused attention on rigidities in Europe, including rigidities in the labour market. If wages were as flexible and workers as mobile as in the U.S., it was argued, much could be done to increase economic growth and to reduce unemployment in Europe [3b].

15. Virtually from the beginning of the post-1973 era, the trade unions found themselves the major force, internationally, in expressing disagreement, even alarm, at the policies on which governments were embarking. They did not disagree that inflation was a dangerous enemy which must be defeated but they were generally of the view that priority should be given to growth, and with it to employment. In this campaign, public expenditure (increasingly a source of concern to governments) was a force for good, not only satisfying social needs but also providing employment.

16. There was of course, international coordination of trade union views on economic policy long before 1974 but such concertation as was possible was frequently expressed in somewhat vague and simplistic terms. As tough national economic policies took effect, as scarce finance and declining trade hit enterprises and strengthened the opposition of employers to wage claims, and as unemployment grew, it became increasingly important to unions to argue against what they saw as policies for stagnation. International trade union coordination was therefore strengthened. Efforts continued through the International Confederation of Free Trade Unions (ICFTU); the World Confederation of Labour (WCL), and the International Trade Secretariats (ITS); but increasingly the lead was taken by an able and influential group of union economists working through the Trade Union Advisory Committee to the OECD (TUAC); and, for Europe, the European Trade Union Confederation (ETUC), and the European Trade Union Institute (ETUI).[4] The alternative international economic policies thus developed were given wide exposure, including being urged on world leaders by presentations on

---

3b. For the argument about labour market flexibility see *Report of Group of Experts* (the Dahrendorf Report), *on Labour Market Flexibility*, OECD, Paris 1986, and for a technical analysis, *Flexibility in the Labour Market, The Current Debate*, OECD, Paris, 1986.

4. Among the first publications of the Institute, in 1979, were *The Economic Situation in West Europe in 1979* and: *Keynes Plus: Towards a Participative Economy*.

the eve of 'summit' meetings – of the European Community; of the seven major market economies (the meetings initiated by President Giscard d'Estaing of France at Rambouillet in 1974), and the annual Ministerial Council of the OECD.

17. This trade union urging had little apparent impact on most governments, who felt that, even if in some ways the outcome of their economic strategies was disappointing, economies were mainly moving in the right direction, though restrictive policies were still necessary.

III. INDUSTRIAL RELATIONS AND GOVERNMENT ECONOMIC POLICIES

18. Industrial relations are a social sub-system and hardly an end in themselves. It is clearly desirable that they should work smoothly but there is no simple way of measuring their success or the impact of their malfunctioning on a country's economic and social advance. It can broadly be said that at most times in most countries – though by no means all – since the war industrial relations systems have satisfied the goal of meeting the needs of employers and workers and of translating economic growth and rising social expectation into workplace life in a tolerably satisfactory way. Whether industrial relations systems have served to facilitate desirable organisational and technological change as much as they might is more doubtful but at least most systems have not served to block such change. Lastly, on the test of whether industrial relations systems have produced wages and working conditions and practices which are consistent with the needs of national economic policies, the verdict must vary from 'poor' to 'rather good'.

19. In the nineteenth century, industrial relations were widely regarded as almost entirely the province of employers and workers. The role of the State was generally seen as providing a basic (often minimal) legal framework; setting a few minimum standard conditions of employment and safety regulations; and, in some countries, providing peacemaking facilities. Wartime apart, the wages and other elements of labour cost that might come about in industry rarely troubled the minds of governments, beyond the need to cope with occasional particularly disruptive national disputes. While the role of the State tended to widen out over the first half of the twentieth century it was not until after the second World War that a number of governments came to find in peacetime that collective bargaining was tending to produce settlements which, by lacking justification in higher productivity or profitability, or improved terms of trade, seemed to threaten the plans of economic policy-makers for price stability, economic growth, full employment and a satisfactory balance of payments.

20. It is, of course, natural and wholly justifiable for workers to seek to increase their wages and to improve other conditions of employment. That some at least of their demands should be met may be socially desirable and economically sound. But, however desirable, if demands produce increases in labour costs which cannot be met through increased productivity or out of profits the results are likely to lead to higher prices. If goods can be sold at the new prices the customer will suffer or will try to pass on his increased cost. If they cannot, contraction of employment will follow. What happened increasingly, in a good number of countries in the years of growth and tight labour markets, was that employers tended to find it possible and preferable to make even economically disadvantageous concessions in collective bargaining rather than to face up to a strike or other industrial action, thereby often adding to inflation. This is not to say that increased labour costs were the sole cause or even the main cause of inflation – there were many causes – but they frequently added to it and collective bargaining proved a ready instrument for turning price increases into wage increases.

21. In countries where increases in labour costs seemed likely to have harmful economic effects the response of governments varied according to the circumstances. In some cases the situation was judged so serious as to necessitate 'freezing' wages (and commonly prices), though it was found that freezing wages was often only effective over relatively short periods and freezing prices rather ineffective anyway. Sometimes statutory limitation of wage increases, often with permitted or approved (e.g. increases for low-paid workers) exceptions were applied. In both of these cases undesirable after effects and side effects were commonly encountered. In other cases less legalistic incomes policies, indicating the desirable limits to increases, were promulgated, frequently in agreement with trade unions and employers. Of course governments also used restrictive monetary and fiscal policies to dampen the expectations of collective bargainers and to support incomes policies.

22. Sometimes institutional machinery, commonly but by no means always involving unions and employers, was introduced to monitor the operation of incomes policies. Several countries introduced machinery to ensure that their economic problems were widely understood and, in some cases, could be discussed on a regular basis with trade unions and employers, occasionally by bringing in other groups as well.[5]

23. Though incomes policies enjoyed some success during the period of postwar reconstruction later policies had rather less effect.[6] Much depended upon union views on the importance of the need, and on their degree of sympathy with the government in power, but even with positive support

5. M. Cooper, *The Search for Consensus*, OECD, Paris, 1982.
6. See P. Schelde Andersen and P. Turner, *Incomes Policy in Theory and Practice*, (Occasional Study, published with the OECD *Economic Outlook*, Paris, July 1980). For a thorough evaluation of incomes policy, see A. Romanis Braun, *Wage Determination and Incomes Policy in Open Economies*, International Monetary Fund, Washington, D.C., 1986.

from trade union centres incomes policies frequently had no more than a short term moderating effect, which might be followed by a surge of wage increases when the policy was relaxed. With the onset of higher inflation in the 1970s, government interest in restraint in collective bargaining became more widespread and more inconsistent.

24. To avoid the disadvantages of formal wage controls the practice developed in several countries of governments seeking consensus with unions, or unions and employers, on the desirable development of wages, commonly in the context of a range of related economic and social policies. Though it was often difficult to achieve consensus, the outcome was modestly successful in a number of cases.[7] A notable recent example of consensus incorporating wage moderation was the Accord instituted by the Hawke government in Australia in 1983 which, with certain modifications along the line and some controlled relaxation in the autumn of 1986, was still operative at the beginning of 1987.

25. In the last few years particularly collective bargaining in several countries seems to have lost something of its propensity to cause anxiety amongst economic policy makers. Indeed in some countries real wages have fallen slightly in particular years. Undoubtedly this tendency has reflected weakened trade union bargaining power in a time of recession and high unemployment. But the underlying problem of avoiding conflict between the results of collective bargaining and the needs of economic policies has not been solved and will again become widely apparent should countries achieve their objectives of a return to sustained growth and full employment.

26. Two questions spring from the experience of different countries in respect of collective bargaining in the recent cold economic climate. Why, in some countries, has the outcome of collective bargaining responded more quickly to new economic conditions than in others and, most importantly, what is the explanation of the great differences between countries as to the extent of mismatch between collective bargaining and economic policies?

27. The speed of response depends partly on the degree of centralisation of collective bargaining. There is a great variety of bargaining levels, and combinations of bargaining levels, in different countries. There are clearly advantages in national-central or national-industrial bargaining. The negotiators are well placed to understand, and pay regard to, national economic needs (very important in ensuring that unions and employers are viable

---

7. *Socially Responsible Wage Policies and Inflation*, 1975, *Wage Policies and Collective Bargaining Developments in Finland, Ireland and Norway*, 1979; *Collective Bargaining and Government Policies*, 1979, and *Collective Bargaining and Government Policies in Ten Countries*, 1979; (all OECD, Paris.)

interlocutors to government) and relate them to social objectives, and to ensure desirable distribution of what improvements can be afforded. On the other hand bargaining at this level is often slow and cumbersome and insensitive to the widely differing circumstances of individual enterprises. It can lead to gaps between leadership and rank-and-file members and conditions may be such that leaders cannot guarantee the compliance of members.

28. If enterprise bargaining is the predominant level there are clear advantages in respect of relating negotiations to productivity, profitability, and the conditions of local labour markets. Union negotiators are necessarily close to their members. But enterprise bargaining makes it difficult to ensure that regard is paid to overall national needs (though arrangements can be made to articulate bargaining levels, as has been done in Sweden) and workers who have a powerful bargaining position, perhaps because of their ability to disorganise complex, integrated production schedules, or highly capitally intensive operations, or to put perishable commodities at risk, are likely to gain advantage at the expense of the weak to an extent that offends public opinion (though it should be added that the strong may be doing no more than to pursue their interests in accordance with sound economic principles).

29. Speed of response is not, of course, only a function of bargaining level. The size of the country and whether it is federal or unitary in structure are also significant in this respect. And, directly or less directly, collective bargaining demands are a function of workers' assessment of what it is possible to achieve at the particular time, which reflects not only the circumstances of their employer but also their perception of the economic and social policies pursued in their countries.

30. The key question, however, is why the problem of mismatch has been so much greater in some countries than in others. Throughout nearly all the postwar period Austria, the Federal Republic of Germany, Japan and Switzerland stand out as countries in which collective bargaining has operated freely without producing results such as to call for intervention by government. By international standards these countries all have excellent records of price stability and have enjoyed more or less steady growth – indeed Japan has long been a world leader in terms of economic growth. All of these countries except FR Germany also enjoy relatively low levels of unemployment and all, generally speaking, of strikes (which in Austria and Switzerland have been insignificant for many years).

31. To draw a contrast from the experience of two other major countries, the corresponding profile for Italy is one of continuing and anxious negotiations between government and unions about wage development and a relatively poor record of price stability, unemployment and strikes, though the growth record is generally good. The United Kingdom has just about the poorest growth record of the major industrialised countries; a history of government intervention in collective bargaining over the postwar period (at least until early 1979); and, in recent years, one of the highest rates of unemployment among the OECD countries.

32. True, these differences may be regarded as no more significant than the differences between countries at any other stage of development. All history is a record of the rise and fall, success and failure of nations. But in the sense that all of the major countries reviewed here are advanced industrialised countries with mature industrial structures confronted with external economic forces which, though they and their effects differ according to the circumstances of individual countries, include substantial common elements, one can well ask why their industrial relations systems – admittedly differing widely but virtually all built on a preference for free collective bargaining – have thrown up such different bargaining results.

33. To go more deeply into this aspect would be to go beyond the scope of this paper but it is arguable that the key lies not in the institutions of industrial relations but in the operation of those institutions, this in turn reflecting the input, or amalgam of attitudes, desires, needs and resolution which workers, unions and employers bring to the system. In this context it is interesting and may be significant, that the successful countries mentioned have in common that in each the mass of workers appear broadly satisfied with the economic and social goals of government, and the way it is proposed to achieve them, while opinions are strongly divided in both Italy and the United Kingdom.

IV. Impact of Economic Change on the Institutions and Practices of Industrial Relations

34. The history of the institutions of industrial relations, like that of other human institutions, is one of constant adaptation to changing external forces and the changing needs of the participants: responsiveness to change is one indicator of the success of an industrial relations system. Naturally adaptation is not only one-way: the industrial relations systems itself, and its operation, produces change in other systems with which it interacts. This section outlines, in a general fashion, the ways in which the institutions and practices of industrial relations have changed under the economic, social, and technological, pressures of the postwar era. It does not attempt a survey of industrial relations: merely of their adaptation.

35. In the postwar years, unprecedented economic growth has been reflected by equally unprecedented gains in the material benefits enjoyed by workers – improved real wages, shorter weekly working hours, longer vacations, more holidays, and substantially more extensive gains in fringe benefits. Higher material rewards for work done have been accompanied by fairly general greater job security and by (in a good number of European countries in particular) greater participation by workers in decision-making. It is probable, at least in some countries, that quite a lot of workers have also, at least until recently, improved their position in relation to the nature and control of their immediate work and work load. Work tasks themselves are difficult to evaluate but the (largely post-war) development of the behavioural sciences has pointed paths to successful new ways of doing work, though for a variety of reasons this knowledge has not been widely utilised.

36. Trade unions in many countries (though not all) have lost members over the last few years – substantially in the U.S. and in Britain – but membership is still commonly considerably higher than it was, say, 25 years ago. Trade union influence in national life generally has followed much the same trend. In countries where union activity used to be mainly at the national- or regional-industry level but has become more decentralised, unions have increasingly sought to initiate or improve services and representation within the enterprise. Unions now face severe challenges. Continuing high unemployment, the shift from old-established heavy industries to services and high-tech industries (usually with smaller-sized enterprises and often located outside traditional industrial areas), and the increased proportion of part-time workers in the labour force, add up to difficult terrain for trade-union activity. Amongst employers, the most substantial changes have occurred in the U.S. American employers have not hesitated, in straitened economic circumstances, to demand concessions from their workers. A few have instituted two-tier wages and working conditions, engaging new workers on less favourable terms than those applied to existing workers. Some employers too have sought to discourage union membership amongst their employees. European employers generally have tended to remain on the defensive, though in Europe too there are numerous cases where individual employers have tightened up labour management to secure higher productivity.

37. Collective bargaining has shown its adaptability – and limitations – in responding to changing needs. In North America it has changed relatively little over the last 30 years. Japanese practice too has not changed very much over, say, the last 20 years. In Australia the traditional tasks of collective bargaining have largely been shouldered by the statutory conciliation and arbitration machinery: the scale and significance of collective bargaining have varied according to circumstances and there has been relatively little since the Accord of 1983.

38. In Europe collective bargaining has shown some appreciable changes over the postwar period. The subjects of bargaining have, in several European countries, widened out to include matters traditionally regarded as within the prerogatives of management. The levels at which bargaining is conducted have tended to change in most European countries, in part towards national-central bargaining but more towards bargaining at the level of the enterprise or plant.

39. The record of industrial conflict has been erratic.[8] Most of the 1950s and early 1960s were a period of peace, compared with earlier times, to the point at which two scholars who examined the international picture could speak of the 'withering away' of the strike.[9] There followed, from 1968 on, a considerable increase in time lost through labour disputes in many countries, including (temporarily) some which had hitherto been remarkably free from such disputes. Even where the increases were most severe, however, the time lost in disputes rarely topped pre-war figures and by the 1980s the figures had fallen considerably in many countries.

40. One of the most notable changes of the postwar period has been in the role of government, very substantially increased in nearly all countries compared with the 1930s. Exceptionally, however, in Portugal and Spain, when the corporate form of state gave way to pluralist democracies, government successfully withdrew from the dominating position it had occupied in industrial relations and encouraged the growth of free trade unions and collective bargaining. Both governments have, of course, found it necessary to play an active part in establishing new industrial relations systems and they have been closely concerned with the outcome of collective bargaining in relation to their economic and social policies.

41. In a few countries – the Federal Republic of Germany, Japan and Switzerland, for example – governments continue to regard industrial relations as the responsibility of employers and trade unions and limit themselves to the minimal role described earlier in this chapter. They want very much to keep it that way. Indeed, throughout the post-war era there have been few cases of governments wishing to intrude further in the relationship: in OECD countries governments have intervened not out of a desire to extend control but because they felt impelled to do so on account of anxiety about the outcome of collective bargaining or because of the malfunctioning of the system. The role of government in industrial relations has also increased, of course, in the sense that directly (as in the case of the civil service) or indirectly (as in nationalised industries) the State has in almost all countries become a considerably larger employer itself – usually the largest employer in a country. The problems of reconciling the role of the State as

8. J.D. Reynaud 'Industrial Relations and Political Systems: Some Reflections on the Crisis in Industrial Relations in Western Europe', and R.O. Clarke, 'Labour–Management Disputes: a Perspective', both in *British Journal of Industrial Relations*, March, 1980 and chapter 18 in the present volume.

9. A.M. Ross and P. Hartmann, *Changing Patterns of Industrial Conflict*, Wiley, New York, 1961.

guardian of national economic interest (another role which has increased substantially since the war) with the role of employer and the role of industrial peacemaker, have sometimes been great. In the 1980s governments in several countries have found it necessary to enforce strict control over the development of pay in the public service, both because of severe constraints in public expenditure and, to some extent, to set an example from bargainers in the private sector. There have also been problems where public and private sector workers compete to achieve the highest wage increase, as strikes in Sweden and Finland in 1986 showed.

42. Lastly, the international dimension of industrial relations has grown. This is most notable in the considerable growth of multinational enterprises and the number of workers which they employ, and it has led to the development, particularly from the mid-1970s, of international guidelines for the conduct of the multinationals. But it can also be seen in the growing sophistication of international policy discussion among the trade unions. Transnational collective bargaining has also been quite extensively discussed, though it has not been practised beyond a handful of isolated cases.

V. ANALYSIS: AND THE POTENTIAL CONTRIBUTION OF INDUSTRIAL RELATIONS SYSTEMS

43. The last section examined some of the changes in industrial relations systems, and their product, since the war. The present section tries to point to some of the reasons for changes and to show some important challenges which some or most of the systems presently face.

44. Most of the changes outlined have flowed from the three main external and interrelated forces mentioned at the outset – economic, social and technological. Rapid economic growth went hand in hand with new technology and also necessitated considerable change in industrial structures, including the size, organisation, and capital-intensivity of many individual enterprises. Change at the enterprise level necessitates adjustment where the most important present level of interaction in industrial relations happens to be national. Such changes commonly meant disturbance for workers, who often reacted by trying to build fences of job security and job control around themselves.

45. Economic growth made possible the great post-war improvements in living standards and in publicly-provided social benefits and protection. People, in their 'working' as in their 'consuming' and their 'social' capacities, looked for improvements at work which reflected the improvements they found outside the workplace. The new generation of workers were better educated than their parents, and often they had been educated to question rather than to take their environment for granted. They now

51

enjoyed the safety net of the welfare state and, in most countries for most of the time since the war until 1974, full employment, at least by pre-war standards. Added together these factors made for a more confident and demanding workforce and fuelled the demand for workers' participation in management.

46. Until 1973 economic development permitted a considerable measure of fulfilment of workers' expectations. At times, as in France in 1968; the Italian 'hot autumn' of 1969; the strike waves in several countries in 1969 and 1970; and in the British mining strike of 1974; one could see a flexing of muscles as workers tested an existing social order, including sometimes the leadership of their own trade unions. Indeed, though this chapter has, for convenience, treated the dividing point in the postwar years as 1973, an alternative structure might have been:
(a) 1948 to 1967, the years of economic growth;
(b) 1968 to 1973, the years of social challenge;[10] though this did not affect all countries, and
(c) 1974, the years of efforts to readjust.
(d) 1980 on, the years of recession, structural adjustment, and changed bargaining power.

47. Had the trends of the fifties and the sixties continued it is likely that the expectations and confidence of workers would have continued to reflect the possibilities opened up by economic growth and social evolution and to have led to quite radical changes, not only in industrial relations' but also in political and economic systems. As it was, the check of 1974 to economic growth, and the changed balance of bargaining power that came with higher unemployment and with employers being unable to afford many concessions, deflected the development of industrial relations systems from the line it had followed for 25 years. And workers commonly became too concerned with maintaining their living standards and keeping their jobs to devote their energies to societal change, though the possibility has to be borne in mind that exceptionally high unemployment, particularly if it were coupled with further economic shocks, could seriously damage the social fabric in some countries.

48. The speed with which the systems reacted to the new circumstances varied considerably from country to country. In the great open market and individualistic societies of the United States and Canada, adjustment of collective bargaining outcomes to harder times was rapid. American workers collectively lost some of their purchasing power in some years and by 1982 some of the best-off American workers were prepared to give up some of

10. S. Barkin (ed.), *Workers' Militancy and its Consequences*, 2nd edition, Praeger, New York, 1975. C. Crouch and A. Pizzorno (eds.), *The Resurgence of Class Conflict in Western Europe since 1968*, Macmillan, London, 1978.

their benefits in order to keep jobs. In Japan, except for a wage round in 1974 which proved inflationary, the habit of consensus quickly related workers' gains to what the economy could afford. In FR Germany too unions took a long-sighted view of their members' interests and contented themselves with modest immediate gains in the interest of price stability and long term improvements. In the United Kingdom and a few other countries, on the other hand, collective bargaining continued for several years to produce gains which had little basis in economic terms and which inevitably added to inflation.

49. By the early 1980s it had become apparent that the changed circumstances which started in 1974 were not a temporary setback but the beginning of a new, less stable and less predictable, economic environment. Industrial relations systems could only influence this environment positively by encouraging greater efficiency and facilitating adaptation to change, both of which factors depended more on the attitudes and understanding of managers and workers than on the institutional structures of industrial relations – though the 'rationalisation agreements' made in some countries from the late 1960s on, and later, various agreements for dealing with the new wave of technological change, were useful innovations.

50. The effect of the economic environment on the working of industrial relations was more predictable. As of the beginning of 1987, unemployment was expected to continue for some time to come at high levels in the great majority of countries, in many of them at the highest continuing levels since the 1930s. A prime, if not the prime, objective of trade union efforts therefore had to be to reduce unemployment. One means to this end was seen by unions as the reduction of working time (shorter working week, longer holidays, earlier retirement, etc.) to which it was considered that employers might be the more receptive because of the commonly low level of business activity. Several campaigns were mounted to secure reduced hours – one of them, in the Federal Republic of Germany in 1984, in the metals and printing industries, led to the biggest dispute of the post-war era in that country. Pressure for reduced hours seems likely to continue but increasingly reductions are being coupled with steps to ensure that plant utilisation times are not decreased on some form of flexible working hours.

51. On wages, be it because the money was simply not obtainable, or because the relationship of wage increases to unemployment became increasingly evident to bargainers, there has been growing moderation in wage bargaining in many countries. For the future, union efforts will naturally continue to be to seek gains wherever circumstances permit (and here it is necessary to remark that although the present economic environment is still harsh by the standards of the golden age of growth most of the countries considered here are achieving *some* growth nearly every year, though usually appreciably less than they used to expect – the growth of real GNP for all OECD countries in 1985 was 3.0 per cent). Otherwise, unions will concentrate on defending members' jobs and present living standards.

52. Finally a word by way of summary. After the war the industrialised market economies entered a period of economic and social advance which continued for a generation. The international economic environment then deteriorated and economic growth, and progress on those aspects of social advance which were dependent on it, slowed considerably. Industrial relations systems adapted to the new situation at different speeds and with varying degrees of success. After some years it became apparent that no early return to steady growth could be expected and that industrial relations systems would need to accommodate to poor possibilities for improving wages and working conditions and to structural adjustment sometimes involving threats to job security and acquired gains in working practices which might be deleterious to efficiency. Much of private industry, faced with poor trading conditions, high interest rates and low investment, was generally quickly affected by the tougher climate but in many countries the public sector too came to find the going hard. The stronger stance of the employer in the public sector was tellingly illustrated by the defeat of the 1981 strike by air traffic controllers in the United States and by the strikes in Belgium and the Netherlands in the autumn of 1983, and by the mining dispute in Britain in 1984–5.

53. At the national level of the problem common to many countries of reconciling the outcome of collective bargaining with economic needs tended to recede slightly, as unemployment grew; as union efforts were diverted towards the protection of jobs and conditions and to job creation; and as, in some countries, union membership fell. As pointed out above, in some countries the problem was never more than small. Where it was and remained substantial, governments either adopted a strict monetary policy or sought to arrive at understandings with unions and employers as to an acceptable outcome of collective bargaining in the context of consensual governmental economic and social policies.

54. Against this background little structural change in industrial relations systems seems likely in the near future. Collective bargaining still enjoys wide confidence as the most democratic and appropriate – or at any rate the least worst – means of regulating wages and working conditions and practices. There is equally fairly common agreement that trade unions are continuing to fulfil necessary and constructive functions. Such change as may be expected will probably reflect a changing power balance between employers and unions, together with related economic imperatives, and is to be seen in the output from industrial relations systems rather than in their structure.

Technological change will present problems – and not least will have their effect on employment – but such problems can be managed by use of the kind of consultative and negotiating machinery now to be found in industrial relations systems in a considerable number of countries, for dealing with the effects of change. Returning to the economic situation, if the emphasis of governmental policies moves from countering inflation to promoting growth and hence employment, it is likely to be necessary, in some countries, to build institutions to reduce conflict between bargaining outcomes and economic needs: such conflict is likely to be potentially substantial where strong divisions exist in a country, particularly between governments and unions, as to economic goals and the means of attaining them.

SELECT BIBLIOGRAPHY

K. Armingeon et al., *Les Syndicats Européens et la Crise*, Presses Universitaires de Grenoble, Grenoble, 1981.
C.L. Barber and J.C.P. McCallum, *Controlling Inflation: Learning from Experiences in Canada, Europe and Japan*, Canadian Institute for Economic Policy, Ottawa, 1982.
A. Romanis Braun, *Wage Determination and Incomes Policy in Open Economies*, International Monetary Fund, Washington, D.C., 1986.
S. Barkin, (Ed), *Worker Militancy and Its Consequences*, (2nd Edn.), Praeger, New York, 1983.
A. Bortho, (Ed), *The European Economy, Growth and Crisis*, Oxford University Press, Oxford, 1982.
R.F. Elliot and J.F. Fallick, *Pay in the Public Sector*, Macmillan, London, 1981.
R.J. Flanagan, D.W. Soskice and L. Ulman, *Unionism, Economic Stabilisation, and Incomes Policies: European Experience*, Brookings Institution, Washington, D.C., 1983.
J.H. Goldthorpe, (Ed), *Order and Conflict in Contemporary Capitalism*, Clarendon Press, Oxford, 1985.
International Labour Organisation, *Collective Bergaining: A Response to the Recession in Industrialised Market Economy Countries*, ILO, Geneva, 1984.
L.N. Lindberg and C.S. Maier, (Eds), *The Politics of Inflation and Economic Stagnation*, Brookings Institution, Washington, D.C., 1985.
Organisation for Economic Co-operation and Development, 1. *Collective Bargaining and Government Policies*, 2. *Collective Bargaining and Economic Policies in Ten OECD Countries*. Both OECD, Paris, 1979.
D. Robinson and K. Mayhew, (Eds), *Pay Policies for the Future*, Oxford University Press, Oxford, 1983.

Chapter 4. Labour Law and Industrial Relations in the Third World

J. Schregle

I. INTRODUCTION

1. Terms and institutions of labour law and industrial relations such as trade unions, employers' organisations, collective bargaining, conciliation, arbitration, workers' participation, employment relationship etc. originated in Western Europe and North America from where they spread all over the world. As pointed out by Blanpain in the first edition of this book[1] the convergence theory, according to which industrialisation would gradually bring labour relations systems closer to one another, is increasingly being contested in the developing countries.

In fact, an increasing number of countries, particularly in Asia and Africa, in which it is very strongly felt that labour law and industrial relations are but one aspect of a national society, seek to have the conditions, traditions, values, needs, objectives and aspirations of their societies better reflected in their labour relations systems.

2. It is the purpose of the present paper to show which particular characteristics must be taken into account when considering labour law and industrial relations phenomena and developments in the Third World.

Needless to say, any generalisation about Third World countries which does not take into consideration the great differences which exist between countries and regions is not only risky but wrong. It is very problematic indeed to compare Singapore with Bangladesh, or Kenya with Chad, or Argentina with Bolivia, to give a few examples of extreme differences within given regions. And if one compares things interregionally doubts are permitted about whether one can usefully compare labour law and industrial relations in Latin America with those in Southern Asia, Africa or the Arab World.[2]

Hence, the present article cannot depict the labour law and industrial relations system of the Third World as such (which is inexistent) nor can it

---

1. R. Blanpain, Comparativism in Labour Law and Industrial Relations, in *Comparative Labour Law and Industrial Relations*, 1982, p. 17.
2. For detailed information on the labour law and industrial relations situation in particular countries see R. Blanpain ed., *International Encyclopaedia for Labour Law and Industrial Relations*. It is impossible in the present paper to give bibliographical references for individual countries.

describe the system of any particular country, region or subregion. The purpose of the paper is rather to give a rapid overview of some of the characteristic features of the systems of a number of more or less representative developing countries and try to bring out some of the major elements and factors which act upon labour law and industrial relations systems in the Third World and which will, in all likelihood, increasingly determine such systems in the future.

II. Main Factors Determining Labour Law and Industrial Relations in Developing Countries

3. Differences between North and South must not make us forget that labour law and industrial relations systems as such have much in common, irrespective of the economic, political, cultural or social characteristics of the country concerned. By definition the basic role and purpose of labour law and industrial relations are the same everywhere: to protect the worker as the weaker party in the employment relationship, and to organise in an orderly fashion the relations between employers and workers and between their organisations, with one another and with the public authorities. In this sense, labour law and industrial relations must be seen within the context of a national society. On the other hand, a labour relations system is the reflection of a given society, its values, traditions and patterns of behaviour. On the other hand, a labour relations system is an instrument or a tool for the shaping of a national society. This is, of course, applicable to all countries, North or South. But the factors which determine a national society differ from country to country and, projected into the North–South comparison, there are certain factors which are typical of developing countries and which distinguish them from the highly industrialised countries. Some such factors are of a general nature while others are more regional in character.

A. *General Factors*

4. There are first those factors which, though not applicable to every developing country, are of a general nature in the sense that they are not typical or specific of particular regions.

1. Development Policies

5. What all developing countries have in common is the existence of a national development plan. Such plans are more or less lengthy documents, prepared by the planning authorities and adopted by the competent political bodies, generally the legislature, in which the country concerned sets out its development objectives and targets which it strives to attain within a given period of time, often a three to five year period. While in the past most development plans had been directed mainly towards growth and rapid industrialisation there has in recent years been a shift of emphasis in development objectives towards a more equitable distribution of wealth and income, more employment and the elimination of poverty.

Of course, the balance between production and distribution is difficult to establish. The fundamental role of labour law and industrial relations in this area is obvious.[3] Small wonder, therefore, that a number of development plans make direct references to labour relations. The Indian Development Plan refers to the need of a comprehensive law on industrial relations, the Plan of Ecuador supports the idea of industry-wide collective bargaining. Societies which believe in the systematic planning of their economic and social future feel that they cannot leave the fixing of wages to the free interplay between trade unions and employers but that the government must exercise some control over trade unions, collective bargaining and strikes. We shall revert to these questions later.

2. Scope and Coverage of Labour Law and Industrial Relations

6. Another characteristic feature of most developing countries is the fact that their labour relations systems are applicable only to a relatively very small portion of the population, i.e. employers and workers in the so-called modern sector of the economy, industry, transport, plantations, banks, hotels etc., a sector which employs only a very small minority of people. Furthermore, larger enterprises where labour law and labour relations can play an effective role are very rare. In India, for instance, labour law applies to no more than 5 per cent of the population. By and large, the huge masses of the population in the rural areas, and in the villages who are not a party to an employment relationship in the labour law concept are left outside of the labour legislation. But also in the big cities (e.g. Mexico City has more than 15 million inhabitants) the large majority of people, engaged in the so-called informal sector, is not covered by the national system of labour and industrial relations.

3. Cultural Influences

7. As stated above several Third World countries are more and more anxious to establish a link between labour law and industrial relations and the characteristic features of their respective national societies by having the latter increasingly reflected in their national labour relations system. The Lagos Plan of Action for the Economic Development of Africa (1980–2000)

---

3. A more detailed discussion is contained in ILO, *The Role of Labour Law in Developing Countries*, Labour–Management Relations Series, No. 49, Geneva, 1975.

adopted by African Heads of State lists among a series of development commitments 'to ensure that our development policies reflect adequately our socio-cultural identity'.[4] The development plans of several African and Asian countries (e.g. Pakistan, Malaysia, Thailand, Kenya, Tanzania) refer explicitly to cultural objectives, the main target being the preservation of national self-reliance and identity. Projected in the field of labour law such basic behavioural elements as the way in which decisions are taken or the way in which disputes are resolved in a given society are examined with a view to developing labour law procedures and institutions more commensurate with national characteristics. This trend is particularly visible in Islamic countries. In a number of Asian countries in particular, Western labour law approaches are seen as being too much based on controversy and opposition of interests and people are more and more 'looking East' (as suggested by the Malaysian Prime Minister) to find more congenial, more 'Asian' labour law formulae in Japan. All these trends and currents are still very vague and imprecise but any student of labour law and industrial relations must be aware of their existence and growing influence.

4. Outside Influences

8. The efforts made by developing countries to mould systems of labour law and industrial relations which are an expression of their respective societies should not make us forget the existence of powerful influences exerted by factors from outside the countries concerned. In a general way, the ongoing contacts between labour law specialists, labour administration officials, employers and trade unionists of different countries maintain a permanent flow of information and international exchange of views and experience which influence the shaping of labour law everywhere. Such outside influences are particularly strong in the Third World.

9. Influences of the labour law system of former colonial powers are particularly strong in the French-speaking African countries whose labour codes are still very much under the impact of French labour law doctrine. In Latin America labour lawyers are very much looking for guidance from Italy, Spain and other European countries. As mentioned above, Japanese influence is increasingly felt in the labour law systems of several South-East Asian countries; examples are Singapore, Malaysia and the Philippines.

10. Another type of influence from abroad is that exercised by multi-national enterprises, particularly as regards the organisation of labour–

---

4. *Lagos Plan of Action for the Economic Development of Africa* – 1980–2000, Organisation of African Unity, published by the International Institute for Labour Studies, Geneva, 1981. See also: Organisation of African Unity, *What Kind of Africa by the Year 2000?* Addis Ababa, 1979.

management relations at the enterprise level and personnel policies. The labour law of socialist countries in the Third World (e.g. Cuba, Ethiopia) is strongly influenced by that of socialist countries in Central and Eastern Europe. Last but by no means least mention must be made of the influence exercised by the policy of the ILO, particularly that embodied in international labour conventions and recommendations and by the conclusions of regional conferences.

B. Regional Factors

11. In addition to these general factors of influence there are those that are specific to certain regions and that operate mainly in the form of mutual influences or a sort of cross-fertilisation between countries of the region concerned. When looking at regional characteristics the great differences between systems of labour law and industrial relations which exist among Third World countries become apparent.

1. Latin America

12. The geographical region with the highest degree of homogeneity (as far as labour law and industrial relations are concerned) is Latin America. A common colonial heritage, a common language (Latin Americans of Spanish and Portuguese language have no difficulty in understanding each other) and, to some extent, comparable economic and social conditions, have helped in bringing about close similarity between the labour law systems of the countries concerned. Historically speaking, the labour codes of Mexico and Chile, both promulgated in 1931, have greatly influenced the labour legislation of the other countries, acting together with the labour law doctrine of Spain, Portugal, Italy, France and FR Germany, to name those European countries with the strongest influence on Latin America. Regular and very close contacts between Latin American labour law specialists, facilitated by the Ibero-American Association of Labour Law and Social Security, ensure close mutual adjustment of labour law developments. Latin America is also the only region of the Third World which considers itself, culturally speaking, as part of the Western European and Christian civilisation – with obvious consequences for labour law and industrial relations.[5]

---

5. For details see Efren Córdova, *Las relaciones colectivas de trabajo en America latina*, ILO, Geneva, 1981; H.H. Barbagelata, *Introduction aux institutions du droit du travail en Amérique latine*, Leuven, 1980.

2. Africa

13. In contrast to Latin America, Africa is a divided continent. The Sahara desert divides the continent into the Arab north and black centre and south. In addition there are the dividing lines established between the colonial territories of mainly France and the United Kingdom, and Belgium, Portugal and Spain. In the French-speaking countries south of the Sahara the former French Labour Code for Overseas Territories of 15 December 1952 continues in force in the form of the national labour codes; the labour legislation of Morocco, Tunisia and Algeria also has been strongly influenced by France. The labour law of the former British territories still follows British labour law thinking although the industrial relations, trade unions and trade disputes acts, as well as the factories acts, of English-speaking African countries have since independence introduced new formulae (e.g. government control of trade unions, compulsory conciliation and arbitration, wage control etc.) which have become an expression of the development objectives of the countries concerned. By and large French-speaking African countries are more similar to each other in the area of labour law than the English-speaking countries. But in labour law the dividing line between French and English-speaking countries is still very determinant in spite of all the efforts of the Organisation of African Unity (OAU) which tries to overcome the linguistic colonial barriers.[6]

3. Asia

14. Asia is also a divided continent. The countries of West-Asia, characterised by their Arab-Islamic background, try to adapt their labour legislation to their (very different) political orientations. Efforts of the Arab Labour Organisation, which also includes the Arab countries of Northern Africa, to harmonise the labour law of the various countries have not been successful. The labour law of the five countries of the South-Asian subcontinent (Pakistan, India, Sri Lanka, Nepal and Bangladesh) has a common base in the labour legislation of former British India but recently each country went its own way. Malaysia and Singapore also have a British colonial background. Indonesia's labour law goes back to Dutch origins, the labour law of the Philippines contains important elements of the United States. Thailand, the only country of the region that had never been under colonial rule, enacted modern labour legislation in recent years. These examples show that in Asia, more than in Latin America and Africa, each country en-

---

6. There is no comprehensive study on industrial relations and labour law in all African countries. For the period before independence of most countries see ILO, *African Labour Survey*, Geneva, 1958, and ILO, *Labour Survey of North Africa*, Geneva, 1980. See also ILO, *Labour Relations in Africa*: *English-speaking Countries*, Labour–Management Relations Series, No. 64, Geneva, 1983. For French-speaking countries see Martin Kirsch, *Le Droit du Travail africain*, *Travail et profession d'outre-mer*, Paris, 1976.

deavours to work out its own labour law. It is also in Asia that people are – more than in other regions – conscious of the need to adjust their labour law to the particular traditions and values of their culture. It is not surprising that, as mentioned above, many Asian countries are looking for guidance and inspiration to Japan, the one Asian country with a tremendous economic success, which is largely ascribed to its system of labour management relations.[7]

III. SPECIFIC ASPECTS OF LABOUR LAW AND INDUSTRIAL RELATIONS IN THE THIRD WORLD

15. It is against the background sketched out on the preceding pages that one must look at the substantive contents of the various labour law and industrial relations systems of Third World countries. Certainly, the differences between the various regions and countries are such that generalisations are possible only within limits. Some of the more typical aspects of labour law and industrial relations which many (though not all) developing countries have more or less in common are briefly referred to on the following pages. Here again, we can only consider certain general features and trends the relevance and importance of which differ widely from country to country. One must never forget that the labour law and industrial relations system of every country, wherever it is situated, is unique. However, certain general considerations are possible. They are presented on the following pages.

A. Role of Employers' and Workers' Organisations

16. The right of employers and workers to form and join organisations for the collective representation and defence of their respective interests is recognised in most developing countries and often explicitly guaranteed in the constitution or legislation. However, it must not be forgotten that historically speaking the liberal concept of 'freedom of association' had originated in Europe from where it was transplanted to the countries situated in the Southern Hemisphere. The role of the ILO in the promotion of freedom of association in developing countries was and is decisive.

The real problem arising from the operation of employers' and workers' organisations in Third World countries arises from the need to strike a balance between the role which these organisations play as representatives of their members' interests (a role which is nowhere contested), and the role which they are expected to play as parties to national development policy.

---

7. For details see: J. Schregle, *Negotiating Development: Labour Relations in Southern Asia,* ILO, Geneva 1982; ILO, *Industrial Relations in Asia,* Labour–Management Relations Series, No. 52, Geneva, 1976.

In this respect the problems affecting employers' organisations and those affecting workers' trade unions are by no means the same.

1. Employers' Organisations

17. In a somewhat simplified fashion one could say that the difficulties facing employers' organisations in developing countries stem less from governments than from the enterprises, their actual or potential members. Apart from a few Third World countries which have opted for a socialist orientation of their economy and which therefore sometimes deny or restrict the right of private employers to organise (to the extent to which a private sector is permitted to exist at all) governments of most Third World countries, which are committed to the principle of private enterprise and a market economy, create no obstacle to the free development of employers' organisations. In fact, governments have an obvious interest in being able to deal with a strong and representative spokesman for employers' interests in national development.

However, in practice particularly the heads of larger firms are sometimes reluctant to accept that an employers' organisation speaks and acts on their behalf. Employers' organisations in many developing countries exercise only an advisory and consultative role *vis-à-vis* their member firms and individual firms are often not willing to abdicate to an employers' organisation the right to bargain collectively with trade unions or public authorities. But there is, at least in a number of countries, a clear trend to strengthen the position of employers' organisations, as regards both their relations with their own members and those with trade unions and governments. In many developing countries the real problem for employers' organisations is the difficulty to convince small enterprises. handicraft shops, etc. of the need and usefulness to join an employers' organisation.

18. Another difficulty which exists for employers' organisations in an important number of developing countries is the question of whether or not publicly owned industrial and commercial enterprises (apart from units of the public administration) should join, or should be admitted to, employers' organisations established by private initiative. In many developing countries the government is in fact the biggest employer, not only in the public service but as owner of public corporations or as sole or majority shareholder of enterprises or companies in industry, mining, banks, airlines, etc. While in some developing countries such public enterprises are admitted to employers' organisations, in others employers' organisations, concerned about their independence from government influence, do not permit such affiliation or restrict it to those publicly-owned enterprises which are operated in accordance with management principles applicable to private business and whose management enjoys a measure of autonomy *vis-à-vis* the government authorities.

19. Another problem concerns the affiliation to national employers' organisations of enterprises belonging to foreign-based firms, the so-called multinational or transnational enterprises. In some of the former colonial territories employers' organisations were initiated by expatriate employers. While foreign-owned firms are by and large welcome to join employers' organisations in developing countries differences in interests may arise and the influence of employers' organisations on national development will be stronger if they can ensure that they represent primarily national interests.

2. Workers' Organisations

20. The difficulties which trade unions in developing countries must face are of a very different kind and comparatively much bigger. Apart from the hostile attitude of certain employers who take anti-union measures (attitudes and practices which are by no means characteristic of, or limited to, developing countries) the main difficulty for trade unions in the Third World arises from their relations with governments.

21. There is, first, the question of the representative character of the trade union movement since, as we have seen, wage earners who are the traditional members of trade unions are often found only in the larger enterprises in the modern sector and represent, if compared with trade unions in the highly industrialised countries, only a small minority of the population. The accusation addressed to trade unions that they represent only the interests of a small 'privileged' minority and ignore those of the large segments of the poor in the rural areas and in the so-called 'informal sector' is vehemently rejected by trade unions which claim that the really privileged classes are outside the wage earning population, that the wage of a worker in the modern sector is often the only income for a large family and that inflation and recession lead to a rapid erosion of the workers' purchasing power. Furthermore, trade unions in a number of developing countries try to extend their activities to the poor in the rural areas and in the informal sector.

22. The second major problem confronting trade unions in the Third World countries is the fact that the traditional form of trade union activity, i.e. collective bargaining with employers and governments for higher wages and better conditions of work, is as we shall see in the next section, often restricted by law in developing countries; and where collective bargaining is possible trade unions often lack the strength, coherence and power to obtain substantial gains at the bargaining table. This leads in many countries to a situation where trade unions do not see their only or primary role in wage-bargaining but in other forms of social services for their members including legal aid, cooperatives, welfare services, etc.

23. Thirdly, in a great number of developing countries the structure of the trade union movement presents a major problem. Countries in which unions speak with one voice or are grouped in one national trade union confederation, which at the same time is independent from the government, are the rare exception. In those countries in which there exists only one national trade union body such organisation is often affiliated to, or otherwise closely related with, the political party in power. This is particularly the case in those countries, in Africa and elsewhere, with a one-party system. But even in such a situation the trade unions have an important function to perform as defenders of workers' interests at various levels of the economy.

24. At the other end of the spectrum are those developing countries in which the trade union movement is divided into several organisations which are often affiliated to different political parties and which therefore compete with each other. Typical examples are India, Bangladesh and Sri Lanka. This situation of 'trade union multiplicity' or 'trade union politicisation' often leads to restrictive measures by governments which see in certain parts of the trade union movement a form of political opposition. Governments tend to reduce influences which politicians exert on trade unions, for example, by prohibiting or limiting political activities of trade unions, restricting trade union leadership by outsiders, prohibiting international affiliation of trade unions, interdicting the affiliation of public servants' associations with general trade unions, etc. In some cases government instituted procedures for trade union recognition, certification or registration are used to control the development of trade unions.

25. In a general way, it would be correct to say that governments would wish to see trade unions integrated into the national development process to which they are expected to make an important contribution by instilling in the workers the need to co-operate. On the other hand, trade unions argue that their role as development partners – which they accept – can be carried out effectively only to the extent to which they are truly independent from governments and employers and can genuinely represent workers' interests. The discussion about the role of trade unions in the Third World centres mainly on this basic issue.

B. Collective Bargaining, Labour Disputes and Workers' Participation

26. It follows from the preceding considerations that institutions and procedures through which employers and employers' organisations as well as trade unions in Third World countries deal with each other, i.e. essentially collective bargaining and labour disputes and their settlement, must be studied within the overall context of development policies.

1. Collective Bargaining

27. Collective bargaining as a process leading to the conclusion of collective agreements on wages, working conditions and labour relations is widely accepted in developing countries. Copied from Western models, collective bargaining is regulated in the labour legislation of practically all Third World countries and collective agreements, some of which take the form of comprehensive and voluminous documents, have been concluded in many countries in Asia,[8] Africa[9] and Latin America.[10] However, such agreements exist mostly in the larger enterprises of the modern sector (public or private). In some countries collective agreements concluded with expatriate firms resemble very much collective agreements in Western Europe or North America. But, as emphasised above, the number of workers covered by such agreements is in most developing countries proportionately very small.

This means that, in order to protect workers who are left outside the collective bargaining process, practically all developing countries have enacted detailed labour legislation, setting out minimum standards for hours of work, annual and public holidays, maternity protection, safety and health, special conditions for women and young workers, protection against the hardships arising from dismissal, etc. Similarly, a large number of Third World countries have enacted legislation on minimum wages, either by fixing statutory minimum wage rates (e.g. in the Philippines) or by creating special wage boards, councils or committees for the fixing of minimum wages (most developing countries).

Such substantive wage rates and working conditions are conceptually and in their protective function not different from similar provisions contained in the labour legislation in the North. The big contrast between North and South lies in the extent to which such statutory provisions are enforced in practice. In many developing countries government authorities entrusted with the application of labour legislation, especially labour inspection services, are insufficiently equipped, with the result that statutory labour protection is often not implemented in practice.

28. While, as pointed out before, the role of collective agreements as instruments for the fixing of wages and working conditions is much more limited in the South than in the North there is one form of collective bargaining which has recently made considerable progress in many parts of the Third World. In an effort to associate employers' and workers' organisations with national development many governments have promoted the

---

8. ILO, *Collective Bargaining and Labour Arbitration in the ASEAN Region*, Bangkok, 1977; ILO *Collective Bargaining and Labour Arbitration in South Asia*, Bangkok, 1979.
9. B.C. Roberts and L. Greyfié de Bellecombe, *Collective Bargaining in African Countries*, International Institute for Labour Studies, Macmillan, London, 1967.
10. ILO, *Some Aspects of Labour–Management Relations in the American Region*, Labour–Management Relations Series, Nos. 11 and 11(a), Geneva, 1961 and 1962.

negotiation of economy wide basic agreements, codes of conduct or industrial relations charters, i.e. documents in which employers' and workers' organisations, and sometimes also governments, have agreed on certain principles which are to determine their relationships. Examples are the Code of Practices for the Promotion of Labour Relations in Thailand (1981), the Industrial Relations Charter of Kenya (1980), the Basic Agreement of Fiji (1981), the Code for Industrial Peace and the Code for Enhanced Productivity of Zambia (1967), the Code of Practices for Industrial Harmony in Malaysia (1975) and the Industrial Relations Charter agreed in 1971 in Sierra Leone.[11] In these and in similar instruments adopted in other developing countries an effort was made to integrate industrial relations in the national development process. The fact that such basic agreements or joint statements are less frequent in Latin America (a notable exception is Mexico) is primarily due to the political polarisation existing in many of these countries.

29. The real problem is the implementation of such economy-wide agreements at the enterprise level. In many of the countries concerned the generally agreed principles are only insufficiently applied at the shopfloor level. Obviously, the gap between agreements reached between national employers' and workers' confederations and the government, on the one hand, and the reality of labour relations in the enterprises, on the other hand, is too large. An intermediary level could be industry-wide or branch or regional agreements but they are rare in most developing countries, except for certain branches (e.g. plantations in Malaysia or Sri Lanka) and for the industry-wide agreements in some French-speaking African countries.

2. Strikes and Lock-outs

30. From the preceding discussion it is not surprising that there is not one developing country whose labour law would recognise the unrestricted right to strike. In fact, the right to strike and limitations of its exercise are at present one of the central and most publicised problems of the industrial relations debate in Third World countries. The main arguments used in government and employer circles are that strikes are incompatible with the pursuit of a national development policy and that, furthermore, work stoppages are disturbances of law and order and a threat to the often precarious stability of national societies. In some countries where the trade union movement is divided according to ideological and political lines, with close affiliations between trade unions and political parties, the fear is often

---

11. The text of some of these agreements has been reproduced in ILO, *Selected Basic Agreements and Joint Declarations on Labour–Management Relations*, Labour–Management Relations Series, No. 63, Geneva, 1983.

expressed that strikes may be used as a political weapon against the government in power.

The trade unions in developing countries do, of course, reject these arguments and allegations, invoking the right to strike as a basic human right and as a necessary corollary to effective collective bargaining.

31. In the law of many developing countries this discussion has resulted in various forms of strike limitations. First, almost all developing countries provide under their industrial relations legislation for some form of compulsory arbitration; this means that labour disputes which cannot be settled by way of conciliation may be referred to an arbitration board or court for final and binding settlement. The modalities of such procedures vary very much from country to country. Second, many developing countries prohibit strikes for certain categories of workers (e.g. public servants or public employees) or empower the government to interdict strikes which threaten the public security (or similar general formulae). In a large number of countries strikes are prohibited in essential services or vital industries. In such cases the main problem is how to define the term 'essential services'. While sometimes the term applies only to public utilities (e.g. electricity and water supply, hospitals, certain transport enterprises, etc.), in others it extends to industry or other important branches of economic activity (e.g. mines, banks, plantations). In the Philippines the term 'vital industries' (in which strikes are not permitted) includes all industries working for export.

3. Procedures for the Settlement of Labour Disputes

32. It follows from these considerations that institutions and procedures for the prevention and settlement of labour disputes constitute in many Third World countries the backbone of the national industrial relations system. To appreciate the different role of courts in different countries one must turn to the typology of labour disputes established by labour legislation. While most English-speaking countries[12] (most countries of Asia, half of Africa and the Caribbean) still follow the British model under which a 'trade dispute' is any labour dispute, whether individual or collective, whether over rights or over interests (with the consequence that the industrial courts, labour courts, arbitration tribunals or even industrial relations commissions acting as part of the judiciary deal with all types of disputes), in those countries which follow the Latin mode (Latin America and French-speaking Africa[13]) a

---

12. *Industrial Courts in English-speaking Developing Countries*, International Institute for Labour Studies, Geneva, 1976; ILO, *Conciliation and Arbitration of Industrial Disputes in English-speaking Countries of Africa*, Labour–Management Relations Series, No. 37, Geneva, 1970.
13. *Les tribunaux du travail en Afrique francophone*, International Institute for Labour Studies, Geneva, 1978.

distinction is often made between collective and individual disputes, and sometimes also between disputes over interests and disputes over rights, the latter being submitted to labour courts.

33. All this has led in many developing countries to a high degree of legalism and, consequently, a preponderant role of lawyers in industrial relations. This trend is surely most pronounced in Latin America but it is also widespread in Africa, particularly in its French-speaking parts, and has also been denounced in some Asian countries (e.g. India and the Philippines). Case law created by labour court decisions is in many Third World countries an important source of labour law. Surely, the concept of avoiding or settling labour disputes by a binding decision handed down by a judicial body is very attractive to governments which want to avoid open conflicts and promote social justice.

34. But, at least in some quarters, especially in Asia and Africa, where much thought is given to linking labour law with national values and traditions, there are people who ask whether litigation before a court is really in line with national patterns of behaviour. Some people argue that the very idea of judicial decisions in labour cases was imported from the West and stems from a conflictual concept of labour–management relations. It is therefore felt that a strengthening of conciliation procedures which aim at bringing about amicable or agreed solutions, with in-built face-saving devices, would be more in line with local values and traditions. These ideas have not yet found their expression in concrete measures in labour law and industrial relations but they are increasingly discussed in a number of countries in Africa and Asia.

4. Workers' Participation in Enterprises

35. It is often assumed, particularly in Europe, that schemes for workers' participation in enterprise decision-making are a characteristic feature of a long-established, 'mature' industrial relations system, based on extensive experience and solidly rooted institutions such as trade unions and collective bargaining. People holding this view are therefore often surprised when they learn in many Third World countries workers' participation at the enterprise level is a very topical issue of the present industrial relations debate.

In fact, workers' participation in management has for many years been a much discussed proposition in India where the principle has even been enshrined in the constitution of the country. Similarly, workers' participation is provided for in the labour legislation of Pakistan, Sri Lanka and Bangladesh. Specific forms of workers' participation have been introduced in Singapore and the Philippines. In Africa, workers' participation schemes are prescribed in Algeria and Tanzania to name only a few examples, and form one of the basic concepts of the industrial relations policy of Zambia. In Latin America experience with workers' participation arrangements was made, for instance, in Peru and Venezuela.

36. What most of these endeavours have in common are two essential aspects. One is the fact that workers' participation in developing countries has, as a general rule, been entrusted to works committees, works councils, employees' councils or similar bodies, established mostly by law, at the enterprise level and composed of elected workers' representatives, which have been given certain rights and functions, mainly of a consultative or advisory nature, to co-operate with management. The second feature which most Third World countries in which workers' participation schemes are tried out have in common is the origin of such schemes. As distinct from Western Europe where workers' participation goes back to the initiative of the labour movement, in most Third World countries the drive for workers' participation goes back to government initiative and not trade union pressure. Governments feel that through an association of workers with management decisions they can replace opposition and conflict by co-operation and thus enlist workers' support for national development.

37. This leads then often to trade union opposition to government plans to introduce workers' participation schemes as trade unions fear – sometimes with, sometimes without justification – that the establishment of works councils or similar bodies outside of and alongside with the trade union movement may be used, or may even be intended, as a means to weaken or undermine the trade union position in the enterprises. Furthermore, trade unions often fear that the existence of works councils or works committees with advisory functions may interfere with the collective bargaining process which, as we have seen, is in most developing countries concentrated at the enterprise level and the conduct of which trade unions consider to be their prerogative.

C. Employment Relationships

38. The questions discussed so far belong to the area of collective labour law or, in other words, industrial relations. If we now take a quick look at the individual employment relationship we must make a sharp distinction between the English-speaking countries (i.e. those in which the British colonial model is still determining labour law concepts) and those countries (in Latin America and French-speaking Africa) whose labour law doctrine goes back to Roman law (or civil law) traditions. In the former there is usually no detailed legal regulation of the individual employment relationship while the labour codes or other labour law enactments of the latter group usually contain very comprehensive standards on the contract of employment, its conclusion and termination, rights and duties of the parties, etc. All this is, as we have seen, – in both types of countries – supplemented by protective labour legislation.

39. In practice the most topical and also controversial aspect of the employment relationship is, in the large majority of developing countries, the question of dismissal. It is not surprising that, at a time of economic recession and in the light of mass unemployment or underemployment in most Third World countries, workers and trade unions should seek to protect workers against arbitrary dismissal and, where dismissal is unavoidable, for example as a result of work force reductions, to mitigate the hardships for the workers concerned, by providing for special severance payments, indemnities, etc. In a large number of developing countries therefore, including Mauritius, Peru, Mexico, Senegal, Ethiopia, Sri Lanka and many others, legislation was enacted or amended in recent years to make dismissal more difficult or to provide for special benefits for dismissed workers. It must be remembered that the absence of unemployment benefit schemes in almost all Third World countries makes the loss of a job a particularly harsh measure, especially where the many members of a large family must live on the wage of one person.

40. If we look at the employment relationship in Third World countries from a conceptual point of view, searching for deeper-going characteristics which may be different from the West, we find that in some quarters in Asia and also in Africa people ask whether the contractual concept prevailing in Western Europe is in line with their own value system and with their own attitudes and patterns of behaviour. The Secretary of the Ministry of Labour of Sri Lanka once remarked to me that in his view the basic difference between West and East in the labour relations field is that in the West the employment relationship is conceived mainly in terms of mutual legal rights while in Asia the emphasis is on mutual ethical obligations. In the West paternalistic concepts have a bad connotation but in Asia and also in some parts of Africa the recruitment of a worker is not conceived as the conclusion of a contract between two equal parties but as the acceptance of a new member in the family of the enterprise.

41. This is clearly the basic idea of the Japanese employment relationship and it is therefore not surprising that the Japanese labour relations model should attract so much attention in the developing countries in South and South-East Asia. While people in the West think, also in the area of labour relations, more in terms of individuals (with their rights and obligations) certain quarters in Asia and Africa, studying the roots and values of their own societies, see people more as members of a group. Admittedly, these ideas are still very vague and imprecise but anyone who tries to understand the present and future labour relations discussion in Asia and Africa must be aware of their existence.

IV. CONCLUDING REMARKS

42. This rapid overview of certain features which characterise, though to varying degrees, the industrial relations and labour law systems of Third World countries is merely intended to promote understanding for the particular characteristics of developing societies which are also reflected in their approach to labour relations. There is surely a need for developing countries to work out labour relations systems which are in line with their development needs but such development needs must not be invoked against the existence and furtherance of universal workers and trade union rights. 'Africanisation' or 'Asianisation' of labour relations is surely a legitimate goal but 'Africanisation' or 'Asianisation' must not be used as a pretext for the undermining or limitation of basic human freedoms. To strike a balance between development-oriented labour relations systems and the promotion of universal human rights is the basic challenge of labour law and industrial relations in the Third World, today and tomorrow.

International Developments

Chapter 5. International Labour Law

N. Valticos

I. INTRODUCTION

A. Definition

1. International labour law covers the substantive rules of law which have been established at the international level, as well as the procedural rules relating to their adoption and their implementation.

B. Historical Development

2. From the origin of labour law it was felt that national legislation on labour matters could not be solidly established in individual countries if not supported by parallel standards adopted internationally. The moves toward international labour conventions date back to the beginning of the nineteenth century. The first two Conventions were adopted by a diplomatic Conference held in Bern in 1906. The 1919 Peace Treaties provided for the establishment of an International Labour Organisation to adopt Conventions and Recommendations.

3. Since then the International Labour Conference has met regularly, normally once a year, and adopted 162 Conventions and 172 Recommendations.

In 1944 in Philadelphia it adopted a Declaration which again defined the aims and purposes of the Organisation and this was incorporated in the ILO Constitution. The Declaration reaffirmed, in particular, that labour is not a commodity, that 'freedom of expression and of association are essential to sustained progress', that 'poverty anywhere constitutes a danger to prosperity everywhere' and that 'all human beings, irrespective of race, creed or sex, have the right to pursue both their material well-being and their spiritual development in conditions of freedom and dignity, of economic security and equal opportunity'.

C. The Purpose of International Labour Law

4. Various arguments have been advanced in support of international labour law.[1]

1. For more details, see N. Valticos, *International Labour Law*, Deventer, 1979.

The first argument related to *international competition*. It was felt that international agreements in the field of labour would prevent international competition from taking place to the disadvantage of workers and would constitute a form of code of fair competition. Later it was realised that costs and the competitive value of products depend on many factors other than labour costs. Nevertheless, the argument of international competition was used more recently for countries where conditions were similar and were not influenced by tariff barriers. Conversely, it has been suggested that the observance by developing countries of minimal labour standards would reduce the risk of unfair competition and would facilitate international trade.

At the end of the First World War, a second argument appeared, namely that action against social injustice serves the *cause of peace*.

5. However, the driving force behind the idea of international labour law has simply been the concept of *social justice* for its own sake. Although there has been marked improvement in the condition of workers in developed countries since the first period of industrialisation, social conditions still involve hardship in the greater part of the world. More generally, the notion of social justice is constantly evolving. It is now understood in its widest meaning and embraces the general welfare of mankind.

6. Apart from these three basic purposes, the function of international labour law is also to promote balanced economic and social progress, to regulate labour questions having an international character and to serve as a source of inspiration to governments, as a basis for the claims of workers and as a guide for the policy of employers.

II. The Sources of International Labour Law

A. *ILO Sources*

1. The Constitution of the ILO

7. The Constitution of the ILO lays down a number of principles, such as freedom of association and non-discrimination, which are regarded as a direct source of law.

2. Conventions and Recommendations

8. Conventions are instruments designed to create international obligations for the States which ratify them, while Recommendations aim at providing guidelines for government action.

ILO Conventions have a number of specific features due to the fact that they are adopted in an institutional framework, that the Conference which adopts them has a 'tripartite' structure and that the system was designed to be more effective than that of normal diplomatic treaties. The provisions contained in ILO Conventions and Recommendations are described as international labour standards.

9. Conventions and Recommendations are adopted in the framework of the ILO. The ILO has 150 Member States. It has a 'tripartite' structure, i.e., it is not composed only of government representatives but also of representatives of employers and of workers. This structure has given rise to a number of difficulties which related, on the one hand, to the designation of workers' representatives by countries in which there is trade union pluralism and by those where there is no real freedom of association and, on the other hand, to the designation of employers' representatives by communist countries. In spite of these difficulties, the tripartite structure of the ILO has certainly been a source of vigour for the Organisation.

10. The ILO comprises three main bodies, the most representative being the International Labour Conference, which meets normally once a year and consists of delegations which should have four members each, i.e. two Government delegates, one Employers' and one Workers' delegate. The latter two delegates must be nominated in agreement with the most representative organisations of employers or workers of their countries. Every delegate votes individually. The second body of the ILO is the Governing Body which is selected every three years by the Conference and comprises 56 members, 28 representing Governments and 14 each the Employers and Workers. Ten of the 28 Government members are appointed by the members of chief industrial importance. In 1986, the Conference adopted an important amendment to the ILO Convention, relating mainly to the composition of the Governing Body. This amendment will come into force when it receives some hundred ratifications. The third body of the ILO is the International Labour Office which is the permanent secretariat of the Organisation. Its Director-General is appointed by the Governing Body.

11. Conventions and Recommendations are adopted by the International Labour Conference following a 'double discussion', i.e. a discussion at two successive annual sessions of the Conference. The International Labour Office prepares preliminary reports setting out the law and practice in the different countries on the questions concerned, and the matter is first considered by a special technical committee appointed by the Conference. Ultimately Conventions and Recommendations must be adopted by the Plenary of the Conference and a majority of two-thirds of the delegates attending the Conference is required.

12. The main problem encountered in framing international labour standards relates to the diversity of national (economic, social and political) conditions in the various countries of the world. However, it has been felt that ILO instruments should remain universal in character and that regional standards, while useful by supplementing universal standards, cannot replace them altogether. In order to take account of the diversity of conditions in the world, recourse was had to various types of flexibility clauses inserted in the Conventions of universal character.[2]

13. Other problems relate to the level of the standards – which should be relevant to the greatest number of countries, while representing some substantial advance upon average existing practice – and to the drafting of the standards, which should not be too strict or detailed.

14. The question of the choice between a Convention and a Recommendation is often discussed. The role of Recommendations is mainly to deal with subjects which are not yet ripe for a Convention, or to supplement a Convention laying down the basic rules, or to deal with matters which do not lend themselves to the adoption of Conventions entailing international obligations.

15. The changes in needs and conceptions may make it necessary to revise international labour standards. Most ILO Conventions contain clauses providing that a new revising Convention does not entail the abrogation of the original instrument, that the original instrument ceases to be open to ratification as from the entry into force of the new Convention, and that ratification by a State of the later involves the denunciation of the original one. Over 40 Conventions have been revised by subsequent instruments: in some cases the aim was to make the Convention more flexible, in other cases, on the contrary, it was to raise the earlier standards.

3. Less Formal Instruments

16. In some cases, standards are laid down in instruments less formal than Conventions and Recommendations, such as *resolutions* adopted by the International Labour Conference, etc.

4. Interpretation

17. The ILO Constitution provides that any question or dispute relating to the interpretation of the Constitution or a Convention must be submitted to the International Court of Justice. There has only been one such case, in 1932.

2. See McMahon, 'The Legislative Technique of the ILO', *British Year Book of International Law*, 1965–66, pp. 31–68,
   Valticos, *op. cit.*, pp. 51–54.

On the other hand, the Director-General is frequently consulted by governments as to the interpretation of Conventions and the opinions which he gives are communicated to the Governing Body of the ILO and published in the *Official Bulletin*. Legal opinions are also given in memoranda by the Director-General or the Legal Adviser of the ILO.

5. Case Law

18. In the course of the years, the supervisory bodies[3] have progressively built up a body of case law as to the precise scope and meaning of various ILO Conventions.

6. Instruments Adopted by Special Conferences under the Auspices and with the Co-operation of the ILO

19. In a number of cases, special governmental Conferences have dealt with questions which concerned only a limited number of countries (such as the *Agreements concerning Rhine Boatmen* of 1950 and the *European Convention concerning Social Security for Workers Engaged in International Transport* of 1956). In two other cases, instruments have been adopted by Conferences convened by other organisations (UNESCO, etc.) with the co-operation of the ILO.

B. United Nations Instruments

20. While the UN does not deal with labour matters as such, it has touched on such matters, mainly in the instruments concerning human rights. The 1948 *Universal Declaration of Human Rights* and the two 1966 *International Covenants* contain various provisions relating to labour matters. Reference should also be made to the 1965 *Convention on the Elimination of All Forms of Racial Discrimination*.

C. European Instruments

1. Council of Europe Instruments

21. The most comprehensive of the instruments adopted by the Council of Europe on social questions is the 1961 European Social Charter which has been ratified by 13 of the Member States of the Council of Europe. Its ratification is subject to the acceptance of at least ten of the 19 articles or 45

---

3. See below under IV, 'The implementation of international labour standards'.

of the 72 paragraphs of Part II of the Charter. Its most original feature is that it recognised the right to strike, subject to some restrictions.

The 1950 *European Human Rights Convention* deals essentially with civil and political rights, including the prohibition of forced labour and the right to form trade unions.

The Council of Europe has also adopted a number of social security instruments, the basic ones being the 1964 *European Code of Social Security*, which is based on the ILO Convention No. 102, and the 1972 *European Convention on Social Security*.

2. European Communities Standards

22. While the main purpose of the European Communities is of an economic nature, they have also set themselves a number of social objectives. Provisions of a social character are to be found both in the basic treaties of the Communities and the various types of acts provided under the Communities' legal system.[4]

D. *Other Regional Instruments*

23. In other geographical and political frameworks, various instruments have also been adopted concerning labour matters. In Eastern Europe, the Council for Mutual Economic Assistance, established in 1949, is authorised to pass recommendations on matters of economic and technical co-operation. In the American region, a Social Security Convention was adopted in 1967 by the Organisation of Central American States, and the countries of the Andean group adopted in 1977 an instrument on social security and another on the migration of workers. The Organisation of American States also adopted in 1969 an American Convention on Human Rights. In the Middle East, Conventions on various labour matters have been adopted by the League of Arab States and, more recently, by the Arab Labour Organisation. In Africa, a General Social Security Convention was adopted in 1971.

E. *Bilateral Treaties*

24. Bilateral treaties in the labour field aim at regulating the admission to and conditions of employment in each of the contracting countries of nationals of the other country. Such treaties are based on the principle of equality of treatment of the nationals of each contracting State to the nationals of the other State in which they reside. The number of these

4. See Ribas, *La politique sociale des Communautés européennes*, Paris, 1969.

treaties is large and their scope has broadened over the years. They include treaties on limited subjects or groups, labour treaties of a more general type, conventions on migration and social insurance treaties.

F. Relations between the Sources

25. The plurality of these international sources of labour law made necessary various measures of co-ordination and consultation aimed at preventing the adoption of standards which would be in conflict with one another. In cases of conflict, preference should be given to the standard which is the most favourable to the workers.

III. The Content of International Labour Law

A. Freedom of Association for Trade Union Purposes

26. Freedom of association has a special importance for workers as it is an essential means for them to defend their interests. The principle of freedom of association is mentioned in the *constitutional provisions* of the ILO.

The basic instrument in this field is the *Freedom of Association and Protection of the Right to Organise Convention*, 1948 (No. 87), which has been ratified by 98 States. This Convention provides that 'workers and employers, without distinction whatsoever, shall have the right to establish and to join organisations of their own choosing without previous authorisation.'

The Convention also provides that the organisations should have the right to draw up their own constitution and rules, to elect their representatives and to organise their activities. The freedom of action of trade union organisations depends to a great extent on the civil liberties which are recognised in each country. This was stressed in a resolution adopted in 1970 by the International Labour Conference. The Convention also provides that trade union organisations shall not be liable to be dissolved or suspended by administrative authority, that they shall have the right to establish federations and confederations, and that all such organisations shall have the right to affiliate with international organisations.

While Convention No. 87 does not deal expressly with the right to strike, a case law on that matter has been progressively developed by the supervisory bodies.

27. The 1949 *Right to Organise and Collective Bargaining Convention* (No. 98) provides for adequate protection of workers and trade union leaders against acts of anti-union discrimination and against interference in trade union matters. It also aims at the promotion of voluntary negotiation between employers and workers.

83

28. More recently, a 1971 Convention (No. 135) and Recommendation (No. 143) provide for the protection and facilities to be afforded to workers' representatives in the undertaking. In 1975, the *Rural Workers' Organisations* Convention (No. 141) and Recommendation (No. 149) provided for policies of active encouragement to these organisations. In 1978, the *Labour Relations (Public Service)* Convention (No. 151) and Recommendation (No. 159) concerned themselves with the right to organise of public employees. Finally, in 1981, a Convention (No. 154) and a Recommendation (No. 163) dealt with the promotion of collective bargaining.

B. Forced Labour

29. There are two important Conventions on forced labour. The 1930 Convention (No. 29), which is the most widely ratified (by 128 States) provided for the progressive suppression of forced labour and, meanwhile, its use only for public purposes and as an exceptional measure, subject to a number of conditions and guarantees. After the Second World War, the Abolition of Forced Labour Convention, 1952 (No. 105), which has been ratified by 109 States, called for the immediate and complete abolition of any form of forced labour for five purposes: as a means of political coercion or education, as a punishment for holding or expressing views ideologically opposed to the established political, social or economic system; as a method of mobilising and using labour for purposes of economic development; as a means of labour discipline; as a punishment for having participated in strikes; or as a means of radial, social, national or religious discrimination.

The application of the forced labour Conventions has given rise to problems which have varied according to the period and the countries concerned.

C. Discrimination in Employment

30. The main instrument relating to discrimination in employment and occupation is a 1958 Convention (No. 111) which has been ratified by 108 States. The Convention defines discrimination as including any distinction, exclusion or preference made on the basis of race, colour, sex, religion, political opinion, national extraction (which may not mean nationality) or social origin, which nullifies or impairs equality of opportunity or treatment in employment or occupation. Certain distinctions are not deemed to be discrimination, such as those based on the inherent requirements of a particular job, those affecting an individual who is justifiably suspected of or engaged in activities prejudicial to the security of the State (provided that the individual concerned shall have a right to appeal) and some special measures of protection or assistance. The Convention and the Recommendation describe the methods designed to eliminate discrimination. In 1981, a

Convention and a Recommendation dealt with men and women workers with family responsibilities (see also below paragraph 43 *in fine*).

31. In the field of *apartheid* in labour matters, which is practised in South Africa, the International Labour Conference adopted unanimously, in 1964, a *Declaration*, which was updated in 1981. In this Declaration, the International Labour Conference condemned the policy of apartheid and called upon the Government of South Africa to renounce it. The ILO also established a detailed programme for the elimination of apartheid in labour matters. Special reports on the policy of apartheid are submitted each year to the International Labour Conference.

D. Employment

32. Many Conventions have been adopted in the field of employment. The most important was the 1964 *Employment Policy Convention* (No. 122) which provides the obligation, for ratifying States (71 up to now), to declare and pursue, as a major goal, an active policy designed to promote full, productive and freely chosen employment. The Convention was supplemented by a more detailed Recommendation and these standards have been further supplemented at the 1984 Session of the Conference. Moreover, in 1969 the ILO launched a World Employment Programme aiming at promoting employment, and in 1976 it convened a Tripartite World Conference which adopted guidelines for a Programme of Action in this field. In 1984, the Conference adopted an Employment Policy (Supplementary Provisions) Recommendation (No. 169).

33. Other ILO instruments dealt more specifically with unemployment (Convention No. 2 of 1919), organisation of public works (in 1937 and 1944), the abolition of fee-charging employment agencies (Convention No. 96 of 1949) and the maintenance of Employment Services (Convention No. 88 of 1948). Various instruments were also adopted in the field of apprenticeship, vocational guidance, vocational rehabilitation and training.

E. Wages

34. While the precise amount of wages can naturally not be regulated internationally, various Conventions and Recommendations were adopted in 1928 and in 1951 concerning minimum wage-fixing machinery, and they were followed in 1970 by a Convention (No. 131) and a Recommendation (No. 135) which providie that States should establish a system of minimum wages to cover all groups of wage earners whose terms of employment are such that coverage would be appropriate. Moreover, the protection of wages and the more specific question of labour clauses in public contracts have been covered by instruments adopted in 1949.

F. General Conditions of Work

35. The first Convention to be adopted by the ILO, in 1919, was the Hours of Work (Industry) Convention, which provided that, subject to various exceptions, working hours should not exceed eight in the day and 48 in the week. While this Convention was not ratified by the major industrial countries, it exercised a considerable influence in the world. In 1935, the ILO adopted the Forty-Hour Week Convention, (No. 47) and a number of special Conventions also based on the standard of the 40-hour week. In 1962, the Reduction of Hours of Work Recommendation (No. 116) set the principle of the progressive reduction of normal hours of work with a view to attaining the social standard of the 40-hour week. In the special field of road transport, a Convention and a Recommendation were adopted in 1979.

36. Weekly rest of not less than 24 hours per week was provided for by a 1921 Convention (No. 14) relating to industry and by a 1957 Convention relating to commerce and offices. A 1957 Recommendation (No. 103) advocated that the period of rest be at least 36 hours.

37. The first Convention on Paid Leave (No. 52) was adopted in 1936 and provided for an annual holiday of at least six days. In 1954, a Recommendation (No. 98) set the standard at 2 weeks and in 1970 a revised Convention (No. 132) raised it to three weeks at least. In 1974, a Convention (No. 140) and a Recommendation (No. 148) introduced the new concept of *paid educational leave*.

38. A considerable number of instruments relate to hygiene and safety. Some of these instruments have dealt, over the years, with specific risks, while other standards concerned special branches of activity. There were also a number of Recommendations dealing with methods and institutions for the prevention of industrial accidents and the protection of worker' health. Recently, in 1981, a Convention (No. 155) and a Recommendation (No. 164), with a general scope, were adopted to cover the matters of occupational safety and health.

Apart from the prevention of occupational accidents and diseases, it was also necessary to establish standards relating to their compensation. The system of compensation organised by ILO standards (Conventions Nos. 18, 42, and 121 of 1925, 1934 and 1964 respectively) is based on a list of diseases which should be considered as being occupational when they affect workers engaged in specified trades, industries or processes.

39. The matters of workers' spare time, welfare facilities for workers and workers' housing have been dealt with in Recommendations adopted, respectively, in 1924, 1956 and 1961.

G. Social Policy

40. Certain instruments relating to social policy as a whole (in particular Convention No. 117 of 1982) were adopted in order to encourage governments to pursue systematic action in this field. More specific standards dealt with questions arising out of technological progress. In 1977, the ILO Governing Body adopted a Tripartite Declaration of Principles concerning Multinational Enterprises and Social Policy.

H. Social Security

41. From 1919 to 1936, a series of distinct instruments based on the notion of social insurance were adopted to protect given categories of workers against a certain number of risks. From 1944, the standards were based on the wider concept of social security, which aimed at providing a basic income for all those who need such protection, as well as full medical care. The main Convention in this field is the 1952 Convention concerning Social Security (Minimum Standards) (No. 102). The Convention defines the scope of protection and it establishes a minimum standard as regards the benefits. Since then, the ILO has adopted at regular intervals a number of further instruments to supplement and revise previous ones, and sometimes to provide for a higher degree of protection than Convention No. 102.

I. Industrial Relations

42. Following the adoption of the main Conventions on freedom of association described above, the ILO dealt – mainly in the form of Recommendations – with various aspects of industrial relations, such as collective agreements, voluntary conciliation and arbitrarion, co-operation at the level of the undertaking, consultation at the industrial and national level, and communications and examination of grievances in the undertaking. In 1963, the ILO Conference also adopted a Recommendation concerning Termination of Employment (No. 119). It was revised in 1982 by a Convention (No. 158) and a Recommendation (No. 166).

J. Work of Women

43. In the field of women's employment international action has been guided by two main considerations: originally the desire to protect women

against excessively arduous conditions of work and also, at a later period, the concern to ensure equality of rights and of treatment between women and men (see also above under discrimination). The main 'protective' instruments relate to *maternity protection* (Conventions Nos. 3 and 103, of 1919 and 1952).

Another protective Convention relates to the *prohibition of night work*. Apart from a 1906 Convention, there were three ILO Conventions on the subject (in 1919, 1934 and 1948) as a result of revisions made to render the standards more flexible. While these standards are still considered in a number of countries as being necessary, doubts are currently expressed in certain quarters as to their suitability in the light of the principle of equality.

Other Conventions refer to the employment of women in *unhealthy or dangerous occupations*.

The most important instrument aiming at ensuring equality is, apart from the Discrimination Convention, the *Equal Remuneration* Convention, 1951 (No. 100) which lays down the rule that each State should promote and, in so far as consistent with the methods in operation in its country, ensure the application of the principle of equal remuneration for men and women workers for work of equal value.

Finally, the question of *employment of women with family responsibilities* was dealt with in a 1965 Recommendation (No. 123), which was followed, in 1981, by a Convention (No. 156) and a Recommendation (No. 165) of a wider scope on men and women *workers with family responsibilities*.

K. Work of Children and Young Persons

44. Child labour was one of the first fields in which standards were adopted. These standards related mainly to the minimum age for admission to employment. Starting in 1919, a number of Conventions set the general standard at 14 years. Later, in 1936 and 1937, the minimum age was raised to 15 years. After ten Conventions in succession were adopted in this field, a consolidated general standard was set in Convention No. 138 of 1973 which linked minimum age to school-leaving age, provided that it should not be less than 15 years – or 14 as an initial step for developing countries – and that it should be 18 years for unhealthy and dangerous work. A supplementary recommendation set the target at 16 years.

Conventions were also adopted to prohibit night work and to provide for medical examinations.

L. Older Workers

45. In 1980, Recommendation No. 162 introduced standards on equality of opportunity and treatment for older workers, on their protection in employment and on preparation for and access to retirement.

M. Special Categories of Workers

46. More than 50 Conventions and Recommendations deal with various aspects of maritime work. They are adopted through a special procedure and there are special conditions for their entry into force. One can refer in particular to a Convention (No. 147) adopted in 1976 to deal with the general question of minimum labour standards for merchant ships. Some analogous standards were adopted in respect of fishermen.

47. Special standards were framed for workers in agriculture. In some cases these standards aimed at extending to agricultural work the rules applying to industry and in other cases, they were adopted to take into account the special features of work in agriculture. Special standards have also been laid down as regards plantation workers (Convention No. 110 of 1958) and tenants, sharecroppers, etc. (Recommendation No. 132 of 1968).

48. Indigenous workers and workers in non-metropolitan territories were in particular need of protection because of the level of their development and of their political and social status. The purpose of the instruments concerning *indigenous workers* has been to protect them in regard to recruiting, contracts of employment and penal sanctions for breaches of contract of employment. As regards *workers in non-metropolitan territories*, in favour of whom the 1930 Forced Labour Convention had mainly been framed, a series of special instruments were adopted from 1944 to 1947, to extend to them a number of standards of a more general nature or to adopt special standards in the field of social policy, right of association, labour inspection and labour standards. In 1957, an important Convention (No. 107) and a Recommendation covered a wide range of subjects in respect of *indigenous and other tribal and semi-tribal populations*, with the co-operation of the UN and the specialised agencies concerned.

49. In 1978, the ILO adopted a Convention (No. 151) and a Recommendation (No. 159) relating to labour relations in the public service. Reference can also be made to two 1977 instruments relating to Nursing Personnel.

N. Foreign and Migrant Workers

50. The most important of the various Conventions dealing with the situation of foreign and migrant workers is the 1949 Migration for Employment Convention (Revised) (No. 97). It applies to migrant workers without discrimination in respect of nationality, race, etc. The Convention aims mainly at granting to immigrants lawfully within the territory treatment no less favourable than that which it applies to its own nationals in respect of labour matters. The Convention is supplemented by a Recommendation.
  A more recent Convention (No. 143) and Recommendation were adopted

in 1975 to deal with migration in abusive conditions and to promote the equality of opportunity and treatment of migrant workers.

Other Conventions of a general character contain special provisions on foreign workers. Conventions which do not contain any provision on foreign workers are considered as being applicable to them.

O. Labour Administration

51. A number of instruments deal with matters of labour administration, and in particular *labour inspection*, the basic instruments being Convention No. 81 of 1947 – for industry and commerce – and two 1969 instruments – for agriculture. In 1978, the Conference adopted a Convention (No. 150) and a Recommendation (No. 158) on labour administration. Other instruments relate to labour statistics (in 1938, to be revised shortly) and to tripartite consultation relating to standards (Convention No. 144 and Recommendation No. 152 of 1976).

P. The Review of Existing Standards[5]

52. As ILO standards have been adopted during a period of over 65 years, a review of existing standards was recently carried out by the Governing Body of the ILO and completed in 1979. Following this in-depth review it was considered that, out of 310 instruments adopted by the ILO up to 1978, 154 retain their validity and should be promoted on a priority basis. Thirty instruments were listed in the category of instruments to be revised. As regards the remaining instruments, some are obsolete and others remain valid as temporary objectives for countries which are not yet able to accept the most recent standard. Finally, the Governing Body identified over 40 subjects on which the adoption of new standards might be considered. This exercise was repeated in 1985–1986 with similar results.

IV. THE IMPLEMENTATION OF INTERNATIONAL LABOUR STANDARDS

A. Obligations in Respect of Standards

53. The ILO Constitution provides that all Member States are bound, in all cases, to *submit* ILO Conventions and Recommendations to their competent authorities (normally the Parliament) within a year or 18 months of their adoption. The Constitution also provides that States should *supply reports* not only on Conventions which they have ratified but also, at the request of the Governing Body of the ILO, on unratified Conventions and on Recom-

---

5. See N. Valticos, 'The future prospects for international labour standards', *International Labour Review*, Nov.–Dec. 1979, pp. 679–697.

mendations, to indicate the position of their law and practice, the difficulties encountered and future prospects.

B. Ratification of Conventions

54. It is by ratifying a Convention that a State undertakes to give effect to it. The ratification of an ILO Convention cannot be accompanied by reservations. ILO Conventions have been the subject of close to 5,300 ratifications as of 31 December 1986. Generally, the coming into force of a Convention is conditional on the receipt of two ratifications. Conventions can be denounced, at certain intervals, by States which have ratified them. The number of denunciations is very small.

International labour Conventions and Recommendations are minimum standards and they cannot affect any law, custom or agreement which is more favourable for workers.

C. Reports on Ratified Conventions

55. Each State is required by the ILO Constitution to supply reports on the measures it has taken to give effect to the Conventions which it has ratified. Reports are now requested every two or four years, according to the importance of the Convention concerned, but in the case of serious problems of application or of observations made by organisations of employers or workers, reports can be requested ealier than they would normally be due.

D. The Incorporation of International Conventions into National Law as a Result of Ratification

56. In a number of countries, the ratification of a Convention makes it part of national law and directly enforceable at the national level. However, to be effectively applied in such cases, a Convention must be self-executing. This is not the case for Conventions which require supplementary acts or regulations for their application.

V. The General Supervisory Machinery of the ILO

57. The ILO has established a diversified system of supervision. The existing procedures fall into two main groups.

A. Procedures Based on the Examination of Periodic Reports

58. The reports supplied by governments on the application of Conventions

and of Recommendations are examined in the first place by a *Committee of Experts*, which is composed of independent personalities. The comments of this body take the form either of 'observations' contained in its printed report or of 'requests' addressed directly to the governments concerned. The Committee also prepares general surveys on particular Conventions.

The reports of the Committee of Experts are submitted to a Tripartite Committee on the Application of Conventions set up at each session of the International Labour Conference. This body discusses with the representatives of the governments concerned the most important discrepancies noted by the Committee of Experts.

In 1968, a procedure of 'direct contacts' was introduced. Under this procedure, representatives of the ILO visit the countries concerned with the agreement of the government, to discuss special difficulties in the implementation of ILO standards. This procedure has been applied to some 300 cases relating to 30 countries. During the past 22 years, there have been over 1,600 cases concerning more than 150 countries in which governments have taken account of the comments of supervisory bodies.

B. Procedures Based on the Examination of Complaints

59. The ILO Constitution makes provision for two kinds of complaints. Firstly, *complaints* proper may be filed by any Member State against another Member State in connection with the application of a Convention which both have ratified. They may also be initiated by the Governing Body of the ILO either on its own motion or on the receipt of a complaint from a delegate at the Conference. Thirteen complaints have thus far been filed. Seven of these complaints were submitted to Commissions of Inquiry, composed of independent personalities. These Commissions hear witnesses and, when necessary, visit the country concerned. All governments concerned, except one, have co-operated in these procedures.

60. Secondly, *representations* may be made by employers' or workers' organisations on the grounds that a State does not secure the application of a ratified Convention. They are considered by a three-member Committee of the Governing Body, and then by the Governing Body as a whole. Twenty-four representations have thus far been submitted.

C. Special Machinery in the Field of Freedom of Association[6]

61. In the field of freedom of association special machinery was set up by

6. See Jenks, *The International Protection of Trade Union Freedom*, London, 1957; Cassese, 'Il controllo internazionale della libertá sindcale', *Communicazione e Studi*, Milan 1966, pp. 293–418; Valticos, 'Les méthodes de la protection internationale de la liberté syndicale', *Rec. Cours Académie droit international*, 1975-I, pp. 77–138.

the ILO in 1950 in agreement with the Economic and Social Council of the United Nations. This procedure is based on complaints by governments or by employers' or workers' organisations, the latter case being by far the most frequent. Complaints may even be made against States which have not ratified the freedom of association Conventions. The machinery comprises two bodies:

The Committee on Freedom of Association[7] is a tripartite body of nine members, appointed by the Governing Body from among its members and presided over by an independent personality. It has dealt with over 1,400 cases relating to a wide range of aspects of freedom of association. It has gradually built up an important body of opinion.[8] More recently, it has resorted to the procedure of 'direct contacts', mentioned above, and such visits took place, in particular, to Uruguay, Bolivia, Argentina, Chile, Canada, Nicaragua, Tunisia, Turkey and Poland between 1980 and 1988.

The Fact-Finding and Conciliation Commission is the more formal body of this special machinery. It is composed of independent persons. In principle, a case may not be referred to the Commission without the consent of the government concerned. In the early years, some governments refused to give their consent but subsequently many agreed to have cases concerning their countries brought before the Commission. The most important cases were those of Japan, in 1964, and Chile, in 1974.

D. Special Studies and Inquiries, Promotional Measures and Technical Co-operation

62. Apart from the supervisory procedures proper, studies and inquiries are frequently undertaken by the ILO in the field of labour standards. Many have been concerned with freedom of association, either as regards the situation in given countries or regions or as regards the membership of the ILO as a whole. There have also been investigations and studies in the field of forced labour from 1951 to 1959.

More recently, missions of ILO officials have visited Israel and the occupied Arab territories every year since 1978 in order to consider the situation of Arab workers of these territories.

Implementation of ILO standards is also sought by means of various educational and training measures, seminars, and the like.

Finally, technical co-operation may serve as a means of helping governments to reach the level of international standards.

---

7. See von Potobsky, 'Protection of Trade Union Rights – Twenty Years' Work by the Committee on Freedom of Association', *International Labour Review*, April 1972, pp. 69–83.
8. See *Freedom of Association. Digest of Decisions of the Freedom of Association Committee of the Governing Body of the ILO*, Geneva, Second edition, 1976.

VI. SUPERVISORY MACHINERIES ESTABLISHED BY OTHER INTERNATIONAL ORGANISATIONS

63. In respect of instruments adopted by international organisations other than the ILO, and in particular the United Nations, the Council of Europe and the European communities, more or less elaborate supervisory procedures have been introduced. In the first two cases, provisions for implementation are not included in the Constitutional Charter of the Organisation, but in each of the separate instruments. In most of these cases, supervision is based on the supply of reports by governments and their examination by different types of organs. As regards the European Social Charter, the arrangements are largely based on the ILO system.

SELECT BIBLIOGRAPHY

The Impact of International Labour Conventions and Recommendations, ILO, Geneva, 1976.
W. Jenks, *The International Protection of Trade Union Freedom*, London 1957.
– *Human Rights and International Labour Standards*, New York, 1960.
E.A. Landy, *The Effectiveness of International Supervision. Thirty Years of ILO Experience*, New York, 1966.
G. Scelle, *L'Organisation internationale du Travail et le BIT*, Paris; 1930.
N. Valticos, *Droit international du travail*, Paris, 2nd edn., 1983.
– *International Labour Law*, Deventer, 1979; Suppl. 1984.

Chapter 6. Conflict of Laws in Employment Contracts and Industrial Relations

F. Gamillscheg

I. Introduction

1. Where an employment contract involves one or more foreign contracts, it must be determined which of the different laws governs the contract before litigious questions can be resolved.

For example, if an American company hires an engineer in Brussels of American (Belgian/Swiss) nationality for work to be executed in Bolivia, a dispute may arise as to whether he may claim compensation for unfair dismissal.

The question is answered by Conflict of Law rules. Every country has its own set of such rules. They are also known as Private International Law, though these rules are not 'international', but national in character. Truly international sources governing conflicts of law in our field are still rare.

2. The conflict of law rule is dependent upon the essence of the subject matter, i.e. labour law norms. In substantive labour law we distinguish three categories of norms:

(1) As a rule the employment relationship, as established by the employment contract, forms part of the general law of contract. The norms governing the employment relationship are mandatory; they cannot be abrogated by contract. Yet it is left to the employee to claim his rights through the courts or grievance procedures. In continental European law this category of norms is classified as private law.

(2) A number of issues (safety at work, protection of children or pregnant mothers, or of handicapped persons, maximum hours, non-discrimination etc) are often considered to be of such fundamental importance that special authorities (factory inspectorates, social security officials etc) are organised to insure compliance with the rules governing these issues, if necessary by means of compulsion. The enforcement of these norms may even take place against the will of the protected employee. For example, an employee may prefer to work overtime in order to generate increased income. In countries with a Roman law tradition these protective rules (or at least the associated regulations on penal sanctions and plant closures etc.) are classified as rules with the

95

character of 'public law'. The distinction between these two modes of enforcement is also known in Anglo-Saxon countries.

(3) Industrial relations are also governed to a growing extent by legal norms. They are often classified as 'collective' norms. The phenomenon of collective labour law does not fit very well into the distinction between private and public law. It resembles the latter (e.g. the duty of fair and equal treatment, the mandatory nature of industrial norms contained in collective agreements, etc.), yet without being subject to state control.

3. The distinction between labour law rules, as described in paragraph 2, is reflected in international labour law. The conflict of laws of the employment contract is regarded as forming a part of the conflict of laws of the contract in a search for the appropriate law, foreign or domestic, controlling the contract. The rule thus indicating the proper law of the contract belongs in the category of so-called *multilateral conflict norms*.

For example, suppose that the employment contract were governed by the law of the place where the work is done/or where the seat of the enterprise is located/or by the law chosen by the parties concerned. In all these cases the applicable law may be foreign, if the place of work/seat of the enterprise/chosen law is foreign. If in our first example above the dismissal is governed by Bolivian law, then there is no difficulty for American or Belgian judges to apply that law.

In the field of public law as described above each authority only applies its own law, and the sole question is whether or not the respective norm is to be applied. If the answer is no, the authority refrains from action. As a rule – this is universally accepted – the application of these protective norms is contingent on the fact that the work is executed within national boundaries. The conflict of law norm is *unilateral*. For example, the German factory inspectorate (Gewerbeaufsicht) is only responsible and German safety regulations only apply if the work is done in Germany. Work done abroad (i.e. beyond the border) lies outside the jurisdiction of such authorities even if German citizens are working there (*infra* paragraph 19).

As concerns collective labour law, most of the answers are still uncertain; only a few sets of rules are generally accepted (*infra* paragraph 26).

II. Sources

A. *International Sources*

4. Written norms in International Labour Law which relate to the employment relationship or to individual aspects thereof may be found in certain conventions of the ILO and in bilateral treaties.[1] In 1980 the EEC proposed a

1. Cf. M. Simon-Dépitre, Acts of the 2nd International Congress of Labour Law 1957 (Geneva, 1961) p. 332; Stefan Szászy, *International Labour Law*, p. 23.

Convention Regarding the Law Applicable to Contractual Obligations (hereinafter: EEC-Draft) which also applies to the labour relationship.[2] It is based on the preparatory work of numerous experts (see the report of Prof. Lagarde and Prof. Giuliano). In addition, the EEC submitted a proposal in 1972 for a regulation to unify International Labour Law within the Community which, however, was highly criticised; a second version was no better received.[3] The project seems to have been abandoned for the moment; however, Article 20 of the EEC-Draft provides that future provisions in the legal rules governing the EEC shall not be affected by the Convention. This is doubtless evidence of an intention to enact the regulation at some point in the future.

B. National Sources

5. A number of states possess *written* multilateral conflict *norms*, mostly contained in a general code of Private International Law. Thus, Article 32 of the Polish Law on Private International Law (1965) grants the parties the right to choose the applicable law. In Austria, Article 44 of the 1978 Austrian Law refers to the law at the place of work; Article 27 of the East German Law on the Application of Law (Rechtsanwendungsgesetz) refers to the seat of the enterprise ('Sitz des Betriebes'). A similar solution is found in section 51 of the Hungarian Law on Private International Law. Written conflict norms are also contained in the respective codes of Spain, Czechoslovakia, Albania, and Kuwait.

Numerous norms determine the scope of application of this or that particular law. They cannot be listed here. They generally provide that the norm must be applied to all work executed within the territorial boundaries of that country regardless of the nationality of the parties. For example, this is the case with section 41 of the British Employment Protection (Consolidation) Act.

6. Norms such as the following are not genuine sources of Private International Law: for example section 92c of the German Commercial Code provides that the mandatory provisions for the protection of the commercial agent are freely negotiable if his place of business is located abroad. Section 7(2)(g) of the British Sex Discrimination Act permits the non-engagement of

---

2. OJ no. L 266 of 9 October 1980. The draft has been incorporated into the Draft of the Law on Private International Law for the Federal Republic of Germany (currently before the Federal Diet); cf. F. Gamillscheg, *Zeitschrift für Arbeitsrecht*, 1983, p. 307.
3. Text of the first version OJ 1972 C 49/26 and 1973 C 4/14; text of the second version Kom (75) 653 final; on the criticism, cf. F. Gamillscheg, *Rabels Zeitschrift für ausländisches und internationales Privatrecht*, 1973, p. 284, and *Recht der Internationalen Wirtschaft*, 1979, p. 225 (234); G. Beitzke, *Gedächtnisschrift Rolf Dietz* (1973) p. 127; A. Philip, *Contracts of Employment in the law of conflicts of laws of the EEC*, Festschrift für F.A. Mann (1977) p. 257.

a woman because of her sex when the position involves tasks which, according to the law or customs of the place of work, cannot be performed by a woman. Such norms are not conflict rules. They apply when German or British law is the proper law. Whether this is the case is a preliminary question and an issue in itself. But of course their very existence may be taken into consideration when the conflict rule itself is being elaborated by the judge.

7. In general, International Labour Law is a product of *case law*; to what extent it has achieved the status of *customary law* must be determined in a country-by-country survey. Many industrial nations, such as the USA, GB, FR Germany, France, Finland, Sweden, and others have no written rules on international contracts. In Germany, this area was expressly consigned to the realm of case law and academic law by the legislature in 1900. The spectrum of opinions and solutions is accordingly broad. But this has the advantage that, in the course of the years, certain standard solutions have been developed for certain typical recurrent situations. It is especially fascinating for the scholar of comparative law to uncover how, on this basis, the same solutions have simultaneously gained acceptance in different countries totally independent of one another, which of course is an indication that the solution satisfies the interests of the parties involved.

Codification of Private International Law or of International Labour Law would only disrupt this development. The European initiatives were the result of the laudable motive of unifying the law of the member states. However, comparative law research reveals that the solutions used in Europe hitherto are not as divergent from each other as they are sometimes presented. On the other hand, it can be predicted that judicial interpretation of the many indefinite terms in the draft-codification would be so diverse in the different member-states that legal uniformity would hardly be served.

III. The Proper Law of the Employment Contract

8. There are three main approaches to resolving the question of the applicable law:
(1) the classical method;
(2) the territorial connecting factor;
(3) the compromise as embodied in Article 6 of the EEC-Draft.

A. *Autonomy of the Parties*

9. The prevailing opinion in many industrialised countries such as the USA, FR Germany, Switzerland, Sweden, and Greece, still adheres to general international contract law and thus the principle of *party autonomy*. This principle provides that the parties to the employment contract have the right

to choose the law governing the contract. If they fail to do so, other substitute criteria apply (*infra* paragraph 14).

German practice is illustrated by the decision of the Federal Court of Labour of 9 November 1977,[4] where the parties – an American journalist working for Radio Free Europe in Munich – agreed on the application of the law of New York. In the United Kingdom general opinion also supports the precedence of the will of the parties in determining the proper law; on the other hand, a series of new protective laws (Employment Protection (Consolidation) Act, Sex Discrimination Act *et al.*) each contain an independent norm limiting their application to work performed at home – regardless of the proper law. That the proper law is not to be superseded by these special norms can be seen definitively in section 153(5) EP(C)A, where it is written that the proper law of a labour contract 'apart from this Act' can be English or foreign law.[5]

10. As a rule, an *implied choice* of law is as effective as an express one. Such a choice exists when the parties intended to submit their contract to a particular legal system but this intention can only be derived from other circumstances. For example, in a contract relating to country A and country B the six-week period of notice is referred to as the 'legal period' of notice. This would be evidence of the intention of the parties to submit the contract to the law of country A if the legal notice period in country B is only four weeks.[6] A reference to the rules of tax or of social insurance law may also be an indication of a tacit choice of law, but this is not necessarily so.

11. Article 3 of the EEC-Draft is satisfied with 'sufficient certainty' of the choice of law; section 44 paragraph 3 of the Austrian Law on Private International Law requires, on the other hand, an express choice (which may, however, be verbal).

12. In general international contract law it is disputed whether the choice of law must be made from among those systems to which the contract entertains material bonds. This does not have to be resolved here; no cases have, as yet, been found where the parties to the employment contract have chosen a totally unrelated legal system. In practice the choice lies exclusively between the law of the place of work and the law at the seat of the enterprise. One must be careful, however, not to misinterpret the required 'close' or 'legitimate' connection of the contract to the chosen law as a purely territorial connection. The work is carried out in a place where the legal system is of course of the greatest significance for its execution, but the issue still remains essentially one of the employment relationship. A legal

---

4. *Arbeitsrechtliche Praxis*, Nr. 13, Internationales Privatrecht Arbeitsrecht.
5. Cf. Bob Hepple and Paul O'Higgins, *Employment Law*, (4th ed. 1981) section 21; Dicey/ Morris (Collins), *The Conflict of Laws* (10th ed. 1980), II, p. 870.
6. Cf. Rechtbank Amsterdam 7. May 1957, *Ned. Jur.* 1957, No. 646.

relationship has its roots not in a place but in a legal system. The law does have a sphere of territorial validity, where it is the *lex fori*; however, this territorial factor is but one of several potentially relevant determining aspects. The place of work is an important point of consideration but far from being the only one.

13. Article 3, paragraph 1 of the EEC-Draft, which was incorporated in this respect into Article 27 of the German Draft, permits the parties to select the governing law 'applicable to the whole or a part only of the contract'. This is, however, not a good solution. It is a perversion of party autonomy to allow them to *select* portions of *different legal systems* and to construct for themselves out of these a mosaic to suit their own tastes. This may be tolerable for general International Contract Law – even here I have my doubts – where parties are of equal economic strength. In Labour Law, however, this would lead to all the dangers which the opponents of party autonomy always, unjustly, conjure up (*infra* paragraph 16). For example, it would be bad law to allow the parties to submit their contract to German law in general and to the law of X for all the questions concerning employee inventions or pension rights. Partial references which take into consideration certain peculiarities of the place of work, e.g., hours of work or holidays, which the employer for practical reasons cannot avoid, are of course not excluded.

14. When the parties *omit to choose the proper law*, a number of written norms state which law applies. In Italy, Article 25 d.p. (disposizioni preliminari al Codice Civile) refers to common nationality of the parties, and, in the absence of this, to the place of conclusion of the contract. Article 10, No. 6 of the Spanish Civil Code refers to the place of performance, as do section 16 of the Czechoslovakian Law on Private International Law and Article 33 of the Polish Law, each with further details.

To the extent that the law is silent, the determination of the proper law becomes the responsibility of the judiciary and the academic community. A number of different approaches have been worked out.

(1) The search for general connecting factors. In early days, Romanic and Anglo-Saxon countries regarded the *locus contractus* as the substitute connecting factor for contracts in the absence of choice by the parties. Savigny replaced the place of contract with the place of performance and found many supporters. Even today there are decisions based on these two rules. As standard criteria for all conceivable cases, however, they fail to satisfy the wide spectrum of interests involved. They have not been generally accepted.

(2) Eminent scholars have for a long time required that every type of contract should have the connecting factor that is most appropriate to it. This is said to be the place of the characteristic performance, a formula set forth in section 29 of the Hungarian law on Private International Law and now also to be found in Article 4 paragraph 2 of the EEC-Draft.

For an employment contract the characteristic factor would be the place of work. To date, however, this proposition has not prevailed because there are too many cases in which the acknowledged interests of the parties require other solutions.

(3) In the practice of many important industrial countries another method still predominates. It endeavours to find the suitable connecting factor for every single contract as such. This theory aspires to a maximum of individual case justice, purchased, to be honest, with a high measure of uncertainty: for, in the final analysis, it is the judge who subsequently decides on the predominant connecting factor and with it on the proper law. This method has recourse to a stock of typical criteria. If one of them is especially germane, i.e. 'most significant', or, where many factors arise, if these all point to the same law, then this is taken to be the *centre of gravity* of the contract and thus leads to its proper law. It is an 'English', 'French' or 'German' contract, therefore English, French or German law applies.

Examples of typically recurrent connecting factors in a legal system are the place of performance; the seat of the enterprise; common nationality; reliance on prior contracts; the place of contract; the place of origin of payment or of instructions; agreements as to currency used for payment; participation in pension plans of the parent enterprise; language of the contract; etc.

In another variation of this method it is not the cumulation of connecting factors but rather a decision on the *alleged intent of the parties* based on these connecting factors that is emphasised. This so-called 'subjective' theory arises from the assumption that the parties had a free choice of law; since they failed to exercise it, the judge makes the choice in their stead as he deems they reasonably and fairly would have done. Both methods lead, as a rule, to the same result. The objective approach is more generally accepted. The subjective has, on the other hand, certain advantages.[7]

On the basis of these methods a number of principles have been developed and applied by the courts, without their relinquishing the prerogative to decide otherwise. According to these principles the place of work emerges as the most relevant connecting factor. If the centre of gravity is the place where the work is usually done, the proper law of the contract does not change merely because the work is temporally completed elsewhere. An example would be a travelling salesperson, working within the FR Germany who takes a trip to Austria.

For persons hired at the seat of the enterprise specifically for work abroad the seat of the enterprise prevails as the connecting factor. This line of thought is even more dominant when the employee is a citizen of the 'sending State' (common nationality being an additional element). The argument which supports this decision is that the legal system at the place of work may be unknown and unfamiliar, often for both parties, so that they, if

7. Cf. Gamillscheg, *International Encyclopaedia of Comparative Law*, l.c., No. 18.

only for this reason, would prefer their own law. Executive and management personnel, for whom transferrals are common, are usually subject to the law at the seat of the enterprise. This connecting factor best corresponds to their vital interest that the proper law does not change with every new place of work.

For sailors the rule still prevails that the law of the flag is to be applied, but this is a very doubtful solution.[8]

B. *Lex loci laboris*

15. A strong trend among scholars and judicial bodies which has also found its way into a number of statutes, such as section 51 of the Hungarian Act, deny the parties the option of choosing the law applicable to the employment contract and demand instead a link independent of their intention. The employee – according to the basic idea behind this view – is economically too weak to resist the choice of law imposed by the employer. Thus, this choice would typically deprive the employee of the protection afforded by the law which would normally be applicable. 'Normaly applicable' means the *law of the place of work*.

Many arguments have been assembled to support this view: the oldest explanation is that labour laws are so-called *lois d'ordre public*. This means that they are so important and so closely related to the social order of the state of the forum that their application is mandatory and independent of the proper law of the contract. The effect is the same when labour laws are characterised as *lois de police et de sureté*, a notion derived from Article 3 paragraph 1 of the French Civil Code. Labour laws as *lois de police* are, above all, protective labour laws with public law reinforcement, but not exclusively. Frequently, all mandatory norms, especially those against dismissal, are included under this designation. Another premise is the notion of territoriality. Courts and authors often rely, without further discussion, on the explanation that labour laws are 'territorial'. Yet this notion is very unclear: 'Nobody knows exactly what this means'.[9] Finally, in the context of present judicial trends attention must be drawn to a modern theory, connected, above all, with the names of, *inter alia*, Francescakis, de Nova, Malintoppi, de Winter which categorises norms such as labour law norms into a special class of 'norms with direct applicability'. This dogmatic construction has found its way into Article 7, paragraph 2 of the EEC-Draft and consequently into the German Draft as well.

As already mentioned, the main idea is to protect the worker against an

---

8. Cf. Kahn-Freund, *Rabels Zeitschrift für ausländisches und internationales Privatrecht* 1958, p. 200; Gamillscheg, Internationales Arbeitsrecht, p. 137.
9. So Blanpain/Dumortier, Belgian National Report to the 11th International Congress of Comparative Law, Caracas, 1982, p. 16.

abuse of power by the employer. This fear of abuse with regard to the freedom of contract is enhanced with a growing distrust of large multinational enterprises. So, English legislation, which prescribes the application of the new protective laws to work performed within its boundaries, independent of the proper law, was justified by the wish to extend the advantages of these laws to the employees of the American multinational enterprises working in England.[10]

16. Yet the criticism of party autonomy is unfounded. Freedom of contract under substantive law and the choice of the governing law under the conflict rules are not comparable. When in substantive law a protective norm is excluded (e.g.: severance pay for unfair dismissal), the employee does not receive this protection: instead of X, there is non-X. When, on the other hand, through a choice of law, X (e.g., the law at the place of performance) is excluded in favour of Y (the law at the seat of the enterprise), non-X is, to be sure, still valid, but Y applies with all its protective provisions. We must now, until there is evidence to the contrary, assume that X and Y offer equivalent protection. With this assumption, however, the employer's incentive to abuse his economic and intellectual advantage through the choice of law is lost. On the other hand, the mandatory application of the *lex loci* may be hazardous to an employee who is sent to a country with (a) insufficient social protection; or (b) which delegates the regulation to collective agreements which do not apply *in casu*. Here the protection, which, for fear of abuse, the denial of the freedom of choice is intended to assure, results in the reverse.

Furthermore, even when the legal system at a distant place of work is socially comparable, it is often an unknown factor for all involved. This uncertainty concerning the legal position may deter an employee, even more than is already the case, from seeking judicial vindication of his rights, and his union will only rarely be in a position to give proper advice and assistance. The judge, for his part, will be compelled to obtain costly expert opinions on the foreign law involved even when the dispute concerns a matter that is clear under domestic law and the ties to the overseas place of work have long been disrupted. Finally, it should be borne in mind that in all developed labour law systems judges are accustomed, in one form or another, to reviewing the fairness of the provisions contained in the employment contract, so that agreements through which the interests of the employee may be unfairly violated are treated as null and void. On the other hand, rigid reliance on the legal provisions at the place of work will, in comparison, give the employer the same possibilities for abuse. Many important employee issues, such as protection against dismissal, competition after termination of the employment relationship, rights to employee inventions, pensions, etc. could be manipulated by say, sending an employee – especially professional and managerial employees – to countries which offer

---

10. Cf. Hepple/O'Higgins, *op. cit.*, no. 731.

less protection. When it is within the employer's power to direct such a transfer the employee will be obliged to comply. Evidence that the transfer was made *in fraudem legis* will not be adducible in all cases.

C. Article 6 of the EEC-Draft

17. Still distrusting party autonomy as such for fear of abuse by the employer, yet mindful of the deficiencies of the place of work as the only connecting factor, the EEC-Draft steers a middle course which seeks to offer the employee a maximum of protection: Party autonomy is not excluded, but it works only in favour of the employee. The *proper law* as such, in the absence of choice, is determined in the following way, Article 6, paragraph 2 EEC:

> '. . . an employment contract shall, in the absence of choice in accordance with Article 3, be governed:
> (a) by the law of the country in which the employee habitually carries out his work in performance of the contract, even if he is temporarily employed in another country; or
> (b) if the employee does not habitually carry out his work in any one country, by the law of the country in which the place of business through which he was engaged is situated;
> *unless* it appears from the circumstances as a whole that the contract is more closely connected with another country, in which case the contract shall be governed by the law of that country.'

Thus the authors of the Draft no longer insist upon the place of work as the sole connecting factor. Another country may be more closely connected with the contract.

Note: The place of work is not only rejected where the other connecting factor is 'manifestly' more intrinsic to the contract. Of two connecting factors the more intrinsic one is adopted.

Yet there is no doubt that the place of work is the rule and the 'unless'-clause the exception.

The 'unless'-clause will permit the actual practice to continue of applying the law of the home State of the employment contracts of people who are sent abroad by their company (permanently or with the intention of returning to continue work at home).

The case is open when an employer of X engages a co-citizen of X in country Y where the employee resides, as when an American company engages in Brussels an American citizen living in Brussels for work in Belgium.

Whether this employee's contract is more closely connected with the United States or with Belgium may depend on additional factors; thus the judge will be more inclined to apply American law with a high-ranking manager than with a blue-collar worker.

18. If the parties choose a law other than that which is described in Article 6, paragraph 2, the choice is valid, but '. . . shall not have the result of depriving the employee of the protection afforded to him by the mandatory rules of the law which would be applicable under paragraph 2 in the absence of choice' (Article 6, paragraph 1).

Thus a new idea, the *principle of the most favourable law*, has achieved a breakthrough. Its purpose is to prevent abuse of the freedom of contract as well as to allay misgivings about submitting the employment contract to an unfamiliar or underdeveloped local law. This theory involves the joint application of both legal systems. The employee is entitled to claim the norm more favourable to him. In this way the well-known Labour Law principle of the most favourable law seems to be incorporated into Conflict Law. This solution has also been adopted in section 44, paragraph 3 of the Austrian Law on Private International Law and Article 74 of the Argentinian Draft of a Law of Private International Law.

Yet reliance on the principle of the more favourable law is not a good solution. In substantive labour law it is used to decide when norms and formative factors in the labour relationship of different levels of authority require simultaneous application: The statute (conferring e.g. a minimum of three weeks vacation) gives way to the more favourable rule agreed upon at a lower level (i.e. collective agreement or employment contract: four weeks). On the other hand, in German law, where these questions have been dealt with most thoroughly, it is undisputed that this principle is not valid when norms on an equal level (e.g. two collective agreements) conflict. This is particularly true of temporal succession: a new collective agreement replaces the former even if the former was more favourable to the employee. Where two concurring collective agreements are simultaneously in effect, there are also several ways of handling the problem; but the principle of the most favourable law is expressly excluded as a possible solution.

The same must apply in a clash between two legal systems existing side by side. They are, as explained above, considered to be in principle equal, even though different in their respective norms. System A might extend less protection against dismissal, but on the other hand a higher standard wage intended to cover this risk. System B emphasises job security with a lower salary level. It would not be reasonable to suggest that the few employees who enter into a legal relationship with contacts to A and B should enjoy the advantages of both legal systems, higher salaries *and* absolute job security.

Another example may be furnished by paid holidays. Suppose that in the state of common nationality ('the sending state') the national law of which has been agreed upon by the parties, some 12 Christian holidays are to be kept without loss of pay, whilst work is done in a Muslim State with 10 other paid holidays: Is our worker entitled to 22 such luxurious days? Or, to push the example to the absurd: is a construction worker working in an Arab country under a German employment contract entitled to weekly rest on Friday (like the rest of the people working on the site) and to the 50 per cent bonus for Sunday work according to the collective agreement that was settled in the home country? The answer is clearly no in both cases.

The objection to the cumulation of advantages could only be avoided by comparing the legal systems in question as a whole. Such a global comparison is, however, impossible. It would be arbitrary in the extreme to suggest that the English or the German or the law of New York or that of Saudi Arabia were best.

Where the principle of the most favourable law to be introduced, the employer would lose all interest in a choice of law, for that would only cost him money. What would remain would be the rule of the law of the place of work with all the disadvantages described above (combined according to Article 6 of the European Draft with all the uncertainties of the 'unless' clause).

IV. THE SPHERE OF APPLICATION OF THE PROTECTIVE NORMS WITH PUBLIC LAW CHARACTER

19. Most legal systems are familiar with the above (*supra* paragraph 2) described classification of protective labour law norms into (1) mandatory norms to be enforced by courts or through the ordinary grievance procedure; and (2) protective provisions of such social and political importance that their enforcement is entrusted to special authorities (factory inspectorates, governmental agencies etc.), including penalties for non-observance and extending to closure of the plant. These categories remain in use even though the distinction between private and public law, as such, is not universally accepted. We should now attempt to bring the application of both these types of provisions into a coherent system.

(1) The *jurisdiction of domestic authorities* is limited territorially. Each authority enjoys the power of enforcement only within the boundaries of the state which has set it up: Any direct activity abroad, such as supervision of violations of domestic legislation at a place of work beyond the frontiers, would be a violation of the sovereignty of that state where the work is being carried out. For example, a factory inspector of state A may not cross the border into state B in order to close a site there because of its insalubrity, even if the majority of persons employed there are border-crossers (citizens of state A).

(2) The limitation sub (1) does not mean that the local authority or court is prevented from trying to obtain results abroad through pressure exercised at home. Employers may, indeed, be compelled to act in the desired manner by means of all appropriate measures. For example, a company the seat of which is in country A may be penalised in order to compel it to introduce the necessary hygienic standards at the site in B.

(3) This does not mean that the courts and authorities extend at will the scope of their own public labour law. It goes without saying that no one wants to establish a world law. Therefore, in practice the concept prevails that public protective labour law or its equivalent and administrative labour law may in principle only be applied if the work is *performed within the state*. The sphere of validity and sphere of application, the jurisdiction of the factory inspectorate and the execution of the norm all come together.

(4) At times, a protective public law norm only concerns the relationship between the employer and the state (e.g. the obligation to allow factory inspectors on the premises or to maintain a register). Most often, however, it includes prohibitions and obligations in favour of the employee, which could just as well be included in the employment contract (e.g. prohibition of employment for more than eight hours daily). This *private law core* of the public law norm may form a part of the employer's duty of care and therefore be a part of the appropriate law. This situation opens the way for the application of public law to work performed (mostly by nationals) abroad. Of course the extent to which protective domestic norms are to be included in the appropriate law depends on the conditions at the place of work and cannot be addressed by a general rule. In any case, in the absence of an analogous norm abroad (or when the norm in effect there does not apply *in casu*), nothing prevents its being enforced as part of the duty of care or even as an implied provision of the employment contract.

(5) Officials may neither exercise their authority nor perform administrative acts in a foreign state, nor will local authorities act on their behalf unless obliged to do so under an active treaty between the two states.

Whether local courts take into consideration the orders and prohibitions in effect at a foreign place of performance depends upon the nature of these norms. Here, too, the protective social provisions will have what we have called a 'private core'. In so far as this core affects the relation between employer and employee, consideration may be given to it by the judge of the forum and an attempt must be made to harmonise this set of rules with the proper law of the contract.[11]

20. The EEC-Draft, though it does not contain any precise rules on these questions, nevertheless opens the gate for consideration of all the propositions described above (1)–(5). As concerns the public (or otherwise cogent) norms of the forum, Article 7, paragraph 2 declares:

'Nothing in this Convention shall restrict the application of the rules of the law of the forum in a situation where they are

---

11. For more details see Gamillscheg, Internationales Arbeitsrecht, l.c. paragraph 11 (= Revue critique de droit international privé 1961, pp. 265, 477, 677).

mandatory irrespective of the law otherwise applicable to the contract.'

With regard to the application of the private core of the respective norms of the foreign place of work, Article 7, paragraph 1 reads:

'When applying under this Convention the law of a country, effect may be given to the mandatory rules of the law of another country with which the situation has a close connection, if and in so far as, under the law of the latter country, those rules must be applied whatever the law applicable to the contract. In considering whether to give effect to these mandatory rules, regard shall be had to their nature and purpose and to the consequences of their application or non-application.'

The words 'effect may be given' emphasise that all is left to the discretion of the judge, so that there is no obstacle to the development of sensible rules in this unexplored field of conflict of laws.

V. THE SCOPE OF THE PROPER LAW

21. Questions of *qualification*, e.g. the correct classification of the relevant legal issue or norm into the categories of private international law, are not infrequent in international labour law. For example, unjust dismissal may be viewed under one system as a breach of the labour contract, in another as a tort, in a third as a question of industrial relations and in still another as a breach of a collective agreement.

It is generally accepted that such questions of classification are decided according to the *lex fori*. This means that the ideas of the law of the forum govern. Of course this is, like every aspect of private international law, highly controversial.

22. In many systems, the *legal capacity* to conclude contracts is determined separately. Thus, e.g. the continental European systems rely on the nationality of the subject; in other countries, like the United States, legal capacity is determined by the proper law.

International labour law is in keeping with this rule. The question is not unimportant since employment contracts are often entered into by minors and the legal systems concerned facilitate the conclusion of such contracts by various means, e.g. by reducing the age limit or presuming the existence of parental consent.

Local rules on legal capacity are often held to be applicable in order to protect local commerce, cf. Article 11 of the EEC-Draft. In the field of employment law, the solution is, however, open to doubts: it does not sufficiently take into consideration that the protection of commerce must be weighed against the protection of the under-aged employee.

23. According to general opinion the *form* of the employment contract or other agreements and declarations (e.g., agreement on competition; notice, etc.), is based on the principle *locus regit actum* together with any supplementary provisions, cf. Article 9 paragraph 1 of the European Draft. In so asserting, it is overlooked that this rule owes its origin to the desire to facilitate the conclusion of contracts (*favor negotii*), while in labour law the purpose of form stems primarily from the desire to protect the worker. The result is that any relaxation of the formal requirements in the conclusion of transactions runs directly counter to the purposes of the law. Consequently, the principle embodied in Article 9, 1.c. should be rejected.

24. The following key-words are meant to give the reader an idea of the *subject matter* covered by the proper law of the employment contract: conclusion, nullity, rescission and interpretation of the contract; payments for work completed in the event of void contracts; the employee's obligations of performance and loyalty; limitations on liability for defective work; agreements in restraint of competition; the employer's duty of care; salary; equal treatment; the obligation to pay salaries in the event of non-performance of work (in cases which are covered by social security different solutions may impose themselves); liability of the employer; employee inventions; periods of notice; justification of dismissal, compensation, reinstatement with or without backpay; company pensions, and others.

25. In most countries the application of a foreign law is not left to the discretion of the judge or the parties, though the judge may refer to the parties in order to ascertain the content of the foreign law. Yet foreign law is not to be applied in every case: if it would lead to a result which *in casu* (even taking into consideration that the case is closely connected with the foreign country where a system of different cultural values may exist) would violate elementary principles of justice, it will not be applied: objection of *public policy, ordre public*, the so-called reservation clause. Cf. Article 16 of the EEC-Draft: 'The application of a rule of any country . . . may be refused only if such application is manifestly incompatible with the public policy ("ordre public") of the forum.'

The *ordre public* device functions as an emergency valve alleviating the uncertainty of the content of the foreign law which is to be applied according to the conflict rules. Whether the result is manifestly incompatible with our standards is a question to be answered above all in the light of the fundamental rights and liberties of the employee and the basic principles of a good social order.

Examples would be discrimination based on race, sex or nationality, etc.; failure to compensate for deprivation of vested rights; life-long labour contracts; usury wages; excessive periods of notice or agreements not to compete; insufficient protection against dismissal; excessive penalties; right of the husband to interfere with the wife's employment contract, and so forth. The reservation clause does not apply when the foreign proper law is merely somewhat less favourable than the *lex fori*; it must be a 'manifest' disadvantage. For instance, it has been decided that the Belgian *ordre public* was not violated when a commercial agent under German law received no severance pay or again, when a period of notice under Nigerian law was reduced to one day. German courts have often applied American law in regard to notice, even though the German law would have granted somewhat broader claims. Differences between the political systems in East and West are not sufficient reason to fall back on the public policy device.[12]

VI. COLLECTIVE LABOUR LAW (INDUSTRIAL RELATIONS)

26. Up until now the international aspects of collective labour law have been widely neglected. Few attempts to elucidate the subject have been made. It would be premature, therefore, to present a set of rules; however, a number of suggestions may be proffered.[13]

27. Not infrequently *collective agreements* on the regulation of work done abroad are concluded in a specific country between unions and employer organisations or companies. Thus, the collective agreement receives an extra-territorial quality. No 'territoriality' or similar concept should be a hindrance to this. A separate question is how far a general agreement concluded to regulate work within the country extends to employees working for the company (temporarily or habitually) abroad.

28. Strikes and lock-outs are so closely related to the public order of the place of the dispute that no other legal system could possibly apply. Hence, the law relating to industrial disputes is territorial. This law also determines the private law consequences of participation in the dispute. Nevertheless, a more favourable regulation included in the proper law should prevail.

29. The sphere of application of the legislation on *works constitution* is usually unilaterally determined according to the principle of territoriality in a statutory system, as in FR Germany or France. Thus the German Works Constitution Act governs enterprises in FR Germany, the French provisions enterprises in France, and so forth. No universal rule envisaging the

---

12. See textbooks on private international law; Gamillscheg, Internationales Arbeitsrecht, l.c., par. 7; Dumortier, l.c., *passim*.
13. Cf. also Lyon-Caen/Lyon-Caen, l.c.; Birk, *Rabels Zeitschrift*, l.c., p. 404; *idem*, Internationales Tarifvertragsrecht, in: Festschrift für Günther Beitzke (1979) p. 831; *idem*, Grenzüberschreitende Streikabwehr, in: Internationale Gedächtnisschrift für Otto Kahn-Freund (1980) p. 21; Gamillscheg, Internationales Arbeitsrecht, l.c., paras. 16, 17.

application, or even consideration, of some kind of foreign plant representation law has yet, so far as I know, been developed.

In consequence, the Federal Labour Court has declared void the dismissal in FR Germany of a foreigner employed under foreign law on the grounds that the works council was not consulted, as required under German law. The authority of the works council also covers employees transferred abroad temporarily, but does not cover those employees who are permanently working abroad. The mere fact that their employment relationship is subject to German law makes no difference.

Under section 106 of the Works Constitution Act, the information due to the works council in economic matters is delegated to the so-called economic committee (*Wirtschaftsausschuß*). If the seat of the company is situated abroad, an economic committee cannot be formed there or meet there; but if the enterprise has one or more domestic factories with a work force totalling more than 100, the smallest number under section 106, then the economic committee must be established for the benefits of the domestic staff, the information being limited to matters affecting and concerning them. If an enterprise with its seat of business abroad has several plants in France, a central work's council (*Comité central d'enterprise*) must be set up for them.[14]

The private international law aspects for *co-determination* of the employees in the Supervisory Board of the company are questions of international company law. The composition of such a board is, in principle, a question to be decided by the law at the seat of the enterprise. Another option would be to apply the law under which the company was incorporated.

Thus, the sphere of application of the German legislation on co-determination is limited: an enterprise with its seat abroad is not subject to a German 'Mitbestimmung', even where its domestic plants are concerned. On the other hand, enterprises with their seat in the FR Germany are, of course, subject to the act. Nevertheless, there are two important limitations: it is prevailing opinion, with regard to the 1976 Co-determination Act, that persons employed in the foreign plants of a specific enterprise are not to be included in computing the minimum number of employees required under section 1 (2000 employees) and that any such employees have no voting rights in the Supervisory Board elections.

14. See decision of the French Cour de Cassation of 29 June 1973, Droit social 1974, p. 48, and the comments of Francescakis, L'arrêt Compagnie Internationale des Waggons-Lits, *Revue critique de droit international privé* 1974, p. 273, and Dumortier, l.c., p. 346.

F. GAMILLSCHEG

SELECT BIBLIOGRAPHY

Acts of the 11th International Congress of Comparative Law, Caracas, 1982 (forthcoming).

R. Birk, 'Das internationale Arbeitsrecht der Bundesrepublik Deutschland', *Rabels Zeitschrift für ausländisches und internationales Privatrecht*, 1982, pp. 384–420.

J. Dumortier, *Arbeidsverhoudingen in het Internationaal Privaatrecht*, 1981, Antwerpen, 409 pp.

F. Gamillscheg, *Internationales Arbeitsrecht (Arbeitsverweisungsrecht)*, 1959, Tübingen, 454 pp.; *idem, International Encyclopaedia of Comparative Law*, vol. III, *Private International Law*, ch. 28 *Labour Contracts*, Tübingen/Paris. 28 pp.; idem, 'Rules of public order in private international labour law', *Académie de Droit International*, La Haye, Recueil des Cours, vol. 181, pp. 289–347.

O. Kahn-Freund, 'Notes on the conflict of laws in relation to employment in English and Scottish law', *Selected Writings* (1978), London, pp. 259–272.

G. and A. Lyon-Caen, *Droit social international et européen* (5th ed.), 1980, Paris, 423 pp.

F. Morgenstern, *International Conflicts of Labour Law*, 1984. Geneva, 129 pp.

S. Szászy, *International Labour Law*, 1968, Budapest, 465 pp.

Chapter 7. European Communities

G. Schnorr

I. The Contribution of the EC to the Comparison and Integration of Labour Law and Industrial Relations

A. The Legal Foundation

1. The European Communities, i.e. the European Community for Coal and Steel, the European Atomic Community, and the European Economic Community, originally were not instruments for a wide-spread harmonisation or assimilation of national labour law upon the basis of a minimum standard as is the ILO. Their purposes are economic. Nevertheless, the Treaty founding the European Economic Community (EEC Treaty) provides for a limited competence of the organs of the Community in social policy in as far as the achievement of the economic aims of the Common Market depends on the solution of social problems. As far as this connection of economic and social problems is concerned, comparison and integration of the labour law systems and industrial relations of the Member States have also become evident within the EC.

2. Thus Article 117 of the EEC Treaty affirms in a general manner that the Member States agree to the necessity of promoting an improvement in living and working conditions, hence making possible their harmonisation in a progressive direction. But at the same time there is an economic link, for the Member States express in the second paragraph of Article 117 their view that such social development will result from the efficiency of the Common Market, as well as from the harmonisation of legal and administrative provisions.

3. There are, furthermore, several specific functions of the Community organs aiming at a closer integration of national labour law systems, although with a different intensity (see paragraphs 9–12). According to Article 118 EEC Treaty the Commission has the general function of promoting close co-operation between the Member States in social affairs. Article 119 of the EEC Treaty obliges the Member States to apply and to maintain the principle of equal pay for men and women for equal work in accordance with the principle of the rate for the job; and Article 120 of the EEC Treaty obliges the Member States to maintain existing national policies on paid holidays. Articles 48 and 49 of the EEC Treaty instituting free movement of workers and a common labour market not only provide

113

for administrative measures but also touch national labour law, mainly as far as equal legal treatment of foreign workers in relation to indigenous workers is concerned.

4. There are, finally, certain economic provisions of the EEC Treaty which imply powers for harmonising the respective labour law of the Member States. Thus Article 75 subsection 1c of the EEC Treaty empowers the Council to issue all regulations necessary to achieve the aims of a common traffic policy. There can be no doubt that this power also covers the issue of regulations on labour law for professional drivers in so far as their social situation will be affected by the common policy on motor-vehicles; for as long as the national provisions obliging employers in traffic to workers' protection differ from one another, they will hinder the efforts for a common policy on international traffic. Indeed the EC Court of Justice has stated that the issue of labour law traffic provisions by the competent organs of the EC is covered by the warrant of Article 75 of the EEC Treaty and, therefore, not contrary to it if the labour law provisions at the same time are connected with road safety.[1] Similarly, according to Article 39 of the EEC Treaty the optimal use of agricultural manpower is one of the aims of a common policy on agriculture. In order to achieve this aim, Articles 41 lit. a and 43 subsection 2 of the EEC Treaty imply measures for an efficient co-ordination of vocational training in agriculture.

5. During the first decade of the EC all these social provisions were interpreted restrictively. European politicians and officials believed that social problems would be solved automatically by increasing economic integration, as Article 117 subsection 2 of the EEC Treaty[2] had foreseen. This was an error.

Experience has shown that economic integration also creates situations which are unfavourable for social development and which, therefore, are contradictory to the necessity of promoting an improvement in the living and working conditions as provided for in Article 117 subsection 1 of the EEC Treaty. Therefore, the joint Presidents and Premiers of the Member States at their 'summit conference' in Paris in October 1972, elaborated principles for wider activities of the EC in the social field. These principles were laid down in detail in the *'programme on social activities'* concluded by the Council on 21 January 1974.[3]

6. The consequence of this social program is that measures for the comparison and harmonisation of the labour law of the Member States have steadily increased within the framework of the EC. On the one hand, the obligation of Article 117 subsection 1 of the EEC Treaty to promote an improvement

1. EC Court of Justice No. 97/98, Collection 1978, p. 2311.
2. For a theoretical discussion of the meaning of Article 117 EEC Treaty see G. Schnorr and J. Egger, *IELL* (European Communities), 1984, paragraphs 57–62.
3. OB 1974, C 13.

in living and working conditions and hence make possible their progressive harmonisation achieves *a more independent importance*. On the other hand, *subsidiary functions* which allow the Community organs to legislate even in the absence of specific jurisdiction if this becomes necessary either for the institution or the functioning of the Common Market (Article 100 of the EEC Treaty) or for realising the aims of the Common Market (Article 235 of the EEC Treaty) become more relevant to labour law.

7. Thus we see that comparison and integration of labour law is a task of the EC, based on a complicated system of international contractual rules of the EEC Treaty and intimately connected with the economic situation of the Common Market.

B. Practice

1. The Specific Means of Comparison and Integration

8. A most important difference between the theoretical method of comparing law and the practical functions of the EC must be viewed. Whereas theoretical comparison permits contemplation of the systematic whole, the functions of the EC in the field of comparison and integration of labour law are sporadic. They depend on various imponderables such as socio-economic necessity within the limits of competence indicated above; the opportunity to achieve a particular political result; the estimation of the importance of the subject by the managing functionaries of the Community organs; and so forth.

9. The visible and proper aspects of the EC in the field of labour law consist in creating a uniform or at least harmonised labour law by *supra-national legislation*. The means for this are directives and regulations. Both are obligatory. But whereas directives only indicate the aims to be achieved and oblige the Member States to issue the necessary legislative measures, regulations are binding in full upon individuals living within the Common Market. These are 'transnational'. (See Article 189 of the EEC Treaty.) In labour law, the possibilities of harmonisation by directives outweigh the possibilities of harmonising through regulations.

10. But it would be illusory to think that the activities of the EC in comparing and harmonising labour law rest exclusively with supra-national legislation. There is a wide field of activities which can be subordinated under the theme of this text.

11. First of all, the *annual social report* elaborated by the EC Commission is not only an account of the activities of the Community, but it also compares the development of labour legislation and working conditions within the

particular Member States. Thus, EC policy may in time find remedies to imperfect socio-economic evolutions. In 1980, for instance, the reduction of working hours in connection with the problem of unemployment as well as the problem of achieving a greater humanisation of work stood at the centre of the comparative element of the review of labour conditions.[4]

12. Furthermore, many activities of the EC Commission and its experts[5] do not generate supra-national legislation immediately, but they aim in part at improved *co-operation of national legislators in labour law*, in part at the *issuing of programmes or recommendations* accentuating the standpoint of the Community on a certain subject, in part at finding *new ideas* in developing a common labour law. An example of the first activity is the planned 'guidelines for common action in the field of temporary work'.[6] An example of the second activity is the very important 'activities programme on safety and protection of workers' health' of 29 June 1978.[7] The third activity is manifested by many of the juridical and sociological studies, often unpublished, elaborated by the above-mentioned experts. All these activities are based on the function of the EC Commission according to Article 118 EEC Treaty to promote closer co-operation between the Member States in labour law.

2. The Process Itself: Political rather than Legal

13. We will not describe the formal path of an action for harmonisation before it becomes effective. This has been done in chapter 1 'Comparativism in Labour Law and Industrial Relations' of this book. Rather we shall describe the background of this process and the problems it raises.

14. First of all each harmonising action of the Community implies intervention in the structure of national labour law. It is clear that every Member State wants its national labour law to be modified as little as possible by actions of the Community. Each Member State regards its labour law as reflecting its best interests. As the Community organs do not perform their actions authoritatively – but only after long discussion with national experts, the Governmental representatives of the so-called standing group, and the European trade unions and employers' associations – the results are often *political compromises* which do not completely correspond to the strictly systematic view of a theorist of comparative law. This means that the

---

4. EC Commission, *Report on Social Development*, 1980, paragraphs 137–145.
5. See above, chapter 1.
6. See *Social Report* 1980, paragraph 11. On 7 May 1982 the Commission transmitted a proposal for a Directive on the harmonisation of the provisions of the Member States on temporary work (OB 1982, C 128, in the wording of the amended proposal of OB 1984, C 133).
7. OB 1978, C 165.

process of comparison and integration of labour law within the EC cannot be measured by the exact methods of comparativism but only by the dynamic views of politicians.

15. This political point of view is reflected in elaborating *drafts of directives*. There is discussed how much detail the content of a directive should entail, and what scope should remain to the national legislation of the Member States. Some hold that the content of directives must be limited to the aims to be achieved by them; the means to realise these aims must be left to national legislators. This was long the view of the 'legal service' of the EC Commission. But we think, with most politicians and officials of the EC, that directives may also contain principles or alternatives regarding the means to be employed in achieving the prescribed aims. This is necessary unless the Member States are to be encouraged to choose those means which are inefficient in achieving the specified aims solely in order to protect their national legislative system against the requirements of the EC.

16. The answer to the question of how much detail the content of a directive must entail to be efficient depends, on the one hand, on the subject to be regulated and, on the other hand, on the political situation. Generally speaking, we can distinguish *three alternatives*.

17. It may be that different models of the subject whose regulation the EC intends already exist in the legislation of some Member States. In this case it is often difficult to agree on a single model. Here the EC limits itself to issuing a directive which regulates the *subject in a rather flexible way* which covers all existing models. The purpose of such a directive is, on the one hand, to prevent a Member State from abolishing their regulation of the subject and, on the other hand, to compel those Member States which have not yet regulated it, to decide on one model for their legislation. A significant example is Directive No. 80/987/EEC[8] by which the Member States are obliged to establish institutions to satisfy unmet claims of workers as a result of the insolvency of the employer. Considering that such institutions already exist in the majority of the Member States, although with differences, the directive permits a wide choice of alternatives in regulating them.

18. On the other hand, it may be that a regulation existing by means of Community law or by means of national law may not function satisfactorily. In this case the EC sees itself as obliged to issue directives which regulate the *subject in detail*. Thus, equal treatment as well as non-discrimination against men and women with regard to pay and employment did not function adequately within the Member States, despite the fact that the EC Court of Justice had stated that the principle of equal pay would be a

---

8. OB 1980, L 283.

directly binding right in the Member States according to Article 119 of the EEC Treaty, that the concerned litigant parties could appeal to it through domestic courts, and that the latter would be obliged to apply it to all facts.[9] The EC, therefore, issued two directives to regulate this problem, especially the legal consequences of a violation of the right to equal treatment.[10]

19. The greatest difficulty arises when an idea is to be realised at Community level which does not yet form part of the common experience of the Member States. A significant example is the achievement of uniform co-determination of workers' representatives in the enterprises (see below paragraph 43ff). Another example is the uniform guarantee of claims to or prospects of old age pension systems supplementary to the legal old age pensions of the social security systems. In these cases the Community organs often limit themselves to a *vague encouragement to the Member States to consider appropriate measures*. See, for instance, Article 8 of Directive No. 80/987/EEC by which the Member States are only obliged to ascertain that, in the event of insolvency of an employer, 'necessary measures may be taken to protect the interests of the employees and persons respective to their claims to or prospects of industrial or supra-industrial supplementary old age pension systems'. This is too vague to expect rapid harmonisation on this question.

3. The Role of Participants (Governments, Trade Unions, Employers' Associations, Organs and Departments of the EC)

20. As we have noted, the process of integration within the EC is a political rather than a juridicial one. Hence it follows that all participants in this process play their proper political roles. A new project for integration is, as a rule, initiated by the competent service of the Commission, especially by its senior civil servants who know best when the provisions of the EEC Treaty make integration necessary. But, although seldom, such initiatives also come from interpellations of the members of the European Parliament or the Economic and Social Committee. Thus, the discussions continuing for the past ten years on harmonising national provisions on temporary work[11] were originally initiated by an interpellation to the European Parliament arguing that temporary workers did not enjoy equal security of their living standards with ordinary workers. This interpellation led first to a volumi-

---

9. EC Court of Justice No. 43/75, Collection 1976, p. 455.
10. Directive No. 75/117 on the harmonisation of the provisions of the Member States on the application of the principle of equal pay for men and women (OB 1975, L 45), and Directive No. 76/207 on the realisation of the principle of equal treatment of men and women concerning access to occupation, vocational education and vocational rise and also concerning terms of employment (OB 1976, L. 39).
11. See '*Social Report 1980*' *op. cit.*, paragraph 11.

nous study of harmonisation in 1971 which has been translated into several languages.[12]

21. The groups of national experts who are asked by the competent service of the Commission to perform comparative analysis and to elaborate a draft instrument for harmonisation still do this in a theoretical and systematic way. But subsequently, the hearings of the standing group of Governmental representatives and, above all, of the trade unions and the employers' associations reveal basic political contradictions. Not only are national interests accentuated within the standing group of Governmental representatives but also in the hearing of the trade unions and the employers' associations are contrary opinions expressed. Thus, the introduction of European co-determination in certain enterprises has been wrecked by opposing views, some wishing independent enterprise committees of workers to be introduced, while others required a central role for trade unions in co-determination within enterprises, for they feared that politically aligned trade unions would be overshadowed by independent enterprise committees. Thus, only a compromise could lead to harmonisation.

II. THE LACK OF A SYSTEMATIC BASIS FOR COMPARISON

22. As the EC have limited power in the sphere of labour law, the legal system of labour law and industrial relations as well as the determination of fundamental terms remains at the discretion of the Member States. The EC, therefore, can never achieve a uniform supra-national labour law but must limit itself to more or less intermittent supra-national legislation justified by the provisions of the EEC Treaty. Hence a problem arises; for the efficiency of the execution of supra-national legal instruments depends on how adequately they may be incorporated into the system of national labour law as a whole. We may illustrate this by two examples:

23. The *definition of labour law* as well as of the terms 'employers' and 'employees' has been left to national legal regulation. The supra-national legal instruments of the EC do not, therefore, provide definitions. Thus it may occur that the same supra-national legal instrument is differently applied according to the different definitions of labour law in the Member States. Thus, there are various conclusions as to whether or not domestic servants, apprentices, or persons who work personally independently but who are economically independent on an employer are employees under the provisions of labour law.

---

12. G. Schnorr, 'Le Travail Temporaire – Analyse du droit des Etats membres des Communautés européennes et propositions relatives à un rapprochement des législations', *Cahiers de droit européen*, 1973, pp. 131–183.

24. Again, the Commission of the EC has long endeavoured to achieve a uniform co-determination of workers' representatives in the organs of commercial companies. This is dealt with in a 'Green Paper on Employee Participation and Company Structure in the EC. The problem here is whether co-determination can be realised without *harmonising the national law of commercial companies* or whether a unification of the different national structures of company law is a condition for such regulation of co-determination.

25. This shows how complex is the problem of harmonisation or unification of labour law. We think that its resolution may arise from many different sources.

26. Firstly, experience shows an increasing assimilation of the fundamental categorieis of labour law. This seems to be caused both by similar socio-economic situations and by the operations of the ILO, the harmonising effects of which have also become evident within the EC.[13] A significant example here is the evolution of labour law in the United Kingdom. Here we can observe a turning away from traditional common law in favour of the enacting of specific labour law provisions by Parliament.

27. Secondly, the EEC Treaty itself has some regard to the possibilities of creating conditions for efficient supra-national labour legislation. Thus, the above-mentioned problem of co-determination of workers in the organs of commercal companies can be regarded in connection with Article 220 of the EEC Treaty, which promotes bargaining between the Member States in respect of improving the international functioning of commercial companies. Indeed, since 1972 there has existed a draft convention between the Member States, based on Article 220 of the EEC Treaty, which will regulate international mergers of joint-stock companies.

28. Thirdly, the role which the EC Court of Justice could play in harmonising fundamental definitions in labour law should not be undervalued. It is true that this Court has up to now had no occasion for such fundamental jurisdiction. But the jurisdiction which the Court has developed in similar arena of social security affirms that this is not beyond all probability. In this field the Court established uniform definitions of 'employers' and 'employees' by interpretations which seem acceptable at European level. As there is great similarity between definitions in labour law and the law on social security, it seems likely that those definitions could also be useful for labour law.

---

13. An opinion of the Economic and Social Committee deals with the harmonising effect of the ILO Conventions, especially between the EC and the 'Third World' (OB 1980, C 230).

III. PROJECTS, RESULTS, SUCCESS

A. *Collective Labour Law and Industrial Relations*

29. There has been little supra-national legislation up until now. There are, however, facts, projects, and models which are worth mentioning.

1. Employers' Associations and the Trade Union Movement
   at the European Level

30. Employers' and employees' associations already exist at EC level. They are formed by the affiliated national confederations of employers' associations and of trade unions and function as their European central organisations. Each national confederation delegates representatives to them.

31. Whereas the *employers* possess a *number of organisations* at the level of the EC, the most important of which is the 'Union of Industries of the EC' (UNICE), the *employees* adopted the principle of a *'unitary trade union movement'*, represented by the 'European Trade Union Confederation' (ETUC). There are, however, few intermediary or branch trade unions at the European level.[14]

32. The functions of European employers' associations and trade unions are not comparable to those of the national ones, as there is neither collective bargaining nor co-determination at supra-national level. However, they do play an important role in their consultations with the organs of the EC and especially as pressure groups.[15]

2. European Collective Bargaining

33. The possibilities of achieving European collective bargaining have been discussed since 1961. Then a group of experts at the EC Commission dealt with them for the first time. A second attempt to master the problem was made by a meeting of experts organised by the Commission in December 1969 at Milan. The promotion of collective bargaining on the European level as an obligation of the organs of the EC is also an element of the 'programme on social activities' of 1974 (see above paragraphs 5 and 6). But the problems are too great for any hope of immediate realisation.

34. These problems concern the capacity for concluding European collective agreements, the methods of collective bargaining (by European model

14. See chapters 6 and 11 for details.
15. See E.J. Kirchner, *Trade Unions as a Pressure Group in the European Community*, Farnborough, 1978.

collective agreements or by directly binding European collective agreements), the mandatory effects of European collective agreements and, finally, their relations to mandatory national legislation.[16]

35. Discussions have taken place as to how far the working conditions are worth regulating by European collective agreements. It is clear that most working conditions are so inter-connected with the different standards of living and economic situations in the particular countries and regions that they could not be treated uniformly by supra-national provisions.

36. As a matter of fact, there are two attempts to realise European collective agreements. Firstly, the organisations in agriculture, COPA and EFA, have agreed upon *European model collective agreements on particular conditions of work in agriculture*, above all on working time. Secondly, the draft regulation on a *Statute for a European Company*[17] confers on the European Company in its Articles 146 and 147 the capacity to contract European collective agreements with the trade unions represented in its enterprises and provides that such collective agreements are obligatory for all members of the participating trade unions. The problems will be similar to those described above.[18]

3. Workers' Participation

37. As to workers' participation in enterprise management, the differences between the labour law systems of the Member States are so great[19] that harmonisation at European level must be supported by new ideas which will be acceptable to all Member States. Thus the organs of the EC promote workers' participation in a cautious manner. It is not the institutions – shop stewards or independent works councils – which are the main point of discussion. This can be left to the discretion of national legislation. But the *functions* of the workers' representatives in the enterprises, their decision-making power, is a problem for harmonisation. The possibilities vary between the two positions of *joint consultation*, on the one hand, and of *co-determination* or co-decision, on the other. The former type only requires that workers' representatives be consulted by management in certain social or economic areas, without the necessity of agreement and without a binding effect of the opinion of workers' representatives. With co-determination or co-decision, on the contrary, the management may not take

---

16. See for details G. Schnorr, *Arbeits- und sozialrechtliche Fragen der europäischen Integration*, Berlin, 1974.
17. *Bulletin* of the EC, Supplement 4/1975.
18. See G. Schnorr, 'Die Kollektivvertragsfähigkeit der Europäischen Aktiengesellschaft – Modell oder Illusion?', *Festschrift für G. Weiszenberg*, Wien/München/Zürich, 1980, pp. 201–215.
19. See below, chapters 11–13.

certain measures without the consent of the workers' representatives. In other words: joint consultation is non-competitive, its results are non-obligatory. Co-determination is competitive, it is a condition of legally effective decision-making by management.

38. The present attempts of the Community organs to introduce uniform participation of workers' representatives vary between joint consultation and co-determination. They are, moreover, limited to such cases of international concern in which changes of the organisation of the enterprise cause social hardship for the employees. Thus, Article 6 of the *Directive No. 77/187* of 14 February 1977, *on the harmonisation of the provisions of the Member States on the protection of workers' claims in the case of the transfer of enterprise, factories or parts of factories*[20] provides that both the transferrer and the transferee of an enterprise, a factory or part of a factory must inform employees of the planned transfer, especially of the motive for transfer, its legal, economic, and social consequences for the employees, and the measures to be taken concerning them. If on the occasion of the transfer modifications of the terms of employment are taken into account the transferrer or respectively the transferee must through consultation aim at agreement with the workers' representatives to avoid or to mitigate the social consequences of transfer. The obligation of the management to reach agreement with the workers' representatives is surely more than a joint consultation. But if the agreement fails there is no sanction in the Directive to compel the parties to come to an agreement. In this case the transferrer or respectively the transferee is free to take the measures which seem appropriate. This, on the other hand, is less than co-determination. The question of whether such compulsion by an authority to agree is given must be answered by the different national laws.

39. This has become a model for other draft instruments of the Community organs. Thus, the proposal of the Commission for a Regulation on the *European Co-operative Association*[21] provided in its arts. 1a and 16a that the associating companies or persons must inform their employees concerning the planned constitution or dissolution of the Co-operative Association and reach agreement with the workers' representatives in order to avoid or to mitigate social hardship caused by the constitution or dissolution. Nevertheless, *Regulation No. 2137/85 of July 25, 1985,* on the now renamed *European Association of Economic Interest*[22] has cancelled the mentioned arts. 1a and 16a, but emphasizes that labour and social law provisions laid down in the legal orders of the EC and the Member States still are effective although not covered by Regulation No. 2137/85. Another interesting example is *Draft EC Directive on procedures for informing and consulting*

20. OB 1977, L 61.
21. OB 1978, C 103.
22. OB 1985, L 199.

employees (the 'Vredeling Directive').[23] According to this draft the central board of a parent company must inform the managements of its subsidiaries of details such as structure, economic and financial situation, presumptive development of business-, production-, marketing-, employment situation and investment, etc., once every year at least. The management of each subsidiary must pass this information to their workers' representatives. If a decision would, in the view of the workers' representatives, directly influence the terms of employment, the management of the subsidiary company is obliged, after providing further information, to consult with a view to reaching agreement with the workers' representatives. This proposal goes a step further. It obliges the Member States to provide for measures which enable workers' representatives to have their interests protected by a national court of justice or authority. After many discussions, the Commission has been requested by the Council[24] to reopen consultations about the 'Vredeling Proposal' early in 1989 and to observe the development of relevant provisions in the Member States meanwhile.

40. Co-determination in a strict sense has been provided for by the draft Regulation on a *Statute for European Companies* (arts. 100–136).[25] In this new form of supra-national commercial company the German model of codetermination is adopted. In every European Company which has enterprises or workshops in different Member States independent work councils are to be constituted as representatives of the employees.

They are competent in matters which concern two or more enterprises or workshops in different Member States if such subjects cannot be regulated by the workers' representatives constituted according to national law. This means that these 'European works councils' are genuine *supra-national workers' representatives*. Besides the right to information and joint consultation, measures have been provided for which cannot be taken by the management except with consent of the European works council, including principles regulating the appointment, vocational advancement and dismissal of employees; vocational training; the principle and methods of remuneration; industrial safety; the constitution and administration of social welfare institutions; principles governing working time; principles for the distribution of annual vacations. In the event of lack of agreement a *compulsory arbitration procedure* will be carried out. This project is much discussed. The German delegation urges its realization as they fear the escape by German commercial companies to the form of the European company if the latter displays less co-determination than that provided by German law. Other delegations reject it, as they in turn fear a diminution of the autonomy of

---

23. OB 1980, C 297, modified by the Commission's Proposal of 13 July 1983, OB 1983, C 217; see for details Blanpain, '*The Vredeling Proposal*', Deventer, 1983 and Nowak, *Die EWG-Richtlinie über die Unterrichtung und Anhörung der Arbeitnehmer*, Heidelberg, 1985.
24. OB 1986, C 203.
25. Bulletin of the EC, Supplement 4/1975.

national trade unions.[26] In 1988 the Commission plans to propose a new draft on a Statute for European Companies.

41. A special form of co-determination instead of or supplementary to the co-determination of works councils is the representation and co-decision of workers' representatives on the governing boards of companies. This has also been provided for by the Statute for European Companies.[27] It was much discussed by a group of experts of the EC Commission entrusted to elaborate a draft convention on the international fusion of companies.[28] Rejected there, it was again discussed in the 'Green Paper on Employee Participation and Company Structure in the EC',[29] mentioned above (para. 24).

For improving the legal situation of the individual Member States on 9 October 1978, the Council has passed a *Third EC Directive under company law No. 78/855 on the (national) fusion of companies*[30] by which a far reaching coordination of the fusion of joint stock companies has been achieved in the national legal orders of the Member States.

Furthermore, the draft of a *Fifth EC Directive regarding the structure of companies and the powers and obligations of their organs* which has been transmitted by the Commission to the Council on 28 July 1983[31] takes in an outstanding place in the discussion on workers' participation within the EC.[32] This draft gives the national legislator the option to elect between different forms of representation and co-decision of workers' representatives on the governing board of companies according as *dual board systems* (supervisory board and management board are separated) or *single board systems* (board of directors as a management board) are in question. This Directive is said to be passed in 1988.

On EC Directive No. 78/855 a new draft of a *Tenth EC Directive on a fusion of companies beyond the frontiers*[33] is based on, which is said to be passed by the Council in 1987. Art. 1 subsect. 3 of this draft lays down a proviso in favour of workers' participation: until the date of passing of the Fifth EC Directive the Member States are not obliged to apply provisions laid down in the 10th EC Directive so far as such application would involve

---

26. See for details K.M. Wagner, *Die wirtschaftliche Arbeitnehmermitbestimmung in einer Europäischen Aktiengesellschaft*, Frankfurt/Main, 1977; R. Birk, 'Europäische Aktiengesellschaft und nationales Betriebsverfassungsrecht', *Zeitschrift für Arbeitsrecht*, 1984, pp. 47–81; Kolvenbach, 'Die Europäische Gemeinschaft und die Deutsche Mitbestimmung', *Der Betrieb*, 1986, pp. 1973–1978 and 2023–2026.
27. Arts. 74a, 137–145.
28. Bulletin of the EC, Supplement 13/1973.
29. Bulletin of the EC, Supplement 8/1975.
30. OB 1978, L 295.
31. OB 1983, C 240.
32. See for details Blanpain, 'Workers' Participation in the European Community, The Fifth Directive', *Bulletin of Comparative Labour Relations*, No. 13, 1984.
33. KOM (84) 727; see for details Lutter, 'Europäisches Gesellschaftsrecht', *Zeitschrif. für Unternehmens- und Gesellschaftsrecht*, Sonderheft 1, 2 ed., 1984, p. 505.

125

that an enterprise does not fulfil conditions for representation of workers' representatives on the governing boards any longer.

B. *Individual Labour Law – Industrial Relations*

1. Labour Relations in General

42. Whereas collective labour law constitutes a unitary system because of its close relation to the European development of company law, individual labour law is more diffuse because of its regard to economic necessities. Here the EC tries to achieve harmonisation by particular recommendations to national legislators, such as Recommendation No. 75/457 of 22 July 1975, on the principle of the 40-hour week and the principle of 4 weeks' annual paid holiday.[34] This lack of a uniform supra-national system of individual labour law will be compensated by an interesting project of the EC Commission: A group of experts has elaborated a *model of a European individual employment contract* which is intended to become a *European code of practice* for parties to the employment contract. Its details are described in Chapter 21 below.

43. A *Convention* of the EC Council *on the law to be applied to contractual obligations*,[35] not yet ratified, also regulates in its Article 6 international private law for contracts of employment. We can distinguish three principles: Contracts of employment are, as a rule, governed by the legal order freely chosen by the contracting parties. In the absence of contractual choice the law of that State in which the employee regularly works is applicable. Exceptions are provided for in special cases. But mandatory law operative at the regular place of work excludes the free choice of law if it grants the employee better protection than the chosen legal order. This draft convention does not apply until ratification by the Member States.

2. Security of Employment

44. There are two socio-economic reasons why the EC deals with security of employment: the negative development of full employment on the common labour market and the danger of the loss of employment as a result of transfers of enterprises.

---

34. OB 1975, L 199; on 18 December 1979 the Council passed a Resolution on the adaption of working time including alternative training, overtime work, flexible age limit, part time employment, temporary work, shift work and diminution of yearly working time (OB 1980, C 2).
35. OB 1980, L 266.

45. The first problem will be dealt with by *Directive No. 75/129 of 17 February 1975, on the harmonisation of the provisions of the Member States on mass dismissals.*[36] Besides the obligation of the employer to consult with workers' representatives in order to achieve agreement on the prevention of mass dismissals, the most important element of the Directive consists in government intervention into the right of dismissal. The employer is obliged to inform the competent internal authority about all intended mass dismissals. National legislation must provide that at least for 30 days after the receipt of the information by the authority any mass dismissal is illegal. This period must be used by the authority to look for a resolution of the employment problems caused by the intended mass dismissal.

46. The second problem is dealt with by *Directive No. 77/187 of 14 February 1977 on the harmonisation of the provisions of the Member States on the protection of workers' claims in the case of the transfer of enterprises, factories, or parts of factories.*[37] At the centre of this Directive stands the legal principle that the existing contracts of employment with the transferrer of an enterprise, a factory, or a part of a factory will automatically pass to the transferee with all rights and duties and even with the obligatory of the collective agreements binding the hitherto existing contracts of employment between the employee and the transferrer. Transfer is as such, moreover, no reason for dismissal, so that illegal dismissals must be regarded as void according to national law. For the provisions on co-determination in cases when modifications of the terms of employment become necessary because of the transfer (for instance the 'whole-sale reduction' of social costs as an urgent industrial requirement) see above paragraph 38. As most of the Member States already had similar regulations, this Directive is more a factor of legal stability than an eminent innovation at the European level.

3. Equal Treatment – Prohibition of Discrimination

47. A distinction must be made between the principle of non-discrimination in the common labour market and non-discrimination in employment relations.[38]

48. Equal treatment in the common labour market aims at removing impediments to workers' free movement which result from special provisions of national laws towards foreigners. The prohibition of discrimination as regulated by Regulation No. 1612/68 of 15 October 1968, on the freedom of movement for workers within the Community (Articles 7–9)[39] is, therefore,

36. OB 1975, L 48.
37. OB 1977, L 61.
38. See for details J. Egger, Equality and Prohibition of Discrimination in Employment, *Bulletin of Comparative Labour Law Relations* XIV, 1985, pp. 39–52.
39. OB 1968, L 257; see also the modifying Regulation No. 312/76 of 9 February 1976 (OB 1976, L 39).

limited to discrimination on grounds of nationality. Other distinctions, as for instance on the basis of professional ability or duration of employment, are not affected by these provisions. But as to nationality, the prohibition of discrimination is absolute. It gives the nationals of the other Member States equal rights to employment with natives. It grants the right to the nationals of the other Member States to elect and to be elected as workers' representatives and to become members of local trade unions. Above all, provisions in employment contracts, factory agreements, and collective agreements which infringe the principle of non-discrimination are void.

49. The prohibition of discrimination in employment relations concerns above all, unjust distinctions between men and women. There is Article 119 of the EEC Treaty which, according to the jurisdiction of the EC Court of Justice (see above footnote 9), gives female workers a direct claim to equal pay for equal work in accordance with the rate for the job principle. Prohibitions of other forms of discrimination on grounds of sex, although in a different way, are provided for in national law. But the realisation of such provisions in practice was insufficient. The EC, therefore, issued two directives which deal with the definitions and implementing of equal rights for men and women in labour law: *Directive No. 75/117 of 10 February 1975, on the harmonisation of the provisions of the Member States on the application of the principle of equal pay for men and women*[40] and *Directive No. 76/207 of 9 February 1976, on the realisation of the principle of equal treatment of men and women concerning access to occupation, vocational education and vocational rise and also concerning terms of employment.*[41] The central idea of these Directives is that the claim of women to equal pay and treatment is to be understood in a comprehensive fashion including prohibition of indirect discriminations, such as because of marriage, family status, or distinctions between equivalent work. Distinctions on grounds of sex which are, on the contrary, allowed are exhaustively enumerated by the Directives: the proviso of occupations for the practice of which sex is an inevitable condition, and special provisions for the protection of women.

As to the consequences of infringements, the Directives provide uniformly for the nullity of provisions in employment contracts, factory agreements, and collective agreements; the right to action before domestic courts; and the illegality of notices or dismissals by the employer solely because the employee insists on pursuing his or her claim or brings an action.

4. Industrial Safety

50. The harmonisation of industrial safety, i.e. the prevention of industrial accidents and of occupational diseases, is most advanced in labour law. But,

40. OB 1975, L 45.
41. OB 1976, L 39.

actually, this is less a question of the harmonisation of law than of the *harmonisation of technical standards and their adaptation to technical development*. The Community organs found their respective activities on two bases: They argue that different technical standards in industrial safety would hinder the free trade of materials and machines beyond the frontiers and, therefore, prejudice the functioning of the Common Market in the sense of Article 100 of the EEC Treaty. Secondly, they say that harmonisation with the aim of improved protection of employees' health is covered by Article 117, paragraph 1 of the EEC Treaty. (See above paragraphs 5 and 6.)

51. It is not our task to explain the technical details of the numerous regulations, directives, and recommendations.[42] We will limit ourselves to the following fundamental princicples: On 29 June 1978, the EC Council issued a comprehensive and detailed 'activities programme of the EC on safety and protection of workers' health'. According to this nearly all legislation on industrial safety and occupational health should be harmonised by the end of 1982. A first consequence of this programme is the issuè of *Directive No. 80/1107 of 27 November 1980, on the protection of workers against danger from chemical, physical and biological agents at work.*[43] This Directive contains a technical framework which is to be implemented by particular directives for the various agents. Also a similar directive on the *risks of serious accidents in certain industrial activities* is in force.[44] A Resolution of the Council on a *second activities programme on safety and protection of workers' health*[45] plans, up to the end of 1988, the realisation of 20 actions of priority in the field of protection against work accidents, dangers and dangerous substances.

Supra-national boards consisting of representatives of the Member States and one representative of the EC Commission as chairman will control the usefulness of the technical data stated in the directives with regard to technical development.

5. Remuneration

52. Remuneration as such is not a subject which is appropriate for supranational regulation. But the question of how to protect the employee's claim to remuneration against loss or diminution can certainly be of common interest. One example is the European-wide insolvencies of multinational enterprises. The EC Commission, therefore, plans to harmonise the national

---

42. See on this point G. Schnorr and J. Egger, *op. cit.*, paragraphs 169–181.
43. OB 1980, L 327.
44. OB 1982, L 230.
45. OB 1984, C 67.

laws on failure. A consequence of this was the issuing of *Directive No. 80/987 of 20 October 1980, on the harmonisation of the provisions of the Member States on the protection of workers in the case of insolvency of the employer.*[46] The Member States are thereby obliged to establish institutions to satisfy the unfulfilled claims of workers as the result of the insolvency of the employer. These institutions must be independent of the trading capital of the employer, and they must be mainly contributed by the employer. The Member States are also to take measures to avoid default on the workers' claims to social security as a consequence of non-performance of the employer's duty to contribute. As the majority of the Member States already have such institutions, the Directive leaves a wide scope for organising alternatives: the principle of special funds in connection with labour market administration (Belgium, Denmark, Germany, United Kingdom); defrayal by means of unemployment insurance (Netherlands); establishment of insurance defrayed by the employers' and employees' associations (France). Such Member States as have no such institutions now have to decide on one of these or a similar system.

C. Common Labour Market

53. The wide-spread supra-national legislation on the common labour market and the free movement of workers beyond the frontiers according to Articles 48–51 EEC Treaty is, in its proper sense, less a subject of harmonisation but rather a subject of a new form of labour market administration in connection with the full right of the nationals of the Member States to be exchanged to and to be engaged by the employers in any other Member State.[47] The main legislation consists in the *Regulation No. 1612/68 of 15 October 1968, on the freedom of movement for workers within the Community.*[48] For the harmonising effect in relation of equal treatment concerning the terms of employment see above paragraph 48.

54. It should, nevertheless, be mentioned that this right to free movement within the common labour market has *indirect effects on national administrative law for foreigners.* Thus, by a number of directives and regulations the EC has regulated the rights of the nationals of the Member States to free entry, residence, and exit, to stay after the end of occupation, to bring in their families etc. in a common sense.[49]

55. The policy of full employment in the common labour market is supported by *financial aid from the European Social Fund* according to Articles

---

46. OB 1980, L 283.
47. See for details G. Schnorr and J. Egger, *op. cit.*, paragraphs 129–148.
48. OB 1968, L 257, modified by the Regulation No. 312/76 of 9 February 1976 (OB 1976, L 39).
49. See for details G. Schnorr and J. Egger, *op. cit.*, paragraph 139.

123ff of the EEC Treaty and its many implementing regulations. Being, in the first place, an instrument of social policy it influences indirectly the national legislation on the promotion of employment.

SELECT BIBLIOGRAPHY

L.E. Troclet, *Elements de droit social européen*, Bruxelles, 1963.
M. Shanks, *European Social Party, Today and Tomorrow*, Oxford, 1977.
P. Kapteyn, *The Social Policy of the European Communities*, Leyden, 1977.
G. Lyon-Caen, *Droit social international et européen*, 5th ed., Paris, 1980.
G. Schnorr, and Egger, J., 'European Communities' in: *International Encyclopaedia for Labour Law and Industrial Relations* (ed. R. Blanpain), Deventer, 1984.

Chapter 8. Guidelines for Multinational Enterprises and Labour Relations

R. Blanpain

R. Blanpain

I THE NEED FOR GUIDELINES

1. Endeavours to draw up a code of good conduct, or guidelines, or a declaration of principles concerning multinational enterprises and social policy were undertaken by the UN, ILO, OECD and the EC. The OECD was the first to promulgate its 'Guidelines for Multinational Enterprises', on 21 June 1976. In November 1977, the ILO governing body adopted a declaration of principles.

On 20 September 1977 the Governments of the then nine Member States of the European Communities adopted a Code of Conduct for companies with interests in South Africa.

Why the need for Guidelines and Codes of Conduct for Multinational Enterprises which have been or are being drawn up in different international organisations?

A. The Balance of Powers – Central Decision-Making

2. The reasons are rather obvious: multinational enterprises may through central decision-making change the balance of power between labour and management and thus affect the hard core of industrial relations, of which power relations are an underlying element, in the sense that industrial relations concern the decision-making power of employers, which is countered by the display of power by employees through, for example, strikes, sitting on boards of companies and the like. Central decision-making is at the heart of the multinational enterprise. The OECD Guidelines for MNE's state that 'these usually comprise companies or other entities . . . established in different countries and are so linked that one or more of them may be able to exercise a significant influence over the activities of other . . .'.

Although the degree of central control differs considerably from one enterprise to another, it is widely accepted that most multinational enterprises have a centralised decision-making process covering investment and technology. Pension funds are often centrally controlled and in some cases there is significant central intervention when subsidiaries are engaged in

133

industrial conflict. Some multinationals have also laid down broad principles concerning labour–management relations and the setting of wages and working conditions; others have developed uniform practices or standard policies over the years (e.g. on dealing with international trade secretariats, or the introduction of check-off clauses and the like). As an ILO study observes, 'there is also the fact that a certain type of behaviour is expected of the members of local top management who are generally selected and appointed by headquarters'. In some enterprises local managers are allowed to negotiate only within certain financial limits.

It must be recognised that national industrial relations systems and legal rules often leave considerable flexibility for a company to conduct its own industrial relations policy, which may make it more difficult for the trade union or the representatives of the employees to operate effectively if it differs significantly from established local custom and practice. From these considerations the following conclusion can be drawn: centralised decision-making, especially in respect of decisions affecting employment in the broad sense, the organisation of work, the introduction of a central company philosophy which may be foreign and alien to local customs into industrial relations and consequently, in some cases, the lack of an *interlocuteur valable* can undoubtedly affect the balance of power between management and labour. Multinationals thus escape the national social network and may become, or seem to become, inaccessible to the local government and union(s). The balance of power can also be affected by the size of a multinational enterprise. The size of a firm, whether national or multinational, is an important element in its power. Although small firms can also be powerful, there is no doubt that the larger enterprises, as measured by the number of workers employed or the amount of the invested capital, command more resources and thus generally possess more power in the sense that they have more options open to them and have greater endurance under pressure than smaller ones. Some unions express the fear 'that a particular operation of a multinational enterprise constitutes so small a part of the company's worldwide operations that it can be treated almost casually. As a consequence, the parent company can close down a given subsidiary in reprisal for a strike or what the company deems unreasonable labour conditions . . . '.[1]

3. Although multinationals in general are in the forefront of industrial relations and wages and working conditions, there are some exceptions which because of the importance of the firm concerned became so notorious in their magnitude that they may cast a damaging shadow on the behaviour of others.

1. *Multinationals in Western Europe: the Industrial Relations Experience*, Geneva, ILO, 1975, p. 20.

B. Countries

4. Moreover, small and even bigger countries feel that the multinational enterprises escape them and wish to ensure their sovereignty over the multinationals. They fear the possible abuses of multinationals 'in the facilities they have to allocate their functions (such as production, research, financing and exportation) geographically, to distribute costs and profits between affiliates and to respond with greater freedom than domestic enterprises to policy objectives of home and host countries'.[2] But on their own, small and even bigger countries cannot do much. They need the investment, especially the technology, and know that national measures may drive multinationals away; so they strive in general for international rules; these may also be necessary to help resolve disputes which may arise between home and host countries. Most countries want especially to safeguard an 'open and stable environment for international investment', emphasising that the basic orientation towards international investment should be promoted since these increase general welfare.

C. Trade Unions

5. The greatest demand for Guidelines obviously comes from the trade unions. In trying to restore the balance of power and in order to be able to influence decisions taken at headquarters, there are basically two ways for the trade union movement to confront the multinationals:
(1) To strengthen the international trade union movement, especially the industrial internationals, and to coerce multinational headquarters on the basis of that strength to hold meetings, leading to collective bargaining.
(2) To appeal to political power by getting the help of governments and (or) international organisations in order to impose upon the multinational enterprise rules favourable to labour.

6. As a general rule however no bargaining at international level has taken place; international solidarity of workers, bans on overtime and the like, have proved to be the exception and not a lever greatly to influence managerial decision-making.[3]
The reasons for this failure are manifold, but essentially they are structural in nature. These reasons are well known by now: ideological diversity, organisational conflicts, financial weakness and, above all, a conflict of interest between the unions themselves.

---

2. T. Vogelaar, Special Consultant on Multinational Enterprises, OECD, Speech, 13 December 1976.
3. See H. Northrup and R. Rowan, *Multinational Collective Bargaining Attempts*, Philadelphia, 1979.

7. Most unions want to compensate this lack of trade union strength by putting pressure upon their national governments to do something at international level, and here the relationships between trade unions and political parties are obviously of the utmost interest. These relationships are of particular importance in the European countries; but also at this level safeguards are built in: countries do not want to harm their own multi-nationals by rigid rules.

8. The overall point is, however, that the trade union movement has to pressurise international organisations to adopt measures to control multina-tional enterprises as a means of building up trade union strength.[4] Unions try to get more grip on multinational enterprises by the establishment of international rules governing, for example,
– outward conditions on investment;[5]
– recognition of trade unions and collective bargaining;
– information;[6]
– access to headquarters and to the actual decision-makers;
– consultation on investment decisions;
– countering of departing firms;
– legalisation of international trade union action and
– the making of a legally binding code.

D. Multinationals

9. It is not only governments and unions – whether or not for different reasons – which favour the adoption of certain guidelines or rules concern-ing international investment, but many multinationals, weary of what they consider to be unjustified and often conflicting criticism, and consequently not always sure themselves what course of action is indicated from the overall societal point of view, also support the idea of Guidelines, which, if adhered to, would elevate their conduct above the level of undue criticism. The condition is that the Guidelines be constructive; that they also recognise the positive contribution of multinational enterprises; that they be consistent with international law and do not discriminate between multinational and national enterprises.

---

4. See the ICFTU's 'Charter of Trade Union Demands for the Legislative Control of Multinational Companies', (Mexico, 1975), *Bulletin of Comparative Labour Relations*, No. 7, 1976, pp. 405–450.
5. Trade unions express concern about investment in countries which do not respect human and trade union rights.
6. Information on the multinational as a whole, and information in advance. See further A. Morgan and R. Blanpain, *The industrial Relations and employment Impacts of multinational Enterprises. An Inquiry into the Issues*, OECD, 1977.

II. THE OECD GUIDELINES

A. The Content of the Guidelines

10. The Guidelines[7] contain, in addition to an introduction, which constitutes an integral part, seven sections, namely:
(1) General policies;
(2) Disclosure of information;
(3) Competition;
(4) Financing;
(5) Taxation;
(6) Employment and Industrial Relations;
(7) Science and Technology.
From the labour relations point of view the Introduction and the chapters on disclosure of information and obviously employment and industrial relations are of particular importance.

B. Nature and Binding Character of the Guidelines

11. The Guidelines contain rules of conduct for multinational enterprises; they lay down standards for the activities of these enterprises. (Introduction, No. 6).

12. Observance of the Guidelines is 'voluntary and not legally enforceable'.
   Voluntary does not mean that multinational enterprises are free to choose whether they accept the Guidelines or not. The Guidelines constitute recommended behaviour, since they are recommendations jointly addressed by member countries to the multinational enterprises. The Guidelines carry that weight and represent a firm expectation of Governments for MNE behaviour. Both business and labour have accepted the Guidelines as 'the' behaviour to expect from enterprises, and this means that the Guidelines constitute 'the' rules of conduct which society as a whole requires the multinational enterprises to live up to. In this sense they are 'morally' binding: they indeed relate to societal principles of right and wrong in behaviour, which constitutes the essence of morality. Whether an enterprise has determined to follow the Guidelines or not is in fact irrelevant. On the contrary, the Guidelines are not legally enforceable, which means that they cannot as such be sanctioned by the courts, although they could acquire in the course of time the legal character of a custom and become legally enforceable 'as custom'.

13. Difficult questions arise concerning the relationship between these moral obligations and the legal obligations under the law of the land.

---

7. See Annex, 'The OECD Guidelines for Multinational Enterprises', *IELL*.

Paragraph 7 of the introduction states, and this is obvious, that 'the entities of a multinational enterprise located in various countries are subject to the laws of these countries'.

National law then comes first, confirming the sovereignty of the State; consequently, the Guidelines cannot compel enterprises to do anything which would be in conflict with national law. However, the Guidelines do place obligations on multinationals which go beyond what is strictly required by law.

14. The Guidelines are also relevant for domestic enterprises. Indeed, as paragraph 9 of the introduction indicates, they 'reflect good practice for all'. Accordingly, 'multinational and domestic enterprises are subject to the same expectations in respect of their conduct whenever the Guidelines are relevant to both'. Consequently, the Guidelines do contain moral obligations for national enterprises, e.g. national enterprises as well as multinationals are expected to give reasonable notice to employees in the case of a major change in their operations, as required in Guideline 6 of the Employment and Industrial Relations chapter. This rule of equal treatment is inspired by a strong political will not to discriminate between national and multinational enterprises. The employers especially have insisted on equal treatment.

15. The introductory part of the Guidelines forms an integral part of the Guidelines and is necessary for a proper comprehension of the nature of the whole exercise.

Let us finally indicate that the Guidelines recommend the use of appropriate mechanisms for resolving international disputes, including arbitration, as a means of facilitating the resolution of problems arising between enterprises and Member countries (No. 10 of the Introduction) and that the Member Countries have accepted the obligation to fulfil their responsibilities to treat enterprises equitably in accordance with international law and international agreements, as well as the contractual obligations to which they have subscribed.

C. The (Non-) Definition of the Multinational Enterprise

16. The Guidelines indicate in paragraph 8 of the Introduction that a precise legal definition of multinational enterprises is not required for the purpose of the Guidelines. In fact, paragraph 8 contains a definition, one which is particularly appropriate from the point of view of labour relations; paragraph 8 defines the multinational as follows:

'These usually comprise companies or other entities whose ownership is private, state or mixed, established in different countries and so linked that one or more of them may be able to exercise a significant influence over the activities of others and, in particular, to share knowledge and resources with the others. The degree of autonomy of each entity in relation to the other varies widely from one multinational enterprise to another, depending on the nature of the links between such entities and the fields of activity concerned'

and it concludes: 'The word "enterprise" as used in these guidelines refers to these various entities in accordance with their responsibilities'. The essential element in the definition is found in the words 'to exercise a significant influence', which refers to the element of central control, centralised decision-making, which constitutes the backbone of the multinational enterprise. The mere sharing of knowledge and resources is insufficient (C.A. case).

III. THE GUIDELINES AND LABOUR RELATIONS

A. *The Heart of the Matter*

17. There is no doubt that during the 1976–1986 period labour relations were at the *centre of the attention* of the OECD's IME Committee (Committee on International Investment and Multinational Enterprises). The clarification of the scope and the meaning of the Guidelines given by the Committee and consequently the experience with the follow-up procedures and the ensuing developments in that area were largely inspired by these discussions concerning issues of industrial relations.

One can speculate about the reasons for this focus on industrial relations. One is obviously the fact that one of the two advisory bodies, namely the Trade Union Advisory Committee (TUAC) has its main interests in that area. TUAC certainly wants to augment the impact of Guidelines on multinational enterprises and has taken an important number of initiatives in that field, amongst others, the introduction of cases and issues for clarification. The IME Committee agreed, after initial hesitation, to discuss them has devoted much of its time to examining these cases and to formulating clarifications of issues, which these cases brought up.

B. *Cases and Issues*

18. Nearly all the cases discussed in the IME Committee were introduced by TUAC. Five cases were also introduced by Governments, two by the Belgian Government, namely the Badger and the Michelin case; one by the Danish Government, the Hertz case; one by the Dutch Government, the Batco case and one by the British Government, the Bankers' Trust case. These individual cases and the general issues they involved were examined by governments in the IME Committee and in the Working Group on the

Guidelines, as well as with BIAC and TUAC during the formal and informal discussions they had with the IME Committee and the Working Group respectively.

These discussions in fact served two purposes: first as an input for the review of the Guidelines, secondly in order to obtain clarification of certain Guidelines. The reviews led to two amendments of the Guidelines and changes in the follow-up procedure, while the IME reports also contains an important number of clarifications.

The most important cases, issues and their outcome are described in International Labour Law, Case Law, IELL.

C. Exchange of Views. Impact of Business and Labour

19. Such clarification was the *result of extensive 'exchanges of views'*, let us say negotiations, between Governments in the IME Committee. There was, however, considerable input from Business and Labour. Indeed, paragraph 4 of the 1984 Revised Decision of the Council on the Guidelines for Multinational Enterprises foresees that the IME Committee 'shall periodically invite the Business and Industry Advisory Committee to OECD (BIAC) and the Trade Union Advisory Committee to OECD (TUAC) to express their views on matters related to the Guidelines and shall take account of such views in its reports to the Council'. In execution of that decision, formal and informal consultations with BIAC and TUAC have been held. It was during these consultations that the cases were introduced.

20. These consultations proved to be very constructive and rewarding since they performed a number of important functions, which in fact went beyond 'the expression of views of the parties' as indicated in the decision. This development however corresponds to the intention of the founding fathers of the Guidelines, since the exercise was from the beginning seen as – and proved to be – an evolutionary process.

During the contacts with IME and the Working Group, TUAC and BIAC not only expressed their 'views' on matters related to the Guidelines within the framework of the review of the 1976 package in 1979 and 1984; business and labour took the occasion to indicate their general philosophy toward the Guidelines, their expectations, their support for the Guidelines and the difficulties in implementing them. The discussion of cases led to far-reaching exchanges of views on the Guidelines, which in turn resulted in better understanding and clarification of the Guidelines, two amendments of them and a substantial change in the follow-up procedures as indicated before.

D. The Role of the IME Committee

21. The Committee used the cases as illustrations of issues arising under the Guidelines. It was thus the *issues*, the general questions and *principles*, on which a debate took place. It is the idea that *cases* should in principle be settled at national or bilateral level. The Committee has no intention of being a semi-court, judging the individual behaviour of companies.

For this reason proposals for *fact finding* have not been retained and the word *clarification* is used instead of interpretation, since fact finding and interpretation might bring the Committee too close to a judicial role. The Committee is, for the same reason, not entitled under the revised consultation procedure to request an enterprise to appear before it or to make a presentation in writing. This does not however alter the fact that when issues or questions of principle are discussed, the members of the Committee are informed about the case and have it in mind; nor that the way in which a discussion evolves and clarification is given may well indicate whether certain behaviour coincides with the Guidelines or not and whether certain enterprises may have to change their conduct.

E. The Clarification Process

22. The clarification process is obviously more a political than a judicial one. Clarification is still the result of tough negotiations between governments, business and labour, with their interests taken into account; this process of give and take, of adjusting fundamental national interests, is still too much in the political arena to entrust interpretation and the resolution of disputes to an independent panel of experts.

23. The Committee's discussions and the report's clarification may be summarised and commented upon as follows.
(1) The Guidelines are addressed to entities which can be considered as enterprises (private, state, mixed), 'established in different countries and so linked that one or more of them may be able to exercise a significant influence over the activities of others and, in particular, share knowledge and resources with the others'. *These criteria cover a broad range of multinational activities and arrangements*, which can be based on equity participation according to the traditional approach to international direct investment, but the same result could be achieved by other means not necessarily including an element of capital equity.
(2) Multinationals should *adapt to local law and practice* and not try to transplant those principles of head office which do not respect the local climate.
(3) Multinational enterprises should not interfere with the *rights* of the employees *to organise*. An anti-union attitude, policies, or instructions by headquarters to go non-union are contrary to this approach. The employers should in fact take a neutral attitude. This does not take away that the employer has the right to express an opinion on the matter, but this should not amount either to threats or to anti-union policies (CITIBANK-CITICORP).
(4) The Guidelines are neutral on the question of *International Trade Secretariats*. It is however obvious that the ITS's are *bona fide* workers'

organisations. Yet the point is that the Guidelines indicate that the conditions under which recognition or bargaining are exercised are a matter of national law, regulations and practices. Thus ITS's must use the possibilities of national law and practice to effect their claims.

(5) The Guidelines are equally neutral on the point of *international collective bargaining*. This means in consequence that international collective bargaining belongs to the autonomous relationship between labour and management and will become a reality when two conditions are fulfilled: (1) the necessity to bargain at that level; (2) when the trade unions (at national level) desire it and exert enough force to push the multinational enterprises to the bargaining table.

(6) The problem of '*access to the real decision makers*' goes to the heart of the multinational matter, given the centralised decision-making structure of the multinational enterprise. This decision-making structure may have as a consequence that strategic decisions, affecting the livelihood of the employees, are taken in far away headquarters, with the possibility that even local managers are not informed about decisions which affect the subsidiary they manage, until after such decisions are taken. The Guidelines are clear and have as a consequence that multinational enterprises will eventually have to adapt their decision-making structures.

In the VIGGO case the IME Committee clarified the position as follows: Paragraph 9 was carefully worded to avoid the need for defining the *locus* of the negotiations or the proper level of management to be involved in such negotiations which would depend upon the decision-making structure in each MNE. The basic purpose of paragraph 9 is to ensure that negotiations conducted under national practice take place in a meaningful manner with representatives of management in a position to directly influence decisions on investment matters and to negotiate in an effort to reach agreement. Where negotiations are defined by national practice in a way that management, in case of disagreement, remains free to make the final decision, these negotiations should still provide employee representatives the opportunity to discuss with representatives of management having a real impact upon the final decision.

In carrying out their responsibilities as discussed above on issues relating to future production and investment plans, management of the enterprise as a whole would seem to have a range of possibilities among which it would choose or that it could combine, taking into full account the need to respect prevailing labour relation practices in the country where the negotiations have been initiated. Its choice depends on various circumstances, such as the matters under discussion, the decision-making structure within the enterprise, and the importance of the decisions to be taken. A number of possibilities are open to this end without suggesting any order of preference. Examples of such possibilities include:

– to provide the management of the subsidiary with adequate and timely information and to ensure that it has sufficient powers to conduct meaningful negotiations with representatives of employees;

– to nominate one or more representative of the decision-making centre to the negotiating team of the subsidiary in order to secure the same result as in the preceding example;
– to engage directly in negotiations.

The Committee also considered that general provisions of the Guidelines, such as paragraphs 1 and 8 of the Introduction together with item (i) of the chapter on Disclosures of Information ('structure of the enterprises'), could not be seen to imply a general right of employees to be informed on the decision-making structure within the enterprise.

It was agreed, however, that as stated on earlier occasions, it was the basic purpose of paragraph 9 of the Employment and Industrial Relations Guidelines to ensure that negotiations take place in a meaningful manner with the relevant representatives of management. For this purpose employee representatives, under the Guidelines, have a legitimate interest to be informed about the decision-making structure within the enterprise but such a right of information is confined to negotiating situations referred to in the Guidelines, and in particular in paragraph 9 of the chapter on Employment and Industrial Relations of the Guidelines.

The question of access to real decision makers comes also up in paragraph 6 of the Employment and Industrial Relations chapter. Indeed paragraph 6 indicates that in considering important changes, multinational enterprises should 'co-operate with the employee-representatives so as to mitigate to the maximum extent adverse effects'. The question arises as to which representatives of management the employees should cooperate. At the occasion of the 1984 Review Report the IME Committee made the following clarification:

'A further area where concerns have been raised by employees and their representatives is that of access to management representatives with sufficient authority to take any decisions which might be called for in the circumstances. The specific concerns in the field of co-operation between management and labour relating to changes in operations which would have major effects on the livelihood of employees are addressed by paragraph 6 of the Employment and Industrial Relations Guidelines. The special character of multinational enterprises is also recognised in this regard, as in other matters related to the Guidelines, in paragraph 8 of the Introduction to the Guidelines, which states that "Guidelines are addressed to the various entities within the multinational enterprise (parent companies and/or local entities) according to the actual distribution of responsibilities among them on the understanding that they will co-operate and provide assistance to one another as necessary to facilitate observance of the Guidelines". The Committee has provided a clarification to paragraph 9 of the Employment and Industrial Relations Guideline regarding different ways in which, when negotiations or collective bargaining or labour management relations issues are concerned, firms can ensure that management representatives who participate in such negotiations "are autho-

143

rised to take decisions on the matters under negotiation". Regarding paragraph 6, which states that, in considering changes in their operations, enterprises should "provide reasonable notice of such changes" and "co-operate with the employee representatives and appropriate governmental authorities so as to mitigate to the maximum extent practicable adverse effects", the Committee has indicated, by means of a clarification, its opinion that it would be in conformity with the intention of paragraph 6 of the Employment and Industrial Relations Guideline if representatives of management participating in the process of co-operation addressed in this paragraph had sufficient authority to co-operate in good faith and consistent with paragraph 8 of the introduction to the Guidelines, to take the decisions that might be called for as required by the circumstances' (Ford Motor Cie Case).

(7) The rules applying to the *disclosure of information* to employees are still mainly national, but the Guidelines may be regarded as supplementary and may recommend additional rules, especially in countries where national law or practice does not contain the obligation to disclose information in view of collective bargaining. It is, however, extremely important that headquarters ensure that the subsidiaries receive sufficient information in due time in order to be able to fulfil their obligations under national law, practice and the Guidelines. Representatives of employees should also receive 'specific information on the group as a whole', as well as on allocation of markets and products among entities in the group.

(8) Paragraph 6 of the Employment and Industrial Relations chapter has been one of the most frequently invoked Guidelines. Following that paragraph, multinational enterprises should, in considering changes in their operations which would have major effects upon the livelihood of their employees, as collective dismissals, transfer, concentration, introduction of new technologies, *provide reasonable notice and co-operate . . . so as to mitigate to the practicable maximum adverse affects*. The wording of the paragraph 'in considering changes' could seem to indicate that information should be given prior to the given decision. Specific circumstances of each case have to be taken into account; in particular, compelling reasons of business confidentiality may prevent early information. But this should be the exception rather than the rule. '*Co-operation*' means consultation, '*mitigation*' includes looking for alternative solutions; the banning of overtime; job-sharing; re-employment; the postponement of dismissals; fewer dismissals; terms of notice; golden handshakes and the like (BADGER CASE).

The Guidelines provide that enterprises should, within the framework of national law, regulations and prevailing labour relations practices, 'respect the right of their employees to be represented by trade unions and other bona fide organisations of employees'. Nevertheless, enterprises may on occasion be faced with a situation where their employees are not represented by trade unions or other bona fide organisations of employees. Paragraph 6 of the Employment and Industrial Relations Guidelines does not address such situations. Nevertheless, it would be consistent with the aims of the Guidelines if, in such situations, enterprises would take all practical steps towards addressing the concerns underlying paragraph 6 of the Employment and Industrial Relations chapter of the Guidelines within the framework of national laws, regulations and prevailing labour relations practices.

In relation to the question concerning the notion of reasonable notice, the Committee recalled that the Guidelines are not aimed at introducing rigid rules that would make the tasks that there may be circumstances in which the sensitivity of business decisions and/or of particular jobs, in terms of possible serious damage to the enterprises concerned, is such that it would render it difficult for them, when considering changes in their activities which would have major effects on the livelihood of their employees, to give the representatives of employees early notice of such changes. However, it is the view of the Committee that such circumstances would be exceptional. In particular, there is no business sector or activity where it could be considered that such circumstances would usually prevail (Bankers' Trust Case).

The key notions in this paragraph of the Guidelines are the 'reasonable notice' to be given of such changes and actions by management and co-operation with employee representatives and appropriate governmental authorities 'so as to mitigate to the maximum extent practicable adverse effects', and 'it has seemed to the Committee that there is a link between these two notions. The notice given has to be sufficiently timely for the purpose of mitigating action to be prepared and put into effect: otherwise, it would not meet the criterion of "reasonable". It would be in conformity with the general intention of this paragraph, in the light of the specific circumstances of each case, if management were able to provide such notice prior to the final decision being taken'. (Michelin Case)

(9) The Guidelines do not prevent a subsidiary of a multinational enterprise from *adapting wages to economic and financial difficulties* experienced by the firm if such conduct under local law and practice would be accepted in the country for national enterprises under comparable circumstances (WAGNER-LAMBERT CASE).

(10) Managers of multinational enterprises should adopt a co-operative *attitude* towards the participation of employees in international meetings for consultation and exchanges of views among themselves, provided that the functioning of the operations of the enterprises and the normal procedures which govern relationships with representatives of

145

the employees and their organisations are not thereby prejudiced. This second condition means in practice that the attendance by employees must be sponsored by the responsible trade union (PHILIPS CASE).

(11) The use of strike breakers in the sense of a *transfer of workers from foreign affiliates* in order to influence negotiations or to hinder the right to organise was not originally covered by the Guidelines. Paragraph 8 of the Employment and Industrial Relations Chapter was amended to that end.[8]

Paragraph 8 has however definite limits. It refers to threats to transfer the whole or part of an operating unit from the country concerned in order to influence . . . 'unfairly'. This paragraph only covers existing plants and equipment; not threats not to invest of disinvestment; neither are the transfer of products, materials, extra-overtime or other measures covered. Transfer of workers from one subsidiary to another within the same country also seems, in the actual clarification, not to be covered by Guidelines 8. The key notion in paragraph 8 is the word 'unfair'. 'Unfair' does not take away the employer's right to inform the employees about what he thinks to be the possible effect of certain actions on the viability of the enterprise. Yet management should be prepared to provide information in order to support this claim (HERTZ CASE).

(12) The Guidelines do not prevent a multinational enterprise from *closing down a subsidiary*, *even a profitable one*; the responsibility and the power to do so remain entirely with the management of the multinational enterprise. The enterprise in doing so must of course take local law and practice into account, as well as the policy objectives of the countries in which they operate. It is advisable, sometimes obligatory, to inform and consult with the government and with the employees and their representatives. Member States are of course free to regulate the closing down of enterprises but must do so taking international obligations (free flow of investment and capital) into account, as well as the obligation to treat enterprises equitably and not to discriminate between national and multinational enterprises (BATCO CASE).

(13) The problem of the *co-responsibility of the parent company* for the obligations of its subsidiaries goes equally to the heart of the question since it also involves the central decision-making structure of the multinationals, which constitutes, as repeatedly stressed, the essence of the multinational enterprise. The IME Committee has accepted certain exceptions to the principle of limited responsibility, which is a well established one in the laws of OECD's member countries. The Com-

---

8. The text of the Guidelines was, for the sake of credibility and stability, *only slightly amended*, to cover an issue that was not foreseen when the Guidelines were drafted. It was accepted by most that the 1976 deal constituted a fragile package, the delicate balance of which had to be maintained. The credibility – in the sense of stability -- of the Guidelines required that after such a short period no changes would be made. The two changes, obviously again a compromise since more changes were asked for, indicate that changes which are needed are possible, which is also necessary for the same 'credibility'.

mittee does in fact distinguish between two kinds of responsibilities: non-financial and financial responsibility. In the *non-financial* area the parent company should see to it that the local affiliate is in a position to respect local law and practice and the Guidelines, especially paragraphs 3 (information), 6 (reasonable notice, co-operation to mitigate . . .), and 9 (access to the real decision-makers) of the Employment and Industrial Relations chapter. As important, if not more so, is the problem of the *financial* responsibility of headquarters for the debts of its subsidiaries. The Committee has accepted that there is, as an exception to the general rule, a principle of parent company responsibility, qualified in the light of such factors as aspects of the relationship between the parent company and the subsidiary and the conduct of the parent company. This responsibility of the parent company is of particular relevance in the cases set out in paragraph 6 of the chapter on Employment and Industrial Relations, relating to important changes in the operation of a firm and its co-operation as to the mitigation of resulting adverse effects (BADGER CASE).

(14) Negotiations, consultation, co-operation or provision of information imply effective communication between the parties concerned. As a general rule it is expected that *communication* will take place *in a language effectively understood by employees*. Nevertheless in case 5 where it may be unreasonably difficult to do so adequate interpreter and translation facilities should be provided. (Citibank)

V. FOLLOW-UP PROCEDURES – THE 1990 REVIEW

24. The *1979 review* concentrated on the *follow-up* procedures. Of the utmost importance in this respect is the recommendation of the IME Committee to all enterprises concerned that they indicate their acceptance of the Guidelines, preferably in their annual reports, and include in those reports brief statements of their experience with the Guidelines, which may contain mention of steps taken with respect to their observance as well as any difficulties experienced in this respect. As important is the setting up by national governments of facilities for handling enquiries (national contact points) and for discussions with the parties concerned on matters related to the Guidelines. As a matter of general principle such contacts should take place at national level before matters are raised at the international level.

25. The IME Committee, which has in practice interpreted its mandate in an evolving and dynamic manner, will remain the forum par excellence in which governments will have the opportunity to exchange views on all matters relating to the Guidelines and the experience gained in their application and to receive views on these matters from business and labour. The Committee is competent to discuss issues introduced by governments,

BIAC or TUAC and intends to respond in a timely manner to further requests for clarification.

26. Another important element in the follow-up is the bi-annual reporting by governments. These national reports will enable the Committee to assess the extent of acceptance and observance of the Guidelines; the action taken within OECD Member Countries by governments, business and labour organisations, and the companies themselves to give effect to them; and the areas where problems are being encountered.

27. The next *formal review* will take place in 1990. This provision does not preclude – in theory at least – an earlier review or certain modifications to these instruments before the end of the six-year period, but these are not likely.

28. Whether the impact of the Guidelines on life in the enterprises will increase will depend largely on the uses which labour and management make of the Guidelines, i.e. on whether in their negotiations and settlement of disputes, reference to the Guidelines is made. Much will depend on whether or not business and labour, especially the latter, which is a major driving force behind the Guidelines, will make use of the facilities, both at national and international level, by the introduction of cases and issues. The social partners must help Governments to see to it that their exchange of ideas continues to reflect the problems of the real world. The new follow-up procedures provide enhanced opportunities to that end.

Lately, however, fewer cases and requests for clarifications have been introduced and fewer clarifications have been given. This has undoubtedly to do with the spirit of the time which reflects the apprehension that further elaboration of rules, or an inclination to engage in that direction, may have counter-productive effects as far as investments and thus potential jobs are concerned.

One wonders what the Guidelines would look like if they were to be negotiated today.

SELECT BIBLIOGRAPHY

R. Blanpain, *The Badger Case and the OECD Guidelines for Multinational Enterprises*, Deventer, 1977, 211 pp.
The OECD Guidelines for Multinational Enterprises and Labour Relations: 1976–1979, Deventer, 1979, 309 pp.; 1979–82, 1983, 248 pp. 1982–1984, 1985, 202 pp.
International Labour Law, Case Law, IELL.
H. Günter, *IELL* (The Tripartite Declaration of Principles concerning Multinational Enterprises and Social Policy), 1983, 42 pp.
N. Horn, *Legal Problems of Codes of Conduct for Multinational Enterprises*, Deventer, 1980, 590 pp.
R. Smith, *IELL* (Codes of Conduct for Multinational Enterprises Operating in South Africa), Deventer, 1983, 46 pp.

Chapter 9. The International Trade Union Movement

J.P. Windmuller

I. Historical Overview

A. To 1914

1. Trade unions are preeminently national institutions. They pursue their primary tasks of defending and improving the conditions of life and work of their members within the confines of national systems of industrial relations. Yet for well over a century trade unions have also had international interests and commitments many of which they have expressed through international trade union organisations.

2. Two different types of international trade union organisations established themselves securely in the last decade of the nineteenth century and the first decade of the twentieth. One was based on an identity of interests among individual national unions for specific crafts, trades and industries in various countries and resulted in the formation of so-called International Trade Secretariats. The other type was of a broader character, for its members consisted of the central federations of trade unions, also called national centres.

3. International Trade Secretariats (often abbreviated as Secretariats or ITSs) first became established in 1889 with the creation of the International Federation of Boot and Shoe Operatives. Its constituent bodies were unions of workers engaged in boot and shoe manufacturing in several European countries. Organisations composed of unions in other trades and industries followed the example in the next few years, including those for miners (1890), clothing workers (1893), typographers (1893), metal workers (1890), textile workers (1894), transport workers (1896), and many others. By 1914 close to 30 ITSs existed. While acknowledging their support of long-range socialist aims, their main efforts were devoted to such practical tasks as disseminating trade information, helping travelling journeymen, and discouraging the international transport of strike-breakers.

4. The second type of international trade union organisation, composed of central trade union federations, emerged from conferences in Copenhagen (1901), Stuttgart (1902), and Dublin (1903). First known as the International

Secretariat of Trade Union Centers, the organisation called itself the International Federation of Trade Unions (IFTU) from 1913 on. Before the outbreak of war put an end to its activities, it claimed as affiliates about 20 central trade union federations with some 7,700,000 individual members, mostly from Europe, but also including the American Federation of Labor (AFL).

B. From 1914 to 1939

5. After the war the IFTU reorganised itself in 1919 under a new constitution at a meeting held in Amsterdam, while many ITSs, too, re-established their organisations. Another important development at this time was the establishment of two new organisations: the Red International of Labor Unions (RILU) and the International Federation of Christian Trade Unions (French initials: CISC). The RILU came into existence in 1921 when the leaders of the Communist Party in the Soviet Union decided to create a competing worldwide trade union international, often also called the Profintern. The formation of the so-called Popular Front in 1935 put an end to the activities of the RILU. At that time Communist parties and trade unions throughout the world were ordered by Moscow to co-operate with and join democratic political and trade union organisations to stem the advance of Nazi and fascist movements. The formal dissolution of the RILU, however, occurred only in 1943 when the Comintern was disbanded.

6. The creation of a separate Christian trade union international (CISC) in 1921 was the culmination of many years of organisational work among Christian workers in several European nations, particularly Germany, Italy, France, and the Low Countries. First organised at local or regional and then at national levels, the Christian trade unions offered an organisational and philosophical alternative to those believing Catholic and Protestant workers for whom membership in socialist unions, with their anticlerical and even anti-religious sentiments, was unacceptable.

7. Of the three international federations – IFTU, RILU, and CISC – the IFTU was the largest and certainly the most representative, even though its membership fluctuated from a peak of well over 20,000,000 in the immediate post-World War I period to fewer than 10,000,000 after the destruction of the German unions by the Nazi regime. When World War II broke out in 1939, the IFTU's affiliates claimed a total of about 14,000,000 members, including the American Federation of Labor.

C. After 1939

8. World War II did more than merely disrupt the functioning of interna-

tional trade union organisations. It also created the opportunity to reconsider fundamentally the international trade union structure. For many organisations, post-war labour unity in place of pre-war division became a key objective. A world labour conference, meeting in London in February 1945, decided to disband the IFTU and establish a new and all-encompassing world labour organisation, the World Federation of Trade Unions (WFTU). Its principal initiators were the British TUC, the Soviet AUCCTU, and the American CIO. The founding congress was held in Paris in October 1945. The most important absentee was the American Federation of Labor which as a matter of principle refused to be associated with unions controlled by governments of political parties, specifically with unions in Communist countries and more generally with Communist-dominated unions anywhere.

9. Other organisations that declined to join the WFTU were the affiliates of the Christian international labour federation (CISC). That rather small body re-established itself after the war on a scale even smaller than before 1939, due to the loss of important affiliates in Germany, Austria, and Italy where post-war drives favouring labour unity had led to the formation of all-encompassing trade unions. In the ensuing decades the CISC gradually abandoned its traditional ties to the Church and adopted a secular programme. In 1968 it adopted the name of the World Confederation of Labor (WCL).

10. In the WFTU the coexistence of organisations representing entirely different conceptions of the role of trade unions in society was of relatively short duration. When disagreements over the Marshall Plan and over other political and trade union issues became unbridgeable, unions from Western countries severed their ties with the WFTU in 1949. Later in the same year they launched a new organisation: the International Confederation of Free Trade Unions (ICFTU). In this endeavour the unions that disaffiliated from the WFTU were joined by the AFL.

11. The divisions that came about in the early post-war years have been maintained. There still exist currently three international trade union federations: the ICFTU, the WFTU, and the WCL. Given their worldwide scope, the three may be referred to as global internationals. They are, however, not in sole possession of the field, for there are quite a few other international trade unions serving specific regional or industrial interests, some of whom are of considerable importance. Clearly the world of international labour, limited though it may be, does not suffer from a shortage of organisations. On the contrary, the structures are profuse, and the relationships between the various parts are complex. Consequently one of the main objectives of the account which follows must be to establish a certain measure of order out of a rather chaotic situation.

II. The International Confederation of Free Trade Unions

12. By any measure except size the ICFTU is the most representative of the three global trade union internationals, especially since the American AFL-CIO decided to rejoin it in 1981 after an absence of 12 years. Not only are the ICFTU's affiliates the largest trade union organisations in almost every Western European country as well as in North America and Australasia, but the ICFTU also has sizable followings in Asia and Latin America. Only in Africa, for reasons to be explained, is it now sparsely represented. (See paragraph 24.) Of course in the Communist countries of Eastern Europe and elsewhere (Cuba, Vietnam, North Korea, the PR of China) it has no members at all. Ideologically the ICFTU is open to trade unions of various views – socialist, social-democratic, pragmatic. The only stipulation is that the affiliated organisation have reasonable freedom from domination by governments, political parties, or other external forces. Similarly wide is the range of members in terms of their countries' level of economic development: the ranks of the ICFTU include unions from the world's most highly industrialised countries and from some of the least developed ones.

A. Aims and Activities

1. Overall Goals

13. Because of the diversity of its membership the ICFTU has always taken care to formulate its basic aims in fairly general terms and to avoid taking sides on issues likely to be divisive, such as the nationalisation of basic industries or the transformation of society from capitalism to socialism. Instead it emphasises those beliefs and values that are shared by the largest possible number of constituents, including firm opposition to totalitarian regimes, support for all genuine efforts to safeguard world peace, endorsement of the struggle for social justice, and demands for the fair distribution of wealth and incomes at national and international levels. Within these basic aims there is room for more specific objectives whose formulation and priority are to some extent subject to changing circumstances. For example, calls for employment-creating measures are bound to be given more emphasis in periods of severe economic crisis than in times when job opportunities are plentiful.

2. Representational Work and Services

14. Most ICFTU activities can be divided into one of three categories: representation, organisation, and services. Representational work consists of the use of public forums, reports, resolutions, and similar means to express concerns and protests on a wide range of issues, from restrictions on freedom of association to the plight of migrant workers. In its representational capacity the ICFTU thus acts as a kind of international labour conscience, calling attention to injustices committed by governments or employers and appealing to the international community to exert its moral authority and pressure on behalf of a particular principle, cause, organisation, or individual, as in the case of an unjustly imprisoned trade union leader.

15. The organisational work of the ICFTU is directed chiefly to the promotion and strengthening of trade unionism in areas where unions are weak and vulnerable, thus mostly in countries of the Third World. The object is to strengthen those organisations which share the philosophy of trade unionism represented by the ICFTU. Assistance may include training programmes for union officials, direct financial subsidies, although this is now usually avoided, gifts of equipment, and study trips for selected leaders. Although the organisational work is a key activity, it is limited by available resources and must be co-ordinated with parallel activities conducted bilaterally by certain national trade union federations, including the American AFL-CIO, the German DGB, the Swedish LO, and several others.

16. The third set of ICFTU tasks, the provision of services, is closely linked to the representational and organising work. It includes not only conventional types of workers education, research, informational and public relations programmes, but has expanded in recent years into so-called 'extra-budgetary' development projects among which vocational training, medical and health care, employment promotion and the development of workers' co-operatives are particularly prominent.

B. *Structure and Government*

1. Membership and Finances

17. In the main the ICFTU is composed of national trade union centres, and as a rule only of one centre from one country. There are, however, exceptions. In some instances two national centres of similar scope, but separated by political or philosophical differences, have been accepted into membership. Italy (CISL and UIL) and India (INTUC and HMS) are apt examples. In other instances dual affiliation stems from the existence of separate organisations for blue-collar and white-collar workers, as in the case of Sweden (LO and TCO) and Denmark (LO and FTF). Individual unions are not generally eligible for membership, but some exceptions have been made for unions not affiliated with their national centre (the United Mine Workers in the United States) and for unions whose national centre does not belong to the ICFTU (Sohyo in Japan).

153

18. ICFTU membership figures are best regarded as rough estimates, since they are likely to be somewhat inflated by the claims of affiliates in countries where such data are usually unreliable. Figures for 1986 showed a total of 146 affiliates in 99 countries with an overall individual membership of about 82,000,000.[1] Europe has always been in first place in the geographic distribution of ICFTU membership, followed at some distance by North America, Asia, and Latin America (including the Caribbean). Africa and the Middle East are only weakly represented. In these two areas most governments discourage or prohibit affiliation.

19. To support its core activities the ICFTU until fairly recently depended essentially on two sources of income: regular affiliation fees from all members and voluntary contributions from the more affluent ones. Regular affiliation fees make up about two-thirds of the total, roughly $5 million out of $7.5 million, based on a rate that in 1986 was set at about $110 per 1,000 members, per year. This means that an organisation with some 9.5 million members, such as the British TUC, would be paying about $1 million in annual contributions. It is possible, however, to negotiate reductions where justified by special circumstances, such as unfavourable exchange rates, low levels of local dues, or restrictions on foreign currency transfers. In fact, a substantial number of affiliates, mostly in less developed countries, pay contributions at substantially reduced rates. As regards the voluntary payments, they have averaged about $2.5 million per year recently, and they serve to maintain the so-called International Solidarity Fund.

20. In the last decade a third source of income has become available which has greatly eased the ICFTU's financial position: the so-called extra-budgetary funds. These funds represent to some extent grants made by private organisations such as foundations, as well as intergovernmental agencies such as the International Labor Organisation, but to a much larger extent they consist of indirect allocations from the treasuries of various national governments, especially the Netherlands, the Scandinavian countries, and Canada. As part of their aid programs to less developed countries these governments have consented to support certain ICFTU-administered development programmes either by funding them directly or by making allocations to their own central trade union federations which, in turn, then pass on all or part of the amount provided to the ICFTU. (In several instances, extra-budgetary funds have also been made available to support the development work of the International Trade Secretariats which are discussed below.) In the first two or three years of the 1980s, the ICFTU's income from extra-budgetary funds averaged $3.5 million annually, a very sizable amount relative to the income contributed by affiliated organisations. In fact, because the availability of such large sums from government sources may create a variety of problems, the ICFTU has deemed it wise to

---

1. *ICFTU Report on Activities 1979–1982* (Brussels, 1983), p. 31.

adopt a special set of rules governing the acceptance and use of extra-budgetary funds.[2]

2. Governing Bodies and Secretariat

21. Policy-making responsibilities in the ICFTU are divided among several bodies. Supreme authority is vested in a congress which meets every four years. Because of their relatively large size and the long intervals between meetings, the congresses cannot be the key decision-making bodies. That role belongs to the Executive Board and particularly to certain committees of the Board. The membership of the Board currently consists of 37 titular representatives and an equal number of first and second substitutes, all chosen so as to ensure the widest possible geographic distribution. The general secretary is a Board member *ex officio*, and the International Trade Secretariats are entitled to be represented by four non-voting members. Normally the full Board meets twice a year. Urgent matters arising between Board sessions are placed before a subcommittee of about ten members. A special position is held by the Board's Finance and General Purposes Committee, whose voting members represent the ICFTU's most important affiliates in Europe, North America, and Asia. That committee has a broad mandate for allocating ICFTU resources, which are of course a key item in decision making.

22. Day-to-day ICFTU activities are the responsibility of a secretariat headed by a general secretary who is elected by the congress. Currently the position is held by John Vanderveken, a Belgian national, who has been associated with the ICFTU in several capacities since 1951. Of the five general secretaries who have held that office since 1949, four have been nationals of the Low Countries. This is not unusual; nationals of smaller countries tend to be regarded as neutrals in the contest for power or influence that sometimes develops between large constituents.

3. Regional Organisations

23. The ICFTU was the first international trade union body to foster the formation of regional organisations. This innovative idea was designed both to create a mechanism through which trade unions could join forces to cope with problems specific to their area of the world and also to avoid an excessive concentration of authority at ICFTU headquarters. The implementation of the idea, however, has been quite divergent. The ICFTU's regional organisations in Asia and the Western Hemisphere – known respec-

2. See the statement on 'Handling, Purposes and Manpower Implications of Projects Financed by Extrabudgetary Means' approved by the 12th ICFTU Congress in Madrid, November 1979.

tively as ARO and ORIT – have in the course of time become self-starting organisations, due largely to the presence, in their areas, of important national trade union federation able to provide leadership, direction, and financial support. To be sure, their efforts to develop a set of independent regional activities have not always proceeded smoothly, largely because their aspirations to regional autonomy have on occasion clashed with the central body's insistence on its own ultimate authority. But this is probably an inevitable problem, one that involves conflicting interests and priorities. For example, in the late 1970s the ICFTU Executive Board refused to approve a new constitution adopted by ORIT, the regional organisation for the inter-American region, because practically all references to ORIT's status as an ICFTU regional body had been dropped from the document, as had the references to the ultimate authority of the ICFTU Executive Board. A revised and more acceptable version did ultimately secure approval.[3] Similar examples could be cited to show the existence of occasional tensions between ICFTU headquarters and ARO, the Asian regional organisation.

24. Entirely different has been the experience in Africa. There the ICFTU's regional organisation (AFRO) has never developed sufficient momentum, nor has it ever had the resources, to become even a moderately autonomous body. A key obstacle to its development has been the opposition of most African governments to a regional trade union organisation under non-African authority, that is, one whose resources would depend largely on funds contributed from outside the African area. Most likely they fear that such a body would encourage a degree of independence and claims-making ability among trade unions that would go well beyond the point that the governments are willing to tolerate at this time.

25. Experience with regional organisations in Europe has taken still another course. Although it was in this area where the ICFTU established its first regional organisation (ERO), and although ERO easily had the potential for becoming a powerful body, its national trade union constituents decided to support the establishment of an even more widely based European trade union federation, one that would be open both to ICFTU affiliates and non-affiliates, but also therefore necessarily separate from the ICFTU. As a result of this decision, made in the early 1970s, ERO was dissolved and a nearly all-inclusive European Trade Union Confederation (ETUC) put in its place. Because the ETUC is independent from the ICFTU, it belongs to a separate section of this account.

III. THE WORLD FEDERATION OF TRADE UNIONS

26. Ever since the departure of a substantial portion of the WFTU's

3. *Report of the ICFTU 12th World Congress, 1979* (Brussels, 1979), p. 196.

affiliates in 1949 its principal constituents have been the labour organisations in countries that are governed by Communist parties. In addition the WFTU contains a substantial number of labour organisations from non-Communist countries, although most of these groups are of only secondary importance on their home grounds. One may, therefore, characterise the WFTU as being largely the international trade union body of the Soviet Bloc.

A. Aims and Activities

27. Under the terms of its constitution the WFTU's overall aim is 'to improve the living and working conditions of the people of all lands.' This is to be achieved by the organisation and unity of the world's working class, assistance to unions in less developed countries, opposition to war, and an unremitting struggle against fascism. Although that is a very broad mandate, the inability of trade unions in Communist countries to play an adversary role in domestic affairs has severely circumscribed the field of action of the WFTU inside the Bloc. That explains why the WFTU agenda is concerned to a very large extent with events and situations outside the Soviet orbit.

28. A foremost WFTU objective has always been firm support for the foreign policy goals of the Soviet Union. The lone and almost inexplicable exception was the WFTU secretariat's rebuke of the 1968 invasion of Czechoslovakia by the Warsaw Pact powers, but that singular deviation was quickly redressed and those responsible for it removed from their official positions. More characteristic are the uniformly optimistic accounts in WFTU publications of working conditions and trade union activities in the Soviet Union and other Communist countries, together with exposures of brutal violations of trade union freedoms and human rights in Western countries and a carefully selected group of Third World countries. An important WFTU activity, conducted in co-operation with certain affiliates, consists of training programmes for trade union leaders and activists from less developed countries. Considerable importance is also attached to the WFTU presence at United Nations headquarters and in the specialised UN agencies, especially the International Labour Office (ILO).

B. Structure and Government

1. Membership and Finances

29. Only recently has the WFTU published a list of membership figures since 1949, but there has never been any doubt about its claim to be the largest international labour federation. In 1982 its 90 affiliates contained, according to the WFTU, a total of 206,000,000 members. The number of union members claimed to be represented by the 810 participants at the

157

WFTU's 1982 Congress in Havana was 269,000,000. Whatever the proper figure may be, the Soviet labour federation (AUCCTU) accounts for over half of the total. It should be noted, of course, that union membership in Communist countries is usually close to the total non-agricultural labour force, if only because social benefits and various entitlements (access to vacation resorts, social insurances, etc.) are often administered by the unions. In other words, union membership confers important advantages.

30. Not all Communist-led countries are represented in the WFTU. Yugoslavia's unions were expelled in 1950 after that country had rejected Soviet hegemony. They were later invited to return but declined, although they have been sending observers to WFTU congresses and exchanging trade union delegations with Soviet Bloc countries. The unions in China and Albania exited in the mid-1960s, after the break between their countries and the USSR became irreparable. A more recent non-affiliate was Poland's now suppressed trade union, Solidarity. Also absent now, but for a different reason, are the Italian trade union federation CGIL and its Spanish counterpart, the CCOO. Both are indubitably under Communist leadership, but they happen to be closely linked to Communist parties whose ideological position may best be described as Eurocommunism. (The CGIL disaffiliated from the WFTU in 1978 after over 30 years of membership.) The French labour federation CGT also at one time considered disaffiliation but decided against it when the French Communist party lost interest in Eurocommunism.

31. Very little is known about the WFTU's finances. It is likely that its income stems mostly from affiliation fees and voluntary contributions, but the amounts involved and the rates are not available. Some years ago the budget figure for 1976 was very exceptionally made public and apparently amounted to $1.6 million.

2. Governing Bodies and Secretariats

32. In its internal government the WFTU follows the usual pattern of most international trade union bodies. Supreme authority is vested in a Congress which in recent decades has been meeting at four-year intervals. (In order to strengthen the impression that it is a widely representative organisation, the WFTU encourages attendance and participation by non-member organisations in the proceedings of its congresses.) The second echelon is filled by the General Council, whose composition indicates that it is a smaller version of the Congress. Still smaller is the Executive Bureau which has a membership of about 30 delegates chosen from the major affiliates. Finally there is the secretariat which consists of a general secretary – currently Ibrahim Zakaria, a national of the Sudan – and five secretaries, including always one from the Soviet Union.

3. Trade Unions International

33. Ostensibly to serve the industrial interests of its membership the WFTU has established eleven Trade Unions International (TUI) for individual economic sectors such as mining, metals, and transport. But whether the TUIs actually perform industrial functions is questionable, for in countries governed by Communist parties the main tasks assigned to trade unions are production-oriented. Only secondarily are the unions concerned with conventional protective and claims-making activities. The tenuous industrial role of the TUIs was once acknowledged by the head of the TUI for the textile industry who wrote in the WFTU's own journal, the *World Trade Union Movement*:

> The question of the relationship between the political and trade interests of the TUIs is often the subject of study. Various discussions are underway to see if the political problems and general resolutions are not predominant in the work of the TUIs, with matters relating to the particular branches of industry relegated to a back-seat position.[4]

34. TUI policies and activities are determined, at least in a general sense, by the WFTU, for the TUIs are not autonomous bodies. Moreover, their expenses are financed by allocations from the WFTU rather than by dues collected directly from their own member unions.

IV. THE WORLD CONFEDERATION OF LABOUR

A. *Membership*

35. When the World Confederation of Labour (WCL) abandoned its Christian identity in the mid-1960s, it adopted a militant secular programme based on a mixture of humanist, socialist, and syndicalist ideas. It also sought to alter the traditional balance of its programme and the composition of its membership by enlarging its activities in the less developed countries. At the time these key decisions were made, the core of the WCL's dues-paying membership consisted of a few affiliates in Belgium, the Netherlands, and France. Other affiliated organisations were scattered mostly among Third World countries where they usually ranked far below the affiliates of the ICFTU and the WFTU in terms of membership.

36. In the last few years, the already small nucleus of dues-paying European organisations has shrunk even further, and little if any compensatory growth has occurred in the outlying regions. The French CFDT, an important trade

---

4. *World Trade Union Movement*, No. 11, 1981, p. 4.

union federation in its own country, left the WCL's ranks in 1978. One of the two Dutch federations, the Catholic NKV, departed two years later. Both departing organisations had urged the WCL to engage in serious merger negotiations with the ICFTU, but to no avail.

37. The adverse financial consequences of their departure were substantially neutralised, however, by the availability of an indirect subsidy from the Dutch government's foreign economic aid program. The WCL was thus able to add to its income a sizable amount of 'extra-budgetary funds' – $600,000 in 1982 alone. This sum, together with funds contributed by the WCL's affiliates in Belgium and the Netherlands and by Catholic organisations in FR Germany, goes far to explain the remarkable survival of what is, all things considered, an exceedingly weak organisation.

B. Aims and Activities

38. Since its transformation in the 1950s the WCL has sought to emphasise its status as an ideological alternative both to the Marxist–Leninist materialism of the WFTU and the social-democratic welfare orientation of the ICFTU. It rejects the model of Soviet society almost as resolutely as it opposes 'international capitalism.' In place of either it propagates a system based on democratic planning, worker participation in decision-making, and trade union independence from any form of external control. According to its vision of the future, 'real democracy' and 'true socialism' will in due course become the earmarks of a genuinely egalitarian society, although nowhere in the WCL's programmatic statements have 'true socialism' and 'real democracy' ever been defined in concrete terms.

39. WCL activities focus on educational and social programs in the less developed countries. The organisation is also represented at most ILO meetings, but it has not been strong enough to gain even a single seat among the worker delegates on the ILO Governing Body. Its few remaining European affiliates participate in the work of relevant EEC agencies and European trade union bodies – including the ETUC.

C. Organisation and Structure

40. The WCL's arrangements for internal government follow a conventional four-tiered structure: a congress, a council, a confederal board, and an executive committee. The first three are composed of elected delegates from affiliated organisations, while the executive committee is made up mainly of full-time WCL officials: the general secretary and five assistant general secretaries.

41. Regional WCL organisations currently exist for Latin America (CLAT) and Asia (BATU). CLAT is militantly anti-establishment, anti-capitalist, and anti-American, and has concentrated its efforts particularly among peasants and agricultural workers. The European regional body (EO) was dissolved in 1974 when the WCL's European affiliates joined the new European trade union body – the ETUC. In the same year, the WCL's African organisation (PAWC) dissolved itself under pressure from African governments but continues to lead a shadowy existence as FOPADESC (Pan-African Foundation for Economic, Social and Cultural Development).

V. INDEPENDENT REGIONAL FEDERATIONS AND RELATED BODIES

42. The three international confederations reviewed in the preceding sections seek to attract eligible members in almost all parts of the world and for that reason may be referred to as global organisations. A more limited territory is claimed by an increasing number of regional and subregional trade union bodies, functioning not as affiliates of one of the global organisations but as independent entities. Of special importance are the European Trade Union Confederation (ETUC), the Organisation of African Trade Union Unity (OATUU), the Trade Union Advisory Committee to the Organisation for Economic Co-operation and Development (TUAC-OECD), and the Council of Nordic Trade Unions. Mention should also be made of the International Confederation of Arab Trade Unions (ICATU), which is an essentially political rather than trade union body, the fairly recently formed Commonwealth Trade Union Council, and the Council of Trade Unions linked to the ASEAN area (Association of South-East Asian Nations).

43. Regional organisations owe their existence to a multiplicity of reasons. Some were founded to express, in the domain of labour, the regional hegemonic aspirations of a particular country or ruler or to propagate a particular ideology, perhaps even both. Others came into existence mainly to articulate the joint economic interests of trade unions in a particular region or to meet a need for bringing the special concerns of workers to the attention of a regional intergovernmental entity such as the European Economic Commission. By and large political considerations have generally been dominant in the less developed areas and economic considerations have weighed more heavily in industrialised areas.

A. The European Trade Union Confederation

44. Currently by far the most important trade union body at European regional level is the European Trade Union Confederation (ETUC). It came into being in 1973, but had several forerunners which cannot be reviewed here.[5] The ETUC currently has 35 affiliates in 21 countries with a total membership of over 43 million. Headquarters are in Brussels where most European agencies of concern to the ETUC have their central office.

45. The ETUC is an entirely independent body organisationally and financially. Its membership includes almost all trade union federations in Western European countries (with a few exceptions noted below), and most of its activities are centred on the defence of joint trade union interests in the European Economic Community and other European-wide bodies.

46. The policies of the ETUC closely reflect the common concerns of its members. At present these are converging, above all, on the struggle against unemployment and persistent pressure on governments to adopt employment-oriented economic policies. Insofar as the Common Market countries co-ordinate their economic and social policies, the ETUC seeks to ensure that labour's top priorities are taken into account. The ETUC thus acts as a regional lobby in the context of a supranational agency, supplementing and to a certain extent harmonising the separate national efforts of its member organisations. Other areas of recent concern to the ETUC have included the extension of industrial democracy throughout the Common Market, the adoption of integrated energy policies, proposals to improve the work environment, and efforts to eliminate discriminatory treatment of the weaker segments of the labour force (women, young workers, migrants, the handicapped, etc.).

47. Political issues have generally been of secondary importance in ETUC activities, though the organisation regularly adopts formal resolutions expressing its support of political freedom, democratic forms of government, strict observance of human and trade union rights, peaceful coexistence, and negotiated steps toward disarmament. If differences on some of these issues exist, they tend to be matters of emphasis rather than principle and can usually be overcome by judicious formulations.

48. More difficult has been the question of eligibility for ETUC membership by Communist-led trade union organisations in Italy, France, Spain, and Portugal. Here the views of several key ETUC affiliates have diverged quite sharply. One group, led by the British TUC, considers all-inclusiveness to be more important than ideological compatibility and has favoured their admission, while another group, headed by the German DGB, has opposed it on grounds of principle. The outcome so far has been mixed. The Italian CGIL has been taken in, but the Communist-led organisations in France, Spain, and Portugal have had their requests denied or indefinitely deferred. Every time the issue has been raised it has brought on a major controversy.

5. See John P. Windmuller, 'European Regionalism: A New Factor in International Labour,' *Industrial Relations Journal*, Vol. 7, No. 2 (Summer 1976), pp. 35–48.

49. To round out its structure the ETUC has promoted the establishment of individual industry committees to represent the European-wide interests of workers and their unions in particular economic sectors, especially in metals, mining, agriculture, and communications. The industry committees act as lobbies and pressure groups, but may some-day seek to become bargaining agents for their constituents within a European-wide system of industrial relations.

50. The relationship of the ETUC's European industry committees to the International Trade Secretariats has raised certain jurisdictional problems that may be difficult to resolve. Some industry committees operate chiefly under ETUC auspices, while others are linked more closely to the ITSs in their particular economic sector. The conflicting pulls and the competitive channels of authority have been a source of considerable tension.

B. *The Organisation of African Trade Union Unity*

51. Although trade unionism in most African countries is of relatively recent origin, several regional organisations for Africa have already appeared and then disappeared – some oriented toward Western conceptions of trade unionism, others more compatible with the WFTU trade union model. Most African governments have shown little tolerance for trade union pluralism or for trade unions independent of government control, and with their support the intergovernmental Organisation of African Unity (OAU) in 1973 established a regional trade union organisation – the Organisation of African Trade Union Unity (OATUU) – that was intended to be an all-inclusive and unitary regional trade union body for Africa. But in recent years the OATUU's claim to exercise a regional monopoly has received several setbacks, and an increasing number of African trade unions have affiliated with the ICFTU or WFTU, depending on their ideological orientation.

52. Despite its exclusionary mandate, the OATUU maintains working relations with the ICFTU, WFTU, and WCL and co-operates with them in various activities such as labour education programmes. But it also hews closely to the political and ideological positions adopted by the OAU. Consequently the OATUU has adopted a position of so-called 'positive neutrality' in world affairs and proclaims itself to be an anti-capitalist, anti-imperialist, anti-colonialist, and anti-Zionist organisation. The major targets of its criticism are forces external to the region, in particular multinational corporations and their governments in Western countries. By contrast, African governments and their sometimes very harsh labour and social policies are treated with much circumspection. Of the obscure financial arrangements in the OATUU it can be said with confidence only that it is not supported solely or even chiefly by contributions from its own

163

affiliates and that government subsidies from Libya and perhaps elsewhere are of considerable importance in balancing the books.

C. The Trade Union Advisory Committee to the OECD (TUAC-OECD)

53. When the Marshall Plan for European economic recovery from the ravages of World War II neared completion in the early 1960s, the participating governments in Europe and North America decided to maintain certain supra-national structures that had played a key role in the administration of the programme. That decision accounts for the existence of the Organisation for Economic Co-operation and Development (OECD) and its trade union 'satellite,' the Trade Union Advisory Committee (TUAC-OECD).

54. TUAC represents trade union interests at the OECD in about the same way as the ETUC represents trade union interests in the Common Market agencies. Its constituents are some 40 trade union federations from 24 OECD member countries in the European area, North America, and Japan. Virtually all TUAC members are affiliates of the ICFTU or the WCL, but no affiliates or former affiliates of the WFTU have ever been admitted to membership.

55. Because the OECD itself is basically a research-oriented, idea-producing, and consensus-seeking organisation in key areas of economic policies rather than an action agency, TUAC's foremost objective is to ensure that adequate consideration is given to trade union viewpoints in the preparation of OECD reports, studies, and policy recommendations to member governments. In recent years OECD agenda items of chief interest to TUAC have included employment creation, manpower and human resource development programmes, trade and tariff issues, and the development and supervision of international guidelines for the conduct of multinational companies – an area in which the OECD has done some pioneering work.[6]

D. Subregional Bodies

56. Regional coalitions of countries seem to lead, sooner or later, to the emergence of parallel coalitions of trade unions. That tendency holds not only for genuine regional alliances, as in the case of the European Common Market, but also for inter-regional and subregional groupings. For example, the Commonwealth (formerly called the British Commonwealth of Nations),

6. See Duncan C. Campbell and Richard L. Rowan, *Multinational Enterprises and the OECD Industrial Relations Guidelines* (Philadelphia: The Wharton School, University of Pennsylvania, 1983).

which is a loose association of states based chiefly on a shared historical attachment to the former British Empire, has recently (1980) spawned a Commonwealth Trade Council whose declared purpose it is to ensure that 'trade union views are taken into account by Commonwealth governments and institutions.' A similar instance is the ASEAN Council of Trade Unions, a recently formed alliance of trade union federations in the five member countries of the Association of South East Asian nations.

57. A flourishing group of this kind is the Council of Nordic Trade Unions, a subregional association of trade union federations in the five Nordic countries (Sweden, Norway, Denmark, Finland, Iceland), founded in 1972, whose membership is expressly limited to organisations affiliated both with the ICFTU and ETUC. (That rule is designed to exclude federations representing the special interests of professional and managerial employees.) With a budget of about $600,000 and a full-time staff of seven professionals, the Nordic Council co-ordinates the policies of its member organisations on socioeconomic and labour market issues of concern to the Nordic governments, such as free labour mobility, social welfare, social insurance, and international trade; prepares research papers and policy positions on these matters; and serves as a device for reaching an identity of views among Nordic trade unions participating in international labour bodies. By acting as a unified bloc in the ICFTU, ETUC, TUAC, ILO, and similar organisations, the unions of the Nordic countries increase their weight by a considerable margin. Moreover, their joint views carry greater force in bilateral contacts with sister organisations elsewhere, such as the British, German, and American labour federations.

VI. INTERNATIONAL TRADE SECRETARIATS

58. The organisations to be reviewed in this section, the International Trade Secretariats (ITSs), differ from those in the preceding sections in that they are composed of individual national unions grouped according to major sectors of industry. Their mandate is primarily an economic or industrial rather than a political one, and their focus is on developments and problems in particular economic or industrial sectors. Consequently they are sometimes referred to as industrial internationals.

A. *Organisation and Structure*

1. Relations with Global Internationals

59. The ITSs are autonomous and self-governing organisations. Collectively their relationship to the ICFTU is based on the so-called Milan Agreement of 1951 (revised in 1969) under which the ITSs agree to follow the ICFTU's lead on broad policy issues, while the ICFTU recognises the General Conference of the ITSs as the joint representative of ITS interests and grants non-voting representation to the ITSs in all ICFTU governing organs.

60. The principle of autonomy determines not only the relations between the ITSs and the ICFTU but also among the ITSs themselves. Their formal link is a General Conference, a loosely structured body which meets about once a year for a review of common problems and interests. Informal contracts are, of course, far more extensive, both among top ITS officials and between them and the ICFTU leadership. They are, after all, constituent parts of the same general labour movement, sharing identical or at least very similar values and conceptions with regard to the position of trade unions in society.

2. Membership and Finances

61. There are currently 14 ITSs. The number has declined over the years, mostly due to mergers. On the other hand, mergers plus successful recruitment efforts have considerably increased the size of almost all ITSs. The largest organisation by far is the International Metalworkers' Federation with about 140 affiliated organisations distributed among some 70 countries and representing about 14,000,000 workers. Other ITSs with at least 4,000,000 members include the Commercial and Clerical Workers, Public Service Employees, Chemical Workers, Textile Workers, and Transport Workers. Although Western Europe and North America account for the bulk of ITS membership (with the exception of the Plantation Workers), most ITSs contain affiliates from almost all parts of the world except the Communist-ruled countries.

62. In order to be truly independent, trade unions must be financially self-reliant. With one or two exceptions the ITSs meet that condition. Each ITS has its own source of income. Average current dues are probably about $0.75 per individual member per year, but each ITS has a dues structure of its own. For those ITSs that are engaged in particularly extensive activities in Third World countries, special levies and supplemental outside funding constitute important sources of extra income. Special grants for educational and union-building programmes have been made available by the ILO and the foreign aid agencies of European and North American governments. Some ITSs, however, have declined such external support to avoid jeopardising their independence.

3. Governing Bodies and Trade Groups

63. Although each ITS operates under its own system of internal government, a fairly common pattern prevails which usually includes a general assembly or congress, an executive board, and the elected officers and staff. The congresses, although not of great decision-making importance, are useful occasions to cement the ties between the ITS and its affiliated organisations, particularly those affiliates which are not sufficiently large and important to occupy a seat on the executive board. Unfortunately, however, the intervals between ITS congresses have become increasingly longer in the last few decades and now average three to four years. A key role in each ITS is played by its top full-time official, the general secretary. Indeed, the calibre of the general secretary is the main determinant of the effectiveness with which an ITS performs its functions.

64. When the ITSs were first established toward the end of the nineteenth century and the beginning of the twentieth, many covered only a single occupation or a limited industrial sector. That is no longer the case. Mergers and the rise of new industries have transformed most ITSs into multi-industrial or multi-occupational bodies whose component sub-groups sometimes face entirely different challenges in their spheres of activity. To cope with this diversification several ITSs have established separate industrial sectors. The Metal workers ITS, for example, whose industrial jurisdiction includes automotive manufacturing, basic steel, mechanical engineering, electrical and electronic products, shipbuilding and several other sectors, has established an equivalent number of trade groups to meet the varying needs of its affiliated unions, especially unions in countries where the structure of unionism is relatively fragmented and specialised, as in Britain and the United States.

B. Aims and Activities

65. Advancing the joint interests of their constituents, and particularly their economic interests, remains the principal aim of the ITSs. They do, of course, also declare their support of the search for a more just social order, the protection of human and trade union rights, the extension of democratic forms of government, and the maintenance of peace with freedom. But their traditional orientation and their structural make-up leads them to stress practical trade union work, and this they perform in a variety of ways.

1. Solidarity and Organisational Work

66. Mobilising international support on behalf of an affiliated organisation involved in a major domestic conflict is one such activity. Support may be expressed in various forms: moral encouragement, appeals to member organisations to extend financial assistance (the ITSs usually do not maintain strike funds of their own), co-ordination of international boycott actions against employers, or public condemnation of a government for particularly harsh anti-union measures.[7]

67. A major portion of ITS activities since the early 1950s has been the organisational work in Third World countries. The aim is the establishment or reinforcement of individual unions to the point where they can effectively represent the interests of their members and at the same time contribute to the development and modernisation of their societies.

2. Information and Research

68. Disseminating information about economic conditions and terms of employment in particular industrial sectors has long been one of the most useful services which the ITSs provide to their members. Some of the larger ITSs have recently begun to compile and computerise data on the financial condition and terms of employment of large individual firms, particularly multinational firms, so as to be able to make this information readily available to affiliates for use in collective bargaining. Some ITSs have initiated research on the long-term economic outlook for the industries in which they operate, with special attention to prospective changes in the volume and structure of employment. Increasingly, too, several ITSs are attending to problems of occupational health and safety in their sectors.

3. Multinational Companies

69. As long as collective bargaining remains primarily a national rather than an international activity, the influence which the ITSs can exert on the outcome will be a relatively modest one. However, the expansion of multinational companies during the past few decades and the adoption by the OECD and other international bodies of international codes of conduct for employers raise the possibility that international bargaining structures may emerge in which the ITSs could become a key participant on the employee side. Some initial steps in that direction have already been taken. The Metalworkers' ITS, for instance, has established several so-called corporation councils for a substantial number of multinational companies (General Motors, Ford, etc.) to facilitate some bargaining co-ordination among unions in different countries whose numbers are employed in the subsidiaries of these corporations. Although the process of creating a world-wide united front on the union side is likely to be extremely slow,

---

7. For an ITS engaged in an unusually broad range of activities on behalf of employee interests see Herbert R. Northrup and Richard L. Rowan, *The International Transport Workers and Flag of Convenience Shipping* (Philadelphia: The Wharton School, University of Pennsylvania, 1983).

attempts to achieve regional co-operation as a first step may yield results more quickly, especially at European level.

70. Co-ordinated international union action may also result from the appointments of leading ITS officials to membership on corporate boards of directors under national co-determination laws. This has been happening on a modest scale in the FR Germany, where some industrial unions have named top ITS officials to board seats assigned by law to employee representatives. (German law does not require board members to be German citizens.) A few board seats may not make much difference, especially not when the firms involved are subsidiaries of multinationals headquartered outside FR Germany. But if the German pattern of co-determination is ever extended to other Common Market countries, as has been proposed, the presence of ITS officials on corporate boards could become a factor in the internationalisation of industrial relations.

VII. Concluding Observations

71. Although trade unions must generally operate within national economic, social, political, and legal contexts, they have nevertheless established a complex even if fragmented network of international associations. To some extent the fragmentation is caused by the functional distinctions between the broad political concerns of national trade union federations and the more specific industrial concerns of individual national unions. But that is only a partial explanation, for ideological commitments and regional attachments have become even more important determinants of separatism and fragmentation.

72. Ideological differences of a fundamental nature separate the international bodies of trade unions in democratic countries with market-oriented economies from international labour organisations in planned economies under Communist party direction. This is a division that is likely to persist, for it is linked to transcending differences over the organisation of society and the principles that should govern the relations between individuals, institutions, and the state.

73. An increasingly important factor contributing to fragmentation is regionalism. It extends, as we have seen, not only to the new countries of the Third World, but has also spread to the older regions, as shown by the emergence of an independent European Trade Union Confederation and the Nordic Council of Trade Unions, both being active and independent organisations strongly supported by their affiliates. Regionalism is likely to remain a decisive factor shaping the structure of international trade unionism.

74. There is no need to inflate the importance of international trade union bodies. On the whole they are auxiliaries and agents rather than principals. Those among them that are *bona fide* organisations will probably continue to play a constructive role in promoting the extension of trade union and human rights, encouraging as far as their means permit the growth of trade unions in developing areas, representing the viewpoints and interests of workers before international agencies, and mobilising trade union efforts to establish an international system of industrial relations. It is not spectacular work, but it is useful and deserves more attention than it usually receives.

SELECT BIBLIOGRAPHY

B. Barnouin, *The European Labor Movement and European Integration*, London, 1986.
A.P. Coldrick and Philip Jones, *The International Directory of the Trade Union Movement*, London and New York, 1979.
L.L. Lorwin, *The International Labor Movement: History, Policies, Outlook*, New York, 1953.
S. Mielke (ed.), *Internationales Gewerkschaftshandbuch*, Opladen, 1983.
R. Miotto, *Les Syndicats Multinationaux*, Rome: Instituto per l'Economia Europa, 1976.
R. Neuhaus, *International Trade Secretariats: Objectives, Organization, Activities*, Bonn, 1982.
E. Piehl, *Multinationale Konzerne und Internationale Gewerkschaftsbewegung*, Frankfurt, 1973.
R.L. Rowan, *et al.*, *Multinational Union Organizations in the White-Collar, Service, and Communications Industries*, Philadelphia, 1983.
R. Rowan, *et al.*, *Multinational Union Organizations in the Manufacturing Industries*, Philadelphia, 1980.
J.P. Windmuller, *The International Trade Union Movement*, Deventer, 1987.

Comparative Studies

Chapter 10. Freedom of Association

A. Pankert

1. In the present monograph, the expression 'freedom of association' refers to the right of workers and employers to organise for the defence of their occupational interests. The expression will be taken in its broad sense, which means that it will not only include the right to set up associations but also a number of other rights without which the right to organise would lose much of its meaning (e.g. the right of the associations to organise their administration and activities freely).

2. Freedom of association is a basic feature of any pluralist society. If it is accepted that decisions on economic and labour issues should not be monopolised by the State but that workers and employers should also play an important role in this respect, it is self-evident that the latter must be given the right to set up organisations for the defence of their occupational interests and that these organisations must be granted the rights which are necessary for them to act effectively. Although the basic principles of freedom of association apply to workers and employers alike, it will be seen below that in practice most problems have arisen in connection with trade unions rather than with employers' organisations. The main reason for this is probably that many governments are more concerned about the potential influence of trade unions on national life and have therefore attempted to control them more closely.

I. LEGAL SOURCES

A. National

3. In many countries, there is a *constitutional basis* for freedom of association. Several national constitutions merely recognize, in a general way, the right of all citizens to set up associations of any kind (e.g. United States). Others specifically establish the right of workers and employers to organise for the defence of their occupational interests (e.g. FR Germany). Among the latter constitutions, some refer to such implications of freedom of association as the right to bargain collectively or the right to strike (e.g. France), but most of them only mention the right to organise in general terms.

4. A great number of countries in all parts of the world have detailed *legislation* on various subjects which are concerned with the external activities of workers' and employers' organisations such as collective bargaining. The situation is different with regard to the establishment and the internal functioning of the organisations concerned as well as with regard to one particular aspect of their external activities, i.e. the right to strike and to lock out. While a number of developing countries in Africa, Asia and Latin America have enacted comprehensive legislation on these subjects, the majority of highly industrialised countries have only adopted a small number of provisions in this respect. The aim of these provisions is either to set out, in general terms, the basic principles to be observed in the areas concerned or to deal with specific issues which have caused particular problems (e.g. the closed shop and trade union immunities in the case of labour disputes in the United Kingdom).

B. *International*

5. The best known international standards on freedom of association are those adopted by the *International Labour Organisation* (ILO). These standards have a considerable impact at the national level. One reason is that the basic instruments in this field have received an exceptionally high number of ratifications. Another reason is that their application is monitored by a highly sophisticated supervisory machinery. It seems therefore appropriate, before engaging in any comparative analysis of national legislation and practice, to provide some brief information on the contents of ILO standards as well as on the supervision of their application.

6. The most important ILO instruments on freedom of association are Convention (No. 87) concerning Freedom of Association and Protection of the Right to Organise, 1948 and Convention (No. 98) concerning the Application of the Principles of the Right to Organise and to Bargain Collectively, 1949. Convention No. 87 – which does not apply to the armed forces and the police – contains four main provisions. The first provides that workers and employers, without distinction, shall have the right to establish and to join organisations of their own choosing, without previous authorisation. The second states that workers' and employers' organisations shall have the right to draw up their constitutions and rules, to elect their representatives, to organise their administration and activities and to formulate their programmes. The third prohibits the suspension and dissolution of workers' and employers' organisations by administrative authority. The fourth provides that workers' and employers' organisations shall have the right to establish and join federations and confederations – which shall have the same rights as their constituent organisations – and to affiliate with international organisations of workers and employers. Convention No. 98 – which does not apply to the armed forces, the police and public servants engaged in the administration of the State – aims at the protection, on the

one hand, of workers against anti-union discrimination in respect of their employment and, on the other hand, of workers' and employers' organisations against interference by each other. It also calls for measures, appropriate to national conditions, to encourage and promote the full development of collective bargaining.

7. Other important ILO instruments on freedom of association are Convention (No. 135) and Recommendation (No. 143) concerning Protection and Facilities to be Afforded to Workers' Representatives in the Undertaking, 1971, Convention (No. 141) and Recommendation (No. 149) concerning Organisations of Rural Workers and their Role in Economic and Social Development, 1975, Convention (No. 151) and Recommendation (No. 159) concerning Protection of the Right to Organise and Procedures for Determining Conditions of Employment in the Public Service, 1978 as well as Convention (No. 153) and Recommendation (No. 164) concerning the Promotion of Collective Bargaining, 1981. The objective of Convention No. 135 and Recommendation No. 143 is to protect workers' representatives in the undertaking – whether designated by the trade unions or elected by the workers – against any act prejudicial to them, including dismissal, which is based on their trade union status or activities and to give them such facilities as are appropriate to enable them to carry out their functions. Convention No. 141 and Recommendation No. 149, taking into account the particular difficulties encountered with regard to the organisation of rural workers, recall the basic principles of freedom of association contained in Conventions Nos. 87 and 98 and prescribe or suggest the adoption of measures designed to promote the effective development of rural workers' organisations. Convention No. 151 and Recommendation No. 159, which apply to those public employees who are not covered by Convention No. 98, include protective measures against anti-union discrimination and against interference by public authorities in the affairs of public employees' organisations. Convention No. 151 also contains provisions on various other issues such as the facilities to be afforded to the representatives of public employees' organisations and the procedures for determining the terms and conditions of employment of public employees, whether through collective bargaining or otherwise. Convention No. 153 and Recommendation No. 164 contain prescriptions and suggestions on the implementation of the general principle of encouraging collective bargaining already contained in Convention No. 98.

8. There are several procedures for supervising the application of ILO standards on freedom of association. In the first place, the general supervisory procedures, which are applicable to all ILO conventions and which are described in detail in another monograph of the present text,[1] apply of course to the conventions on freedom of association. In the second place,

1. See above, chapter 5.

there are special supervisory procedures in the area of freedom of association. Governments as well as national and international workers' and
employers' organisations may submit complaints against a government which
allegedly does not observe the principles of freedom of association. These
complaints may be addressed either to the Committee on Freedom of
Association of the ILO Governing Body or, under certain conditions, to the
Fact-Finding and Conciliation Commission. Such complaints may be
directed even against a government which has not ratified the ILO conventions on freedom of association. The reason is that ILO membership is
conditional upon the acceptance of the obligations set out in the ILO
Constitution, which enunciates, although in general terms, the principle of
freedom of association. The Committee on Freedom of Association has so
far examined more than 1,300 cases and has thus played a far more
important role than the Fact-Finding and Conciliation Commission, which
has only examined five cases. It must be emphasised in this respect that the
number of complaints addressed to the Committee on Freedom of Association has dramatically increased in recent years. While the vast majority of
complaints is still concerned with the situation in developing countries, the
number of those relating to industrialised countries (and, more particularly,
to the restrictive wage policies initiated by the governments of many of these
countries during the last decade or so in order to fight inflation and
unemployment) is also on the increase. The Committee on Freedom of
Association, which was set up in 1951, is of a tripartite composition. Its
functions are of a quasi-judicial nature. It submits its conclusions and
recommendations to the Governing Body for adoption. Over the years, the
Committee has developed a voluminous and detailed case law which has a
world-wide influence.

9. A number of *other international organisations* have also adopted standards on freedom of association. These standards are less detailed than
those of the ILO. In addition, the machinery for supervising their application, if any, is less well developed than the ILO machinery. Provisions on
freedom of association are included in several United Nations instruments,
i.e. the 1948 Universal Declaration of Human Rights (Articles 20 and 23,
paragraph 4), the 1966 International Covenant on Economic, Social and
Cultural Rights (Article 8) and the 1966 International Covenant on Civil and
Political Rights (Article 22). Among the regional instruments containing
provisions on freedom of association are the 1948 American Declaration of
the Rights and Duties of Men, adopted at the Ninth International Conference of American States in Bogota (Article 22), the 1950 European Convention for the Protection of Human Rights and Fundamental Freedoms
(Article 11) and the 1961 European Social Charter (Part II, Articles 5 and
6), both of which were adopted within the Council of Europe. All the
above-mentioned instruments recognise the right to organise in general
terms. A number of them also refer to the right to strike (e.g. the
International Covenant on Economic, Social and Cultural Rights and the

European Social Charter) or to other matters related to freedom of association such as collective bargaining (e.g. the European Social Charter).

It is clear from the above survey of national and international legal sources that the issue of freedom of association presents many different aspects. For reasons of space, it will not be possible to deal with all of them here. An attempt will however be made to examine the most important ones, with a geographical coverage which is world-wide, but excluding countries with a centrally planned economy. This comparative analysis of national legislation and practice will be based to a large extent on the conceptual framework used in the ILO instruments on freedom of association. Mention will also be made of the positions adopted by the ILO Committee on Freedom of Association with respect to the various subject matters dealt with below.

II. ESTABLISHMENT OF ORGANISATIONS, FEDERATIONS AND CONFEDERATIONS

A. *The Right of Workers and Employers to Establish and Join Organisations of their own Choosing without Previous Authorisation*

1. The Right to Organise

10. The issue dealt with in this section is whether the various categories of workers and employers have or do not have the right to organise. Consideration will be given later to cases where this right exists but where the free choice of organisations is restricted, for example because workers of a certain category may not set up a trade union together with workers of a certain other category.[2]

11. Convention No. 87 grants the right to organise to all workers and employers but, according to Article 9, 'the extent to which the guarantee provided for . . . shall apply to the armed forces and the police shall be determined by national laws and regulations'.

12. If one sets aside instances where trade unions have been suspended or dissolved as a consequence of dramatic changes in a country's political situation, it may be said that the right to organise of most categories of workers and employers covered by Convention No. 87 is generally recognised. In Africa, Asia and Latin America there are examples of discriminatory provisions based on such criteria as race, nationality or political activities, but they are small in number. By far the most important problem – particularly but not exclusively in the developing regions of the

---

2. See paragraphs 14–21 below.

world – concerns public employees.[3] In a certain number of countries, the right to organise is still denied to this category of personnel (e.g. Ethiopia, Liberia and several Latin American countries). In the majority of countries, however, the right to organise is nowadays granted to public employees; but here too there are nevertheless prohibitions or severe restrictions of various kinds, not only for the armed forces and the police but sometimes also for firemen (e.g. Gabon, Japan), prison staff (e.g. Mexico, Nigeria, Pakistan) and public employees occupying managerial, supervisory or confidential positions (e.g. Colombia, Egypt, Singapore).

13. The right of agricultural workers to organise is usually recognised in law, but the extent of their organisation is actually less developed than that of industrialised workers for reasons such as lack of education, dispersal, difficulties of communication in the countryside and the migratory nature of the workforce in certain cases. An exception to this general rule is the plantation sector, mainly because it is characterised by a high concentration of labour. As mentioned earlier, Convention (No. 141) and Recommendation (No. 149) concerning Organisations of Rural Workers and Their Role in Economic and Social Development, 1975 were adopted to promote the effective development of rural workers' organisations. For reasons which are to a certain extent similar to those just mentioned with regard to the agricultrual sector, trade unionism is also less well implanted in small industrial or artisan-type undertakings in both rural and urban areas. Since these undertakings, together with the agricultural sector, represent a very high percentage of the economic activity of most developing countries (where they are usually called the 'informal sector'), the problems dealt with in this paragraph are particularly serious in these countries.

2. The Choice of Organisation

14. The right of workers and employers to establish and join organisations *of their own choosing*, which is embodied in Convention No. 87, has hardly raised any serious problems in highly industrialised countries. In a number of developing countries, on the contrary, difficulties have arisen on several issues, which concern either the composition and structure of organisations or the question of trade union monopoly.

---

3. The definition of the concept of 'public employee' raises many difficult problems which cannot be dealt with here for reasons of space. We may note however that in some countries the concept only covers employees who, by their function, are directly engaged in the administration of the State, whereas in other countries it also covers other persons employed by the public authorities, persons employed by autonomous public bodies or even persons employed by public undertakings. For more details, see *ILO, Freedom of Association and Procedures for Determining Conditions of Employment in the Public Service*, Report VII(1) submitted to the 63rd Session of the International Labour Conference, 1977, pp. 5–14.

a. Composition and Structure of Organisations

15. The legislation of many countries contains minimum membership requirements for trade unions, which are expressed either in absolute figures or in percentages. No objections have been raised against these requirements by the Committee on Freedom of Association of the ILO Governing Body, provided they are set at a 'reasonable rate'. According to the Committee, a 50-member requirement would be too high for an enterprise union.

16. In several countries, membership of trade unions is restricted to persons belonging to similar branches of activity or occupations (e.g. Brazil, Kuwait, Malaysia). The Committee on Freedom of Association has accepted such regulations, provided that primary organisations may join federations or confederations whose membership is not restricted to any particular category of workers. The same principle applies where public employees may not belong to the same trade unions as workers of the private sector (e.g. Malaysia). According to the Committee on Freedom of Association, there may on the contrary be problems of compatibility with Convention No. 87 where the legislation does not only restrict union membership to workers of similar branches of activity or occupations, but also fixes the structure, by branches of activity or occupations, of the trade union movement (e.g. Libya, Iraq).

17. A particular problem has arisen in respect of managerial staff, who are precluded from joining the same union as lower echelon employees in several countries (e.g. Japan, Mexico). The Committee on Freedom of Association has considered that such provisions are in line with Convention No. 87, provided the staff concerned have the right to set up their own organisations and provided the concept of managerial personnel is defined very narrowly.

b. Trade Union Monopoly

18. The legislation of some countries provides that there may only be one trade union for the workers of a given unit or category – such as an undertaking, a branch of activity or an occupation – it being understood however that these unions may freely federate and confederate (e.g. Colombia, Panama). In other countries, the number of which has been on the increase in recent years, legislation prescribes a single trade union structure at all levels, including the federal and confederal levels (e.g. Egypt, Ethiopia, Kenya, Tanzania, Zambia).

19. It is obvious that the provisions mentioned in the preceding paragraph generally have technical as well as political objectives. Technically, their purpose is to avoid trade union multiplicity, which may have many negative consequences in the field of labour relations. Usually these provisions also pursue, however, a political aim, which is to permit a certain amount of control of the trade union movement by the public authorities. It may be noted in this connection that most of the countries which have imposed a single trade union structure at all levels only have one political party and that there are usually close links between the latter and the trade union movement. The Committee on Freedom of Association has made it clear that provisions which impose a trade union monopoly at whatever level are at variance with the principle of freedom of association. Convention No. 87 does not prescribe trade union diversity, but it requires this diversity to remain possible. It may be to the advantage of the workers to avoid trade union multiplicity, but a single trade union structure may not be imposed by law.

20. The Committee of Freedom of Association has similarly considered that the right of workers and employers to set up organisations of their own choosing is denied if the registration of a trade union may be refused by the competent authority because there already exists another union of the same category of workers (e.g. Malaysia, Singapore).

21. The legislation of several countries, both developing and highly industrialised, provides that in a given bargaining unit the right to bargain may only be exercised by one single trade union. This union is generally called the 'sole bargaining agent' and must represent a certain percentage – normally an absolute majority – of the workers concerned (e.g. Canada, Mexico, Pakistan, United States). In other countries, the right to bargain collectively is limited to all unions which fulfil certain conditions of representativeness laid down by law and which are usually called 'most representative unions' (e.g. France, Belgium). The Committee on Freedom of Association has raised no objections against such provisions, provided that the representative character of the unions concerned is ascertained in accordance with objective criteria and that minority unions are allowed to function and have at least the right to make representations on behalf of their members and to represent them in cases of individual grievance.

3. Previous Authorisation

22. Convention No. 87 provides that employers and workers must have the right to set up organisations 'without previous authorisation'. In the majority of countries, a number of formalities – such as the deposit of rules, registration or the acquisition of legal personality – are compulsory. In other countries, which are few in number, these formalities are optional, it being understood however that an organisation which does not comply with these formalities loses such important advantages as fiscal immunities, the right to have recourse to the existing dispute settlement machinery or the right to obtain recognition as the sole bargaining agent (e.g. Australia, Pakistan). In still other countries, most of which belong to the highly industrialised parts of the world, there are no special formalities required (e.g. Belgium, Denmark, FR Germany, Italy, Sweden, Switzerland). The Committee on Freedom of Association has pointed out that the establishment of organisations may be made subject to certain formalities, but that these requirements may not be such as to be equivalent to previous authorisation or even to a prohibition. The Committee has also underlined that whenever an administrative authority has refused authorisation, an appeal should be possible to the judiciary and that the latter should be competent to re-examine the grounds for the administrative decision.

B. The Right of Workers Not to Join a Union

23. With regard to the right of workers not to join a trade union, it appears from the discussions prior to the adoption of Convention No. 87 'that Article 2 of the Convention leaves it to the practice and regulations of each State to decide whether it is appropriate to guarantee the right of workers not to join an occupational organisation or, on the other hand, to authorise and, where necessary, to regulate the use of union security clauses in practice. . . . The situation is altogether different when union security ceases to be based on clauses freely agreed upon between workers' unions and employers but is imposed by the law itself on workers. This is the case when the law makes it compulsory to join a union or when it designates a specific trade union as benefitting from the system, or when the law establishes the system of compulsory trade union contributions in circumstances such that the same aim is achieved. Such provisions are similar in their results to those establishing a trade union monopoly and are not compatible with the right of workers to establish and join organisations of their own choosing'.[4]

24. None of the international instruments listed in paragraph 9 above explicitly mentions the right of workers not to join a trade union. Discussions on whether or not the Universal Declaration of Human Rights guarantees such a right are still going on. As far as the European Social Charter is concerned, it is spelt out in its Annex that the relevant provisions of the Charter 'shall not be interpreted as prohibiting or authorising any union security clause or practice'. The issue of negative freedom of association has never been raised during the *travaux preparatoires* of the International Convenant on Economic, Social, and Cultural Rights. During the discussion preceding the adoption of the International Covenant on Civil and Political Rights and of the European Convention for the Protection of Human Rights and Fundamental Freedoms, it was proposed to insert provisions guaranteeing the negative freedom of association, but these

---

4. *Freedom of Association and Collective Bargaining*, General Survey by the Committee of Experts on the Application of Conventions and Recommendations, Report III (Part 4B) submitted to the 69th Session of the International Labour Conference, ILO: Geneva, 1983, pp. 47–48.

proposals were rejected. According to many scholars the two last-mentioned instruments do nevertheless prevent the signatory States from setting up compulsory unionism. It should also be mentioned that the European Court of Human Rights has recently considered at least the later introduction of a closed shop system to be, an infringement of Article 11 of the European Convention for the Protection of Human Rights and Fundamental Freedoms.[5] The case referred to a situation where certain workers had been terminated because of their refusal to become members of a union which had gained a closed shop agreement after the date on which these workers had been recruited by the enterprise concerned.

25. In some countries, the law guarantees, explicitly or implicitly, the right of workers not to join a union (e.g. several countries of the European continent such as Austria, France and Italy, most French-speaking African countries and several Latin American countries), whereas in others union security clauses are allowed to a varying degree. In the latter group of countries, law and practice differ so much with regard to the type of permissible union security arrangements and their detailed mode of operation that only a very rough outline of the situation can be given in the present discussion.

26. The three main types of union security clauses are the closed shop, the union shop and the agency shop. The first is an arrangement whereby the employer is required to hire only employees who are union members. Under the second, non-union members may be recruited but have to become union members within a specified period after recruitment. Under the third, workers, without being required to become union members, are obliged to pay dues to the union.

27. There are several rationales for trade union security arrangements. Although it may be somewhat artificial to establish a clear-cut separation among them, it would seem that, in chronological order, the main objectives pursued have been
(1) to enable the unions to control access to jobs (as did the medieval European guilds);
(2) to strengthen the position of the unions in a hostile environment (because of employers' anti-union attitudes or recruitment difficulties in sectors with an unstable workforce such as construction and docks);
(3) to force outsiders to share the financial burden of the operation of the trade union; and
(4) to strengthen trade unions as an indispensable partner for the effective operation of the industrial relations system.
   Originally, trade union security arrangements were practised almost ex-

---

5. European Court of Human Rights, *Case of Young, James and Webster – Judgment*, Council of Europe: Strasbourg, 13 August 1981.

clusively in the Anglo-Saxon world (e.g. Australia, Canada, New Zealand, United Kingdom, United States), mainly with the first two above-mentioned objectives. Later, as the two last-mentioned objectives were added to the previous ones, the practice spread to other countries, especially in the developing regions of the world. During this second phase, public authorities, particularly in developing countries, have often favoured union security clauses whereas, during the first stage, these clauses were generally the exclusive result of militant trade union action.

28. To give a few examples of national situations, it may be mentioned that in the United States the closed shop is illegal under federal law. The union shop and the agency shop – two institutions which it is difficult to distinguish, if not in law at least in practice – are, as a rule, permitted by federal legislation, but the scope of this principle is severely limited by a number of provisions. According to one of them, it would be an 'unfair labour practice' for a union to invoke a union shop clause in order to have an employee discharged for non-membership where the employee was denied or lost union membership for reasons other than the failure to pay dues. According to another provision, all types of union membership or support clauses can be made unlawful by state law, which happened in twenty states through so-called 'right-to-work laws'. In the UK, the lawfulness of union membership agreements has been made subject to a number of restrictions in recent years. Among the most important ones are the provisions which make it 'unfair' for an employer to dismiss a worker who 'genuinely objects on grounds of conscience or other deeply held personal convictions to being a member of any trade union whatsoever or of a particular trade union',[6] or to dismiss any worker if the union membership agreement has not been approved in a secret ballot, held within the five years preceding the time of dismissal, by 80 per cent of the workers entitled to vote or 85 per cent of those who actually voted. In addition, there are important obstacles to new closed shops. In Canada, agency shop clauses, based on the so-called 'Rand formula' seem to cover about one-third of employees in the manufacturing sector. In Switzerland, where compulsory unionism is outlawed, there is a special form of agency shop. There, collective agreements may require contributions from non-union members who benefit from the collective agreements concerned, it being understood that these contributions may only be used for certain specific purposes.

29. In developing countries, closed shop and union shop agreements have been practised for many years in Mexico. More recently, union shops were introduced in various forms in several countries (e.g. the Philippines, Tanzania) whereas several formulae for agency shops appeared in some others (e.g. Argentina, Colombia, Panama). It should be noted that in some

---

6. Employment Act 1982, section 3.

of these countries (e.g. Tanzania), union security is imposed or may be imposed under certain conditions by the public authorities.

30. The Committee on Freedom of Association has pointed out that where union security arrangements operate which require membership of a given organisation as a condition of employment, there might be an unfair discrimination if unreasonable conditions were to be imposed upon persons seeking such membership and if members were to be arbitrarily expelled from the organisation concerned. Legal provisions dealing with this problem exist only in a few countries (e.g. United Kingdom) and are usually worded in very general terms. One reason is that such provisions could very easily interfere with the right of employers' and workers' organisations to function freely, which is guaranteed by Convention No. 87 and which will be examined later in this study.[7]

C. *The Right of Organisations to Establish Federations and Confederations and the Right of International Affiliation*

31. Convention No. 87 provides that workers' and employers' organisations shall have the right to establish and join federations and confederations – which shall have the same rights as their constituent organisations – and that any such organisations, federations and confederations shall have the right to affiliate with international organisations of workers and employers. As a rule, all the principles applying to primary organisations also apply *mutatis mutandis* to higher-level organisations. There are, however, several specific problems with regard to federations and confederations, particularly in a number of developing countries.

32. One of the most serious problems relates to the restrictions imposed by law on the free establishment of federations and confederations in a trade union monopoly system. We have already dealt with this problem.[8]

33. Another serious problem, some aspects of which have already been examined,[9] arises in countries where the establishment of federations and confederations is confined to constituent organisations of the same or similar branch(es) of activity or occupation(s) or of the same region, and where inter-occupational and/or inter-regional organisations may therefore not be set up (e.g. Kuwait, Malaysia). It should be noted that in some of the countries concerned inter-occupational or inter-regional organisations have nevertheless been established, but they do not have all the rights which usually belong to a trade union or an employers' organisation. Similar

7. See paragraphs 38–50 below.
8. See paragraphs 18–21 above.
9. See paragraph 16 above.

184

problems – but limited to a specific category of workers – arise in those countries where it is explicitly or implicitly provided that organisations of public employees may not affiliate with federations or confederations which are also open to private sector organisations (e.g. Malaysia).

34. Other restrictions concerning federations or confederations result from provisions requiring a minimum number of trade unions or federations for the establishment or at least registration of organisations of a higher level (e.g. Brazil, the Philippines) or from provisions making affiliation to a federation subject to the consent of the registrar of trade unions (e.g. Malaysia).

35. Besides the above-mentioned restrictions, there are some others which concern the activities of federations and confederations, particularly their right to bargain collectively and/or their right to strike (e.g. Chile, Colombia).

36. The right to affiliate with international organisations of workers and employers is generally recognised. In some countries, however, international affiliation is subject to prior authorisation by the public authorities (e.g. Brazil, Libya, Zambia) or is otherwise limited (e.g. Ethiopia, where only the sole central organisation may sign agreements with international organisations on the basis of the principle of proletarian internationalism).

37. All the restrictions mentioned in paragraphs 32 to 36 above have been considered by the Committee on Freedom of Association as being incompatible with Convention No. 87.

III. FUNCTIONING AND ACTIVITIES OF ORGANISATIONS, FEDERATIONS AND CONFEDERATIONS

A. *The Right of Organisations, Federations and Confederations to Function Freely*

38. Convention No. 87 provides that workers' and employers' organisations shall have the right to draw up their constitutions and rules, to elect their representatives in full freedom and to organise their administration.

1. Drawing Up of Constitutions and Rules

39. In a number of countries there are no legal provisions relating to the content of the constitutions and rules of workers' and employers' organisations. In many other countries, however, particularly in the developing regions of the world, legislation enumerates the subjects to be dealt with in

185

these documents or provides more detailed indications on how various issues, such as the election of officers and the management of funds, should be regulated in these documents (or should be dealt with in actual practice). The issues concerned will be examined in more detail in subsequent paragraphs. It may however be mentioned at this stage that the Committee on Freedom of Association has expressed the general opinion that such provisions are compatible with Convention No. 87 to the extent to which they are designed to protect the right of individual members or to provide for sound administration of the organisation. The Committee on Freedom of Association has however also pointed out that such provisions are at variance with Convention No. 87 whenever they are of such a nature as to impede the normal running of an organisation (which can be the case, for example, when the provisions concerned are excessively detailed).

2. Election of representatives

40. The two main problems arising in this field relate to the qualifications for eligibility as well as to the procedures for the election and the suspension and removal of representatives.

41. As far as the qualifications for eligibility are concerned, difficulties have arisen with regard to legal requirements concerning the nationality, the occupational status, the political belief or activities and the criminal record of candidates as well as the re-election of officers.

42. In many countries, particularly of the developing world, nationality of the country concerned is a condition of eligibility for trade union office. The Committee on Freedom of Association has considered that such provisions may involve the risk that certain categories of workers will be denied their right to freely elect their representatives, particularly in a context of increasing migration of workers. The Committee has therefore considered it desirable, where necessary, to relax legislation in order to permit foreign workers to hold trade union office.

43. Under the legislation of several developing countries, trade union officers – or at least a certain percentage of them – must work in the occupation represented and/or must have been engaged in it for a certain period prior to their election (e.g. India, Sri Lanka, Zambia). This issue of the role of 'outsiders' in trade union leadership has given rise to many controversial opinions. Some governments have stated that the essential purpose of the occupational requirements is to prevent trade unions from being used as tools of politicians. It has, however, also been stressed that in many developing countries the labour force still lacks sufficient education to be able to provide a qualified leadership completely from within its own ranks. In addition, the requirement of current engagement in the occupation would make it impossible for anyone to be a full-time trade union official or would automatically expel from trade union office any worker dismissed by an employer. In view of the various above-mentioned considerations, the Committee on Freedom of Association has expressed the view that the relevant provisions should be flexible, i.e. admit as candidates for trade union office persons who have been previously employed in the occupation concerned and exempt from the occupational requirements a fairly large proportion of the officers concerned.

44. In certain countries, ineligibility for trade union office may result from activities of a subversive nature (e.g. Australia), or from activities in support of a party which is considered as being contrary to the national interest (e.g. Brazil). Such provisions raise extremely complex problems which must be examined on an *ad hoc* basis. The Committee on Freedom of Association decided for example in one case that 'legislation which debars from trade union office . . . any person taking part in political activities of a communist character . . . may involve a violation of . . . Convention No. 87'.[10] In another case, the Committee took the view 'that a law is contrary to the principles of freedom of association when a trade unionist can be barred from union office and membership because in the view of the minister his activities might further the interests of communism'.[11]

45. In many countries, there are provisions which disqualify from trade union office persons who have been convicted of specified crimes which are considered to be of such a nature that the guilty person can no longer hold a position of trust such as a trade union office. In several developing countries, such disqualification applies for almost any type of criminal offence (e.g. Chile, Madagascar). According to the Committee on Freedom of Association, only the first type of provision is compatible with Convention No. 87.

46. In a few developing countries legislation contains provisions which prohibit or limit re-election to trade union office (e.g. Mexico, in so far as public servants are concerned). The Committee on Freedom of Association has taken the view that such provisions are at variance with Convention No. 87.

47. Statutory provisions on trade union elections – which are more common in developing than in highly industrialised countries – are generally designed to ensure due respect for the rights of the membership and to avoid disputes as to the result of the election. According to the Committee on Freedom of Association, such provisions are in line with Convention No. 87. There is,

10. *Freedom of Association, Digest of Decisions of the Freedom of Association Committee of the Governing Body of the ILO,* ILO: Geneva, third edition, 1985, paragraph 311.
11. *Ibid.,* paragraph 312.

on the contrary, undue interference in the election procedure, amongst others where the election must be approved by the minister (e.g. Liberia), where the top executive of the workers' confederation has been appointed by the Chief of State (e.g. Kenya) or where the authorities have actually made recommendations or expressed their view with regard to certain candidates. Referring to the legislation of a number of African and Latin American countries, the Committee on Freedom of Association has also pointed out that administrative authorities should neither be involved in the supervision of elections (e.g. through the counting of votes), nor in the procedures to be followed in case of contested elections. According to the Committee, such functions should only be exercised by the judicial authorities.

48. In some developing countries, trade union officers may be suspended or removed by decision of the administrative authorities (e.g. Colombia). The Committee has indicated that only the Courts should be empowered to take such decisions. In addition, the legislation should specify in a detailed manner the reasons which justify the suspension or removal of trade union officers.

3. Internal Administration

49. The most serious problems concerning the internal administration of workers' and employers' organisations have arisen with respect to the financial administration of these organisations.

50. In many countries in all parts of the world, the law provides for the filing of periodic financial reports with the competent authorities, it being understood that these authorities often have the power to investigate further any matter which is not clear to them. The Committee on Freedom of Association has taken the view that such special investigatory measures should be limited to exceptional circumstances, such as presumed irregularities, and that they should only be ordered and implemented under the control of judicial authorities. In a number of countries, especially in the developing regions of the world, the legislation also contains provisions on certain other matters such as the sources of union funds or the internal control of these funds. The general principle applied by the Committee on Freedom of Association in this respect is that such provisions are acceptable as long as their purpose is to prevent abuses and to protect members against mismanagement. In the light of this principle, the Committee has raised objections to several categories of provisions such as those fixing minimum contributions (e.g. Ecuador) or those requiring approval of trade union financial rules by the public authorities (e.g. Syria).

B. The Right of Organisations, Federations and Confederations to Organise their Activities Freely

51. The main restrictions on the activities of workers' and employers' organisations which are to be found in national legislation concern collective bargaining, the right to strike and the political activities of the organisations concerned.

1. Collective Bargaining

52. The purpose of the present section is not to compare national legislation and practice in the field of collective bargaining, since this subject is dealt with elsewhere in this text.[12] Its objective is rather to summarise very briefly the main conclusions which the Committee on Freedom of Association has drawn from Article 4 of Convention No. 98, which states that 'measures appropriate to national conditions shall be taken, where necessary, to encourage and promote the full development and utilisation of machinery for voluntary negotiation between employers or employers' organisations and workers' organisations with a view to the regulation of terms and conditions of employment by means of collective agreement'.

53. The most important principles adopted in this respect by the Committee on Freedom of Association can be summarised as follows:
– the right to bargain collectively is a fundamental trade union right;
– legislation excluding certain matters from the field of collective bargaining or providing that collective agreements may not grant more favourable terms and conditions than those set out in the law are contrary to Convention No. 98;
– legislation according to which collective agreements must be approved by the public authorities before becoming effective are contrary to Convention No. 98;
– governments may feel in certain cases that the economic situation of the country calls for stabilisation measures during the application of which it would not be possible for wage rates to be fixed freely by means of collective bargaining. Such a restriction, however, should only be imposed as an exceptional measure and to the extent necessary, without exceeding a reasonable period, and it should be accompanied by adequate safeguards to protect workers' living standards.
It should be mentioned in this connection that, since the beginning of the economic crisis in 1973, the Committee on Freedom of Association has had to examine an increasing number of cases where governments of highly

12. See below, chapter 15.

industrialised countries have adopted economic stabilisation programmes which included temporary limitations of free wage bargaining. On these occasions, the Committee has particularly insisted on the need for these measures to be strictly limited in time and on the need for all possibilities of negotiation to be exhausted prior to the imposition of compulsory measures.[13]

2. The Right to Strike

54. The right to strike is explicitly recognised in the International Covenant on Economic, Social and Cultural Rights and in the European Social Charter. There is, on the contrary, no mention of the right to strike in the Universal Declaration of Human Rights (several amendments aiming at the recognition of this right were rejected during the *travaux preparatoires*), in the International Covenant on Civil and Political Rights (the issue was never discussed during the *travaux preparatoires*) and in the European Convention for the Protection of Human Rights and Fundamental Freedoms. According to several decisions of the European Court of Human Rights, the European Convention grants the right to strike at least to a certain extent.

55. As far as ILO instruments are concerned, Conventions Nos. 87 and 98 do not mention the right to strike. The Committee on Freedom of Association has however recognised this right with certain restrictions. The present section does not aim to describe national legislation and practice with regard to the right to strike, since this issue will be examined elsewhere.[14] Its purpose is rather to explain very briefly to what extent the right to strike has been recognised by the Committee on Freedom of Association. The basic principles adopted by the Committee are as follows:
– a general prohibition of strikes, unless imposed as a transitory measure in a situation of acute national emergency, is contrary to Convention No. 87;
– provisions under which public authorities may prohibit all strikes which they consider prejudicial to the public order, the national interest or economic development are not admissible, because they are drafted in too general a way;
– prohibition of purely political strikes is admissible;
– temporary restrictions are admissible, for example during conciliation and arbitration procedures, during the currency of a collective agreement, or before the lapse of a strike notice;
– restrictions with regard to public employees and workers working in essential services (i.e. those whose interruption could endanger the existence or well being of the whole or part of the population) are admissible,

13. For more details, see: A. Pankert, Government Influence on Wage Bargaining: The Limits set by International Labour Standards, *International Labour Review*, September–October 1983, pp. 579–591.
14. See below, chapter 19.

provided that appropriate compensations are given to the persons concerned under the form of impartial and speedy conciliation and arbitration procedures;
– restrictions aimed at ensuring compliance with statutory safety requirements are normal restrictions.

3. Political activities

56. Legislative provisions regarding the political activities of trade unions are mainly to be found in developing countries. In some of these countries, trade unions are prohibited from engaging in party politics (e.g. Brazil, Colombia) or in any political activity whatsoever (e.g. Kuwait). The Committee on Freedom of Association has considered such a general prohibition to be incompatible with Convention No. 87 and unrealistic in practice. According to the Committee, states should rather, if they so wish, entrust to the judicial authorities the task of repressing the abuses which might be committed by organisations which have lost sight of the fact that their fundamental objective should be the economic and social advancement of their members.

57. In several other countries of the developing world (e.g. Tanzania), trade unions are closely associated with the political party through legislative or other means. The Committee on Freedom of Association has pointed out in this respect that governments should not attempt to transform the trade union movement into an instrument for the pursuance of political aims.

IV. Protection Against Acts of Anti-Union Discrimination and Acts of Interference

A. *Protection Against Acts of Anti-Union Discrimination*

58. Convention No. 98 provides that workers should enjoy protection against acts of anti-union discrimination, both at the time of taking up employment and in the course of the employment relationship. Similar provisions are contained in Convention No. 151 with regard to public employees. Since the main problem at the national level is not to adopt adequate provisions on anti-union discrimination but rather to enforce them, Convention No. 98 also requires the establishment, where necessary, of appropriate machinery for that purpose. Taking into account that trade union representatives in the undertaking are particularly exposed to acts of anti-union discrimination, Convention No. 135 and Recommendation No. 143 prescribe or suggest special protective measures in their favour.

59. In the large majority of countries, workers are protected against acts of anti-union discrimination at the time of recruitment and during employment. In quite a number of countries, a wider protection is afforded to trade union representatives. There are, however, a few countries (e.g. Australia, Finland) where there are apparently no specific provisions concerning the protection of workers at the time of engagement. There are also some other countries (e.g. Switzerland) where there are no special provisions protecting workers against dismissal for reason of trade union membership or activity and where employers are usually not bound to give reasons for dismissals. The machinery for enforcing existing provisions varies considerably according to national law and practice. While this machinery is sometimes aimed at preventing anti-union discrimination (e.g. where a previous authorisation is needed in case of dismissal of a trade union representative), it normally has the purpose of providing compensation or of imposing penal sanctions. In many countries, anti-union discrimination is dealt with by the courts and tribunals or through normal labour disputes settlement procedures. In some other countries (e.g. Canada, Japan, Pakistan, United States) cases of anti-union discrimination are dealt with by certain administrative bodies with quasi-judicial functions (which also perform other functions related to the administration of existing labour relations legislation, such as the organisation of secret ballots to determine the most representative union). It should also be mentioned that several legislations (e.g. Australia, New Zealand) have placed on the employer the onus of the proof that the dismissal is not connected with trade union membership or activity.

B. Protection Against Acts of Interference

60. Convention No. 98 provides that workers' and employers' organisations shall enjoy adequate protection against acts of interference by each other or each others' agents or members in their establishment, functioning or administration. Although this provision applies equally to workers' and employers' organisations, the protection provided is primarily intended for trade unions. That is the reason why the provision concerned goes on to describe particular acts of interference which are designed to promote the establishment of workers' organisations under the domination of employers' organisations or to support workers' organisations by financial or other means with the object of placing them under the control of employers or employers' organisations. Convention No. 151 contains similar provisions with regard to public employees.

61. In a number of countries, both developing and highly industrialised, there are provisions for the protection of workers' organisations against acts of interference by employers or employers' organisations. These provisions are sometimes of a fairly general and sometimes of a more specific nature. The latter provisions refer for example to the refusal of registration of a trade union or its deregistration if it is not independent of employers, the refusal of bargaining rights to a non-independent trade union or the prohibition of payments by employers to trade union representatives (e.g. Australia, Japan, Mexico, United Kingdom, United States, Venezuela). The machinery to enforce these provisions varies from one country to another and may consist in the intervention of an administrative authority, a judicial authority or the special bodies which are referred to in paragraph 59 above and which are also competent to deal with anti-union discrimination.

62. Specific protective provisions are less frequent with regard to acts of interference than with regard to acts of anti-union discrimination. One reason seems to be that in a number of countries the development and strength of the trade unions are such that there is in practice no real danger of acts of interference.

V. Suspension and Dissolutions of Organisations, Federations and Confederations

63. Convention No. 87 provides that workers' and employers' organisations shall not be liable to be suspended or dissolved by administrative authority. The reason is that such measures would not provide all the requisite guarantees, which can only be ensured by judicial procedure. The Committee on Freedom of Association has made it clear that a mere right of appeal to the judiciary against administrative decisions is not enough. According to the Committee, such decisions should not take effect until the expiry of the statutory period for lodging an appeal or until the confirmation of the decisions concerned by a judicial authority. The Committee has also pointed out that the courts should be empowered to re-examine the grounds for the administrative decision.

64. In many countries, both developing and highly industrialised, the legislation provides that suspension and/or dissolution of organisations can only be ordered by the judiciary on the grounds of infringement of the law. In some other countries however – mainly in Africa and Latin America – administrative suspension and/or dissolution is possible (e.g. Bolivia, Colombia, Kenya). In the latter countries, the situation varies widely with respect to the possibility of an appeal to the courts and to the effects of such appeal. In certain cases, it is even not clear whether an appeal is at all possible and whether it holds up the execution of the administrative decision.

65. In a number of countries, most of which belong to the African and Asian continent, the registrar of trade unions may, under certain conditions, cancel the registration of an organisation (e.g. Kenya, India, Malaysia, Singapore). The Committee on Freedom of Association has pointed out that such a decision may have the same effect as a suspension or a dissolution and should be treated in the same manner.

66. In several countries, it has happened that trade unions have been suspended by a special law or decree rather than on the basis of ordinary trade union legislation (e.g. Nigeria, Turkey). In some countries (e.g. Kenya, Tanzania), such measures were taken in order to replace a nation-wide organisation by a new organisation with a structure established by law or a constitution prepared by the public authorities. In other countries, the measures concerned were taken as a sanction because of strike action or for political reasons. The Committee on Freedom of Association has made it clear that such measures are contrary to Convention No. 87.

VI. FREEDOM OF ASSOCIATION AND CIVIL LIBERTIES

67. Convention No. 87 contains a provision according to which 'the law of the land shall not be such as to impair nor shall it be so applied as to impair, the guarantees provided for in this Convention'. The implications of this principle are particularly relevant when considering the interaction of trade union rights and civil liberties. The Committee on Freedom of Association has recalled on many occasions that a genuinely free and independent trade union movement can develop only under a regime which guarantees fundamental human rights. The International Labour Conference has summed up these opinions in a Resolution concerning Trade Union Rights and Their Relation to Civil Liberties, adopted in 1970. According to this Resolution and according to the experience of the Committee on Freedom of Association, the main problems seem to arise in connection with freedom from arbitrary arrest and the right to a fair trial as well as freedom from arbitrary interference with privacy. The purpose of the present section is not to give a comparative view of national legislation and practice with regard to the relationship between freedom of association and civil liberties, but rather to summarise the main decisions of the Committee on Freedom of Association in this respect.

68. The most important principles adopted by the Committee on Freedom of Association concerning the interaction of freedom of association and civil liberties are as follows:
– *Freedom of assembly*. Occupational organisations should have the right to meet freely on their own premises without the need for prior notification to or authorisation from the public authorities and without the attendance of these authorities. Public meetings also constitute an important trade union right, but the unions should comply with the general formalities which uniformly apply to all gatherings of this kind.
– *Freedom of expression and opinion*. The full exercise of trade union rights calls for a free flow of information, opinions and ideas at union meetings, in union publications and in the course of union activities. This right would be affected by prior censorship of all means of communication and

publication of trade unions' views. Measures such as the refusal or revocation of licences should be subject to judicial review.

– *Freedom from arbitrary arrest and the right to a fair trial.* Trade unionists should not of course be arrested on account of normal trade union activities. Besides, the detention of trade unionists in any circumstances runs the risk of involving serious interference with the exercise of trade union rights, unless there are appropriate judicial safeguards. Every government should therefore ensure the observance of specific guarantees for citizens in general with regard to such matters as arrest, detention and trial.

– *Freedom from arbitrary interference with privacy.* While trade unions cannot claim immunity from search of their premises, any such search should only be made following the issue of a warrant by the appropriate judicial authority and should be restricted to the purpose for which the warrant was issued. The protection of the property of trade unions is essential for the normal exercise of trade unions rights.

69. One of the most obvious conclusions which can be drawn from the information provided above is that many developing countries have experienced more difficulties than the vast majority of highly industrialised countries in the implementation of the basic principles laid down in Convention No. 87 and Convention No. 98. The main reason is probably that in many developing countries it is considered by the government that freedom of association in the broad sense of the term – which includes the right to bargain collectively and the right to strike – may conflict with requirements of economic development. It must also be recalled in this respect that, in a number of highly industrialised countries, governments have felt obliged, since the beginning of the recession in 1973, to limit, at least on a temporary basis, the right to free wage bargaining in order to stabilise the economic situation. While the Committee on Freedom of Association is very much aware of these problems and has made efforts to take into consideration the fears expressed by the governments concerned, it has also considered it necessary to uphold the basic principles of Conventions Nos. 87 and 98 on the grounds that any concession on a fundamental point might subsequently open the door to unacceptable abuses.

SELECT BIBLIOGRAPHY

ILO, *Freedom of Association and Collective Bargaining*, General Survey by the Committee on the Application of Conventions and Recommendations, Report III (Part 4B) submitted to the 69th Session of the International Labour Conference, 1983 (Geneva, 1983).

ILO, *Freedom of Association*, Digest of Decisions of the Freedom of Association Committee of the Governing Body of the ILO (third edition, Geneva, 1985).

Max-Planck-Institut für ausländisches öffentliches Recht und Völkerrecht, *Die Koalitionsfreiheit des Arbeitnehmers/The Freedom of the Worker to Organize/La Liberté syndicale des salariés* (Springer-Verlag, Berlin, Heidelberg, New York, 1980), 2 vols.

Chapter 11. National Trade Union Movements

G. Cella and T. Treu

I. Introduction

1. National trade union movements are fundamental elements of any developed industrial relations and labour law system. Yet, as H. Clegg[1] points out, 'there exists no systematic theory of trade unionism and – even less – of national labour movements.' This section will focus on national trade unions. Reference will be made to broader aspects of the labour movement when they are indispensable for an understanding of unionism.

For analytical purposes the models will be presented and interpreted as follows:
(1) union membership (or density), structure and internal organisation;
(2) union presence or influence at the workshop level;
(3) forms of union action;
(4) political action and relations with political parties;
(5) trade unions and state intervention in industrial relations.
Each aspect will be considered in terms of the present situation along with basic historical references as needed. Finally, an attempt will be made to give an overall appraisal and interpretation of the models and trends.

II. Trade Union Structure

2. A first series of elements for the identification of the various models of unionism concerns structural characteristics such as the quality and quantity of trade union membership, patterns of union organisation and their internal government (i.e., internal structure, regulations). These elements are all related in part to the characteristics of the labour force, on the one hand, and to the methods used by organised labour to achieve its aims on the other.

A. Craft-Occupational Unions

3. The first type traditionally identified is the *craft union*, composed of workers in the same trade able to control the labour supply and hence

---

1. H. Clegg, *Trade Unionism under Collective Bargaining*, Oxford, 1976, p. 1.

unilaterally to impose their conditions and terms of work on the employers. The craft union flourished in the numerous industries of the nineteenth century which relied on a rather small number of highly skilled workers and formed the backbone of the oldest trade union movements, led by Britain and the United States, where it later survived the development of mass production industry, the consequent standardisation of labour and the decline of traditional skills. On the contrary, in continental Europe craft unionism, in the true sense of the term, has hardly gone beyond the early stages of union history or very limited areas of the labour force. In most late developing countries the timing and conditions of industrialisation – plus the absence of a significant guild tradition – tended to exclude the basic prerequisites for such a model.

4. However, over the past few decades craft (or, more generally, *occupational*) unions have undergone a profound change in order to survive. Besides adopting collective bargaining as the major method of action (like their competitors, the industrial unions), they expanded, or attempted to expand, into weakly organised industries and occupations with little regard for original boundaries (in much the same way as general unions, see below). This accounts in part for the highly complex organisation of these trade union movements.

B. White-Collar Unions

5. An equally important development is the rapid and widespread growth of another type of occupational union: the organisation of white-collar employees. It developed in all countries much later than blue-collar unionism and is still much less widespread in the private sector. Attempts to organise manual and white-collar employees into the same union have rarely been totally successful, not even in those countries dedicated to industrial unionism, for example FR Germany and Sweden. This is particularly true for employees with medium standards of professional qualifications, who continue to grow increasingly disenchanted with the general objectives and attitudes of national labour movements. They were the first to create separate organisations or confederations (the French CGC is among the best known), but in most countries are not organised at all in the private sector. Managerial personnel are in a similar situation (often the law forbids their unionisation in the same organisation as other employees).

6. The types of white-collar organisations are as variable as those of blue-collar. Some white-collar unions cover the relevant occupation within a single sector or industry: e.g. most national or local government employees in the public service. Others are more strictly occupational, since they group one or several occupations separately from the others within the same sector (e.g. airline pilots, assistants and air controllers in many countries). Some of

the largest unions organise white-collar occupations across industrial boundaries, even beyond the industrial sector, e.g. the two largest unions affiliated to the Swedish TCO.

Finally, some unions tend to organise white-collar employees across industrial boundaries *and* irrespective of occupation: for example, the Austrian and Danish white-collar employees' unions. The area of organised white-collar employees in some countries tends to extend to middle and even upper management in the public service – although chiefly through separate occupational unions. The trend is more uncertain in the private sector.

C. Industrial Unions

7. The second major historical model is the industrial union, organising all workers of the same branch of the economy, irrespective of occupation. This type of union has developed in most industrialised countries since the turn of the century, along with the rapid growth of mechanisation and mass production industry. Recruitment is based mainly on the mass of semi- and unskilled workers, a typical product of this industry.

In some of the first industrialised countries (Britain, the United States, but also FR Germany) where its growth was strongly resisted by craft unionism, the industrial union developed in those (separate) areas which craft unions had failed to occupy. One of the best examples is the competition and distribution of influence of the AFL and CIO in the United States. In these industrialised countries the two models *coexist*.

8. Industrial unions developed more easily, soon becoming the dominant structure, particularly among blue-collar workers where strong craft unions had no time to grow, e.g. in most continental European countries (from Sweden, to FR Germany, to Italy). Most European labour movements also initially endorsed industrial unionism as the ideal type of organisation for ideological reasons as well (the promotion of proletarian unity). Industrial unionism is likewise endorsed as the dominant model in planned economies. Pragmatic rather than doctrinal considerations account for the more recent trend – common to most industrialised countries – toward the amalgamation of craft unions into industrial (or general) unions,[2] arising, for example, from the need to enhance the bargaining power and quality of services or to reduce jurisdictional disputes.

9. The process of amalgamation and the underlying structural changes in modern economies (growing interdependence among sectors, importance of services) tend to blur the distinction between the two models. On the one

---

2. J.P. Windmuller, Concentration Trends in Union Structure: An Inter-Trade unionism under collective bargaining, 35, 1981, p. 54.

hand, the growth of occupational unions reduces the total coverage of industrial unions from within; on the other, industrial unions are forced to cover new fields. Thus they are often better defined as multi-industrial or conglomerate (if not general) unions.[3]

10. Whereas the extension of industrial unionism in the earliest industrialised countries was limited by the existence of strong occupational unions, the influence of this model in most newly developing nations has been reduced by the lack of structural preconditions (delayed and limited industrial growth, an industrial labour force smaller than the agricultural one). Even where industrial unions do exist – as in most cases – they are far from dominant, tending to leave room for another model of organisation: the territorial type.

D. General Unions

11. Mass production favoured not only industrial unions but, under given circumstances, a third pattern of organisation, i.e. general unions. They can be defined negatively as unions which organise employees irrespective of their occupation and industrial boundaries. This pattern is found first and foremost in countries with a history of strong occupational unions which 'as collective bargaining developed . . . promoted general unions'.[4] Some of the oldest and most famous general unions originated as such, including the American Teamsters, the British Transport and General Workers' Union (TGWU) and General and Municipal Workers, the Australian Workers' Union. But many originally craft unions have acquired the characteristics of a general union by recruiting in new areas and absorbing other occupational unions (e.g. the International Association of Machinists in the United States).

12. The expansion of the general union is still further reduced among blue-collar workers in countries adopting industrial unionism. But even in these countries, the balance is shifting with the development of private and public services where mostly white-collar employees (the fastest growing manpower group) operate. In these services, the productive identity of the branch and the occupational connotations of the groups tend to be less clear-cut, thereby creating favourable structural conditions for the development of general or multi-occupational unions. Indeed, the same trend has also been noted in some unions organising mostly blue-collar workers. The former district 50 of the American Mineworkers is one of the first and finest examples.

The above-mentioned elements, especially the growth of employment in

3. Windmuller, *op. cit.*, p.
4. Clegg, *op. cit.*, p. 39.

services, explain why general and white-collar unions – more so than the traditionally industrial ones – are strengthening their position as leaders among the largest national unions in many industrialised countries.[5]

E. Territorial Structures

13. Territorial or horizontal structures can be found in most trade union movements, usually not as an exclusive form of organisation but together with others, as a way of grouping or co-ordinating them. The importance and functions of the horizontal model of organisation – at the decentralised and central level (where the structure is usually called a confederation) – vary in different countries and during different periods within the same country. At one extreme the 'horizontal' structure is only a loose co-ordinating body with a substantially non-bargaining role, fewer powers than the federated unions. Often it does not even include all the major unions of the country, as has traditionally been the case with the American AFL and later the AFL-CIO. In other countries, horizontal structures and particularly the central confederations have substantial financial and staff resources, a high degree of control over the most important activities of the federated unions and are included in bargaining, sometimes operating as bargaining agents with respect to the employers and public institutions.

14. This significant power of the horizontal structure is often correlated with the structural characteristics of the country and its labour movement. The late development of industry and of trade unions in general, the fragmented nature of the economy and of the labour market, traditionally high unemployment levels and an extreme political orientation of the labour movement stress the importance of the unity of the working class and union pursuit of general goals, of which the horizontal structure is the natural expression. In fact, these factors serve to explain the traditionally central position of these structures in the history of European countries such as France, Italy, Belgium and, *mutatis mutandis*, may account for the strong territorial basis of trade unions in many developing countries. This form was the most effective means to promote the initiative of a weak and often divided labour movement on both the economic and political fronts.

15. But it would be simplistic to correlate the emergence of the territorial organisational pattern, with the weakness and sometimes the political divisions of the trade union movement. This is particularly true for the role of the central confederations.

In fact, confederations more than decentralised territorial structures,

---

5. See the table in Windmuller, *op. cit.*, p. 55. The concentration of trade union structures seems to be a general trend in most developed countries, favoured also by public authorities (see below).

prove to have a crucial position in countries with a history of strong, politically united trade union movements, such as Scandinavia, Austria and to, a lesser extent, FR Germany. The influence of central confederations is reported to be growing as a general trend even in countries with a long tradition of organisational complexity and independence of single unions (e.g. Great Britain). Here the correlation can be made, and should be more accurately tested, with elements which generally account for the centralisation of industrial relations, namely growing state intervention in economic and social affairs and increased union recourse to the political arena, where economic decisions are also made with greater frequency. Both factors favour the role of central horizontal (rather than peripheral) union structures capable of mobilising large sectors of the labour movement on an inter-industrial or inter-occupational basis.

16. A further distinction can be made as to whether
(a) the central horizontal structure, the confederation, groups the entire trade union movement or the vast majority of it (like the British TUC, the German DGB, the Austrian OGB); or
(b) there are separate confederations, each grouping mainly white-collar and blue-collar unions (TCO and LO in Sweden, ACSPA and ACTU in Australia); or whether
(c) the pluralism of the confederation basically follows political and ideological lines (France, Italy, Belgium, the Netherlands).
In these latter cases political and ideological elements influence the entire trade union movement, irrespective of other organisational criteria, amounting to a kind of separate principle of organisation.

F. Enterprise Unionism

17. Many countries have a history of enterprise unionism (distinguished here from enterprise sections of national unions). Western labour movements looked upon it with diffidence. However, many developing countries have a wide experience of enterprise unions (e.g. Latin America). This is due both to the economic structure (fragmentation of the labour force and concentration in few large enterprises) and to government and employers' action, which was opposed to national union organisation for fear of excessive politicisation and mass conflictual pressure (general strikes). A significant exception in this respect among developed countries is Japan, where enterprise unionism has been the dominant form of organisation since World War II.

The information of this pattern is explained by the peculiar situation of the immediate post-war period when unions were organised within enterprises (and not from the outside as usually occurred in other labour movements), with no resistance either from the government or from the employers. Efforts made by the national trade union centres to overcome enterprise unionism and strengthen industrial unions have been unsuccessful except for a few cases. National unions in Japan are a federation of enterprise unions more than a compact organisation, and some enterprise unions are directly affiliated to the national centre. In fact, the most important functions (above all bargaining) are vested at the enterprise level even taking into account the importance acquired by the spring offensive in national wage negotiations. Local or enterprise sections are also highly autonomous in other countries for example the USA, but the national federations maintain a decisive role in supporting and enlarging union presence in new areas.

The expansion and endurance of enterprise unionism in Japan beyond its origins must be considered in light of the nature of Japanese industrial relations. First of all, the lifetime employment system and the consequent enterprise-wide type of bargaining for which the employees remain tied to the specific enterprise; second, the harmonics relationship which has developed within enterprises between management and employees, based on interests that are common to the well-being of the enterprise.

III. MEMBERSHIP AND INTERNAL GOVERNMENT

A. *Membership*

18. Reference has already been made to the different degrees of unionisation in different manpower sectors, even in countries with similar economic and political patterns.

The most common features are a rather low trade union density in private white-collar employment with few notable exceptions (such as Sweden and Austria) and a relatively high density in public employment for developed countries, once again with significant exceptions (the US, first and foremost). Private manual employment shows the greatest variation, ranging from very low minima – (France (less than 25 per cent) and many developing countries) – to high maxima (over 90 per cent in most Scandinavian countries; nearly total membership in many countries with public or quasi-public unionism: see below).

19. An interesting attempt to explain divergencies in union density in six countries linked them to the extent and depth of collective bargaining and to the support of union security from employers or collective agreements.[6] State intervention, in such forms as pressure on employers to recognise unions and protection of organising rights, played a decisive role, in particular for 'latecomers' in promoting unionisation. The high trade union density and the apparent trend to expansion in most countries may well be explained by the structural characteristics of public services: high concentra-

6. Clegg, *op. cit.*, p. 12 ff.

tion of undertakings, direct government control, bureaucratic organisation favouring collective bargaining and control of rulings on employment conditions.

20. A positive relationship – not disproving the argument above – has been found in OECD countries between trade union density and (predominant) levels of bargaining, where increasing density goes hand in hand with increasing centralisation of the bargaining structure. A somewhat similar relationship has also been ascertained between (the degree of) centralisation in the bargaining structure and that of the trade unions and employers' associations, measured by the extent of the union, the number of federations and the control and bargaining powers vested in central union bodies. Sweden, Norway and Austria are among those countries with highly centralised bargaining structures, a prevalence of national bargaining and the highest degree of trade union centralisation. Japan, the United States and Canada lie at the opposite end of the scale.[7]

B. Government

21. The structure of trade unions appears to point to increasing centralisation in many developed countries. Hypotheses have been advanced to the effect that since this trend is related to the predominant bargaining level, it is influenced by the increasing government involvement in industrial relations (incomes policies in particular). On the contrary, it has also been argued that government intervention and control over bargaining could reduce the bargaining power of central bodies (unions and employers), catalysing reactions from the rank and file and emphasising the need for safety valves (i.e. decentralised activities).[8]

22. Another theory (H. Clegg) maintains that the collective bargaining structure, and hence trade union behaviour and organisation in general, are under the primary influence of employers' forms of organisation (and behaviour). This correlation might well explain the centralisation of collective bargaining and trade unions, as well as the internal coherence of organisation in countries like Sweden (where employers' associations have been similarly centralised and strong); the territorial structure of bargaining in France and FR Germany (which corresponds to employers' association levels); the fragmented structure of bargaining and trade unions in the United States, Britain and Australia (where large employers' associations are weak or non-existent). But the value of this theory can be questioned in Italy, for example, where the structure and initiatives of employers' orga-

---

7. C. Blyth, 'The Interaction between Collective Bargaining and Government Policies in Selected Member Countries', in *Collective Bargaining and Government Policies*, Paris, 1979, p. 90 ff.
8. Blyth, *op. cit.*, p. 75.

nisations have tended to respond to, more than originate, those of the trade union. Moreover, Clegg's basic assumption relating trade union behaviour to collective bargaining needs discussion and specification, particularly when analysing the political action of trade unions and its central role in some countries (see below).

23. Internal rules and methods of administration vary not only among countries but within the same system, according to the type of union, its size and degree of centralisation. Internal union government in a small highly decentralised occupational union is likely to be different from that of a large centralised general or industrial union in terms of: the degree of direct member participation in union affairs, the powers of elected bodies and general meetings *vis-à-vis* the bureaucracy, the position and tenure of officers, the degree of autonomy of peripheral bodies, the ratio of officers to members, etc. They may have a few basic principles in common, often deriving from the general rules of representative organs: the plurality of decision-making bodies; voting procedures for decision and majority rule; election of governing bodies and officers, although there are many exceptions (probably the most widely adopted method, at least in Europe, is that delegate conferences elect chief officers and governing bodies which in turn appoint and control full-time officers).

24. Financial resources are also differentiated. At one extreme some unions (in many developing countries) can rely only on contributions collected *ad hoc* from members and/or a few occasional contributions, at the other, unions in countries such as FR Germany, Sweden, the USA, have strong financial positions, based on stable generalised check-off systems, and administer considerable funds for various purposes.

25. The predominant influence of collective bargaining patterns and dimensions on union behaviour, analysed by H. Clegg, has also been related to some aspects of union structure, such as the distribution of power and factionalism within the union. The theory maintains that since power is concentrated at the seat of collective bargaining, centralised industry-wide bargaining concentrates power in the centre, promoting integrated bureaucratic government, whereas decentralised bargaining establishes an independent power centre at a lower level (particularly that of the workshop) which can serve as a basis for factions.[9] Clegg also concedes, however, that the origins of factionalism may not be solely bargaining-structural in nature. The motives may also be political (in European countries such as Italy and France, in Australia, in many developing countries). More generally, the concentration of power at confederate levels in many countries cannot be explained merely on the basis of a bargaining role; it is inevitably concerned with the growing importance of political functions.

9. Clegg, *op. cit.*, p. 40 ff.

IV. Unions and Workplace Organisations

26. Workplace organisations are considered here in light of their possible relevance to the trade union movement. (Their connection with the problems of workers' participation is covered in chapter 13.)

Four basic situations can be found in principle and in fact:

(a) workplace organisations not directly related to trade unions;
(b) workplace organisations which are formally or in fact an integral part of trade unions (such as plant union sections);
(c) workplace organisations of both types (dual forms of employee representation);
(d) absence of any substantial forms of workplace organisation.

27. The oldest labour movements, of Great Britain and the United States, historically took root within the productive units. Workplace organisations in these two countries are still basically integrated in their trade unions and among the most important centres of union power, although British shop stewards have shown greater militancy and autonomy from the external trade union organisation. But the same single channel formula also applies to continental Europe, in such different cases as the Italian delegates and factory committees and Swedish plant committees. (Although other forms of specific employee representation have been recognised.) The situation is even more clear-cut in Japan, where enterprise unions have since become the basis of trade unionism and the only form of workers' representation at the enterprise level. The single (union) channel of representation can also be found in Latin American countries for the reasons above mentioned and for different reasons in socialist countries, where unionism is organised under public control (a public system of unionism tends to exclude pluralism).

28. Forms of employee representation not directly related to trade unions are traditionally common in continental Europe (France, FR Germany, Belgium, the Netherlands, Italy until 1970). The origins of these 'works councils', 'enterprise committees' etc. go back to the early history of trade unionism. These origins are linked to the features of the labour movements in these countries: extreme weakness, political orientation and occasional division, centralisation and lack of roots within productive units. And, indeed, this model of (employee) representation (not directly related to unions) is also present in many of the developing countries of Africa, East Asia (India, Singapore) with much the same type of unionism (above a minimum degree of unionisation which is a prerequisite for union presence within plants).[10] The model appears to be a more 'diluted' form of collective

---

10. See further information in *Workers' Participation in Decisions within Undertakings*, Geneva, ILO, 1981.

representation than the plant union section, more acceptable to employers and more easily legitimated by law (for the very fact that it is the representation of all workers and not only of union members).

29. A common characteristic may be that they are a substitute for the remoteness of trade unions from the plant and, in cases of political division, an elementary form of workers' unity as far as the direct relationship with employers is concerned.

Attempts – more successful in FR Germany and Austria than in other countries – have been made to distinguish their functions of general workers' representation and co-operation with management from the conflictual and bargaining role supposedly typical of unions. On the other hand, this type of representation has survived well beyond the early stages of immaturity and division of the labour movement, acquiring new powers (as in FR Germany) or being set up (or extended) by law even in countries with no such tradition (such as the developing countries). They indicate the increasing importance of collective forms of action which are different from traditional collective bargaining (participation, information, control and the like), felt to be handled better by direct employees' representatives than by union organs. This dual channel formula is in fact rejected by labour movements more directly rooted at the enterprise level and dedicated to collective bargaining (as in Britain, the United States, Italy). Even when they accept forms of participation different from collective bargaining, they tend to use instruments (specialised or mixed committees) composed of union representatives.

30. In European countries where these forms of representation are most firmly established, unions often tend to control them, and thus an important reason of their success. On the other hand work councils are often an important centre of power and can condition union action (e.g. in FR Germany); so that the relationship is not one way. In the same countries trade unions have not given up their objective of being directly present at the workshop level in different forms (union trusted persons in FR Germany, union plant sections in France, etc.). Results have been inconsistent. The success and development of direct employee representative bodies have sometimes hindered the development of effective union plant structures. The growth of the two forms of representation appears to be inversely proportionate, so that a perfect dual channel of representation is never fully implemented, and one form usually prevails. FR Germany is a clear example, where works councils, which in fact exercise most important negotiating functions, dominate and where union control over them is still the most effective vehicle of presence in the plant. The opposite is true in the Swedish and Italian system, where union structures are unequivocally dominant. In France the various forms of union and employees' representation are all relatively feeble institutions, because collective action at the plant level is also traditionally weak.

31. In conclusion, the correlation between the type of workplace organisation and prevailing forms of trade union organisation at the national level
and degrees of decentralisation is a partial one. It can only be said that the
decentralisation of bargaining structures tends to promote the role of
workplace organisations within the unions (as in Great Britain, the United
States, Japan, Italy) and favour the single channel formula. The reverse is
partially confirmed: centralisation leaves room for dual channels of representation (with important exceptions such as Sweden and, to some extent,
Italy). On the other hand, the dual channel may be used to decentralise
collective action and union presence insofar as employees' representative
bodies – indirectly linked to unions – serve as important vehicles of such
action, including collective bargaining.

V. Forms of Trade Union Action and Objectives

32. In most developed countries unilateral regulation, originally the basic
method of craft unionism, now ranks as a minor form, even for occupational
associations (apart from e.g. restrictive practices by some of these unions).
Collective bargaining has instead become the dominant instrument for
regulating terms of employment *vis-à-vis* the employer. Strikes and other
forms of pressure are also fundamental methods of action in 'Western'
countries, where they are used in different patterns and to different degrees
(see chapter 18).

A. Collective Bargaining and Political Action

33. At present, probably the most relevant basic variance is not between
collective bargaining and unilateral action but, roughly speaking, between
bargaining and political action (depending on whether union pressure is
exerted on the labour and economic markets or on political institutions
(parties, legislatures, etc.)). The balance or combination of the two
methods – which are not alternatives in principle but may be in fact – can be
seen on a continuum. At one extreme the unions of some countries have
come to rely on collective bargaining as almost the exclusive way to
represent members' interests and regulate terms of employment *vis-à-vis* the
employer.

34. On the other hand, in many developing nations particularly when
unions are weak in the labour market and an integrated part of the broader
national movement, collective bargaining (as an adversary process with
private employers ending in an agreement) is almost unknown and/or hardly
accepted.
   The regulation of employment terms or other settlement of employees'
interests, including broad social reforms, is reached either through legisla-

tion or through administrative and political decision-making on which unions may exert different degrees of influence. This is also the case, but for different reasons, in centrally planned economy countries, where decisions affecting the workers' position and production are made according to publicly directed forms of economic planning rather than after market evaluations. In both cases, the lack of union market power or the non-existence of a (fully operating) market account for the union's quasi-total reliance on political, legislative or administrative action.

35. Most situations in democratic industrialised countries fall somewhere in between these two extremes. Political action is used in varying degrees and forms, partly as a substitute but more generally as a complement than an alternative to economic bargaining. Likewise, trade union objectives tend to be broader than those traditionally prevailing in the first group of cases.

36. A change of attitude towards political action and a trend towards a wider use of this method developed early in the majority of these countries, even in those traditionally the most dedicated to pure unionism. Indeed, the most immediate and customary recourse to legislative action points to issues and aims which are clearly compatible with collective bargaining: setting minimum standards for employment conditions, generalising conditions beyond the areas covered by collective bargaining, providing support and recognition for unions as bargaining agents. More recently, political action appears not only to widen but also to change its meaning. The objectives and issues of union political action extend well beyond the reach of traditional collective bargaining and of possible employers' concessions (even in a broad sense), such as welfare, income distribution, full employment and related policies (industrial labour market policies, etc.), which are coming more and more under direct public influence. On the other hand, the 'complementary' relationship between collective bargaining and state intervention is altered mainly by a recurring use of the latter, even in countries traditionally dedicated to *laissez-faire*, to control wage bargaining in particular.

37. No simple argument sufficiently explains this trend. The determinant factors are much the same as those previously mentioned with respect to the growing role within trade union movements of the central confederations, which are also the political centres of unions (section II, E). In the first group of cases, the importance which has always been given to political action is a counterbalance (necessary or believed to be so) to an unfavourable market situation. But the results may differ, depending on the political system itself (in particular, government attitudes toward organised labour). In most of the European and developing countries mentioned here, when this attitude is unfavourable and the labour movement often divided and antagonistic, the use of political action is predominantly 'defensive'.

209

38. Under different conditions, countries such as Austria and Scandinavian countries show an effective use of political action on reformist targets through strong, united, fully recognised trade union movements. These unions may even be reluctant to use their market power, even for conflicts with employers, preferring political bargaining and trade-offs. Participation in political and economic decisions is the major trade-off made to unions (and employers) by the state as a counterpart to self-restraint in the use of market power.

Some conditions are advisable for this trade-off to work: (in addition to) the reformist attitude of the trade unions themselves, a *pro-labour government* or, generally, a political system in a position to guarantee trade union benefits for the organisation and the rank and file; an effective *centralisation* of industrial relations, in particular the ability of trade unions to mobilise mass pressure and, at the same time, to control peripheral behaviour in exchange for political benefits. These latter conditions in particular tend to reinforce one another. A decentralised system of industrial relations can hardly bear any weight on political action; centralisation is a common feature of trade union movements using both 'defensive'- and 'reformist'-oriented political action.

B. Collective Bargaining and Participation

39. Another basic variance in union methods of action is that between collective bargaining (in a strict sense) and various forms of participation (or control or co-determination, etc.). The meaning and different aspects of participation are discussed in chapter 13. Here the focus will be on trade union attitudes towards the problem. The following types of situation may be identified.

1. Collective Bargaining

40. Trade unions traditionally more dedicated to collective bargaining (USA, Britain) tend not only to reject the most institutionalised and committing forms of co-determination (such as representation on enterprise managing bodies), but also to resist less binding solutions such as joint or mixed consultation and the like. The reasons are much the same: fear of being involved in responsibilities which limit their autonomy rather than grant them real powers, of interference in the union bargaining role, of a possible reduction in the scope of union representation (where a dual channel exists: see section IV above).

41. Trade union movements with a firm, often antagonistic political orientation and less of a bargaining tradition share this diffidence, partly for the same reasons, partly for ideological motives. (France, Italy, some developing countries, but also Australia.) Some of the previously mentioned characteristics of these labour movements constitute potential obstacles to institutional participation. In the first group traditional roots in the enterprise, highly decentralised and effective bargaining; in the second, centralisation, weakness at the workshop level, political division and radicalisation. In the first case the need for an alternative method to collective bargaining is reduced, and the stress is on adapting or enlarging the latter; in the second effective collective bargaining is yet to be fully practised and recognised.

42. A common argument by most unions in these countries is that – as experience demonstrates – no distinct line can be drawn between what is suitable for collective bargaining and what is suitable for 'participation' – meant here as a non-adversary type of process – on matters of 'common interest' between management and labour or a mere consultative type of union intervention in company 'internal affairs'. The very distinction between the two methods is questioned and all collective dealings between workers and management are seen as a form of trade union activity, and therefore under direct trade union control. According to this position, the best way to promote industrial democracy is to improve the process and enlarge the scope of bargaining.

Interestingly enough, this traditional diffidence towards union participation is less pronounced (beyond the enterprise level) in public bodies, particularly those active in social security and on the labour market.

2. Self-Management

43. A different and more drastic approach towards industrial and economic democracy is that of self-management. Among socialist countries Yugoslavia has experimented with self-management, not only as a direct form of workers' participation in company economic decision-making, but as a means of making the originally rigid method of publicly-planned direction of the economy more flexible and open to the market. Significant, although limited, experiments in self-management are also present in countries with market economies, from the well-known kibbutz of Israel, to the mainly agricultural experiments in newly independent African and South American countries, Algeria and Peru; to trade union self-management in France, Italy, Belgium, Japan and even the United States as a response to the threat of enterprise bankruptcy; to the recent interest shown by some European trade unions in workers' participation in capital formation as a means of shifting power in the economy and among other things, to support industrial co-operatives and self-management.

3. Institutional Participation

44. The widest application of institutional forms of participation, in particular workers' representation on company supervisory or managing boards that are accepted or even supported by trade unions, can be found in a group of countries originally and still mainly concentrated in continental Western Europe. These systems are characterised by a strong and politically integrated union movement, by centralised bargaining, narrowly practised on specific workshop or internal enterprise matters. Organic participation may be used here as a functional equivalent or substitution for collective bargaining, more so than for the third type of participation (see above). It may also be experimental with, as with other forms of participation, in addition to collective bargaining, particularly in countries where the latter has developed effectively.

45. Apart from variants in forms, the model of workers' representation in managing bodies of the enterprise is slowly expanding to some developing countries (India, Pakistan, Iraq, Congo Republic, Venezuela) and to those of the first group mentioned above (Britain, France, Belgium), both mostly in public enterprise or the like, where the nature of the enterprise reduces traditional trade union diffidence towards these formulas and. obviously, management resistance.

4. Works Council

46. In almost all these countries, 'intermediate' forms of participation (through works councils or similar consultative committees, specialised joint bodies, etc.) are probably the most widely adopted, fastest growing solutions. They are even accepted by those unions most reluctant to follow patterns of 'organic participation'. Their intermediate and at times ambivalent position may account for their expansion. For unions they are less compromising and risky, yet useful for obtaining information and often for bargaining or establishing bargaining grounds. For management they may serve to channel discussion and consultation on matters of common and crucial interest, such as productivity, mobility, welfare, or the management of industrial restructuring beyond a strictly adversary process. The economic crisis stresses the importance for both parties of such joint handling of these matters.

VI. POLITICS AND RELATIONS WITH POLITICAL PARTIES

47. Relationships with political parties are crucial for all trade unions. No major union has reached the present day without recognising the necessity for some sort of party relationship. The two extreme doctrines – complete self-sufficiency of trade unions in an anarchist or quasi-syndicalist perspective, and sheer business unionism – have for the most part been rejected in principle and in practice.

A. No Stable Relationship

48. A practice closer to the second extreme was originally dominant in the United States, where trade unions by tradition not only have no formal allegiance but not even a stable relationship with the national parties (often unstable organisations themselves). But even here political practices of the AFL-CIO very soon showed a preferential link with the Democrats: endorsement of candidates, financial assistance (even though legally restricted), and the voting patterns of members. More than formal relations, influence on single issues is sought according to the traditional political pattern of this country. Some strongly politically-oriented labour movements like the French, Italian and Spanish have barely managed to obtain this result, even in light of their stronger and more autonomous growth.

B. Dependence

49. The historical weakness, division and lack of legitimacy, combined with a stronger party organisation and presence in public life (plus the division of left-wing parties), have tended to subordinate these European trade union movements to the parties, mainly left-wing but with important exceptions. It is not by chance that they have repeatedly been tempted by syndicalist or quasi-syndicalist behaviour, particularly as a reaction to Communist dominance; nor that they have recently tried to act directly on the political system, bargaining with Parliament and (not necessarily pro-labour) governments.

50. An even more radical position in this direction can be seen in a number of developing countries of Africa and Latin America. As the first organisation with a relatively modern, or at least concentrated, working class and an educated leadership, the trade union movements have played a direct and initially dominant role in the push towards political, cultural and economic emancipation of the population (examples range from Algeria, to Kenya, to Peru). The growth of national political movements and the relative strengthening of political systems appear to eliminate or restrict the substitution of trade unions for direct party roles in these countries. Indeed, this relationship may change into the opposite model of organic subordination of trade unions to the same national political movements, for reasons similar to those indicated for European countries. These organic ties of subordination may even be stronger or more complete than in the European cases due to the often extremely limited basis and development of trade unions and to the nature of the national political systems.

51. In centrally planned economy countries organic subordination and integration of trade unions with respect to the party is the absolute model, linked to the very basis of the political system. Their subordination is a consequence of the original identity of their basic role with that of the party and of the state (in turn identified), all directed to implement the general objectives of Socialism, although with specific functions. The fact that trade union and party functionnaires are completely interchangeable bears witness to this integration. The specific trade union function is not to represent particular employees' interests, different from or *vis-à-vis* the party, but, under party-state supervision, to help organise the utilisation of the labour force and satisfy the basic needs (welfare, education, etc.) to achieve these objectives better.

C. Inter-Dependence

52. The relationship between trade unions and political parties is more balanced in most industrialised countries with market economies compared to the two cases just discussed. More than the formal connection (trade union affiliation or non-affiliation with a political party), the degree of dependence–independence is significant. Independence is never absolute, apart from formal affiliations. The best-known cases of direct affiliation with a (labour) party (Britain, Sweden, Australia) involve trade union movements with a long tradition of strong unitary organisation, full recognition, reformist orientation and fruitful relations with a stable political system and a *united* pro-labour political party. In these three cases there are some common characteristics indicative of a relative union predominance in the relationship: namely, union financing of the party, control of votes at the party conference, union officers elected to Parliament. But even here positive union influence may be reduced (the power of veto remains) when the labour party is in government. A tendency to increase interdependence can be seen in other European countries – such as Italy, France, the Netherlands, particularly in cases of non-communist trade unions (but it is much contrasted). A major obstacle to the stability of trends and relations is the division among left-wing parties which has historically caused a division among trade unions.

VII. Unions and State Intervention in Industrial Relations

53. Historically, the initial attitude of the state and of the law with respect to organised labour has been one of prohibition.

A. Repression

In most of the oldest industrialised countries of Europe, coalition and conflict were originally sanctioned as criminal law. This position (also seen in countries where unionism developed later on) was substituted by an attitude of relative tolerance towards organised labour, first in Great Britain then, during the second half of the nineteenth century, in most European countries. Different factors contributed to this tolerance. The pressure of the rising socialist parties and of the trade union movements themselves, economic growth and the self-confidence of liberalism which allowed governments to extend their basic principles of freedom of initiative to organised labour. It took time, however, for this evolution to be completed. Even after the abolition of general criminal sanctions, collective union actions, in particular conflict, remained unlawful in many respects (e.g. under civil law) and fell under possible limitations by the courts.

54. The timing and nature of this evolution generally reflect the economic and political development of each country. Economic difficulties, political instability and divisions slowed down the process toward legal tolerance and recognition of trade union action, at times even causing a reversal in trends. The most blatant cases are the Nazi and Fascist periods in Germany, Italy and Spain, where the totalitarian state excluded all sorts of trade union freedom and conflict as a crime against the national economy.

55. Repression or heavy restrictions of trade union action (especially strikes) are the basic attitudes of nations run by authoritarian regimes and, more generally, where trade union movements are considered public bodies or the direct expression of the state is ruling bureaucracy. Such is the case in some developing countries of Latin America (Chile, Brazil, Colombia) and Africa. In centrally planned economy countries the important public functions that comprise the trade union's position within the state structure exclude the possibility and legality of trade union conflictual action.

In the above-mentioned cases legal restrictions correspond to a situation whereby unions are excluded from the decision-making process of the country, while in the latter they reflect the tight integration into state institutions.

B. Tolerance

56. In many developed countries state tolerance towards trade union action has long been a fundamental tenet. This attitude has several implications, not always coexistent. The most common is that trade unions are considered private voluntary associations, not recognised by law and in principle exempted from direct legal regulation of their internal affairs. In most 'Western' developed countries (but the same is true of Japan and Australia), trade unions have been rather successful in avoiding this type of legal control, more so than public or legal interventions on other aspects of industrial relations, such as collective bargaining and conflict. Even here the immunity is hardly ever total, because some judicial control of the most

215

crucial union affairs (discipline, democratic procedures, etc.) has been exerted even in the absence of legislation in order to guarantee minimum standards of fairness and democracy to its members.

57. The *laissez-faire* model in its broadest implications, including lack of special legislation on collective bargaining and strike, has long prevailed in Great Britain, considered its homeland. It has also been periodically adopted in countries with different traditions, e.g. Italy from 1960 to 1970. The success, partial or complete, of this model has usually been sustained by a stronger desire for voluntarism and autonomy of the parties, trade unions and employers, than the need for state assistance. However, a prerequisite (met in a minority of cases) is that the trade union be strong enough to win a minimum bargaining role and recognition from the employers without state intervention.

C. Intervention

58. In almost all developed nations, in fact, state abstention from industrial relations has been followed – and substituted – by a position of heightened intervention. A major effect and role of this state action – which in some countries goes back to the early twentieth century – has been to support the formation and growth of trade union movements, through such different measures as support of individual employees on the labour market (protective legislation varied in content), indirect incentives for collective bargaining (e.g. by public conciliation, mediation and arbitration, by union rights to organise at plant level), pressures on employers to make them recognise unions or bargaining agents, direct imposition on employers of bargaining duties with trade unions on working conditions.

59. Some distinctions may be made according to
(1) the focus or direction of state support; and
(2) the instruments and conditions of support.
Their influence on trade union developments is different. State support may be directed at promoting trade union organisation mostly from within the plant and enterprise or from the outside.[11] Trade union rights and protection as stipulated in the 1935 Wagner Act, and subsequently extended to Japan, France, Italy, etc., or in the Australian legislation of 1904 belong to the first type. The promptness and results of such state recognition vary according to the same factors influencing union growth: conditions of the labour market, structure of the economy, attitude and organisation of employers.

11. J.S. Valenzuela, *A Conceptual Framework for the Analysis of Labour Movement Developments*, unpublished paper.

60. Legal rights which strengthen union organisation outside the plant are those to hold funds and property, to use them (also) for political purposes, to designate representatives on public agencies or administrative bodies. They are now part of the legal system of most developed countries. The latter are particularly diffuse in the European experience of the last decades regarded as evidence of its inclination towards neo-corporatist models.

61. The legal forms of union recognition are important for the relative mix of rights versus restrictions implied therein. In most developed countries unions may receive support without – or with limited – interference in their internal affairs and activities (see above). However, the law usually permits selection among unions, e.g. giving support only to those with certain standards of representativeness (hence it indirectly controls them). This is the case with most continental European systems and also Japan, where representativeness is controlled 'from the outside' on the basis of general criteria (size, activities, etc.).

A much stricter influence is exerted under the USA's legal pattern of exclusive representation. In this country control over trade union and collective bargaining has been further extended – well beyond the limits of most other developed Western countries – by the Taft Hartley and Landrum Griffin Acts and by court interpretation of the duty to bargain. Somewhat similar controls are granted to federal industrial courts in Australia.

62. A vehicle of direct state control on unions is typically the registration or recognition procedure introduced in some European countries, in spite of union opposition and hence with scarce effectiveness. The British Industrial Relations Act and its subsequent failure, are the most evident case. The widely adopted registration law has given control authorities broad powers of intervention in union life in many developing countries of Latin America, Asia and Africa where they often go back to periods of pre-independence and where the law has usually played an important or decisive role in shaping the trade union movement.

63. The mix of promotion versus restriction depends once again on many factors (see above) related to the political system itself. It may be argued that the most lasting and trouble-free recognition processes are granted in either of two ways. By political coalitions, which exclude the labour movement's leadership but are, however, inclined (or forced) to recognise it (e.g. the case of Britain but also of Italy); or by pro-labour governments, provided that they are in power for a relatively long period (after recognition), that union leadership is not linked to a Marxist left, and that recognition of leadership is combined with substantial benefits to the rank and file (typical of Northern European countries, excluding FR Germany, and of the successful state-sponsored unionism of Mexico, Brazil and Argentina under Peron's first government).

D. Neo-Corporatism

64. As already mentioned, state intervention in industrial relations has grown and changed in most developed countries during the last decade, becoming more directly involved in the social and economic governing process. Unilateral or authoritative solutions in crisis management are hardly feasible in Western countries. In fact, attempts by the state to impose binding incomes policies on the social parties have only lasted for short periods, usually substituted by the search for stabilisation through consensual solutions. Again success has been uneven. Even so, restrictions on union bargaining freedom may be quite severe; certainly they are more stringent than traditional instruments such as mere voluntary guidelines or state-oriented mediation in industrial disputes.

65. This trend has often been analysed through conceptual categories, such as 'political trade-off' or 'neo-corporatism'. The debate on their usefulness and meaning is open.[12] Important distinctions must of course be made among countries where politicisation and growing involvement in economic decision-making are underway. A number of elements usually attributed to the corporatist model can be found in countries such as Austria, Sweden and, to a substantial extent, FR Germany. Trade union involvement in tripartite deals on major economic issues – which substitute in part the traditional political decision-making process – has been widely practised with stabilising effects: It has guaranteed by stable links with pro-labour parties and central control of industrial relations, although the degree of institutional and legal constraints differs – greater in FR Germany than in Sweden. At the other extreme, the model can hardly be applied to cases like Britain and Italy, where any stable institutionalisation of tripartism and political trade-off lacks the basic conditions, such as centralisation of industrial relations, social and political stability (see section V, A). Here the state can win a consensus from trade unions and employers mostly through case by case bargaining. Its stabilising effects are limited and the process of political trade-off is often blocked.

Summary and Conclusions

66. In this chapter we have analysed different models of organisation, action and relationships in contemporary national trade union movements. The dimensions of union behaviour, using Clegg's terminology, which have been considered above concern: union structure, density, degree of centralisation, workshop organisation, types of union action, relationship with

12. See *inter alia* N. Lehmbruch, 'Liberal Corporatism and Party Government', *Comparative Political Studies*, vol. 10, 1977; T. Wilensky, *The 'New Corporatism', Centralisation and the Welfare State*, London, 1977.

political parties – plus industrial conflict and relationship with the state and political system.

The first dimension pertains to the trade union structure (A). Organisational models are the following:

(1) Craft (early period of USA and British unionism, with cases still existing);
(2) Occupational (private and public white-collar unionism in most industrialised countries).
(3) Industrial (predominant model in continental mid-northern Europe);
(4) General (deriving from Craft in USA and Great Britain);
(5) Territorial or Horizontal (France, Italy and many 'latecomer' countries);
(6) Enterprise (Japan).

67. The second dimension is union density (B). Taking into account union membership as a proportion of the employed labour force, three categories can be considered:

(1) High density (more than 50 per cent: Scandinavian countries, Australia, Austria and the socialist countries of Eastern Europe);
(2) Medium density (30–50 per cent: Great Britain, FR Germany, Italy, Japan);
(3) Low density (less than 30 per cent: USA, France, developing countries).

68. The third dimension is the degree of centralisation of union internal government and, given the close correlation with it, of collective bargaining structure (C). Here too three major models can be identified:

(1) High centralisation (Scandinavian countries, Austria);
(2) Bipolar or mixed structures or medium centralisation (FR Germany, Italy);
(3) Decentralisation (in decreasing order Japan, Britain, USA).

69. The fourth dimension, more qualitative than the former, has to do with the types of workplace organisation (D). The typical models are the following:

(1) No organisation (underdeveloped countries and the early periods of most European countries);
(2) Single non-union organisation (France and Italy in the fifties);
(3) Single union structure (Britain, USA, Japan, Italy, socialist countries with the possible exception of countries with experiences of self-management);
(4) Dual channel (FR Germany, the Netherlands, Austria, Sweden).

70. The fifth dimension indicates types of union action (E). Here the typology is necessarily more complex and corresponds to the following models:

(1) Collective bargaining only (USA and Britain until the First World War);
(2) Collective bargaining and participation at the enterprise level (Japan);

(3) Collective bargaining and occasional partnership, in economic and political decision-making (Britain and Italy);
(4) Collective bargaining, co-determination and institutional partnership (FR Germany, Scandinavian countries, Austria);
(5) Institutional partnership (socialist countries of Eastern Europe and other cases of unionism state-sponsored);
(6) Political opposition (early periods of unionism in continental Europe, some underdeveloped countries).

In model E.4 co-determination and partnership reinforce each other, making union action qualitatively different from that prevailing in E.2 and E.3.

71. The sixth dimension is industrial conflict (F), measured on the basis of the number of days lost for strikes per 100,000 workers. Four categories can be considered:
(1) High conflict (over 50,000 days' lost in the period 1969–76: Italy, Australia, USA);
(2) Medium conflict (between 10,000 and 50,000 days' lost: Britain, Denmark, France, Japan);
(3) Low conflict (less than 10,000 days' lost: Sweden, Norway, FR Germany);
(4) Official conflict non-existent.

72. The seventh dimension concerns the relationship with political parties (G). Three patterns can be identified:
(1) No relationship or no stable organised relationship or 'bargaining' relationship related to specific political circumstances (USA, Italian CISL);
(2) Interdependence with labour parties, on an equal basis or with union predominance (FR Germany, Scandinavian countries, Britain);
(3) Dependence on communist or nationalist parties (French CGT, Italian CGIL, many unions in underdeveloped countries).

73. The last dimension pertains only indirectly to union behaviour, being related indeed to the context of industrial relations: it indicates their relationship with the state and political system. This dimension (H), which identifies therefore the role of the state, can be seen in four models:
(1) Repression due to exclusion of unions from the system (early period of unionism in industrial countries and also authoritarian conservative political systems);
(2) Repression due to integration (socialist states and also some underdeveloped countries recently independent);
(3) *Laissez-faire* or state abstensionism (an historical pattern of Britain and Italy of the sixties);
(4) Organised or controlled and supported pluralism (Britain, USA, Italy, Japan);
(5) Neo-corporatism (Austria, Sweden, the Netherlands, FR Germany).

74. On the basis of these dimensions an attempt can be made to identify general models of the trade union movement or typical patterns of union behaviour and industrial relations' which are present in contemporary society. It is not within the purpose of this chapter to expound a general theory of unionism or of union behaviour (for which basic knowledge is still lacking). Therefore we have left in the background the determinants and origins of different models and of the historical experiences of unionism which correspond to them. The table presented here has therefore no definite theoretical value; it is only an instrument for a synthetic appraisal of contemporary unionism.

75. The models of trade union movements which have been identified are the following five: opposition, business (or domestic), competitive, participation, state-sponsored.

Opposition unionism is typical of the history of some European countries and, of a different nature, of some developing countries; it is mainly organised on a territorial basis, since its main resource is represented by the general mobilisation and organisation of the labour force on political grounds and occasions.

Business unionism, originated in the Anglo-American tradition and still characteristic of the North American experience, is identified for its mainly economic objectives, pursued strictly through collective bargaining, outside stable political initiatives, and by relying mostly on direct organisation at the workplace.

Competitive unionism: its objectives are broader; they include basic socio-economic reforms and are pursued by initiatives both on the economic and political fronts, often highly conflictual, with close but not necessarily institutionalised relationship with the political system (Britain and Italy being typical cases).

Participatory unionism operates in neo-corporatist environments and is an essential actor in the system of economic and political tripartite bargaining which characterises these environments; this implies high institutional involvement both at the enterprise and labour market level (the clearest cases being countries such as FR Germany, Austria and the countries of Scandinavia).

State-sponsored unionism is related to a system of industrial relations strictly controlled by the state and operates towards objectives defined at the State level with public or quasi-public functions, which exclude proper bargaining and conflictual action (socialist countries and some developing nations).

76. A final problem is that of ascertaining how the different dimensions influence the general models of unionism, i.e. which dimensions are most decisive or comprehensive. Trade union structure is certainly not decisive. Almost all types of unionism are compatible with different organisational structures. For example, business and competitive unionism are compatible

PATTERNS OF UNIONISM	A Union structure	B Union density	C Coll. bargaining and union structure	D Workplace organisation	E Union action	F Industrial conflict	G Relations with polit. parties	H Relations with polit. system
Opposition unionism (France: CGT; Italy: CGIL) some developing countries	horizontal	low	bipolar or medium central	none (single) non-union	opposition	medium low	dependence	repression (*laissez-faire*)
Business unionism (USA)	craft industrial general enterprise	low	decentralised	single-channel union	coll. bargaining (coll. barg. + part.)	high medium	none (or occasional)	*laissez-faire*
Competitive unionism (Britain; Italy)	all models	medium	bipolar or medium central	single-channel union	coll. barg. + occasional partnership	high medium	inter-dependence	pluralism
Participatory unionism (FR Germany: Austria; Scandinavians)	occupational industrial territorial	high	centralised (bipolar)	dual	coll. barg. + participation + partnership	low	inter-dependence	neo-corporatism
State sponsored unionism (Socialist Countries)	(occupational) industrial territorial	high	centralised	single-channel union	partnership	none	dependence	integration

* Models in brackets are not typical.
** Japan is in some respects a typical: some characters of low conflict, participation and partnership at the enterprise level are typical of the *participatory* pattern (even if decentralised bargaining structure, lack of corporatist relating with political parties and political systems are more typical of *business unionism*.

with organisational models 1, 3, 4, and 6. More important is the influence of union density. To each model of unionism there corresponds only one degree of union density, with a positive correlation (increasing density) from opposition to competitive to state-sponsored unionism. Collective bargaining structure (or, more precisely, its degree of centralisation) has a more decisive influence than that of union structure on different models. However, the existence of bipolar structures makes it less easy to identify the direction of influence of the bargaining structure. Much the same can be said of the influence of union action; this is likewise due to the complexity of this dimension (moreover, similar types of union action, such as participation, acquire different meanings in different contexts). Levels of industrial conflict do not *per se* define the model of unionism: more than one level is compatible with one model. Workplace organisation on the contrary identifies precisely the various models, each model being compatible with only one type of workplace organisation.

A definite influence can be attributed to political variables too: to the unions' relationship both with political parties and with the political system as a whole. In conclusion, short of establishing precise cause-effect relationships, it can be said that the most decisive variable affecting models of unionism are union density, workplace organisation, relations with political parties and with the political context of industrial relations. These variables should be mostly considered in comparative analysis of national labour movements.

VIII. Epilogue: Trade Unions and the Crisis

77. The persistent economic crisis which is affecting most countries of the world has exerted a profound influence on trade union structures and behaviour. These changes have led some observers to forecast a future of deunionized societies, where labour relations will be (again) governed by market individualism and there will be less and less room for organised collective action. Workers' organisations will lose their traditional strongholds – mass production industries – and have few opportunities to make gains in new sectors of production. In developing countries – where recession implies a reduction in the production and costs of exported raw material – the economic crisis has affected labour movements which are generally characterised by weak financial and organisational structures and are not as well equipped to meet the challenge of economic difficulties. In developed societies national trade union movements will be obsolete, and in developing countries they will be incapable of reaching the threshold of stability. These forecasts for the future of labour movements seem excessively pessimistic. However, trade unions are certainly facing serious problems of adjustment to changed economic, social and political conditions which affect the structure and behaviour of national trade union movements: high inflation and unemployment; profound modification in productive and economic structures; deep productive, organisational and technological re-conversion; wide and enduring changes in the qualitative and quantitative composition of the labour force; relaunched government policies of neo-*laissez-faire* implying extensive deregulation and a drive towards maximum flexibility of the labour market. The possible influence of these elements on the dimensions of union behaviour can be analysed as follows:

A. Trade Union Structure

78. The process of concentration of trade unions common to developing and developed countries has continued in the form of reduction in the number of trade unions affiliated to national labour movements. But the process is counteracted in many countries by the growth of associations representing some categories of (mainly) professional employees of cadres, with quasi-union status and objectives, and by the reactivated initiative of independent unions, particularly in service industries. Industrial unionism remains the dominant type in developed countries and is on the rise in developing countries as well. However, it is losing its vitality due to the decline of traditional industrial sectors (e.g. steel) and the reduction of manpower following technological innovations (e.g. auto).

Industrial unions in some countries are trying to recruit members in different areas, often quite foreign to their original jurisdiction (see UAW in the USA) and are behaving more and more like general unions. The most vital type seems to be the occupational unions of mainly white collar employees as a result of the expansion of the tertiary, both private and public. In almost all developed and developing countries the only consistent-ly growing unions are those of public employees: see, for example, the American Federation of State Council and Municipal Employees in USA and the Mexican Federation of Trade Unions of Government Employees, which have both reached one million members.

79. In some European countries, such as Italy, Spain, France and Belgium, characterised by multiple unionism due to ideological and political divisions, the process of trade union concentration also shows a decline in the efforts during the '70s toward unity, a reopening of old rivalries and increased competition among different wings of the trade union movement.

The proximate cause of this trend lies in the attitude towards austerity and restriction policies adopted to different degrees by the governments of the countries mentioned above.

Ideological and political rivalries continue to fragment and divide the labour movement in many developing countries, especially in Asia.

B. Membership and Internal Government

80. The decline of unionisation is one of the clearest indicators of the difficulties faced by national trade union movements. It is pronounced in industrial sectors and is only partly compensated by the growth in some (new) sectors of the tertiary, with Scandinavia probably the only important exception. In developing countries, too, unionisation rates have been affected by the economic recession and inflation, even in some trade union movements which had reached a fairly high membership, like those of some Caribbean countries.

Decline is more pronounced in countries with a decentralised structure of bargaining and industrial relations in general (e.g. the USA and Great Britain, where from 1979 to the end of 1983 TUC members dropped from over 12 million to 10,076,000 (-17 per cent)) and in countries where union bargaining power has been traditionally weak with respect to both employers and governments (France and Spain). In Italy and FR Germany, with their bipolar or mixed structure or medium centralisation, unionisation seems to have decreased at a slower rate. These data appear to confirm the positive relationship – indicated above – between trade unions and the degree of centralisation of the bargaining structure.

The question remains open whether these variations in trade union density are a cyclical fluctuation in a long term trend towards expansion common to the post-war period[13] or an indication of a real reversal of trend. The latter hypothesis may not be unfounded.

81. As to the composition of union membership, there is a general increase in the number of unionised white-collar workers, due both to their increased presence in industrial unions and to the expansion of occupational unions in the tertiary sector, especially of public services. This trend is found in countries so different as Australia, FR Germany and the UK.[14] The growth of unionisation of women workers, particularly in northern European countries, is partially related to this phenomenon.

82. As far as forms of trade union government are concerned, two annotations can be added to the trends already indicated. In the first place, the trends towards an increase in power of the central bodies of trade unions (and employers' associations) seem to have stopped as a result of the growing difficulties in central bilateral or tripartite neo-corporatist bargaining, even in countries with the longest tradition of this practice (Scandinavia, FR Germany, Austria). This phenomenon of relative decentralisation, when it does not imply a reduction of union power altogether, has not been counter-balanced by an increased authority of national industrial unions but it seems to favour more decentralised union structures at the local or enterprise level.

In the second place, signs of dissent are visible in the attitude of the rank and file towards central leadership, particularly as a reaction to the trade

13. G. Bain and R. Price, *Profiles of Union Growth*, Oxford, 1980.
14. G. Griffin, *White Collar Unionism* 1969–1981: some determinants of Growth, the Journal of ind. relations (Kensington, Aus.) vol. 25, 1, March 1983.

unions' acceptance of wage policies (Italy, Spain), profound industrial restructuring (France, UK) or the practice of concession bargaining (USA). These reactions do not necessarily imply a decreased responsiveness of central union structures, but rather they indicate an obvious problem in the functioning of democratic union procedures and practices.

C. Unions and Workplace Organisations

83. No major structural change has modified the situations of workplace organisation illustrated above. Union representation at the workplace level is however having problems of initiative and identity. These seem to be related to the reduced scope of economic bargaining common to all systems and to the increased pressure for greater employee involvement in the joint handling of crucial matters such as productivity, industrial restructuring and the like, for which union representatives are traditionally unequipped. For this reason it might well be that the dual channel type of employee representation will prove better able to face the coming challenge than the single union channel.

D. Forms of Trade Union Action and Objectives

84. Collective bargaining remains the dominant method of trade union action in developed and some developing countries. However it faces major obstacles due to the reduced scope for economic gains, the weakening of union organisational power, the resurgence of employers' initiative, the push to return to market regulation and the intervention of some governments which tends to limit union bargaining action to various degrees.

It is probable that a period which lasted several decades has now come to an end: the period of continuous development of collective bargaining based on the acquisition of ever-increasing economic gains for employees and on the rigid regulation of working conditions. Almost everywhere real wages have stabilised or more often have begun to decrease; collective limits on working conditions are either diminishing or being replaced by some flexible forms of control.

Only one new collective bargaining objective seems to emerge: the reduction of working time as a means of defending employment. The major example in this direction is the collective action of FR Germany's IG Metall to obtain the 35 hour week.

85. A second common phenomenon is the slow down or halt, if not the reversal, of a trend towards centralised bargaining which seemed to be general during the '70s.

In most cases the pressure for decentralisation comes from the employers, often with government support. Here again the most obvious signs come from countries which already had a relatively weak decentralised bargaining structure: the USA in the first place, and the UK to a large extent. They include the fragmentation of, and increase in, the number of bargaining units and the relaxing of the forms of multi-employer bargaining co-ordination or pattern-setting effects. But difficulties in central bargaining practices due to employer opposition are also reported by countries such as Sweden (1982–83), which has had the longest tradition in this respect. Italy and Spain, two relative latecomers to centralisation, are among the few countries where important cases of central bargaining are reported in 1983–84.

A clear decline in the various forms of industrial action is also observed everywhere. With the exception of Australia, and in part Sweden, all indicators of industrial conflict from 1974 to 1982 (yearly average) are lower than the figures for the period 1968–73.

The difficulties of collective bargaining are not counterbalanced by a renewed vigour of political action or by an increased intensity and effective-ness of various forms of worker participation. Whereas in the past decade workers' participation was most often intended and promoted as a supple-ment or expansion of collective bargaining, cases are reported where em-ployee consultation and concerted action have begun to be used by manage-ment as an alternative to collective bargaining and as a direct form of relationship with employees outside union channels (USA, Great Britain). Here again, significant exceptions can be found in the Swedish legislation (1983) on worker participation in capital formation (Workers' Funds) and in the extensive French legislation (1983–84) promoting union rights and worker participation in public and private enterprises.

E. Politics and Relations with Political Parties

86. In general, the current economic recession has seemed to increase tensions and difficulties in relations between trade unions and pro-labour political parties. Controversial issues are either the attitude towards auster-ity policies implemented by pro-labour governments or behaviour with respect to conservative governments. The former is the case, for example, of Spain, France and Italy, where tensions are mounting among the major confederations, as a consequence of the rapprochement of Communist-dominated trade unions (CCOO in Spain, CGT in France, CGIL in Italy) with the Communist Party and the party's critical attitudes towards the governments. The latter is the case e.g. of Great Britain and Belgium.

The attempt by the American AFL-CIO to tighten its links with the Democratic Party during the 1984 presidential campaign does not contradict this trend.

In many countries a possible growing influence on or interference by political parties with trade unions is envisaged, parallel to the relative decline of trade union market power.

F. Unions and State Intervention in Industrial Relations

87. The types of state intervention in industrial relations basically remain those indicated above (section VII), although a few important changes are noticeable. This does not necessarily hold true for the nations where repression of trade union action is the dominant attitude. Such are the commonly reported cases of Chile, whose regime has continued to implement heavily repressive policies, and Poland, whose authoritarian policies have seen the rise of the widest autonomous labour movement in any of the countries with centrally planned economies.

Marked changes can be seen in countries corresponding to our models B (Tolerance) and C (Intervention). In Great Britain and the USA, two examples of countries with a longer tradition of *laissez-faire*, the conservative government and republican administration respectively are adopting forms of intervention that clearly restrict trade union action. The Thatcher legislation of 1984 is the best example. In some countries with a strong tradition of intervention, restriction of control policies tend to prevail over promotion measures. This applies not only to conservative governments (Belgium) but to some extent to pro-labour governments (France, Spain) as well.

Countries with a longer neo-corporatist experience seem to be relatively stable. However, the practice of union involvement in tripartite deals on major economic issues has slowed down on occasion due either to the change of political balance in government (FR Germany, Austria) or to strong employer opposition (Sweden). Union participation in public administrative institutions remains solidly entrenched.

The models of trade union movements are still the ones identified in our conclusions, because, among other things, the relative positions of the various trade unions with respect to the most decisive variables (union density, workplace organisation, relations with political parties and with the political context) have not changed significantly.

The trade union movements which seem to be able to face the challenges of economic crisis and change better are those adhering to the model of participatory unionism. Serious difficulties seem to be affecting the models of business unionism (the heaviest hit by market monetarism and deregulation) and competitive unionism (weakened by profound rivalry in the case of organisation pluralism and by restrictive state intervention).

SELECT BIBLIOGRAPHY

H. Clegg, Trade Unionism under collective bargaining. A theory based on comparison of six countries, Oxford, 1976.
E. Kassalow, Trade unions and industrial relations: an international comparison, Scranton, 1969.
J.T. Dunlop and Galenson W. (eds.), Labor in the Twentieth Century, New York, 1978.
E. Gördova, Workers' organisations in market economics: a world wide view, 1983 (mimeo).
In general, National Monographs of *IELL*, Deventer.

Chapter 12. Employers' Organisations

J.J. Oechslin

INTRODUCTION: DEFINITION

1. Employers' organisations will be defined as formal groups of employers set up to defend, represent or advise affiliated employers and to strengthen their position in society at large with respect to labour matters as distinct from economic matters. They may conclude collective agreements but this is not a formal rule and cannot be an element of their definition. Unlike trade unions, which are composed of individual persons, employers' organisations are composed of enterprises.

2. This concept does not imply a particular legal form and the expression 'employers' association' has been avoided for this reason. Most legal definitions of a trade union apply to them: they are combinations whose principal object is to regulate the relations between workmen and masters (British definition), they are associations for the defence of economic interests (French definition) . . .

In many countries, the legal form of a trade union is open for an employers' organisation. If it is so, they may and do choose sometimes other legal forms – or no form at all – to suit their purposes. Often, especially initially, the function of an employers' organisation is assumed by a body created for another purpose, for instance a Chamber of Commerce. In this chapter, an employers' organisation will be defined by its functions, which are the result of historical development. In a second stage, the structure of the oganisation will be analysed in the light of the analysis of functions.

I. HISTORICAL DEVELOPMENT

From Guilds to Employers' Organisations

3. It is often said that employers' organisations have usually been established in reaction to union power and are therefore a more recent phenomenon than workers' organisations. They have, however, roots in a more remote past if we accept that they are, to some extent, successors to the guilds of the Middle Ages and Classical times. But contrary to them, employers' organisations are normally freely constituted organisations, representing enterprises in competition with one another and dealing on an equal footing with workers' organisations, especially for the establishment of

229

the 'price' of labour, even if the modern 'labour market' is no longer really a market.

4. A market economy and a liberal organisation of the economy and the political and social structure were initially regarded as incompatible with the guild system. The evolution was more radical in some countries, such as France, more gradual in others. In France, the celebrated Le Chapelier Act of 14–17 June 1791 forbade members of the same trade to form associations in defence of 'their so-called common interests'. The logic of the market system leads an employer to consider other employers as rivals or competitors. The workers very soon realised that competition between fellow workers was a weakness and an advantage for the other party. But Adam Smith had already observed in 1776 that 'we rarely hear . . . of the combination of matters, though frequently of those of workmen. But whoever imagines, upon this account, that masters rarely combine, is as ignorant of the world as of the subject. Masters are always and everywhere in a sort of tacit, but constant and uniform combination, not to raise the wages of labour above their actual rate'.[1]

5. Certainly entrepreneurs, individualists by nature and by function, have a weaker spirit of association than other social groups. They do not easily accept a discipline that may interfere with their technical or commercial operations. Liberty of action is regarded as an essential element of production. Any restriction on this liberty has to be justified by circumstances. The first associations of heads or undertakings, industrialists or tradesmen, were more clubs or social institutions, convenient for exchanging views or opinions. The members were divided on questions of manufacturing or foreign trade, while labour questions simply did not arise. The situation began to change at the turn of the century.

6. With the end of the century came the end of 'laissez-faire', i.e. of a certain neutrality of the State in respect of economic and labour questions. The first element was the recognition of trade unionism and the legitimacy of industrial action which led to labour unrest and the first big strikes. In addition, employers began to experiment with the development of a labour legislation, which may appear to-day as particularly benign but was considered at the time as an intolerable encroachment on freedom of enterprise.

7. Many sectoral employers' federations were created before the First World War. This is also the case with a few central employers federations, for instance in the Nordic countries (Denmark 1896, Norway 1900, Sweden 1901, Finland 1905) as in Germany where two organisations merged in 1913 to form a Confederation not so different from the present organisation, despite the interruption of the Nazi regime.

1. Adam Smith, *The Wealth of Nations*, Pelican Series, London, 1970, p. 169.

In all these countries, organisations specialised in labour matters (employers' organisations) have remained distinct from the economic organisations. In other European countries, central organisations are a later development. In France, such an organisation was founded in 1920 to become after some changes of name and an eclipse during the war, the National Council of French Undertakings (Patronat). In the United Kingdom, the present Confederation of British Industry was founded as late as 1965 from a merger of three organisations, only one specialised in labour matters. In these two countries, the employers' organisation deals also with economic matters.

In non European countries, some employers' organisations are very old: for instance the Union Industrial Argentina has been founded in 1887. Many of these organisations, particularly in the Americas, were not established in the context of industrial relations but mainly to deal with such questions as fiscal legislation or foreign trade. They have assumed the functions of an employers' organisation *stricto sensu* when it became necessary to respond to a government policy or to the development of the trade union movement. In some Latin American countries business organisations have been set up by law in the thirties with a compulsory membership. Others are free associations. In other parts of the world, newly independent nations have followed the pattern of their former Colonial Power: for instance 'Employers' federations' based on the British model of the time have proliferated in English-speaking African and Asian states. The main problem of organisations in developing countries has been the difficulty of integrating a very heterogeneous membership: small national businessmen, state enterprises, subsidiaries of multinationals, as well as to securing the means necessary to enable them to play a significant role as representative of the productive sector of the economy.

II. FUNCTIONS OF EMPLOYERS' ORGANISATIONS

A. Functions of Defence and Promotion

8. Employers' organisations were generally established at the same time as trade unions. In general, however, they did not try to defend their members by direct dialogue with the workers' unions but rather by approaching government leaders. In early times it could suffice to make discreet representations to the political authorities, statesmen, or senior civil servants. Very soon, like all interests groups, employers' organisations tried to find a place in the democratic decision-making process. Employers are not numerous and therefore are not in a privileged position in a modern society based on mass institutions. They are however influential by virtue of their economic control and because they influence – or appear to be able to influence – a large number of people.

231

9. Employers as such are not considerably well represented in parliaments. On the other hand, there are no political parties formally linked with an employers' organisation as, for instance, the Labour party is linked with the British trade unions. The more informal relations existing between most socialist parties and unions have no equivalent on the other side. Conservative parties are often ideologically close to the employers but without formal relations. The employers' influence on parliaments or some parliamentary fractions is genuine but difficult to analyse. It is based less on formal structures than on personal contacts and the weight of expertise in matters dealt with, the same type of influence that can be exerted on civil servants.

10. This traditional way of protecting members' interests is still of value but is now considered as insufficient. The first reason for a new approach is the need to go to the root of the decision-making process in democratic societies – the formation of public opinion. Press campaigns are not a new form of action for employers' groups, but a systematic effort to influence public opinion in general is a rather new development. The target groups to which it is felt important to send a message include notably the employees of one's own enterprises, leaders in community groups, school teachers, churches, and particularly, those people who can influence the media.

11. Another important aspect is the involvement of employers' organisations in social policy rather than to react to specific issues. Workers' unions also increasingly offer a general view of the social order and not only claims for the improvement of definite labour conditions. The political debate in most nations involves alternative choices of society and a global view calling into question the social order. Employers' organisations are therefore also expected to present a coherent view of the socio-economic structure. Information and formation of public opinion appear therefore as a prerequisite to negotiation or specific action on particular issues.

12. These functions correspond to those of a 'pressure group'. The term is often rejected by occupation and organisations because it seems to imply a negative value judgement. It certainly reflects an important aspect of the functions of an employers' organisation as well as of any interest group. But in modern societies, employers' organisations are also expected to participate in various decisions as a consequence of their representative character.
I propose to call that aspect the representative function of organisations.

B. Function of Representation

1. Representative Function in the Political Structure

13. A government department may take the initiative in seeking the advice of an interest group (in the preceding section the initiative came from the interest group). The meaning of such a step is the recognition of the technical expertise of the group and of its representative character. It is felt necessary to gauge the preliminary reaction of the group if the decisions to be taken are to be implemented correctly. This system developed at the beginning of the century as a necessary corollary to the growing state interventionism in social and economic questions. In Switzerland this concept was recognised in the Federal Constitution in 1947. Its Article 32, al. 3, states that 'interested economic groups shall be consulted in the preparation of implementing regulations'. This applied only to the articles determining the competence of the Confederation in general economic matters but reflects a practice generally accepted by most governments.

14. This practice leads to an important question: how to choose the organisation to be consulted. In some countries the reply is straightforward. In others the choice is not clear and this may enable the consulting authorities to choose to consult the organisation whose reply will support their own views. An important function of an employers' organisation is therefore to be representative in order to be able to represent its membership and to participate in consultation. The appreciation of this representative character is often more difficult than for other groups. Members of employers' organisations are not individual persons but enterprises of different sizes and natures. The simple arithmetic of adding units is not enough. Representation has to be appreciated in consideration of the final result: is the organisation able to present the real views of those who will have to implement the decision in its final stages.

15. This representative function assumed a new dimension when consultation became formalised in tripartite or bipartite institutions. The International Labour Organisation, created in 1919, gave the most striking illustration of tripartism with its unique structure associating employers' and workers' delegates on an equal footing with representatives of governments. Before and mainly during the First World War, some form of tripartite machinery was established in the United Kingdom, France and Germany, especially in the management of the war economy. It has influenced many countries, especially among developing nations which have benefited from its technical co-operation activities. In most countries, numerous government committees associate employers' representatives with other partners but usually in a consultative capacity. It is not often however that this association leads to participation in the decision-making process.

16. The idea of representing economic and social interests finds its most obvious expression in Economic and Social Councils, as in France, French-speaking Africa, in Latin America, and in the Netherlands. There is also an Economic and Social Committee in the European Community. But if these bodies are integrated elements of political structures, they remain consultative and are kept independent of political representative bodies elected by the citizens. The presence of interest groups in legislative assemblies is a sign of a corporatist system, and the function of such groups is so changed that it is no longer possible to call them employers' organisations as here understood.

17. Other examples could be provided, especially the participation of employers' organisations in national planning, a process more concerning developing than developed countries (except France). In some Third World countries with a single-party system, employers' organisations are sometimes associated with the ruling party, together with other 'national organisations'. Tripartism is also often applied to management of social security schemes.

2. Representative Function in the Industrial Relations System

18. It is in collective bargaining that the representative character of employers' organisations is most apparent. However, in many countries employers' organisations do not bargain with unions. It is therefore necessary to distinguish various models.

19. The first model is typical of the Nordic countries. Global negotiations are undertaken at national level. This does not imply that agreement is always achieved at this level. In any case, negotiations are continued at branch level to apply the centrally-agreed provisions. It is clear that such a system implies a strong centralised employers' organisation. To be accepted at intermediate or enterprise level, it is also necessary for the organisation to be structured in a way that enables the negotiators to be fully aware of the needs of all the constituents. The central organisation should also dispose of all necessary elements – economic and statistical data – which can only be provided if the headquarters are adequately equipped. There is also a need for firm discipline based on a guarantee that individual members will not suffer from a decision taken at central level. A mutual strike insurance system is therefore an essential element of the system.

20. In the opposite model, collective bargaining takes place only at the enteprise level. Does this mean that the employers' organisations have in such case no role in industrial relations? The situation of Japan illustrates a negative reply. The Japanese Federation of Employers' Associations (Nikkeiren) does not negotiate, but considers as its main mission the formulation of guidelines for employers elaborated by its policy-making bodies in which major corporations are represented. This work is prepared by extensive research by economists on the staff. On the other side of the table, unions also try to concert their action in the undertakings. In North America, negotiation is generally (but not always) at enterprise level. Employers' group are numerous and well organised but the two main associations, the National Association of

Manufactures and the Chamber of Commerce of the United States, very active in legislative and political action, do not intervene in collective bargaining.

20bis. Another model, which may be called the German model, is based on negotiations at the level of national branches of industry. There are no other levels of negotiation. Typically, participation and consultation in the enterprise is not collective bargaining *stricto sensu* nor does it embrace items dealt with in industrial agreements. On the other hand, relations between top organisations of workers and employers are limited to common participation in various tripartite bodies or to informal contacts. As a rule, no formal agreements are concluded between them. The central organisation: has the task of co-ordinating the policy of its members, which are not too numerous and may easily be assembled around a table. This model implies well-organised branch organisations able to assume at their level the functions ascribed to the national body in the first model. The function of the Confederation is more to ensure a certain common approach based on internal consultation and research.

21. The last model, typical for instance of France, Belgium or Italy, is different from 'the three previous ones because it is based on several levels of negotiation. The emphasis in the negotiation structure is still on the branches of industry but this does not exclude the conclusion of agreements at the national multi-industry level. These agreements may consist of broad statements on general policy or they may deal with more specific problems such as hours of work, the unification of the status of white- and blue-collar workers, wage indexation, additional social security benefits and the like. Frequently these agreements only set out general principles which have to be further implemented at the branch or enterprise level.

On the other hand, negotiations in the enterprise may supplement agreements concluded at a higher level. Such a system based on a chain of negotiations is difficult to monitor. The structure of the employers' organisations as a whole has to be based on frequent liaison between all the levels involved in the negotiating process.

C. *Internal Functions of Employers' Organisations*

22. It is not always easy to draw a line between activities supporting the functions described above and those undertaken for the members in their interest. Research, for instance, is necessary before action directed to government or public opinion or to furnish the negotiators with good arguments. But enterprises also need research to help them in their operations. Most organisations undertake for the benefit of their members various types of enquiries and surveys on wages or fringe benefits, based on national and international data. They help managers confronted with a growing flow of information and elaboration of guidelines on industrial health and safety. At a time when management principles and techniques are questioned outside and inside the business community, employers' organisations provide an essential forum for the discussion of new approaches. Many new concepts – like participative management, communications with the workforce, continuous training – have been developed through reflection by heads of undertakings in their organisations.

It is also in this framework that common views have emerged on such general issues as workers' participation, income policies, role of trade unions in collective bargaining . . . The difference of national conditions makes it almost impossible to make international comparisons of the positions taken by employers' organisations.

23. Employers' organisations are now important training institutions. They help in developing among their members an interest in training in general and in elaborating common policies on the subject. These activities are especially oriented towards management training or the training of leaders of personnel departments. The biggest organisations have established well-organised management development centres but modest associations in developing countries are also conscious of the necessity of involvement in training and have appointed one or several training officers. The training of other categories is also often taken care of by employers' organisations, generally by industry branch associations which have set up or sponsored apprentice training centres, adult training schemes or similar activities.

24. Employers' organisations have also been active in social work. For instance workers' housing development has often been initiated by employers. In France, family allowances were introduced during the First World War by employers and the schemes, compulsory from 1932, continued to be administered until 1945 by equalisation funds set up by the employers. Most of these functions have been taken over by social security institutions, but not all, and not everywhere.

25. Enterprises, especially the small and medium-sized ones, also expect direct services from their organisation. They ask information and advice to guide them or their personnel officers through the labyrinth of legal obligations deriving from regulations and agreements. In some countries, employers' organisations assist the employers before labour courts or similar institutions or help them to solve specific labour problems in the enterprise. Advice on method to improve management and productivity is more and more sought, particularly in developing countries.

III. STRUCTURE OF EMPLOYERS' ORGANISATIONS

26. The study of the structure of an employers' organisation in isolation is not a very fruitful exercise. How does one compare a local trade association with a confederation? We will rather consider the overall structure of the

employers' organisation as a system to evaluate how they are adapted to the main functions described above. The variations from country to country will depend on the weight of the different functions and especially on the degree of centralisation of the industrial relations system as a whole. In this respect there should be some parallelism between employers' and workers' organisations. Other variables are dependent on factors external to the industrial relations system, such as the size of the country and its form of government. The employers' structures in India are different from the one prevailing in Mauritius. A federal state leads normally – but not always – to a decentralised employers' organ-isation. Account has also to be taken of the degree of economic development. The degree of sophistication of employers' organisations in Nordic countries cannot be reached in a developing economy. A diversified industry, based on small and medium-sized enterprises calls for a different type of organisation than a country based on one or few basic branches. But the more important differentiations are based on history. A slow and peaceful development leads to a structure more complex and less rational than that in a country, which has been rebuilt after complete collapse, such as Germany or Japan, or even than in an emerging nation.

A. Unity of the Central Organisation at National Level

1. Economic and Social Organisations

27. As well as the functions of employers' organisations as defined above, or 'social questions', enterprises are also grouped for other purposes such as the regulation of domestic and foreign trade, customs policies, company taxation or investment promotion, usually defined as 'economic questions'. In the Nordic countries, FR Germany, Switzerland, Ireland, and in most countries which experienced British colonisation, these functions have been assumed by separate organisations. Many of them have the word 'industry' in their titles or are called in English-speaking parts of the world Chambers of Industry and/or Commerce. (In French-speaking and other countries Chambers of Commerce are public establishments, with compulsory membership, run by organs elected by all industrialists and by businessmen.) In other countries, especially Belgium, France, Italy, and some Latin American countries, the two groups of functions are assumed by a single organisation called a federation of Industry, of enterprises or, in France 'patronat'. The British themselves have joined this camp since the Confederation of British Industry came into being in 1965. In the Netherlands also, the Federation of Dutch Enterprises has replaced two organisations responsible in the social field and the economic field respectively.

28. Of course it is sometimes rather difficult to make a clear-cut division between 'social' and 'economic' questions. Tax laws or inducements to investment have consequences for wage or employment policies. The

intermingling of functions makes it hard for organisations responsible in both fields to distinguish among their own staff those in charge of each function. Participation in national planning and global economic and social policy implies an integrated approach to economic and labour issues. However, in countries where the dual structure has been maintained, employers justify it, indicating that it is easier to maintain cohesion in labour matters than in the economic field where the opposition of interests is greater. In any case, there is need for close co-operation.

2. Coverage of the Central Organisation

29. The coverage of the central organisation varies very much from country to country. It is difficult to propose criteria but it seems that wide coverage is easier to achieve in an organisation specialised in labour matters. In one group of countries (FR Germany, UK, New Zealand . . .) only a single organisation exists, open to all sectors of the economy, including agriculture. In another group the central employers' organisation covers all sectors, except agriculture where there is a special organisation (France, Tunisia). In Malaysia, there are separate organisations for both mines and agriculture. In a larger group of countries, the central organisation embraces a sizeable number of groups in the secondary sector – mostly manufacturing – while the tertiary sector – and sometimes also building, transport or mining – form different organisations. It is often difficult to associate manufacturing and commerce in the same organisation. In Switzerland, membership of the central organisation extends to cover banks, insurance companies and the large department stores but not the wholesale and retail trade. In Belgium, however, it has been possible to merge the organisation for industry and for the tertiary sector. It is certainly an advantage for an organisation to dispose of wide coverage even if it results in more differences of opinion and a differing capacity to contribute to the cost of operations.

3. Parallel Organisations

30. In few cases, there is more than one employers' organisation with some over-lapping among them. This is the case in the United States with the National Association of Manufactures and the Chamber of Commerce of the US, both with very similar functions. In India, one organisation includes the big enterprises, including the multinationals, the other smaller national businesses. In the two cases, the duality is explained by history and has no rational justification. In India, a joint Council has been established by two bodies, particularly for international representation. In Australia, a very complex situation has led to the creation of an apex body, the Confederation of Australian Industry. In the Netherlands, there are also two organisations, both covering almost all sectors, one non-denominational and another

Christian (resulting from the merger of a Catholic and a Protestant organisation). It is the only country where an employers' organisation has been set
up on a denominational basis.

31. It is true that associations of Christian employers exist in other countries, forming the national sections of UNIAPAC (International Christian
Union of Business Executives) but their purpose is more to define a certain
approach to social problems than to act as representatives of employers.
Their members are persons acting as individuals, and not as enterprises.
Therefore they are not employers' organisations. Groups of employers have
also established associations based on the same shade of opinion but which
do not pretend to a representative character. Their aim is the discussion of
social topics or the promotion of certain ideas (for instance profit-sharing).
They are sometimes associate members of the central organisation but
should not be confused with representative organisations.

B. Membership of Employers' Organisations

1. Small and Medium-Sized Enterprises

32. The concept of small and medium-sized enterprises is widely accepted
but difficult to define in quantitative terms. It refers to an enterprise where
the manager is normally the owner of the majority or a large part of the
capital and maintains direct and permanent relations with the employees.
The climate of industrial relations is therefore quite different, and formal
institutions of workers' representation are often impracticable. They are also
financially more vulnerable and more reluctant to accept increases in labour
costs. They also lack expert staff and need more advice from their organisation. These enterprises have specific needs. Are they better met by the
creation of special organisations or by their inclusion within the over-all
system of employers' organisation? As a matter of fact the great majority of
central employers' organisations is open to all undertakings irrespective of
their size. Restrictions, where they exist, apply to very small firms which can
be described as handicrafts. It appears however that they cover a less
representative number than is the case with large undertakings and that
their leaders are less active in the various decision-making bodies. The
policy of the central organisation is generally to have a large membership in
small enterprises to ensure more political influence and to avoid the creation
of splinter groups but this implies an effort to associate them in decisions, to
increase the direct services to members and to adapt the scale of contributions.

33. Nevertheless parallel organisations catering solely for smaller undertakings are to be found in some countries. A typical example is France where
all 'General Confederation of Small and Medium Sized Enterprises' has

been in existence since 1946 and is considered as representative of the category. It has at times been a member of the CNPF but is now separate. Most of its members are nevertheless still represented in the central organisation through the branch trade associations in which they remain members and they are covered by collective agreements concluded at the branch level.

2. Public sector enterprises

34. Free enterprise being at the core of employers' organisations' ideology, the principle of membership of enterprises in the public sector should have raised a difficult issue. On the other hand, the State sector employs in most countries a growing number of people and has indeed become the biggest employer. Employers' organisations have taken in this respect a pragmatic attitude. In very few countries – such as the United States and Switzerland – the employers' organisations are closed to public enterprises – typically countries where this sector is very small indeed. In very few countries also, organistions are open to any such undertakings, especially in English-speaking Africa. For instance the Nairobi City Council, the Post Office and Harbour Authorities are members of the Federation of Kenya Employers. In most cases, organisations adopt a selective approach which is of great interest in elucidating the concept of enterprise as understood by employers' organisations.

35. The general attitude of employers' organisations towards public sector undertakings is that of limiting membership to publicly-owned companies largely run on the same economic principles as private companies. This would normally exclude state monopoly sectors like postal, telegraph and telephone services, radio and television, rail transport or, less frequently, coal mines or electricity power. A characteristic of these undertakings is that the price of their products does not result from a competitive market but is determined by the government. The result of this situation makes the position of management in the collective bagaining process quite different. Another criterion might be the degree of autonomy of the management in relation to government authorities. Public sector undertakings may be not very different from ministerial department without even a special budget or companies with State participation may have practically the same freedom of action as private groups. The appreciation of this situation varies from country to country.

36. In very few cases, the State has prohibited public sector undertakings from joining the employers' federations. For instance, in Italy, an Act of 1956 prohibits companies in which the State has a direct or indirect interest from affiliating to trade or regional associations affiliated to the General Confederation of Italian Industry. In India, there is also a special organisation for public enterprises, but it is a member with the two others of the Council of Indian Employers. Such government decisions have, as a rule, been regretted by employers' organisations.

C. Employers' Organisations at the Sectoral and Regional Levels

37. In very small countries, it is possible to have a single employers' organisation to which the individual employers are directly affiliated. This is of course impracticable in most countries. Usually individual firms are grouped under trade and/or regional associations with the latter directly affiliated to the central oganisation. In one group of countries, including the Nordic countries, Belgium, the Netherlands and a few others, trade associations alone are affiliated. This is typical of medium-sized centralised countries with an industrial relations system based on an emphasis on negotiation at branch level. In a few federal countries, with negotiation at enterprise level, member associations are all regional. In a larger group trade and regional associations are members and most firms are themselves affiliated both to a trade and a regional unit (with possibility of any form of intermediary groups). The number of direct members may vary between a dozen and a few hundred.

38. In most organisations, the branch structure has more weight than the regional one due to the fact that major labour questions are dealt with at the branch level. But the general trend is towards the reinforcement of regional structures. This is linked with the need to maintain closer contacts with the smaller firms without headquarters in the capital city but also to facilitate the framing of employers' policy on regional problems – a trend which illustrates also the new function of employers' organisations to contribute to a global approach to economical and social problems in their local environment. This new stress on regions may be applied by a reinforcement of regional associations or by the establishment of regional offices and a decentralisation of activities (for instance in organising important meetings in different parts of the country). A regional policy is an essential means of preserving the cohesion of the institution.

39. These intermediate structures contribute to the decision-making process. In this respect, employers' organisations meet specific problems compared with most other associations. It has already been stressed that their members are not physical persons but artificial entities – enterprises which are of very different size. A simple application of the democratic principle – one man, one vote – would not be very practicable and ultimately not very democratic. The problem is not so different in the international organisations of States.

40. It is necessary to give more weight to bigger enterprises but on the other hand not to reduce to a minimum the influence of small enterprises which should have a feeling of genuinely belonging to the organisation. It is therefore necessary to ensure a proper balance between different categories in the decision-making bodies by formal arrangements or by consensus.

41. The formalisation of the employers' structure may lead to a certain remoteness of central organisation from the actual employers. A way to correct this disadvantage has been to admit individual firms as members of the central organisation along with associations. This is for instance the rule in the Confederation of British Industry. A drawback is that this may lead to a weakening of the branch organisations and a certain imbalance in so far as it gives more weight to bigger firms than to smaller, which remain affiliated only through their associations.

D. Means and Resources

42. To fulfil all the functions described above, the employers' organisations need resources, particularly human resources. They need expertise which can be given by a permanent staff of lawyers, economists, sociologists, public relations specialists, statisticians, political scientists, but also experts in the running of employers' organisations, which has become a profession. Many employers' organisations have set up special institutions for the training of their staff and organise career development for their personnel. But on the other hand, an employers' organisation also needs a real contribution by actual employers. Usually (there are a few exceptions), presidents and chairmen of committees are honorary functionaries. It is not too easy to find businessmen willing to spare their time – free of charge – for rather exhausting jobs involving for instance long negotiations and proceedings. Employers' organisations should also be represented in a growing number of various tripartite and consultative bodies. The running of an employers' organisation is based on close co-operation between elected chairmen and professional staff members. To cover the cost of their operations – mainly staff costs – the employers' organisations need resources. Usually they consist of contributions paid by enterprises either directly or through the branch or regional organisations. In a very centralised system (for instance in the Nordic countries), the contributions are paid directly to the central body which returns a fraction of it to the branch federations, but this is rather exceptional. The contributions are based on the wage bill (less often on the number of employees) in pure employers' organisations. For 'economic and social' organisations, account is also taken of such data as turnover, sales, value added . . .

IV. INTERNATIONAL EMPLOYERS' ORGANISATIONS

A. *Historical Development*

43. The first international meeting of representatives of central employers' federations, as understood here, was held in 1912 in Turin on the occasion of a World Labour Exhibition. It recommended the creation and promotion of employers' associations in their own countries and the study of the possibility of establishing an international group. It was in fact the first ILO Conference in 1919 which provided a new opportunity for a gathering of employers' representatives at international level. In 1920 the 'International Organisation of Industrial Employers' was created with headquarters in Brussels. After the Second World War, the organisation changed its name to 'International Organisation of Employers'.

44. Between the two World Wars, the IOIE remained active almost solely within the framework of the ILO. The development of international federations of Trade Unions in the twenties had no real counterpart on the employers' side. After 1945, the development of international institutions in the United Nations System led to a reinforcement of the IOE, whose headquarters were moved in 1964 from Brussels to Geneva.

B. *International Employers' Organisations at World Level*

1. General Description

45. As in many national situations, there are two organisations representing the interests of employers at international level, one in charge of so-called social questions, the International Organisation of Employers (IOE), and one specialised in economic questions, the International Chamber of Commerce (ICC). An agreement exists between the two organisations establishing a division of work. It is a fact, however, that the borderline between the two types of questions is becoming blurred, for instance in the current debate on the role of transnational corporation.

46. Other groups aim at representing special categories of enterprises. For instance, an 'International Association of Crafts and Small and Medium-Sized Enterprises was founded in 1947 and has members in 22 countries. Other organisations have been set up at sectoral level', like the International Shipping Federation. National federations of building and civil engineering employers are grouped in three regional federations which set up in 1973 a 'Confederation of International Contractors' Associations'. These associations are rather active in labour matters, especially in the context of the ILO. Other sectoral organisations, such as the Road Transport Union, the International Iron and Steel Institute, the International Textile Manufacturers' Federation, deal mainly with scientific or technical issues and only occasionally with labour matters.

2. The International Organisation of Employers (IOE)

47. The members of the IOE, 95 in 90 countries, are 'central employers' federations'. This means that undertakings cannot be in direct membership even if they are multinational enterprises. It should also be noted that the members are national multi-industry groups – normally one per country – in practice the most representative organisation called upon to nominate the employer's delegate to the International Labour Conference, in accordance with the ILO Constitution. International sectoral organisations cannot be members but working arrangements have been concluded. Contrary to most national organisations, the IOE is based on territorial units and not on industrial branches.

48. IOE members also have to fulfil special conditions. They have 'to be composed exclusively of employers or employers' organisations, to stand for and defend the principle of free enterprise and to be a free and independent organisation, not subject to control or interference of any kind from any governmental authority or any outside body'. These conditions exclude corporatist structures like those in Fascist Italy, the French 'Charte du Travail' or the Spanish 'sindicatos' during the Franco regime. They also exclude industrial organisations from fully or predominently socialised economic systems. It may be questioned whether such enterprises are really representing employers, i.e. parties to a contract of employment. However 'free enterprise' is not a synonym for private enterprise. Many IOE members include public corporations as mentioned above when this type of membership does not appear to affect the independence of the organisation.

49. The internal structure of the IOE is based on a General Council, where all members are represented, an Executive Committee and a permanent Secretary General. Most members who actually take part in the deliberations of the Executive Committee are at the same time employer members of the Governing Body of the ILO. Its chairman is – and has been most of the time – employers' vice-chairman of the ILO Governing Body and, as such, the leader of the employers at major ILO meetings, including the General Conference.

50. This symbiotic relationship between the IOE and the Employers' Group of the ILO (with the exception of Eastern Europe) illustrates the fact that the ILO is the main concern of the IOE. The international trade union federations also organise the workers' group but they are divided and their other activities are more extensive or better known by the public. The IOE also maintains activities not related to the action of intergovernmental institutions, especially in the field of mutual information on labour issues and discussion of topics of special interest to members. These studies are as a rule restricted to members' organisations. The ILO also provides assistance to employers in developing countries, for instance by organising seminars or by sending experts to help them with organisational problems.

51. The IOE is one of the organisations enjoying full consultative status with the ILO (as well as with the UN). But its main function, in an organisation where employers' (and workers') delegates are able to express directly the point of view of enterprises, is to maintain the cohesion of the group and to make sure that the delegates are well informed about the substance of the issues and about procedures. Through the employers' delegates, the IOE contributes to the process of elaboration of ILO instruments and to the development of technical co-operation. As the majority of IOE members come from developing countries they are particularly interested in general training, management training, and industrial safety. The ILO has now introduced a programme of assistance to employers' organisations, parallel to the workers' education programme, operated in close liaison with the IOE.

C. Regional Organisations

52. The international scene is also occupied by a number of regional employers' associations. Some of them are mainly but not exclusively concerned with economic questions, like the Inter-american Council of Commerce and Production or the Association of Industrialists of Latin America. At the sub-regional level, some employers' organisations *stricto sensu* have been constituted, often following ILO meetings, for instance in the Caribbean and in South East Asia (ASEA group). The development of a tripartite regional organisation is of course an incentive for the establishment of an employers' organisation. For instance, the existence of an Arab Labour Organisation has induced the General Union of Chambers of Commerce, Industry and Agriculture for Arab Countries to establish a standing Committee for Social Affairs.

53. This tendency to establish employers' organisations to represent the views of enterprises before intergovernmental institutions can also be noted in Europe. In this way, the Council of European Industrial Federations (CIFE) was created in 1949 to make possible direct consultations with the Organisation for European Economic Co-operation (OEEC). When the latter disappeared in 1961 and was replaced by the OECD, most activities of the CIFE were taken over by the Business and Industrial Advisory Committee (BIAC). In the early phases of the development of the European Community, employers' affairs were taken care of in the framework of CIFE but a 'Union of Industries of the European Community (UNICE) was formally created in 1958 with the national employers' federations of the six countries.

54. The CIFE had as a matter of fact a wider representation than that of the OEEC, since Spain and Finland were members in spite of the fact that, in the beginning, they had remained outside of the intergovernmental organisation. In the UNICE the same situation has arisen: as early as 1962 the Federation of Greek Industry was associated with its work. In 1972–1973 the Employers' organisations of the three new EEC State Members, the UK, Denmark and Ireland, joined the UNICE but a little later employers' organisations from West European countries remaining outside the Community decided also to become associate members. UNICE is now more than an organisation of EEC employers but also an organisation of European employers. It has now members in 19 countries.

55. UNICE, like CIFE and BIAC, is competent both in the social and in the economic field, reflecting the scope of activities of the EEC.

The model of organisation at European level is different from the dualist system at international level. On the other hand, UNICE representativeness is limited to 'industry' although most of its members have a wider coverage. The function of spokesperson of the employers in general is assured by an Employers' Liaison Committee (CLE) associating UNICE with other federations representing Commerce, Insurance, Banking, Handicrafts. The UNICE provides the secretariat and being by far the better organised part of CLE, retains a leading position. Agriculture is also organised separately, as is the public sector through the European Centre for Public Enterprises (CEEP). This is rather paradoxical because most members of UNICE are open to the public sector and there is no special oganisation covering it except in Italy.

56. The variety and complexity of EEC competence and its supra-national character lead to a structure of UNICE characterised by the daily involvement of its members and the relative importance of the services provided. The organisation is run by a President elected by the Council of Presidents (of the member federations), an Executive Committee composed of the Managing Directors of Members' Federations, a Committee of Permanent Delegates, in constant contact with the Secretary General and with most of them residing near the headquarters in Brussels.

57. The co-operation between the UNICE and Community institutions is often informal but regular. In addition, the EEC structure includes an Economic and Social Committee made up of persons representing employers, workers and other groups. The members are appointed in a personal capacity and do not necessarily reflect the view of UNICE, which however provides them with experts and documentation. Other EEC standing fora include representatives of employers and workers, such as the

Standing Committee on Employment, created in 1970, and the Tripartite Conferenecess. The employers, like workers members, are then direct representatives of UNICE and other European Employers' Federations.

58. In these different instances, UNICE meets European workers' organisations and also has occasional direct relations with them. These relations do not so far lead to a situation of collective bargaining. The UNICE is not empowered with this function and its members are not yet prepared to give it this competence. This can be explained by legal and political reasons, and especially by the fact that many UNICE members are not themselves empowered to bargain.

59. UNICE is, then, the international employers' organisation which is more like a national federation. Its structure is more complex than that of many national bodies in developing countries. It remains however of a different nature because it deals with a community which is not yet fully integrated and where the realities of social debate are still to be found in the States. This illustrates the basic fact that employers' organisations' functions and structures are to be appreciated in the context of a general political framework and of an overall industrial relations system.

Select Bibliography

J. Oechslin, Employers' organisations: Current Trends and social responsibilities; *International Labour Review* Vol. 121, September-October, 1982.
J.P. Windmuller and A. Gladstone (eds.), *Employers Associations and Industrial Relations – A Comparative Study*, Oxford, 1984.
I.L.O. Labour Relations Series
   No. 39 – Role of Employers' Organisations in Asian Countries, Geneva, 1971.
   No. 42 – Role of Employers' Organisations in English Speaking African countries, Geneva, 1973.
   No. 53 – Role of Employers' Organisations in English Speaking Caribbean Countries, Geneva, 1977.
   No. 46 – Rôle des oganisations d'employeurs dans les pays d'Afrique francophone, Geneva, 1975.
   No. 54 – Rôle des organisations d'employeurs dans les pays arabes, Geneva, 1978.
   No. 51 – Papel de los organizaciones de empleadores en America Latina, Geneva, 1976.

Chapter 13.   Employee Participation in the Workshop, in the Office and in the Enterprise

T. Hanami and J. Monat

Introduction

1. In spite of the diversity of its institutional arrangements, employee participation – or to put it another way employees' influence on decisions which may affect them – is attracting renewed attention in both industrialised societies and developing countries due, among other factors, to increasing international and internal competition as well as to the spread of new technologies. In this chapter, the main forms of participation, with the exception of collective bargaining, dealt with in chapter 15 will be examined. At the same time, it would appear appropriate to briefly describe why different institutions play a dominant role in different countries so as to provide an insight into the various forms of participation, their interrelationship with one another and the relationship between these forms and collective bargaining.

2. Most of the chapter will be devoted to what is referred to as indirect or ascending participation (i.e. employee participation through their representatives or their organisations), but some attention will also be paid to direct participation or the involvement of individual employees, (referred to as descending participation, i.e. arrangements for associating employees with the determination of work organisation at shopfloor level and the way in which their own work is to be carried out).*

I. Rationale and Meaning of Employee Participation in the Industrial Relations Systems and Historical Background

3. There are many reasons for the interest in employee participation in the world today, as will be seen below, but the idea that the workforce should have a share in decisions which affect the operation of the enterprise had already found a certain expression in some of the social doctrines that emerged in the nineteenth century.

* See also chapter 14 on Quality of Working Life.

249

4. The objectives assigned to employee participation in decisions within enterprises vary from country to country and have sometimes undergone certain changes. Moreover, they need not be mutually exclusive – indeed, at the origin of many schemes or experiments, a whole range of considerations have come into play.

5. Initially, the emphasis was on ethical or moral considerations reinforced by notions of equity and social justice, the aim being to contribute to the all-round development of the individual. This general proposition has been elaborated in various doctrinal statements – papal encyclicals, national constitutions (the right to participation in one form or another now exists in the constitutions of countries as different as *Czechoslovakia*, *Ecuador*, *German Democratic Republic*, *India*, *Italy*, *Norway*, *Portugal*, *Romania*, *Spain*, the *USSR* and *Yugoslavia*), the programmes of trade union movements, management statements, etc.

6. One of the arguments behind the ethical approach is that – as the employees play their part in production, sometimes at the risk of their own health and life, spending a major part of each day at work to support themselves and their families – they have some right to be heard on matters connected with the running of the enterprise. As the 'Green Book' published by the Commission of the EC put it, 'Decisions taken by or in the enterprise can have a substantial effect on their economic circumstances, both immediately and in the long term; the satisfaction which they derive from work; their health and physical condition; the time and energy which they can devote to their families and to activities other than work; and even their sense of dignity and autonomy as human beings. Accordingly, continuing consideration is being given to the problem of how and to what extent employees should be able to influence the decisions of enterprises which employ them'.[1]

7. It has also become clear in most countries today, that the younger generation is increasingly unwilling to accept authority and decisions in which they have had no share and hence are determined to have a say in the decisions that are taken. This is no doubt due to increased educational levels and to the development of students' critical faculties in post-primary schooling, as well as to more participative methods of education which encourage initiative, creativity and readiness for individual or collective responsibility.

8. At the same time, political and social objectives have become increasingly important. These are frequently put forward as a means of promoting 'industrial democracy'. In election periods leading personalities in radio or

---

1. 'Employee participation and company structure in the European Community', *Bulletin of the European Communities* (Luxembourg, Office for Official Publications of the European Communities), Supplement 8/75, p. 9.

television broadcasts emphasise the importance of every citizen's vote for the conduct of public affairs and it is often argued that, since workers have the same rights as any other citizen, at the political level in democratic system it is paradoxical that they have no say in the making of decisions directly affecting them at enterprise level. In 1978, the Economic and Social Committee of the EC unanimously agreed that employee participation in the broadest sense of the term 'is a desirable development in a democratic society'. It is even not uncommon that the issue of employee participation is stated in terms of distribution or redistribution of power in the enterprise as between the employees and the employer (in any case the power of decision of the 'employer' may be exercised to a large extent, not by the owners or shareholders but by professional managers who are themselves salaried employees)[2] or in the wider sense of 'economic democracy'.

9. It may also be observed that in countries which have a relatively complete socialised economy, collective ownership of the means of production is one of the foundations of the workers' right to participate in decisions. The centrally planned economies have often resorted to increased worker participation at the enterprise level to raise productivity, output and delivery, and consequently the standard of living.

10. There is, in addition, a general drive, noticeable in many developing countries, towards a closer association of workers and their trade unions with national economic development at various levels. Southern Asian governments, for instance, which are trying to develop employee participation often do so with the declared objective of enlisting workers' support for national development through improved labour–management relations. Governments expect that through such an involvement, it will be possible to reduce conflicts, to enhance co-operation between employers and employees, to increase productivity and, most important of all, to make labour disputes and work stoppages unnecessary. The increasing interest in employee participation as a means of improving the functioning of public enterprises will be examined in more detail in another part of the present chapter.

11. Generally, economic objectives relate directly or indirectly to increasing the efficiency of the enterprise. By associating the workforce with the decisions taken, it is hoped to improve the quantity and quality of output and the utilisation of labour, raw materials (less waste and rejects) and equipment (less idle time and better maintenance, especially useful when replacement or spare parts are difficult to import), as well as facilitate the introduction of new technologies. There is growing awareness of the fact

2. See, for instance, 'Worker participation in the European Community', in *European Documentation* (Luxembourg), No. 1977/3, p. 4.

that the knowledge, experience and intelligence of those who actually do the work is insufficiently utilised for improving industrial organisation and methods.

12. Inflation in itself seems to have contributed directly or indirectly to the spread of participation: directly by increasing the demand for information and negotiation at the level of the enterprise in order to restore the purchasing power of wages as soon and as much as the enterprise capacity to pay permits; indirectly, because greater participation in decisions is sometimes regarded, according to some observers, as partial compensation for the restricted ability of unions to obtain wage increases. Similarly, concession bargaining to restore competitivity and save employment has often implied more participation in decisions for employees and their representatives and/or financial participation.

13. Apart from ideological considerations, certain modern management methods have contributed in their way to the growth of employee participation. Based on criteria of efficiency and influenced by industrial experience, social psychology (particularly in-depth motivation studies by well-known authors such as Maslow, Herzberg and McGregor)[3] and industrial sociology (e.g. the socio-technical approach pioneered by Norway and Sweden and the UK), such methods have promoted the decentralisation of authority and of responsibility, more comprehensive consultation and what is generally referred to as shopfloor participation. At the same time, as it has been pointed out, the alternatives to employee participation in the shape of misunderstanding, resistance, low morale and suspicion are all too prevalent.

14. While a majority of employers continue to oppose board representation of employees and other forms of institutionalised participation in management, involving joint decision-making, employers generally now tend to take a more positive attitude to employee participation in the organisation of their work and the determination of their conditions of employment. In line with an increasing individualisation of labour relations, they often introduce participative personnel policies or so called 'human resources management'.

15. In any case, there is no doubt that there is a common need in every society to cope with new problems caused by drastic changes in technology and economic structures, which are difficult to deal with by means of

3. Cf. A.H. Maslow, *Motivation and Personality* (New York, Harper and Row, 2nd Edition 1970); F. Herzberg, B. Mausner and B.B. Snyderman, *Motivation to Work* (New York, Wiley, 1959) and F. Herzberg, *Work and the Nature of Man*, (Cleveland and New York, the World Publishing Company, 1966), D. McGregor, *The Human Side of Enterprise* (New York, McGraw-Hill, 1960), and *Leadership and Motivation* (Cambridge, Mass., M.I.T., 1966).

established industrial relations systems. Employee participation should therefore be examined as a process for coping with contemporary problems rather than a mere institution or system. On the one hand it is possible to recognise the extension and development of industrial relations issues, and in particular, the large number which are not easily settled through an absolute approach.

In fact, the role of the trade unions on the industrial relations scene has been reinforced by worker directors, works councils and other bodies, while at the same time collective bargaining issues have been extended and supplemented by other forms of participation such as consultation or co-decision. On the other hand, the growing importance of participation reflects the efforts by both sides of industry to cope with economic difficulties experienced by individual enterprises and national economies.

16. Initially, in most industrialised countries, collective bargaining has been regarded as the orthodox and almost exclusive way of expressing the employees' voice. In contrast, employee participation was based on the assumption that there exist certain common interests between labour and management. Thus, various institutions of the works council type were established in some European countries around the end of the First World War and lost impetus after prospering for some years. During the Second World War joint production committees were set up in several English-speaking countries. After the war, works councils were established or re-established in many European countries either by law or by agreement (in Scandinavia). In the FR Germany, employee representation on supervisory boards introduced on a minority basis at the beginning of the 1920s became parity representation in the coal and steel industries, according to an Act of 1951, although limited to one-third in other industries by further legislation in 1952. After the mid-60s and especially after 1970, renewed interest in employee participation[4] (apart from collective bargaining) has emerged in almost every European country and various developing countries.

17. While, to some extent, employee participation is still viewed in certain quarters as the opposite of confrontation and conflict, significant conceptual changes have recently taken place. The original emphasis on the existence of a community of interests and on the setting up of machinery for associating employees and management in joint efforts to solve industrial problems has given way to a broader view of participation. This view includes collective bargaining and other forms of negotiations as participatory processes and thus embraces both collaborative and the conflictual types of interaction as participation. The accent is, moreover, placed on participatory means aimed at ensuring that labour's views will be taken into account in all centres of

4. See for instance, J. Monat and H. Sarfati (ed.): *Workers' Participation: A voice in decisions,* *1981–85* (Geneva, International Labour Office, 1986).

decision, rather than merely in the identification of suitable areas of co-operation or in the collaborative implications of certain systems. Stress is laid nevertheless on the fact that, irrespective of the approach followed, there is an element of rational understanding and an accommodation of interests that will eventually diminish open and systematic conflict. Even collective bargaining itself, which was originally conceived and is still considered as an adversary process, nowadays shows some clear integrative elements.

18. Because of differences in the historical context of the industrial relations system in different countries, the role of trade unions and especially the function of collective bargaining has varied. In other words, in certain countries at a given historical juncture, unions and collective bargaining play a greater role at certain levels and in certain areas (issues or subjects of collective bargaining). In some countries bargaining is mainly or exclusively carried out at the industrial level. The trade union role at enterprise level is very limited. In such cases, works councils or shop stewards have to make up the gap at enterprise level. In other countries collective bargaining takes place at enterprise level but only handles matters of conflicting interest between labour and management and is mainly an *ex post facto* phenomenon being to a large extent limited to social consequences of key management decisions already taken or intervenes just in a periodic or sporadic fashion and is generally a time-consuming exercise. Other forms of employee participation may occur almost continuously and at each stage and level of decision making, and there is an increasing tendency to consider this type of participation complementary to collective bargaining. However, one of the main problems raised by employee participation remains its relationship with trade unions in the context of the power relationship with the employer.

Trade unions may remain suspicious of the idea of employee participation where they see it as a device to promote the integration of employees into the enterprise; they may be reluctant to share responsibility and afraid of losing their independence. As for employers, the attitude towards participation depends to a considerable extent on the levels, subject areas and the type or machinery of participation.

II. The Levels of Operation

19. Even if there is often some relationship or interaction between decisions taken at various levels any in-depth study of employee participation may benefit from a clear distinction between its levels of operation. Only practical analysis of centres of decision can show where responsibilities lie and suggest how to introduce greater industrial and economic democracy. An enterprise which seems to outsiders to have only one centre of decisions may in fact comprise a whole web of centres of responsibility.

20. As will be seen throughout the present chapter the concept of employee participation in decisions within enterprises may cover one, several or all of four main levels: (1) shop floor; (2) department, plant or establishment; (3) company or corporate level; (4) group of companies or multinational companies.

21. It has to be recalled that even if such levels are beyond the subject of the present chapter, there is often a relationship with other levels – industry, regional, national – where there may also be participation (as provided for in the ILO Consultation (industrial and national levels) Recommendation, 1960 (No. 113)).

III. AREAS OF EMPLOYEE PARTICIPATION

22. As regards the areas of decision-making in which employee participation may operate, there are four major categories to be considered:
– technical questions relating to production, organisation, equipment, work methods and performance;
– personnel questions concerning the individual at work and in some cases outside work: selection, recruitment, allocation and distribution of work, job classification and evaluation, remuneration, fringe benefits, promotion and career policy, working conditions, hours of work and holidays, safety and health, welfare (sometimes a very large area including works medical services or dispensaries, canteens, reduced-price stores, housing, day nurseries, rest homes, children's holiday camps, sports facilities and clubs and other kinds of social and cultural activities), training at various levels, further training and retraining, discipline, individual and collective lay-offs and dismissals, relations with personnel representatives and settlement of grievances;
– economic and financial policy of the enterprise (forecasts, programmes, investments, sales, pricing and distribution of profits);
– questions of general policy relating to the very existence of the enterprise and to its structure: appointment of managers, partial or total shutdowns, mergers, transfers of plant and other reorganisation measures or structural changes.

23. It appears to be in the last two categories that the pressure to maintain decisions within the scope of so-called 'management prerogatives' is the strongest in employers' and shareholders' circles.

24. Nevertheless, in practice the different categories of decisions are not fully separable since one type of decision may greatly influence others, e.g. a change of production programme may have considerable repercussions on personnel matters such as job security and hours of work.

25. Some decisions are taken at the highest echelons – by the general manager, the board of directors, the supervisory board, or even the general meeting of shareholders – whereas others are taken at various lower echelons. The degree of participation may vary with the particular class of decisions, i.e. in one and the same enterprise there may be co-decision by collective bargaining as regards terms and conditions of employment, consultation on organisation of work, information on business policy and administration of welfare schemes directly by the employees.

IV. Various Types of Employee Participation

26. In addition to various possible stages of operation – basically preparation of decisions, decision-taking and follow-up of decisions – a distinction will have to be made here between the main types of employee participation in decisions: information, consultation, co-decision in works councils or similar bodies which may imply actual (even if informal) negotiation and other forms of trade union action, board representation, self-management and related systems such as co-operatives, workers' buy outs and enterprises owned and managed by trade unions, shopfloor participation not speaking of financial participation (profit sharing, workers share ownership) which in spite of its expansion in recent years, has seldom a direct relationship with participation in decision-making as such.

A. Information

27. The meaning of the word 'information' seems rather simple: it is 'the communication of . . . knowledge'.[5] Disclosure of information to employees means that the employer provides information about which explanation may be sought and questions can be raised; information which will eventually be discussed. It may be noted from the outset that consultation, and even more so co-decision and collective bargaining, can only be reasonably performed if the right kind of information is provided.

28. The obligation of employers to provide information finds its origin in sometimes overlapping, even opposed values and aims, as diversified as the promotion of collective bargaining, the promotion of collaboration between employers and employees (integrative) or workers' control (polarising). It is self-evident that these different aims, as well as ensuing strategies, have their bearing on the type and level of information, the recipients of information, secrecy and the like. Various factors may have an influence such as the timing of information delivery, its clarity, the opportunity to

---

5. *Webster's Dictionary*, 1965, p. 433.

examine books, accounts and other documents and possible recourse to inside and/or outside experts.

29. In addition to collective bargaining procedures, information is given to employee representatives – mostly to works councils, specialised committees such as safety and health committees, sometimes union delegates – in order to allow these representatives to fulfil their role, and to keep employees informed about the enterprise, its prospects and the situation of the work-force.

30. Contrary to certain cases of information disclosure for collective bargaining purposes where trade unions have to request the information (as in the USA and the UK),[6] the systems in which documentation must be given to works councils is entirely automatic: the employer has the (legal) obligation to provide information. Works councils have, as a general rule, been set up with the idea of promoting collaboration between employees and employers. This is explicitly stressed in the Works Constitution Act of January 1972 in the FR Germany which emphasises 'that employer and works council have to work together in a spirit of mutual trust'. The basic idea is that the employees, as members of the enterprise, have a self-evident right to know and to be informed. This is also clearly expressed in Article 3 of the 1973 Belgian decree on economic and financial information to be given to the works council: 'the purpose of this information is to give the employees a clear and correct view of the situation, its evolution and the projects of the unit or group to which it belongs'. The same is the case for employees and/or trade unionists who are members of supervisory boards or boards of directors of private companies, in the FR Germany, Austria, Denmark, Norway, Sweden and Luxemburg. These members are entitled to the same information as the shareholders' representatives.

31. In Italy, important national agreements have introduced clauses making it compulsory for employers or employers' associations to inform local unions or 'delegates' about investment programmes and long term business policies influencing employment and working conditions and to examine these matters in conjunction with the unions.[7] The scope of discussion and consultation – on the basis of that information – has been expanding; so that, whereas in other countries this kind of development has been introduced by law, in Italy it has come about through collective bargaining, particularly in larger firms.

32. In order to evaluate the kind of information which is given to employees, a number of questions must be asked; the most important concern: (1) the subject matter; (2) the entity about which information has to be

6. *IELL*, USA, paragraph 496; Great Britain, paragraphs 451–453.
7. *IELL*, Italy, 1981, paragraph 440.

given; (3) when information has to be given; (4) to whom information has to be given; (5) the obligation of headquarters to help subsidiaries; and (6) the problems concerning confidentiality.

1. Subject Matter

33. Examining the range of topics on which information is required to be given, it is easy to be baffled by the wide diversity and differences between the different (national) systems and provisions. There is, however, a clear trend for information to cover economic and financial decisions. The Draft Statute on European Companies by the EC indicates that 'the Board of Management shall provide written information on any matter, which, in the opinion of the European Works Council, affects the fundamental interests of the S.E. (Societas Europea) or its employees . . .' (Article 113).[8]

34. The ILO Communication Within the Undertaking Recommendation, 1967 (No. 129) contains a non-exhaustive list of information items of particular importance. The trend towards the provision of greater information is also clearly confirmed in the social EC directives on collective dismissals[9] and acquired rights as well as the ILO's Termination of Employment Convention and Recommendation adopted in 1982;[10] the proposed EC directive on procedures for informing and consulting employees foresees that at least once a year, at a fixed date, the management of a parent undertaking shall forward general but explicit information giving a clear picture of the activities of the parent undertaking and its subsidiaries as a whole to the management of each of its subsidiaries in the Community, with a view to the communication of this information to the employees' representatives. For the same purpose, the management of the parent undertaking shall forward to the management of each subsidiary concerned specific information on a particular sector of production or geographical area in which the subsidiary is active.

35. Where the management of a parent undertaking proposes to take a decision concerning the whole or a major part of the parent undertaking or of a subsidiary in the Community which is liable to have serious consequ-

----

8. See 'Worker's Participation in the European Company', *Bulletin of Comparative Labour Relations*, No. 8, 1979, Deventer, p. 254.
9. Article 2, 3 provides that the employer will supply the workers' representatives with all relevant information, and in any event in writing the reasons for the redundancies, the number of workers to be made redundant, the number of workers normally employed and the period over which redundancies are to be effected.
10. Article 6, 1 indicates that the employer is required to inform of the following:
    – the reasons for the transfer;
    – the legal, economic and social implications of the transfer for employees;
    – measures envisaged in relation to employees.

ences for the interests of the employees of its subsidiaries in the Community, it shall be required to forward precise information to the management of each subsidiary concerned in good time before the final decision is taken with a view to the communication of this information to the employees' representatives.

36. The ILO tripartite Declaration of principles concerning multinational Enterprises and Social Policy adopted in 1977 contains similar language. As regards information on changes of operations, paragraph 26 of the Declaration reads: 'In considering changes in operations (including those resulting from mergers, take-overs or transfers of production) which would have major employment effects, multinational enterprises should provide reasonable notice of such changes to the appropriate government authorities and representatives of the workers in their employment and their organisations so that the implications may be examined jointly in order to mitigate adverse effects to the greatest possible extent. This is particularly important in the case of the closure of an entity involving collective lay-offs or dismissals'. The OECD Guidelines contain a similar principle, namely in the Employment and Industrial Relations chapter (Guideline No. 6).

37. However, in general the employer's duty to inform can be waived if other values come into play, such as the prejudicial effect on the enterprise, national interest[11] and privacy. The question then remains: who in cases of conflict decides whether information is of a prejudicial nature, of national interest, of a private nature, etc.? This may be a court or, as in Belgium, a government official.

2. The Involved Entity

38. Although in most cases information will be limited to the local entity or to the national group of enterprises (e.g. in the FR Germany), there is a discernible trend to give information on the (international) group as a whole. This is not only the case in Belgium, but also true for international instruments. The OECD Guidelines in the Annex to the Declaration of 21 June 1976 by Governments of OECD Member Countries on International Investment and Multinational Enterprises espouse the idea that '. . . the complexity of these multinational enterprises and the difficulty of clearly perceiving their diverse structures, operations and policies sometimes give rise to concern.' The chapter on 'Disclosure of Information' recommends that companies provide information – to the public at large – on the enterprise as a whole, while the Employment and Industrial Relations Chapter, indicates that they should provide representatives of employees with 'information which enables them to obtain a true and fair view of the entity or,

---

11. See also the ILO Collective Bargaining Recommendation, 1981 (No. 163).

where appropriate, the enterprise as a whole...' (Guideline No. 3). As indicated, a similar principle can be found in the ILO declaration on multinationals. As already noted earlier, the proposed EC directive on information calls most clearly on enterprises to give information on the enterprise as a whole.

3. When?

39. A most crucial question is, of course, when information should be given. Usually, employers try to ensure that the actual decision to invest in new equipment or processes remains the exclusive prerogative of the management. However, bringing in new equipment without first informing employees and their representatives, if only to prepare them psychologically for the changes involved and for any necessary training or retraining, is always something of a risk. Obviously, if employees are to have an opportunity to influence certain management decisions which will affect them or to prepare for their social implications, the giving of information only makes sense if it is done in advance. This certainly is the case with collective dismissals, substantive modifications of activity and the like. Different expressions are used to convey this idea.

40. In Belgium if an employer has to resort to collective dismissals, the works council must be informed immediately and in any event before the actual decision has been taken.

The EC directive on acquired rights (1977) provides that information must be given '...in good time, before the transfer is carried out,...in any event before his employees are directly affected by the transfer as regards their conditions of work and employment (Article 6, 1)'. The proposed EC directive on information and consultation also requires information on major decisions 'in good time' (Article 4, 1) or 'without delay' (Article 4, 3).

41. The OECD Guidelines for multinationals provide that advance information should be given. 'Management', states the OECD's IME Committee, 'is encouraged... to adopt an open and co-operative attitude to the provision of information to employees relevant to the objective of this paragraph, which could include information on future plans'.[12] Obviously, the specific circumstances of each case have to be taken into account; especially compelling reasons of confidentially may prevent early information.

12. *Review of the 1976 Declaration and Decisions on International Investment and Multinational Enterprises (Report by the Committee on International Investment and Multinational Enterprises to the Council)*, Paris, 1979, paragraph 64.

4. Information to Whom

42. Here again there are different possibilities, which are covered by the term 'employee representatives'. These can be the trade unions (especially in cases of collective bargaining), or employees of the firm through their representatives – a union delegation (shop stewards), a works council, a safety and health committee, or economic committee (FR Germany and France), or representatives on the supervisory board (or board of directors) of enterprises. In certain cases, (e.g. in the FR Germany), specific information has to be given to individual employees or general information has to be periodically provided to the whole workforce of the enterprise at a general meeting. It is obviously important to whom information is given as the impact and outcome will be affected by the attitudes of the recipients involved.

5. The Obligation of Headquarters to Help its Subsidiaries

43. The employer, responsible for the entity involved, has the duty to provide the required information. This will generally be, depending on national law and/or practice, the local manager. The IME Committee of the OECD addressed itself to this problem: '. . . if an entity in a given country is not able to provide information to the employees in accordance with paragraphs 2(b) and 3, the other entities of the enterprise are expected to co-operate and assist one another as necessary to facilitate observance of the Guidelines. Since representatives of employees may experience difficulties in obtaining such information at the national level, this provision of the Guidelines introduces a useful supplementary standard in this respect'.[13] Headquarters must therefore ensure that the subsidiaries get sufficient information in due time in order to be able to fulfil their obligations under national law and practice and the Guidelines.

6. Problems of Confidentiality

44. In all systems, employee representatives are in one way or another bound to observe discretion or secrecy with respect to certain types of information provided by the employer. In Sweden 'in respect of information which the enterprise wishes to keep secret, . . . under the Act on Board Representation, . . . the worker representative acquires information in his capacity as a member of the board and is placed under the same duty of confidentiality as the rest of the directors'.[14] In Belgium. when communicating information to the works council, the employer should mention – when

13. *Ibid.*, paragraph 65.
14. F. Schmidt, *Law and Industrial Relations in Sweden*, Stockholm, Almquist & Wiksell, 1977, p. 118.

necessary – any confidential aspect of that information, the diffusion of which would create problems for the company. If there is a disagreement in the works council concerning this matter, the confidential nature of the information should be submitted to an official of the Department of Commerce for a decision. In Luxemburg, the director of the Labour Inspection Service will, in cases of conflict over confidentiality, make a binding decision.[15]

45. The proposed EC directive on information and consultation provides similar obligations. Confidentiality entails a great dilemma: how can the rank and file participate in a meaningful way if the information given to a minority of them must be kept secret? Is there (real) participation if, for instance, only 30 employees – members of a council – out of 9,000 employees are informed? Personnel meetings, in which the works council meets in the presence of the employer (every three months in the FR Germany), have an important function in overcoming some of these difficulties. Regarding the question of confidentiality, it has sometimes been stressed that, in the case of minority representation at board level, it would be appropriate for employee representatives in reporting on decisions with which they were in disagreement, to give both the background to the decisions and the stand which they themselves took up.

46. The present chapter cannot pretend to be either complete or exhaustive. Therefore, it will not attempt to deal with certain other important aspects such as informal ways of providing information, training for the handling of information, (evoked in paragraph 6 of ILO Recommendation No. 129), the increasing resort to outside experts, e.g. for new technologies, the special costs involved and the like.

B. Consultation

47. Consultation takes place mostly, but not exclusively, in the framework of works councils and other comparable committees. It is obvious that trade unions can also have 'consultative' status. However, consultation is not competitive but integrative in nature. Consultation means that advice is given to the employer, alternative courses of action may be proposed but that the decision-making power is left intact after having listened to the views of the employee representatives.

1. Subject Matter

48. The subject matter of consultation is usually not so wide as the subject matter of information.[16] The same is true for the consultation provided for

15. See *Workers' Participation in Decisions within Undertakings*, Geneva: ILO, 1981, p. 215.
16. One exception in the European Works council which can give its opinion on any matter, which effects the fundamental interests of the SE or of the employees (Article 123).

in the social EC directives, and the other international instruments already cited (ILO Declaration paragraph No. 26; OECD Guideline 6 Employment and Industrial Relations Chapter). The requirement or practice of consultation refer in general to subjects such as closures, collective dismissals, structural changes, mergers and the like. The consultation will usually be limited to the mitigation of the adverse effects of managerial decision-making. For example, the EC directive on collective dismissals states: 'the consultation shall, at least, cover ways and means of avoiding collective redundancies or reducing the number of workers affected, and mitigating the consequences' (Article 2,2).[17] Similarly, the ILO's Termination of Employment Convention (No. 158) of 1982 stipulates inter alia that employers contemplating terminations 'for reasons of an economic, technological, structural or similar nature shall provide the workers' representatives concerned in good time with relevant information' and give them 'an opportunity for consultation on measures to be taken to avert or to minimise the terminations' or 'to mitigate their adverse effects'. More generally, the Recommendation (No. 166) adopted the same year states that, when an employer contemplates the introduction of 'major changes' in an enterprise that are likely to entail terminations, he should 'consult the workers' representatives concerned as early as possible on, inter alia, the introduction of such changes, the effects they are likely to have and the measures for averting or mitigating the adverse effects of such changes'. Even if new technologies do not lead in all cases to workforce reduction when introducing them, the kind of issues that need tackling are usually redeployment, how to keep retrenchment to a minimum when it cannot be avoided altogether (e.g. by adopting a 'social plan' in several stages or at least by introducing the technology progressively, so as to take advantage of attrition, organised transfers, early retirement, retraining for alternative employment, etc), the problems raised by deskilling and the need for training and retraining facilities to adapt the workers to the new processes and equipment. They may also cover new job classifications and career prospects, job satisfaction, the impact of new technology on working conditions including safety and health, the monitoring of staff made possible by sophisticated equipment, the privacy of personal data and the use of subcontracting arrangements. Vocational training and retraining, as well as job evaluation, are areas in which workers' participation, whether institutionalised or not, has been steadily growing.

2. The Involved Entity. Access to Decision Makers

49. The employer, obliged to consult, will be mostly the local employer, but could also be someone else, when the local manager is not the real decision

---

17. See also OECD Guideline 6 of the Employment and Industrial Relations Chapter and principle No. 56 of the ILO declaration, and paragraph 3 of ILO Recommendation No. 129.

maker. According to the OECD Guideline 9, Employment and Industrial Relations Chapter and the ILO Declaration, employees should have access to decision makers, i.e. representatives of management who are authorised to take decisions on the matters under negotiation.[18]

3. When? To Whom? Confidentiality

50. Here there is really no fundamental difference with what has been said in relation to information and we refer to that part in this chapter.

C. Co-decision and Other Types of Participation

51. Co-decision – including that resulting from a veto power – has been, as will be seen below, expanding in the context of works councils of some countries where it is provided for, mostly for various personnel policy matters, either by legislation or by agreement.

52. It must be noted that co-decision amounts, in practice, to some kind of informal negotiation in a number of cases, since it can imply a give and take phenomenon. Moreover, formal consultation has often become very close to co-decision and informal negotiation (some observers such as Gerard Adam have spoken of an intermediate procedure where more than mere consultation occurs and less than bargaining in its traditional meaning[19] and in his country – France – lawyers tend to admit nowadays a new category of 'quasi-agreements').

53. Other observers, in particular in the FR Germany which has the longest experience of co-decision within works councils, have stressed the importance of the statutory conciliation procedure or recourse to a court decision if not formal arbitration in case of lack of agreement on a matter which has to be co-decided. Although seldom used in practice partly because lengthy and expensive, such a possibility may promote consensus. An appeal to the tripartite national Social and Economic Council in case of veto by the shareholders' general meeting or the works council of the appointment of a supervisory board member in the Netherlands is resorted to very seldom.

54. Similarly, while board representation on a minority basis might be assimilated to high level consultation and on a parity basis to co-decision, the experience of the FR Germany shows a predominance of decisions by

---

18. On the 'when', for the Netherlands see H. Bakels; *op. cit.*, p. 201; for France, N. Catala, *L'entreprise*, Paris, 1980, p. 799: 'Ces avis doivent être préalable à la décision envisagée et résulter d'un libre débat.'
19. Gérard Adam: 'La négociation collective en France: Eléments de diagnostic', in *Droit social* (Paris), Dec. 1978, p. 443; see also *ibid.*, p. 448.

agreement within supervisory boards. In any case, in the opinion of some observers, discussions between representatives of the employees and of shareholders within a board of directors or supervisory board often constitute a kind of bargaining.[20]

55. In addition to formal collective bargaining, there are also various forms of trade union action within undertakings, in particular by shop stewards in the framework of grievance procedures, in their relationship with management in Eastern Europe (notably through the plant trade union committee and its specialised sub-committees but other forms are developing, e.g. joint management councils in most medium-sized or large enterprises in Hungary) or as described later in the present chapter in a country such as Japan where labour relations are largely based on an enterprise unionism structure.

56. As will be seen below, one of the main problems of works councils, in particular their consultation and, possibly, co-decision powers, has been the relationship with collective bargaining. In fact, this is mostly a problem of the relationship between such bodies and trade unions both as far as membership and forms of action are concerned.

57. As a concept, 'self-management' or 'workers' management' of enterprises, certainly represents the most far-reaching attempt to involve the workers in decision-making and managerial responsibilities, by having the workers designate the members of the managerial body and by deciding how the income from their work is to be shared out (the entrepreneurial motivation of workers' management is linked with the right to allocate the profits or the net income of the enterprise, or a part thereof – for reinvestment, social and cultural activities or for direct distribution in the form of extra remuneration). Normally, these systems are based on a general law applying to public-sector enterprises, under which managerial rights but not ownership rights are transferred to those working in them. The rights are given to the workers (manual, office or staff) collectively, and the 'collective' exercises them through a body elected by the entire workforce (e.g. in Yugoslavia which has the longest experience and is the most well-known example, the 'workers' council' periodically elects the managers) – though a recent tendency has been noted in some self-management systems for greater weight to be given to the general meeting of workers (or of workers' representatives in large enterprises) assisted by specialised committees.

58. In addition to Yugoslavia, self-management has been, to varying degrees, experienced in Israeli kibbutzim, in Algeria (at the time of independence and then limited to the large estates of the modern agricultural sector), in Poland, mostly between 1956 and 1958, in Portugal in various small and

20. See, for instance, Johannes Schregle: 'Co-determination in the Federal Republic of Germany: A comparative view', in *International Labour Review*, Geneva: ILO, Jan.-Feb. 1978, pp. 90–92.

medium-sized undertakings, at the time of the 1974 Revolution, in the biggest enterprise of Malta (the Drydocks Corporation) from 1975 onwards, in the Libyan Arab Jamahiriya after the publication by the Head of State of his 'Green Book,[21] and in Romania. The concept is spreading in a few other Eastern European countries, e.g. Bulgaria. In Peru the 'social ownership sector' experiment with self-management remained rather limited. In the People's Republic of China, too, the management of industrial enterprises reflects the political development of the country in that, since the cultural revolution, it has been moving towards a far-reaching system of self-management, interrupted when Mao Zedong died by a definite strengthening of the power of managers, followed by a significant return to workers' participation with, in particular, workers' assemblies in enterprises but more recently in putting managers under the general so-called 'responsibility system'.

59. In the recent past, there have been a few cases in certain industrialised countries with a market economy, such as Belgium, France, Italy, Japan and the UK, of employees undertaking a form of self-management when an enterprise has been about to close down on account of serious economic difficulties. In circumstances of this kind, some enterprises have been transformed into producers' co-operatives, sometimes with State help, or all shares sold at exceptionally low prices to the workforce or at least the managerial staff, e.g. in the USA.

60. A form of self-management that is rarely classified as such but where the workers can directly control the running of the enterprises is the producers' co-operative. These are to be found in a number of industrialised countries and in various developing countries, both in agriculture and in manufacturing and services. The members of a genuine producers' co-operative are simultaneously workers, owners and directors of an enterprise managed by a committee and staff elected or appointed by them.

61. The enterprises owned and managed by trade unions are another related system of workers' management of enterprises by their very nature. Those of the central trade union organisation (Histadrut) in Israel have, since the adoption of a participation charter in 1968, gone further by progressively introduced parity representation for manual and office workers on the boards. There has been some development of union-owned and managed enterprises in Australia, Austria, the FR Germany, Japan and Sweden, but also in varying degrees (in addition to workers' education, training and credit institutions and even home construction and other welfare facilities) in various developing countries, e.g. Argentina, Ghana, India, Malaysia, Malta, Panama, Singapore and Tunisia. There have also

---

21. Muammar Al Qadhafi: *The Green Book* (Tripoli, Public Establishment for Publishing, Advertising and Distribution, no date, 3 vols).

been cases of trade unions buying out enterprises or investing in them (a growing practice in Mexico and Venezuela, for instance).

62. In addition to workers' management of enterprises' welfare activities a few observers tend to consider that in a number of experiments of shopfloor participation dealt with below there is an element of self-management by individual employees or small groups of them as concerns the organisation of their work within certain limits such as fixed output targets (which themselves may have been discussed and mutually agreed) and dates of delivery.

V. THE MACHINERY OF PARTICIPATION

A. Employee Representation in Managerial Bodies

63. Nowadays, a number of countries have employee representatives who are recognised as full members on the supervisory board or board of directors administering the company, undertaking or establishment in which they are employed. This arrangement is often called a 'management participation system', 'co-determination', 'co-supervision', or 'co-management'. A distinction should, however, be made between representation on a supervisory board (two-tier system), a board of directors (one-tier system) and a management board where such representation is much less common than in the other two types of body. A supervisory board usually appoints and can dismiss the management board or management team responsible for day-to-day running of the enterprise and lays down the general policies of the company. It may disapprove certain proposals or have the final decision on matters of major importance for the company.

64. A distinction can also be drawn between systems under which managers are not allowed to be members of the board of directors (or at least for the managing director to chair it) or of the supervisory board (the commonest situation) and those systems in which such membership is allowed. On the other hand, it must be borne in mind that in practice, in a given country, some boards of directors are functioning more in the way of a supervisory board or *vice versa*. Another distinction is made between cases in which employee representatives on these bodies are equal in number to those of shareholders (the parity model) and cases in which they are a minority (the minority model) but we will see that in a few cases, in particular, since an Act of 1976 in the FR Germany, a type of quasi-parity has been introduced. In most countries, only company employees are entitled to employee representation on the board while in others, in particular the FR Germany, seats may be attributed to trade union representatives from outside. There are also cases where State representatives sit on the board (e.g. in the banking and insurance sectors of some Scandinavian countries) or of 'gener-

267

al interest' (e.g. consumers' representatives) as proposed, *inter alia*, in the Draft Statute for a European company or applied in the public sector of various countries.

65. It seems that in the industrialised countries more attention has generally been paid to employee representation on boards of directors or supervisory boards in the private sector (where it has raised various objections in employers' circles – especially when shareholders' representatives would not be in the majority – such as infringement of private ownership, jeopardizing of market economy, excessive power given to trade unions, or interference with collective bargaining)[22] than in the public sector, where there is most often greater employment security and easier access by employee representatives to information. In the developing countries, on the other hand, interest in this form of participation is greater in government or nationalised enterprises.

66. Employee representatives on managerial bodies are so far mainly a Western European phenomenon in the private sector. In other areas, they are either in the experimental stage, as in Japan, or appear only as isolated cases, as in the USA. In developing countries, several reasons are noted for such rarity in private enterprises.[23] Some of these include: fears of putting off foreign investors, trade union preference for collective bargaining, the weakness of trade unions reluctant to be 'captives of management', the multiplicity of trade unions which may cause difficulty in designating their representatives.

67. In addition to the FR Germany, whose system will be described later, Austria is one of the rare countries with a two-tier system having introduced employee representation in supervisory boards for a number of years (this representation remained limited to a minority but was extended to one-third by an Act of 1973). In France where either a two-tier or one-tier system (by far the most common) may be chosen, with the exception of a few voluntary experiments, board representation in private companies was since the second world war, limited to delegates of the works council in an advisory capacity. A minority board representation with voting rights is provided for such companies but not imposed by an enabling legislation of 1986.

68. Over the first half of the past decade, four West European countries have passed laws providing for employee minority representation on the boards of directors of private companies exceeding a certain size: Denmark, under two Acts in 1973 amended by a 1980 Act increased the proportion to one-third; Norway, under a 1972 Act for certain industries, and through agreements and orders-in-council for other industries, and lastly by an Act

---

22. See *op. cit.* ILO, pp. 29–36.
23. *Ibid.*, pp. 111 ff.

of 1976; Sweden also, under an Act of 1972 for a three-year experimental period later confirmed by a 1976 Act which extended the scope to companies with 25 employees or more; and Luxemburg, under a 1974 Act applying to companies with over 1,000 employees and companies holding a concession from or partly financed by the State. In Norway, the legislation also provides for a 'corporate assembly', one-third of which consists of employee representatives and which appoints the board of directors and must take major decisions on investment, rationalisation or reorganisation. In Sweden, there is a provision (often disregarded in practice) according to which worker directors may not take part in board discussions concerning a labour dispute or negotiations which may result in a collective agreement.

69. This minority representation in the private companies of these three Scandinavian countries is not automatic. In Norway, it must be requested by one-third of the 'corporate assembly' and exceptions are provided for. In Denmark, it must be requested by a majority of the works council (the so-called 'co-operation committee') or by one or more unions representing one-tenth or more of the employees or else by one-tenth of the enterprise workforce. In Sweden, it depends on a request being made by the union representatives in the enterprise. In practice, such requests have been made in most cases and this minority representation – with the exception of the 'corporate assembly' (a national Committee report suggested making it optional but proposed to extend board representation to smaller companies) – seems well accepted in the three countries both by shareholders and trade unions which do not seem to have lost their bargaining power while employee representatives have gained some influence on boards which according to various surveys have often become more active. It must be emphasised that this introduction of employee representation on the board of directors of private companies in Scandinavia was accompanied by a comprehensive and intensive programme of appropriate training for such representatives, as well as information and training programmes for managers and shareholder representatives, in order to prepare them for the implementation of such a new scheme. In several instances, joint sessions for employee, managerial and shareholder representatives have been and are being organised.

70. Lastly, a system for co-opting members of the supervisory board was introduced in the Netherlands by a 1971 Act that came into force in 1973. Under this Act, the works council can – like the management and the general meeting of shareholders – propose candidates who are not employees or members of the union with which collective bargaining takes place, and has also (like the general meeting of shareholders) a right to veto nominations (in which case there is a possibility of appeal to the tripartite Social-Economic Council of the Netherlands as indicated above). The aim is to ensure that those appointed to the supervisory board enjoy the confidence both of the shareholders and of the personnel.

269

71. Introduction of employee representatives on boards of private companies was the subject of public debate during the seventies in various countries in Western Europe, including Finland, France and Switzerland and in the UK following a 1973 trade union report as well as the controversial 'Bullock Report' published in January 1977. The Commission of the EC has prepared a draft statute for a European Company, already referred to above, and a proposal for a Vth directive with a view to harmonising the laws governing joint stock companies in member states. These texts, initially inspired by the West German system of minority employee representation and the Dutch system described above, have been revised and made more flexible, especially the Vth directive proposal providing for at least information and joint consultation in the enterprise, but their adoption by the Council of Ministers is not likely in the near future.

72. As mentioned above, employee representation at board level is much less common in the private sector of developing countries. It is provided for in the legislation of Benin, Egypt and Pakistan but in practice is limited to Algeria, Iraq and the Syrian Arab Republic and some experiments e.g. in Malta and Senegal. The system of 'industrial communities' linking a profit sharing scheme with a progressive number of seats for worker directors up to a limit of 50 per cent of the board, introduced in Peru in private companies in 1970, has gradually lost its importance and concentrated on the profit sharing aspect. Employee representation on boards of directors of some or all public enterprises is widespread in developing countries (about a dozen in Africa and several in Asia, Near and Middle East and Latin America). But there is presently a trend towards privatisation of at least part of the public sector, in particular in Africa.

B. Works Councils and Similar Bodies

73. Works councils, works committees, joint consultation committees or similar bodies remain by far the commonest form of employee participation. In many countries, these bodies are set up by legislation. The most representative cases are those of Austria, Belgium, France, the FR Germany, Luxemburg, the Netherlands and Spain in Western Europe; Burundi, Gabon, Mauritania, Somalia, the Sudan, Swaziland, Tanzania, Tunisia, Zaire, Zambia and Zimbabwe in Africa; Bangladesh, Burma, the Republic of Korea and Pakistan in Asia; and Iraq in the Near and Middle East or Panama in Latin America (mainly for dealing with grievances). In other countries such as Denmark and Norway, they have been established by agreement between the national workers' and employers' organisations. In many other countries, they have been set up not by national agreements but by agreements at industry or enterprise level, or even at the employer's own initiative. Such is the case in Australia and New Zealand, Canada, Ireland, Japan, Switzerland, the UK and the USA; and in some developing countries

such as Brazil, Cyprus, India, Jordan, Malaysia, the Philippines, Singapore, Venezuela and various English-speaking countries in Africa such as Ghana, Kenya, Nigeria and Sierra Leone. In Bahrein, Mauritius, Nepal, Portugal, the Sultanate of Oman, Thailand, Uruguay and the USA, there exists legislation which provides for the setting up of works councils but does not make them compulsory or encourages the creation of such bodies. In some countries, works councils exist in a certain limited area of the economy, for instance, in a given industry or in the public sector, e.g. in Morocco and Sri Lanka.

1. The Level of Operation

74. As for employee participation in general, several levels are possible: the production unit, establishment or department; the enterprise; the group of enterprises or the multinational level.[24] The level at which works councils are set up is generally the level of the enterprise or more often the level of the establishment of an enterprise such as the factory or branch when these are independently operating organisational units and have more than a certain number of employees. For instance, in the FR Germany, a central works council is set up in enterprises with more than one works council, i.e. in all enterprises with more than one factory. The members of this central council comprise two representatives from each plant-level works council. A group works council is set up if endorsed by a majority of the central works councils in the group. Each central works council delegates two of its members to the group council. Similarly, for several years now, a central works council has had to be established in France if establishment committees existed due to the size of their respective workforce and recently so-called group committees have been introduced by legislation in groups of enterprises. In a case in which works councils are set up by national agreement, such as Norway, departmental committees are established within enterprises for departments employing over a certain number of persons and having their own management.

2. Composition, Election

75. The composition of works councils is divided into two main types. One represents the workers collectively and on its own initiative, deals with all the tasks within their competence, communicates with the management, or meets the employer or manager as in Austria or the FR Germany. Such a formula of works councils composed exclusively of employee representatives has been introduced in recent years by Dutch and Spanish legislation. The

24. See Roger Blanpain, 'The influence of Labour on Management Decision-Making: a General Introduction', *Bulletin* 8, 1977, Institute for Labour Relations–Catholic University of Leuven, p. 19.

other type provides for direct co-operation with the employer, who is present at all meetings of the council; sometimes the employer normally chairs meetings, as in Belgium, France, Tunisia or Zaire, for instance. However, in the second type, there is usually no question of equality of numbers – the employer-chairman being often the only representative of management in cases of councils established by law, except in some countries, such as Belgium, where several representatives of management may belong to the works council. In contrast, in works councils set up by agreements the principle of parity is more prevalent and the chairman is chosen from among management members and the vice-chairman from among employee members. In Norway, unless otherwise agreed, the chairman is designated by the representatives of the management and of the employees alternatively.

76. As regards employee members, a certain number of seats are reserved for certain categories of employees, for example salaried, young, supervisory, or technical employees. It may happen that separate councils exist for different categories of employees as, for instance, in Austria, where above a certain number, wage earners and salaried employees have separate councils. The employee members are in most cases elected by secret ballot from among the workforce in general or from several electoral colleges if they have separate representatives. In some countries, trade unions have an exclusive right to put forward candidates, as in Belgium, or priority in this respect, as in France, Tunisia and Zaire. In other countries where law does not give such privileges to trade unions, they exercise substantial influence on the election of employee members. In fact, a large majority of members in such countries as Austria and the FR Germany, for instance, are elected from persons proposed by trade unions or are themselves active trade union members. In Denmark and Norway, the trade union representatives of the enterprise or chief shop stewards are *ex officio* members of the works council. In Japan·the trade union when it exists in the enterprise has a monopoly of the appointment of employee representatives on the joint consultation committee. These examples show that different formulae have managed to reduce or overcome the reluctance of trade union in certain countries, as indicated above, to bodies of the works council type. Similar reluctance has, however, been experienced as far as their functions are concerned *vis-à-vis* trade union action including collective bargaining.

3. Power and Functions

77. The competence of works councils used to cover mainly social matters. In recent years, however, there has been a trend in industrialised countries towards including, at least in so far as information disclosure is concerned, such fundamental management matters as the general, economic and financial outlook of the enterprise, including employment prospects; investment forecasts; rationalisation through the introduction of new methods or processes; production changes (including closing down or transfer of activities), as well as company structure and so on. Such information disclosure is sometimes the subject of precise regulation, e.g. in Belgium, as are the standards governing the confidentiality of certain information in countries where the establishment of works councils is required by law.

78. The right to information is now often accompanied by a right to consultation. The employer has to indicate the measures to be taken to avoid or to soften the impact of especially unfavourable consequences for the personnel, and the works council is entitled to discuss these forecasts and proposals and to suggest alternative solutions. This is especially the case concerning workforce reductions and collective dismissals following an EC directive and new ILO standards on termination of employment adopted in 1982. In countries where works councils have no legislative base and are set up by agreement or on a voluntary basis, works councils and similar bodies mainly play a consultative role as in the case of the UK. In Denmark an agreement on works councils lists among their duties that of participating only in decisions of principle, but not the actual decisions on the organisation of local conditions of work, safety and welfare, and on the enterprise's personnel policy.

79. In the recent past there has been a strong tendency in some West European countries such as Austria, Belgium, the FR Germany and the Netherlands to extend the co-decision powers of the works councils, especially with regard to welfare and personnel matters. The brief description which is given below of the West German system of workers' participation offers concrete examples of such co-decision powers. The legislation of a few developing countries, in particular Tanzania and Zambia, has given some consultation and even co-decision powers, in the case of the latter country, to the works councils.

80. These three functions of the works council, namely information, consultation and co-decision, each involve a different degree of participation, information being the weakest and co-decision being the strongest. The recent trend is that the areas of coverage are becoming broader while at the same time the degree has been increased. In addition, in some countries, works councils may sign works agreements with management as a result of either co-decision or even of consultation. In practice the borderline between co-decision and traditional collective bargaining is now blurred and may cause conflict between the works councils and trade unions in spite of the fact that legislation has often tried to distinguish their respective fields of competence. But on the whole, the trend is towards an enlargement of the scope of negotiation and an extension of the degree of employee participation regardless of which institution plays a greater role. The bulk of the functions of works councils would be shifted either to consultation or co-decision depending on the given conditions and industrial relations needs in a particular country at a given time. In the case of the FR Germany, where as a rule there is no trade union structure formally recognised at the enterprise level, and where collective bargaining takes place normally at

273

industry, regional or national levels, works' agreements are signed by works councils which have no right to resort to strike pressure. Various rules are applicable in order to avoid actual conflict between such works' agreements and collective agreements which may even provide for supplementary company agreements (e.g. in a recent past concerning hours of work). In the Netherlands when certain questions, subject to co-decision have already been settled in a collective agreement, there is no need to request the consent of the works council. In Spain, while the recent legislation only gave a priority to the works councils in the negotiation of collective agreements at enterprise level, in fact they became generally the bargaining body. In Japanese enterprises, surveys show that there is, in fact, no clear distinction between consultation, co-decision and collective bargaining, the kind of participation depending on the subject dealt with and consultation being often a preliminary to bargaining in the absence of quick agreement. Here again, the experience of various countries seems to show that there are various possibilities in order to avoid difficulties between works councils and trade union action.

81. Obviously when trade unions are not supposed to be directly represented in works councils, they have, in many cases, been reluctant to give them full support out of fear of being by-passed by such bodies which might appear as a substitute to collective bargaining and other forms of trade union action. In some countries, workers have also shown little interest in bodies which dealt mostly with trivial matters. Lastly, employers were often reluctant to envisage any infringement on management prerogatives and to give detailed financial and commercial information for fear that such bodies may, at a later stage, press for collective bargaining benefits if not becoming a new bargaining body. This occurred, for instance, on many occasions in India as well as in a number of other developing countries where only a few works councils have been created or have seldom functioned efficiently. Nevertheless, for some employers' and government circles, works councils or similar joint consultation bodies are considered to represent a step towards participation, especially where collective bargaining is not sufficiently developed. Furthermore, employee participation, through joint machinery notably in the management of welfare services, in addition to its intrinsic value, provides a good opportunity for the training of employee representatives in participation.

82. In any case, it was clear from the ILO worldwide Symposium on Workers' Participation held in the Hague in 1981 that during recent years works councils have staged an impressive comeback.[25]

C. Specialised Bodies

83. The same ILO worldwide Symposium also noticed a marked trend

25. See E. Córdova: 'Workers' participation in decisions within enterprises: recent trends and problems', in *International Labour Review*, March–April 1982, pp. 125–140.

towards an expansion of specialised participatory bodies which in some countries of Latin America – a region where introducing joint bodies of the works council type often encountered difficulties – constitute the main institutional arrangements of employee participation at enterprise level in addition to collective bargaining. A well-known form of specialised body is the Safety and Health Committee, some of which have undergone an enlargement of their scope to cover the working environment in general (in France bodies dealing with working conditions have been merged by law with safety and health committees, while in Norway in practice and by agreement a number of work environment committees merged with works councils). Other specialised bodies are dealing with productivity, promotion or job classification, grievance settlement, etc. There are a few countries (Austria, Belgium, the FR Germany, Luxemburg and the Netherlands) which have either special bodies or delegates within the enterprise to represent young workers *vis-à-vis* the works council.

84. Increasingly, technology committees appear with the introduction of new technology. Similarly to safety delegates (which in Eastern Europe and Scandinavia are allowed to stop work in case of serious danger to the life or health of the workers), there are also 'technology delegates' in some countries. Due very often to the high level of training required – a problem which may be reduced in countries where engineers, technicians and other supervisory personnel are largely unionised – they have not always been as successful as initially expected. Here again recourse to outside experts and/or well equipped trade unions appears to be of particular importance.

D. Shop Stewards and other Employee Representatives

85. Shop stewards and other union representatives who perform some of the functions of a works council could be regarded as an extension of the union's function in the form of collective bargaining. However, if we understand the function of collective bargaining fundamentally as the determination of terms of employment and standards of working conditions, the role of shop stewards and other employee representatives is broader than that of collective bargaining. Especially when there are no works councils, works committees or similar bodies in a country or, at any rate none in small enterprises, the varied activities of such representatives are quite similar to those of works councils and other bodies already described in the previous section. Traditionally shop stewards play an important role concerning grievances within enterprises, and as with works councils in most countries one of their major functions is to keep an eye on the application of legislation and collective agreements.

86. In most French-speaking African countries 'employee representatives', who are generally elected by the workers of the enterprise from among candidates proposed by the trade union, are also active in grievance procedures. They inform the labour inspectorate of infringements to legislation or collective agreements and transmit their own suggestions and those of workers to the management.

87. In countries or small enterprises where works councils do not exist, such representatives carry on some of their functions, in particular with respect to welfare activities.

88. In some European and developing countries, the role of shop stewards or other trade union representatives and bodies within enterprises has increased at the expense of the works councils or joint consultation committees. For example, in Finland, the works councils set up under the name of production committees by an Act of 1949 are due to go out of existence as a result of the 1978 Act which has increased consultation and bargaining opportunities for trade union representatives in the enterprise. The employer is obliged to supply them with information on certain matters and to consult with them before taking decisions on important changes in the activities of the company. They must also receive at specific intervals information on the economic situation of the enterprise, its programmes and future plans, as well as an annual plan relating to personnel. The employer must consult the personnel or their representatives before taking any decisions which are likely to have repercussions on the employees such as substantial changes in the organisation of work or production, closure or relocation of the enterprise or of a department, rationalisation, lay-offs, etc. In Sweden the agreement on works councils was terminated by the unions pending a review of their functions in the light of the 1976 Act extending information and bargaining rights within enterprises. In Italy the 'factory councils' that developed spontaneously at the end of the sixties became the union's basic organisational unit in the enterprise, usually replacing the 'internal committees' set up earlier under a national agreement even if they seem less active in various cases than during the 1970s. Delegates who are members of such councils are elected in each small shop (one per 40–50 employees) by all workers but are considered as union representatives to all intents and purposes. They handle bargaining at the shop and enterprise levels and also handle information and consultation procedures, information and consultation rights being provided for in most national collective agreements. In public enterprises of the IRI group an agreement tried on two occasions to expand the role of joint committees. In Algeria, the trade union branch of an enterprise in the private sector plays, according to the legislation, a role similar to that of the works council in other countries. Such a trend has also been observed in the People's Republic of Congo. In Tanzania, the works' councils continued to function in parastatals and large enterprises after the establishment of the trade union branches which replaced the former system of workers' committees at the level of the enterprise.

89. As far as international labour standards are concerned, protection against acts prejudicial to them, including dismissal, based on their status or activities as employee representatives and facilities (such as time off etc.) to be afforded in order to enable them to carry out their functions efficiently, are dealt with in ILO Workers' Representatives Convention (No. 135) and Recommendation (No. 143) adopted in 1971.

E. Shopfloor Participation

90. In the recent past and in particular during the 1970s, there have been a number of experiments on shopfloor level participation for involving employees directly in the determination of work organisation (including pace of work and layout of premises) in most Western European countries as well as in Australia, Canada, Japan, New Zealand and the USA.[26] Within the framework of an industrial democracy programme, Norway has done much of the pioneering work in this field[27] after important research and experiments corresponding to a 'socio-technical' approach have been carried out in the UK.[28] Some of the Swedish experiments[29] such as those in the Volvo company are internationally well-known. These experiments are generally based on the concept of group production methods, where small teams of employees, often called semi-autonomous groups, have a wide margin of autonomy and freedom of planning, scheduling and organising their work, to the extent of introducing job rotation among themselves. They also took care of ensuring a certain degree of quality control and simple maintenance of plant equipment. In several experiments, workers carried on their activities without first-line supervisors or the latter became mostly advisers and trouble-shooters.

91. This new form of shopfloor participation departed fundamentally from the Tayloristic system of work organisation which often produces stress and monotony (and possibly absenteeism or turnover) and does not take into account individual capacities of speed at work, creating bottlenecks, etc. It provided more autonomy and responsibility to individual employees as members of small groups and therefore more chances for job satisfaction, job enrichment, self-development, initiative and creativity, as well as versatility. It has expanded also in the service sector, especially in banks, insurance companies and postal services. In various industrialised countries, the new generation of blue-collar workers in particular stood to benefit from these schemes for satisfying its rising expectations for a better working life

26. Cf. *inter alia*, ILO International Centre for Advanced Technical and Vocational Training: Seminar on the Effects of Group Production Methods on the Humanisation of Work – *Proceedings*. J.L. Burbidge, Ed. (Turin, June 1976); *New forms of work organisation* (Geneva, ILO, 1979), 2 vols. and *Industrial Democracy in Europe, a Business International Report* (Geneva, Business International, 1974).
27. The first phase of this programme was described by F.E. Emery, Einar Thorsrud and Eric Trist in *Form and Content in Industrial Democracy* (London, Tavistock, 1969).
28. See Tavistock Institute, *Characteristics of Socio-Technical Systems*, Document 527, 1959; E. Thorsrud, *Socio-Technical Approach to Job Design and Organizational Development*, Oslo, Work Research Institutes, 1967 and F.E. Emery, *Systems Thinking*, Penguin Modern Management Readings, 1969.
29. See *inter alia*, SAF – Swedish Employers' Confederation, *Job Reform in Sweden* (Stockholm, SAF, 1975).

(a number of experiments were launched in the framework of quality of working life – QWL-programmes – as indicated below and employees were unwilling to revert to traditional forms of work organisation, while on the other hand, marked productivity increases were often observed). Up to the beginning of the seventies, manpower shortages contributed to such experiments while nowadays new technologies are often conducive to participative forms of work organisation.

92. However, up to now, only very few such experiments have been undertaken in developing countries in spite of their possibilities.[30] In India, a wide-scale experiment was introduced in the Calico Mills Company, a textile firm, as early as the 1960s and in 1977, some 16 action-oriented studies on participative redesign of work systems were carried out in the heavy electrical engineering industry and in the service sector. In recent years, increased responsibility in work organisation, output and delivery within small teams of workers (brigades) has been expanding in the USSR and to varying degrees in other countries of Eastern Europe including Poland. In most industralised countries and new industrialising countries there is now a mushrooming of 'quality circles' or similar formulas which to a large extent correspond to a modernised form of suggestion schemes, based on small groups of volunteers, and considered as an important factor of the economic success of Japan where they are very widespread. In France, the 1982 Act which introduced an individual and collective 'right of expression' of employees on their working conditions on an experimental basis, was definitely confirmed by an Act of 1986 which enlarged the mandate of 'expression groups' to quality problems.[31]

F. The Case of Japan and the FR Germany

93. Enterprise unionism, which is a basic feature of the trade union movement in Japan, is a participatory type of unionism in a category by itself. Members of an enterprise union are recruited only from employees of that particular enterprise. Furthermore, in most cases they are regular employees who are expected to remain in that enterprise until retirement age after having been employed straight from school. Thus, all members are ready and often willing to participate in decisions of management, since the fate of their entire lives depends very much on the fate of the company. Collective bargaining is carried out almost exclusively at enterprise level. Enterprise unions are very conscious of the economic condition of the enterprise when they establish working conditions. Collective bargaining to establish standards of working conditions for a particular craft or industry is unknown in Japan except in a very few cases. Not only collective bargaining but also almost all of the functions of enterprise unions are participatory in nature.

30. Cf. G. Kanawaty, E. Thorsrud et al.: 'Field experience with new forms of work organisation' in International Labour Review, May–June 1981, pp. 263–277 and G. Kanawaty (Ed.) Managing and developing new forms of work organisation (Geneva, ILO, Management Development Series, No. 16, 1980).
31. For model regulations of such brigades, see ILO Legislative Series 1984 – USSR.

1. Collective Bargaining and Works Councils etc.

94. Works councils are established by agreements between enterprise unions and management. Members of the workers' side are appointed by the union and some of them are the same union officers who represent the union in collective bargaining sessions. The relationship between collective bargaining and works councils is rather obscure. In nearly half of the cases the subjects of both bargaining and works councils overlap with one another and in more than half of the cases the issues are submitted to bargaining if settlement has not been reached at the works council. Grievance procedures are also introduced in some 40 per cent of enterprises, while works councils are set up in over 50 per cent of the enterprises surveyed by the Labour Ministry in 1977. Grievance procedures mainly handle grievances regarding wages, working hours, working environment, dismissal, discipline, transfer and the like. Here again when the matter is not settled by these procedures it may be handled by collective bargaining in nearly 70 per cent of the surveyed relevant enterprises. This rather obscure but perhaps flexible interrelationship between collective bargaining and other forms of participation is quite unique to enterprise unionism. One reason for this flexibility is the fact that the labour side of all these institutions is the same union organised in the undertaking.[32] Another is the functional diffuseness of all modern Japanese institutions.[33]

2. The Level of Operation

95. Enterprise unions are mainly organised at enterprise level, but in the case of larger enterprises with several plants or offices of a significant size, they are organised in each such establishment. Those organisations of independent production sections or facilities may be either a branch of an enterprise union or independent unions by themselves. Collective bargaining is carried out by an enterprise union and the management of the enterprise in regard to the matters which affect the entire enterprise. Plant unions or branch organisations also bargain with plant management. Works councils and grievance procedures may also be set up at either the enterprise or plant level by agreements between either of these parties.

3. Composition, Election

96. Bargaining is done by union officers elected by members of the union or by their delegates in case of larger enterprises. Members of works councils are mostly appointed by the executives of the unions. In most cases they consist of an equal number of members of both workers and management.

32. However, this might not be so unique to Japan since British shop stewards, American union agents and Italian shopfloor delegates are virtually, though not formally, union representatives.
33. See T. Hanami, Labor Relations in Japan Today, Tokyo: Kōdanska International, 1979, pp. 45 ff.

Grievance procedures are also conducted by members of both labour and management. Labour members are appointed by union executives.

4. Power and Functions

97. Theoretically collective bargaining is understood to cover all matters concerning undertakings in so far as they affect the working conditions of workers. In fact, not only working conditions but also issues of managerial decision such as changes in the activities of the undertakings, could be handled by collective bargaining. As mentioned above, grievances often become the subject of collective bargaining, especially when they are not settled by grievance procedures. However, employers have been reluctant to discuss important management decisions in the forum of collective bargaining. In fact this is one reason why works councils were set up, although the parties in these two institutions are exactly the same in most cases. Thus, the main function of works council is not co-decision but information and consultation. The jurisdiction of works councils is divided into
(1) matters affecting management and production;
(2) personnel affairs;
(3) matters of welfare;
(4) working conditions; and
(5) others.
The functions of works councils are often different depending on the different categories of their subject matter. Functions are divided into
(1) information;
(2) seeking opinions;
(3) consultation; and
(4) co-decision.
Very few agreements require co-decision in matters of management and production.

In Japan some big firms have recently introduced workers' representatives on certain management bodies, including the introduction of special bodies such as 'production committees' for that purpose. However, in spite of some positive opinions among unions and management, these are seen as rather negative trends by trade unions, perhaps because supervisory board's function is rather limited within the supervision of accounting of the company only and even boards of directors also have no real power, which is normally in the hand of a small number of full-time directors.[34] In addition, without the introduction of former system of this effect it is reported that already in 1978 in a survey by the Federation of Japanese Employers' Association two-thirds of the 352 large firms surveyed had ex-members of the trade union committee on their management board, in an average proportion of about 16 per cent.

98. A far-reaching system of employee participation in decisions is also that applied in both private and public enterprises of the FR Germany since the

---

34. See the series of articles by Tadashi Hanami and others on participation in Japan in *Japan Labor Bulletin*, 1 January, 1 August and 1 September, 1977.

beginning of the fifties. It was already discussed to some extent more than a century ago and introduced on a minority basis at board level in the years which immediately followed the First World War. This system has been the object of numerous studies and has attracted special attention in many countries.

99. By an Act of 1951, equal representation of employees was established on the supervisory boards of large iron and steel and coal and iron-ore mining enterprises. These boards generally include five employee representatives (one worker and one salaried employee nominated by the works council from among members of the personnel of the enterprise, and three representatives nominated by the trade union organisations, one of whom must come from outside the enterprise and the unions concerned), five representatives of the shareholders, and an eleventh member nominated by mutual agreement (or, in the absence of such an agreement, by the relevant court) who plays in practice the role of a mediator. In addition, one of the members of the management board, namely the 'labour director', who is responsible for personnel questions and social affairs, may only be nominated or dismissed in agreement with the majority of the workers' members of the supervisory board. He also participates on an equal footing in all general decisions within the competence of the management board as a whole[35].

100. An Act of 1952 introduced workers' representation equal to one-third of the total membership on the supervisory boards of companies not belonging to the above industries (with the exception of companies owned by only one person or family-owned companies with less than 500 employees). Employee representatives on the supervisory board are elected directly by and from the workforce from employee and works council nominations. Such representation is still applicable in companies with less than 2,000 employees.

101. For some time, and with increasing insistence in the 1970s, the German Confederation of Trade Unions has been demanding equal representation of employees on the supervisory boards of companies in sectors other than iron and steel and mining industries, at least for enterprises of a certain size or with a certain financial turnover. This demand met with strong opposition on the part of the German Employers' Confederation, which saw in it, among other things, an attack on property rights as well as a threat to the market economy and to the autonomy of the parties in collective bargaining. Finally, a compromise was reached within the then coalition government of social democrats and liberals and an Act was adopted by a large majority in the Federal Parliament, which came into force on 1 July 1976. It was

35. The number of employees in the industries covered by this legislation is declining. Moreover due to cases of diversification of activities, an Act was passed in 1981 requiring enterprises ceasing to meet one of the criteria under this legislation to continue applying the parity board system for another six years (for more details on the origins of this 1981 Act, see J. Monat and H. Sarfati, ed., *op. cit.*, pp. 11, 183–184).

submitted in 1977 by some employers' organisations and companies to the constitutional court. This Act, applicable to joint-stock and limited companies which have more than 2,000 employees, provides that shareholders and employees are to be represented in equal number of the supervisory board, having a total of 12, 16 or 20 members according to the size of the enterprise. Among the employee members of the board, trade unions are represented by two persons (out of six or eight) in companies with up to 20,000 employees, and by three persons (out of ten) in large companies, the other employee representatives being employees of the company. The supervisory board elects a chairman and a vice-chairman from among its own members by a majority of two-thirds of the total number of members of which it is required to be composed. Where this majority is not attained, a second vote is taken. In this vote, the shareholders' members of the supervisory board elect the chairman and the workers' members elect the vice-chairman in each case by the majority of the votes cast. The members of the management board are elected by the supervisory board with a two-thirds majority. If that is not possible, a mediation committee of the board will try to reach a compromise. If necessary, the chairman has the deciding vote. This is not regarded by the unions as genuine parity since, among other things, the chairman with a casting vote is virtually always a shareholders' representative under the rules, and the employee representatives on the supervisory board are now required to include at least one representative of managerial personnel.

102. The employer and the works council, which is elected by the whole personnel and compulsory under West German legislation in each enterprise employing five persons or more, meet at least once a month for an exchange of views and to settle any disputes; they may conclude company agreements, except on wages and other conditions of employment determined, or normally determined by collective agreement (unless the latter expressly provides for supplementary company agreements).

103. The works council receives prior information and is consulted, in particular, on recruitment, promotions, transfers, individual and collective dismissals (in specified cases it is entitled to object to them on certain grounds, and in the event of a dispute its opinion is communicated to the tribunal or other authority); it receives prior information and is consulted on the construction and transformation of premises, installations, processes and workplaces. The council has a right of co-decision, in particular in regard to directives concerning selection of personnel for recruitment, transfers and dismissals, and on hours of work and rest and holiday periods, disciplinary matters, determination of the principles to govern remuneration, the adoption of new remuneration methods, vocational training, and the organisation and management of welfare services. When major changes are contemplated which would lead to unfavourable repercussions for the personnel, such changes must be the subject of a compromise and a 'social plan'.

104. In principle, the council reports on its activities every quarter to a general meeting of the personnel to which the employer is invited; representatives of the trade unions may attend this meeting in an advisory capacity and the employer may be accompanied by a representative from his employers' association. Separate meetings by sectors may be organised, if necessary. Each year, the employer or his representative must report to a general meeting of the personnel on the situation of the enterprise and on personnel matters.

105. An economic committee appointed by the works council must receive information from the employer each month on production methods and plans, the financial situation of the enterprise, production and sales. It must be informed of investment plans, structural changes and any project appreciably affecting the interests of the personnel. It reports to the works council and, with the latter, is consulted by the employer regarding the information on the situation and prospects of the enterprise which must be supplied every quarter to all members of the personnel.

106. On the whole, it appears that participation at company board level coupled with the works council at plant level constitutes an important element in the smooth operation of the West German system according to legal provisions in force (filled in and interpreted by a host of court decisions), in practically all the companies concerned. Although the appeal and arbitration procedures have been made use of in a limited number of cases, no major breakdown in the management structure has been reported. Indeed, it is a common finding that the employee representatives in most companies have found it possible to collaborate quite closely with other board members in drawing-up policies and in the decision-making process. It may also be noted that employee representatives on supervisory boards have the same rights and duties as shareholders' representatives, receiving the same emoluments but they refund a certain percentage (fixed by the trade unions) into the assets of a special foundation financing research and training in the field of participation. On the supervisory boards of iron and steel or mining enterprises, decisions have generally been taken unanimously. In fact, one of the criticisms that has sometimes been made is of over frequent resort to compromise and give and take. The importance of the informal decision-making process in various instances, i.e. informal contacts or preliminary meetings of bargaining groups, has also been pointed out. On the other hand, the labour directors on management boards have been, in most cases, able to develop a working arrangement with the two other members and to cope with the management functions within their own sphere of competence. According to various surveys, a considerable proportion of the chairmen of works councils who are, in general, members of supervisory boards, have held those posts for more than ten years which leads to a risk of their becoming professional 'representers' and losing contact with the rank and file. On the other hand, several observers have stressed that, in general, rank and file workers seem more aware of and interested in works councils' activities which are closer to them than those of the supervisory board which are more long-term and remote. However, such problems exist in any participation system.

283

Conversely, it has been emphasised that being a member both of the works council and of the supervisory board gives one a very thorough understanding of the daily realities of the enterprise, which the shareholders' representatives seldom have and this leads to a better discussion on the supervisory board. Possible delays in the decision-making process, an often repeated criticism, do not seem to have resulted in serious and frequent difficulties in the day-to-day running of enterprises if one considers the impressive economic record of the country. It should also be recalled that the supervisory board which elects the management board and may dismiss or not re-elect its members intervenes only in connection with the major decisions depending on the by-laws of each individual company (e.g. it has to approve decisions on plant closures, major product changes, large invest-ments, etc.). Its terms of reference include general policy guidance and supervision of the activities of the company concerned. It does not meet more than four or five times a year. In addition, there is an industry-based structure of trade unions without trade union rivalry and there is a broad consensus of opinion in favour of the existing economic and social structure. It has been underlined that 'accommodation and integration, as well as order and authority occupy an important place in the national system of values'.[36] Furthermore, as a rule, collective bargaining takes place at industry instead of enterprise level.

VI. Some Prominent Contemporary Issues

107. It may appear from this overview of developments in 'employee participation' that, with the exception of the public sector of both industrial-ised and developing countries, employee representation at board level in general has not been expanding since the second half of the previous decade. Several factors have probably played a role in this regard such as a shift in the balance of power in a situation of severe unemployment and economic crisis as well as a reluctance of certain trade unions to be involved in some sort of co-responsibility especially *vis-à-vis* decisions which in difficult economic periods may have negative social consequences. Con-versely, works councils and specialised bodies have assumed a wider role, with reinforced rights of advance information and far-reaching consultation, (e.g. in the case of introduction of new technology and/or workforce reductions,) which correspond to recent EC and ILO standards on dismis-sals. Joint consultation bodies set up on a voluntary basis have made a comeback in countries and industries facing a severe crisis such as iron and steel and automobiles e.g. in the USA (often under the label of 'employee involvement') and in a number of industries in the United Kingdom.

108. In various countries in Western Europe, participation formulae or bodies specifically set up for middle management have been experimented, at a time when the unionisation of this category of employees is increasing.

---

36. Johannes Schregle, *op. cit.*, p. 88.

109. Formulae aimed at introducing participation arrangements in small and medium sized enterprises have been tried recently, e.g. in France and the Netherlands, but the limited results seem to show how difficult it is to extend institutionalised participation to this type of enterprise, in spite of the fact that the number of small plants is increasing with new technologies, outsourcing and subcontracting as well as of small establishments in the service sector.

110. Shopfloor participation experiments, which were expanding at the end of the 1960s and at the beginning of the 1970s, have not been used so much in recent years. In spite of a marked and sustained movement in favour of the quality of working life (QWL) there have been failures and disappointment in various cases. Nevertheless, with an improvement of the economic situation, it might well be that shopfloor participation in one way or another and new forms of work organisation will again take place among priorities for new generations of workers and managers. Even now the mushrooming of 'quality circles' shows how much 'participative management' and various features of Japanese participation retain attention.

111. The controversies around the EC Fifth Directive and Vredeling proposals show how harmonisation on such sensitive subjects is difficult. On the other hand, ILO and OECD principles and guidelines highlight of the importance nowadays of multinational companies.

112. Collective bargaining has proved its adaptability to difficult times and new issues. However, due, *inter alia*, to its periodic nature and to its usual level in the decision-making process, it might well be that after some time of economic recovery the debate on employee participation at board level will resume and as Efren Córdova wrote following the ILO Symposium in the Hague, in a long-term perspective 'one nevertheless has the impression that the whole movement is approaching a crucial stage in which the various forms of workers' participation will come to complement each other and a more coherent and articulate system will appear'.[37] The active search for flexibility within enterprises in recent years (e.g. size of workforce, type of employment contracts, working time arrangements) to adapt more quickly and efficiently to changing and highly competitive markets, at a time when the balance of power is shifting in their favour and trade unions in many countries are seeing a decrease in traditional membership, may also offer new opportunities for introducing different forms of participation. The latter might facilitate a less unilateral implementation of 'human resource management policies' in many enterprises and a more cooperative problem-solving approach.

37. E. Córdova, *op. cit.*, p. 139.

Chapter 14. The Attitudes of Employers and Trade Unions Towards the Quality of Working Life Movement*

J. Rojot

I. THE CONCEPT OF QUALITY OF WORKING LIFE IN PRACTICE

1. Firstly, it should be pointed out that the quality of working life is not a clearly defined concept. It is interpreted as having different meanings in different contexts. Different individuals or organisations use the same term at different opportunities, with different contents and while referring to different themes.

This fuzzy character is evidenced by the fact that many of the themes encompassed by the generic term of quality of working life often used by the academic community are referred to under different headings, commonly used by governments, unions and employers' associations, in different countries.[1] If the accepted term in the USA is most often the 'quality of life at work', or 'quality of working life', it becomes 'improvement of conditions of work' in France, 'humanisation of work' in FR Germany, 'work restructuring' in the Netherlands, 'improvement of the working milieu' in Scandinavian countries, 'task restructuring or task enrichment' in the United Kingdom, 'ambiance and organisation of work' in Italy, etc. . . . This variety of terms used to label concepts gathered around a common concern, illustrates 2 points: on the one hand, whatever the differences due to the intrinsic nature of the language used and the vagaries of translation, the concepts in each country are far from identical. On the other hand, the issues covered in each country under the national heading are distributed with more or less variance around a central concern: work, life at work and efforts to improve it.

2. Secondly, the area covered by QWL, as time passed, has seemed to grow and encompass more and more issues which were earlier considered as

---

* This paper is based primarily on a survey of the literature published by labour organisations and employers' associations, as well as on interviews carried out by the author. Secondary sources from academic publications have also been used and are listed in an annex.
1. This was first pointed out by J.D. Reynaud, *Problèmes et perspectives de la négociation dans les pays membres de la Communauté*, Série Politiques Sociales No. 40, Commission des Communautés Européennes, Bruxelles, 1979.

separate. For instance, at the conference on 'Quality of Working Life and the 80's' held in Toronto in August 1981, some of the papers presented dealt with topics which alternatively could have been described as belonging to the area of participation in decision-making, participative management or even industrial democracy.

Different groups of researchers and academics draw fine distinctions between various schools, such as job enrichment, job design, socio-technical systems, etc. However, to most practitioners, whether from the management or labour side, those divisions are irrelevant and the interest centres around the broadest possible definition focused on the results of QWL. In the terms of a study commissioned by the New Stock Exchange,[2] 'QWL covers not only participation in decision-making but more general efforts . . . by making (workers') jobs interesting, giving them more control over their own activities, and providing them with a direct stake in their companies' futures'. Thus, in that definition, it is even broad enough to also include financial participation.

3. In this framework, a list can be drawn up of issues touched upon in the quality of working life movement by compiling the various issues which are discussed under that heading in the literature issuing from employees' and managerial associations and union organisations. The list is, of course, non-exhaustive and not all issues are covered within each country, but it may help focus on what can be meant by the quality of working life in practice. Most of the issues arising under this heading can be grouped under a certain number of main themes as follows. It should be pointed out that the list is presented without any specific order due to the importance or recurrence of given topics.

(1) *Wage, salary and type of wage*: For instance, change in the wage payment method, such as moving from piece work to hourly pay, or from an hourly to monthly wage. Such issues as guaranteed annual wage, participation of employees in profit and/or ownership of companies, etc. . . .

(2) *Hygiene and Safety*: At the most basic level, holding a job which is safe, protected from hazards, dangers and occupational disease is the basis of the quality of working life.

(3) *Physical conditions of the performance of work*: This applies in terms of period of work (shift work or night work) but also in terms of job content (effort, tiredness, ergonomics analysis of the job) or productivity (assembly line speed, measured time method, work pace) and workload (physical or mental).

(4) *Environment of the job site*: Apart from problems related purely to health and safety, this covers areas such as temperature, noise, aeration, dust, etc., as well as cleanliness and comfort of the job site.

(5) *Duration of work*: This concerns not only the sheer quantity, the hours

2. *People and Productivity, A Challenge to Corporate America*, NYSE, 1982.

per day or week of work, but part-time or flextime as well, and even the distribution of breaks over the working period.

(6) *Organisation of work* contains issues related to the content of tasks too repetitive or parcellised, but also the type of supervision over the work accomplished (narrow, tight, authoritarian, more or less arbitrary).

(7) *Interest in tasks accomplished*, which can be intrinsically varied, interesting or boring, demanding or not the use of general or specialised knowledge, challenging or not. Also the job held may or may not be on a career ladder, offer opportunities for promotion to better jobs, for further on-the-job training, etc.

(8) *Control over one's own work* in terms of work pace, selection of tasks, etc. . . .

(9) *The social environment of work* may or may not offer the opportunity of contacts with others, whether fellow workers, customers or the general public.

(10) *Participation in decision-making*, where the employee has a chance to express himself with more or less weight upon matters which affect his work place. He is given a chance to take part in the making of these decisions, either directly or indirectly.

(11) *Social oganisation of production*, when the traditional division between conception, management and execution can be altered, and when the hierarchical and managerial structure of the organisation can be modified.

(12) Finally, *the environment of life at work* is concerned. In other words, the life of the employee outside the place and hours of work. This may refer, in particular, to facilities for social activities, public transportation between home and place of work, facilities related to personal or family life such as day care centres, etc.

4. At first glance, an obvious comment can be drawn from this list: to a larger or lesser extent, some of the areas covered have long since been the focus of interest from the labour or management side. The themes related to the amount of wages and duration of hours have consistently been the subject matter of collective bargaining and/or statutory labour laws.

However, some areas are different and have come to the forefront of attention of labour relations more recently. The most obvious case here is the one concerning areas related to trying to improve jobs whose content consists of boring, parcellised tasks, where little meaning can be found in the job itself which offers no intrinsic interest or satisfaction. These types of jobs are often viewed as the consequence of and organisation geared to mass production and/or separating the task of conception and execution, whether in blue- or white-collar jobs, and their existence is often ascribed to methods of organisation originating with Taylorism.

5. Thus the quality of working life movement proposes to tackle these questions and to remedy this state of affairs by actions addressing all the areas of concern listed above. Whatever the scientific or academic school concerned, and without entering the debates surrounding the alleged or real benefits of various programmes or methods, actions towards the improvement of the quality of working life in its larger sense can be roughly grouped into four categories:

(1) Restructuring of tasks or work methods, which aims to change the content of work.
(2) Rearrangement of the technology which has produced the job, or a modification of the environment of the job site.
(3) Redesign of the organisational structure, including the hierarchical structure and the locus of decision-making.
(4) Financial participation.

Of course, specific quality of working life programmes can include any combination of methods pertaining to each of the four categories thereof, depending on the nature of the industry concerned, the constraints issuing from technology, market, etc. The individual solutions implemented in practice in enterprises range from simple improvement on the job itself, such as introducing buffer zones on an assembly line, to a complete overhaul of the social and technical organisation of new plant, combining autonomous groups of workers (without supervision) and the suppression and replacement of the assembly line by individual carriers moving at the worker's pace. The complete range of programmes is too large to be listed here, but it includes provisions so diverse and varied as job rotation, job enlargement, job enrichment, flextime, quality circles, ergonomically designed new machines, non-mandatory grievance procedures, shares distribution to employees, etc. . . .

II. Managerial and Employees' Attitudes towards Quality of Working Life

6. Management attitudes towards QWL, defined in the broadest terms outlined above, vary of course from case to case. Firstly, a list of outside factors affect their position. Different national environments foster different attitudes, in turn stressing different aspects of life at work. Besides, within each country, industries operate under very different conditions in terms of market demand, financial margins, value-added, labour costs, etc. From the point of view of QWL, in particular, it is clear that operating in a labour intensive or capital intensive industry makes a great difference. Very different attitudes on the part of management can be expected in cases where labour costs represent either 10 per cent or 60 per cent of total costs. The skill content of the jobs also has an important impact. Operating in a high technology industry where most of the employees are highly skilled, if not professionals, graduate engineers and technicians, certainly sets a particular framework of operation for management in terms of life at work. Within each industry, geographical regional differences can also be felt. Finally, some companies are profitable, some less so, some are losing money and some may be near bankruptcy. But it would be a mistake to believe that these differences in the position of a company directly dictate its attitude towards QWL. It has long been discovered that technological determinism is not enough, alone to explain corporate strategies.[3]

A. The Growth of Interest in QWL

7. Each corporate, and each plant, management holds its own value system where the place granted to QWL may vary enormously. It is clear that some managers care little about, or do not believe in the part QWL has to play. Just as Henry Ford I put Taylor's theories into their best-known illustration with the model T assembly line, he is credited with having said that 'all that people want is to be told what to do and be paid for it'. Assembly line and Taylorism are still very much with us. Indubitably, a very large part of the goods and machines manufactured in the present world are produced according to such methods. In the same way, the concommitant spirit which holds QWL as a useless loss of time and a flash in the pan is also very much present. QWL, even if its importance is growing and if it has grown over the experimental stage, represents only presently a relatively small part in the concerns surrounding the production and sales of goods and services.

However, the interest towards the quality of working life seems to be increasing fast in managerial and employers' circles. Several factors seem to bear witness to that.

For instance, out of the 1700 participants in the Toronto conference 'QWL and the 80's', 1000 were managers. Also, the study carried out by the New York Stock Exchange estimates that 14 per cent, or 7000 out of 49 000 corporations with 100 or more employees in the USA, had programmes relating to the broad concept of QWL defined above. It can also be noted that the French employers' federation, the CNPF, has included among the 8 targets of its action plan developed at its congress of Villepinte in December 1984 'to develop the participation of all within the undertaking'. Associations of employers for the development of various aspects of QWL have appeared, such as the AFCERQ in France or the Work in America Institute in the USA.

8. Also, several governments have established national agencies to help business establish and monitor quality of working life programmes,[4] probably answering an existing demand. Finally, and tellingly, the quality of working life has expanded beyond the restricted field of academic publications and has taken over, both in Europe and the USA, the field of

---

3. See, for instance, P.R. Lawrence and J.W. Lorsch, *Developing organisations, diagnostic and action*, Massachusetts, 1969.
4. Such as the Work Research Unit in the UK, the ANACT in France, or the Ontario Quality of Working Life Center in Canada, to list only a few.

managerial publications with a primarily managerial readership, where it has flourished.

B. *The Range of Employers' and Management Attitudes*

9. Therefore it is of primary importance to understand the attitudes towards QWL on the part of management and employers who demonstrated an interest in using programmes related to it.

It is clear that, as we pointed out above, any individual company's management will adopt a specific attitude based on features unique to that specific firm. Nevertheless, general categories of attitudes can be outlined. Very often, at plant-level, the initiative for operations to improve the quality of working life has been taken by management. In almost 100 per cent of cases in France, in a large number of cases in the USA, although this should be qualified in the Scandinavian countries and FR Germany where some specific goals expressly qualified as related to the quality of working life have been pursued by the labour movements.

There are several reasons put forward by employers and management to promote such activities. They range from tinted with ethical views to very pragmatic and practical. The ones most often advocated can be listed as follows:

10. The concern to 'make the company a better place to work in' occurs rather often.[5] Here the motivation on the part of the management is purely ethical and caused by a benevolent attitude towards the work force. The company has a duty towards its employees to provide them with the best possible working conditions, and while knowledge and research progresses and discovers new means of improving the quality of working life, the company should avail itself of them.

11. We also find social concerns related to the larger world causing a need felt to adapt the company to changes in the environment. It is, for instance, pointed out that a totalitarian disciplinary system within a production unit may have a hard time surviving in an increasingly democratic society,[6] which for some reason would see the rights and privileges of its members cease at the plant gates. We have also noted that Taylorian type methods of production are prevalent, and thus traditional jobs, with little change in their content over generations of employees, are still in the majority. But younger workers who have benefited from a longer, better, more liberal

5. M. Macoby, 'Helping labor and management set up a quality of worklife program', *Monthly Labor Review*, March 1984.
6. Jenkins, *QWL, Current Trends and Directions*, Ontario Quality of Working Life Center, occasional paper No. 3, 1981, Toronto, Ontario.

292

education than their forebears, may be adapting very badly to these jobs[7] and cause widespread industrial relations problems.

12. Management may also have noted some disturbing trends among their existing work force. In one case,[8] the following feelings were reported: dissatisfaction with the technology used, too much supervisory control, a belief that the employees were mismanaged and pushed too hard, a concern that the spirit of service was eroded by the pursuit of profit, deteriorating the quality of the service provided by the company. That dissatisfaction may be materialising in tell-tale signals, such as very high rates of absenteeism or even turnover, even in the presence of a loose labour market, as was the case for a study carried out by the Volvo Corporation.

13. Moving further towards pragmatic motivations, it has also been put forward, in particular by the President of the IOE,[9] that in order to survive, companies must perform at the highest level. This implies a high level of technology, of management and of innovation. But this cannot be obtained in an authoritarian way. It can only come through decentralisation and by letting the employees fully express themselves, in order that they feel concerned. This pronouncement clearly puts forward the use of the quality of working life as a means of providing for a better use of the labour force. It can be a way to have employees go beyond 'a fair day's work for a fair day's pay' and go further. Faced with increased competition,[10] companies need quality products efficiently produced. An employee whose job is more than just a way to earn a living, but provides him with intrinsic satisfaction, may be ready to involve himself more in helping provide a top quality product, at a faster rate.

14. It is also certainly a way to tap potential resources, as yet unacknowledged and unreachable, within the work force. An employee who, according to the classic division of labour, is told to do a job, instructed exactly how to do it and paid consequently, has no incentive and even has some disincentives into promoting a more efficient design or work method. But few people know a job better than the person who is doing it and has done so for the past several years. If he applies himself to the task, he may be likely to come up with several improvements in work methods and work processes, likely to produce improved quality and savings. Here, quality of working life programmes are viewed as a way to tap these resources.

15. Also, there is a feeling, whether grounded in fact or not, that an employee with a more pleasant life at work will be more motivated to

7. *Idem.*
8. Macoby, *op. cit.*
9. J.J. Oeschlin, 'Les employeurs dans le monde actuel', address to the Biannual Assembly of Employers of New Zealand, UIMM, Paris, May 1981.
10. CNPF, *Pour une Paticipation Active dans l'Entreprise*, ETP, Paris, 1983, Jenkins, *op. cit.*

produce more and better. Besides, there may also be a feeling that people have a natural tendency to do a job better when they are left alone and not told how to do it and checked constantly.[11]

16. There also exists a recognition of the fact that, notwithstanding how much care has been exercised in designing jobs and tasks and in cutting down work in pre-established parts, not all situations are flexible and that at same point a problem will appear, resulting in delays or faulty operation that can only be solved if the operator is able and willing to display initiative and creativity. He probably most often is able to do so, but may not be willing or even permitted to or rewarded if he does so. The quality of working life programmes are a means of encouraging that creativity and initiative. It may also be recognised that, whether combined with the introduction of new technology or not, quality of working life programmes may provide for more flexibility in the work force and therefore a more productive use of plant, whether this takes the form of flextime, part-time replacement for shift work, or polyvalent workers, who can be assigned to different skilled jobs according to the demand issuing from diversified products manufactured in short runs.

17. It is also clear that some operations to improve the quality of working life, such as autonomous work groups, job rotation, etc., may increase the flexibility in the use of the work force. The traditional assembly line or standardised method of production was and is well fitted to long production runs of identical objects. However, changes in demand issuing from a more sophisticated and increasingly diversified market have brought some firms to reconsider this mode of production. Also, in leaner economic times management has felt the need to move closer to and to anticipate the market better, as well as to change production faster to react to shifts in demand. Therefore, this strategy of production, for many consumer goods, implied on the one hand a move to shorter runs, and on the other hand to often modify or recombine plant and equipment. Thus the flexibility and adaptability of manpower became crucial.

18. In this light, in managerial eyes, QWL programmes became not only a useful tool to attract and keep a qualified work force, but also, by adapting selected programmes, a way to tap the benefits of a more flexible and adaptable work force able to follow these shifts in production equipment. The traditional manpower, either unskilled or semi-skilled, was little prepared and little willing to adapt. Job rotation, job content change, some autonomous work groups, etc., upgraded its possibility of adapting[12] to the new production needs,

---

11. Jenkins, *op. cit.*
12. For a Marxist analysis of the process see J. Kelly, 'Pratiques patronales de restructuration du travail: procès de travail, marché de l'emploi et débouchés commerciaux', *Sociologie du Travail*, 1984, No. 1, pp. 268.

C. Some Consequences

19. In conclusion, by referring to and combining the French employers federations' objectives and the NYSE study, a good summary of employers' and management attitudes to QWL is obtained. Of course, it concerns only that part of management which feels concerned by QWL and considers it has some potential, as was pointed out earlier.

Three dominant themes appear:

(1) A philosophical concern that it is part of the role of management and the employer to provide a working environment where the employees can express themselves and reach their full potential.

(2) The need to react and to adapt to a changing environment: a different, more educated, differently structured work force with new expectations, and tougher economic conditions.

(3) The improvement of competitiveness by cost cutting, higher productivity, better quality of product, etc.

Therefore, the attitude of management toward QWL, which was reserved if not clearly dubious only 10 years ago, now seems to be more favourable for a growing number. QWL programmes are no longer only a sprinkling of marginal cases and/or experiments, but concern a larger number of enterprises, still a minority, though, but a sizeable one.

This may perhaps, as the NYSE report suggests, be linked with turnover in management, when, as in the labour force in general, a new generation emerges, also with different expectations, also with a different training.

However, this new emphasis may, after a first initial step forward, need some reconsidering. Participation and QWL, although including many facets, gather around a central issue; the individual employee or group of employees, and how much power he or they have in their work and conditions of work.[13]

20. Thus, a central concern becomes power in the organisation. It should be clear that the introduction of quality of working life programmes will tamper with all structures of power within an organisation, both formal and informal. By altering or changing the relationship between an employee and his job and job conent, the relationship with his supervisor is changed. Not only the hierarchical structure is affected, but all power relationships: union, work councils if they exist, as well as various levels of management. This has been pointed out by various case studies.[14] Even in the case of relatively modest consultative experiments, successful quality of working life experiments start a dynamic move, which reaps benefits but also produces an increased demand towards more QWL and also more participation in

---

13. For participation in decision-making see K. Walker, 'Participation in decision-making', *Revue de l'Institut International d'Etudes Sociales*, No. 10, Geneva, 1973, who pointed this out.
14. See in particular *Metalinter* case study by J. Rojot, *CEDEP*, Fontainebleau, France.

related areas. This point is often overlooked in the launching stage of a programme of QWL, but should be taken into account, and preparations for the follow-up period must be made. In other words, changes will occur in the organisation and the organisation should be ready to accommodate them. This implies consequences and adaptions in terms of training, manpower policy, Human Resources Management policies, eventually even Industrial Relations policy.

A car manufacturer's personnel manager's inteview sums up accurately the problems that may then arise[15] after the successful establishment of quality circles; he is quoted as saying that he was 'completely unprepared for the enthusiasm (of the work force)'. He predicts that 'they may eventually cause a fundamental change in the hierarchical structure at the plant. We want to enrich jobs . . . but we do not want to lose control'.

III. LABOUR'S ATTITUDE TOWARDS QWL

21. If we turn now to the labour side, it is not surprising that we meet very different attitudes.

It should come as no surprise that the attitude of labour movements towards the quality of working life finds its roots in different preoccupations to those of the employers.

A. *QWL as a Field for Labour's Action*

22. Of course, all the domains we defined above as pertaining to the area of the quality of working life have, to some extent, been of concern to the labour movement in general. Together with wages and employment, they have constituted, with a more or less marked emphasis depending on the domain, the field of action and demands by unions.

Besides, this concern is not recent. Action for improved conditions of health and safety or shorter work duration is as old as the labour movement itself. A wide consensus, ranging from the AFL-CLO in the USA to the GGT in France, could at least be reached on the point that for 150 years, the unions have had improvement of working life as a target, and that this concern predates by far the weakest scope of interest in such an activity on the part of management and government. J. Peel[16] typically adds that, although it may seem evident, it is however necessary to recall and remember this.

However, union demands have long centred around traditional areas. From wage and hours laws they have moved into health and safety and

---

15. *Business Europe*, 12 June 1981, p. 186.
16. J. Peel, 'European Trade Unions and the Quality of Working Life', in Cooper and Mumford (eds.), *The Quality of Working Life in Western Europe*, London, 1979.

larger areas of nationwide concern, such as social security, for instance. Nevertheless, the new arising trends in quality of working life, including task restructuring, rearrangement of technology and organisational redesign, have raised problems and specific questions as to what the unions' response should be and to related problems. For instance, should the labour movement integrate within its set of demands such types of issue? Can it use its classic tools of collective bargaining and industrial action as far as they are concerned? What should be the attitude if management, or government, unilaterally attempt to conduct such programmes? From the outset, the unions' response has been varied, with a different emphasis not only in each country, but also almost from case to case.

B. Labour Movement's Concerns with QWL

23. Some specific isolated cases of union attitudes can be singled out, such as the participation in joint programmes of QWL by the Communication Workers of America, or the UAW, who described their experience at the Toronto conference on the Quality of Working Life in the 80's. Such instances remain, however, quite isolated. Most unions have found problems of a varying nature in dealing with the newest programmes for improvement of the quality of working life.[17]

It is useful to list and briefly describe these problems in order to account for and try to explain the unions' attitudes towards QWL.

24. Firstly, QWL programmes may raise again the lingering memories, sometimes recent enough, of paternalistic employers' behaviour and traditions. These had their roots in a generous impulse to improve the lot of the employees, but their actual implementation not only did not include the existence of a union, but also often had the explicit goal of forestalling or fighting a trend towards organisation among employees.

In this tradition, the union is considered to be an outsider trying to wedge itself within the working community of the enterprise, constituted of the employer and *his* employees. The real interests of both parties would actually be convergent and the union as a third party and a foreign body would compromise this peaceful state of affairs. Therefore, an operation to improve the quality of the employees' working life may lead the union to fear that this has the goal of eliminating it. It may constitute a weapon

---

17. Earlier efforts to account for union attitudes in this field include Y. Delamotte, 'Union attitudes towards the quality of working life', in L. Davis and A. Cherns (eds.), *The Quality of Working Life*, NY, 1975; J. Boeweg, *The Quality of Working Life, an Industrial Relations Perspective*, paper presented to the IRRA 33rd Annual Meeting, Denver, 5–7 September 1980. We should also mention numerous national monographs edited by ANACT (Paris) and IILS (Geneva), and a comparative study carried out by the European Trade Union Institute (Brussels), to which we shall largely refer later on. The present paper builds upon such work.

against the union, either directly by overpassing it in establishing a direct link between management and the employees, or indirectly by demonstrating to the employees that the union is useless, because management is enough to take care of the employees' interests, which it has at heart. All related attempts to 're-establish a direct link of communication' between management and employees are, in the same way, often considered by the union as a thinly disguised means of turning employees away from union representation. One of the former leaders of the French CGT wrote: 'Employees capitalise upon the fact that the subjective and natural conditions (at the work place) already call for direct democracy on the definition of working conditions, and normal employee expectations hardly go farther . . . and if the union reacts clumsily we shall be close to the point where the majority of the employees would turn against it.'[18]

Along the same lines, it should be underlined that several US consultants specialising in union decertification programmes, or in maintaining a non-union environment in corporations, often advocate jointly with other procedures the implementation of a quality of working life programme.[19]

25. Quality of working life operations may constitute the source of a certain number of risks for the union, even if they are not strictly meant as an anti-union device. They may, for instance, mislead the union onto a wrong track, which will later cost it dearly in influence among employees and membership. If it agrees to jointly take part in sponsoring an operation to improve the quality of working life, it may appear to have been co-opted by management as an additional tool, in order to enlist employees towards the exclusive aims of the employer. The union may lose its essential characteristic of appearing as an independent organisation with its own goals.

Representatives of German and Italian unions express a similar concern, although in very different terms: one notes the 'ambivalence of an agreement dealing with the quality of working life, which risks imposing limits on additional demands',[20] whilst the other calls attention to 'the damage of an operation of involvement (of the union) . . . (with) a risk of integration, of auto-control within the group of employees'.[21]

26. The programmes for improvement of the qualtiy of working life are often marked by an individualistic approach to problems. Cases are dealt with employee by employee, one by one, and such a process is in opposition to the traditional labour attitude of dealing with collective situations, of putting forward collective demands, of generating a general rule applicable to a whole group. Generally, the union strategy is based on presenting itself

18. J.L. Moynot, 'Le Mouvement Syndical en France', *Dialectiques*, No. 28.
19. For instance, see the chapter in 'Job Design', C.R. Hughes, *Making Unions Unnecessary*, New York, 1976.
20. ANACT, *Organisation et Conditions de Travail en République Fédérale d'Allemagne*, Université de Lille III et Maison des Sciences de l'Homme, Paris, 1977, p. 9.
21. *Ressegna Sindicale*, No. 64–65, January–April 1977.

in front of management as the spokesman for all the employees, or all of a group of employees. The union represents, or claims to represent, all the employees in a collectivity. Besides, its very existence and survival rest upon the solidarity of that collectivity. In this light, the individualistic approach threatens the union. Thus the European Trade Union Institute calls attention to the fact that 'the effort of the employers towards individualisation of production . . . seriously jeopardises the spirit of material co-operation on the shop floor'.[22] This same report[23] underlines that quality of working life operations may have even more far-reaching results and create tensions among individual employees within working groups.

It is to be noted that in practice such tensions may appear in somewhat different ways. Sometimes it occurs between the group of employees who are participating in the programme and the other workers, but other situations may also appear. It may be the case that conflict arises between competing autonomous working groups, or even within a single working group, when some employees cannot, or will not, follow a pace set by the majority of the group. Also, a consequence of task restructuring is to enlarge or enrich the basic work of the employee, but in doing so the work of other categories of employees, such as supervisors or maintenance men, may be poorer as a result. Thus, a conflict will result between these groups of employees.

27. The historical tradition of many labour movements often does not include dealing in a paritary way with management. Even though they have very different roots and ideological rationales, the adversary collective bargaining tradition of the USA labour movement and the class warfare tradition of part of the Italian and French labour movements have the same result on this point. However different they are, these 2 types of attitude are equally not conductive to a paritary treatment of issues allowing for a large degree of co-operation.

28. The quality of life at work maybe no longer appears to unions as still being a concern of primary importance and a forefront objective. The topic appeared and flourished in the late 60's and early 70's. Since then, after the 2 oil shocks of 1974 and 1979, the international financial and economic crisis has pushed other issues ahead, which may now appear as requesting priority over these problems. Inflation, unemployment, the impact of new technologies on job structures seem now to be the prevalent problems to be dealt with by labour. Indeed, the issues addressed by quality of working life programmes are linked with these problems, but these links may appear tenuous and complex. The need felt to deal first with what is more urgent may push it into the background.

22. Institut Syndical Européen, *Nouvelles formes d'organisation du travail: les expériences en Europe occidentale*, Bruxelles, 1980, p. 9.
23. *Idem*, p. 109.

Besides, labour organisations must be responsive to the concerns of members, and not only to their leadership's objectives. To give a priority to quality of working life at the present time would imply 3 successive requirements. Firstly that, with a large majority, most employees be really dissatisfied with the work they are performing, and the design of their job and organisation within which they work; secondly, that these employees believe that it is actually possible to change this present condition for the better; and thirdly, that innovative improvements in this domain can be effective and efficient. For lack of adequate information, it is impossible to find out if each of these 3 successive requirements is fulfilled. However, it is by far not clear that most union leaders believe that they are. On the contrary, the majority opinion among them might well be that, for most wage earners, what is really still a priority nowadays is basic health and safety, and increasing wages is still the best way to improve their quality of working life.

29. The union may be tempted to consider that programmes of improvement of quality of life at work are only a disguise for the true concerns of management. In other words, even if management has accepted the union presence on the shop floor, and if such programmes are not aimed against its existence, they may nevertheless have hidden objectives detrimental to union members and/or all the employees. The real goal of management, far from improving the quality of working life, being to harden working conditions.[24] The programme, for instance, may actually speed up the pace of work and try to increase the amount of work for the same or a lesser wage. For example, a longer work cycle may make the job more interesting, but it may also impose a faster work speed. Quality of working life may also constitute a managerial argument to deny a wage increase. A new job design, consisting of added elementary tasks, may not be much more interesting than the former job, but may help management save the cost of hiring a new employee, or may make some present employees redundant.

Besides, some labour movements agree that the programmes for improvement of the quality of working life are simply an alternative response to the economic crisis on the part of the employers.

In face of the gains achieved by workers and the labour movement since 1945, it is alleged that employers have put together a response since 1973. This response includes several facets and notably rationalisation investments, together with a decrease in labour costs stemming from a faster work pace and productivity improvements. Besides the use of traditional methods to implement these goals, management is alleged to have introduced 2 new specific processes.

Firstly, the introduction of new technology. This in itself constitutes a separate concern, but it is intimately linked with the quality of working life. On the one hand, investments in new technologies decrease the volume of

24. The Belgian FGTB and French CFDT reports to the Trade Unions European Institute contain such arguments.

employment, for they are rationalisation investments and labour saving. On the other hand, they may worsen working conditions, either by speeding the work process or by introducing new working methods. The central computer linked to the work stations may, for instance, allow an increased and permanent control of the presence and work speed of employees (cashiers in a department store is a prime example). Besides, computer work from screens may be dangerous for the health of operators.[25] Also, and more generally, the introduction of new technology by definition carries a reshuffling of work duties and a redefinition of tasks, which the management operate to their advantage and which results in an increased work load.

Secondly, the employer's response has another new specific feature. Under the cover of improvement of the quality of life at work, it really aims to obtain an increased degree of flexibility in the organisation of labour. It aims to recreate a work process less constrained by narrow definitions of tasks, specific shells, technical constraints linked to the use of conventional technology. But this new flexibility jeopardises some of the traditional aspects of the job beneficial to the employee; for instance, established and agreed upon skill categories, workers' control upon the work process or speed, etc.

In that light, it is alleged that quality of working life programmes actually bring, not an improvement, but a worsening of conditions of work.

30. A large number of European unions[26] tend to consider that operations for improving the quality of life at work, even if they do not directly aim at worsening conditions of work, nonetheless have at least mixed objectives. Among the various objectives behind an employer's decision to implement such a programme, the unions try to establish which are the priority ones and classify them into 3 categories: suspicious, mixed, and finally those which can be beneficial to the employees, but should be bargained against employer's concessions and not automatically flow from a unilateral decision.[27]

Whatever the circumstances, behind any such employer's decision lays a prerequisite to increase or maintain productivity. This productivity increase can be direct and result from additional output per worker, or indirect and result from better flexibility, better quality or less rejects, savings in materials, etc.

Thus the perception by an employee of an actual improvement in his working conditions may well be associated with invisible detrimental consequences: job restructuring may suppress some jobs; job rotation may be paid at the rate of the lowest paid job; new responsibility without compensation may fall on individual employees. For instance, the actual results of the introduction of some autonomous work groups may indeed be less boring

25. See *Syndicalisme CFDT*, 1981, 'Les Dossiers de l'Ecran'.
26. This position is outlined in detail in the European Trade Institute Report, *op. cit.*
27. *Idem.*

jobs, but it may also result in more complex and heavier tasks for each member of the group, associated with self-supervision and the suppression of a job for a supervisor or leadman. In the same way, job enrichment may allow management to eliminate the better paying jobs, job enlargement may result in a lower net take-home pay if it replaces a piece work wage rate, etc.[28]

Therefore, the union may be careful that if there are any benefits to be reaped by the employees, this be the case without any of these detrimental consequences taking place. Increases in productivity are not bad in themselves; however, they should not be paid for by the employees only.[29]

31. It was clearly pointed out that successful operations for improving the quality of working life tend to modify existing organisational structures and power relationships within the enterprise. Just as it was noted that management may want to stay in control, the union may be wary of such changes. The union is also conscious that the final result of the operation is quite impossible to foresee. A member of the German I G Metall pointed out that 'of course we certainly are always in favour of humanisation of work, but the problem here is that nobody knows how things may end up in each case'.[30]

32. Labour unions have, in each case, their own specific structure taking root in specific historical or technical circumstances. The carrying out of operations for improvement of life at work may threaten these structures or fit badly with them. For instance, a job enlargement or enrichment scheme may raise delicate problems of jurisdictional competence for craft unions, in the building trades for example.

Besides, the structure of labour organisations is generally inspired by the structure of democratic organisations where 'power ultimately comes from the membership'. Thus, this results in a rather complex and relatively heavy decision-making structure, which may demand time lags before a course of action is selected. This prevents chancy actions, but also rapid evolutions. This is not a handicap for traditional union activities, for historically the initiative has come from the employer in the domain of industrial relations. The union had to be reactive, seldom proactive. However, this model is ill-adapted to operations dealing with the quality of working life, which often involve rapid change and demand that initiatives be taken quickly at decentralised levels. This is hardly compatible with the traditional decision-making process in unions.

33. Classic systems of job control by unions might be threatened. For instance, these systems are based roughly upon qualifications in France,

28. Interview by the author, French CFDT, German Union of Wood Workers.
29. *Idem.*
30. Interview by the author.

302

classification (category) in Italy, job description and promotion ladders in the USA, etc. An operation for improvement of quality of life at work may well put in question and take exception to a traditional set of rules, customs, practices which are instrumental to the local union action at plant level. The union officers will have to develop new strategies. The meaning of seniority job ladders, job evaluation will need to be re-evaluated and re-established. In fact, the union will have to face a renegotiation of a new set of guarantees, for the older rules lie open to question, and thus often have had to negotiate the acceptance and implantation of the operation for improvement of the quality of working life.

34. The unions may not be well equipped to deal with issues related to the quality of working life. The classic 'bag of tools' of the labour movement may not fit the nature of the new problems arising. In particular, collective bargaining, which was the typical mechanism geared to deal with common demands in a collectivity raised at separate time intervals, may not adapt itself well to deal with situations and problems centred around the individual and subject to constant change.

Besides, the level of negotiations will not be the one where quality of working life issues arise and have to be solved. Also, the union may foresee problems of implementation, even if an agreement is reached. How in practice will it be possible to make sure and check that the management's part of the agreement is carried out and kept that way? In fact, here the management not only has the initiative for acting first, as usual, but it also enjoys a monopoly on initial implementation. It may be too late to react later for the union and to regain the lost ground. This may often be the case when a project for improving the quality of working life is linked to the introduction of new technology and implies huge investments, such as computerisation, etc.

In the same way, there may also exist a feeling, on the union side, that 'all the experts sit on the other side'. In several countries, shop stewards and union officials are often little aware, other than by their own practical experience, of developments in participation and quality of working life. They often lack training and theoretical knowledge in this area. Thus, they may on first impulse have little trust in operations of this kind. At the extreme, they may be tempted to automatically oppose such initiatives because of lack of knowledge, rather than risk compromising their negotiating position or having to rely on an outside expert whom they must trust little as far as his actual knowledge of work and plant-floor conditions is concerned.

Such negative reactions are likely in the cases where the union has to face a ready-made plan, already prepared by an academic or a consultant, without having been involved at the preparation and conception stage, and with the choice of either accepting or rejecting the whole plan without any power, or the necessary information, to mitigate, alleviate or change any part of it.

Union representatives[31] note that programmes for the improvement of the quality of working life are most often initiated, planned and implemented by management alone. What is required from the union and/or the employees is mostly to blindly trust the goodwill and intentions of the management.

Even when a certain degree of paritarism and union involvement has taken place, it is noted that the amount of time dedicated to the planning phase and the joint search for alternatives and solutions is too limited, and often considered by management as an unproductive chore to be faced without benefit.[32]

35. The introduction of quality of working life operations may also decrease the efficiency of the existing tools of union action. For instance, setting up semi-autonomous work groups may disrupt in-company formal and informal channels of union communication. It may help decrease the link between employee and union. It may, in the minds of employees, cancel 'the big picture' of the plant-wide work force and promote small group specific interests. For the union, quality of working life issues, like any other, are rooted in a power relationship with management. But the dominant approach in these issues presently consists of, sometimes naively, denying conflicts and opposition of interests, and of promoting joint benefits exclusively.

36. Finally, it should also be remembered that some unions' ideology may be *a priori* opposed to the principle of promoting joint operations or programmes with the employer. For instance, the US dominant ideology of collective bargaining leaves little room for co-operation and is essentially adversary. In Europe, some labour movements refer exclusively to the class struggle, and do not think it possible to take into account any behaviour from an employer other than driving to straight project maximisation and increased exploitation of the working class.

IV. CONCLUSION

37. The attitudes of employers and unions towards the quality of working life movement are presently in a condition of change.

Employers and management, after considering it for a long time to be a matter of mostly academic interest, are turning in increasing numbers towards one or several schemes related to it under the impact of the factors we have outlined above. However, these increasing numbers still constitute a minority and some of the schemes may have only a marginal impact.

31. Wallenbury, Huisman and Vantoor, 'Nouvelles formes d'organisation du travail et qualité du lieu de travail, un point de vue du syndicat aux Pays Bas', *Travail et Société*, Volume 4, No. 2, April 1974.
32. European Trade Union Institute, *op. cit.*, p. 13.

Moreover, a concern over the long-range effects of such schemes on company structure begins to emerge.

Organised labour is also conscious that, whatever its reservations, quality of working life operations may also bring real benefits to the work force. Besides, a union would clearly be hard pressed to explain to its members or to the public at large its refusal to agree to what appears to be an effort in favour of the conditions of work of its members. Also in most cases, quality of working life operations can be introduced unilaterally by management, and will take place whether the union likes it or not, tries to influence them or not. It should be added that for a segment of the labour movement, it may also constitute an opportunity to influence in the long-term the managerial principles of organisation and management in favour of a 'democratised' work place. The principles and operations of quality of working life imply that a given state of technology does not dictate a given traditional type of management and organisation, and therefore QWL opens a new field for union action at plant level to attempt to influence it.

It should be underlined that, in any case, it is not certain that the spread of quality of working life operations carries compulsorily with it a spirit of increased co-operation with management. If that were the case, it would be necessary to assume that there are 'mutual' benefits which have no effect on the organisation and power relationships. Clearly, both parties are aware that this is not the case. However, if there is no co-operation as far as the long-term goals are concerned, there may be a degree of co-operation in the methods to be used in order to improve the quality of working life of the employees, for the reasons outlined above. A new zone of common interest between management and labour may appear, with a dimension varying case by case. Beyond that, power relationships will appear again. B. Trentin[33] even sees in it stakes including the social control of production.

It should be clear that, for each party, the quality of working life will be an element integrated into their global strategy. For management in general it will be an asset towards increased productivity and flexibility and better work-place relationships with employees. For different labour movements in different countries, it will be integrated into the main demands and specific characteristics of each. It is revealing that the quality of working life is referred to within a framework of co-determination for German unions, of industrial democracy for Swedish unions, of self-management for the CFDT in France, of the unity of the working class around 'professionality' in Italy, and finally as an objective to be bargained collectively for the section of the North American labour movement which concerns itself with it.

33. *Rassegna Sindicale, op. cit.*

SELECT BIBLIOGRAPHY

ANACT, *Organisation et Conditions de Travail en République Fédérale d'Allemagne*, Université de Lille III et Maison des Sciences de l'Homme, Paris, 1977, p. 9.

J. Boeweg, *The quality of working life, an industrial relations perspective*, paper presented to the IRRA 33rd Annual Meeting, Denver, 5–7 September 1980.

F. Chiaromonte, *Nuove forme di organizzazione del lavoro*: job enlargement, job rotation, con esempi di applicazione in imprese americane, Milan, 1975.

J.M. Clerc, *Expériences en vue d'une organisation plus humaine du travail industriel*; compte rendu d'un colloque international qui s'est tenu à Paris les 26 et 27 janvier 1973, Paris, 1973.

CNPF, *Pour une Participation Active dans l'Entreprise*, Jenkins, ETP, Paris, 1983.

L. Davis and A. Cherns (eds.), *The Quality of Working Life*, New York, 1975.

Y. Delamotte, 'Attitudes of French and Italian trade unions to the humanisation of work', *Labour and Society*, Geneva, pp. 49–62.

Y. Delamotte and K.F. Walker, *Humanisation of work and the quality of working life*: trends and issues, Bulletin, International Institute for Labour Studies, Geneva, 1973.

European Association of Personnel Management, Institute of Personnel Management, London, *Humanisation of Work in Western Europe*, London, 1979.

R. Greve, *Selected and partially annotated bibliography on certain aspects of the quality of working life, with special reference to work organisation (1970–1975)*, III, Geneva, 1976.

Institut Syndical Européen, *Nouvelles formes d'organisation du travail*: les expériences en Europe occidentale, Bruxelles, 1980, p. 9.

Jenkins, *QWL, Current Trends and Directions*, Ontario Quality of Working Life Center, occasional paper No. 3, Toronto, 1981.

M. Macoby, 'Helping labor and management set up a quality of worklife program', *Monthly Labor Review*, March 1984.

M. Mine, 'Quality of Working Life in Japan: Trends and Characteristics', *Labour and Society*, 1982, pp. 265–278.

New York Stock Exchange, *People and Productivity, A Challenge to Corporate America*, NYSE, 1982.

J.J. Oeschlin, 'Les employeurs dans le monde actuel', address to the Biannual Assembly of Employers of New Zealand, UIMM, Paris, May 1981.

Ontario Quality of Working Life Centre, Ministry of Labour, *Perspectives on the quality of working life*; proceedings of a conference, 15 October 1980, Toronto, Onario.

Organisation et Conditions de Travail en Grande-Bretagne, January 1981, 198 p.

Organisation et Conditions de Travail en RFA, January 1978, 102 p.

Organisation et Conditions de Travail en Suède, February 1980, 288 p.

R.N. Ottoway, *Humanising the Work Place: New Proposals and Perspectives*, London, 1977.

J. Peel, 'European Trade Unions and the Quality of Working Life', in Cooper and Mumford (eds.), *The Quality of Woking Life in Western Europe*, London, 1979.

Pour une nouvele organisation: la méthodologie ARPES (de Rome), June 1982.

Rassegna Sindicale, No. 64–65, January–April 1977.

K.M. Srinivas, 'Humanisation of Worklife in Canada: Progress, Perspectives and Prospects', *Journal of Occupational Behaviour*, pp. 87–118.

Le syndicat et l'organisation du travail, l'exemple de la CGT italienne, Octobre 1978, 272 p.

S.I. Takezawa, 'Changing Worker Values and Management Innovations in Japanese Industry', *Labour and Society*, Geneva, 1979, pp. 129–141.

S. Timperley and D. Ondrack, *Humanisation of Work*, II, London, 1982.

K. Walker, 'Participation in decision-making', *Revue de l'Institut International d'Etudes Sociales*, No. 10, Geneva, 1973.

Wallenbury, Huisman and Vantoor, 'Nouvelles formes d'organisation du travail et qualité du lieu de travail, un point de vue du syndicat aux Pays Bas', *Travail et Société*, Volume 4, No. 2, April 1974.

World Federation of Trade Unions, *International Impact of Micro-Technology on Workers*, Prague, 1981.

Chapter 15. Collective Bargaining

E. Córdova

I. THE MEANING OF THE TERM

1. There are two meanings of the term collective bargaining – a broad and a narrow one. In its broad sense, collective bargaining is a process of interest accommodation which includes all sorts of bipartite or tripartite discussions relating to labour problems and directly or indirectly affecting a group of workers. The discussions may take place in different fora, with or without the presence of governments, and aim at ascertaining the view of the other party, obtaining a concession or reaching a compromise. Obviously, the lines dividing this notion of collective bargaining from various institutional and non-institutional forms of consultation, co-operation and concert are rather difficult to draw.

2. A narrower but more precise meaning of collective bargaining views it only in connection with the bipartite discussions leading to the conclusion of agreements. Collective bargaining here, involves a process of negotiations between individual employers or representatives of employers' organisations and trade union representatives, as well as the conclusion, in case of accord, of a written agreement. Negotiations are usually conducted at periodic intervals and the agreement is, as a rule, regarded as a document which binds not only its signatories but also the groups they represent. The main purpose of both negotiations and agreements is the determination of wages and other conditions of employment in an enterprise or industry, but other objectives including the regulation of relations between the parties, the settlement of disputes and the promotion of workers' participation may also be pursued.

3. The broad and the narrow sense of collective bargaining roughly correspond to what has also been called in France the informal and formal types of negotiation ('négociation officieuse et négociation officielle')[1] and in the UK the 'permanent' or 'dynamic' and the contractual methods.[2] A broad interpretation of the term collective bargaining might also entail the need to

---

1. Commission des Communautés Européennes, *Problèmes et perspectives de la négociation collective dans les pays membres de la Communauté*, Brussels, 1979 (edition provisoire), p. 183.
2. See B.A. Hepple, *IELL* (Great Britain), Kluwer, 1980, p. 33.

include some forms of political bargaining and tripartite co-operation, in addition to collective bargaining proper.

Although the broad, informal and political types have tended to grow in recent years and their development has no doubt affected the traditional view of negotiations, emphasis will be placed in this chapter on the narrower sense. Many aspects of the broad meaning of collective bargaining are in effect discussed in other chapters of this book.

II. HISTORICAL BACKGROUND

4. Collective bargaining appeared at the early stages of the Industrial Revolution as a means of fixing wages and a few other conditions of employment. It was mainly conceived in order to replace unilateral decision-making by the employer and to overcome the weak bargaining position of individual workers. The new procedure also fitted well into the sociological features of manufacturing industries which concentrated large groups of wage earners doing similar tasks in one single workplace, and gave practical expression to the nascent feelings of solidarity among workers. Such feelings, which were first directed in a somewhat sporadic fashion towards the declaration of strikes, were later channelled in a more systematic manner towards the establishment of a common rule in a given undertaking or industry.

5. Despite its manifest *raison d'être*, collective bargaining was not able to play an important rule during the nineteenth century, mainly because the bargaining agent on the workers' side – the trade union – was not recognised by most governments and employers but also because legal systems were not yet able to comprehend the nature of the agreement that usually came out of negotiations. Negotiations were then conducted in an atmosphere of crisis under the pressure of strikes or lockouts and collective agreements had only a *de facto* validity. They were frequently concluded by a mere coalition of workers likely to be subsequently disbanded.

6. When trade unions grew in strength and were able to obtain recognition, at the turn of the century in some European countries and a few decades later in other industrialised and developing countries, collective bargaining promptly acquired sizeable dimensions and became a key element of industrial relations systems. Such development was also made possible by the incorporation of collective agreements in the legal system of various European countries as a new source of rules and regulations in the field of labour. This process was started by the Dutch Civil Code (1907) and the Swiss Code of Obligations in 1911 and followed by the adoption of specific legislation in Norway (1915), Germany (1918), France (1919), Finland (1924) and the Netherlands (1927). This legislation acknowledged that collective agreements constituted a valid and suitable way of determining conditions of employment for a collectivity of workers. Further developments came about a few years later when the National Labor Relations Act of the United States introduced, in 1935, principles governing the orderly conduct of negotiations and the prohibition of unfair labour practices. A third major contribution was represented by the seminal influence of the United Kingdom in respect of the voluntary character of negotiations and the respect for the autonomy of the bargaining parties.

7. Not only have these influences contributed to shape the prevailing national models but they have also found reflection in the instruments adopted by the International Labour Organisation. The British emphasis on voluntarism probably inspired the reference to 'machinery for voluntary negotiations' contained in one of the key provisions of Convention No. 98 on the Right to Organise and to Bargain Collectively (1949). The continental model served no doubt to frame most of the provisions on effects, interpretation and extension of agreements included in Recommendation No. 92 on Collective Agreements (1951). Finally, some elements of the American penchant for regulating collective bargaining procedures can be found in Recommendation No. 130 concerning the Examination of Grievances within Undertakings, as well as in Convention No. 154 and Recommendation No. 163 concerning the Promotion of Collective Bargaining (1981).

8. No single, universally valid model of collective bargaining has emerged, however, from the above-mentioned influences. In the UK and a few other English-speaking countries, collective agreements are not legally binding unless so specifically requested by the parties; if such request is not made, and if the agreement is not in writing, it is simply considered as a 'gentleman's agreement' whose enforcement hinges on the good will or relative strength of the parties. In a few other European countries, collective agreements bind only affiliated members of the signatory union. A third group of countries have preferred not to regulate the process of negotiations out of concern for the wish of the social partners to preserve the autonomy of collective bargaining and avoid any form of government intervention. It should nevertheless be noted that the notion of a gentleman's agreement is increasingly being discarded, that in practice agreements are applied to the ensemble of workers even in countries where they are supposed to bind only trade union affiliates and that, in the absence of legislative provisions, rules dealing with the process of negotiations are created by jurisprudence, the social partners or industrial practices.

III. A Multifaceted Role

9. It follows from the above that, in practice, collective bargaining serves various purposes and can be regarded nowadays as a multifaceted institution

which, in addition to determining wages and working conditions, performs other functions dealing with the settlement of disputes, the regulation of relations between the parties and the promotion of workers' participation.

10. Rule-making concerns the inclusion in the agreement of provisions governing the various employment relationships that obtain in the bargaining unit. These provisions are deemed to become part of all the individual contracts of employment, including in most countries those concluded by workers who were not members of the union at the moment at which the agreement was concluded or who only later joined the bargaining unit; the individual contracts cannot in turn contain any stipulation contrary to the collective agreement. While in most countries individual workers and the employer may improve the standards fixed by collective agreements, in a few others such specific improvements might be regarded as an undue departure from the common rule. A similar but inverse relationship obtains between collective agreements and statutory provisions. The latter prescribe minimum standards of protection which can be improved for the benefit of the workers by collective agreements. However, collective agreements cannot in turn detract from the level of legislative standards and cannot contravene a public policy provision contained in the laws.

11. The rule-making functions of collective bargaining go well beyond the limits of a bargaining unit. Working conditions established in collective agreements apply frequently to workers who were not members of the union or were excluded from the bargaining unit and sometimes through extension procedures to non-signatory and non-unionised undertakings in a given industry. They may also serve to influence the evolution of labour legislation: improvements first introduced in collective agreements are later incorporated into the statutory books. The dynamic nature of collective bargaining, and its ability to adapt quickly to changing circumstances, equip it well to act as an instrument of innovation and change.

12. The capacity of collective bargaining to create standards of a general application is an indication of both the power of groups to provide for their own internal regulation and of the limits of the sovereign power of the State. It is in this respect that collective bargaining can be regarded as an expression of pluralism. The fact that joint regulations take the place of authoritarian decision-making also means that collective bargaining is an effective vehicle for the democratisation of industrial life.

13. As a conflict resolution device, collective bargaining usually precedes the intervention of third parties and has also developed into an important problem-solving technique. Negotiations may serve to solve disputes arising from the interpretation or application of existing legal or contractual provisions, i.e. disputes over rights. They may also be used to overcome deadlocks in the bargaining process, i.e. disputes over interests, as it is normally the prerogative of the parties to decide at any point in the operation of the dispute settlement machinery to return to direct negotiations in order to overcome possible areas of disagreement.

14. Between the rule-making and the conflict resolution functions, collective bargaining also plays an important part as a regulator of relations between the employer or employers' organisation concerned and the workers' organisation which is also signatory to the agreement. As trade unions entered the factory gates and established themselves as a recognised and permanent feature of industrial relations, and as employers made clear their intention to retain their basic function of managing the undertaking, it became necessary to provide for the mutual accommodation of these two social forces. Collective bargaining sought to do this, firstly, by determining the lines of demarcation of management prerogatives and providing for the security and effective functioning of the trade union and, secondly, by setting out internal procedures for bargaining and/or administering the agreement. To the extent that collective bargaining thus became a mechanism for the orderly distribution of powers within different levels of economic activity, it has no doubt made a significant contribution to industrial peace and the stabilisation of labour relations.

15. Although the principal functions of collective bargaining described above are carried out on the workers' side by trade union officials or other workers' representatives, the whole bargaining process entails a significant quantum of workers' participation. Workers are involved, for example, in the determination of their conditions of employment, first, when they make suggestions and approve the list of demands in the relevant trade union meetings, next, when they elect the team of negotiators and, finally, when they are called upon to ratify the agreement entered into by the said negotiators. These various forms of participation are particularly visible when negotiations take place at the shop, plant or undertaking level, where workers normally exert a direct influence on the course of negotiations. They are less relevant in the case of industry-wide, regional or national negotiations which are conducted by top-level officials, usually mandated by delegates or representatives of federations. One could therefore conclude that the lower the level of negotiations the greater the opportunities for direct workers' participation. This may perhaps help to explain why other forms of workers' participation, such as employee representation on company boards, have developed in countries where collective bargaining is largely conducted at the industry level.

16. But even when negotiations are carried out at the enterprise level, the value of collective bargaining as a form of workers' participation should not be over-emphasised. For one thing, negotiations are conducted in periodic or sporadic fashion and both the conclusion of the agreement and its subsequent administration are the business of a relatively few shop stewards

311

and trade union officials. For another, the coverage of collective bargaining is rather limited in some countries as we shall see shortly. For a third, collective bargaining is on many occasions an *ex post facto* proposition which comes relatively late into the labour relations picture and deals with matters that have already been decided upon by management.[3]

IV. COVERAGE

17. A rule-making and conflict resolution process, a form of worker participation, a forerunner of labour legislation, an instrument of peace and stability, a reassertion of pluralism and a means of democratising industrial life – all these are indications of the qualitative impact of collective bargaining in contemporary society. But which is its real quantitative impact? What is the extent of its coverage and actual presence in today's industrial relations? Most statistics refer in this connection to the number of agreements concluded and the number of workers covered by the agreements. However, the first yardstick is somewhat misleading because a few industry-wide or national agreements may carry more weight than a relatively high number of enterprise or plant agreements.

In the Netherlands, for instance, there were at the end of the 1970s some 160 industry-wide agreements but they covered more than 80 per cent of the total labour force.[4] Likewise, in the FR Germany and Sweden, the figures concerning national and industry-wide agreements seem modest but the corresponding coverage is even higher than in the Netherlands (more than 90 per cent).[5] Norway also has a rather centralised system of collective bargaining which covers about three-quarters of the labour force.[6] In the USA, on the contrary, there are approximately 178,000 agreements in force but their over-all coverage does not exceed 28 per cent of the labour force.[7] In Japan, the number of agreements in 1980 was around 53,000, which covered approximately 25 per cent of the total labour force.[8] In Canada, where 90 per cent of the approximately 10,000 agreements negotiated every year are concluded at the enterprise level, about 50 per cent of the work force is covered by collective agreements.

The number of agreements may be even more impressive at levels lower than the enterprise. In the UK, where the number of shop stewards is around 250,000, it is often said that each one of them negotiates every year an agreement on behalf of his fellow workers in the shop or department

3. E. Córdova, 'Workers' Participation in Decisions within Enterprises: Recent Trends and Problems', *International Labour Review* (Geneva), March–April 1982.
4. M.H.L. Bakels, *IELL* (The Netherlands), p. 59.
5. ILO 'Collective Bargaining in Industrialised Countries', *Labour–Management Relations Series*, No. 5 (Geneva, 1978), p. 82.
6. *Labour Relations in Norway* (Oslo, 1975), p. 46.
7. Author's estimate.
8. Ministry of Labour, 1981 *Basic Survey of Trade Unions* (Tokyo, 1981).

concerned. Needless to add that these are rather informal and mostly verbal agreements.

18. However, a full appraisal of the weight of collective bargaining in industrial relations systems would require the introduction of another element which will be discussed later, namely, the content of agreements. While most national agreements contain basic principles and industry-wide agreements include minimum rates, enterprise-level agreements provide for a wider and more detailed spectrum of standards. The quantitative and qualitative elements are thus interconnected and questions of coverage tie up with questions of level and content of agreements.

19. Whatever may be the over-all impact of collective agreements some general indications can be given in respect of their coverage: this is larger in industrialised than in developing countries and more significant in the secondary sector than in the others. Both findings clearly correspond to the number of large enterprises, which is particularly high in the industrial sector of industrialised countries, but are also a consequence of the degree of implantation of trade unions. Recent increases in the coverage of collective bargaining have come about, however, as a result of its inception and development in the public sector. Either *de jure* or *de facto* collective bargaining is being increasingly used in public enterprises and in the public service proper as a means of determining conditions of employment. Canada offers an example of an over-all increase in the coverage of agreements due largely to the extension of collective bargaining to the public service: in 1967, just before negotiations were authorised at the federal level, 44 per cent of all employees were covered by collective agreements; in 1978 this percentage had increased to 58.[9]

20. In developing countries the coverage of collective bargaining is rather uneven. In Latin America, for instance, while in Mexico there are approximately 60,000 agreements in force and one single Argentinian collective agreement covered more than one million workers,[10] only 12 per cent approximately of the economically active populations are covered by collective agreements in Ecuador' and in Brazil it was only after 1978 that collective bargaining acquired a relative significance. One can safely say, however, that in some developing countries (e.g. Argentina, Malaysia, Mexico, Philippines, Singapore and Venezuela) collective bargaining is already approaching an extent comparable to that of many industrialised countries, while in others (e.g. Colombia, Ghana, India, Kenya, Nigeria and Sri Lanka) it is more slowly reaching significant proportions. However,

9. See the corresponding issues of *The Current Industrial Relations Scene in Canada* published by the Industrial Relations Centre of the Queen's University at Kingston.
10. See A. Bronstein, *Collective bargaining* in Efrén Córdova, *Industrial Relations in Latin America* (New York, 1984), p. 89.

313

coverage is still below 10 per cent of the labour force in the majority of developing countries.

21. The coverage of collective bargaining usually expands in times of prosperity and declines in periods of recession. In the UK, for instance, collective agreements covered 71.8 per cent of employees in 1973 and 68.6 in 1978, and then declined substantially in subsequent years.[11] Although the extent of collective bargaining has also experienced some setbacks, particularly in developing countries, as a result of political vicissitudes which frequently affect freedom of association and the functioning of trade unions, there is no doubt that, on the whole it has been expanding consistently in both industrialised and developing countries. Conventional forms of collective bargaining catering to blue-collar workers in industry now co-exist with a wide range of other forms of negotiations which have even developed their own character: professional negotiations covering teachers, the performing arts, nurses, air traffic controllers, etc.; public sector negotiations involving public servants or employees in public enterprises; and multipartite forms of negotiation embracing farmers, fishermen and other self-employed people, in addition to wage earners. Collective bargaining is, in fact, one of the few forms of workers' participation which cuts across ideological and national boundaries and can be found almost everywhere in the world. Among the industrialised market-oriented countries, only Australia and New Zealand have placed collective bargaining in a secondary position (next to arbitration awards) as a rule-making device.

21bis. Mention should however be made of a recent phenomenon which may affect the future of collective bargaining as well as that of traditional forms of workers' representation, namely the growth of atypical kinds of employment. Most of these new modalities of work (temporary work, part-time jobs, home work, work in mini-enterprises, clandestine work, etc.) do not lend themselves to the practice of negotiation and conclusion of agreements. Workers engaged in these activities have a different mentality and lack the feelings of solidarity and the propensity to look for collective-like approaches that normally lead to the occurrence of negotiations. The very nature of their work environment is also an obstacle to trade union action. Few collective agreements have in fact been negotiated by atypical workers which are also characterised by their low rates of unionisation.[11bis]

V. The Parties to Collective Bargaining

22. As the very name of the institution suggests, the process of collective bargaining requires two parties linked in one way or another to a collectivity

11. See B.C. Roberts, 'Recent Trends in Collective Bargaining in the United Kingdom', *International Labour Review*, 1984, pp. 289–290.

11*bis.* E. Cordova, 'From full-time wage employment to atypical employment: A major shift in the evolution of labour relations, *International Labour Review*, Vol. 125, no. 6, November-December 1986.

of workers. While individual employers already meet *per force* this requirement, the bargaining agent on the workers' side necessarily supposes a
group of workers or an organisation representing such a group. Given the
difficulties involved in discussing, concluding and administering an agreement directly with a whole group of wage earners, workers' representation is
normally entrusted to a trade union organisation. Unions are almost everywhere regarded as the natural bargaining agent and collective bargaining
has, in turn, become one of the main functions of a workers' organisation.
However, the efficiency of a trade union in discharging this function
depends to a large extent on the size of its membership, its financial
resources, the degree of support of its affiliates and their willingness to
engage in industrial action in case of a deadlock, all of which constitute the
basis of the unions bargaining power.

23. Although trade unions assume in the majority of cases the role of
bargaining agent, there are at least two additional forms of workers'
representation. In some developing countries (Colombia, Costa Rica, Chile,
Peru, Sri Lanka, Thailand, Uruguay and Venezuela) non-organised groups
of workers are also entitled to negotiate. This is usually permitted only in
the absence of a trade union and provided that certain requirements
concerning the number of workers, the appointment of a team of negotiators and the form of the agreement are met. In some countries these
requirements are stricter than those applicable to trade unions.

24. The other form of workers' representation obtains in some European
countries where works councils or other enterprise bodies perform some
bargaining functions. In the majority of cases, negotiations deal with non-
wage questions or are conducted on a *de facto* basis since the law has tried
to separate the bargaining functions of trade unions from the participative
responsibilities of works councils.

25. On the employers' side, negotiations can be carried out by individual
employers, as happens in countries where enterprise-level bargaining prevails, or by an employers' organisation which is the case of countries with
industry-wide bargaining. Multi-employer bargaining carried out outside an
employers' organisation is also known in a few countries but its occurrence
is relatively rare. In general, the role of employers' organisations is becoming increasingly important as they also frequently act as clearing-houses of
information and advisers to individual employers in cases of enterprise-level
bargaining. Some problems have arisen, however, with regard to the authority of employers' organisations to conclude collective agreements on behalf
of their members at the industry level (see below paragraph 62). As
mentioned in chapter 11, in some countries employers' organisations do not
actually engage themselves in industry-wide negotiations but limit themselves to a co-ordinating role.

26. Both parties appoint their negotiating committees, usually composed of high-level trade union officers and corporate officials, assisted frequently by lawyers and, in the case of local unions, by senior representatives of the national unions federations. In some countries, e.g. Chile and Spain, the number of negotiators cannot exceed certain limits (12 persons for instance). Employers' and workers' negotiators are, as a rule, authorised to conduct collective bargaining discussions with an adequate margin of autonomy. It is important that they be regarded not as simple conveyors of proposals and counterproposals but as real negotiators. As indicated by ILO Recommendation No. 163 concerning the promotion of collective bargaining, 'parties to collective bargaining should provide their respective negotiators with the necessary mandate to conduct and conclude negotiations, subject to any provisions for consultations within their respective organisations'.

27. Mention should finally be made of the role of government as a possible third party in collective bargaining. In principle, governments should limit themselves to the establishment of an institutional framework within which the parties should feel free to operate without outside pressures or restraints. In practice, however, governments are increasingly involved in negotiations, sometimes in overt fashion as a party to national agreements, as happened recently in Ireland (1980), Italy (1983), Norway (1974) and Spain (1982 and 1984) and more frequently in an indirect and informal manner. Labour ministries, particularly in developing countries, seek to influence collective bargaining by acting as promoters, regulators, moderators and conciliators. Their officials are often called upon to sit in at some critical negotiations and assist the direct participants. Other indications about the role of government in negotiations will be given in the final section below.

VI. LEVELS OF BARGAINING

28. Collective bargaining may take place at different levels. The more common ones are the undertaking, the craft, the industry and the national levels. On some occasions, bargaining may come down to the level of the plant and even the shop; there are also cases of negotiations limited to specific groups of workers belonging to the same craft. In some countries, e.g. Brazil, France and Italy, and in the construction industry of the United States, bargaining levels may also include geographic units, and negotiations are held at the local, regional, provincial and national levels. While national-level bargaining aims in some cases, particularly in the public service, at the determination of substantive conditions of employment, it is for the most part concerned with the regulation of matters of general interest, e.g. wage indexation and retirement benefits, or the establishment of the basic 'rules of the game'. These rules are intended to regulate and facilitate subsequent processes of bargaining at lower levels; substantive standards

constitute the minimum that must be observed in industry-wide and enterprise-level negotiations.

29. An even higher level of negotiation would be represented by multinational bargaining. However, there have only been a few cases of real
multinational bargaining arrangements (e.g. between the International
Transport Workers Federation and the shipping industry in various countries and in the European recording, radio and television industries).

The other examples that are often cited by some international trade
secretariats correspond more properly to the area of multinational union–
management consultation or to simple exchanges of information.[12]

30. By far the more significant levels of negotiation are the undertaking and
the industry. Each of these levels presents its own advantages and disadvantages which explains why countries usually prefer one or the other. A
historic attachment to the enterprise or industry level also reflects geographic and economic circumstances as well as other factors regarding the
structure of employers' and workers' organisations and the evolution of
labour relations. Smaller countries and relatively homogeneous sectors may
find it convenient to emphasise negotiations covering whole branches of
economic activity. Trade union movements in which the locus of power is at
the top of the organisation have traditionally pushed for industry-wide
bargaining whereas decentralised union structures tend to bring about
enterprise negotiations. Employers' preferences and reluctances have also
contributed to influencing bargaining structures, as could be seen in France
until recently with the development of inter-occupational agreements. In
some countries levels tend also to shift according to the economic conjunc-
ture: in times of prosperity workers and trade unions favour enterprise-level
bargaining so as to maximise their benefits by negotiating directly with
prosperous employers, while in periods of crisis they tend to stress solidarity
and secure minimum levels of protection at the level of a whole branch of
the economy. The law may obviously influence the level of bargaining by
making mandatory or giving priority to negotiations at a certain level. The
preference of most Latin American countries for enterprise level bargaining,
as well as the predominance of industry-wide negotiations in Argentina and
Brazil, were basically the result of the legal approaches contained in the
labour codes. In the case of France the establishment in 1982 of the legal
obligation to negotiate every year in all enterprises where a trade union
representation exists – though not fully implemented yet – has already
brought about a decline of sectoral agreements and an increase in the
number of enterprise agreements which reached 4,850 in 1983.

---

12. H.R. Northrup and Richard L. Rowan, *Multinational Collective Bargaining Attempts*: *The
Record, the Cases and the Prospects*, University of Pennsylvania: The Wharton School,
Industrial Research Unit, 1979.

31. The advantages of negotiating at the local level are apparent. It allows for an adaptation of collective bargaining to the specific needs and circumstances of each enterprise; the parties are thus in a position to agree on a comprehensive set of standards and regulations which would constitute 'the law of the enterprise'. They would also be in charge of administering the provisions that they themselves have created which would presumably lead to greater stability, more effective implementation and mutual understanding. As mentioned earlier, decentralised bargaining also encourages worker participation. It may also signify, however, that on a one-to-one basis unions may at time feel weak or impotent, particularly in a smaller undertaking. Enterprise-level bargaining also entails the need to spread thin the potentialities of the trade union movement in terms of skilful negotiators and adequate preparations. Some studies carried out in Canada and the USA have found that a highly decentralised collective bargaining structure may bring about a greater frequency of strike activity. Finally, fragmented forms of negotiation make it rather difficult to bring considerations of general interest into each and every one of the numerous bargaining exercises that would take place in a country.

32. Negotiations at a higher level make it possible to take account in a more feasible fashion of government economic policies. They also reduce the degree of personal animosity that may obtain in enterprise bargaining and enable trade unions to make a more rational use of their human and financial resources. More importantly, trade union negotiators can pursue more egalitarian objectives and give rise to benefits for all workers, including those employed in small undertakings. A larger coverage is frequently attained, however, at the expense of the quality and quantity of such benefits which are often fixed in the light of the economic capacity of smaller or marginal enterprises. This would inevitably result in a wage drift or in the recognition of the need to supplement industry-wide bargaining with local negotiations.

33. Most European countries have traditionally opted for industry-wide bargaining while Canada, the United States and Japan except for the maritime industry have highlighted enterprise bargaining. Among developing countries preference usually goes to the latter form, although Argentina and Brazil in Latin America, Nigeria, Ghana, Zambia and the French-speaking countries in Africa and a few exceptional cases in Asia (like the plantations sector in Malaysia and Sri Lanka and the steel and coal industries in India) have given priority to industry-wide bargaining.

34. There has in recent times been a trend towards the diversification of bargaining levels.[13] A number of European countries have witnessed the

13. See E. Córdova, 'A Comparative View of Collective Bargaining in Industrialised Countries'. *International Labour Review*, Vol. 117, No. 4, July–August 1978, p. 427.

appearance of new forms of negotiations at the enterprise level, notably in Ireland, Italy, the Netherlands, Sweden and the United Kingdom. In the FR of Germany of the 38,537 agreements registered in 1980, 64 per cent were industry-wide agreements and 36 per cent were enterprise agreements.[14] At the same time, other countries with a decentralised system are moving towards the inception of certain forms of industry-wide bargaining. In the USA the current trend appears to favour consolidations in bargaining, organisational mergers, company-wide bargaining and even industry-wide bargaining in certain sectors (transport, steel, aluminium, automobile, farm implements, etc.)[14bis] There has also been a move towards the growth of national-level negotiations, although they may not always lead to formal agreement. In Belgium, Spain, the UK and several other countries collective bargaining takes place today at all levels. This trend towards the institutionalisation of more than one level of bargaining responds to the recognition of the fact that there are certain questions which lend themselves to specific treatment at different levels, i.e. to local, industry or national discussions. Questions of supplementary social security benefits or over-all wage policy, for instance, seem appropriate for centralised national negotiations. Work schedules or payment by results, on the other hand, should preferably be discussed at the local level.

35. The existence of various levels of negotiation poses a problem of co-ordination between them. There is a need to spell out which issues are going to be discussed at what levels, to foresee the sequence of negotiations and to provide for various types of protection and guarantees. Italy devised in the early 1960s a system of articulated bargaining which sought to co-ordinate the enterprise, industry and national levels; in 1983 a tripartite basic agreement established procedures governing the different negotiating levels. Sweden and other Scandinavian countries have also developed some techniques of articulated bargaining which apply largely to the national and industry levels. Both experiences have relied on successive delegations of authority as a means of ensuring an appropriate distribution of competence. Such an objective presupposes a measure of centralisation and self-discipline in the trade union movement as well as a widespread acceptance of the peace obligation and the criteria for distribution of competence. These conditions are not easy to meet and this may account for the limited success of the said experiences. One should not forget, however, that the alternative to an effective co-ordination of bargaining levels is a return to one-level bargaining or an admission that any matter can be discussed at any level.

14. F. Furstenberg, 'Recent Trends in Collective Bargaining in the Federal Republic of Germany,' *International Labour Review*, 1984, p. 620.

14bis. Stephen G. Peitchinis, *Issues in Management-Labor Relations in the 1990s*. (New York, St. Martin Press, 1985), pp. 47–48.

VII. THE BARGAINING PROCESS

36. As collective bargaining grows, and its repercussions acquire greater dimensions, rules and procedures are developed to govern its process, which thus becomes more complex and institutionalised. A full-fledged process of negotiations usually nowadays includes six different stages:

 (i) the definition of the appropriate bargaining unit;
 (ii) the mutual recognition of the parties;
(iii) the preparation and submission of demands;
(iv) the actual conduct of negotiations;
 (v) the conclusion of the agreement; and
(vi) its registration.

In certain countries there is an additional step appearing towards the end of the bargaining process, but before registration, namely the ratification of the agreement. Some of these stages are carefully regulated in many countries by law so as to provide for an institutional framework within which collective bargaining can be carried out in an orderly fashion. In other countries, which refrain from any legislative regulation of collective bargaining, there are nevertheless some commonly accepted rules established by basic agreement or by tradition. Only in some developing countries, where collective bargaining is still at an incipient stage, is the process of negotiations conducted in a rudimentary and unstructured manner.

37. Identifying an appropriate bargaining unit is an indispensable preliminary step, although the importance attached to this determination varies considerably from country to country. In a few industrialised and developing countries where collective bargaining takes place at the undertaking level this is done in a rather formal fashion as part of the representation procedures.. A special board is vested with authority to determine the appropriate bargaining unit and criteria are developed to guide its rulings. The three basic rules that have traditionally been used by the US National Labor Relations Board, for instance, are:

 (i) the desires of the parties;
 (ii) the bargaining history; and
(iii) the commonality of interests.

In other countries, however, no formal procedures are set forth in this respect and the determination of the bargaining unit is simply the result of customary practices or tacit understanding based on the structure of trade unions and employers' organisations.

38. Another preliminary step is represented by the employers' recognition of the workers' organisation concerned. Such recognition is usually based on certain proof of representativeness and should be distinguished from the registration of unions for the acquisition of legal personality, which is usually made in the labour ministry or some other government office and requires only the fulfilment of minimum requirements.

Four major systems or recognition for bargaining purposes are discernible in comparative labour legislation, namely:
  (i) exclusive bargaining representation for the majority union (e.g. Canada, the Philippines, Trinidad and Tobago and the United States);
  (ii) non-exclusive bargaining rights accorded to the most representative unions (Belgium, the Netherlands);
  (iii) multiple representation of various unions on the basis of a joint negotiating committee (Spain and Ecuador); and
  (iv) multiple representation of various units with concurrent bargaining rights (Japan).[15]
Because multiple representation entails more difficult and time-consuming negotiations as well as the possible adoption of different conditions of employment for a similar group of workers and a complex administration of the agreement, the trend is, particularly in countries with enterprise-level bargaining, to move away from multiple representation towards exclusive bargaining rights.

39. Several procedures, both mandatory and voluntary, have been established to ascertain the representative character of a union. Mandatory procedures are established by law, mainly in countries where exclusive bargaining representation or most representative systems have been introduced. They rely heavily on elections by secret ballot or evidence of substantial membership support (usually the majority of workers or voters concerned, although lower and higher percentages are also known). Other criteria may also be used, including an appraisal of the experience, independence and stability of the union. In some countries, independent agencies have been set up to handle representation cases, while in others this task is performed by the ministry of labour or the labour courts. It should be added that according to ILO standards the determination by public authorities of the union entitled to negotiate should be based on 'pre-established and objective criteria'.

Voluntary procedures set out in basic agreements or codes of discipline have also been tried by a number of countries but with limited success.

40. The need for appropriate representation procedures is particularly evident in countries where multiplicity of unions is acute and bargaining takes place at the enterprise level. While multiplicity means that workers have a choice between different unions, it also means problems of inter-union and intra-union rivalry as well as possible recognition strikes, all of which may harm sound collective bargaining. Enterprise-level bargaining entails, in turn, a more direct challenge to the authority of individual managers, who may be more inclined to resist the recognition of bargaining rights to several unions than employers' organisations.

15. See A. Gladstone and M. Ozaki, 'Trade Union Recognition for Collective Bargaining Purposes', *International Labour Review*, Vol. 112, Nos. 2–3, August–Sepember 1975.

41. Although the bargaining process is not an entirely rational exercise, as we shall see later, efforts are being made in many countries by both parties to devote greater attention to preparations for bargaining, to collect and collate background information, and to produce suitable lists of demands and counterproposals. Union demands are usually discussed first at general meetings of the local union or at higher councils of union delegates, then analysed by the officials in charge of conducting the negotiations, who may sometimes decide to resubmit them to a general meeting before their final presentation to the employer. Some unions in industrialised countries avail themselves of computerised information with a view to detecting trends in negotiations or ascertaining comparisons with other groups. Others approach collective bargaining in a more empirical and sometimes improvised fashion. Employers proceed, in turn, to cost out economic and non-economic demands and possible counterproposals to compare current and projected agreements costs to devise appropriate bargaining strategies.

42. The actual process of bargaining is governed in some countries by a set of ground rules or procedures aimed at providing for the orderly development of negotiations. Two institutional models seem to emerge from the experience of industrialised countries. One is the model followed by some Western European countries with industry-wide bargaining which tends to emphasise the importance of *machinery* and the other is the North American type which pays particular attention to *procedures*.

43. The European approach has resulted, for instance, in the creation of permanent bilateral bodies (e.g. joint committees in Belgium, employee–labour conferences in Ireland, the Foundation of Labour in the Netherlands and the joint industrial councils in the United Kingdom) entitled to settle wages and other conditions of employment and to fix their own procedural rules. The American model, which has been followed by several developing countries, is based on two major pillars: the duty to bargain in good faith and the prohibition of unfair labour practices. While the latter presupposes a specific enunciation of certain types of conduct which are deemed to militate against collective bargaining, the former is a somewhat vaguer notion that usually requires further elaboration by the courts or the enforcement agencies. In the USA the good-faith bargaining duty was advanced as early as 1921 in a case submitted to the Railway Labor Board. As developed by the Taft-Hartley Act and the decisions of the NLRB, bargaining in good faith would include at least four duties: the duty to meet and confer at reasonable intervals; the duty to engage in meaningful discussions over all negotiable issues; the duty to show the reason why certain demands cannot be accepted; and the duty to make counterproposals. It may be noted that elements of the duty to bargain in good faith have slipped into the legislation of other industrialised countries, e.g. Japan, Luxemburg and Spain, and have influenced the labour relations law of many developing countries.

44. An important additional component of the duty to bargain in good faith is the provision of information. What was regarded in the past as a management prerogative or a procedural matter to be discussed prior to actual negotiations is now considered as an employer's obligation and sometimes also as a union's duty. The USA was the first country to introduce the notion that bargaining in good faith involved the duty to provide the other party with certain information necessary for meaningful negotiations. However, this applied mostly to the information needed by the union to prepare its wage proposals. A more complete definition of this duty was contained in the Civil Service Reform Act of 1978 which refers to the information "which is reasonably available for full and proper discussion, understanding and negotiation of subjects within the scope of collective bargaining". The two other countries where disclosure of information for collective bargaining purposes has developed in the most advanced fashion are Sweden (1976 Act on Joint Regulation of Working Life) and the UK (The Employment Protection Act, 1975). Belgium has a sophisticated system of periodic and ad hoc information but as indicated in another chapter of this book this information is provided to the works council. Although the principle is still far from being universally accepted, it can also be found in the legislation of a few developing countries (Jamaica, Tanzania and Zambia) and has reached international recognition through the OECD Guidelines for Multinational Enterprises (1976), the 1977 ILO Tripartite Declaration of Principles concerning Multinational Enterprises and Social Policy and the above mentioned Recommendation 163 concerning the Promotion of Collective Bargaining. The latter instrument indicates that 'public and private employers should, at the request of workers' organisations, make available such information as is necessary on the economic and social situation of the negotiation unit and the undertaking as a whole, to the extent to which its disclosure is not prejudicial to the undertaking'.

45. Beyond legal requirements and established procedures, collective bargaining is a complex relationship based on power, reason, tactical skills and sometimes even emotional factors. The threat of a strike or a lockout acts, no doubt, as one of the moving forces behind negotiations. The parties are accordingly forced to make constant comparisons between the economic significance of the concessions they will have to make or the demands they may obtain and the cost of disagreement. Their behaviour is also guided to a certain extent by the degree of maturity of the existing labour–management relations. Where the parties feel that they are placed in a purely adversarial position, their reaction would differ sharply from that which characterises the more integrative and co-operative relationships.

46. Irrespective of these limitations, employers and trade unions use different tactics and techniques in order to minimise sacrifices and maximise possible advantages. Bluffing, haggling, formulating over-inflated demands, hard bargaining, package deal offers, and splitting the difference, are some of the most common tactical approaches used by the parties. Such practices must, however, be attuned in some countries to a statutory duty to bargain in good faith and/or to court decisions concerning the nature and scope of such a duty.

47. Since most negotiations are initiated by the union, collective bargaining discussions concentrate as a rule on the union's list of demands, and eventually on the employer's counterproposals. These two elements provide the basis for the drafting of the agreement once an accord is reached. Given the scope and complexity of the issues nowadays involved in collective bargaining, agreements are normally made out in writing. Some legislation (e.g. Denmark, Japan and the UK) still permits the conclusion of verbal collective agreements but this is a rather exceptional practice. In fact, many collective agreements in large undertakings are now printed documents. Provision is made in some countries for the distribution of copies of the agreement among the workers concerned or for other appropriate forms of dissemination of information about its contents.

48. Submission of the agreement for ratification by the workers concerned is a relatively frequent occurrence in Canada and the USA and to a lesser extent in Japan and the UK. Ratification seems more feasible in countries where enterprise-level bargaining prevails, which explains why it is less common in continental European countries, although there are cases of negotiations subject to a referendum in Belgium (by a national committee of union delegates), Finland, the FR Germany and Switzerland. Nor is ratification foreseen in the majority of trade union constitutions in developing countries, despite their preference for enterprise-level bargaining. In the USA the rate of rejection of agreements subject to ratification fluctuates considerably but can be estimated, as an average, at around 10 per cent. In several countries there has recently been an increase in the frequency of employee refusals to ratify agreements. Among the reasons advanced to explain this increase the most important ones seem to be the failure of union leaders to communicate effectively the terms of the proposed agreements, internal union politics and dissatisfaction of special groups of workers within the organisation. In developing countries the chief reason relates to the gap between rising expectations and deteriorating economic realities.

49. The process of bargaining generally concludes with the registration of the agreement in the ministry of labour, an industrial or labour court, or other government office. Registration is in some countries a mere formality provided for in the law for statistical purposes or to facilitate proof of the existence and content of the agreement. In a number of countries, registration has a more substantive implication and is made following a verification of the content of the agreement in the light of legal requirements concerning the inclusion of certain mandatory clauses and the compatibility of the agreement with public law provisions or the minimum standards of protection. Concern for development and inflation problems have given rise, particularly in some developing countries, to a third type of registration in which government authorities check also on the conformity of the agreement with existing wages and incomes policy.

VIII. CONTENT OF AGREEMENTS

50. The content of agreements is obviously determined by the scope of negotiable issues, i.e. the definition by law or basic agreement of the areas liable to be jointly regulated by the parties. Within those limits, the content of agreements is influenced by various forces which are sometimes simultaneously at work. Union pressures to expand the scope of collective bargaining are frequently counterbalanced by employers' resistance and their attachment to management prerogatives. Governments seem to play an ambivalent role, sometimes favouring an expansion of collective bargaining by providing that certain subjects should be the object of negotiations and sometimes pre-empting the domain of collective bargaining by enacting an extensive protective labour legislation.

Economic factors can force the parties to respond in their negotiations to new challenges and changing conditions but they may also restrict the scope of collective bargaining by pushing governments to take some questions off the bargaining table.

51. In the long run, however, there is a trend towards the expansion of the content of collective agreements. Management prerogatives have increasingly been eroded by trade union power; experience has also shown that many questions affecting the management and operation of the undertaking are virtually indistinguishable from working conditions. In Japan, for instance, it is generally admitted that in principle employers have the obligation to bargain about all aspects of managerial decisions affecting conditions of employment. Sweden established in 1976 a primary duty to bargain which made practically everything negotiable. In the United States, the distinction between mandatory, permissible and prohibited subjects of negotiation has actually worked in favour of a constant expansion of the content of the agreements.

52. What was thus originally limited to 'wages, hours and other terms and conditions of employment' has come today to include a broad range of questions. At the level of the undertaking, for instance, one can easily find collective agreement clauses dealing with the following questions:
   (i) preliminary provisions concerning the identification of the parties, the bargaining unit and the groups excluded from the agreement;
   (ii) working conditions dealing with the wage and effort bargaining (wages, hours of work, rest periods, vacation, night work, overtime, etc.);

   (iii) other terms and conditions directly relevant to the employment relationship (recruitment, job security, manning levels, seniority, training,
etc.);

   (iv) management questions indirectly affecting conditions of employment
(subcontracting, investments, changes of technology, etc.);

   (v) provision of social services, welfare measures and other matters affecting the workers' conditions of life (canteens, recreation, transportation
etc.);

   (vi) social security provisions (sick leave, complementary retirement
benefits, maternity leave, etc.);

   (vii) other fringe benefits including dependents' allowances, Christmas
bonuses, medical and dental plans;

 (viii) quality of life matters, including physical working conditions and
participation;

   (ix) regulation of relations between the contracting parties (peace obligation, management prerogatives, union security, duration of the agreement, etc.);

   (x) provisions regarding the administration of agreements (grievance procedure and rules concerning the interpretation of their clauses.

Obviously, not all these questions are always found in the same document; specific agreements are sometimes devoted to one or several of the
subject matters listed in numbers (ii) to (x). Industry-wide and national-level
bargaining have also expanded to cover nowadays such matters as the
organisation of the labour market, vocational training, the avoidance and
settlement of industrial disputes, and macro-economic trade-offs regarding
employment and the over-all level of wages.

53. Parallel to the trend towards expanding the content of agreements,
industrialised countries have recently witnessed a shift from wage increases
and other material benefits to questions of job security, quality of life and
the promotion of workers' participation. Non-economic benefits and further
involvement in management decisions are thus gaining momentum at the
expense of more traditional clauses. Collective bargaining is thus ceasing to
be considered as an alternative to other forms of workers' participation
(works councils and representation on company boards, for instance) and is
gradually becoming a means of promoting them.

54. These quantitative and qualitative changes in the context of agreements
have been brought about by the dynamic nature of collective bargaining and
its capacity to innovate and evolve according to changing circumstances. The
net result of this process is that agreements have evolved from simple
documents specifying a wage scale and hours of work into much more
complex, elaborate and voluminous documents.

55. Although the variety of subjects now dealt with in collective agreements
does not lend itself to clear-cut classification, some attempts have been

made to group them in distinct categories. The more generally accepted classification distinguishes two major groups: the normative and the contractual clauses. Normative clauses refer to the terms and conditions of work which must be observed in all the individual employment contracts in the enterprise or industry concerned. Within a given bargaining unit they are the equivalent of substantive legislative provisions at the national level. Their purpose is to provide standards of protection and advancement to individual workers. Contractual clauses (also known as obligatory clauses) include all provisions spelling out rights and duties of the parties to the agreement. They tend to provide greater stability to labour relations and have acted both as a counterpart and a driving force to the expansion of normative clauses.

56. It may be noted, however, that contractual provisions, such as union security or check-off clauses, may also have normative effects as they establish a triangular relationship implying rights and duties for individual workers as well as the contracting parties. There are also other clauses frequently found in recent agreements, e.g. protection of the environment, organisation of social services and participation rights which are in fact neither normative nor contractual. This realisation has prompted some experts to propose the addition of new categories of clauses, including institutional clauses (to cover union security and check-off). In the UK the Donovan Commission proposed in 1968 to distinguish between substantive and procedural clauses (to include in the latter grievance procedures and provisions regarding duration and renewal of agreements). Others have tried to distinguish between economic, social, union-related and general provisions. It may be safer, however, to conclude that the normative-contractual classification, first popularised in the 1920s by German scholars, is still relevant and useful but cannot pretend to cover all the different modalities now contained in the practice of collective agreements.[16]

57. While collective agreements have spearheaded numerous significant improvements in substantive labour law, the impact of its innovative character is at least equally visible in respect to the contractual provisions. Two of these provisions have in fact had far-reaching effects in the practice of industrial relations: the peace obligation and the union security arrangements.

58. The peace obligation has been regarded by some experts as a natural effect of collective bargaining, agreements of fixed duration, which are supposed to bring stability to labour relations and put an end during the term of the agreement to all the various issues that have arisen between the parties. There are, however, two kinds of peace obligation: the absolute one which obliges the parties to refrain from all sorts of industrial action during the period of validity of the agreement and the relative peace obligation which limits such obligation to the matters dealt with in the agreement. The

16. Although Hueck and Nipperday had already foreseen the existence of some 'normative collective' clauses; see *Lehrbuch des Arbeitsrechts*, Berlin and Frankfurt, 1963.

absolute peace obligation is less frequent than the relative one and would require a specific clause to that effect. It has nevertheless been used with considerable success in Switzerland since 1937. The relative peace obligation, included in the law in Austria and the FR Germany and in many collective agreements in a number of other countries, offers trade unions the advantage of safeguarding their right to formulate new demands if and when substantive changes in the socio-economic environment have taken place.

Although both clauses have made an important contribution to the development of industrial relations, their application presupposes a measure of internal discipline and has encountered some difficulties in cases where large groups of workers engage in unauthorised action and the employer requests the union to initiate disciplinary action against them. Moreover, in a number of countries including France and Italy, peace obligation clauses are seldom included in collective agreements as they are regarded as a limitation of the right of strike.

59. Union security arrangements appeared in countries where trade unions confronted serious difficulties of recognition and survival. They aimed at obtaining certain guarantees and facilities *vis-à-vis* the employer and at overcoming the apathy of certain groups of workers or the particular characteristics of certain labour markets where turnover was frequent or the work force dispersed. Two variants developed in this connection: while some clauses sought to strengthen unions by making membership a condition of employment (closed shop and union shop), others provided for a compulsory payment of union contributions (agency shop and compulsory check-off). These clauses developed mainly in the UK, USA and other English-speaking countries. More recently, however, union security arrangements have been introduced in some developing countries and have experienced a change in their rationale, which relates now to the recognition of the important functions that unions perform in modern societies, particularly as collective bargaining agents. However, as discussed in chapter 9, union security arrangements are regarded in other countries as an infringement of the freedom not to belong to a union and many existing legal provisions limit or prohibit their use.

IX. Effects of the Agreement

60. While in some countries the effects of agreements are still limited, at least in theory, to workers affiliated to the union on whose behalf they were concluded, in the great majority of countries a specific law or established practice has determined that collective agreements are applicable to all workers in the bargaining unit. Already in 1951, ILO Recommendation No. 91 pointed out that the stipulation of a collective agreement 'should apply to all workers of the classes concerned employed in the undertakings covered by the agreement, unless the agreement specifically provides to the contrary'.[17]

17. Article III, 4.

61. This general acceptance of the '*erga omnes*' effect of agreements was due, in part, to the recognition in labour law doctrine of their special nature and also, in part, to the realisation that if employers were to limit the application of the agreement to union members, they would be either indirectly promoting unionisation or fostering the collapse of the union, or establishing embarrassing discrimination in their treatment of personnel.

62. The situation is different with respect to non-signatory employers who are not deemed to be bound by the agreement unless they are members of the employers' organisation concerned or voluntarily decide to adhere to the provisions of the agreement. Even if an employer belongs to the contracting organisation, there must be a relevant provision in its by-laws or a special authorisation empowering the organisation to bargain on his behalf.

63. A number of European countries (e.g. Austria, Belgium, Denmark, France, FR Germany, Spain, and Switzerland), as well as several Latin American and most French-speaking African countries, have nevertheless devised a procedure of extension of collective agreements, whereby workers and employers who do not belong to the contracting organisations but who belong to the sector of activity covered by the agreement, may be bound by its provisions, provided that certain requirements be met. The original rationale of this procedure was the need to avoid unfair competition from non-unionised enterprises; however, other considerations regarding the promotion of collective bargaining and the pursuit of more egalitarian and solidaristic goals were later taken into account.

64. Extension procedures generally start with a meeting convened by the ministry of labour, on its own initiative or, more frequently, on the request of representative unions. Employers' and workers' organisations affected by the proposed extension are invited to attend the meeting and to make observations on the suitability and implications of the extension.

Extension orders are issued by the minister only when the agreement or agreements in force already cover a substantial proportion of employers and workers in the industry or trade concerned and when they include a minimum of substantive provisions. In some countries, additional proof is required in respect of the difficulties confronted by the workers to negotiate an agreement in the enterprises or industries to which the extension would apply.

X. DURATION OF AGREEMENTS

65. Collective agreements can be concluded for a fixed or indefinite duration. Agreements of indefinite duration refer, for the most part, to the basic or procedural kinds of agreements, although there may also be some ordinary substantive agreements of indefinite duration, usually with a renewal clause. Whatever their nature, most legislation provides that a collective agreement of indefinite duration can always be terminated by giving advance notice of termination.

66. The period of validity of collective agreements of fixed duration is sometimes governed by legal provisions setting forth minimum and maximum limits. The former respond to the need to provide for a measure of stability and certainty in the labour–management relationship. The latter take account of possible one-sided bargaining relationships in which the employer may succeed in fixing an excessively long duration likely to frustrate the *raison d'être* of collective bargaining. Minimum limits are normally set at one year. Maximum limits range in industrialised countries from three years (New Zealand) or four years (Finland) to five years (France as regards job classification).

67. While there has been a secular trend towards longer contracts, the average duration of agreements is likely to experience some changes in accordance with economic circumstances. In periods of prosperity, agreements tend to be of shorter duration, as unions seek to exploit more frequently the greater ability to pay of employers. In periods of crisis, workers' organisations prefer to obtain longer-term guarantees and protection. Inflation also affects the duration of agreements since it introduces an element of uncertainty and the need to catch up with increases in the cost of living, all of which result in shorter periods of validity.

68. The average currency of collective agreements in industrialised and developing countries should now be estimated at around two years. Where longer periods of validity prevail, it is customary to insert appropriate clauses for reopening wage negotiations after one or two years. In Mexico it is the law which prescribes that wage clauses should be revised every year. In FR Germany collective agreements are normally for one year if they involve wages and of longer duration if they concern other matters.

In the UK collective bargaining resolutions are open-ended to all issues, which are settled as they arise. In contrast, in the USA, outside the railroad and airline industries, collective agreements are for a specific duration usually ranging from one to three years. In 1985 fifty per cent of the agreements were for three years.

XI. Administration of the Agreement

69. The period of validity of an agreement is also the period of its administration. Once the quasi-legislative functions are over, there is room for some administrative and judicial activities. Many substantive provisions of the agreement hardly require any administration as they are automatically incorporated into the individual contracts of employment. But other clauses may provide for the setting up of committees in charge of certain functions concerning job classification, safety and health, promotions, etc., or for the joint administration of social services.

Some disputes may also arise over the interpretatio
certain clauses and this would require a system of intern
cedures. The North American practice of collective barg
developing in this connection some sophisticated proced
of grievances which were later extended to other coun
tional level the ILO adopted in 1967 Recommendatio̶n̶ ..̶
the Examination of Grievances within the Undertaking which contaɪɪɪ
general principles thereon. Grievance procedures involve different levels of
internal discussions in which individual workers and representative of the
parties to the agreement seek to settle the disputes. A settlement reached
jointly by the worker and management representatives is generally regarded
as final and binding.

70. Failure of the parties to reach agreement at the conciliatory or internal
stages of a grievance procedure leads in the North American model to
grievance arbitration, i.e. final and impartial determination by a private
arbitrator. Some 90 per cent of all collective agreements in the USA make
provision for grievance arbitration which has been regarded as 'one of the
outstanding success areas of USA industrial relations'.[18]

Outside Canada and the USA, private arbitration is practised *inter alia* in
Jamaica, Malaysia, New Zealand, Panama, the Philippines and Zambia.
The majority of other countries have followed the European model of
enforcement which entrusts the interpretation and implementation of agreements to labour courts or in some instances to ordinary courts.

Individual workers and trade unions can appear directly before the court
and sue for the implementation of normative provisions. Employers and
trade unions are also entitled to claim damages in connection with contractual provisions. On some rare occasions each organisation may sue its own
members for not observing the agreement. The European approach does
not preclude, however, prior attempts at a direct settlement of the dispute.
In Italy, for instance, the large majority of cases arising from the interpretation and implementation of collective agreements are settled through conciliation, either following a grievance procedure or before the tripartite
commissions attached to the labour offices.

XII. Collective Bargaining and Economic Problems and Policies

71. Collective bargaining was conceived for the defence of sectoral and
group interests. Neither employers' nor workers' organisations are supposed
to have direct responsibility for the protection of the general interest,
although they would probably prefer not to harm it in their negotiations.
Governments, on their part, may include the promotion of collective bargaining among its social objectives, but must give priority to their primary
obligation concerning the safeguarding of the public interest. This initial
divergence of objective may obviously lead to some conflicts between the

18. G. Strauss and P. Feuille, 'Industrial Relations Research in the United States', in Peter B.
Doeringer, ed. *Industrial Relations in International Perspective*, London, 1981, p. 114.

tcome of collective bargaining and the economic policies set out by government. Such conflicts become particularly acute in periods of economic crisis and may reach serious dimensions when both inflation and unemployment appear as important elements of the crisis.

72. Generally speaking, there are three possible ways of avoiding conflicts between collective bargaining and economic policies:
(1) the parties themselves may seek to exert moderation in their negotiations;
(2) governments may decide to take unilateral action using its fiscal, monetary or incomes policies;
(3) governments, employers and trade unions may join forces and try to work out some appropriate responses to their sectoral and national problems.

73. The first solution has been frequently tried in a number of industrialised and developing countries. The parties usually respond to the dual challenge of inflation and government concern for economic stability by, *inter alia*, stipulating wage indexation provisions, exerting moderation and restraint in their wage negotiations, stressing non-economic demands and linking wage cuts to reductions in the price of the products. Responses to unemployment problems have also included a variety of formulas including: reduction in hours of work, promotion of early retirement and part-time employment, control of overtime, increases in vacation periods, and internal transfers and re-adjustments. Experience shows, however, that faced with accelerated inflation and massive unemployment, these measures can only provide limited and temporary relief. There are also serious difficulties of implementation and co-ordination, particularly when collective bargaining is limited and temporary relief; moreover, some forms of wage indexation have frequently been accused of fueling inflation. There are also serious difficulties of implementation and co-ordination, particularly when collective bargaining is decentralised and the trade union movement is divided according to ideological lines.

74. Government efforts to reconcile collective bargaining with its own economic policies include a full range of approaches, some voluntary such as exhortations, voluntary guidelines and using the public sector as a means of setting examples, and others of a statutory nature, like fixing wage ceilings, ordering a wage freeze, providing for wage indexation or seeking to control wage movements and sometimes other incomes and prices by legislation or executive action. The most important and controversial are, of course, the statutory ones and more specifically the income policies. Although they have sometimes been effective during short periods, the experience of some countries shows that the temporary suppression of inflation is frequently followed by periods of wages explosion. It is also generally agreed that incomes policy cannot be successfully operated without the support of employers' and workers' organisations. While trade unions tend to reject any attempt to impose only wage controls, without similar control over

prices, governments have found if difficult to operate an effective supervision of prices.

75. There is, finally, the problem of a possible violation of the principle of free collective bargaining. It should be noted in this regard that the ILO Committee on Freedom of Association has considered that 'where intervention by the public authorities is essentially for the purpose of ensuring that the negotiating parties subordinate their interests to the national economic policy pursued by the government, irrespective of whether they agree with that policy or not, this is not compatible with the generally accepted principles' in the field of freedom of association.[19]

As regards more particularly the problem of government influence on wage fixing, the Committee has also recalled on several occasions in recent years that 'if, as part of its stabilisation policy, a government considers that wage rates cannot be settled freely through collective bargaining, such a restriction should be enforced as an exceptional measure and only to the extent that is necessary, without exceeding a reasonable period, and it should be accompanied by adequate safeguards to protect workers' living standards'.[20]

76. The relative failure of the voluntary approaches and the shortcomings of the statutory measures have led some governments to seek agreements or understandings with employers' and workers' organisations with a view to limiting the inflationary impact of collective bargaining or to make it more compatible with economic policies in general.

The appearance of national tripartite agreements has also been prompted by the realisation of the potentialities that joint efforts by the three social partners might present to tackle economic problems.

77. National agreements to which the government is also a party in addition to employers' and workers' organisations usually contain a series of trade-offs intended to avoid unacceptable or uncompensated sacrifices on the part of anyone of the social partners. Some of these agreements limit themselves to the fight against inflation, e.g. the 1972 Dutch agreement and the Finnish agreement of 1974 and subsequent years. Others have sought broader aims, including increasing employment, combating price rises and helping low-paid workers. The 1980 and 1981 Irish National Understanding for Economic and Social Development, for instance, embraced policies on employment, pay, taxation, education, health and social welfare.

More recent tripartite agreements concluded in Italy in 1983 and 1984 and Spain in 1984 have sought to control inflation by limiting the application of wage indexation (Italy) or setting the parameters of wage increases (Spain). The Spanish 1984 Economic and Social Agreement, intended to be applied in 1985 and 1986 included provisions on investments, fiscal policies, job creation and the conduct of industrial relations. As noted by a recent

19. ILO, *Freedom of Association*, Digest of Decisions of the Freedom of Association Committee of the Governing Body of the ILO (Geneva, 1976), paragraph 284.
20. *Ibid.*, paragraph 288.

publication 'a common denominator of tripartite approaches was the recognition of the need to combine industrial relations and non-industrial relations elements as a means of alleviating or diminishing the economic crisis'.[21]

78. The co-ordination of collective bargaining and government policies can also take place outside the negotiation of formal agreements, through the discussions that are held in tripartite informal bodies such as the Contact Committee in Norway, the Concerted Action Mechanism in the Federal Republic of Germany, the Wage and Price Committee in Austria and the Labour–Management Round Table (Sanrokon practice) in Japan. This approach corresponds to the broad meaning of collective bargaining mentioned at the beginning of this chapter, and represents a relatively mild form of government intervention, particularly in comparison with the practice of some developing countries where collective agreements are sometimes supposed to follow the specific wage adjustments periodically fixed by government (some Latin American countries) or to observe general guidelines on wage policy laid down by a tripartite body (Singapore) or their validity is subject to approval by an industrial court or some other government agency in charge of ascertaining whether the content of the agreement is in conformity with established economic policies (Kenya, Nigeria and Trinidad and Tobago). Whatever the degree of government intervention, all these recent developments point, no doubt, to a trend towards the appearance of new forms of *tripartism* in the conduct of collective bargaining relationships. They also mean that the narrow meaning of collective bargaining, i.e. the negotiation of formal agreements, is bound to be increasingly influenced by the broad forms of preliminary, tripartite collective bargaining discussions.

79. In recent years a combination of monetary, fiscal and social policies which, as a rule, include elements of wage moderation, has succeeded in lowering the levels of inflation in most industrialised countries. Some of them are even approaching a deflationary situation. However, the level of unemployment is still high in the majority of these countries. Attempts to reduce unemployment rates through a variety of statutory and collective bargaining approaches, as the solidarity contracts in France and Italy and the flexibilisation policies instituted in these and other European countries, have met with rather limited success.

While inflation has ceased to be a major problem in most industrialised countries, price instability and even hyper inflation continue to rage in number of developing countries. In Argentina, Bolivia, Brazil and Peru, where inflation reached three or four digits, drastic measures consisting of devaluation and change of currency coupled with the freezing of wages and prices, were adopted in 1985 and 1986 to avoid economic catastrophe. Although the results of these policies have initially been satisfactory, inflation is resurfacing in Argentina, difficulties have arisen in connection with the control of prices in Brazil and Bolivia and doubts remain as to the

21. ILO, *Collective Bargaining: A Response to the Recession in Industrialised Market Economy Countries* (Geneva, 1984), p. 3.

long-run efficacy of the restrictive measures. This fact, coupled with the high levels of unemployment, seems to indicate that wage controls are not in themselves enough to combat inflation and unemployment whose root causes are complex and multifarious. It is generally believed today that collective bargaining may contribute to transmit or perpetuate an inflationary process started elsewhere in the economy but that it rarely constitutes its main determining factor.

SELECT BIBLIOGRAPHY

John P. Windmuller, *Collective Bargaining in Industrialised Market Economies*, Geneva, ILO 1976.

E. Córdova, 'A Comparative View of Collective Bargaining in Industrialised Countries,' *International Labour Review*, Vol. 117, No. 4, July–August 1978.

ILO, *Promotion of Collective Bargaining*, Report V (1) (Geneva, 1979).

OECD, *Collective Bargaining and Government Economic Policies*, Paris, 1979.

Chapter 16. Settlement of Disputes over Rights

B. Aaron

I. GENERAL CLASSIFICATION OF SYSTEMS FOR SETTLING DISPUTES OVER RIGHTS

1. This chapter deals with various procedures for the settlement of disputes in the private sector over rights, which are also referred to in different countries as grievances or legal disputes. This type of dispute is to be distinguished from conflicts over interests, sometimes called social or economic conflicts, which are dealt with in chapter 17.

As the term implies, disputes over rights involve the interpretation or application of existing rights created by statutes, individual contracts of employment or collective bargaining agreements; theoretically, at least, they are not concerned with efforts to achieve rights that concededly are not presently in being. However, the line between disputes over rights and conflicts over interests is not always an impregnable wall; rather, it sometimes is more analogous to a semi-permeable membrane, through which disputes that are nominally of one type pass and are handled under procedures usually reserved for disputes of the other type. Thus, in certain contexts conflicts of interests are disposed of through grievance and arbitration procedures supposedly reserved for disputes over rights, whereas the processes of conciliation and mediation, which in some countries are primarily employed in conflicts of interests, are in other countries routinely applied to disputes over rights.

2. Although the organisation, jurisdiction, composition, and procedures of labour disputes-settlement mechanisms vary widely in minor details throughout the world, they can be subsumed under a relatively few systems of disputes settlement: labour courts; industrial tribunals; administrative agencies; organs of arbitration; and ordinary courts. Each has been developed to a relatively advanced degree in one or more countries. The distinction between ordinary courts and labour courts is, of course, self-evident. The distinction between labour courts and organs of arbitration is more complex. The principal difference is that the arbitration process is not self-enforcing; in the absence of voluntary compliance the injured party must turn to the courts for relief or rely upon self-help. In addition, the parties generally play a role in determining the composition of arbitral tribunals. Other differences relate to the jurisdiction and procedures of labour courts, industrial tribunals, and administrative agencies, on the one hand, and arbitral tribunals on the other.

3. This chapter focuses primarily upon a few countries in which a particular mechanism for the settlement of disputes over rights has been highly developed.

4. Most countries make use of more than one procedure for the settlement of disputes over rights. To mention a few conspicuous examples, the labour-court countries of the FR Germany and Sweden also permit, in varying degrees, resort by the parties to arbitration; Britain, which also may be classified as a labour-court country, provides a rich variety of mechanisms, including organs of conciliation, mediation, and arbitration, as well as industrial tribunals, for the resolution of rights created both by statutes and by private agreements; and the USA, although relying almost exclusively on private, consensual arbitration of grievances, also has elaborate administrative and judicial mechanisms for adjudication of certain statutory rights.

II. Labour Courts and Industrial Tribunals

A. *Brief Description of the Respective Systems*

5. Among the countries of the world, labour courts appear to be the most common mechanism used for the settlement of disputes over rights. This is particularly true in Western Europe, where labour costs play major roles in the disputes-settlement procedures of Austria, Belgium, Denmark, the FR Germany, Finland, Norway, Spain, Sweden, and Britain. They are also found in Switzerland and Turkey. Varieties of labour courts (although bearing different names) exist in the socialist countries of Eastern Europe: Bulgaria, Czechoslovakia, GDR, Hungary, Poland, and the USSR. Outside Europe, labour courts have been established in many Latin American countries, including Argentina, Brazil, Colombia, Mexico, Uruguay, as well as in Israel and other Middle Eastern countries, and in a number of African and Asian countries.

6. In all of the labour-court countries there are statutory requirements of eligibility to serve both as professional judges or as lay judges. The required qualifications of the judges differ widely among countries.

Generally, the lay representatives, variously called wingmen or assessors, are either appointed by some government official from lists of nominees prepared by their respective organisations, or are elected by their constituencies. In most cases they are expected to decide objectively and in a non-partisan fashion; they cannot represent the interests of the parties to the dispute in terms of their organisation.

7. In many countries labour courts have jurisdiction only of disputes over rights; in others the jurisdiction encompasses, either explicitly or implicitly, both disputes over rights and conflicts over interests.

Similar variations are found in the jurisdiction of individual and collective disputes. In some countries the formal jurisdiction of the labour courts is limited to collective disputes, that is, between employers and unions as entities.

8. French labour courts (*conseils de prud'hommes*) are essentially bipartite. The judges (*conseillers*) are elected representatives of employers and of employees, in equal numbers. Each labour court has five sections, devoted respectively to industry, commerce, agriculture, miscellaneous occupations, and *cadres*, a group generally defined as upper-level supervisory, technical, or managerial employees, who hold positions of high responsibility in the enterprise.

9. Decisions of French labour courts are made by majority vote. In case of a tie, another meeting is held in which a judge from the *tribunal d'instance*, the local regular court composed of a single professional judge, participates. If the regular members of the court deadlock again, he casts the deciding vote.

10. The labour courts of the FR Germany are tripartite. The local courts and the appellate courts usually consist of one or more panels, each composed of two knowledgeable lay judges (*Richter*), and one professional judge. The Federal Labour Court (*Bundesarbeitsgericht*) has multiple divisions. Each division consists of two labour specialists and three professional judges.

11. The industrial tribunals of Britain enforce a variety of laws, including the Equal Pay Act 1970, the Sex Discrimination Act 1975, the Employment Protection Act 1975, the Race Relations Act 1976, the Employment Protection (Consolidation) Act 1978, and the Employment Act 1980. They are, in fact, quite similar to the labour-court systems of other countries. An industrial tribunal consists of a chairman and two wingmen.

12. The Swedish Labour Court is tripartite. It consists of not more than three chairmen, three vice-chairmen, and 16 other members.

13. Although the primary organs for the settlement of rights disputes in the Eastern European countries are known by various names ('labour disputes commissions', 'arbitration commissions', 'arbitration committees', and 'disputes committees') and although none of these bodies is called a 'labour court', they all function essentially in the manner of labour courts.

14. Most labour disputes in the USSR are handled initially by labour disputes commissions composed of an equal number of permanent representatives of the factory or workshop trade union committee and of the undertaking's administration. The number of representatives on each side is determined by agreement.

15. In Czechoslovakia disputes over rights are considered by 'arbitration commissions' composed exclusively of workers. A commission must have at least seven members.

16. The French labour courts are competent to deal only with *individual* disputes, as opposed to *collective* disputes, arising out of the employment relation. This distinction is difficult to apply in practice because the case law which established the distinction does not originate from a single hierarchical court system, but from several authorities, each determining the scope of its own jurisdiction. Labour and ordinary courts under the authority of the *Cour de Cassation* have defined the meaning of individual disputes, while ordinary courts and arbitrators have elaborated the concept of collective disputes. Consequently, it is at least theoretically possible that a dispute may not be covered by either definition, or may be covered by both.

17. A labour conflict is individual if it involves one employer and one employee, without affecting a group or collectivity on either side. Thus, an individual dispute involves rights only, and typically arises out of an individual contract of employment. However, because terms of a collective agreement are frequently incorporated into individual contracts of employment, disputes over the interpretation or application of collective agreements are commonly heard by a French labour court as a result of their having arisen from individual contracts of employment.

18. The labour courts of the FR Germany, which are generally regarded as special civil courts, have virtually exclusive jurisdiction over both individual and collective disputes. They are empowered to deal with a variety of issues connected with the establishment and functioning of works councils, representational disputes, individual disputes between an employer and an employee, and individual disputes among employees arising out of common employment, including tort actions. The labour courts, additionally, have jurisdiction over both dispositive and mandatory provisions of collective agreements, as well as disputes over attempts of either employers' associations or unions to coerce membership.

19. In Britain the jurisdiction of the industrial tribunals since 1966, especially that concerning unfair dismissals (which in 1978 accounted for over 80 per cent of all applications made to tribunals), has involved, with few exceptions, disputes between individual employees and employers. Exclusive jurisdiction over claims arising out of a contract of employment, such as common law injury suits, remains with the ordinary courts. Moreover, as in

340

the case of France, the line between individual and collective disputes has not been easy to draw. Despite the original intention to make the tribunals available to large numbers of employees for whom no voluntary machinery existed, some of the statutes subsequently enacted provide that unions and employers may apply to have a group of workers excluded from the coverage of specific statutory provisions on the ground that adequate, alternative, voluntary machinery does exist, as in the case of redundancy payments, or unfair dismissal, or guarantee payments.

20. As a general rule, the Swedish Labour Court is the first and final court deciding labour disputes involving the relationship between parties to a collective bargaining agreement, disputes relating to conditions of employment of a union member, and most matters concerning the 1976 Co-determination Act. It also hears cases involving the rights of safety delegates and damages suits for illegal industrial actions.

21. The majority of cases for which a Swedish district court is the appropriate court of first instance, and from which appeals may be taken to the Labour Court, involve industrial disputes between unorganised workers and their employers, or between organised workers whose trade union is unwilling to bring or pursue an action (not based on a collective agreement) on their behalf.

22. As in the case of other socialist countries of Eastern Europe, the jurisdiction of the labour disputes commissions in the USSR appears to be exercised almost entirely in individual rights disputes. Under the prevailing political and social systems in those countries, there is deemed to be no need to establish separate organs for the settlement of conflicts of interest.

23. A labour disputes commission in the USSR has compulsory jurisdiction over all labour disputes arising in an undertaking, institution or organisation between wage and salary earners and the management, except for disputes within the primary jurisdiction of a district people's court or of a higher-level authority and those falling within specified exceptions. In addition, a labour disputes commission has compulsory jurisdiction over other labour disputes relating to the application of labour legislation, collective agreements, contracts of employment and works rules, except for certain disputes explicitly excluded from such jurisdiction. The latter include disputes relating to determination of output standards, state social insurance benefits, qualifying periods for employment benefits, reinstatement of dismissals, and living accommodation.

24. The compulsory jurisdiction of an arbitration commission in Czechoslovakia extends to termination and disciplinary actions and claims of workers while still employed. A commission is barred, however, from considering matters involving a manager's duties or employment.

341

B. Strengths and Weaknesses of the Respective Systems

25. In evaluating the strengths and weaknesses of a given labour-court system, there is a natural tendency to compare it both with the labour courts of other countries and with an arbitration system. The strengths of the French labour-court system are the law's concern for individual rights and the relative success of the bipartite *conseils de prud'hommes* in settling large numbers of individual disputes quickly and inexpensively. In these respects the French system is superior to the arbitration systems of the USA and Canada.

26. There are, however, a number of offsetting weaknesses. Many employees have no access to labour courts; until recently, only 40 per cent of the population live within areas covered by *conseils*. Appeals go to the regular appellate courts, and it is doubtful that even the social chambers of those courts have the kind of expertise possessed by the employer and employee members of the *conseils de prud'hommes*. On the other hand, it would simply not be feasible to retain the bipartite composition of the labour courts at the appellate level, because any specialised tribunal at the appellate level would almost certainly be headed by a professional magistrate.

27. Another weakness is the scope of judicial review in France, which is much broader than in the USA and Canada. Also the French pluralistic system of worker representation, which permits more than one union to represent the workers in a single enterprise or establishment, as well as the virtually unfettered right of individual workers to strike, or to ignore grievance procedures and take complaints directly to the labour courts, tends to limit the importance of the unions' role in the settlement of disputes over rights, at least in comparison with their counterparts in the USA and Canada. This is not necessarily a 'weakness'; rather, it represents a conscious choice to provide maximum freedom of action to the individual worker, and correspondingly less power to unions.

28. In respect of the matter of unjust dismissal, the French worker is better off than the unorganised worker in the USA, but probably less protected than organised workers in the USA and Canada, where the remedy of reinstatement is provided as a matter of course. The French worker must usually settle for damages, despite the 'historic' decision of the *Cour de Cassation* on 14 June 1972, approving a court of appeals ruling ordering the reinstatement of a shop steward.

29. Finally, the bipartite structure of the French labour courts may be considered, from one point of view, to contain an intrinsic weakness, namely, a tendency to make the disputes-settlement process political rather than judicial. *Conseillers* are expected to deliver decisions which will favour

the interests of their constituencies. In corresponding bodies in other countries, whether they be labour courts, arbitration or industrial tribunals, or administrative agencies, the presence of neutrals introduces an element of objectivity and impartiality that seems to be lacking, or at least present to a lesser degree, in the *conseils de prud'hommes*.

30. The labour-court system of the FR Germany has most of the strengths of the French system: protection of individual rights, fairly effective conciliation techniques, and relatively expeditious and inexpensive procedures. In addition, unlike the situation in France, there are labour courts at all levels of the system. Thus, the litigants are assured of tripartite consideration of their disputes at every state of the proceedings.

31. One major criticism of the German system is that it apparently provides insufficient protection against retaliation by the employer against a worker who files a claim against him whilst the employment contract is still in effect. As a rule, therefore, workers do not generally bring cases before the labour courts until their employment relations with the defendant employers have expired.

32. As in France, reinstatement is not a common remedy for unjust dismissal in the FR Germany. Normally, the employer cannot unilaterally remove a worker. Not requirements and works council consultation entitle the dismissed worker to remain on the job during the initial stages of revision. Once a worker is removed, however, the Federal Labour Court has held that in dismissal cases there can be no reinstatement as long as the lawsuit is pending. If the worker wins his case, however, he has the legal right to both back pay and reinstatement. Nevertheless, because such a relatively long time elapses before the final disposition of such cases when they are litigated in the courts, in most instances the worker will have found another job and will not wish to return to the one from which he was wrongfully dismissed.

33. Although one criticism of the French labour-court system is that its bipartite structure encourages settlement according to politico-economic considerations, the labour-court system in the FR Germany has been criticised on the ground that the courts co-opt the employer and union representatives as agents of the state, and do not adhere strictly in their judgements to the constitution, statutes, collective bargaining agreements and employer–worker council agreements. This latter claim probably has been leveled, however, in every country at every court exercising the power of judicial review.

34. Also as in France, the distinction in the FR Germany between individual and collective disputes cannot always be observed in practice and on occasion leads to an overlapping jurisdiction of labour courts and arbitration boards. Thus, although a dispute over the interpretation of an individual

343

contract of employment is a matter for the labour court, from time to time one has been submitted to arbitration by the parties to a collective agreement when the agreement so provided.

35. The role of the industrial tribunals in Britain is quite similar to that of the labour courts in the countries of Western Europe and with the NLRB in the USA. The industrial tribunals have as yet narrower and more specialised jurisdictions than that of the labour courts, but, taken together, a broader jurisdiction than that of the NLRB. Both the labour courts and the industrial tribunals provide speedier and cheaper means of resolving the disputes brought before them than does the NLRB, and their proceedings are more informal.

36. When it comes to providing a remedy for unfair dismissal, however, only the NLRB regularly orders reinstatement with back pay and obtains court enforcement of its orders when necessary (subject, of course, to the reviewing court's power to vacate or modify the Board's order). On the other hand, the industrial tribunals and the labour courts have the power, which the NLRB lacks, to impose what amounts to damages in lieu of reinstatement. Moreover, employers in the USA sometimes trade their right to appeal from an NLRB reinstatement order in return for the unfairly dismissed employee's agreement to accept back pay without reinstatement.

37. The incidence of appeals from decisions of the British industrial tribunals seems to be less than that of appeals from decisions of labour courts or of the NLRB. Whether this is properly attributable to general satisfaction with the tribunals' decisions, to a reluctance to appeal on the part of the typical complainant, or to the requirement that appeals be generally confined to points of law is not certain.

Appeals to courts of the second instance on both the law and the facts are permitted in France and the FR Germany, and appeals from decisions of the NLRB may be taken to the federal circuit courts of appeals in the USA, which uphold the findings of the Board on questions of fact, if they are supported by 'substantial evidence on the record considered as a whole'.

38. Much of the British system is attractive to societies which place a high value on voluntarism, as opposed to governmental compulsion. Still, the actual operation of the system reveals serious flaws. What seems to be lacking is the development and observance of procedures at plant level that will effectively replace industrial action as the ultimate weapon to resolve disputes for which such a weapon is inappropriate. Treating all disputes as problems to be solved, without regard to whether they involve 'rights' or 'interests', does not necessarily imply either that a single procedure can accommodate all types of disputes equally well, or that a resort to economic force is an acceptable way to resolve all types of disputes.

39. The Swedish labour court system has some obvious advantages over those of France and the FR Germany. For most disputes within its jurisdiction it is a court of first and last instance; this insures greater speed of disposition, as well as greater consistency of judicial policy. It has consistently sought to confine itself to the enforcement of the legislative will; the occasional criticisms of its judgements in that respect have been that it has been too legalistic. Another strength of the Swedish labour court system is its compatibility with private arbitration, which is well established in Sweden.

40. With the possible exception of the Labour Court's procedural formalities, which may inhibit somewhat the settlement of cases by conciliation after they have been filed, there appears to be no weakness of any consequence in the Swedish system for settlement of rights disputes. This is a reflection, however, more of the climate of industrial relations than of the procedures employed. Many more things are possible when, as in Sweden and in the FR Germany, for example, employers and unions are in general agreement on the fundamental principles that should govern their relationship and have a mutual respect for the rule of law.

41. Despite superficial differences, the rights disputes mechanisms of the socialist countries of Eastern Europe are, in essence, sufficiently similar to warrant consideration of them as a group. All are based on the same political, economic, and social philosophy, which, among other things, gives considerably more legal power to unions than is granted by most other countries. Each has a variant type of labour jurisdiction under which most cases are initially heard and disposed of at the plant or enterprise level. All of these systems share the twin advantages of settling labour disputes over rights promptly and with no cost to the worker.

42. Commentators in the Eastern European countries seem to share the view that, as their respective disputes settlement systems mature, the number of disputes will tend to decline. In the last two decades the labour laws of those countries have been modified and clarified, but reliable data on the incidence of labour disputes are unavailable, which is also true for most other countries.

43. One of the principal features that vary between Eastern European socialist countries is the composition of the organs of disputes settlement. In Bulgaria and the GDR, and also in Czechoslovakia, these organs are, in the first instance, unipartite, that is composed solely of workers' representatives; whereas in the USSR and Hungary they are bipartite, that is, composed of equal number of representatives of workers and of management. Their status is thus more similar (although not identical) to the wingmen on the tripartite Austrian, FR Germany, and Swedish labour courts and British industrial tribunals.

44. The jurisdiction of the GDR disputes committees is somewhat broader than that of their Eastern European conterparts; it embraces all workers, irrespective of their function, including foremen and directors of public-owned enterprises.

III. Organs of Arbitration

45. Although used as the principal method of settling disputes over rights in only a few countries (USA, Canada, and Australia), arbitration is employed as an alternative or supplementary means of resolving such disputes in a relatively small number of other countries. Thus, it is provided for and used in varying degrees in France, FR Germany, Britain, and Sweden. On the other hand, the 'arbitration commissions' of Czechoslovakia and Hungary function more like labour courts and industrial tribunals than like the organs of arbitration in the USA and Canada. Other labour court countries in which arbitration plays a subordinate but important role in the settlement of disputes over rights include Austria, Finland, Britain, and Israel. Arbitration is also used to some extent in Italy, where the main body of labour disputes reaching adjudication is handled by the ordinary civil courts. The discussion of arbitration in this chapter, however, will be devoted to the principal models: the USA, Canada, and Australia. The two North American countries have a sufficient number of at least superficial similarities to permit them to be linked together; but Australia is unique and must be treated separately.

A. *United States and Canada*

46. In both the USA and Canada arbitration of disputes over rights (commonly known as 'grievances'), arising out of the interpretation of existing collective bargaining agreements, is widespread. In the USA this method of disputes settlement, although entirely voluntary, is provided for in over 95 per cent of all collective agreements in the private sector. In Canada, except in the province of Saskatchewan, all collective agreements are required by law to include a provision for the arbitration of grievances.

47. Although both the USA and Canada have federal systems of government, the applicable laws governing arbitration are quite different in the two countries. In the USA, the applicable substantive law is federal; individual state laws apply only in respect of minor procedural details. In Canada, federal law applies only to such interprovincial or foreign activities as shipping, railroads, canals, telephone, and telegraph; all other activities are governed by provincial laws.

48. In addition to its pervasiveness, perhaps the most distinctive feature of grievance arbitration in the USA is its diversity. Arbitration provisions in

collective agreements (most of which are with single plants) reveal a remarkable variety of arrangements in respect of coverage, structure, procedure, and scope of authority of the arbitrator, umpire, impartial chairman, or board. Although many arbitration provisions are similar, no standard arbitration clause can be said to exist, except sometimes among the several agreements between a single union and the firms comprising an entire industry.

49. There is no standard definition of a 'grievance'; some agreements define it narrowly, others broadly. It may be limited to disagreements over application or compliance with the provisions of the agreement, or it may be expanded to include any question relating to the wages, hours of work, and other conditions of employment.

50. The provincial statutes of Canada show greater similarity. Considered as a group (with the exception of Quebec and Saskatchewan) they require with only minor variations, that every collective agreement contains a provision for final and binding settlement without stoppage of work, by arbitration or otherwise, of all differences between the parties or persons bound by the agreement, concerning its meaning, interpretation, application, administration, or alleged violation, including any question of arbitrability.

51. In both the USA and Canada the union selected by a majority of employees in an appropriate bargaining unit becomes the exclusive bargaining representative for all employees in that unit; thereafter, bargaining between the employer and another union on behalf of those employees or directly between the employer and individuals or groups of those employees is forbidden by law. The union achieving the status of exclusive bargaining representative thus has control of the grievance and arbitration procedure: so long as it acts in good faith and without hostile discrimination, it has the right to decide whether to process a grievance or to appeal it to arbitration if the matter cannot be settled in the grievance procedure.

52. In Canada strikes over rights disputes are forbidden by law. In the USA, there is no such proscription on strikes, except in the railroad and airline industries. Nevertheless, about 90 per cent of the major collective agreements in the USA include restrictions on strikes and lockouts during the term of the agreement. Slightly less than 50 per cent specify an absolute ban on all strikes; in the remainder the strike ban is limited most frequently to those disputes that are subject to arbitration.

53. The oft-repeated dictum of the United States Supreme Court that 'the agreement to arbitrate grievance is the *quid pro quo* for an agreement not to strike'[1] is not always true in practice. Whether this precise equilibrium can

1. Textile Workers v. Lincoln Mills, 353 US 448, 455 (1957).

be achieved depends upon the relative bargaining strength of the parties. Thus, if an employer is significantly stronger than the union, the collective agreement may contain an absolute ban on all strikes for the duration of the agreement, whilst at the same time excluding one or more types of disputes from the arbitration procedure. Conversely, if the union is significantly stronger than the employer, the agreement may provide for the arbitration of all grievances, but may contain no commitment by the union not to strike, or only a limited commitment. The Supreme Court has ruled, however, that to the extent that a labour agreement provides for the arbitration of unresolved grievances, an agreement not to strike over such arbitrable grievances will be implied.[2] In relations between large and powerful employers and unions, however, issues excluded from arbitration are also likely to be excluded from the no-strike clause.

54. About 43 per cent of the major agreements banning either all strikes or lockouts, or those over arbitrable grievances, make the ban contingent on compliance by the parties with some or all provisions of the agreement. Such clauses may declare non-compliance by either party to constitute a waiver of the ban against a strike or lockout, as the case may be, or (rarely) the grounds for terminating the agreement.

55. In a relatively small number of collective bargaining relationships in the USA, the parties use a permanent umpire or impartial chairman to arbitrate all cases arising during the term of the agreement. Such an arrangement is practicable only when substantial numbers of grievances are filed each year. Moreover, the appointment of a permanent umpire or chairman indicates a desire by the parties to employ an arbitrator who either has already acquired an extensive knowledge of the enterprise or industry, or who may be expected to accumulate such knowledge over time. The term 'permanent', however, is misleading. The unquestioned right of either party to dismiss the arbitrator at any time, for any reason or no reason, is widely regarded by all participants as one of the great strengths and safety valves of the system. The role played by the umpire or impartial chairman is largely determined by the parties themselves. They may restrict him to the performance of purely adjudicatory functions, or they may invite him to assume the role of mediator and adviser.

56. The great majority of grievance arbitration in the USA, however, is of the *ad hoc* variety; that is, aribtrators are chosen only for a particular case or group of cases. The *ad hoc* arbitrator is thus frequently unacquainted with the parties or with the problems in the enterprise; he may, indeed, be unfamiliar with the type of problem in dispute. For this reason, *ad hoc* arbitrators almost never undertake to mediate a case submitted to them, and are likely to be resisted by the parties if they attempt to do so. The principal

2. Local 174, Teamsters Union v. Lucas Flour Co., 369 US 95 (1962).

emphasis in *ad hoc* arbitration is on the relatively strict interpretation of the language of the collective agreement and its application to the grievance involved.

57. Regardless of which type of arbitration is used, a further choice must be made between arbitration by a single neutral person or by a tripartite board. In the latter type the neutral chairman is flanked by one or more representatives of the disputants, who are normally voting members of the arbitration board. In most cases the partisan board members are closely associated with the parties to the dispute.

58. In almost all instances a decision of the board must be by majority vote. The reasons are set forth in a written opinion, which is usually prepared and signed only by the neutral chairman. The role of the partisan members in the decision-making process varies according to local practice. Under some arrangements it is customary for partisan members to participate actively – questioning witnesses and participating in procedural rulings during the hearing, and meeting in private session with the chairman after the hearing has been closed to discuss the evidence and the proposed award. In others the participation of partisan members is nominal. Upon receipt of the chairman's proposed award and opinion, they either concur or dissent, usually without comment. Between these two extremes there are a number of varying degrees of involvement by the partisan members.

59. Under all Canadian statutes, the parties are free to submit disputes over rights either to a single arbitrator or to an arbitration board; in over 75 per cent of the cases, they choose tripartite arbitration boards. The chairmen of such boards are typically chosen on a rotating basis from a panel of names jointly selected by the parties. Unlike the situation in the USA, most provincial statutes provide that if there is no majority, the decision of the chairman becomes the decision of the board, unless the parties have agreed on another arrangement.

60. In the USA, both agreements to arbitrate and arbitration awards are enforceable in the courts. In the great majority of cases the former are observed and the latter are accepted by both parties. The US Supreme Court has developed a series of rules which the courts are obliged to follow in the relatively small number of cases involving refusal to arbitrate or to abide by an arbitrator's award that do come before them. Those rules, which manifest a high degree of judicial restraint, are binding on all federal and state courts. They require that the courts refrain from interfering with arbitration procedures incorporated in collective agreements. All doubts about arbitrability must be resolved in favour of coverage. If the minimum conditions are met, the court must order arbitration, even if it feels that the grievance is trivial, frivolous, or wholly devoid of merit. Similarly, such questions as whether all the procedural steps of arbitration have been

349

completed in a timely fashion must also be left for the sole determination of the arbitrator.

61. In respect of enforcement of arbitration awards, courts must refrain from considering the merits, and must limit their review to the question whether the arbitrator confined his decision to the issue submitted and based it on the terms of the collective agreement. If he does so, his decision may not be set aside because of mistakes of law or fact.

62. The situation in Canada is quite different. Despite language in both the federal and provincial statutes to the effect that arbitration awards are final and binding, and not subject to questioning or review by any court, the Canadian courts have continued their traditional practice of intervention and refusal to defer to the arbitration process. Thus, the courts will exericise what they consider to be their inherent jurisdiction to review such awards, and they will do so even in the face of an agreement by the parties to be bound by the award and not to seek judicial review. The grounds for vacating an award include bias, fraud, denial of 'natural' justice, acting in excess of jurisdiction, and an error of law on the face of the record.

63. The principal strengths of the grievance arbitration system in the USA are its largely voluntary nature and flexibility, and the opportunity it provides employees, through their unions, to participate in a process so vital to their employment. All collective bargaining parties in the private sector are free to decide for themselves whether they wish to use arbitration as the method for the final settlement of grievances. That the overwhelming number of them have chosen to do so is itself evidence that, despite its defects, the system has proved to be generally satisfactory.

64. Because the system is largely voluntary and not subject to statutory restriction other than the requirement that if it is used, it must be applied fairly to all employees, the parties are free to introduce as much flexibility and diversity as they choose. To mention only one conspicuous example, the sharp distinction between disputes over rights and disputes over interests, although generally observed, is frequently ignored by parties who find it necessary to resort to a calculated ambiguity in the negotiation of their collective agreements. Rather than precipitate a strike or lockout following an impasse over the wording of a key contract provision, they prefer to adopt ambiguous language that can be interpreted to support either of the opposing positions. If a dispute arises during the contract period over the meaning of the provision, the arbitrator functions as a legislator rather than as a judge. In some situations, usually when the arbitrator is a full-time umpire jointly employed by the parties, he may function as a mediator, attempting to effect the agreement between the parties that eluded them during their contract negotiations.

65. The collective bargaining parties are also free to make their arbitration procedures as formal or informal as they wish.

66. As practised in the USA, grievance arbitration makes it possible for individual employees, whether or not they are union members, to have at least limited access to direct participation in the grievance arbitration procedures, although such access is far less than that available in the labour-court countries. Despite the fact that the union 'owns' the grievance, many local unions vote, after open discussion at a union meeting, whether to take a grievance to arbitration. Moreover, in most arbitration hearings the grievant is present; with the union's permission, which is almost invariably granted, he has the privilege of testifying in his own behalf, and even more important, he has the chance to observe his immediate superiors, and perhaps their supervisors, being examined by a union representative and required to account for their behaviour.

In many instances, employees and management representatives, although not involved in the case, are allowed to attend the arbitration hearing as spectators. The hearing thus serves as a catharsis for the aggrieved employee and as a means of educating employees and management personnel in the administration of the collective agreement.

67. Finally, remedies available through arbitration in the USA tend to parallel statutory remedies available in the courts. For example, a grievant found to have been unjustly dismissed is almost always reinstated with back pay and without loss of seniority rights. Compensatory damages for serious violations of a collective agreement by either party are also sometimes awarded. The chief difference between judicial and arbitral remedies is that the former sometimes include punitive damages, whereas the latter almost never do.

68. There are two main types of weaknesses in the grievance arbitration system in the USA: one type is incidental; the other fundamental. The principal incidental weaknesses are high costs and delays; but these weaknesses are remediable, and many efforts are currently being made, with varying degrees of success, to lower costs and reduce the average total time required to process a grievance to finality.

69. There are at least two fundamental weaknesses of the system, however, for which no satisfactory remedies have been found. The first is a defect of the entire structure of collective bargaining in the USA, namely, that it applies, by its very nature, only to those who have no collective bargaining representative, as distinguished from those who, although not union members, are nevertheless represented by a union. Thus, in the USA, unorganised workers have less constitutional and statutory protection against economic risks and unfair treatment than do workers in most industrialised nations of the world.

70. Even where collective bargaining is firmly established in the USA no satisfactory solution has yet been found for the problem of the individual employee or group of employees who are in bad favour with the exclusive bargaining representative, either because they have refused to join, or because, though members, they are considered by the union leaders to be disloyal, troublesome, or politically dangerous. For practical purposes, their only recourse against the employer is through the contract grievance procedure controlled by the union, which has broad latitude to decide whether, or in what manner, to present a grievance in arbitration. Even if a grievant wants only to sue his employer for damages for violating the collective agreement, he cannot go directly to court, but must first exhaust his remedies under the agreement. An adverse arbitrator's award cannot be successfully appealed on the merits save in the relatively rare instance when an arbitrator clearly exceeds his authority. And should the grievant believe that the union, individually or in collusion with the employer, has violated its duty of fair representation, he must carry the formidable burden of proving his allegations before he can recover against either of them.

71. Despite its weaknesses, the system of grievance arbitration in the USA seems largely successful and well adapted to the economic, social, and political environment of that country. Objectively, it compares unfavourably with most of the other industrialised nations in terms of coverage, cost, and total time required to dispose of even minor grievances. Its greatest defect – limited coverage – is the result of the singular failure to enact any legislation protecting unorganised employees in general, such as a law against abusive discharge. Its procedures, though costly and slow compared to those of the labour-court countries, are cheaper and more rapid than those of either the courts of administrative agencies in the USA.

72. Yet, in a country in which organised labour and management remain in disagreement and often active opposition over basic principles accepted long ago by unions and employers in other countries, it is remarkable that agreement between them does exist that collective agreements should be for fixed terms and enforceable in the courts; that, with few exceptions, strikes and lockouts for the term of a collective agreement should be foresworn; and that unresolved grievances should be submitted to final and binding arbitration.

73. The Canadian traditions of compulsory conciliation of conflicts of interests, compulsory arbitration of rights disputes, and general acceptance of collective bargaining in both the private and the public sectors have given their present system of settling disputes over rights a distinctive character that is quite different from the prevailing system in the USA, despite the superficial similarities.

74. Because the American doctrine of federal supremacy and pre-emption

has no parallel in Canada, patterns of labour relations in the latter country are more diverse than in the former. In Canada both federal and provincial laws are characterised by flexibility and a commendable spirit of experimentation.

75. On the other hand, because the arbitration of disputes over rights is encouraged in the USA and has been voluntarily adopted in most collective agreements, the possibility of striking legally over a rights dispute during the period of an effective collective agreement is somewhat greater in the USA than in Canada. But it seems likely (precise statistics are lacking) that the number and impact of such strikes is not very great in either country.

76. In many ways Australia represents the most interesting and idiosyncratic of the variations on the arbitration theme. Initially, the federal government, which was concerned primarily with major national disputes only, elected in the first Commonwealth Conciliation and Arbitration Act, 1904, not to adopt either a system of disputes-settlement controlled completely by the government or one left to the free forces of collective bargaining. Instead, it opted for a system of 'compulsory arbitration' that borrowed from all, but which was essentially different in character from each.

77. Australia has a federal form of government, and considerable powers relating to the settlement of labour disputes reside with the six states. Limitations of space, however, permit only a discussion of the federal government's disputes-settlement procedures in this chapter.

78. In order for a labour dispute to be arbitrable in the federal jurisdiction, the dispute must involve an 'industry' and be of an interstate character. But no dispute requiring interpretation of the Act or of a prior award or decision may be brought before an arbitral body.
Finally, any arbitral award must be within 'ambit', that is, within the highest terms demanded and the lowest terms offered by the parties.

79. The federal Act was amended in 1956 to establish a Conciliation and Arbitration Commission and an Industrial Court, replacing the single Court of Conciliation and Arbitration established in 1904, and since renamed the Australian Conciliation and Arbitration Commission (ACAC).
The jurisdiction of the Industrial Court was transferred, in 1976, to the Federal Court of Australia, also established in that year.

80. In the *Boilermakers' Case*,[3] it was held that in as much as the Commonwealth Court of Conciliation and Arbitration both made and enforced awards, the federal judges were acting both as judges and as legislators, and thus had offended against the doctrine of separation of powers. The making

3. R. v. Kirby; *ex parte* Boilermakers Society of Australia (1956), 94 CLR 254.

353

of awards was declared to be beyond the constitutional power of the federal judiciary.

81. In Australia the term 'arbitration' theoretically applies exclusively to a process of interests-disputes settlement, which is compulsory and quasi-legislative in character, and which results in an 'award'. An arbitration award looks to the future; it does not address itself to the interpretation or application of established rights under previous or existing awards or agreements. The latter function is viewed as essentially judicial, and is accordingly assigned to the Federal Court of Australia, which renders 'decisions'. The ACAC is the chief federal award-making body.

82. The jurisdiction of the ACAC extends to interstate disputes over issues as widely divergent as basic wage rates and the alleged improper dismissal of an employee in violation of the Act. The ACAC has no general power over dismissal cases, however, because disputes over dismissals are rarely interstate in character and involve judicial matters which are exclusively for the Federal Court.

83. One of the difficulties inherent in the Australian federal system of disputes settlement is that an award is usually made for an industry, or at the very least, binds a number of employers and employees scattered over a very wide area.

The award, although aiming at uniformity, often must recognise that different conditions obtain in different places. Further, there will often be minor disputes arising between parties to the award at a local level. Thus, to ensure that the award made continues to be an effective settlement, a means must be available whereby the potential sources of trouble can be instantly tackled.[4]

The means adopted by Parliament is the board of reference, appointed by the ACAC. A board may consist of or include a commissioner. Once reference boards are set up by authority of award provisions, either party may convene a board as occasion requires.

84. Most Commission awards provide for boards of reference, with authority and instruction to settle industrial disputes arising thereunder. Settlements of such disputes, however, may not be judicial determinations; for the boards of reference, like the ACAC, may not exercise any part of the judicial power of the federal government. By the same token, boards of reference, like the ACAC, are not supposed to 'interpret' awards, but only to 'apply' them, the point being that interpretation is a purely judicial function. That awards cannot be applied without being interpreted is obvious; thus, the entire question of the authority of boards of reference lies mired in a Serbonian bog of semantics.

4. E. Sykes and H. Glasbeek, *Labour Law in Australia*, Sydney, 1972, p. 496.

85. Although the weight of informed Australian opinion appears to be that boards of reference may not deal with disputes over rights, it appears that they do so anyway and have proved to be effective. The whole idea, in fact, is to avoid the necessity of any findings by a board of reference, the primary function of which is that of mediation and conciliation.

86. In contrast to both the USA and Canada, Australian collective agreements do not generally provide for the settlement of unresolved grievances by arbitration; neither do they establish detailed grievance procedures. No-strike clauses are a rarity. Consequently, 'a far larger proportion of all strikes in Australia than in the USA are short, "quickie" walk-offs precipitated by intraplant differences lacking ready means of peaceable adjustment, and . . . the majority of those unadjusted disputes are over rights'.[5]

87. To the foreign observer, the Australian system of settling disputes over rights is one of profound and pervasive ambiguity. Although theoretically applied primarily, and often exclusively, to conflicts of interests, it is apparently, in practice, applied routinely, though often illegally, to disputes over rights. No sharp distinction is drawn between the two types of disputes, as in the USA and Canada; indeed, this distinction is virtually unknown in Australia.

88. All commentators have observed that there is a significant difference in the Australian system between appearance and reality. Conciliation always precedes arbitration, and many disputes are settled at the former stage.

89. To draw an analogy from natural history, the Australian system of compulsory arbitration is like that country's duck-billed platypus, which combines features of several different birds and animals. It survives and works with at least moderate success, it would seem, in defiance of inherent inconsistencies. To some the 'brooding omnipresence' of the courts appears to be a major handicap, but as Sykes observes, 'Australians are far less critical of government control than are Americans (and, one might add, the British) and the field of labour relations has always been regarded by them as one fit for governmental regulation.'[6] Whether the general absence of formal grievance procedures in collective agreements to deal with minor grievances at plant level is a serious drawback is a matter for consideration.

IV. ORDINARY COURTS

90. Italy, Japan, and the Netherlands have in common the characteristic that they leave to the regular courts the task of deciding disputes over rights.

5. P. Brissenden, *The Settlement of Labor Disputes on Rights in Australia*, Los Angeles, 1976, p. 119.
6. E. Sykes, 'Labor Arbitration in Australia', 13, *Amer. J. Comp. L.*, 1964, pp. 216, 248.

As previously noted, arbitration plays a minor role in the settlement of disputes in Italy, but it is practically unknown in the other two countries. Conciliation, however, has become increasingly important.

In Japan the distinction between disputes over rights and conflicts of interests is recognised but is difficult to observe in practice. Japan has also adopted the concept of unfair labour practices – a legacy of the American Occupation Forces in the immediate post-World War II period.

Some reference must also be made to the disputes-settlement functions of the Japanese labour relations commissions. The Netherlands, alone among the three countries, entrusts exclusively to its regular courts the task of deciding all labour disputes that cannot be settled by the parties themselves. The disputes-settlement procedures in the three countries are sufficiently dissimilar to require brief separate treatment.

A. Italy

91. In Italy labour disputes fall under the jurisdiction of the civil courts. Special courts, and implicitly labour courts, are prohibited by Article 102 of the Constitution; this proscription appears to be a legacy of the former fascist regime, during which the use of special courts was abused. Article 102 does authorise, however, 'specialised sections of the ordinary courts for specific subjects' in which 'qualified citizens not drawn from the judiciary may participate.' Prior to the 1970s, there was some agitation for establishment of such specialised sections for labour disputes; but since enactment of procedural reforms in 1973, interest in that proposal has almost completely vanished, the reason being that 'the ordinary civil courts, and in particular the *pretori* (usually young and open-minded judges) have been seen to handle efficently and competently the growing number of often very delicate labour disputes which have been brought to the judiciary under the new regulation enacted during this period.'[7]

92. The *pretore*, which is not a specialised court within the meaning of Article 102 of the Constitution, has general first instance jurisdiction in all labour disputes in the private sector. Where the local office of *pretore* is made up of several divisions, only labour disputes are customarily assigned to one or more *pretori*.

93. Appeals against decisions of *pretori* involving at least a minimum statutory amount are heard by the *tribunale*, a panel of three professional judges. Appeals in cases involving less than the statutory minimum are not allowed. Appeals against decisions of the *tribunale* are heard by a special section of the Supreme Court (*Corte di Cassazione*).

---

7. T. Treu, *IELL* (Italy), 1978, p. 86.

94. Designed to increase speed, informality, and accessibility, proceedings before the *pretore* differ significantly from those in ordinary civil practice. The *pretore* has extensive investigative powers and may gather evidence independently of the parties involved. Oral evidence prevails over written evidence, and the court's decision must be pronounced immediately upon the conclusion of the final hearing. A judgement that a worker has been unjustly dismissed and must be reinstated is automatically temporarily enforceable.

95. Act 533 of 11 August 1973 institutionalised a prior informal conciliation procedure for the settlement, *inter alia*, of rights disputes under collective agreements. Permanent commissions of conciliation were established in each province. The commissions are tripartite. Their jurisdiction may be invoked by any individual worker or employer, or by a labour organisation of the worker's own choosing. If conciliation is successful, the record, authenticated by the president of the commission, can be enforced immediately by a 'decree' of the *pretore*. The same result can be achieved through a written agreement between an employer and a union without the intervention of a conciliation commission.

96. The Italian system of settling rights disputes is similar to that of a number of civil law countries which rely upon labour courts at least to the extent of protecting the right of the individual worker to control the handling of his own grievance, although union participation in the process, largely in the form of assistance rather than direction, is certainly permitted, if not encouraged. Another similarity with some labour-court countries (e.g. France and the FR Germany) is the emphasis on conciliation throughout the various phases of a labour dispute. Thus, the vast majority of rights cases are settled by the tripartite commission or by conciliation before the court. Very few cases actually go through formal litigation process in Italy.

B. Japan

97. In Japan both individual and collective disputes, if adjudicated, are handled by the ordinary courts. The distinction between disputes over rights and conflicts of interests is never very clear because the law courts often give rulings on questions of appropriateness as well as on strictly legal issues. The court may also play the role of a mediator, especialy in respect of the appropriateness of such matters as collective dismissals or the procedural problems of bargaining sessions. Whether the matter before the court requires only a ruling on appropriateness or a legal decision depends largely on how it is raised. The reason for this confusing situation is that the Japanese, like the British, regard labour contracts as 'gentlemen's agreements'. Negotiation of differences is much favoured over formal adjudication, and only rarely are disputes not resolved by mutual agreement. When this method fails, however, 'the parties tend to move on to final confrontation, appealing to the Courts or resorting to drastic action such as strikes or other acts of dispute.'[8]

98. Disputes-settlement procedures in Japan reflect both the eclecticism that characterises much of its labour law and the profound influence of its own culture, which differs in so many respects from that of the Western world. Given the strong cultural preference for compromise rather than legal confrontation, the monopoly of disputes-settlement mechanisms by the government and the absence of voluntary, private arbitration is rather surprising. The explanation offered by Tadashi Hanami is 'the virtual impossibility of finding a third party with authority and influence over both parties to a dispute; whereas in traditional Japanese society disputes are often settled by men of influence with sufficient authority who can and do appeal to sentiment rather than to any universal norm.'[9]

C. The Netherlands

99. Among the Western European countries, the Netherlands is unique in assigning responsibility to the ordinary courts for adjudicating unresolved civil disputes connected with individual contracts of employment or collective agreements. Labour courts, as such, do not exist; there are no administrative boards or agencies to share part of that burden, nor does the law provide for compulsory arbitration or recognise voluntary private arbitration of disputes over rights.

100. As in the USA, some of the most important terms of employment are provided in the Netherlands by collective or individual agreements, rather than by statute; legislation often sets only minimum standards, which are raised through collective bargaining; and statute law may itself be a product of collective bargaining.

101. A lower court judge sits alone; the court is one of first instance for all civil disputes connected with individual contracts of employment or collective agreements, without regard to the amount of the claim. Its decisions are subject to appeals to the district court, which generally consists of three judges. Decisions of all subordinate courts are subject to 'appeal in cassation' to the Supreme Court, comprised of five judges. Like the French *Cour de Cassation* the Supreme Court is bound by the facts as established by the lower court, and may decide only on questions of law. It must either dismiss the appeal or quash the decision of the lower court. In the latter event, it must either remand the case to the lower court or render final judgment.

---

8. T. Hanami, *IELL* (Japan), 1978, p. 140.
9. *Idem* at 141.

102. In the absence of statistical evidence, it is impossible to state categorically that the somewhat skeletal framework for the adjudication of disputes over rights in the Netherlands is adequate for the job. Although originally intended to be simple and speedy, lower court procedures have not met that expectation. For example, if appeals to the district court and the Supreme Court are exhausted, a dismissal case can take five years or more until final adjudication. In the view of Bakels, 'The absence of an informal quick-working Labour Court is . . . a serious drawback of the Dutch labour law system . . . Nor is there, strangely enough, any convincing evidence that this gap is being filled by the use of grievance procedures in collective agreements.'[10]

SELECT BIBLIOGRAPHY

B. Aaron, ed., *Labour Courts and Grievance Settlement in Western Europe*, Los Angeles, 1971.
American Arbitration Ass'n, *The Future of Labor Arbitration in America*, New York, 1976.
R. Blanpain, ed., *International Encyclopaedia for Labour Law and Industrial Relations*, Vols. 1–10.
O. Kahn-Freund, *Labour and the Law*, 2nd ed., London, 1977.
M. McAuley, *Labour Disputes in Soviet Russia 1957–1965*, Oxford, 1969.
E. Sykes and H. Glassbeek, *Labour Law in Australia*, Sydney, 1972.
P. Weiler, *Reconcilable Differences: New Directions in Canadian Labour Law*, Toronto, 1980.

10. H. Bakels, *IELL* (The Netherlands), 1979, p. 23.

Chapter 17. Settlement of Disputes over Interests

A. Goldman

I. Overview of Models for Interest Disputes Settlement

1. To a considerable degree, the processes of notice, information exchange and consultation, discussed in earlier chapters, serve to avoid disputes over interests. This chapter examines and compares seven basic models for the resolution of such disputes when they do arise. These models are:

(1) Acquiescence in Unilateral Action;
(2) Governmental Fiat;
(3) Political Discipline;
(4) Adjudication;
(5) Voting;
(6) Negotiation; and
(7) Conciliated Negotiation.

Each model has variations in structure. Though each model at times is used independently to resolve an interest dispute, at other times two or more are involved either simultaneously or sequentially in dispute settlement.

2. Some might argue that Acquiescence in Unilateral Action is not a model for interest dispute settlement but rather represents the absence of such disputes. However, the failure of a party to assert displeasure concerning employment interests does not necessarily mean that that party is satisfied with the nature, level or assortment of those interests. Acquiescence in Unilateral Action occurs if the acquiescing party either does not think it has any way to influence the resolution of those differences or does not wish to exercise its power to influence the result. Accordingly, the differences do not go unresolved; they are resolved, but the resolution results from one side submitting to the other's initiative.

3. An essential characteristic of every social unit is the ability to establish, alter and enforce behavioural norms. Societal units have greater ability than do individuals or informal groups to achieve adherence to norms. In addition to inducements, social units generally can legitimately resort to a variety of coercive techniques including manipulating psychological ties of group loyalty. When all members of a social unit are committed to conformity with a particular behavioural norm, we can speak of that norm as a law or a rule of governance.

4. The norms established and maintained by social units sometimes are the product of prior individual autonomy that has developed into a generally imitated pattern of behaviour. Such patterns are known as customs or tradition. Other norms are determined at the discretion of those who control the prerogatives of the societal unit. For our purposes, the establishment or modification of a social unit's behavioural norms, when imposed by those responsible for exercising the unit's prerogatives, will constitute the Governmental Fiat model for conflict resolution.

5. In some political systems the coercive power of the state treats nonconformity with a political party's doctrine as a crime against the state itself. The political party thereby can wield the power of Governmental Fiat. A political party can also assert influence to the extent that it can offer economic opportunities. Generally, such patronage benefits are available to the party in power with respect to at least some government jobs. Often some employment opportunities with government-owned, controlled or influenced enterprises are also reserved for members of the dominant political party. Opportunities to do business with the government similarly may be reserved for loyal supporters of the party in power. Generally, beneficiaries of such patronage comply with the dictates of those who control the party. The party's influence over its members also may be enhanced by the psychological and ideological ties of its supporters. Whatever the source of that influence, the party's ability to control its members' conduct constitutes its power of Political Discipline. Of course, the more dominant the political party's role in a nation's affairs, the more significant its role in resolving interest disputes through Political Discipline.

6. Adjudication is the model by which one or more individuals having no direct personal interest in a dispute resolve those differences on the basis of settled principles.

7. Arbitration is a special form of Adjudication that receives wide use as a means of settling interest disputes in some labour relations systems. In arbitration the neutral tribunal that decides the dispute is selected with the participation of the disputing parties; its members are not governmental officials appointed by the state or elected by the public to wield authority over disputes.

8. Voting is a format for collective self-determination by which each participant makes an unequivocal choice from among specific alternatives. Essentially, voting is a fact finding process by which individuals record their preferences.

9. Negotiation is the process by which two or more parties through some form of communication mutually resolve to alter, or refrain from altering, the relationship between or among themselves or their relationship with respect to an object or group of objects. The process involves clarification of issues, sharing information, exploring alternative settlements, examining the consequences of not settling, persuasion and accommodation. It covers a broad range of formats. In the FR Germany, for example, the term 'bargaining' is used to connote a settlement reached under pressure of a work stoppage. Clearly, though, this process is Negotiation. The term 'co-determination' is used in the FR Germany to connote settlements reached through the deliberations of supervisory boards having joint representation and of work councils. These institutions, too, largely rely on the Negotiation process in reaching their decisions.

10. As previously noted in this book, there is an uncertain line between consultation and Negotiation. In its pure form, consultation aims at dispute avoidance. It accomplishes this through the exchange of information, persuasion and even accommodation. However, if that exploration fails to avoid a dispute, and if the issue is not reserved for unilateral resolution, consultation is readily transformed into Negotiation.

11. When negotiating parties are unable to agree, neutral third parties sometimes try to assist the negotiators in reaching a settlement. The resulting Conciliated Negotiation can involve the third party serving as a communications conduit or can involve the more active role of third party fact-findings or suggested formulas for agreements. In the area of disputes concerning employment interests, government agencies often offer or mandate the aid of mediators or conciliators.[1]

12. Before comparing applications of the foregoing models for settling interest disputes, two points are worth reiterating.

The first is that each model has its variations. The second is that the basic models for interest dispute settlement can operate simultaneously or sequentially. For example, if the legislative branch of government imposes a solution to the parties' differences based upon its objective collective judgment respecting a fair balancing of the parties' competing equities, the dispute is resolved through the simultaneous application of the Adjudicative and Governmental Fiat models. An example of the sequential operation of interest dispute settlement models would be where the Negotiation model is used by the parties' representatives to reach an agreement but the completion of that agreement is contingent upon the approval of the parties' constituents by means of a ratifying vote.

---

1. The terms 'mediation' and 'conciliation' are used interchangeably. Some scholars distinguish the terms using 'conciliation' to refer only to efforts to assist in communications while using 'mediation' to refer to the additional effort of formulating and proposing suitable settlement terms. In Denmark 'conciliator' is used for the more intrusive, rather than the less intrusive, third party role.

II. ACQUIESCENCE IN UNILATERAL ACTION

13. Market theorists argue that the ultimate determination of employment interests is the law of supply and demand. The underlying assumption is that, in the absence of interference with the free movement of workers, those who seek to labour move to jobs offering more favourable employment benefits and that management provides those benefits necessary to attract and retain a work force of the size and ability it requires. As the supply of labour increases in relationship to the demand, competition for jobs enables management to reduce employment benefits; when the supply decreases in relationship to the demand, competition for workers forces management to increase employment benefits. In the first instance the market places management in the dominant position so that workers must acquiesce; in the second situation labour is in the dominant position and it is management that must acquiesce. Thus, the free market system for establishing work benefits is an example of Acquiescence in Unilateral Action.

14. Most market theorists recognise that, at least in industrially advanced societies, considerable economic effort is directed toward avoiding the free play of market forces. One reason is that the result often does not satisfy concepts of social justice. Only those who find ethical virtue in the law of natural evolution can take comfort from the impact of the free market upon those who labour. In contrast, those who adhere to competing concepts of social justice often seek to restrain, control, or eliminate the free market for labour through modifications ranging from the restraints upon competition inherent in collective negotiation to the imposition of a settlement by means of Governmental Fiat so as to eliminate market considerations altogether.

15. In some economies, Acquiescence in Unilateral Action resolves many interest disputes despite the attempted imposition of settlements by Governmental Fiat. Accordingly, in Mexico it is estimated that about half of all workers covered by minimum wage laws are paid less than the minimum. In India the lack of adequate law enforcement personnel, plus the gratitude of workers for obtaining any employment, often results in employers unilaterally eliminating fringe benefits they are legally required to provide when engaged in performing government contracts. Similarly, in the USA and elsewhere, illegal aliens often acquiesce in accepting wages below the rate required by law or by the employer's collective agreement.

16. Many labour relations systems preserve the individual bargaining opportunity for various classes of employees by excluding them from collective bargaining. In such situations, differences respecting employment interests often will be settled using the model of Acquiescence in Unilateral Action. Thus, in Canada and the United States those exercising managerial decision-making authority, including shop floor supervisors, and persons who serve in a confidential capacity with regard to those who formulate the enterprise's labour relations policies, are normally excluded from the collective bargaining process. As a result, generally they acquiesce in the benefits unilaterally bestowed from above or seek other employment. Similarly, as a result of being excuded from minimum wage standards adopted by Governmental Fiat, domestic workers in the USA, Brazil, Thailand and France, among other nations, can be expected to settle interest disputes largely by Acquiescence in Unilateral Action.

17. The Acquiescence in Unilateral Action model is available, too, in situations in which workers are collectively represented. To illustrate, shop floor workers through informal collective action frequently set a work pace which goes unchallenged by management. In like manner, a new work assignment policy might be discussed with the works council and then be immediately instituted in the absence of the council's opposition, or in the absence of its emphatic opposition.

18. In those labour relations situations in which one side plays a wholly dominant role, whether as a result of the structure of the legal relationship, the great imbalance in economic positions, or through physical or psychological coercion, the model of Acquiescence in Unilateral Action constitutes the principal method for resolving interest disputes. At most, the dominated party's participation in the outcome is limited to calling attention to the existence of its desires concerning the particular employment interest. In law or effect the worker in such a subservient position is in a property-type relationship with the employer.

19. While either through internal law, ratification of international conventions, or both, most nations have outlawed slavery, the most complete property-type employment relationship, the system of owned workers has not been totally eradicated. The dowry system practised in the Asian sub-continent has been characterised as a slavery-like system and exploitation of prostitutes in developed as well as developing economies has been similarly characterised. Debt bondage, or peonage, though outlawed in India, continues and in South Africa the system known as Apartheid, by severely limiting the economic opportunities of a racial group, converts their market position into what has been called a 'collective form of slavery'.[2]

20. Similarly, because of their reduced ability to resist domination, children are ready victims of a subservient system. Although legislation at the international as well as national levels has been designed to protect young workers, these protections are not always enforced, generally do not provide

2. For a summary and analysis of the periodic reports of the UN Economic and Social Council, Commission on Human Rights, Sub-Committee on Prevention of Discrimination and Protection of Minorities, see D. Ziskind, 'Forced Labor in the Law of Nations', *Comparative Labor Law*, 1980, vol. 3, p. 253. See also, R. Goldfarb, *Migrant Workers: A Caste of Despair*, Iowa City, 1981; C. Johri, *IELL* (India), 1980, paragraph 714.

protection beyond the early stages of puberty, and frequently make exceptions for employment within family enterprises.

21. The significance of labour being treated as property is that the subservient employee is unlikely to resort to the Adjudicative model, even if it is available, is unlikely to seek enforcement of any applicable Governmental Fiat, and lacks the bargaining leverage with which to enter into negotiations. Thus, the subservient worker can merely plead his differences and accede to the unilateral solutions imposed by his dominating employer.

22. For the most part, rules of substantive law prohibit workers from placing management in a subservient position. Accordingly, in most nations if workers seize the authority for determining the operations of a sea-going vessel they can anticipate severe punishment for the crime of mutiny. Similarly, seizing control of a business establishment in the form of a sit-in, sit-down, or work-in action is an illegal trespass in Belgium, France, Italy, and the USA, among other nations. Nevertheless, there are situations in which employees can, through the exercise of economic dominance, dictate a settlement of differences regarding employment interests and anticipate employer acquiescence in the result. Examples of this are sometimes encountered in the rules of professional conduct adopted by professional organisations or craft rules adopted by a trade union as an internal regulation of its membership. A very different form of worker domination is the Indian tactic of *gherao* – a human blockade of managers which isolates them from all amenities and sustenance until they accede to the workers' demands. Although illegal and no longer used with frequency, the tactic persists.

23. In every labour relations system one can find evidence of some reliance upon Acquiescence in Unilateral Action for settling interest disputes. As a method of dispute resolution, this model has the virtue of efficiency. The result is reached promptly with a minimum of resources required to permit the model to function. Also, it can be tailored to meet the needs of the particular situation – at least as perceived by the dominant party. One drawback is that the level of underlying discontent is likely to remain undisclosed until such time as the dominated party is prepared to sever the relationship or resort to violence in an effort to reverse the roles. Another drawback is that the unilaterally imposed solution, while tolerable, may not be the most advantageous settlement for either side because it is unlikely that there has been full utilisation of the process of deliberation, rationalisation and information exchange by all affected or informed parties.

III. Government Fiat

24. Governments often stand ready to enforce norms established by custom and tradition. The Anglo-American systems refer to this as common law, but the practice is found in other legal systems as well. To illustrate, in

France the period of required dismissal notice, if not specified by collective agreement, is determined by the customs of the locality or the industry. In Israel the very right to receive advance notice of discharge is derived from custom. And Treu explains that in Italy 'custom can be applied when legislation and collective agreements are lacking and, if it is more favorable to the workers, it can prevail over non-imperative provisions of law not over provisions of collective agreements.[3]

25. Governmental Fiat often takes the form of a formal document such as a statute or regulation. As is illustrated by the above reference to custom in Italian labour law, Governmental Fiat does not always preclude a different settlement by means of some other model for settling interest disputes. Moreover, in reality even when Governmental Fiat is supposed to prevail over all other determinations, the parties may find ways to evade or avoid the law or may adopt some other norm of conduct as a result of lack of knowledge of the law.

26. Often Governmental Fiat is used to structure the relationship between workers' representatives and enterprise management. For example, in the USA the collective bargaining system is structured largely by statute. In Belgium, the collective bargaining structure under which workers' interests are represented by the 'most representative organisations' (the Christian, the Socialist and Liberal union organisations), is recognised by a legislative act. In contrast, the Danish system of collective bargaining operates without legislative management of its structuring. Both in the case of Belgium and the USA, the legislative structuring did not introduce a new institution. Rather, the enactments largely formalised and expanded approaches that had become customary.

27. Governmental Fiat, similarly, often provides the structure and procedural rules for other dimensions of the industrial relationship such as works councils, grievance machinery and co-determination.

28. Perhaps the most characteristic of all disputes involving employment are those concerning remuneration. The role played by Governmental Fiat in settling such disputes in any particular nation provides considerable insight into the nature of that labour relations system.

29. Minimum wage laws and laws requiring overtime differentials are common. The underlying dispute resolved by such laws is the competition between management's goal of higher profits and the collective interest of workers in being shielded from market forces that might otherwise drive wage levels down to or below survival standards. In more prosperous nations minimum wage laws usually leave actual wage adjustment to the Negotiation and Acquiescence in Unilateral Action processes so long as the result is no less advantageous than the minimum standards established by

3. T. Treu, *IELL* (Italy), 1985, paragraph 49.

the government. An example of this relatively unobtrusive degree of governmental intervention is encountered in Japan where specified minimum wage rates are set by a commission and have been established only for traditionally low wage industries and where overtime hours and wage differentials are regulated only in the most hazardous industries. In the FR Germany provision is made for the states to establish minimum wages but, except for home workers, no minimum standards have been adopted. In Britain, although there is no general minimum wage legislation, the Secretary of State may set up a Wages Council consisting of equal numbers of employer and union representatives plus a number of independent members. The Wages Council, which is established for a particular industry, may adopt orders fixing minimum pay levels. Less than a sixth of the labour force is affected by Wage Council orders. Minimum wage and overtime differential legislation is far more pervasive in the USA, where the federal standard is sometimes supplemented by even more protective state regulations. Although the minimum wage level directly affects only a small portion of the American work force, overtime pay requirements have a direct impact on most non-managerial employees.

30. One might expect to find government imposed minimum wage standards prevalent in developing countries inasmuch as other interest dispute settlement models are unlikely to provide an effective barrier to exploitation of large numbers of desperate workers. On the other hand, the presence of those same large numbers of desperate workers is likely to lead to wide evasion of government standards. As a result of these conflicting forces, the extent to which Governmental Fiat has been used to establish minimum wage standards in developing economies is quite varied. For example, in India minimum pay standards have been established by judicial decree as well as by state-administered regulations which vary according to job, industry and region. However, often workers are unaware of the existence of such protections. In addition, the enforcement machinery is inadequate, especially in rural areas. Burma has established minimum wages for only two industries and Indonesia has been gradually introducing them.

31. The determination of whether employees will receive particular days as paid holidays or of the duration and level of annual vacation benefits is resolved by Governmental Fiat in a number of countries including Austria, Brazil, France, Italy, Finland, and Belgium, among others. Similarly, Governmental Fiat often mandates paid leave for performing civic duties.

32. As an interest dispute settlement model, Governmental Fiat has the virtue of holding out the promise that the result will accurately reflect the society's notions of social and economic justice. In addition, if the government functions efficiently and honestly, its prestige and power in support of the settlement has the stabilising benefit of assuring that workers and managers will in fact abide by the settlement. Moreover, because the

governmental decision-makers often have no direct involvement in the interest dispute, there is enhanced opportunity for an objective, rational result that serves the needs of the total community, not just those of the interested parties.

33. On the other hand, Governmental Fiat is a cumbersome process if carried out with responsibility, objectivity and reason; too cumbersome to deal with more than a small fraction of the interest disputes that arise in the course of a nation's employment relations. Moreover, Governmental Fiat can become arbitrary or corrupt. In addition, Governmental Fiat is a relatively inflexible device, incapable of adjusting to special or momentary needs. Often it can deal effectively with questions of broad principle but not with problems requiring responsiveness to minute detail or frequent variation. And, settlement imposed by Governmental Fiat is unlikely to satisfy either side if the authorities do not enjoy the disputing parties' trust. Finally, a settlement imposed by Governmental Fiat does not add to the parties' skill in developing or sustaining a harmonious relationship.

IV. Political Discipline

34. The Political Discipline model for conflict resolution is not confined to political entities. It is available to other partisan alliances whose foundations are ideological, emotional, economic or opportunistic. Labour and business entities can use Political Discipline to gain their goals within a political party as can partisan factions functioning within a labour or business organisation. In addition, Political Discipline is an especially important model for interest dispute resolution in those nations in which a single political or religious alliance is the exclusive reservoir of collective authority. (Such nations, however, are beyond the scope of this book's examination.)

35. In many countries there is a strong link between one or more political parties and various labour organisations. In Denmark the Social Democratic Party and the major federation of national unions are closely related. Each organisation has representatives on the other's governing bodies. The link is sufficiently close so that the seamen's union, which is dominated by the Communist Party, was expelled from the federation for refusing to aid the federation-owned Social Democratic Party newspaper. The link between the Labour Party and the central union federation in Britain is less formal than in Denmark, but a regular liaison is maintained. About half of the member unions of the British federation are affiliated with the Labour Party and constitute a critical voting block in determining party policies. A different sort of inter-relationship is found in Israel where the numerous political organisations vie for their candidates' election to the National Convention of the Histadrut, the dominant labour federation, in much the same way as they vie for election to the national legislature.

36. Employer and managerial organisations also have the potential for exercising the Political Discipline model. Members often share common ideological and economic ties and can wield patronage power in the form of willingness or unwillingness to engage in business with one another or alert each other to business opportunities with others. These organisations are likely to carry influence within the more conservative political parties and are prone to be more co-operative in carrying forward the programmes of such parties when they are in power.

37. Political Discipline is a means, as well, by which decisions that impose managerial will upon subservient workers are themselves shaped by peer group norms and preferences. Thus, it has been observed that the representatives of supervisory personnel, a component of the employee delegation on supervisory boards in FR Germany, are far more inclined to share the views of management than are other employee representatives. This, too, is evidence of the impact of Political Discipline.

38. The most obvious opportunity for Political Discipline to serve as a model for interest dispute settlement is in the shaping of employment and labour relations policies carried out through Governmental Fiat. To illustrate, the Industrial Relations Act adopted in Britain in 1971 sought to modify the very structure of labour–management relations as well as alter, to some degree, the parties' respective power positions. The Act had the support of employers' organisations and the Conservative Party, which was in power. However, it was opposed and resisted by most unions. The Trade Union and Labour Relations Act, adopted by the Labour government when it had regained power in 1974, repealed most of the 1971 reforms.

39. A different sort of example of Political Discipline resolving interest disputes is found in the employment of some local government workers in the United States. By working diligently in the campaigns for the election of local officials, and soliciting the votes of relatives and friends, government workers in many localities have made their support an essential element in any serious candidate's election effort. These 'loyal' supporters then have special claims upon the elected officials' highly sympathetic consideration of the workers' position respecting their employment interests.[4]

40. Similarly, the choice of demands which a labour or employer organisation makes can reflect the dispute settlement model of Political Discipline. Thus, if the goal of the partisan group, whether allied with labour or with management, is to create an atmosphere of harmony, issues might be avoided or dealt with in vague or incomplete ways. Whereas, if the goal is to

---

4. Such activity often violates statutory and constitutional restrictions. See *Branti v. Finkel*, 445 US 507 (1980) and *US Civil Service Commission v. National Association of Letter Carriers*, 413 US 548 (1973).

create or aggravate an atmosphere of crisis or a sense of ineffectiveness, then positions can be adjusted to serve that purpose. This is illustrated by the posture taken by Australian unions in connection with the 1983 federal election. The government imposed a wage freeze several months prior to the election. Although the labour unions opposed the freeze, they refrained from industrial actions so as to avoid creating an issue that would weaken the Australian Labour Party's campaign prospects. When the Labour Party prevailed at the polls, the unions continued to exercise restraint – this time in order to give their political allies breathing space in establishing the new government.

41. Another example of Political Discipline as a method of settling interest disputes is the impact of the *Zaikai* in Japan's economy including the resolution of labour–management disputes. *Zaikai* is a group representing the leaders of Japan's financial institutions, employer associations and other business organisations. It is said that together 'with several informal clubs of influential business leaders they are believed to make and break governments.'[5] Through the *Zaikai*, employers influence government as well as employer representatives in the tripartite deliberations which shape economic planning and public employee relations. Japanese employer associations additionally have had some success in closing ranks and co-ordinating employer responses to *Shunto*, the labour movement's annual 'Spring Struggle'.

42. Depending upon the respective political influence of the parties, and the strength of a political party within the economic and social system, Political Discipline can be a central or an inconsequential model for settling employment disputes. It can have the virtue of expediency and of promoting social harmony. But it can as easily have the vice of confusing employment interests with other social and economic concerns and can promote settlements that lack economic or social rationality, that are inflexible and that give too little consideration to the needs of some affected persons who are not part of the controlling alliance.

V. Adjudication

43. The distinguishing feature of interest dispute settlement through Adjudication is the assumption that the result will be a principled decision. One variable in the adjudicative process, therefore, is the nature and source of the guiding principles. Should they reflect only the goals of the disputing parties or should they reflect the broader concerns of social and economic policy?

5. S. Levine, 'Employer Associations in Japan', in *Employer Associations and Industrial Relations* (J. Windmuller and A. Gladstone, eds.), 1984, pp. 318, 324, 326–27, 343–45, 353.

44. Another variable in the Adjudication model is the structure and source of the tribunal. Additional variables are the number and training of tribunal members, the permanency or *ad hoc* nature of the appointment of tribunal members, whether submission of the dispute is voluntary or compelled, or whether the award is advisory or binding. Other variables include the formality or informality of procedures, the stage of dispute development at which Adjudication is invoked, and its co-ordination with or independence from other dispute settlement efforts.

45. When discussing Adjudication of interest disputes, one must begin with the foremost examples, Australia and New Zealand, where Adjudication plays a principal role in interest dispute settlement. The use of the Adjudication model for interest dispute settlement has been an important feature of both countries' labour relations systems since the late nineteenth century.

In New Zealand the process begins upon either party's application to submit an interest dispute to a conciliation council. That body consists of an equal number of representatives of both sides and is presided over by a government official carrying the title 'conciliator'. In the event that the parties' representatives are equally divided, the conciliator casts the deciding vote in reaching the council's decision. Therefore, inasmuch as the council's decision is binding on the parties, the conciliator, despite the title, may ultimately wield adjudicative power by casting the deciding vote. As an alternative to submitting a case to a conciliation council, the parties may submit it to the Court of Arbitration. This tribunal consists of two legally trained judges and four lay members selected on the nomination of the central workers' and employers' organisations. Hearings may be by a single judge and two lay members. The Court of Arbitration may refuse to hear a dispute if it finds that the parties have not made a genuine attempt to settle. It has an additional power, under the General Wage Orders Act, by general order to amend rates of remuneration fixed by awards and collective agreements so as to reflect what it deems just and equitable. This power is exercisable only after a hearing in which the union, employer and local government federations, and the Minister of Finance, have an opportunity to be heard.

In fixing wage rates the Court weighs specified factors including the promotion of industrial harmony, Consumer Price Index changes, and the goals of full employment and a vigorous export trade. The awards of the conciliation and arbitration tribunals are legally enforceable.

46. In Australia, because of its federated structure and the significant role that state governments play in much of the employment relations area, the available Adjudication machinery varies depending upon which set of laws control a particular employment relationship. Yerbury and Isaac divide the various tribunal structures into three classes: curial types, tripartite boards, and a mixture of the two.[6] The curial type bodies are presided over by

6. D. Yerbury and J. Isaac, 'Recent Trends in Collective Bargaining in Australia', in ILO, *Collective Bargaining in Industrial Market Economies*, 1973, pp. 173, 176.

legally trained judges assisted by lay members called commissioners. These tribunals operate with greater formality than the tripartite boards which consist of equal representatives from each side and are presided over by a neutral. Whatever the tribunal, its awards are enforceable in the manner of legislative enactments. Interest disputes may be brought to an arbitral tribunal either on the initiative of a party or through the tribunal's own intervention. Once the arbitral process has been initiated, the parties generally proceed to negotiate a settlement, with or without the aid of government conciliators. However, negotiated settlements often are submitted for award certification since only certified arbitration awards are judicially enforceable. Applications for such consent awards are rejected if the Commission finds that they would have an undesirable impact or otherwise would be contrary to national interests. Although federal arbitration awards in Australia are enforceable only against the participating parties, awards of state tribunals can be extended to all others similarly situated within the jurisdiction.

47. Frances Raday observed that in Australia and New Zealand there has been a cyclical relationship between employment standards adopted in arbitral awards and collective agreements. At various times awards have either appeared to provide the lead for the bargaining process or have taken their cues from that process.[7]

48. In Canada, several provincial governments and the federal government give the Minister of Labour authority to require parties to submit interest disputes to binding third party resolution if the disputes result in an impasse in the parties' efforts to reach their first collective agreement. A major factor that appears to guide the tribunal members is their finding respecting prevailing employment conditions for organised employees doing similar work. It has been observed that, in 'British Columbia, the jurisdiction with the longest experience administering this type of provision, . . . very few of these "trial marriages" have matured into a permanent relationship.'[8]

49. With respect to its own workers, the federal government in Canada requires the representative union to elect, prior to commencing negotiations, to resolve impasses either by conciliation subject to an ultimate right to strike, or by compulsory arbitration by a tribunal consisting of a labour and a management representative plus a neutral drawn from permanent panels.

50. When the arbitration/strike option approach was first introduced to federal workers in Canada, the unions preferred the arbitration alternative. After a dozen years of experience with the approach, a majority of labour organisations were electing in favour of the conciliation–strike option. At first, most unions selecting the arbitration route successfully negotiated new

7. F. Raday, *Adjudication of Interest Disputes*, 1983, p. 180.
8. H. Arthurs *et al.*, *IELL* (Canada), 1980, paragraphs 520–522.

collective agreements without having to resort to that impasse procedure. In time, though, there has been a growing dependency upon arbitration among those who have continued to select that impasse option.

51. Traditionally, interest arbitration has played a minor role in labour-management relations in the USA. At times it has been available by contractual arrangement in a few industries, including steel, and is used to resolve impasses concerning the individual compensation rates for athletes in some professional sports.

52. The most common use of interest arbitration in the USA is in the employment relations of government workers. Impasses in collective bargaining for postal workers, for example, are required to be submitted to interest arbitration if fact finding and conciliation efforts fail. The mandated arbitration procedure requires each side to designate an arbiter with a third to be selected by those two arbitrators. The parties equally share the costs and have the right to adopt an alternative procedure by mutual consent.

53. A variety of interest arbitration formats have been adopted as mandatory settlement procedures for state and local government workers in the USA. A few state courts have rejected such legislation on the grounds that it violates the constitutional prerogatives and responsibilities of executive and legislative officers. Among the states in which impasse arbitration has survived judicial scrutiny, several limit mandatory arbitration to certain groups of workers such as police and fire fighters. A few states use a tripartite format while others provide for determination by a single arbiter. In some instances the tribunal must choose between each side's final bargaining offer package while in other jurisdictions the tribunal must separately choose between each side's last offer with respect to each disputed issue. In the state of Iowa, the tribunal may select from among the parties' last offers or the fact finder's recommendation to the parties. (Fact finding and conciliation generally are earlier mandated stages of the procedure under these state laws.) In still other states the tribunal may shape the award without restriction respecting the parties' bargaining positions. There is a movement in the direction of legislatively providing a list of criteria to be weighed by such tribunals as the basis for decision.

54. Several studies attempt to assess the impact of interest arbitration upon government employee labour relations in the USA. One observation is that while collective bargaining continues to be the dominant model for resolving such disputes, even when arbitration is available, some parties become dependent upon arbitration if available. An explanation for this dependence is the presence of special problems regarding the parties' respective power positions and political or personal pressures. In any event, the difference in results between negotiated settlements and arbitral awards does not appear to be very great.[9]

9. P. Feuille, 'Selected Benefits and Costs of Compulsory Arbitration', *Industrial and Labor Relations Review*, 1979, vol. 33, pp. 64, 74–76.

55. In Britain, Parliament has established an independent agency called the Central Arbitration Committee (CAC) consisting of a chairman and members drawn from both union and management representatives. It normally sits as a three member panel. Parliament has established another independent body known as the Advisory Conciliation and Arbitration Service. It is composed of equal numbers of employer, union and public members. For some purposes it sits as an adjudicative tribunal. In that capacity it may impose mandatory terms and conditions of employment upon an enterprise that is failing to carry out its obligation to recognise a labour organisation for collective bargaining. Violations of the award issued by the Service are brought as claims to the CAC. The Service and Committee also have competence to entertain certain claims involving alleged failures to provide minimum standards of employment. Such matters are submitted to conciliation by the Service and, if necessary, to arbitration by the CAC.

56. Many nations have policies that give preference to Adjudication machinery that is established by the disputing parties. For example, in the USA impasses concerning postal worker interest disputes are submitted to a statutory arbitration tribunal only if the parties have not agreed to their own arbitral mechanism. In Kenya, Tanzania, Trinidad and some other developing nations, the labour ministry must refer reported disputes back to the parties' own binding conflict resolution procedures before considering any governmental steps to end the dispute.

57. The Adjudication model is used infrequently or never in some other labour relations systems. Even in countries in which it is not in general use, often Adjudication is a method of interest dispute resolution utilised in some segments of the economy. Thus, in the Swedish printing industry the parties have had long term agreements for the submission of impasses first to mediation and then to arbitration. The textile industry in one region of India arbitrates interest disputes under an arrangement influenced by Mohandas Gandhi in the 1920s. Israel has both voluntary and mandatory interest arbitration structures but they are not often utilised. The FR Germany has no laws compelling submission of the disputes to arbitration. There are some agreements between the employer and labour organisations for such impasse machinery but very few industries resort to these processes. While interest arbitration is legally possible in Belgium, it is not used. Similarly, in Japan it is available but seldom resorted to in the private sector because of the cultural preference for the promotion of harmony through mutual resolution of differences. However, there is some public sector use of arbitration in Japan. Thus, the postal system's wage rates are determined by a tripartite commission through an arbitration process that is guided by the comparable wages paid by private industry.

58. The acceptance of the Adjudication model for settling interest disp[...] has largely been a result of wanting to avoid an alternative of prolo[...] economic warfare or wanting to prevent work stoppages on the part o[...] who provide public services. The Adjudication model, even when[...]

through the generally informal processes of arbitration, is relatively time consuming because the arbiters need to be appointed, or at least notified, the issues must be framed, and the decision-makers must be educated concerning the competing contentions and considerations. Moreover, to the extent that there are neutral principles to be applied, at best they are vague and broad. There is always the danger, too, that the 'neutral' will harbour secret biases or will reach an impractical solution. On the other hand, because there is no precise science of social or economic justice, the benefit of having a method available to definitively resolve the parties' differences often outweighs the disadvantages and dangers of relying upon a neutral third party's imposed decision. Unresolved interest differences are costly when they create open economic warfare; they can be equally costly when they fester in the form of uncertainties or repressed discontent.

VI. VOTING

59. Although voting is a fact finding process, the facts that are found can be influenced by the choice of procedural variables for structuring the process. One such variable is the choice of those who will participate – the electors. Another structural variable is the degree of secrecy of the ballot. Still another is the choice of the time and place for balloting. The result can be influenced, too, by the manner of phrasing the question to be decided and by the number or proportion of votes needed to resolve the question or selection. Finally, the method of counting and weighing ballots are yet added variables that can affect the outcome.

The most obvious use of voting to settle interest disputes is in the determination of who will represent those interests. Representatives to works councils, safety and health committees, shop stewards, negotiating committees, and the like, often are selected by a majority vote of the workers whose interests are affected by the conduct of those representatives.

60. A broader use of Voting to resolve interest disputes is illustrated by the operations of socially owned undertakings in Peru. All personnel of such undertakings are required to meet annually to elect the board of directors. In addition, the workers vote to ratify or reject the proposed general ⌐ager, the proposed annual programme, and the balance sheet. All of ⌐e by secret ballot.

⌐al structures of shop level joint committees and au-
Voting is likely to serve as the model for settling
⌐ants are unable to resolve them through
allow them to be resolved through Ac-
Voting is also often used in determining
ges and other actions respecting unresolved

62. When Negotiation is the principal model used for resolving an interest dispute, frequently the result is subject to a ratifying vote by the affected workers. This is the practice in the FR Germany where rejection of the negotiated agreement is rare. Rejection is less rare in the USA, where ratification votes generally are required under the labour organisation's constitution or by-laws. Finnish labour organisations, too, often condition their collective agreements upon approval by the membership.

63. Voting provides an efficient means for ascertaining the preferences of interested parties and for enabling groups to be self-governing. Also, Voting gives every affected member a chance to participate in determining the outcome and in this way it provides a sense of personal identification with the settlement. That personal identification can be expected to promote individual commitment to carrying out whatever settlement has been reached. On the other hand, Voting involves regulation based upon power differences rather than the balanced, reasoned accommodation of competing and conflicting goals. Often minority interests are ignored and the process is subject to manipulation. In the latter case, Voting can be but a facade for the resolution of disputes through Political Discipline.

VII. Negotiation

64. At the shop floor level it is probably impossible to wholly eliminate at least some resort to Negotiation as a method of interest dispute settlement. In many systems Negotiation is used frequently at all levels and the determination of whether and when to bargain and the subject matter of bargaining is left entirely to the parties' discretion. This essentially is the situation in the FR Germany and in Denmark, among other countries.

In the USA, in contrast, important details concerning bargaining procedure are regulated under the duty to bargain provisions of the National Labour Relations Act, and the potential subjects of bargaining have been classified by the courts into the categories of mandatory (either side may compel good faith discussion), permissive and illegal.

65. Interest disputes can be divided into three classes: integrative, distributive and mixed. Integrative disputes are those in which the parties' interests are not in conflict. The dispute is of a problem solving nature – how can the mutual interests of the parties be best satisfied. Much of the Negotiation within an autonomous work group is of this nature. Distributive issues involve those situations in which the parties' interests conflict – one side's gain is the other's loss. How much of an enterprise's income will be distributed in wages, how much will be reinvested, how much will be distributed to the owners is largely a dispute of this category. The mixed category of interest disputes covers those situations in which there are both distributive and integrative elements. An example of the mixed category of

interest dispute would be the issue of how to schedule individual vacations among a group of employees without shutting down operations.

66. The choice between settling a dispute by Political Discipline, by Governmental Fiat, or by Negotiation, may at times be affected by whether the nature of the dispute is integrative or distributive. As between the parties immediately involved, an integrative dispute is not likely to concern questions of economic or social justice. Hence there likely will be less prospect for settlement by Political Discipline or by Governmental Fiat. Distributive issues, in contrast, largely involve questions of social and economic justice. Therefore, if the labour relations system exists in a society which is governed by fixed *non-laissez faire* concepts, intervention in settling those differences is more likely to be imposed by government or political authorities.

67. The attitude of the parties toward the Negotiation process affects both the outcome and the availability of the method as a means of resolving interest disputes. In some nations there is a tradition of looking upon the negotiating process as an opportunity for the parties to accommodate their differences in a conciliatory and harmonious way. Japan probably is the prime example of such an orientation among the industrial nations. Accordingly, many of the 'acts of dispute' utilised by Japanese workers in support of their bargaining demands are designed not so much to place economic or political pressure on the enterprise as to emphatically communicate the absence of harmony and need for further exploration and mutual adjustment. In the USA, in contrast, there is a tradition of adversarial approach to the bargaining table. Although the intensity of bargaining table adversity is probably less today than it was 50 years ago in the USA, a common concern of the parties' representatives is that their constituents will question their integrity and determination if the relationship begins to reflect too much accommodation and trust.

68. Attitudes toward Negotiation can change with political and social trends. Thus, in Belgium for a long period after the Second World War negotiations were approached with a considerable degree of mutual trust and willingness to compromise, but in recent years a more adversarial tone has come to characterise the relationship.

VIII. CONCILIATED NEGOTIATION

69. When negotiating parties have difficulty adjusting differences through their own efforts, it often helps to introduce an outside party whose goal is to facilitate reaching agreement. At the least intrusive level of such intervention a private outside party is invited by the negotiators to assist in efforts to communicate. More intrusive are those situations in which the third party is a government official whose presence is mandated. Still more intrusive is the third party whose assigned task is to make findings of fact respecting

the matters at issue and report those findings to the parties or even to the public. Finally, there is third party intervention in the form of one whose responsibilities include proposing terms of settlement.

70. In Belgium collective bargaining is carried on through a joint committee chaired by a civil servant. If joint negotiations fail, the parties convene in the form of a conciliation committee. Again the parties are equally represented and chaired by a civil servant but his role at this stage is to actively seek their agreement.

71. Denmark has a Public Conciliation Service consisting of three conciliators and an alternate. Each conciliator has responsibility for a particular bargaining sector. The Danish conciliator's role is very influential because the conciliator can propose a solution and require that the proposal be submitted for vote by the negotiating parties' memberships. Normally a conciliator does not submit questions to a membership vote unless the parties' representatives have requested this action. The Service must be informed of bargaining disputes and the appropriate conciliator can intervene by request or on his own initiative. The conciliators are assisted by a corps of mediators who are assigned to aid the parties in negotiating differences of local interest. If unsuccessful, the mediator submits a written report to the conciliator who can then elect to intervene personally. The parties must jointly consent to the participation of a mediator, but this consent is rarely withheld if requested by the conciliator. Similarly, countries as diverse as Indonesia, Zaire, Ghana, and Venezuela also use multistage conciliation, usually with the first stage being conducted by a single mediator and later ones being conducted by a board or a higher ranking government officer. Another feature of the Danish system that is encountered in some other countries (e.g., New Zealand and Norway) is the prohibition against lawyers presenting the parties' positions to the conciliators.

72. In the FR Germany in most industries the parties have established conciliation arrangements for dealing with impasses in industry-wide bargaining. Also, there are a few examples of state-sponsored conciliation efforts but as a practical matter the only significant conciliation carried out is the unofficial intervention of high government officials in major industrial disputes. Such conciliation by 'political mediators' is a significant institution in Italy where local government officials and even the Labour Ministry intervene in local, national and enterprise bargaining by offering highly publicised settlement proposals. The accompanying public pressure often forces acceptance of these third party proposals with the result that the technique sometimes is described as 'quasi-arbitration'.

73. Ireland provides government conciliators to assist the parties if they desire. Similarly, voluntary conciliation by government mediators generally is available in the USA. However, in some instances it is compulsory. One such situation is where the dispute involves a health care institution. Conciliation is also compulsory in the USA for the railroad and airline industries and in situations in which a court, upon Presidential request, has issued a decree temporarily halting a strike found to threaten national health or safety. A variety of mandatory conciliation and fact finding procedures are also required in the USA in disputes involving govenment workers.

74. In India conciliation officers are entitled to intervene if there is a threat to industrial peace. They must intervene if a notice of strike or lockout is given and the dispute involves a public utility. Similarly, in Israel government conciliation may be imposed at the discretion of the Chief Labour Relations Officer if the parties seek to resort to work stoppages. Once appointed, an Israeli conciliator is given some investigatory authority. Investigatory power is given to conciliators as well in Finland, Sweden, Denmark, India, Peru, and Zaire, among other countries. Generally, information thereby obtained must be treated as confidential.

75. Among its several responsibilities, the British Advisory Conciliation and Arbitration Service provides assistance to parties in resolving collective disputes. Officials of the agency act as bargaining facilitators. However, if the parties seek the more intrusive aid of third party recommendations ('mediation' in British usage), the agency appoints outside independent experts. Intervention is based upon the parties' consent. Although in the 1960s there was growing resentment to government intervention through pre-Service institutions, in recent years there has been evidence of increasing willingness to utilise the assistance of the Service.

76. Krislov and Galin have surveyed union and management attitudes toward conciliation in Britain, Ireland, Israel and the USA. The respondents in all four countries overwhelmingly indicated their feeling that such third party intervention is consistent with mature collective relationships. Greater reluctance to accept conciliation enthusiastically was expressed by the British respondents than by those in the other three countries. Similarly, except in Britain, the respondents generally supported the view that absent conciliation, work stoppages would be more frequent. With the exception of the Israeli respondents, a majority indicated that they favoured forceful conciliators and in all four countries there was a favourable impression of the third party's knowledge and understanding of the bargaining process.[10] In contrast, a separate study by Krislov indicates that in India conciliation is unpopular among larger employers and unions. Moreover, the conciliators are not held in high regard on either side of the bargaining table.[11]

77. Both the Negotiation and Conciliated Negotiation models provide disputing parties with a goal directed opportunity to gain a better understand-

---

10. J. Krislov and A. Galin, 'Comparative Analysis of Attitudes Towards Mediation', *Labor Law Journal*, 1979, vol. 30, p. 165.
11. J. Krislov, 'Supplying Mediation Services in Five Countries', *The Columbia J. of World Bus.*, Summer 1983.

ing of each other's needs and values. If they are amenable to improving the harmony of their inter-relationship, these models provide a means with which this can be achieved. Moreover, these models allow the flexibility needed to examine complex, multifaceted problems and adjust competing values and goals in such a way that the dignity and worth of all participants are acknowledged and the result is tailored to meet their unique needs. In addition, negotiated solutions can be innovative; they can explore previously untried adjustments of differences. Finally, Negotiation can take account of unofficial norms (e.g., deference to the interests of longer term workers) and can accommodate competing norms (e.g., promotion based on ability versus promotion opportunities for loyal, long-term workers). On the negative side, Negotiation and Conciliated Negotiation pose an opportunity for sacrificing the interests of the weak and for reaching expedient settlements that satisfy the desires of the participants but ignore the demands of social and economic interests (including official norms) not represented at the bargaining table. However, where the role of the conciliator is mandatory and the conciliator occupies a governmental position, there is an opportunity to introduce larger concerns of national need and principles of justice into the deliberations.

Interestingly, labour law in nations with developing economies have been particularly emphatic about the need to take economic and social adjustment considerations into account in shaping settlements.[12] Sceptics, nevertheless, may question whether in such situations the lofty goals of justice and national policy in fact ever effectively displace the parties' self-interests in shaping their settlement.

SELECT BIBLIOGRAPHY

B. Aaron, J. Grodin, J. Stern, eds. *Public-Sector Bargaining*, Washington, DC, 1979.
R. Blanpain, ed., *International Encyclopaedia for Labour Law and Industrial Relations*, Deventer.
J. Degivry, 'Prevention and Settlement of Labour Disputes other than Conflicts of Rights', in O. Kahn-Freund, ed., *International Encyclopaedia of Comparative Law*, Tubingen, 1978, vol. XV, ch. 14.
A. Goldman, *Processes for Conflict Resolution*, Washington, DC, 1972.
T. Hanami, 'The Settlement of Labour Disputes in Worldwide Perspective', *Int'l Soc. Sci. J.*, 1980, vol. 32, p. 490.
T. Hanami and R. Blanpain, *Industrial Conflict Resolution in Market Economies*, Deventer, 1984.
EEC, *Prevention and Settlement of Industrial Conflict in EEC Countries*, Brussels, 1982.
ILO, *Conciliation and Arbitration Procedures in Labour Disputes*, Geneva, 1980.
F. Raday, *Adjudication of Interest Disputes – The Compulsory Arbitration Model*, Jerusalem, 1983.
J. Schregle, *Negotiating Development: Labour Relations in Southern Asia*, Geneva, 1987.

12. ILO, *Conciliation and Arbitration Procedures in Labour Disputes*, Geneva, 1980, p. 14.

Chapter 18. Industrial Conflict: Perspectives and Trends

R.O. Clarke[1]

I. The Nature and Manifestation of Industrial Conflict

1. Employers and employees usually come together in a common workplace to make products or provide services for an unspecified time. Employers who are not satisfied with workers can, at least if the action can be objectively justified, discharge them. Workers who find their jobs intolerable are free to quit. However, the usual intention in offering and accepting employment is to enter into a continuing relationship.

2. But continuing relationships – be they marital, business partnerships, or employment – are vulnerable to changing, sometimes diverging, interests, perceived or real. In other words, employment is liable to conflict, both individual and collective. Such conflict may be clear-cut, as when a group of workers are convinced that they are underpaid, or it may be diffuse and not readily apparent, say, some dissatisfaction amongst workers with the style of management in an enterprise. If it is latent and not overt an untoward incident, unimportant in itself, may be enough to set off a major dispute. Thus the apparent cause of an industrial dispute is not always the true cause.

3. Sources of conflict are not confined to the conditions of employment in the employing enterprise. Workers commonly identify their interests with those of workers elsewhere, to the point of being willing to strike in support of them. As members of trade unions which may have both political and broad industrial objectives, workers may use the leverage that withholding their labour gives them to exert pressures on governments or on employers collectively.

4. The manifestations of conflict are varied. The strike is the most obvious form but conflict can equally show itself in high absenteeism – even a high rate of sickness or accidents – or labour turnover, shoddy work, or difficult-to-measure low morale. Concerted action too may take various forms. Overtime may be banned. There may be a refusal to do particular tasks. A

---

1. Mr. Clarke is a Principal Administrator in the Social Affairs and Industrial Relations Division of the OECD, Paris. The views expressed in this chapter are Mr. Clarke's own and do not necessarily represent the views of the OECD.

'go-slow' may be called, or (which in practice comes to the same thing), a 'work-to-rule'. Workers have been known to engage in a 'sick-out', i.e. to absent themselves collectively, declaring that they are sick. At least one British union has been known to announce that its members intended to 'work without enthusiasm' and another that its members would 'withdraw co-operation'. Sterner measures have on occasion included sabotage of plant or products (though this has almost always been confined to individual incidents), 'sit-ins', where workers go to their place of work during normal hours but do not work, and, in a few countries, occupation of the workplace and even sequestration of the management. In support of workers elsewhere workers may refuse to handle products made by a firm in dispute (blacking). Some conflicts are essentially between workers, such as strikes to claim the right to do particular work (demarcation disputes), the employer often being no more than an innocent but afflicted bystander.

5. Industrial conflict is not, of course, a one-way process. But employers are not in the same position as workers. Management may have its divisions of view but it represents one decision-making entity compared with workers. If employers, individually or collectively, are determined to reduce wages or to change established practices, and the workers do not accept, the employers may simply go ahead with the changes – though arbitrary action may well precipitate a strike. And the employers too are in a position to apply sanctions. They may decide that the enterprise should go out of business, or that its production should be transferred elsewhere. They may dismiss strikers. But their most obvious sanction, the mirror image of the strike, is the lockout.

6. The incidence of lockouts is low, compared with strikes. They are likely to be expensive to the employer as well as the workers. Their main use is as a response to a partial action by workers. Thus, if one section of a union's members goes on strike, to minimise the cost to the union, the employer(s) may respond by locking out the rest of the union members. In multi-employer disputes it is often difficult to persuade individual employers to form a common front and, once agreed, to ensure that it is held. Nevertheless, the lockout has continued to be used effectively notably in Sweden and the FR Germany.

7. Unfortunately, statistical data is rare about most of the forms of conflict discussed here. There is, however, considerable data and documentation about strikes and, for that reason, and because they can reasonably stand proxy for industrial conflict generally, most of what follows in this chapter will be based on this one form of action.

8. But even a strike is commonly not so simple in practice. It is rarely a straightforward stoppage of work by x workers for d days. Many strikes are hesitant affairs, starting with a small number of strikers, and later joined by

others. Others start with a large number but weaken as workers drift back to work. Others still are 'in' and 'out' affairs, as workers return to resume negotiations but strike again when they do not get satisfaction. Some strikes are merely mass demonstrations of dissatisfaction, or warning strikes, limited to a day, or even an hour. Some strikes are spontaneous, others carefully planned. In some, only sections of union members are brought out at any one time, the strikers being chosen, by function or, in an industry or multi-plant enterprise, by area, (rotating strikes), so as to bewilder or inflict the maximum damage on the employer at the least cost to the union.[2] In many strikes the stoppage of work is virtually complete. In others it is partial and the employer is able to keep his enterprise in operation. In some cases the refusal of some workers to join a strike ('loyal staff' to the employer, 'scabs' or 'blacklegs' to the strikers) leads to long-lasting bitterness between workers.

9. Conflict is news and peace is not, so the media tend to dwell on strikes but not report cases where differences of interest are resolved in a peaceful and statesmanlike way. There is also some tendency to describe strikes as rather regrettable affairs. So some of them may be but the natural and positive aspects should not be overlooked. Thus most strikes are, basically, merely a natural continuation of the process of collective bargaining. If workers had not been prepared to strike in the past many gains leading to real social progress might never have been made. Then too, some strikes have the effect of releasing tensions and resolving long-fermenting sources of discontent, thus helping social stability.

II. THE MEASUREMENT AND COSTS OF STRIKES

A. Counting

10. It might be thought a relatively simple matter to quantify the frequency and dimensions of strikes but this is far from being the case and the difficulties are multiplied as soon as we try to compare one country's experience with that of another.

11. First, a decision has to be made about what should be counted as a strike. Potentially this raises both qualitative and quantitative questions. Should demonstration stoppages, or strikes with a political objective be counted? Should a series of five half-day stoppages (or two long stoppages several weeks apart) on the same or related subjects be counted as one strike or five (or two)? Should stoppages only be counted as a strike if they last more than h hours or involve n workers and/or involve a loss of x

2. For a consideration of types of strike see D. Weiss, *Les Relations du Travail*, 5th Edition, Paris, 1983, chapter 2.

working hours? In the event of a strike occurring at the same time in more than one workplace of an enterprise, perhaps on the same subject, should it count as one or more strikes?

12. The number of workers striking runs up against the problem that in many strikes the total changes daily. A further problem is whether to count workers not on strike but idled as a result of it.

13. The duration of strikes carries similar problems. Should a strike be counted as starting from the time the first worker stopped or as continuing until the last striker returns, irrespective of what the bulk of the workforce does?

14. What is probably the most useful measure, total working days not worked (though each indicator has its uses), compounds the problem of both the number and duration of strikes. And to make the resultant figures comparable between countries of different size the working days not worked must be calculated on an employment base, typically in practice per 1,000 of the labour force, the total employed population, or the workforce in, say, the manufacturing, construction and transport industries, or in all industries minus agriculture.

15. To add to all these difficulties, the accuracy and comparability of the statistics will depend on the assiduity and accuracy of the arrangements for reporting strikes. The reality underlying present statistics is that many small strikes, and some which come above the threshold for reporting, pass unnoticed.

16. The foregoing difficulties have been posed to illustrate the problems which have to be taken into account in assessing the recording of strikes. They have been fully analysed elsewhere and that analysis need not be repeated here.[3] A helpful factor is that as long ago as 1926 the ILO conducted a full examination of what was being recorded, and what it was desirable to record, and issued a well thought out set of guidelines[4] which, though the guidelines were not mandatory, had a considerable influence in assuring at least some uniformity about the bases of national statistics.

---

3. A comprehensive analysis is to be found in M.R. Fisher, *The Measurement of Labour Disputes and their Economic Effects*, OECD, Paris, 1973. For later reviews see M. Shalev, 'Lies, Damned Lies, and Strike Statistics: the Measurement of Trends in Industrial Conflict', in C. Crouch and A. Pizzorno (eds.), *The Resurgence of Class Conflict in Western Europe Since 1968*, London, 1978, Vol. 1, also Appendix II to that volume, *Problems of Strike Measurement*; and K. Walsh, *Strikes in Europe and the United States*, London, 1983.
4. Resolution concerning Statistics of Industrial Disputes adopted by the Third International Conference of Labour Statistics, ILO, Geneva, 1926.

B. The Cost of Strikes[5]

17. From the strikers' point of view the cost of a strike is normally the income foregone less any income they may secure from the social security system, union strike payments, or from other employment during the strike. Lessened liability to income tax may also have to be taken into account. Workers may make up some of their losses on returning to work through overtime payments or decreased absenteeism. They expect that their investment in the strike will be repaid (at least in the typical case of a wage claim) by increased remuneration following the strike. They have to remember, however, that a strike can be a two-edged weapon in that, insofar as it seriously damages the employer's business, it not only makes him less able to meet future demands but the strike, or the cost of what has been conceded, may force him out of business altogether.

18. It is very difficult to assess the real cost of a strike to the employer. The cost often cited is that of foregone production. Thus, in an automobile plant where all the scheduled production is lost the value of that production may be cited as the cost of the strike. This is clearly misleading. It is by no means certain that the planned productions would have been achieved if there had not been a strike. Further, though customers may be lost, though many overhead expenses – including, perhaps, the wages of non-striking workers idled by the strike – continue during the strike, there are also savings on the costs of normal production: raw material is not used, the wages of strikers are not paid, the workplace may not be heated, etc. The employer's costs will also depend upon whether he has planned ahead, stockpiling products, should that be possible. Costs will vary according to whether the strike occurs at a critical time (transport on the eve of a holiday or a toy factory the month before Christmas, for example). A strike may even help an employer's costs, if it takes place at a period when stocks are high and demand low.

19. But a strike affects more than the struck employer and his workers. A resultant wage increase may be reflected in consequent 'whipsawed' increases in other enterprises. Customers may incur costs because needed products do not arrive and workers may have to be laid off because of lack of work both in the customers' and in suppliers' works. Ultimately some of the costs of the strike are likely to be passed on to the employer's customers in the form of higher prices for goods or services. If the strike is substantial the trade of local shopkeepers may be hit. There will also be costs to the national purse, both in lost income tax (and some indirect taxes because of lower purchases) and in foregone social security contributions, also in social security payments made to strikers and/or their dependants.

---

5. See Fisher, *op. cit.*, pp. 179 ff, for a detailed analysis of the costs and benefits of strikes.

387

20. One aspect of costs is the comparison often made between time lost through strikes and time lost through sickness, with the implication that the very much greater extent of sickness absence shows strike absence to be relatively unimportant. This is quite fallacious. In the case of sickness absence, a fairly small proportion of workers are normally absent at any one time and their colleagues try to ensure that all essential work is carried out. The net effect on production is usually small. In the case of a strike, every effort is made by the strikers to ensure that the cessation of work is complete.

III. TRENDS OF STRIKES

21. We turn now to the strike pattern across countries, as it is today, as it has changed over recent years, and as it may develop. Table 1 shows annual average working days lost per thousand of the total employed for four selected consecutive sub-periods, running from 1960, in 19 OECD countries.

Table 1. Labour Disputes

Working Days Lost per 1,000 of Labour Force (Annual Average)

	1960–1967	1968–1972	1973–1979	1980–1984
Australia	154	384	572	394
Austria	44	5	8	1
Belgium	76	189	196	n.a.
Canada	311	745	837	587
Denmark	160	20	291	94
Finland	120	359	458	393
France	136	144[1]	169	77
Germany, Federal Republic	14	37	39	46
Ireland	336	535	564	349
Italy	569	1038	1063	653
Japan	89	85	80	11
Netherlands	19	22	35	21[3]
New Zealand	71	156	272	295
Norway	65	13	48	54
Spain	14[2]	53	735	437
Sweden	15	63	22	225
Switzerland	3	1	2	1
United Kingdom	121	487	456	318
United States	319	578	286	178
Average for the above 19 countries	139	259	323	230

1. Excluding 1968 strike wave.
2. Data not applicable for years 1960 to 1962 included.
3. 1984 NA.

Sources: ILO, Yearbook of Labour Statistics, Industrial disputes table;
OECD Labour Statistics, Total employment table 1986.

22. The sub-periods were selected as reflecting particular economic circumstances. Thus, in 1960–1967 the industrialised market economies were enjoying sustained economic growth and the post-war spell of industrial peace was still generally prevalent. 1968–1972 was characterised by the French *événements* and largely unexpected outbursts of industrial conflict in Italy, FR Germany, Sweden and Belgium.[6] 1973–1979 covers the economically uncertain years starting with the first oil shock. Finally, 1980–1987 was a period of recession and growing unemployment, and a widespread drive to achieve higher productivity on the part of employers. How, then, did strikes evolve, at least in terms of time lost, over these years?

23. From 1960–1967 the time lost was indeed the lowest of the four sub-periods considered here and was followed by a much more turbulent time. But instead of falling, time lost continued to increase over the difficult years of 1973–1979. It would seem that the underlying surge of militancy manifesting itself in 1968 carried over and was strengthened by the conflict between workers' continuing expectations of steadily improving pay and conditions and the hard economic realities which followed the first oil shock and made it impossible to satisfy those expectations. In the final sub-period, on the other hand, with disappointing economic conditions, working time lost fell substantially, falling in 14 of the 18 countries for which figures are available in fact for all except the three Scandinavian countries, Denmark, Norway and Sweden; in two of the four exceptions, Germany and Sweden, the increase reflected one major dispute. It seems likely that the fall was due to the now heavy unemployment and the realisation by workers that there was little to be had and that if they sought improvements nonetheless they were likely to meet determined resistance by employers.

24. It would not be correct to assume from Table 1 that we live in a strike-prone age. Table 2 compares the annual average days lost, 1980–1983, with the highest previous recorded figures for five of the major countries for which time series are available, showing vastly greater losses in earlier times – and in days when the employed population was much smaller than it is today.

25. As to changes in the occupational mix of strikers the ILO has noted, in an international survey, that there has been a reduction of days lost in mining, but an increase in strikes by teachers, in the tertiary sector, and public services.[8] It is notable that a greater number and variety of workers

---

6. Industrial conflict during these years is particularly well documented. See, for instance, Crouch and Pizzorno, *op. cit.*, and J.-D. Reynaud, 'Industrial Relations and Political Systems: Some Reflections on the Crisis in Industrial Relations in Western Europe', in: *British Journal of Industrial Relations*, March 1980.
7. This is a warning in relation to interpreting strike statistics that one massive strike can lead to an inaccurate concept of the normal degree of industrial conflict in a country.
8. *World Labour Report*, Vol. 2, ILO, Geneva, 1985.

Table 2. Labour Disputes

	Annual Average Working Days Lost 1980–1983	Previous Highest Recorded Working Days Lost in Any One Year	
	(Thousands)	(Thousands)	(Year)
France (omitting 1968)	1,755	23,112	1920
Germany (1980–1983 figures for Federal Republic)	61	36,198	1924
Japan	650	15,075	1952
United Kingdom (omitting 1926)	6,324	85,872	1921
United States	16,069	116,000	1946

are nowadays involved in strikes than in earlier years.[9] It would seem that there has been an undermining of normative barriers to strike action which existed in the past. Hibbs has ascribed changes in strike volume to changes in the locus of the struggle over distribution.[10]

26. Open to extensive qualification as the statistics are, some significant facts are readily apparent. Thus we can note the substantial extent to which countries maintain roughly the same position in the 'league table'. For example Italy, Canada, Australia (until recently) and Ireland are normally to be found near the head of the table and Switzerland and Austria at the bottom. There are few dramatic moves over time from high to low position or *vice versa*. (The exceptional cases in Table 1, Spain and Sweden, are accountable to the political change of 1977 in the first case and the major dispute of 1980 in the second. If, however, the table were extended backward, to the 1920s, it would be seen that changes can take place; thus Sweden was commonly a high-strike country in the inter-war years, until management and unions, weary of conflict, determined, through the famous Saltsjöbaden Agreement of 1938, to find a more peaceful way of regulating their differences. Switzerland too experienced some turbulent years before a new era began with the Industrial Peace Agreement in the metal industry of 1937 – an Agreement which has been regularly renewed to the present day.)

27. The second fact to note is the enormous differences between the almost negligible loss of working time through strikes in, say, Austria or Switzerland compared with Italy and Canada.

28. The general impression gained from Table 1 is that the incidence of time lost through strikes has tended to reflect the changing economic and social

9. See Shalev, 1979, *op. cit.*, pp. 7 and 8.
10. D.A. Hibbs, Jnr., 'On the Political Economy of Long-Run Trends in Strike Activity', in: *British Journal of Political Science*, Vol. 8, No. 2, p. 165.

environment[11] but that it is difficult to infer any marked change of a structural kind. In this respect it is useful to look back to the major international review published by Ross and Hartman in 1960.[12]

29. Ross and Hartman based their work on the experience of 15 non-communist countries from 1900 to 1956. Their findings suggested a gradual decline in the proportion of union members going on strike and in the average duration of strikes in all the countries. They spoke of 'the withering away of the strike, the virtual disappearance of industrial conflict in numerous countries where collective bargaining is still practised', and of the transformation of the strike from a test of economic strength into 'a brief demonstration of protest'. The volume of industrial conflict, they concluded, would continue to diminish in the long run.[13] They did not, however, expect the strike to wither away in the United States.

30. The primary reasons for the changed pattern of strikes, as Ross and Hartman saw it, were that employers had 'developed more sophisticated policies and more effective organisations'; that the state had 'become more prominent as an employer of labour, economic planner, provider of benefits, and supervisor of industrial relations'; and that in many countries (but not in the USA) the labour movement had been 'forsaking the use of the strike in favour of broad political endeavour'.[14]

31. Ross and Hartman were writing at a time when most industrialised countries, including the USA, had first gone through a somewhat turbulent period, following the war, and then entered a relatively quiescent period, starting in the early 1950s. Their basic expectations have plainly been proved wrong, and both the logic of their findings and their methodology have been questioned,[15] but at the time their broad argument that strikes were decreasing as industrial relations machinery became better able to resolve conflict and the role of state changed seemed reasonable enough.

32. With this historical perspective, what can be said about present and likely future trends in strikes?

33. The determinants of strike activity can be divided into environmental and structural. The principal environmental determinant in recent years has

11. See, for a comprehensive review of strike movements, M. Shalev, 'Strikes and the Crisis: Industrial Conflict and Unemployment in the Western Nations', in *Economic and Industrial Democracy*, 1983, Vol. 4, pp. 417–460.
12. A.M. Ross and P. Hartman, *Changing Patterns of Industrial Conflict*, New York.
13. *Op. cit.*, pp. 6, 181.
14. *Op. cit.*, p. 42.
15. See, for instance, J.E.T. Eldridge, *Industrial Disputes, Essays in the Sociology of Industrial Relations*, London, 1968, ch. 1, and G.K. Ingham, *Strikes and Industrial Conflict, Britain and Scandinavia*, London, 1974, ch. 1.

undoubtedly been the economic situation, and this seems likely to continue to be dominant. Many workers have recently gone through a period of constraint, so far as the yields of collective bargaining are concerned, and have quite widely had to accept a tightening up to working practices. Economic improvement is likely to bring efforts by workers to restore past losses and achieve new gains, particularly once unemployment starts to fall. Such efforts are not likely to be strife-free. Secondly, in most countries sweeping changes are taking place in industrial structures, as old industries decline and new ones spring up. Such change often bears hardly on workers and is likely to present many points of friction. A third environmental factor is the current major wave of technological change: much depends on how well it is handled but it is in any case a potential source of dispute. In short, the level of strike activity in the years to come may be depressed by high unemployment but there is not likely to be any substantial reduction.

34. As the relative hierarchical stability in the 'league table' suggests, other determinants of strike activity are peculiar to each country and largely unchanging. The general factors mentioned above seem to have the least weight in the countries which have the lowest proportion of days lost and, here, too, there is no reason to expect any substantial change in the near future, since no major relevant changes are taking place in the economic circumstances or political or social structures in these countries.

35. A study[16] of whether there is *prima facie* evidence of relationships between strikes and particular economic indicators, in 1980, suggested that high-strike countries are also high-inflation countries, and tend to be high-unemployment countries. No clear relationship was found between strikes and economic growth.

36. As to the possible relationship of strikes and inflation, unemployment and economic growth apart, it is difficult to see any clearly identifiable common factors amongst the high-strike countries on the one hand or among the low-strike countries on the other. Perhaps the only generalisation that can be made is that Austria, the FR of Germany, Japan and Switzerland (all consistently among the lowest-ranking countries in Table 1 above) are what might be called 'consensual' countries, whereas Italy, Canada and Australia (among the highest-ranking countries in the table) might be called 'conflictual' countries. It should be said that 'consensual' is used here in the sense that the bulk of the population is broadly in agreement as to the economic and social goals at which the country should aim, and how to achieve them. It by no means supposes an absence of dissent but only that dissent is markedly less noticeable than common purpose. Conversely,

16. R.O. Clarke, 'Labour-Management Disputes: a Perspective', in: *British Journal of Industrial Relations*, March, 1980.

'conflictual' denotes countries where there are substantial disagreements between groups of the population on economic and social policies.

37. But are strikes, or industrial conflict in general, so very important? The importance of strikes can indeed be, and often is, overstressed and, as we have noted above, a large volume of strikes seems to have little effect on economic growth. Nevertheless, some strikes involve economic costs and disruption of the day to day business of the community which are clearly out of all proportion to the issues at stake, and in any case it is difficult to disagree that if disputes can be resolved without recourse to strikes, lock-outs, or other forms of industrial action, so much the better. It is in this spirit that our societies have sought to rationalise conflict and, as Barbash has put it, 'substituted procedural and substantive rules for trial-by-ordeal and confrontation'.[17] The next section reviews, from the point of view of industrial relations institutions and practices, the peaceful means adopted to avoid and resolve disputes.

IV. THE AVOIDANCE AND RESOLUTION OF DISPUTES

38. Since most forms of conflict resolution are fully discussed from a legal standpoint in the chapters by Professors Aaron, Goldman and Birk in this volume the treatment in this chapter will be brief and concentrated on non-legalistic procedures.

39. In principle any issue arising between management and workers or their unions could be dealt with by legislation; through an ordinary or special court of law or tribunal; by a process of third-party conciliation; or through a procedure instituted by employers' associations (or individual employers) and unions to formalise their relationship and to deal with questions arising in it.

40. Both legal or quasi-legal and what we may call by contrast voluntary procedures established by the parties have different advantages and dis-advantages. Thus, legalistic procedures are equitable; they are even-handed, not unduly favouring those with strong bargaining power; and they build a body of case law which helps all concerned to know just where they stand. The disadvantages are that they tend to be slow, cumbersome and that their existence may discourage the parties from trying to resolve their own disputes, sometimes expensive, and that they may produce decisions which one or the other party finds unacceptable.

41. The advantages of voluntary procedures established by the parties are that they are largely aimed at producing settlements with which both

17. See J. Barbash, *The Elements of Industrial Relations*, Madison, Wisconsin, 1984, p. 132.

disputants can live; they are flexible both as to their findings and their method of operation; they can be tailored to suit particular circumstances; and they are less tied by precedent than legalistic procedures. As the authors of the procedures, and because conflict imposes costs on them, the parties have a vested interest in making them work. On the other hand, voluntary procedures tend to be susceptible to the balance of bargaining power at the expense of equity or efficient working.

42. Countries in which an important proportion of labour disputes are settled through agreed procedures include Belgium, Canada, the FR Germany, Sweden, Switzerland, the UK and the USA. In some countries, such as Belgium, Denmark, the Netherlands, the UK, and USA, the use of voluntary procedures goes back to the nineteenth century – indeed in the UK such procedures were discussed in the 1830s and the first joint board of lasting importance was set up as early as 1860, for the hosiery trade in Nottingham.[18]

43. Common to the great majority of procedures is the assumption – with the force of law in many countries and incorporated in collective agreements in others – that the process provided is intended to replace or at least defer a trial by force, so that there is no justification for any departure from normal working to enforce a claim during the time that discussions are in progress.[19] As Prof. Birk points out, in the following chapter, this peace obligation may be general or confined to the specified life of an agreement.

44. The existence of an agreed procedure for resolving disputes is not always in practice a guarantee that peace will be maintained. Workers may feel so strongly about an issue that they strike contrary to a procedure agreement (wildcat strikes) – and sometimes outside the rules of their own union (unofficial strikes). Such strikes are particularly likely if events arrive which were not foreseen in existing agreements, if management has acted in what workers consider to be an arbitrary and unacceptable manner, or where there has been dilatoriness in operating the agreed procedure.

45. How severely wildcat strikes are viewed varies according to national attitudes. Clearly they are blameworthy on moralistic grounds, though it is best to suspend judgement on particular cases until all the circumstances are known. Pragmatically, they often have a value as a safety valve, drawing attention to a source of grievance which should be quickly redressed. If

18. See R. Blanpain, 'Prevention and Settlement of Collective Labour Disputes in the EEC Countries', in: *Industrial Law Journal*, June and September 1972; 'Conciliation and Arbitration in Labour Disputes', ILO, Geneva, 1980; and, for early British experience, Ian G. Sharp, *Industrial Conciliation and Arbitration in Great Britain*, London, 1950.
19. B. Aaron and K.W. Wedderburn (eds.), *Industrial Conflict*, London, 1972, ch. 3, gives a good account of the peace obligation in a study of five European countries and the United States.

there are frequent wildcat strikes the main fault may lie in bad management or in the inadequacy of the formal procedural arrangements.

46. When a prescribed bipartite voluntary procedure has been exhausted, unless a reference to arbitration or some other form of third party involvement has been stipulated either party is free to take arbitrary action to enforce his will or support his position. At this point – if not before if the dispute is a costly one – the question arises as to whether the community interest demands some form of intervention in the dispute by the state.

V. The Role of the State

47. The prime responsibility of the state in relation to labour disputes is to provide a legal framework for their conduct. Beyond this the rationale for the state taking an active part in relation to them has two bases. The more general case is that a peacemaking service for disputants is worthwhile in that it may diminish the cost of disputes to the community. This aspect has been well put in the American Labor Management Relations Act, 1947, in the words: 'the settlement of issues between employers and employees through collective bargaining may be advanced by making available full and adequate government facilities for conciliation, mediation, and voluntary arbitration. . .'

48. Secondly, there is the particular case that a dispute may be deemed so serious as to pose an unacceptable threat to the interests of the community.

49. On these bases a whole array of services for the use of the parties have been built up in different countries over the years.[20] They include assisting the parties by information, and by advisory, research and educational services, and providing conciliation, mediation and arbitration services.

50. The extent of these services varies considerably between countries. In France the main agent of state involvement in disputes is the labour inspector, whose principal function, as in other countries, is ensuring observance of protective and other labour legislation. In the FR Germany there is a strong conviction that disputes are for unions and employers themselves to sort out, in an orderly manner, and there are no legal provisions for federal conciliation or arbitration. (In practice in very important disputes in the FR Germany people prominent in political life may be named as mediators.) Japan has a tripartite labour relations commission system. The UK has a history of state services in relation to disputes going back to the nineteenth century. The publicly-funded but autonomous ACAS

---

20. For a useful survey see 'Conciliation and Arbitration Procedures in Labour Disputes', *op. cit.*

has a general duty to promote improvement of industrial relations and provides conciliation services, responding to requests but acting on its own initiative to approach disputants when it thinks fit. It also administers a voluntary arbitration service. In the USA the role of the FMCS is to help the parties to a dispute whenever it judges that the dispute threatens a substantial interruption of commerce.

51. The main argument against the provision of services by the state is that it diminishes the incentive to employers and trade unions to resolve their disputes.

52. Lastly, we come to the role of the state in respect of those disputes which affect essential services or are otherwise potentially damaging to the national interest, commonly known as emergency disputes.[21] The ILO has pointed out that: 'Practically all countries have provisions that prohibit strikes in essential services or, at least, restrict recourse to strikes in order to ensure that truly vital services can continue to operate'.[22] The range of options open to governments in respect of emergency disputes includes:
(a) establishing an inquiry into the dispute by a court or committee, which may or may not make recommendations;
(b) compulsory conciliation, mediation or arbitration;
(c) forceful intervention.

53. Commenting on these possibilities in turn, the value of an official inquiry is that by establishing the facts relating to a dispute, not only does it bring the pressure of public opinion to bear on the disputing parties, but, in practice, the process of inquiry often produces a change of view in one or more of them. The use of inquiries is not, of course, confined to emergency disputes but can be particularly useful for such disputes since the public interest adds weight to their significance. As Prof. Birk notes in the following chapter, the American Labor Management Relations Act, 1947, requires fact-finding to be carried out in respect of a dispute designated by the President as damaging to national health or safety. In Britain the Secretary for Employment has the power to set up a court of inquiry into a dispute, though, because of the existence of ACAS, the power is sparingly used.

54. Outside the special form existing in Australia, compulsory conciliation, mediation or arbitration, in relation to disputes is uncommon in industrialised market economies, though widely used in developing countries. The exception is that in some cases they are used for certain classes of public employees for whom a strike would be harmful to the community – firemen, police, etc. In Canada, compulsory arbitration is one of two procedures used

---

21. The following discussion draws on *Labour Disputes: a Perspective*, OECD, Paris, 1979.
22. *World Labour Report*, Vol. 2, ILO, Geneva, 1985.

for the civil service, the other procedure leading to strike action and the choice of procedure being optional for a bargaining group. In Denmark and Sweden official conciliators have the power to summon the parties to appear before them in the event of a serious labour dispute.

55. Forceful intervention by the State is now somewhat rare. It may conclude:
(a) seizing and operating the enterprise or industry in dispute;
(b) drafting the workers concerned into public service and requiring them to carry on work;
(c) using the armed forces to carry on the strikers' work; and
(d) legislating the terms of a settlement.

56. The main example of the government temporarily taking over an enterprise or industry is in the USA, though it has not been used for many years. Under Presidential seizure strikers were required to continue work under the prevailing conditions with the state assuming control of operations (and profits if any) until agreement could be reached.

57. The enforced continuation of essential work by conscripting the workers concerned into public service, and instructing them to carry on with their normal work, as M. Briand did in the famous French railway strike of 1910, is rare nowadays, though it has been done in Spain.

58. The use of troops to safeguard essential services is also less common than it used to be but it is sometimes applied in cases such as operating ambulance or fire-fighting services or clearing uncollected garbage. Particularly notable has been the use of military personnel to keep flights running during strikes by air traffic controllers, for instance in France and the USA.

59. Finally, government-legislated settlements have sometimes been applied, notably in Denmark, in the case of major obdurate wage claims. Normally, however, the processes of legislation are too slow and too insensitive to the nuances of industrial usage for the method to be used frequently.

60. The mention of legislated wage settlements recalls that one of the most notable post-war developments in industrial relations has been the increased tendency, in many countries, for wage settlements to exceed levels which economic policy-makers regard as consistent with anti-inflationary policies. This tendency has had two implications relevant to the present chapter. Firstly, it has often caused governments to intervene – sometimes with and smetimes without the agreement of trade unions and employers' associations – in the wage determination process, be it by a general freeze on wages for specified periods, by halting or slowing the results of indexation of wages on prices, where that is practised, or by setting limits which wage

increases should not exceed. Secondly, state conciliation services have been faced with problems, in some countries, where they have been concerned with cases where their traditional even-handed aptitude to the parties has been suspected of breaking down because a claim is in conflict with the announced policies of government. This is one of the reasons which has prompted separation of state conciliation services from direct administration by a ministry, as in the case of the United Kingdom where the Advisory, Conciliation and Arbitration Service was created in 1975, as an autonomous body, but assumed functions earlier carried out by the Department of Employment.

VI. CONCLUDING COMMENTS

61. This chapter has briefly reviewed, from an institutional standpoint, the nature and manifestation of industrial strife, trends in strike activity, and institutions and procedures for the resolution of disputes. There has, in recent years been little change in the nature and manifestation of conflict. The volume of strikes first increased, starting near the end of the 1960s, and went on increasing until it declined, over 1980–1985. Though strikes may continue to decrease somewhat, while unemployment remains high and inflation relatively low, there are plenty of likely points of friction and there is certainly no likelihood of their 'withering away' in any country.

62. It is difficult to see a likelihood of any sweeping change in the ways in which conflict is mediated. There is nothing new about the successful resolution of industrial conflict: it remains, as it has always been, a function of good management and a simple, expeditious, effective and trusted set of procedures for dealing with the terms of collective relations and individual grievances. In these regards there is plenty of room for improvement.

63. The role of the state in relation to industrial conflict is a difficult one. In many countries the state is at the same time responsible for setting the legal framework, for protecting the national economic interest, and often for serving as industrial peacemaker. In addition it has come to have a greatly enlarged role as an employer, direct and indirect, itself. Integrating the various elements of this role is not likely to become any easier in the foreseeable future. But for dealing with major disputes, or disputes in key sectors, experience has provided a range of procedures sufficiently large and varied to cope with most problems.

SELECT BIBLIOGRAPHY

C. Crouch and A. Pizzorno (eds.), *The Resurgence of Class Conflict in Western Europe since 1968*, Macmillan, London, 1978.
P.K. Edwards and H. Scullion, *The Social Organisation of Industrial Conflict*, Blackwell, Oxford, 1982.

E.W. Evans and S.W. Creigh (eds.), *Industrial Conflict in Britain*, Cass, London, 1977.

T. Hanami and R. Blanpain (Eds), *Industrial Conflict Resolution in Market Economies*, Kluwer, Deventer, 1984.

R. Hyman, *Strikes*, Fontana-Collins, London, 1972.

G.K. Ingham, *Strikes and Industrial Conflict*: *Britain and Scandinavia*, Macmillan, London, 1974.

ILO, *Conciliation and Arbitration in Labour Disputes*, Geneva, 1980.

A. Kornhauser, R. Dubin and A.M. Ross (eds.), *Industrial Conflict*, McGraw-Hill, New York, 1954.

OECD, *Labour Disputes*, Paris, 1979.

M. Shalev, 'Strikes and the Crisis', in: *Economic and Industrial Democracy*, November 1983.

K. Walsh, *Strikes in Europe and the United States*, Pinter, London, 1983.

H. Wheeler, *Industrial Conflict. An Integrative Theory*, University of South Carolina Press, Columbia, SC, 1985.

Chapter 19. Industrial Conflict: The Law of Strikes and Lock-outs

R. Birk

1. Conflict is a necessary consequence of industrial relations. Such conflict arises both within groups of workers, within the individual employment relationship or between a group of workers and a group of employers. Here we are concerned only with the latter type of industrial conflict, namely collective industrial conflict. The conflict is revealed in more or less frequent industrial action. Its most common manifestation is the strike. Sometimes the employers reply with a lock-out of the workers.

2. The form and extent of such conflict and action differ; they are by no means always the same. This depends not only on varying social conditions but it is also a product of the law itself. The law on industrial action, both conceptually and in detail, displays striking and considerable differences.

3. The comparative analysis and evaluation of the legal regulation of strikes and lock-outs as a legal model for the solution of industrial conflict is the subject of this chapter.[1] However, lack of space does not permit a comprehensive and detailed description. In addition, we have no reliable factual or legal material in regard to a number of states.[2] Often the law on industrial

1. The literature on this topic in English is very small. Only B. Aaron *et al.*, *Industrial Conflict – A Comparative Legal Survey*, London, 1972, is of some relevance.
2. For various countries there are monographs on the legal problems of industrial conflict. The following selection is not exhaustive:
Austria: Th. Tomandl, *Streik und Aussperrung als Mittel des Arbeitskampfes*, Wien/New York, 1965.
Belgium: M. Rigaux, *Staking en bezetting naar Belgisch recht*, Antwerpen, 1979.
Denmark: P. Jacobsen, *Kollektiv arbejdsret*, 3rd edn., Copenhague, 1982.
FR Germany: H. Seiter, Streikrecht und Aussperrungsrecht, Tübingen, 1975; H. Brox/B. Rüthers (ed.), *Arbeitskampfrecht*, 2nd edn., Stuttgart, 1982; W. Däubler (ed.), *Arbeitskampfrecht*, Baden-Baden, 1984.
France: R. Latournerie, *Le droit français de la grève*, Paris, 1972; B. Teyssié, *Les conflits collectifs du travail*, Paris, 1981; H. Sinay/J.-Cl. Javillier, *La grève*, 2nd edn., Paris, 1984.
Italy: D. Garofalo/P. Genoviva, *Lo sciopero*, Torino, 1984.
Netherlands: P. Zonderland, *Recht en plicht bij staking en tegenstaking*, 2nd edn., Deventer, 1974.
Portugal: B. Xavier, *Direito da greve*. Lisboa, 1984.
Spain: M. Alonso Garcia, *La huelga y el cierre empresarial*, Madrid, 1979; J. Garcia Blasco, *El derecho de huelga en Espana*, Madrid, 1983.
United Kingdom: O. Kahn-Freund, *Labour and the Law*, 3rd edn., London, 1984; P. Davies/M. Freedland, *Labour Law*, 2nd edn., London 1984, p. 693 ff.

action does not go beyond certain programmatic declarations. General legal regulation in effect does not exist. This is because in modern democracies such rules which necessarily imply some limitations on freedom of action are not always politically feasible. Therefore the legislature often wraps itself in silence and leaves its duty to the courts (e.g., FR Germany, France, Italy).

I. METHODS AND FORMS OF INDUSTRIAL ACTION

4. Industrial action manifests itself above all in the stoppage of work in order to exert pressure on the opponent. The strike and the lock-out are the chief weapons of pressure and counter-pressure.

A. *Definitions*

5. Strikes and lock-outs may be defined in a wider or more restricted sense. For legal purposes however we need the greatest possible precision. We cannot rest with the individual choice of every author. The subsuming of a certain situation under the concept of strike is no verdict on its lawfulness or unlawfulness but means that in principle the relevant legal rules on industrial conflict and their legal limits are applicable. Concept formation therefore does not have a descriptive but a normative function.

6. Most legal systems regard a *strike* as the organised or co-ordinated full or partial stoppage of work by a group of workers in order to exert pressure on the employer for fulfilment of certain demands. According to the circumstances, purpose and organisational execution there are several, legally relevant forms such as the wage strike, protest strike, token strike, sympathy strike, work-to-rule, official strike, wildcat strike and others.

7. The lock-out involves the reverse situation. As an essential weapon of the employer, it is a work stoppage caused by one or more employers closing down a plant in order to exert pressure on the workers to abandon their demands or to accept the demands of their employers. As with the strike, we can also subdivide the lock-out into various types.

8. Normally the strike is an aggressive weapon while the lock-out has a defensive function against the demands of the workers.

9. Although a number of legal systems define strikes and/or lock-outs by legislation, the reason is frequently not to facilitate concept formation but to specify the means of application of the relevant statute.[3] Nevertheless such definitions are of general interest.

---

3. Cf. J. de Givry, 'Prevention and Settlement of Labour Disputes, Other Than Conflicts of Rights', in O. Kahn-Freund, ed., *International Encyclopedia of Comparative Law*, Vol. XV, ch. 14, pp. 3–4.

Strikes and lock-outs can be regarded as *primary* industrial actions. They are often accompanied and complemented by *secondary* industrial action such as boycotts, picketing, neutrality and sympathy strikes.

B. Different Types of Strike and Lock-out

10. The more broadly one defines the concept of strikes the more various are its forms. The lock-out is not so differentiated however.

1. Forms of Strike[4]

11. The classification of strikes depends on the criteria of differentiation, for example purpose, target, duration, autonomy, form and extent of work stoppage. Which forms of strike are existent in a specific country depends on the structure of industrial relations. In any case some forms always exist, but rarely are all types to be found.

a. The Purpose of a Strike

12. One may distinguish between a situation where the strikers exert pressure on an employer and one in which the main aim is to provide a warning or demonstration of a certain attitude. Thus we may distinguish between strikes to wring a concession, warning or token strikes and demonstration strikes.

b. Tactics

13. The extent of a strike is often determined by tactical aspects. The general strike which embraces all workers is rare even when the area affected is very small. In many states the partial strike or 'whipsaw strike' is of more importance. Both concepts often signify the same state of affairs: either a strike in part of a plant, e.g., in one of several departments, or a strike against only some employers in a certain area. If the strike consists of a number of outbreaks over time we have a successive strike of which there are many variations in different countries.

c. The Adversary

14. Not every strike is intended to support a demand directed towards an employer. The latter case is referred to as a strike on labour matters. If a demand can be met only by the parliament or the government, then we speak of a *political strike*. The political strike has often taken the form of a *general strike*.

---

4. For the international strike see R. Birk, *Die Rechtmäßigkeit gewerkschaftlicher Unterstützungskampfmassnahmen*, Stuttgart, 1978, pp. 127 ff.

403

A special case is the *jurisdictional strike* as it is known in the USA. The work stoppage takes place because of inter-union conflicts; it does not aim at improving labour conditions.

d. Primary and Secondary Strikes

15. If the strikes have purposes of their own but support a foreign strike, the so-called primary strike or principal strike, then they are involved in a *sympathy* or *solidarity* strike and therefore in a secondary strike. The delimitation of the various types, as well as the terminology of such supportive strikes are indeed not always clear.

The American and British characterisation of primary and secondary strikes is somewhat different. If workers direct their action against their employer, this is normally referred to as a primary strike. If action is directed against a supplier or customer of the employer in order to bring pressure to bear on the latter, this is called secondary action or a secondary boycott.

In particular Great Britain (section 17 Employment Act 1980) and the USA (section 8(b)(4) National Labour Relations Act) handle these questions in an extremely detailed and complicated manner. It is therefore hardly possible to give a correct, general statement. The secondary strike is the strike which is directed against the supplier or customer of the primary strike employer. Sometimes the distinction is not drawn between a secondary boycott and a secondary strike. The typical case of a secondary strike is the sympathy strike. Sympathy strikes and secondary boycotts can coincide.

e. Behaviour During a Strike

16. A strike does not consist merely in work stoppage resulting from absence in a plant. When workers are present at their work place, a strike may take the form of a sit-in or occupation of the plant.

But strikers may refuse only certain types of work, e.g., they may refuse to work overtime as an overtime ban. Other kinds of a partial work stoppage are the go-slow, work-to-rule, or mass absenteeism.

f. The Administration of a Strike

17. A distinction which is of great practical importance is whether or not a strike is organised by a union. A strike organised by a union is an *official strike*. A strike which is not organised by a union is often called a *wildcat* or unofficial strike. The difference is important because in many countries the unofficial strike is not legal (e.g., FR Germany, Sweden).

2. Types of Lock-out

18. A typology of the lock-out parallels that of the strike. Because of the far fewer number of lock-outs, however, it does not play the same role.

While the strike is normally regarded as an offensive, the lock-out is normally defensive.

When a lock-out is organised by an employers' association it is an association lock-out. In the FR Germany this is the most important type and it is used against strikes organised by trade unions.

3. Other Methods of Industrial Action[5]

19. In addition to the strike, which is practically and theoretically the most important weapon of industrial action, boycotts and picketing also play a significant role. However, their relevance varies considerably from country to country. The *boycott* is not used primarily as an autonomous weapon, on the contrary its practical significance is to support a strike, and therefore as a *secondary boycott*. As a primary weapon it occurs where strikes have no or not much chance of success because of the special situation of industrial relations – e.g., in the shipping industry.

In Scandinavia a boycott by workers is called a 'blockade'.

20. Picketing, on the other hand, is very common, and especially in the Anglo-American area: it constitutes an important method of industrial action. In other countries it is limited mainly to a plant on strike and is directed to non-striking colleagues and to win them to the strike by psychological pressure. Picketing at the same time also implies a boycott of strikers directed against outside workers to prevent the latter from seeking work in the plant or enterprise which is on strike.

In the USA and in Britain firms and plants which are not on strike are also picketed: the objective of picketing is often to impede the supply and transport of goods, raw materials and energy in order to exert further pressure on the employer. In Britain section 16 Employment Act 1980 (cf. also sections 8 and 9 Code of Practice: Picketing (1980) and Annex) permits picketing only of the primary employer. In the USA this will be further extended when the premises are shared by other employers (common situs picketing).[6]

II. General Legal Attitudes to Industrial Action

21. No legal order can be totally indifferent to industrial conflict; it is thus a legal problem. Its respective standpoint depends much on political, social and economic factors which cannot be described, not only because of the lack of space but also for lack of sufficient evidence. Equally varied is the regulation and in accordance with what principles.[6a] Here *three models of*

---

5. Cf. for aspects of comparative law see R. Birk (N. 4).
6. Cf. Goldman, *IELL* (USA), 1983, pp. 174 ff.
6a. Cf. the comparative survey of R. Birk, 'Gesetzliche und autonome Regelung des Arbeits-kampfrechts im Ausland', *Recht der Arbeit*, 1986, p. 205–216.

state behaviour and therefore of legal order may be identified:[7] The law of a state may disapprove, tolerate or recognise industrial action.

None of the three variants has, however, been systematically elaborated as a theoretical concept. One can identify only certain basic ideas.

A. Suppression of Industrial Action

22. An explicit legal or factual prohibition of the strike cannot be found in any democratic state. It would be incompatible with the principles and maxims of democracy. In an *authoritarian state* industrial action is a danger to the established order, and therefore prohibited.

23. The *socialist state* as a state with a centrally planned economy is also hostile to industrial action. It not only disturbs or prevents central planning but it also denies ideological presumptions, since no one can strike against him/herself. Industrial actions are thus in theory impossible.

B. Freedom to Strike

24. Freedom of strike means that the strike is legally permitted but no special privileges are granted. In this case the strike does not need special rules. The legal *limits* of the freedom to strike are hence a consequence of the *general legal order*. The strike is tolerated but not privileged. This does not however prevent certain aspects from being regulated. A typical example is *Britain*.[8] The participation of a worker in a strike normally entails a breach of the employment contract, it is not normally allowed as long as the contract is valid. On the other hand, collective action was protected by the negative immunity in 'trade disputes' given to those who organise industrial action. Recently, this immunity has been further restricted by statute (e.g., section 15 ff. Employment Act 1982).[9]

25. The freedom to strike differs also from the freedom to organise although both are linked to a certain extent. Only a democratic state with – at least partial – market economy and independent labour organisations can tolerate strikes.

C. The Right to Strike

26. The right to strike differs from the freedom to strike when the legal order evaluates the pursuit of collective interests more highly than the opposed individual obligations of the employment contract. The strike is

---

7. Cf. T. Tomandl, 'Grundprobleme des Arbeitskampfrechts in rechtsvergleichender Sicht', *Zeitschrift für Arbeitsrecht*, 1974, pp. 187 ff.
8. Kahn-Freund, *op. cit.*, pp. 227 ff.
9. Cf. Davies/Freedland, *Labour Law*, 2nd ed., London, 1984, pp. 790 ff, 817 ff.

therefore privileged. If the right to strike is guaranteed the legal order of a state must hence take precautions to ensure the exercise of this right and not to impede it.

The detailed regulation of the right to strike may vary considerably in conditions and extent.

27. The legal regulation of the collective pursuit of interests by means of industrial action depends essentially on the legal relationship between collective bargaining and the right of strike, i.e. whether there is a strong or loose connection between them. This relationship has consequences for the question of parity, the peace obligation, the lockout or the wildcat strike. This also raises the question of whether comprehensive legal regulation of *industrial action* is possible or only of *strikes*.

28. Essentially we can find *three* different answers in modern industrialised states:
(1) the right to industrial action consists substantially in a comprehensive right to strike (France, Italy);
(2) the right to industrial action includes both parties in the labour market (USA, Canada);
(3) the right to industrial action is part of a comprehensive law of industrial action; this law of industrial action and the collective autonomy to conclude agreements are closely connected (FR Germany, Sweden).

1. The Comprehensive Right to Strike

29. The French and Italian constitutions guarantee the right to strike[10] within limits to be determined by statute, as yet neither France nor Italy has enacted such a statute. This doctrine refuses parity between the trade unions and employers' associations on the level of collective bargaining on the grounds that workers are less powerful than employers. Therefore only the right to strike is privileged; the lock-out is merely tolerated. The distinction between an official and unofficial or wildcat strike is legally insignificant. The peace obligation of trade unions is suspect. Only a strike suspends the obligations of the employment relationship. A lock-out entails a breach of contract.

2. Equality of the Strike and the Lock-out

30. In the USA and in Canada the legislature to some extent gives trade unions and employers the same opportunities in industrial conflict. This is deemed necessary for the workability of the system and for the procedure of collective bargaining.

---

10. 'Il diritto di sciopero si esercita nell' ambito delle leggi che regolano'.

3. Comprehensive Law on Industrial Action

31. The third type of regulation exists in the FR Germany[11] and in Sweden.[12] Strikes and lock-outs are respected both as weapons of the same value in industrial conflict. In this respect there is parity between trade unions and employers' associations.

In the FR Germany the legal basis are the decisions of the Federal Labour Court; in Sweden it is based on the constitution, statutes and agreements concluded between the trade union congress and the central employers' association.

32. In both countries the strikes administered by trade unions are privileged, while unofficial strikes are unlawful. The individual obligation outweighs collective interests in this respect. The peace obligation is in Sweden explicitly regulated for the parties to a collective agreement and their members by statute. In the FR Germany it is only applicable on the basis of judge-made law and the dominant doctrine, and it applies only to the parties to a collective agreement but not to their members.[13]

Parity in industrial action and with regard to the peace obligation are regarded as necessary conditions of the workability of the collective bargaining process. Whereas in the FR Germany the law on industrial action is totally judge-made, in Sweden at least some principles are laid down by statute, while associations of workers and employers have reached agreement regulating the area in detail.

III. THE LEGAL REGULATION OF INDUSTRIAL ACTION

33. Up until now almost no legal order which permits industrial action has been able to regulate extensively by statute the admissibility and the limits of industrial action. Political considerations largely explain this. On the other hand there have also been efforts at the international level to guarantee the right to strike by means of conventions. Generally one may conclude that the regulation of industrial action by statute is limited; sometimes the situation may be improved by collective agreements. But often only the courts have worked out and applied the basis and limits of the collective pursuit of interests.

A. Legal Sources

34. Legal sources may be categorised as international law, constitutional law, statutes, and collective agreements.

11. Cf. T. Ramm, *IELL* (Federal Republic of Germany), 1979, pp. 191 ff.
12. F. Schmidt, *Law and Industrial Relations in Sweden*, Stockholm – New York, 1977, pp. 160 ff.
13. Cf. the comparative work of Aubert, *L'obligation de paix du travail*, Genève, 1981.

1. International Law

35. The most widely ratified international instrument is Article 8 of the International Covenant on Economic, Social and Cultural Rights of 19 December 1966. The parties to this convention oblige themselves to guarantee the right to strike 'in conformity with the laws of the particular country'. The ILO was neither in Convention No. 87[14] nor in Convention No. 98[15] occupied explicitly with the right to strike.[16a]

36. Some regional organisations also protect the right to strike and partially even industrial actions by employers. Article 43 lit. c of the Charter of the Organization of American States obliges the Member States to guarantee workers the right to strike in accordance with the appropriate statutes. The formulation of the obligation in part II Article 6 No. 4 of the *European Social Charter* of 18 October 1961, which recognises 'the right of workers and employers to collective action in cases of conflicts of interest, including the right to strike, subject to obligations that might arise out of collective agreements previously entered into' is somewhat broader.[16b]

2. Constitutional Law

37. A number of constitutions guarantee strikes only, but within the limits of special statutes (France, Greece, Italy, Spain, Portugal). In some legal systems the courts regard the protection of the freedom of association as including the right to strike and the right to lock-out (e.g., FR Germany).

An explicit prohibition of the lock-out is contained in Article 60 of the Portuguese constitution.[16] But some American constitutions, like that of Mexico, explicitly recognise the lock-out (Article 123 XVII/XIX).[17] The constitution of Spain in Article 28, subsection 2 is not so clear, it definitely protects only the right to strike but in the case of employers it speaks merely

---

14. 'Concerning Freedom of Association and Protection of the Right to Organise.'
15. 'Concerning the Application of the Principles of the Right to Organise and to Bargain Collectively.'
16. 'Lock-outs shall be prohibited.'
16a. The Committee of Experts on the Application of Conventions and Recommendations has the opinion that the right of strike is implicitly guaranteed by the relevant convention (cf. *Freedom of Association and Collective Bargaining*, ILO, 1983, No. 200 ff.). The same point of view is found in the decisions of the Freedom of Association Committee of the Governing Body of the ILO (cf. *Freedom of Association, Digest of decisions and principles of the Freedom of Association Committee*, 3rd edn., ILO, 1985, No. 360 ff).
16b. The relevant case law of the Committee of Independant Experts of the European Social Charter is summarized in Council of Europe-Social Affairs (edn.), *Case Law on the European Social Charter*, Strasbourg, 1982, p. 57 ff. The later practice of this committee will be found in *Conclusions*, vol. VIII, Strasbourg, 1984, pp. 95 ff.
17. Article 123 XVIII: 'The laws shall recognise strikes and lock-outs as rights of workmen and employers.'

of a right to collective action (Article 37, subsection 2).[18] Chapter 2, §5 of the Swedish constitution gives workers and employers the right to industrial action only through their associations.[19] In sum, certain constitutions make it clear that they tend to guarantee only the right to strike, while others imply a certain parity in industrial disputes.

3. Statutes

38. Detailed and exhaustive regulation of industrial action, in particular of the strike and lock-out, is extremely rare. Frequently, however, statutes deal with separate aspects of industrial action, mainly with its effects in labour and civil law but not with its presuppositions.

a. Comprehensive Statutes

39. No industrial nation has yet established a comprehensive legal regulation of strikes and lock-outs. Faced with the political weakness of the modern democracies one cannot expect regulation by legislation. Only the interested parties, hence the trade unions and employers, have the opportunity to determine rules for industrial conflict and action. This is the case to a greater extent in Denmark, Sweden and in Switzerland.

Only Turkey has a comprehensive statute on the law of industrial action: the Act No. 2882 respecting collective labour agreements, strikes and lock-outs of 5 May 1983 regulates strikes and lock-outs in detail (section 25 ff).[20] Also the prescriptions in *Portugal* (Statute No. 65/77 of 26 August 1977) and *Spain* (Decreto-Ley of 4 March 1977) are comparatively extensive.

b. Occasional Legislation

40. In many countries only particular aspects of the law on industrial action are regulated, mainly in regard to the consequences and effects of industrial action for other legal questions, not its particular conditions and limits.

---

18. Article 28 (2): 'The right of workers to strike in defence of their interests is recognised. The law which regulates the exercise of this right shall establish precise guarantees to ensure the maintenance of essential services of the community.'
    Article 37 (2): 'The right of the workers and employers to adopt measures concerning collective conflict is recognised. The law which shall regulate the exercise of this right, without prejudice to the limitations it may establish, shall include precise guarantees to ensure the functioning of the essential services of the community.'
19. 'Any trade union and any employer or association of employers shall have the right to take strike or lock-out actions or any similar measures, except as otherwise provided by law or ensuing from a contract.'
20. Reprinted in ILO, *Legislative Series*, 1983 – Tur. 2.

c. The Role of the Judiciary

41. The main source of the law on industrial action is the judiciary. This applies particularly to all industrialised nations. *Judge-made law* plays the paramount role even where in statutes certain individual aspects are regulated in more detail (e.g., USA and Britain).

The courts of the FR Germany, above all the Federal Labour Court, have developed the essential principles of a comprehensive law on industrial action with no statutory basis. A similar situation occurs in all the industrialised countries of the West because the legislature has in general proved politically incapable of acting.

B. The Structure of Legal Regulation

42. In so far as one can speak of the legal regulation of strikes and lock-outs two points seem to be of particular interest:
(1) Is the strike – and perhaps also the lock-out – seen as a freedom or a right?
(2) Who disposes of this freedom or of this right, and who can exercise it?
It should not be surprising that the answer to both of these questions will not be the same in all legal systems.

1. Freedom or Right?

43. From the historical point of view the *freedom to strike* is older. The strike is not privileged by the legal system, it is merely not prohibited. The United Kingdom is a typical example. It is questionable whether such an attitude is in harmony with international guarantees of the right to strike.

The freedom to strike however implies that the strikers, at least at the time of the strike, must give notice of termination of their contracts of employment if they are not to be in breach of contract. The same is true for the lock-out. Neither the strike nor the lock-out gives the right to breach of the contract of employment or to violate other rights. Section 3 of the British Trade Disputes Act of 1906 however conceded to the trade unions immunity in tort which subsequently has been removed by the Employment Act 1982.[21]

44. In most countries the *right to strike* exists. Under the special conditions and circumstances which each legal system can establish, the exercise of these legal freedoms may not be totally restricted.

The strike is therefore privileged. It does not infringe the individual obligation to work based on the contract of employment. The strike sus-

---

21. The trade unions are now liable according to the sections 15–17 of the Employment Act 1982.

pends it and is therefore a collective justification of the individual breach of contract.

2. Competence and Exercise

45. For the freedom to strike as for the right to strike the same question arises in principle: who is the bearer and who can exercise it: the bearer alone or only together with other people? Must a legal evaluation consequently begin with the individual worker or a group of workers, e.g., a trade union?

These questions are not yet clarified in many countries. The problem becomes particularly clear in the case of the wildcat or unofficial strike. If the right to strike is only conferred upon a union and not the individual worker, as is the case in the FR Germany and in Sweden, then the right is limited only to a *group*.

46. But when the right to strike is granted to the individual worker – as does Article 40 of the Italian constitution –, then the unofficial strike is not unlawful. The question merely arises whether the exercise of the right to strike presupposes co-operation with other workers, i.e. a common work stoppage. In this case an individual right could be exercised only in and by a group or collective. A single worker is indeed unable to strike. This concept is dominant almost everywhere.

Nor does the characterisation of the right to strike as an individual right alter the fact that it can only be exercised collectively. It depends on the restrictive legal order whether this can only be done in a trade union (e.g., FR Germany) or in any group of workers (e.g., Italy). Ownership and exercise do not coincide therefore in the case of the right to strike.

If a single worker stops work without reference to a collective industrial conflict he does not exercise the right to strike. But from the legal standpoint he probably has a right of retention against his employer.

IV. GENERAL LEGAL PRINCIPLES

47. Are there general legal conditions and principles for industrial action which can found throughout various legal systems? Or are they excluded because of their different points of departure? Or have all three models of regulation certain common legal features?

This last question may be partially answered in the affirmative. It concerns first of all rules on the conditions and limits of industrial action, namely of the strike. Such principles include compliance with the peace obligation, parity between the parties to industrial action, the proportionality of weapons.

A. The Peace Obligation

48. The obligation of the parties of a collective agreement not to strike before its expiration or not to lock-out exists in many countries. But in other countries its existence is not quite clear (e.g., France). Some other refuse it as an unlawful waiver of the right to strike (e.g., Italy).[22] The peace obligation itself is based either on *statute* or on special *agreement*. In general it binds merely the parties of the collective agreement but not the single worker, except in Sweden. The Swedish Act on the Joint Regulation of Working Life lays down explicitly the peace obligation in §41. On the other hand, in the FR Germany it is derived from the function of the collective agreement as a 'peace convention'. This last concept is dominant also in Austria and Switzerland.

49. The general agreement between the central associations of trade unions and employers' associations contains the peace obligation in Denmark.[23]
   This differs from the specific agreement of a peace obligation by a no-strike-clause in a collective agreement which can be found in many countries (e.g., USA). For in these countries the parties to collective agreement are not bound by a general peace obligation in as far as no peace obligation is implied.

50. The peace obligation is normally a *relative* one; it exists only for the duration of the collective agreement. An *absolute* peace obligation as a continuous waiver of industrial action can be laid down only by agreement. In Switzerland such an agreement exists in the metal industry.

B. Parity in Industrial Action between Trade Unions and Employers' Associations

51. Less universal than the peace obligation is the principle of parity in industrial action between trade union on the one hand and employers' association or individual employers on the other. This means first of all that the strike and the lock-out are conceded to be weapons of equal value (FR Germany, Denmark, Sweden, USA).
   In France and Italy this principle is rejected on the grounds that only the strike guarantees the necessary balance in the collective bargaining process. Making the lock-out lawful would however result in the preponderance of the employers.

22. Cf. G. Giugni, 'The peace obligation', in Aaron *et al.*, *op. cit.*, pp. 127 ff.
23. Reprinted (in Danish) in P. Jacobsen, *Kollektiv arbeijdsret*, pp. 705 ff.

C. *The Principle of Proportionality*

52. Regarding the necessity of the strike (and of the lock-out) as well as their extent, certain demands are made by the several legal systems; this is particularly true in regard to effects on outsiders. German terminology here uses the concept of the principle of proportionaltiy.[24] The phenomenon itself is recognised in other countries if a strike cannot be initiated before certain measures are taken or when a particular industrial action exceeds certain limits and thereby constitutes an abuse of the right to strike.

1. The Need for Strikes and Lock-outs

53. Strikes are not always immediately allowed in all cases of industrial conflict, even when no peace obligation or conciliation procedure is prescribed or agreed.

The judiciary in the FR Germany has decided that the strike must be the *ultima ratio*. Collective bargaining must have failed. But a strike is not necessary and therefore disproportional if the conflict can be decided by the courts. Some countries do not allow strikes until a strike *ballot* among the workers has been held; or a strike may not be called without *previous announcement*.

2. Extent and Administration of Strikes

54. The extent and administration of industrial action are in most countries subject to certain restrictions. These may be a consequence of the fact that certain behaviour is not regarded as a strike or that certain forms of strike are unlawful. The latter is the case in France and Italy but not much is however clarified in detail.

If a strike or boycott extends to an employer from whom no higher salary or improvement of the conditions of employment is demanded, then such actions (e.g., sympathy strike, secondary boycott) are generally more restricted than other strikes.

In such cases the strike must be fair. An unfair strike is a disproportional method of interest promotion. Equally some tactics (e.g., the whipsaw strike) may be legally doubtful.

D. *Injunctions*

55. A central question in the law on industrial action refers to the problem of whether and to what extent an injunction can interfere in a forthcoming or existing strike action. Such intervention probably impairs the chances of the workers in the industrial conflict. An interrupted strike can never be revived and resumed under the same circumstances and conditions. It is

24. Cf. T. Ramm, *op. cit.*, p. 197.

therefore not surprising that in nearly all industrialised countries this question is discussed. This debate has been very intensive in the USA,[25] in France, Britain and in the FR Germany.[26] But discussion has not yet resulted in clarification; however a total prohibition of a strike by an injunction is not generally accepted.

V. Lawful and Unlawful Strikes

56. The answer to the question of whether a strike is lawful or unlawful has relevance in several respects: As a norm of the behaviour of the participants and as a norm for the judge to decide legal conflicts, e.g., the liability for unlawful strikes.

The criteria of the lawfulness and unlawfulness of a strike are determined first of all by the respective type of legal regulation. Lawfulness may be determined at various legal levels. The following legal levels may restrict the lawfulness of either strikes or lock-outs: the level of constitutional law, that of collective and individual labour law, and that of general civil law. These levels exist not as independent strata; they are obviously linked. A strike permitted by collective labour law will not generally be prohibited by the law on contracts of employment.

A. Constitutional Limits

57. Where the constitution explicitly or indirectly guarantees the right to strike (France, Italy, Portugal, Spain, Sweden), the question arises as to how the constitution itself delimits such a right. In a democratic community the *political strike* is in question. Except in Italy where the Italian Constitutional Court has allowed them in certain cases, political strikes are regarded as unlawful. Such pressure on parliament and on government does not accord with the free and unduly influenced decision of politically responsible institutions. Even the constitutional grant of the right to strike does not alter this because the right is conceded mainly through regulation by particular statute.

Thus Constitutions do not grant the right to strike for political purposes. But which other purposes can be achieved is hereby not yet decided.

B. Collective Labour Law: Prerequisites and Limits

58. The more detailed elaboration and definition of the right to strike is a genuine duty of collective labour law, though other legal strata also have some influence on it. The essential questions are the following: Who can strike, when, what for and how?

25. See Frankfurter/Green, *The Labor Injunction*, New York, 1930, for the time before World War II.
26. R. Birk, 'Boykott und einstweilige Verfügung im grenzüberschreitenden Arbeitskampf', *Arbeit und Recht*, 1974, pp. 289 ff with further references.

1. Unofficial, Unconstitutional or Wildcat Strike

59. Who can strike? The answer to this question means to whom the right to strike is granted. We have discussed this aspect above.

Wildcat strikes are generally permitted; the strike is characterised as a weapon for the improvement of the conditions of employment or collective bargaining but the purpose of the strike must not be to conclude a collective agreement. Exceptions are the FR Germany[27] and Sweden[28] where the wildcat strike is unlawful.

2. Purpose of the Strike

60. For which purpose can a strike be called? According to all legal systems improvement of the *conditions of employment* demanded from their employer for the strikers themselves or exceptionally for other workers (sympathy strikes) are a lawful purpose. However, there is no general answer to the question if certain *economic decisions* by the employer are demanded by strike. A *protest strike* against such decisions and measures also covering personnel policy is, however, tolerated by most legal systems.

In general the purpose of the strike must not be the conclusion of a collective agreement. It must have a more or less narrow connection with industrial relations. The conditions in German and Swedish law are however more rigid. On the other hand the *jurisdictional strike* would be legally doubtful outside the USA.

3. Conflicts of Rights and Conflict of Interests[29]

61. Normally the purpose of a strike is not to enforce existing rights but to create them. The strike serves therefore to resolve *conflicts of interests* between labour and management. *Disputes over rights* of workers are mostly decided by the courts, especially the labour courts if such exist. The rigorous differentiation between the pursuit of conflicts of interests and conflicts of rights is not always observed. But conflicts of rights may also be settled by strikes. This applies particularly to the 'unfair-labour-practice-strike' in the USA, as a lawful strike caused by the unlawful conduct of the employer.[30]

When the workers intend to achieve the reinstatement of an unlawfully dismissed worker, then in the FR Germany only the respective worker has the opportunity to bring his case before the labour court. But strikes for such purposes are not permitted.

27. T. Ramm, *op. cit.*, p. 196.
28. F. Schmidt, *op. cit.*, pp. 179 ff, 221 ff.
29. See also chapters 16 and 17.
30. For more details see B. Aaron, 'Methods of Industrial Action', in Aaron *et al.*, *op. cit.*, pp. 97 ff.

4. Initiation of a Strike

62. Sometimes a *strike ballot* must precede a strike; this is required by sections 10 and 11 of the British Trade Union Act 1984. Many union rules have similar provisions. The violation of such union rules does not affect the legality of the strike.

The situation is quite different concerning the *obligation to announce a strike* in advance. The French statute of 31 July 1963 prescribes for public employees the announcement for a strike five days in advance. Such an announcement may be provided by agreements between trade unions and employers' associations. If the legally provided announcement is lacking, then a strike is unlawful.

A general legal duty to announce a strike (or lock-out) does not exist either in France nor in other countries with the exception of *Sweden*, where §45 of the Act on the Joint Regulation of Working Life requires those undertaking industrial action 'to notify the other party in writing at least seven days in advance'.

5. Extent of the Strike

63. How, to what extent and how long an association of workers intends to strike is its autonomous decision. The *temporal* and *spatial extent* of the strike as well as its *form* are left to the discretion of the trade union. However there are limits to ensure a certain minimum protection of the affected employers and the general public against excessive damages.

64. As far as the spatial extent of a strike is concerned the area of the strike depends – in states where the strike is regarded as an institution connected with the autonomy of collective bargaining (FR Germany, Sweden) – on the required collective agreement. If an agreement extends merely over a part of the national territory or covers a single enterprise. Where such a strict relation to the collective agreement does not exist, as is the case in most countries, there are no explicit criteria for its restriction.

When in one or several plants only individual departments are on strike (a partial strike) then the courts have set certain but obscure limits to this tactic. It is not allowed to disturb the organisation of the plant or enterprise severely, and the damage should not threaten the existence of the employer. In *France* and in *Italy* such partial and successive strikes in different departments of the same plant or in the same department at short intervals are in general not lawful.[31]

65. The extension of the strike to third parties (sympathy strikes) or their inclusion in the industrial action by *secondary boycott* or *picketing* is permitted only within narrow limits. In the *USA* the section 8(b)(4) National

31. M. Despax and J. Rojot, *IELL* (France), 1979, p. 210.

Labor Relations Act prohibits the secondary boycott; in *Britain* section 17 of the Employment Act 1980 does the same. In several other countries the judiciary tries in a similar way to set limits where the third party is neutral towards the primary strike.

66. There is no express time limit for a strike. The initiation of a strike may however be restricted as outlined above; namely by the peace obligation or by the duty to announce the strike in advance.

An obligatory *minimum period* for the strike is exceptional. According to the French statute of 31 July 1963 a strike in the public sector must have a duration of at least one day. The general public is thus better prepared for the interruption of public services.

67. In so far as a certain kind of strike is not already prohibited because of temporal and spatial reasons *the form* of the work stoppage produces some restrictions. The main case in this connection is that the workers either perform their duty only in part (e.g., work to rule); or fully cease work but justify it with sickness; or link the work stoppage to other behaviour, as when they remain for instance in the plant but do not work (sit in, occupation).

All these cases are nowhere clearly characterised as lawful or unlawful strikes. The work-to-rule is sometimes conceptually regarded as not constituting a strike. In the case of occupation of the plant, in France the question is debated if the *juge des référés* is able to prohibit it because on the one hand the property of the employer is affected and on the other the *liberté du travail* of the non-strikers.[32] Therefore with regard to the collective conditions and limits of the strike one finds in all industrialised nations somewhat obscure limits. More detailed limits are exceptional; they are based either on individual statutes and are not a consequence of a general concept of legal regulation of industrial action or they are an outcome of the idea which confers a more limited role on industrial action.

C. Individual Labour Law

68. Collective and individual labour law must be more co-ordinated in order to avoid contradictions. In the case of the strike difficulties result however from the circumstance that individual labour law dominates the simple freedom to strike because according to it, work stoppage means a breach of contract. On the other hand, collective labour law proves to be stronger if a right to strike is granted. Its privilege contains a justification of the nonperformance of the obligation to work. Collective labour law transcends individual labour law.

Where only the freedom to strike is accorded to the workers the strike does not mean a breach of contract in so far as the employment relationship

32. Cf. Latournerie, *op. cit.*, pp. 194 ff.

is previously dissolved. Although in Britain the strike is not privileged by the law of contracts the situation is unclear.[33]

Where however the workers have the right to strike, the lawful strike is no breach of contract and it suspends the obligation to work.

D. Law of Torts

69. A necessary consequence of each strike is the causation of more or less serious economic damages to the employer but also to third persons and to the national economy. On the one hand the question is up to what limit do such damages have to be tolerated by the persons affected; on the other hand, who is liable for a strike with unlawful damages? There is no problem that in general damages caused by an unlawful strike have to be compensated. An unlawful strike is not legally privileged and is subject in all legal systems to the rules of the law of tort. An original lawful strike may become unlawful because of disproportional employer's damages.

Great Britain constituted an exception until 1982. Trade unions were excepted from tort liability (originally section 4 Trade Dispute Act 1906, later section 14 Trade Union and Labour Relations Act 1974). This virtually absolute immunity was removed in 1982 by section 15(1) Employment Act and thus brought the position of the union into line with the liability provided for individuals. Both trade unions and individuals are now restrictively liable in tort.[34]

But a lawful strike does not legally infringe the property or enterprise of the employers. Even when the strike as a whole is lawful then particular actions during its performance may be unlawful under the liability aspect (e.g., the damage of machines, vehicles or buildings).

VI. Lock-Outs[35]

70. The lock-out of the workers by the employer on his own initiative or by order of the employers' association has theoretically and practically two essential aspects:
(1) Does the employer generally dispose of the lock-out as a weapon? or
(2) Is the lock-out only a defence against unlawful strikes?

A. The Lock-out: A Consequence of the Parity Principle?

71. If the legal system gives the employer a means of defence against a

---

33. Cf. M. Freedland, *The contract of employment*, Oxford, 1976, pp. 102 ff.
34. Cf. Davies/Freedland, *Labour Law*. pp. 818 ff.
35. For comparative aspects see R. Birk, 'Die Aussperrung in rechtsvergleichender Sicht', *Zeitschrift für Arbeitsrecht*, 1979, pp. 231 ff.

lawful strike, this is a question of the general evaluation of their position and function in industrial action.

Those who believe that the strike alone provides a balance between trade unions and employers must see in the lock-out a disturbance of this balance and refuse it as a weapon of equal value (France, Italy, Portugal). However those who grant both sides the same chance in industrial action because of the principal freedom to engage in industrial action, or in the case of the right to strike of the danger of excessive workers' strength, will allow the lock-out in principle.

72. In many countries this is the case (Canada, Denmark, FR Germany, Great Britain, Israel, Sweden, USA). In FR Germany and in Sweden the lock-out organised by the employers' association prevails. The employers' associations will attack first of all whipsaw strikes. Because of these strikes the trade unions can win with comparatively low risk broad effects, the employers of the same area against whom there is a strike also lock-out non-striking workers in order to hit the trade unions financially. In this case of both strike and lock-out, they support their members. The German Federal Labour Court regards it not as a sympathy lock-out but as *a defensive lock-out* which corresponds in general to the principle of proportionality.[36]

In countries in which the strike is regarded primarily as a means to achieve the conclusion of a collective agreement and both partners to the contract should have the opportunity to influence its conclusion and content (FR Germany, Sweden), the lock-out has for industrial action as a whole a function only in the system of collective agreements. The employer should be allowed to reject a demand of the workers. Even where the defensive lock-out is permitted the offensive lock-out has no practical importance with the exception of the USA. Lock-outs may be used there also offensively to place economic pressure upon an union in order to gain its submission to an employer's bargaining position.

B. The Lock-out: As a Defence against Unlawful Strikes

73. France, Italy and Portugal refuse the lock-out. They recognise it at most as a freedom to lock-out but not as a right to lock-out. The lock-out is not privileged. While Portugal categorically rejects the lock-out in Article 60 of its constitution, France and Italy reject the parity between strike and lock-out with special reference to the exclusive constitutional guarantee of strikes. The lock-out is therefore characterised as a breach of the employment contract.

But when the worker has already violated his employment contract by an unlawful strike then French and Italian law permits the employer to enforce

---

36. Cf. T. Ramm, *op. cit.*, p. 198.

this violation of a right not only before the courts but also – and more effectively – by a lock-out. The lock-out is allowed as a *defence against unlawful attacks*;[37] it is a special kind of self-help. Therefore one may doubt the appropriateness of the term 'lock-out' because it concerns a special kind of the enforcement of a right but not of the pursuit of interests.

C. Similar Phenomena

74. The behaviour of an employer during a strike can – by the conscious exclusion of the workers from their work places and by refusal to pay wages – come very close in result to a lock-out.

This phenomenon is known in all industrialised countries. If merely a section of the workers of the enterprise is on strike, or if the enterprise has because of the strike no raw materials or semi-finished products so that the employer has no opportunity to maintain production, then he has the right to shut the firm (shut down, *chômage* technique,[38] *messa in libertà*). With reference to the 'risk of enterprise' the law of the FR Germany permits an employer to refuse the payment of wages.[39] The details are controversial.

VII. EXCLUSION AND RESTRICTION OF STRIKE AND LOCK-OUT

A. General Remarks

75. Nearly all industrial countries recognise some restrictions on industrial action for the protection of the general public. The effects of the strike on third parties and on the community should be diminished and essentials and vital services maintained.

The restriction or the exclusion of the right to strike or the freedom to strike will be only accepted as suitable in the system of collective bargaining if conflicts are solved by compulsory conciliation, arbitration or automatic salary increase. A good example of an *Ersatzlösung* (alternative) is Canada in the case of the prohibition of strikes for hospital personnel.[40]

B. Exclusion and Restriction of the Strike

76. As a consequence of an agreement between a trade union and employer strikes can be generally prohibited. But these agreements are very rare. The

---

37. G. Pera, *Diritto del lavoro*, 2nd ed., Padova, 1984, pp. 348 ff; R. Birk (N. 35), *op. cit.*, pp. 257–258.
38. See especially Ramin, *Le lock-out et le chômage technique*, Paris, 1977.
39. Cf. T. Ramm, *op. cit.*, pp. 115–116.
40. Section 4 Hospital Labour Disputes Arbitration Act (Ontario).

peace convention of the Swiss Metal Industry of 1937[41] does, however, contain an *absolute peace obligation*.

77. Prohibitions of the strike for certain groups such as policemen, firemen, doctors, hospital personnel or civil servants are of great interest. These should guarantee services for the general public which modern society will not waive. Which services are involved in prohibition? The answer to this questions varies, however, from country to country because evaluation and historical conditions differ considerably. *Strikes by civil servants* are not allowed in *FR Germany* according to the dominant doctrine.[42] The civil servant has a special status which cannot be comprehended by the criteria of the labour law. The particular conception of the civil servant's function is decisive for the strike prohibition. Public employees and workers have the right to strike. Other states make no distinction.[43]

78. The *French* restriction of strikes by civil servants by the statute of 31 July 1963 depends on functional arguments. *Britain* provides for some *categories of public services* (police, post) a restriction of the freedom to strike; these are so-called 'essential services'.[44]

C. Emergency Laws

79. Emergency laws play a special role in the framing of restrictions of the right to strike in several states. The best known rules are laid down in the Taft Hartley Act 1947 in the USA. If in the opinion of the American President a forthcoming or actual strike/lock-out 'affecting an entire industry or a substantial part thereof' will 'imperil the national health or safety', then he may apply for an injunction against the strike before the competent federal court. The national emergency dispute injunction can impose a 'cooling off' period up to 80 days (section 209(b) Labor Management Relations Act).

VIII. LAWFULNESS OF OTHER FORMS OF INDUSTRIAL ACTION

80. The workers may protect their interests not only by strikes. Other weapons belong to their arsenal, including boycotts, secondary boycotts,

---

41. Cf. Jaeger, *Beiträge der Rechtsordnung zur Sicherung des Arbeitsfriedens*, Bern, 1981, pp. 106 ff.
42. See Federal Constitutional Court – Official Report of its decisions (BVerfGE) vol. 8, p. 1 (17).
43. A general survey on the right to strike in the public service is provided by an ILO-paper: International Labour Conference, 63rd Session 1977, Report VII(2): *Freedom of association and procedures determining conditions of employment in the public service*, pp. 86–102.
44. Cf. especially G.S. Morris, *Strikes in Essential Services*, London and New York, 1986. See also Articles 28(2) and 37(2) of the Spanish Constitution which will ensure the maintenance of essential services in the case of the industrial action.

picketing and the refusal of hot-cargo-work. Sometimes boycotts and picketing are autonomous means of industrial action. Secondary boycotts and hot cargo depend on a primary industrial action.

A. Boycott

81. As an autonomous industrial action the boycott is not frequent. It is found particularly in the shipping industry where longshoremen refuse the loading or unloading of a ship in support of nonstriking or striking seamen. The *German* Federal Labour Court considers such a boycott as lawful.[45] It has to satisfy similar requirements as the strike. In *Scandinavia* the opinion regarding its lawfulness is not unanimous.[46]

Between the boycott as a general industrial action and the ordinary consumer boycott, lies the consumer boycott organised by a union against the products of the primary employer as one finds frequently in the USA.

B. Secondary Boycott

82. The secondary boycott extends industrial action to a third party in order thereby to increase the pressure. Such an extension of industrial action is rejected by most legal systems. *Britain* (section 17, Employment Act 1980) and the *USA* (section 8(b)(4) National Labor Relations Act) explicitly prohibit this kind of industrial action.

So simple as the principle sounds its limits are difficult to determine. The border between the primary and secondary employer is often not easily defined because both are either legally or economically intertwined with each other. Even a neutral employer can lose his neutrality and become an 'ally' when he aids the primary employer in the industrial conflict. On a construction site or in a building used by several employers neutral employers frequently may be drawn into an industrial conflict of another employer. This may occur when the employer is picketed. The US Case law has developed complicated rules for common situs picketing which cannot be outlined.[47]

C. Picketing

83. Picketing is intended primarily to deter persons from working so as not to diminish the effect of a strike. In the USA picketing is a general weapon in industrial conflicts. Specific types include organisational and recognitional

---

45. Cf. R. Birk (N. 4), *op. cit.*, pp. 17 ff.
46. See F. Schmitt, *Politiska strejker och fackliga sympatidtgarder*, Stockholm, 1969; idem, *Law and Industrial Relations in Sweden*, p. 175.
47. Cf. especially Goldman, *IELL* (USA), 1983, pp. 174 ff.

picketing and consumer picketing. In general it is not legal to picket an employer who is not the primary employer (secondary picketing).

In *France* picketing must be peaceful because the *liberté du travail* of non-strikers is protected by penal law. Section 15 of the Employment Act 1980 expressly requires 'peaceful picketing' in *Britain*. The legal regulation of picketing in the USA is very detailed but nevertheless not very clear. Unlawful picketing is an unfair labour practice.

D. Hot Cargo

84. The lawfulness of refusal of work from an establishment on strike seems not in dispute. The problems are discussed more fully in *FR Germany*, *Britain* and in the *USA*. But there are hardly definite rules.[48]

In the USA as well as in the FR Germany the distinction is drawn between a refusal to do struck work (*direkte Streikarbeit*) and a refusal to handle the work produced at the struck bargaining unit (USA) or section of a plant (FR Germany) (*indirekte Streikarbeit*). The general legal view can be summarised as follows: It is permissible to refuse to do struck work but it is illegal to refuse to handle products produced by a struck employer.[49]

IX. The Impact of a Lawful Strike and Lock-Out on the Individual Employment Relationship[50]

85. As far as the influence of industrial action on the employment contract is concerned two types of regulation may be distinguished: In the case of the freedom to strike the strike is mostly characterised as a breach of contract, but the right to strike does not infringe the employment contract.

A. Freedom to Strike and to Lock-out: Great Britain

86. Since industrial action does not prevail over the law of contracts, strikes and lock-outs are breaches of contract unless the employment contract was already terminated at the onset of the industrial action. But the legal situation is, in detail, not yet fully clarified.[51]

B. Right to Strike and Freedom to Lock-out: France, Italy

87. The strike suspends the employment contract. The employment rela-

---

48. Cf. R. Birk (N. 4), *op. cit.*, pp. 117 ff.
49. For the USA cf. Goldman, *IELL* (USA), 1983, pp. 177 ff, also for the question of hot cargo agreements.
50. For more details see Blanc-Jouvan, 'The effect of industrial action on the status of the individual employee', in Aaron *et al.*, *op. cit.*, pp. 175 ff.
51. Cf. M. Freedland, *op. cit.*, pp. 102 ff.

tionship remains but the obligation to work and to pay wages are suspended.[52,53]

The lock-out is a breach of contract unless the employment contract was not previously dissolved. The general law of contract provides for particular legal effects. The employer has in general the obligation to pay wages to workers who are locked-out.

C. Right to Strike and Right to Lock-out: FR Germany

88. Strikes and lock-outs are treated equally concerning their legal effects. Both suspend the principal obligations of the employment contract. If a strike and lock-out coincide then the strike suspends the employment contract. The effect of a lock-out is under such circumstances non-existent.

The previous conception of the dissolving effect of the lock-out has been abandoned by the Federal Labour Court.[54]

D. The Impact on Non-strikers

89. The effects of industrial action on non-strikers of the same plant or enterprise are manifold. They can be locked out lawfully (FR Germany) or the employers may refuse to pay wages (FR Germany, if there is no lock-out; France, Italy).

Non-strikers have the opportunity to refuse struck work. This is also true for temporary workers, as far as they are used as strikebreakers or blacklegs.

X. Neutrality of Government in the Industrial Conflict

90. States and governments do not interfere in disputes of interests by legislation or individual acts where the industrial action is not prohibited. Only where the Commonwealth is involved or exposed to danger does this principle no longer apply.

This demand of non-interference or of *neutrality* appears in legislation in different connections.

The public offices (e.g., the German employment office) should not pay *unemployment benefits*[55] to strikers and thereby to support the strike in

---

52. M. Despax and J. Rojot, *op. cit.*, pp. 212–213.
53. L. Riva Sanseverino, *Diritto sindicale*, 3rd ed., Torino, 1976, pp. 394 ff.
54. Cf. Federal Labour Court, Decision of 21 April 1971, quoted by Ramm, *op. cit.*, p. 198.
55. §17 (2) Arbeitsförderungsgesetz.

disadvantage to the employer (FR Germany,[56] Great Britain[57]). But the payment of supplementary benefits is not excluded.

Cases which prohibit a strike by legislation or individual for the benefit of the general public are exceptional. But they result from the nature of the modern state which will and must offer to its citizens certain services, thus taking into consideration its social and political liability. Neutrality is therefore not an end in itself.

SELECT BIBLIOGRAPHY

B. Aaron *et al.*, *Industrial Conflict – A Comparative Legal Survey*, London, 1972.

T. Hanami/R. Blanpain (ed.), *Industrial Conflict Resolution in Market Economies – A study of Australia, The Federal Republic of Germany, Italy, Japan and the USA*, Deventer, 1984.

56. § 116 Arbeitsförderungsgesetz.
57. Section 8 Schedule 2 of the Social Security Act 1980.

Chapter 20. Different Categories of Workers and Labour Contracts

H. Barbagelata

I. INTRODUCTION

1. The expression 'worker' like its corresponding word in all languages does not have a single universal meaning in social and labour law. In a broad sense a worker is one who performs personal services in return for a promise of economic compensation. But individual employment law and sometimes the law of collective labour relations narrows down this definition of 'worker'. In most countries regardless of the economic legal and political system, labour law and industrial relations apply only to those workers who are in a subordinate employment relationship with an employer, so-called *employees*, as distinct from independent workers, the so-called self-employed.

2. In most systems the chief source of the individual employment relationship is the *contract of employment*. But this concept does not explain much. Personal services can also be rendered under other contracts, such as those by an independent contractor, an agent or with a partner. For this reason individual contracts of employment have to be carefully differentiated from other forms of contract and this is of great practical importance as well as a source of considerable difficulty.

3. In truth the definition of the 'employee' and the 'contract of employment', as distinct from other voluntary relationships where personal services are rendered in return for money, is not determined by a single criterion. There is, however, a convergence in modern legal doctrine towards he recognition of submission of the employee to the employer's command or control as to the time, place and manner in which the work is to be done as a necesary criterion. This criterion of subordination or dependency is of Continental European origin and was originally distinct from the Common Law test of control derived from the old law of master and servant. But the conception of a power of control in the Common Law countries has been influenced by the Continental doctrines of subordination and integration, especially as a result of the work of the late Sir Otto Kahn-Freund. This implies a functional dependency inherent in the employment relationship.

The criterion is not sufficiently precise and consistent to be of practical use in every case. It must be kept in mind that the degree and quality of control, authority, direction, etc. of the employer over the worker are subject to change due to a number of facts, such as the nature of the job, the size and complexity of the employer's organisation, the professional qualifications of the worker etc. This is illustrated by the limited possibilities of command or control by managers or executives over highly-qualified technicians as to the way in which a certain job is to be done.

4. Because of this, in most countries the criterion used to determine the quality of the employee based on subordination and control tends to be determined according to the particular context of legislation and is also subject to constant revision by case law. After a period during which there was constancy as to the importance of subordination and control (and subordination is expressly mentioned as a definitive factor in the Civil Codes of Italy and of the Netherlands and of most Latin American countries, while the Belgian law on labour contracts of 1978 mentions authority, direction, etc.) a number of new social and economic criteria have recently become significant. These include factors such as the method of performance, the manner of payment of wages, the ownership of the tools of production, the chance of profit and the risk of loss. The idea of alienation was expressed by the old Spanish Law on Labour Contracts of 1931 and although omitted in later texts it was taken up again in case law and is currently to be found in the Spanish Workers' Statute of 1980. The concept of workers belonging to the employer's organisation (sometimes called the organisation or integration test) is used either separately or jointly with others (mixed or multiple test) by British courts and in countries such as Israel and with less clarity in India. In any event legislation has often accepted and consolidated the case law in order to widen the concept of employees. However, some laws have been passed to counteract this expansive tendency, such as the French law of 1977, which ruled that 'collaborating lawyers' were not salaried. Moreover legislation has been used to prevent *fraudem legis*, e.g. Article 21 of the Mexican Workers' Statute creates a presumption of an existing contractual labour relationship between the party who performs personal services and the party for whom work is done.

Legislation has been used to defend the conditions under which workers whose status has been questioned, such as apprentices, homeworkers, commercial travelers and professional sportsmen, are to be regarded as employees.

5. In several countries the regime of individual employment relationships has remained confined to the sphere of private activities. This excludes from the coverage of ordinary labour law certain categories of workers in the service of the State. The classic example is the German *beamte*. However, discrimination between workers in the public and private sectors is of relatively little importance in some countries such as the UK and certain other countries under British influence. Moreover, in the socialist labour codes of Eastern Europe ordinary labour law is applicable to both private and public enterprises (e.g., GDR and Czechoslovakia) but in Poland it is acknowledged in the Labour Code that a labour relationship stemming from an act of nomination contains elements of administrative law and is partially ruled by special regulations. Differences in the treatment of public and private sector workers have tended to disappear even in countries where they were once strongly marked, such as Latin America. The tendency is for the situation of workers employed by the State and public corporations to become similar to that of workers under contracts of employment with private enterprises.

6. The status of members of co-operative organisations or self-managed ones varies. Under some legislation they are assimilated to employees with refinements (e.g., Cyprus, GDR, Israel, Uruguay). Under others none of these workers are regarded as employees (e.g., Poland) and they are expressly excluded from this status, the situation being similar to that of civil servants.

7. The following paragraphs deal first with the principal categories of employees which have emerged. Three groups may be identified. The first contains categories basd on their type of work, the second those based on the peculiarities of their respective activities and the third on the different ways of acquiring a professional qualification. Obviously this outline excludes categories based on age, sex or nationality of the worker (women, young persons and foreign workers are often subject to special regulations) because these factors are currently more relevant in dealing with problems stemming from protection against discrimination in employment discussed in chapter 21.

Second, what follows deals with categories of contracts of employment rather than of employees. Two large categories, based on the duration of the relationship are: indefinite contracts and contracts for a definite period. This categorisation is important for comparative law because it is universal and because of its repercussions for job security in most systems. Of late, some complexities have developed around the rendering of temporary services. Also, the fact that an employer may contract with an employee to work only part-time may seriously affect the law relating to the contract of employment and this justifies the use of part or full-time as differential criteria. Other categorisations may be addd to these. Among the most important ones are those which, in accordance with the custom and legislation of countries like India, Israel and the Philippines, categorise contracts of employment according to the regularity, permanence or stability of the relationship and connected questions. However, these categorisations usually run parallel with that based on duration, which is more general. Yet another categorisation of contracts of employment that should be mentioned, is the 'group contract' or contract with a group taken as a whole, as contrasted with the individual contract. Such contracts receive special treatment in some legislation, like the Spanish Statute of Workers.

II. CATEGORIES

A. Categories Based on the Type of Work

8. The categorisation of some employees as white collar workers as opposed to blue collar workers is loaded with notorious social implications. It highlights not only those characteristics which are derived from the type of work done, but also the social stratification of the groups concerned. It tends to propagate a difference in treatment which is contrary to the movement towards uniform treatment in modern legislation which frequently contains declarations against differences based on the type of work. Studies of social status show that the income security of white collar workers, their chances of obtaining professional promotion as well as other cultural factors make the average status of the white collar worker higher than that of the blue collar worker. This is especially true in those communities where manual work occupies a low place in a scale of values.

9. This differentiation is the result not only of tradition but is also entrenched in many countries by the structure of trade unions and the coverage of collective agreements. This is often reflected in legislation which differentiates between regular and temporary employment or between salaried workers and wage-earners or between skilled and unskilled workers. It must also be remembered that in some countries the differentiation between blue and white collar workers results from the legal tradition of affording white collar workers the protection of commercial codes on matters such as accidents at work and illness which did not extend to blue collar workers. Moreover the emphasis in contracts of employment with white collar workers has tended to be on co-operation and loyalty as reflected in the covenant against competition.

10. There is, however, a tendency in both legislation and collective agreements (e.g. Italy from 1973 onwards) towards reducing the differences. Recent legislation like that of 1978 in Belgium and 1980 in Luxemburg in which the distinction between blue collar and white collar workers in *summa divisio* is certainly exceptional. However, the distinction still exists in many countries, including some of the socialist countries, and its importance should not be minimised.

11. Among the outstanding problems in this connection is the regularity and periodicity of payment. This is reflected in a difference between 'salaried' employees (paid monthly) and wage earners paid according to the labour days worked within the week, the fortnight or the month. The efforts of the

blue collar unions chiefly in several European countries has been to obtain monthly payment of wages. Other important distinctions between blue collar and white collar workers relate to trade union structure and this is reflected in collective bargaining, the different position of organisations representing white collar personnel, and sometimes the constitution and competence of labour courts. The working conditions of white collar workers are often superior to those of blue collar workers in respect of the length of the working day, weekly rest, enjoyment of holidays and even the length of the probationary period, and such matters as termination of employment and compensation in lieu of notice. There are other matters as well such as personal relationships within the enterprises and the enjoyment of welfare facilities. But these tend to be effaced as time goes by and they differ greatly from one country to another.

12. However, neither the socio-legal base nor the legal techniques have managed to elaborate a consistent criterion for the definition of both categories. The traditional criterion based on the assumption of a dichotomy resulting from the nature of the work or the type of activity, manual or non-manual, does not withstand a moderately exacting analysis and lacks the consistency necessary to include a growing number of workers, even when an attenuated formula referring to the predominant element is used. Other criteria proposed are periodicity of payments, work milieu, the ease with which the worker may be replaced, the degree of co-operation with this employer, the distance from the centre of power, the types of interactions with management, the direct contact with the materials of production, the social status of the worker, and a combination of one or more of these matters. However, these criteria where they deviate from the traditional one have not been successful even in those countries where a marked difference of regime between categories exists.

Some laws provide a list of employees who must be considered white collar workers (e.g. Luxemburg). But it is inevitable that such a list cannot cover all possibilities and may itself create new problems. Finally in this respect it is to be noted, that only in a few countries, and there it is heavily criticised, is the category of white collar worker fixed according to a certain ceiling of remuneration (e.g. Hong Kong).

13. However, alongside the broad and vague categories based on type of work a tendency has grown towards recognising other categories which result from the complexity of the division of labour in modern enterprises. The traditional foremen and oversers, who belong to the world of manual labour, and whose authority in managerial responsibilities used to be circumscribed to the production line and exerted over other blue collar workers, have been changing their functions, drawing nearer to the legal and social status of the white collar worker and have come to be considered as a different group. Also, employees with managerial and commanding functions over white collar workers to which group they originally belonged

431

now comprise a complex range of hierarchical positions ranging from the top to the lower levels of management. In any event employees classifiable as supervisory personnel, although generally understood to be included in the white collar category and sometimes expressly included in it so long as manual work is not their main activity (e.g. Finland), should not be fully identified with ordinary white collar workers and are in fact distinguishable from them. In view of their position in industrial relations, supervisory personnel are sometimes listed in labour laws among the exceptions to benefits and privileges. These limitations are related chiefly to their freedom to organise their tasks, free schedules and the greater importance given to trust and confidence in their employment relationship. Many norms exclude this category from rigorous working day regulations and those on weekly rest or vacations. They are sometimes restricted (e.g. in Malaysia, Pakistan and Singapore) in the right to form trade unions or in representation by works councils. In an extreme position India and Burma deny an executive with power the character of employee.

14. Another category or rather an amalgam of categories, not very clearly distinguishable at its lower levels from supervisors, is that of executives and managers. This category has become increasingly relevant in new forms of industrial organisation of enterprises. In some countries it is regarded as a fundamental category, subject to special rules, such as in the socialist countries of Eastern Europe. The difficulty is to determine the point of management at which those who represent the corporate employer in industrial relations should be catalogued as employees. This question and the possible solutions are of great theoretical and practical interest, but a general tendency towards a uniform solution cannot be found. A similar problem arises in determining to what extent high level technicians may be regarded as managerial employees even when they do not manage.

B. *Special Categories Related to their Activities*

15. The activity of the employer for whom the services are rendered determines the existence of workers, subject to special rules, differing from the basic rules of labour law. These rules are sometimes more, sometimes less advantageous than the 'usual' employment contract. The variation may be due to tradition or collective bargaining or to other reasons such as the special characteristics of the work. The differential status of particular categories of activity may be derived from collective bargaining or from legislation; it is to some extent a reflection of the weakness of the bargaining power of certain sectors that they are specially regulated by the state. The following paragraphs refer to statutes most frequently found but this is by no means exhaustive. Other categories, more commonly subject to special regulation, include artists, bank employees, bakers and confectioners, hotel and catering workers, journalists, miners, nurses and medical workers, post and telecommunication workers, teachers, transport workers and of course civil servants and public employees.

1. Agricultural Workers

16. Agricultural workers who render services under conditions which are not always recognised as contracts of employment represent a sizeable labour force in countries of low industrial development. They are subject to working conditions generally inferior to those of urban workers. This is partly because in many countries less favourable rules on working hours, rest, wages and dismissals subsist partly because of ineffective enforcement and partly because of the poor development of trade unions and inefficient administrative control.

Currently these differences are being reduced. The tendency is towards eliminating special rules and covering matters such as housing and food, medical attention, recruitment (particularly of migrant and seasonal plantation workers) and protection of income in a way similar to general labour law. In some countries in Latin America, where agricultural work is of great importance, employers are charged with special obligations such as the maintenance of schools. In Latin America, besides, the tendency is to establish the main characteristics in a few provisions of the labour code or general labour law. However, Argentina has recently passed a detailed and full text on agricultural work, which remains outside the general law on labour contracts.

17. There is no uniform approach to the regulation of rural wage earners such as partners and tenants of smallholdings, who personally cultivate their land or are assisted by family groups. In some countries the courts identify these workers with employees, whenever an economic dependency is found (e.g. Panama), but some legislation expressly excludes this possibility (e.g. Chile). Finally in some countries like Argentina certain categories of partner have a special regime, similar to that of employees, which ensures the worker's percentage of earnings, the relative stability of employment and the amount of indemnity for wrongful dismissal. This does not exclude the use of hired help by the partner. In this case the landowner is liable for indemnities owed to those who help a partner who is dismissed unjustly.

2. Commercial Travellers (Sales Representatives)

18. A commercial traveller who meets certain requirements found in laws, collective agreements, professional custom and case law is acknowledged as an employee in a significant number of countries. However, criteria on this subject differ widely. The essential feature is that the representative must personally perform services such as visiting clients to obtain orders or closing deals by proxy for his or her principal. The most important variations are factors such as the permanence of the activity, abstention from business on his/her own account, rendering exclusive services to the employer, working within a fixed radius and complying with certain formalities, the keeping of registers etc., and thereby developing a bond of dependency with the employer.

In certain countries some of these requisites, such as exclusiveness, are imposed by law and collective agreements not so much for acknowledging the quality of employee as for ensuring him certain rights, such as minimum wages, reimbursement of expenses etc. In some others like France commercial travellers who receive only regular fixed wages constitute a subcategory with a somewhat different regime.

The distinction between sales persons and other independant business agents is a matter of controversy. The presumption of the quality of employee established by legislation in some countries when one or more objective traces is present is often a *praesumptio iuris tantum*.

19. Persons occupied in this type of activity and who are recognised as employees are entitled to rights and obligations substantially similar to those of other employees. However, laws, collective agreements and professional practice have introduced certain refinements, relating to work hours, weekly rest and annual vacations. It is also usual for remuneration to be integrated wholly or partly with commission calculated in relation to the amount of work done at given rates. However, in many countries it is established by practice, law and collective agreements that basic fixed wages are paid or an average level of earnings guaranteed.

Another characteristic of the regime for travelling salespersons is that they are usually entitled to commission on sales which are made with their customers even if the salesperson took no part in the sales. There are definite rules on accepting and rejecting orders transmitted through a sales representative and also on terms for accounting and paying commission, excluding or strictly limiting in most legislation participation of the employee in the risk of the client's failure to comply.

20. Other important peculiarities of the regime relating to commercial travellers are related to the termination of the relation between employer and employee, e.g. the circumstances under which the employee may be regarded as having been wrongfully dismissed and so entitled to an indemnity. In some legislation (e.g. Argentina, Belgium, France, Uruguay) the commercial traveller receives not only the normal indemnity in the relationship when it terminates but also another indemnity for the loss of customers which is calculated in different ways. In some countries it is a percentage of the usual indemnity or a round sum fixed in accordance with average remuneration and seniority. In general usage the indemnity is paid only when the employer terminates the employment directly or indirectly. In Argentina and other countries indemnity is due even when the employment relationship is terminated by the employee.

21. There are some special rules relating to covenants of non-competition which limit the activity of the employee even after a relationship is terminated. Solutions of law and collective agreements and also court decisions, applying general principles of commercial law are varied.

In almost all European countries with a market economy the covenants are accepted under reasonable conditions. The period of restraint may be limited (e.g. a maximum of three years in Switzerland and Italy) but in some other countries such as Uruguay the law declares that such covenants are null and void since they limit the worker's right to work.

3. Domestic Servants

22. Domestic servants are excluded from the category of employees in some countries and they are generally less well protected especially in relation to working hours and young persons' labour, dismissal, minimum wages and collective agreements. This is so in many different countries but it is obvious that their traditional exclusion from British labour law is less important than that in other countries, such as those of Latin America and Asia, because of the importance of the market in fixing the conventional conditions of these workers. Domestic servants are distinguished by virtue of working in the home of their employer; by contrast these very circumstances have led to the establishment of special protection such as limiting the duration of the obligtion assumed by the employee or ensuring the preferment of the obligation of schooling for young persons (e.g. Philippines and Ecuador). Because it is understood that the legislation on domestic servants deprives them of benefits in comparison with those enjoyed by other workers, the law circumscribes this condition to persons who in the home of the employer look after the comfort of that family. That is to say, any lucrative activity is left out of the definition and so are private chauffeurs, nurses and personnel of apartment buildings. In Chile, however, the statute on domestic servants includes those workers who discharge tasks serving in charitable institutions, while in Nigeria drivers of privately used motor cars are included.

4. Dockers

23. The situation of workers at dock, loading and unloading ships, has claimed special consideration in many countries since it is dangerous and heavy work and only foremen and a few others enjoy a permanent relationship with the employer. Traditionally each loading or unloading operation is negotiated succesively for different agents who do not always have a clear identity. For this reason laws have been passed to identify those liable for the performance of obligations towards dockers and to acknowledge the dockers' quality as employees with adequate general rules to serve their special characteristics and to give them protection akin to that of other employees.

435

The norms also tend to ensure an equitable distribution of working opportunities, the organisation of docking operations, prevention of accidents, discipline of personnel and quick settlement of individual disputes. To serve all these purposes dockers' activities are carried out under a complex of domestic and international laws and regulations, collective agreements, awards, and usage in practices of the respective ports.

5. Homeworkers

24. This refinement is traditionally important in the garment industry and related activities. The work is done for an industrial or business manager, outside the premises of the establishment, generally at the worker's home. This category has its own rules. It is a system which precedes the growth of factories and so is of particular importance in the developing countries. In the developed countries it has also come under the attention of labour law because of the possibilities for abusing the general regulations applicable to factory workers. New activities including the application of new technology in the developed countries are being undertaken by forms of homework. There is today talk of 'intellectual homeworkers'. A special feature of this type of employment is the predominance of women.

25. The statutes concerning these workers in different countries reflect the common purpose of ensuring their protection as employees by adapting the legislation affecting employees to their needs and preventing managerial abuses. Restrictions for reasons of public health are also frequent. The laws on minimum wages also tend to require remuneration akin to those of workers in the same activity who work on the employer's premises and to limit working days and working weeks. Their annual vacations are often financed by percentage overcharges on tasks accomplished. Usually there is a system of payment similar to that of employees when the 'employer' or work distributor terminates the work relationship unfairly. However, the different countries are not in accord about collaborators within the family of the homeworker and their maximum number. In this status some legislation recognises as homeworkers the head of the family workshop who at times acts as an agent of the employer. But in other legislation the prohibition of intermediaries in work distribution is stricter.

6. Offshore Workers

26. The statutes concerning offshore workers (mainly seafarers but also including workers on oil rigs etc.) shows the influence of other preoccupations besides that of protecting the security of the ship and its cargo. In many countries the work of seafarers is regulated by laws and customs of the sea and it is usual to have special statutes regulating seafarers and offshore workers such as those developing the exploration of the resources of the seabed. In many respects the labour relations of the masters and seafarers aboard ships are ruled by international norms and collective agreements, but some owners and shipping agents try to avoid these by placing their ships under flags of convenience of countries whose rules are less strict.

27. The seafarer's contract must usually be in writing and contain more formalities than most other contracts of employment. The contract for the term of a certain voyage is common, as is the establishment of conditions for terminating the contract prematurely or during the voyage, indemnities in cases of shipwreck are also foreseen, as are measures to repatriate members of the crew for various reasons including sickness. Limitations of the working day, weekly rest or vacations are recognised, but are differently formulated from those of other employees. The statutes concerning these workers traditionally prescribe when salaries should be paid and lay down special guarantees for the payment of such salaries. It is understood, even in countries like the USA where collective bargaining is very important, that these measures may not be weakened by collective conventions.

28. In many countries the crew of some ships like fishing vessels are generally remunerated by participation in the result of operations without losing their quality as employees. This form of remuneration goes back to Byzantine law but its practical applicability varies greatly.

In a few countries high sea navigation, pilotage and internal navigation and fishing are ruled by special statutes, which limit the applicability of norms on maritime work to personnel discharging activities specially defined.

7. Professional Sportsmen

29. Professional sportsmen have only recently been recognised as employees and this only in a few countries. In some, like Brazil, the law contemplates exclusively the contract of employment of the soccer player. In others these norms have a wider range; and in some like Venezuela and Mexico they have been incorporated in codes or general labour laws; mostly because of the great abuses in restraining freedom to work, found in this field, and to establish restrictions on the maximum duration of the contract, to regulate the termination of employment, to state under what conditions services may be transferred to other employers and what benefits the worker may obtain from the transfer. Among the subjects of regulation are: the minimum time which must elapse between the events in which the sportsman participates, enjoyment of gratifications and even, as in Belgium, minimum remuneration priodically adjusted by administrative authorities.

This work relationship presents other peculiarities such as the fact that the law expressly refers to statutes and regulations of national and international

437

leagues; and considerations of discipline are frequently left to their discretion. Besides this in some legislation, like that of Peru, the professional sportsman remains duty bound under threat of severe sanctions to enter national competitions with his national team. Although contracting out of the jurisdiction of labour courts is forbidden, as a matter of public policy it is effective in practice because of the imposition of regulations by the great international federations. In order to protect sportsmen who may well become defenceless, some laws and collective agreements have prescribed arbitration procedures and 'sports courts' have been created by law (e.g. in Brazil).

C. Special Categories Related to Acquiring Professional Proficiency

30. When workers perform within a relationship established with a view to acquiring a professional qualification or as practical work experience, it gives rise to a series of special categories of workers. A basic form is the traditional apprenticeship but this is now usually regarded as inadequate for modern production conditions. Besides it has generated abuses reflected in the growing resistance of the young. For these reasons considerable changes are being introduced and new incentives have been established. New legal institutions have been created for young people, especially those out of work, to complete their training in real jobs. Simultaneously an effort is being made, particularly noticeable in countries with centralised economies, to integrate study and work at all levels.

1. Apprenticeship Contracts

31. In a number of countries the apprenticeship contract is regulated by recent or recently amended laws, but in other countries no regulations exist or the existing statutes are insufficient and must be complemented by way of court decisions. In any case, a few apprenticeship contracts are regarded as void, illegal or unenforceable, when they transgress mandatory labour law and minimum wages law (e.g. USA) or when they are expressly excluded from the labour code (e.g. Mexico) but even then analogous relations may be validly agreed.

32. From the legal definitions it may be concluded that apprenticeship contracts are generally regarded as contracts of employment of a special type, since their purpose is training; but in various countries with different characteristics – such as Belgium, PR China, Czechoslovakia, the Netherlands and Nigeria – the traditional concept of training as an aim is so strong that it prevents the relationship from being treated as a contract of employment. In a way French legislation is eclectic, because apprenticeship is defined as a form of education and the contract guaranteeing training within an enterprise is 'a labour contract of a special type'. The legal regulation of the apprenticeship is varied. Several statutes allow administrative authority to regulate basic aspects of the relationship. This is generally assisted by specialised organs which in some cases (e.g. New Zealand) may be designated by an arbitration court. However, as a rule the maximum duration of the relationship (two or three years usually) is fixed, as is a minimum or maximum age for the apprentice (the maximum is generally fixed at 18). Other requisites besides those resulting from the apprentice being under-age include the completion of obligatory schooling. Sometimes the employer must obtain previous authorisation from the authorities. In Danish law of 1956 an employer employing a person who has not reached the age of 18 years in an enterprise where work is performed which, according to the Act is approved as a trade or as belonging to such a trade, has an obligation to conclude a contract of apprenticeship with the person before he starts work.

33. The written form is practically a universal requirement for the apprenticeship contract and in many legal texts the penalty for omission of this or other formalities (e.g. registration or authorisation) is the nullity of the apprenticeship and the application of the normal rules of the labour contract. In relation to working hours the time spent in training centres is counted as real working time. As to wages, it is usual to permit pay inferior to the minimum of an ordinary worker, pay scales have progressively reduced differentials but in some countries (e.g. Costa Rica) the employer must put the differential into an official institution for professional training to finance scholarships. In other countries remuneration payable during the apprenticeship is ruled by the norms adopted by authorities (e.g. Libya, Gabon, USSR) or by a special collective agreement or by a board's award for each trade activity (e.g. Norway). It is normal practice to apply to apprenticeship contracts the rules relating to termination of the ordinary contract of employment, especially those for a fixed term introducing certain modifications. In any case in countries where the apprentice is considered as an employee all restrictions on his rights including dismissal may be held to be unconstitutional (e.g. Italy). In British law and that of other countries like New Zealand the unfair dismissal of an apprentice may result not only in compensation for loss of wages but also for loss of future opportunities. It is usual in several countries to count time spent as an apprentice towards seniority when the employer remains the same; but when the employer is obliged to include a certain percentage of apprentices in the workforce (an equivalent of 5 per cent of working personnel in Latin America) the apprentice can only expect a certificate of proficiency according to his ability and the limited hope of obtaining effective work in the establishment where he was trained as an apprentice. In régimes like those of GDR and Czechoslovakia the labour code lays down the right of a trained worker to obtain a job appropriate to his qualifications.

439

2. New Forms of Training

34. In recent decades, new types of institutions for training have emerged in many countries. They are much nearer to the world of labour than the old vocational schools. This has given rise in developed countries like Denmark and France, but also in less developed ones like those of Latin America, to the alternative of training workers in centres or in large enterprises. The 'apprentice' is bound to the employer by an apprenticeship contract and thereby receives wages from him, but he is entirely trained in the centre. The very concept of an apprenticeship contract is changing. In developed countries different systems are appearing, integrated with policies and programmes of continuing education; while in less developed countries the change comes from programmes of employment and training of young people with development in view.

In West European countries the fight against unemployment starting in the mid-seventies, especially against that of young people, also reflects itself in new schemes, like 'stagiaires', 'educational contracts', 'employment training' and other different forms of employment like 'activities of collective interest'. The new schemes differing from the old ones are addressed directly to young people who are already qualified, even at high academic levels; the age group is considerably older; the relation is relatively brief and in several countries employers are amply subsidised with public funds if they comply with given requirements.

III. Categories of Labour Contracts

A. *Contracts Containing a Trial Clause*

35. The categorisation of contracts about to be made, as was said in the introduction, is primarily related to duration. In this context, however, a specific type of employment, that of the so-called probationary employee will be considered first. The situation of these employees arises from a special stipulation (*trial clause*) which, usually for a specified time, partially stops the functioning of the rules relative to termination of the contract of employment, while the parties get to know each other. Sometimes, though less frequently, the trial clause relates to a promotion or to a particular assignment rather than to the continuation of the employment relationship between the parties. This usage is rarely found in laws (Venezuela Labour Law, Article, 33) but it is given attention in collective agreements. The trial clause is important in practice and deserves some attention before going on to the other categories of contracts, especially because, although it is usually held to validly create a contract for a fixed term, it is not always treated as such in law. While the aim remains the same such clauses may function differently, as different laws specifically provide.

36. Provisions with respect to trial clause are not frequent and not very detailed in legislation, and this causes confusion. In extreme cases, like Mexico, their omission from mention by the law is interpreted as forbidding such clauses; while French jurisprudence widely accepted them under the old Labour Code. In British law, the lack of any law dealing explicitly with trial clauses has been made up for by using general principles of contract law. In any event, when such clauses are allowed they are frequently limited in their maximum duration; and sometimes in their minimum duration, as in Belgium. In Japan there is a two week term separating the first part of the trial, which may end without previous notice; and the second part, which has no fixed limit but during which 30 days notice must be given. The terms of trial clauses, however, differ greatly according to the worker's category or the duration of the engagement, quite apart from qualification periods for the enjoyment of certain benefits, which should not be confused with periods of trial relating to employment as such. The maximum period permitted is two weeks in some countries, for example in Panama for all employees, in Belgium for blue collar workers, in France for short term contracts and in Poland for all personnel save managerial. But in Laos the trial clause may extend to six months because of professional custom. Six months is the absolute ceiling in Italy. In Belgium the maximum period for white collar workers now is twelve months. But three months is the period most accepted: in Brazil, Ecuador, Finland, Hungary, Jamaica and Peru for example, and in Poland for managerial personnel.

An extension of the period set is possible under certain circumstances in some countries, or up to the legal maximum in others; but generally a repeat of the period of trial is not permitted, for example in term contracts in Peru, for unskilled workers in Panama or for qualified workers with diploma in Iraq.

This variety of situations and the need to find a way to state that the maximum term of trial must be limited. Led to the inclusion by the OIT Conference, in Article 2.2.b. of Convention 158, of a formula which permits limitations on job security only by a trial clause 'whose duration has been previously fixed and is reasonable'.

37. Even when the law is silent it is generally understood that the rights and obligations of probationary employees are the same as those of other employees except in aspects specifically affected by the trial clause. Normally such a clause grants the employer a greater freedom of dismissal without justification and eliminates or reduces the requirement of previous notice. However, in some legislation a proportional indemnity for dismissal is due (Peru); when the contract is for a fixed term (Brazil) there may be indemnity for non-justified early termination. The jurisprudence of various countries tends to treat that the employer's power to dismiss during or at the end of trial period without justification as only attenuated, not absolute. Iraq (Labour Code Article 71), for example, an employer who terminates a

441

probationary relationship is liable unless he can prove the worker's incompetence.

When an employees' performance during his trial period has been expressly approved or when he is simply kept on in employment beyond the legal trial period the contract converts into a normal contract of employment, retroactive to the beginning of the relationship. That is to say the trial period counts for seniority.

38. As to formality, almost all laws regulating trial clauses require a written document previous to the begining of the employment. Otherwise the trial clause is a nullity and the contract is treated as a normal contract of employment. Exceptionally, in some countries there is a legal presumption of a trial period in the contracts of domestic workers (Belgium and Peru, the first two weeks) or of appentices (Colombia, the first three months).

B. Contracts for an Indefinite Period

39. Currently the basic or normal contract of employment is the contract for an indefinite period. Undoubtedly there have been common reasons or common causes but there have been different paths to this situation. Moreover indefiniteness of the period of employment contracts has not always or everywhere been perceived as leading to permanent employment or as contributing to job security.

The civil and commercial codes of the nineteenth century favoured the contract for a fixed term. Systems deriving from such codes arrived at the present situation in indirect and varied ways, including extended previous notice, a theory of abuse of rights, refusal of approval, restriction of justifying causes and presumption of an intent to establish a permanent relation. Most obviously the concept of the contract for an indefinite period as a precarious relationship which could be terminated at any time by either party without cause and only brief notice was finally overcome by the prohibition of dismissal without cause.

Countries following the British system have arrived at the common position that contracts of employment are normally of indefinite duration, terminable for cause or upon reasonable notice, after living for years with the concept that an indefinite term was presumed to show an intent that the contract be for a year. This term was not adequate for conditions which had ceased to be predominantly agrarian. In varying degrees, depending on the country, guarantees of job security have been added through law or collective agreements.

40. Contracts for an indefinite period maintain their eminence in practically all countries, no matter what their juridical, political or economic system may be. However, recent measures, like those supporting contracts for temporary work and other forms of limited employment, suggest that this basic type of employment contract has lost some favour in the eyes of lawmakers. Nevertheless, it is widely understood that such contracts make it possible for workers to hold their jobs throughout their active lives, while keeping their freedom to terminate the relationship for proper reasons. Such employment contracts are the norm in the sense that there is a legal presumption that when any other type fails the relationship reverts to these terms. Departure from this norm is often restricted. In the legislation of many countries, like Mexico and other Latin American countries, limits on the term of an employment contract must be expressly permitted by law or justified by the type of work to be done.

Employment contracts of indefinite duration require less formalities than all other types and may be more easily proved, unless they include special clauses like provisions for trial periods or incompetence.

Restrictions on freedom to contract for an indefinite period are infrequent and they deal mostly with apprenticeship contracts or contracts for particular tasks or jobs specified by law. Legal guarantees of minimum duration are also exceptional and do not affect the nature of the contract. Where such gaurantees do exist they benefit specific categories of workers. For example in Italy there is two-year minimum term prescribed for certain agricultural workers.

C. Contracts for a Definite Period and Related Contracts

41. In spite of what has been said, there are cases in which the specific character of the task or other factors limit the possible duration of a labour relationship, or both parties may simply wish to contract for a definite period. Because of the general preference of both legislators and courts for contracts of indefinite term a major concern has been to limit the range of employment relationships that are treated as inherently incapable of being for an indefinite term. But it has also been a major concern to allow for a reasonable margin of free will in this field, while ensuring that real or apparent contractual job security does not undermine job security statutes. This explains the differing degrees of acceptance of contracts for fixed periods in various legal regimes and the greater or lesser concern for formalities and conditions imposed. These variations principally relate to the term of the contract of employment but also extend to the treatment of redundancy and collective dismissals. In any case it is understood that the situation of employees under contracts of other than indefinite term and containing special conditions cannot be below minimum legal labour standards. Often the way in which annual vacations or Christmas bonus must be calculated for such employees, that they receive proportionate treatment, is expressly provided for.

42. The most important variations in this category of contracts are those in which:

(1) the term is fixed by the free will of the parties;
(2) the term is determined by the task to be discharged;
(3) the term suits the rhythm of the activity of which the job is a part.

All these have in common the fact that ending the relationship on the basis foreseen does not make either party liable. However in Argentina, Ecuador, Italy and Peru, for example, indemnities or premiums must be paid depending on the term of the contract. In almost all jurisdictions either legislation or jurisprudence clearly provides that a contract for a definite term is converted into one for an indefinite term if the employment relationship continues beyond the term or the end of the task contracted for.

1. Contract for a Definite Period

43. The possibility of making a valid contract of employment for a fixed term is subject to restrictions in most countries; and if such a contract is made fraudulently it is treated as a contract for an indefinite term. This is clear in the legislation of Hungary, Italy and Portugal and accords with Article 2.3 of International Convention 158 and numeral 3.2 of Recommendation 166.

Most legislation seems to favour the idea that a valid contract for a definite period must necessarily contain a very specific term, precisely fixed from the moment the contract is concluded. Sometimes this excludes certain legal arrangements allowed by civil law. This is also, apparently, the criterion applied by courts of various countries, like France, which introduced into the Labour Code a provision to that effect. But when there is no express prohibition, in some systems, like the British, there is some degree of uncertainty. In some countries, principally in Latin America where a marked resistance to this type of contract is found, legislation sets a maximum term, however variable it may be, from a year in Mexico, Costa Rica or Panama to five years in Argentina. In Finland observing the total term is obligatory only on the employer. The worker may terminate the relationship after the first year of contracted service has elapsed. In some countries, like Portugal, there is a minimum duration of six months unless custom determines a shorter period or the transient nature of the task motivating the contract is proved. (Law 781/76, Article 1(2).)

44. Along the same lines, reducing a contract for an indefinite term to a definite term is usually expressly prohibited or restricted. This is true in the legislation of a number of countries in Latin America and in other countries, although several do allow successive extensions of contracts for fixed terms as long as the extensions are not unreasonable. (See for example LCT of Argentina, Article 90, last a.)

Extensions may also be accepted if they are proved to be justified 'by the nature of the work or other legitimate reasons' (Belgian law on labour contracts 1978, Article 10) or if they do not go beyond the duration permitted by law (Portuguese law *cit.*, Article 3.1.). In some legislation where the general principle is the conversion of the contract for a definite term into a contract for indeterminate term, a first and only extension is tolerated. (For example Brazil CLT, Article 451.)

In some countries these restrictions are expressly applicable to the making of successive contracts for a fixed term when these are not separated by a sensible or prudent lapse.

Colombian legislation constitutes a very real exception because although it provides a maximum term, recontracting, even tacit, is allowed under identical conditions any number of times.

45. When extension is not for an objectively justified cause, when it damages the worker (for instance, in Hungary) or when an unacceptable fetter is intended (for instance in Austria), the courts, even in absence of an express term, may transform a contract for a fixed term into a contract for an indefinite term. In general, however, jurisprudence does not pronounce contracts for fixed terms possible or impossible by any one criterion. Exceptionally, before the legislative reforms which reduced the possibility of making successive labour contracts for fixed terms, the French Court of Cassation had elaborated a doctrine according to which successive labour contracts for fixed terms, created a whole, an entirety, of indeterminate duration which could not be interrupted without complying with the requirements for indeterminate contracts. However each contract making up that entirety maintained its nature as a contract for a definite term and had to be observed as such.

46. As with employment contracts that depart from the basic scheme, the contract for a fixed term must usually be written and failure to comply with this requirement and any other formalities imposed by law leads automatically, or almost automatically, to the treatment of the contract as one of indeterminate term. Exceptionally, some legislation dispenses with these formalities for contracts of short duration; for instance in Hungary (less than 30 days), Italy (less than 12 working days), or German Democratic Republic (less than a week).

47. Reference to period of notice is omitted from the text of most laws or is expressly excluded (for example Norway or Hungary). Others however, including Argentina, Ecuador, Finland, France, Portugal, require notice, at least under certain circumstances.

48. Subject to certain exceptions, where a contract for a set term is allowed the term must be observed by both parties, but the strictness of this requirement is not always the same. In many countries the sanction for failure to comply is greater for the employer than for the employee. The damage payment due to the worker in such a case of premature termination is sometimes equivalent to at least the amount of pay due to the end of the

445

agreed term (Colombia, Nicaragua and Portugal) but in some countries significant reduction is provided for (50 per cent in Brazil and Ecuador). In still others the amount of damages and any other sanction against the guilty party is left to judicial assessment.

49. Generally doctrine provides that when a contract of apparently limited duration contains a clause authorising one of the parties, or both, to reject it at any time without good legal reasons it is to be treated as a contract of indeterminate duration and not as a contract for a fixed term.

50. In short, one may conclude that the current tendency in the jurisdictions compared is towards permitting the parties to make employment contracts for fixed terms, but within narrow limits, as to qualifying circumstances, the extent of the term and its renewal. In general workers may not by this means be excluded from benefits accorded by legislation or resulting from collective bargaining or practice to those with contracts of indeterminate term.

It seems that jurisprudence will more and more frequently deny validity to any clause fixing a term, when invoked by the management, if it does not clearly serve the interests of both parties or appear reasonable in the circumstances.

It is very clear that the tendency is toward requiring notice of termination, not only when the worker is not in a position to know beforehand when the contract will end, but also in the contracts for a fixed term, to confirm with precision and reasonably well ahead of time that the relationship will not continue.

All this does not prevent provision for fixed term contracts in the statutes governing certain professions, such as professional sportsmen, artists and other workers in show-business, seamen, fishermen and, sometimes, highly-qualified technicians and executives.

In setting legal damages for repudiating a term contract before due time the tendency is to put the employee as completely as possible in the position he would have been had the contract been performed and to minimise his responsibility if he is the party responsible for repudiating the contract.

It seems to be increasingly common that the expiry of the term does not deprive the worker of damages for dismissal calculated in relation to seniority, and the like.

2. Contract for a Specific Task

51. In most legislation labour contracts which are neither permanent nor for a definite period are allowed when they are for transient tasks or tasks normally performed by a worker temporarily absent from his job (replacement or substitution) or generally in cases where the job ends automatically. Such laws are sometimes very strict, for example in Mexico. In other instances only a general reference is found and custom governs (Sweden) or judges apply a relatively broad standard of reasonableness.

52. International Convention 158 expressly refers to two varieties of contracts for specific tasks: those expressly thus qualified, which are included in the group of determinate duration, and those qualified as 'occasional during a short period', mentioned by inc. C of Article 3.2. as another category of employed persons from which some or all of the guarantees for job security may be excluded.

53. The cases of specific tasks most frequently mentioned by law are the substitute which in India represents a category called *baldi*, and those employed for construction work. The main variation on the basic type of contracts for a definite term results from indeterminacy in the term:
(a) In some jurisdictions there is greater requirement of notice (for instance Finland, or German Democratic Republic).
(b) In general, legislation and jurisprudence provide that when the employer party claims that workers are under contract for transient jobs the exception is valid only when they are employed for a reasonably brief term and their occupation is well recognised as an aspect of the employer's enterprise.
(c) Where the temporary worker is kept on after the owner of the job is back, or after the task is finished, the relationship changes into a contract of indefinite term, as is the case with contracts for fixed term.

3. The Season Contract

54. Contracts for a season are, according to some legislation, only one of the possible variations of the contract for a definite period or they are mentioned separately among the exceptions to legal job security.

Due to the fact that the same personnel is usually employed for successive seasons the jurisprudence, legislation and collective contracts (of some countries) has tended to develop the seasonal contract as an independent concept and to recognise in it some traits which differentiate it from contracts for a specific task. This is especially so with respect to the hotel business in summer resorts. The trend is towards restricting the concept of 'season' to those cases in which the rhythm of the occupation is substantially affected by natural factors known in advance and reoccurring regularly. In such cases the relationship of the employee who continues to work for several seasons is treated as if it were for an indefinite term, with suspension only permitted between seasons. This approach is taken by Argentina and by the law of the *Estatuto de los Trabajadores* of Spain (Article 15.1.e), among others.

447

D. Contract for Temporary Work

55. The contract for temporary work, also known as the employment leasing relationship, is characterised by the participation in it of a labour contractor, an enterprise or agency whose activity consists in leasing to other agencies workers for transient or temporary tasks.

The answers of law and jurisprudence to the development of this activity and the making of such contracts has been varied and contradictory. In some countries it is expressly forbidden (Spain, Italy and Sweden) or indirectly so (Mexico); in some others it is understood to be forbidden because an interpretation that affirms that (in the countries that have ratified it) enterprises providing temporary workers fall under the interdiction of International Convention 96, dealing with the prohibition of paid placement agencies. On the other extreme, the laws of the FR Germany, France, the Netherlands, Denmark, Norway, Belgium, Brazil and other countries have especially regulated the activity of these agencies with a view to protecting temporary workers, safeguarding the interests of permanent workers, protecting clients or users and preventing the infringing of norms on work by aliens. There are, moreover, several countries where this sort of arrangement is very comon which have no law at all about it (USA).

56. Regulations of the sort most frequently adopted vary markedly in the degree to which they accept the idea that there may be a special labour contract between a qualified labour contractor and employees which is adjusted to provide for the discharging of temporary tasks for the clients, the lessees. The relationship between the employees and the labour contractor does not disappear or change its nature merely because during particular assignments the worker is under control of the lessee; nor is this an obstacle to the applicability in each case of the appropriate rules with respect to wages, and all other rules contained in laws, regulations or conventions proper to the place of the contract.

In the various laws on this particular relationship conditions that must be met by enterprises are clearly specified; the formalities that must be fulfilled to make the temporary work contract valid, the rules for recognising seniority within the temporary work enterprise and its obligations with respect to social security. In some laws, like the FR Germany 1982 (section 10), the effects of nullity of the contract between the labour contractor or lessor and the worker are provided for in detail, as is the fact that that contract may automatically convert into a labour contract between the employee and the client. Of course then the lessor is liable for indemnities in favour of the employee who expected his contract of temporary work to be valid.

57. French legislation relative to ruling of temporary work is specially significant. In 1982 the socialist government dictated a text meant to establish restrictions to temporary work (Ordonnance 82–131). And among the disposition adopted by the right-center government which substituted

the former in 1986, measures reforming the labour code are found, which are meant to make it easier for enterprises to use this type of contract, and that of contracts for an established period of time and contracts for Part-time Work, and (Ordonnance 86-948 of 11 August 1986, dictated in relation to Habilitation Law of 2 July 1986, which permits the adoption by ordonnance of several economic and social measures).

Current legislation has eliminated from the French Labour Code the taxative list of cases in which temporary work may be used for the execution of a *mission*. However there exists a limit imposed by a principle: the temporary work contract's object cannot be that of providing a durable employment linked to the normal and permanent activity of the enterprise that makes use of it (New Art. L.124-2 of the Code du Travail. So the decision as to whether the situation in question respects, or not the principle to which we have just referred, tests with the Labour Courts.

Besides, if, in general terms, the duration of the mission of a temporary worker must have a fixed span determined with precision in the contract, three situations may arise according to French law in which the temporary worker may not have a fixed term:

1. When he has to replace an absentee worker or one whose contract is suspended;

2. When the job is seasonal and;

3. When the work is such that the common practice is not to use contracts of indeterminate duration because of the nature of the activity and the temporary nature of that employment.

As to the duration of this type of contracts the current French law has extended it to a maximum of 24 months.

The conditions for the renewal of such contracts, when the maximum above mentioned is respected, must be established beforehand, and in any case, only one renewal is accepted.

Some aspects of the previous legislation are still in force. For instance, these forms may not be used when dealing with contracts suspended by a strike, nor can a workman whose contract has ended, be replaced (there are some exceptions) immediately, by this means, before a certain time has elapsed.

It must be underlined that the liberalisation of the ruling of this contract in France, has not altered the social statute of the temporary worker. – Identical remuneration to that of the permanent worker of the same qualification is still requested; when the contract ends, the worker receives an indemnity because of the precarious nature of the job; the contract must be written; and when the rulings for the category of contracts for temporary work are not observed, the régime for the contract of indeterminate duration must be applied.

E. *Contract of Part-time Work*

58. It is normal for an employee to occupy all his active time with the same employer; however, there are some jobs, like those related to cleaning offices or homes, where it is traditional for an employee to work a limited number of hours each day for several different employers. Women with family responsibilities, housewives, etc., often prefer part-time or half-time jobs. This is also a way for workers whose job does not take up all their time to improve their income (professors, journalists, civil servants, etc.). In general part-time employment follows the ordinary rules except for the working hours contracted for. Although steps may be taken against part-time work as a cause of unemployment it does not cause legal problems, except for possible disputes between employers during an employee's time or because the total working hours involved may exceed the number tolerated by law.

59. However, in some countries according to common law or legislation labour laws are applicable only to full-time workers or, at least, only they may benefit from certain types of measures, like reinstatement under the Peruvian law of 1973. In Danish Law, generally speaking, a wage-earner cannot quality in a category with the legal status of *'functionnaire'* unless requirements relating to a minimum number of working hours are met.

60. In Spanish law, however, temporary provisions of the Statute of 1980 express the wish of the legislator, at least while 'present circumstances of employment persist', to direct offers of this type of work towards particular categories of workers, such as those who receive unemployment benefits, those who, having exhausted their benefits, are still unemployed, unemployed workers from rural sectors and young people under 25 years of age. However, with respect to this last category Dec. No. 1362 of 1981 on part-time labour contracts provides that under the circumstances set out above a young person under 25 years of age with a permanent job may enter a part-time contract only when the time put in on the two jobs together does not exceed an ordinary work day in the sector to which his principal work belongs.

61. Lately in the USA, where part-time work is widespread, and also in some countries of Western Europe, new forms have developed. One of them is *job-sharing*, in which two or more workers share the same job, taking turns in the day's work or in the days of the week. Analysts point out that the real difference between this arrangement and traditional part-time work lies in the compact between the *twin workers*, which makes them responsible for the division of working time and for taking charge of the whole job in case of the absence of one of them, without demanding extra pay for hours exceeding their own working time.

These techniques have not been specifically legally regulated up to now and their acceptability may be subject to the fulfilment of certain conditions. For instance, in France the acceptance of job-sharing as a type of the so-called *'contracts de solidarité'* would depend on the fulfilment of legal requirements for this type of contracts, which charge the employer with

contracting with the respective enterprise committee and c
an employment (Ordinance 40/1982).

62. The persistent crisis affecting the labour market in developed countries
and in those in process of development, and the poor success of other
procedures used to boost the labour market, have again brought to question
the real benefits obtained through labour law rulings. And so, labour
flexibility has been claimed from various sectors, especially from European
organisations of employers. The objective pursued by this *flexibility* is,
among others, to put an end to dissuasive rulings for the use of differential
forms of labour relations, such as Contracts for a Definite Period and
Related Contracts, the Contracts of Part-time Work and the Contracts for
Temporary Work (ILO, Social and Labour Bulletin, Na 5/85).

63. The subject is of course open to debates, as much so in academic circles
as in the professional and the political. Currently, it is included in the
agenda of congresses and similar events at national and international levels;
it is feeding the production of documents and studies and is being included
in the programs of political parties.

In France, for instance, one of the very first decisions adopted by the
coalition which took over the government in 1986, was to use one of the
measures most frequently claimed under the signs of flexibility or flexibilisation: the suppression of administrative objections or red tape to free
dismissals.

Within ILO, flexibility had been alluded to in the *Report of the Director-
General* to the International Labour Conference, 71st session (1985). It was
considered anew in his Report to the 72nd session (1986) and this motivated
commentaries which, especially in the case of the delegations of workers,
insisted on the danger held by vague concepts and the risk of 'sliding
backwards in social conquests'.

64. This process has not been totally legal, as was the case of France; in
several countries one can detect new flexibilisation through what USA calls
Concession Bargaining.

In highly developed countries, specially in the Netherlands there has been
observed a quantitative advance in the rates of a modality auspiciated by the
partisans of flexibilisation: for instance, part-time work. There are others
and they tend to spread into an ever greater number of countries.

In countries under process of development, however, the current characteristics, aside from the atypical modalities which are also to be found, are:
the impressive development of *independent marginal work*, which deprives
workers of the protection of labour law and also, frequently, of social
security. In countries where labour law is sufficiently developed, and the
organisation of workers holds considerable power (e.g. Argentina) it is

estimated that these independent marginal workers represent several million people, of which almost one half does not have monthly earnings equivalent to minimum vital salary.

65. The evolution of modalities of labour contract in the future, is always difficult to foresee, but for the moment everything points towards an accent of flexibilisation of the individual labour relations to what the growing weakness of the negotiation power of the syndicates is certainly contributing.

The decree of flexibility to be reached will surely vary in different countries according to their political, economical and social orientation and the strength of their professional organisations.

In any case, compared law shall surely go on showing simultaneous advances and setbacks in the ruling of labour contracts. This is proved by the fact that, while France approved the most flexible rules on 'licenciement', Peru (4 June, 1986) adopted almost simultaneously a new law of stability much stricter than the one in force at the moment.

SELECTED BIBLIOGRAPHY

C.S. Aronstein (Editor), *Handbook on Contracts of Employment*, Deventer, 1976.
R. Blanpain (Editor in Chief), *International Encyclopaedia for Labour Law and Industrial Relations*, Deventer, Kluwer.
F. Gamillscheg, 'Labour Contracts', 1973, in *International Encyclopaedia of Comparative Law*, vol. XV, ch. 28.4.
O. Kahn-Freund, *Labour and the Law*, 2nd edn., London, 1977.
K.W. Wedderburn, *The Worker and the Law*, 2nd edn., Harmondsworth, 1971.

Chapter 21. Equality and Prohibition of Discrimination in Employment*

R. Blanpain

I. Historical Development: A Fundamental and Universal Principle

1. Individual equality is a long-standing aspiration, underlying *inter alia* the American declaration of Independence of 4 July 1776 which proclaimed 'that all men are created equal, that they are endowed by their Creator with certain inalienable rights' . . . and the French Declaration of Human Rights of 1789 which stated that 'all men are and shall be born free and equal before the law. Social differences may only be established for the good of all. Undoubtedly words had a different meaning than they have today, since the word 'men' was not understood to include all human beings; 'men' meant only white males: indeed the United States Constitution of 1789 tolerated slavery, while French women were excluded from political rights.[1] However, with both Declarations important steps were taken. 'Equality before the law' found its way into the constitutional history of the nineteenth century. By way of Belgium – the constitution of 1831 of that country served as an important link between France and other countries – it reached Prussia and the German Empire of 1871[2] and developed further.

2. At present equality, that is, the absence of discrimination, – equality and non-discrimination are two sides of the same coin – is accepted as a fundamental and universal principle not only in a significant number of national Constitutions, but also in a considerable number of far-reaching international instruments.

---

* This chapter contains mainly the introductory remarks and general overview which I wrote based on international and national monographs on *equality and prohibition of discrimination* which were published in the *Bulletin of Comparative Labour Relations*, No. 14 (Kluwer Law and Taxation, 1985). Contributors to this study were I. Asscher-Vonk (The Netherlands), R. Birk (FR Germany), V. Brajic (Yugoslavia), J. Egger (EEC), B. Flodgren (Sweden), T. Hanami (Japan), B. Hepple (Great Britain), H. Jain (Canada), J. Jones (USA), L. Nagy (Hungary), J. Rojot (France), C. Rossillion (ILO), T. Treu (Italy) and J. Walgrave (Belgium).
1. T. Ramm, 'Introduction' in F. Schmidt, ed., *Discrimination in Employment*, Stockholm, 1978, p. 37.
2. *Ibid.*, p. 32.

453

3. The *Charter of the United Nations of 1945* and the *Declaration of Human Rights of 1948* are among the most significant. The Declaration of 1948 provides in Article 2 that everyone is entitled to all the rights and freedoms which are set forth in the Declaration 'without distinction of any kind, such as race, colour, sex, language, religion, political or other opinions, national or social origin, property, birth or other status'. A provision in similar terms is formulated in the *International Covenant on Economic, Social and Cultural Rights* and in the *International Convenant on Civil and Political Rights of 1966.*

4. The *Charter of Economic Rights and Duties of the Organization of American States of 1974* declares that 'it is the right and duty of all States, individually and collectively, to eliminate colonialism, apartheid, social discrimination, neo-colonialism and all forms of foreign aggression, occupation and domination, and the economic and social consequences thereof, as a prerequisite for development' (Article 16, 1).

5. Further, in 1965 the United Nations adopted an *International Convention on the Elimination of all Forms of Racial Discrimination.* More than 100 States are parties to this convention. Following this instrument States undertook 'to prohibit and to eliminate racial discrimination in all forms and to guarantee the right of everyone, without distinction as to race, colour, or national or ethnic origin, to equality before the law'.

Among the rights the convention refers to, are economic, social and cultural rights, and in particular the right to work, to free choice of employment, to just and favourable conditions of work, to protection against unemployment, to equal pay for equal work, to just the favourable remuneration, the right to form and join trade unions, the right to housing, the right to public health, medical care, social security and social services and the right to education and training.[3]

6. The ILO likewise established the principle of non-discrimination in the *Declaration of Philadelphia* (1944) and incorporated it in its Constitution. This declaration affirms that 'all human beings, irrespective of race, creed or sex, have the right to pursue both their material well-being and their spiritual development in conditions of freedom and dignity, of economic security and equal opportuntity'. Although the ILO dealt with discrimination in a number of instruments, in 1958, following a resolution of the Economic and Social Council of the UN, it adopted an overall comprehensive *Convention and a Recommendation concerning Discrimination in Employment and Occupation* (No. 111).

ILO Convention No. 111 and Recommendation refer to 'employment and occupation'; they provide that these terms include access to vocational

3. N. Valticos, *IELL*, (International Labour Law), 1979, p. 113.

training, access to employment and to particular occupations, and terms and conditions of employment.

7. Important instruments were also adopted at European level. Thus the *European Convention for the Protection of Human Rights and Fundamental Freedoms of 1950,* Article 14 of which forbids discrimination on grounds of 'sex, race, colour, language, religion, political or other opinions, national or social origin; association with a national minority, property, birth or other status'. It should also be noted that the *European Social Charter of 1961* refers in its preamble to the principle of non-discrimination.

8. The EC's law also contains a number of important rules imposing non-discrimination, thus the right to non-discriminatory treatment of workers from other Member States both on equal pay and equal treatment of men and women concerning employment, which we will also discuss in detail later.

9. Although the goal of equality and the prohibition of discrimination constitutes a long-standing and fundamental aspiration of many nations, it is only recently that a number of countries have taken positive steps aiming at its concrete implementation.

France may be one country illustrating such a development. For a long period the Declaration of 1789 and general provisions in the Constitution were the only available basis of judicial protection against discrimination in general. It is only recently that France has adopted a large number of legal texts covering different kinds of discrimination, namely in 1972, in 1975, and especially in 1982 and 1983.

One wonders whether these developments are at a turning point? The equality movement is likely to become at least blocked, at the worst eroded, by the overall embracing deregulation mood, urging for market flexibility for the very sake of employment and job creation and thus doing away with protective legislation, equally in the name of freedom.

II. Discrimination: A Definition

10. The term discrimination has recently acquired a pejorative meaning,[4] namely the *unjustified unequal treatment of human beings.* Justified unequal treatment is called differentiation. ILO Convention 111 defines the term 'discrimination' as including 'any distinction, exclusion or preference made on the basis of race, colour, sex, religion, political opinion, national extrac-

---

4. M. Bossuyt, *L'interdiction de la Discrimination dans le Droit international des Droits le l'Homme,* Bruxelles, 1976, p. 26.

tion or social origin, which has the effect of nullifying or impairing equality of opportunity or treatment in employment or occupation'.

11. There are different types of discrimination. The first is *direct* discrimination, that is 'less favourable treatment on forbidden grounds'. For some, direct discrimination covers both equal opportunity and equality of outcomes. This may not be fully the case in all countries. British legislation for example is based rather on the notion of equal opportunity.

The definition of direct discrimination in most cases covers both intentional and unintentional practices.

12. The second type of discrimination is indirect discrimination or discrimination by effects. In the *USA* the concept of indirect discrimination was articulated by the Supreme Court in the Griggs v. Duke Power Co. case in 1971. In the *USA*, 'the disparate impacts or disparate effects, or the consequences theory holds that a facially non-discriminatory employment practice that disproportionally screens out a higher percentage of protected class members is an unlawful employment practice unless it can be demonstrated . . . that the practice is required by business necessity or has a manifest relationship to job performance. The disparate impact concept has been used to invalidate a wide range of recruitment, assignment, hiring, promotion, discharge, testing and supervisory selection practices.'

13. In order to establish indirect discrimination the complainant in *Great Britain* must prove that the respondent applied a requirement or conditions, applied to all work-seekers or employees and which constitutes an absolute bar; the proportion of the complainant groups, who can comply with that requirement is considerably smaller than the proportion of persons who do not belong to that group. It is then up to the respondent to prove that the requirement or condition is 'justifiable'. The *British* concept of justifiability is far broader than the *American* touchstone, which is 'business necessity'. It follows that if the defence of justifiability is too wide, the objective of the legislation will be easily defeated. In the *British* context, some of the most important examples of indirect discriminatory requirements or practices would include minimum height requirements; prohibition on wearing certain types of clothing (such as turbans by Sikhs); language proficiency in manual jobs; a refusal to accept foreign qualifications; maximum age limitations; experience or training in *Britain*; recruitment by personal referrals within the existing work force, sometimes called 'word of mouth hiring'; and recruitment through a network of contacts which excludes ethnic minorities, women, etc.

The *US* Griggs approach has been adopted in *Canada* in both equal pay and equal employment cases. The final resolution of impact vs intent as an element of the definition of discrimination is now before the Supreme Court of Canada.

14. In other countries, for example *Japan*, the difference between direct and indirect discrimination has been less discussed. It seems, however, that any indirect discrimination which brings separate treatment as a result without reasonable grounds is regarded as prohibited discrimination.

15. The concept of equal employment opportunity is that employment opportunities and benefits should be determined by individual performance or functional characteristics and should not be influenced by the worker's status identification.

16. Another element of the definition obviously refers to the *areas* and *persons* to which it applies: to employees as well as the self-employed, to all or only some aspects of the employment relationship. The *ILO* and the *EC* instruments cover a wider field. Recommendation No. 111 specifies as follows the matters in respect of which all persons should, without discrimination, enjoy equality of opportunity and treatment (paragraph 2):
 (i) access of vocational guidance and placement services;
 (ii) access of training and employment of their own choice on the basis of individual suitability for such training or employment;
 (iii) advancement in accordance with their individual characters, experience, ability and diligence;
 (iv) security of tenure of employment;
 (v) remuneration for work of equal value;
 (vi) conditions of work including hours of work, rest periods, annual holidays with pay, occupational safety and occupational health measures, as well as social security measures and welfare facilities and benefits provided in connection with employment.
It also points out that there should be no discrimination in respect of admission to, retention of membership in or participation in the affairs of employers' and workers' organisations.

An *EEC* Directive No. 76/207 of 9 February 1976 deals with equal treatment as regards access to occupation, vocational training and promotion and working conditions.

In *Canada* the relevant statutes apply to employers, employment agencies, trade unions and in some jurisdictions to self-governing professions. Discrimination is prohibited with respect to advertising, the terms and conditions of employment, including promotion, transfer and training.

In other countries one may have different instruments, which cover each a different area and/or actor. For *Japan*, the courts protect workers against discrimination only after employment, but not in hiring.

III. GROUNDS

17. Some grounds, which do not justify different treatment, are more or less universally covered.

In the international rules and countries studied *race* and *sex* are most prominent on the list of prohibited grounds. *Religion*, *political opinion* and *marital status* (which is closely linked with sex), rank second. Then follow *colour* (close to race), *nationality* and related *grounds* as *national extraction*, *ethnic origin*, as well as *social origin*, *trade union* involvement and *age*. *Handicap* is gaining in importance as a prohibited ground, as well as *private life*.

Less prominent are *pregnancy* (also related to sex), *ideological opinion*, *social status*, *family responsibilities*, *sexual orientation*, *pardoned offence* and *language*. But most of these grounds can however be brought under the umbrella of other more widely prohibited grounds.

18. This brings us to the first problem, namely the fact that the meaning of some of the terms employed is not at all clear, so that different words are used to point to a diversified reality, which may contain shades of differences in relation to one another. This leads to the possibility of grouping certain grounds. One can distinguish the following groupings:
(1) Race, colour, ethnic origin, national extraction, nationality, social origin, status; and
(2) Sex, pregnancy, marital status, family responsibilities;
(3) Political and ideological opinion, religion and trade union involvement;
(4) Age;
(5) Handicap;
(6) Private life, sexual orientation, pardoned offences.

The charts on pages 457 and 458 give an overview of the prohibited grounds as they are enumerated in 14 different international instruments (I) and in the ILO, the EC, as well as in 12 countries (II).

Let us consider some of these grounds, which due to the vagueness of the terms do to a certain extent overlap, in more detail.

A. Race, Colour ... Nationality

19. A common feature of these various grounds of discrimination is the fact that they are generally linked to the existence of different ethnic groups.

The words '*ethnic origin*' have been given a wide interpretation as meaning a group which is a segment of the population distinguished from others by a sufficient combination of shared customs, beliefs, traditions and characteristics derived from a common or presumed common past, even if not drawn from a common 'racial stock'.

The concept of *race* stems from perceptions in difference or primary stock.

Even though 'race' and '*colour*' refer to two different kinds of human characteristics, it is the visibility of skin colour – and of other physical traits associated with a particular colour or group that marks individuals out. 'Most people do not know the difference between race and ethnic group,

Chart 1. Forbidden Grounds in 14 Different International Instruments

Number of instruments mentioning the category	GROUNDS	Declaration of Philadelphia	UN Charter	Constitution UNESCO	Constitution OMS	American Declaration	Universal Declaration Polit.–Social Pacts	European Convention	Convention Refugees	ILO 111	Convention UNESCO	European Social Charter	Racial Declaration	Racial Convention	American Convention
(17)	Race (17)	×	×	×	×	×	×××	×	××	×	×	×	×	×	×
	Colour (12)						×××	×		×	×	×	×	×	×
(14)	Religion (12)		×		×		×××	×	××	×	×	×			×
	Creed (2)	×				×									
(12)	National Origin (7)						×××	×			×			×	×
	Birth (6)						×××	×			×				×
	Country of Origin (2)								××						
	National Extraction (2)									×		×			
	Ethnic Origin (2)												×	×	
	Descent (1)													×	
	National Minority (1)							×							
(12)	Sex (12)	×	×	×		×	×××	×		×	×	×			×
(10)	Social Origin (8)						×××	×		×	×	×			×
	Wealth (4)						×××	×							
	Any Other Situation (4)						×××	×							
	Economic Conditions (3)			×	×						×				
	Social Conditions (2)			×	×										
	Economic Status (1)														×
	Any Other Social Conditions (1)														×
(9)	Political Opinion (9)				×		×××	×		×	×	×			×
	Other Opinions (6)						×××	×			×				×
(8)	Language (8)		×			×	×××	×			×				×
(1)	Any Other Factor					×									
	Number of grounds in each instrument	3	4	4	5	5	12	13	3	7	11	7	3	5	12

Source: Bossuyt op. cit.

Chart II. Forbidden grounds in ILO, EC and 12 countries

	ILO	EEC	Belgium	Canada	France	FR Germany	Great Britain	Hungary	Italy	Japan	Netherlands	Sweden	USA	Yugoslavia	Total	Subtotal
I. Race	×	×	×	×	×	×	×	×	×	×	×	×	×	×	14	53
Colour	×			×		×	×				×	×	×		7	
Ethnic origin				×			×	×	×		×	×	×		7	
Language				×											1	
Nationality		×	×	×		×	×	×				×	×	×	9	
National extraction	×			×		×	×					×			5	
Social origin	×			×	×			×	×	×	×	×			8	
Social status										×	×				2	
II. Sex	×	×	×	×	×	×	×	×	×	×	×	×	×	×	14	32
Family responsibilities	×	×	×		×				×						5	
Marital status	×	×	×	×	×		×	×	×	×	×				10	
Pregnancy									×	×			×		3	
III. Ideological opinion									×						1	27
Political opinion	×		×		×				×	×	×	×	×	×	9	
Religion	×			×	×	×		×	×	×	×		×		9	
Trade Union Involvement	×		×		×	×			×	×	×			×	8	
IV. Age	×		×	×	×			×	×				×		7	7
V. Handicap	×			×	×								×	×	5	5
VI. Pardoned offences				×											1	8
Private life			×		×					×			×	×	5	
Sexual orientation				×	×										2	
TOTAL	12	5	9	14	12	7	7	8	12	10	10	8	11	7	132	

between *nurture* and *nature*. It makes for an economy of thought to ascribe peculiarities of appearance, custom, values, to race. It is simpler to attribute differences to heredity than to juggle all the complex social grounds for differences that exist'.

20. National origin includes in the *USA* 'the denial of employment opportunity because of an individual's, or his or her ancestors', place of origin; or because an individual has the racial, cultural, or linguistic characteristics of a national origin group. It also includes consideration of whether opportunities have been denied because of marriage to or association with persons of a national origin group, or membership in or association with an organisation so identified, attendance or participation in schools, churches, temples or mosques generally used by persons of a national origin group and because an individual's name or spouse's name is associated with such a group.'

The term 'national origin', which is a protected class under the principal federal law, does not prohibit a private employer from discriminating on the basis of an employee's lack of citizenship. However, the failure to include the term 'ancestry' does not reduce the scope of coverage as the term national origin is considered to include ancestry.

Social origin refers to situations where there exist divisions of society into classes or castes or hierarchic traditions or distinctions resulting from the educational methods which are employed.

National extraction covers distinctions with reference to naturalised persons of foreign origin or between communities with ties to different national cultures.

21. Access to most labour markets is restricted for *foreigners*, who need a *work permit* in order to take up a job. A notable exception is to be found in the *EC* treaty which provides for the right of free circulation of workers inside the Community, with as *ratio legis* the establishment of a Common Labour Market. Nationals of the Member Countries can claim admission to vacant positions on the same basis as native workers. Foreign workers are to be treated equally. Convention No. 143 (1975) of the ILO providing for equality of opportunity and treatment of migrant workers has not been widely ratified.

The *EC* treaty specifies that only discrimination on grounds of nationality is forbidden. The Court of Justice has indicated however that indirect discrimination, referring e.g. to origin or domicile are equally prohibited. Equal treatment in the EC also benefits family members.

The knowledge of a given *language* may be a permitted ground if justified objectively. In *Sweden* the labour court did not accept an employer's argument that Swedish was a prerequisite for safety reasons.

B. Sex

22. Discrimination based on sex – which means in practice discrimination

461

against women – is certainly the form of discrimination which is most frequently encountered, both in the area of equal pay and equal treatment.
The legal protection in many countries, mainly due to the action of the ILO
and the EEC, seems at first glance quite complete and covers not only
direct, but also indirect discrimination, including that linked to pregnancy,
marital status and family responsibilities. In many cases the legislation
concerned represents an attempt at 'social engineering' in a situation in
which there is no real consensus.

23. Marital status is defined in *Ontario* (Canada) as the status of 'being
married, single, widowed, divorced and separated' and expressly includes
'living with a person of the opposite sex in conjugal relationship or outside
marriage'. In *Italy*, to give another example, Act 7/1963 nullifies any clause
in agreements or factory rules providing that the employment relationship
be terminated because of marriage or for any dismissal of a female employee
occurring between the banns and one year after the marriage. In *Great
Britain* dismissal on grounds of *pregnancy* is not covered by legislation on
discrimination on grounds of sex since that legislation applies legally to men
and women and men cannot become pregnant. In the *USA* an amendment
to the 1964 Civil Rights Act was added in 1978 defining the terms 'because
of sex' to include on the basis of pregnancy, childbirth or related medical
condition.

24. Notwithstanding wide-ranging legislation, discrimination because of sex
still exists. Differentials in income remain in certain cases considerable. The
reasons for these differences depend on historical tradition and are multi-
dimensional. The problem is to overcome historical sex segregation by
opening up traditionally male professions to women through education and
training; another aspect is the under-valuing of certain kinds of jobs, which
are female-dominated. Lack of social organisation may be another factor.
These factors, Treu concludes, can only be redressed by positive action
rather than by the legal prohibition of formal discrimination.

25. Discrimination on grounds of sex is perhaps the most significant field of
discrimination in contemporary *Japan*, also due to a constant increase of a
number of female employees. There has been a traditional practice of
discrimination. Some companies employed women mainly for temporary,
part-time or lower jobs. Some of them had earlier retirement for women on
marriage, pregnancy or childbirth. Most companies discriminated regarding
promotion and average wage differentials were considerable.
   Recently however an Equal Employment Opportunity Act was adopted
May 1985 which aims to promote welfare and equality of opportunity and
treatment for women workers in employment. The Act covers recruitment
and hiring, job assignment and promotion, education and training, welfare,

mandatory retirement age and dismissals. Forbidden grounds of discrimination are sex, marriage, pregnancy or childbirth.

26. Obviously economic crises and especially rising unemployment have an impact. In the *FR Germany* the courts tend toward the view that the decision of an employer does not represent inadmissible discrimination against a married woman if he terminates her employment contract instead of that of a married man when she is in a secure economic position due to her husband's job.

In other instances commercial interests are in play: in *France* the dismissal of an employee whose husband was hired by a competitor was deemed justified. This may be remedied by recent legislation which protects against dismissal for reason of marital status.

C. Political Opinion . . . Religion and Trade Union Involvement

27. These grounds relate to the right to freedom of opinion and conscience in general. In some countries discrimination on those grounds is forbidden on the basis of general, fundamental legal principles; thus in *France* the civil code provides that all persons should enjoy the right of protection to their private lives. Thus when hiring, inquiries concerning political opinion or political and trade union affiliation are forbidden. In other countries these grounds are *explicitly* prohibited. Thus the *Italian* workers' statute of 1970 stipulates that 'it is unlawful for an employer, with a view to admitting a worker into his employment, and for so long as the employment relationship continues, to conduct or cause to be conducted any inquiry into the worker's political, religious, or trade union opinions, or concerning any fact not connected with an assessment of the worker's aptitude for this occupation.'

In *Canada* there is – and this is probably true for most countries – no clear indication whether *religion* and *creed* include only beliefs in a supreme being or a broader spectrum including a personal philosophy, political beliefs, agnosticism, atheism and others. Legal decisions have thus far only addressed a narrow range of issues such as dress and safety requirements, sabbath observance and the like.

28. In the *USA* the Civil Rights Act of 1964 was amended in 1972 to define the term 'religion' to include all aspects of religious observances and practice as well as belief, unless an employer demonstrates an inability to accommodate reasonably an employee's or prospective employee's religious observance or practice without undue hardship.

In a number of countries it is accepted that enterprises with a special political, religious or ideological vocation may demand specific requirements from their employees to match their purposes. Those exceptions to equality are however to be interpreted in a restrictive manner.

In *Sweden* women are now allowed to hold positions as clergy within the

Swedish Church. The question remains whether clergymen may refuse to hold services together with female colleagues.

D. Age

29. In times of growing unemployment the question of age becomes increasingly important in the discussion who should get and retain the jobs that are available. In quite a number of countries there is no specific protection against discrimination because of age, interpreted to include younger workers, as well as older ones.

Canadian laws set varying protected age groups: 45 to 65, 40 to 65, 18 to 64. In the *USA* age groups 40 to 69 are protected. In *France* the Labour Code provides that job offers cannot include an upper age limit. In *Japan* there are special measures to promote the employment of aged workers (45–65 years) and some quotas have been set by the government for workers older than 55 years.

Seniority benefits and compulsory retirement seem exempted from prohibited discriminatory practices, notwithstanding the ILO recommendation regarding the latter; lately in many countries older workers have been pushed out, voluntarily or involuntarily, in order to make room for younger workers, for whom, in many countries preferential measures are taken. Neither seem different retirement ages for men and women to be looked upon as contrary to the goals of equality. The Supreme Court of *Canada* (1982) ruled that in order for employers to deny employment on the basis of age, two standards must be met. One is based on production and economic reasons and the other is related to public safety. There must be objective evidence relating to performance in order to claim exception.

E. Handicap

30. Specific protection of handicapped people, from the point of view of equality, is a more recent concern, as expressed in the 1983 ILO Convention No. 159 and Recommendation 168.

In *France*, as in some other countries, handicapped persons benefit from positive discrimination, as legislation imposes a quota of 3 per cent of the work force to be compulsorily hired in enterprises of over 10 employees. In *Japan* the government has set a quota, a prescribed percentage of handicapped workers, as well as providing funds to employers who employ or train them. In *Yugoslavia*, V. Brajic reports, certain jobs and working tasks are reserved exclusively for disabled persons. In the *USA* certain contractors with the Federal Government and recipients of federal funds are prohibited from discriminating against the handicapped and some 47 of the 50 states have some form of handicapped law.

F. Private Life

31. In most countries discrimination in employment for reasons related to an employee's private life is not covered by specific texts and therefore is covered by the general principles of law providing that all persons enjoy protection in their private life. One consequence is that recruitment tests and inquiries have to be job related.

Although private lives and jobs are to be treated separately, one cannot escape the fact that they have an important impact upon each other. This differs from person to person and job to job. It differs for a priest teaching religion in a religious school on the one hand and for a painter in an automobile factory on the other. Just as a job may make certain demands upon an individual's private life, so privacy must also be protected at the workplace: thus the right of non-smokers to fresh air, freedom of dress (within reasonable limits). The rule which is more and more generally accepted is that private life is only relevant to a job if in consequence the adequate performance of the job is seriously threatened and/or undermines considerably the credibility of the employee. Examples of such facts include criminal charges, extramarital relationship(s), or homosexuality. Sexual harassment at the workplace has been recently highlighted as a form of unacceptable conduct at the workplace.

Alcoholism, drug addiction and gambling may also have an important impact on job performance and may constitute reasons for disciplinary action, including dismissal. In *Sweden*, however, the Labour Court (1979) reversed the decision of the Lund City Council, which suspended a painter with seniority of more than 30 years for 14 days because he had arrived drunk at work on two occasions. The Court ruled that the employee was chronically sick and could therefore not be subjected to damages for the period of suspension. It seems 'that the original moralistic approach is giving way to the reverse attitude, aiming at rehabilitating the addicted to normal working life'.

IV. EXCEPTIONS

A. *Bona fide occupation qualifications*

32. Both international and national regulations do indicate measures which are not deemed to be discriminatory; or put otherwise, constitute differences in opportunity or treatment which are justified.

First there come to mind *bona fide occupational qualifications* (BFOQ). In *Belgium* a limited list of professions for which the gender of an employee is a decisive element due to the particular nature of the job was drawn up: actors, singers, dancers, artists and models and also jobs which are reserved for a particular sex in countries which are not members of the EC.

465

33. In *Great Briatin*, the list also includes toilet attendants, hospital and prison staff, personal welfare counsellors. The Race Relations Act allows exceptions for jobs for which a person of a particular race is required 'for reasons of authenticity' (e.g. Chinese Restaurants).

Also in *Italy* BFOQ's are related to the nature of the work: it would be illegal to exclude women as salespeople for reason of insufficient agressiveness or unsuitability of the business environment. Certain physical requirements such as minimum height or weightlifting were considered to be irrelevant.

In *Sweden* moral or cultural values or respect for integrity justify that only women are employed in the social home service. It is in *Sweden* uncertain whether an employer may select a person of a certain sex simply because of a belief that his business would so benefit. As in *Great Britain* natural origin (e.g. of ethnic chefs) may be a BFOQ in *Sweden*.

34. Similarly, political and religious opinion may be a BFOQ for instance for a political secretary of a political party, a chief editor of a newspaper, a clerical position of different kind. Following the ILO a religious requirement should not apply to the holding of all jobs in an institution connected with the religion concerned; the nature of the particular job must be taken into account.

In the *USA* while the 1964 Act recognises a BFOQ for religion, sex, and national origin, there is no BFOQ exemption for race or colour. The law declares that it shall not be an unlawful employment practice for an employer or other covered entity to classify on the basis of religion, sex, or national origin in those certain instances where religion, sex, or national origin is a *bona fide* occupational qualification reasonably necessary for the normal operation of that particular business or enterprise. The age discrimination laws also contain specific *bona fide* occupational qualification exceptions.

The burden of proof of a BFOQ rests with the employer. In *Canada* the Supreme Court found that mandatory retirement of firefighters at age 60, although honestly imposed, was not objectively based and constituted discrimination on the basis of age.

35. In *Yugoslavia* there are additional requirements for certain jobs; e.g. judges, public prosecutors and policemen should have moral-political capabilities.

B. Security of the State

36. Security of state is another ground justifying separate treatment. Following the ILO this exception relates to individual activities and not merely to the basis of membership of a particular group or community; the concept of

State security must be interpreted in a sufficiently strict sense. Criticising the policy of the Government is not in itself an activity against the security of the State.

37. Usually civil service jobs are reserved to nationals. The *European* Court of Justice has ruled that this exception to the free movement of labour in the EEC has to be interpreted restrictively and only concerns functions which have to do with the exercise of public power. In *Hungary* the safety of the State emphasises Hungarian citizenship and a clean record. In *FR Germany* civil servants are expected to have a positive attitude towards the Constitution. In *Japan* the National Civil Service and the Local Service law disqualify from employment those who engage in activities which extend to destroy by violence the Government based on the Constitution. Public employees should be political neutral. In the *Netherlands* security reasons were explicitly mentioned by the government in the case of a homosexual who applied for a job as social worker in the Royal Household; he was rejected on the grounds that he had kept his homosexuality secret in the course of the selection procedure and that a homosexual who keeps his nature a secret is vulnerable and thus can be considered a security risk. In *Sweden* certain positions which are 'essential for the total defence of the country or for the security of the State in general' may be classified as sensitive positions. For those functions checks are made regarding civil reliability and may be reconsidered every five years.

In the *USA* members of the Communist Party are looked upon as security risks. One should in the context of this exception to equal treatment mention that the ILO advocates the guarantee of the existence of a right of appeal to a competent body.

C. Special Protective Measures

38. A third category of exceptions may be found in *special measures of protection.* The *ILO* indicates that each country may define as non-discriminatory other 'special measures designed to meet the particular requirements of persons, who for reasons such as sex, age, disablement, family responsibilities or social or cultural status are generally recognised to require special protection or assistance'. Also the *EEC* accepts special provisions for the protection of women, especially the protection of motherhood. It is above all in the area of discrimination on the basis of gender that problems have arisen and the question arises whether some protective measures are still justified in the light of the goals of equality and modern technological evolution.

39. In *Belgium* maternal protection is confined first to the 14 weeks of compulsory rest in case of childbirth; education of children, in the sense of leave of absence for family reasons, parental leave and the like are not covered and equal treatment is the rule. In *Belgium* a list of jobs which are considered to be dangerous for mother and/or child has also been drawn up. In such a case the employer must do the utmost to provide another (healthy) job.

There are also specific rules on night work. In this area there reigns a lack of consensus: trade unions distrust social regression for the sake of equality; employers want equality for the sake of more flexibility and female night work.

40. In the *FR Germany* the legislature has embodied a series of additional protective measures for women, juveniles and severely disabled persons. Also in *Great Britain* the Sex Discrimination Act and Equal Pay Act preserve the special protective legislation which applies to women; much of the nineteenth and twentieth century legislation relating to the hours of work, holidays and safety of women in factories, mines and certain other places of employment remains in force. The absolute prohibition of employment underground has been modified. However, it is still impossible for a woman to become a face-worker in a coal mine but she could become an engineer or join any other occupation which does not involve spending a significant proportion of her time underground. In *Hungary* special protection concentrates on pregnant women, mothers, and the handicapped. In *Italy* too protective measures in favour of women workers were traditionally rather widespread. The criticism claiming that this legislation was at least partly responsible for women's disadvantaged position and thus indirectly conducive to discrimination, has been almost totally accepted by the law. Italian law now, Treu reports, encompasses more than is required by the EEC. The way the changes are introduced is interesting: a flexible arrangement is set up by an interplay between the law and collective bargaining. Thus the prohibition of heavy work was lifted by Act 903 but at the same time the law empowered collective agreements to restore the prohibition of 'particularly heavy jobs'. A different approach was followed with respect to night work: Act 903 maintains the prohibition but empowers collective agreements to deviate. For heavy work no more than 20 agreements were reported; for night work over 200.

The major protective legislation still in force in *Italy* concerns pregnancy and maternity. Some rights reserved to the mother have been granted to the father when the children are in his custody.

41. In *Japan* the traditional special protective standards have been amended by the Equal Employment Opportunity Law of May 1985. Prohibition of working overtime and on Public Holidays have been abolished for certain specified managers or professionals. Regulation on overtime for two hours a day has equally been abolished for manufacturing workers while overtime and work on holidays for non manufacturing workers will be regulated within the limits set by the Ministry of Labour. The prohibition of night work has been amended for certain specified managers and shorthour workers, who are required to work at night due to the nature of the job. Maternity leave and menstruation leave remain protected, while expectant mothers may not perform certain jobs which may cause harm to pregnancy, child delivery and child-rearing. In *Sweden* equality prevails: both parents have a right to parental leave. The only difference which remains on grounds of gender is the obligatory rest in case of maternity and time for breast-feeding.

V. Legal Consequences

42. The question arises as to the legal consequences of rules or acts that are discriminatory. The *EEC* regulation on free movement of labour provides that provisions in individual labour contracts, work rules and collective agreements which are discriminatory are null and void. The same goes for *Belgium*: all provisions and practices contrary to the principle of equal treatment are void, which mean that they are null, *ex tunc*, and are to be invoked by the judge *ex officio*. Also in the *FR Germany* the sanction of illegal acts is nullity. The same is true for *Italy* and other countries.

VI. Affirmative Action and Reverse Discrimination

43. Affirmative action programmes are designed to correct the consequences of past and continuing discrimination. They involve a series of steps in order to remove barriers to employment and achieve measurable improvement in recruiting, hiring, training and promotion of worker groups who have in the past been denied assess to certain jobs. In *Japan* affirmative action is only a matter of theory. In other countries, like *Italy*, this area of law is hardly developed. In still other countries, like *Belgium*, *FR Germany* and the *Netherlands* the idea is accepted, but no concrete action of any importance is undertaken, except for some isolated actions in individual enterprises. In *Great Britain* the Commission of Racial Equality has issued a Code of Practice recommending trade unions and employers to take positive measures to provide encouragement and training where there is under-representation of particular groups in particular jobs. A similar Code has been drafted by the Equal Opportunities Commission in respect of sex discrimination. In *France* temporary measures to the benefit of women, in order to re-establish equality of opportunity between men and women, and particularly to remedy current *de facto* inequalities, are allowed. They may be initiated by the government, by extended collective agreements or by enterprise plans. These plans can benefit from governmental subsidies up to 35 per cent of the capital investment needed and 50 per cent of other expenses.

44. It is especially in *Canada* and in the *USA* that substantial affirmative action programmes have been set up and tested in the courts. The Canadian National Railways, to give one example, was ordered by Court to hire women for one in four non-traditional (blue-collar) jobs in the region until they hold 13 per cent of such jobs. The CN is also required to implement a series of other measures, ranging from abandoning certain mechanical aptitude tests to modifying the way it publicises available jobs.

The affirmative action programmes in the *USA* are impressive. Governmental rules require that companies take affirmative action to ensure equality of employment opportunity and prepare and maintain an affirmative action plan. This plan requires self-analysis and determination of areas of under-utilisation of women and minorities and the establishment of goals and timetables to achieve appropriate utilisation of the excluded classes in the job categories in which they are found lacking. The rules require the 'government contractor' to make an effort in good faith. Nothing in the plan requires the employers to hire unqualified individuals. Voluntary programmes – e.g. between a company and a trade union – are equally legal and it seems that the principle of affirmative action is constitutionally secure.

VII. Enforcement

45. It is obvious that the mechanism provided for the enforcement of any law is an important as the substantive rights sought to be protected by the legislation. Otherwise a law tends to be more symbolic than substantive, especially in an area where there is a likelihood of non-voluntary compliance with legal goals.

An analysis of the different reports confirms this observation. This is e.g. the case in *Belgium*, the *FR Germany, and Italy*, where the normal, usual procedures apply. The limited implementation of the law is due in part of the weakness of the enforcement system.

A. Proof

46. A key point in the enforcement concerns the proof of discrimination. In quite a number of countries the normal rule *'actori incumbit probatio'*, namely that a plaintiff has to prove his or her point, has been reversed.

In *France* e.g. without going to the extreme of reverting the burden of proof (employer would then have to prove that he did not discriminate) the law prohibiting sex discrimination now provides that the judge, who has knowledge of the elements of proof of discrimination claimed by the plaintiff, will also have the employer furnish elements of proof justifying the absence of discrimination. The judge may order all provisions deemed necessary (experts and the like) before reaching a decision. If a doubt remains it should benefit the employee. In the *FR Germany* the burden of proof lies with the employer, who must prove that his decision was based on other reasons than sex, if the employee can satisfactorily show that there is a presumption of sex discrimination by the employer. In *Great Britain* the formal burden of proof is on the complainant; the tribunals however adopt a flexible attitude: if the primary facts indicate that there has been discrimination of some kind, the ball is in the camp of the employer.

47. In *Italy* courts appear reluctant to admit statistical evidence as *prima facie* evidence of discrimination. In *Japan* courts often switch the burden of proof to the dependant when the plaintiff has reasonably convinced the court of the probability of discrimination. Even with this shift it is very hard to prove discrimination, especially in cases of hiring or promotion, since the courts acknowledge extensive freedom to employers in such cases. In *Sweden* an applicant who did not get a job (and who claims that sex discrimination has taken place) first has to make evident that he/she has better qualifications than the person of the opposite sex who got the job. If such is found to have been the case, the assumption is made that the employer has discriminated due to sex. The burden of proof then falls on the employer to exculpate himself or herself. S/he must demonstrate that the decision was not due to the person's sex, or that it was part of a conscious affirmative action programme or that there was some other *bona fide* reason for the decision. If s/he does not manage to prove this, sex discrimination shall be found to have taken place.

48. In the *USA* the Supreme Court, in establishing the order and allocation of burdens of proof for disparate treatment under Title VII of the 1964 Act, has declared that the plaintiff in order to establish a *prima facie* case needs to show membership in a protected class, qualification for the position or promotion in question, application for consideration of some, and that he or she was passed over the some other unprotected class person accepted or that the employer continued to seek persons of the skills which the plaintiff has. Once a *prima facie* case has been established, the defendant may 'articulate a non-discriminatory reason for the action'. The burden would then shift to the plaintiff to establish that the purported reason is a pretext for discrimination or is unworthy of credence. For disparate impact – or effects discrimination –, a plaintiff needs to show that a disproportionate number of his or her class is affected; the employer must prove that his action is job-related and necessary.

B. The Role of the Representatives of the Employees

49. *France* is one of the few countries where specific measures have been taken to enhance the role of the representatives of the employees in the pursuit of equality. In *France* recently certain steps have been taken,

enhancing the role of the *workers' representatives*. First, the employer must give the works council a written report on the comparative situation regarding the general conditions of employment and training of women and men in the enterprise. This report must include 'a quantitative analysis evidencing, for all categories of employers the respective situation of men and women as far as are concerned "hiring, training, promotion, qualifications, classification, conditions of work and actual pay".' Besides, the report must enumerate all provisions taken during the past year with a view to ensuring occupational equality, objectives for the following year, and it must define quantitatively and qualitatively specific actions towards that goal and an evaluation of their cost. If actions asked for by the committee or forecast by the report of the preceding year did not take place, the report should also explain why. Also the works council has, in French law, the right to give its advice on the plan for employee training established by the employer, which must compulsorily amount to a minimum of 1.2 per cent of the wage bill. Before deliberating the council has to be given, three weeks in advance, a set of documents to which are now added the 'provisions to be taken to ensure occupational equality between women and men within the enterprise.' In *France* it is now compulsory to bargain annually over wages and every five years over scales. The parties are to examine them by sex.

Next trade unions are allowed to embark on law suits in favour of an employee without being empowered to do so by the employee, but only provided that the employee has been warned and has not opposed the suit within a period of 15 days. The employee retains the right to join the suit later.

C. *Ombudsman*

50. In *Sweden* an equality ombudsman tries to persuade employers to voluntarily comply with the equal treatment legislation. The policy of the ombudsman – in fact it is a women – is voluntarism and co-operation.

D. *Equal Opportunity Commissions*

51. In a few countries specific enforcement organs have been set up. In the *Netherlands* the officially established Committees for Equal Treatment have only very limited power and resources. Their judgment has no binding effect. Also in *Italy* a Committee for Equality has been established. It has however only rather theoretical powers. The *British* Equal Opportunities Commission and the Commission for Racial Equality are empowered to conduct investigations and to take action to remove unlawful practices. They may apply to an industrial tribunal and seek injunctions in the County Courts. The Commissions have made relatively little use of their powers.

In the *USA* the Equal Employment Opportunity Commission has substantial enforcement authority through the judicial process. The agencies have authority to investigate, hold hearings and to attempt to resolve disputes by conciliation. There are also substantial efforts to assist the parties voluntarily to resolve such issues.

E. Remedies

52. In many countries remedies remain rather weak. In the *FR Germany*, e.g., the plaintiff is only entitled to the damage s/he can prove. If the plaintiff can prove s/he was not hired for reason of discrimination s/he is entitled to compensation for the costs of the application. The European Court of Justice (1984) has declared this sanction insufficient, without however indicating what constitutes an appropriate compensation.

In *Great Britain* the remedies which the tribunal may award under the terms of the Sex Discrimination and Race Relations Acts are far less effective than those to be found in corresponding *USA* legislation. The tribunal may
  (i) make an order declaring the rights of the parity;
 (ii) award compensation which is subject to a maximum at present of £8,500, including a sum in respect of injured feelings (usually in the vicinity of £150); and
(iii) recommend that the respondent take within a specified period action appearing to the tribunal to be practicable for the purposes of obviating or reducing the adverse effect of the unlawful discrimination on the complainant.
There is no power to order reinstatement or re-engagement or that the next job be offered to the complainant, although these measures may be recommended. If a recommendation is not complied with without reasonable justification, the amount of compensation may be increased but not so as to exceed the overall limit of £7,500.

53. In *France* on the contrary the dismissed employee is to be reinstated, or at his or her choice be compensated by the usual severance pay, augmented by a sum equal to a minimum of six month's wages. In *Hungary* the employment relationship will be considered to continue in case of termination on basis of discrimination. In *Sweden* discrimination in the case of hiring may lead to damages; in the case of firing to reinstatement. Again, the *USA* provides for reinstatement – including orders for hiring – with back pay. Where reinstatement does not seem appropriate the individual is compensated in an adequate way.

EVALUATION

54. Even in countries where some positive efforts have been undertaken towards more equality, overall results are often meagre. The earning gaps

473

remain. Very little use is made of legal remedies. In *Great Britain* the number of cases are decreasing and those who use the law have little chance of success. Even in the *USA*, where substantial legal instruments are in place, attempting to ensure equality of employment, the macro-figures demonstrate clearly that much remains to be done. Inequality, more than equality, seems the rule.

The lesson is clear. Equal opportunity legislation, although more than necessary, may not be sufficient for the elimination of inequality between majority and minority groups within the labour force. Legal approaches are limited because they operate only on the demand side of the problem (i.e. employer side) and do little to change supply, (i.e. education and training of minorities). Free and equal access to education and professional training is the essential condition for the realisation of the right to work and employment. This suggests the need for supportive politics in education and training, together with continued vigilence.

SELECT BIBLIOGRAPHY

A. Cook and H. Hayashi, *Working Women in Japan, Discrimination Resistance and Reform*, New York, 1981.
Equal Opportunities for Women, Paris, OECD: 1979.
H.C. Jain and P.S. Sloane, 'Race, Sex and Minority Group Discrimination. Legislation in North America and Britain', *Industrial Relations Journal*, 1978, pp. 38–55.
J.E. Jones, 'Reverse Discrimination in Employment. Judicial Treatment of Affirmative Action Programmes in the United States', *International Labour Review*, 1980, pp. 453–472.
J.E. Jones, W.P. Murphy and R. Belon, *Discrimination in Employment*, 1987.
F. Schmidt, ed. *Discrimination in Employment*, Stockholm, 1978.
Special National Procedures Concerning Non-Discrimination in Employment – A Practical Guide, Geneva, ILO: 1975.
Women and Labour: A Comparative Study, Bulletin of Comparative Labour Relations, No. 9, 1978.
Equality and Prohibition of Discrimination, Bulletin of Comparative Labour Relations, No. 14, 1985.
International Society for Labour Law and Social Security, 10th International Congress, *Position of Women in Labor and Social Security*, Vol. III, 1984.

Chapter 22. Security of Employment

B. Hepple

I. What is Meant by 'Security of Employment'?

A. The 'Right to Work'

1. The Nature of the 'Right'

1. Job security is everywhere in the news. In the industrialised market economies and in the developing countries there are sharp political debates about macro-economic and social policies for ensuring full employment. It is common to speak of an abstract 'background' right of the individual requiring the state to maintain a full employment policy, to protect the opportunity of every worker to earn his living in an occupation freely entered upon, to establish and maintain free employment services for all workers and to provide for and maintain vocational training. This is the sense in which the European Social Charter, Article 1, describes the 'right to work' as do the Constitutions of some industrialised market economies such as Article 4 of the Italian Constitution and Article 27, section 1 of the Constitution of Japan.

2. The Constitutions and Labour Codes of the European socialist countries also proclaim such a 'right to work' in the sense of the guarantee of employment. This is not the right to any particular job but – in words of Article 40 of the USSR Constitution of 7 October 1977 – is in accordance with the 'abilities, training and education' of the individual and 'with due account of the needs of society'. Moreover, it is a 'right' only in the sense of a political goal because it is said 'to be ensured by the socialist economic system, steady growth of the productive forces, free vocational and professional training, improvement of skills, training in new trades or professions and development of the systems of vocational guidance and job placement'.

3. What distinguishes the 'right to work' in the socialist countries from the 'right to work' in the European Social Charter and similar Western declarations, apart from the fundamentally different political and economic methods used to achieve full employment, is that in those countries there corresponds to the abstract background 'right to work' a concrete legal duty to work and strictly to observe labour discipline. 'Evasion of socially useful work', declares Article 60 of the USSR Constitution, 'is incompatible with the principles of socialist society'. Any such legal duty to work does not – indeed cannot – form part of the legal system of a 'capitalist' market economy except in times of war or emergency when the state assumes the role of directing labour. While in the socialist countries the duty to work is derived from the abstract 'right to work' and forms a fundamental part of labour law, in the Western market economies the duty to work forms a part only of social security law since it is usually a condition for the receipt of various social benefits that a person is not voluntarily unemployed, has not been dismissed due to misconduct and is available for employment. In other words, the duty to work corresponds only to a right to social security, and not to a right to work.

2. Strategies

4. The measures adopted by governments to achieve the 'right to work' in this broad sense fall within the realm of economic and social policy and not of individual legal rights and obligations. For example there are differences between the 'monetarists' and the neo-Keynsians in Great Britain and the USA whether to pursue a strategy of fiscal and other measures to bring down inflation and encourage higher profits and investment, or a strategy of subsidising job creation. The first strategy is attacked because of its damaging short – and medium – term social effects, involving a selective approach to job preservation and an increasing burden of welfare expenditure to support rising numbers of unemployed. The second strategy is frequently criticised for harmful effects on profitability, productivity and inflation. In practice many governments have tried to steer a middle course between these strategies. This chapter is not concerned with the macro-economic strategies themselves but instead with the more limited, yet vitally important question of the various ways in which job security is pursued by law and the practice of industrial relations. Even in the most non-interventionist countries, such as the USA, there is a developing body of law and practice of job security.

5. The measures adopted are deeply rooted in the political, social and economic traditions of each country. This, together with the enormous diversity of job security measures, makes it impossible to present any kind of comprehensive summary. Even where common minimum standards have been adopted – for example, the Member States of the EEC – it is striking how divergent are the methods used to implement these common obligations. The mixture between law and collective bargaining is different; the methods of legal enforcement are extremely varied; and the standards are reflected in many baffling forms. Moreover, in each country one hears frequent complaints that the measures being adopted are *ad hoc* responses to particular events, that they are contradictory and unco-ordinated. However, three main trends characterised developments in the 1970s:
(1) a substantial growth of state intervention in labour markets;

(2) growing emphasis on participation by employers and trade unions in the formation of policy and on diversity of forms of worker participation in enterprises and plants; and

(3) an increasing reliance on law to create job rights outside the sole control of the employer by means of independent scrutiny of the substantive grounds and procedural form of dismissals from employment.

In the 1980s, as a response to the economic crisis, the general trend has been towards deregulation, or what might be called market regulation rather than state regulation, in the industrialised market economies. Indications of this trend are the abolition of the requirement of prior authorisation of redundancies by public authorities (France), the introduction of greater flexibility in the use of fixed-term contracts (e.g. Belgium, FR Germany, Sweden, Spain, Italy) and the reduction of employers' obligations in respect of notice periods (e.g. Belgium) and unfair dismissal protection (e.g. Great Britain, FR Germany). In some, but certainly not all, of these countries (e.g. Great Britain, Belgium) this has been accompanied by a reduction in legal support for workers' participation in the control of jobs.

B. Termination of Employment at the Initiative of the Employer

1. The Idea of 'Ownership of Jobs'

6. While the 'right to work' is a broad abstract 'right' which includes the creation and continuity of jobs as well as their termination, a narrower sense in which the concept of 'security of employment' is frequently used is to describe the control of termination of employment at the initiative of the employer. Laws and practices of this kind are sometimes characterised as 'job property' laws.

7. Frederic Meyers, in his classic study covering Mexico, France, Britain and the USA, *The Ownership of Jobs*,[1] utilised the analogy of 'property' in the sense of a right to retain undisturbed possession of one's job:

> 'If employment is property, or analogous thereto, undisturbed possession means the right to continue in employment at the will of the employee. Protection against involuntary dismissal is a crucial characteristic to be sought if a system may be said to have property-like rights in employment.'[2]

His conclusion, on the basis of evidence gathered in these 4 countries, was that:

> 'Workers do in fact tend to regard themselves as having some kind

1. Frederic Meyers, *The Ownership of Jobs*, Los Angeles, 1964.
2. *Op. cit.*, p. 1.

of right of possession in a job, and to devise institutions which invest control over incumbency from the hands of the employer and which express objectively a vesting of property-like rights in the workers. The devices by which this trend is expressed and the rate of change vary, of course, from country to country. In the United States, it is expressed primarily through the device of the collective agreement, and it may be farthest advanced in those jobs in the United States in which collective bargaining determines the basic character of the relationship of workers and employers to jobs. On the other hand it is undoubtedly least far advanced in the unorganised segments of American industry, in which little has changed, so far as job control is concerned, since 1870.'[3]

2. Law, Collective Agreements and Strikes as Devices

8. Meyers noted that in France and Mexico the primary device was the law. Indeed the well-known labour article (Article 123 section XXIII) of the Mexican Constitution of 1917 is the first modern legal guarantee of protection of the employee against dismissal by the employer 'without just cause'. In Britain, on the other hand, at the time of Meyers' study (1964) the formal institutions of law and collective agreements were not the primary devices through which job security was enhanced, although some collective agreements existed; instead, he found that unofficial (wildcat) strikes by groups of workers were a common method of securing reinstatement for dismissed workers. Since Meyers' study there have been dramatic changes in Britain with the result that law is now a primary device, although collective agreements and industrial action supplement this. In the USA there is pressure for a legislative approach to job security because of concern for the unorganised sector and the fact that the organised sector, enjoying job security through collective agreements, is declining as a proportion of the total labour force.

9. These trends of the past decade illustrate the point that the devices for improving job security tend to change depending upon factors such as unemployment and alterations in the relative strength of management and of organised labour. It is always necessary to examine the precise social and economic context into which job security laws have been injected in order to understand their social function.

3. Disciplinary Dismissals and Workforce Reductions Distinguished

10. The international instruments and national legislation and practices on

3. *Op. cit.*, p. 112.

dismissals generally draw a distinction between
(1) the power of the employer to terminate the employment relationship when the job itself will continue to exist; and
(2) the power of the employer to make workforce reductions for economic, technical or organisational reasons.

The first is mainly concerned with what are termed disciplinary dismissals, i.e. on grounds of the conduct or capacity of the worker. The second is often subject to special rules, because workforce reductions may affect sizeable numbers of workers and create serious social and economic problems for the community.

11. A variety of concepts are used to describe the situations in which these special rules apply. For example EEC Directive 77/187 on the acquired rights of employees in the event of transfers of undertakings permits dismissals for an 'economic, technical or organisational reason entailing changes in the workforce'.[4] Such reasons may result from market conditions such as changes in demand, or from foreign competition, or technical innovations or changes in work processes. These causes may interact with each other, for example a decline in demand may lead to reorganisation or technical changes in order to increase efficiency. In Britain the concept of 'redundancy' has acquired the technical legal meaning of a dismissal by reason of either the employer ceasing to carry on business at the place where the employee worked, or a reduction in the requirements of the employer for employees to do work of a kind which the employee was engaged to do.[5] This may be compared with the wide interpretation which was given to 'economic' dismissals in the French Law of 3 January 1975, to include changes in the organisational structure of the enterprise even if not directly caused by a change in business activity. Since 1987, however, all distinctions in France between 'economic' and 'structural' reasons for dismissal have been dropped. In the USA and Canada and concept of 'layoff' is used in collective agreements to denote a suspension of the employment relationship with the maintenance of certain rights regarding seniority and the right to recall when work again becomes available, but no right to wages. After a certain time, sometimes specified in the collective agreement, a worker 'laid off' will no longer be entitled to these rights and the employment relationship will be considered as ended. In some Scandinavian countries and India, 'layoff' is a concept restricted to temporary workforce reductions, while dismissal is the usual method of making a permanent reduction, with different rules applying to each of these techniques.

12. The special rules relating to workforce reductions are of various kinds, but they generally aim at two objectives:
(1) avoiding or minimising compulsory workforce reductions as far as practicable; and

4. Article 4, OJ No. L 61/26, 5 March 1977.
5. Employment Protection (Consolidition) Act 1978, s. 81(2) (Great Britain).

(2) taking measures to mitigate the consequences for the workers concerned.

These objectives are principally sought through various procedural obligations (see Parts III and IV below) involving public authorities and workers'
representatives.

II. The Conflicting Demands of Economic Adjustment and Job Security

A. Labour Markets

13. In recent years industrialised market economies and many developing
countries have shared the problems of high and generally rising unemployment and a decline in the number of jobs available coupled with an increase
in the population of working age, particularly women. The average length of
time a person can expect to be unemployed has increased.

14. The effects of unemployment are not shared equally among the working
population. It is a mistake to think of only two situations: employment and
unemployment. There is a hierarchy of ranks in the labour market from
whole-time secure employment through less secure forms of whole-time
employment, part-time employment, and casual and temporary work to
continuous unemployment. In several countries there has been a tendency
for inequality to grow between these ranks. The nature of the demand for
labour and the inequalities of collective bargaining power have led to the
often-observed phenomenon of segmented and dual labour markets with a
'primary' sector in which unions are strong and pay and job security are
relatively high, and a 'secondary' sector in which unions are weak and pay
and job security are relatively low. Individuals and social groups, such as
ethnic minorities, migrant workers, women, and others who lack collective
bargaining power have less access to the opportunities and benefits of
employment than those in strong unions in key sectors of the economy. The
'secondary' labour market of casual, temporary and part-time workers
disguises the true level of unemployment in many countries, as do immigra-
tion controls in countries which rely on migrant labour.

15. When evaluating the principal models of state intervention (Part III),
collective bargaining (Part IV) and laws (Part V) one may ask whether the
measures adopted (including the anti-discrimination laws discussed in chapter 21 help to eliminate inequality in the labour market and the poverty of
those in the lower ranks, or do they instead legitimate an elite section of the
working population in the primary segment of the labour market? This
question was posed by Hugo Sinzheimer, a founder of the labour law of the
German Weimar Republic, as he witnessed the crisis and collapse of that
system of workers' rights in 1933:

'What meaning does Labour Law have, if it is at most just a law for an elite of workers, who have the good fortune to remain in work, if alongside the existence of Labour Law an economic graveyard of "structural unemployment" opens up?'[6]

16. One might compare, in this respect, three different models: a labour market of an industrialised market economy which segregates life-time and temporary employees (Japan); a developing country with a small protected sector and a large unprotected one (India); and a planned economy which aims at full employment but underutilises labour (China).

17. The segmented nature of labour markets is increasingly formalised as a result of the attempts to resolve the competing claims of economic adjustment and of job security. In a nutshell, the conflict is between management whose interests lie in preserving the flexibility to hire and fire – as epitomised in the non-unionised sector in the USA where management is free to terminate employment at will – and the trade unions whose interests lie in preserving the jobs of the existing permanent workforce, sometimes at the expense of those in the secondary labour market such as young people, women and foreign workers.

18. The pressure for economic adjustment is experienced by management in the face both of economic recession and of technological change including such major innovations as microprocessors. In Europe acute problems are being felt in low productivity, low wage economies such as the UK, Italy and Spain. The persistent claims by management in these countries that there is 'overmanning' has resulted in a multiplicity of schemes at company and plant level to facilitate redundancies – for example by severance payments, transfer payments, and promises of priority of re-engagement in the event of vacancies.

B. The Evolution of Common Rules

1. Measures to Minimise Workforce Reductions

19. In practice unions generally take a step by step defensive approach to infringements of job security. There is a preference for collective bargaining, but where unions find themselves lacking industrial power they tend to rely on their political power to obtain legal measures and other state intervention to preserve jobs. There are striking similarities between the common rules which have emerged in different countries aimed at minimising workforce reductions and mitigating the consequences for the established labour force.

6. Hugo Sinzheimer, 'Die Krisis des Arbeitsrechts' (1933) *Arbeitsrecht und Rechtssoziologie,* Band I, Frankfurt, 1976, p. 145 (my translation).

The various procedural obligations relating to workforce reductions will be reviewed in Part IV. Legislation or generally applicable collective agreements between central organisations of employers and workers regarding consultation in a number of countries (e.g. Austria, Belgium, France, Ireland, Italy, Portugal and the UK) or 'social plans' agreed between employers and works councils (e.g. FR Germany, France) provides that one of the objectives of consultation is to minimise workforce reductions or mitigate the consequences for the workers concerned. The following are some of the common rules which have emerged.

2. Reduction of Staff without Compulsory Redundancy

20. The measure most frequently resorted to is the reduction of staff size by voluntary means, or 'natural wastage' as it is sometimes called. This includes a freeze or restrictions on engagement of new staff to fill vacancies, spreading the reduction over a period of time so as to allow natural departures to reduce staff to the desired levels and internal transfers with training for the transferred workers. In some countries the policy of internal transfer is a matter of legislation (e.g. Yugoslavia, GDR) and in others a matter of collective bargaining. In several countries (e.g. Norway, Sweden) a worker may be dismissed for a reason related to the operational requirements of the enterprise only if the employer is unable to transfer him to other suitable employment. Another measure used is to stimulate voluntary departures by offering financial incentives such as early retirement on full or partial pensions or generous severance allowances, with state assistance (e.g. FR Germany, Spain).

3. Reduction of Working Time

21. In situations of a temporary fall in demand a frequently used measure is spreading the available work over the existing workforce by reducing the number of hours worked. This may be achieved, for example, by reducing overtime, by shortening the working week or by short-term lay-offs. In some countries the employer is obliged to pay part of the wages for the normal hours not worked.

The precise circumstances in which such payments have to be made vary considerably. For example, in FR Germany, compensation is payable only where the reduction in work arises from economic causes during a continuous period of at least 4 weeks and where a minimum of one-third of employees are idle for more than 10 per cent of normal weekly working time. In the Netherlands, on the other hand, compensation is payable simply because work cannot be carried out due to economic difficulties. Benefit levels are linked to a variety of factors such as previous earnings and family status, and the period for which payment must be made is often limited (e.g. 5 days in any three-month period in Great Britain) but sometimes is almost unlimited (e.g. Italy). In some countries, compensation for short-time working is simply an extension of state unemployment benefits (e.g. Belgium, Ireland, Norway, Spain); in others (e.g. France) special compensation schemes exist.

22. In a number of countries there are central funds which are used to subsidise payment of part of the wages for normal hours not worked under such schemes. This is the case for example in Austria, Canada, France, FR Germany, Italy, Japan and the UK. Problems can arise when such funds come under excessive demands. This occurred in Italy with the Supplementary Guarantee Fund (CIG) which is largely state-financed. In order to reduce recourse to this Fund and to safeguard jobs in 'crisis' situations, new forms of negotiated company or plant collective agreements – known as 'solidarity contracts' – were concluded. These provide for the reduction of working-time and in pay. This was deliberately borrowed from the French 'solidarity contracts'. However, unlike the French contracts which are made between government officials and companies, the Italian 'solidarity contracts' are negotiated between companies and local unions as a means of averting dismissals and reducing the drain on public funds. Where such contracts are concluded supplementary wage payments amounting to 50 per cent of pay lost due to a reduction in working hours for up to 2 years may be made available from CIG. In non-crisis situations, where 'solidarity contracts' are used to reduce working hours with reduction in pay in order to create *new* jobs for named workers, employers may claim special payments from an unemployment fund for 3 years. Subsidies of this kind may be compared with fiscal means, many of which have no maximum time limit, such as tax relief or rebates of social security contributions which help employers continue permanent employment.

4. Criteria for Selection of Workers for Dismissal

23. When compulsory redundancies cannot be avoided it is in the interests of management and workers to have clear rules as to the selection of workers to be dismissed. In some countries this is done by legislation and in others it is done by collective agreements, or in works rules. In the Netherlands criteria are established by the administrative authorities responsible for authorising dismissals. Legislation against unjustified dismissal sometimes provides that on a complaint by an individual worker the court or tribunal must determine whether the selection was in breach of criteria specified in a collective agreement or customary arrangement in which case it is automatically unlawful.

24. Among the criteria most frequently specified are
(a) length of service or seniority, which may be supplemented by other

criteria such as priority for retention of those with the greatest number of family dependants (Algeria), expectant mothers and trade unions officials (Panama) or the oldest workers (Sweden and the Netherlands);

(b) occupational qualifications or ability, supplemented in the case of equal ability by length of service (USA) or family responsibilities or being a disabled veteran (USSR);

(c) variety of other criteria such as age, being in a protected category such as disabled workers or workers' representatives.

Sometimes the rules negotiated between employers and trade unions may indirectly discriminate against women workers or ethnic minorities and for this reason may be unlawful. For example, in the UK a collective agreement providing for the selection first of part-time employees has been held by an industrial tribunal to be in contravention of the Sex Discrimination Act because its impact is greater on women than on men.

5. Priority of Re-Employment

25. Legislation and collective agreements frequently stipulate that workers dismissed for economic reasons should be given priority when the employer again needs to engage workers or that part-time workers should have priority when full-time vacancies occur. Sometimes priority of recall is limited to workers in the category in which new vacancies have occurred, and often the priority is limited in time (between 3 months and 2 years). Collective agreements are more likely than legislation to stipulate that workers who are recalled retain or accumulate seniority rights.

6. Finding Alternative Employment and Training

26. Legislation and collective agreements frequently impose obligations on the employer to assist the worker in finding new employment, including time off for this purpose. One method is by requiring the employer to give prior notification of dismissals to the public authorities (see Part III) to enable them to help. Another, as in France, is for employers to enter into training contracts under which workers are kept on (for a maximum of 5 months) until regraded, while drawing an allowance equal to 70% of their former gross pay from the unemployment insurance fund. A further device is for courts and tribunals when considering complaints by individual workers to treat a dismissal as unjustified if the employer has failed to take reasonable steps to find alternative employment and retraining for the employee in the enterprise.

7. Severance Allowances and Income Maintenance

27. Much attention has been devoted to levels of financial compensation to workers both in the context of collective bargaining and of legislation. There are two main kinds of scheme: (a) Severance allowance; and (b) Income maintenance.

a. Severance allowances

These may also be called redundancy payments, indemnities, length-of service allowances, gratuities, etc. These generally increase with length of service and are payable as a lump sum. In some countries they are payable only for specified reasons, such as redundancy in the UK and Ireland, or collective dismissal due to closure or redundancy in Portugal, or the operating requirements of the enterprise in Spain. However, in most countries where there is provision for a severance allowance it is payable whatever the reason for dismissal, other than serious misconduct. In some it is payable even in the case of resignation by the worker for whatever reason or in case of termination by *force majeure*. In many cases, a severance allowance is not payable on reaching normal retiring age, but it may be replaced, as in France, by an end-of-career indemnity. The conditions of entitlement to a severance allowance differ considerably from country to country.

28. There has been much discussion about the nature of severance allowances. Are they an element of wages, payment of which has been postponed? Or are they the worker's 'share' in the undertaking, increasing with his length of service? Or a valuation of his 'job property' rights? Or simply a means of income protection during a period of unemployment, helping him to adjust and move to new employment? The answer to these questions depends on the terms of the specific legislation and collective agreements in each country, and the result may have practical consequences. For example if the allowance is regarded as income protection during unemployment the worker may lose his entitlement for a time to state unemployment benefits. If it is regarded as a capital payment it may not be subject to taxation. If it is not a 'wage' it may not have preferential status on the bankruptcy of the employer. These allowances should be distinguished from wages in lieu of notice (below paragraph 50) and compensation for unjustified dismissal (below paragraph 65).

b. Income maintenance

29. In some of the industrialised countries dismissed workers are provided by employers with periodical payments which are intended to be supplementary to state unemployment benefits or to support the worker during a period of retraining. In Belgium, for example, an interoccupational collective agreement provides for an allowance additional to unemployment insurance following a collective dismissal equal to half the difference between the unemployment insurance benefits and the previous monthly wage (subject to a maximum and certain deductions). In France, a worker with at least 2 years' service dismissed for reasons of an economic nature is entitled,

subject to certain conditions, to a percentage of his former gross salary for up to one year of unemployment. In FR Germany, the worker may claim compensation from the employer for up to one year for any economic disadvantages due to collective redundancies. This is in addition to any special payments due under a 'social plan' negotiated between the employer and works council, or failing agreement, worked out by a joint conciliation committee. (Forthcoming legislation in FR Germany will exclude new firms from 'social plan' obligations during their first four years of business.)

C. Avoidance and Evasion

1. 'Black' Markets

30. Strict legal regulation has encouraged the growth in some countries of clandestine or 'black' labour markets, including illegal use of child labour, as in Italy. In France, the inflexibility and complexity of statutory regulation led to agreements, whose legal validity was uncertain, between employers and unions for workers to quit 'voluntarily', in return for a lump sum bonus in order to avoid the legal provisions against dismissal. Jacques Rojot writes[7] that 'one might suspect that there might be something wrong with the law of dismissal when both employees and employers agree to evade it as is the case for (these) "negotiated dismissals".' Eventually, there was a major reform of French redundancy procedures in 1986.

2. Temporary Work through an Intermediary

31. Another method of avoiding the law and collective agreements is by the use of temporary or casual workers. A distinction must be drawn between temporary work in the broad sense of anyone who is engaged to work for a limited period of time or to perform a specific task of short duration, and temporary work in the narrow sense of a triangular relationship in which a temporary work organisation supplies a worker to a user for a limited period of time.

32. The latter kind of temporary work, of which the Belgian concept of *travail intérimaire* is the prototype, was relatively rare until the late 1950s but is now an established feature of the labour market in many countries.

In relatively few countries (e.g. Italy, Greece, Spain, Sweden) the law forbids fee-charging employment agencies. The countries which authorise the existence of temporary employment businesses fall into two categories. In the first category are those countries (e.g. USA, Canada, Finland and some Latin American states) where law and practice allow these businesses the same freedom as other services. In the second category are those

7. Jacques Rojot, 'France', *Bulletin of Comparative Labour Relations*, No. 11, 1980, p. 100.

countries where specific legislation has been passed to regulate these businesses and to protect temporary workers (e.g. Belgium, Denmark, France, FR Germany, Ireland, the Netherlands, Norway and the UK). The UK and Ireland are in a rather unique position in this group, however, because in these countries employment businesses are often also placement agencies. This makes it difficult to measure, identify and compare the activities of employment businesses in the UK and Ireland with those in the rest of Western Europe, and was one of the reasons why the UK objected to a draft EEC directive on temporary work in 1982. In the second category of countries, with specific legislation, three main purposes can be gathered for the legislation. The first is to ensure that only reputable and solvent businesses are engaged in supplying temporary workers. In most countries, this involves applying for a licence, usually to a government ministry but in Belgium to a tripartite commission which includes representatives of existing employment businesses, before the business begins to operate. The EEC draft directive would require temporary employment businesses, before authorisation, to show evidence of adequate financial resources and of the good character of their managers, and would make the user undertaking jointly liable for wages etc. in the event of default by the temporary employment business. The second purpose of legislation is to give temporary workers, broadly speaking, the same protection as permanent workers. So most countries require certain clauses to be included in the contract between the temporary employment business and the worker, such as equality of treatment with workers in the user undertaking. The third purpose of legislation is to protect the permanent workforce in the user undertaking. In the words of the draft EEC directive: 'permanent employment must remain the rule' and 'recourse to temporary labour should therefore be confined to situations where it is economically justified and restricted in terms of duration of contract'. In some countries, temporary employment businesses are not allowed to operate at all in certain industries. In others the precise circumstances in which temporary workers can be used are specified (e.g. under the law of 1982 in France, to cover for the temporary absence of a permanent employee; to fill in between the time one permanent employee leaves and is replaced by another; to ensure that emergency work is carried out immediately to avoid any safety hazards, and to cope with exceptional and temporary increases in work, with labour inspectorate approval). The recent trend (e.g. in Belgium and France) has been to allow employers greater flexibility in the use of temporary replacement contracts.

3. Fixed Term Contracts

33. Temporary work in the broad sense (*travail temporaire*) of work for a short duration has also come under legal regulation in many countries. For example in Italy Act No. 230 of 1962 strictly controls contracts for fixed periods of time, allowing them to be used only in very limited situations such as for specified seasonal activities, and for temporary replacement of an employee whose job security is guaranteed and who is absent from work. Amendments in 1977 and 1978 lifted the restrictions to some extent in the fields of tourism, commerce and show business to respond to the need for flexibility, and the validity of an education contract for a limited period was also recognised. Further amendments in 1984 allowed short-term training contracts for workers aged 15–29 on a named recruitment basis for up to 2 years in certain circumstances. The trend in Western Europe has been towards greater flexibility in the use of fixed-term contracts. For example, the Employment Promotion Act 1985 in FR Germany allows fixed-term contracts for up to 18 months, without special justification (24 months in new firms with no more than 20 employees), provided they are new appointments or with those who were previously on training contracts. In Spain, amendments in 1984 to the Workers' Statute allow new enterprises to resort to fixed-term contracts of up to 3 years' duration, but with a severance payment similar to that in France. In Belgium, legislation in 1984 has made it easier for employers to recruit on a fixed-term basis to replace permanent employees whose contracts have been suspended in certain circumstances for up to 2 years; the new provisions also allow greater flexibility in the recruitment of persons under 30 for training.

4. Part-time Contracts

34. Voluntary part-time work has become increasingly popular in recent decades. In the Member States of the EEC part-time work represents about 9 per cent of the Community labour force, although the proportion varies from 2–3 per cent in some countries to 15–20 per cent in others. In most Member States, the overwhelming majority of these part-time workers are women. Part-time work has attractions for employers, offering greater flexibility, and also meets the needs of married women and some persons near to retiring age who do not want full-time work. Legal definitions of 'part-time' vary, usually being between two-thirds and four-fifths of normal working hours. One of the problems arising from the use of part-time work is the tendency for this to be associated with insecure forms of employment such as temporary contracts, or the denial of employment protection rights. State-subsidised job creation measures usually result in part-time jobs of limited duration. A draft EEC directive in 1981 aimed to improve the status of part-time workers by requiring Member States to give them equality of treatment with full-time workers. This principle of non-discrimination already exists in some countries (e.g. France, FR Germany, Spain), but at present the proposed directive is being blocked by some Member States who believe that it will have the effect of reducing employment opportunities, by making part-time work unattractive to employers.

5. Small Employers

35. It is difficult to enforce laws and agreements where there are large numbers of small units of production. Governments are also under pressure to encourage small businesses. Research has indicated that most new job opportunities are generated by small businesses. One finds institutionalised recognition of this in the practice of exempting small enterprises from employment protective laws. 'Small' is a relative concept, for example covering 35 or less persons in Italy, 20 or less in the UK and 5 or less in FR Germany.

III. The Role of Public Authorities

A. *Employment and Training Services*

36. The most common form of state intervention in the labour market, acceptable even to dogmatic supporters of the free market, is to attempt to achieve a better match between supply and demand, in particular for skilled workers and to improve occupational and geographical job mobility. The measures adopted include public employment services, occupational retraining schemes, grants to workers to encourage them to move and regional development subsidies to encourage investment and employment. These cannot be discussed within the confines of this chapter.

B. *Job Creation Measures*

37. Similarly it is not possible here to analyse the various measures which have been taken in response to the economic crisis, such as subsidies to employers to continue the employment of workers who otherwise would be made redundant, schemes to support the employment of young workers, and state-supported early retirement to provide vacancies. One particular tension which must be noted in the context of job security, is that many of these schemes encourage short-term employment. For example, in Belgium and the UK 'work experience' type programmes have been designed to give workers a short spell at work. The trade unions in both countries have criticised this type of programme as providing employers with temporary 'cheap' labour instead of stimulating the creation of permanent jobs. The unions would prefer genuine vocational training schemes financed by government.

C. Information Requirements

38. In recent years there has been a tendency for public authorities to become increasingly involved in workforce reductions. The commonest form is legislation requiring the employer to inform the public authority of a proposed reduction in workforce. The information may be used for statistical purposes, and also to give the authorities the opportunity to help find jobs or provide training for the dismissed workers and sometimes to provide conciliation to resolve disputes about planned reductions. Control of dismissals might be ineffective if the employment services could not, at the same time, exert influence over engagements and so in some countries (e.g. Sweden, the Netherlands) there is a duty to notify vacancies to the authorities. This also enables the public authorities to encourage special treatment for disadvantaged groups such as older workers and disabled persons.

39. Recent trends have been to reduce the level of formal regulation. In France, for example, the role of the labour inspectorate in checking the grounds for redundancy was substantially reduced with effect from January 1987. In Italy, the legal grounds for intervention in the past have been described as being weak and hardly significant, but employers and unions have persistently had recourse to almost entirely informal public conciliation and mediation, particularly by regional governments. The strength of the informal approach is that it relies on social acceptability for its effectiveness. Its weakness is that it tends to result in a series of *ad hoc* and *ex post facto* interventions lacking co-ordination and leaving the weakest unprotected. In Italy, there have been recent moves, for example in a decree of December 1979, to counteract these shortcomings.

D. Consent Requirements

40. It is now highly unusual to find a legal duty on employers to seek *prior approval* by the authorities of engagements and dismissals. In France the requirement for prior authorisation by the labour inspectorate in respect of redundancies was abolished by a law of 3 July 1986, and more flexible procedures, increasing managerial power, were agreed by unions and employers in October 1986.

41. The Netherlands provides the classic example of a 'licensing' approach to dismissals. The Extraordinary Decree on Labour Relations of 1945 provides that neither employer nor employee can terminate employment without the consent of the Director of the District Labour Office, with certain exceptions such as termination by mutual consent, justified summary dismissal, or dismissal during a trial period. The Director must be satisfied that the dismissal is reasonable, in accordance with official guidelines. A dismissal without the Director's consent is void, which means that the employer must go on paying wages as long as the employee is willing to work. In practice, the statistics indicate that the Director of the District Labour Office refuses permission in only about 5 per cent of requests.[8] Professor H.L. Bakels concludes that the Director of the District Labour Office fulfils much the same function by 'pseudo judicial decision' as does the independent Advisory, Conciliation and Arbitration Service in Great Britain by conciliation in individual cases of dismissal.[9] It must be borne in mind that the grounds on which a dismissal may be examined *ex post facto* by the courts in the Netherlands are narrower than in Great Britain.

42. In some countries, such as Belgium, FR Germany and Luxembourg, the power of the public authorities is limited to that of postponing the date of dismissal, or of authorising earlier dismissal. In most countries, however, there are still no powers of direction. A Deregulation Commission (1984) in the Netherlands, thought that such direction hindered economic growth, partly because of the delays it causes in rationalising the labour force. They also considered that this kind of control violates the constitutional principle that differences over civil rights should be decided by the judiciary. Against this, it can be argued that ex *post facto* penalisation of the employer for unjustified dismissal through judicial decisions in individual cases is unable to take proper account of factors such as the temporary or permanent nature of the difficulties of the enterprise and cannot achieve a co-ordinated manpower policy combining job creation and job preservation measures for firms in economic difficulties. A 'licensing' type system can (but does not necessarily) assist planned utilisation of manpower. *Ex post facto* control by judicial bodies, on the other hand, is usually more appropriate in the case of disciplinary dismissals.

IV. THE ROLE OF WORKERS' REPRESENTATIVES

A. Direct Action

43. At plant and company level one can find examples almost everywhere of directed industrial action by workers to prevent closures and redundancies. The forms of action are diverse including occupations, 'work-ins' (in which production is continued) and strikes. In most countries these forms of self-help, particularly where they infringe employers' property rights, are considered unlawful. The results of direct action have been uneven. In Italy and the UK, for example, there have been a few cases where solidarity among workers has been generated and public sympathy has been won so that closures have been averted. But by and large these actions have been

---

8. T. Havinga, *Sociaal Maandblad Arbeid*, No. 40, Jan. 1985, p. 27.
9. H.L. Bakels, 'Het Engels en Nederlands Arbeids- en Ontslagrecht', *Sociaal Maandblad Arbeid*, No. 36, July/Aug. 1981, p. 538.

unsuccessful as a means of preserving jobs. This reflects the fact that the key decisions about closures, transfer of undertakings and investment are taken at enterprise or company level and not at plant or shop floor level. The response to the inadequacy of bargaining at enterprise level has commonly been to increase the rights of worker representatives to receive information and be consulted on job security issues.

B. Procedures Involving Workers' Representatives

44. The rights of workers' representatives to delay and their factual power to prevent individual dismissals, workforce reductions and other major changes in the undertaking affecting job security is closely related to the more general question of workers' participation. Only a brief description of the main models relevant to job security can be given here. The forms of participation include:
(1) information;
(2) consultation and negotiation; and
(3) consent or co-determination.
The information and consultation model is laid down as a minimum standard in I.L.O. Convention 158 of 1982, Article 13, and I.L.O. Recommendation 166 of 1982, Article 20.

The consent or co-determination model is found in relatively few countries. In the USSR and some other European socialist countries (Czechoslovakia, GDR, Romania) the prior consent of the trade union committee is required to individual dismissals and also workforce reductions. In Yugoslavia an elected disciplinary commission of the work unit must consent to disciplinary dismissals. In FR Germany (in provisions which can be traced back to the Weimar Republic), the works council has the right to refuse consent to recruitment and transfer of employees in certain circumstances (this consent may be substituted by the decision of the labour court) and also the right to be heard before every dismissal.

In terms of subject matter the procedures may cover.
(1) all kinds of individual dismissals (e.g. Austria, FR Germany, Norway, Poland and Sweden);
(2) disciplinary dismissals (e.g. Portugal);
(3) workforce reductions (e.g. in legislation in Belgium, FR Germany, France, the Netherlands, Norway, Spain, Sweden, UK and collective agreements in Italy, and the USA and industrial awards in Australia and New Zealand); and
(4) major changes in the undertaking, such as closure, mergers, rationalisation (e.g. in legislation in FR Germany and Sweden, in collective agreements in Denmark and Norway).
The representatives may be the works council (e.g. FR Germany, Belgium) or enterprise committee (e.g. France), the competent trade union committee (e.g. USSR) or the recognised independent trade union (e.g. UK). The

obligations are frequently limited to medium-sized and large undertakings (e.g. in the case of workforce reductions 21 or more workers in FR Germany and Ireland).

V. Individual Legal Rights and Remedies

A. *The Liberal Contractual Approach*

45. In the countries with a civil (Roman) law tradition as well as those of the English common law tradition, legal thinking in the nineteenth century and the first half of the twentieth century was dominated by the liberal concept of freedom of contract. The French Revolution removed the relics of mediaeval work obligations (which had included an element of job security) and in their place the Napoleonic Codes established general principles applying to all contracts. In theory employer and employee became free and equal contracting parties with reciprocal rights and obligations. Similarly in Great Britain, after the abolition by Act of Parliament in 1875 of criminal sanctions for breach of contract by a deserting servant, and in the USA, after the post Civil War constitutional amendments had rendered invalid state laws enforcing labour other than by way of civil suit for damages, the contractual principles of equality and reciprocity were established in relation to contracts of employment.

46. Article 1780 of the French Civil Code, designed to prevent slavery or peonage, provided that a person could not hire his services except for a specific period or to a specific employer. There is no similar prohibition on lifelong employment in the English common law, but involuntary servitude offends against judge-made public policy. Article 1780 of the French Civil Code (later Article 23.1 of the *Code du Travail*) enshrined the principle that 'the hiring of services for an indefinite term can always be brought to an end at the will of one of the contracting parties'. Article 1142 provided that an obligation to act or refrain from acting could be resolved only by damages. This was the French counterpart of the English rule that the courts cannot specifically enforce contracts of employment. Reinstatement as a remedy for breach of contract by the employer has been unavailable in French and English courts since the 'obligation to do' can be remedied only in the same way as the employee's obligation, by payment of money.

B. *Termination by Notice*

1. The Concept of Notice

47. Contracts of employment for a definite duration end when the period expires. Contracts of indefinite duration can generally be terminated only with advance notice. This is a principle established in the civil and commercial codes of most countries applicable to various types of contract such as leases and also employment contracts. In the English common law, a presumption of yearly hiring was applied (in theory until as late as 1969) to most classes of servants but this could easily be rebutted by proof of a custom of the trade allowing a shorter period in specific cases. The rule developed that all hirings could be terminated upon reasonable notice and in the case of manual workers this could be as short as two hours to terminate at the end of a workday in the construction industry. It is a striking fact, however, that in the United States, where the English rules were originally adopted, a rule developed at the end of the nineteenth century and has been maintained in the twentieth century (except where ousted by collective agreements), that the employer may terminate at will. The doctrine has undoubtedly made dismissal cheaper for the employer in the non-unionised sector in the USA than it is in Western Europe.

48. The concept of 'notice' has two meanings:
(1) it may indicate the formal unilateral notification that the contract is to end (in French: *le congé*); or
(2) it may also signify the period of time between the notification and the time when the notice expires (*délai-congé* in France, *delais de prevais* in Belgium).
For a long time the length of notice was implied by custom: in France as a survival of the practices of the guilds in the older trades, in Belgium depending upon the period of payment of wages (daily, weekly or monthly), and in Italy termination at will was permitted by the *Probiviri* only if notice of customary or 'reasonable' length was given in advance. These customary lengths of notice were, however, of little value in the newer occupations where such customs did not exist. It was only towards the beginning of the twentieth century that European countries began to adopt specific legislation on notice, starting with the French Law of 27 December 1890, followed by the Belgian Act of 1900 (manual workers) and 1922 (white-collar workers), all of which referred to the customary periods of notice.

2. Length of Period of Notice

49. In modern legislation provisions as to notice vary greatly. There is a general tendency to regard notice as a reciprocal obligation of employer and employee. The German courts at one time forbade agreements for unequal periods of notice as *contra bonos mores*, but section 622 V of the Civil Code of FR Germany now allows the parties to fix different terms. This is, however, still subject to a prohibition on the period for termination by the employee being longer than that by the employer. Another general tendency is to apply the provisions as to notice only to contracts of indefinite duration, but in a few countries a period of notice is required for the

494

termination of fixed-term contracts, which are deemed to be renewed by the parties in the absence of notice (e.g. under awards in Australia and legislation in some Canadian provinces). In some countries (e.g. France), when a fixed-term contract is renewed it becomes one of indefinite duration, requiring notice to terminate.

50. A distinction may be drawn between those countries in which *minimum* periods of notice are laid down by law which may be increased by collective agreement, usage or individual contract, and those in which the law provides for periods of notice only in the absence of contractual provisions, leaving the parties free to agree upon shorter or longer periods of notice. The length of the minimum period of notice in countries of the first category is fixed in a variety of ways such as whether the worker is manual (blue-collar) or salaried (white-collar), or in the private or public sector, or it may depend upon the amount of pay, or it may increase with the length of service or age (e.g. Sweden). As an example of a country in which periods of notice play an important part in the overall approach to termination of employment, one may cite Belgium, where white-collar workers are entitled to substantially longer periods of notice than blue-collar workers, although reforms which came into force in 1985 have made it easier and less expensive for the employer to dismiss recently recruited white-collar employees. This may be contrasted with those countries where the length of notice is uniform for all categories of workers, and is either fixed (e.g. one week in New Zealand, one month in Japan) or increases with length of service (e.g. one week for the first 2 years and then one week for every year of service up to 12 years in the UK).

51. Usually the employer failing to give the prescribed notice must pay compensation in lieu of notice, or damages for breach of contract as fixed by court. This is distinct from a severance allowance (above paragraph 27) or compensation for abusive (paragraph 54) or unjustified dismissal (paragraph 56).

3. Loss of Right to Notice: Summary Dismissal

52. In all countries the right to notice may be lost in certain circumstances. In some countries this is where the worker is guilty of 'serious fault' (e.g. France) or fundamental breach of contract (e.g. UK) or reasons attributable to his fault (e.g. Japan). In some other countries (e.g. FR Germany, Finland, Italy, the Netherlands, Switzerland) the test is whether it would be unreasonable to expect the relationship to be maintained for the duration of the notice period, and this is the standard prescribed in I.L.O. Convention 158 of 1982, Article 11. In some (e.g. most European socialist countries, Finland, the Netherlands and Sweden) the conduct justifying summary dismissal is defined in considerable detail, including matters such as dishon-

t to superiors and fellow-workers, habitual violation or
l negligence and habitual bad time-keeping.

~~. A number of countries have legislation which provides for the worker to
have such time off, without loss of pay, as is 'reasonable' or 'necessary' to
seek new employment. In some countries (e.g. UK) this is limited to cases
of dismissal on grounds of redundancy. It is a widespread practice to oblige
the employer to issue the employee with a certificate including information
on the dates of engagement and dismissal, but containing nothing unfavourable to the worker. I.L.O. Recommendation 166 of 1982, Article 17, says
that, at the request of the worker, an evaluation of his conduct and
performance may be given in this certificate or in a separate certificate.

C. Requirements of Justification for Dismissals

1. Abusive Dismissal

54. Provisions as to notice are compatible with the liberal doctrine of
freedom of contract. They leave intact managerial freedom to hire and fire
for any reason or without assigning a reason. It was in France between 1859
and 1890 that a legal and political controversy first developed over the
desirability of providing some job security for workers in newer occupations,
in particular those on the railways, who were not protected by the customs
of the older trades. The inferior courts applied the civil theory of abuse of
the law to the unilateral termination of the contract of employment.
However, the highest court (*Cour de Cassation*) never approved these
decisions. The Act of 27 December 1890, while reaffirming the basic
principle that a contract of indefinite duration may always be terminated at
the will of one of the parties, modified Article 1780 of the Civil Code by
adding the important proviso: 'nevertheless the breaking of a contract by the
will of only one of the parties may open the right to damages'. This gave a
legislative basis for the development of actions for damages for abusive
dismissal, and an Act of 19 July 1928 made a clear distinction between pay
in lieu of notice and damages for abuse of the right to terminate. However,
the concept of abusive dismissal remained a judicial creation. As developed
by the courts it may occur not only when the employer acts maliciously,
which is extremely difficult to prove, but also when the employer acts with
culpable negligence (*légèreté blamable*), which is somewhat easier to establish. Examples are the dismissal of an employee offered 'stable' employment
who has incurred substantial moving expenses and is then dismissed without
justification, or the lay-off of a manual worker without following customary
seniority procedures. The real difficulty is that the burden of proving the

abusive nature of the dismissal is generally on the employee. The trade unions criticised the law on abusive dismissal as insufficient to protect employees, and this led to the reforms introduced by the Act of 13 July 1973 providing compulsory procedures and requiring genuine and serious reasons for dismissal.

55. In some other countries in the French tradition (e.g. Luxembourg and Tunisia) legislation still appears to be limited to protection against abusive dismissal. In Greece and Switzerland the civil law concept of 'abuse of right' is sometimes applied. Recently in the USA, there have been decisions in some states utilising common law tort and implied contract theories to provide remedies for workers dismissed in bad faith or by way of victimisation. It is, however, only in Japan that the concept of abusive dismissal has been systematically developed. The constitutional protection of job security and the lifetime employment system have influenced the courts to regard the exercise of the employers' right of dismissal as abusive if the employer fails to show a 'just cause'. Professor Hanami writes that 'the courts have adopted a rather strict attitude towards admitting the existence of a "just cause". From the general trend of the legal precedents it would seem that Japanese employers are not allowed to dismiss workers just because of their inefficiency, laziness or any minor misconduct.'[10]

2. Objectively Valid Reasons for Dismissal

56. The great majority of countries today have explicit legislative requirements that dismissals must be for justified reasons. As pointed out earlier, the first legal statement of the need for 'just cause' was in the Mexican Constitution of 1917, and this was followed by the Labour Code of 1922 of the Russian Soviet Federated Socialist Republic and Cuban Legislation of 1934 and 1938. The Germany Protection against Dismissals Act 1950 introducing the concept of 'socially unjustified' dismissals was an influential post-war landmark, but most of the legislation dates from the 1960s and was strongly encouraged by the ILO Recommendation No. 119 of 1963. This has now been superseded by I.L.O. Convention No. 158 of 1982 concerning termination of employment at the initiative of the employer. Article 4 of this Convention provides that 'the employment of a worker shall not be terminated unless there is a valid reason for such termination connected with the capacity or conduct of the worker or based on the operational requirements of the undertaking, establishment or service'.

57. In some countries collective agreements have played the central part in subjecting dismissals to the 'just cause' requirement. In Canada and the USA most collective agreements (in the USA covering about 19 per cent of

10. T.L. Hanami, *IELL* (Japan), 1978, paragraph 146.

the non-agricultural labour force) require 'cause' or 'just cause' for discharge or discipline and disputes are submitted to private arbitration. The case law of the arbitrators indicates that similar standards have been evolved to those applied under European legislation. In Denmark, Finland, Sweden and Italy basic agreements including this type of protection were concluded at central level in the 1960s. In Italy and Sweden this has largely been superseded by legislation, while in Denmark it has been supplemented by legislation for salaried employees. In Canada (federal jurisdiction and some provinces) there is now legislative protection for workers not covered by collective agreement, but in the USA the non-unionised sector remains without protection.

58. The types of valid reason for dismissal generally fall within ILO Convention No. 158's concepts of 'capacity or conduct of the worker' and 'operational requirements of the undertaking, establishment or service', although it must be noted that in several Latin American countries 'just cause' or 'justification' is defined to cover only misconduct. Among other reasons enumerated in legislation as justifying dismissal are imprisonment beyond a certain minimum period (e.g. European socialist countries and Mexico), statutory requirements prohibiting the employment of the worker (e.g. a driver following a disqualification in the UK), and the attainment of retiring age (e.g. Sweden; in the UK, Ireland and Italy this excludes persons from protection altogether).

59. It is widely accepted, either in the legislation itself or in judicial decisions, that not only must dismissal be for one of the valid reasons but it must be sufficiently serious to justify dismissal. In France this is expressed as a 'genuine and serious reason', and in the United Kingdom as a 'sufficient reason' 'having regard to equity and the substantial merits of the case'. However, the general approach of courts and tribunals is to allow the employer a degree of discretion in deciding whether or not a particular reason is sufficient to justify dismissal, and the dismissal will only be regarded as unjustified if no reasonable employer could have dismissed for that reason. In many countries (e.g. Italy) the burden of proof of 'justifiable reasons' is on the employer. In FR Germany the onus of proving the facts on which the dismissal was based generally rests upon the employer; however, if the dismissal arises from the 'urgent operating requirements of the enterprise' the worker will have to make out his case that the social considerations did not justify his dismissal. In France before 1973, a dismissal was presumed to be justified until the contrary was shown, but since the Act of 13 July 1973 the judge makes the evaluation on the basis of the evidence of the parties and, if necessary, after conducting additional enquiries. In the United Kingdom since the Employment Act 1980 a middle course has been adopted by requiring the employer to show a potentially fair reason for dismissal (conduct, capability, redundancy etc.) which he can do simply by showing the genuineness of his beliefs. It is then for the industrial tribunal to evaluate the 'reasonableness' of his actions in the circumstances, including the size and administrative resources of the employer's undertaking. This so-called 'neutral' burden of proof operates in a different procedural milieu from that in France because the industrial tribunals in the United Kingdom have no power of their own to call witnesses or to order the production of evidence, the procedure being essentially an adversary one.

3. Particular Prohibitions against Dismissal

60. ILO Convention 158 of 1982, Article 5 lists a number of grounds of dismissal which should always be treated as invalid:
(a) union membership or participation in union activities outside working hours, or with the consent of the employer, within working hours;
(b) seeking office as, or acting or having acted in the capacity of a workers' representative;
(c) the filing of a complaint or the participation in a proceeding against an employer involving alleged violations of laws or regulations or recourse to competent administrative authorities; and
(d) race, colour, sex, marital status, family responsibilities, pregnancy, religion, political opinion, national extraction or social origin.
(e) absence from work during maternity leave.
These prohibitions have been widely established in national legislation either as part of the law on unjustified dismissal or in the law relating to matters such as trade union rights and workers' representation. Apart from these grounds, other automatically invalid reasons for dismissal include absence from work due to compulsory military service or other civic obligations or because of age other than reaching normal retiring age. These are mentioned as invalid grounds in ILO Recommendation 166 of 1982, Article 5.

4. Worker's Resignation by Reason of Employer's Conduct

61. Legislation against unjustified dismissal could be easily evaded if an employer were free to put pressure on the employee to resign rather than be dismissed. For this reason many countries give the worker the right to terminate his employment and claim remedies for unjustified dismissal on grounds of the conduct of the employer. Usually the degree of misconduct by the employer sufficient to justify resignation is determined by the courts and tribunals and includes such acts as violence, unlawful withholding of wages, endangering the health and safety of the worker as well as other serious failures to maintain trust and confidence between the parties.

D. Procedural Safeguards

62. Public authorities, courts and tribunals generally feel easier about imposing procedural requirements before or at the time of dismissal than questioning the substantive merits of the employer's decision. One may distinguish two types of procedure: procedural fairness to the employee affected by a disciplinary decision and procedures which involve workers' representatives. The second type of procedures is discussed above, Part IV. Legislation, judicial decisions and collective agreements creating procedures of the first type are to be found in most countries. The procedures usually involve:

(a) investigation of the facts;

(b) the worker's right to a hearing to present his defence and to be accompanied by a fellow worker or trade union official; and

(c) a right of appeal to a higher level of management.

It is also a common requirement that a series of recorded verbal and written warnings should be given to a worker in cases of minor misconduct before dismissal is justified. The worker is often entitled to a written statement of the reasons for dismissal. These standards are reflected in the ILO instruments.

E. Remedies

1. The Right of Appeal

63. Whenever there is protection against unjustified dismissal, there should be a right of appeal to an impartial body which can award remedies. The right of appeal is nearly always vested in the individual worker, but in some countries (e.g. India) legislation allows a trade union as well as the worker to bring a claim. Sometimes the trade union must approve the complaint before it can be heard, or if a works council has expressly consented to the dismissal (e.g. Austria) the worker may not appeal. Where the protection is provided by collective agreement (e.g. USA and Canada) the right to process the grievance belongs solely to the union and not the individual. The competent body to hear appeals is defined by legislation (e.g. a labour court or tribunal or the ordinary civil courts) or collective agreement (private arbitration). In some countries conciliation by a third party, before decision by the competent body, has resulted in the settlement of a high proportion of disputes (e.g. about two-thirds of complaints of unfair dismissal in the United Kingdom are disposed of in this way).

2. Continuation of the Employment Relationship

64. In an increasing number of countries the sole or principal remedy for unjustified dismissal is the continuation of the employment relationship. This may take several forms:

(a) an order annulling the dismissal;

(b) an order for reinstatement in the same job as if the worker had not been dismissed;

(c) an order for re-engagement in a different job, or with an associated employer on such terms as the competent body directs.

The first form is facilitated by legal provisions which suspend the effects of dismissal until the competent body has reached a decision. The suspension may be automatic (e.g. for dismissals with advance notice in the FR Germany, Norway and Sweden) or by order of the court or tribunal (as in several Arab contries). This approach has the advantage of overcoming the psychological barrier which may be caused by the rupture of the relationship by dismissal and encourage the worker to await the decision of the court or tribunal instead of seeking alternative employment. However, it can only work in practice if cases are quickly determined. One may compare in this respect, the relative success of the remedy in Sweden where cases are dealt with in about 6 months, with the situation in the FR Germany where it is estimated that only about 5 per cent of employees whose cases go to the Labour Court are reinstated, partly because cases take 3 or 4 years to reach a decision and so workers do not await the outcome.

65. In the European socialist countries reinstatement is generally the sole remedy for unjustified dismissal with notice.[11] But in most industrialised market economies and developing countries, even where reinstatement or re-engagement is regarded as the primary remedy, the worker can seek compensation in lieu of re-employment. There is an interesting contrast, however, between those countries in which the right not to be unjustifiably dismissed is dependent on collective bargaining (and hence, in the last resort, union support) and those in which it is the creature of legislation. In the USA for example, grievance arbitrators reinstate over one-half of all employees whose dismissals are brought to arbitration by unions. In the United Kingdom, on the other hand, re-employment accounts for only about 2 per cent of remedies agreed by the parties at conciliation stage and just over 1 per cent of remedies granted by tribunals. In Italy, where Article 18 of Act No. 300 of 1970 empowers the *pretore* to order reinstatement, a recent survey based on a broad sample of cases throughout the country showed that although 72 per cent of employees managed to obtain a favourable decision, only a very small percentage of those dismissed is actually reinstated, apart from dismissals for union membership or participation where reinstatement under Article 28 of Act No. 300 is more frequent in practice.[12]

3. Compensation

66. In several countries compensation is the only remedy in law as well as in

---

11. For a comparative evaluation between Poland and the UK see Bob Hepple, 'A Functional Approach to Dismissal Laws', *International Collection of Essays in Memoriam Sir Otto Kahn-Freund*, Munich 1980, pp. 477–491; see too, Wacław Szubert, 'Protection Against Dismissal in Polish Labour Law', *Studia in Honorem Ladislai Nagy Septuagenarii* (Szeged, 1984) pp. 313–323.
12. T. Treu, *IELL* (Italy), 1978, paragraph 218.

practice (e.g. Belgium). Whether compensation is the sole remedy or is in lieu of re-employment, the amount awarded is usually in the discretion of the competent body having regard to factors such as the prejudice suffered by the employee, his age and length of service, but it may be a fixed amount (e.g. in Belgium 3 months' wages for white-collar workers per 5 years' service with the same employer). There is sometimes a minimum amount of compensation (e.g. in France 6 months wages for workers with 2 or more years' service; in Italy 5 months' wages but reducible by 50 per cent for employers with 60 or fewer employees), and sometimes a maximum (e.g. in FR Germany 12 months wages increasing to 15 or 18 months after given ages and lengths of service, the court taking into account both social considerations and the situation of the firm).

4. Social Security Benefits Following Dismissal

67. No account of laws and practices against dismissal would be complete without mentioning some important links with the law of social security, in particular unemployment benefit. First, the conditions of entitlement to unemployment benefit usually strengthen the disciplinary powers of the employer because the worker must not have been dismissed for misconduct or have voluntarily quit his job. Secondly, there have been moves in some countries towards integrating severance payments and other compensation paid by the employer with unemployment benefit schemes, for example by paying special allowances to workers dismissed for economic reasons (e.g. Italy), or allowing the unemployment benefit authority to recover the amount of unemployment benefit from an award of compensation for dismissal so as to avoid double compensation to the employee (e.g. the UK).

SELECT BIBLIOGRAPHY

R. Blanpain (ed.) and various authors, 'Job Security and Industrial Relations', *Bulletin of Comparative Labour Relations*, No. 11, 1980.
J. Gennard, *Job Security and Industrial Relations*, Paris OECD, 1979.
B.A. Hepple, 'A Right to Work?' *Industrial Law Journal*, 10 (1981), pp. 65–83.
F. Meyers, *The Ownership of Jobs*, Los Angeles, 1964.
B.W. Napier, J.-C. Javillier and P. Verge, *Comparative Dismissal Law*, London, 1982.
Jack L. Stieber, 'Protection against Unfair Dismissal: a Comparative View', *Comparative Labour Law*, 3 (1980), pp. 229–240.
Edward Yemin (ed.), *Workforce Reductions in Undertakings*, Geneva ILO, 1982.
Proceedings of the Tenth Internatonal Congress (1982), *International Society of Labour Law and Social Security*, Vol. II, Employee Terminations (published by BNA Books, Rockville, MD, USA 20850).

Chapter 23. Labour Relations in the Public Sector[1]

J. Schregle

I. INTRODUCTION

1. This paper attempts to give a comparative view of labour law and industrial relations in the public sector. It can certainly not present much descriptive detail of the law and practice of various countries in various parts of the world. Its purpose is rather to offer the reader a frame of reference, a typology of labour relations phenomena as they arise in the public sector. In doing this the paper concentrates on the major differences which distinguish the public from the private sector, on the assumption that the other articles in this book are more concerned with the private sector. The central question to be considered is whether labour relations in the public sector diverge from, or converge with, those in the private sector and to what extent the legislators of various countries believe that the particular characteristics of public sector employment warrant a distinct legal treatment.

II. SCOPE AND DEFINITION OF 'PUBLIC SECTOR'

A. Difficulties of Definitions

2. In its wide meaning the expression 'public sector' includes the offices of a government department, municipal employees, publicly owned hospitals and schools, employees (not members) of a parliament, the courts, the police force, fire brigades, government-owned airlines and railways, postal services, garbage collectors and those commercial and industrial enterprises which are run as companies under commercial law and whose shares are wholly or to more than 50 per cent owned by public authorities at the central, regional or local level. The picture becomes further complicated by the different usage and different meaning which the term 'public sector' or its equivalents in other languages have in different countries.

---

1. For previous publications by the same author on labour problems in the public sector see 'Industrial Relations in the Public Sector. An International Viewpoint', in *The Changing Patterns of Industrial Relations in Asian Countries*, Proceedings of the Asian Regional Conference on Industrial Relations (Tokyo 1969), The Japan Institute of Labor, Tokyo, 1969; and 'Labour Relations in the Public Sector', *International Labour Review*, ILO Geneva, November 1974, p. 381.

B. Typology of Public Sector Employment

3. For the purposes of international comparison, the objective of the present paper, it is suggested to make a distinction between three major categories of public sector employees.

1. Government Administration[2]

4. The first category of public sector employees are those employees who are engaged, primarily as officials or civil or public servants, in the central, regional or local administration of the State. This category includes also employees of regional or local self-governing bodies (e.g. provinces, states or cantons of a federal state, municipalities). In many cases employees working in the administration of the State enjoy a special legal status as public servants, civil servants or *Beamte* (in the German-speaking countries) which is not an employment contract like those prevailing in the private sector but a public law status, frequently linked with special benefits (life-time tenure, a pension paid from the State budget) or obligations (e.g. prohibition of the right to strike). However, not all civil servants work in the administration of the State. In some countries some employees in the postal services or even in the railways enjoy the civil servant status. In a general way, the number of government employees has sharply increased during recent years and this trend will in all likelihood continue in the future, with the extension of State responsibility to new areas, particularly in the economy, fiscal measures, administration of justice, social policy, protection of the environment, etc.

2. Public Utilities

5. The second category of public sector employees are the employees of publicly owned and operated utilities, services or agencies providing essential services such as electricity, gas or water supply,[3] hospitals and other medical services, schools, transport (buses, subways, railways, airlines, etc.), harbours and postal services, including telegraph and telephone. Here also the trend appears to be in the direction of expansion. The demand for water and for electricity, gas and other forms of energy, television programmes, the need for hospitals, schools and telecommunications are increasing

---

2. For an international overview of labour relations in the public sector see *Freedom of Association and Procedures for Determining Conditions of Employment in the Public Service*, ILO Geneva, 1976.
3. *Conditions of work and employment in water, gas and electricity supply service*, ILO Geneva, 1982.

sharply as is the demand for transport, ranging from local to international communication.

6. Surely, there has been in recent years, particularly in some of the Western European countries, a new debate about the question of whether public utility services could be provided more efficiently by private enterprises and in some countries some of the services mentioned are in fact furnished by privately owned companies. But if we look at the world as a whole, including the large developing areas in Africa, Asia and Latin America, there can be no doubt that publicly-owned rather than privately-owned operations will increasingly have to provide public utility services, particularly because governments are expected, and accept that responsibility, to make such services available to the community.

3. Publicly-owned Industrial and other Economic Undertakings

7. It is in connection with the third category of public sector employees, i.e. those employed in industrial, commercial or agricultural enterprises which are mainly or entirely owned by the State, that the problem of public versus private enterprise is most keenly debated. What we have in mind here are publicly-owned enterprises irrespective of the legal form of operation and management (e.g. public corporations, joint stock companies with the government as majority shareholder, etc.). This debate, which includes the discussion for or against nationalisation, is not so much about economic efficiency but has clear political and ideological undertones. In other words, the discussion is essentially about power relationships in society.

Nationalisation is at present a political issue, for instance, in France and the UK. While there is a 're-privatisation' debate in the FR Germany no such discussion takes place in Austria which has nationalised after the Second World War important parts of its economy, particularly steel, electricity and banks.

8. In the large majority of Third World countries, especially in Asia and Africa, the public sector of the economy is huge and rapidly expanding.[4] As a result of lack of local private capital and as a consequence of growing national self-assertion and sense of independence, governments of Third World countries often make large-scale investments in mining, plantations, industry, banks, etc. Sometimes also the debate is about the pros and cons of public (i.e. local) capital versus private (i.e. foreign) capital and, in a

---

4. For information on public enterprises in the Third World see *Labour–Management Relations in Public Enterprises in Asia*, ILO-Friedrich Ebert Stiftung, Bangkok, 1978; A. Bronstein, *Las relaciones laborales en las empresas estatales de América latina*, ILO Geneva 1981; *Labour–Management Relations in Public Enterprises in Africa*, Labour–Management Relations Series No. 60, ILO Geneva 1983 (also in French).

general way, about investments of multi-national companies in developing countries. This debate can only be mentioned here in passing. Typical examples are, on the one hand, Singapore which seeks to attract foreign private investors and, on the other, India which is opposed to foreign private investment and has a large publicly-owned industry. Looking at the situation from a world-wide point of view the trend is clearly towards an enlargement rather than a limitation of publicly-owned industry.

III. The Parties

9. Before turning to the various forms and aspects of labour relations it is necessary to have a quick look at the parties concerned, again with a view to bringing out differences or similarities in comparison with private enterprises.

A. The Management Side

10. From the point of view of labour relations the crucial question is the extent to which the government which in the final analysis is the employer deals with employees' representatives, or delegates this authority to management at different levels. Here again we shall examine the situation with regard to the main categories of public sector employment indicated above.

1. Government Administration

11. In most countries the public service has been established as a national system, applicable to all sectors of a country's public administration and the rates of salary or general conditions of work, particularly hours and annual holidays, are fixed at the national level, either by the government itself or, if these measures are taken in the form of legislation, by parliament. This means that organisations of public employees must deal or negotiate with the government at the national level and must therefore organise themselves accordingly. But in some countries with a certain degree of decentralisation, i.e. federal states or countries with a fairly autonomous system of local administration at the municipal level there may be a lesser degree of centralisation in the determination of salaries and general working conditions in the public service as a whole. Furthermore, within the limits of nation-wide salary scales or other benefits schemes or general principles for working hours there may well be, at the level of different government departments or agencies, let alone provincial or local administrations, a certain degree of autonomy to decide on working time arrangements, work organisation, etc. at that level. Hence employees' representatives must also be able to discuss or bargain with employing authorities at that level.

506

2. Publicly-owned Utilities

12. Where publicly-owned utilities are not operated in the form of government departments but either by public corporations or commercial companies wholly or mainly owned by the government or regional or local public authorities the management of such utilities usually enjoys a large measure of autonomy. This, in turn, means that pay rates and working conditions are decided at the level of each utility management, often as a result of bargaining with employees' organisations. But the degree of autonomy or independence of public utility management from government control is seldom completely unlimited. In fact, unions often expect publicly owned utilities to act as pattern setters in labour matters and they often try to influence managements by intervening at the level of the government authority which acts as the owner of the utility concerned. Since public utilities must provide the public with certain services at a reasonable price, the enterprises or corporations providing these services sometimes incur net losses which must then be made up by public subsidies. Here again trade unions will try to influence public utility managements through interventions at the political level.

3. Publicly-owned Industrial and other Economic Undertakings

13. The degree of management autonomy from government control is even greater with regard to publicly-owned industrial and other economic enterprises which, according to a widely held view, should in principle be able to act like management in the private sector. There should therefore be no basic difference between public and private enterprises in the area of labour relations. Conceptually, there need not be any difference because management is answerable to the shareholders irrespective of whether the shares are owned by private citizens, banks or public authorities. However, shareholders' assemblies are not completely without influence on management and, in the public sector, there is furthermore the additional control exercised by the watchful public which will, at least to some extent, hold the government accountable for the way in which public enterprises are managed or mismanaged, particularly where there is a financial deficit. If publicly-owned enterprises were run precisely as private enterprises the question of the *raison d'être* of government involvement in industry would be raised.

The degree of management autonomy in public enterprises will often decide on the links or forms of co-operation and co-ordination between managers in the public and those in the private sector. A concrete consequence of this is the question of whether or not public enterprises can join employers' organisations. While in some countries (e.g. India, Japan, Kenya, the UK) public sector enterprises are members of general employers' organisations, in others (e.g. Italy) they have their own organisations and in still others (e.g. Malaysia, FR Germany) public enterprises do not belong to employers' organisations.

B. *The Employees' Side*

14. There has been over the recent years a considerable growth of public sector unionism. Here it would not be meaningful to make a distinction between the three categories of public sector employment referred to in the preceding sections. The picture presented by trade union structures varies too much from country to country. In a general way, it must be noted that trade unions representing public sector employess have become not only more powerful but also more aggressive in a number of countries. Recent examples were strikes by teachers in Sweden, by doctors in Belgium, by railwaymen in India, by airtraffic controllers in the FR Germany, by postal workers in the USA and, very recently, by workers in the nationalised coalmines in the UK.

15. An important problem for the trade union movement arises from the increasing union membership of white-collar employees employed in the public sector, including especially civil servants. Whether public servants are organised separately from workers in the private sector or whether they belong to the same union as their colleagues in the private sector, the increasing influence exercised by public or civil servants on general trade union policy will inevitably lead to tensions within the trade union movement itself. This phenomenon must be seen as a development which parallels the increasing number of salaried employees or white collar members, accompanied by a proportionate decrease of the number of manual or blue collar workers. The challenge for trade unions to devise new and more efficient forms of trade union structures to take account of these trends is obvious.

When discussing the employees' side of labour relations in the public sector we cannot limit ourselves to the trade union movement. In fact, in a number of countries there exist, at various levels of public administration, employees' or staff councils or committees to represent public employees' interests. Likewise, in publicly-owned enterprises – public utilities and nationalised industry – there are works committees or works councils similar to those established in private sector undertakings. The peculiar feature of public sector enterprises as compared with those in the private sector often is the fact that governments which wish to promote such machinery often seek to introduce it first in public sector enterprises, expecting private enterprises then to follow the example set by the public sector. The result is often a fear on the trade union side that enterprise level machinery for the representation of employees' interests might be used, or is even intended, to undermine or weaken the trade union position. Recent examples of such developments are Sri Lanka and Zambia.

IV. Main Forms of Industrial Relations

16. The way in which the parties to the employment relationship in the public sector deal with each other may, as in the private sector, take different forms. Basically, they are of three different kinds: first, collective bargaining or other forms of employees' association with the determination of pay rates and general working conditions, second, labour disputes, i.e. the situation when direct negotiations fail, and, third, specific forms of workers' participation other than through collective bargaining. These methods are considered in the following paragraphs.

A. Collective Bargaining

17. The term 'collective bargaining' as used here is employed in its widest possible meaning, that is the association of public sector trade unions with the determination of salaries and working conditions. Again we shall look separately at the three categories of public sector employees.

1. Government Administration

18. The real problem here is that governments have never found it easy to accept the notion, and still less the practice, of sharing, except with the legislative bodies, their power to fix salaries and working conditions in the public service. The main obstacle to decision sharing is the sovereign power of government which is answerable only to the electorate. This makes it very difficult for governments to delegate to a joint process such as collective bargaining a part of its decision-making power. The central question is: How can the government, holding the supreme authority of a country which as been vested in it by way of elections, act as an employer of labour and, at the same time, abdicate some of its sovereign power to a process of negotiation with representatives of its employees? It is for these reasons that in a great number of countries the pay and working conditions of civil servants have traditionally been fixed statutorily, by law or government ordinance, and the status of civil servants has long been held to be incompatible with the very concept of collective bargaining.

19. But, as a recent ILO report points out 'a wind of change is blowing and many developments are taking place in the area of employer–employee relations in the public service which would have been thought intolerable only a decade ago'. The same study states 'over the past few decades ... a gradual erosion of the unilateral decision-making power of government authorities has been taking place in many countries. With the accession of public servants to the right to organise and the development of strong associations and organisations of government personnel for the defence of

509

their occupational interests, the latter have been able to bring increasing pressure on the public authorities to consider their views, take cognisance of their claims and negotiate agreements on these matters'.[5]

20. Recent developments in a large number of countries show a shift from formal to informal consultation and negotiation. Fully-fledged collective bargaining for civil servants has in recent years been introduced in a number of countries, including Canada, France, Israel, Norway, Singapore, Sweden and the USA. On the other side of the spectrum are those countries which cling firmly to the traditional special status of civil servants, including Austria, Colombia, the FR Germany and Switzerland. However, in these countries the public servants' trade unions are consulted by the public authorities concerned and often such consultation, although it is not called 'collective bargaining', does in fact come very close to a process of negotiation.

21. A unique procedure for the determination of salaries and conditions of employment in the public service is the Whitley Council system of the UK. This system provides for consultation and for the negotiation of agreements within the framework of legally instituted joint councils. Such councils have been established at three levels (national, departmental, local) where representatives of the authorities (the official side) discuss and negotiate with representatives of the employees' organisations (the staff side). Following the British pattern, Whitley Councils have also been instituted in a number of other countries (e.g. Hong Kong, Ireland, Kenya, Mauritius, Nigeria, Tanzania, Uganda, and other countries) which before independence had been under British rule.

2. Publicly-owned Utilities and other Enterprises

22. As far as collective bargaining is concerned there is basically no distinction between publicly-owned utilities and publicly-owned industrial and other undertakings. In both types of enterprises collective bargaining is widely accepted as the most suitable method of fixing pay rates and general working conditions. There is from this point of view no conceptual distinction if compared with the private sector of the economy.

Differences may arise, however, – in practice more than in law – in those publicly-owned enterprises which embrace a whole industry or a major part of an industry. In such a case collective bargaining which often acts as a pattern setter for the entire industry of the country cannot escape political ramifications. Examples are the nationalised steel industry in Austria, the

---

5. ILO, *Freedom of association and procedures for staff participation in determining conditions of employment in the public service*, Report II, Joint Committee on the Public Service, First Session, Geneva 1971, p. 14.

nationalised coal industry in the UK and the nationalised enterprises belonging to the Italian IRI or ENI groups. Obviously, in such cases the government cannot simply stay out of the bargaining process. One could argue that even a complete government withdrawal from the negotiations does in fact amount to government intervention in favour of the more powerful of the two parties.

In public utilities the situation is by and large the same. However, here the role of the public authorities may even be more important. Since it is the main function of public utilities to provide certain basic services and facilities to the general public, necessary for the life, health and security of the population, if necessary even at the cost of incurring a financial loss, which would then be made up from the budget, taxpayers and the authorities which represent them cannot be indifferent to the outcome of collective bargaining in these enterprises. Again, the problem of the degree of management authority is likely to arise in a more acute form than in nationalised industries.

B. Labour Disputes and their Settlement

23. There are in the public sector of all countries procedures for the settlement of labour disputes and there are third party arrangements, such as courts, arbitrators etc., to which employees can turn for a decision whenever they find that they are not receiving the benefits to which they feel entitled under a law, ordinance, collective agreement, contract of employment or other legally enforceable standard. Such redress procedures for the settlement of legal disputes or disputes over rights are no particular feature of the public sector. They are conceptually not different from those in the private sector. In fact, the procedures and the machinery which administers them are sometimes similar to, or the same as, those operating in the private sector.

The main difference between the private and the public sector in the field of labour disputes lies in the way in which both sectors react to collective labour disputes over economic claims, which may be over wage and salary rates, reduction of staff, hours of work etc. The real issue here is the discussion over the right to strike. We shall therefore in the following paragraphs concentrate on the right to strike, again distinguishing among the three main categories of public sector employment. The last section will consider procedures for the settlement of collective disputes.

1. Public Administration

24. The question of the right to strike in the public service is in many countries a vehemently debated issue. Opinions for and against the right to strike of public servants and about limitations on the exercise of such right

511

where it is recognised in principle have been voiced and debated on so many occasions and have been the subject of so many publications that there is no need here to repeat them in detail.

The main argument advanced against the recognition of the right to strike in the civil service is that it would be incompatible with the functions of the civil service since it would run counter to the sovereign power of government which is derived from the right of the elected lawmakers to pass legislation. It is argued that the special relationship between the government and public servants in government administration is fundamentally and conceptually different from the relationship between employers and employees in private industry. Particularly in those countries where public servants hold office under a statute or statutory regulations not applicable to the private sector the status of civil servants implies a privileged position for them under which they owe the government a special degree of loyalty and allegiance in return for which they receive from the government a guarantee of security of tenure and income and a retirement pension guaranteed by the national budget. The argument then is that under such conditions public servants can be expected to accept a limitation of the right to strike which is available to workers in the private sector. On the other hand, it is argued that there is basically no difference between public and private employment and that the right to strike as a basic human right must be guaranteed for everybody.

25. Whatever argument may prevail, a look at the legal situation in various countries shows a wide variety of approaches to the problem. Countries, which do not recognise the right to strike for public servants and whose legislation therefore often contains a prohibition of that right include Austria, Colombia, the FR Germany, Greece, Japan, Peru, Spain, Switzerland, the USA and Venezuela. Those countries which recognise, explicitly or implicitly, the right to strike in the public service include Canada, Finland, France, Ivory Coast, Mexico, Norway, Portugal, Senegal and Sweden. In another group of countries, including Ghana, Italy, Malaysia, Nigeria, Singapore and Sri Lanka no distinction is made between the public and the private sector as regards strikes. In some countries, which do recognise in principle the right to strike in the public sector, the legislation imposes certain limitations on the exercise of such right. France, for instance, provides for a five day notice period in the case of strikes in the public sector, including the public service. The picture would not be complete without a reference to the fact that even in those countries which prohibit the strike of public servants the legal sanctions for those public servants who actually do participate in work stoppages are not always applied in practice. This happened for instance, in the FR Germany, Japan and the USA.

2. Publicly-owned Utilities

26. In the publicly-owned utilities prohibitions or limitations of strike action where they occur are based on the argument that services and facilities which are essential for the life, health and security of the population must not be interrupted by work stoppages as such interruptions can cause considerable hardship to the general public. Hence strike restrictions are not justified with the particular character of the employment relationship as is the case in the public service but with the 'essential' nature of the utilities concerned.

It has to be borne in mind, however, that enterprises providing essential services or utilities are by no means everywhere in public ownership and that there is no particular type of service commonly held to be 'essential' that could not be run by either publicly or privately owned enterprises. Examples are hospitals, schools, airlines, bus lines, railways, telephone networks, electricity and water supply enterprises, docks, etc. There even seems to be in some countries, of which the United States is an outstanding example, a trend towards providing these or other services by private enterprises. Even postal services which traditionally and commonly are provided by publicly run agencies, often by even government departments or ministries, are now in specific cases, particularly in international business, entrusted to private companies which are said to collect, transport and deliver letters, parcels, etc., more rapidly and more reliably than the government-operated postal services.

However, if we include in our considerations the Third World countries it would be wrong to speak of a trend towards 'reprivatisation'. On the contrary, it would appear that there is rather an expansion of publicly-owned essential utilities.

27. A closer look at the legislation of those countries which prohibit or restrict strikes in essential services shows that the central problem is the way in which the scope of essential services is fixed or the way in which 'essential services' are defined. In many countries, particularly in Africa, Asia, Latin America and the Near and Middle East, the legal definition of 'essential services' is often very broad and includes not only electricity, gas and water supply, health services and fire brigades but, in many cases, also all forms of transport and even branches of industries such as coalmining, oil extraction and even plantations. In fact, sometimes the definition of 'essential services' is so wide or deliberately so vague that it amounts in fact almost to a general prohibition of strikes.

3. Publicly-owned Industrial and other Economic Undertakings

28. There are generally no strike prohibitions or restrictions in the national-ised industries different from those that are also applicable to the private sector. This shows that the mere fact that part of the economy is owned by the government is not considered as a justification for applying principles and rules relating to strikes different from those in force for private enterprises. The situation is of course very different in the socialist or communist countries in which all or most of the means of production are in public or collective ownership. Here it is often argued that the workers who are considered as collective owners of the means of production need no right to strike against themselves. These countries are not considered in this paper which is concerned with a comparison in the treatment of labour relations between the public and private sectors.

4. Disputes Settlement Procedures

29. As indicated above we are dealing here with settlement procedures for collective disputes, i.e. those arising from a collective bargaining deadlock. Such procedures are conceptually only feasible in those countries in which the principle of collective bargaining is recognised.

As regards the public service itself all countries in which public servants have the right to bargain collectively with their employing authorities over pay and working conditions have established institutions and procedures for conciliation or mediation, arbitration and, where appropriate, adjudication of such disputes. One example of such procedures is the Whitley Council system of the UK mentioned above. All these procedures must, of course, be viewed within the general industrial relations context of the country concerned. Since in most of the developing countries in Africa, Asia, the Caribbean, Latin America and the Near and Middle East industrial relations law provides for some form of compulsory arbitration, to be initiated under conditions which vary considerably from country to country, compulsory arbitration in the public service is no exception from the general pattern of the country concerned.

30. With regard to publicly-owned utilities providing for essential services the procedures for the settlement of collective labour disputes are determined by the attitude which the law takes as regards the right to strike. To the extent to which strikes are permitted voluntary settlement procedures apply. In those countries in which strikes in essential services are prohibited (depending on the definition and scope of 'essential services') such interdiction is usually linked with compulsory arbitration or adjudication.

In state-owned industrial and other economic undertakings, including nationalised industry, usually no distinction is made as far as labour disputes settlement procedures are concerned if compared with the private sector. However, we must recall that most developing countries, i.e. the part of the world where the public sector of the economy is proportionately the largest, provide for some kind of compulsory arbitration, at least for the case in which a labour dispute is likely to threaten the stability of the country or the pursuit of its development goals. Here again, the question of whether enterprises are in public or private ownership is not the determinant factor.

C. Workers' Participation

31. The drive for workers' participation in its wide meaning of associating workers with the making of decisions which concern them has also affected the public sector in many countries. In the government administration far-reaching workers' participation schemes are often not considered conceivable because, at least in the view of some, schemes which would go as far as giving the public servants co-decision rights, would be incompatible with their status and with the sovereign power of government. However, arrangements for consultation in the form of employees' councils or committees with mainly advisory functions are frequent. One example is the British Whitley Council system, another example is the statutory staff councils of the FR Germany which exist at various levels of public administration. In this respect there is no fundamental difference between consultation arrangements in the public sector and those in private enterprises.

32. In public utilities and other publicly-owned enterprises, including nationalised industry, the situation is somewhat different. Surely, such enterprises also have consultative committees or councils, but what gives them a special feature is the widespread acceptance of the principle that in such enterprises workers' representatives should be directly involved in the enterprise and company structure. The main argument used against workers' representation on company boards in the private sector, i.e. that such workers' intervention would violate the principle of private ownership, cannot validly be used in publicly-owned undertakings, particularly those providing essential services or other facilities for the general public. Therefore, the admission of worker members to boards of public utility enterprises or of nationalised industry has become a fairly common and well-established practice, the principle of which is generally accepted. To illustrate this point reference could be made to the representation of workers on the boards of public airlines or state railways. Examples are Belgium, France, the FR Germany, Mexico, Nigeria, Switzerland and many other countries. Whether workers' representatives on company boards should be designated by the public authority, nominated by the trade unions or elected by the workers of the enterprises concerned is a difficult problem which is much discussed in a number of countries.

V. CONCLUDING REMARKS

33. As indicated in the introduction the present article is not intended to provide the reader with a host of factual information but rather to offer a frame of reference, a typology of labour relations phenomena in order to facilitate meaningful comparison between the public and the private sectors. Since the term 'public sector' is used and interpreted differently in different countries it is employed in this article in its widest meaning. Three categories of public employment were singled out: public administration, public utilities and publicly-owned industrial and other economic enterprises. With regard to each of these three categories there are similarities and differences in comparison with private employment. While there would seem to be a trend towards reducing these differences to those aspects which justify the difference from the point of view of rational analysis, traditions and opinions derived from history are very powerful. The question concerns basically the role of government within a society, a problem which goes far beyond the field of labour relations.

Authors Index

The number before the oblique stroke refers to the Chapter number; the reference after the oblique stroke refers to the numbered paragraph(s) of that Chapter. e.g. 1/28 refers to Chapter 1, paragraph 28. 10/22, 33–46 refers to Chapter 10, paragraphs 22 and 33–46.

Aaron 2/14, 23; 18/38; 21/14, 71
Adam 13/52
Bakels 22/41
Balzarini 2/14
Barbagelata 2/12
Bar-Niv 2/13
Birk 18/38, 43, 53
Blanc-Jouvan 2/23
Blanpain 2/7, 10, 11, 13, 21; 4/1
Blum 2/12
Bullock 13/71
Clegg 11/1, 22
Coleman 1/1
Córdova 13/112
Davies 2/19
De Gaulle 1/45
De Nova 6/15
De Winter 6/15
Drobnig 2/11
Dunlop 1/1, 25
Ford 14/7
Francescakis 6/15
Galin 17/76
Garanscy 2/8
Giscard d'Estaing 3/16
Giugni 2/23; 21/38, 42
Goldman 1/42; 18/38; 21/35
Giuliano 6/4
Hanami 16/98; 22/55
Harbison 1/1
Hartmann 1/26; 18/28–31
Herzberg 13/13
Isaac 17/45
Jain 2/12
Johri 21/65
Jonczy 2/12
Jones 21/59
Kahn-Freund 1/47, 51; 2/9, 23; 20/3
Kamin 2/12

Kerr 1/1
Krislov 17/76
Lagarde 6/4
Lyon-Caen 2/12
Malintappi 6/15
Mao 13/58
Maslow 13/13
Mazza 22/32
McGregor 13/13
Meyers 22/7, 8
Morgan 2/7
Neal 2/14
Peel 14/22
Pipkorn 1/22
Raday 17/46
Ramm 2/23
Ribas 2/12
Rojot 22/30
Ross 1/26; 18/28–31
Savigny 6/14
Schmidt 2/23; 21/29
Schregle 1/1, 2; 2/21
Séché 2/12
Sherman 1/40
Sinzheimer 22/15
Smith 12/4
Sykes 16/89
Szladits 2/8
Taylor 13/91; 14/7, 11
Trentin 16/37
Treu 17/23; 22/32
Troscanyi 2/18
Valticos 1/2, 15, 18, 19; 2/12; 19/14, 35
Vredeling 7/39
Waschke 2/12
Wedderburn 2/23
Windmuller 2/4
Yerbury 17/45

Geographic Index

The number before the oblique stroke refers to the chapter number; the reference after the oblique stroke refers to the numbered paragraph(s) of that chapter: e.g. 1/28 refers to chapter 1, paragraph 28; 10/22, 33–46 refers to chapter 10, paragraphs 22 and 33–46.

Africa 2/3; 4/1, 2, 7, 13, 14, 23, 27, 32, 33, 34, 35, 40, 41; 5/23; 9/18, 24, 41, 42, 51, 52, 56; 11/28, 50, 55, 62; 12/16, 34; 13/72, 15/33, 63; 16/5; 23/6, 8, 27, 29
Albania 6/5
Algeria 4/13, 35; 11/43, 50; 13/58, 72, 88; 22/24
America 2/3, 12, 17, 18; 5/23; 8/13; 9/8, 15, 57; 3/3; 12/20; 15/42, 43; 17/23; 19/15, 21; 21/1
Amsterdam 9/5
Andean Group 5/23
Arab-Islamic 4/13
Arab States 4/2; 5/23, 62; 12/52
Argentina 4/2; 6/18; 10/29; 11/63; 13/61; 15/20, 30, 33, 79; 16/5; 17/29; 20/42, 43, 47, 54, 64
Asia 2/3, 18; 4/1, 7, 9, 14, 27, 32, 33, 34, 40, 41; 9/12, 18, 21; 3/41, 51; 11/28, 62; 12/52; 13/72; 16/5; 17/18; 20/22; 21/37; 23/6, 8, 27, 29
Australia 1/12; 3/3, 24, 37; 9/12; 11/11, 16, 25, 52, 56, 61, 66, 67, 71, 81, 85; 12/30; 13/61, 73, 90; 15/21; 16/45, 76, 77, 81, 83, 85, 86, 87, 88; 17/40, 45, 46, 47; 18/26, 36, 53; 22/44, 49
Austria 1/6, 20, 28; 3/30; 6/5, 11, 15, 78; 9/9; 11/6, 15, 16, 18, 29, 38, 41, 64, 66, 67, 68, 69, 70, 73, 75, 81, 87; 13/30, 45, 61, 67, 73, 75, 76, 79, 83; 15/63, 78; 16/5, 43, 45; 17/31; 18/26, 36; 19/41; 20/45; 22/19, 22, 44, 63; 23/7, 20, 22, 25

Bahrein 13/73
Bangladesh 4/2, 14, 24, 35; 13/73
Belgium 1/28, 29, 53; 2/9, 10; 3/9, 52; 4/13; 7/52; 8/18; 9/35, 37; 11/16, 43, 45, 79, 86; 12/21, 27, 29, 37; 13/30, 38, 40, 44, 59, 73, 75, 76, 77, 79, 83; 15/34, 38, 43, 44, 48, 63; 16/5; 17/21, 25, 31, 68, 70; 18/22, 42; 20/4, 10, 20, 24, 32, 36, 38, 44, 55, 57; 21/1, 18, 20, 26, 32, 34, 42, 44, 45, 50, 54, 67; 22/5, 19, 21, 29, 32, 33, 37, 41, 44, 66; 23/14, 33
Bern 5/2

Bolivia 4/2; 10/64; 15/79
Brazil 10/16, 56; 11/55, 65; 13/73; 15/20, 28, 30, 33, 79; 17/16, 29, 31; 20/29, 36, 37, 44, 48, 55
Brindisi 2/17
British Columbia 17/47
Brussels 1/50; 2/17, 20; 9/44; 12/44
Budapest 2/17
Bulgaria 13/58, 16/5, 43; 17
Burma 13/73; 20/13
Burundi 13/73

California 2/14
Canada 3/48; 5/61; 9/20; 10/58; 11/18; 13/73, 90; 15/17, 19, 23, 31, 48, 70; 16/25, 27, 28, 45, 46, 47, 50, 51, 52, 57, 62, 73, 74, 86, 87; 17/16, 48, 49, 50; 18/26, 27, 36, 42, 54; 19/29, 30, 73, 76; 21/13, 18, 22, 27, 29, 34, 44, 45, 51; 22/11, 22, 32, 49, 57, 63; 23/20, 25
Caracas 2/17
Caribbean 4/32; 9/18; 11/80; 12/53
Central America 5/23
Chad 4/2
Chicago 2/12
Chile 4/12; 5/61; 10/45; 11/55, 86; 15/20; 20/17, 22
China 9/12; 13/58; 20/32; 22/16
Columbia 1/12; 10/29, 48, 56, 64; 11/55; 15/20, 23; 16/5; 20/38, 44, 48; 23/20, 25
Commonwealth 3/5; 9/56
Congo 11/45; 13/88
Costa Rica 15/23; 20/33, 43
Cuba 4/10; 9/12; 20/33; 22/56
Cyprus 1/20; 13/73; 20/6; 21/58
Czechoslovakia 16/5, 14; 13/5; 6/5, 15, 24, 43, 45; 20/32, 33; 22/44

Denmark 1/20; 2/9; 7/52; 8/18; 9/17, 37; 11/16, 71; 12/7; 13/30, 68, 69, 73, 76, 83; 15/47, 63; 16/5; 17/25, 35, 64, 71; 18/42, 54, 59; 19/40, 50, 52, 73; 20/32, 34, 55, 59; 22/32, 44, 57

Eastern Europe 1/48; 2/17; 5/23; 13/55, 84
Ecuador 4/5; 10/50; 13/5; 15/20, 38; 17/29; 20/22, 36, 42, 47, 48

518

EC 13/5, 8, 33, 40, 45, 71
Egypt 10/12, 16
English-speaking Africa 4/13, 32, 38
Ethiopia 4/10, 39; 10/18, 36
Europe 1/11, 16, 20, 21, 24, 38, 42, 50; 2/3,
    6, 12, 17, 18; 3/5, 14, 35, 36, 38; 4/1,
    16, 27, 35, 36, 40; 5/21, 22, 63; 6/2;
    7/1, 14, 20, 28, 29, 33, 34, 35, 36, 39,
    40, 41, 42, 52, 55; 9/6, 21, 25, 41, 42,
    44, 45, 49, 50, 53, 54, 56, 61, 62;
    11/3, 8, 14, 23, 25, 27, 28, 37, 43, 50,
    53, 61, 62, 69; 12/7, 54, 58; 14/8, 30,
    36; 15/8, 24, 29, 33, 34, 42, 43, 70;
    16/13, 22, 41, 42, 43; 19/31; 20/3, 5,
    11, 14, 21, 34; 22/1

Fiji 4/28
Finland 6/7; 9/57; 10/12; 12/7, 54; 13/71, 88;
    15/6, 48, 66, 77; 16/5, 45; 17/31, 62,
    74; 20/13, 36, 43, 47, 53; 22/32, 52,
    57; 23/25
France 1/2, 28, 33, 39, 42; 2/2, 9, 12, 23; 3/3,
    16, 46; 4/12, 13; 6/7, 15, 29; 7/52;
    8/11; 9/6, 35, 36, 48; 11/14, 16, 18,
    22, 25, 28, 41, 43, 45, 48, 59, 66, 67,
    68, 69, 71, 72, 78, 80, 86; 12/2, 4, 7,
    15, 16, 17, 21, 24, 27, 29, 48; 13/52,
    59, 67, 71, 73, 74, 75, 76, 83, 91;
    14/9, 22, 27, 33; 15/3, 6, 28, 30, 38,
    58, 63, 66, 68, 79; 16/4, 8, 9, 16, 19,
    25, 27, 28, 29, 30, 32, 33, 39, 44, 45,
    96, 101; 17/21, 23; 19/29, 30, 38, 49,
    56, 58, 63, 65, 72, 74, 79, 84, 85, 89,
    91, 92; 18/22, 56; 19/3; 20/20, 34, 36,
    43, 45, 47, 51, 53, 55, 57, 61, 62, 64,
    65; 21/1, 9, 18, 26, 27, 29, 30, 32, 42,
    43, 46, 49, 53; 22/3, 7, 8, 11, 19, 21,
    22, 26, 27, 29, 30, 32, 33, 34, 38, 39,
    40, 44, 48, 49, 52, 54, 58, 59, 64, 66;
    23/7, 20, 25, 32
French-speaking Africa 4/9, 13, 29, 32, 38;
    13/86
FR Germany 1/6, 20, 28, 33, 36, 39, 53; 2/3,
    9, 13, 15, 17, 18, 23; 3/3, 9, 30, 41,
    48; 4/12; 6/6, 7, 9, 13, 18, 29; 7/40,
    52; 8/11; 9/6, 9, 15, 20, 37, 57, 70;
    11/5, 7, 8, 15, 16, 22, 24, 28, 29, 30,
    63, 64, 66, 67, 68, 69, 70, 71, 72, 73,
    74, 79, 80, 81, 87; 12/7, 15, 20, 26,
    27; 13/16, 30, 38, 42, 45, 53, 54, 61,
    64, 67, 73, 75, 76, 79, 90, 83, 98;
    15/6, 17, 34, 48, 56, 63, 68, 78; 16/5,
    18, 30, 31, 32, 34, 37, 39, 40, 43, 45,
    96; 17/9, 28, 31, 37, 57, 62, 64, 72;
    18/22, 36, 42, 50; 19/3, 17, 18, 29, 32,
    33, 39, 42, 46, 47, 49, 52, 53, 54, 56,

60, 61, 63, 67, 73, 75, 78, 82, 90, 91;
    20/5, 55, 56; 21/1, 20, 23, 26, 27, 37,
    40, 42, 43, 45, 46, 51, 52; 22/5, 15,
    19, 20, 21, 22, 29, 32, 33, 34, 41, 44,
    49, 52, 56, 59, 64, 66; 23/4, 7, 14, 20,
    25

Gabon 13/73
GDR 6/5; 13/5; 16/5, 43, 44; 20/6, 33, 46,
    53; 22/20, 44
Geneva 1/27; 2/2, 5, 17, 20; 12/44
Ghana 13/61, 73; 15/20, 33; 17/71; 23/25
Great Britain 1/39, 42; 2/13, 15, 19, 23; 3/36,
    46, 52; 4/13; 6/6, 7, 9; 9/8, 48, 57, 64;
    11/3, 7, 11, 15, 16, 22, 27, 29, 31, 40,
    45, 52, 53, 54, 57, 63, 64, 66, 67, 68,
    69, 70, 71, 72, 73, 75; 11/80, 87; 12/2,
    7, 9, 15, 27, 29, 41; 15/17; 16/4, 5, 11,
    19, 35, 37, 38, 43, 45; 17/28, 35, 38,
    55, 76; 18/53; 19/15, 21, 25, 42, 44,
    56, 63, 66, 69, 70, 73, 79, 83, 84, 85,
    88, 92; 20/4, 5, 11, 22, 23, 39, 43;
    21/11, 13, 18, 23, 33, 40, 43, 44, 46,
    50, 51, 52, 54, 69, 70; 22/4, 5, 7, 8,
    11, 18, 19, 21, 22, 24, 26, 32, 37, 41,
    43, 45, 50, 53, 58, 59, 63, 64, 67
Greece 3/2; 6/9; 19/40; 22/32, 55; 23/25

The Hague 2/17; 13/82
Hamburg 2/11
Heidelberg 2/22
Honduras 1/12
Hong Kong 20/12; 23/21
Hungary 2/8; 6/5, 14, 15; 13/56; 16/5, 43, 45;
    20/36, 43, 45, 46, 47; 21/37, 40

Iceland 1/20; 9/57
India 1/28; 4/5, 6, 14, 24, 33, 35; 11/28, 45;
    12/26, 30, 63; 13/5, 61, 73, 81, 92;
    15/20; 17/15, 22, 29, 57, 73, 74; 20/4,
    7, 12, 53; 21/65; 22/16, 63; 23/13, 14
Indonesia 4/14; 13/73; 17/71
Iowa 17/52
Iraq 10/16; 11/45; 13/72, 73; 20/36, 37
Ireland 1/20; 12/27; 13/73; 15/27, 34, 43, 77;
    17/73, 76; 18/26; 22/19, 21, 27, 32, 44,
    58; 23/21
Israel 2/13; 11/43; 13/58, 61; 16/5, 45; 17/23,
    35, 57, 74, 76; 20/4, 7, 16; 23/20
Italy 1/6, 12, 28, 39, 53; 2/9, 13, 15, 23; 3/2,
    3; 4/9, 12; 6/14; 8/6, 17; 9/9, 17, 48;
    11/8, 14, 16, 22, 25, 29, 31, 41, 43,
    48, 52, 57, 59, 63, 64, 66, 67, 68, 69,
    70, 71, 72, 73, 75, 79, 80, 85, 86;
    12/21, 27, 36, 48; 13/5, 31, 59, 88;
    14/1, 27, 33; 15/27, 28, 34, 35, 58, 69,

77, 79; 16/90, 91, 96; 17/21, 23, 36, 72; 18/26, 27, 36, 50; 19/3, 29, 30, 38, 47, 49, 52, 58, 65, 72, 74, 89, 91; 20/4, 21, 33, 36, 42, 43, 46, 55; 21/20, 23, 27, 33, 39, 40, 42, 43, 45, 47, 51; 22/1, 5, 17, 19, 21, 22, 29, 30, 31, 39, 43, 44, 48, 52, 57, 58, 59, 64, 65, 67; 23/13, 23, 25
Ivory Coast 23/25

Jamaica 13/73; 15/70; 20/36
Japan 1/33, 43, 50; 2/7, 13, 20; 3/3, 9, 14, 30, 37, 41, 48; 4/7, 9, 14, 41; 5/61; 8/13; 9/17, 49, 54; 11/17, 18, 27, 43, 56, 59, 61, 66, 67, 68, 69, 70, 71, 73; 12/20, 26; 13/55, 59, 61, 66, 73, 76, 80, 90, 91, 94, 97; 15/17, 33, 38, 43, 47, 48, 51, 78; 16/90, 97, 98; 17/28, 41, 57, 66; 18/36; 20/36; 21/14, 16, 25, 29, 30, 37, 40, 43, 47; 22/1, 18, 22, 50, 52, 55; 23/13, 25
Jesolo 2/18
Jordan 13/73

Kenya 1/12; 4/2, 7, 28; 10/18, 20, 65; 12/34; 13/73; 15/20, 78; 20/36
Korea 3/6; 11/50; 13/73
Kuwait 6/5; 10/16, 33, 56
Kyoto 2/20

Laos 2/3; 20/36
Lagos 4/7
Latin America 1/12; 2/12; 4/2, 9, 12, 14, 27, 28, 32, 33, 38; 9/12, 18, 41; 10/25; 11/17, 27, 50, 55, 62; 12/16, 27, 47, 52; 13/72, 83; 15/20, 30, 63, 78; 20/4, 5, 16, 22, 33, 34, 40, 43, 44; 22/32, 58; 23/6, 27
Leuven 2/10
Liberia 10/12
Libya 10/16, 36; 13/58; 20/33
London 2/20; 9/8
Luxembourg 1/42; 2/6, 9, 22; 13/30, 44, 68, 73, 83; 15/43; 20/10, 12; 22/42, 55
Los Angeles 2/14
Low Countries 9/6, 22
Lyon 2/17

Madrid 2/17
Madagascar 10/45
Malaysia 1/12; 4/7, 9, 14, 28, 29; 10/16; 12/29; 13/61; 15/33, 70; 20/13; 21/58; 23/25
Malta 13/58, 61
Mauretania 4/39; 13/73
Mauritus 12/26; 13/73; 23/21

Mexico 4/6, 12, 39; 8/12; 10/46; 11/63, 78; 13/61; 15/20; 16/5; 17/15; 19/38, 40; 20/4, 29, 31, 36, 40, 43, 51, 55; 22/7, 8, 56, 58; 23/25, 32
Middle East 5/23; 9/18; 23/27, 29
Milan 7/33; 9/59; 10/16
Morocco 4/13; 13/73
Munich 2/17, 19

Nepal 4/14; 13/73
The Netherlands 1/20, 28, 33, 53; 2/6, 9, 13; 3/3, 52; 4/14; 8/18; 9/15, 20, 35, 36; 11/16, 69, 73; 12/16, 27, 30, 37; 13/53, 70, 73, 80, 83; 15/17, 34, 43, 77; 16/90, 94; 18/42; 20/4, 32, 55, 64; 21/37, 43, 51; 22/21, 23, 24, 32, 38, 41, 42, 52
New Zealand 10/27; 12/29; 13/73, 90; 15/21, 66, 70; 17/45, 47, 71; 20/32, 33; 22/44, 50
New York 14/2, 7
Nicaragua 5/6
Nigeria 10/29, 66; 13/73; 15/20, 33, 78; 23/21, 25, 32
Nordic Countries 1/53; 9/57, 71; 12/19, 26, 27, 37
North 1/1; 4/2, 27; 8/13
North Korea 9/12
Norway 1/20; 9/42, 57; 11/18, 71; 12/7; 13/5, 13, 30, 68, 69, 73, 74, 75, 76, 83, 90; 15/6, 17, 27, 78; 16/5; 17/71; 20/33, 47, 55; 21/62; 22/20, 21, 32, 44, 64; 23/20, 25

Oman 13/73

Pakistan 4/7, 14, 35; 10/21; 11/45; 13/61, 73; 20/13
Panama 10/23, 46; 13/61, 73; 15/70; 20/17, 36, 43; 22/24
Paris 2/20; 9/8
Peru 4/35, 39; 11/50; 13/58, 72; 15/23, 79; 17/60, 74; 20/29, 36, 37, 38, 42, 59, 64; 23/25
Philadelphia 5/3
The Philippines 4/9, 14, 27, 33, 35; 10/29; 13/73; 15/38, 70; 17/29; 20/7, 22
Poland 1/6, 48; 4/2, 9, 12, 14, 27, 28, 32, 33, 38; 6/5, 14; 11/87; 13/58, 91; 16/5; 20/5, 6, 36; 22/44
Portugal 3/2, 40; 4/12, 13; 9/48; 13/5, 58, 73; 20/38, 43, 44, 47, 48, 58, 72, 74; 22/19, 44; 23/25

Quebec 16/50

Romania 13/5, 58; 17/14, 36; 22/44
Rome 1/23
Russia 2/2

Sahara 4/13
Saskatchewan 16/50
Sao Paulo 2/17
Scandinavia 8/12; 9/20, 72; 11/15, 18, 38, 66, 67, 68, 70, 89; 13/16; 14/1, 9; 18/23; 19/82; 22/11
Senegal 4/39; 23/25
Sierra Leone 1/12, 18; 4/28; 13/73
Singapor 1/12; 4/2, 9, 14; 11/28; 13/61; 15/20, 78; 20/13; 23/20, 25
Socialist Countries 4/10
Somalia 13/73
South 1/1; 4/2, 16, 27; 8/13
South Africa 5/31; 8/1; 17/19; 21/24
Southern Asia 4/2; 13/10
Soviet-Union 9/26, 27, 28
Spain 1/6, 12, 20; 2/2; 9/48; 3/2, 9; 4/9, 12, 13; 6/5, 14; 11/79, 80, 85, 86; 12/48, 54; 13/5, 73, 80; 15/26, 27, 34, 38, 43, 63, 77; 16/5; 18/26; 19/38, 40, 58; 20/4, 54, 55, 60; 22/5, 18, 20, 21, 27, 32, 33, 34; 23/25
Sri Lanka 1/28; 4/14, 24, 29, 35, 39, 40; 13/73; 15/20, 23, 33; 23/25
Stockholm 2/17
Strasbourg 1/50
Sudan 13/73
Swaziland 13/73
Sweden 1/20, 39; 2/13, 23; 6/7, 9; 9/15, 17, 57; 11/5, 8, 16, 18, 22, 24, 27, 52, 63, 64, 69, 71, 73, 85, 87; 12/7; 13/13, 30, 44, 61, 68, 69, 88, 90; 15/17, 34, 35, 44, 51; 16/4, 5, 12, 20, 21, 39, 40, 43, 45; 17/74; 18/22, 26, 42, 54, 59; 19/17, 29, 32, 33, 38, 40, 42, 46, 49, 52, 58, 60, 61, 63, 65, 73; 20/51, 55; 21/21, 28, 31, 33, 37, 40, 44, 47, 50, 64; 22/5, 20, 23, 32, 38, 44, 50, 52, 57, 58, 64; 23/14, 20, 25
Switzerland 1/6; 3/30, 41, 53, 54; 6/9; 10/22; 12/13, 27, 29, 34; 13/71, 73; 15/6, 63; 18/26, 27, 36, 42; 20/21; 22/52, 55; 23/20, 25, 32
Syria 10/50; 13/72
Szeged 2/18

Tanzania 4/7, 35; 10/12; 13/73, 79, 88; 15/44; 23/21
Teheran 2/17
Thailand 4/7; 13/73; 14/28; 15/23
Third World Countries 4; 9/28, 62, 67; 17/16
Tobago 1/12; 15/38, 78

Tilburg 1/53
Toronto 14/2, 7
Trinidad 1/12; 15/38, 78
Tunisia 4/13; 5/61; 12/29; 13/61, 73, 76; 22/55
Turin 1/28
Turkey 3/2; 10/12, 66; 19/40

Uganda 23/21
The United Kingdom 1/20; 3/3, 9, 31, 48; 7/26, 52; 8/18; 10/28; 11/81, 85; 13/13, 30, 59, 71, 73, 78, 90; 14/1; 15/3, 6, 7, 8, 21, 34, 43, 44, 47, 48, 56, 59, 68; 18/42, 50; 20/36; 23/7, 13, 14, 21, 22, 29
Uruguay 9/32; 13/73; 15/23; 16/5; 20/5, 20, 21, 33
USA 1/28, 39, 42, 50; 2/13; 3/3, 9, 14, 36, 37, 48, 53; 4/1, 14, 27; 6/7, 9; 9/12, 17, 21, 53, 54, 61, 62, 64; 10/3, 7, 11, 12, 18, 22, 24, 27, 29, 31; 11/18, 31, 40, 43, 48, 61, 66, 67, 68, 70, 71, 72, 73, 75, 76, 80, 81, 85, 87; 12/30, 34; 13/30, 73, 90; 14/7, 8, 9, 22, 27, 33; 15/6, 7, 17, 28, 31, 33, 34, 37, 38, 42, 43, 44, 48, 51, 59, 68, 69, 70; 16/4, 25, 27, 28, 35, 45, 46, 47, 48, 51, 53, 55, 56, 60, 66, 67, 68, 69, 70, 71, 73, 75, 86, 87, 100; 17/15, 16, 21, 25, 28, 39, 51, 54, 56, 62, 64, 67, 73, 74, 76; 18/42, 56, 58; 19/15, 21, 29, 30, 50, 52, 56, 62, 66, 73, 80, 81, 83, 84, 86, 87; 20/55, 64; 21/1, 12, 13, 15, 17, 18, 20, 23, 25, 28, 29, 34, 35, 37, 40, 41, 43, 44, 49, 51, 52, 53, 54, 57, 59, 60, 61, 62, 63, 65, 70, 72; 22/4, 7, 8, 11, 17, 24, 32, 44, 45, 55, 57, 63, 64; 23/14, 20, 25, 61
USSR 13/5, 92; 16/5, 14, 22, 23, 43; 17/30; 20/33; 22/1, 3, 24, 44, 56

Venezuela 4/35; 11/45; 13/51, 73; 15/20, 23; 17/71; 23/25
Vietnam 9/12

Warsaw 2/17
Washington 2/17
Western 1/43; 11/17, 56; 22/3
Western Europe 2/23; 9/12, 28; 11/44; 23/5

Yugoslavia 1/45; 9/30; 11/43; 13/5, 57, 58; 21/30, 35; 22/20

Za ≙ ∧ re 10/11, 12; 13/73, 75, 76; 17/71, 74
Zambia 1/12; 4/28, 35; 10/18; 13/73, 79; 15/33, 70

Subject Index

The number before the oblique stroke refers to the chapter number; the reference after the oblique stroke refers to the numbered paragraph(s) of that chapter: e.g. 1/28 refers to chapter 1, paragraph 28; 10/22, 33–46 refers to chapter 10, paragraphs 22 and 33–46.

Abusive dismissal 22/54–55
ACAC 16/81–84
ACAS 2/19; 17/75; 18/50
Access to real decision makers 8/23;
Acquiescence 17/1, 12–22
ACSPA 11/16
ACTU 11/16
Adjudication 17/6, 43–58
Administrative Tribunal 2/3
Adversarial approach 17/66–67
Affirmative action 21/43–44, 58–65
AFL 9/4, 8, 10; 11/48
AFL-CIO 9/12, 15, 18; 11/7, 13, 86; 14/22
AFRO 9/24
Age 21/29, 45
Agricultural workers 20/16–17
Agriculture 5/47; 7/36
Alcoholism 21/31, 47
Alternative employment 22/26
Amalgamation 11/9
Andean Group 5/23
Annual Social Report 2/6; 7/11
Annual vacation 5/37
Anti-union 5/27; 9/58–59
Apartheid 5/31; 17/18; 21/24
Application 1/19
Apprenticeship 20/31–33
Approval of dismissal 22/40–41
Arab Labour Organisation 12/52
Arbitration 1/12, 42; 4/33; 7/40; 16/45–90;
        17/42–57
ARO 9/23
ASEA group 12/52
Asean Council of Trade Unions 9/53
Assistance 1/14
Atypical 20/64
AUCCTU 9/8, 29
Autonomous work groups 14/30; 17/60, 64
Autonomy 6/9, 15

BADGER 8/23
Bankers' trust 8/23
Bargaining process 15/36–49
Bargaining unit 15/36–49
BATCO 8/23
BFOQ 21/35, 48–51
BIAC 8/18, 19, 20, 25, 12/53
Bibliography 2/4, 5, 6, 8

Bilateral treaties 5/24
Black market 22/30
Blockade 19/20
Blue collar 20/8–12
Boycott 19/19, 82
Bulletin of Comparative Law 2/10
Bulletin of Labour Statistics 2/2
Business unionism 11/75

C & A 8/16
CAC 2/19; 17/55
Case law 2/13; 5/18
Categories of workers 20
CBI 12/7; 13/14
CCOO 9/30
Centre of gravity 6/14
Central decision making 8/2, 23
Central Federation of Trade Unions 9/2, 4
CFDT 9/36
CGS 11/5
CGIL 9/30
CGT 9/30; 14/22, 24
Child labour 5/44
CIO 9/8
CISC 9/5, 6, 7, 9
CISL 9/17;
CITIBANK 8/23
Civil liberties 9/67–68
Civil servants 19/78–79; 20/5
CLAT 9/41
Closed shop 9/4, 24, 26–30;
Closure 22/43
CNFP 3/36; 12/7; 14/7
CNV 9/37
Co-decision 13/51–62, 79–80
Codes of conduct 3/52; 9/69
Co-determination 7/37; 22/44
Codification 6/7
Collective agreements 6/27
Collective bargaining 1/28; 2/6; 3/25–30, 37–
        38; 4/22, 27–29; 5/27–28; 9/52–53;
        11/22, 25, 33–46, 84–85; 12/18–21;
        13/18–94; 15; 17/63–76; 23/17–22
Collective dismissals 7/45; 13/40, 48
Collective disputes 16/16–17, 34
Collective Labour Law 1/52; 6/26–29; 7/29–
        41

Colonial 1/1
Colour 21/19
Commercial travellers 20/18
Commonwealth Trade Union Council 9/56
Communication 14/35
Comparative Labor Law Group 1/39; 2/23
Comparative Labor Law 2/14
Comparativism
    Definition 1/2
    Documentation 2
    Educational visits 1/41
    Group collaboration 1/38
    Horizontal 1/15
    How 1/30–40
    Integrated 1/36
    Transplantability 1/47–52
    Traps 1/41–43
    Uses 1/3–27
    Vertical 1/15
    What? 1/28–30
Competitive unionism 11/75
Concession bargaining 20/64
Compulsory arbitration 16/73; 18/54
Conciliated Negotiation 17/68–76
Conciliation 15/70; 16/90
Conflict 19/1
Conflict of Laws 6
Confidentiality 13/44–45, 49
Conflictual 18/36
Conflict resolution 15/13–14
Consensus 2/6; 18/36
Consultation 7/39; 8/23; 13/47–50, 78
Contract of employment 20/2–3
Contract for a definite period 20/39–41
Contract for an indefinite period 20/41–50
Contract for a specific term 20/51–54
Contractual clauses 15/55
Control 14/2
Convergence 1/1; 4/1
Cooperation Committee 13/69
Co-operatives 20/6
COPA 7/36
Co-responsibility 8/23;
Council for Mutual Economic Assistance
    5/23
Council of Europe 1/20; 2/6; 5/21, 63; 9/9,
    24; 21/7
Council of Nordic Trade Unions 9/37
Coverage of collective bargaining 15/27–21
Covenant of non-competition 20/21
Craft Unions 11/3
Creativity 14/16
Creed 21/27
Crisis 3/5–17; 11/77
CSC 9/37
Cultural 4/7

Decertification 14/24
Deregulation 21/9; 22/42
Development policies 4/5
Developed countries 1/12; 11/78
Developing countries 1/13; 11/34, 78
DGB 9/15; 11/16
Direct discrimination 21/11
Directive 7/9
Directory of Institutes for Labour Studies
    2/5
Disciplinary dismissals 22/10–12
Discrimination 7/49; 21
Dismissal 4/39, 20/63
Disputes over interests 17; 17/64; 19/62;
    23/23–25; 29–30
Disputes over rights 16; 19/62
Dissolution of trade unions 9/63–66
Distributive disputes 17/64
Dockers 20/23
Documentation 2
Domestic servants 20/22
Dowry system 17/18
Duration of collective agreements 15/65–68

EC 1/21, 54; 2/6; 5/22, 63; 6/4, 11, 13, 14,
    15, 17; 7; 8/1; 9/39; 12/53–59; 13/6, 8,
    33–35, 40, 45, 48, 71, 78; 21/8, 9, 16,
    19–20, 22, 28, 32–35, 44, 48; 22/5, 11
EC-Depositary libraries 2/6
Economic 1/42
Economic and Social Council 12/16
Economic Committee 6/29; 13/105
Economic Policies 3/18–33; 15/71–77
Education 1/4
EEOC 21/71
EFA 7/36
Election of trade union representatives
    9/40–47
Emergency laws 19/80
EMF 9/49–50
Employees 20/1–3
Employers' associations 7/30–32;
Employers' Organisations 4/16–19; 12; 19/73
Employment 3/8; 5/32–33; 8/2
Employment Service 22/36
Enforcement 21/45–53; 66–72
Enquiries 21/25
Enterprise unionism 11/17; 13/94–97; 15/30
Environment 14/2
EO 9/41
EP 1/24
Equal opportunity commission 21/51
Equality 21
Equal pay 21/31–36
Equal treatment 7/47–49; 21/21–23
Equity 13/5

ERO 9/25
ESC 1/24
Ethnicity 21/16
ETUC 1/23–24; 9/25, 39, 41, 42, 44–50
European Collective Bargaining 7/33–36
European Company Statute 7/36, 40
European Convention of Human Rights
    1/20; 5/21
European Co-operative Association 7/39
European Documentation Centres 2/6
European Social Charter 1/20; 5/21, 63; 9/9,
    24; 19/36; 21/7; 22/3
European Social Fund 7/55
European Trade Union Institute 14/26
Executives 20/14

Fact finding 17/51–52
Family responsibilities 5/43
Fiat 1/28;
Flexibility 14/30
FMCS 18/50
FNV 9/15
Forced labour 5/29–48
FORD 8/23
Forecast 1/8
Foreign workers 5/50; 7/53–54; 21/21
Formulation 1/18, 22
Free movement 7/53; 21/9
Governmental Fiat 17/4, 24/33
Freedom of association 4/16; 9; 14/25
Freedom to strike 19/25, 43–47
FTF 9/17
Functions 1/28
Functioning of trade unions 9/38–50

General conditions of work 5/35
General Unions 11/11
GHERAO 17/22
Government 11/87
Government administration 23/4
Grievances 15/69–70; 16/49–56, 66, 68,
    70–71
Guidelines for Multinationals 8
Guilds 12/3

Handicap 21/30
Harmonisation 1/21; 7/9–10, 24
HERTZ 8/23
High level technicians 20/14
HMS 9/17
Homeworkers 20/24–25
Human Rights 1/20; 5/20, 23; 9/9, 24; 21/5, 8
Hungarian Academy of Science 2/8
Hygiene-Safety 5/38; 14/2, 22

Ibero-American Association 4/12
ICC 12/45
ICFTU 9/10, 12/24, 51–52
Ideology 1/44–46; 11/79
IELL 2/10; 8/18
IFTU 9/4–5, 7
IG Metall 14/31
IIRA 1/54; 2/20
ILO 1/15–19, 51, 54; 2/2–5; 4/10, 16; 5/7–19;
    6/4; 8/1; 9/28; 9/5–9; 12/43–51; 13/21,
    34–36, 38, 48/49, 78, 82–83; 15/7, 44;
    18/52; 19/36; 21/6, 11, 29, 30, 31;
    22/44, 60
IME Committee 8/17–25
Implementation 5/53–57
Income maintenance 22/29
Income policies 3/23–25; 15/71–77
Indexation 15/73
Indigenous workers 5/48
Indirect discrimination 21/11
Indirect participation 13/2; 21/12
Individual disputes 16/16–17, 34
Individual employment 4/38
Individual employment Contract 2/6; 8/2
Individual Labour Law 7/42–52
Industrial Conflict 18
Industrial Court 1/12; 4/32
Industrial Disputes 1/42
Industrial Relations 5/42; 7/29–41; 8/2
Industrial tribunals 16/5–44
Industrial unions 11/7–10
Industry Committees 9/49
Inflation 3/6
Information 1/28; 7/39; 8/23; 13/27–46, 78;
    15/79; 22/38–39, 44
Injunction 19/56
Insolvency 7/52
Institute for International Law 2/21
Institutional participation 11/44–45
Institutions 1/28
Integrative disputes 17/64
Interference 9/60–62
Internal administration of trad-unions 9/48;
    11/18–25
International Academy for Comparative
    Law 2/17
International Affiliation 9/31–37
International Case Law 2/13
International Collective Bargaining 8/34;
    3/42
International Competition 5/4
International Conventions and Recommen-
    dations 2/4
International Court of Justice 5/17
International Employers' Organisations
    12/43–59

International Encyclopedia of Comparative law 2/11
International Institute for Labour Studies 2/5
International Institute for Temporary Work 2/9
International Labour Documentations 2/4
International Labour Law 2/13; 5; 19/36–37
International Labour Relations 3/42
International Labour Review 2/2
International Minimum Standards 1/15
International Private Labour Law 1/7; 2/12; 6; 7/43
International Society for Labour Law and Social Security 1/39, 54; 2/17–18
International Solidarity Fund 9/19
International Trade Secretariats 1/8; 8/23; 9/2, 3, 5, 20, 51, 58–70
International Trade Union Action 9/70
International Trade Union Movement 9
International Trade Unions 1/8
Interpretation 5/17
INTUNC 9/17
Investment decisions 1/28
IOE 12/45, 47–51
IOIE 12/44

Job creation 22/37
Job enrichment 14/2
Job security 1/32–34; 4/39; 15/53; 22
Job sharing 20/61
Joint committees 15/43
Joint consultation 7/37
Journal of Comparative Labour Law 2/14
Judgments of the Administrative Tribunal of the ILO 2/2
Judicial review 16/27
Jura Europae 2/9
Jurisprudence of International Labour Law 2/13
Just cause 22/57
Justification for dismissal 22/54–60

Labour Administration 5/51
Labour and Society 2/5
Labour Code 1/12
Labour Costs 3/21
Labour Courts 1/30; 4/32; 15/70; 16/5–44
Labour Inspector 18/50
Labour-Management Relations Series 2/2
Labour Market 2/6; 22/13–18
Labour relations in general 7/42–43
Language 1/41–43; 21/21
League of Arab States 5/23
Legislative Series 2/2
Levels of bargaining 15/28–35

Lex fori 6/12
Lex loci laboris 6/15
Lifetime employment 3/3; 4/41
LO 9/15, 17; 11/16
Lock-out 4/30-31; 6/28; 16/54; 18/6; 19; 19/71–80
Locus regit actum 6/23
Lois de police 6/15

Management perogatives 8/23; 13/23; 15/51
Managerial Boards 13/63–72
Managerial employees 20/13
Managers 20/14
Marital Status 21/44
Maritime work 5/46
Market system 17/12–15
Marshall Plan 9/10
Maternity protection 5/43
Mediator 17/70
Medium Sized Enterprises 2/6
Merger 13/48
MICHELIN 8/18, 23
Migrant Workers 5/50
Minimum wage 17/28
Mixed disputes 17/64
Models 1/31
Most favourable law 6/18
Multinational Enterprises 1/8; 2/7; 4/10, 19; 8; 9/69; 13/20, 4315/44
Multinational Labour Relations 1/8–9

National Origin 21/20
Negative freedom of association 9/23
Negotiation 17/1, 9–10, 64–77; 22/44
Neo-corporatism 11/64
Night work 5/43
NKV 9/36
NLRB 16/35–37
Non-metropolitan 5/48
Non-strikers 19/91
Normative clauses 15/55
No-strike clauses 16/86
Notice 22/47–52

OATUU 9/42, 51–52
Occupation 19/68
Occupational Unions 11/3
OECD 1/54; 2/7; 3/2, 14; 8/1, 10–18; 9/53–55; 13/36, 38, 41, 48, 49; 15/44; 18/21
Official Bulletin 2/2; 5/17
Offshore workers 20/26–28
OGB 11/16
Older workers 5/45
Ombudsman 21/50
Opposition unionism 11/75
Ordinary Courts 16/90–102

Organisation of African Unity 4/13
Organisation of American States 5/23; 19/37; 21/4
Organisation of Central American States 5/23
ORIT 9/23
Overtime 7/34; 17/28–29
Ownership of jobs 22/6–7

Paid Educational Leave 5/37
Paid Holidays 6/18
Papal Encyclicals 13/5
Parity in industrial action 19/52, 72–73
Participatory unionism 11/75
Part-time 7/34; 20/58–61; 22/34
Parochialism 1/44–46
Paternalism 14/24
PAWC 9/41
Peace 5/4
Peace obligation 15/57–58; 16/54; 19/49–51
Peonage 17/18
PHILIPS 8/23
Picketing 19/19–20, 84
Plant 13/20
Political action 11/33–36, 86
Political activities 9/56; 12/9
Political discipline 17/5, 34–42
Political Opinion 21/27–28
Political Parties 11/47–52
Postwar Development 3/1–3
Power 14/20
Pregnancy 21/23
Pressure group 12/12
Pretore 16/92
Priority of Re-employment 22/25
Private Life 21/46
Productivity 14/30
Professional sportsman 20/29; 21/20
Profit making 1/45
Profit sharing 13/72
Proofs 21/68
Proportionality 19/53–56
Public Company 1/42
Public sector employees 23/3–4
Public sector enterprises 4/18; 12/34
Public service 5/28, 49
Public utilities 23/5–7, 12, 26–27

Quality of Working Life 13/91; 14
Questionnaire 21/25

Race 21/19–21
Racial Discrimination 5/20; 21/5; 21/18
Ratification 5/54–56; 15/36, 48; 17/61
Recession 3/39
Recruitment 21/25

Reduction of Working Time 22/21–23
Regional 4/11–13
Regulation 7/9
Reinstatement 16/32
Religion 21/27–28
Remedies 1/34; 16/67; 21/72; 22/45–46, 62
Remuneration 7/52
Representative Union 4/21
Research 1/55
Resolution of conflict 18/38–46
Resolutions 5/16
Reverse discrimination 21/58–65
Review 5/52
Review of arbitration 16/62
Rhine Boatmen 5/19
Right to organise 5/26–27; 8/28; 9/10–12
Right to strike 19/27–33, 43–47
Right to work 22/1–5
RILU 9/5, 7
Role of the state 3/19, 40–41; 11/53–65; 15/27; 19/92; 22/36–42
Rule-making 15/10–12
Rural Workers 5/28

Safety 7/50–51; 14/2, 22
Safety and Health Committee 13/89
Salaried employees 20/11
Scope of bargaining 15/50–59
Season (contract) 20/54
Security of Employment 7/44; 22
Security of the State 21/36–37
Selection of Workers for Dismissal 22/23–24
Self-management 11/43; 13/57–62; 20/6
Seniority 14/33
Seiority Wage System 3/3
Severance allowance 11/27–28
Settlement of disputes 4/32; 16; 17
Sex 21/17, 22–26
Shop floor 13/20, 90
Shop stewards 13/85; 17/58
Short-term contracts 22/33
Sit-in 17/21; 19/68; 22/43
Slavery 17/18; 21/1
Small employers 22/35
Social 1/42
Social action programme 7/5
Social and Labour Bulletin 2/2
Social change 1/10–14
Social Europe 2/6
Social justice 5/5; 13
Social Origin 21/20
Social Policy 5/40
Social Policy Series 2/6
Social Security 5/19, 21, 23, 41; 22/67
Social Work 12/24
Sohyo 9/17;

Solidarity 9/30
Solidarity contracts 15/79
Special protective measures 21/55–57
Spring offensive 3/3
State-sponsored unionism 11/75
Strike 3/39; 4/30–31; 5/26; 6/28; 9/54–55;
    16/52–54; 18/3, 8, 10/37; 19
Structures of employers' organisations
    12/26–42
Subordination 20/3–4
Summary dismissal 22/52
Supervisory Machinery 5/57–63; 9/8
Supervisory personnel 20/13
Supervisory Board 1/28; 13/99–102, 106
Suspension of trade-unions 9/63–66
Sympathy strike 19/66

Task enrichment 14/1
TCO 11/6, 16
Teaching 1/55
Teamsters 11/11
Technology 2/6; 5/40; 14/29; 22/18
Temporary work 1/11; 7/34; 20/55–57;
    22/31–32
Terminology 1/43
Territorial trade union structures 11/13–16
Test 21/25
TGW 11/11
Theory formulation 1/25–27
Third World 4
Time of new employment 22/53
Torts 19/70
Trade union action 11/32
Trade Union Freedom 4/20; 5/26, 61–62
Trade Union Membership 11/80
Trade union structure 4/23; 11/2–17, 78
Trade Unions 4/20; 8/5–8; 13/18
Trade Unions Monopoly 9/18–21
Training 12/23; 20/34; 22/36
Transfer of employees 8/23
Transfer of enterprises 7/38–46
Transplantability 1/10, 47–52; 4/8–9
Trial clause 20/35–38
Tribal 5/48
Tripartite Declaration Multinationals 5/40
TUAC 8/18–20, 25; 9/42, 53–55
TUC 9/8, 10, 19, 48; 11/16, 80
TUI 9/33

Twin workers 20/61

UAW 11/78
UIL 9/17;
UN 5/20, 48, 63; 9/28; 9/9
Unconstitutional strike 19/60
Unemployment 22/14
UNESCO 5/19
UNIAPAC 12/31
UNICE 1/23–24; 7/31; 12/54–59
Union density 11/67
Union security clauses 9/26–30; 15/59
United Nations 21/3, 5, 6
Unjust dismissal 16/28
Unofficial strike 18/44; 19/33, 46, 60

VIGGO 8/23
Volkswagen 1/28
VOLVO 13/90; 14/22
Voting 17/8, 59–63
Vredeling proposals 1/50; 7/39

Wage moderation 15/72
Wages 5/34; 14/2
Wages Council 17/28
WAGNER-LAMBERT 8/23
WCL 12; 9/9, 11, 35–41
WFTU 9/8–11, 26–34, 51–52
Whipsaw strike 19/55
White-collar 20/8–12
White-collar Unions 11/5
Wildcat strike 18/44–45; 19/47, 60
Women 5/43
Women at Work 2/2
Work in action 17/21
Work permit 21/21
Workers 20/1
Workers (special categories) 5/46
Workers Participation 1/28, 42; 2/5; 4/35–37;
    7/37–41; 9/39–46; 13; 14/2–34; 15/15,
    53; 23/31–32
Workforce reduction 22/10–12, 21–20
Working time 2/6; 5/36; 7/34; 14/2
Works council 11/28–31; 13/73–83, 94, 102–
    104; 17/58
Young persons 5/44; 17/19
Young workers 2/6